Lecture Notes in Artificial Intelligence   2407

Subseries of Lecture Notes in Computer Science
Edited by J. G. Carbonell and J. Siekmann

Lecture Notes in Computer Science

Edited by G. Goos, J. Hartmanis, and J. van Leeuwen

Springer
Berlin
Heidelberg
New York
Barcelona
Hong Kong
London
Milan
Paris
Tokyo

Robert A. Kowalski

Antonis C. Kakas   Fariba Sadri (Eds.)

Computational Logic: Logic Programming and Beyond

Essays in Honour of Robert A. Kowalski
Part I

Springer

Series Editors

Jaime G. Carbonell,Carnegie Mellon University, Pittsburgh, PA, USA
Jörg Siekmann, University of Saarland, Saarbrücken, Germany

Volume Editors

Antonis C. Kakas
University of Cyprus, Department of Computer Science
75 Kallipoleos St., 1678 Nicosia, Cyprus
E-mail:antonis@ucy.ac.cy

Fariba Sadri
Imperial College of Science, Technology and Medicine
Department of Computing, 180 Queen's Gate
London SW7 2BZ, United Kingdom
E-mail: fs@doc.ic.ac.uk

Cataloging-in-Publication Data applied for

Die Deutsche Bibliothek - CIP-Einheitsaufnahme

Computational logic: logig programming and beyond : essays in honour of
Robert A. Kowalski / Antonis C. Kakas ; Fariba Sadri (ed.). - Berlin ;
Heidelberg ; New York ; Barcelona ; Hong Kong ; London ; Milan ; Paris ;
Tokyo : Springer
Pt. 1 . - (2002)
   (Lecture notes in computer science ; Vol. 2407 : Lecture notes in
   artificial intelligence)
   ISBN 3-540-43959-5

CR Subject Classification (1998): I.2.3, D.1.6, I.2, F.4, I.1

ISSN 0302-9743
ISBN 3-540-43959-5 Springer-Verlag Berlin Heidelberg New York

Springer-Verlag Berlin Heidelberg New York
a member of BertelsmannSpringer Science+Business Media GmbH

http://www.springer.de

© Springer-Verlag Berlin Heidelberg 2002
Printed in Germany

Typesetting: Camera-ready by author, data conversion by Boller Mediendesign
Printed on acid-free paper   SPIN 10873675   06/3142   5 4 3 2 1 0

Table of Contents, Part I

III Software Development

IV Extensions of Logic Programming

V Applications in Logic

Author Index

Table of Contents, Part II

VI Logic in Databases and Information Integration

VII Automated Reasoning

VIII Non-deductive Reasoning

I   Logic for Action and Change

Logic, Language, and Learning

I Computational Logic and Philosophy

Author Index

A Portrait of a Scientist as a Computational Logician

Maurice Bruynooghe[1], Luís Moniz Pereira[2], Jörg H. Siekmann[3], and
Maarten van Emden[4]

[1] Department of Computer Science,
K.U.Leuven,
Belgium
[2] Departamento de Informatica,
Universidade Nova de Lisboa,
Portugal
[3] Saarland University,
German Research Center for Artificial Intelligence (DFKI),
Saarbruecken,
Germany
[4] Department of Computer Science,
University of Victoria,
Victoria, British Columbia,
Canada

Throughout his prolific scientific career, Robert (Bob) Kowalski was motivated by his desire to reshape logic from an abstract mathematical discipline into a working tool for problem solving. This led him towards a wide exploration of logic in computer science, artificial intelligence, cognitive science, and law.

His scientific achievements in these pursuits have become landmarks. To this we should add the enthusiasm and leadership with which he has enrolled into this venture an entire community extending over two generations of researchers.

Below we detail by topic some of his accomplishments.

1 Automated Theorem Proving

Bob's early work was part of the enormous enthusiasm generated by Robinson's discovery of the resolution principle. Bob started off with important technical contributions, with Hayes on semantic trees and with Kuehner on SL resolution. The pinnacle of this line of research is Bob's Connection Graph proof procedure.

Already before the Connection Graph proof procedure, Bob was concerned with the redundancy of unrestricted resolution. He collaborated with workers in operations research applying search techniques to guide resolution theorem-provers.

2 Logic for Problem Solving

A formative episode in Bob's development was the backlash against resolution theorem-proving. Green had shown how goals of plans could be elegantly formu-

A.C. Kakas, F. Sadri (Eds.): Computat. Logic (Kowalski Festschrift), LNAI 2407, pp. 1–4, 2002.
© Springer-Verlag Berlin Heidelberg 2002

lated in logic and that the plans themselves could be read off from the proofs that showed the goals were achievable. On the one hand there was the completeness of resolution that suggested this might be feasible. On the other hand there was the painful fact that no existing resolution theorem-prover could implement this research program. An implicit revolt was brewing at MIT with, for example, the development of Hewitt's PLANNER.

Resolution theorem-proving was demoted from a hot topic to a relic of the misguided past. Bob doggedly stuck to his faith in the potential of resolution theorem proving. He carefully studied PLANNER. He worked with Colmerauer on the representation of grammars in logic, discovering the importance of Horn clauses. In this way it was discovered how proofs could be parses, vindicating part of Green's grand vision according to which proofs could be executions of plans that achieve goals formulated in logic. Thus Logic for Problem Solving was born.

3   Logic Programming

Logic for problem-solving, specifically how to represent grammars in logic and how to parse by resolution proofs, influenced the conception of Prolog by Colmerauer and Roussel. Conversely, Prolog influenced logic for problem-solving so that it spawned a well-defined subset that we now know as logic programming.

The birth of the logic programming paradigm had a great impact. Its elegance, simplicity and generality offered a new perspective on many areas in computer science and artificial intelligence. It resulted in several novel programming languages, led to the development of deductive databases, was the foundation for the influential constraint logic programming paradigm, inspired much innovating work in natural language processing, had great influence on developments within knowledge representation, and was the basis for inductive logic programming, a recent offspring from machine learning.

Bob's influential dictum "Algorithm = Logic + Control" provided fundamental direction for increasing clarity and scope in the description of algorithms and design of new control mechanisms for logic programming languages, namely through meta-programming. His subsequent research revealed the potential of the logic programming paradigm in many areas.

4   Logic across the Children's Curriculum

Bob's research program, born in the dark days around 1971, was vindicated in the programming language area when a prominent member of the MIT AI group said, much later, "Prolog is PLANNER done right". But the research program is more radical: logic is not just a good model for programming languages, but also for the way humans think by nature. To test this wider concept, a project was started at a school in London for a class of children who were about 13 years old. A key ingredient was Micro-Prolog, a version of Prolog that ran on micro-computers (as PCs were then called). This system, at the time a revelation, was developed in Bob's group by McCabe and Clark. Another key ingredient was Ennals, a school teacher, who was trained by Bob in logic programming. Together they developed a curriculum, which was taught on a regular basis for a year by Ennals, with the children writing and running Prolog programs on computers at the school. It showed that with English-like syntax, Horn clauses can be used by children to support their curriculum material in English, mathematics, geography, and history.

5   Logic and Data Bases

Influenced by the pioneering work of Minker, Gallaire, Nicolas and others on the logical analysis and inference techniques for data bases, Bob provided central insight, as well as numerous technical contributions, for this emerging field, that eventually led to the amalgamation of classical data base theory with knowledge representation formalisms in artificial intelligence, logic, and semantic networks. Together with colleagues, Sadri, Sripada and others, he has established significant landmark contributions in various problems such as the frame problem in logic data bases, data base integrity and temporal databases.

6   Logic Programming and the Law

Is mathematical reasoning just typical for proofs of mathematical theorems or can the inspiring vision of Leibniz, that two philosophers in dispute may settle their differences by coding their arguments into an appropriate calculus and then calculate the truth: "CALCULEMUS" be turned into reality?

Bob, in a team effort with Sadri, Sergot and others, showed that the British Nationality Act as well as other highly formalized legislation can be coded into an enchanced logic programming language — and then computed! This insight spawned an interdisciplinary field, logic and law.

7   The Event Calculus

In 1986, at a time when the program of implementing temporal reasoning using Situation Calculus in classical and nonmonotonic logics continued to struggle with conceptual and computational problems, Bob delivered a seminal contribution to the use of logic-based temporal reasoning. In an attempt to overcome the shortcomings of situation calculus, he and Marek Sergot introduced a new ontological concept, the *event* which is an occurrence of an action bound at a specific time point and location. They developed a theory based on this concept, called *Event Calculus* and implemented it in logic programming. This work was very influential and created quite a debate between supporters of the two approaches. Ironically, about ten years later, different researchers including Bob himself showed a close relationship between the event and situation calculi. The work on event calculus is still influential and is applied in the context of AI-applications such as robot control.

8   Common-Sense Reasoning

The naive use of negation in PLANNER and early logic programming was soon replaced by the much deeper insight into the distinction between classical negation and what became known as "negation as failure".

Similarly, the early confusion in expert systems between deduction and abduction led to a more thorough investigation and Bob's collaboration with Eshghi, Kakas, Toni and Fung spawned several papers on this issue. Amongst other things these papers compare abduction with negation as failure and have opened the new area of Abductive Logic Programming. Related to this is also Bob's work, with Dung, Toni and others, on argumentation for formalising nonmonotonic reasoning.

9   Logic Modeling of Agents

The recent world-wide interest in agents and their applications was met by Bob with a challenge to the Logic Programming community to hone their tools to the issues raised. He led the way himself, publishing with Sadri, on the balanced combination of deliberation and reaction, integrated into an original IFF agent cycle framework, in which the agent at turns reacts and reasons with limited resources. His work paved the road for the involvement of the logic programming community in the flurry of activity we have today concerning computational logic agents and societies of agents.

10   Conclusion

Bob's inspiring leadership and expertise was widely appreciated and sought after the whole world over. His bold initiative to organise a first Logic Programming workshop in May 1976 laid the foundation for an enthusiastic community of logic programmers. His advisory role in projects such as the Japanese Fifth Generation Computing Systems and in organisations such as DFKI, the German National Research Center for A.I. was deep and very influential. As coordinator of the ESPRIT Basic Research Action in Computational Logic, as participant to its successor, Compulog2, and as founding chairman of the ESPRIT network of Excellence in Computational Logic (CompulogNet), he had an enormous impact on the European logic programming research community. His leadership and drive for quality was an example for many young researchers. Distinctions and prizes from many countries pay tribute to his role: MIT Distinguished Lecture, Honorary Distinguished Alumnus of Phi Kappa Phi at the University of Bridgeport, the "Docente a titulo individuale" from Bologna, the fellowships of AAAI, City and Guilds of London Institute, DFKI, ECCAI, and ACM.

As this volume illustrates, Bob's work has established logic as a tool for problem solving and has a lasting influence in many areas of computer science.

Bob Kowalski: A Portrait

Marek Sergot

Department of Computing
Imperial College of Science, Technology and Medicine
London SW7 2BZ

Introduction

The hardest part about writing an introductory piece for a celebratory volume
such as this is finding the right opening. It has to hit the right tone straight
away—affectionate, respectful, but not too sweet and cloying. I had tried and
discarded half a dozen attempts when, more in desperation than in any real hope,
I turned to technology and typed 'Bob Kowalski' into a WWW search engine. I
am not sure what I expected to find. Some previously unpublished tidbit perhaps
on which I could build an insightful and original opening. The search yielded
a great many results. On page 12 I came across an entry from the newsletter
of the *Tulsa Thunder*, a girls' football ('soccer') team in the US. According to
one person quoted there: "Bob Kowalski was one of the first influential coaches
I had. He was an all-round good guy." I was about to discard this interesting
observation (it is a different Bob Kowalski) when it occurred to me that in fact
this quotation would serve perfectly as an opening for this piece. I had wanted to
begin with remarks about Bob's inspirational influences and what a good guy he
is, but could not decide which should come first. Bob has certainly been one of
the most influential coaches I ever had, and as the rest of this volume testifies,
an inspirational influence on many, many others too. He is an influential and
inspirational coach, and he is an all-round good guy.

The 'all-round good guy' part was particularly tricky to introduce. How does
one bring this up? For now I will just state it as an assertion, and leave the
reasons to emerge in the course of the article.

The editors encouraged me to give this introduction a personal tone, and so at
this point I display my credentials. Among the many important and long-lasting
contributions Bob Kowalski has made to the development of Computer Science, a
lesser known one is that he is the main reason I decided to stick with Computer
Science myself. In the Spring of 1975 I was halfway through an MSc course
in Computer Science at Imperial College. I was disillusioned and disappointed
and bored. I could not believe there was so little in it. It was like plumbing, but
without the intellectual challenge. I turned up for a research seminar by Bob who
had just moved to the Department of Computing (or Computing and Control
as it was then called) from Edinburgh. Like many others before me and since, I
was inspired—inspired by the prospects of new and exotic applications, a little,
but more by the enthusiasm and energy of the speaker, and most of all, by the

A.C. Kakas, F. Sadri (Eds.): Computat. Logic (Kowalski Festschrift), LNAI 2407, pp. 5–25, 2002.
© Springer-Verlag Berlin Heidelberg 2002

elegance of the logic programming story that he unfolded before us. There was something in computing after all.

Since then I have had the fortune to work closely with Bob, briefly in the summer of 1975, and then more or less continuously since 1979, in close collaborations throughout the 1980s and early 1990s, and then more at a distance as our interests diverged.

The account of Bob's life and work given here is based on my memory of Bob's musings and recollections in casual conversations over the years. Many of our colleagues would recognise these recollections, I am sure. I tried to fill the gaps by conducting subtle interrogations of Bob on the last few occasions I have had the opportunity to chat with him. These interrogations were so subtle that he did not notice and they failed to yield anything at all. By luck, just as this volume was going to press, Bob distributed to a few of us a short autobiographical piece he had written in response to some request or other he had received from a student. I was thereby able to confirm the facts as I had remembered them. I have also taken the liberty of lifting three small quotations from Bob's own version, where I had remembered the gist of what he had said, but where his own words have a particular interest.

I should say that Bob has not had the chance of reviewing this manuscript before it went to press. There may be mistakes in points of detail. Moreover, the opinions expressed are mine, and not necessarily the same as Bob's.

Some Biographical Details

Robert Anthony Kowalski was born on 15 May 1941 in Bridgeport, Connecticut. He has two younger brothers, Bill and Dan. His father was the son of Polish immigrants to the US; his mother, if I recall correctly, came to the US from Poland as a young girl. Although his parents would speak Polish occasionally at home, the boys did not. Bob attended a Catholic primary school attached to the Polish parish and then—much more significantly—a Jesuit High School. This had a lasting influence, clearly, since Bob mentions it often. I was most impressed when I discovered it, because I was educated by another brand of Catholic brotherhood, not nearly so famous, and the products of a Jesuit education have always held a certain cachet for me. Jesuit schools got prominent mentions in our History books. When I think of Jesuit schools in the USA in the 1950s and 1960s I immediately get a mental image of something like the jet fighter-pilot training school in the film *Top Gun* but with intellectual missiles instead of heat-seeking ones. By coincidence, there was another American Jesuit-educated Professor in the Department of Computing at Imperial College, and so I had an opportunity to try to detect the common features. The results were inconclusive.

Bob says that he was not an academically outstanding pupil at High School, until he discovered, or had discovered in him, an aptitude for Latin, in which he represented the school in contests in New England. I have some difficulty in imagining what a Latin contest in New England must be like, but the important thing is that it awakened Bob's academic ambitions, and encouraged him to undertake independent reading, especially in areas of Philosophy and the Philosophy of Science which have remained a lifelong interest.

Bob began undergraduate studies in 1958 at the University of Chicago. He enjoyed the academic and intellectual environment. His courses included introductions to mathematical logic. However, other components of the courses were much more tedious and this, together with aspects of the social life, led him to abandon his studies at the University of Chicago early in his second year, in November 1959.

He resumed his undergraduate studies the following academic year, this time in his home town at the University of Bridgeport. He majored in Mathematics. In 1963 he won Woodrow Wilson and National Science Foundation Fellowships for graduate study and was admitted to the PhD programme (in Mathematics) at Stanford University. Jon Barwise was a classmate and a friend. The academic year 1964-1965 was spent on an exchange programme at the Mathematics Institute of the Polish Academy of Sciences and the University of Warsaw, noted for its work in Mathematical Logic. Besides studies of logic, and meeting and visiting his Polish relatives, in that year Bob learned Polish, he met and married his wife, Danusia, a student in the Mathematics Department at the University, and he discovered that the world was not as he had been led to believe it was.

One of the first conversations I remember having with Bob was of his experiences of that year in Poland. A childhood in the US in the 1950s and an education with the Jesuits had painted a clear picture of what life in Poland would be like. He expected that there would be very severe restrictions on personal and other freedoms. What he found was quite different, and in particular that the people seemed to have much more freedom than he had been told to expect. The discrepancy was so great that he felt he had been badly let down and misled—'cheated' was the word he often uses when speaking of it.

On his return to Stanford with Danusia for the academic year 1965 he found it increasingly difficult to focus on studies of mathematics. The war in Vietnam was escalating, and he became active in the protest movement. I knew that he had participated in marches and demonstrations, and he had told me that his specialty had been in generating new ideas for protests. It was only when I read his autobiographical piece as this volume was going to press that I discovered he also participated actively in some of his own schemes. I discovered, for example, that he devised and with a childhood friend from Bridgeport took part in a 'bombing' campaign to drop leaflets from airplanes. The first sortie nearly ended in disaster. The last mission also stands out. In Bob's own words:

> Our main goal was to 'bomb' the Rose Bowl football game in Los Angeles. Ray and I worked out an elaborate scheme to change the registration number on the side of the plane, ripping the false numbers off in mid-flight, to minimise the chance of getting caught when we made our getaway. Unfortunately, when we landed in the Mojave Desert to change the number, the plane burst a tire, and we were too late to get to the Rose Bowl in time for the game. We bombed Disneyland instead.

Bob decided to leave Stanford in the middle of the academic year in 1966, which gave him a Master's degree. Having looked for work, mostly outside the US, he eventually took a position for a year as Assistant Professor and Acting Head of the Mathematics Department at the Inter-American University in San Juan, Puerto Rico. His first daughter, Dania, was born in Puerto Rico during that year.

In 1967 he accepted an IBM Research Fellowship to undertake PhD studies in the Meta-mathematics Unit directed by Bernard Meltzer at the University of Edinburgh. The research topic was the mechanisation of mathematical proofs. Bob was not particularly enthusiastic about the topic, and even less enthusiastic about Computer Science, but was determined to finish his PhD quickly. Of course we now know that he could not have arrived in a new place at a better or more exciting time. Edinburgh was a world-renowned centre of research in Artificial Intelligence and attracted visiting researchers from all over the world. A major influence was that of Alan Robinson, the inventor of resolution, who was spending a year's sabbatical in Edinburgh. Bob wrote his first research paper[1] on some ideas of Robinson's on semantic trees jointly with another new PhD student, Pat Hayes, now a prominent figure in the field of Artificial Intelligence himself of course.

Bob finished his PhD, on studies in the completeness and efficiency of resolution theorem-proving, in just over two years, and then stayed at Edinburgh on a postdoctoral Fellowship. His two other daughters, Tania and Janina, were born in Edinburgh.

The history of the origins of logic programming have been documented by the main participants elsewhere[2] and I make no attempt to reproduce them here. Bob had been working on the SL form of resolution[3] with Donald Kuehner, a former teacher from the University of Bridgeport whom Bob had persuaded to come to Edinburgh to do his PhD. It was becoming clear that the goal-directed nature of SL-resolution provided a procedural as well as a declarative reading for logic clauses, so giving the basis for a new kind of programming language, and a way of reconciling the debates about procedural and declarative representations that were starting to dominate AI research. In the summer of 1971, and then again in 1972, Bob was invited by Alain Colmerauer to visit him in Marseilles to work on the application of SL-resolution to Colmerauer's work on natural language understanding and question answering. These collaborations focussed initially on the applications of clausal logic and SL resolution to grammars and

[1] Kowalski, R.A., Hayes, P.J. Semantic trees in automatic theorem-proving. In *Machine Intelligence 4* (B. Meltzer, D. Michie, eds), Edinburgh University Press, 1969, pp181–201. Reprinted in *Anthology of Automated Theorem-Proving Papers*, Vol. 2, Springer-Verlag, 1983, pp217–232.

[2] See e.g. Kowalski, R.A. The Early Years of Logic Programming.   *CACM* 31(1):38–43 (1988).

[3] Kowalski, R.A., Kuehner, D. Linear resolution with selection function. *Artificial Intelligence* 2:227–260 (1971). Reprinted in *Anthology of Automated Theorem-Proving Papers*, Vol. 2, Springer-Verlag, 1983, pp542–577.

to parsing, but from them emerged many of the principles for the use of logic as a progamming language, and led Colmerauer to the design and implementation of the logic programming language Prolog in 1972.

The next few years at Edinburgh were spent developing the new logic programming paradigm and laying down its foundations. Edinburgh provided the perfect environment. There were enthusiastic colleagues, notably Maarten van Emden, with whom he developed the fixpoint semantics[4] and ideas for applications, and David Warren, Bob's first doctoral student, who designed and implemented the 'Edinburgh Prolog' compiler. Bob's hugely influential "Predicate Logic as Programming Language" was published in 1974[5]. There were also visiting researchers from institutions around Europe—Maurice Bruynooghe, Keith Clark, Luis Pereira, Peter Szeredi, Sten Åke Tarnlund, among others—with whom Bob formed lasting collaborations and friendships. He travelled extensively, mostly in Europe, spreading the ideas. He completed a long technical manuscript, later to become the core of his book *Logic for Problem Solving*[6]. He also continued to work in automated theorem proving. His connection graph proof procedure was developed during that period.

In January 1975 Bob left Edinburgh to take up a Readership[7] in the Department of Computing and Control at Imperial College, London (now the Department of Computing). The second half of the 1970's was spent finishing his book, producing other milestone papers, such as his famous *Algorithm = Logic + Control*[8], and building up activity in logic programming at Imperial College. Keith Clark, who had been a visitor at Imperial College when I was first there in 1975, had moved from Queen Mary College in London to a permanent position at Imperial by the time I returned in 1979. Chris Hogger had completed his PhD and although still a member of another Department would shortly join the Department of Computing. A number of other colleagues in the Department had been enticed to work in logic programming. The first Logic Programming Workshop, which eventually evolved into the ICLP series of International Conferences on Logic Programming, was held at Imperial College in 1976. I attended that workshop myself, though what I mainly remember about it was the workshop party that was held at Bob and Danusia's home in Wimbledon one evening, and the rolling tobacco that I was induced to try by Danusia's father. All this talk of logic programming made my head spin (though it might have been the tobacco). I didn't even smoke cigarettes. Natural politeness made me accept.

By 1979, the Logic Programming Group at Imperial College consisted of Bob, Keith Clark, Chris Hogger, two or three other members of staff who were starting to work in the area, and six PhD students and research assistants, of which I

---

[4] van Emden, M., Kowalski, R.A. The semantics of predicate logic as a programming language. *JACM* 23(4):733–742 (1976).

[5] *Proceedings of the IFIP Congress, Stockholm*, North Holland, 1974, pp569–574.

[6] North Holland Elsevier, 1979.

[7] A Readership in the UK is a senior academic position, somewhat below the rank of (Full) Professor, and traditionally with an emphasis on research rather than teaching.

[8] *CACM* 22(7):424–436 (1979).

was one. Logic programming, in various guises, was part of the curriculum of the undergraduate and MSc courses. There was also an active group in functional programming with whom we had close contacts and regular joint seminars. There was a constant stream of visitors and speakers. My memory of Bob and Danusia's home in Wimbledon will be that there always seemed to be someone staying there—a brother from the USA, a relative from Poland, a former colleague from Edinburgh, a logic programmer passing through. It was not always easy to tell the difference, except that the brother from the USA and the relative from Poland would usually be sanding down floors or painting the kitchen door. Bob was appointed Professor of Computational Logic at Imperial College in 1982.

I realise that I am starting now to conflate Bob's biography with the fortunes of the Logic Programming Group at Imperial College, but for much of the 1980s and 1990s the two are so inextricably linked that it is impossible to disentangle them.

The 1980s saw a massive expansion of the Logic Programming Group, and of Bob's personal standing and celebrity in Computer Science. The group was already growing with the acquisition of a number of new projects and grants when in 1981 came the announcement by MITI in Japan of the Fifth Generation Computer Project. The project aimed to leapfrog a generation of computer system development in 10 years, to a position of dominance over IBM, and to a new era of advanced knowledge processing applications. Logic programming—to widespread surprise—was identified as the core technology. Various governments, including the UK, were invited to participate. Since we at Imperial College were at that time the largest and most active centre of research in logic programming, we expected that we would be playing a substantial role in the Fifth Generation Project, especially if the UK government decided to accept the invitation to participate.

Bob, who was already a very well-known figure in computer science, became something of a celebrity. At the ICLP conference in Marseilles in 1982 I was chatting to him over breakfast when suddenly a camera was thrust between us and he was asked to pose for photographs. He was photographed at lunchtime, and in the afternoon breaks when we all walked down to swim in the sea, his head was photographed again as it bobbed up and down in the Mediterranean swell.

I hesitate to dwell too long on the Fifth Generation Project and the associated politics of the UK's response since much of the account would be second hand. However, these matters dominated the 1980s in one way or another, and accounted for much of Bob's time and energy for nearly a decade. Bob had been working very hard at putting a case to the Science Research Council for what it called a Specially Promoted Programme (SPP) in logic programming. The argument was not just that logic programming was the enabling technology for new AI and 'knowledge processing' applications, but that it provided a unifying foundation for developments in AI, in programming languages, in formal methods for software engineering, and in parallel computing. The case for the SPP went through several iterations but was eventually swallowed up in the UK's general response to the Fifth Generation Project.

Not everyone in the UK was as enthusiastic about the role of logic programming as the Japanese. The UK government's reaction to the Fifth Generation Project was to set up a committee, chaired by John Alvey, to recommend the best course of action. That committee was advised by another layer of committees drawn from academia and industry. Naturally, most of these advisers saw it as an opportunity to push the importance of their own area of computing. One could hardly have expected anything else. The result was the kind of global behaviour that often emerges from interactions of agents who are seeking to maximize their own local goals. 'Fifth Generation' meant different things to different people. Nearly everyone seemed to have an opinion about what it meant, what key problems it faced, and the best way to address them. Very few seemed actually to have read the published Fifth Generation Project proposals, and indeed regarded them as irrelevant. In his short autobiographical piece, Bob summarises the outcome in these words: "In the end, by the time the Alvey Committee produced its recommendations, virtually every area of Computing and related Electronics was singled out for special promotion."

The UK declined the Japanese invitation to participate in the Fifth Generation Project and set up the Alvey Programme instead. As Bob puts it: "after much more argumentation and discussion, logic programming was identified, along with all the other areas, as worthy of special promotion."

And so, along with many other groups in computing and information technology in the UK, the Logic Programming Group at Imperial College received a large injection of funding under the Alvey Programme—sometimes at the price of forced collaborations that we would not have chosen ourselves—and under the ESPRIT programme of research from the European Commission that followed shortly after. In the mid-1980s the Logic Programming Group had grown to about 50 persons including faculty members, research assistants, PhD students, and support staff. Bob calculates there were 13 separate three-year research grants running at one time, which is my estimate too.

At the time I did not think so much about it, but looking back I stand in awe at the administrative effort that all this required. At the same time, there were new MSc courses being set up in the Department. There were committees, national and international. There were constant demands on Bob's time for invited talks, offers of collaborations, serious and otherwise, letters and articles to respond to (serious and otherwise). There were interviews for newspaper articles. Once, standing in for Bob when he was away, I was interviewed for an article on logic programming and the Fifth Generation for *Vogue* magazine. I declined to unbutton my shirt for the photograph but pouted in the required manner. The industrialist Clive Sinclair was a regular visitor—a version of Frank McCabe's microProlog was eventually released for the Sinclair Spectrum.

There were also difficulties to contend with at the Departmental level. The expansion of the Logic Programming Group, and of some of the other groups in the Department under Alvey and ESPRIT, were causing resentment and some tension. It was perhaps most acute for the Logic Programming Group because we were receiving offers and opportunities to establish ourselves as an independent entity within the Department, and this was not universally regarded as a healthy development. These matters intruded greatly on Bob's time and energy and caused him much personal stress.

I look through Bob's CV and I am astonished that he found time for any research at all during this period. Yet we had regular technical meetings of various sub-groups one or two times a week. Bob participated actively in projects developing computational logic as a language for school children, on representing laws and regulations, on applications in temporal reasoning, on meta-level reasoning, on abduction, on integrity constraints in databases. How he managed to fit all this in with his other commitments remains a mystery to me (though that will not stop me speculating on it later in this article).

Funding agencies, perhaps only in Europe, like to refer to something called 'critical mass'. Much is made of this, and of its importance when building research activity. Whole research strategies and funding programmes are designed with the goal of creating it. I am not sure where the concept came from, but if it does really exist, I think it must be much, much smaller than is generally assumed. In the case of the Logic Programming Group at Imperial we attained critical mass very quickly. Fission followed shortly after. First we lost contact with the functional programming group—no more time for joint seminars, no more time for conversations in the common room or in corridors. Then the Logic Programming Group divided (harmoniously) into two parts: the Parlog group, working on concurrent Prologs, and the rest, working on everything else. Then the second group split again, this time along no obvious technical boundaries.

In the 1990s, the size of the Logic Programming Group began to dwindle as members of the group moved away to take up positions elsewhere and logic programming became less fashionable. We still had a very sizeable presence in the Department, though it is difficult to count exactly because the boundaries had become very blurred. Notable acquisitions included Dov Gabbay who had arrived in 1983 as a Visiting Fellow and then eventually became a Professor in the Department, and Barry Richards who had moved from the Centre for Cognitive Science at Edinburgh to take up another Professorship. Tensions in the Department abated, or rather, shifted to a different battleground.

¿From 1989 to 1991 Bob was co-ordinator of the Compulog project, a large collaborative project funded by the European Commission bringing together the main academic groups working in logic programming in Europe. The project was addressing the topics in computational logic closest to Bob's heart. When asked, and sometimes when not asked, I used to say that the technical objectives of the Compulog project were to develop the second half of Bob's *Logic for Problem Solving*. This was a joke (and an exaggeration) but it is true that the Compulog project allowed Bob to extricate himself from Departmental politics and focus his energies on his favourite research topics. The Compulog project funded a replacement for his teaching duties in the Department. A similar arrangement in a project on abductive logic programming funded by Fujitsu continued to provide an academic replacement for another three years. By the time Bob resumed full duties in the Department, in 1994 or so, his rehabilitation, as he puts it, was complete.

In March 1997 Bob was persuaded to take on the role of Head of the Department of Computing at Imperial College. The Head of Department is essentially a managerial and administrative position, usually for a fixed term, which the Head can organise according to his or her own tastes. It has wide-ranging power and authority but also huge responsibilities for the running of virtually every element of the Department. We were at the time in a period of unrest following the resignation of the previous Head. Bob had gone to speak to the Rector about how the Headship could be resolved, and came back from that meeting finding that he had agreed to take on the job himself. I believe I was the first person he spoke to on his return to the Department. I am not sure which of us was more surprised at the news. The agreement was that Bob's was to be an interim appointment, for three years or so. The Rector's calculation was that Bob's seniority and academic reputation would command authority and respect within the Department. This was a good idea. Bob's calculation was that the time taken away from research for administration and management would be compensated by a reduction in time spent teaching. This was a very good idea in theory. He also thought that it might afford a chance to develop his technical interests, in that it provided an opportunity to test out how ideas from computational logic could serve as a tool in organising the affairs of the Department and in the resolution of conflicts and disputes. This was not such a good idea, even in theory, in my opinion.

Bob threw himself into his new role with typical energy and vigour. The atmosphere in the Department improved considerably. But the day-to-day running of the Department, and a series of obstacles to getting things organised as he wanted, were leaving Bob increasingly frustrated. The theory that time spent on administration and management could still leave time for research was being refuted every day. Eventually, Bob asked to step down as Head of Department after two years not three, and asked to take early retirement. From 1st September 1999 he has been a Senior Research Fellow in the Department of Computing and Emeritus Professor. He has an office in the Department and continues to participate in research projects but has no other duties or responsibilities imposed upon him beyond those he chooses to take on voluntarily. To my eyes, he has attained a kind of blissful state of existence which even his Jesuit teachers might have difficulty claiming could exist.

At some time in the 1980s Bob acquired a small cottage near Petworth in Sussex, which lies in the countryside roughly half-way between London and the South Coast of England. It was a base for weekend breaks and walks in the South Downs. There are several logic programmers around the world for whom that cottage was home during visits spent at Imperial College. Over the years the cottage in Petworth has been extended and developed. Since Bob's retirement, it has been extended again and has now become Bob and Danusia's main residence.

Between taking up invitations for extended visits to research institutes abroad Bob spends his time in Petworth with occasional visits to the Department. He is working on a new book.

Research Themes

Bob's early work was in automated theorem proving, where he made contributions to the technology of resolution theorem proving. His connection graph proof procedure[9] provided a general and very efficient framework for reasoning with (full) clausal form theories. By picking links in the graph in different ways, a wide range of reasoning strategies could be accommodated, for non-Horn as well as Horn clause reasoning. These are demonstrated in *Logic for Problem Solving*.

However, it is the special case of SL-resolution which came to dominate later, of course, and which led to the logic programming model of computation. It should be remembered that the extended case for logic programming as a new foundation for computing was developed not by appeal to novel and exotic applications in knowledge processing but by showing carefully how cleanly and elegantly it dealt with standard computing problems and algorithms. The beauty of Bob's *Algorithm = Logic + Control* lies in the detailed exposition of how both *Logic* and *Control* components can be varied to generate families of algorithms.

However, it has always been Bob's contention—passion—that computational forms of logic have much wider application than to the solution of mere computing problems. The single strongest and most sustained driving force in his research has been the goal of developing appropriate forms of logic to make it an effective tool for improving human affairs and communication, and to present these forms in a way that makes them accessible to the widest possible group. These aims reflect his lifelong interests in problem solving and communication, in epistemology and in the philosophy of science. These elements were already evident in the second part of *Logic for Problem Solving* which addresses knowledge representation, problem solving strategies, temporal reasoning and planning, knowledge assimilation and belief revision. His working hypothesis is that the features which make special forms of logic suitable for computational purposes are also the features that will be most natural and effective for use in human problem solving and communication. Application and testing and refinement of this hypothesis is the recurrent theme in his research.

One clear example of these general aims is the sustained project Bob conducted on developing simplified forms of logic and logic programming for school children[10]. In 1978 Bob started a course of logic lessons for 12 year old chil-

[9] Kowalski, R.A. A proof procedure using connection graphs. *JACM* 23(4):733–742 (1976).

[10] Kowalski, R.A. Logic as a Computer Language for Children. In *Proc. European Conference on Artificial Intelligence*, Orsay, France, July 1982. Reprinted in *New Horizons in Educational Computing* (M. Yazdani, ed), Ellis Horwood Ltd, Chichester, 1984, pp121–144. Reprinted in *Progress in Artificial Intelligence* (L. Steels, J.A. Campbell, eds), Ellis Horwood Ltd, Chichester.

dren at his daughters' school. Logic problems were formulated and then solved using Prolog over a telephone connection to a computer at Imperial College. The project was subsequently maintained for about 5 years from 1980 by grants from the Science Research Council and then the Nuffield Foundation and Sinclair Research. The first phase supported Frank McCabe's developments of his microProlog system for micro-processors and the associated programming and query environment ('SIMPLE'). Richard Ennals conducted the lessons and prepared teaching materials for pupils and teachers. If I recall rightly, there were two groups of children, 8 year olds and 12 year olds, and a smaller group of 17–18 year olds. The aim was not just to teach logic as a programming language, but rather to engage the children in developing its use as a representational and reasoning tool in subjects across the whole curriculum. Richard Ennals's own specialty, for example, was History. I am not in a position to comment on the long term impact of the school lessons on the children. It would be interesting to track them down and ask them now what they thought of those lessons. What is clear is that the schools project was instrumental in driving the developments of microProlog and its associated software environments, and in practical knowledge representation techniques that were subsequently used in a variety of other applications.

One such group of applications was in the representation of laws and regulations. I find myself about to write much more about this topic than the others, but this is because it provides the clearest example of Bob's ideas about the applications of logic programming to the world outside computing, and the clearest example of how his stance has been misinterpreted by some of his critics.

In 1979 Bob was invited to participate in a workshop on Computers and Law held in Swansea, in Wales. Although he could not attend, that invitation led to a number of very valuable contacts in the AI and Law community. It soon became clear to us that logic programming provided a general solution to some problems of representation that were being attacked by low-level programming languages or special-purpose formalisms. Our argument was that logic programming provided a better foundation for such developments. We were able to show, for example, how large and complex bodies of definitional law ('qualification norms') can be represented and executed as logic programs. Our representation of the British Nationality Act 1981 is the best known and most commonly cited example[11]. It was originally suggested by Chris Moss, a member of our group, who had been given a draft copy of the Bill while it was still at an early stage of discussion by Parliament. The Bill was very controversial at the time. It proposed to introduce four new categories of British citizenship to replace the existing definition completely, and had been accused by several political groups of being racist in that it disadvantaged certain groups of potential citizens but not others. One of these pressure groups had suggested to us that a formal representation might help to bring this out. We knew that it could not, since whether the Act

---

[11] Sergot, M.J., Sadri, F., Kowalski, R.A., Kriwaczek, F.R., Hammond, P., Cory, T. The British Nationality Act as a Logic Program. *CACM* 29(5):370–386 (1986).

was racist or not depended on background information about the various categories of persons affected, and that information was not part of the legislation itself. We did subsequently explore, in a different project, whether given the necessary background information, we could predict some of the socio-economic consequences of introducing new legislation, but that was later and was never attempted for the British Nationality Act. However, the British Nationality Act was very suitable for other reasons. It was almost entirely definitional, that is to say, its main purpose was to set out definitions of new legal categories and relationships, which made it amenable to representation as a logic program, yet it was complicated and big so one could see what would be gained from translating it into an executable form. We had already constructed a small demonstration system dealing with the core definitions from Chris Moss's copy of the draft Bill. Frank McCabe, as I recall, was particularly keen that we should continue to develop a larger system dealing with the whole Act to demonstrate that a sizeable application could be implemented using these techniques and his microProlog system. Fariba Sadri, who was about to start a PhD in our group, was employed on funds left over from some other grant to extend the prototype to a more complete representation over two or three months in the summer before she started her PhD. The whole system, including the APES software used to execute the representation, ran on a small micro-computer with only 64K of memory. I used to say that for us at Imperial College, Fifth Generation computing meant any computer with more than 64K of memory.

The work on the British Nationality Act was generally well received and well regarded by the research community in Artificial Intelligence and Law, which shared the pre-suppositions and starting assumptions, and by the lawyers and government agencies with whom we produced various other applications. It did attract negative publicity as well. In the climate of Alvey and the Fifth Generation there was even an article in *The Guardian* national newspaper about it. It repeated a common criticism, that by attempting to represent legal rules as executable logic clauses we were, deliberately or out of ignorance, oversimplifying and mistakenly thinking we could reduce legal decision making to the mechanical application of fixed rules. We were accused of demonstrating a complete ignorance of legal theory and jurisprudence, and a fundamental misunderstanding of the nature of legal reasoning and the process of law. We thought that in describing the work we had identified the background assumptions, and also the limitations of what we had described, but these qualifications had obviously not registered with some critics. That was tiresome enough, but the article went on—to accuse us of being apologists for the racist policies of a right-wing government, and of grabbing government funding for these activities, out of greed or naïvety or both. It even raised the spectre of computers at Heathrow Airport that would decide who would be admitted into the UK and who would not. Even allowing for journalistic licence, these claims were so outrageous (and so completely wrong on every point of fact) that we felt obliged to write a letter of complaint to *The Guardian* in our own defence. I say 'we' though I am not sure now whether Bob wrote on his own or whether it was a joint reply. Perhaps we sent more than one letter. A short flurry of further correspondence ensued.

Bob has used the representation of legislation and regulations as a rich source of motivating examples for developments in the treatment of general rules and exceptions in logic programs[12], and later in his work on the theory of argumentation[13]. He has also been enthusiastic about using examples from legislation to support his views about the value of logic in clarifying and communicating statements of rules in natural language, whether these rules are intended for execution in a computer program or not[14]. It is presumably these general views that have irritated his critics.

For my own part, I learned long ago to avoid making reference to 'AI and law' or to 'logic and law' when asked in casual conversations, at parties and so on, what I am working on. A mention of 'Artificial Intelligence' is often bad enough, but 'Artificial Intelligence and Law' seems to be one of those topics on which everybody has an opinion. Once my car was hit by a Frenchman who drove his car backwards the wrong way out of a one-way street in the area around Imperial College and while we were waiting to sort out the insurance details, he lectured me for half an hour on the futility of AI applied to law. Apparently, I was seriously underestimating the problems. I confess that on that occasion, and others, I have resorted to sarcasm. "Oh no! Ten/fifteen/twenty years I have worked in this area. The law is not just black-and-white? I never noticed. You have opened my eyes. I see now that I have been wasting my time. You are right. I will abandon it." Why any intelligent person should automatically assume that another intelligent person has never noticed that law is not 'black-and-white' and that justice is not dispensed by the mechanical application of fixed rules is the really intriguing question.

It is a facet of Bob's character that he is prepared to take a dose of his own medicine. So for example, at the time he was engaged in Alvey and other grant-awarding committees in the 1980s, he had the idea that the decision making could be improved and made more consistent by formulating clear rules about what projects would or would not qualify for funding. He even formulated a draft set of such rules. He tried essentially the same idea when Head of Department for rationalising teaching and resource allocations. But it is a fundamental misunderstanding of Bob's position to think that such rules are intended to be applied blindly and mechanically. The idea is quite different. One applies the rules to a particular case and examines the conclusion. If the conclusion is unacceptable,

---

[12] Kowalski, R.A., Sadri, F. Logic programming with exceptions. In *Proc. 7th International Conference on Logic Programming* (D.H.D. Warren, P. Szeredi, eds). MIT Press, 1990, pp598–613. Also in *New Generation Computing* 9(3–4):387–400 (1991)

[13] Kowalski, R.A., Toni, F. Abstract argumentation. *Journal of Artificial Intelligence and Law* 4:275–296 (1996). Also in *Logical Models of Legal Argumentation* (H. Prakken, G. Sartor, eds). Kluwer Academic Publishers, 1997

[14] Kowalski, R.A. English as a logic programming language. *New Generation Computing* 8(2):91–93 (1990).

Kowalski, R.A. Legislation as logic programs. In *Logic Programming in Action* (G. Comyn, N.E. Fuchs, M.J. Ratcliffe, eds). Springer-Verlag, 1992, pp203–230.

or if someone wishes to disagree with the conclusion, the burden is to argue why the rules should not apply in this case. If someone wishes to argue that one or other of the conditions should be ignored or altered, the burden is on them to argue why it should be so altered in this case. The rules serve as a device for structuring the discussion. They are intended to expose the arguments and open up the decisions to scrutiny. There is more to it than that—one might examine the reasons why such a reasonable suggestion does not usually work in practice or why it almost always meets with strong resistance—but it is not my purpose here to give a complete account. I just wanted to give some indication of why Bob's views on 'clear rules' are not nearly as unsophisticated as some critics have assumed.

A strand of research that attracted less criticism was our joint work on the event calculus[15], an approach to representing the effects of action and change in a logic programming framework. It is another example of something that is intended to straddle knowledge representation in AI and problems in mainstream computing, such as temporal databases and database updates. The name was coined (by Bob) to draw attention to the contrast with the conception of action and change employed in the situation calculus of McCarthy and Hayes. Instead of thinking primarily in terms of situations—states of the world at which nothing changes—and actions as transitions between situations, we wanted to think first and foremost about the occurrences of actions—events—and the periods of time that they initiate and terminate; situations during which nothing changes are incidental and there is usually nothing interesting to say about them. Although not stressed in more recent presentations of the event calculus, most of the effort went into deriving an effective computational framework from a general account of events and periods of time and their properties. As in much of his other work, Bob was particularly keen that the presentation should be made as generally accessible as possible. I remember more than one discussion about how abstract and technical the presentation should be. The event calculus was generally well received—at least there were no articles in *The Guardian* about it. Variations, applications, and large scale implementations were subsequently developed in a number of other projects, including as a main strand of a European Community ESPRIT project on temporal and qualitative reasoning. Bob's main applied work in that project was an application to air traffic flow management.

The formal treatment of action and change, and the associated problems of default reasoning and exception handling, have been a constant throughout Bob's research career. These questions are as prominent in his latest research on multi-agent systems as they were in his early work on knowledge representation. I can still cite 'Chapter 6' of *Logic for Problem Solving* without having to look at the Table of Contents. These are issues that are at the heart of knowledge representation. Opinions about their relative merits will vary, but together

---

[15] Kowalski, R.A., Sergot, M.J. A logic-based calculus of events. *New Generation Computing* 4(1):67–95 (1986). Reprinted in *Knowledge Base Management Systems* (C. Thanos, J.W. Schmidt, eds). Springer-Verlag, pp23–51.

with the situation calculus (in its many various forms), the event calculus (in its many various forms) continues to be a major driving force for foundational developments in knowledge representation.

In 1981 Bob visited Syracuse University for a short, one academic term, sabbatical. Whilst there he collaborated with Ken Bowen on amalgamating object-level and meta-level logic programming. Their joint paper[16] was frequently cited in later years in the context of 'meta-level programming' and 'meta-level interpreters' though it was really about something quite different. The goal was to combine the two levels in such a way that they could interact, so yielding a very general and very expressive representational and reasoning framework. The main technical problem was to achieve this interaction without introducing inconsistencies. The Bowen-Kowalski paper laid out the basic moves. Bob continued the investigations with a PhD student, Kave Eshghi, and worked at the applications, to default and epistemic reasoning in particular, until about the mid-1990s. Meta-level inference was a strand of the Compulog project—the Goedel language of John Lloyd and colleagues is a direct descendant—and was a main theme of Bob's MSc course on knowledge representation in the 1990s. With Kave Eshghi Bob also investigated alternative accounts of negation by failure[17], combining ideas from the amalgamated object-level/meta-level work and from abductive reasoning.

Abductive logic programming became increasingly important in Bob's research in the 1990s. It was embraced partly to support reasoning from effect to possible causes, but also because the abductive proof procedures, when combined with a treatment of integrity constraints, provided a computational system that could overcome limitations of standard logic programming systems. I have noticed over the years that Bob has a strong distaste for classical disjunctive reasoning. It may be that an attraction of abductive logic programming is that it provides an alternative way of dealing with disjunctive reasoning. Collaborations with Francesca Toni and Tony Kakas developed an abstract account of the abductive framework[18], which in turn made connections to results emerging in the theory of argumentation. The key idea here is that an argument, to be admissible, must be able to defend itself against attack from other arguments and itself. Varying the details yields argumentation frameworks with different technical properties. Work with Francesca Toni, Phan Minh Dung, and Andrei Bondarenko produced an argumentation-theoretic account of negation as failure,

---

[16] Bowen, K., Kowalski, R.A. Amalgamating language and meta-language in logic programming. In *Logic Programming* (K.L. Clark, S-Å. Tarnlund, eds). Academic Press, 1982, pp153–172.

[17] Eshghi, K., Kowalski, R.A. Abduction compared with negation by failure. In *Proc. 6th International Conference on Logic Programming* (G. Levi, M. Martelli, eds). MIT Press, 1989, pp234–254.

[18] Kakas, T., Kowalski, R.A., Toni, F. Abductive logic programming. *Journal of Logic and Computation* 2(6):719–770 (1992).

and then more generally, an abstract argumentation framework which includes many of the schemes for default reasoning as special cases[19].

In recent years Bob's interests have turned to multi-agent systems. Here the aim has been to combine pro-active, rational problem solving with the reactive behaviour of an agent situated in a changing environment through which it also interacts with other agents. This brings together several of the recurring themes of Bob's research: goal-directed problem solving, the treatment of actions and procedures, belief revision and the assimilation of new facts, and a search for a way of reconciling and integrating two apparently conflicting models of computation. With Fariba Sadri, Bob has been developing a general account which combines a logic programming model of execution with a condition-action execution cycle[20]. His longer term plans are to investigate systematic methods for conflict resolution in multi-agent systems.

Some Personal Traits

This portrait would not be complete without some glimpse of Bob's personal characteristics. I make no attempt to identify them all, but three in particular stand out for me. First, there is his dogged determination and self-discipline, and the passion with which he embraces scientific concepts and theories. Second there is his tolerance and sense of fair play, which is also connected to the way he has coped with his celebrity. And third there is the question of his sense of humour.

Bob is the most determined and self-disciplined person I have worked with. He will say, no doubt, that he is not self-disciplined because he has temptations and weaknesses. That is irrelevant. When I looked through his CV in preparation of this article, the list of invited talks and travels alone seemed enough for a full-time occupation. I think what impresses me most in this regard is his discipline in dealing with tedious and time-consuming chores which others might put off or simply fail to discharge conscientiously. Bob seems able to dispatch them all with the minimum of fuss.

I have written papers and grant proposals with many different co-authors and have seen other groups in action. All of them seem to experience the same last-minute frenzy as the deadline approaches (and as the editors of this volume would say, passes and recedes into the distance). Once when in the grip of three

---

[19] Bondarenko, A., Dung, P.M., Kowalski, R.A., Toni, F. An abstract argumentation-theoretic approach to default reasoning. *Journal of Artificial Intelligence* 93(1–2):63–101 (1997).

[20] Kowalski, R.A., Sadri, F. Towards a unified agent architecture that combines rationality with reactivity. *Proc. International Workshop on Logic in Databases*, San Miniato, Italy. Springer-Verlag LNCS 1154, 1996, pp131–150.

Kowalski, R.A., Sadri, F. From logic programming to multi-agent systems. *Annals of Mathematics and Artificial Intelligence* 25:391–419 (1999).

converging deadlines, I was moaning to Bob about the strain and complaining that everyone seemed to pick the same times for deadlines. Bob's reaction was to ask why I did not set myself my own deadline one week before each piece was due and thereby avoid the last-minute stresses. Parkinson's law does not apply to Bob.

Bob recounts that when he was a student at the University of Chicago, he obtained A grades in all his subjects, except for English writing skills in which he did badly. Many of us would have shrugged our shoulders and dismissed it—"I wasn't really trying/taking it seriously", "I am no good at it". Bob's response was to set about an analysis of what had gone wrong, to diagnose the sources of the problem and to devise methods for overcoming them. This was no easy fix but something that he worked at over several years, and indeed continues to think about still from time to time. When he was Head of Department, for example, he set up a voluntary writing class for the PhD students. I do not know what he told them exactly, but it must have been interesting, for eighteen months after his retirement we still see PhD students searching plaintively for the writing class. At the annual meeting at which we ask the PhD students how their lives could be improved, the most common request was for a resumption of the writing classes by Professor Kowalski.

This same determination and single-mindedness is evident also throughout Bob's technical work. His ability to take up an idea and then to apply it and refine it and pursue it relentlessly is a major strength. Which is not to say that he is always right, or refuses to change his views as a matter of principle. As in the case of writing skills, when ideas do not get the same A grades as others, they are subjected to thorough scrutiny and diagnosis and careful correction.

The passion and conviction with which Bob expounds his technical position can be misinterpreted. In invited talks especially, he will sometimes deliberately adopt an extreme point of view in order to provoke debate or to rehearse the arguments that can be put forward for it. This has apparently led some to assume that his views must be based on some kind of irrational emotional attachment, and that with it must come a refusal to acknowledge the worth of alternative points of view. Nothing could be further from the truth.

Bob is a widely recognised figure in computer science. His name appears, deservedly, in most summaries of accomplishments and trends in computer science, and in logic. This is why he receives requests from students asking for biographical details they need for their project assignments.

The other side of celebrity, however, is that it attracts criticism and caricature. For example, one article, in a 1987 volume of collected papers on the sociology of research in AI and what it called the 'AI establishment', went so far as to compare Bob with a now obscure 16th century figure, Petrus Ramus[21].

---

[21] Philip Leith. Involvement, Detachment and Programming: The Belief in Prolog. In *The Question of Artificial Intelligence*, (Brian Bloomfield, ed), Croom Helm, London 1987.

Ramus, according to the article, devised distorted and simplified forms of logic or 'method' which he and his followers vigorously promoted for use across all scholarly disciplines. The Ramist method, now all but forgotten (except perhaps in the sociology of science where references to it seem to be quite common), had a very widespread influence for a considerable time across the post-medieval world. It is generally regarded as a curiosity and something of an aberration in the history of logic and rhetoric, which I suppose is the point of the caricature. So in that article parallels are seen between Bob and the figure of Ramus himself, in the 'close technical analogy with the methods of Ramus and Kowalski', in their widespread influences, particularly over 'impatient and not too profound thinkers', and in the lack of scientific detachment in the disciples of Ramus on the one hand and the esoteric circle of Kowalski's followers on the other hand. The Logic Programming Group at Imperial College is described in these terms:

> Within the academic software teaching and research group it seems—to the outsider—that the entire department is involved in logic programming. Some are involved in the theoretical issues (Clark and Hogger, for example) and some are involved in more practical issues (Ennals, Sergot and Hammond). Kowalski, to some extent, appears to stand above the details of logic programming, leaving the particulars to the group. His role is that of advocate for logic programming, a role which he plays out through academic and commercial contacts and consultancies and through involvement in the provision of research funds as a member of an Alvey advisory committee. It would seem to be difficult for any member of that group to move away from such a logic programming hegemony, for a scientific establishment based upon that logic programming technique must be expected to control its members.

There is nothing in the picture painted here that I recognise. I have no idea where the author got the idea of a hegemony, or what made him think that members were subject to some kind of control. The other facts quoted with such authority are wrong too. Why did the author not bother to check them? The general nature of the remarks in that article, and the repeated references to funding agencies and Bob's influence over the distribution of research funds, leads me to think that the objectives of the article were not entirely scientific.

It is ironic that amongst his most vehement critics are persons whom Bob has defended and supported, usually without their knowledge. And in contrast to the picture painted above, Bob is no seeker of self-publicity. He is very sensitive that collaborators and co-authors should receive their share of recognition for joint work. When the Association for Logic Programming was formed in 1986 it was typical that Bob preferred to take the role of Secretary rather than that of President.

Indeed, if I had any criticism of Bob in this regard, it would be that his sense of fair play can be too acute, and has been taken advantage of. When he was Head of Department, for example, he would never, as a matter of principle, push through by force what he could not obtain by reasoned argument. On occasion, when forming committees or taking advice, he deliberately under-represented his own position and strengthened the representation of opposing views in an effort to give the fairest possible hearing to all. Unfortunately, not everyone is as scrupulous.

I turn finally to the question of Bob's sense of humour. Some of my colleagues will say that making remarks about this is like commenting on the appearance of the current King of France. That is an over-simplification. Bob enjoys jokes very much, but never tells them. He prefers something that might be called the meta-joke.

For example, I remember when Bob was asked to be the Banquet Speaker at the Conference on Automated Deduction (CADE) in Oxford in 1986. Bob had agreed but was far from happy about it. He dislikes this kind of speaking and finds it very awkward. I am not sure why. When he was Head of Department he was often called upon to make little speeches and introductions, and always found a way of doing them with elegance and wit. For the CADE speech Bob asked my advice, or rather, he wanted suggestions for jokes he could include in his speech, ideally but not necessarily something connected with deduction or reasoning. "Don't worry about it", I said. "It's like a wedding. Everyone wants to be amused. Most of them will be half-drunk. Whatever you say they will laugh. The contents don't matter." I suggested a couple of jokes he could use, with the best reserved for the opening and the end. "You also need a packer", I said. "Something to keep things going in the middle. It doesn't have to be very funny. At that point they will all be laughing anyway, and you just need something to keep things moving along. By the time they realise it isn't funny, you will be into your closing part and they won't notice." Bob looked dubious. "Trust me", I said.

I remembered a (not very funny) joke Dov Gabbay had told me about a young man who wants to become the student of a famous rabbinical scholar, an expert in the interpretation of Talmudic texts. The young man goes along and asks if he may be allowed to study at the Master's feet. "Perhaps", says the Master, "but first you must pass a test." The student agrees. "Two men climb down a chimney", says the Master. "One comes out dirty, the other comes out clean. Which one washes?" "That's easy", says the student. "The dirty one." "No", says the Master. "The clean one. For consider: the dirty one will look at the clean one and will think 'If he is clean, I must be clean.' While the clean one will look at the dirty one and will think 'If he is dirty, I must dirty.' So the clean one washes." "Give me another chance", says the student. "Very well", says the Master. "Two men climb down a chimney. One comes out dirty, the other comes out clean. Which one washes?" "I know this", says the student. "It is the clean one who washes." "No", says the Master. "It is the dirty one who washes. For consider: the clean one will look at himself and see that he is clean. While the dirty one will look at himself and see that he is dirty. So the dirty one will wash." "Oh no!" says the student. "But please, give me one more chance." "Very well", says the Master. "Two men climb down a chimney. One comes out dirty, the other comes out clean. Which one washes?" "Ah, I think I have it now", says the student. "The dirty one washes." "No, no", says the Master. "I don't think you are cut out for this line of work. How can two men climb down the same chimney, and one come out dirty, the other come out clean?" This is not much of joke, though it was funny when Dov told it, and it is about reasoning, of a sort. Bob was not convinced. "Trust me", I said. "It is a good packer. It will keep them laughing until you get on to the better stuff. Perhaps you can even work in some remark about legal reasoning, or something like that."

The following Monday Bob was back in the office. "How did your Banquet speech go?" I asked. "Disaster!" said Bob. "No-one laughed. Especially not at that joke about the student and the chimney." I was surprised. "It isn't much of a joke, I admit. But it should have been enough to keep them happy for a while." "Of course", said Bob, "I did simplify it a bit. It seemed to me that it contained a lot of redundancy, so I cut it down." According to Bob, he eliminated the redundancy and moved straight to the line "How can two men climb down the same chimney and one come out dirty, the other come out clean?"

I have told this story to many people who know Bob well. They chortle with delight when I get to the part "Of course, I simplified it a bit. There was a lot of redundancy." This is exactly what Bob would say, which is why I have included it in this piece. But what is the real joke here? Fifteen years after that speech, I do not know what Bob said at that banquet in Oxford. I know he was teasing me with the reference to redundancy, but I do not know whether he made the same remark in his speech, or whether he mentioned the student and the chimney at all. It is a meta-joke, at my expense.

Conclusion

As part of my subtle interrogations for this article, I asked Bob if he could summarise the various phases of his professional career by picking out an event or anecdote that he would associate with each period of time. "What springs to mind when I mention, say, Edinburgh in the 1970s?", I asked. Bob's answers were as follows: Edinburgh in the 1970s—foundations of logic programming; Imperial College in the 1970s—building up the group and finishing the book; 1980s—the Fifth Generation Project and the Alvey Programme; 1990s—realisation that the early promise of logic programming was not going to be fulfilled, disappointment, and retrenchment (my word); the first years of the 21st century—waiting.

Now I could not let this pass without comment. I understand what Bob means when he says 'disappointment'. He is referring to the prospects of logic programming as the unifying foundation for all of computing, and to the influence of computational logic on the world outside computing. But honestly I cannot see anything to be disappointed about.

In recent years Bob has given talks with titles along the lines of "Logic programming: Where did it all go wrong?" or "Why was logic programming a failure?". Of course I know that he is being deliberately provocative when choosing such titles and that the point of the talk is usually to identify the technical reasons why logic programming as originally conceived does not measure up to all requirements now. Perhaps I caught him on a bad day, but on the occasion I heard him deliver this talk I believe I detected a genuine tone of disappointment. The title, on that occasion at least, was not entirely ironic.

I confess that my reaction was to laugh (inwardly, of course). All I could think of was the image of George Best, a very famous ex-footballer ('soccer player') in the UK, and the story he tells about himself on TV chat shows and the like. I hope English readers will forgive me for digging up such a tired old chestnut. I know it is corny but honestly it was the vision that flashed before my eyes at this talk of disappointment. George Best played in the 1960s and early 1970s. He is still internationally regarded as one of the two or three best footballers of all time. His career ended tragically early (tragically for us, not necessarily for him) in alcohol, and nightclubs, and even a short prison sentence. He finished playing when he should have been approaching his peak.

George Best tells the following story about himself. Some years after he had finished playing he was staying at a casino somewhere, in Las Vegas I think, though the details do not matter. He was at that time accompanied by a Miss World, or a former Miss World, or at least a Miss World finalist. I cannot remember. And one evening at this casino he won a considerable sum of money, of the order of $20,000. Again the details do not matter. Back at his hotel suite, while the former Miss World went into the adjoining bathroom, Best spread his winnings, all $20,000 of it, over the bed and phoned room service for champagne. The champagne was delivered by an old Irish waiter who of course recognised George Best immediately. According to Best's story, the waiter looked around the bedroom—the vintage champagne in the ice bucket, the former Miss World emerging from the bathroom, the cash spread all over the bed—and shook his head sadly. "Mr Best," he said, "where did it all go wrong?"

It seems to me that a field which annually has at least one, sometimes two, international scientific conferences devoted to it is not a moribund field. And this is not to count the journals, and the numerous series of workshops and meetings (CLP, LOPSTR, ILP, LPNMR, among others) devoted to specific aspects of logic programming and its applications. While logic programming may not have come to be the foundation for all of computing, that is partly because the conception of computing itself has changed. It is the cornerstone of many important sub-areas of computing, and its influences continue to be felt across all of computer science and AI.

I look at the chapters of this volume spread proverbially across the bed. I think of the many others who would have jumped at the chance to contribute a chapter to this volume. They are the former Miss Worlds peeking around the bathroom door, so to speak. Looking at this I do not shake my head sadly and ask "Where did it all go wrong, Bob?". A better question would be "Where did it all go right, Bob?", except that we know the answer. This volume is a worthy and deserved tribute to someone who has made a lasting contribution to the development of computer science, and ideas far beyond.

An influential coach and all-round good guy. Yes indeed, among many other things.

Directions for Logic Programming

Robert A. Kowalski

Department of Computing,
Imperial College of Science, Technology and Medicine,
180 Queen's Gate,
London SW7 2BZ, UK

Times have changed. Gone are the days when Logic Programming looked ready to take over the world. In these days of the Internet, object-oriented programming, reactive agents and multi-agent systems, we need a better understanding of the possible role of Logic Programming in the future.

The argument for Logic Programming is based in large part on its Logical foundations. But Logic has been subjected to numerous attacks in recent years, and these attacks have, therefore, shaken the very foundations of Logic Programming.

Traditionally, researchers in Logic and Artificial Intelligence focussed on the use of Logic to formalise the thinking process of an individual agent. They paid little attention both to the environment in which the agent was embedded and to the interaction of the agent both with the environment and with other agents.

Logic Without Model Theory

In my own work, I have at times taken an extreme view about the relationship between a logical theory and the environment with which that theory interacts. I now believe that that view has been partly to blame both for some of the limitations of my own work and for some of the limitations of the approach to logic programming I have advocated in the past.

In "Logic Without Model Theory" [4], I wrote:

> In model theory, there is a real world, consisting of real individuals, functions and relations. In the more pragmatic theory, however, there is only an inescapable, constantly flowing input stream of observational sentences, which the agent is forced to assimilate. To inquire into the source of this input stream and to speculate about the nature of the source is both unnecessary and unhelpful. For all the agent can ever hope to determine, the source might just as well be some form of virtual reality.

Although such a view might be logically coherent, it undervalues the importance of the environment. I now believe, differently from before, that the environment is a real world, which gives meaning to an agent's thoughts, in the same way that a model, in the sense of model theory, gives meaning to sentences in logical form.

A.C. Kakas, F. Sadri (Eds.): Computat. Logic (Kowalski Festschrift), LNAI 2407, pp. 26–32, 2002.
© Springer-Verlag Berlin Heidelberg 2002

The Observation-Thought-Action Agent Cycle

My new way of thinking has been inspired in large part by thinking about reactive agents and multi-agent systems. Reactive agents and intelligent agents, more generally, can be understood within the framework of an agent's observation-thought-action cycle.

The agent cycle has emerged, in recent years, as a more comprehensive framework for understanding human and artificial intelligence. It puts logic in its place as one way of thinking; and it highlights the importance of the agent's interactions with the world. The cycle can be put in the simplified form:

> **to cycle,**
> **observe** any inputs,
> **think,**
> **select and commit** to an action to perform,
> **act,**
> **cycle.**

Thus, for an intelligent agent, life is a potentially endless cycle of interacting with the world.

What is important about the agent cycle is that it opens up a thinking agent to the outside world. In fact, it would be more realistic of natural agents and more general for artificial agents to view them as concurrent systems, which observe, think and act concurrently, all at the same time.

Condition-Action Rule Production Systems

Logic programming, and indeed traditional logic more generally, are not obviously well suited to serve as the thinking component of the agent cycle. That distinction belongs instead to the production system model, which, according to [5], is the most widely accepted computational model of human intelligence.

Production systems represent the link between observations and candidate actions by means of **production rules**, which have the form:

> If conditions then actions.

For example:

> If it's raining, then carry an umbrella.

> If it's clear ahead, then step forward.
> If there's an obstacle ahead, then turn right.

> If a car is rushing towards you, then jump out of its way.

Condition-action rules are executed in the forward direction, by matching their conditions with "facts" in the current state, and deriving the corresponding actions as candidates for selection and execution.

If several actions are candidates for selection at the same time, then the agent needs to make a **committed choice**, from which there is no backtracking. For example, if both of the following rules apply at the same time:

If it's raining, then carry an umbrella.
If a car is rushing towards you, then jump out of its way.

then the second rule should take priority over the first.

Although there is no backtracking on the execution of an action, if a candidate action has not been selected in one cycle, it may still be possible to select it in a later cycle. So, for example, if it is raining, and there is a car rushing towards you, and you succeed in jumping out of the way, then you can put up your umbrella afterwards, if it's still raining.

The internal state of an agent might consist entirely of production rules and contain no internal, symbolic representation of the world. In such a case, it has been said that the world serves as its own representation: If you want to find out about the world, don't waste time thinking about it, just observe it instead!

Abductive Logic Programming and the Agent Cycle

The problem with production systems is that they are not very good for reasoning about goals and for reducing goals to subgoals. However, as we all know, this is where logic programming and backward reasoning excel.

But conventional logic programs are closed to changes in the environment. They define all their predicates completely, and have no room for new information. Abductive logic programming [2] solves this problem, by representing observations and actions by means of abducible predicates. Unlike closed predicates, which are completely defined by conventional logic programs, abducible predicates are constrained by integrity constraints, which behave like condition-action rules.

Thus abductive logic programs, as we have argued elsewhere [3], can combine the goal-directed behaviour of conventional logic programs with the reactive behaviour of condition-action rules.

Ordinary integrity constraints in database systems are passive. They merely monitor updates to the database and reject updates that violate the constraints. Integrity constraints in abductive logic programming agents, on the other hand, are active, deriving candidate actions to ensure that integrity is maintained. They also monitor candidate actions, to ensure that integrity would not be violated by their performance. To the best of my knowledge, this latter use of integrity constraints was first used in semantic query optimisation [1].

Thus integrity constraints in abductive logic programming agents can behave, not only as condition-action rules, but also as obligations (to perform actions that maintain integrity) and as prohibitions (to prevent actions that would violate integrity).

The following partial reconstruction of the London Underground Emergency Notice shows one of the ways that integrity constraints and logic programs can be combined:

If there is an emergency then you will get help.
You will get help if you alert the driver to an emergency.
You alert the driver to an emergency if you press the alarm signal button.

The first sentence is an integrity constraint, in which the condition is an observation and the conclusion is a goal that needs to be achieved. The second and third sentences are logic programming clauses, which reduce that goal to an action that needs to be performed.

The World as a Model

The vision of the future that emerges from these considerations is of an agent that uses abductive logic programs, to pursue its own goals, together with integrity constraints, to maintain a harmonious relationship with the world that surrounds it.

The agent cycle can be viewed as a game in which the world and the agent are opponents. The moves of the world are the observations with which the world confronts the agent. In the case of naturally intelligent systems, the agent's own body is part of the world; and the observations an agent receives from the world include bodily sensations, like hunger and pain.

The moves of the agent are the actions that the agent performs, generated by abductive logic programs, either proactively, by reducing goals to subgoals, or reactively, by maintaining integrity constraints. These actions can include actions, like eating, kicking and screaming, that affect the agent's own body.

For the agent, the goal of the game, in this hostile environment, is to survive and prosper for as long as possible: to perform actions that change the world, so that future observations confirm both the truth and the utility of the agent's goals and beliefs.

Thus the world is a Herbrand model, specified, for the purposes of the game, by the ground atomic sentences that the world generates piecemeal as observations for the agent. It is good if the agent's beliefs are true of this world, because then they can be used reliably for goal reduction and action generation. But it is also important that they be useful, in that they give rise to actions that lead to states of the world that achieve the agent's goals.

The World and Multi-agent Systems

In this vision of an agent situated in the world, other agents are just other inhabitants of the shared world. Thus, when agents interact with one another, they do so, as in blackboard systems, by performing actions on their shared environment. A message sent from one agent to another consists of a speech act performed by the first agent on the environment, paired with a corresponding observation made by the second agent.

The shared environment in such a multi-agent system is still a model theoretic structure, which changes over time. It is not part of a logic program or part of a logical theory, which describes actions and events. But it is a structure that actually changes state, so far as anyone can tell, by destructively "overwriting" itself.

Compare this view of multi-agent systems with the conventional logic programming view that programs can be or should be purely declarative. Not only do logic programs lack the assignment statement of imperative programming languages, but they lack the shared environment needed to implement at a high level the kind of multi-agent systems that occur in nature.

No wonder, then, that concurrent logic programming languages have not caught on. They lack the destructive assignment statement of imperative programming languages, and they lack the shared environment needed for high-level multi-agent systems. And all of this is because they can only think declaratively about actions, without actually being able to perform them.

The World, the Frame Problem, and Destructive Assignment

The lack of destructive assignment in pure logic programming languages is a special case of the frame problem: namely the problem of representing and reasoning about changing states of affairs. For example:

> The state of an object after changing its state is its new state.
> The state of an object after changing the state of some other object is exactly what it was before the change took place.

No matter how you do it, using such frame axioms, there is an unacceptable computational overhead involved in reasoning about the current state of affairs. Unfortunately, in pure logic programming languages without destructive assignment, there is no alternative but to incur such overheads.

In closed systems, it might be possible to reason about the changing states of objects. But in open systems, in which objects have a life of their own or in which they can be changed unpredictably by the actions of other agents, it is not even theoretically possible.

The alternative, when all you are concerned about is the current state of an object, is to let the world look after it for you. Since the world is a semantic, rather than a linguistic structure, it does not have to be declarative. It can change destructively without remembering its past. However, in those cases, when you need to reason about the past or the future, observing the current state of the world can be combined with reasoning about it by means of suitable frame axioms.

Thus abductive logic programming can be combined with destructive assignment, in a single more general-purpose programming language for multi-agent systems. The abductive logic programming part of the language can be used to implement the thinking part of individual agents. The destructive assignment part can be used to implement an environment that can be shared with other agents.

In fact, the resulting language is a lot like Prolog with its database of assertions, augmented with integrity constraints. The assertions can be thought of as a Herbrand model, which is an internal simulation of part of the external environment. Like the external environment, it can also change destructively, in this case as the result of actions such as "assert" and "retract".

Conclusions

The view of logic programming that I have just sketched has both engineering and cognitive science implications. From an engineering perspective, it suggests a new kind of general-purpose computer language, which embeds abductive logic programs together with integrity constraints in a perpetual input-output agent cycle, with an interface to an environment with destructive assignment, possibly shared with other agents. The language incorporates a number of features of Prolog that are not catered for by pure logic programming. It also incorporates features of object-oriented and imperative programming.

For the practical purpose of gaining wider acceptance, it might be better, initially, to present the extended language as an implementation language for a specification language such as some kernel UML. In that way, it need not compete with other programming languages or with established programming methodologies. In many cases, of course, the implementation of the specification will be sufficiently efficient that lower programming-level implementation will not be necessary. Logic programming through the back door!

From a cognitive science perspective, the extension goes far beyond the simple logic programming model of problem solving by goal-reduction. It incorporates the condition-action rule model of problem solving as an additional component, and it embeds them both in a sensory-motor system that interacts with an environment that gives meaning to an agent's thoughts.

As a cognitive model, the proposed framework is still only a basic skeleton. It, obviously, needs to be extended further with other problem solving mechanisms, such as learning; and it needs to be reconciled with other cognitive models, such as neural networks. Nonetheless, it seems to me that the framework has the potential to serve as the basis for a more comprehensive symbolic model of cognition.

I know of no other approach that has such potential to serve as a general framework for both computing and cognitive science. Adding this consideration to the other arguments for logic programming in both of these fields, I believe there is good reason to expect logic programming to prosper in the future.

Acknowledgements

Although she may not agree with many of the views presented in this paper, I am indebted to Fariba Sadri for her contributions to most of the ideas presented here. I am also pleased to acknowledge my debt to Jack Minker for the influence of his work on semantic query optimisation, which helped to inspire the combination of logic programs and integrity constraints that lies at the core of the abductive logic programming agent model. Thanks also to Phan Minh Dung, Tony Kakas and Ken Satoh for helpful comments on an earlier draft of this paper.

I am very grateful both to Tony Kakas and Fariba Sadri for editing this collection of papers and to all the authors who took the trouble to contribute to it.

A variant of this paper appeared in the January 2001 issue of the ALP newsletter.

References

1. Chakravarty U. S., Grant, J., Minker, J., "Foundations of Semantic Query Optimization for Deductive Databases" in Foundations of Deductive Databases and Logic Programming, pp.243-273, 1988.
2. Kakas, T., Kowalski, R. and Toni, F., "The Role of Logic Programming in Abduction", Handbook of Logic in Artificial Intelligence and Programming 5, (eds. D. Gabbay, C.J. Hogger, J.A. Robinson) Oxford University Press, pp 235-324, 1998.
3. Kowalski, R. and Sadri, F., " From Logic Programming towards Multi-agent Systems, Annals of Mathematics and Artificial Intelligence , Volume 25, pp. 391-419, 1999.
4. Kowalski, R., "Logic without Model Theory", in What is a logical system?,(ed. D. Gabbay), Oxford University Press, 1995.
5. Thagard, P., "Mind: Introduction to Cognitive Science". A Bradford Book. MIT Press, 1996.

Agents as Multi-threaded Logical Objects

Keith Clark[1] and Peter J. Robinson[2]

[1] Department of Computing, Imperial College, London, England
klc@doc.ic.ac.uk
[2] School of Computer Science and Electrical Engineering, The University of
Queensland, Australia
pjr@csee.uq.edu.au

Abstract. In this paper we describe a distributed object oriented logic
programming language in which an object is a collection of threads de-
ductively accessing and updating a shared logic program. The key features of the language, such as static and dynamic object methods and
multiple inheritance, are illustrated through a series of small examples.
We show how we can implement object servers, allowing remote spawning
of objects, which we can use as staging posts for mobile agents. We give
as an example an information gathering mobile agent that can be queried
about the information it has so far gathered whilst it is gathering new
information. Finally we define a class of co-operative reasoning agents
that can do resource bounded inference for full first order predicate logic,
handling multiple queries and information updates concurrently.
We believe that the combination of the concurrent OO and the LP programming paradigms produces a powerful tool for quickly implementing
rational multi-agent applications on the internet.

1 Introduction

In this paper we describe an object oriented extension of the multi-threaded
Qu-Prolog described in [7]. We show how this can be used to quickly implement
multi-agent applications on the internet in which agents have both reactive and
pro-active behaviours that utilize quite rich inference systems. The different
behaviours execute concurrently, as separated threads of an active object that
implements the agent.

The original Qu-Prolog [12] was developed as an implementation and tactic language for interactive theorem provers, particularly those that carry out
schematic proofs. It has built-in support for the kinds of data values typically
needed when writing a theorem prover in Prolog: object variables - the variables
of the logical formulae being manipulated, substitutions for these object variables, and quantified terms, terms denoting object level formulae with explicit
quantifiers over the object level variables. As further support, the unification algorithm of Qu-Prolog unifies such quantified terms up to alpha-equivalence, that
is it knows about equivalence up to changes of quantifier bound object variables.
It also carries out the occurs checks before binding a variable. This is essential for implementing sound inference systems. Qu-Prolog is the implementation

A.C. Kakas, F. Sadri (Eds.): Computat. Logic (Kowalski Festschrift), LNAI 2407, pp. 33–65, 2002.

language of the Ergo theorem prover [1], which has seen substantial use in the development of verified software.

Motivated by a desire to implement a multi-threaded, multi-user version of Ergo, we then added multi-threading and high-level inter-thread communication between Qu-Prolog threads running anywhere on the internet [7]. Each thread has a internet wide unique identity similar to an email address. It also has a message buffer of received but unprocessed messages which it can periodically search for messages of interest. Communication between threads in different Qu-Prolog processes makes use of the store and forward ICM communications system [17] developed for the April language [18]. This offers robust middleware for distributed symbolic applications. As an example, it can be configured to automatically store messages for threads running on hosts, such as laptops, that are temporarily disconnected, delivering them when the laptop reconnects.

In [7] we describe the multi-threading and the inter-thread communication facilities in detail and show how they can be used to implement a distributed deductive data base in which each data base comprises the clauses of a program being executed by a multi-threaded Qu-Prolog process. The clauses in each data base can contain remote calls that are queries for relations defined in other data bases. Such a remote call takes the form DB?Call, where DB is the global identity of the query interface thread for the other Qu-Prolog process. DB typically has a value such as interface:qupDB@'zeus.doc.ic.ac.uk'. The interface thread can fork a new query thread for each received remote query. Moreover, although we did not illustrate this in [7], different deductive data bases can do inference using a different logic, a non-resolution inference system or even a modal logic. Since each can have rules that call for sub-proofs in other deductive data bases, we can easily implement distributed hybrid reasoning systems.

Threads in different invocations of Qu-Prolog can only communicate using messages, but threads within the same invocation can also communiciate via the dynamic clause data base. Asserting or retracting a clause is an atomic operation with respect to the multi-threading. In [7] we showed how we can use the shared dymamic clauses to implement a Linda-style tuple space manager in Qu-Prolog. In addition, threads can be made to suspend waiting for a particular clause to be asserted. Suspension waiting for a clause of a certain form to be asserted enables one to implement daemons. A daemon is a thread that is launched but which immediately suspends until the trigger clause is asserted.

In [8] we sketched how multi-threaded Qu-Prolog could be used to implement DAI applications. With this type of application in mind, we have recently added a concurrent object oriented layer to Qu-Prolog. This OO layer, which in this paper we shall refer to as QuP++, is transformed into the base Qu-Prolog using the term expansion pre-processing facilities of Qu-Prolog. It allows OO software engineering methodology to be used to construct distributed Qu-Prolog applications, in particular multi-agent applications.

In the next section we give a brief overview of the main features of QuP++. This is followed by section 3 which is an example based introduction to programming in QuP++. In section 4 we show how object servers allowing remote spawning of objects can be defined and used to create and manage mobile objects and agents. In section 5 we introduce the features of Qu-Prolog that allow the implementation of non-resolution inference. We show how they can be used to define a reasoning agent that can do resource bounded inference for full first order predicate logic both to answer questions about what it believes and to check for possible inconsistency before it adds new information to its belief store. We then elaborate the agent to a co-operative reasoning agent that can ask other agents to engage in sub-prrofs on its behalf. In section 6 we conclude with mention of related research.

2   Overview of QuP++

QuP++ is a class based OO language with multiple inheritance. A class is a named collection of static Qu-Prolog clauses with an optional state component comprising a collection of dynamic predicates and state variables, the latter being Qu-Prolog atoms. The stucture of a class definition is:

```
class C isa [S1,.Si-[r/2]..,Sn]  % optional inheritance
state [d/3,a:=9,b,{k(g,h). k(j,1)},...] % state components
clauses{                         % sequence of static clauses
p(...):-  ...
...
p(...):-super?p(...).
....
}private [d/3,..]  % preds that are private
```

The dynamic predicates (of the object state) must be disjoint from the static predicates of the class and any of its super-classes. Instances of the class share the static clauses but *do not* share clauses for their dynamic predicates and *do not* share state variable values.

A class definition with a state component is the template for an object. An object is an instance of the class. The static clauses of the class are the fixed methods of the object. Objects are *active*, each is implemented as one or more independently executing threads. The clauses for the dynamic predicates and the values associated with the state variables are the state of the object. Default initial clauses for the dynamic predicates can be given in the class definition, e.g. the clauses for k/2 above, as can default initial values for the state variables, e.g. a:=9. A default value for a state component given in a class C over-rides any default value given for the same state component in a super-class of C. A state variable value can only be accessed and updated from the methods of the class, and clauses for a dynamic predicate can only be asserted and retracted by a class method. However, the dynamic predicates of an object can be queried in the same way as the static predicates. Externally they look like extra method names. They are methods with dynamic definitions unique to each object.

Static predicate names and state component names can be re-used in different classes, they are treated as distinct names. Inheritance, by default, makes all the static predicates of the super-classes of a class C static predicates of C. If an inherited predicate is redefined in a class, the new definition over-rides the inherited definition. However, the combined superclass definition for a predicate p/n can always be accessed from inside C with a call super?p(...). Using super?p(...) we can make the new definition extend what would have been the inherited definition, as in:

```
p(...):-  ...
...
p(...):-super?p(...).
```

More precisely, the definition for p/n given in a specific super-class S can also be accessed with a call super(S)?p(...). If the predicate p/n is not redefined in C, the definition that is inherited in C is exactly the same as if it were redefined in C as:

```
p(X1,..,Xn):-  super(S1)?p(X1,..,Xn);
               super(S2)?p(X1,..,Xn);
               ...
               super(Sj)?p(X1,..,Xn).
```

Here S1,..,Sj are all the superclasses of C from which inheritance of p/n has not been explicitly suppressed. Inheritance of the clauses for p/n, from a specific super-class S is suppressed by using of S-[p/n], rather than S in the isa list of super-classes.

A call p(...) in a static clause of a class C always denotes a call to the definition for p/n of the class C, even if the call is executed inside an object O that is an instance of a sub-class SubC of C that has redefined p/n. In contrast, a call self?p(...) in a static method of C executed by O will be evaluated using the definition for p/n of SubC.

Inheritance unions the state components of a class C with the state components of all its superclasses. That is, all state variables of a super-class are automatically state variables of C, and all dynamic predicates of a super-class are automatically dynamic predicates of C.

By default, all the static and dynamic predicates of a class are visible, that is they can be used in queries to the object instances of the class. Both static and dynamic predicates can also be declared as private, in which case they can only be called from methods of the class and its sub-classes[1]. Queries to instances of the class cannot access the clauses for the private predicates. Such a call to a private predicate of an object will fail.

An object instance of a calls C is created with a call of the form:

```
new(C,...,O)
```

where O is an unbound variable which will be assigned a system generated globally unique identity for the new object. O is actually the identity of the object's

---

[1] Private predicates are inheritable and can be redefined in sub-classes.

default execution thread. This thread will immediately call the init method of class C, if this is defined. This can be used to launch sub-threads of object O using the QuP^{++} object_thread_fork primitive. The object sub-threads can communicate with one another either by explicit messages using the inter-thread message primitives of Qu-Prolog, or by updating O's dynamic clauses or state variables. Special QuP^{++} self_assert and self_retract primitives enable any thread within an object to update the dynamic clauses of the object. The QuP^{++} primitives *= and := enable any object thread to access and update the value of one of the object's state variables[2]. The init method can also be used to announce the object's presence by remote calls to other objects, for example a call to a directory server registering some description of the object. On termination of the init method, the default thread enters a loop in which it repeatedly accepts and evaluates remote calls for O. It suspends if there are no pending remote calls. It becomes the object's external interface thread - its reactive component.

A remote call is a query Q sent to O from another concurrently executing object, anywhere on the internet. The query can be sent as a call O?Q, or a call O^^Q[3]. (The differences between the two forms of call will be explained shortly.) Q can be an arbitrary Prolog query using any of the visible predicates of the class of O or any Qu-Prolog primitive[4]. Multiple remote calls, whether synchronous or asynchronous, are queued at an object in time order of arrival. The object will respond to them in this order.

A ? call is a *synchronous* communication, the client querying thread Cl suspends until an answer is returned, which may be a fail message. Backtracking in the client thread will generate all solutions of the remote call[5].

A call O^^Q is an *asynchronous* remote call. Q is executed by O as a single solution call. There is no automatic answer response from O to such a query, no client variables in Q will be bound as a result of the call, and on the client side the call always *immediately succeeds*. Usually Q will cause some update of the state of O, or cause O to execute a remote call. This remote call could be either a synchronous or an asynchronous call back to the object from which the query was sent. The architecture of a QuP^{++} object is depicted in figure 1.

During the evaluation of any remote call received by an object O, the global identity of the object QO from which the query came can be found by executing a call caller(QO). This will unify QO with the global identity of the querying

---

[2] Execution of the dynamic clause and state variable update and access primitives is an atomic action. However it is a useful discipline to restrict update of a particular dynamic predicate or state variable to a particular sub-thread and have other threads only access the value.

[3] There is also a O??Q form of call with the semantics as given in [7]. We shall not use this form of call in this paper.

[4] In addition, any predicate of a Qu-Prolog program can be used in Q if we know that it will have been loaded by the Qu-Prolog process in which O is running. To the QuP^{++} application these are seen as extra Qu-Prolog primitives.

[5] For a call O?Q all solutions to Q are immediately found by O using a findall call and returned by O to Cl as a list. There is then local backtracking in Cl over the different solutions in the returned list.

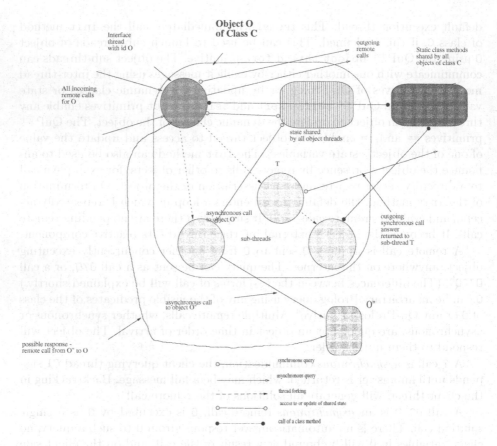

Fig. 1. A QuP^{++} object

object, which remember is the global identity of its interface thread. This will be the case even if the query came from another sub-thread of QO. The pair of calls, `caller(QO),QO^^RCall`, thus sends an asynchronous query RCall to the object QO which sent O the remote call it is currently evaluating. If O executes this pair of calls whilst evaluating an asynchronous call, `O^^Q`, from QO, the return call `QO^^RCall` is effectively a response to QO for the query Q. Use of `^^` remote calls and `caller/1` enables objects to have asynchronous conversations as well as client server interactions. This is particularly useful when the objects implement agents.

Tests on the value returned by a `caller/1` call can also be used to restrict use of certain methods to known objects, or objects satisfying certain properties. For example, a method:

```
p(...):- caller(QO), allowed_to_call_p(QO), ...
```

causes a remote call to p to fail if the querying object is not allowed to call p. `allowed_to_call_p/1` can be a dynamic predicate initialised when the object is created, and perhaps updated by calls to a method:

```
allow_to_call_p(NewO):-caller(QO),allowed_to_call_p(QO),
                        self_assert(allowed_to_call_p(NewO)).
```

from objects already allowed to call p/k.

3 QuP⁺⁺ by Example

Let us begin with a simple example program. This is a class definition for a person
object. In this case there is no inheritance, except from a default system class
that defines a set of standard method predicates for all objects. One of these is
the reflective method predicate/1 which can be used to query an object to find
its visible predicates. A call O?predicate(V), where V is a variable, will return
one at a time the names and arities of O's visible predicates. Another system
class predicate is class/1. A call O?class(C) will unify C with the class name
of O. There are two other reflective predicates: myid/1 and mystate/1 which
are actually used in the above class definition. They can only be called from a
method. myid/1 unifies its argument with global identity of the object that calls
it. mystate/1 returns the entire current state of the object that executes the
call as a list.

```
class person
state [firstname/1,surname/1,age:=0,sex/1,child/1,parent/1]
clauses{
adult :- age*=A,A>18.
family_name(N):-surname(N).
likes(O):-child(O).

new_child(Fn,Sx,O):-
    nonvar(O),!,
    self_assert(child(O)).
new_child(Fn,Sx,O):-
    surname(Sn),
    myid(Me),
    new(person,
        [firstname(Fn),surname(Sn),sex(Sx),{parent(Me). }],
        O),
    self_assert(child(O)).

get_married_to(Sp):-
    myid(Me),
    Sp?(class(person);class(married_person),spouse(Me)),
    mystate(St),
    become(married_person,
                    [spouse(Sp)|St]).

} private {surname/1}.
```

Let us now look more closely at the above class definition. The state declaration:

```
state [firstname/1,surname/1,age:=0,sex/1,child/1,parent/1]
```

tells us that instances of this class will record the state of the object using clauses for five dynamic predicates and one state variable age. The state variable has a default initial value of 0. When we create an instance of the class we can give values for the dynamic predicates and we can override the default value 0 for age. For example, the call:

```
new(person,[firstname(bill),surname(smith),sex(male),age:=23],O1)
```

will create a new instance of the person class, with the clauses given in the state list second argument as initial definitions for its dynamic predicates, and the value 23 for its age state variable. The clauses for the dynamic predicates and the state variable initialisations can be given in any order. Notice that this person object does not have clauses defining parent/1 and child/1.

When an object is created it can be given a set of clauses for some or all of its dynamic predicates and values for some or all of its state variables. For a dynamic predicate these either over-ride or add to any default clauses given for the predicate of the class definition. The choice is signalled by the way the clauses are given in the object creation call. For a state variable any value given in the object creation call always over-rides any default value it might have in the class definition.

new/3 is one of two QuP^{++} primitives for creating new objects. The above call to new/3 returns the global indentity of the person object as the binding for O1. We can access O1's state as recorded by its visible dynamic predicates by queries such as:

```
O1?sex(S)
```

which binds S to male. We cannot directly access the age of O1 since this is recorded as the value of a state variable. However we can use the adult method to indirectly access its value. For example,

```
O1?adult
```

will succeed. The call age*=A in the adult clause uses the QuP^{++} primitive *=/2 to access the current value of the age state variable. This call can only be used in a method. An attempt to use it in a remote call such as O1?age*=A will fail.

A call:

```
O1?predicate(P)
```

will in turn bind P to each of:

```
new_child/3, adult/0, family_name/1, get_married_to/1,
likes/1, firstname/1,  sex/1, child/1, parent/1
```

surname will not be returned as it was declared as private to the class. Its definition can be accessed indirectly via the family_name method. We have a separate family_name definition because, when we define the married_person subclass, we shall redefine this predicate.

```
O1?class(C)
```

will bind C to person.

The person class has a method new_child/3 that both updates the state of the object that executes it and may create a new instance of the person clause, which is the object representing the recorded child. The asserted child/1 clause records the child object's global identity. A new person object is created if the third argument of the new_child/3 method call, the object identity of the child, is given as an unbound variable. Thus, a call:

```
O1?new_child(mary,female,O2)
```

will result in a new person object with the global identity the returned binding for O2 being created with state:

```
[surname(smith),firstname(mary),age:=0,sex(female),parent(O1)]
```

The new_child/3 second clause is used and this calls the dynamic predicate surname/1 to access the surname for object O1 in order to define the surname/1 dynamic predicate of the new person object that it creates. It also calls the QuP^{++} primitive myid to find the global identity of the object executing the method[6]. This is in order to give an initial clause for the parent/1 dynamic predicate of the new person object, which is deemed to be a child of the object executing the new_child method. Finally the new_child/3 method adds the clause child(O2) to the state of O1 using the QuP^{++} primitive self_assert. self_assert rather than assert is used to ensure that the dynamic clauses for the same predicate in different objects are kept distinct.

Now a query:

```
O2?firstname(F)
```

or the equivalent queries:

```
O1?child(C),C?firstname(F)
```

```
O1?(child(C),C?firstname(F))
```

---

[6] In many OO languages the returned binding for Me is denoted by use of the term self. In QuP^{++} self can only be used as the object identity of a call, as in self?p(..). If we want to embed its value as an argument of a remote call, as here, we must find its value using myid/1. As we remarked earlier, a self?p(...) call can be used within a method of a class C to signal that the latest definition of p should be called in case the method is being executed by an instance of a subclass of C which redefines p. This is a standard use of self in OO languages.

can be used to find the first name of the new child object. The last two queries differ with respect to where the call `C?firstname(F)` is executed. In the first query it is executed in the object that executes the call `O1?child(C)`, and in the second it is executed in the object `O1`. The second is a remote call containing a remote call. Remember all the objects are executing as separate threads which repeatedly accept and execute remote calls. The differences between the evaluations of the two queries is depicted in figure 2.

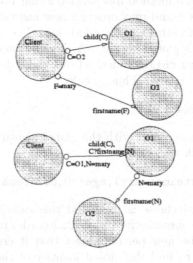

Fig. 2. Remote calls

Let us now look at the method `get_married_to/1`. This does not create a new object but metamorphises the person object that executes it into an instance of the `married_person` class. This is as a result of the call to the the QuP^{++} primitive `become/2`. This can be called by a static method of any object O and when the method that calls it terminates the object O becomes an instance of a new class. Importantly, it retains the same global identity. The first argument of the `become/2` call is the name of the new class, the second is a list, just like the list argument of a `new/3` call, giving values for some or all the state components for the object as an instance of the new class. In the case of the `become/2` call of the `get_married_to/1` method the new state list is the state list returned by executing the system class method `mystate` with the clause `spouse(Sp)` added as a new component. Notice that the method only succeeds if `Sp` is an instance of the person class (i.e. as yet unmarried), or `Sp` is an instance of the `married_person` call that has the person being told to get married (the `Me` returned by the call `myid(Me)`) as its recorded spouse. A call to `mystate/1` unifies its argument with a list giving the current complete state of the object O that executes the call. The state of an object O as a married person is its state as a person object with an extra clause for a new dynamic predicate `spouse/1`.

This clause records the identity of the object to whom the married person is married.

As one can imagine, the married_person class is best defined as a sub-class of the person class. Its definition is given below. The isa person-[get_married_to/1] of the class declaration means that all the static clauses and state components of the person class, except the clauses for get_married_to/1 which is not inherited and family_name/1 and likes which are redefined, are automatically included in the married_person class. Note that the sub-class redefines the likes/1 predicate as:

```
likes(O):- spouse(O);super?likes(O).
```

This redefinition calls the definition that would be inherited so it just extends the person definition for likes/1. Note that get_married_to/1 is removed from the methods of the married_person class.

The sub-class also has a clause for the predicate init. When a class contains a definition for init, which is always deemed as private to the class, it is called immediately after any instance of the class is created, either by a new call, or a becomes call. Only when the init method terminates will the object accept external queries.

```
class married_person isa person-[get_married_to]
state [spouse/1]
clauses {
init:-  spouse(Sp),
        myid(Me),
        Sp?spouse(Me) -> true;
                        Sp^^get_married_to(Me).

likes(O):- spouse(O);super?likes(O).

family_name(N):- sex(male) -> surname(N) ;
                              spouse(Sp),Sp?surname(N).

get_divorced:-
        mystate(St),
        remove(spouse(Sp),St,NSt),
        myid(Me),
        (Sp?spouse(Me)->Sp^^get_divorced),
        become(person,NSt).
}.
```

Let us see what the effect of the init is if we execute the conjunction:

```
new(person,[firstname(june),surname(jones),
            sex(female),age:=20],O3),
O3^^get_married_to(O1)
```

where O1 is the previously created male instance of the **person** class. The call
O3^^get_married_to(O1) is an asynchronous call. It always immediately succeeds whether or not the call get_married_to(O1) succeeds in the object O3. No
answer bindings are ever directly returned from an asynchronous call and so the
query of the call usually contains no unbound variables, as here.

When O3 receives the query it will eventually execute:

```
become(married_person,
       [spouse(O1),firstname(june),surname(jones),
        sex(female),age:=20])
```

and this causes O3 to become an instance of the **married_person** class. This in
turn, will cause the automatic execution of the **init** method of this class by O3.
This will query O1, the recorded spouse of the metamorphised O3, to see if O1
'knows' that its spouse is the object executing the **init** method, i.e. O3. The
init method finds the global identity O3 by executing the call myid(Me). Since
O1 is at this time an instance of the **person** class, it will have no clauses for
spouse, and the call Sp?spouse(Me) will fail. This will result in the execution
by O3 of the asynchronous remote call:

```
O1^^get_married_to(O3)
```

and this will cause O1 to metamorphise into an instance of the **married_person**
class, with recorded spouse O3. Now the **init** call executed when O1 becomes a
married person will find that its spouse O3 does 'know' that it is married to O1
and the distributed activity started by the **init** executed by O3 will terminate.
The **init** method ensures consistency between the state components of the two
married person objects.

Note that it is essential that the remote call to get_married_to/1 of the **init**
method is executed asynchronously. Before the remote call terminates, the object that executes the call will itself be queried. The interaction between O1 and
O3 is as depicted in the figure 3. If O1 executed the remote get_married_to(O1)
query to O3 synchronously, that is if it suspended until the remote query successfully terminated, it would not be able to respond to the synchronous query
spouse(O3) from O3. The two objects would deadlock, and neither would be
able to complete their **init** methods.

Finally let us look at the get_divorced method for a married person. This
causes a **married_person** object O to metamorphise back into a **person** object
and ensures that the recorded spouse, if it 'believes' it is still married to O,
similarly reverts to being a **person**.

4   Object Servers and Mobile Agent Objects

Below is a definition of an object server class. Instances of this class can be
sent messages to remotely spawn objects and can be used as stepping stones by
mobile agent objects.

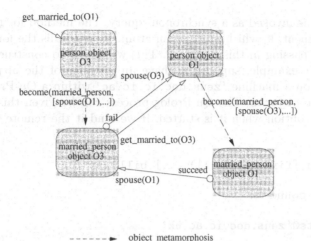

------▶   object metamorphosis

Fig. 3. Object state synchronisation

An `object_server` accepts requests to create new objects for a particular class keeping track of which objects it has created, in which class, in a dynamic predicate `class_of/2`. It also allows objects to be created with given public names, as we shall describe below. It keeps track of these public names in a dynamic relation `used_names`. The two dynamic predicates are not private, so both can be queried by other objects. Use of such an object server assumes that the class definitions for all the classes for which it may need to create instances have been loaded by the Qu-Prolog process in which the object server is running.

```
class object_server
state [class_of/2,used_name/1]
clauses {
  newob(C,Inits,O) :-
      var(O),
      new(C,Inits,O),
      self_assert(class_of(C,O)).
  newob(C,Inits,N,O) :-
      atom(N),
      var(O),
      \+ used_name(N),
      new(C,Inits,N,O),
      self_assert(used_name(N)),
      self_assert(class(C,O)).
}.
```

The class has two methods, one for `newob/3` and one for `newob/4`. The first takes the name of the class and the state components and creates a new object with a system generated identity O that will be returned to the client providing the method was invoked as a synchronous query. The method for `newob/4` has an extra argument, N, which must be an atom. It then calls the four argument new primitive passing in this symbol N. This will use N to construct the global identity O. For example, suppose we have an instance of the `object_server` class running on a machine `'zeus.doc.ic.ic.ac'` within a Qu-Prolog process with the name `objects`. The Qu-Prolog process can be given this name by a command line option when it is started. If we send it the remote synchronous query:

`newob{person,[firstname(bill),...],billS,O)`

then O will be bound to:

`billS:objects@'zeus.doc.ic.ac.uk'`

providing `billS` is not already a used name for an object already created by the object server. (The already used names can be found by querying its `used_names` dynamic relation.) This is a public global identity that can be used to refer to this particular `person` object in any QuP^{++} application. A call:

`billS:objects@'zeus.doc.ic.ac.uk'?family_name(N)`

from any QuP^{++} object, anywhere on the internet, will be routed to the object via the ICM[17] message transport system[7]. The
More usefully, we can give such a public identity to the object servers running on each internet host. We can do this by launching each object server, in a Qu-Prolog process with the name `objects`, with a call:

`?-new(object_server,[],server,_).`

If we do this on the host `zeus.doc.ic.ac.uk`, we can remotely launch an object on this host with a remote call:

`server:objects@'zeus.doc.ic.ac.uk'?newob(person,[...],O).`

or, if we want the launched object to have a public name, with a query:

`server:objects@'zeus.doc.ic.ac.uk'?newob(person,[...],billS,O).`

As we remarked earlier, such a remote launch requires that the class definition for `person` has been loaded on `zeus.doc.ic.ac.uk`. We could, however, elaborate the object server so that it keeps track of which class definitions have been loaded, loading new ones as required. Then all that we need to assume is that we only use a given object server to create objects for classes to which it has access to the class definition.

---

[7] This typically requires ICM processes to be running on each host on which we have a QuP^{++} process running.

Consider now the class definitions:

```
class mobile_object
clauses {
move_to(Host,O):-
  mystate(St),
  class(C),
  server:objects@Host?newob(C,St,O),
  die.
}.
```

`mobile_person isa [person,mobile_object].`

The `mobile_object` class is an abstract class. It will have no direct instances but can be used as a super-class whenever we want some class of objects to be re-locatable. The `mobile_person` class inherits from this class, and the `person` class.

The single method of the `mobile_object` class takes the name of a host machine, `Host` and relocates the object by sending a remote `newob/3` query to the publically named object server on that host. Executed by a `mobile_person` object, the call `mystate(St)` will bind `St` to the person state component and the call `class(C)` will bind `C` to `mobile_person`. The last action of the method, executed if the remote `newob` call succeeds, is `die`. This terminates all the threads executing within the object on the current host.

Suppose `O1` is mobile person object initially created by a `newob/3` query to some object server. If we then execute[8]:

`O1?move_to('pine.doc.ic.ac.uk',O2)`

then, providing there is an object server running on that host, the object `O1` will relocate to become the object with global identity `O2`. This safely relocates an object that only has the default interface thread executing at the time it is relocating and the `move_to` is executed by this thread. If we want to relocate a multi-threaded object we should program it so that all threads but the interface thread have terminated, perhaps after recording information about their execution state in the state of the object, before `move_to` is executed. The object's class should then have an `init` method that will re-launch the additional threads when the object is re-launched on the new host.

Of course, if we are to have objects moving from object server to object server, we should augment the object servers so that they can be informed when an object moves. We should add a new method to the object server class:

```
moved_to(NewHost):-
  caller(O),
  self_retract(class_of(O,C)),
  (O=N:_@_,atom(N)->self_retract(used_name(N));true).
```

---

[8] We can also identify the host using its IP number

and the `move_to/1` method of a mobile object should be:

```
move_to(Host,O):-
  mystate(St),
  class(C),
  server:objects@Host?newob(C,St,O),
  myid(_:objects@CurrHost),
  server:objects@CurrHost^^moved_to(Host),
  die.
```

Notice that the new `moved_to/2` method of the object server uses `caller /1` to find the identity of the local object that is moving, and the `move_to` method finds the identity of the object server that should be informed of the move by massaging the term that is its own global identity. It makes the assumption that all these moving objects are created by `newob` messages to object servers and hence have global identities of the form:

`Name:objects@CurrHost`

This is the case even if the object is not given a public name, `Name` is then an atom such as `object234`.

To many, a mobile agent is a mobile object with a purpose. The purpose manifests itself in proactive behaviour when the agent object arrives at a new site. Below is a class definition for a two threaded generic mobile agent object.

```
class mobile_agent isa mobile_object
state [name,hostlist,script/1,report_to]
clauses {
init:-
    hostlist*=[CH|Hosts], % find where I am -- head of hostlist
    hostlist:=Hosts,      % update hostlist
    report_to*=R,         % find agent to report to
    name*=N,              % find my name
    myid(Me),             % find my current global id
    R^^i_am_now(N,Me),    % inform report_to agent of new id
    object_thread_fork(_,script(CH)). % execute script for CH
                                      % as a separate thread
} private [move_to].
```

It has a state component which is a list of hosts to visit, and a script of what to do as it arrives at each host. The script is given by clauses for the dynamic relation `script/1`. It has another state component, `report_to`, which is the global identity of an agent to which it should report, and one called `name` which is some name by which it can be recognised. Each time it arrives at a host it executes the `init` method. This sends an asynchronous call to the `report_to` agent object giving its current global identity. This is so that the `report_to` agent can send remote queries accessing its current state.

The init method of this class also calls the script progam passing in the name of the current host which is assumed to be the first host on hostlist. The script is executed as a separate object thread so that the main thread of the object can become the default interface thread responding to remote calls, in particular calls from the report_to agent that will have been informed of its current identity. It also updates hostlist by removing the current host name. The called script/1 program will typically end by executing a move_to/1 call on the inherited method of the mobile_object class. To implement a mobile agent we only need to assume that this generic class definition is available on each host that the agent will visit. The actual script for the mobile agent will be passed as part of the state component of the agent and will be agent specific.

```
server:objects@H1?newob(mobile_agent,
          [hostlist:=[H1,...,'zeus.doc...'],report_to:=R,
          {script('zeus....'):- % script for home base
             make_visible(found_pair/2),
             !.                    % terminate script thread
          script(H):-              % script for elsewhere
             make_visible(found_pair/2),
             forall(server:objects@H?
                   class_of(Mp,married_person),
                   (Mp?(sex(male),spouse(Sp)),
                    self_assert(found_pair(Mp,Sp)))),
             hostlist*=[H|_],
             self^^move_to(H,_).}],_)
```

The above call creates a mobile agent that moves to each of the list of hosts [H1,...'zeus.doc...'] reporting to an agent object $\hat{R}$. It is initially created on H1. In all but the last host 'zeus.doc...', which is its home base, perhaps the host on which R resides, it queries all the local married_person objects to create a list of the married_person pairs on that host. It finds the identities of the married_person objects by querying the class_of relation of the local object server. The found married person pairs, if any, are cached in a new dynamic relation found_pair. self_assert can be used to add clauses for dynamic relations that are not declared in the state component of an object's class. By default they become additional private dynamic relations of the object and are automatically collected as part of the state list constructed by mystate/1. So the clauses for these additional dynamic relations will move with the mobile agent. Any private dynamic predicate can be made visible if the object executes a call to make_visible/1. This is what our mobile agent script does at each host, allowing the report_to agent to query the found_pair/2 relation each time the mobile agent reports its new identity. Finally note that the last action of the script, at other than the home host, is an asynchronous call self^^move_to(H,_) to itself. This is instead of of a direct method call move_to(H,_). The direct call would result in the inherited move_to method being executed in the script thread, whereas the asynchronous self call results in its being sent as an asynchronous remote call to the interface thread of the mobile agent. Sending it for execution in the interface thread is cleaner. It means that when it is executed the script thread on the current host will have terminated because it immediately terminates after sending the `self` call. It also means that any remote synchronous call currently being executed by the interface thread, and any such calls that are pending, will be completed before the `move_to` method is executed by this thread. (Remember that remote calls are queued and executed by the interface thread in time order of arrival.)

This is a very simple mobile agent program but the agent, in its ability to concurrently accept queries about the information it has gathered, whilst it is gathering new information, is quite sophisticated. Its activity is as depicted in figure 4. We can use the same program to launch mobile agents with scripts that find out new hosts to visit, adding the host name to `hostnames`. We can also define other mobile agent classes, inheriting from this class, or directly from `mobile_object`, that allow agents to be recalled or given new scripts on their journey.

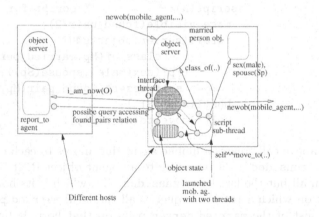

Fig. 4. Simple mobile agent

5   Advanced Reasoning Agents

In this section we show how the Qu-Prolog support for quantifiers, substitutions and object variables can be used to implement powerful reasoning agents that go beyond Prolog inference.

In order to support the programming of such reasoning agents the Herbrand Universe (or object-level) of Qu-Prolog extends that of normal Prolog. Qu-Prolog's Herbrand universe has quantified terms and object level variables. Correspondingly the meta-level of Qu-Prolog includes terms to represent the object-level quantified terms and variables. Object variables (or more strictly object-variable variables) are meta-level variables that range over variables at the object-level. This means that one object variable may be bound to another during unification, but cannot be bound to any other kind of term.

Qu-Prolog also supports a notation for substitution application. Such a meta-level term represents the application of a substitution to a term at the object-level with change of bound variables as required.

Unification in up to alpha-equivalence. In other words, the unification algorithm attempts to find instantiations of variables that make two terms equal up to change of bound variables. We present some example unification problems shortly to illustrate the unification of quantified terms.

Note that, in Qu-Prolog, there is a distinction between substituition and instantiation. When talking about *substitution* we mean variable substitution at the object-level and consequently change of bound variables is required when 'pushing' a substitution into a quantified term (at the object-level). On the other hand, *instantiation* (often called substitution when discussing standard Prolog) is really substitution at the meta-level. Instantiations therefore 'move through' terms representing object-level quantified terms without requiring change of bound variables.

Object variables use the same syntax as Prolog atoms but are distinguished from atoms by declaration. The declaration

```
?- obvar_prefix([x,y]).
```

declares x and y, as well as x and y followed by numbers or underscores and numbers, as object variables. So, for example, x0, y_1 are also object variables.

Quantifier symbols are declared using the same method as declaring operators. So, for example,

```
?- op(500, quant, q).
```

declares q to be a quantifier symbol with precedence 500. Note, however, that this declaration does not give any semantics to the quantifer symbols (other than as an object variable binder) – the semantics are defined by the predicates of the program.

Assuming the declarations above, the following interaction with the interpreter shows Qu-Prolog unification in action.

```
| ?- x = y.
x = y
y = y

| ?- x = a.
no

| ?- q x f(x) = q y f(y).
x = x
y = y
```

```
| ?- q x A = q y B.
x = x
A = [x/y]B
y = y
B = B
provided:
x not_free_in [$/y]B

| ?- [A/x]B = 3.
A = A
x = x
B = B
provided:
[A/x]B = 3
```

The first example shows that object variables can be unified with each other. The second example shows that object variables don't unify with other terms. The third example shows that unification of quantified terms is up to alpha-equivalence – neither x nor y is instantiated by the unification.

The forth example extends the third example – to make the two terms alpha equivalent all free occurrences of y in B are replaced by x. The notation [x/y]B is the application of a substitution to B with this property. Note that, without more information about B, the substitution cannot be evaluated. Also note that the unification adds the constraint x not_free_in [$/y]B (where $ is an atom). This constraint is also required in order to make the terms alpha-equivalent. If x and y represent different object variables then the constraint reduces to x not_free_in B – which says that since the left hand side of the unification has no free x's then neither can the right hand side. On the other hand if x and y represent the same object variable then the constraint becomes true since there are no free x's in [$/x]B. Also, in this case there are no free x's on either side of the unification.

The final example shows a unification problem that delays, that is, becomes a constraint. This is because the unification problem has two solutions: B = 3 and B = x, A = 3. Unification problems that have more than one solution or problems for which it is hard to prove there is only one solution, delay in the hope that some future computation will simplify the problem. The Qu-Prolog release comes with an example program, `incomplete_retry_delays` that attempts to find solutions to delayed unification problems. This program is used in the Ergo prover to eliminate such delays on request and is used in our example below to eliminate any remaining delayed unification problems.

Let us now look at the implementation in QuP^{++} of a reasoning agent whose inference engine is a tableau style prover for full first order predicate logic. The inference engine is given a list of sentences in first order logic and tries to find a contradiction – in other words it tries to show the collection of sentences is unsatisfiable. The inference engine is supplied with a resource bound that limits the number of inference steps.

We begin with a discussion of the inconsistency checker class (the inference engine) and later look at the reasoning agent class.

The inconsistency checker and the reasoning agent and its clients need to represent logical formulae as Qu-Prolog terms and this is aided with the following declarations.

```
?- obvar_prefix([x,y]).
?- op(860, quant, all).   % The universal quantifier
?- op(860, quant, ex).    % The existential quantifier
?- op(810, fx, ~).        % negation
?- op(820, xfy, and).     % conjunction
?- op(830, xfy, or).      % disjunction
?- op(840, xfy, =>).      % implication
?- op(850, xfy, <=>).     % equivalence
```

Following the declarations, the Qu-Prolog parser will then recognize the terms below (for example).

```
all x p(x)
[A/x]B
all x_1 ex x_2 (p(x_1) => q(x_2))
```

The first term represents the quantified term whose quantifier symbol is `all`, whose bound variable is `x` and whose body is `p(x)`. The seond term represents a substitution application where all free `x`'s in B are to be replaced by `A`.

The header for the inconsistency checker class is given below. The state variable `simplifier` is the address of a simplifier agent that the inconsistency checker uses to simplify the formulae.

```
class inconsistency_checker
state [simplifier]
inconsistent(Fs,R,RR):-
    find_contradiction(Fs,R,RR,not_simplified_yet).

% ... clauses for find_contradiction/4 and make_instances/5
} private [find_contradiction/4,make_instances/5]
```

In the only public method of this class, `inconsistent(Fs,R,RR)`, Fs is a list of formulae and R is a resource bound – the maximum number of inference steps allowed in trying to reduce Fs to an obviously inconsistent list of formulae. RR is the remaining sumber of inference steps after an inconsistency is found. The state variable `simplifier` holds the identity of a simplifier agent that can be used, at most once, to do auxilary simplification reductions.

```
find_contradiction(_,0,_,_):- !,fail. %  resource bound exceeded
find_contradiction(Fs,R,RR,STag) :-
    member(~true, Fs),!,
    RR is R-1.
```

```
find_contradiction(Fs,R,RR,STag) :-
    member(~(X=X), Fs),
    incomplete_retry_delays,
    !,
    RR is R-1.
find_contradiction(Fs,R,RR,STag) :-
    member(X, Fs),
    member(~X, Fs),
    incomplete_retry_delays,
    !,
    RR is R-1.
find_contradiction(Fs,R,RR,STag) :- %  Split conjunct.
    member_and_rest(A and B, Fs, Rst),
    !,
    NR is R-1,
    find_contradiction([A,B|Rst],NR,RR,STag).
find_contradiction(Fs,R,RR,STag) :- %  Remove an ex quantifier.
    member_and_rest(ex x A, Fs, Rst),
    x not_free_in Rst,
    !,
    NR is R-1,
    find_contradiction([A|Rst],NR,RR,STag).
find_contradiction(Fs,R,RR,STag) :- %  Branch on disjunct.
    member_and_rest(A or B, Fs, Rst),
    !,
    NR is R-1,
    find_contradiction([A|R],NR,IRR,STag),
    find_contradiction([B|R],IRR,RR,STag).
find_contradiction(Fs,R,RR,STag) :- %  Branch on implication.
    member_and_rest(A => B, Fs, Rst),
    !,
    NR is R-1,
    find_contradiction([~A|R],NR,IRR,STag),
    find_contradiction([B|R],IRR,RR,STag).
find_contradiction(Fs,R,RR,STag) :- % Do   univ. instantiations.
    make_instances(Fs, Fs, NewFs, R, NR),
    NR < R,        % made at least one univ. instantiation
    !,
    find_contradiction(NewFs,NR,RR,STag).

%  Call the simplifier - only if not been called before.
find_contradiction(Fs,R,RR,not_simplified_yet) :-
    NR is R-1,
    simplifier*=S,
    S?simplify(Fs,SFs),      % remote call to simplifier agent
    find_contradiction(SFs,NR,RR,simplified).
```

```
% Make instances of all universal and
% negated existential formulae.
make_instances([], New, New, R, R).
make_instances([H|T], Fs, NewFs, R, NR) :-
    ( H = all x A
      ->
         IFs = [[_/x]A|Fs],
         IR is R - 1
    ;
      H = ~ex x A
      ->
         IFs = [~[_/x]A|Fs],
         IR is R - 1
    ;
         IFs = Fs,
         IR = R
    ),
    make_instances(T, IFs, NewFs, IR, NR).
```

The private method `find_contradiction/4` attempts to reduce its `Fs` argument to a contradictary list and succeeds if it can do this within the resource bound of `R` steps. The last argument is a symbol flag that switches to `simplified` when the `simplifier` agent has been used in a particular inference, preventing another use. The third argument will return the final resource count when a contradiction is found. It is not of interest for a top level call, but it must be used when an inference splits into two sub-proofs to ensure that the second sub-proof uses only the resource left after the first sub-proof succeeds.

The first clause for `find_contradictition/4` causes the call to fail when the resource bound has been reduced to 0. The next three clauses deal with direct contradictions in its list of formulae first argument. The remainder deal with the logical operators and simplification. We only give representitive examples of this last group of clauses. The predicate `member_and_rest(E,L,R)` succeeds if `E` is somewhere on `L` and `R` is `L` with `E` removed.

The sixth clause eliminates existential quantifiers. The call to the built-in predicate `not_free_in/2` constrains `x` to be not-free-in `R` as required.

The universal instantiation rule makes an instance of each universal and negated existential formula and **adds** this to the list of formulae. For example, the formula `all x A` is instantiated to `A` with all free `x`'s in `A` replaced by a new meta-variable representing a yet-to-be-determined instance and this is added as a new formula. Since the universally quantified formulae remain, the rule can be re-applied any number of times providing there is at least one new formula added by its application. Repeated application of the rule to the same formulae is needed because sometimes a proof requires several different instantiations of a universally quantified formula. After each application we can expect that earlier rules will apply to the augmented list of formulae and these will be exhaustively applied before it is re-used. The earlier rules always remove the formula to which they apply.

The universal instantiation rule is made to fail if no universal instantiation is found by the call to the auxiliary predicate `make_instances/5` to prevent repeated, pointless application to lists of formulae which contain no universally quantified formulae. In this case, when the universal instantiation rule is first called and fails, only the simplification rule can be used, as a last resort. After this has been used once, when all the earlier rules have been exhaustively applied and the universal instantiation rule is recalled and again fails, the entire proof fails.

The last clause sends a message to a simplifier agent that attempts to simplify the formula list according to its own simplification rules. The prover agent waits until the simplifier returns a simplified list. This clause demonstrates how one reasoning agent can take advantage of the skills of other reasoning agents in solving its problems. The simplifier might, for example, be a rewrite system for arithmetic subexpressions.

We now give an example of the inference engine in action by showing the sequence of transformations that `find_contradictition` would generate given a list of formulae.

```
(initial list)
[ ~ex x r(x), p(a) or ex x1 q(x1), all y1 ~q(y1),
                              all z1 p(z1) => r(z1)]

(or rule on: p(a) or ..)
[ ~ex x r(x), p(a), all y1 ~q(y1), all z1 p(z1) => r(z1)],

[~ex x r(x), ex x1 q(x1), all y1 ~q(y1), all z1 p(z1) => r(z1)]

(univ. instant. rule on: ~ ex x .., all y1 .., all z1 ..
          of first list)
[~r(X1), p(a), ~q(Y1), p(Z1) => r(Z1), ~ex x r(x),
                   all y1 ~q(y1), all z1 p(z1) => r(z1)],

[~ex x r(x), ex x1 q(x1), all y1 ~q(y1), all z1 p(z1) => r(z1)]

(implies rule on: p(Z1)=>r(Z1) of first list)
[~r(X1), p(a), ~q(Y1), ~p(Z1), ...],

[~r(X1), ~q(Y1), r(Z1), ...],

[~ex x r(x), ex x1 q(x1), all y1 ~q(y1), all z1 p(z1) => r(z1)]

(contradiction rule appied to: p(a),~p(Z1) of first list
                 and to: ~r(X1),r(Z1) of second list)
[~ex x r(x), ex x1 q(x1), all y1 ~q(y1), all z1 p(z1) => r(z1)]
```

```
(ex rule applied to: ex x1 q(x1))
[~ex x r(x), q(x2), all y1 ~q(y1), all z1 p(z1) => r(z1)]

(univ. instant. rule applied to:
        ~ex x r(x), all y1 ~q(y1), all z1 p(z1) => r(z1))
[~r(X2), ~q(Y2), p(Z2) => r(Z2), ~ex x r(x), q(x2), ...]

(contradiction rule applied to: ~q(Y2),q(x2))
success
```

When the `ex rule` is applied the new object variable (which comes from the rule instance) is set to be not free in all the other formulae in the list.

Note that we can use `find_contradiction` to attempt answer extraction during the proof. If, for example, we have the formula `~r(X)`, instead of the formula `~ex x r(x)` in the list of formulas at the start of the above contradiction derivation, a contradiction will also be found generating the binding `X=a`. In fact, if the formulae in the knowledge base are essentially horn clauses and the 'query' formula is of the right form then `find_contradiction` behaves as a Prolog goal evaluator.

However, answer extraction is not always possible. If we take `~ex y r(y)` as the query formula and if the knowledge base consists of the formula `ex x r(x)` or the formula `r(a) or r(b)` then `find_contradiction` will succeed. If, however, the query formula is `~r(X)` then a contradiction cannot be found. In the first case, the use of the rule for existential quantification causes a not-free-in condition to be generated that prevents `X` from being instantiated to `x`. In the second case, two different instantiations are required during the proof.

We now turn our attention to an example of a reasoning agent class. This is the class definition for a reasoning agent. Each reasoning agent object contains a knowledge base of `believes` facts that can be initialised when the agent is created and added to whilst it is alive. Clients of the reasoning agent can use the `ask` method to see if the agent believes the supplied formula. The agent believes the formula if it is in the knowledge base or can be deduced from the knowledge base within the supplied inference step resource bound.

```
class reasoner isa inconsistency_checker
state [believes/1, told/1, mentor/1]
clauses{
init :- object_thread_fork(_,absorb_told_info).

absorb_told_info:-
   thread_wait_on_goal(self_retract(told(F))),
   findall(S, believes(S), Fs),
   ( inconsistent([F|Fs],200,_) ->
       true
   ;
```

```
        self_assert(believes(F))
    ),
    absorb_told_info.
tell(B) :-
    caller(M),
    mentor(M),
    self_assertz(told(B)).
ask(F,_) :-
        believes(F),
        !,
        caller(Cl),
        Cl^^proved(F).
ask(F,R):-
        nonvar(F),
        integer(R),
        R>0,
        caller(Cl),
        object_thread_fork(_,try_to_prove(F, R, Cl)).
try_to_prove(F, R, Cl) :-
        findall(S, believes(S), Fs),
        ( inconsistent([~F|Fs],R,RR) ->
                Cl^^proved(F,RR)
        ;
                Cl^^not_proved(F,RR)
        ).
}
private [try_to_prove/2, absorb_told_info/0, inconsistent/2,
        told/1].
```

As an example use of this program, suppose we execute:

`new(reasoner,[{believes(p(a) or ex x1 q(x1)). ..},..],Ag)`

where the agent is given the formulas:

`p(a) or ex x1 q(x1), all y1 ~q(y1), all z1 p(z1) => r(z1)`

as its initial beliefs. If some other agent Cl then sends the query:

`Ag^^ask(r(X),100)`

Ag will spawn a contradiction sub-proof trying to reduce:

```
[ ~r(X), p(a) or ex x1 q(x1), all y1 ~q(y1),
                        all z1 p(z1) => r(z1)]
```

to a contradiction. Since this will succeed, the reply:

`Cl^^proved(r(a))`

will be sent to the client agent.

The mentor/1 dynamic predicate is used to tell the agent which other agents are allowed to give it new information by calling its tell method. Notice that the method does not immediately add a believes/1 fact. Instead a told/1 fact is asserted and it is the responsibility of the absorb_told_info 'daemon', that runs as a separate thread launched by the init method, to check if the told sentence F is inconsistent with the sentences already in the knowledge base. If it can prove inconsistency within a resource limit of 200 inference steps then the told sentence is ignored. Otherwise the told sentence is added to the knowledge base. This is potentially dangerous since it could produce a knowledge base with 'deep' contradictions, but it is pragmatic. That the agent will not accept tell/1 calls except from its mentors is another safeguard.

The meta-call predicate thread_wait_on_goal, used in the reasoner class definition, causes the thread to suspend until the goal which is its argument succeeds. That is, the argument goal is tried. If it succeeds, the meta-call succeeds and no further solutions of the argument goal are sought on back-tracking. If it fails, the thread executing the meta-call suspends until there is some update to the dynamic clause data base, or the record date base. The argument call is then retried. This try, fail, retry, continues indefinitely until the argument goal succeeds. In this case it will cause the absorb_told_info object thread to suspend until some told(F) fact is asserted by the interface thread. The thread deletes the asserted fact and asserts a believes(F) fact if F cannot be shown to be inconsistent with the agent's current beliefs within 200 inference steps. If it can be shown to be inconsistent with the current beliefs no belief fact is asserted. The absorb_told_info thread then recurses to handle the next asserted told/1 fact.

This is one simple example of a reasoning agent. Another possibility is to define a cooperative reasoning agent that can be used to implement a distributed knowledge base. The system would contain a collection of agents, each with their own local knowledge base, that would cooperate to produce proofs based on the combined knowledge of the group. Each agent could have meta knowledge about which other agents 'know about' particular predicates and hence can be asked to prove or disprove predications (or their negations) containing these predicates.

To achieve this we can define a sub-class coop_reasoner of the reasoner class. This is given below.

It has an extra dynamic predicate:

has_proved_false(L,Ag,RR)

which is used by the agent to record answers to isfalse/2 queries it has sent out to other agents. It also has extra methods for accepting asynchronous calls isfalse(L,R), that cause the agent to try to contradict L within R inference steps, and for accepting asynchronous proved_false(L,RR) replies to such calls that it has sent to other agents. Here RR is the number of inference steps left from the resource R given in the isfalse/2 request.

The three new clauses for find_contradiction/4 add a new way for terminating a contradiction proof. When a literal L is found in the current list of formulas with a predicate P, and the agent believes that some other agent Ag knows about P, providing the complement literal to L is not in the currentl list, Ag is sent an asynchronous isfalse(L,RforAg) call. The proof then continues with asked(L,A) replacing L in the list of formulas. (For this reason we need the second new clause for find_contradiction/4 that terminates a proof when a literal is found for which there is an asked/2 formula mentioning its complement.) RforAg is a number of inference steps that Ag should use in trying to contradict L. It is got by dividing up the remaining inference steps in a manner dependent upon L. We leave this undefined. A suitable default definition would just halve the remaining inference steps, no matter what L is. Notice that when a sub-contracted proof is achieved inside the given resource bound, signalled by the eventual self asserting of a has_proved_false(Ag,L,RR) dynamic clause by the concurrently executing interface thread as a result of a proved_false(L,RR) call, the unused inference steps RR of the sub-contracted proof are added to the still unused inference steps of the main proof to give a more accurate value for the unused the inference steps of the main proof.

The agent's interface thread will concurrently be responding to queries from other agents, including any proved_false(L) reply sent back from Ag. The interface thread will respond to this by self asserting a has_proved_false(L,Ag). These dynamic facts are handled by the second new clause. This second clause looks for asked(L,Ag) reminders left in the current list of formulas. For each such reminder it checks to see if has_proved_false(L,Ag) holds, i.e. if such a fact has been asserted by the concurrently executing interface thread. If any such replies have been received to the sub-contracted proofs, the main contradiction proof immediately terminates.

```
class coop_reasoner isa reasoner
state [has_proved_false/3]
clauses {
find_contradiction(Fs,R,RR,STag) :-
    member_and_rest(L, Fs, Rst),
    literal(L),
    predicate_of(L,P),             % perhaps should sub-contract L
    believes(knows_about(P,Ag)),   % to Ag but should not if
    complement(L,CompL),           % Fs contains complement of L
    \+ member(CompL,Rst),          % or a note that Ag has been
    \+ member(asked(CompL,Ag)),    % asked about its complement
    divide_up(L,R,RforAg,NR),
    !,
    isfalse(L,RforAg)^^Ag,
    find_contradiction([asked(L,Ag)|Rst],NR,RR,STag).
find_contradiction(Fs,R,RR,STag) :-
    member(L, Fs),
    literal(L),
    complement(L,CompL),           % find complement to L
    member(asked(CompL,_), Fs),    % equiv. to having CompL
```

```
        incomplete_retry_delays,
        !,
        RR is R-1.
find_contradiction(Fs,R,CRR,STag) :-
        member_and_rest(asked(L,A),R),
        has_proved_false(L,A,RR),   % reply has come from A about L
        incomplete_retry_delays,
        CRR is R + RR,
        !.
find_contradiction(Fs,R,RR,STag):-
        super?find_contradiction(Fs,R,RR,STag).

proved_false(L,RR):-
        caller(Ag),
        self_assert(has_proved_false(L,Ag,RR)).

isfalse(L,R):-
        caller(Ag),
        findall(S,believes(S),Fs),
        object_thread_fork(_,try_to_contradict(L, R, Ag)).

try_to_contradict(F, R, Ag) :-
        findall(S, believes(S), Fs),
        inconsistent([F|Fs],R) -> proved_false(L)^^Ag ; true.
} private [has_proved_false].
```

6 Related Work

With repect to its OO features the design of QuP^{++} has been much influenced by
L&O [16] and DK-Parlog++ [9]. L&O is an OO extension for a single threaded
Prolog and the objects are not active. However, QuP^{++} borrows its inheritance
semantics from L&O. DK-Parlog++ is an OO extension of a distributed hybrid of Parlog[6] and the multi-threaded IC-Prolog II[10]. DK-Parlog++ classes
have both procedural methods (Parlog clauses) and knowledge methods (Prolog clauses). Object state, as in QuP^{++}, is represented by both state variables
and dynamic clauses. QuP^{++} methods are the equivalent of the DK-Parlog++
knowledge methods. However, DK-Parlog++ has only single inheritance and
does not have built in support for multi-threaded objects where all the threads
can access and update the object's state with atomic operations. It is also restricted to a local area network, whereas QuP^{++} objects can be distributed over
the internet.

DLP [11] is perhaps the closest distributed OO LP language to QuP^{++}. DLP
has classes with multi-inheritance and class instances run as separate threads.
Object state can only be recorded as state variables, not as clauses. Method
invocation is a remote synchronous call. The default is that such a call spawns

a query sub-thread in the target object. This is similar to the O??Q remote call of QuP^{++} that we have not discussed in this paper. For a query O??Q the different solutions are returned by O to the caller C1, one at a time, as required by backtracking within C1. This is distributed backtracking and its QuP^{++} implementation is sketched in [7]. For a O?Q call all its solutions are returned to C1 in a list with local backtracking within C1. DLP does not have the equivalent of the ? and ^^ remote calls. In addition, it appears objects can only be single threaded. An object can have the equivalent of an `init` method but this cannot spawn sub-threads, it can only spawn new objects that have a separate state. Because of this the DLP `init` method must periodically expiclitly interrupt its pro-active execution to accept remote calls. One cannot have QuP^{++} style multi-threaded objects, with one thread accepting remote calls whilst the other threads concurrently engage in their own specific activities interacting, if need be via the shared object state. In addition, neither DLP and DK-Parlog++ have reflective methods such as `class/1` and `mystate/1` and consequently do not allow easy programming of mobile agents. Both are also OO extensions of normal Prolog, with no special support for writing inference systems.

CIAO Prolog is a rich Prolog systems that also has multi-threading[4], with inter-thread communication via atomic updates of the dynamic data base, and a module system which has been used to implement an OO extenssion O'CIAO[5]. O'CIAO supports multiple inheritance between classes with class methods being static clauses and object state being represented as dynamic clauses. Dynamic clauses for the different object instances are distinguished in the same way as in QuP^{++} by adding the object identity as an extra argument to the predicate they define. The objects of O'CIAO are passive objects, the instances do not run as separate threads, however CIAO itself has active modules which can also have state, repesented as dynamic clauses local to the module. These active modules can be given global identities that can be stored in files and client modules can make use of the active module by referencing this file and declaring which predicates it is using from amongst those that are exported by the module. These exported predicates are then called in the normal way within the client module, but the implementation will do a remote call to the active module. The concept of an active module/class could be added to O'CIAO to give it active objects. Also, the multi-threading of CIAO could be used to allow multi-threaded objects sharing the same dynamic clause object state, but this integration of all the features of CIAO has apparently not yet been done. CIAO Prolog also has constraint handling but has no built in support for programming non-clausal theorem provers.

Mozart-Oz[19] is a multi-paradigm distributed symbolic programming language with support for logic programming, functional programming and constraint handling. It is being used for distributed agent applications[22]. It also has passive objects, essentially records of functions which can access and update state local to the record. Mozart-Oz is multi-threaded with the threads sharing a common store of values and constraints. The store is used for inter-thread communication. Constraints are posted to the store and the store can be queried as to whether some particular constraint is entailed by the current constraint store. A thread executing such a query will suspend until the store entails the constraint. This is a generalisation of our use of `thread_wait_on_goal/1` in QuP^{++}.

In Mozart-Oz any data value, including on object or an unbound variable of the constraint store, can be shared across different Mozart-Oz processes by creating a ticket for the data value using a special primitive. The ticket is an ASCII string and is similar to the global identity of an active object in QuP^{++}, which is a term constructed from three symbols. This ticket string can then be used in another Mozart-Oz process to access the value associated with the ticket, even if it is held in a non-local store, by calling another ticket value access primitive.

Active objects can be programmed by using a Mozart-Oz port which can be sent a message from any thread that has access to the port, perhaps via a ticket. A port is rather like an object's message queue in QuP^{++}. Another thread then accesses the messages sent to the port as elements of an incrementally generated list, calling an appropriate method of some local passive object for each accessed message. Such a port/thread/object combination behaves very like a QuP^{++} active object, but the calling of the object's methods and the sending of replies has to be achieved in Mozart-Oz using explict asynchronous message sends to ports and explicit accesses of messages from the port message streams. That is, what we have referred to as the interface thread has to be explictly programmed as a wrapper for an object to make it active. This is how the remote calls of QuP^{++} are implemented, using the inter-thread communication primitives of Qu-Prolog[7], but QuP^{++} presents to a programmer the higher level abstraction of synchronous and asynchronous remote calls directly to an object's methods.

Gaea[20] is a multi-threaded OO Prolog system with active objects which have dynamic methods and modifiable inheritance trees. Gaea is not a class based OO system. Instead each active object, which in Gaea is just a thread with an associated `cell` of clauses, executes in an environment of a list of parent cells for its cell. These parent cells have the role of super-classes, but the list of parent cells can be dynmically constructed as the object is created. Each of these parent cells can itself have an associated list of parent cells. So an object executes in an tree structured environment of ancestor cells rooted at its cell. This is similar to a QuP^{++} object executing in tree structured environment of the static methods of its super classes (the parent hierarchy of Gaea cells) with its own state component of dynamic clauses and state variables (the root cell directly linked with the Gaea object/thread). The difference is that in Gaea, the inheritance structure is created dynamically, as the active object is forked, *and* it can be modified whilst the object is executing. Any parent cell of a cell can be removed and new ones can be added. So the entire inheritance hierarchy for an object is dynamic. These modifications to the inheritance structure can be made by the object itself, or by another object executing in the same Gaea process.

Cells can contain cell variables as well as clauses. The cell variables are similar to the state variables of a QuP^{++} object. The cell clauses can be updated using special cell assert and retract primitives, similar to the self assert and retract of QuP^{++}, as can the cell variables. Objects communicate via the clauses and cell variables of the cells they both have access to. In addition, a call can be evaluated relative to a named cell. When this is the root cell linked with an object, this is equivalent to a call to the methods of that object, even though the call is executed in the caller, rather than the callee. Clearly this is only possible when the different objects execute in the same Gaea process, for only then will each have access to the cell clauses of the other objects. Gaea is not a distributed system.

The ability to modify the inheritance structure of an object is a much more dymamic way of changing an object's behaviour than the `become/2` primitive of QuP^{++}. However, the flexibility may come at a cost of program transparency. Gaea has no special support for writing theorem provers.

λProlog, see for example [2], is a logic programming language with built-in support for λ-terms and consequently can be used as an implementation language for theorem provers in much the same way as is done in Qu-Prolog. λProlog does not, however, appear to provide as much support as Qu-Prolog does for implementing interactive theorem provers, nor does it appear to have support for multiple threads or even high-level communication bewteen different λProlog processes.

In this paper we have shown how simple multi-threaded agents can readily be implemented in QuP^{++}. Since our main concern was illustrating the features of the language we have not developed any complex agent architectures. However, it would be no great effort to implement logic based agent architectures such as those described in [3], [21], [23]. Implementing more complex architectures, with both sophisticated reasoning and reactive capabilities, is the subject of our on-going research.

Bob Kowalski wrote a short paper in 1985 [13] which anticipated many of the ideas now being discussed with respect to logic based agents. In particular, the paper discusses the need for information assimilation by resource bounded reasoning agents, interacting with one another and the world. Our co-operative reasoning agents are a partial realisation of the ideas expressed in that paper. His ideas have since been elaborated in [14] and [15] to allow interleaving of action and reasoning within an agent, in order to reconcile the need for rationality and reactivity. The agent architectures sketched in these more recent papers could also easily be implemented in QuP^{++}.

References

1. Holger Becht, Anthony Bloesch, Ray Nickson and Mark Utting, Ergo 4.1 Reference Manual, Technical Report No. 96-31, Software Verification Research Centre, Department of Computer Science, University of Queensland, 1996.
2. C. Belleannée, P. Brisset, O. Ridoux, A pragmatic reconstruction of λProlog, *Journal of Logic Programming*, 41(1), 1999, pp 67-102

3. M. Bozzano, G. Delzanno, M. Mattelli, V. Mascardi, F. Zini, Logic Programming and Multi-Agent Systems: A synergic combination for applications and semantics, in *The Logic Programming Paradigm*, (eds K. Apt et al), Springer-Verlag, 1999.
4. M. Carro and M. Hermenegildo, Concurrency in Prolog Using Threads and a Shared Database. *Proceedings of ICLP99*, (ed. D. De Schreye), MIT Press, 1999, pp 320-334.
5. A. Pineda and M. Hermenegildo, O'Ciao: An Object Oriented Programming Model for (CIAO) Prolog, Research Report CLIP 5/99.0, (accessible from http://www.clip.dia.fi.upm.es/), Facultad de Informatica, UPM, Madrid, 1999.
6. K. L. Clark, S. Gregory, Parlog: Parallel Programming in Logic, *ACM Toplas* 8(1), 1-49 pp, 1986.
7. Keith Clark, Peter Robinson and Richard Hagen. Multi-threading and Message Communication in Qu-Prolog *Theory and Practice of Logic Programming*, **1**(3), 2001, pp 283-301.
8. Keith Clark, Peter J. Robinson and Richard Hagen, Programming Internet Based DAI Applications in Qu-Prolog, *Multi-agent systems*, (eds. C. Zhang, D. Lukose), Springer-Verlag, LNAI 1544, 1998.
9. K.L. Clark, T.I. Wang, Distributed Object Oriented Logic Programming, *Proceedings of FGCS94 Workshop on Co-operating Heterogeneous Information Systems*, Tokyo, 1994.
10. D. Chu, K. L. Clark, IC-Prolog II: A multi-threaded Prolog system *Proceedings of ICLP93 Post Conf. Workshop on Concurrent, Distributed and Parallel implementations of Logic Programming Systems*, 1993
11. A. Eliens, *DLP, A language for distributed logic programming* Wiley, 1992
12. Richard Hagen and Peter J. Robinson. Qu-Prolog 4.3 User Guide. Technical Report No. 97-12, Software Verification Research Centre, University of Queensland, 1999.
13. R. A. Kowalski, Logic Based Open Systems, *Representation and Reasoning*, Jakob ph. Hoepelmann (Hg.) Max Niemeyer Verlag, Tubingen, 1985, pp125-134.
14. R. Kowalski and F. Sadri, Towards a unified agent architecture that combines rationality with reactivity, *Proc. International Workshop on Logic in Databases*, Springer-Verlag, LNCS 1154, 1996.
15. R. A. Kowalski and F. Sadri, From Logic Programming to Multi-Agent Systems, *Annals of Mathematics and Artificial Intelligence* 25, 1999, pp391-419.
16. F.G. McCabe, *Logic and Objects* Prentice-Hall, 1992.
17. F.G. McCabe, The Inter-Agent Communication Model (ICM), http://www.nar.fla.com/icm/, Fujitsu Laboratories of America Inc, 2000.
18. F. G. McCabe and K. L. Clark. April:Agent Process Interaction Language. *Intelligent Agents*, (ed. N. Jennings, M. Wooldridge), Springer-Verlag LNCS 890, 1995.
19. Mozart-Oz Homepage: www.mozart-oz.org
20. I. Noda, H. Nakashima, K. Handa, Programming language GAEA and its application for multi-agent systems, *Proc. of Workshop on Multi-agent systems and Logic programming*, In conjunction with ICLP'99, 1999.
21. A. Roa, AgentSpeak(L): BDI Agents speak out in a logical computable language, *Agents Breaking Away*, (eds. W. van de Velde and J. W. Perram), Springer-Verlag LNCS 1038, 1996.
22. Peter Van Roy and Seif Haridi, Mozart: A Programming System for Agent Applications, *International Workshop on Distributed and Internet Programming with Logic and Constraint Languages*, 1999. Accessible from http://www.mozart-oz.org/papers/
23. G. Wagner, Artificial Agents and Logic Programming, in *Proc. of ICLP'97 Post Conference Workshop on Logic Programming and Multi-Agent Systems*, 1997.

Logic Programming Languages for the Internet

Andrew Davison

Prince of Songkla University
Dept. of Computer Engineering
Hat Yai, Songkhla 90112, Thailand
dandrew@ratree.psu.ac.th

Abstract. We specify the major characteristics of the Internet under
the headings: heterogeneity, service characteristics, dynamic nature, no
global notions, and unreliability (i.e. security and partial failure). In the
process, we identify five categories of Internet services: hosts, active entities, agents, semistructured data, and passive code.
Logic Programming (LP) languages for the Internet are divided into six
broad groups: shared variables, coordination, message passing, client-
side execution, server-side execution, and integration of heterogeneous
data sources. Within each group we attempt to highlight the advantages
and disadvantages for Internet programming in terms of our Internet
characteristics and services, and describe LP languages that typify the
group.

1 Answering the Challenge

In the mid 1980's, Carl Hewitt argued that Logic Programming (LP) was inadequate for modeling open systems [67]. Hewitt's objections rest on classical
logic's use of a static, globally consistent system which cannot represent dynamic
activities, inconsistencies, and non-global concerns.

At the time, his broadside was addressed by two papers. Kowalski [77] agreed
that model theoretic formulations of logic were lacking, and proposed the use
of knowledge assimilation to capture change, along with additional elements
to deal with belief systems. Kowalski's subsequent work on the event calculus
and reactive and rational agents [78,79] can be viewed as developments of these
ideas. Kahn and Miller suggested concurrent LP as the logical framework for
open systems [75].

Another way of answering Hewitt is to look to the Internet, the World's
largest open system. Among other things, this survey shows that LP is a successful *component* of Internet programming languages, employed for tasks ranging from security semantics, composition of heterogeneous data, to coordination
'glue'. Many approaches have moved beyond first order logic (e.g. to concurrent
constraints, linear logic, higher order), and LP is frequently combined with other
paradigms (e.g. mutable state, objects). Furthermore, many of the programming
concerns for the Internet are still less than fully understood: for example, there
are unanswered problems related to mobility, security, and failure. No single
Internet language, including an Internet LP language, has all the answers *yet*.

A.C. Kakas, F. Sadri (Eds.): Computat. Logic (Kowalski Festschrift), LNAI 2407, pp. 66–104, 2002.

2   From LAN to Internet

Cardelli [25] argues that the Internet is not some scaled-up version of a LAN, but actually violates our familiar assumptions about distributed systems, learnt from multiprocessor and LAN-based applications. We specify the differences under five headings: 1) Heterogeneity; 2) Service Characteristics; 3) Dynamic Nature; 4) No Global Notions; and 5) Unreliability.

2.1   Heterogeneity

Due to wide variations in Internet components, it is impossible to make predictions about overall behaviour. This covers topics such as processor capabilities, available resources, response time, and latency. In particular, bandwidth fluctuations due to unpredictable congestion or partitioning means that any guarantees of services will be guesses at best, and that failure becomes indistinguishable from long delays.

In the next sub-section, we identify five kinds of Internet service: hosts, active entities, agents, semistructured data, and passive code. Each of these exhibit quite different capabilities and behaviours, and have a variety of owners and authors.

2.2   Service Characteristics

Hosts Hosts are services which stay in one (virtual) location, perhaps acting as a Web server, virtual machine, or resource provider. Virtual locations are defined in terms of their position within administrative domains, through which mobile services (e.g. agents) must move. Domains may be nested, and a mobile service must have suitable capabilities to move in and out of those domains it visits.

The utilisation of administrative domains (a non-technical constraint on programming) gives rise to a view of the Internet as a hierarchical set of spaces with non-flat addressing, non-transparent routing, and non-free mobility – a radical departure from a LAN-derived model [26].

Active Entities Typically criteria for an active entity are autonomy, reactivity, concurrency, and non-determinism [67,75].

The arguments for employing the object oriented paradigm as part of an Internet model are so strong that other paradigms, such as LP, must find ways to reconcile themselves with it. Several recent object oriented deductive languages are compared in [82]. An older survey of LP-based object oriented languages is [44].

The disconnected nature of entity communication is often modeled by asynchronous message passing (to decouple communication delay from computation). Other reasons for an arm's length relationship are to maintain security and prevent failure of one entity affecting others.

Active entities may be mobile, deciding for themselves where to go – this is part of their autonomous behaviour. The inclusion of mobility into a programming language and/or system makes network transparency very hard to maintain [19]. Mobile entities require knowledge about current node (or host) connectivity and the location of site-specific resources. Mobility can mean different things: moving the entity's code, moving a reference to the entity (its execution location remaining unchanged), the entity's state, or relocating its computation or closure. Designing suitable abstractions for these approaches, especially inside an open system architecture, are difficult problems.

Agents There are various definitions of agents [60,55], which are considered in more depth elsewhere in this volume. We will not discuss agent theories or languages.

Semistructured Data Semistructured data on the Web/Internet has been investigated extensively by Abiteboul [1]. It has an irregular structure (usually involving nested or cyclic structures), a mix of typed and untyped elements, and parts of the data are implicitly structured or partially specified. Significantly, these kinds of structural requirements are beyond the representational powers of many calculi and algebras.

Two important aspects of semistructured data on the Web is how to query it, and how to combine data from heterogeneous sources.

Passive Code A familiar example of passive code is the Java applet. In terms of functionality, passive code is similar to an active entity, the main difference being its means of mobility. An active entity decides for itself where to go, while another service (e.g. a Web browser) decides whether to download passive code. It is in that sense that the code is passive – it does nothing until another service executes it. Passive data mobility (sometimes called code fetching) is usually implemented via copying, while active entities actually move. This has consequences for the semantics of updates.

2.3 Dynamic Nature

Nothing is permanent on the Internet: all the services described in section 2.2 can change over time, new services appear, others disappear or move. This implies the need for white and yellow page services but, due to the lack of global knowledge, they will never be able to index everything. In any case, administrative domains will hide certain services.

Connectivity will also change, perhaps because of hardware issues, or because logical link information is passed around the system. Assumptions based on topology and routing behaviour will be suspect – for example, that messages arrive in the order they are sent.

2.4   No Global Notions

The Internet has no global time or state (knowledge base). Administrative domains mean there is no single naming scheme. Control/coordination is decentralised: to avoid bottlenecks in communication, because it is more scalable, and due to the impossibility of organising a single locus of control or coordination.

2.5   Unreliability

Security There can be no global trust, which implies the need for security. Until recently, security issues were concerned with the safe handling of messages, including the problems of eavesdropping, masquerading, tampering, and replay [39]. With the growing importance of mobile code, security concerns have become more complex.

Moore [95] identifies two problematic areas of mobility: a host requires protection against malicious mobile services (i.e. active entities, agents, downloaded passive code), and a mobile service must guard itself against dangerous hosts.

Thorn [123] considers four issues in the malicious mobile service category: maintaining the confidentiality of a host's private information, retaining the integrity of its information, preventing denial of service attacks, and visitor authentication. These issues are complicated by security being potentially 'spread' through many layers in a host.

Security is arguably at the heart of mobile entity design, since it defines the boundaries of control and responsibility between the entity and its host's execution environment.

Partial Failure Partial failures of the Internet fall into two main parts: node (host) failure and network link failures, with numerous subdivisions. For example, Coulouris et al. [39] identify node failures where the current state is lost, corrupted, or an earlier state is restored on restart. Other types of error, which may be caused by node or link failure, include message loss, message corruption, or message delay beyond some time limit.

In practice, fault tolerant protocols utilise time-outs and retransmission of messages based on assumptions about the maximum likely response time of a service and the likelihood of repeated message loss. Another approach is to use transactions, either implicitly added to the client by the system, or as a language construct. A popular language solution is to pass detected failures to the client as exceptions.

Waldo et al. [128] names partial failure as one of the four areas which makes distributed computing fundamentally different from local computation (the others are latency, memory accesses, and concurrency). Waldo believes that it is impossible to satisfactorily integrate failure handling for local and remote entities without introducing unacceptable compromises.

3 Let the Games Commence

This survey utilises the classification structure given in Figure 1. Within each category, we identify the advantages and disadvantages for Internet programming, and describe languages which typify that category.

- Shared Variables
  - Concurrent (Constraint) LP
  - Distributed Oz/Mozart
- Coordination
  - Linda and LP
  - Parallel Multiset Rewriting
- Message Passing
  - IC-Prolog II and Friends
  - PVM-Prolog
  - Mercury
- Client-side Execution
  - Libraries
  - Query Languages
  - Web Pages as Programs
  - Java and LP
- Server-side Execution
  - Libraries
  - Modifications to CGI
- Integration of Heterogeneous Data Sources
  - Classical Integration
  - New Wave Integration

Fig. 1. Categories of LP Languages for the Internet.

A useful online resource for Internet and Web programming using LP and constraint LP is http://www.clip.dia.fi.upm.es/lpnet/index.html. It contains links to numerous workshops and other resources.

4 Shared Variables

The languages described here utilise shared logic variables as a communications mechanism between processes. This approach raises many questions: Are shared variables alone expressive enough for the range of communication protocols required? Can such a technique be efficiently implemented? Are shared variables really any better than conventional communications devices (e.g. message passing, mailboxes)? What do the introduction of these ideas do to the semantics of the logic language?

Most research has addressed the communications aspects of using shared variables. Little consideration has been given to partial failure, security or mobility.

4.1 Concurrent (Constraint) LP

We will not discuss the concurrent LP and concurrent constraint LP paradigms in depth, as they are considered elsewhere in this volume; we also recommend [109,122,105]. The impact of concurrent LP on client-side and server-side Web programming is deferred to sections 7 and 8.

Paradigm Features Concurrent LP offers a process reading of logic programs, which is quite different from sequential LP, but well suited for the implementation of reactive, dynamically changing systems with encapsulated mutable state.

There are no global notions in concurrent LP languages: communication is based solely on shared variables which must be explicitly allocated between the processes. A process network is equivalent to a conjunction of AND-parallel goals.

Programs utilise very fine grained parallelism at the level of individual goal reductions. Even in distributed memory multiprocessor implementations, the overhead of goal management (e.g. task creation, migration to a processor, switching, scheduling, communication) compared to the amount of computation in the goal is of concern [5]. Across the Internet, it becomes imperative that task granularity be controlled. One solution is to add extra notation to the language for grouping related predicates and goals.

Programming Techniques The logic variable is an expressive communications mechanism; for instance, it can be used to encode stream communication (sequenced message passing), channels (partially ordered message streams), point-to-point delivery, multicasting, many-to-one links (stream merging), and blackboards.

Logix is a high-level environment/OS for developing FCP programs, written entirely in FCP [68]. Logix offers four layers of control over programs, defined using meta-interpreters. The failure mechanism only catches logical process errors not hardware/node failure.

Meta-interpreters are also used for implementing process to processor mapping [121]. Again a layered approach is utilised, with the program being mapped to a virtual machine topology, and then combined with a separate layer mapping the virtual machine to the physical architecture. At the program level, goals are positioned dynamically on virtual nodes using LOGO-like turtle annotations.

Process to processor mapping is a powerful abstraction away from the physical network. However, its success relies on the closely linked behaviour of the underlying architecture. The less well-ordered topology of the Internet may prove harder to abstract.

Efficient Communication A severe concern for language designers is the cost of output unification. In the case of FCP(:) the tell part of the guard carries out general unification, but this must be undo-able if the clause is ultimately not selected [76]. The cost of such atomic unification is similar to an atomic transaction, only possibly more prohibitive since partial bindings of data structures may be involved.

Strand makes the assumption that there is only one producer for a variable, thereby avoiding the "multiple tellers" problem altogether [58]. Janus is more restrictive in that there must only be one consumer and producer of a binding [106]. Strand and Janus programs cannot fail due to conflict bindings, and so do not have to implement atomic unification. Strand goes further and simplifies output binding to be assignment only.

The designs used in Janus and Strand have major consequences for Internet-based concurrent LP: they show that efficient communication between processes using logic variables is possible (i.e. by using non-atomic publication) while retaining their expressiveness.

PCN (Program Composition Notation) has been described as a hybrid of Strand and C, based around a few concepts: concurrent composition, single assignment variables, and nondeterministic choice [59]. Mutable variables are included, mainly as an optimisation, and to interface to pre-existing code. PCN utilises the mapping mechanisms, scheduling pragma, and virtual and physical topologies found in Strand.

PCN is novel in showing that the single assignment variable can be used as communications 'glue' for code written in non-logic programming languages.

Another approach to the multiple teller problem is to include special-purpose many-to-one communication mechanisms in the languages.

DRL [53] introduces logic channels as an efficient version of shared logic variables. Logic channels can contain messages made up of terms, logic variables, or other logic channels, thereby allowing dynamic reconfiguration of communication paths. This mechanism proved so useful that it was later extracted from DRL to become a coordination model suitable for any type of language [52]. The model also supports a virtual machine layer for grouping processes. PVM is used to implement remote process creation and message passing.

Failure Concurrent LP languages handle logical failure in one of two ways: those from the Concurrent Prolog 'camp' utilise meta-interpreters as described above for Logix. The other method, typified by Parlog, is to use a meta-call primitive [35].

The most developed concurrent LP language for failure handling is Sandra [54]. It borrows the guardian mechanism from Argus as a way of encapsulating processes, mutable state, a communications interface and a many-to-one communication port. A guardian instance represents a fail-stop logical multiprocessor. Every guardian has stable persistent storage (used in the recovery protocol), and can be relocated to a working processor in the event of failure.

Sandra utilises both forward and backward recovery. Forward recovery is based on exceptions (both logical and at the node level), which are processed by a separate handler in each guardian. Its semantics are specified using a meta-interpreter. Backward recovery is based on optimistic recovery using periodic logging and checkpointing.

The following predicate can signal (raise) an exception when a get message cannot be satisfied. no-value exceptions are dealt with by code in resource/2 itself, as are hardware connection errors. Unprocessed exceptions will be passed out to the enclosing handler.

```
resource([get(X)|In], [X|L]) :-      % normal behaviour
   resource(In, L).
resource([get(X)|In], []) :-         % raise exception
   signal( no-value(get(X)) ).

resource(In, L) :-                   % handle exceptions
   otherwise( no-value(get(X)) ) |
   X = nothing, resource(In, L).
resource([_|In], L) :-
   otherwise( connect-error(resource) ),
   emergency_action(resource, In, L).
```

Security Security has been poorly considered by concurrent LP languages, perhaps because of the prevalence of uniprocessor and LAN-based implementations. Shapiro [109] reports that one use for read-only variables in Concurrent Prolog is to protect process communication across trust boundaries. The essential idea is to make the incomplete part of the output data structure read-only to its consumers, and keep write access inside the issuing process.

A related approach, implemented in FCP so that read-only variables could be used, is described in [94]. A protocol similar in style to public key encryption is proposed which uses pairs of unforgeable IDs issued by a dedicated 'locksmith' process.

4.2   Distributed Oz

Distributed Oz (or Oz 3) is a rich mix of paradigms and techniques, including symbolic computation, inference, objects, concurrency, and distribution [66].

Oz 3 introduces distributed programming and fault detection (Mozart is the name of the current implementation [125]). The main aim is to make programs as network transparent as possible – a program should perform the same computation independently of how it is partitioned over the network. In other words, Oz 3 tries to support the illusion of a single network-wide abstract store / address space, making distributed execution indistinguishable from concurrent evaluation. For example, no program level distinction is made between local and remote references.

Distributed Semantics The intention is to make the distributed semantics a natural extension of the centralised (local) meaning of a program, the practical benefit being that a stand-alone program requires virtually no changes to convert it to a distributed application.

Centralised and distributed semantics are presented in [65], and state (mutable pointers) is considered in [126,124]. The main addition to the distributed semantics is site location for program entities.

Logic Variables Oz shows that logic variables can be efficiently supported in a distributed programming language while retaining the expressiveness seen in concurrent (constraint) LP [65]. In addition, Oz can make use of other aspects of the language (e.g. state, search) to improve on these algorithms. An example is the use of ports for many-to-one communication, which have constant time behaviour compared to the cost of concurrent LP merge networks (at best O(log n) for n senders).

Explicit networking benefits of logic variables include increased latency tolerance since producers and consumers are decoupled, and third-party independencies. This arises when two variables have been unified at a site, since that site is no longer involved in the network communication of future bindings.

Logic variables have proved so useful that the Oz group has added them to versions of Java (called CCJava) and ML [65]. Their main use in CCJava is as a replacement for monitors, allowing Java to utilise the dataflow threads techniques of Oz [112]. This requires the addition of statement-level thread creation.

Their approach is very similar to the extensions to C++ in Compositional C++ (CC++) [27], which include single assignment variables (called sync variables) and statement level threads. When a read is attempted on an unbound sync variable it causes the thread to block. CC++ also includes atomic functions, similar to synchronized methods in Java.

Beyond Network Transparency Although network transparency is a commendable design goal for distributing concurrent programs over a network, it seems unlikely to be wholly successful for Internet-based applications, such as mobile agents. However, Oz does support these kinds of programs by means of tickets and functors.

A ticket is a global reference (usually a URL) to an Oz entity (usually a logic variable), stored as an ASCII string. A ticket can be accessed by a system newcomer to obtain a language level communication link.

Functors are module specifications that list the resources that a module needs in order to execute. Their purpose is tied to an Oz programming technique called remote compute servers, which are procedures executed at fixed sites.

This example shows producer and consumer threads communicating via a data stream, with the consumer located remotely on a compute server:

```
proc {Generate N Max L}        % outputs N to Max-1 integers
   if N < Max then L1 in
```

```
      L=N|L1   {generate N+1 Max L1}
   else L=nil end
end

fun {Sum L A}                % return A + sum of L's elements
   case L
   of nil then A
   [] X|Ls then {sum Ls A+X}
   end

local CS L S in
   CS={NewComputeServer 'sinuhe.sics.se'}   % remote server
   thread L = {Generate 0 150000} end       % local producer
   {CS proc {$} S={Sum L 0} end}            % remote consumer
   {Print S}                                % print result locally
end
```

Fault Tolerance Oz 3's support for fault tolerance is based on the assumptions that sites are fail-stop nodes (i.e. that permanent site failure is detectable) and that network failure is temporary. The basic response is to raise an exception when failure is detected, which can either be handled automatically or be processed by a user-defined procedure call. Typical default behaviour for network failure is to attempt to restart the TCP connection using a cache of existing TCP connections.

Van Roy [124] has shown how the centralised and distributed semantics for mutable pointers can be extended to include exception raising when a fault occurs.

The search for higher-level abstractions for fault tolerance in Oz is an active research goal. One approach is the *global store*, a globally fault-tolerant transactional memory, implemented as a Mozart library [6]. Internally, the store uses process redundancy: with n copies of a process it can tolerate up to $n-1$ fail-stop process failures. There is an agent API on top of the store which provides fault tolerance and agent mobility without site dependencies.

Security Security concerns are still under investigation in Oz. Language security centers around lexical scoping, first-class procedures and the unforgeability of variable references.

An interesting point is the appearance of read-only views of variables (called futures). As in Concurrent Prolog, they allow the scope of variables to be limited so that, for instance, a stream cannot be altered by its readers [89]. Unlike Concurrent Prolog, the read-only mechanism imposes no efficiency penalty when it is absent.

Below the language level, Oz uses a byte-code emulator to protect machine resources, and can create virtual sites. A virtual site appears as a normal site, but its resources are under the control of a separate master process on the same machine. If the virtual site crashes, the master is notified, but is not otherwise affected.

5   Coordination

A perceived drawback of the coordination model is the use of a single shared space, which would introduce significant latency and reliability problems if applied to the Internet, as well as being very difficult to manage [98]. This has led to the introduction of multiple spaces to make the mapping to a decentralized architecture easier and scalable. Hierarchical spaces are also useful for representing nested domains with trust boundaries.

A major question is how these richer models should be integrated with existing Internet services. Various solutions include adding spaces as new services, masking Internet services as shared spaces, and introducing special purpose agents to mediate between the shared spaces and services [34].

Another trend has been the augmentation of the coordination laws of the shared space so that its behaviour can be modified. This has proved useful in an Internet setting for creating enforceable 'social behaviour' which malicious entities cannot bypass [51].

Several problems are only starting to be considered: the conflict between coordination (which encourages communication) and security (which restricts it), and partial failure.

Linda Linda supports a shared dataspace, called a tuple space, and a small set of operations for reading, adding, and removing tuples from the space [23].

Multiple flat tuple spaces were introduced quite quickly to facilitate distributed programming [63]. Hierarchical tuple spaces followed, most notably in a major revision to the Linda model by its authors, called Bauhaus Linda [24]. Bauhaus removes the distinction between tuples and tuple spaces, leading to a hierarchy based on multisets. Since tuple spaces are also tuples, they are first class citizens, and so can be moved around easily. The distinction between passive and active data is removed, making it simpler to reposition processes and copy them. Movement between spaces is based on short steps, either to the parent or one of the space's children.

Linda extensions especially for the Web/Internet include JavaSpaces [113], PageSpace [31], and WCL [92].

SeCoS [19] supports secure spaces which allows tuples to be locked with a key. A matching key for unlocking can be passed to other processes. This is quite similar to public key cryptography.

Another popular security device is to assign access rights (e.g. read and write permissions) to tuples. Menezes et al. [92] suggests including group permissions so that capabilities can be supported.

5.1 Linda and LP

Ciancarini [30] suggests four approaches to creating LP coordination models.

The first is to add the Linda primitives and shared dataspace into Prolog. The typical mapping is to represent tuples by terms, and replace pattern matching with unification. Backtracking is not supported for the reading, writing, and removal operations. Terms added to the dataspace are copies, so it is not possible to create dynamic communication links by including variables in the terms shared with other processes.

Several Prolog systems include Linda-style libraries, including BinProlog [16] and SICStus Prolog [110]. The SICStus library has been used widely as an implementation tool (e.g. [97,114]).

An operational semantics for a Linda-like coordination language using ground terms as tuples and unification for pattern matching is presented in [96].

The second approach is a variation of the first, where backtracking is allowed over the primitives. Functionality of this kind is very complex to implement, and difficult to reason about, which may explain why it has never been utilised in a coordination setting.

A third alternative is to create a new abstract machine for Prolog based on the Linda model. This line of research has not been investigated to date.

A fourth possibility is to permit the logic language to use the concurrent process model inherent in the Linda style of programming. Ciancarini and others have concentrated on this approach, resulting in Shared Prolog and its descendents.

In the following we survey the work in the first and fourth categories relevant to Internet programming.

μlog and Its Relatives μlog supports a tuple-based dataspace/blackboard [73]. No distinction is made between passive and active data, the latter being executed as goals, allowing processes to be dynamically created.

The operational and denotational semantics of μlog are investigated in [46,48]. Subsequent versions of the language added multiple named blackboards, primitives with optional guards/constraints, and bulk operations [48].

μ^2log introduced distributed blackboards, and virtual boards as local 'aliases' for boards on remote hosts [47]. Boards are treated as another form of data by the Linda primitives, which allows them to be moved between locations easily.

An operational semantics for μ^2log is outlined in [47].

Multi-BinProlog μ^2log was a strong influence on the design of Multi-BinProlog [49]. It implements the virtual board device using RPCs: a local process transparently communicates with a remote RPC server representing the remote board. It carries out the board operations locally, using a dedicated thread for the request.

LogiMOO LogiMOO is a virtual world framework which rests on top of Multi-BinProlog [120,118]. It supports the notions of places, objects, and agents using the underlying boards and threads of Multi-BinProlog. A place corresponds to a board at a remote site, objects to terms and URLs of Web pages and multimedia, and agents are collections of threads.

BinProlog's binarization preprocessor has been extended to support first order continuations, which are the basis of mobile threads programming [119].

Jinni The on-going integration of BinProlog and Java led to Jinni (the Java INference engine and Networked Interactor) [117]. It uses Prolog engines (coded in Java) to execute goals, with each engine in a separate thread. If a thread wants to communicate with a remote board it must move to its place by utilising first order continuations and socket links.

A suggested Jinni solution to malicious hosts is to have a thread take its own interpreter with it when it moves. This is feasible due to the small size of Jinni's Prolog engine. Also, returning threads can be checked since they are first order entities.

Shared Prolog and Its Descendents Shared Prolog supports the creation of parallel processes consisting of Prolog programs extended with a guard mechanism [18]. The processes communicate via a shared dataspace of terms, using unification for matching.

ESP and Polis Extended Shared Prolog (ESP) [20] is based on the Polis model [30,32] which introduced the notion of multiple tuple spaces and the storage and manipulation of rules inside the dataspaces as first-class entities (called program tuples).

A tuple space (called a place or sometimes a theory) is represented by a named multiset of tuples; operations are annotated with the place name where they are to occur. Names can be freely passed around inside tuples, so allowing dynamic reconfiguration. Places can be dynamically created by a process.

The following is a Polis theory called `eval_f` which consumes a tuple `tuple(Input)`, calls `f/4`, then produces a result `tuple(Ouput)` and recurses.

```
theory eval_f(State) :-
eval
    { tuple(Input) }  -->              % consume
    f(input, State, Output, NewState)   % process
    { tuple(Output), eval_f(NewState) } % output
with
    f(I, S, O, NS) :- ...      % Prolog defn
```

Later versions of the language allowed spaces to be distributed [30]. This was implemented on top of a network version of Linda (Network-C-Linda) that supports clusters of workstations

The Polis model was further extended to support hierarchies of multiple tuple spaces [32]. It uses a naming mechanism similar to Bauhaus Linda to allow a multiset to refer to its parent and children.

An operational semantics for Polis and a formal semantics using a temporal logic of actions are presented in [32]. An alternative approach is to specify place behaviour using a chemical interpretation in which 'molecules' float, interact, and change according to reaction rules [29].

ACLT and Tuple Centers Processes in ACLT (Agents Communicating through Logic Theories) interact with named logic theories (tuple spaces holding Prolog clauses) [97]. One mode of interaction is via Linda operations, which may cause the theory to change. The other mode uses demo-style predicates to execute goals against the theory. This means that ACLT spaces can be interpreted either as communication channels or as knowledge repositories.

Later work on ACLT [51] introduced a separate first order logic language called ReSpecT (Reaction Specification Tuples). ReSpecT reaction rules are used by the ACLT coordination model to define the behaviour of its theories in response to communication operations. Logical theories are now called tuple centers because of their programmable coordination feature.

For instance, the following reaction

```
reaction(out(p(_)), (
   in_r(p(a)), in_r(p(X)), out_r(pp(a,X)) ))
```

is triggered whenever a new p/1 tuple is inserted into the tuple space. Its intended effect is to replace two p/1 tuples (one of them should be p(a)) with a single pp/2 tuple.

This approach has the advantage (and disadvantage) of allowing the normal meaning of a Linda operation (e.g. an out) to be varied. The most important benefit is that additional coordination logic can be located in the tuple center itself, augmenting the standard behaviours of operations. This makes it easier to specify enforceable global coordination behaviours for processes.

Another advantage of reaction rules is that less communication operations are required to implement nonstandard protocols (which is important in a network setting). Rules can also support security features such as the cancellation of an illegal agent operation.

TuCSoN TuCSoN (Tuple Centers Spread over Networks) extends the tuple center approach to the Internet [41]. The Internet is viewed as a hierarchical collection of locality domains [42]. A mobile entity must dynamically acquire information about the location of resources and their availability (to that entity) as it moves over the network. There may be parts of the network with restricted access, which requires a means to authenticate entities and allocate them permissions.

Tuple centers are located on Internet nodes, and are used as the building blocks for coordination, and for resource control and access. An Internet domain is defined in terms of a gateway which controls access to places inside the domain and to subdomains gateways.

The following example outlines how an agent might explore a domain inside TuCSoN:

```
<goto d>                  % migrate to gateway d
<identify>                % authenticate agent with d
?rd(places)               % get places info
?rd(commspaces)           % get tuple centres
<for pl in places do>
  <goto pl>               % visit place pl
  <for tc in commspaces do>
    tc?op(tuple)          % ask tuple centre tc of place pl
                          % to execute op(tuple)
```

5.2   Parallel Multiset Rewriting

Parallel multiset rewriting gained wide notice in Gamma [15]. A program is a collection of condition/action rules which employ a locality principle – if several conditions hold for disjoint subsets of the multiset being processed then the actions can be carried out in parallel.

One of the benefits of this programming style is its chemical solution metaphor. The multiset is the solution, and rules specify chemical reactions which work on distinct parts of the solution, changing sets of molecules into others [14].

LO   Linear Objects (LO) [10] was originally proposed as a merger of LP and object oriented programming. It extends Prolog with multi-headed formulae which work on a multiset of terms. OR-parallelism can be used for rule evaluation, which implies the atomic removal of terms from the multiset. Later versions of LO include the ability to clone new multisets and to terminate a multiset [9]. A broadcast operator can send a copy of a term to all the multisets.

Around this time, Interaction Abstract Machines (IAMs) were developed as a model for concurrent multi-agent worlds [9]. The IAM can be used as a computation model for LO.

CLF   CLF (Coordination Language Facility) utilises parallel rewrite rules as a scripting language for specifying and enacting the coordination of distributed objects [8].

A typical coordination action consists of the atomic removal of a number of resources from some objects, followed by the insertion of resources into other objects. This atomic removal and insertion is captured succinctly by rewrite rules.

The objects refereed to in the rules can contain sophisticated protocols for extracting resources from distributed services (e.g. based on negotiation, atomic performance). The objects also locate suitable services, which may be distributed over the Internet.

6   Message Passing

Most LAN and Internet-based message passing languages utilise existing communication protocols (e.g. TCP/IP) or libraries (e.g. PVM). This supplies useful functionality immediately, such as guarantees of service in TCP and failure detection in PVM, as well as support for interaction across heterogeneous platforms and processes written in varied languages. However, there are several disadvantages, related to the mismatch between the LP paradigm and the low-level (imperative) viewpoint offered by these protocols and libraries.

Invariably, the LP level must restrict the use of logic variables in messages in order to maintain the uni-directional nature of the message passing at the lower levels. This usually means renaming variables as they are transmitted, so eliminating the possibility of dynamic communication channels. Backtracking is also ruled out since the underlying primitives are deterministic. Some libraries, such as early versions of MPI [62], do not support dynamic process creation, which naturally affects process support in the LP layer

The typical unit of computation is a sequential Prolog process, which promotes a coarser grained parallelism than in concurrent LP. This may be a benefit since it makes it easier to justify the communication costs of distributing tasks between machines. Several languages also support threads, often for handling subtasks inside a process.

6.1 IC-Prolog II and Friends

IC-Prolog II can create concurrently executing Prolog threads, possibly spread over separate machines [28]. Threads are independent, sharing no data, but can communicate using pipes if the threads are on the same host, or with primitives utilising TCP/IP if the threads are on different machines. The messaging operations are non-backtrackable and send/receive terms with variables renamed.

A concurrent server example using TCP:

```
conc_server(Port) :-
  tcp_server(Port, Socket),    % listen for connections
  multi_serve(Socket).

multi_serve(Socket) :-
  tcp_accept(Socket, New),     % get a connection
  fork( service(New) ),        % create thread to service it
  multi_serve(Socket).         % look for more connections
```

Processes can employ mailboxes; a message is sent to a mailbox by referring to its ID or name, which is globally unique. Mailboxes can be linked so that messages placed in one box are automatically copied to other boxes. Links allow the creation of arbitrary communication topologies.

April April is a concurrent language, offering distributed objects as lightweight processes [88]. Each process has a globally unique handle, which can be registered with DNS-like April name servers. The communications model is point-to-point, being based on TCP/IP. A receiving process can use pattern matching to search for a suitable incoming message stored in a message buffer.

A server which executes a task:

```
server([any]{}?T) {
  repeat {
    [do,any?arg] -> {          % request a task using arg
       T(arg);                 % execute it
       done >> replyto         % reply when finished
    }
  } until quit                 % server continues until a quit
};
```

The server is forked and its name (server1) is registered with the local name server:

```
server1 public server(taskName)
```

Processes can send messages to the server at its location (foo.com for example):

```
[do,taskArg] >> handle?server1@foo.com
```

April combines several paradigms, including LP. It includes a variety of data types based on tuples and sets, higher-order features such as lambda, procedure and pattern abstractions, real-time support, and an expressive macro language.

Qu-Prolog Qu-Prolog has been extended with April-like communication support and multi-threading [38]. Threads located on the same machine can utilise Linda-style operations on a shared dynamic database.

Qu-Prolog extends Prolog with support for qualified terms, object variables, and substitutions, which allows it to easily express inference rules for many kinds of logics, and implement theorem provers efficiently. These features are particularly suited for building agent systems.

QuP++ is an object oriented layer on top of the Qu-Prolog/April work [37]. It offers a class-based language with multiple inheritance, where a class is a collection of static (unchangeable) and dynamic clauses and state variables, and an object is a collection of one or more independently executing threads. Synchronous and asynchronous remote method calls are available, including a form of distributed backtracking.

Go! Go! is a higher order (in the functional programming sense), multi-threaded LP language, making use of April's symbolic message communication technology [36]. Go! does not support Prolog's meta features for interpreting data as code; instead of `assert` and `retract`, Go! has a restricted assignment mechanism.

6.2   PVM-Prolog

PVM-Prolog can create distributed Prolog processes communicating by message passing [43]. It differs from the other Internet-based languages described here in that it uses the PVM messaging library [61].

The principle advantages of PVM over TCP/IP are that it offers a higher level communications layer (messages rather than byte streams), a virtual machine, and plentiful commands for process/resource management (e.g. for fault tolerance).

PVM-Prolog has two components – the Parallel Prolog Virtual Machine (PPVM) and a process engine (PE). The PPVM acts as a LP interface to PVM; for instance, it supports Prolog terms as messages. A PE executes Prolog processes, and several may be created on a single virtual machine.

In a later version of PVM-Prolog, threads were introduced to support fine-grain concurrency within a process [107]. Each thread represents an independent query over the process' database, but they can interact via shared term queues.

6.3   Mercury

Mercury is a pure logic/functional programming language, utilising a strong type system with parametric polymorphism and higher-order types, mode declarations on predicates, extra determinism information, and a module system.

MCORBA is a binding to the CORBA distributed object framework for Mercury [74]. The approach is made possible by utilising Mercury's type classes and existential types. A type class offers a form of constrained polymorphism which is quite similar to a Java interface – the class is specified in terms of method signatures which can be instantiated later. An existential type allows a predicate to return a variable whose type is constrained to be of a particular type class but not an actual concrete type instance. This is useful for supporting CORBA functions that return generic objects which are later 'narrowed' to a specific object type.

A compiler back-end is being developed for Mercury which targets Microsoft's .NET Web services framework. This will allow components coded in Mercury to inter-operate with other .NET elements programmed in C#, Visual Basic, C++, and other languages. Preliminary details are available at
http://www.cs.mu.oz.au/research/mercury/information/dotnet/
mercury_and_dotnet.html.

7   Client-side Execution

Sections 7 and 8 are complementary since they describe client/server mechanisms, which are still the most common way of using the Web (e.g. a Web browser communicating with a server).

In general, client-side code can be more closely integrated with the browser and so can offer more sophisticated user interfaces than server-side solutions. Also, once client-side code is downloaded it does not need to communicate with the server, thereby avoiding networking problems that can affect server-side applications. Only the code which is needed for the current task has to be downloaded and, since it is a copy of the original, it can be changed or combined with other code without affecting the original.

A disadvantage of the client-side approach is security when running foreign code locally.

We consider four topics: libraries, query languages, Web pages as programs, and the combination of Java and LP. Parts of this section previously appeared in [83].

7.1   Libraries

Most modern Prologs contain libraries for creating TCP and UDP sockets (e.g. SICStus, BinProlog, Amzi, LPA, Quintus). With these it is possible to code support for protocols such as HTTP and NNTP. System calls to `telnet` can also be employed as a foundation for network functionality.

PiLLoW   PiLLoW is the most elaborate Web library [21]. The main client-side predicate, fetch_urls/2, downloads a page corresponding to a URL with additional options specifying such things as a timeout limit, the maximum number of retries before the predicate fails, and user ID and password details for protected sites. PiLLoW's parsing predicates extract HTML tag attributes and values from a page string, returning them as Prolog terms. It is possible to convert an entire page into a list of terms, making it more amenable to manipulation.

The following call fetches two documents, also getting the type and the size of the first, and checking for non-fatal errors in the second, and allowing only one socket to be used:

```
fetch_urls([ doc('http://www.foo.com',
    [content(D1), content_length(S1), content_type(T1)] ),
            doc('http://www.bar.com/drinks.htm',
    [content(D2), errors(non_fatal,E)] )     ],
        [sockets(1)]
    ).
```

Streaming Download   Davison [45] models page retrieval using a stream-based approach, in the context of a concurrent LP language. download/4 returns a page incrementally as a partially instantiated list (stream) of characters, and includes Parlog meta-call arguments for status reporting and control. download/4 can be used as a building block for AND- and OR- parallel Web search, time-outs, repeated attempts to download, and the cancellation of slow retrievals.

A retrieval predicate with a time-out facility (using deep guards):

```
mode timeout(?, ?, ^, ^, ?).
timeout(_Time, Request, Text, Result, Stop) :-
    download(Request, Text, Result, Stop) : true.
timeout(Time, _, _, err(timeout), _) :-
    sleep(Time) : true.
```

`download/4` executes the request and returns the text of the page, unless it is stopped or the second clause succeeds because the timeout has expired.

Webstream, a macro extension to April, also views Web page downloading as incremental stream-based retrieval [69]. It extends the idea with a pipelining mechanism (reminiscent of UNIX pipes) which allows stream data to be filtered concurrently.

7.2 Query Languages

A more abstract approach to client-server computation is to view the Web as a vast heterogeneous collection of databases, which must be queried in order to extract information.

In fact, in many ways the Web is *not* similar to a database system: it has no uniform structure, no integrity constraints, no support for transaction processing, no management capabilities, no standard query language, or data model.

Perhaps the most popular data model for the Web is the labelled graph, where nodes represent Web pages (or internal components of pages) and arcs correspond to links. Labels on the arcs can be viewed as attribute names for the nodes. The lack of structure in Web pages has motivated the use of semistructured data techniques, which also facilitate the exchange of information between heterogeneous sources.

Abiteboul [1] suggests the following features for a semistructured data query language: standard relational database operations (utilising a SQL viewpoint), navigational capabilities in the hypertext/Web style, information retrieval influenced search using patterns, temporal operations, and the ability to mix data and schema (type) elements together in a query.

Many languages support regular path expressions over the graph for stating navigational queries along arcs. The inclusion of wild cards allows arbitrarily deep data and cyclic structures to be searched, although restrictions must be applied to prevent looping.

Query Computability The question of query computability is considered in [3,91]. Mendelzon and Milo [91] focus on two aspects that distinguish Web data access from database manipulation: the navigational nature of the access, and the lack of concurrency control. They investigate the Web Calculus, a query language quite similar to WebSQL, under the assumption that the Web is static (no updates), and the more realistic dynamic case.

The main open problem is how to characterize queries which definitely terminate. One sufficient condition is to avoid the use of the regular expression * pattern in paths.

Abiteboul and Vianu [3] differ from Mendelzon and Milo in assuming that the Web is infinite, an assumption which seems somewhat dubious. They examine the computability of first order logic, Datalog, and Datalog with negation.

Queries Languages for HTML Pages

Relational WebSQL models the Web as an extremely large relational database composed of two relations: Document and Anchor [12]. Document contains one tuple for each Web document, and the Anchor relation has one tuple for each anchor in each document.

An interesting feature of the language is its use of regular expressions involving URL links to define paths between documents. For example, '->' denotes a link between two pages at the same site, while '=>' is a link to a page at another site. Chains of links (called *path regular expressions*) are created using sequential, alternating, and multiplicative operators.

For example, suppose we want to find a tuple of the form (d,e), where d is a document stored on our local site (http://www.foo.com), and e is a document stored elsewhere. The query to express this is:

```
SELECT d.url, e.url
FROM   Document d SUCH THAT  "www.foo.com" ->* d,
       Document e SUCH THAT d => e
```

d is bound in turn to each local document, and e is bound to each document directly reachable from d.

Datalog, F-logic WebLog utilises a Datalog-like language to retrieve information from HTML documents and to build new documents to hold the results [80]. It represents links as first class entities, specified using molecular formulas (somewhat like F-logic terms). A molecular formula for a URL lists attribute/value pairs for the relevant data inside the page. Attributes can be keywords, page substrings, links or tags. Backtracking allows alternative matching URLs to be found.

This example collects all the links in the page http://www.foo.com, and retrieves the titles of the pages pointed to by the links. It stores the results in a new Web page ans.html.

```
ans.html[title->"All Links", hlink->>L, occurs->>T] <--
    http://www.foo.com[hlink->>L],            % a molecule
    href(L,U), U[title->T].
```

FLORID is a prototype deductive object oriented database using F-logic, containing builtins for converting Web documents and their links into objects [86].

The FLORID database corresponds to a labelled graph where nodes are logical object IDs (OIDs) and object and class methods are labelled edges.

FLORID provides general path expressions, very similar to those in Lorel (discussed below), which simplify object navigation and avoids the need for explicit join conditions. The operations (e.g. *, +, ?, |) are specified and implemented in F-logic, making them amenable to simplification rules and to being extended (e.g. with path variables).

Web documents are modeled by two classes: `url` and `webdoc`. `url` represents a link and has a `get()` method for retrieving the referenced page as a `webdoc` object. The `webdoc` class has methods for accessing the text in a page, its links, and various meta-level details.

The program below collects the set of Web documents reachable directly or indirectly from `http://www.foo.com` by links whose labels contain the string "database".

```
("www.foo.com":url).get.(Y:url).get <-
  (X:url).get[ hrefs@(L) =>> {Y} ],
  substr("database",L).
```

The Web->KB Project The Web->KB Project [40] demonstrates the potential of using machine learning techniques for extracting knowledge bases from Web sites. The best approach uses a combination of statistical and relational rule learners; for example, a Naive Bayes text classifier combined with FOIL. This merger is well suited to the Web/hypertext domains because the statistical component can characterise text in terms of word frequency while the relational component can describe how neighbouring documents are related by hyperlinks [111].

Labelled Graph Models Much of the present research on semistructured data query languages centers on object models for edge-labelled directed graphs. Little of the work is logic-based, but the proposals embodied by these languages are sufficiently important to strongly influence logic programming approaches. To some extent this can be seen in FLORID.

Lorel is a query language in the style of SQL and OQL [2], originally used within the TSIMMIS system (discussed in section 9.1). Its object model, OEM (Object Exchange Model), is an extension of the structured object database model ODMG.

Lorel offers regular path expression, with wild cards and path variables, for specifying navigation over the graph. Path expressions extend Lorel's functionality beyond that of SQL and OQL.

The following Lorel query finds the names and zipcodes of all the "cheap" restaurants in a `GoodFood` database.

```
SELECT GoodFood.restaurant.name,
       GoodFood.restaurant(.address)?.zipcode
WHERE  GoodFood.restaurant.%grep "cheap"
```

The "?" makes the address part optional in the path expression. The wildcard "%" will match any sub-object of restaurant, which is then searched with `grep` to find the string "cheap".

Queries to Pages Using XML or RDF XML (eXtensible Markup Language) is a notation for describing labelled ordered trees with references [130]. It is possible to type portions of XML data with DTDs (Document Type Definitions). A DTD defines the types for elements, and what attributes can appear in each element. The specification is written using regular expressions.

Specifying a query language for XML is an active area of research, much of it coordinated through a W3C (the World Wide Web Consortium) working group [127]. The suggested features for such a language are almost identical to those for querying semistructured data [56].

It is hardly surprising that most proposals utilise models which view XML as an edge-labelled directed graph, and use semistructured data query languages (e.g. Lorel). The main difference is that the elements in an XML document are sometimes ordered.

Relational Models Shanmugasundaram et al. [108] investigate the possibility of using a traditional relational database engine to process XML documents conforming to DTDs. Problems with query translation center on handling regular path expressions which frequently translate into many SQL queries and expensive joins. This suggests that while regular path expressions are high-level, they are also costly to execute in many cases.

Functional Programming Approaches XDuce is a tree transformation language, similar to functional programming languages, but specialized for XML processing [70]. It adds regular expression types and regular expression pattern matching, similar to pattern matching in ML. The result is that XML document fragments can be manipulated as XDuce values.

XMλ is a small functional language (very close to Haskell) which maps DTDs into existing data types [90]. Document conformance to a DTD becomes a matter of type correctness.

Declarative Description Theory The Declarative Description Theory (DDT) is an extended definite clause logic language where substitution is generalised to specialization [4]. Specializations permit language elements to have specific operations for variable expansion and instantiation.

DDT is utilised in [11] to define a specialization system for XML elements and attributes. This allows clauses to use variables which may be partially instantiated XML elements or attributes, containing further variables. Pattern matching and binding use the specialization operators to manipulate these variables according to their XML definitions.

RDF RDF (Resource Description Framework) is an application of XML aimed at facilitating the interoperability of meta-data across heterogeneous hosts [131].

The SiLRi (Simple Logic-based RDF interpreter) utilises an RDF parser (called SiRPAC) to translate RDF statements into F-logic expressions [50].

Metalog is a LP language where facts and rules are translated and stored as RDF statements [87]. Facts are treated as RDF 3-tuples, while rule syntax is supported with additional RDF schema statements for LP elements such as head, body, if and variable.

7.3 Web Pages as Programs

LogicWeb The LogicWeb system [83] resides between the browser and the Web. As pages are downloaded, they are converted into logic programs and stored locally.

A Web page is converted into several predicates, including facts holding meta-level information about the page, a fact containing the page text, and page links information. Programs can be composed together using operators inspired by work on compositional LP, implication goals, and contextual LP. There is a context switching operator which applies a goal to a program specified by its ID. If the program required by the goal in the context switch is not in the local store, then it is transparently downloaded. This behaviour hides low-level issues concerning page retrieval and parsing.

The query:

```
?- subject_page("LP", "http://www.foo.com", P).
```

will bind P to a URL which is related to "LP" and is linked to the starting page. subject_page/3 is defined as:

```
subject_page(Subject, StartURL, URL) :-
    lw(get,StartURL)#>link(_, URL),
    lw(get,URL)#>h_text(Source),
    contains(Source, Subject).
```

The lw/2 call retrieves the starting Web page using an HTTP GET message and selects a link URL. The source text of that page is examined to see if it contains "LP"; if it does not then a different link is selected through backtracking.

An extension of the LogicWeb system deals with security aspects of client-side evaluation [84] – LogicWeb code can be downloaded with a digital signature. This is decrypted using the page's public key in order to authenticate the code. The decrypted signature is also used as an ID to assign a policy program to the code during its evaluation.

A concurrent LP version of LogicWeb is outlined in [45]: it allows queries to be evaluated using parallel versions of the composition operators. It utilises the download/4 operator described in section 7.1, and requires an atomic test-and-set primitive so that the client-side program store is updated atomically.

W-ACE and WEB-KLIC The concurrent constraint-based LP language W-ACE has explicit support for Web computation [101]. Some of its novel ideas include representing Web pages as LP trees and the use of constraints to manipulate tree components and the relationship between trees.

The following predicates extend the current HTML graph (GraphIn) with all the documents linked to Page, resulting in GraphOut.

```
update(Page, GraphIn, GraphOut) :-
  Links = { X : ref(X) <= Page},    % make a links set
  addLks(Links, Page, GraphIn, GraphOut).

addLks(0, _, GIn, GOut) :- GOut = GIn.
addLks(X:Rest, Page, GIn, GOut) :-
  get_url(X,Tree), !,          % get the page tree for X
  GNew = {(Page,Tree)} U GIn,
  addLks(Rest, Page, GNew, GOut).
addLks(X:Rest, Page, GIn, GOut) :-
  GNew = {(Page,dead)} U GIn,       % dead link info.
  addLks(Rest, Page, GNew, GOut).
```

W-ACE also contains modal operators for reasoning about groups of pages, and composition operators very similar to those in LogicWeb.

The authors of W-ACE have been working on a Web version of the concurrent LP language KLIC, called WEB-KLIC [98]. Their primary goal has been the augmentation of its CGI facilities (i.e. for server-side computation).

7.4   Java and LP

A spate of Java/LP systems have appeared in recent years. A connection to Java gives an LP language immediate access to a very wide range of classes for GUIs, imaging, multimedia, business components, and networking support. However, there are some serious disadvantages, the main one being the mismatch between the Java programming model (imperative/object oriented) and LP, which occurs in all multi-paradigm approaches. For instance, how should traditional control flow be combined with non-determinism, how should destructive assignment be reconciled with logic variables, and how are the variety of data structures/types/classes in Java mapped to atoms and terms? How should garbage collection be handled in a hybrid environment?

Calejo [22] categories Java and LP systems into two broad camps: "Prolog in Java" and "Prolog+Java". URLs for most of the current systems can be found at his Web site: http://dev.servisoft.pt/interprolog/systems.htm.

Prolog in Java The 'in' crowd can be divided into those systems that compile Prolog code into Java (e.g. jProlog, LLPj, MINERVA), and those that utilise a Prolog interpreter as a Java class (e.g. BirdLand Prolog, DGKS Prolog, JavaLog, Jinni, W-Prolog).

A benefit of "Prolog in Java" is the close integration, which permits Prolog code to more directly employ Java functionality, and be downloaded to browsers alongside Java applets.

Prolog+Java The "Prolog+Java" camp consists of systems which link Prolog and Java via their foreign language interfaces (e.g. Amzi! Prolog, Jasper, JIPL,

JPL, NanoProlog), and systems which use a network link (usually socket based), such as InterProlog.

The following fragment shows how the Jasper package in the SICStus library can be used by Java. A Prolog query connected("Wilmslow","Stockport", Route) is constructed, passed to the Prolog engine which applies it to the program in train.ql, and all the different possible routes are printed back on the Java side.

```
SICStus sp = new SICStus(argv,null);    % Prolog engine
sp.load("train.ql");

SPPredicate pred = new SPPredicate(sp, "connected", 3, "");
SPTerm to = new SPTerm(sp, "Wilmslow");
SPTerm from = new SPTerm(sp, "Stockport");
SPTerm route = new SPTerm(sp).putVariable();


SPQuery q = sp.openQuery(pred,
            new SPTerm[]{from, to, route});    % build query
while (q.nextSolution())
   System.out.println( route.toString() );
```

An obvious disadvantage of "Prolog+Java" over "Prolog in Java" is the requirement to have two distinct systems running for any application. This makes programs harder to write, debug, maintain, and complicates portability.

CCJava A somewhat different perspective on combining Java and LP is embodied in CCJava [112]. As mentioned earlier in the section on Distributed Oz (section 4.2), it adds single assignment variables and statement-level threads to Java as a way of enhancing its thread communication features. This permits a Java program to use techniques such as incremental and back communication popularized in concurrent LP.

8   Server-side Execution

Server-side evaluation typically involves the user in completing a form on their browser, which is submitted across the network to a Web server to be processed. The most widespread server-side evaluation mechanism is the Common Gateway Interface (CGI) which delivers form details to programs, and routes any output from the code back to the user.

In general, server-side software is ideal for controlling resources such as databases which cannot be sent over the Web for various reasons. Also, having all users communicate with a central location makes it easier to program applications with more complex communication requirements, such as chat systems or market places.

One disadvantage of server-side programming is the difficulty of extending the user interface. For instance, it is not possible to intercept the activation of a hypertext link or to augment the forms interface with additional GUI elements. Also, since server-side scripts are usually located on different machines from the forms which use them, communication latency can be a problem. A further drawback is the load on the server caused by multiple clients running scripts.

Parts of this section previously appeared in [83].

8.1   Libraries

There are many libraries which enable Prolog programs to process information from CGI input, and generate suitable replies (typically, new Web pages) [7,21,85].

The following server-side program uses the PiLLoW library [21] to extract a name from CGI input, call a user-defined **response/2** predicate to get an answer, and then construct a Web page.

```
main(_) :-
   get_form_input(Input),         % read CGI input
   get_form_value(Input, person_name, Name),
   response(Name, Response),      % lookup response
   output_html([ form_reply, start,
      title('Response'),
      heading(2, 'Response'),
      Response, end ]).
```

get_form_input/1, get_form_value/3, and output_html/1 are PiLLoW library predicates.

8.2   Modifications to CGI

A CGI script is newly invoked for each query from a client, which can be a problem if the script has to load very large support software. Much of this overhead can be avoided by using shared dynamically linked libraries, and utilising compilers which generate fast object code and small executables. Also, it is far from clear whether the poor performance of a particular Prolog CGI script is due to its coding in Prolog, or because of network and machine overheads, and/or the slowness of CGI.

A related issue is that the client-server model allows a server to process several clients concurrently, which implies that several invocations of the same script may need to be running simultaneously. This may not be practical because of the size of the system, and also makes changes to shared resources more complicated.

Separating Interface and Process Another server-side solution is to separate query processing into two parts: a light-weight CGI script which acts as an interface to a separate heavy-weight task process. A key feature of the task process is that it is continually running, and so only needs to be loaded once. In the context of LP, this process might be a Prolog system or logic database.

This approach is used in the EMRM knowledge base of medical records, which utilises the OR-parallel Aurora system to process multiple queries at once [115].

The PiLLoW/CIAO library supports a higher level communications layer between the interface and task processes based on Active modules. Each invocation of the interface script communicates with the task process as if it was calling a module [21]. The authors speculate on using &-Prolog/CIAO to parallelise their Prolog engine.

Another problem, addressed in the EMRM system, is how to deal with lengthy browser interactions, which require the task process to suspend while the user enters further details. A related difficulty, peculiar to LP systems, is how to deal with backtracking to a previous stage in the user interaction. The ProWeb system [85] records the pages associated with earlier stages, and can redisplay them as required. Backtracking may also make it necessary to rollback changes to (shared) resources. These problems can occur with any multi-user LP application, but are compounded by the forms-based user interface supplied by CGI, and the stateless nature of the HTTP protocol.

Replacing the Server A third server-side technique is to completely replace the traditional Web server by software which combines the functionality of a server with the particular task.

A notable LP solution in this style is the ECLiPSe HTTP server library, which allows a basic server framework to be customized for different communication protocols [17]. Indeed, the major advantage of this technique is the way that the server can be specialized for specific applications and communication modes. The main drawback is the large amount of work required to implement a fully featured server with concurrency control, error handling, administrative tools, and so on.

9   Integration of Heterogeneous Data Sources

The issues related to data integration on the Web/Internet are similar to those for integrating heterogeneous database systems, but are arguably more complex due to the large number, and evolving nature, of Web sources, the lack of meta-data (i.e. schema) about the sources, and the degree of source autonomy. Semantic heterogeneity – the representation of the same or overlapping data in two or more ways – is a difficult problem.

Hull [71] identifies a number of data management architectures: mediation systems (integrated read-only views of data), mediation with updates (which introduce the view update problem, federated systems, and work flow architectures.

Research on Web data integration focuses on mediation, and borrows from the DARPA I3 reference architecture [72]. Wrappers are employed at the lowest level to translate between a Web source's local language, model and concepts and the global concepts embodied by the system. Mediators obtain information from the components below them (which may be wrappers or other mediators).

The wrapper and mediator architecture has two distinguishing features over integrated heterogeneous databases: a mediator does not directly communicate with a source, instead interacting with its wrapper, and a user does not pose queries in the schema of the data sources, instead using the mediated, global schema. This last point requires the mediator to reformulate queries using some kind of source description.

There are two main approaches to specifying a mediated schema and its reformulation, which Hull terms "classical integration" and the "new wave" [71].

Classical integration defines global, mediated schema as views over the local schema. Query reformulation becomes very simple – view unfolding or partial evaluation until the query is expressed in terms of the local schema elements. A survey of this approach, as applied to heterogenous databases, can be found in [93]. Many Web-based systems use classical integration (e.g. TSIMMIS [100], described below).

The new wave considers global schema to be independent of the local schema to a large extent. Data held at the sources are expressed as views over the chosen global schema, to specify how mediated schema relations are to be translated. An advantage is the ease of adding/removing sources since they do not require a view mechanism to be altered at the mediator level.

Many new wave systems utilise description logics as glue between local and global schema (e.g. Information Manifold [81], described below). A description logic is typically a subset of first order logic with specialized syntax that makes it suitable for describing and reasoning about entities and relationships. It is often combined with a Datalog-based query language which handles other aspects of inference.

Two good sources of papers on this topic are the 1999 Workshop on LP and Distributed Knowledge Management [99], and the recent JLP special issue on logic-based heterogeneous information sources [104].

9.1   Classical Integration

TSIMMIS TSIMMIS (The Stanford-IBM Manager of Multiple Information Sources) implements a mediator hierarchy, where a mediator may converse with sub-mediators or with wrappers [100]. The system concentrates on the querying of semistructured or unstructured data, and utilises the OEM (Object Exchange Model) data model. The query language is MSL (Mediator Specification Language), which is also used to describe mediators and wrappers in various ways.

MSL is an object logic with a Datalog-like syntax. Mediators are specified using MSL rules. Each rule maps a set of objects at a source into a 'virtual' object at the mediator. Mediator objects with the same OID are fused together in ways specified by the rules. Mediator rules are like a database view since the sources are only queried for objects when a query arrives.

For example, the rule *paper* is defined as:

```
<paper { <title T><author A><abstract B><conf C> }> :-
  <entry { <title T><author A><abstract B> }>@s1,
  <entry { <title T><conf C> }>@s2.
```

paper is essentially a join of the views exported by sources s1 and s2, with `title` being the join attribute. The head consists of an OEM object with the label `paper`, and a list of sub-objects describing the `title`, `author`, and so on.

MSL without negation and OIDs can be considered a variant of Datalog. Full MSL can be converted to Datalog with function symbols and negation.

A query is evaluated by expanding the applicable mediator rules using unfolding until the query is expressed in terms of source information only. This can lead to exponential growth in the rule set as m query conditions unify with n rules to produce n^m expanded rules. TSIMMIS employs a range of techniques to limit such growth.

Medlan The Medlan system [13] implements a declarative analysis layer on top of a commercial GIS. The layer consists of multiple logic theories which can be composed together using meta-level operations, which form a program expression for the resulting collection of theories. A goal can be executed against a program expression. The operations in Medlan and LogicWeb (discussed in section 7.3) are similar.

9.2   New Wave Integration

Information Manifold New wave integration is typified by Information Manifold [81] which provides uniform access to a heterogeneous collection of more than 100 information sources, most of them on the Web. Its query language is based on a dialect of the description logic CARIN, which offers a fragment of first order logic almost equivalent to non-recursive Datalog. The Information Manifold architecture is based on global predicates, where each information source has one or more views defined in terms of those predicates.

Context Interchange The context interchange strategy primarily addresses the issue of semantic heterogeneity, where information sources have different interpretations arising from their respective contexts [64].

The global domain utilises the COIN data model; the COINL language offers a mixture of deductive and object oriented features, similar to those in F-logic.

Elevation axioms say how source values are mapped to semantic objects in the global domain. Context axioms include conversion functions which state how an object may be transformed to comply with the assumptions of a context. Conversion functions are crucial for allowing semantic objects to be moved between contexts.

An interesting feature of query rewriting in this approach is the use of abduction. Initially domain model axioms, elevation axioms and context axioms are rewritten as Horn clauses, with the addition of generic axioms defining the abductive framework and other integrity constraints. The abductive rewriting of the query is achieved through backward chaining until only source relations (and builtins) are left. Backtracking is used to generate alternative rewrites.

The abductive process is implemented using ECLiPSe and its Constraint Handling Rules (CHR) library. However, the authors remark on the suitability of Procalog for this purpose. Procalog is an instantiation of the work of Wetzel, Kowalski, and Toni on unifying abductive LP, constraint LP, and semantic query optimisation [129].

10   Conclusions

LP is a natural choice when a programming task requires symbolic manipulation, extended pattern matching, rule-based representation of algorithms, inference/deduction, a high degree of abstraction, and notation which reflects the mathematical basis of computation. It is not surprising that LP languages have found wide usage in the Internet domain.

A crucial requirement for Internet programming is a clear, unambiguous model of the Web/Internet. The most popular is the labelled graph, where nodes represent Web pages (or parts of them) and arcs correspond to links. This model can be directly translated into a LP framework, as seen for example in LogicWeb [83] and FLORID [86].

Logic variables are a powerful *and* efficient communications mechanism (e.g. see Janus [106], Strand [58], Distributed Oz [66]), and one which offers benefits to non-LP paradigms (e.g. see PCN [57], CC++ [27], CCJava [112]). One benefit is the possibility of using concurrent (constraint) LP programming techniques such as incomplete messages, bounded buffers, and short circuits.

(LP) coordination languages are sometimes discounted for being unable to encompass the size and complexity of the Web/Internet. Development of richer dataspaces based on multiple, hierarchical domains, the introduction of first order representations of tuple spaces, and the cross-fertilization of ideas from parallel rewrite systems has shown this view to be wrong. Coordination languages seem certain to play an important role in representing and controlling mobility, and in the integration of heterogeneous data sources.

Message passing languages illustrate the advantages of building on existing protocols and systems (e.g. TCP/IP, PVM, CORBA), and thereby gaining features like fault tolerance and reliable communication. The downside of using existing protocols is that it is difficult to retain LP elements such as logic variables.

Joining Java and LP is a growth area at present, although frequently driven only by the wish to gain access to Java's extensive libraries. However, CCJava shows how Java can benefit from logic variables [112], and Jinni is a close integration of Java and Prolog in a blackboard setting [117].

The server-side execution of LP code has been standardised into libraries which make it easy to develop CGI-based applications [21]. However, several issues remain concerning the suitability of combining LP and HTTP. One of these is the interaction between backtracking in the LP code and the 'backtracking' possible in a typical multiple forms interface.

Many query languages for semistructured data seem quite distant from LP, concentrating on relational database manipulation, information retrieval search techniques, temporal operators, and navigation based on regular path expressions. Nevertheless, Datalog and F-logic (and their many variants) are popular tools, although sometimes hidden behind SQL-like syntax (e.g. Lorel [2]).

There seems to be little LP involvement in the current development of query languages for XML. This contrasts with the rather active participation of the FP community, which have found interesting ways of using types to capture the regular expression aspects of DTDs.

Datalog and F-logic (and variants) are widely used for the integration of heterogeneous data sources, and there is much work to be done on applying results from heterogeneous database integration to the semistructured domain. Of particular note is the use of abduction in the context interchange strategy [64], and the deployment of inductive LP ideas for information discovery and data mining [40]. Also, as mentioned above, there seems scope for the application of LP coordination languages.

Failure handling is a difficult problem in an Internet setting; Sandra [54] and Distributed Oz [66] both offer a range of practical proposals. Approaches based on the meta-call also are worth further investigation.

Security is another under-developed topic, although we noted the use of read-only variables from FCP [94], and the meta-interpreter for client-side security in LogicWeb [84]. An approach with great flexibility is the tuple center [41] for enforcing 'social behaviour' as coordination laws.

The importance of mobility is being increasingly recognised: Distributed Oz takes an implicit view [66], while languages like TuCSoN [41], Jinni [117], and TeleLog [116] make mobility explicit. It appears that a visible notion of mobility is suited to most Web/Internet applications, where resources have stated locations.

One thread running through this paper is the utility of meta-level ideas. For example, meta-level mechanisms are used to specify security in LogicWeb, which can be viewed as a more expressive way of defining Java-like 'sandbox' restrictions [84]. Meta-level programming is at the heart of layered program approaches (e.g. in Logix [68]) and in process-to-processor mapping notations. Meta-level features often facilitate language extensions.

One Internet trend if the rise of components (e.g. ActiveX controls, JavaBeans) as the building blocks of applications. A key element of the component architecture is *reflection* – the ability of a component to manage its own resources, scheduling, security, interaction, and so on. Meta-level concepts are central to reflection, and so LP seems an ideal way of building such components.

References

1. Abiteboul, S. 1997. "Querying Semistructured Data", In *Proc. of the Int. Conf. on Database Theory (ICDT)*, Delphi, Greece, January.
2. Abiteboul, S., Quass, D., McHugh, J., Widom, J., and Wiener, J. 1997. "The Lorel Query Language for Semistructured Data", *Int. Journal on Digital Libraries*, Vol. 1, No. 1, April, pp.68-88.
3. Abiteboul, S. and Vianu, V. 1997. "Queries and Computation on the Web", In *Proc. of the Int. Conf. on Database Theory (ICDT)*, Delphi, Greece, January.
4. Akama, K. 1993. "Declarative Semantics of Logic Programs on Parameterized Representation Systems", *Advances in Software Science and Technology*, Vol. 5, pp.45-63.
5. Alkalaj, L., Lang, T., and Ercegovac, M. 1990. "Architectural Support for the Management of Tightly-Coupled, Fine-Grain Goals in Flat Concurrent Prolog", In *Int. Symp. on Computer Architecture*, June, pp.292-301.
6. Alouini, I. and Van Roy, P. 2000. "Fault Tolerant Mobile Agents in Mozart", Available at http://www.mozart-oz.org/papers/abstracts/asama2000.html.
7. Amzi! Prolog. 1996. "Internet and Web Tools", Available at http://www.amzi.com/internet.htm.
8. Andreoli, J.-M., Arregui, D., Pacull, F., Riviere, M., Vion-Dury, J-Y., Willamowski, J. 1999. "CLF/Mekano: A Framework for Building Virtual-Enterprise Applications", In *Proc. of EDOC'99*, Mannheim, Germany, September.
9. Andreoli, J.-M., Ciancarini, P., and Pareschi, R. 1993. "Interaction Abstract Machines", In *Research Directions in Concurrent Object Oriented Programming*, G. Agha, P. Wegner, A. Yonezawa (eds.), MIT Press, pp.257-280.
10. Andreoli, J-M. and Pareschi, R. 1991. "Linear Objects: Logical Processes with Built-in Inheritance", *New Generation Computing*, Vol. 9, Nos. 3-4, pp.445-473.
11. Anutariya, C. 1999. "A Declarative Description Data Model for XML Documents", Dissertation Proposal, CSIM, Asian Institute of Technology, Bangkok, Thailand, September.
12. Arocena, G.O., Mendelzon, A.O., Mihaila, G.A. 1997. "Applications of a Web Query Language", In *6th Int. WWW Conf.*, April, Available at http://atlanta.cs.nchu.edu.tw/www/PAPER267.html.
13. Aquilino, D., Asirelli, P., Formuso, A., Renso, C., and Turini, F. 2000. "Using MedLan to Integrate Geographical Data", In [104], pp.3-14.
14. Banatre, J.-P., and Le Matayer, D. 1993. "Programming by Multiset Transformations", *Communications of the ACM*, Vol. 36, No. 1, January, pp.98-111.
15. Banatre, J.-P., and Le Matayer, D. 1996. "Gamma and the Chemical Reaction Model: Ten Years After", In *Coordination Programming: Mechanisms, Models and Semantics*, J.-M. Andreoli, C. Hankin, and D. Le Metayer (eds.), Worl Scientific, pp.1-39.
16. BinProlog. 2000. "BinProlog Linda Library Manual", Available at http://www.binnetcorp.com/BinProlog/index.html.
17. Bonnet, Ph., Bressan, S., Leth, L., and Thomsen, B. 1996. "Towards ECLiPSe Agents on the Internet", In *Proc. of the 1st Workshop on Logic Programming Tools for Internet Applications*, P. Tarau, A. Davison, K. De Bosschere, and M. Hermenegildo (eds.), JICSLP'96, September, pp.1-9.
18. Brogi, A. and Ciancarini, P. 1991. "The Concurrent Language, Shared Prolog", *ACM Trans. on Programming Languages and Systems*, Vol. 13, No. 1, January, pp.99-123.

19. Bryce, C., Oriol, M., and Vitek, J. 1999. "A Coordination Model for Agents Based on Secure Spaces", In *Coordination Languages and Models: Coordination 99*, Amsterdam, April.

20. Bucci, A., Ciancarini, P., and Montangero, C. 1991. "Extended Shared Prolog: A Multiple Tuple Spaces Logic Language", In *Proc. 10th Japanese LP Conf.*, LNCS, Springer-Verlag.

21. Cabeza, D., Hermenegildo, M., and Varma, S. 1996. "The PiLLoW/CIAO Library for INTERNET/WWW Programming", In *Proc. of the 1st Workshop on Logic Programming Tools for Internet Applications*, P. Tarau, A. Davison, K. De Bosschere, and M. Hermenegildo (eds.), JICSLP'96, September, pp.43-62.

22. Calejo, M. 1999. "Java+Prolog: A Land of Opportunities", In *PACLP'99: The 1st Int. Conf. on Constraint Technologies and Logic Programming*, London, pp.1-2.

23. Carriero, N. and Gelernter, D. 1989. "Linda in Context', *Comms. of the ACM*, Vol. 32, No. 4, April, pp.444-458.

24. Carriero, N., Gelernter, D., and Zuck, L. 1996. "Bauhaus Linda", In *Object-based Models and Languages for Concurrent Systems*, P. Ciancarini, O. Nierstrasz, A. Yonezawa (eds.), LNCS 924, Springer-Verlag, July, pp.66-76.

25. Cardelli, L. 1999. "Abstractions for Mobile Computation", In *Secure Internet Programming: Security Issues for Mobile and Distributed Objects*, J. Vitek and C. Jensen (eds.), LNCS 1603, Springer-Verlag, pp.51-94.

26. Cardelli, L. and Gordon, A.D. 1998. "Mobile Ambients", In *FoSSaCS'98*, LNCS 1378, Springer-Verlag, pp.140-155.

27. Chandy, K.M. and Kesselman, C. 1993. "CC++: A Declarative Concurrent Object-oriented Programming Notation", In *Research Directions in Concurrent Object Oriented Programming*, MIT Press.

28. Chu, D. and Clark, K.L. 1993. "IC-Prolog II: A Multi-threaded Prolog System", In *Proc. of the ICLP'93 Post Conf. Workshop on Concurrent, Distributed and Parallel Implementations of LP Systems*, Budapest.

29. Ciancarini, P. 1991. "Parallel Logic Programming using the Linda Model of Computation", In *Research Directions in High-level Parallel Programming Languages*, J.P. Banatre and D. Le Metayer (eds.), LNCS 574, June, pp.110-125.

30. Ciancarini, P. 1994. "Distributed Programming with Logic Tuple Spaces", *New Generation Computing*, Vol. 12, No. 3, May, pp.251-284.

31. Ciancarini, P., Knoche, A., Tolksdorf, R., Vitali, F. 1996b. "PageSpace: An Architecture to Coordinate Distributed Applications on the Web", *Computer Networks and ISDN Systems*, Vol. 28, pp.941-952.

32. Ciancarini, P., Mazza, M., and Pazzaglia, L. 1998. "A Logic for a Coordination Model with Multiple Spaces", *Science of Computer Programming*, Vol. 31, Nos. 2-3, pp.231-262.

33. Ciancarini, P. and Rossi, D. 1998. "Coordinating Java Agents over the WWW", *World Wide Web Journal*, Vol. 1, No. 2, pp.87-99.

34. Ciancarini, P., Omicini, A., and Zambonelli, F. 1999. "Coordination Technologies for Internet Agents", *Nordic Journal of Computing*, Vol. 6, pp.215-240.

35. Clark, K.L. and Gregory, S. 1986. "Parlog: Parallel Programming in Logic", *ACM Trans. Programming Languages and Systems*, Vol. 8, No. 1, pp.1-49.

36. Clark, K.L. and McCabe, F.G. 2000. "Go! – A Logic Programming Language for the Internet", *DRAFT*, July.

37. Clark, K.L. and Robinson, P.J. 2000. "Agents as Multi-threaded Logical Objects", November. Available at http://www-lp.doc.ic.ac.uk/~klc/qp3.html.

38. Clark, K.L., Robinson, P.J., and Hagen, R. 1998. "Programming Internet Based DAI Applications in Qu-Prolog", In *Multi-agent Systems*, LNAI 1544, Springer-Verlag.
39. Coulouris, G., Dollimore, J., and Kindberg, T. 1994. *Distributed Systems: Concepts and Design*, Addison-Wesley, 2nd ed.
40. Craven, M., DiPasquo, D., Freitag, D., McCallum, A., Mitchell, T., Nigam, K., and Slattery, S. 1998. "Learning to Extract Symbolic Knowledge from the World Wide Web", In *Proc. of the 15th Nat. Conf. on AI (AAAI-98)*.
41. Cremonini, M., Ominici, A., and Zambonelli, F. 1999. "Multi-agent Systems on the Internet: Extending the Scope of Coordination towards Security and Topology", In *Proc. of the 9th European Workshop on Modelling Autonomous Agents in a Multi-Agent World (MAMAAW'99)*, LNAI 1647, Springer-Verlag, pp.77-88.
42. Cremonini, M., Ominici, A., and Zambonelli, F. 2000. "Ruling Agent Motion in Structured Environments", In *HPCN Europe 2000*, LNCS, May.
43. Cunha, J.C. and Marques, R.F.P. 1996. "PVM-Prolog: A Prolog Interface to PVM", In *Proc. of the 1st Int. Austrian-Hungarian Workshop on Distributed and Parallel Systems, DAPSYS'96*, Miskolc, Hungary.
44. Davison, A. 1993. "A Survey of Logic Programming-based Object Oriented Languages", In *Research Directions in Concurrent Object Oriented Programming*, G. Agha, P. Wegner, A. Yonezawa (eds.), MIT Press.
45. Davison, A. 1999. "A Concurrent Logic Programming Model of the Web", In *PACLP'99: The 1st Int. Conf. on Constraint Technologies and Logic Programming*, London, pp.437-451.
46. De Bosschere, K. and Jacquet, J.-M. 1992. "Comparative Semantics of μlog", In *Proc. of the PARLE'92 Conf.*, D. Etiemble and J.-C. Syre (eds.), LNCS 605, Springer-Verlag, pp.911-926.
47. De Bosschere, K. and Jacquet, J.-M. 1996a. "μ^2log: Towards Remote Coordination", In *1st Int. Conf. on Coordination Models, Languages and Applications (Coordination'96)*, P. Ciancarini and C. Hankin (eds.), Cesena, Italy, LNCS 1061, Springer-Verlag, April, pp.142-159.
48. De Bosschere, K. and Jacquet, J.-M. 1996b. "Extending the μlog Framework with Local and Conditional Blackboard Operations", *Journal of Symbolic Computation*.
49. De Bosschere, K. and Tarau, P. 1996. "Blackboard Extensions in Prolog", *Software–Practice and Experience*, Vol. 26, No. 1, January, pp.49-69.
50. Decker, S., Brickley, D., Saarela, J., and Angele, J. 1998. "A Query and Inference Service for RDF", In *W3C Workshop on Query Languages for XML*, Available at http://www.w3.org/TandS/QL/QL98/pp/queryservice.html
51. Denti, E., Natali, A., and Omicini, A. 1998. "On the Expressive Power of a Language for Programming Coordination Media", In *Proc. of the 1998 ACM Symp. on Applied Computing (SAC'98)*, February, pp.167-177.
52. Diaz, M., Rubio, B., and Troya, J.M. 1996. "Distributed Programming with a Logic Channel-based Coordination Model", *The Computer Journal*, Vol. 39, No. 10, pp.876-889.
53. Diaz, M., Rubio, B., and Troya, J.M. 1997a. "DRL: A Distributed Real-time Logic Language", *Computer Languages*, Vol. 23, Vol. 2-4, pp.87-120.
54. Elshiewy, N.A. 1990. *Robust Coordinated Reactive Computing in Sandra*, Thesis for Doctor of Technology, Royal Institute of Technology KTH and Swedish Institute of Computer Science (SICS), RIT (KTH) TRITA-TCS-9005, SICS/D-90-9003.

55. Etzioni, O. and Weld, D.S. 1995. "Intelligent Agents on the Internet: Fact, Fiction, and Forecast", *IEEE Expert*, pp.44-49, August.
56. Fernandez, M., Simeon, J., and Wadler, P. (eds.). 2000b. "XML Query Languages: Experiences and Exemplars", Available at http://www-db.research.bell-labs.com/user/simeon/xquery.html
57. Foster, I. 1992. "Information Hiding in Parallel Programs", Tech. Report MCS-P290-0292, Argonne National Lab.
58. Foster, I. and Taylor, S. 1989. *Strand: New Concepts in Parallel Programming*, Prentice Hall.
59. Foster, I. and Taylor, S. 1992. "A Compiler Approach to Scalable Concurrent Program Design", Tech. Report MCS-P306-0492, Argonne National Lab.
60. Franklin, S. and Graesser, A. 1996. "Is it an Agent, or just a Program?: A Taxonomy for Autonomous Agents", In *Proc. of the 3rd Int. Workshop on Agent Theories, Architectures and Languages*, Springer Verlag. Available from http://www.msci.memphis.edu/~franklin/AgentProg.html
61. Geist, G.A. Beguelin, A., Donjarra, J., Jiang, W., Manchek, R., and Sunderam, V. 1994. *PVM: Parallel Virtual Machine A Users' Guide and Tutorial for Networked Parallel Computing*, MIT Press. Available at http://www.netlib.org/pvm3/book/pvm-book.html.
62. Geist, G.A., Kohl, J.A., and Papadopoulos, P.M. 1996. "PVM and MPI: A Comparison of Features", *Calculateurs Paralleles*, Vol. 8, No. 2.
63. Gelernter, D. 1989. "Multiple Tuple Spaces in Linda", In *Proc. PARLE'89: Parallel Architectures and Languages Europe*, June, pp.20-27.
64. Goh, C.H., Bressan, S., Madnick, S., and Siegel, M. 1999. "Context Interchange: New Features and Formalisms for the Intelligent Integration of Information", *ACM Trans. on Info. Systems*, Vol. 17, No. 3, July, pp.270-293.
65. Haridi, S., Van Roy, P., Brand, P., Mehl, M., Scheidhauer, R., and Smolka, G. 1999. "Efficient Logic Variables for Distributed Computing", *ACM Trans. in Programming Languages and Systems*, Vol. 21, No. 3, May, pp.569-626.
66. Haridi, S., Van Roy, P., Brand, P., and Schulte, C. 1998. "Programming Languages for Distributed Applications", *New Generation Computing*, Vol. 16, No. 3, May, pp.223-261.
67. Hewitt, C. 1985. "The Challenge of Open Systems", *Byte*, April, pp.223-233.
68. Hirsch, M., Silverman, W., and Shapiro, E.Y. 1987. "Computation Control and Protection in the Logix System", In *Concurrent Prolog: Collected Papers, Vol. 2*, E.Y. Shapiro (ed.), MIT Press, Chapter 20, pp.28-45.
69. Hong, T.W. and Clark, K.L. 2000. "Concurrent Programming on the Web with Webstream", August. Avalable at: http://longitude.doc.ic.ac.uk/~twh1/longitude/.
70. Hosoya, H. and Pierce, B.C. 2000. "XDuce: A Typed XML Processing Language", Preliminary Report, Dept. of CIS, Univ. of Pennsylvania, March 8th.
71. Hull, R. 1997. "Managing Semantic Heterogeneity in Databases: A Theoretical Perspective", Invited tutorial at *16th ACM Symp. on Principles of Databases Systems (PODS'97)*, Available at http://www-db.research.bell-labs.com/user/hull/pods97-tutorial.html.
72. I3 Program. 1995. *Reference Architecture for the Intelligent Integration of Information*, Version 2.0 (draft), DARPA. Available at http://dc.isx.com/I3/html/briefs/I3brief.html.
73. Jacquet, J.-M. and De Bosscher, K. 1994. "On the Semantics of μlog", *Future Generation Computer Systems*, Vol. 10, pp.93-135.

74. Jeffery, D., Dowd, T., and Somogyi, Z. 1999. "MCORBA: A CORBA Binding for Mercury", Tech. Report., Dept. of CSSE, Univ. of Melbourne, Australia.
75. Kahn, K.M., and Miller, M.S. 1988. "Language Design and Open Systems", In *The Ecology of Computation*, B. Huberman (ed.), North Holland.
76. Klinger, S., Yardeni, E., Kahn, K., and Shapiro, E.Y. 1988. The Language FCP(:,?), In *Proc. of the Int. Conf. on 5th Generation Computer Systems*, pp.763-773.
77. Kowalski, R. 1985. "Logic-based Open Systems", Technical Report, Dept. of Computing, Imperial College, September.
78. Kowalski, K., and Sadri, F. 1996. "Towards a Unified Agent Architecture that Combines Rationality with Reactivity", In *Proc. of Int. Workshop on Logic in Databases*, San Miniato, Italy, Springer-Verlag.
79. Kowalski, K., and Sadri, F. 1999. "From Logic Programming to Multi-Agent Systems", *Annals of Mathematics and Artificial Intelligence*, Vol. 25, pp.391-419.
80. Lakshmanan, L.V.S., Sadri, F., and Subramanian, I.N. 1996. "A Declarative Approach to Querying and Restructuring the World-Wide-Web", In *Post-ICDE Workshop on Research Issues in Data Engineering (RIDE'96)*, New Orleans, February. Available as `ftp://ftp.cs.concordia.ca/pub/laks/papers/ride96.ps.gz`.
81. Levy, A.Y., Rajaraman, A., and Ordille, J.J. 1996. "Querying Heterogeneous Information Sources using Source Descriptions", In *Proc. of the Int. Conf. on Very Large Databases*, September.
82. Liu, M. 1999. "Deductive Database Languages: Problems and Solutions", *ACM Computing Surveys*, Vol. 31, No. 1, March, pp.27-62.
83. Loke, S.W. and Davison, A. 1998. "LogicWeb: Enhancing the Web with Logic Programming", *Journal of Logic Programming*, 36, pp.195-240.
84. Loke, S.W. and Davison, A. 2001. "Secure Prolog Based Mobile Code", *Theory and Practice of Logic Programming*, Vol. 1, No. 1, To Appear.
85. LPA 1997. LPA ProWeb Server. Available at `http://www.lpa.co.uk/`.
86. Ludascher, B., Himmeroder, R., Lausen, G., May, W., and Schlepphorst, C. 1998. "Managing Semistructured Data with FLORID: A Deductive Object-Oriented Perspective", *Information Systems*, Vol. 23, No. 8, pp.1-25.
87. Marchiori, M. and Saarela, J. 1998. "Query + Metadata + Logic = Metalog", In *W3C Workshop on Query Languages for XML*, Available at `http://www.w3.org/TandS/QL/QL98/pp/metalog.html`
88. McCabe, F.G. and Clark, K.L. 1995. "April: Agent PRocess Interaction Language", In *Intelligent Agents: Theories, Architectures, and Languages*, M. Wooldridge, N.R. Jennings (eds.), LNAI 890, Springer-Verlag, pp.324-340.
89. Mehl, M., Schulte, C., and Smolka, G. 1998. "Futures and By-need Synchronization for Oz", Tech. Report, Programming Systems Lab, DFKI and Univ. des Saarlandes, May.
90. Meijer, E. and Sheilds, M. 2000. "XMLambda: A Functional Language for Constructing and Manipulating XML Documents", Tech Report, Oregon Graduate School.
91. Mendelzon, A.O. and Milo, T. 1997. "Formal Models of Web Queries", In *Proc. of the ACM SIGACT-SIGMOD-SIGART Symp. on Principles of Database Systems (PODS)*, May, pp.134-143.
92. Menezes, R., Merrick, I., and Wood, I. 1999. "Coordination in a Content-Addressable Web", *Autonomous Agents and Multi-Agent Systems*, Vol. 2, pp.287-301.

93. Meng, W. and Yu, C. 1995. *Query Processing in Multidatabase Systems*, Addison-Wesley.

94. Miller, M.S., Bobrow, D.G., Tribble, E.D., and Levy, J. 1987. "Logical Secrets", In *Logic Programming: Proc. 4th Int. Conf. (ICLP'87)*, pp.704-728.

95. Moore, J.T. 1998. "Mobile Code Security Techniques", CIS, Univ. of Pennsylvania, May.

96. Omicini, A. 1999. "On the Semantics of Tuple-based Coordination Models", In *Proc. of the 1999 ACM Symp. on Applied Computing (SAC'99)*, February, pp.175-182.

97. Omicini, A., Denti, E., and Natali, A. 1995. "Agent Coordination and Control through Logic Theories", AI*IA'95: In *Proc. of the 4th AI*IA Congress*, LNAI 992, Springer-Verlag, pp.439-450.

98. Papadopoulos, G.A. and Arbab, F. 1998. "Coordination Models and Languages", In *Advances in Computers*, Vol. 46, Academic Press, pp.329-400.

99. Pappas, A. (coordinator) 1999. *Workshop on Logic Programming and Distributed Knowledge Management*, ALP-UK/ALP/Compulog-net Tutorial/Workshop at PA Expo99, London, April.

100. Papakonstantinou, Y., Abiteboul, S., and Garcia-Molina, H. 1996. "Object Fusion in Mediator Systems", In *Proc. of the Int. Conf. on Very Large Databases*, September.

101. Pontelli, E. and Gupta, G. 1997. "W-ACE: A Logic Language for Intelligent Internet Programming", ICTAI'97, In *Proc. of the IEEE 9th Int. Conf. on Tools with AI*, pp.2-10. A much expanded version of this paper can be found at `http://www.cs.nmsu.edu/lldap/pri_lp/web/`.

102. Pontelli, E. and Gupta, G. 1998. "WEB-KLIC: A Concurrent Logic-based Unified Framework for Internet Programming", *AITEC Contract Research Projects in FY 1998: Proposal*, Tokyo, Japan, Available at `http://icot10.icot.or.jp/AITEC/FGCS/funding/98/plan07.html`.

103. Ramakrishnan, R. and Silberschatz, A. 1998. "Scalable Integration of Data Collections on the Web", Tech. Report, Univ. of Wiscosin-Madison.

104. Ramakrishnan, R. and Subrahmanian, V.S. (guest editors) 2000. *Journal of Logic Programming Special Issue on Logic-based Heterogeneous Information Systems*, Vol. 43, No. 1, April.

105. Saraswat, V.J. 1993. *Concurrent Constraint Programming*, MIT Press.

106. Saraswat, V.M., Kahn, K., and Levy, J. 1990. "Janus: A Step towards Distributed Constraint Programming", In *North American Conf. on LP*, MIT Press, October, pp.431-446.

107. Scroeder, M., Marques, R., Wagner, G., and Cunha, J.C. 1997. "CAP – Concurrent Action and Planning: Using PVM-Prolog to Implement Vivid Agents", In *PAP'97: The 5th Int. Conf. on the Practical Applications of Prolog*, London, pp.271-289.

108. Shanmugasundaram, J., Tufte, K., He, G., Zhang, C., DeWitt, D., and Naughton, J. 1999. "Relational Databases for Querying XML Documents: Limitations and Opportunities", In *Proc. of the 25th VLDB Conf.*, Edinburgh, Scotland.

109. Shapiro, E.Y. 1989a. "The Family of Concurrent Logic Programming Languages", *ACM Computing Surveys*, Vol. 21, No. 3, September, pp.413-510.

110. SICS. 1999 "SICStus Prolog Manual", Swedish Institute of Computer Science, Kista, Sweden, Available at `http://www.sics.se/sicstus/`.

111. Slattery, C. and Craven, M. 1998. "Combining Statistical and Relational Methods for Learning in Hypertext Domains", In *Proc. of the 8th Int. Conf. on Inductive LP*.

112. Sundstrom, A. 1998. *Comparative Study between Oz 3 and Java*, Master's Thesis 1998-10-01, CS Dept., Uppsala University, Sweden.
113. Sun Microsystems, 1999. "The JavaSpaces Specification", Available at `http://java.sun.com/docs/books/jini/javaspaces`.
114. Sutcliffe, G. and Pinakis, J. 1992. "Prolog-D-Linda", Technical Report 91/7, Dept. of CS, Univ. of Western Australia, Western Australia.
115. Szeredi, P., Molnár, K., and Scott, R. 1996. "Serving Multiple HTML Clients from a Prolog Application", In *Proc. of the 1st Workshop on Logic Programming Tools for Internet Applications*, P. Tarau, A. Davison, K. De Bosschere, and M. Hermenegildo (eds.), JICSLP'96, September, pp.81-90.
116. Taguchi, K., Sato, H., and Araki, K. 1998. "TeleLog: A Mobile Logic Programming Language", Tech. Report, Chikushi Jyogakuen Univ. Japan.
117. Tarau, P. 1999. "Jinni: Intelligent Mobile Agent Programming at the Intersection of Java and Prolog", *Proc. of PAAM'99*, London.
118. Tarau, P. and Dahl, V. 1998. "A Coordination Logic for Agent Programming in Virtual Worlds", In *Coordination Technology for Collaborative Applications - Organizations, Processes, and Agents*, W. Conen and G. Neumann (eds.), Springer-Verlag.
119. Tarau, P. and Dahl, V. 1998. "Mobile Threads through First Order Continuations", In *Proc. of APPAI-GULP-PRODE'98*, Coruna, Spain, July.
120. Tarau, P., De Bosschere, K, Dahl, V., and Rochefort, S. 1999. "LogiMOO: An Extensible Multi-User Virtual World with Natural Language Control", *Journal of Logic Programming*, Vol. 38, No. 3, March, pp.331-353.
121. Taylor, S., Av-Ron, E., and Shapiro, E.Y. 1987. "A Layered Method for Process and Code Mapping", *New Generation Computing*, Vol. 5, No. 2.
122. Tick, E. 1995. "The Deevolution of Concurrent Logic Programming Languages", *Journal of Logic Programming*, 10th Anniversary Special Issue, Vol. 23, No. 2, p.89-123.
123. Thorn, T. 1997. "Programming Languages for Mobile Code", *ACM Computing Surveys*, Vol. 29, No. 3, pp.213-239, September.
124. Van Roy, P. 1999. "On the Separation of Concerns in Distributed Programming: Application to Distribution Structure and fault Tolerance in Mozart", In *Int. Workshop on Parallel and Distributed Computing for Symbolic and Irregular Applications (PDSIA'99)*, July.
125. Van Roy, P. and Haridi, S. 1999. "Mozart: A Programming System for Agent Applications", In *Int. Conf on Logic Programming (ICLP'99), Int. Workshop on Distributed and Internet Programming with Logic and Constraint Languages*, November.
126. Van Roy, P., Haridi, S., Brand, P., Smolka, G., Mehl, M., and Scheidhauer, R. 1997. "Mobile Objects in Distributed Oz", *ACM Trans. on Programming Languages and Systems*, Vol. 19, No. 5, September, pp.804-851.
127. Wadler, P. 2000. "XML: Some Hyperlinks Minus the Hype", Bell Labs, Lucent Technologies, Available at `http://cm.bell-labs.com/cm/cs/who/wadler/xml/`.
128. Waldo, J., Wyant, G., Wollrath, A., and Kendall, S. 1994. "A Note on Distributed Computing", Tech Report SMLI TR-94-29, Sun Microsystems Lab, November.
129. Wetzel, G., Kowalski, R.A., and Toni, F. 1995. "A Theorem Proving Approach to CLP", In *Proc. of the 11th Workshop on LP*.
130. W3C. 1998. *Extensible Markup Language (XML)*, W3C Recommendation, 10th February, REC-xml-19980210 Available at `http://www.w3.org/TR/REC-xml`.
131. W3C 2000b. *Resource Description Framework (RDF)*, 5th May, Available at `http://www.w3.org/RDF/`.

Higher-Order Computational Logic

John W. Lloyd

Computer Sciences Laboratory
Research School of Information Sciences and Engineering
Australian National University
jwl@csl.anu.edu.au

Abstract. This paper presents a case for the use of higher-order logic as a foundation for computational logic. A suitable polymorphically-typed, higher-order logic is introduced and its syntax and proof theory briefly described. In addition, a metric space of closed terms suitable for knowledge representation purposes is presented. The approach to representing individuals is illustrated with some examples, as is the technique of programming with abstractions. The paper concludes by placing the results in the wider context of previous and current research in the use of higher-order logic in computational logic.

1   Introduction

In 1974, Robert Kowalski published the seminal idea that predicate logic could be used as a programming language [10]. The setting for Kowalski's idea was first-order logic, in fact, the Horn clause fragment of that logic. Since 1974, there has been an explosion of research activity that has pushed the fundamental idea in many different directions.

Once the idea that logic can be used as a programming language is appreciated, it is natural to ask what other logics might be useful in this context. Indeed, one can ask the question more generally: what logics are useful as a basis for the field of computational logic, where computational logic is to be understood broadly as the use of logic in Computer Science? There are a number of good answers to this question that depend to some extent on which part of computational logic one wishes to study. Some of these are explored elsewhere in this volume. In this paper, I make a case for the use of higher-order logic as the theoretical basis for computational logic.

I begin by giving an overview of a suitable higher-order logic. This logic has its origins in Church's simple theory of types [4], but is significantly extended by a polymorphic type system that is needed for its application to declarative programming languages. I briefly describe the syntax and proof theory of the logic. Next I introduce a metric space of certain closed terms. This space is highly suitable for modelling individuals in diverse applications and, unusually, includes certain abstractions that represent (finite) sets and multisets. A much more detailed account of the logic, including its semantics and the proofs of all the propositions in this paper, is contained in [13].

A.C. Kakas, F. Sadri (Eds.): Computat. Logic (Kowalski Festschrift), LNAI 2407, pp. 105–137, 2002.

I then turn to some more practical issues. First, there is a discussion, illustrated by two examples, of the approach to the representation of individuals. This knowledge representation issue is crucial in many applications. For example, in machine learning, there are individuals about which something has to be learned (for example, a classification or a regression value) and these individuals can have complex internal structure for which the full power of the higher-order logic is needed to represent them. In particular, it is often necessary to use lists, sets and multisets, all of which are provided directly by the logic. The second practical issue is the technique of programming with abstractions which is illustrated with some examples. This technique provides an elegant and convenient method of processing sets and multisets.

The last section sets the contributions of this paper in the context of previous and current research in the use of higher-order logics for computation. In particular, I discuss briefly three higher-order declarative programming languages Haskell [9], λProlog [15], and Curry [8]. The paper ends with some suggestions for future research in higher-order computational logic.

2   Types

Definition. An *alphabet* consists of four sets:

1. A set $\mathfrak{T}$ of type constructors.
2. A set $\mathfrak{P}$ of parameters.
3. A set $\mathfrak{C}$ of constants.
4. A set $\mathfrak{V}$ of variables.

Each type constructor in $\mathfrak{T}$ has an arity. The set $\mathfrak{T}$ always includes the type constructors 1 and Ω both of arity 0. 1 is the type of some distinguished singleton set and Ω is the type of the booleans. The set $\mathfrak{P}$ is denumerable (that is, countably infinite). Parameters are type variables and are typically denoted by $a, b, c, \ldots$. Each constant in $\mathfrak{C}$ has a signature (see below). The set $\mathfrak{V}$ is also denumerable. Variables are typically denoted by $x, y, z, \ldots$. For any particular application, the alphabet is assumed fixed and all definitions are relative to the alphabet.

Types are built up from the set of type constructors and the set of parameters, using the symbols $\rightarrow$ and $\times$.

Definition. A *type* is defined inductively as follows.

1. Each parameter in $\mathfrak{P}$ is a type.
2. If T is a type constructor in $\mathfrak{T}$ of arity k and $\alpha_1, \ldots, \alpha_k$ are types, then $T \, \alpha_1 \ldots \alpha_k$ is a type. (For $k = 0$, this reduces to a type constructor of arity 0 being a type.)
3. If α and β are types, then $\alpha \rightarrow \beta$ is a type.
4. If $\alpha_1, \ldots, \alpha_n$ are types, then $\alpha_1 \times \ldots \times \alpha_n$ is a type. (For $n = 0$, this reduces to 1 being a type.)

$\mathfrak{S}$ denotes the set of all types obtained from an alphabet ($\mathfrak{S}$ for 'sort'). The symbol $\to$ is right associative, so that $\alpha \to \beta \to \gamma$ means $\alpha \to (\beta \to \gamma)$.

Definition. A type is *closed* if it contains no parameters.

Notation. $\mathfrak{S}^c$ denotes the set of all closed types obtained from an alphabet.

Note that $\mathfrak{S}^c$ is non-empty, since $1, \Omega \in \mathfrak{S}^c$.

Example. In practical applications of the logic, a variety of types is needed. For example, declarative programming languages typically admit the following types (which are nullary type constructors): 1, Ω, *Int* (the type of integers), *Float* (the type of floating-point numbers), *Char* (the type of characters), and *String* (the type of strings). Another useful type in applications is *Nat* (the type of natural numbers).

Other useful type constructors are those used to define lists, trees, and so on. In the logic, *List* denotes the (unary) list type constructor. Thus, if α is a type, then *List* α is the type of lists whose elements have type α.

Use will be made later of the concept of one type being more general than another.

Definition. Let α and β be types. Then α is *more general than* β if there exists a type substitution ξ such that $\beta = \alpha\xi$.

Note that "more general than" includes "equal to", since ξ can be the identity substitution.

Example. Let $\alpha = (List\ a) \times \Omega$ and $\beta = (List\ Int) \times \Omega$. Then α is more general than β, since $\beta = \alpha\xi$, where $\xi = \{a/Int\}$.

3   Terms

Definition. A *signature* is the declared type for a constant.

Notation. The fact that a constant C has signature α is sometimes denoted by $C : \alpha$.

I distinguish two different kinds of constants: *data constructors* and *functions*. In a knowledge representation context, data constructors are used to represent individuals. In a programming language context, data constructors are used to construct data values. In contrast, functions are used to compute on data values; functions have definitions while data constructors do not. In the semantics for the logic, the data constructors are used to construct models. As examples, the constants $\top$ (true) and $\bot$ (false) are data constructors, as is each integer, floating-point number, and character. The constant : (cons) used to construct lists is a data constructor. The constants $\subseteq$ and *concatenate* introduced in examples below are both functions.

The set $\mathfrak{C}$ always includes the following constants (where a is a parameter).

1. $()$, having signature 1.
2. $=$, having signature $a \to a \to \Omega$.
3. $\top$ and $\bot$, having signature Ω.
4. $\neg$, having signature $\Omega \to \Omega$.
5. $\wedge$, $\vee$, $\longrightarrow$, $\longleftarrow$, and $\longleftrightarrow$, having signature $\Omega \to \Omega \to \Omega$.
6. Σ and Π, having signature $(a \to \Omega) \to \Omega$.

The intended meaning of $=$ is identity (that is, $= x \, y$ is $\top$ iff x and y are identical), the intended meaning of $\top$ is true, the intended meaning of $\bot$ is false, and the intended meanings of the connectives $\neg$, $\wedge$, $\vee$, $\longrightarrow$, $\longleftarrow$, and $\longleftrightarrow$ are as usual. The intended meaning of Σ is that it is true iff its argument is a predicate that is true on *some* domain element, and the intended meaning of Π is that it is true iff its argument is a predicate that is true on *every* domain element.

Note. In this paper, the equality symbol '$=$' is overloaded. On the one hand, '$=$' is a constant in the alphabet of a higher-order logic. On the other hand, '$=$' is a symbol of the informal meta-language in which the paper is written with the intended meaning of identity. The meaning of any occurrence of the symbol '$=$' will always be clear from the context. Equality is nearly always written infix.

Data constructors always have a signature of the form $\sigma_1 \to \cdots \to \sigma_n \to (T \, a_1 \ldots a_k)$, where T is a type constructor of arity k, $a_1, \ldots, a_k$ are distinct parameters, and all the parameters appearing in $\sigma_1, \ldots, \sigma_n$ occur among $a_1, \ldots, a_k$ ($n \geq 0$, $k \geq 0$). Furthermore, for each type constructor T, I assume that there does exist at least one data constructor having a signature of the form $\sigma_1 \to \cdots \to \sigma_n \to (T \, a_1 \ldots a_k)$.

Example. The data constructors for constructing lists are $[]$ having signature $List \, a$ and $:$ having signature $a \to List \, a \to List \, a$, where $:$ is usually written infix. $[]$ represents the empty list. The term $s : t$ represents the list with head s and tail t. Thus $4 : 5 : 6 : []$ represents the list $[4, 5, 6]$.

The next task is to define the central concept of a term. In the non-polymorphic case, a simple inductive definition suffices. But the polymorphic case is more complicated since, when putting terms together to make larger terms, it is generally necessary to solve a system of equations and these equations depend upon the relative types of free variables in the component terms. The effect of this is that to define a term one has to define simultaneously its type, and its set of free variables and their relative types.

Definition. A *term*, together with its type, and its set of free variables and their relative types, is defined inductively as follows.

1. Each variable x in $\mathfrak{V}$ is a term of type a, where a is a parameter.
   The variable x is free with relative type a in x.
2. Each constant C in $\mathfrak{C}$, where C has signature α, is a term of type α.

3. (Abstraction) If t is a term of type β and x a variable in $\mathfrak{V}$, then $\lambda x.t$ is a term of type $\alpha \rightarrow \beta$, if x is free with relative type α in t, or type $a \rightarrow \beta$, where a is a new parameter, otherwise.

   A variable other than x is free with relative type σ in $\lambda x.t$ if the variable is free with relative type σ in t.

4. (Application) If s is a term of type $\alpha \rightarrow \beta$ and t a term of type γ[1] such that the equation
   $$\alpha = \gamma,$$
   augmented with equations of the form
   $$\rho = \delta,$$
   for each variable that is free with relative type ρ in s and is also free with relative type δ in t, have a most general unifier θ, then $(s\ t)$ is a term of type $\beta\theta$.

   A variable is free with relative type $\sigma\theta$ in $(s\ t)$ if the variable is free with relative type σ in s or t.

5. (Tupling) If $t_1, \ldots, t_n$ are terms of type $\alpha_1, \ldots, \alpha_n$[2], respectively, such that the set of equations of the form
   $$\rho_{i_1} = \rho_{i_2} = \ldots = \rho_{i_k},$$
   for each variable that is free with relative type ρ_{i_j} in the term t_{i_j} ($j = 1, \ldots, k$ and $k > 1$), have a most general unifier θ, then $(t_1, \ldots, t_n)$[3] is a term of type $\alpha_1\theta \times \ldots \times \alpha_n\theta$.

   A variable is free with relative type $\sigma\theta$ in $(t_1, \ldots, t_n)$ if the variable is free with relative type σ in t_j, for some $j \in \{1, \ldots, n\}$.

The type substitution θ in Parts 4 and 5 of the definition is called the *associated* mgu.

Notation. $\mathfrak{L}$ denotes the set of all terms obtained from an alphabet and is called the *language* given by the alphabet.

Definition. A term is *closed* if it contains no free variables.

Example. Let M be a nullary type, and $A : M$ and *concatenate* : *List* $a \times$ *List* $a \rightarrow$ *List* a be constants. Recall that $[] :$ *List* a and $(:) : a \rightarrow$ *List* $a \rightarrow$ *List* a are the data constructors for lists. I will show that $(concatenate\ ([], [A]))$ is a term. For this, $([], [A])$ must be shown to be a term, which leads to the consideration of $[]$ and $[A]$. Now $[]$ is a term of type *List* a, by Part 2 of the definition of a term. By Parts 2 and 4, $(:\ A)$ is a term of type *List* $M \rightarrow$ *List* M,

---

[1] Without loss of generality, one can suppose that the parameters in $\alpha \rightarrow \beta$, taken together with the parameters in the relative types of the free variables in s, and the parameters in γ, taken together with the parameters in the relative types of the free variables in t, are standardised apart.

[2] Without loss of generality, one can suppose that the parameters of each α_i, taken together with the parameters in the relative types of the free variables of t_i, are standardised apart.

[3] If $n = 1$, (t_1) is defined to be t_1. If $n = 0$, the term obtained is the empty tuple, $()$, which is a term of type *1*.

where along the way the equation $a = M$ is solved with the mgu $\{a/M\}$. Then $((:\ A)\ [])$ (that is, $[A]$) is a term of type $List\ M$ by Part 4, where the equation $List\ M = List\ a$ is solved. By Part 5, it follows that $([], [A])$ is a term of type $List\ a \times List\ M$. Finally, by Part 4 again, $(concatenate\ ([], [A]))$ is a term of type $List\ M$, where the equation to be solved is $List\ a \times List\ a = List\ a \times List\ M$ whose mgu is $\{a/M\}$.

Example. Consider the constants $append : List\ a \to List\ a \to List\ a \to \Omega$ and $process : List\ a \to List\ a$. I will show that $(((append\ x)\ [])\ (process\ x))$ is a term. First, the variable x is a term of type b, where the parameter is chosen to avoid a clash in the next step. Then $(append\ x)$ is a term of type $List\ a \to List\ a \to \Omega$, for which the equation solved is $List\ a = b$. Next $((append\ x)\ [])$ is a term of type $List\ a \to \Omega$ and x has relative type $List\ a$ in $((append\ x)\ [])$. Now consider $(process\ x)$, for which the constituent parts are $process$ of type $List\ c \to List\ c$ and the variable x of type d. Thus $(process\ x)$ is a term of type $List\ c$ and x has relative type $List\ c$ in $(process\ x)$. Finally, we have to apply $((append\ x)\ [])$ to the term $(process\ x)$. For this, by Part 4, there are two equations. These are $List\ a = List\ c$, coming from the top-level types, and $List\ a = List\ c$, coming from the free variable x in each of the components. These equations have the mgu $\{c/a\}$. Thus $(((append\ x)\ [])\ (process\ x))$ is a term of type Ω.

Notation. Terms of the form $(\Sigma\ \lambda x.t)$ are written as $\exists x.t$ and terms of the form $(\Pi\ \lambda x.t)$ are written as $\forall x.t$ (in accord with the intended meaning of Σ and Π). In a higher-order logic, one may identify sets and predicates – the actual identification is between a set and its characteristic function which is a predicate. Thus, if t is of type Ω, the abstraction $\lambda x.t$ may be written as $\{x \mid t\}$ if it is intended to emphasise that its intended meaning is a set. The notation $\{\}$ means $\{x \mid \perp\}$. The notation $s \in t$ means $(t\ s)$, where t has type $\alpha \to \Omega$ and s has type α, for some α. Furthermore, notwithstanding the fact that sets are mathematically identified with predicates, it is sometimes convenient to maintain an informal distinction between sets (as "collections of objects") and predicates. For this reason, the notation $\{\alpha\}$ is introduced as a synonym for the type $\alpha \to \Omega$. The term $(s\ t)$ is often written as simply $s\ t$, using juxtaposition to denote application. Juxtaposition is left associative, so that $r\ s\ t$ means $((r\ s)\ t)$. Thus $(((append\ x)\ [])\ (process\ x))$ can be written more simply as $append\ x\ []\ (process\ x)$.

For the later definition of a statement, the concept of one term being type-weaker than another will be needed.

Definition. Let s be a term of type σ and t a term of type τ. Then s is *type-weaker* than t, denoted $s \precsim t$, if there exists a type substitution γ such that $\tau = \sigma\gamma$, every free variable in s is a free variable in t, and, if the relative type of a free variable in s is δ, then the relative type of this free variable in t is $\delta\gamma$.

Example. Let $s = y$ and $t = f\ x\ y$, where $f : M \to N \to N$. Let $\gamma = \{b/N\}$, where b is the type of y. Then $b\gamma = N$ and s is type-weaker than t.

Example. Let $s = y$ and $t = f\ y\ x$, where $f : M \to N \to N$. Then s is not type-weaker than t since no suitable γ exists.

Definition. Two terms s and t are *type-equivalent*, denoted $s \approx t$, if they have the same types, the same set of free variables, and, for every free variable x in s and t, x has the same relative type in s as it has in t (up to variants of types).

4 Schemas

The above definition of terms is sufficient for many knowledge representation tasks. However, it turns out that a more flexible notation on top of the term syntax is needed in some applications, the prime example of which is programming languages. Here is an example to motivate the ideas.

Example. Consider the programming problem of writing some code to implement the subset relation between sets. Here is a possible definition of the function $\subseteq : (a \to \Omega) \to (a \to \Omega) \to \Omega$, which is written infix.

$$\{\} \subseteq s = \top$$
$$\{x \mid x = u\} \subseteq s = u \in s$$
$$\{x \mid \boldsymbol{u} \vee \boldsymbol{v}\} \subseteq s = (\{x \mid \boldsymbol{u}\} \subseteq s) \wedge (\{x \mid \boldsymbol{v}\} \subseteq s).$$

At first sight, all these equations look like terms. However, closer inspection of the third equation reveals that $\boldsymbol{u}$ and $\boldsymbol{v}$ there are not ordinary variables. Intuitively, these are intended to stand for expressions (possibly) containing x as a free variable. Technically, they are syntactical variables in the meta-language that range over object-level terms. Syntactical variables are distinguished from (ordinary) variables by writing them in bold font.

   This use of syntactical variables is common in the presentation of axioms for logics. The third equation in the above example is thus a schema rather than a term in which the syntactical variables $\boldsymbol{u}$ and $\boldsymbol{v}$ range over object-level terms.

   The definition of a schema can be obtained from the previous one for a term by also allowing syntactical variables to appear. The details are given in [13].

   A schema can be reified to obtain a term.

Definition. A *reifier* is a finite set of the form $\{\boldsymbol{x}_1/t_1, \dots, \boldsymbol{x}_n/t_n\}$, where each $\boldsymbol{x}_i$ is a syntactical variable, each t_i is a term, and $\boldsymbol{x}_1, \dots, \boldsymbol{x}_n$ are distinct.

Definition. Let s be a schema whose syntactical variables are included in $\{\boldsymbol{x}_1, \dots, \boldsymbol{x}_n\}$ and $\Psi = \{\boldsymbol{x}_1/t_1, \dots, \boldsymbol{x}_n/t_n\}$ a reifier. Then $s\Psi$, the *reification* of s by Ψ, is the expression obtained from s by replacing each occurrence of a syntactical variable $\boldsymbol{x}_i$ in s by the term t_i, for $i = 1, \dots, n$.

   Under certain natural conditions discussed in [13], $s\Psi$ is a term. The concepts of type-weaker and type-equivalence for schemas will be needed.

Definition. Let s be a schema of type σ and t a schema of type τ. Then s is *type-weaker* than t, denoted $s \precsim t$, if there exists a type substitution γ such that $\tau = \sigma\gamma$, every free variable in s is a free variable in t and, if the relative type of a free variable in s is δ, then the relative type of this free variable in t is $\delta\gamma$, and every syntactical variable in s is a syntactical variable in t and, if the relative type of a syntactical variable in s is ρ, then the relative type of this syntactical variable in t is $\rho\gamma$.

Definition. Two schemas s and t are *type-equivalent*, denoted $s \approx t$, if they have the same types, the same set of free variables and, for every free variable x in s and t, x has the same relative type in s as it has in t, and the same set of syntactical variables and, for every syntactical variable $\boldsymbol{x}$ in s and t, $\boldsymbol{x}$ has the same relative type in s as it has in t (up to variants of types).

5   Statements and Statement Schemas

Next the definition of a class of terms (and schemas) that can serve as statements in declarative programming languages whose programs are equational theories is presented.

Definition. A *statement* is a term of the form $h = b$, where h has the form $f\, t_1 \ldots t_n$, $n \geq 0$, for some function f, and b is type-weaker than h.

The term h is called the *head* and the term b is called the *body* of the statement. The statement is said to be *about* f.

Example. Consider the function $append : List\ a \times List\ a \times List\ a \to \Omega$. Then the following term is a statement about $append$.

$$append\,(u,v,w) = (u = [\,] \wedge v = w) \vee$$
$$\exists r.\exists x.\exists y.(u = r : x \wedge w = r : y \wedge append\,(x,v,y)).$$

The head has type Ω and the free variables u, v, and w have relative type $List\ a$ in the head. The body also has type Ω and its free variables u, v, and w have relative type $List\ a$ in the body. Thus the body is type-weaker than (in fact, type-equivalent to) the head.

Usually, the head and the body of a statement are type-equivalent, but this is not always the case.

Example. Consider the statement

$$concatenate\,([\,], x) = x$$

about the function $concatenate : List\ a \times List\ a \to List\ a$. Here h is $concatenate\,([\,], x)$ and b is x. Then h has type $List\ a$ and b has type a', for some parameters a and a'. Thus b is type-weaker than h with $\gamma = \{a'/List\ a\}$.

Schemas should also be allowed to appear in programs.

Definition. A *statement schema* is a schema of the form $h = b$, where h has the form $f\, s_1 \ldots s_n$, $n \geq 0$, for some function f, and b is type-weaker than h.

The schema h is called the *head* and the schema b is called the *body* of the statement schema. The statement schema is said to be *about f*.

Each statement is a statement schema.

Example. Consider the function $\subseteq$ studied earlier.

$$\{\} \subseteq s = \top$$
$$\{x \mid x = u\} \subseteq s = u \in s$$
$$\{x \mid u \lor v\} \subseteq s = (\{x \mid u\} \subseteq s) \land (\{x \mid v\} \subseteq s).$$

The first two are statements, while the third is a statement schema. In the first statement, the body is type-weaker than the head, but not type-equivalent to the head because of the extra variable s. For the second statement and the third statement schema, the body is type-equivalent to the head.

Example. Consider the function *powerset* $: (a \to \Omega) \to (a \to \Omega) \to \Omega$. The following is a statement schema in which the head is type-equivalent to the body.

$$powerset\; \{x \mid if\; u\; then\; v\; else\; w\} =$$
$$if\; v\; then\; powerset\; \{x \mid u \lor w\}\; else\; powerset\; \{x \mid \neg u \land w\}.$$

The condition that the body of a statement (or statement schema) be type-weaker than the head is needed to prove the important property that run-time type checking is unnecessary in the computational model [13].

Definition. The *definition* of a function f is the collection of all statement schemas about f, together with the signature for f.

Definition. A *program* is a collection of definitions.

6 Proof Theory

I now turn to the proof-theoretic aspects of the logic. The main goal here is to define a suitable operational behaviour for programs in declarative programming languages whose programs are equational theories. Throughout this section, I assume that each definition is given in the context of some program. Two terms are said to be α-equivalent if they differ only in the names of their bound variables.

Definition. A *redex* of a term t is an occurrence of a subterm of t that is α-equivalent to either an instance of the head of a statement or an instance of a reification of the head of a statement schema.

Example. Consider the function $\subseteq$ again.

$$\{\} \subseteq s = \top$$
$$\{x \mid x = u\} \subseteq s = u \in s$$
$$\{x \mid u \vee v\} \subseteq s = (\{x \mid u\} \subseteq s) \wedge (\{x \mid v\} \subseteq s).$$

The term

$$(\{\} \subseteq \{D\}) \wedge (\{y \mid (y = A) \vee (y = B)\} \subseteq \{A, C, D\})$$

has two redexes. The first is

$$\{\} \subseteq \{D\},$$

which is an instance of the head of the first statement by the substitution $\{s/\{D\}\}$. The second is

$$\{y \mid (y = A) \vee (y = B)\} \subseteq \{A, C, D\},$$

which is α-equivalent to an instance of a reification of the head of the third statement schema. The reifier is $\{u/(x = A), v/(x = B)\}$ and the substitution is $\{s/\{A, C, D\}$.

Definition. Let $\mathfrak{L}$ be the set of terms constructed from the alphabet of a program and $\mathfrak{DS}_{\mathfrak{L}}$ the set of subterms of terms in $\mathfrak{L}$ (distinguished by their occurrence). A *selection rule* S is a function from $\mathfrak{L}$ to the power set of $\mathfrak{DS}_{\mathfrak{L}}$ satisfying the following condition: if t is a term in $\mathfrak{L}$, then $S(t)$ is a subset of the set of outermost redexes in t.

A redex is *outermost* if it is not a (proper) subterm of another redex. Typical selection rules are the parallel-outermost selection rule for which all outermost redexes are selected and the leftmost selection rule in which the leftmost outermost redex is selected. The choice of using outermost redexes is motivated by the desire for evaluation strategy to be lazy.

Definition. A term s is obtained from a term t by a *computation step* using the selection rule S if the following conditions are satisfied:

1. $S(t)$ is a non-empty set, $\{r_i\}$, say.
2. For each i, the redex r_i is α-equivalent to either an instance $h_i\theta$ of the head of a statement $h_i = b_i$ or to an instance of a reification $h_i'\Psi\theta$ of the head of a statement schema $h_i' = b_i'$.
3. s is the term obtained from t by replacing, for each i, the redex r_i by $b_i\theta$ or $b_i'\Psi\theta$, respectively.

Note that a computation step is essentially a (multiple) application of the inference rule of type theory (Rule R) [1, p. 164]. Each computation step is decidable in the sense that there is an algorithm that can decide for a given subterm whether or not there is an instance of the head of a statement or an instance of a reification of the head of a statement schema that is α-equivalent to the subterm. This algorithm is similar to the (first-order) unification algorithm. In particular, the undecidability of higher-order unification [16] is not relevant here because α-equivalence is demanded rather than $\beta\eta$-equivalence (or β-equivalence) for higher-order unification.

Definition. A *computation* from a term t is a sequence $\{t_i\}_{i=1}^n$ of terms such that the following conditions are satisfied.

1. $t = t_1$.
2. t_{i+1} is obtained from t_i by a computation step, for $i = 1, \dots, n-1$.

The term t_1 is called the *goal* of the computation and t_n is called the *answer*.

7 Normal Terms

Next I identify a class of terms, called *basic* terms, suitable for representing individuals in diverse applications. For example, this class is suitable for machine learning applications. From a (higher-order) programming language perspective, basic terms are data values. The most interesting aspect of the class of basic terms is that it includes certain abstractions and therefore is much wider than is normally considered for knowledge representation. These abstractions allow one to model sets, multisets, and similar data types, in an elegant way. Of course, there are other ways of introducing (extensional) sets, multisets, and so on, without using abstractions. For example, one can define abstract data types or one can introduce data constructors with special equality theories. The primary advantage of the approach adopted here is that one can define these abstractions *intensionally* as shown in Section 13.

The definition of basic terms is given in several stages: first I define normal terms, then define an equivalence relation on normal terms, and finally define basic terms as distinguished representatives of equivalence classes. Before getting down to the first step of giving the definition of normal terms, some motivation will be helpful. How should a (finite) set or multiset be represented? First, advantage is taken of the higher-order nature of the logic to identify sets and their characteristic functions, that is, sets are viewed as predicates. With this approach, an obvious representation of sets uses the connectives, so that $\lambda x.(x = 1) \lor (x = 2)$ is the representation of the set $\{1, 2\}$. This was the kind of representation used in [12] and it works well for sets. But the connectives are, of course, not available for multisets, so something more general is needed. An alternative representation for the set $\{1, 2\}$ is the term

$$\lambda x.if\ x = 1\ then\ \top\ else\ if\ x = 2\ then\ \top\ else\ \bot$$

and this idea generalises to multisets and similar abstractions. For example,

$$\lambda x.if\ x = A\ then\ 42\ else\ if\ x = B\ then\ 21\ else\ 0$$

is the multiset with 42 occurrences of A and 21 occurrences of B (and nothing else). Thus I adopt abstractions of the form

$$\lambda x.if\ x = t_1\ then\ s_1\ else\ \ldots\ if\ x = t_n\ then\ s_n\ else\ s_0$$

to represent (extensional) sets, multisets, and so on.

However, before giving the definition of a normal term, some attention has to be paid to the term s_0 in previous expression. The reason is that s_0 in this abstraction is usually a very specific term. For example, for finite sets, s_0 is $\perp$ and for finite multisets, s_0 is 0. For this reason, the concept of a default term is now introduced. The intuitive idea is that, for each closed type, there is a (unique) default term such that each abstraction having that type as codomain takes the default term as its value for all but a finite number of points in the domain, that is, s_0 is the default value. The choice of default term depends on the particular application but, since sets and multisets are so useful, one would expect the set of default terms to include $\perp$ and 0. However, there could also be other types for which a default term is needed. For each type constructor T, I assume there is chosen a unique *default data constructor C* such that C has signature $\sigma_1 \to \cdots \to \sigma_n \to (T\ a_1 \ldots a_k)$. For example, for Ω, the default data constructor could be $\perp$, for *Int*, the default data constructor could be 0, and for *List*, the default data constructor could be $[]$.

Definition. The set of *default terms*, $\mathfrak{D}$, is defined inductively as follows.

1. If C is a default data constructor having signature $\sigma_1 \to \cdots \to \sigma_n \to (T\ a_1 \ldots a_k)$ and $t_1, \ldots, t_n \in \mathfrak{D}$ $(n \geq 0)$ such that $C\ t_1 \ldots t_n \in \mathfrak{L}$, then $C\ t_1 \ldots t_n \in \mathfrak{D}$.
2. If $t \in \mathfrak{D}$ and $\lambda x.t \in \mathfrak{L}$, then $\lambda x.t \in \mathfrak{D}$.
3. If $t_1, \ldots, t_n \in \mathfrak{D}$ $(n \geq 0)$ and $(t_1, \ldots, t_n) \in \mathfrak{L}$, then $(t_1, \ldots, t_n) \in \mathfrak{D}$.

There may not be a default term for some closed types.

Example. Assume the alphabet contains just the nullary type constructors M and N (in addition to *1* and Ω) and the data constructors $F : M \to N$ and $G : N \to M$. (Recall that each type constructor must have an associated data constructor.) Let G be the default data constructor for M. Then there are no *closed* terms of type M and hence there is no default term of type M.

However, if it exists, one can show that the default term for each closed type is unique.

Proposition 7.1. *For each $\alpha \in \mathfrak{S}^c$, there exists at most one default term having type more general than α.*

Now normal terms can be defined. In the following, $\lambda x.s_0$ is regarded as the special case of

$$\lambda x.if\ x = t_1\ then\ s_1\ else\ \ldots\ if\ x = t_n\ then\ s_n\ else\ s_0$$

when $n = 0$.

Definition. The set of *normal terms*, $\mathfrak{N}$, is defined inductively as follows.

1. If C is a data constructor having signature $\sigma_1 \to \cdots \to \sigma_n \to (T\ a_1 \ldots a_k)$ and $t_1, \ldots, t_n \in \mathfrak{N}$ $(n \geq 0)$ such that $C\ t_1 \ldots t_n \in \mathfrak{L}$, then $C\ t_1 \ldots t_n \in \mathfrak{N}$.

2. If $t_1, \ldots, t_n \in \mathfrak{N}$, $s_1, \ldots, s_n \in \mathfrak{N}$ $(n \geq 0)$, $s_0 \in \mathfrak{D}$ and

$$\lambda x. if\ x = t_1\ then\ s_1\ else\ \ldots\ if\ x = t_n\ then\ s_n\ else\ s_0 \in \mathfrak{L},$$

then

$$\lambda x. if\ x = t_1\ then\ s_1\ else\ \ldots\ if\ x = t_n\ then\ s_n\ else\ s_0 \in \mathfrak{N}.$$

3. If $t_1, \ldots, t_n \in \mathfrak{N}$ $(n \geq 0)$ and $(t_1, \ldots, t_n) \in \mathfrak{L}$, then $(t_1, \ldots, t_n) \in \mathfrak{N}$.

Part 1 of the definition of the set of normal terms states, in particular, that individual natural numbers, integers, and so on, are normal terms. Also a term formed by applying a constructor to (all of) its arguments, each of which is a normal term, is a normal term. As an example of this, consider the following declarations of the data constructors *Circle* and *Rectangle*.

$Circle : Float \to Shape$

$Rectangle : Float \to Float \to Shape.$

Then (*Circle* 7.5) and (*Rectangle* 42.0 21.3) are normal terms of type *Shape*. However, (*Rectangle* 42.0) is not a normal term as not all arguments to *Rectangle* are given. Normal terms coming from Part 1 of the definition are called *normal structures* and always have a type of the form $T\alpha_1 \ldots \alpha_n$.

The abstractions formed in Part 2 of the definition are "almost constant" abstractions since they take the default term s_0 as value for all except a finite number of points in the domain. They are called *normal abstractions* and always have a type of the form $\beta \to \gamma$. This class of abstractions includes useful data types such as (finite) sets and multisets (assuming $\perp$ and 0 are default terms). More generally, normal abstractions can be regarded as lookup tables, with s_0 as the value for items not in the table.

Part 3 of the definition of normal terms just states that one can form a tuple from normal terms and obtain a normal term. These terms are called *normal tuples* and always have a type of the form $\alpha_1 \times \ldots \times \alpha_n$.

Proposition 7.2. $\mathfrak{D} \subseteq \mathfrak{N}$.

It will be convenient to gather together all normal terms that have a type more general than some specific closed type.

Definition. For each $\alpha \in \mathfrak{S}^c$, define $\mathfrak{N}_\alpha = \{t \in \mathfrak{N} \mid t \text{ has type more general than } \alpha\}$.

The intuitive meaning of $\mathfrak{N}_\alpha$ is that it is the set of terms representing individuals of type α. Note that $\mathfrak{N} = \bigcup_{\alpha \in \mathfrak{S}^c} \mathfrak{N}_\alpha$. However, the $\mathfrak{N}_\alpha$ are not necessarily disjoint. For example, if the alphabet includes *List*, then $[] \in \mathfrak{N}_{List\ \alpha}$, for each closed type α.

8 An Equivalence Relation on Normal Terms

Several syntactically distinct terms in $\mathfrak{N}$ can represent the same individual. For example,

$$\lambda x.\text{if } x = 1 \text{ then } \top \text{ else if } x = 2 \text{ then } \top \text{ else } \bot,$$
$$\lambda x.\text{if } x = 2 \text{ then } \top \text{ else if } x = 1 \text{ then } \top \text{ else } \bot,$$

and

$$\lambda x.\text{if } x = 3 \text{ then } \bot \text{ else if } x = 2 \text{ then } \top \text{ else if } x = 1 \text{ then } \top \text{ else } \bot$$

all represent the set $\{1, 2\}$. To reflect this, a relation $\equiv$ is defined on $\mathfrak{N}$.

Definition. The binary relation $\equiv$ on $\mathfrak{N}$ is defined inductively as follows. Let $s, t \in \mathfrak{N}$. Then $s \equiv t$ if there exists $\alpha \in \mathfrak{S}^c$ such that $s, t \in \mathfrak{N}_\alpha$ and one of the following conditions holds.

1. $\alpha = T\ \alpha_1 \ldots \alpha_k$, for some $T, \alpha_1, \ldots, \alpha_k$, and s is $C\ s_1 \ldots s_n$, t is $C\ t_1 \ldots t_n$ and $s_i \equiv t_i$, for $i = 1, \ldots, n$.
2. $\alpha = \beta \to \gamma$, for some β, γ, and
   s is $\lambda x.\text{if } x = t_1 \text{ then } s_1 \text{ else } \ldots \text{ if } x = t_n \text{ then } s_n \text{ else } s_0$,
   t is $\lambda y.\text{if } y = u_1 \text{ then } v_1 \text{ else } \ldots \text{ if } y = u_m \text{ then } v_m \text{ else } s_0$
   and, $\forall r \in \mathfrak{N}_\beta$,
   $(\exists i, j.\ r \equiv t_i \wedge r \not\equiv t_k(\forall k < i) \wedge r \equiv u_j \wedge r \not\equiv u_m(\forall m < j) \wedge s_i \equiv v_j) \vee$
   $(\exists i.\ r \equiv t_i \wedge r \not\equiv t_k(\forall k < i) \wedge r \not\equiv u_j(\forall j) \wedge s_i \equiv s_0) \vee$
   $(\exists j.\ r \not\equiv t_i(\forall i) \wedge r \equiv u_j \wedge r \not\equiv u_m(\forall m < j) \wedge s_0 \equiv v_j) \vee$
   $(r \not\equiv t_i(\forall i) \wedge r \not\equiv u_j(\forall j)).$
3. $\alpha = \alpha_1 \times \ldots \times \alpha_n$, for some $\alpha_1, \ldots, \alpha_n$, and s is $(s_1, \ldots, s_n)$, t is $(t_1, \ldots, t_n)$ and $s_i \equiv t_i$, for $i = 1, \ldots, n$.

Proposition 8.1. *For each $\alpha \in \mathfrak{S}^c$, $\equiv|_{\mathfrak{N}_\alpha}$ is an equivalence relation on $\mathfrak{N}_\alpha$.*

Later I will need the following concept.

Definition. Let t be $\lambda x.\text{if } x = t_1 \text{ then } s_1 \text{ else} \ldots \text{if } x = t_n \text{ then } s_n \text{ else } s_0 \in \mathfrak{N}_{\beta \to \gamma}$ and $r \in \mathfrak{N}_\beta$. Then $V(t\ r)$ is defined by

$$V(t\ r) = \begin{cases} s_i \text{ if } r \equiv t_i \text{ and } r \not\equiv t_k(\forall k < i) \\ s_0 \text{ if } r \not\equiv t_i(\forall i) \end{cases}$$

Intuitively, $V(t\ r)$ is the "value" returned when t is applied to r.

9   A Total Order on Normal Terms

The equivalence relation $\equiv$ was introduced because several syntactically distinct terms in $\mathfrak{N}$ can represent the same individual. Rather than deal with all the normal terms in an equivalence class in some $\mathfrak{N}_\alpha$, it is preferable to deal with a single representative from the equivalence class. For this purpose, a (strict) total order on normal terms is introduced.

Recall that a (strict) partial order on a set A is a binary relation $<$ on A such that, for each $a, b, c \in A$, $a \not< a$ (irreflexivity), $a < b$ implies $b \not< a$ (asymmetry), and $a < b$ and $b < c$ implies $a < c$ (transitivity). In addition, a (strict) partial order is a (strict) total order if, for each $a, b \in A$, exactly one of $a = b$ or $a < b$ or $b < a$ holds.

If $<$ is a (strict) total order on a set A, then $<$ can be lifted to (strict) total order, also denoted by $<$, on the set of sequences of elements in A by $a_1 \ldots a_n < b_1 \ldots b_m$ if either
(i) $a_1 = b_1, \ldots, a_n = b_n$ and $n < m$, or
(ii) there exists j such that $1 \le j \le n$, $a_1 = b_1, \ldots, a_{j-1} = b_{j-1}$ and $a_j < b_j$.
The order $<$ on the sequences is called the *induced lexicographic* ordering.

In the definition of the binary relation $<$ below, it is assumed that, for each $T \in \mathfrak{T}$, there is defined a (strict) total order $\prec_T$ on the set of all data constructors associated with the type constructor T. For standard types, such as *Int* and *Float*, the usual order provides an appropriate total order. To simplify the statement of the definition, the concept of the trace of an abstraction will be useful.

Definition. Suppose that s is a normal abstraction

$$\lambda x. if \ x = t_1 \ then \ s_1 \ else \ \ldots \ if \ x = t_n \ then \ s_n \ else \ s_0.$$

Then the *trace* of s, $trace(s)$, is the sequence $t_1 \, s_1 \, t_2 \, s_2 \ldots t_n \, s_n$. (For the normal abstraction $\lambda x. s_0$, the trace is the empty sequence ε.)

Definition. The binary relation $<$ on $\mathfrak{N}$ is defined inductively as follows. Let $s, t \in \mathfrak{N}$. Then $s < t$ if there exists $\alpha \in \mathfrak{S}^c$ such that $s, t \in \mathfrak{N}_\alpha$ and one of the following conditions holds.

1. $\alpha = T \, \alpha_1 \ldots \alpha_k$, for some $T, \alpha_1, \ldots, \alpha_k$, and s is $C \, s_1 \ldots s_n$, t is $D \, t_1 \ldots t_m$ and either $C \prec_T D$ or $C = D$ and there exists j such that $1 \le j \le n$, $s_1 = t_1, \ldots, s_{j-1} = t_{j-1}$ and $s_j < t_j$.
2. $\alpha = \beta \to \gamma$, for some β, γ, and $trace(s) < trace(t)$, where $<$ is the induced lexicographic ordering.
3. $\alpha = \alpha_1 \times \ldots \times \alpha_n$, for some $\alpha_1, \ldots, \alpha_n$, and s is $(s_1, \ldots, s_n)$, t is $(t_1, \ldots, t_n)$ and there exists j such that $1 \le j \le n$, $s_1 = t_1, \ldots, s_{j-1} = t_{j-1}$ and $s_j < t_j$.

Proposition 9.1. *For each $\alpha \in \mathfrak{S}^c$, $<|_{\mathfrak{N}_\alpha}$ is a (strict) total order on $\mathfrak{N}_\alpha$.*

10   Basic Terms

Finally, the definition of the key concept of a basic term can be given.

Definition. The set of *basic terms*, $\mathfrak{B}$, is defined inductively as follows.

1. If C is a data constructor having signature $\sigma_1 \to \cdots \to \sigma_n \to (T \ a_1 \ldots a_k)$ and $t_1, \ldots, t_n \in \mathfrak{B}$ ($n \geq 0$) such that $C \ t_1 \ldots t_n \in \mathfrak{L}$, then $C \ t_1 \ldots t_n \in \mathfrak{B}$.

2. If $t_1, \ldots, t_n \in \mathfrak{B}$, $s_1, \ldots, s_n \in \mathfrak{B}$, $t_1 < \ldots < t_n$, $s_i \notin \mathfrak{D}$, for $1 \leq i \leq n$ ($n \geq 0$), $s_0 \in \mathfrak{D}$ and

$$\lambda x. \text{if } x = t_1 \text{ then } s_1 \text{ else } \ldots \text{ if } x = t_n \text{ then } s_n \text{ else } s_0 \in \mathfrak{L},$$

then

$$\lambda x. \text{if } x = t_1 \text{ then } s_1 \text{ else } \ldots \text{ if } x = t_n \text{ then } s_n \text{ else } s_0 \in \mathfrak{B}.$$

3. If $t_1, \ldots, t_n \in \mathfrak{B}$ ($n \geq 0$) and $(t_1, \ldots, t_n) \in \mathfrak{L}$, then $(t_1, \ldots, t_n) \in \mathfrak{B}$.

The basic terms from Part 1 of the definition are called *basic structures*, those from Part 2 are called *basic abstractions*, and those from Part 3 are called *basic tuples*.

Proposition 10.1. $\mathfrak{D} \subseteq \mathfrak{B} \subseteq \mathfrak{N}$.

As for normal terms, the basic terms of a particular type can be gathered together.

Definition. For each $\alpha \in \mathfrak{S}^c$, define $\mathfrak{B}_\alpha = \{t \in \mathfrak{B} \mid t \text{ has type more general than } \alpha\}$.

Proposition 10.2. *For each* $\alpha \in \mathfrak{S}^c$, $\mathfrak{B}_\alpha \subseteq \mathfrak{N}_\alpha$.

The next result shows that, for basic terms, the equivalence relation $\equiv$ reduces to the identity relation.

Proposition 10.3. *Let* $s, t \in \mathfrak{B}$. *Then* $s \equiv t$ *iff* $s = t$.

The next proposition justifies restricting attention to basic terms for knowledge representation purposes.

Proposition 10.4. *If* $s \in \mathfrak{N}_\alpha$, *for some* $\alpha \in \mathfrak{S}^c$, *then there is a unique* $t \in \mathfrak{B}_\alpha$ *such that* $s \equiv t$.

Definition. Let $s \in \mathfrak{N}_\alpha$, for some $\alpha \in \mathfrak{S}^c$. The unique $t \in \mathfrak{B}_\alpha$ such that $s \equiv t$ is called the *basic form* of s.

Here is an example to illustrate how the basic form can be computed.

Example. Let s be the normal term

$$\lambda x. \text{if } x = 3 \text{ then } \perp \text{ else if } x = 2 \text{ then } \top \text{ else if } x = 1 \text{ then } \top \text{ else}$$
$$\text{if } x = 3 \text{ then } \top \text{ else } \perp.$$

Assume that the total order on the integers is the usual order. In the first step, each of $1, 2, 3$, and $\top$ and $\perp$ are replaced by their basic form. Since each of these is already a basic term, this step has no effect. Second, the component of the if-then-else containing the duplicated occurrence of $x = 3$ is dropped to obtain

$$\lambda x. \text{if } x = 3 \text{ then } \perp \text{ else if } x = 2 \text{ then } \top \text{ else if } x = 1 \text{ then } \top \text{ else } \perp.$$

Third, the component containing the occurrence $x = 3$ is dropped since the corresponding value is $\perp$ to obtain

$$\lambda x. \text{if } x = 2 \text{ then } \top \text{ else if } x = 1 \text{ then } \top \text{ else } \perp.$$

Finally, the sequence 2 1 is ordered according to the total order and the components of the if-then-else are reordered accordingly to obtain

$$\lambda x. \text{if } x = 1 \text{ then } \top \text{ else if } x = 2 \text{ then } \top \text{ else } \perp,$$

which is the basic form of s.

11   A Metric on Basic Terms

For a number of reasons, it is important to have a metric defined on basic terms. For example, in instance-based learning, such a metric is needed to determine those terms that are "nearby" some given term [14, Ch.8]. Thus I give now the definition of a suitable function d from $\mathfrak{B} \times \mathfrak{B}$ into $\mathbb{R}$, where $\mathbb{R}$ denotes the set of real numbers.

The definition of this function depends upon some given functions ρ and φ. The real-valued function ρ is defined on the product of the set of data constructors with itself and is assumed to satisfy the following conditions:

1. For each type constructor $T \in \mathfrak{T}$, ρ is a metric on the set of data constructors associated with T.
2. For the set of data constructors associated with a type constructor for which there is at least one data constructor of arity > 0, ρ is the discrete metric.

For example, the type constructor *List* has two data constructors : (of arity > 0) and [], and so $\rho([], :) = 1$. In contrast, *Nat* has only nullary data constructors and hence the second condition does not apply. As will become apparent in the definition below of the function d, it is only necessary to be concerned about the value of $\rho(C, D)$ for those data constructors C and D that are associated with the *same* type constructor. The next example gives typical choices for ρ.

Example. For the types 1 and Ω, ρ could be the discrete metric. For the types *Nat*, *Int*, and *Float*, one could use $\rho(n, m) = |n - m|$. For a type constructor like *Shape* in Section 7, it is natural to employ the discrete metric on the set of data constructors $\{Circle, Rectangle\}$.

The second function φ must be a non-decreasing function from the non-negative reals into the closed interval $[0, 1]$ such that $\varphi(0) = 0$, $\varphi(x) > 0$ if $x > 0$, and $\varphi(x + y) \leq \varphi(x) + \varphi(y)$, for each x and y.

Example. Typical choices for φ could be $\varphi(x) = \frac{x}{1+x}$ or $\varphi(x) = \min\{1, x\}$.

Definition. The function $d : \mathfrak{B} \times \mathfrak{B} \to \mathbb{R}$ is defined inductively on the structure of terms in $\mathfrak{B}$ as follows. Let $s, t \in \mathfrak{B}$.

1. If $s, t \in \mathfrak{B}_\alpha$, where $\alpha = T\,\alpha_1 \ldots \alpha_k$, for some $T, \alpha_1, \ldots, \alpha_k$, then

$$d(s, t) = \begin{cases} \rho(C, D) & \text{if } C \neq D \\ (1/2) \max_{i=1,\ldots,n} \varphi(d(s_i, t_i)) & \text{otherwise} \end{cases}$$

   where s is $C\,s_1 \ldots s_n$ and t is $D\,t_1 \ldots t_m$.
2. If $s, t \in \mathfrak{B}_\alpha$, where $\alpha = \beta \to \gamma$, for some β, γ, then

$$d(s, t) = \sum_{r \in \mathfrak{B}_\beta} d(V(s\,r), V(t\,r)).$$

3. If $s, t \in \mathfrak{B}_\alpha$, where $\alpha = \alpha_1 \times \ldots \times \alpha_n$, for some $\alpha_1, \ldots, \alpha_n$, then

$$d(s, t) = \sum_{i=1}^{n} d(s_i, t_i),$$

   where s is $(s_1, \ldots, s_n)$ and t is $(t_1, \ldots, t_n)$.
4. If there does not exist $\alpha \in \mathfrak{S}^c$ such that $s, t \in \mathfrak{B}_\alpha$, then $d(s, t) = 1$.

In Part 1 of the definition, if $n = 0$, then $\max_{i=1,\ldots,n} \varphi(d(s_i, t_i)) = 0$. The purpose of the function φ is to scale the values of the $d(s_i, t_i)$ so that they lie in the interval $[0, 1]$. Thus $\max_{i=1,\ldots,n} \varphi(d(s_i, t_i)) \leq 1$. The factor of $1/2$ means that the greater the "depth" to which s and t agree, the smaller will be their distance apart. So for lists, for example, the longer the prefix on which two lists agree, the smaller will be their distance apart.

In Part 2 of the definition, the sum $\sum_{r \in \mathfrak{B}_\beta} d(V(s\,r), V(t\,r))$ is finite since s and t differ on at most finitely many r in $\mathfrak{B}_\beta$. In the case of sets, $\sum_{r \in \mathfrak{B}_\beta} d(V(s\,r), V(t\,r))$ is the cardinality of the symmetric difference of the sets s and t (assuming that ρ is the discrete metric for Ω).

It should be clear that the definition of d does not depend on the choice of α such that $s, t \in \mathfrak{B}_\alpha$. (There may be more than one such α.) What is important is only whether α has the form $T\,\alpha_1 \ldots \alpha_k$, $\beta \to \gamma$, or $\alpha_1 \times \ldots \times \alpha_n$, and this is invariant.

The definition given above for d is, of course, only one of a number of possibilities. For example, one could use instead the Euclidean form of the metric (with the square root of the sum of the squares) in Part 3 or a more specialised metric for lists in Part 1. For a particular instance-based learning application, such fine tuning would be almost certainly needed. These variant definitions for d are likely to share the following properties of d; in any case, the proofs of these properties for d show the way for proving similar properties for the variants.

Example. Suppose that ρ is the metric given by $\rho(n, m) = |n - m|$ for *Int* and *Float*. Then $d(42, 42) = 0$, $d(21, 42) = 21$ and $d(42.1, 42.2) = 0.1$.

Example. Suppose that ρ is the discrete metric for *List* and also for the set of data constructors $\{A, B, C, D\}$ (of some unnamed type) and that $\varphi(x) = \frac{x}{1+x}$. Let s be the list $[A, B, C]$ and t the list $[A, D]$. (See Figure 1.) Then

$$
\begin{aligned}
d(s, t) &= d([A, B, C], [A, D]) \\
&= \frac{1}{2} \max\{\varphi(d(A, A)), \varphi(d([B, C], [D]))\} \\
&= \frac{1}{2}\varphi(d([B, C], [D])) \\
&= \frac{1}{2}\varphi(\frac{1}{2} \max\{\varphi(d(B, D)), \varphi(d([C], []))\}) \\
&= \frac{1}{2}\varphi(\frac{1}{2} \max\{\varphi(1), \varphi(1)\}) \\
&= \frac{1}{2}\varphi(\frac{1}{2} \cdot \frac{1}{2}) \\
&= \frac{1}{2} \cdot \frac{\frac{1}{4}}{1 + \frac{1}{4}} \\
&= \frac{1}{10}.
\end{aligned}
$$

Example. Let *BTree* be a unary type constructor, and *Null* : *BTree a* and *BNode* : *BTree a* $\rightarrow$ *a* $\rightarrow$ *BTree a* $\rightarrow$ *BTree a* be data constructors. Here *BTree a* is the type of binary trees, *Null* represents the empty binary tree, and *BNode* is used to represent non-empty binary trees. Let $A, B, C, D : M$ be data constructors. Suppose that ρ is the discrete metric on M and $\varphi(x) = \frac{x}{1+x}$. Let s be

BNode (BNode Null A Null) B (BNode Null C (BNode Null D Null)),

a binary tree of type *BTree M*, and t be

BNode (BNode Null A Null) B (BNode Null D Null).

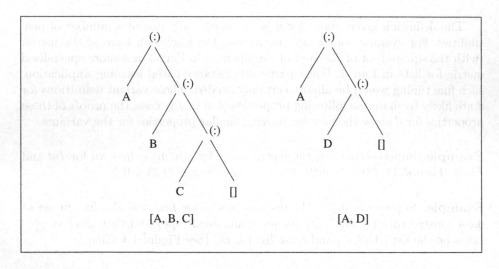

Fig. 1. Two lists

(See Figure 2.) Then

$$d(s,t) = \frac{1}{2}\max\{\varphi(d(\textit{BNode Null A Null}, \textit{BNode Null A Null})), \varphi(d(B,B)),$$
$$\varphi(d(\textit{BNode Null C (BNode Null D Null)}, \textit{BNode Null D Null}))\}$$
$$= \frac{1}{2}\varphi(d(\textit{BNode Null C (BNode Null D Null)}, \textit{BNode Null D Null}))$$
$$= \frac{1}{2}\varphi(\frac{1}{2}\max\{\varphi(d(\textit{Null}, \textit{Null})), \varphi(d(C,D)),$$
$$\varphi(d(\textit{BNode Null D Null}, \textit{Null}))\})$$
$$= \frac{1}{2}\varphi(\frac{1}{2}\max\{\varphi(1), \varphi(1)\})$$
$$= \frac{1}{2}\cdot\varphi(\frac{1}{4})$$
$$= \frac{1}{2}\cdot\frac{\frac{1}{4}}{1+\frac{1}{4}}$$
$$= \frac{1}{10}.$$

Notation. The basic abstraction $\lambda x.\textit{if } x = t_1 \textit{ then } \top \textit{ else } \ldots \textit{ if } x = t_n \textit{ then } \top$
$\textit{else } \bot \in \mathfrak{B}_{\beta\rightarrow\Omega}$ is a set whose elements have type more general than β and is
denoted by $\{t_1, \ldots, t_n\}$.

Example. Suppose that ρ is the discrete metric for Ω. If s is the set $\{A, B, C\} \in$
$\mathfrak{B}_{\beta\rightarrow\Omega}$ and t is the set $\{A, D\} \in \mathfrak{B}_{\beta\rightarrow\Omega}$, then $d(s,t) = \sum_{r\in\mathfrak{B}_\beta} d(V(s\ r), V(t\ r)) =$
$1+1+1 = 3.$

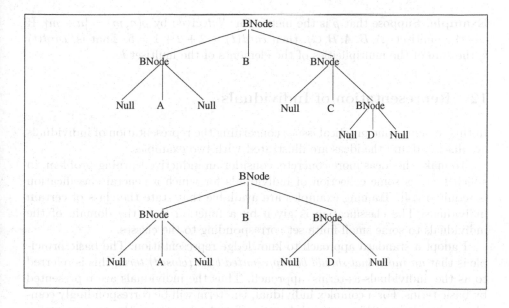

Fig. 2. Two binary trees

Notation. The basic abstraction $\lambda x.if\ x = t_1\ then\ m_1\ else\ \ldots\ if\ x = t_n\ then\ m_n\ else\ 0 \in \mathfrak{B}_{\beta \to Nat}$ is a multiset whose elements have type more general than β and is denoted by $\langle t_1, \ldots, t_1, \ldots, t_n, \ldots, t_n \rangle$, where there are m_i occurrences of t_i, for $i = 1, \ldots, n$. (That is, the number of times an element appears in the expression is its multiplicity in the multiset.) Obviously, this notation is only useful for "small" multisets.

Example. Suppose that ρ is the metric for Nat given by $\rho(n, m) = |n - m|$. If s is $\langle A, A, B, C, C, C \rangle \in \mathfrak{B}_{\beta \to Nat}$ and t is $\langle B, C, C, D \rangle \in \mathfrak{B}_{\beta \to Nat}$, then $d(s, t) = \sum_{r \in \mathfrak{B}_\beta} d(V(s\ r), V(t\ r)) = 2 + 1 + 1 = 4$.

Proposition 11.1. *For each $\alpha \in \mathfrak{S}^c$, $(\mathfrak{B}_\alpha, d)$ is a metric space.*

I now give a generalised definition of cardinality for basic abstractions.

Definition. Let t be $\lambda x.if\ x = t_1\ then\ s_1\ else\ \ldots\ if\ x = t_n\ then\ s_n\ else\ s_0 \in \mathfrak{B}_{\beta \to \gamma}$. Then the (generalised) cardinality of t is defined as follows:

$$card(t) = \sum_{r \in \mathfrak{B}_\beta} d(V(t\ r),\ s_0).$$

The function *card* measures how much a basic abstraction deviates from being constant.

Example. Suppose that ρ is the discrete metric for Ω. If t is the set $\{A, B, C\}$, then $card(t) = 3$. That is, $card(t)$ is the cardinality of the set t.

Example. Suppose that ρ is the metric for Nat given by $\rho(n, m) = |n - m|$. If t is the multiset $\langle A, B, A, B, C\rangle$, then $card(t) = 2 + 2 + 1 = 5$. That is, $card(t)$ is the sum of the multiplicities of the elements of the multiset t.

12   Representation of Individuals

In this section, some practical issues concerning the representation of individuals are discussed and the ideas are illustrated with two examples.

To make the ideas more concrete, consider an inductive learning problem, in which there is some collection of individuals for which a general classification is required [14]. Training examples are available that state the class of certain individuals. The classification is given by a function from the domain of the individuals to some small finite set corresponding to the classes.

I adopt a standard approach to knowledge representation. The basic principle is that *an individual should be represented by a (closed) term*; this is referred to as the 'individuals-as-terms' approach. Thus the individuals are represented by basic terms. For a complex individual, the term will be correspondingly complex. Nevertheless, this approach has significant advantages: the representation is compact, all information about an individual is contained in one place, and the structure of the term provides strong guidance on the search for a suitable induced definition.

What types are needed to represent individuals? Typically, one needs the following: integers, floats, characters, strings, and booleans; data constructors; tuples; sets; multisets; lists; trees; and graphs. The first group are the basic types, such as *Int*, *Float*, and Ω. Also needed are data constructors for user-defined types. For example, see the data constructors *Abloy* and *Chubb* for the nullary type constructor *Make* below. Tuples are essentially the basis of the attribute-value representation of individuals, so their utility is clear. Less commonly used elsewhere for representing individuals are sets and multisets. However, sets, especially, and multisets are basic and extremely useful data types. Other constructs needed for representing individuals include the standard data types, lists, trees, and graphs. This catalogue of data types is a rich one, and intentionally so. I advocate making a careful selection of the type which best models the application being studied.

Consider now the problem of determining whether a key in a bunch of keys can open a door. More precisely, suppose there are some bunches of keys and a particular door which can be opened by a key. For each bunch of keys either no key opens the door or there is at least one key which opens the door. For each bunch of keys it is known whether there is some key which opens the door, but it is not known precisely which key does the job, or it is known that no key opens the door. The problem is to find a classification function for the bunches of keys, where the classification is into those which contain a key that opens the door and those that do not. This problem is prototypical of a number of important practical problems such as drug activity prediction [5], as a bunch corresponds to a molecule and a key corresponds to a conformation of a molecule, and a molecule has a certain behaviour if some conformation of it does. I make the following declarations.

> $Abloy, Chubb, Rubo, Yale : Make$
>
> $Short, Medium, Long : Length$
>
> $Narrow, Normal, Broad : Width.$

I also make the following type synonyms.

> $NumProngs = Nat$
>
> $Key = Make \times NumProngs \times Length \times Width$
>
> $Bunch = \{Key\}.$

Thus the individuals in this case are sets whose elements are 4-tuples. The function to be learned is

> $opens : Bunch \to \Omega.$

Here is a typical example.

> $opens \; \{(Abloy, 4, Medium, Broad),$
>
> $\qquad (Chubb, 3, Long, Narrow),$
>
> $\qquad (Abloy, 3, Short, Normal)\} = \top.$

For further details on this example, see [2] or [3].

As another example of knowledge representation, consider the problem of modelling a chemical molecule. The first issue is to choose a suitable type to represent a molecule. I use an undirected graph to model a molecule – an atom is a vertex in the graph and a bond is an edge. Having made this choice, suitable types are then set up for the atoms and bonds. For this, the nullary type constructor $Element$, which is the type of the (relevant) chemical elements, is first introduced. Here are the constants of type $Element$.

> $Br, C, Cl, F, H, I, N, O, S : Element.$

I also make the following type synonyms.

> $AtomType = Nat$
>
> $Charge = Float$
>
> $Atom = Element \times AtomType \times Charge$
>
> $Bond = Nat.$

For (undirected) graphs, there is a "type constructor" $Graph$ such that the type of a graph is $Graph \; v \; e$, where v is the type of information in the vertices and e is the type of information in the edges. $Graph$ is defined as follows.

> $Label = Nat$
>
> $Graph \; v \; e = \{Label \times v\} \times \{(Label \to Nat) \times e\}.$

Here the multisets of type *Label* → *Nat* are intended to all have cardinality 2, that is, they are intended to be regarded as *unordered* pairs. Note that this definition corresponds closely to the mathematical definition of a graph: each vertex is labelled by a unique integer and each edge is uniquely labelled by the unordered pair of labels of the vertices it connects. Also it should be clear by now that *Graph* is not actually a type constructor at all; instead *Graph v e* is simply notational sugar for the expression on the right hand side of its definition.

The type of a molecule is now obtained as an (undirected) graph whose vertices have type *Atom* and whose edges have type *Bond*. This leads to the following definition.

Molecule = *Graph Atom Bond*.

Here is an example molecule, called d1, from the mutagenesis dataset available at [17]. The notation $\langle s, t \rangle$ is used as a shorthand for the multiset that takes the value 1 on each of s and t, and is 0 elsewhere. Thus $\langle s, t \rangle$ is essentially an unordered pair.

$$(\{(1, (C, 22, -0.117)), (2, (C, 22, -0.117)), (3, (C, 22, -0.117)),$$
$$(4, (C, 195, -0.087)), (5, (C, 195, 0.013)), (6, (C, 22, -0.117)),$$
$$(7, (H, 3, 0.142)), (8, (H, 3, 0.143)), (9, (H, 3, 0.142)),$$
$$(10, (H, 3, 0.142)), (11, (C, 27, -0.087)), (12, (C, 27, 0.013)),$$
$$(13, (C, 22, -0.117)), (14, (C, 22, -0.117)), (15, (H, 3, 0.143)),$$
$$(16, (H, 3, 0.143)), (17, (C, 22, -0.117)), (18, (C, 22, -0.117)),$$
$$(19, (C, 22, -0.117)), (20, (C, 22, -0.117)), (21, (H, 3, 0.142)),$$
$$(22, (H, 3, 0.143)), (23, (H, 3, 0.142)), (24, (N, 38, 0.812)),$$
$$(25, (O, 40, -0.388)), (26, (O, 40, -0.388))\},$$
$$\{(\langle 1, 2 \rangle, 7), (\langle 1, 6 \rangle, 7), (\langle 1, 7 \rangle, 1), (\langle 2, 3 \rangle, 7), (\langle 2, 8 \rangle, 1),$$
$$(\langle 3, 4 \rangle, 7), (\langle 3, 9 \rangle, 1), (\langle 4, 5 \rangle, 7), (\langle 4, 11 \rangle, 7), (\langle 5, 6 \rangle, 7),$$
$$(\langle 5, 14 \rangle, 7), (\langle 6, 10 \rangle, 1), (\langle 11, 12 \rangle, 7), (\langle 11, 17 \rangle, 7),$$
$$(\langle 12, 13 \rangle, 7), (\langle 12, 20 \rangle, 7), (\langle 13, 14 \rangle, 7), (\langle 13, 15 \rangle, 1),$$
$$(\langle 14, 16 \rangle, 1), (\langle 17, 18 \rangle, 7), (\langle 17, 21 \rangle, 1), (\langle 18, 19 \rangle, 7),$$
$$(\langle 18, 22 \rangle, 1), (\langle 19, 20 \rangle, 7), (\langle 19, 24 \rangle, 1), (\langle 20, 23 \rangle, 1),$$
$$(\langle 24, 25 \rangle, 2), (\langle 24, 26 \rangle, 2)\}).$$

Having represented the molecules, the next task is to learn a function that provides a classification of the carcinogenicity of the molecules. One way of doing this is to build, using a set of training examples, a decision tree from which the definition of the classification function can be extracted. The most important aspect of building this tree is to find suitable predicates to split the training examples. The search space of predicates is determined by the type of the individuals and the constants that appear in the corresponding alphabet. The higher-order facilities of the logic are used to structure this search space. More details can be found in [2] and [3].

13   Programming with Abstractions

In this section, the paradigm of programming with abstractions, introduced in [12], is illustrated with some examples.

But first some motivation. One approach to the problem of designing and implementing a declarative programming language that integrates the functional programming and logic programming styles is based on the observation that the functional programming language Haskell [9] is a highly successful, modern declarative programming language that can serve as the basis for such an integration. Haskell provides types, modules, higher-order programming and declarative input/output, amongst other features. With Haskell as a basis, the problem then reduces to identifying the extensions that are needed to provide the usual logic programming idioms. In this section, I illustrate how the paradigm of programming with abstractions can provide these extensions.

Consider the definitions of the functions *append*, *permute*, *delete*, and *sorted* given in Figure 3, which have been written in the relational style of logic programming. The intended meaning of *append* is that it is true iff its third argument is the concatenation of its first two arguments. The intended meaning of *permute* is that it is true iff its second argument is a permutation of its first argument. The intended meaning of *delete* is that it is true iff its third argument is the result of deleting its first argument from its second argument. The intended meaning of *sorted* is that it is true iff its argument is an increasingly ordered list of integers. As can be seen, the definition of each function has a declarative reading that respects the intended meaning.

What extra machinery needs to added to Haskell to enable it to run the definitions in Figure 3? First, the constructor-based assumption of Haskell has to be relaxed to allow λ-abstractions and functions to appear in arguments in the heads of statements. Also, (free and bound) variables have to be allowed to appear in redexes. The most crucial idea behind these extensions is the introduction of λ-abstractions in arguments in heads and so this programming style is termed 'programming with abstractions'.

The notable feature of the definitions in Figure 3 is the presence of existential quantifiers in the bodies of the statements, so not surprisingly the key statement that makes all this work is concerned with the existential quantifier. To motivate this, consider the computation that results from the goal *append* $([1], [2], x)$. At one point in the computation, the following term is reached:

$$\exists r'.\exists x'.\exists y'.(r' = 1 \,\wedge\, x' = [] \,\wedge\, x = r' : y' \,\wedge\, append\ (x', [2], y')).$$

An obviously desirable simplification that can be made to this term is to eliminate the local variable r' since we have a "value" (that is, 1) for it. This leads to the term

$$\exists x'.\exists y'.(x' = [] \,\wedge\, x = 1 : y' \,\wedge\, append\ (x', [2], y')).$$

Similarly, one can eliminate x' to obtain

$$\exists y'.(x = 1 : y' \,\wedge\, append\ ([], [2], y')).$$

$$append \ : \ List \ a \times List \ a \times List \ a \to \Omega$$

$$append \ (u, v, w) \ = \ (u = [] \ \land \ v = w) \ \lor$$
$$\exists r.\exists x.\exists y.(u = r : x \ \land \ w = r : y \ \land \ append \ (x, v, y))$$

$$permute \ : \ List \ a \times List \ a \to \Omega$$

$$permute \ ([], x) \ = \ x = []$$

$$permute \ (x : y, w) \ = \exists u.\exists v.\exists z.(w = u : v \ \land \ delete \ (u, x : y, z) \land permute \ (z, v))$$

$$delete \ : \ a \times List \ a \times List \ a \to \Omega$$

$$delete \ (x, [], y) \ = \ \bot$$

$$delete \ (x, y : z, w) \ = \ (x = y \land w = z) \ \lor \ \exists v.(w = y : v \ \land \ delete \ (x, z, v))$$

$$sorted \ : \ List \ Int \to \Omega$$

$$sorted \ [] \ = \ \top$$

$$sorted \ x : y \ = \ if \ y = [] \ then \ \top \ else \ \exists u.\exists v.(y = u : v \ \land \ x \leq u \ \land \ sorted \ y)$$

Fig. 3. List-processing functions

After some more computation, the answer $x = [1, 2]$ results. Now the statement that makes all this possible is

$$\exists x_1. \cdots \exists x_n.(\boldsymbol{x} \land (x_1 = u) \land \boldsymbol{y}) = \exists x_2. \cdots \exists x_n.(\boldsymbol{x}\{x_1/u\} \land \boldsymbol{y}\{x_1/u\}),$$

which comes from the definition of $\Sigma : (a \to \Omega) \to \Omega$ and has λ-abstractions in its head.

The above ideas, plus some carefully chosen definitions, are all that are needed to allow Haskell thus extended to encompass the relational style of logic programming. The definitions of predicates look a little different to the way one would write them in, for example, Prolog. A mechanical translation of a Prolog definition into one that runs in this extended version of Haskell simply involves using the completion [11] of the Prolog definition. The definition here of *append* is essentially the completion of the Prolog version of *append*. Alternatively, one can specialise the completion to the [] and (:) cases, as has been done here for the definitions of *permute*, *delete*, and *sorted*. One procedural difference of note is that Prolog's method of returning answers one at a time via backtracking is replaced here by returning all answers together as a disjunction (or a set). Thus the goal

$$append \ (x, y, [1])$$

reduces to the answer

$$(x = [] \land y = [1]) \lor (x = [1] \land y = []).$$

However, the idea of programming with abstractions can be pushed much further to enable direct programming with sets, multisets and other abstractions, a facility not provided by either Haskell or Prolog. First, I deal with sets. Consider the definition of the function *likes* in Figure 4. This definition is essentially a database of facts about certain people and the sports they like.

$Mary, Bill, Joe, Fred : Person$

$Cricket, Football, Tennis : Sport$

$likes \ : \ Person \times Sport \to \Omega$

$likes \ = \ \{(Mary, Cricket), (Mary, Tennis), (Bill, Cricket), (Bill, Tennis),$
$$(Joe, Tennis), (Joe, Football)\}$$

Fig. 4. A database to illustrate set processing

Here are some examples of set processing. Consider first the goal

$$\{Mary, Bill\} \cap \{Joe, Bill\}.$$

Using the statement

$$s \cap t \ = \ \{x \mid (x \in s) \wedge (x \in t)\}$$

in the definition of $\cap \ : \ (a \to \Omega) \to (a \to \Omega) \to (a \to \Omega)$, one obtains

$$\{x \mid (x \in \{Mary, Bill\}) \wedge (x \in \{Joe, Bill\})\},$$

and then

$$\{x \mid (if \ x = Mary \ then \ \top \ else \ if \ x = Bill \ then \ \top \ else \ \bot) \ \wedge$$
$$(if \ x = Joe \ then \ \top \ else \ if \ x = Bill \ then \ \top \ else \ \bot)\},$$

by β-reduction. After several uses of the statements

$$(if \ u \ then \ v \ else \ w) \wedge t \ = \ if \ u \wedge t \ then \ v \ else \ w \wedge t$$
$$t \wedge (if \ u \ then \ v \ else \ w) \ = \ if \ t \wedge u \ then \ v \ else \ t \wedge w$$
$$v \wedge (x = u) \wedge w \ = \ v\{x/u\} \wedge (x = u) \wedge w\{x/u\}$$

from the definition of $\wedge$, the answer $\{Bill\}$ is obtained. In this example, the main novel aspect compared to Haskell is the simplification that has taken place *inside* the body of a λ-abstraction.

For a second example, consider the goal

$$\{x \mid \forall y.(y \in \{Cricket, Tennis\} \longrightarrow likes \ (x, y))\},$$

which reduces via the steps

$$\{x \mid \forall y.((\text{if } y = \textit{Cricket then } \top \textit{ else if } y = \textit{Tennis then } \top \textit{ else } \bot) \longrightarrow \textit{likes } (x, y))\}$$

$$\{x \mid \forall y.(((y = \textit{Cricket}) \vee (\text{if } y = \textit{Tennis then } \top \textit{ else } \bot)) \longrightarrow \textit{likes } (x, y))\}$$

$$\{x \mid \forall y.((y = \textit{Cricket}) \longrightarrow \textit{likes } (x, y)) \wedge$$
$$\forall y.((\text{if } y = \textit{Tennis then } \top \textit{ else } \bot) \longrightarrow \textit{likes } (x, y))\}$$

$$\{x \mid \textit{likes } (x, \textit{Cricket}) \wedge \forall y.((\text{if } y = \textit{Tennis then } \top \textit{ else } \bot) \longrightarrow \textit{likes } (x, y))\},$$

and so on, to the answer

$$\{\textit{Mary}, \textit{Bill}\}.$$

During this computation, use is made of the statements

$$\forall x_1. \cdots \forall x_n.(\boldsymbol{x} \wedge (x_1 = u) \wedge \boldsymbol{y} \longrightarrow \boldsymbol{v}) =$$
$$\forall x_2. \cdots \forall x_n.(\boldsymbol{x}\{x_1/u\} \wedge \boldsymbol{y}\{x_1/u\} \longrightarrow \boldsymbol{v}\{x_1/u\})$$

$$\forall x_1. \cdots \forall x_n.(\boldsymbol{u} \vee \boldsymbol{v} \longrightarrow \boldsymbol{t}) =$$
$$(\forall x_1. \cdots \forall x_n.(\boldsymbol{u} \longrightarrow \boldsymbol{t})) \wedge (\forall x_1. \cdots \forall x_n.(\boldsymbol{v} \longrightarrow \boldsymbol{t}))$$

$$\forall x_1. \cdots \forall x_n.((\text{if } \boldsymbol{u} \text{ then } v \text{ else } \boldsymbol{w}) \longrightarrow \boldsymbol{t}) =$$
$$\text{if } v \text{ then } \forall x_1. \cdots \forall x_n.(\boldsymbol{u} \vee \boldsymbol{w} \longrightarrow \boldsymbol{t}) \text{ else } \forall x_1. \cdots \forall x_n.(\neg \boldsymbol{u} \wedge \boldsymbol{w} \longrightarrow \boldsymbol{t})$$

from the definition of $\Pi : (a \to \Omega) \to \Omega$.

The example in the previous paragraph is reminiscent of list comprehension in Haskell. In fact, one could set the database up as a list of facts and then give Haskell a goal which would be a list comprehension analogous to the set goal above and obtain a list, say $[\textit{Mary}, \textit{Bill}]$, as the answer. Substituting lists for sets in knowledge representation is a standard device to get around the fact that few programming languages support set processing in a sophisticated way. However, sets and lists are actually significantly different types and this shows up, for example, in the different sets of transformations that each type naturally supports ([2], [3]). Consequently, I advocate a careful analysis for any particular knowledge representation task to see what types are most appropriate and also that programming languages support a full range of types, including sets and multisets.

Another point to make about the previous example is that it is an illustration of *intensional* set processing. Extensional set processing in which the descriptions of the sets manipulated are explicit representations of the collection of elements in the sets is commonly provided in programming languages. For example, it is straightforward in Haskell to set up an abstract data type for (extensional) sets using lists as the underlying representation. A language such as Java also provides various ways of implementing extensional sets. But the example above is different in that the goal is an intensional representation of a set (in fact, the set $\{\textit{Mary}, \textit{Bill}\}$) and the computation is able to reveal this. The ability to process intensional sets and the smooth transition between intensional and extensional set processing are major advantages of the approach to sets advocated here. Similar comments apply to programming with other kinds of abstractions such as multisets.

Consider next the problem of giving a definition for the powerset function that computes the set of all subsets of a given set. Here is the definition.

$$powerset \; : \; (a \rightarrow \Omega) \rightarrow (a \rightarrow \Omega) \rightarrow \Omega$$
$$powerset \; \{\} \; = \; \{\{\}\}$$

$$powerset \; \{x \mid if \; \boldsymbol{u} \; then \; v \; else \; \boldsymbol{w}\} \; =$$
$$\qquad\qquad if \; v \; then \; powerset \; \{x \mid \boldsymbol{u} \vee \boldsymbol{w}\} \; else \; powerset \; \{x \mid \neg \, \boldsymbol{u} \wedge \boldsymbol{w}\}$$
$$powerset \; \{x \mid x = t\} \; = \; \{\{\}, \{t\}\}$$
$$powerset \; \{x \mid \boldsymbol{u} \vee \boldsymbol{v}\} \; = \; \{s \mid \exists l. \exists r. (l \in (powerset \; \{x \mid \boldsymbol{u}\})) \wedge$$
$$\qquad\qquad\qquad\qquad (r \in (powerset \; \{x \mid \boldsymbol{v}\}) \wedge (s = l \cup r))\}.$$

The first and second statements cover the cases of an empty set and a 'non-empty' one, where the set is represented by a basic term. (Non-empty is quoted since $\{x \mid if \; \boldsymbol{u} \; then \; v \; else \; \boldsymbol{w}\}$ can represent an empty set if both v and $\boldsymbol{w}$ are $\perp$, for example.) The third and fourth statements are needed to handle calls which arise in the second statement. They could also be used if the representation of the set is not a basic term, but has an equality or disjunction at the top level in the body. Of course, if the representation of the set does not match any of the statements, then it will have to be reduced (by using the definitions of other functions) until it does. One can see immediately that each statement in the definition is declaratively correct.

Note the analogy between set processing as illustrated by *powerset* and list processing in which the definition of a list-processing function is broken up into two statements – one for the empty list and one for a non-empty list. In the case of sets, it is convenient to have four cases corresponding to where the body of the set abstraction has the form $\perp$, *if* $\boldsymbol{u}$ *then* v *else* $\boldsymbol{w}$, $x = t$, or $\boldsymbol{u} \vee \boldsymbol{v}$. The third and fourth cases arise because of the richness of the set of functions on the booleans. For other kinds of abstractions typically only the first two cases arise, as is illustrated below for multisets.

As an illustration of the use of *powerset*, the goal

$$powerset \; \{Mary, Bill\}$$

reduces to the answer

$$\{\{\}, \{Mary\}, \{Bill\}, \{Mary, Bill\}\}.$$

This section concludes with an illustration of multiset processing. Suppose one wants to compute the pairwise minimum $s \sqcap t$ of two multisets s and t, where

$(s \sqcap t) \ x = min \ (s \ x) \ (t \ x)$. Now recall that a multiset is represented by a basic term, that is, an abstraction of the form

$$\lambda x.if \ x = t_1 \ then \ s_1 \ else \ \ldots \ if \ x = t_n \ then \ s_n \ else \ s_0,$$

where the type of each s_i is Nat. In particular, the empty multiset is represented by the abstraction $\lambda x.0$.

How can one compute the function $\sqcap$? The idea is to consider two cases: one in which the first argument to $\sqcap$ is the empty multiset and one in which it is not. This leads to the following definition.

$$\sqcap : (a \rightarrow Nat) \rightarrow (a \rightarrow Nat) \rightarrow (a \rightarrow Nat)$$

$$\lambda x.0 \ \sqcap \ m \ = \ \lambda x.0$$

$$(\lambda x.if \ x = t \ then \ v \ else \ \boldsymbol{w}) \ \sqcap \ m \ =$$
$$\lambda x.if \ x = t \ then \ min \ v \ (m \ t) \ else \ (\lambda x.\boldsymbol{w} \ \sqcap \ m) \ x.$$

The first statement just states that the pairwise minimum of the empty multiset and any multiset is the empty multiset. The second statement is the recursive case in which the minimum of the multiplicity of the first item in the first argument and its multiplicity in the second argument is computed and then the rest of the items in the first argument are considered. Note once again the similarity with the definitions of many list-processing functions that consist of a statement for the empty list and one for a non-empty list.

As an illustration of the use of $\sqcap$, the goal

$$(\lambda x.if \ x = A \ then \ 42 \ else \ if \ x = B \ then \ 21 \ else \ 0) \ \sqcap$$
$$(\lambda x.if \ x = A \ then \ 16 \ else \ if \ x = C \ then \ 4 \ else \ 0)$$

reduces to the answer

$$\lambda x.if \ x = A \ then \ 16 \ else \ 0.$$

14   Discussion

At this point, I summarise what has been achieved and put the developments into a wider context.

I started from the position that higher-order logic provides a suitable foundation for computational logic. A particular higher-order logic, based on the simple theory of types, was then presented. This logic is suitable for use as a basis for declarative programming languages. Next the issue of knowledge representation was discussed and a suitable class of terms, the basic terms, was identified as appropriate for representing individuals. The set of basic terms is a metric space in a natural way and hence provides a context in which metric-based machine learning can take place. The approach to representation was then illustrated with a couple of applications that arise in machine learning. Finally, the technique of programming with abstractions was illustrated with some examples. In this development, the higher-order nature of the logic was essential: as a foundation for the functional component of declarative programming languages, since functions can take other functions as arguments; in the use of the logic for knowledge representation, since sets and similar abstractions are needed; and for programming with abstractions, since abstractions can appear as arguments in function definitions.

However, the advantages of using higher-order logic for computational logic have been advocated by others for at least the last 30 years. Here I remark on some of this work that is most relevant to the present paper.

First, the functional programming community has used higher-order functions from the very beginning. The latest versions of functional languages, such as Haskell98 [9], show the power and elegance of higher-order functions, as well as related features such as strong type systems. Of course, the traditional foundation for functional programming languages has been the λ-calculus, rather than a higher-order *logic*. However, it is possible to regard functional programs as equational theories in a logic such as the one I have introduced here and this also provides a satisfactory semantics.

In the 1980's, higher-order programming in the logic programming community was introduced through the language λProlog [15]. The logical foundations of λProlog are provided by almost exactly the logic introduced earlier in this paper. However, a different sublogic is used for λProlog programs than the equational theories proposed here. In λProlog, program statements are higher-order hereditary Harrop formulas, a generalisation of the definite clauses used by Prolog. The language provides an elegant use of λ-terms as data structures, meta-programming facilities, universal quantification and implications in goals, amongst other features.

A long-term interest amongst researchers in declarative programming has been the goal of building integrated functional logic programming languages. A survey of progress on this problem up to 1994 can be found in [7]. Probably the best developed of these functional logic languages is the Curry language [8], which is the result of an international collaboration over the last 5 or so years. To quote from [8]: "Curry is a universal programming language aiming to amalgamate the most important declarative programming paradigms, namely functional programming and logic programming. Moreover, it also covers the most important operational principles developed in the area of integrated functional logic languages: 'residuation' and 'narrowing'. Curry combines in a seamless way features from functional programming (nested expressions, higher-order functions, lazy evaluation), logic programming (logical variables, partial data structures, built-in search), and concurrent programming (concurrent evaluation of expressions with synchronisation on logical variables). Moreover, Curry provides additional features in comparison to the pure languages (compared to functional programming: search, computing with partial information; compared to logic programming: more efficient evaluation due to the deterministic and demand-driven evaluation of functions)."

There are many other outstanding examples of systems that exploit the power of higher-order logic. For example, the HOL system [6] is an environment for interactive theorem proving in higher-order logic. Its most outstanding feature is its high degree of programmability through the meta-language ML. The system has a wide variety of uses from formalising pure mathematics to verification of industrial hardware. In addition, there are at least a dozen other systems related to HOL. On the theoretical side, much of the research in theoretical Computer Science, especially semantics, is based on the λ-calculus and hence is intrinsically higher-order in nature.

I finish with some remarks about open research issues. I believe the most important open research problem, and one that would have a major practical impact, is that of producing a widely-used functional logic programming language. Unfortunately, there is a gulf between the functional programming and logic programming communities that is holding up progress. A common programming language would do a great deal to bridge that gulf. More specifically, the logic programming community needs to make much greater use of the power of higher-order features and the related type systems. Furthermore, higher-order logic has generally been under-exploited as a knowledge representation language, with sets and related data types rarely being used simply because they are not so easily provided by first-order logic. Having sets directly available (as predicates) in higher-order logic is a big advantage.

Just over 25 years ago, Robert Kowalski started a major stream of research in Computer Science with the Horn clause subset of first-order logic. The natural and ultimate setting for that research stream is clearly higher-order logic – every contribution towards that goal would be valuable.

References

[1] P.B. Andrews. *An Introduction to Mathematical Logic and Type Theory: To Truth Through Proof.* Academic Press, 1986.

[2] A.F. Bowers, C. Giraud-Carrier, and J.W. Lloyd. Classification of individuals with complex structure. In P. Langley, editor, *Machine Learning: Proceedings of the Seventeenth International Conference (ICML2000)*, pages 81–88. Morgan Kaufmann, 2000.

[3] A.F. Bowers, C. Giraud-Carrier, and J.W. Lloyd. A knowledge representation framework for inductive learning. Available at http://csl.anu.edu.au/~jwl, 2001.

[4] A. Church. A formulation of the simple theory of types. *Journal of Symbolic Logic*, 5:56–68, 1940.

[5] T.G. Dietterich, R.H. Lathrop, and T. Lozano-Pérez. Solving the multiple instance problem with axis-parallel rectangles. *Artificial Intelligence*, 89:31–71, 1997.

[6] M.J.C. Gordon and T.F. Melham. *Introduction to HOL: A Theorem Proving Environment for Higher Order Logic.* Cambridge University Press, 1993.

[7] M. Hanus. The integration of functions into logic programming: From theory to practice. *Journal of Logic Programming*, 19&20:583–628, 1994.

[8] M. Hanus (ed.). Curry: An integrated functional logic language. Available at http://www.informatik.uni-kiel.de/~curry.

[9] S. Peyton Jones and J. Hughes (editors). Haskell98: A non-strict purely functional language. Available at http://haskell.org/.

[10] R. A. Kowalski. Predicate logic as a programming language. In *Information Processing 74*, pages 569–574, Stockholm, 1974. North Holland.

[11] J.W. Lloyd. *Foundations of Logic Programming*. Springer-Verlag, second edition, 1987.

[12] J.W. Lloyd. Programming in an integrated functional and logic language. *Journal of Functional and Logic Programming*, 1999(3), March 1999.

[13] J.W. Lloyd. Knowledge representation, computation, and learning in higher-order logic. Available at http://csl.anu.edu.au/~jwl, 2001.

[14] T.M. Mitchell. *Machine Learning*. McGraw-Hill, 1997.

[15] G. Nadathur and D.A. Miller. Higher-order logic programming. In D.M. Gabbay, C.J. Hogger, and J.A. Robinson, editors, *The Handbook of Logic in Artificial Intelligence and Logic Programming*, volume 5, pages 499–590. Oxford University Press, 1998.

[16] D.A. Wolfram. *The Clausal Theory of Types*. Cambridge University Press, 1993.

[17] Home page of Machine Learning Group, The University of York. http://www.cs.york.ac.uk/mlg/.

A Pure Meta-interpreter for Flat GHC, a Concurrent Constraint Language

Kazunori Ueda

Dept. of Information and Computer Science, Waseda University
3-4-1, Okubo, Shinjuku-ku, Tokyo 169-8555, Japan
ueda@ueda.info.waseda.ac.jp

Abstract. This paper discusses the construction of a meta-interpreter of Flat GHC, one of the simplest and earliest concurrent constraint languages.

Meta-interpretation has a long history in logic programming, and has been applied extensively to building programming systems, adding functionalities, modifying operational semantics and evaluation strategies, and so on. Our objective, in contrast, is to design the pair of (i) a representation of programs suitable for code mobility and (ii) a pure interpreter (or virtual machine) of the represented code, bearing networked applications of concurrent constraint programming in mind. This is more challenging than it might seem; indeed, meta-interpreters of many programming languages achieved their objectives by adding small primitives into the languages and exploiting their functionalities. A meta-interpreter in a pure, simple concurrent language is useful because *it is fully amenable to theoretical support including partial evaluation*.

After a number of trials and errors, we have arrived at *treecode*, a ground-term representation of Flat GHC programs that can be easily interpreted, transmitted over the network, and converted back to the original syntax. The paper describes how the interpreter works, where the subtleties lie, and what its design implies. It also describes how the interpreter, given the treecode of a program, is partially evaluated to the original program by the unfold/fold transformation system for Flat GHC.

1 Introduction

1.1 Meta-interpreter Technology

Meta-interpreter technology has enjoyed excellent affinity to logic programming since the seminal work by Bowen and Kowalski [5]. It provides us with a concise way of building programming systems on top of another. This is particularly useful for AI applications in which flexibility in designing and modifying inference mechanisms is of crucial importance. Interactive programming environments such as debuggers or visualizers are another example in which interpreters can play important rôles. Extensive survey of meta-interpretation in logic programming can be found in [11], Chapter 8.

A.C. Kakas, F. Sadri (Eds.): Computat. Logic (Kowalski Festschrift), LNAI 2407, pp. 138–161, 2002.

Critics complain of performance degradation incurred by the interpreter technology, but the speed of system prototyping with interpreters and symbolic languages cannot be matched by any other methodologies. Hardwiring all design choices into a lower-level language such as C may be done, but at the latest possible stage and to the least extent. Indeed, due to Java and scripting languages, interpreter technologies – including bytecode interpreters and its optimization techniques such as just-in-time compilers – are now quite ubiquitous outside the world of symbolic languages. Java demonstrated that poor initial performance of non-optimized interpreters was acceptable once people believed that the language and the system design as a whole were the right way to go.

1.2   Concurrency and Logic Programming

The *raison d'être* and the challenge of symbolic languages are to construct highly sophisticated software which would be too complicated or unmanageable if written in other languages. Logic programming has found and addressed a number of such fields [4]. While many of those fields such as databases, constraints, machine learning, natural languages, etc., are more or less related to Artificial Intelligence, concurrency seems special in the sense that, although somewhat related to AI through agent technologies, its principal connection is to distributed and parallel computing.

Distributed and parallel computing is becoming extremely important because virtually all computers in the world are going to be interconnected. However, we have not yet agreed upon a standard formalism or a standard language to deal with concurrency. Due to the lack of appropriate tools with which to develop networked applications, computers communicate and cooperate much more poorly than they possibly can.

Concurrent logic programming was born in early 1980's from the process interpretation of logic programs [34]. Relational Language [7], the first concrete proposal of a concurrent logic language, was followed by a succession of proposals, namely Concurrent Prolog [20], PARLOG [8] and Guarded Horn Clauses (GHC) [27]. KL1 [29], the Kernel Language of the Fifth Generation Computer Systems (FGCS) project [22], was designed based on GHC by featuring (among others) *mapping* constructs for concurrent processes. To be precise, KL1 is based on Flat GHC [28], a subset of GHC that restricts guard goals to calls to test predicates.

The mathematical theory of these languages came later in the generalized setting of concurrent constraint programming (CCP) [18] based on Maher's logical interpretation of synchronization [12]. Grand challenges of concurrent logic/constraint programming are proposed in [32].

Although not as widely recognized as it used to be, Concurrent Prolog was the first simple high-level language that featured channel mobility exactly in the sense of π-calculus [15]. When the author proposed GHC as an alternative to Concurrent Prolog and PARLOG, the principal design guideline was to retain channel mobility and evolving process structures [22], because GHC was supposed to be the basis of KL1, a language in which to describe operating systems of Parallel Inference Machines as well as various knowledge-based systems. The readers are referred to [22] for various researchers' personal perspectives of the FGCS project.

1.3 Meta-interpretation and Concurrency

Another guideline of the design of GHC was the ability to describe its own meta-interpreter. Use of simple meta-interpreters as a core technology of system development was inspired by [5], and early work on Concurrent Prolog pursued this idea in building logic-based operating systems [21].

A key technology accompanying meta-interpretation turned out to be partial evaluation. Partial evaluation of a meta-interpreter with an additional "flavor" with respect to a user program will result in a user program with the additional "flavor" that runs almost as efficiently as the original user program [24].

This idea, though very elegant, has not become as popular as we had expected.

One reason is that before the booming of the Internet, a program ran either on a single processor or on parallel processors with a more or less uniform structure, where a hardwired approach was manageable and worked. However, software for distributed computing environments is much harder to build, configure and reconfigure, and run persistently. Such software would not be manageable without a coherent solution to the difficulties incurred by heterogeneous architectures, process and code mobility, and persistence.

Another reason is that the languages and the underlying theories were not mature enough to allow full development of the idea. Meta-interpreters of many programming languages achieved their objectives by adding small primitives into the language and exploiting their functionalities. Those primitives were often beyond the basic computational models of the languages. We believe that *pure* symbolic languages are the right way to go in the long run, because only with theoretical support we can expect a real breakthrough.

1.4 Goal of This Paper

In this paper, we discuss how we can construct a meta-interpreter of Flat GHC, one of the simplest and earliest concurrent constraint languages. Our objective is to design the pair of

1. a representation of programs suitable for code mobility and interpretation, and
2. a pure, simple interpreter of the represented code.

One of the motivations of the work is to use concurrent logic/constraint programming as a concise tool for networked applications. There are strong reasons to choose concurrent logic/constraint programming as a framework of distributed computing.

First, it features channel mobility, evolving process structures, and incomplete messages (messages with reply boxes), all essential for object-based concurrent programming.

Second, it is unlike most other concurrency frameworks in that data structures (lists, trees, arrays, etc.) come from the very beginning. This means that there is little gap between a theoretical model and a practical language. Actually, a lot of applications have been written in concurrent logic/constraint languages, notably in KL1 and Oz [23].

Third, it has been extremely stable for more than 15 years. After GHC was proposed, the main variation was whether to feature *atomic tell* (publication of bindings upon commitment) or *eventual tell* (publication after commitment). However, by now both concurrent logic programming and concurrent constraint programming seem to converge on *eventual tell*, the simpler alternative [22][26]. Indeed, concurrent constraint programming with *ask* and *eventual tell* can be thought of as an abstract model of Flat GHC.

Last, as opposed to other parallel programming languages, it achieves clear separation of concurrency (concerned with logical aspects of programs) and parallelism (concerned with physical mapping of processes). We regard this separation of concerns as the most important achievement of KL1 and its parallel implementation [29]. In other words, by using logical variables as communication channels we had achieved 100% network transparency within system-area networks (SAN). The fact that programs developed and tested on sequential machines ran at least correctly on parallel machines has benefited us enormously in the development of parallel software. We believe that this feature should be explored in distributed software as well.

Addressing networked applications using interpreters as a core technology is promising because flexibility to cope with heterogeneity is more important than performance. However, it is not obvious whether we can write a reasonably simple interpreter in a pure concurrent logic/constraint language such as Flat GHC. A meta-interpreter in a pure, simple concurrent language is fully amenable to theoretical support including partial evaluation and verification. Also, it can help *analytic approach* to language design [32], because meta-interpretation is considered an acid test of the expressive power of the language. The rôle of an interpreter technology in networked applications should be clear since an interpreter is just another name of a virtual machine.

2 Previous Work

Meta-interpreters of symbolic languages date back to a Lisp interpreter in Lisp around 1960 [13]. Prolog interpreters in Prolog were available and widely used in 1970's; an example is the interpreter of the *de facto* standard DEC-10 Prolog.

Meta-interpreters of Concurrent Prolog can be found in various papers. Figure 1 shows two versions, the first one in [20] and the second in [17].

Program (a) is very similar to a Prolog interpreter in Prolog, but it relies on the "large" built-in primitive, clause/2 (clause with two arguments), that performs synchronization, evaluation of clause guards, and committed choice. The only thing reified by the interpreter is parallel conjunction. Program (b) takes both a program and a goal as arguments, and reifies the unification of the

```
reduce(true).
reduce((A,B)) :- reduce(A?), reduce(B?).
reduce(A) :- A\=true, A\=(_,_) | clause(A?,B), reduce(B?).
```

(a) Without a program argument

```
reduce(Program,true).
reduce(Program,(A,B)) :-
    reduce(Program?, A?), reduce(Program?, B?).
reduce(Program,Goal) :-
    Goal\=true, Goal\=(A,B),
    clause(Goal?,Program?,Body) |
    reduce(Program?,Body?).
clause(Goal,[C|Cs],B) :-
    new_copy(C?,(H,G,B)), Goal=H, G | true.
clause(Goal,[C|Cs],B) :-
    clause(Goal,Cs?,B) | true.
```

(b) With an explicit program argument

Fig. 1. Meta-Interpreters of Concurrent Prolog

goal with clause heads and the evaluation of guards. Note, however, that most of the important operations are called from and performed in clause guards. In particular, clause/3 calls itself recursively from within a clause guard, forming a *nested (or deep) guard*.

While Concurrent Prolog employed read-only annotations as a synchronization primitive, GHC replaced it with the rule that no bindings (constraints) can be published from the guard (including the head) of a clause to the caller of the clause.

Figure 2 shows a GHC interpreter in GHC in [27]. Here it is assumed that a built-in predicate clauses/2 returns in a *frozen* form [16] a list of all clauses whose heads are potentially unifiable with the given goal. Each frozen clause is a ground term in which original variables are indicated by special constant symbols, and it is *melted* in the guard of the first clause of resolve/3 by melt_new/2. The goal melt_new(C, (A :- G|B2)) creates a new term (say T) from a frozen term C by giving a new variable for each frozen variable in C, and tries to unify T with (A :- G|B2). However, this unification cannot instantiate A because it occurs in the head of resolve/3.

The predicate resolve/3 tests the candidate clauses and returns the body of arbitrary one of the clauses whose guards have been successfully solved. This many-to-one arbitration is realized by the multi-level binary clause selection using the nested guard of the predicate resolve/3. It is essential that each candidate clause is melted after it has been brought into the guard of the first clause of resolve/3. If it were melted before passed into the guard, all variables

```
call(true  ) :- true | true.
call((A, B)) :- true | call(A), call(B).
call(A      ) :- clauses(A, Clauses) |
    resolve(A, Clauses, Body), call(Body).

resolve(A, [C|Cs], B) :- melt_new(C, (A :- G|B2)), call(G) | B=B2.
resolve(A, [C|Cs], B) :- resolve(A, Cs, B2) | B=B2.
```

Fig. 2. Meta-Interpreter of GHC

in it would be protected against instantiation from the guard. We must protect variables accessible from outside but allow local variables to be instantiated.

Again, this GHC meta-interpreter calls `resolve/3` from within a guard recursively. However, our lesson is that, except for meta-interpreters, we can dispense with general nested guards. To put it more precisely, we can dispense with guard goals that may instantiate local variables; restricting guard goals to calls to *test* predicates is a more realistic choice. Test predicates are predicates defined in terms of clauses with no body goals. A nice property of test predicates is that they deterministically succeed or fail depending on their arguments. They are regarded as specifying conditions, as opposed to predicates for specifying concurrent processes. Test predicates defined using guarded clauses may call themselves recursively from guards, but unlike general nested guards, there is no need to maintain multiple layers of variable protection to implement synchronization. In this sense, languages with restriction to test predicates have been called *flat* languages. In most implementations of flat languages, test predicates are further restricted to predefined ones.

Later development of concurrent logic languages can be phrased as *devolution as evolution* [26][32] in the sense that it focused on high-performance, compiler-based implementation of flat languages. Strand [9], KL1 and Janus [19] all belong to this category. Accordingly, there was less work on meta-interpreters for the last 10 years. Huntbach [11] shows a meta-interpreter that implements *ask* using `match/2`, a special primitive discussed in detail in Sect. 3.3. Although using `match/2` to implement *ask* is a natural idea, `match/2` turns out to have properties not enjoyed by other goals definable in concurrent logic languages. This motivated us to design a meta-interpreter that does not use `match/2`.

Distributed computing based on concurrent constraint programming is not a new idea. The Oz group has done a lot of work in this direction [10]. However, code mobility in Oz is based on bytecode technology, and Oz has added to CCP a number of new constructs including ports (for many-to-one communication), cells (value containers that allow destructive update), computation space (encapsulated store, somewhat affected by nested guards of full GHC and KL1's *shoen*), and higher-order. This is in sharp contrast with the minimalist approach taken in this paper.

3   The Problem Statement

Now let us state the goal and the constraints of our problem precisely. Our goal is to design a binary Flat GHC predicate, say `exec`, that

- takes
    1. a multiset G of goals (represented as a list) to be executed and
    2. a ground representation of the program P to execute G, and
- behaves exactly like G running under the ordinary compiled code for P.

The predicate `exec/2` is sometimes called a *universal* predicate because it can be tailored, at run time, to whatever predicate you like.

The only built-in primitives the `exec/2` program is allowed to use are those definable using (a possible infinite number of) guarded clauses. Other primitives are considered extralogical and are ruled out. Observing this constraint will enable the resulting interpreter to run on KLIC [6], which is in our context considered as a (Flat) GHC-to-C compiler and its runtime system. Flat GHC and KLIC carefully rule out extralogical built-in primitives because they can potentially hamper efficient implementation and theoretical support.

A solution to the problem is not obvious because Flat GHC and KLIC do not have general nested guards, on which the interpreter of full GHC in Sect. 2 depends in a fundamental way.

Some remarks and discussions on our requirements are in order, which are (1) representation of code, (2) representation of runtime configuration, and (3) primitives for *ask* (matching) and *tell* (unification).

3.1   Representation of Code

Meta-interpreters vary in the representation of programs. Some retrieve programs from the internal database using primitives like `clause/2`. This is not suited to our goal of code mobility and persistence. Some use a list of clauses in which variables are represented using variables at the level of the interpreters. This is considered misuse of variables, as criticized by later work on meta-programming, because those variables are improperly scoped and awkward to handle. One solution is to use a higher-order construct as in Lambda Prolog [14], and another solution is to come up with a ground representation of variables. Although the higher-order approach gives us the most natural solution, the difference between the two solutions is not large when the programs to be represented have no nested scope, which is the case with Prolog and Flat GHC.

As we will see later, we have chosen to represent a variable in terms of a reserved unary constructor with an integer argument. This could be viewed as a de Bruijn notation as well.

3.2   Representation of Runtime Configuration

In a rule-based language where programs (rewrite rules) are given separately from expressions (goals), how to represent runtime configurations and how to represent the programs are independent issues. The two alternatives for the representation of runtime configurations are

1. to reify logical variables and substitutions and handle them explicitly, and
2. not to reify them but use those at the interpreter level.

We adopt the latter, because

- an interpreted process must be *open-ended*, that is, it must be able to communicate with other native processes running in parallel with the interpreter,
- the reification approach would therefore require 'up' and 'down' predicates to move between the two levels of representation and (accordingly) a full-fledged meta-programming framework in the language, and
- explicit representation can cause performance degradation unless elaborate optimization is made.

3.3 Primitives for Matching/Ask and Unification/Tell

In the CCP terminology, Prolog and constraint logic languages in their basic forms are *tell*-only languages because unification or constraint solving is the attempt to publish bindings (constraints) to the binding environment (constraint store). In contrast, concurrent logic/constraint languages are *ask+tell* languages which additionally feature matching (in algebraic terms) or the asking of whether a given constraint is entailed (in logical terms) by the current store. So how to implement *ask* and *tell* in an interpreter is a key design issue.

The Prolog and GHC versions of *tell* are unification over finite trees and can be written as $\mathrm{unify}(G, H)$ or $G = H$. This has the following properties:

1. *Immediate* — It either succeeds or fails and does not suspend.
2. *Monotonic* — Its success/failure can depend on the current store; that is, $\mathrm{unify}(G, H)$ that succeeds under some store can fail under a store augmented with additional constraints. However, if we consider failure as a over-constrained store, $\mathrm{unify}(G, H)$ can be thought of as an operator that monotonically augments the current store.
3. *Deterministic* — The conjunction of all *tell*s generated in the course of program execution deterministically defines the current store.

Now we consider the properties of *ask*, which appears in concurrent logic languages as matching between a goal and a clause head. Let σ be the current store under which the *ask* is performed. We suppose $\mathrm{match}(G, H)$

- *succeeds* when there exists a substitution θ such that $G\sigma = H\sigma\theta$,
- *suspends* when there is no such θ but $G\sigma$ and $H\sigma$ are unifiable, and
- *fails* when $G\sigma$ and $H\sigma$ are non-unifiable.

Clearly, $\mathrm{match}(G, H)$ is not immediate. Furthermore, it is neither monotonic nor deterministic with respect to suspension behavior:

- match(X, Y) will succeed when Y is uninstantiated but may suspend when Y is instantiated. This behavior is opposite to that of ordinary CCP processes which can never be suspended by providing more constraints.
- match(X, Y) ∧ match(3, Y) under the empty store succeeds if executed from left to right but suspends if executed from right to left.

When simulating matching between a goal G and a clause head H using match/2, H must have been renamed using fresh variables, and H is therefore immune to σ. If this convention is enforced, match/2 enjoys monotonicity, that is, if match/2 succeeds under σ, it succeeds under $\sigma\sigma'$ for any σ'. The convention guarantees determinism as well.

The lesson here is that the scope of the variables in H, the second argument of match/2, should be handled properly for match/2 to enjoy reasonable properties. As suggested by [12], the proper semantics of match(G, H) would be whether σ interpreted as an equality theory *implies* $G = \exists H$. Thus the second argument should specify an existential closure $\exists H$ rather than H. However, then, the second argument would lose the capability to *receive* matching terms from G. For instance, the recursive clause of append/3 in GHC is

```
append([A|X],Y,Z0) :- true | Z0=[A|Z], append(X,Y,Z).
```

while the CCP version of the above clause would be less structured:

```
append(X0,Y,Z0) :- ask(∃A,X(X0=[A|X])) |
    tell(X0=[A|X]), tell(Z0=[A|Z]), append(X,Y,Z).
```

To summarize, while implementing *tell* in an interpreter is straightforward, implementing *ask* without introducing new primitives is a major design issue.

4   A Treecode Representation

In this section, we discuss the design of our treecode representation of Flat GHC programs, which is interpreted by the treecode interpreter described in the Sect. 5.

4.1   Treecode

Treecode is intermediate code in the form of a first-order ground term which is quite close to the original source code. It is more abstract and "structured" than ordinary bytecode sequences that use forward branching to represent if...then ...else. Trees are much more versatile than sequences and are much easier to represent and handle than directed graphs. Indeed, the booming of XML tells us that standard representation of tagged trees has been long-awaited by a great number of applications, and XML trees are little more than first-order ground terms.

Of course, the control flow of a program forms a directed graph in general and we must represent it somehow. Directed graphs could be created rather easily by unification over rational terms, but we chose to dispense with circular structures by representing recursive calls (that form circularity) using explicit predicate names. When the interpreter encounters a predicate call, it obtains the code for the predicate using an appropriate lookup method. An optimizing interpreter may create a directed graph by "instantiating" each predicate call to its code before starting interpretation.

An alternative representation closer to source code is a set of rewrite rules. However, it turns out that a set (represented as a list) of rewrite rules is less suitable for interpretation. This is because GHC "bundles" predicate calls, synchronization and choice in a single construct, namely guarded clauses. While this bundling simplifies the syntax and the semantics of Flat GHC and captures the essence of concurrent logic programming, guards – even flat guards – can specify arbitrary complex conditions that may involve both conjunctive and disjunctive sets of multiple synchronization points. Programmers also find it sometimes cumbersome to describe everything using guarded clauses exactly for the reason why Prolog programmers find that the (P -> Q ; R) construct sometimes shortens their programs considerably.

As we will see soon, treecode still looks like a set of clauses, but the major difference from a set of clauses is that the former breaks a set of guards down to a tree of one-at-a-time conditional branching. In this sense, treecode can be regarded as *structured intermediate code*.

4.2   Treecode by Example

Now we are in a position to explain how treecode looks like. Throughout this section we use append/3 as an example. The treecode for append/3 is:

```
treecode(6,
  [c(1=[], b([<(2)= <(3)],[])),
   c(1=[>(4)|>(5)],
           b([<(3)=[<(4)|>(6)]],[append(5,2,6)]))])
```

The first argument, 6, stands for the number of variables used in the treecode, and the second argument is the main part of the treecode.

The readers may be able to guess what it does basically, since it is quite similar to the original source code:

```
append(X, Y,Z ) :- X=[] | Y=Z.
append(X0,Y,Z0) :- X0=[A|X] | Z0=[A|Z], append(X,Y,Z).
```

In this simple example, the treecode still looks like a list of clauses, with heads (with mutually disjoint variables) omitted and variables represented by positive integers. The constructor c/2 forms a case branch by taking an *ask* and another treecode as arguments. The list of case branches forms a *casecode*.

The constructor b/2 forms a *bodycode* by taking a list of *tells* and a list of calls to user-defined predicates. The former is understood by the interpreter, while the latter involves code lookup.

A *treecode* is either a casecode or a bodycode. Figure 3 shows the syntax of treecode.

$$\begin{aligned}
\langle treecode \rangle &::= \langle casecode \rangle \mid \langle bodycode \rangle \\
\langle casecode \rangle &::= \text{list of } \langle choice \rangle\text{'s} \\
\langle choice \rangle &::= \text{c}(\langle ask \rangle, \langle treecode \rangle) \\
\langle ask \rangle &::= \langle reg \rangle = \langle term \rangle \mid \langle reg \rangle \langle relop \rangle \langle term \rangle \\
\langle bodycode \rangle &::= \text{b}(\langle tells \rangle, \langle goals \rangle) \\
\langle tells \rangle &::= \text{list of } \langle tell \rangle\text{'s} \\
\langle tell \rangle &::= \langle annotatedreg \rangle = \langle term \rangle \mid \langle annotatedreg \rangle := \langle term \rangle \\
\langle goals \rangle &::= \text{list of } \langle goal \rangle\text{'s} \\
\langle goal \rangle &::= \langle pred \rangle(\langle reg \rangle, \ldots) \\
\langle annotatedreg \rangle &::= [\langle annotation \rangle]\langle reg \rangle \\
\langle annotation \rangle &::= \text{<} \mid \text{<<} \mid \text{>} \\
\langle reg \rangle &::= 1 \mid 2 \mid 3 \mid \ldots \\
\langle term \rangle &::= \langle functor \rangle(\langle annotatedreg \rangle, \ldots) \\
\langle relop \rangle &::= \text{>} \mid \text{<} \mid \text{>=} \mid \text{=<} \mid \text{=:=} \mid \text{=\textbackslash=}
\end{aligned}$$

Fig. 3. Syntax of Treecode

4.3 Representing and Managing Logical Variables

The unary constructors '<' and '>' have two purposes. First, they distinguish integer representation of variables from integer constants in the program to be interpreted. Second, they tell whether a variable has occurred before and whether it will occur later. *Initial mode*, denoted, '>', means the creation of a new variable, while *final mode*, denoted '<', means the final access to an already created variable. In append/3, each variable occurs exactly twice, which means that all accesses are either initial or final accesses. For variables that are read more than once, we use another reserved unary constructor, '<<', to indicate that they are accessed in *intermediate mode*, that is, they are neither the first nor the last occurrences.

The first occurrence of a variable in each case branch (1 in the case of append/3) and the arguments of user-defined predicates are supposed to be final-mode. These are the only places where mode annotations are omitted for ease of interpretation.

Representing variables by positive integers suggests the use of arrays to represent them. We use a constructor g/n to represent goal records, where n is the number of variables in the treecode that works on the goal. The structure g/n can be regarded as a *register vector* as well.

Let a be the arity of the predicate represented by the treecode. The first ath arguments of g/n are the arguments of the original goal, while the remaining arguments are local variables of the original goal. Thus this structure can be regarded both (i) as a concretization of goals that makes housekeeping explicit and (ii) as an abstraction of implementation-level goal records. When the structure is created, the first ath arguments are initialized to the arguments of the original goal, while the remaining arguments are initialized to the constant 0. The value of a is not recorded in the treecode itself. It is the responsibility of the predicate try/3 to "apply" treecode to a goal record, as will be described in Sect. 5.

The distinction between initial, intermediate and final modes not only makes interpretation easier but also allows the reuse of the same register for different variables. For example, the code for append/3 could be written alternatively as:

```
[c(1=[], b([<(2)= <(3)],[])),
 c(1=[>(4)|>(1)],
         b([<(3)=[<(4)|>(3)]],[append(1,2,3)]))]
```

because

- Variable 1 in the second branch, holding the first argument of the caller, will not be accessed after its principal constructor has been known, and
- Variable 3 in the second branch, holding the third argument of the caller, will not be accessed after it has been instantiated to an non-empty list.

This is register allocation optimization which is optional in our treecode. Without it, different numbers represent different single-assignment variables and the code is more declarative. With it, the size of goal records can be reduced.

5   Structure of the Treecode Interpreter

This section describes, step by step, how our treecode interpreter works on a goal record. We focus on basic *ask* and *tell* operations. The actual interpreter handles arithmetic built-in predicates for comparison (guard) and assignment (body), but it is straightforward to include them.

The two main predicates of the interpreter are exec/2 and try/3. The predicate exec/2 takes a multiset G of goals and a program $\mathcal{E}$ for executing them. We call the program an *environment* because it associates each predicate name with its treecode. The goal exec$(G, \mathcal{E})$ resolves predicate names in G into their corresponding treecode, and invokes try/3 for each goal in G after preparing a goal record for the goal. The predicate try/3 takes a goal record, a treecode and an environment, and applies the treecode to the goal record. The more interesting aspects of the interpreter lie in try/3.

5.1   Deterministic and Nondeterministic Choice

When the treecode given to try/3 is *casecode*, it deterministically chooses one branch as follows: It picks up the first case branch of the form c(*Ask, Treecode*), where *Ask* is of the form $n = T$. This causes the interpreter to wait for the principal constructor of the nth argument, and when it is available, it is matched against the constructor of T. The n's in each case branch must be identical; thus casecode has exactly one synchronization point for all its top-level *ask*s and is therefore deterministic.

When some guard involves the asking of more than one symbol, it is compiled into nested casecode. For instance, the program

```
part(_,[],      S, L ) :- true | S=[], L=[].
part(A,[X|Xs],S0,L ) :- A>=X | S0=[X|S], part(A,Xs,S,L).
part(A,[X|Xs],S, L0) :- A< X | L0=[X|L], part(A,Xs,S,L).
```

can be compiled into:

```
[c(2=[], b([[<(3)=[],<(4)=[]],[])),
 c(2=[>(5)|>(2)],
   [c(1>= <<(5), b([[<(3)=[<(5)|>(3)]],[part(1,2,3,4)]])),
    c(1< <<(5), b([[<(4)=[<(5)|>(4)]],[part(1,2,3,4)]]))])]]
```

Note that the matching of the second argument with [X|Xs] has been factored, as would be done by an optimizing compiler.

Nested casecode is still deterministic because it has at most one synchronization point (i.e., the variable on whose value the interpreter suspends) at any time. Our experience with Flat GHC/KL1 programming has shown that the majority of predicates are deterministic.

Nondeterministic predicates are those which contain *disjunctive* wait, namely wait for the instantiation of one of several variables. Some of the predicates people write are nondeterministic, but most of them involve binary choice only. For instance, the following stream merging program

```
merge([],Ys,Zs) :- true | Zs=Ys.
merge(Xs,[],Zs) :- true | Zs=Xs.
merge([X|Xs],Ys,Zs0) :- true | Zs0=[X|Zs], merge(Xs,Ys,Zs).
merge(Xs,[Y|Ys],Zs0) :- true | Zs0=[Y|Zs], merge(Xs,Ys,Zs).
```

has two disjunctive synchronization points, namely the principal constructor of the first argument and the principal constructor of the second argument.

In this paper we focus on binary nondeterministic choice, which is simpler to implement than general multiway choice. It can be expressed in terms of two nondeterministic branches in the interpreter. By extending our treecode in Fig. 3, the treecode for merge/3 can be written as follows:

```
treecode(4,
   (1->[c(1=[], b([[<(2)= <(3)],[])),
        c(1=[>(4)|>(1)], b([[<(3)=[<(4)|>(3)]],[merge(1,2,3)]]))])
 + (2->[c(2=[], b([[<(1)= <(3)],[])),
        c(2=[>(4)|>(2)], b([[<(3)=[<(4)|>(3)]],[merge(1,2,3)]]))])])
```

The extended syntax of treecode is:

$$\langle treecode\rangle ::= \langle casecode\rangle \mid \langle bodycode\rangle \mid \langle nondeterministiccode\rangle$$
$$\langle nondeterministiccode\rangle ::= (\langle reg\rangle \rightarrow \langle treecode\rangle) + (\langle reg\rangle \rightarrow \langle treecode\rangle)$$

where the form $(n_1 \rightarrow treecode_1) + (n_2 \rightarrow treecode_2)$ causes the goal to wait disjunctively upon variables n_1 and n_2.

5.2   Interpreting Casecode

The *ask* part of a casecode of the form $n = T$, where T is a non-variable term whose arguments are all *annotatedregs*, is interpreted by the following piece of code:

```
try_one(A0,Rn=T,B,Cs,Env) :- true |
    setarg(Rn,A0,AORn,ARn,A), functor(AORn,AORnF,AORnN),
    functor(T,TF,TN), test_pf(AORnF,AORnN,TF,TN,Res),
    try_match(Res,T,AORn,ARn,A,B,Cs,Env).

test_pf(F1,A1,F2,A2,Res) :- F1=F2, A1=:=A2 | Res=yes(A1).
otherwise.
test_pf(F1,A1,F2,A2,Res) :- true | Res=no.

try_match(yes(N),T,AORn,ARn,A0,B,Cs,Env) :- true |
    ARn=0, getargs(1,N,T,AORn,A0,A), try(A,B,Env).
try_match(no,      T,AORn,ARn,A, B,Cs,Env) :- true |
    ARn=AORn, try(A,Cs,Env).

getargs(K,N,T,AORn,A0,A) :- K> N | A0=A.
getargs(K,N,T,AORn,A0,A) :- K=<N |
    arg(K,T,Tk), setarg(K,AORn,AORnk,0,AORn1),
    getputreg(Tk,A0,AORnk,A1),
    K1:=K+1, getargs(K1,N,T,AORn1,A1,A).

getputreg(<(Rk), A0,ARk,A) :- true | setarg(Rk,A0,ARk,0,A).
getputreg(<<(Rk),A0,ARk,A) :- true | setarg(Rk,A0,ARk,ARk,A).
getputreg(>(Rk), A0,ARk,A) :- true | setarg(Rk,A0,_,ARk,A).
```

This is almost a Prolog program with a cut in every clause. KL1's built-in predicate, $\mathrm{setarg}(I,T,X,X',T')$, is like Prolog's $\mathrm{arg}(I,T,X)$ except that T' is bound to T with its Ith element replaced by X'. This is a declarative array update primitive and used extensively in the interpreter to read data from, and write data to, goal records.

The try_one/5 program first retrieves the Rnth variable in the goal record A0, binding it to AORn. Then it checks if AORn is instantiated and its principal constructor matches that of T, using functor/3 and test_pf/5. If the matching succeeds, the first clause of try_match/8 stores (by using getargs/6) the top-level arguments of AORn to the goal record A0 according to the prescription template T. Then it executes the bodycode B under the updated goal record A and the environment Env. The first goal AR0=0 binds the Rnth element in A to 0; this is to explicitly discharge a pointer from the goal record to the top-level structure that has just been *ask*ed. The interpreter uses the constant 0 as a filler when some element of a goal record does not contain a meaningful value, that is, before a meaningful value is loaded or after a meaningful value is taken away.

5.3 Interpreting Bodycode

Bodycode performs *tell*s and the spawning of user-defined body goals:

```
try(A0,b(BU,BN),Env) :- true | tell(A0,BU,A), spawn(A,BN,Env).
```

The *tell*s are not only to instantiate variables passed from the caller; it is also used to prepare non-variable terms to be passed to user-defined body goals, and to unify two variables to create a shared variable between two body goals. How `tell/3` manipulates data is quite similar to how `getargs/6` gets data from a non-variable goal argument. A *tell* of the form $n = T$ manipulates the nth element of the goal record according to the template T:

```
tell(A0,[(Rn=T)|BU], A) :- true |
    getputreg(Rn,A0,A0Rn,A1), tell_one(T,A0Rn,A1,BU,A).
tell(A0,[],            A) :- true | A=A0.

tell_one(<(Rk),  A0Rn,A1,BU,A) :- true |
    getputreg(<(Rk),A1,A0Rn,A2), tell(A2,BU,A). /* load Rk */
tell_one(>(Rk),  A0Rn,A1,BU,A) :- true |
    getputreg(>(Rk),A1,A0Rn,A2), tell(A2,BU,A). /* store Rk */
tell_one(T,      A0Rn,A1,BU,A) :- integer(T) |
    A0Rn=T,  tell(A1,BU,A).
otherwise.
tell_one(T,      A0Rn,A1,BU,A) :- true |
    functor(T,F,N), new_functor(A0Rn0,F,N),
    putargs(1,N,T,A0Rn0,A0Rn,A1,A2), tell(A2,BU,A).

putargs(K,N,T,A0Rn0,A0Rn,A0,A) :- K> N | A0Rn0=A0Rn, A0=A.
putargs(K,N,T,A0Rn0,A0Rn,A0,A) :- K=<N |
    arg(K,T,Tk), setarg(K,A0Rn0,_,A0Rnk,A0Rn1),
    getputreg(Tk,A0,A0Rnk,A1),
    K1:=K+1, putargs(K1,N,T,A0Rn1,A0Rn,A1,A).
```

Note that the two functionalities of Prolog's `functor/3` are provided by different KL1 built-ins, `functor/3` and `new_functor/3`. While `functor/3` suspends on the first argument and examines its principal constructor, `new_functor/3` creates a new structure with a constructor specified by the second and the third arguments. The major difference between `new_functor/3` and its Prolog counterpart is that the arguments of the structure are initialized to 0 rather than fresh, distinct variables. This is because we have found that initializing its elements to a filler constant and replacing them using `setarg/5` shows much better affinity with a static mode system that plays various important rôles [30] in concurrent logic programming. As discussed in [31], strong moding is deeply concerned with the number of access paths (or references) to each variable (or its value). It prefers variables with exactly two occurrences to those with three or more occurrences by giving the former more generic, less-constrained modes. Our `setarg/5` does not copy or discard the (direct or indirect) access paths to the elements of an array, including the element to be removed and the element with which to fill in the blank.

Linearity analysis [33] for Mode Flat GHC is more directly concerned with the number of access paths. Under reasonable conditions, it enables us to implement setarg/5 as destructive update as long as the original structure is not shared.

Both mode and linearity systems encourage *resource-conscious programming*. Resource-conscious programming means to pay attention to the number of occurrences of each variable and to prefer variables with exactly two occurrences. This is not so restrictive as it might seem, and our static analyzer *klint* [33] and an automated debugger *kima* [2][3] support it by detecting – and even correcting – inadvertently too many or too few occurrences of the variables. Resource-conscious programs are easier to execute on a distributed platform because they can benefit more from compile-time garbage collection.

Finally, we show the definition of spawn/3 for spawning body goals according to the bodycode and the current goal record:

```
spawn(A, []      ,Env) :- true | true.
spawn(A0,[B0|BN],Env) :- true |
    functor(B0,F,N), setargs(1,N,B0,A0,B,A),
    exec_one(B,Env), spawn(A,BN,Env).

/* registers once read are cleared */
setargs(K,N,B0,A0,B,A) :- K> N | B=B0, A=A0.
setargs(K,N,B0,A0,B,A) :- K=<N |
    setarg(K,B0,Bk,ABk,B1), setarg(Bk,A0,ABk,0,A1),
    K1 := K+1, setargs(K1,N,B1,A1,B,A).
```

Note that concurrent execution of body goals is realized by the concurrent execution of exec_one's.

5.4 Summary

Now we have almost finished the description of our interpreter. To be self-contained, here we show all the remaining predicates.

```
/* The interpreter's top-level */
exec([],Env)        :- true | true.
exec([G|Gs],Env) :- true | exec_one(G,Env), exec(Gs,Env).

exec_one(G,Env) :- true |
    retrieve(G,Env,TC), prepare_goalrec_body(G,TC,A,B),
    try(A,B,Env).

retrieve(G,Env,TC) :- true |
    functor(G,P,N), retrieve(P,N,Env,TC).
retrieve(P,N,[P/N-TC0|_],TC) :- true | TC=TC0.
otherwise.
```

```
retrieve(P,N,[_|Env],TC) :- true | retrieve(P,N,Env,TC).

prepare_goalrec_body(G0,treecode(N,B0),A,B) :- true |
    B=B0,
    functor(G0,_,Ng), new_functor(A0,g,N),
    transfer_args(1,Ng,G0,A0,_,A).

transfer_args(I,N,G0,A0,G,A) :- I> N | G=G0, A=A0.
transfer_args(I,N,G0,A0,G,A) :- I=<N |
    setarg(I,G0,Gi,0,G1), setarg(I,A0,_,Gi,A1),
    I1 := I+1, transfer_args(I1,N,G1,A1,G,A).

/* Simply a case branch based on the syntax of treecode */
try(A,[c(G,B)|Cs],Env)                 :- true |
    try_one(A,G,B,Cs,Env).
try(A,(Rn1->Cs1)+(Rn2->Cs2),Env) :- true |
    try_two(A,Rn1,Cs1,Rn2,Cs2,Env).
try(A0,b(BU,BN),Env)                   :- true |
    tell(A0,BU,A), spawn(A,BN,Env).

/* Binary disjunctive wait */
try_two(A0,Rn1,Cs1,Rn2,Cs2,Env) :- true |
    setarg(Rn1,A0,A0Rn1,ARn1,A1), setarg(Rn2,A1,A0Rn2,ARn2,A),
    try_two(A,A0Rn1,ARn1,A0Rn2,ARn2,Cs1,Cs2,Env).

try_two(A,A0Rn1,ARn1,A0Rn2,ARn2,Cs1,Cs2,Env) :- wait(A0Rn1) |
    ARn1=A0Rn1, ARn2=A0Rn2, append(Cs1,Cs2,Cs), try(A,Cs,Env).
try_two(A,A0Rn1,ARn1,A0Rn2,ARn2,Cs1,Cs2,Env) :- wait(A0Rn2) |
    ARn1=A0Rn1, ARn2=A0Rn2, append(Cs2,Cs1,Cs), try(A,Cs,Env).

append([],   Y,Z ) :- true | Y=Z.
append([A|X],Y,Z0) :- true | Z0=[A|Z], append(X,Y,Z).
```

The restrictions of the above interpreter and possible solutions to them are
as follows:

1. Three unary constructors, '<', '>' and '<<', are reserved. This can be easily
   circumvented by wrapping non-variable as well as variable symbols by some
   constructors, but we did not do so for the readability of treecode.
2. Currently, the only built-in predicates provided (but not shown above) are
   those for arithmetics. However, other built-ins such as those used in the
   interpreter itself can be easily provided.
3. A nonlinear clause head, namely a head with repeated occurrences of a variable, cannot be compiled into treecode. Extending the interpreter to deal
   with nonlinear heads is straightforward and left as an exercise. However, the
   use of a nonlinear clause head to check the equality of arguments is discour-
   aged, because it is the only construct that may take unbounded execution

time by comparing two terms of arbitrarily large sizes. For distributed and real-time applications, it is desirable that the execution time of every primitive language construct is bounded.

4. The only construct whose support requires non-straightforward hacking on the interpreter is non-binary disjunctive wait. Since n-ary disjunctive wait is essentially n-ary arbitration, this could be supported by implementing an n-ary arbiter which observes variables $x_1, \ldots, x_n$ and returns an arbitrary k such that x_k has been instantiated.

The interpreter is not self-applicable in its present form, but the discussions above indicate that we are quite close to a self-applicable meta-interpreter. Note that the `otherwise` construct to specify default cases can be expressed implicitly using casecode because the *ask* parts of its branches are tested both deterministically and sequentially.

6   Partial Evaluation

How can one be assured that interpreted treecode behaves exactly the same as its original code?

Instead of showing a translator from Flat GHC to treecode and its correctness, here we illustrate how the treecode for `append/3` applied to our interpreter can be partially evaluated to its original Flat GHC code.

The rôle of partial evaluation in our framework is twofold. First, the receiver of treecode can figure out what Flat GHC code it represents. Second, although the interpreter itself is not directly amenable to static analysis because its behavior depends on the treecode given, the original code restored by partial evaluation is amenable to static analysis. In this way we can attach various kinds of type information (including mode and linearity) to the arguments of a goal whose behavior is determined by treecode.

For partial evaluation, we use unfold/fold transformation rules described in [28]. The rules consist of the following:

1. *Normalization* — executes unification goals in a guard and a body so that each clause reaches its unique normal form. A normal form should have no unification goals in guards, and all residual unification body goals should be to instantiate head variables of the clause.
2. *Immediate Execution* — deals with the unfolding of a non-unification body goal which does not involve synchronization. That is, the rule is applicable only when, for each clause C in the program and each goal g to be unfolded, either g is reducible using C or, for all σ, $g\sigma$ is irreducible using C.
3. *Case Splitting* — deals with the unfolding of non-unification body goals of a clause C which may promote *ask*s from the guards of clauses used for the unfolding to the guard of C. The clause C must not have unification body goals.

   To see how the Case Splitting of C works, consider a goal g that is about to be reduced using C. For g to generate some output, at least one more reduction (of one of the body goals of C) is necessary because C has no unification body goals. Case splitting enumerates all the possibilities of the first such reduction.

4. *Folding* — which is essentially the same as the Tamaki-Sato folding rule [25].

The major difference from the Tamaki-Sato rule set is that unfolding is split into two incomparable rules, *Immediate Execution* and *Case Splitting*, to deal with synchronization.

Let $\mathcal{E}$ be the treecode for `append/3`:

```
[append/3-treecode(6,
   [c(1=[], b([<(2)= <(3)],[])),
    c(1=[>(4)|>(1)], b([<(3)=[<(4)|>(3)]],[append(1,2,3)]))])]
```

To show that `exec_one(append(X,Y,Z),`$\mathcal{E}$`)` behaves the same as `append(X,Y,Z)` under its standard definition, let us start with a clause

```
append(X,Y,Z) :- true | exec_one(append(X,Y,Z),E).
```

and start applying Immediate Execution to its body goal. Using `exec_one/2` shown in Sect. 5.4, we obtain

```
append(X,Y,Z) :- true |
   retrieve(append(X,Y,Z),E,TC),
   prepare_goalrec_body(append(X,Y,Z),TC,A,B), try(A,B,E).
```

With two more applications of *Immediate Execution*, first to the goal `retrieve/3` and the second to the primitive `functor/3`, we obtain

```
append(X,Y,Z) :- true |
   P=append, N=3, retrieve(P,N,E,TC),
   prepare_goalrec_body(append(X,Y,Z),TC,A,B), try(A,B,E).
```

which can be normalized to

```
append(X,Y,Z) :- true |
   retrieve(append,3,E,TC),
   prepare_goalrec_body(append(X,Y,Z),TC,A,B), try(A,B,E).
```

With several steps of *Immediate Execution* and *Normalization*, we arrive at

```
append(X,Y,Z) :- true |
   transfer_args(1,3,append(X,Y,Z),g(0,0,0,0,0,0),_,A),
   try(A,[c(1=[],b([<(2)= <(3)],[])),
      c(1=[>(4)|>(1)],b([<(3)=[<(4)|>(3)]],[append(1,2,3)]))],E).
```

where `transfer_args/6` "loads" the arguments X, Y, Z to the goal record and returns the result to A. Further steps of *Immediate Execution* and *Normalization* lead us to

```
append(X,Y,Z) :- true |
  functor(X,AORnF,AORnN),
  test_pf(AORnF,AORnN,[],0,Res),
  try_match(Res,[],X,ARn,g(ARn,Y,Z,0,0,0),b([<(2)= <(3)],[]),
    c(1=[>(4)|>(1)],b([<(3)=[<(4)|>(3)]],[append(1,2,3)])),ℰ).
```

This is the first point at which we can't apply *Immediate Execution* or *Normalization*.

We regard the primitive `functor/3` as comprising clauses such as:

```
functor([],   F,N) :- true | F=[],   N=0.
functor([_|_],F,N) :- true | F='.',  N=2.
functor(f(_), F,N) :- true | F=f,    N=1.
```

There is one such clause for each constructor available, but without loss of generality we can focus on the above three clauses, of which the third one is meant to be a representative of all constructors irrelevant to the current example.

Now we apply *Case Splitting* and obtain the following:

```
append([],Y,Z) :- true |
  AORnF=[], AORnN=0,
  test_pf(AORnF,AORnN,[],0,Res),
  try_match(Res,[],[],ARn,g(ARn,Y,Z,0,0,0),b([<(2)= <(3)],[]),
    c(1=[>(4)|>(1)],b([<(3)=[<(4)|>(3)]],[append(1,2,3)])),ℰ).
append([H|T],Y,Z) :- true |
  AORnF='.', AORnN=2,
  test_pf(AORnF,AORnN,[],0,Res),
  try_match(Res,[],[H|T],ARn,g(ARn,Y,Z,0,0,0),b([<(2)= <(3)],[]),
    c(1=[>(4)|>(1)],b([<(3)=[<(4)|>(3)]],[append(1,2,3)])),ℰ).
append(f(X),Y,Z) :- true |
  AORnF=f, AORnN=1,
  test_pf(AORnF,AORnN,[],0,Res),
  try_match(Res,[],f(X),ARn,g(ARn,Y,Z,0,0,0),b([<(2)= <(3)],[]),
    c(1=[>(4)|>(1)],b([<(3)=[<(4)|>(3)]],[append(1,2,3)])),ℰ).
```

That is, we unfold `functor/3` and promote its *ask*s to the guards of `append/3`. The *Case Splitting* rule dictates that we should unfold `test_pf/5` and `try_match/7` as well; however, unfolding `test_pf/5` using its first clause, for instance, would promote two *ask*s, `AORnF=[]` and `AORnN=:=0`, which can never be satisfied because the two variables don't occur in the head of `append/3`. Clauses with unsatisfiable *ask*s are deleted finally. Note that clauses below the `otherwise` directive (such as the second clause of `test_pf/5`) implicitly perform all *ask*s in the clauses above the `otherwise`.

Now we come back to applying *Normalization* and *Immediate Execution*, which leads us via

```
append([],Y,Z) :- true |
  try_match(yes(0),[],[],ARn,g(ARn,Y,Z,0,0,0),b([<(2)= <(3)],[]),
```

```
  c(1=[>(4)|>(1)],b([<(3)=[<(4)|>(3)]],[append(1,2,3)])),E).
append([H|T],Y,Z) :- true |
  try_match(no,[],[H|T],ARn,g(ARn,Y,Z,0,0,0),b([<(2)= <(3)],[]),
    c(1=[>(4)|>(1)],b([<(3)=[<(4)|>(3)]],[append(1,2,3)])),E).
append(f(X),Y,Z) :- true |
  try_match(no,[],f(X),ARn,g(ARn,Y,Z,0,0,0),b([<(2)= <(3)],[]),
    c(1=[>(4)|>(1)],b([<(3)=[<(4)|>(3)]],[append(1,2,3)])),E).
```

to the following:

```
append([],Y,Z) :- true |
  getargs(1,0,[],[],g(0,Y,Z,0,0,0),A),
  try(A,b([<(2)= <(3)],[]),E).
append([H|T],Y,Z) :- true |
  getargs(1,2,[>(4)|>(1)],[H|T],g(0,Y,Z,0,0,0),A),
  try(A,b([<(3)=[<(4)|>(3)]],[append(1,2,3)]),E).
append(f(X),Y,Z) :- true | try(g(f(X),Y,Z,0,0,0),[],E).
```

Here, the rules as stated in [28] do not allow *Immediate Execution* of the third clause because we cannot form any unfolded clause to replace it. However, a close look at the reason why assures us that this clause *can* indeed be removed. The removal of a clause C whose body goal can never proceed changes the behavior of a goal g when there is another clause C' that can reduce g. However, the three clauses of append/3 above don't overlap with one another; that is, any goal that can be reduced using the third clause and then gets stuck will get stuck without it.

By steps of *Immediate Execution*, we can "load" necessary values to registers:

```
append([],Y,Z) :- true |
  try(g(0,Y,Z,0,0,0),b([<(2)= <(3)],[]),E).
append([H|T],Y,Z) :- true |
  try(g(T,Y,Z,H,0,0),b([<(3)=[<(4)|>(3)]],[append(1,2,3)]),E).
```

Now we have restored the guards of the original append/3, which is much more than halfway to our goal. It remains to restore the bodies, and this can be done by repetitive application of *Immediate Execution* and *Normalization*:

```
append([],Y,Z) :- true | Y=Z.
append([H|T],Y,Z) :- true |
  Z=[H|AORn], exec_one(append(T,Y,AORn),E).
```

Finally, we fold the body goal of the second clause using the clause we coined initially, and obtain the following:

```
append([],   Y,Z) :- true | Y=Z.
append([H|T],Y,Z) :- true | Z=[H|AORn], append(T,Y,AORn).
```

We anticipate that the significance of partial evaluation in our context is it enables us to use available tools for "just-in-time" static analysis. For faster execution, designing an optimizing compiler from treecode to machine code would be more appropriate than going back from treecode to Flat GHC source code.

7   Conclusions

We have described an interpreter of Flat GHC treecode in Flat GHC. The interpreter uses only *pure* built-in primitives, that is, those whose behavior can be defined using a set of guarded clauses (e.g., `functor/3`, `setarg/5`, etc.) or by simple source-to-source transformation (`otherwise`). The interpreter is only 39 clauses long (without arithmetics), and runs directly on KLIC.

Treecode is very close to source code but is designed so that it can be easily interpreted, transmitted over the network, and stored in files. The major differences from most bytecode representations are that it is more structured and, more importantly, that it is inherently concurrent.

The design of an interpreter involves decisions as to what are reified and what are not. To allow interpreted processes to freely communicate with non-interpreted, native processes, we made the following design choices:

- *Reified*: code, reduction, concurrency and nondeterminism; goal records, argument registers and temporary registers; control structures
- *Not reified*: logical variables and substitutions (constraints); heaps; representation of terms.

Although our initial objective was to have an 100% pure interpreter of Flat GHC, the outcome can be viewed also as a virtual machine working on register vectors. The three annotations, '>', '<', and '<<', are reminiscent of the distinction between put and get instructions in the Warren Abstract Machine [1].

Translation from source code to treecode is straightforward for most cases. For deterministic programs, its essence is to build a decision tree for clause selection. Some complication arises only when a predicate has both conjunctive and disjunctive synchronization points. The paper did not show a concrete translation algorithm, but instead illustrated how a treecode could be translated back to its source code using partial evaluation. Note that the source code could be restored because the interpreter was a *meta*-interpreter. Partial evaluation thus ensures the applicability of program analysis to interpreted code. Type analysis is important for an interpreted process to communicate with a native process running with no runtime type information. It is also important in building a stub and a skeleton of a (marshaled) logical stream laid between remote sites.

Our primary future work is to deploy those technologies to demonstrate that concurrent logic/constraint programming can act, possibly with minimal extensions, as a high-level and concise formalism for distributed programming. Another important direction is, starting with treecode, to develop an appropriate intermediate code representation for optimizing compilers. This is important for another application of concurrent languages, namely high-performance parallel computation.

Acknowledgment

Comments from anonymous referees were useful in improving the presentation of the paper.

References

1. Aït-Kaci, H., *Warren's Abstract Machine: A Tutorial Reconstruction*. The MIT Press, Cambridge, MA, 1991.
2. Ajiro, Y., Ueda, K. and Cho, K., Error-Correcting Source Code. In *Proc. Fourth Int. Conf. on Principles and Practice of Constraint Programming (CP'98)*, LNCS 1520, Springer-Verlag, Berlin, 1998, pp. 40–54.
3. Ajiro, Y. and Ueda, K., Kima – an Automated Error Correction System for Concurrent Logic Programs. In *Proc. Fourth Int. Workshop on Automated Debugging (AADEBUG 2000)*, Ducassé, M. (ed.), 2000.
   http://www.irisa.fr/lande/ducasse/aadebug2000/proceedings.html
4. Apt, K. R., Marek, V. W., Truszczynski M., and Warren D. S. (eds.), *The Logic Programming Paradigm: A 25-Year Perspective*. Springer-Verlag, Berlin, 1999.
5. Bowen, K. A. and Kowalski, R. A., Amalgamating Language and Meta-Language in Logic Programming. In *Logic Programming*, Clark, K. L. and Tärnlund, S. Å. (eds.), Academic Press, London, pp. 153–172, 1982.
6. Chikayama, T., Fujise, T. and Sekita, D., A Portable and Efficient Implementation of KL1. In *Proc. 6th Int. Symp. on Programming Language Implementation and Logic Programming (PLILP'94)*, LNCS 844, Springer-Verlag, Berlin, 1994, pp. 25–39.
7. Clark, K. L. and Gregory, S., A Relational Language for Parallel Programming. In *Proc. ACM Conf. on Functional Programming Languages and Computer Architecture (FPCA'81)*, ACM, 1981, pp. 171–178.
8. Clark, K. L. and Gregory, S., PARLOG: Parallel Programming in Logic. *ACM. Trans. Prog. Lang. Syst.*, Vol. 8, No. 1 (1986), pp. 1–49.
9. Foster, I. and Taylor, S., Strand: a Practical Parallel Programming Tool. In *Proc. 1989 North American Conf. on Logic Programming (NACLP'89)*, The MIT Press, Cambridge, MA, 1989, pp. 497–512.
10. Haridi, S., Van Roy, P., Brand, P. and Schulte, C., Programming Languages for Distributed Applications. *New Generation Computing*, Vol. 16, No. 3 (1998), pp. 223–261.
11. Huntbach, M. M., Ringwood, G. A., *Agent-Oriented Programming: From Prolog to Guarded Definite Clauses*. LNCS 1630, Springer-Verlag, Berlin, 1999.
12. Maher, M. J., Logic Semantics for a Class of Committed-Choice Programs. In *Proc. Fourth Int. Conf. on Logic Programming (ICLP'87)*, The MIT Press, Cambridge, MA, 1987, pp. 858–876.
13. McCarthy, J., *Lisp 1.5 Programmer's Manual*. MIT Press Cambridge, MA, 1962.
14. Miller, D. and Nadathur, G., Higher-order Logic Programming. In *Proc. Third Int. Conf. on Logic Programming (ICLP'86)*, LNCS 225, Springer-Verlag, Berlin, 1986, pp. 448–462.
15. Milner, R. *Communicating and Mobile Systems: the Pi-Calculus*. Cambridge University Press, 1999.
16. Nakashima, H., Ueda, K. and Tomura, S., What Is a Variable in Prolog? In *Proc. Int. Conf. on Fifth Generation Computer Systems 1984 (FGCS'84)*, ICOT, Tokyo, 1984, pp. 327–332.
17. Safra, M. and Shapiro, E. Y., Meta Interpreters for Real, In *Information Processing 86*, Kugler, H.-J. (ed.), North-Holland, Amsterdam, pp. 271–278, 1986.
18. Saraswat, V. A. and Rinard, M., Concurrent Constraint Programming (Extended Abstract). In *Conf. Record of the Seventeenth Annual ACM Symp. on Principles of Programming Languages (POPL'90)*, ACM Press, 1990, pp. 232–245.

19. Saraswat, V. A., Kahn, K. and Levy, J., Janus: A Step Towards Distributed Constraint Programming. In *Proc. 1990 North American Conference on Logic Programming (NACLP'90)*, The MIT Press, Cambridge, MA, 1990, pp. 431–446.
20. Shapiro, E. Y., Concurrent Prolog: A Progress Report. *IEEE Computer*, Vol. 19, No. 8 (1986), pp. 44–58.
21. Shapiro, E. Y. (ed.), *Concurrent Prolog: Collected Papers*, Volumes I+II. The MIT Press, Cambridge, MA, 1987.
22. Shapiro, E. Y., Warren, D. H. D., Fuchi, K., Kowalski, R. A., Furukawa, K., Ueda, K., Kahn, K. M., Chikayama, T. and Tick, E., The Fifth Generation Project: Personal Perspectives. *Comm. ACM*, Vol. 36, No. 3 (1993), pp. 46–103.
23. Smolka, G., The Oz Programming Model. In *Computer Science Today*, van Leeuwen, J. (ed.), LNCS 1000, Springer-Verlag, Berlin, 1995, pp. 324–343.
24. Takeuchi, A. and Furukawa, K., Partial Evaluation of Prolog Programs and Its Application to Meta Programming. In *Information Processing 86*, Kugler, H.-J. (ed.), North-Holland, Amsterdam, 1986, pp. 415–420.
25. Tamaki, H. and Sato, T., Unfold/Fold Transformation of Logic Programs. In *Proc. Second Int. Logic Programming Conf. (ICLP'84)*, Uppsala Univ., Sweden, 1984, pp. 127–138.
26. Tick, E. The Deevolution of Concurrent Logic Programming Languages. *J. Logic Programming*, Vol. 23, No. 2 (1995), pp. 89–123.
27. Ueda, K., Guarded Horn Clauses. ICOT Tech. Report TR-103, ICOT, Tokyo, 1985. Also in *Logic Programming '85*, Wada, E. (ed.), LNCS 221, Springer-Verlag, Berlin, 1986, pp. 168–179.
28. Ueda, K. and Furukawa, K., Transformation Rules for GHC Programs. In *Proc. Int. Conf. on Fifth Generation Computer Systems 1988 (FGCS'88)*, ICOT, Tokyo, 1988, pp. 582–591.
29. Ueda, K. and Chikayama, T. Design of the Kernel Language for the Parallel Inference Machine. *The Computer Journal*, Vol. 33, No. 6 (1990), pp. 494–500.
30. Ueda, K. and Morita, M., Moded Flat GHC and Its Message-Oriented Implementation Technique. *New Generation Computing*, Vol. 13, No. 1 (1994), pp. 3–43.
31. Ueda, K., Experiences with Strong Moding in Concurrent Logic/Constraint Programming. In *Proc. Int. Workshop on Parallel Symbolic Languages and Systems (PSLS'95)*, LNCS 1068, Springer-Verlag, Berlin, 1996, pp. 134–153.
32. Ueda, K., Concurrent Logic/Constraint Programming: The Next 10 Years. In [4], 1999, pp. 53–71.
33. Ueda, K., Linearity Analysis of Concurrent Logic Programs. In *Proc. Int. Workshop on Parallel and Distributed Computing for Symbolic and Irregular Applications*, Ito, T. and Yuasa, T. (eds.), World Scientific, Singapore, 2000, pp. 253–270.
34. van Emden, M. H. and de Lucena Filho, G. J., Predicate Logic as a Language for Parallel Programming. In *Logic Programming*, Clark, K. L. and Tärnlund, S. -Å. (eds.), Academic Press, London, 1982, pp. 189–198.

Transformation Systems and Nondeclarative Properties

Annalisa Bossi[1], Nicoletta Cocco[1], and Sandro Etalle[2]

[1] Dipartimento di Informatica, Università di Venezia
via Torino 155, 30172 Venezia, Italy
{bossi,cocco}@dsi.unive.it
[2] University of Twente and CWI, Amsterdam
Department of Computer Science
PO Box 217, 7500 AE Enschede, The Netherlands
etalle@cs.utwente.nl

Abstract. Program transformation systems are applied both in program synthesis and in program optimization. For logic programs the "logic" component makes transformations very natural and easy to be studied formally. But, when we move to Prolog programs, the "control" component cannot be ignored. In particular we need to cope with termination properties which are essential for ensuring the reachability of solutions for a given query.
We give an overview of the main proposals in the field of transformation systems for logic programs and we emphasize how they cope with those properties of logic programs which are not strictly declarative. We focus in particular on how the transformation can affect the termination of a program.

1 Introduction

Virtuous programming methodology, which consists in focusing on correctness of programs at first and on their efficiency only afterwards, fits particularly well with the logic programming paradigm, as stated by the famous motto: *Algorithm = Logic + Control* [Kow79]. This encourages the application of *transformation systems* to logic programs both for synthesizing a correct program from a logic specification [Dev90] and for optimizing it [TS84].

The main requirements for a practical transformation systems are on one hand to guarantee the preservation of interesting program properties and on the other hand to be supported by an automatic or semi-automatic tool. The most important program properties are characterized by the "Logic" component, namely declarative semantics describing the intended results of computations. But nondeclarative properties, the "Control" component, namely the actual behaviour of the interpreter, are extremely relevant.

The logic programming paradigm, in its pure form, knows *two sources of nondeterminism*:

ND1 The choice of the atom in the query (selection rule),
ND2 The choice of the clause to resolve it.

A.C. Kakas, F. Sadri (Eds.): Computat. Logic (Kowalski Festschrift), LNAI 2407, pp. 162–186, 2002.

The Prolog interpreter however gives up the first one by employing a fixed left-most selection rule, and the second one with a fixed top-down selection method. This latter nondeterminism is recovered (thought not entirely, for the possibility on nontermination) by the use of backtracking. Between pure logic programming and pure Prolog, we find the well-studied paradigm of "logic programming + leftmost selection rule", which is of theoretical relevance.

The influence of (ND1) and (ND2) varies according to the kind of *observable behaviour*, *observable* for short, we focus on. For instance, if the observable is the *Success Set* of the program, then, by the well-known result of the independence from the selection rule, (ND2) can compensate for the absence of (ND1). For other observables this does not apply: for instance, if one observes the *Finite Failure Set* of the program, then (ND1) is of influence, while (ND2) is not. The same holds for *(universal) termination*.

A program transformation system is characterized by a set of *basic transformation operations* and a *strategy* which combines them for a given aim. The transformation operations are generally constrained by *applicability conditions* which ensure their *correctness*, that is, the preservation of the observables of interest. These applicability conditions should balance between the need to capture the majority of cases and the need to allow for a simple verification, if possible they should be purely syntactical in order to be automatically verified by the system. Similarly, the strategy should strike a balance between being powerful and being automatizable, thus reducing interactions with the user to the minimum.

When transformation techniques, formulated for logic programs in general, are applied to real programs, Prolog's choices wrt (ND1) and (ND2) become relevant for preserving the observables one is interested in. Useful observables usually represent the results of computation, which for Prolog programs can be characterized by the *Computed Answer Substitutions* [FLMP93] and the *Finite Failure Set* (when negation is used). But since Prolog replaces (ND2) by backtracking, also termination properties are essential, as they guarantee the effective reachability of solutions.

In this paper we intend to give an overview of some of the transformation systems which have been proposed for logic programs and we look at how they influence the observables of a program. We shall look especially at nondeclarative properties, and at termination in particular. In fact, transformation systems preserving termination are suitable to deal with pure Prolog programs. We think that the field is mature enough to allow for a comparison and a classification of such systems by considering the basic transformation operations, the preserved termination property, the purpose and the level of automatization.

The paper is organized as follows. In Section 2 we give some notation on general logic programs and briefly recall the major termination properties. In Section 3 we define the simplest unfold/fold transformation system, which is common to the majority of transformation systems. We illustrate the properties of both the basic operations, unfold and fold, and we discuss the problems related to preserving termination and the proposed solutions. We also discuss the need of reordering literals in clause bodies during transformations and define a switch operation. In Section 4 we introduce the powerful replacement operation, discuss its properties and the proposals for preserving termination. A short conclusion follows in Section 5.

2   Preliminaries

2.1   General Programs and LDNF-resolution

Let $\mathcal{P}$ be a finite set of *predicate symbols* (or *relations*). An *atom* is an object of the form $p(t_1, \ldots, t_n)$ where $p \in \mathcal{P}$ is an n-ary predicate symbol and $t_1, \ldots, t_n \in \mathcal{T}$. A *literal* is either an atom A (a *positive literal*) or the negation of an atom $\neg A$ (a *negative literal*). A *general query* is a possibly empty finite sequence of literals $L_1, \ldots, L_n$ $(n \geq 0)$. Following the convention adopted by Apt in [Apt97], we use bold characters (e.g. **B**) to indicate sequences of objects, typically **B** indicates a sequence of literals, $B_1, \ldots, B_n$, **t** indicates a sequence of terms, $t_1, \ldots, t_n$, and **x** denotes a sequence of variables, $x_1, \ldots, x_n$. A *general clause* is a construct of the form $H \leftarrow \mathbf{B}$ where H is an atom (the *head*) and **B** is a general query (the *body*). When **B** is empty, $H \leftarrow \mathbf{B}$ is written $H \leftarrow$ and is called a *unit clause*. A *general program* is a finite set of general clauses.

Apart from this, we use the standard notation of Lloyd [Llo87] and Apt [Apt97]. In particular, given a syntactic construct E (so for example, a term, a literal or a set of equations) we denote by $Var(E)$ the set of the variables appearing in E. Given a substitution $\theta = \{x_1/t_1, \ldots, x_n/t_n\}$ we denote by $Dom(\theta)$ the set of variables $\{x_1, \ldots, x_n\}$, and by $Ran(\theta)$ the set of variables appearing in $\{t_1, \ldots, t_n\}$. Finally, we define $Var(\theta) = Dom(\theta) \cup Ran(\theta)$.

A substitution θ is called *grounding* if $Ran(\theta)$ is empty, and it is called a *renaming* if it is a permutation of the variables in $Dom(\theta)$. By $Pred(E)$ we denote the set of predicate symbols occurring in the expression E.

We use a notation introduced in [AP93], and we say that a predicate p *is defined in the program* P iff there is a clause in P that uses p in its head.

Definition 2.1 Let P, Q be programs, which define different predicates, and p, q relations in $Pred(P)$.

(i) We say that p *refers to* q *in* P if there is a clause in P that uses p in its head and q in its body.

(ii) We say that p *depends on* q *in* P, and write $p \sqsupseteq q$, if (p, q) is in the reflexive, transitive closure of the relation *refers to*.

(iii) We say that P *extends* Q, $P \sqsupseteq Q$, if there is no $q \in Pred(Q)$ which refers (in Q) to a predicate p defined in P.

(iv) Let B be an atom, by $P|_B$ we denote the set of clauses of P that define the predicates which the predicate of B depends on. Similarly by $P|_p$ we denote the set of clauses of P that define a predicate p and all the predicates which it depends on. $\square$

We consider SLDNF-resolution with Prolog selection rule, that is the leftmost selection rule. As usual, we call this form of resolution *LDNF-resolution*.

Following Apt and Pedreschi's approach in studying the termination of general programs [AP93], we view the LDNF-resolution as a top-down interpreter which, given a general program P and a general query Q, attempts to build a search tree for $P \cup \{Q\}$ by constructing its branches in parallel. The branches in this tree are called *LDNF-derivations* of $P \cup \{Q\}$ and the tree itself is called *LDNF-tree* of $P \cup \{Q\}$. Negative literals are resolved using the negation as failure rule which calls for the construction of a *subsidiary LDNF-tree*. If during this subsidiary construction the interpreter diverges, the (main) LDNF-derivation is considered to be infinite. An LDNF-derivation is finite also if during its construction the interpreter encounters a query with the first literal being negative and non-ground. In such a case we say that the LDNF-derivation *flounders*. An LDNF-tree is called *non-floundering* if none of its derivations flounders.

By termination of a general program we actually mean termination of the underlying interpreter. Hence in order to ensure termination of a query Q in a program P, we require that all LDNF-derivations of $P \cup \{Q\}$ are finite.

We use the following abbreviations for a program P: M_P for the least Herbrand model of P, and $comp(P)$ for Clark's completion of P [Cla78].

2.2   Termination Properties

We recall in this section some important termination properties for logic programs which have been studied in the literature. We refer all definitions to general programs.

Definition 2.2 (Terminating Program) A program P is called *terminating* iff all SLDNF-derivations of P starting in any ground query are finite.

This is a very strong termination property since it must hold for any selection rule. If we consider only the leftmost selection rule of Prolog, namely LDNF-resolution, the following property of left termination is more appropriate.

Definition 2.3 (Left Terminating Program) A program P is called *left terminating* iff all LDNF-derivations of P starting in any ground query are finite.

For verifying a termination property on a program, a common technique is to find a measure on queries which, under certain conditions, can only decrease during the computation. Such measure is based a *level mapping*, namely a map from ground literals to natural numbers. Two important classes of programs had been characterized by means of properties of level mappings: *Acyclic programs* and *Acceptable programs*.

Acyclic programs were introduced by Cavedon [Cav89] and have been further studied by Apt and Bezem [AB91]. An acyclic program is characterized by the fact that for any ground instance of any clause, the level mapping of the head is greater than the level mapping of each literal in the body.

We can relate acyclic and terminating programs: If P is an acyclic program then P is terminating. Moreover if P is a definite program, then P is terminating iff P is acyclic. When negation is allowed in clause bodies, there are programs which are terminating but not acyclic. This is caused by the presence of floundering derivations, since non-ground negative literals are not selected and some infinite branches of the search tree cannot be explored [AB91]. Note that if a program is terminating or acyclic, it is also left terminating.

The concept of *acceptable program* generalizes the one of acyclic program and had been introduced by Apt and Pedreschi in [AP90, AP93] to characterize left terminating programs.

In the two previous definitions, all ground queries were requested to terminate. Vasak and Potter in [VP86] introduced two different termination properties which refer to a specific query $\mathbf{Q}$ in a program: Universal termination and existential termination.

Definition 2.4 (Universal and Existential Termination)

- A query $\mathbf{Q}$ is *universally terminating* in P iff all LDNF-derivations for $\mathbf{Q}$ in P are finite.
- A query $\mathbf{Q}$ is *existentially terminating* in P iff there exists at least one LDNF-derivation for $\mathbf{Q}$ in P which is finite.

Note that if every ground query universally terminates in a program P, then P is left terminating. Conversely, if P is left terminating then every ground query is universally terminating in it.

In order to characterize programs where every query is universally terminating, we introduced also the following very strong termination property.

Definition 2.5 (Always Left Terminating Program) A program P is called *always left terminating* iff all LDNF-derivations of P starting in any query are finite.   □

In an always left terminating program no computation can diverge. These programs are generally defined by clauses which are not recursive or by built-ins and used to perform some checks.

Note that if a program is always left terminating, then it is also left terminating. Hence the class of left terminating programs includes the ones of terminating, acyclic and always left terminating programs.

Another interesting class of queries we will refer to, and which contains all the ground ones, is the class of *well-moded* queries. Modes are extensively used in the literature on logic programs, usually they indicate how the arguments of a relation should be used. A *mode* is a function that labels as *input* (+) or *output* (-) the positions of each predicate in order to indicate how the arguments of a predicate should be used. Most predicates have a natural moding, which reflects their intended use. For example, the natural moding for the usual program append, when used for concatenating two lists, is append(+,+,-). When talking about moded programs, we assume that each predicate symbol has a unique mode associated to it; multiple modes may be obtained by simply renaming the predicates. If Q is a query, we denote by $In(Q)$ (resp. $Out(Q)$) the set of terms filling in the input (resp. output) positions of predicates in Q.

The concept of *well-moded program* is essentially due to Dembinski and Maluszynski [DM88]. Intuitively a program is well-moded when the modes of literals in each clause, which reflect the dataflow taking place in it, are consistent with the left-to-right selection rule. The definition of well-moded program and query has been given for definite programs but it can be extended to general programs, as in [BCER01]. *Moded level mappings* are introduced in [EBC99], they do not take into account output terms, but only input terms. The relevance of well-moding and moded level mappings for termination is studied for definite programs in [EBC99]. We give here an extended definition for general programs.

Definition 2.6 (Well-Terminating Program) A program is called *well-terminating* iff all its LDNF-derivations starting in any well-moded query are finite.

Notice that a well-terminating program is also left terminating.

3   A Simple Transformation System: Unfold and Fold

In their seminal papers [TS84, ST84], Sato and Tamaki adapted to definite logic programs the ideas on program transformations firstly introduced by Burstall and Darlington for functional programs [BD77]. They defined *the basic unfold/fold transformation system*, based on the operations of *new definition, unfold and fold*. Then they made it more powerful with *replacement* and further with *clause addition* and *clause deletion*. They studied the system wrt to a declarative semantics given by the least Herbrand model. This was the starting point for a number of studies on transformations preserving properties of logic programs, both definite and general, which can be expressed by a declarative semantics, such as: Success Set, Computed Answer Substitutions and Finite Failures Set, see for example [Mah87, KK90, Sek91, GS91, BCE92, AD93, BC93] just to quote some of these efforts.

We start by considering the basic operation: Unfold. From now on, standardization apart is always assumed.

3.1   Unfold

Unfold is the fundamental operation for partial evaluation [LS91] and it consists in applying a resolution step to an atom in a clause body, by using all possible resolving clauses.

Definition 3.1 (Unfold) Let $cl : H \leftarrow \mathbf{J}, L, \mathbf{K}$. be a clause of a program P, L a positive literal and $\{A_1 \leftarrow \mathbf{B}_1., \ldots, A_n \leftarrow \mathbf{B}_n.\}$ the set of clauses of P whose heads unify with L, by mgu's $\{\theta_1, \ldots, \theta_n\}$.

- *unfolding* L *in* cl consists of substituting cl with $\{cl_1', \ldots, cl_n'\}$, where, for each i, $cl_i' = (H \leftarrow \mathbf{J}, \mathbf{B}_i, \mathbf{K})\theta_i$.

L is the *unfolded atom*, $\{A_1 \leftarrow \mathbf{B}_1., \ldots, A_n \leftarrow \mathbf{B}_n.\}$ are called the *unfolding clauses* and $\{cl_1', \ldots, cl_n'\}$ are the unfolded clauses (*unfoldings* for short). □

There are a few slightly different versions of this operation. A more powerful definition of unfold for definite programs has been given in [Gal91] where the unfold operation is based on partial evaluation, namely it consists in building a finite (incomplete) SLD-tree for the body of a clause $H \leftarrow \mathbf{B}$. and in getting the resultants $H\alpha_i \leftarrow \mathbf{G}_i$. as unfoldings. With such a "multi-step" unfold it is possible to obtain unfoldings which are not obtainable through a series of one step unfoldings.

Note that we define the unfold only for positive literals (atoms). In some proposals also a negative literal can be unfolded: For example in [GS91], if $L = \neg A$ with A ground, and A has a finitely failing SLDNF-tree, then unfolding L is done by deleting L from the clause cl. On the other hand if A has a successful derivation, then the same operation yields the removal of cl. In [AD94] another unfold for negative literals is defined in the context of a well-founded partial evaluation: Any negative literal $\neg p(\mathbf{t})$ in the program is replaced by an atom $notp(\mathbf{t})$, where the new predicate $notp$ is defined as the negation of the completed definition of p.

Declarative Properties Thanks to its correspondence to a resolution step, the unfold operation in Definition 3.1, is safe wrt basically all the declarative semantics available for logic programs: The least Herbrand model, as shown already in [TS84], the Success Set and the Computed Answer Substitutions semantics and this was shown by [KK90]. When used alone, unfold preserves also the Finite Failure Set, while in combination with other transformation operations, such as fold, this is no more preserved [Sek91].

Fixing the Selection Rule Let us discuss now what happens when we are interested in preserving more procedural properties as termination ones. In this Section we analyze what happens when we give up on (ND1) by fixing the selection rule.

Let us start by considering termination. *For definite programs*, in [BC94] we proved that *unfold preserves universal termination of a query* and as a consequence it preserves also left termination and well-termination. Unfortunately this reasoning does not carry over to general logic programs, due to the possibility that they terminate by floundering. Consider:

```
p  ← not(trigger(X)), q(X), p.
trigger(a).
q(b).
```

This program is left terminating. Notice however that the query p terminates by floundering. Now, if we unfold q(X) in the first clause, we obtain a program containing the clause p ← not(trigger(b)), p. In this program the query p does not left terminate any longer.

This has to do with the fact that Definition 3.1 of *unfold allows for a left-propagation of the bindings*: The atoms on the left of the unfolded atom might be instantiated during the unfolding (i.e. J becomes instantiated). In the above example this happened to not(trigger(X)). This implies that after the unfold operation some "calls" might be more instantiated than before the unfold.

On the other hand, *for general programs* we can say that *the unfold operation maintains acyclicity* [BE94] *and acceptability* [BCE96b]: If P is acyclic (resp. acceptable wrt a certain level mapping $| \; |$ and a model M) and P' is obtained from P by the application of an unfold operation, then P' is acyclic as well (resp. acceptable wrt $| \; |$ and M as well).

Another consequence of the already mentioned left-propagation of the bindings is that *unfold can "increase termination"*, namely the transformed program can terminate with a failure also for queries which are non-terminating in the original program. Consider the trivial program:

```
c1:   q ← p.
c2:   p ← p, r.
```

If we unfold r in $c2$ we obtain the one-line program q ← p. for which all queries terminate since they finitely fail. This can happen also when the unfolded atom is not finitely failing. Consider the non-left terminating program:

```
q ← p(X), r(X).
p(s(X)) ← p(X).
r(a).
```

In this program the query q does not left terminate, however, by unfolding r(X), we obtain a left terminating program.

Pure Prolog We now see what happens when we substitute (ND2) by a fixed clause selection augmented with backtracking. In this setting the order of the clauses in a program becomes relevant, and we intend to consider more procedural observables. We notice the following: *Unfold can change the order of the computed answer substitutions*. Consider:

```
c1:   p(X) ← q(X), r(X).
c2:   q(a).
c3:   q(b).
c4:   r(b).
c4:   r(a).
```

The query p(X), with a Prolog interpreter, has the sequence of computed answer substitutions $\{X = a, X = b\}$. If we unfold r(X) in c1 we obtain:

```
c1': p(X) ← q(b).
c2': p(X) ← q(a).
       :
```

Now the query p(X) returns first the answer X=b and then the one X=a.

Even in the absence of non-logical predicates, this apparently minor fact can have annoying consequences. In particular, unfold can deteriorate the performances of a program. Consider:

```
p ← heavy(X), q(X).
heavy(X) ← lots_of_calculations, X is b.
q(a).
q(b)
```

By unfolding q(X), we obtain.

```
p ← heavy(a).
p ← heavy(b).
heavy(X) ← lots_of_calculations, X is b.
```

In the second program, the query p generates two calls to heavy, while in the first one heavy was called only once.

Thus *the left-propagation of bindings can deteriorate efficiency and/or spoil termination*. Partial evaluation systems have different ways for dealing with this. Gallagher, [Gal91] for the SP system introduces the concept of *determinate unfolding*. Roughly speaking, an unfolding is determinate if it returns no more than one clause (more precisely, no more than one *live* clause, where dead clauses are those that contain an immediately failing atom). This guarantees that the amount of nondeterminism is not increased, which would be harmful for the efficiency. Determinate unfolding is also used in the ECCE partial evaluation system [LMS98].

In [PP91] Pettorossi and Proietti propose two restrictive definitions of unfold for definite programs: *Unfold of the leftmost atom*, which is clearly not harmful wrt any semantics (as it trivially cannot cause any left-propagation), and *deterministic non-left-propagating unfold*.

Definition 3.2 (Deterministic Non-Left-Propagating Unfold) The unfolding of a clause $cl : H \leftarrow \mathbf{J}, A, \mathbf{K}$. wrt the atom A is *deterministic non-left-propagating* iff

1. there exists exactly one clause whose head is unifiable with A via an mgu θ;
2. $(H \leftarrow \mathbf{J})\theta$ is a variant of $H \leftarrow \mathbf{J}$.

They proved that both such restrictive unfold operations preserve the "sequence of answer substitution semantics" (a semantics for Prolog programs, defined in [JM84, Bau89], which takes into account also the order of the computed answer substitutions, together with their multiplicity). This guarantees that if the initial program is left terminating, then the resulting program is left terminating as well.

Also *partial evaluation systems for real Prolog generally forbid left propagation of the variable bindings.* Mixtus [Sah93], for instance exploits disjunction for unfolding Prolog programs.

Definition 3.3 (Unfold in Mixtus) Let $cl : H \leftarrow \mathbf{J}, L, \mathbf{K}$. be a clause of a program P, L a positive literal and $\{A_1 \leftarrow \mathbf{B}_1., \ldots, A_n \leftarrow \mathbf{B}_n.\}$ the set of clauses of P whose heads unify with L, by mgu's $\{\theta_1, \ldots, \theta_n\}$.

– *unfolding L in cl* consists of substituting cl with
$cl' : H \leftarrow \mathbf{J}, (\bigvee_{i=1}^{n} (L = A_i, \mathbf{B}_i)), \mathbf{K}$.

This unfold guarantees that no left-propagation is performed, which in turn ensures that the system is correct also in the presence of extra-logical predicates.

A conceptually similar approach is used in the PADDY system [Pre92] for partial evaluation, but the disjunction is obtained by means of the introduction of a new definition.

Prolog When extra-logical features are involved, unfold can create further problems. One of them is the possible *loss of computed answer substitutions*, as shown in the following examples. Let us consider the program

```
c1:   p(X)  ← q(X).
c2:   p(a).
c3:   q(b)  ← !.
c4:   q(c).
```

for the query p(X) we get the computed answer substitutions $X = b, X = a$. By unfolding q(X) in c1 we get

```
d1:   p(b)  ← !.
d2:   p(c).
c2:   p(a).
c3:   q(b)  ← !.
c4:   q(c).
```

Now, for the query p(X), we obtain only $X = b$. Similarly let us consider

```
c1:   p(X)  ← var(X), q(X).
c2:   q(b).
c3:   q(c).
```

for the query p(X) we obtain the computed answer substitutions $X = b, X = c$. But if we unfold q(X) in c1, for the same query p(X) we now have a failure.

These problems are deeply connected with the left-propagation of bindings, and are automatically avoided if one employs a definition of unfold such as Definition 3.2 or 3.3.

Unfolding in Prolog has been studied in the context of partial evaluation systems also in [LS88, BR89, Pre93]. They proposed either to restrict unfold on extra-logical features or to transform the program before unfolding, in order to eliminate such extra-logical features or at least to have them only in a standard form.

3.2   Fold

Fold is possibly the transformation operation for which we find the most different definitions. In order to approach it, we first define the concept of transformation sequence.

Definition 3.4 (Transformation Sequence) A *transformation sequence* is a sequence of programs $P_0, \ldots, P_n$, $n \geq 0$, such that each program P_{i+1}, $0 \leq i < n$, is obtained from P_i by applying a basic transformation operation to a clause of P_i. $\qquad \square$

The simplest transformation systems (and then sequences) include only three basic operations which allow for a reasonable set of transformations: *new definition, unfold and fold*. In the literature we can find many different definitions for these operations. Here we are forced to choose one and we try to choose it in the most general way, giving a short description of other proposals. Actually, in [TS84] the *new definition* operation is not explicitly considered as a transformation operation; rather, all new definitions are assumed to be present at the beginning of the transformation. Here we follow the same syntax and we assume that every transformation process starts from an *initial program* which already contains new definitions expressed as Prolog clauses.

Definition 3.5 (Initial Program) We call a program P_0 an *initial program* if it can be partitioned into two programs P_{new} and P_{old} such that the following conditions are satisfied:

(I1) $P_{new} \sqsupseteq P_{old}$;
(I2) P_{new} is not recursive.

P_{new} contains the *new definitions*, that is the completed definitions of the predicates defined in P_{new} which are called *new* predicates. The predicates defined in P_{old} are instead the *old* ones. Similarly we say that a literal is a *new* (resp. *old*) literal iff its predicate symbol is.

We now give the most "classical" definition of fold, equivalent to the one by Tamaki and Sato [TS84]: Fold is the inverse of unfold when one single unfold is possible, and it consists in substituting an atom A for an equivalent conjunction of literals $\mathbf{B}$ in the body of a clause cl. The transformation sequence and the fold operation are defined in terms of each other.

Definition 3.6 (Fold) Let $P_0, \ldots, P_i$, $i \geq 0$, be a transformation sequence and P_0 an initial program, $cl : H \leftarrow \mathbf{J}, \mathbf{B}, \mathbf{K}$. be a clause in P_i, and $d : D \leftarrow \mathbf{B}'$. be a clause in P_{new}. *Folding* $\mathbf{B}$ *in* cl *via* τ consists of replacing cl by cl' : $H \leftarrow \mathbf{J}, D\tau, \mathbf{K}$., provided that τ is a substitution such that $Dom(\tau) = Var(d)$ and such that the following conditions hold:

(F1) d is the only clause in P_{new} whose head is unifiable with $D\tau$;
(F2) If we unfold $D\tau$ in cl' using d as unfolding clause, then the result of the operation is a variant of cl;

(C1) Either cl defines an *old* predicate, or at least one atom of cl is the result of a previous unfolding.

Notice that the clause used for folding, d, does not necessarily belong to the program P_i in which the folding is performed. The following example is inspired by one in [Sek93].

Example 3.7 Consider the initial program

```
c1:   path(X,X,[X]).
c2:   path(X,Z,[X|Xs])  ← arc(X,Y), path(Y,Z,Xs).
c3:   goodlist([]).
c4:   goodlist([X|Xs])  ← good(X), goodlist(Xs).
c5:   goodpath(X,Z,Xs)  ← path(X,Z,Xs), goodlist(Xs).
```

$P_{new} = \{c5\}$, thus goodpath is the only new predicate. The query goodpath(X,Z, Xs) can be employed for finding a path Xs starting in the node X and ending in the node Z which contains exclusively "good" nodes. As it is now, goodpath works on a "generate and test" basis: First it produces a whole path, and then it checks whether it contains only "good" nodes or not. Of course this strategy is quite naive: Checking if the node is "good" or not *while* generating the path would noticeably increase the performances of the program. We can obtain such an improvement via an unfold/fold transformation. By unfolding path(X, Z, Xs) in the body of c5, we obtain

```
c6:   goodpath(X,X,[X])  ← goodlist([X]).
c7:   goodpath(X,Z,[X|Xs])  ← arc(X,Y), path(Y,Z,Xs),
      goodlist([X|Xs]).
```

In the above clauses we can unfold goodlist([X]) and goodlist([X|Xs]). The resulting clauses, after further unfolding goodlist([]) in the clause obtained from c6, are

```
c8:   goodpath(X,X,[X])  ← good(X).
c9:   goodpath(X,Z,[X|Xs])  ← arc(X,Y), path(Y,Z,Xs), good(X),
      goodlist(Xs).
```

Let $P_2 = \{c1, c2, c3, c4, c8, c9\}$. Now we have reached a crucial step in the transformation: According to Definition 3.6 we can *fold* path(Y, Z, Xs), goodlist(Xs) in c9. The result is the following recursive clause:

```
c10:  goodpath(X,Z,[X|Xs]) ← arc(X,Y),good(X),goodpath(Y,Z,Xs).
```

Let $P_3 = \{c1, c2, c3, c4, c8, c10\}$. Notice that this definition is now directly recursive and it checks the "goodness" of the path while generating the path itself. □

A different definition of fold is given in [Mah87] and in [GS91]: Both cl, the folded clause, and d, the clause used for folding, are in P_i and they must be different clauses (hence conditions **F1** and **F2** must hold in P_i, while **C1** can be dropped). This fold is normally regarded as weaker than the Tamaki-Sato's one, in fact it cannot produce all the same transformed programs, but its correctness wrt the least Herbrand model, the Success Set and the Computed Answers Substitutions is easier to prove. The disadvantage of this fold operation is that it does not allow us to introduce direct recursion in a definition (as done in Example 3.7), which is generally regarded as the key aspect of the folding operation.

We should mention another definition of fold, strictly stronger than Definition 3.6. It allows for simultaneous folding of different clauses and has been proposed in [PP94a] by extending the idea of fold as the inverse of unfold to the case when multiple unfoldings are possible.

Declarative Properties Of course, it is of primary importance to ensure the correctness of an unfold/fold system from a declarative point of view. For the system presented here the following properties hold in case of definite programs:

- the least Herbrand Models of the initial and final programs coincide [TS84];
- the Success Sets of the initial and final programs coincide [KK90];
- the Computed Answers Substitutions of the initial and final programs coincide [KK90].

The first unfold/fold transformation system was later generalized to general logic programs, and proved correct wrt the well-founded semantics [Sek93]. Aravindan and Dung proved in [AD93] that it preserves also the so-called *semantic kernel*, that guarantees that the transformation is correct wrt a number of semantics for programs with negation.

On the other hand, the Finite Failure Set is not preserved. Consider the following example.

Example 3.8 Let P_0 be the program

```
c1:   p ← q, h(X).
c2:   h(s(X)) ← h(X).
```

Where $P_{old} = \{c_2\}$ and $P_{new} = \{c_1\}$. Notice that there is no definition for predicate q, so p and q finitely fail. By unfolding h(X) in c1 we obtain a variant of c1:

```
c3:   p ← q, h(Y).
```

Now, we can fold q, h(Y) in c3, using clause c1 for folding. The result is

```
c4:   p ← p
```

The Finite Failure Set has changed: p does not finitely fail any longer.   □

This problem was addressed and fixed by Seki, who in [Sek91] provides a *modified fold* operation for stratified general programs which requires that **C1** be modified into

(**C2**) either *cl* defines an old atom, or all the literals in the folded part of the clause *cl*, **B**, must result from a previous unfolding.

This restriction is sufficient to guarantee that the Finite Failure Set of the initial and of the final programs are the same. Seki also introduces *a labelling of literals in clause bodies in order to keep track of the ones coming from previous unfolding and to make syntactically checkable this condition.*

Termination Properties We discuss now what happens when we are interested in preserving more procedural properties such as termination ones.

If we consider termination wrt *all* selection rules, then the system we present here is correct: In [BE94] we proved that if the initial program is (definite and) terminating for all selection rules, then the transformed program is terminating for all selection rules as well. This result extends also to general programs by considering the concept of *acyclic program*: If the initial program is acyclic then the resulting one is acyclic as well.

However, many usual programs are not terminating wrt all selection rules, and it is clearly of interest to see what happens for instance to *left termination* when we apply a fold-unfold transformation sequence. First of all note the obvious fact that *when we fix the selection rule, the order of literals in the bodies becomes relevant*. This is in contrast to the way the transformation rules were originally defined in [TS84, Sek91]. For instance in the last transformation step of Example 3.7 we have actually *swapped* the two atoms `path(Y,Z,Xs)`, `good(X)` before applying the fold operation. Since Definition 3.6 is given modulo reordering of the body atoms, this does not pose any problem in applying it. On the other hand, if one fixes the selection rule, such a swapping can easily introduce non-termination: For instance think about swapping the two atoms `fail, loop` in a clause body. Thus, in order to apply the fold operation to Prolog or pure Prolog programs, one has to give a definition for it which takes into account the order of the literals in clause bodies.

A first relevant result in the direction of an unfold/fold transformation system which preserves left termination was presented by Proietti and Pettorossi in [PP91]. They propose a transformation system for definite programs which is similar to [TS84] with three additional conditions: (a) no reordering of the atoms is allowed, (b) unfolding is allowed only for the leftmost atom of a clause or in the case of a deterministic non-left propagating atom, and (c) folding is allowed if **C1** is modified as:

(**C3**) either *cl* defines an old atom, or the leftmost atom of the folded clause is the result of a previous unfolding. [1]

They proved that this system preserves a very strong semantics, namely, the *sequence of answer substitutions semantics* (a semantics for Prolog programs,

---

[1] These are not *exactly* the conditions proposed in [PP91], but a conservative approximation of them in terms of the concepts we have introduced so far. We do this in order to avoid introducing too much notation and to make it easier to compare the different approaches.

defined in [JM84, Bau89]). This guarantees also that if the initial program is left terminating, then the resulting program is left terminating as well. While this system has rather restrictive applicability conditions (e.g. the transformation of Example 3.8 is not possible within it), we believe that in order to preserve such a strong semantics it is hardly possible to do any better.

In our works on unfold/fold transformations systems which preserve left termination [BC94, BC97, BCE96b, BCE00] we have explored two different approaches:

- In [BC94, BC97] we have considered the preservation of universal termination for definite programs, based on the (semantic) concept of *non-increasing operation*.
- In [BCE96b, BCE00] we show that the crucial aspect in preserving left termination is the reordering of the atoms in a clause and we provide – among other things – novel applicability conditions for reordering which in some cases are purely syntactic, hence of practical nature. These will be discussed in Section 3.2.

In [BC94] we studied the preservation of universal termination for a query with *LD-resolution*. In order to capture computed answer substitutions plus universal termination, we defined an appropriate operational semantics for definite programs and split the equivalence condition to be satisfied between the original and the transformed program wrt a query into two complementary conditions: A "completeness" condition, which ensures that successful LD-derivations for the query are preserved, and the condition of being "non-increasing". This second condition is very operational since it compares the lengths of corresponding partial LD-derivations of the query in the initial and the transformed program. Its validity ensures that a transformation cannot introduce infinite derivations. We proved that, by appropriately restricting the version with no reordering of Tamaki-Sato's system, based on new definition, unfold and fold, the whole transformation sequence is non-increasing and then it preserves also universal termination for a query. As a consequence, left termination of programs is also preserved by such a restricted transformation sequence. The restriction we introduce into the unfold/fold transformation system imposes that fold can be performed only after a "decreasing" unfold of the clause to be folded. Namely let $cl : H \leftarrow \mathbf{J}, \mathbf{B}, \mathbf{K}$. be the clause to be folded in $\mathbf{B}$, we require instead of **C1** the condition:

(C4) either cl defines an old atom, or at least one reachable atom in $\mathbf{J}, \mathbf{B}$ comes from a previous unfolding,

where an atom is called *reachable* when it has no finitely failing or diverging atom to its left in cl. Clearly condition **C4** is not decidable in general, even if there are sufficient conditions for it, for example condition **C3**.

Another related work is [Amt92], where Amtoft gives a unified treatment of conditions for preserving termination properties in transformation systems based on unfold and fold. He sets up a model, parametrized with respect to the evaluation order, which allows one to reason about termination in an algebraic fashion. In such a model he can represent most of the previous results in the literature as a special case: He can represent the condition of folding wrt a *new* predicate in [TS84, KK90], the condition **C2** of [Sek91], namely that all the atoms in the folded part of the body have to be labelled (i.e. they must result from a previous unfolding), or the weaker one, **C3**, in [PP91] for Prolog leftmost selection rule, namely that at least the leftmost atom in the clause to be folded is labelled.

Folding + Switching We have already stressed that unfold/fold transformations might at some point require a reordering of body literals in order to perform a fold operation. Such a reordering can harm the termination of a program, and – because of this – we have seen that unfold/fold systems for (pure) Prolog programs do not allow for any permutation of literals in the clause's bodies. This restriction limits sensibly the effectiveness of a transformation system; to alleviate this problem, in [BCE96b, BCE00] we have addressed the problem of introducing in the transformation system a *switch* operation for reordering the body literals and of finding suitable applicability conditions for such operation in order to guarantee persistency of left termination: If the original program is left terminating, then the transformed program is left terminating as well. We now give a brief summary of those results, starting by the obvious definition of switch.

Definition 3.9 (Switch) Let $cl : H \leftarrow \mathbf{J}, A, B, \mathbf{K}.$ be a clause of a program P. *switching A with B in cl* consists of replacing cl with $cl' : H \leftarrow \mathbf{J}, B, A, \mathbf{K}.$ □

   The switch operation can be seen as a replacement (discussed in the next Section) which *trivially maintains all the declarative properties of a program.* On the other hand, the *switch does not preserve left termination.* For instance if we take the contrived program

   p ← q, p.

we have that at the moment the program is terminating (q fails), however, if we swap the two atoms in the body of the clause, we get a program which is not terminating. Another typical situation is the one in which we have in the body of a clause a combination such as   ...p(X,Y), q(Y,Z)... , where the rightmost atom uses Y as input variable; in this case, bringing q(Y,Z) to the left of p(X,Y) can easily introduce non-termination, as q(Y,Z) might be called with its arguments not sufficiently instantiated. In the context of an unfold/fold transformation system, this situation is further complicated by the presence of the other operations, in particular of fold which may introduce recursion and hence non-termination. Consider the following example.

Example 3.10 Let P_0 be the following initial program.

```
c1:   z ← p, r.
c2:   p ← q, r.
c3:   q ← r, p.
```

Where $P_{new} = \{c1\}$ and $P_{old} = \{c2, c3\}$. Notice that r is not defined anywhere, so everything fails and this program is left terminating. By unfolding p in c1 we obtain the following clause:

```
c4:   z ← q, r, r.
```

By further unfolding q in c4 we obtain:

```
c5:   z ← r, p, r, r.
```

Now we switch the first two atoms, obtaining:

```
c6:   z ← p, r, r, r.
```

Notice that this particular switch operation *does preserve left termination*. However, if we now fold the first two atoms, using clause c1 for folding, we obtain the following:

```
c7:   z ← z, r, r.
```

which is not left terminating any longer.   □

Here, we have a situation in which the switch operation does preserve left termination in a *local* way while left termination will subsequently be destroyed by the application of the fold operation. Notice also that such a fold operation satisfies any of the conditions **C1**, ..., **C4**. This shows that the switch operation requires applicability conditions which guarantee more than the termination properties of the actual program.

In [BCE96b] we propose a transformation system for definite programs based on unfold, fold and switch, which when applied to a left terminating moded program, yields a program which is left terminating as well. For this, we employ a new condition for the fold operation. Namely if $cl : H \leftarrow \mathbf{J}, \mathbf{B}, \mathbf{K}$. is the clause to be folded in **B**, instead of **C1**, we require that:

(C5) either cl defines an old atom, or one of the atoms in **J** or the leftmost in **B** comes from a previous unfolding.

(actually, this is not exactly the condition reported in [BCE96b], however, it is substantially equivalent to it, and this formulation allows us to compare it to the other ones reported here). This condition is clearly stronger than **C1** but weaker than **C3**. Then, the concept of transformation sequence is extended so that it includes the switch operation, for which specific applicability conditions are devised. The first applicability condition, introduced in [BCE96b] applies to moded programs and states that switching the atom A with B in the clause $cl : H \leftarrow \ldots, A, B, \ldots$. is *allowed* if

(SW2) A is an *old* literal, $Var(Out(A)) \cap Var(In(B)) = \emptyset$, and A is *non-failing* in cl,

where *non-failing in cl* means that any instance of A, selected by the leftmost selection rule when cl is used in the resolution process, will eventually succeed[2]. The intuitive idea is that if A is non-failing, then it cannot "hide" any potential loops of the following atoms, hence we are allowed to move it to the right. A drawback is that the condition of being non-failing is generally non-computable, but for very particular classes of programs and queries [BC98], *noFD programs and queries*, which cannot have finitely failing LD-derivations, the non-failing property can be trivially guaranteed.

In [BCE00] we extend this transformation system for definite programs, by using the dual reasoning: If an atom B "never loops" then we should be able to move it *leftward*. This intuitive reasoning is not entirely true (the counterexample is still Example 3.10), however, it yields a new syntactic-based condition for guaranteeing the preservation of left termination, provided that the definition of B is never modified by the transformation. For this we need a new definition of initial program:

Definition 3.11 (Initial Program) We call a program P_0 an *initial program* if it can be partitioned into three programs P_{new}, P_{old} and P_{base}, such that the following conditions are satisfied:

(I1) $P_{new} \sqsupseteq (P_{old} \cup P_{base})$ and $P_{old} \sqsupseteq P_{base}$;
(I2) P_{new} is not recursive;
(I3) all the literals in the bodies of the clauses of P_{old} are labelled "f", with the exception of literals defined in P_{base}; no other literal of the initial program is labelled.

We assume that the transformation does not affect the clauses in P_{base}. Then we obtain this new applicability condition for the switch operation: Switching the literal A with B in the clause $cl : H \leftarrow \dots, A, B, \dots$. is *allowed* if

(SW1) B is a *base* literal.

This condition allows for a complex theorem which has a number of different modular results on termination. To mention two of them which apply to definite programs: Let $P_0, \dots, P_n$ be a transformation sequence in our system (where every fold satisfies **C5** and in which every switch operation is allowed) then we have that

- If P_0 is left terminating and P_{base} always left terminating, then P_n is also left terminating.
- If P_0 is well moded and left terminating and P_{base} well-terminating, then P_n is also left terminating.

---

[2] Again, this is a conservative approximation of the more complex notion of non-failing used in [BCE96b].

Summarizing, in [BCE96a, BCE00] we propose a transformation system for definite programs with fold satisfying **C5** and a switch operation with special applicability conditions. Such system – intuitively speaking – maintains left termination together with the usual declarative properties.

Our system is appropriate for the paradigm *logic programming + leftmost selection rule*. At the same time it is not suitable for Prolog with built-ins: For instance it employs an unfolding operation which allows for left-propagation. Moreover *the switch operation can cause permutations in the sequence of answers substitutions*, which, as we have seen before, in the case of full Prolog can have serious consequences on the operational behaviour of the program.

Prolog and Partial Evaluation In general, the term partial evaluation indicates a transformation system which does not include the fold operation. To this rule there are important exceptions. In the first place, the PADDY system [Pre92] employs a fold operation which is based on the system of Proietti-Pettorossi [PP91] (yet with a different unfolding). Sahlin's Mixtus [Sah93] is an automatic partial evaluator for *full* Prolog which incorporates a fold operation. The latter operation employs further restrictions, among which that the folded conjunction (**B** in Definition 3.6) must consist of only one atom. Sahlin states: "Our experience indicates that the most important class of programs to be partially evaluated, the interpreters, folding for composite goals does not seem to be required for getting satisfactory results".

Finally, we should mention the work on *conjunctive partial deduction*. [SGJ+99]. Partial deduction in its usual form (i.e. without a fold operation) cannot achieve certain optimizations which are possible by unfold/fold transformations. Conjunctive partial deduction is an extension of partial deduction which allows for optimizations which are typical of an unfold/fold system, for instance tupling and deforestation. Intuitively speaking, this is achieved by extending the paradigm to one in which a head of a clause might consist of a *conjunction* of atoms. In its pure form, conjunctive partial deduction is correct wrt the declarative semantics of a program (basically wrt the least Herbrand model and the Computed Answer Substitutions semantics, however Finite Failure and other declarative semantics can also be accommodated). Clearly, these semantics are independent of the selection rule.

The authors in [SGJ+99] address also the problem of conjunctive partial deduction in presence of a fixed left-to-right selection rule. Interestingly, the authors come to the conclusion that one should "limit the splitting to contiguous atoms only", otherwise one might degrade program's performances or even introduce non-termination. Without getting into the details of the splitting operation, we notice that this is very similar to *forbidding any switching* of two atoms.

4   An Extended System: Replacement

We can obtain a much more powerful transformation system by adding to unfold and fold a further transformation operation: The replacement. Replacement allows one to substitute a sequence of literals in a clause body by an "equivalent" sequence of literals. What "equivalent" means depends on the chosen observables. We give here a very general definition.

Definition 4.1 (Replacement) Let $\mathbf{B}'$ be a sequence of literals defined in P, $c : H \leftarrow \mathbf{A}, \mathbf{B}, \mathbf{C}$. be a clause in P and let $c' : H \leftarrow \mathbf{A}, \mathbf{B}', \mathbf{C}$.
Let X be the set of *common variables* and Y be the set of *private variables in* $\mathbf{B}$ *and* $\mathbf{B}'$, namely $X = Var(\mathbf{B}) \cap Var(\mathbf{B}')$ and $Y = Var(\mathbf{B}, \mathbf{B}') \setminus X$.
Replacing $\mathbf{B}$ *by* $\mathbf{B}'$ *in* c consists in replacing c by c' if

(R1) *the variables in* Y *are local wrt* c *and* c', *that is* $Var(H, \mathbf{A}, \mathbf{C}) \cap Y = \emptyset$;
(R2) $\mathbf{B}$ *and* $\mathbf{B}'$ *are equivalent wrt the chosen semantics*, that is (with an extended notation on existential quantifiers) $\exists Y \mathbf{B} \equiv_S \exists Y \mathbf{B}'$, where S is a specified semantics.

Replacement may be used for applying algebraic laws as shown in the next example.

Example 4.2 Let a program P contain the clause

$c:$ p$(l_1, l_2, l_3, \mathbf{Z})$ $\leftarrow$ app$(l_1,\ l_2,\ \mathbf{Y1})$, app$(\mathbf{Y1},\ l_3,\ \mathbf{Z})$.

where *app* is the usual append predicate and l_1, l_2, l_3 are lists of fixed length. Let $\mathbf{B} = app(l_1, l_2, Y1), app(Y1, l_3, Z)$ and $\mathbf{B}' = app(l_2, l_3, Y2), app(l_1, Y2, Z)$. Replacing $\mathbf{B}$ by $\mathbf{B}'$ in c satisfies both the syntactic condition and the equivalence one. In fact this replacement corresponds to applying the *associative property* of append.

Replacement can also be used to eliminate or add literals to a clause body, what is called respectively *thin* and *fatten* operation in [BC93].

Clearly a transformation system including replacement has a much greater power and it allows for a deep restructuring of the initial program. A typical use of replacement is transforming non-linear recursive predicates into linear ones by introducing accumulators or difference-lists. It is also clear that such transformations are less automatizable and require more guidance from the programmer.

Notice also that fold can be considered as a special case of replacement. A transformation system containing replacement could then drop the fold operation. This was actually done by Cook and Gallagher in [CG94]. In fact they propose an elegant transformation system for definite programs based on two basic operations only: A particular form of unfold that we already described in Section 3.1 and replacement. The basic difference between folding and replacement is that in the first one there has to be a *folding clause*, which makes the operation of "syntactic nature", on the other hand, the replacement allows one to exchange any two sequences of literals, provided he can prove their equivalence. It is then a very general operation, whose applicability is typically undecidable.

Declarative Properties The first requirement in Definition 4.1 is syntactic correctness, namely private variables Y must not produce different bindings of **B** and **B**′ with their contexts c and c'. The second requirement imposes the equivalence of **B** and **B**′ wrt common variables in the chosen semantics. Many different instances of this second condition can be found in the literature.

- [GS91] requires that for all grounding θ, $P \models \mathbf{B}\theta$ implies $P \setminus \{c\} \models \mathbf{B}'\theta'$ and vice-versa that for all grounding θ, $P \models \mathbf{B}'\theta$ implies $P \setminus \{c\} \models \mathbf{B}\theta'$, where θ and θ' coincide on the variables occurring in $H, \mathbf{A}, \mathbf{C}$. This guarantees the preservation of the least Herbrand Model, M_P. They study replacement also in the context of general programs.
- In [Mah87], given that no predicate in **B** and **B**′ depends on $Pred(H)$, the equivalence must be provable in $comp(P)$; then it guarantees the preservation of the Success Set and of the Ground Finite Failure set in definite programs.
- In [BCE96a] a simultaneous replacement of many sequences of literals in many clauses is defined. The (rather complex) condition to be satisfied allows for dependencies between replaced sequences of literals and modified clauses and still it guarantees to preserve the Fitting's and Kunen's semantics of general programs.
- In [PP94b] the equivalence condition is parametric wrt the semantics and it depends on $P \setminus \{c\}$. In order to prove it, Pettorossi and Proietti propose unfold/fold proofs for definite and gneral programs which are naturally parametric wrt the semantics.

Termination Properties Let us consider now more procedural properties such as termination ones. First notice that when we consider control issues, the order of literals in the bodies becomes relevant also for replacement. Note also that replacement itself can be used for reordering literals.

As previously mentioned, Cook and Gallagher in [CG94] define a transformation system for definite programs based only on a particular unfold and replacement. Such replacement depends on (semantic equivalence +) termination analysis, namely it requires a property of termination (or left termination if we consider the Prolog leftmost selection rule) which must hold on the resulting program. This condition ensures that the system preserves the Success Set. If a similar termination property is required also on the program to be transformed, then the system preserves also the Finite Failure Set. The authors suggest to check such termination properties a posteriori, by means of any known technique for verifying termination properties, but they also claim that one could devise sufficient conditions for the applicability of such replacement.

In [BC97] we extend our simple unfold/fold system for definite programs presented in [BC94], which preserves universal termination of a query with *LD-resolution*. For reordering atoms in the bodies, we introduce also a replacement operation. In order to guarantee the non-increasing property also for replacement, besides conditions **R1** and **R2** (referred to the semantics given by Computed Answer Substitutions plus universal termination for a query), we impose a further restriction on replacement, namely that

(R3) B' *is non-increasing in c wrt* **B** *in P*.

This basically means that for any substitution θ, instantiating only common variables, any partial LD-derivation of $\mathbf{B}'\theta$ is not longer than a corresponding one of $\mathbf{B}\theta$.

We also study how typing information and the well-typing property can simplify the verification of such applicability conditions for replacement. In fact the major problem is how to verify in practice such applicability conditions for preserving universal termination since they are semantic conditions and operational in style, not decidable in general.

5   Conclusions

Virtuous programming methodology which consists in focusing on correctness of programs at first and on their efficiency only afterwards, fits particularly well with logic programming [Kow79, Dev90]. This encourages the application of transformation systems to logic programs both for synthesizing a correct program from a logic specification and for optimizing it.

The main requirements for a practical transformation systems are on one hand to guarantee the preservation of interesting program properties and on the other hand to be supported by an automatic or semi-automatic tool. Among interesting properties the most basic are captured by declarative semantics, but nondeclarative properties are also extremely relevant, such as the termination of the program.

In this paper we give a short description of the systems proposed for logic program transformation. In particular, we focus on systems able to preserve termination and other nondeclarative properties in Prolog programs.

We consider at first simple unfold/fold systems and then more powerful ones including the replacement or at least the switch operation. Transformation systems can include other basic transformation operations, either obtainable through a combination of the previous ones or completely independent from them. Since any transformation system proposes his own set of basic operations, we decided to restrict our comparison only to the main ones: New definition, unfold, fold and replacement. Such set of operations gives rise to systems which are powerful enough for dealing with most applications of program transformation.

Since we focus on nondeclarative properties of Prolog programs, we have not given a detailed account of the various results on declarative semantic, neither we consider transformation systems dealing with extended logic programming paradigms, such as CLP, or with modified interpreters. For a rather complete panorama of recent proposals in the field of logic programs transformations the LOPSTR proceedings are a good reference [LOP].

References

[AB91]   K. R. Apt and M. Bezem. Acyclic programs. *New Generation Computing*, 9(3&4):335–363, 1991.

184   Annalisa Bossi, Nicoletta Cocco, and Sandro Etalle

[AD93]   C. Aravidan and P. M. Dung. On the correctness of Unfold/Fold transfor-
            mation of normal and extended logic programs. Technical report, Division
            of Computer Science, Asian Institute of Technology, Bangkok, Thailand,
            April 1993.
[AD94]   C. Aravidan and P. M. Dung. Partial Deduction of Logic Programs w.r.t.
            Well-Founded Semantics. *New Generation Computing*, 13:45–74, 1994.
[Amt92]   T. Amtoft. Unfold/fold transformations preserving termination proper-
            ties. In *Proceedings PLILP'92*, number 631 in Lecture Notes in Computer
            Science, pages 187–201. Springer-Verlag, 1992.
[AP90]   K. R. Apt and D. Pedreschi. Studies in pure Prolog: termination. In J.W.
            Lloyd, editor, *Symposium on Computional Logic*, pages 150–176, Berlin,
            1990. Springer-Verlag.
[AP93]   K. R. Apt and D. Pedreschi. Reasoning about termination of pure Prolog
            programs. *Information and Computation*, 106(1):109–157, 1993.
[Apt97]   K. R. Apt. *From Logic Programming to Prolog*. Prentice Hall, 1997.
[Bau89]   M. Baudinet. *Logic Programming Semantics: Techniques and Applications*.
            PhD thesis, Stanford University, Stanford, California, 1989.
[BC93]   A. Bossi and N. Cocco. Basic Transformation Operations which preserve
            Computed Answer Substitutions of Logic Programs. *Journal of Logic Pro-
            gramming*, 16(1&2):47–87, 1993.
[BC94]   A. Bossi and N. Cocco. Preserving universal termination trough un-
            fold/fold. In G. Levi and M. Rodríguez-Artalejo, editors, *Proc. Fourth
            Int'l Conf. on Algebraic and Logic Programming*, volume 850 of *Lecture
            Notes in Computer Science*, pages 269–286. Springer-Verlag, Berlin, 1994.
[BC97]   A. Bossi and N. Cocco. Replacement can preserve termination. In J. Gal-
            lagher, editor, *Proc. Sixth Workshop on Logic Program Synthesis and
            Transformation*, volume 1207 of *Lecture Notes in Computer Science*, pages
            104–129. Springer-Verlag, Berlin, 1997.
[BC98]   A. Bossi and N. Cocco. Programs without failures. In R. Fuchs, editor,
            Proc. Seventh Workshop on Logic Program Synthesis and Transformation,
            volume 1463 of *Lecture Notes in Computer Science*, pages 28–48. Springer-
            Verlag, Berlin, 1998.
[BCE92]   A. Bossi, N. Cocco, and S. Etalle. Transforming Normal Programs by
            Replacement. In A. Pettorossi, editor, *Meta Programming in Logic - Pro-
            ceedings META'92*, volume 649 of *Lecture Notes in Computer Science*,
            pages 265–279. Springer-Verlag, Berlin, 1992.
[BCE96a]   A. Bossi, N. Cocco, and S. Etalle. Simultaneous replacement in normal
            programs. *Journal of Logic and Computation*, 6(1):79–120, February 1996.
[BCE96b]   A. Bossi, N. Cocco, and S. Etalle. Transformation of Left Terminating Pro-
            grams: the Reordering Problem. In M. Proietti, editor, *LOPSTR95 – Fifth
            International Workshop on Logic Program Synthesis and Transformation*,
            number 1048 in LNCS, pages 33–45. Springer-Verlag, 1996.
[BCE00]   A. Bossi, N. Cocco, and S. Etalle. Transformation of Left Terminating
            Programs. In A. Bossi, editor, *Ninth International Workshop on Logic
            Program Synthesis and Transformation*, number 1817 in LNCS, pages 156–
            175. Springer-Verlag, 2000.
[BCER01]   A. Bossi, N. Cocco, S. Etalle, and S. Rossi. Termination in a hierarchy
            of general logic programs. Technical Report CS-2001-05, Dipartimento di
            Informatica, Università Ca' Foscari Di Venezia, Italy, March 2001.
[BD77]   R.M. Burstall and J. Darlington. A transformation system for developing
            recursive programs. *Journal of the ACM*, 24(1):44–67, January 1977.

[BE94]   A. Bossi and S. Etalle. Transforming Acyclic Programs. *ACM Transactions on Programming Languages and Systems*, 16(4):1081–1096, July 1994.

[BR89]   M. Bugliesi and F. Rossi. Partial evaluation in Prolog: Some improvements about cut. In E.L. Lusk and R.A. Overbeek, editors, *Logic Programming: Proceedings of the North American Conference 1989, Cleveland, Ohio, October 1989*, pages 645–660. MIT Press, 1989.

[Cav89]   L. Cavedon. Continuity, consistency and completeness properties for logic programs. In G. Levi and M. Martelli, editors, *6 International Conference on Logic Programming*, pages 571–584. MIT press, 1989.

[CG94]   J. Cook and J.P. Gallagher. A transformation system for definite programs based on termination analysis. In F. Turini, editor, *Proc. Fourth Workshop on Logic Program Synthesis and Transformation*, pages 51–68. Springer-Verlag, 1994.

[Cla78]   K. L. Clark. Negation as failure rule. In H. Gallaire and G. Minker, editors, *Logic and Data Bases*, pages 293–322. Plenum Press, 1978.

[Dev90]   Y. Deville. *Logic Programming. Systematic Program Development*. Addison-Wesley, 1990.

[DM88]   W. Drabent and J. Maluszynski. Inductive assertion method for logic programs. *Theoretical Computer Science*, 59:133–155, 1988.

[EBC99]   S. Etalle, A. Bossi, and N. Cocco. Termination of well-moded programs. *Journal of Logic Programming*, 38(2):243–257, 1999.

[FLMP93]   M. Falaschi, G. Levi, M. Martelli, and C. Palamidessi. A Model-Theoretic Reconstruction of the Operational Semantics of Logic Programs. *Information and Computation*, 102(1):86–113, 1993.

[Gal91]   J. P. Gallagher. A system for specializing logic programs. Technical Report 91-32, University of Bristol, 1991.

[GS91]   P.A. Gardner and J.C. Shepherdson. Unfold/fold transformations of logic programs. In J-L Lassez and G. Plotkin, editors, *Computational Logic: Essays in Honor of Alan Robinson*. MIT Press, 1991.

[JM84]   N. Jones and A. Mycroft. Stepwise Development of Operational and Denotational Semantics for Prolog. In Sten-Åke Tärnlund, editor, *Proc. Second Int'l Conf. on Logic Programming*, pages 281–288, 1984.

[KK90]   T. Kawamura and T. Kanamori. Preservation of Stronger Equivalence in Unfold/Fold Logic Programming Transformation. *Theoretical Computer Science*, 75(1&2):139–156, 1990.

[Kow79]   R. Kowalski. Algorithm = Logic + Control. *Communications of the ACM*, 22(7):424–436, 1979.

[Llo87]   J. W. Lloyd. *Foundations of Logic Programming*. Symbolic Computation – Artificial Intelligence. Springer-Verlag, Berlin, 1987. Second edition.

[LMS98]   M. Leuschel, B. Martens, and D. De Schreye. Controlling Generalisation and Polyvariance in Partial Deduction of Normal Logic Programs. *ACM Transactions on Programming Languages and Systems (TOPLAS)*, 20(1):208–258, 1998.

[LOP]   International Workshops on Logic Program Synthesis and Transformation. http://www.cs.man.ac.uk/ kung-kiu/lopstr/.

[LS88]   G. Levi and G. Sardu. Partial evaluation of metaprograms in a multiple worlds logic language. *New Generation Computing*, 6(2,3):227–247, 1988.

[LS91]   J. W. Lloyd and J. C. Shepherdson. Partial Evaluation in Logic Programming. *Journal of Logic Programming*, 11:217–242, 1991.

[Mah87]   M.J. Maher. Correctness of a logic program transformation system. IBM Research Report RC13496, T.J. Watson Research Center, 1987.

[PP91]   M. Proietti and A. Pettorossi. Semantics preserving transformation rules
           for Prolog. In *ACM SIGPLAN Symposium on Partial Evaluation and
           Semantics-Based Program Manipulation (PEPM '91), New Haven, CT
           (U.S.A.) (SIGPLAN NOTICES, Vol.26 (9))*, pages 274–284. ACM press,
           1991.
[PP94a]   A. Pettorossi and M. Proietti. Transformation of Logic Programs: Foun-
           dations and Techniques. *Journal of Logic Programming*, 19(20):261–320,
           1994.
[PP94b]   M. Proietti and A. Pettorossi. Total correctness of a goal replacement rule
           based of the unfold/fold proof method. In M. Alpuente, editor, *Proc. 1994
           Joint Conference on Declarative Programming GULP-PRODE'94*, pages
           347–358. Springer-Verlag, 1994.
[Pre92]   S. Prestwich. The PADDY partial deduction system. Technical Report
           92-6, ECRC GmbH, Munich, Germany, 1992.
[Pre93]   S. Prestwich. An Unfold Rule for full Prolog. In K.K. Lau and T. Clement,
           editors, *Proceedings LOPSTR'92*, Workshops in Computing, pages 199–
           213. Springer-Verlag, Berlin, 1993.
[Sah93]   D. Sahlin. Mixtus: An automatic partial evaluator for full Prolog. *New
           Generation Computing*, (12):7–51, 1993.
[Sek91]   H. Seki. Unfold/fold transformation of stratified programs. *Theoretical
           Computer Science*, 86(1):107–139, 1991.
[Sek93]   H. Seki. Unfold/fold transformation of general logic programs for the Well-
           Founded semantics. *Journal of Logic Programming*, 16(1&2):5–23, 1993.
[SGJ⁺99]   D. De Schreye, R. Glück, Jesper Jørgensen, M. Leuschel, B. Martens, and
           M. H. Sørensen. Conjunctive partial deduction: foundations, control, algo-
           rithms, and experiments. *Journal of Logic Programming*, 41(2-3):231–277,
           1999.
[ST84]   T. Sato and H. Tamaki. Transformational logic program systhesis. In
           *International Conference on Fifth Generation Computer Systems, Tokyo,
           Japan, November 1984*, pages 195–201. ICOT, 1984.
[TS84]   H. Tamaki and T. Sato. Unfold/Fold Transformations of Logic Programs.
           In Sten-Åke Tärnlund, editor, *Proc. Second Int'l Conf. on Logic Program-
           ming*, pages 127–139, 1984.
[VP86]   T. Vasak and J. Potter. Characterization of Terminating Logic Programs.
           In *Proc. Third IEEE Int'l Symp. on Logic Programming*, pages 140–147.
           IEEE Comp. Soc. Press, 1986.

Acceptability with General Orderings

Danny De Schreye and Alexander Serebrenik

Department of Computer Science, K.U. Leuven
Celestijnenlaan 200A, B-3001, Heverlee, Belgium
{Danny.DeSchreye, Alexander.Serebrenik}@cs.kuleuven.ac.be

Abstract. We present a new approach to termination analysis of logic programs. The essence of the approach is that we make use of general orderings (instead of level mappings), like it is done in transformational approaches to logic program termination analysis, but we apply these orderings directly to the logic program and not to the term-rewrite system obtained through some transformation. We define some variants of acceptability, based on general orderings, and show how they are equivalent to LD-termination. We develop a demand driven, constraint-based approach to verify these acceptability-variants.

The advantage of the approach over standard acceptability is that in some cases, where complex level mappings are needed, fairly simple orderings may be easily generated. The advantage over transformational approaches is that it avoids the transformation step all together.

Keywords: termination analysis, acceptability, orderings.

1 Introduction

It is not uncommon in research to have different research communities that tackle a same problem from a very different perspective or using totally different techniques. In some cases, such communities may co-exist for many years without much integration, cross-fertilisation or even decent comparison of the relative merits and drawbacks of competing approaches.

In the context of termination analysis of logic programs, two such sub-communities are those who develop and apply "transformational" approaches and those working on "direct" ones. A transformational approach first transforms the logic program into an "equivalent" term-rewrite system (or, in some cases, into an equivalent functional program). Here, equivalence means that, at the very least, the termination of the term-rewrite system should imply the termination of the logic program, for some predefined collection of queries[1]. Direct approaches do not include such a transformation, but prove the termination directly on the basis of the logic program.

Besides the transformation step itself, there is one other technical difference between these approaches. Direct approaches usually prove termination on the

---

[1] The approach of Arts [5] is exceptional in the sense that the termination of the logic program is concluded from a weaker property of *single-redex normalisation* of the term-rewrite system.

A.C. Kakas, F. Sadri (Eds.): Computat. Logic (Kowalski Festschrift), LNAI 2407, pp. 187–210, 2002.
© Springer-Verlag Berlin Heidelberg 2002

basis of a well-founded ordering over the natural numbers. More specifically, they use a *level mapping*, which maps atoms to natural numbers, and, they verify appropriate decreases of this level mapping on the atoms occurring in the clauses. On the other hand, transformational approaches make use of more general well-founded orderings over terms, such as reduction orderings, or more specifically simplification orderings, or others (see [14]).

At least for the direct approaches the systematic choice for level mappings and *norms*—functions which map each term (module variable renaming) to a corresponding natural number—instead of general orderings, seems arbitrary and ad hoc. More generally, the relative merits and drawbacks of these two lines of work are not well understood. This has been the main motivation for this paper. We present an initial study on the use of general well-founded orderings as a means of directly proving the termination of logic programs—without intermediate transformation. In particular,

- we study whether the theoretical results on acceptability can be reformulated on the basis of general orderings,
- we evaluate to what extent the use of the general orderings (instead of level mappings) either improves or deteriorates the direct approaches.

To illustrate the latter point, consider the following program, that formulates some of the rules for computing the repeated derivative of a linear function in one variable u (see also [16]) :

Example 1.

$d(der(u), 1).$

$d(der(A), 0) \leftarrow number(A).$

$d(der(X + Y), DX + DY) \leftarrow d(der(X), DX), d(der(Y), DY).$

$d(der(X * Y), X * DY + Y * DX) \leftarrow d(der(X), DX), d(der(Y), DY).$

$d(der(der(X)), DDX) \leftarrow d(der(X), DX), d(der(DX), DDX).$

We are interested in proving LD-termination, i.e., finiteness of the SLD-tree constructed using the left-to-right selection rule of Prolog, of the program above together with the queries of the form $d(t, v)$, where t is a term, expressing a derivative of a linear function in one variable u, such as $der(der(u * u * u + 3 * u * u + 3 * u + 1))$, and v is a fresh variable, that will be unified with the result of the computation.

Doing this on the basis of a level-mapping is hard. For this example, a level-mapping that decreases between two sequential calls of d is a non-linear function. In particular, a level mapping $| \cdot |$, and a norm $\| \cdot \|$, such that: $|d(X, Y)| = \|X\|$, $|number(X)| = 0$, $\|der(X)\| = 2^{\|X\|}$, $\|X + Y\| = max(\|X\|, \|Y\|) + 1$, $\|X * Y\| = max(\|X\|, \|Y\|) + 1$, $\|u\| = 2$, $\|n\| = 2$,   if n is a number, would be needed. No automatic system for proving termination on the basis of level mappings is able to generate such mappings. Moreover, we believe, that it would be very difficult to extend existing systems to support generation of appropriate non-linear mappings.   □

Although we have not yet presented our general-well-founded ordering approach, it should be intuitively clear, that we can capture the decrease in ordering between the $der(X)$ and DX by using an ordering on terms that gives the highest "priority" to the functor der.

On the other hand, using level mappings and norms allows sometimes to explore more precise information on atoms and terms, that cannot be expressed by general orderings, such as arithmetical relations between terms. This information can sometimes be crucial in proving termination as the following program from [10, 13] demonstrates.

Example 2.

$$conf(X) \leftarrow delete_2(X, Z), delete(U, Y, Z), conf(Y).$$
$$delete_2(X, Y) \leftarrow delete(U, X, Z), delete(V, Z, Y).$$
$$delete(X, [X|T], T).$$
$$delete(X, [H|T], [H|T1]) \leftarrow delete(X, T, T1).$$

Note that by reasoning in terms of sizes of terms, we can infer that the size decreases by 2 after the call to $delete_2$ predicate in the first clause and then increases by 1 in the subsequent call to the $delete$ predicate. In total, sizes allow us to conclude a decrease. Reasoning in terms of ordering relations only, however, does not allow to conclude the overall decrease from the facts that the third argument of $delete$ predicate is smaller (with respect to some $>$) than the second one and that the first argument of $delete_2$ predicate is greater (with respect to $>$) than the second one. □

As can be expected, theoretically both approaches are essentially equivalent. We will introduce a variant of the notion of acceptability, based on general orderings, which is again equivalent to termination in a similar way as in the level mapping based approach. On the more practical level, as illustrated in the two examples above, neither of the approaches is strictly better: the general orderings provide a larger set of orderings to select from (in particular, note that orderings based on level mappings and norms are general orderings), the level mapping approach provides arithmetic, on top of mere ordering.

In the remainder of this paper, we will start off from a variant of the notion of *acceptability with respect to a set*, as introduced in [11], obtained by replacing level mappings by orderings. We show how this variant of acceptability remains equivalent to termination under the left-to-right selection rule, for certain goals. Then, we illustrate how this result can be used to prove termination with some examples. We also provide a variant of the *acceptability* condition, as introduced in [4], and discuss advantages and disadvantages of each approach. Next, we discuss automation of the approach. We elaborate on a demand-driven method to set-up and verify sufficient preconditions for termination. In this method, the aim is to derive—in, as much as possible, a constructive way—a well-founded ordering over the set of all atoms and terms of the language underlying the program, that satisfies the termination condition.

2   Preliminaries

2.1   Logic Programs

We follow the standard notation for terms and atoms. A *query* is a finite sequence of atoms. Given an atom A, $rel(A)$ denotes the predicate occurring in A. $Term_P$ and $Atom_P$ denote, respectively, sets of all terms and atoms that can be constructed from the language underlying P. The extended Herbrand Universe U_P^E (the extended Herbrand base B_P^E) is a quotient set of $Term_P$ ($Atom_P$) modulo the variant relation.

We refer to an SLD-tree constructed using the left-to-right selection rule of Prolog, as an LD-tree. We will say that a goal G *LD-terminates* for a program P, if the LD-tree for (P, G) is finite.

The following definition is borrowed from [2].

Definition 1. *Let P be a program and p, q be predicates occurring in it.*

- *We say that p refers to q in P if there is a clause in P that uses p in its head and q in its body.*
- *We say that p depends on q in P and write $p \sqsupseteq q$, if (p, q) is in the transitive, reflexive closure of the relation refers to.*
- *We say that p and q are mutually recursive and write $p \simeq q$, if $p \sqsupseteq q$ and $q \sqsupseteq p$.*

2.2   Quasi-Orderings and Orderings

A *quasi-ordering* over a set S is a reflexive and transitive relation $\geq$ defined on elements of S. We define the associated equivalence relation $\leq\geq$ as $s \leq\geq t$ if and only if $s \geq t$ and $t \geq s$, and the associated *ordering* $>$ as $s > t$ if and only if $s \geq t$ but not $t \geq s$. If neither $s \geq t$, nor $t \geq s$ we write $s\|_{>}t$. Sometimes, in order to distinguish between different quasi-orderings and associated relations we also use $\succeq$, $\succ$, $\preceq\succeq$ and $\|_{\succ}$.

An ordered set S is said to be *well-founded* if there are no infinite descending sequences $s_1 > s_2 > \ldots$ of elements of S. If the set S is clear from the context we will say that the ordering, defined on it, is well-founded. We'll also say that a quasi-ordering is well-founded if the ordering associated with it, is well-founded.

Definition 2. *Let $\geq$ be a quasi-ordering on a set T. A quasi-ordering $\succeq$ defined on a set $S \supseteq T$ is called a proper extension of $\geq$ if*

- *$t_1 \geq t_2$ implies $t_1 \succeq t_2$ for all $t_1, t_2 \in T$.*
- *$t_1 > t_2$ implies $t_1 \succ t_2$ for all $t_1, t_2 \in T$.*

The study of termination of term-rewriting systems caused intensive study of orderings on terms. A number of useful properties were established.

Definition 3. *Let* $>$ *be an ordering on* $U_P^E \cup B_P^E$.

- $>$ *is called* monotonic *if* $s_1 > s_2$ *implies* $f(\bar{t}_1, s_1, \bar{t}_2) > f(\bar{t}_1, s_2, \bar{t}_2)$ *and* $p(\bar{t}_1, s_1, \bar{t}_2) > p(\bar{t}_1, s_2, \bar{t}_2)$ *for any terms* s_1 *and* s_2, *sequences of terms* $\bar{t}_1$ *and* $\bar{t}_2$, *function symbol* f *and predicate* p.
- $>$ *is said to have the* subterm property *if* $f(\bar{t}_1, s, \bar{t}_2) > s$ *holds for any term* $f(\bar{t}_1, s, \bar{t}_2)$.

We extend the definition above to quasi-orderings.

Definition 4. *Let* $\geq$ *be a quasi-ordering on terms.*

- $\geq$ *is called* monotonic *if*
  - $s_1 \geq s_2$ *implies* $f(\bar{t}_1, s_1, \bar{t}_2) \geq f(\bar{t}_1, s_2, \bar{t}_2)$ *and* $p(\bar{t}_1, s_1, \bar{t}_2) \geq p(\bar{t}_1, s_2, \bar{t}_2)$ *for any terms* s_1 *and* s_2, *sequences of terms* $\bar{t}_1$ *and* $\bar{t}_2$, *function symbol* f *and predicate* p *and*
  - *the associated ordering is monotonic.*
- $\geq$ *is said to have the* subterm property *if the associated ordering has the subterm property.*

The following are examples of orderings: $>$ on the set of numbers, lexicographic ordering on the set of strings (this is the way the entries are ordered in dictionaries), multiset ordering and recursive path ordering [14]. The following are examples of quasi-orderings: $\geq$ on the set of numbers, $\supseteq$ on the power set of some set.

For our purposes monotonicity and subterm properties are too restrictive. Thus, we assign to each predicate or functor a subset of argument positions, such that for the argument positions in this subset the specified properties hold. We will say that a predicate p (a functor f) is monotone (has a subterm property) on a specified subset of argument positions. The formal study of these weaker notions may be found in [27].

Example 3. Let f be a functor of arity two, and a, b two terms, such that $a > b$. Let f be monotone in the first argument position. Then, $f(a, c) > f(b, c)$ holds for any term c, but there might be some term c, such that $f(c, a) \not> f(c, b)$.

3   Order-Acceptability with Respect to a Set

In this section we present and discuss some of the theory we developed to extend acceptability to general orderings. In the literature, there are different variants of acceptability. The most well-known of these is the acceptability as introduced by Apt and Pedreschi [4]. This version is defined and verified on the level of ground instances of clauses, but draws its practical power mostly from the fact that termination is proved for *any bounded* goal. Here, boundedness is a notion related to the selected level mapping and requires that the set $\{|G\theta| \mid \theta \text{ is a grounding substitution for goal } G\}$ is bounded in the natural numbers, where $|\cdot| : B_P \to \mathcal{N}$ denotes the level mapping.

Another notion of acceptability is the "acceptability with respect to a set of goals", introduced in [11]. This notion allows to prove termination with respect to any set of goals of interest. However, it relies on procedural concepts, such as calls and computed answer substitution. It was designed to be verified through global analysis, for instance through abstract interpretation.

A variant of acceptability with respect to a set that avoids the drawbacks of using procedural notions and that can be verified on a local level was designed in [13]. This variant required that the goals of interest are *rigid* under the given level mapping. Here, rigidity means that $|G\theta| = |G|$, for any substitution θ, where $|\cdot| : B_P^E \to \mathcal{N}$ now denotes a generalised level mapping, defined on the extended Herbrand base.

Comparing the notions of boundedness and rigidity in the context of a level mapping based approach, it is clear that boundedness is more general than rigidity. If the level mapping of a goal is invariant under substitution, then the level mapping is bounded on the set of instances of the goal, but not conversely.

Given the latter observation and given that acceptability of [4] is a more generally known and accepted notion, we started our work by generalising this variant.

However, it turned out that generalising the concept of boundedness to general orderings proved to be very difficult. We postpone the discussion on this issue until after we formulated the results, but because of these complications, we only arrived at generalised acceptability conditions that are useful in the context of well-moded and simply moded programs and goals.

Because of this, we then turned our attention to acceptability with respect to a set. Here, the generalisation of rigidity was less complicated, so that in the end we obtained the strongest results for this variant of acceptability. Therefore, we first present order-acceptability with respect to a set of goals. We need the following notion.

Definition 5. *[12] Let P be a definite program and S be a set of atomic queries. The* call set, *$Call(P, S)$, is the set of all atoms A, such that a variant of A is a selected atom in some derivation for $P \cup \{\leftarrow Q\}$, for some $Q \in S$ and under the left-to-right selection rule.*

To illustrate this definition recall the following example [2, 13].

Example 4.

$$permute([], []).$$
$$permute(L, [El|T]) \leftarrow delete(El, L, L1), permute(L1, T).$$
$$delete(X, [X|T], T).$$
$$delete(X, [H|T], [H|T1]) \leftarrow delete(X, T, T1).$$

Let S be $\{permute(t_1, t_2) | t_1$ is a nil-terminated list and t_2 is a free variable$\}$. Then, $Call(P, S) =$

$S \cup \{delete(t_1, t_2, t_3) | t_1, t_3$ are free variables and t_2 is a nil-terminated list$\}$.

Such information about S could for instance be expressed in terms of the rigid types of Janssens and Bruynooghe [21] and $Call(P, S)$ could be computed using the type inference of [21]. □

The following definition generalises the notion of acceptability with respect to a set [12] in two ways: 1) it generalises it to general quasi-orderings, 2) it generalises it to mutual recursion, using the standard notion of mutual recursion [2].

Definition 6. *Let S be a set of atomic queries and P a definite program. P is order-acceptable with respect to S if there exists a well-founded quasi-ordering $\geq$, such that*

- *for any $A \in Call(P, S)$*
- *for any clause $A' \leftarrow B_1, \ldots, B_n$ in P, such that $\mathrm{mgu}(A, A') = \theta$ exists,*
- *for any atom B_i, such that $rel(B_i) \simeq rel(A)$*
- *for any computed answer substitution σ for $\leftarrow (B_1, \ldots, B_{i-1})\theta$:*

$$A > B_i \theta \sigma.$$

The following establishes the connection between order-acceptability with respect to a set S and LD-termination for queries in S.

Theorem 1. *Let P be a program. P is order-acceptable with respect to a set of atomic queries S if and only if P is LD-terminating for all queries in S.*

Proof. For all proofs we refer to [27].

We postpone applying the Theorem 1 to Example 4 until a more syntactic way of verifying order-acceptability with respect to a set is developed.

To do this, we extend the sufficient condition of [13], that imposes the additional requirement of rigidity of the level mapping on the call set, to the case of general quasi-orderings.

First we adapt the notion of rigidity to general orderings.

Definition 7. *(see also [8]) The term or atom $A \in U_P^E \cup B_P^E$ is called rigid with respect to a quasi-ordering $\geq$ if for any substitution θ, $A \leq \geq A\theta$. In this case $\geq$ is said to be rigid on A.*

The notion of the rigidity on a term (an atom) is naturally extended to the notion of rigidity on a set of atoms (terms). In particular, we will be interested in quasi-orderings that are rigid on $Call(P, S)$ for some P and S.

We also need interargument relations based on general orderings.

Definition 8. *Let P be a definite program, p a predicate in P with arity n. An interargument relation is a relation $R_p \subseteq \{p(t_1, \ldots, t_n) \mid t_i \in Term_P\}$. R_p is a valid interargument relation for p if and only if for every $p(t_1, \ldots, t_n) \in Atom_P$: if $P \models p(t_1, \ldots, t_n)$ then $p(t_1, \ldots, t_n) \in R_p$.*

Usually, the interargument relation will be defined based on a quasi-ordering used for proving termination. However, in general, this need not be the case.

Example 5. Consider the following program.

$$p(0, []).$$
$$p(f(X), [X|T]) \leftarrow p(X, T).$$

The following interargument relations can be considered for p: $\{p(t_1, t_2) \mid t_2 > t_1 \vee t_1 \leq \geq t_2\}$, valid if $\geq$ is a quasi-ordering imposed by a list-length norm, $\| \cdot \|_l$. Recall, that for lists $\|[t_1|t_2]\|_l = 1 + \|t_2\|_l$, while the list-length of other terms is considered to be 0. On the other hand, $\{p(t_1, t_2) \mid t_1 > t_2 \vee t_1 \leq \geq t_2\}$ is valid, if $\geq$ is a quasi-ordering imposed by a term-size norm.

Using general (non-norm based) quasi-orderings, $\{p(t_1, t_2) \mid t_1 > t_2\}$ is valid, for example, for the recursive path ordering [14] with the following ordering on functors: $f/1 \succ ./2$, where $./2$ is a function symbol defining lists, and $0 \succ []$. Alternatively, $\{p(t_1, t_2) \mid t_2 > t_1\}$ is valid, for example, for the recursive path ordering with the following ordering on functors: $./2 \succ f/1$ and $[] \succ 0$. □

Using the notion of rigidity we state a sufficient condition for order-acceptability with respect to a set.

Theorem 2. *(rigid order-acceptability with respect to S) Let S be a set of atomic queries and P be a definite program. Let $\geq$ be a quasi-ordering on U_P^E and for each predicate p in P, let R_p be a valid interargument relation for p. If there exists a well-founded proper extension $\succeq$ of $\geq$ to $U_P^E \cup B_P^E$, which is rigid on Call(P, S) such that*

- *for any clause $H \leftarrow B_1, \ldots, B_n \in P$, and*
- *for any atom B_i in its body, such that $rel(B_i) \simeq rel(H)$,*
- *for any substitution θ, such that the arguments of the atoms in $(B_1, \ldots, B_{i-1})\theta$ all satisfy their associated interargument relations $R_{rel(B_1)}, \ldots, R_{rel(B_{i-1})}$*

$$H\theta \succ B_i\theta$$

then P is order-acceptable with respect to S.

The stated condition is sufficient for order-acceptability, but is not necessary for it. Indeed, consider the following example:

Example 6.

$$p(X) \leftarrow q(X, Y), p(Y).$$
$$q(a, b).$$

Query $\leftarrow p(X)$ terminates with respect to this program. Thus, Theorem 1 implies the program is order-acceptable with respect to $\{p(X)\}$. However, the conditions of Theorem 2 do not hold. If $\geq$ is a quasi-ordering that satisfies these conditions, then $p(a) \leq \geq p(b)$ is implied by rigidity and $p(a) > p(b)$ is implied by the decrease, contradicting the definition of $>$.

We continue the analysis of Example 4 and show how Theorem 2 is used.

Example 7. Let $\succeq$ be a well-founded quasi-ordering on $U_P^E \cup B_P^E$, such that:

- for all terms t_1, t_{21} and t_{22}: $permute(t_1, t_{21}) \preceq\succeq permute(t_1, t_{22})$.
- for all terms $t_{11}, t_{12}, t_2, t_{31}, t_{32}$: $delete(t_{11}, t_2, t_{31}) \preceq\succeq delete(t_{12}, t_2, t_{32})$.
- for all terms t_{11}, t_{12} and t_2: $[t_{11}|t_2] \preceq\succeq [t_{12}|t_2]$.

That is, we impose that the quasi-ordering is invariant on predicate argument positions and functor argument positions that may occur with a free variable in $Call(P, S)$. Furthermore, we impose that $\succeq$ has the subterm and monotonicity properties at all remaining predicate or functor argument positions.

First we investigate the rigidity of $\succeq$ on $Call(P, S)$, namely: $G\theta \preceq\succeq G$ for any $G \in Call(P, S)$ and any θ. Now any effect that the application of θ to G may have on G needs to be through the occurrence of some variable in G. However, because we imposed that $\succeq$ is invariant on all predicate and functor argument positions that may possibly contain a variable in some call, $G\theta \preceq\succeq G$.

Associate with *delete* the interargument relation $R_{delete} = \{delete(t_1, t_2, t_3) \mid t_2 \succ t_3\}$. First, we verify that this interargument relationship is valid. Note, that an interargument relationship is valid whenever it is a model for its predicate. Thus, to check whether R_{delete} is valid, $T_P(R_{delete}) \subseteq R_{delete}$ is checked. For the non-recursive clause of *delete* the inclusion follows from the subset property of $\succeq$, while for the recursive one, from the monotonicity of it.

Then, consider the recursive clauses of the program.

- *permute.* If $delete(El, L, L1)\theta$ satisfies R_{delete}, then $L\theta \succ L1\theta$. By the monotonicity, $permute(L, T)\theta \succ permute(L1, T)\theta$. By the property stated above, $permute(L, [El|T])\theta \preceq\succeq permute(L, T)\theta$. Thus, the desired decrease $permute(L, [El|T])\theta \succ permute(L1, T)\theta$ holds.
- *delete.* By the properties of $\succ$ stated above: $delete(X, [H|T], [H|T1]) \succ delete(X, T, [H|T1])$ and $delete(X, T, [H|T1]) \preceq\succeq delete(X, T, T1)$. Thus, $delete(X, [H|T], [H|T1]) \succ delete(X, T, T1)$.

We have shown that all the conditions of Theorem 2 are satisfied, and thus, P is order-acceptable with respect to S. By Theorem 1, P terminates for all queries in S.

Observe, that we do not need to construct the actual ordering, but only to prove that there is one, that meets all the requirements posed. In this specific case, the requirement of subterm and monotonicity on the remaining argument positions is satisfiable. □

4   The Results for Acceptability with Respect to a Model

In this section we briefly discuss some of the results we obtained in generalising the acceptability notion of [4, 17]. Since these results are weaker than those presented in the previous section, we do not elaborate on them in full detail.

For a predicate p with arity n, a *mode* is an atom $p(m_1, \ldots, m_n)$, where $m_i \in \{in, out\}$ for $1 \leq i \leq n$. Positions with *in* are called *input positions*, and positions with *out* are called *output positions* of p. We assume that a fixed mode is associated with each predicate in a program. To simplify the notation, an atom written as $p(\mathbf{s}, \mathbf{t})$ means: $\mathbf{s}$ is the vector of terms filling the input positions, and $\mathbf{t}$ is the vector of terms filling the output positions. Furthermore, by $Var(\mathbf{s})$ we denote the set of variables occuring in vector of terms $\mathbf{s}$ [2].

Below, we assume that modes for the program and goal are given. For any atom A and a mode m_A for A, we denote by A^{inp} the atom obtained from A by removing all output arguments. E.g., let $A = p(f(2), 3, X)$ and $m_A = p(in, in, out)$, then $A^{inp} = p(f(2), 3)$.

Definition 9. *Let $\geq$ be a quasi-ordering relation on B_P^E. We say that $\geq$ is output-independent if for any two moded atoms A and B: $A^{inp} = B^{inp}$ implies $A \leq \geq B$.*

The first class of the programs we consider, are *well-moded* programs.

Definition 10. *[2]*

1. *A query $p_1(\mathbf{s_1}, \mathbf{t_1}), \ldots, p_n(\mathbf{s_n}, \mathbf{t_n})$ is called* well-moded *if for $i \in [1, n]$*

$$Var(\mathbf{s_i}) \subseteq \bigcup_{j=1}^{i-1} Var(\mathbf{t_j}).$$

2. *A clause $p_0(\mathbf{t_0}, \mathbf{s_{n+1}}) \leftarrow p_1(\mathbf{s_1}, \mathbf{t_1}), \ldots, p_n(\mathbf{s_n}, \mathbf{t_n})$ is called* well-moded *if for $i \in [1, n+1]$*

$$Var(\mathbf{s_i}) \subseteq \bigcup_{j=0}^{i-1} Var(\mathbf{t_j}).$$

3. *A program is called* well-moded *if every clause of it is.*

For well-moded programs, order-acceptability in the style of [4] can now be defined as follows.

Definition 11. *Let P be a well-moded program, $\geq$ an output-independent well-founded quasi-ordering and I a model for P. The program P is called* order-acceptable *with respect to $\geq$ and I if for all $A \leftarrow B_1, \ldots, B_n$ in P and all substitutions θ, such that $(A\theta)^{inp}$ and $B_1\theta, \ldots, B_{i-1}\theta$ are ground and $I \models B_1\theta \wedge \ldots \wedge B_{i-1}\theta$ holds: $A\theta > B_i\theta$.*

P is called *order-acceptable* if it is order-acceptable with respect to some output-independent well-founded quasi-ordering and some model. Note the similarity and the difference with the notion of *well-acceptability* introduced by Etalle, Bossi and Cocco [17]—both notions relay on "ignoring" the output positions. However, the approach suggested in [17] measures atoms by level-mappings, while our approach is based on general orderings. In addition [17] requires a decrease only between atoms of mutually recursive predicates. Similarly, one might use the notion of order-acceptability that requires a decrease only between atoms of mutually recursive predicates. This definition will be equivalent to the one we used, since for atoms of non-mutually recursive predicates the dependency relation, $\sqsupset$, can always be used to define an ordering. Since every level mapping naturally gives rise to the ordering on atoms, that is $A_1 \succ A_2$ if $\mid A_1 \mid > \mid A_2 \mid$, we conclude that *every well-acceptable program is order-acceptable*.

The following theorem states that order-acceptability of a well-moded program is sufficient for termination of well-moded goals with respect to this program. Etalle, Bossi and Cocco [17] call such a program *well-terminating*.

Theorem 3. *Let P be a well-moded program, that is order-acceptable with respect to an output-independent well-founded quasi-ordering $\geq$ and a model I. Let G be a well-moded goal, then G LD-terminates.*

Note that if the requirement of well-modedness of the program P is dropped then the theorem no longer holds.

Example 8.

$$p(a) \leftarrow q(X).$$
$$q(f(X)) \leftarrow q(X).$$

We assume the modes $p(in)$ and $q(in)$ to be given. This program is not well-moded with respect to the given modes, because $p(a)$ calls $q/1$ with a free variable, but it satisfies the remaining conditions of order-acceptability with respect to the following quasi-ordering $\geq$ on terms $p(a) > q(t)$ and $q(f(t)) > q(t)$ for any term t and $t \leq\geq s$ only if t and s are syntactically identical, and the following model $I = \{p(a), q(a), q(f(a)), q(f(f(a))), \ldots\}$. However, note that the well-moded goal $p(a)$ is non-terminating. □

Unfortunately, well-modedness is not sufficient to make the converse to hold. That is, there is a well-moded program P and a well-moded goal G, such that G is LD-terminating with respect to P, but P is not order-acceptable.

Example 9. Consider the following program

$$p(f(X)) \leftarrow p(g(X)).$$

with the mode $p(out)$. This program is well-moded, the well-moded goal $p(X)$ terminates with respect to this program, but it is not order-acceptable, since the required decrease $p(f(X)) > p(g(X))$ violates output-independence of $\geq$. □

Intuitively, the problem in the example occured, because some information has been passed via the output positions, i.e, P is not *simply moded*.

Definition 12. *[3]*

1. *A query* $p_1(\mathbf{s_1}, \mathbf{t_1}), \ldots, p_n(\mathbf{s_n}, \mathbf{t_n})$ *is called* simply moded *if* $\mathbf{t_1}, \ldots, \mathbf{t_n}$ *is a linear family of variables and for* $i \in [1, n]$

$$\mathrm{Var}(\mathbf{s_i}) \cap (\bigcup_{j=i}^{n} \mathrm{Var}(\mathbf{t_j})) = \emptyset.$$

2. *A clause* $p_0(\mathbf{s_0}, \mathbf{t_0}) \leftarrow p_1(\mathbf{s_1}, \mathbf{t_1}), \ldots, p_n(\mathbf{s_n}, \mathbf{t_n})$ *is called* simply moded *if* $p_1(\mathbf{s_1}, \mathbf{t_1}), \ldots, p_n(\mathbf{s_n}, \mathbf{t_n})$ *is simply moded and*

$$\mathrm{Var}(\mathbf{s_0}) \cap (\bigcup_{j=1}^{n} \mathrm{Var}(\mathbf{t_j})) = \emptyset.$$

3. *A program is called* simply moded *if every clause of it is.*

Indeed, if P is simply moded the second direction of the theorem holds as well. This was already observed in [17] in the context of well-acceptability and well-termination. The following is an immediate corollary to Theorem 5.1 in [17]. As that theorem states for well-moded simply moded programs, well-termination implies well-acceptability. Therefore, well-terminating programs are order-acceptable.

Corollary 1. *Let P be a well-moded simply moded program, LD-terminating for any well-moded goal. Then there exists a model I and an output-independent well-founded quasi-ordering $\geq$, such that P is order-acceptable with respect to I and $\geq$.*

To conclude, we briefly discuss why it is difficult to extend the notions of order-acceptability to the non well-moded case, using a notion of boundedness, as it was done for standard acceptability [4]. In acceptability based on level mappings, boundedness ensures that the level mapping of a (non-ground) goal can only increase up to some finite bound when the goal becomes more instantiated. Observe that every ground goal is trivially bounded.

The most naive approach to generalisation of boundedness is replacing comparisons of level mappings with orderings, that is defining an atom A to be *bounded* with respect to an ordering $>$, if there exists an atom C such that for all ground instances $A\theta$ of A, $C > A\theta$. Unfortunately, this definition is too week to impose termination.

Example 10.

$$q \leftarrow p(X).$$
$$p(f(X)) \leftarrow p(X).$$
$$p(a).$$

Goal $p(X)$ is bounded with respect to the quasi-ordering such that $q > \ldots > p(f(f(a))) > p(f(a)) > p(a)$. Similarly, the decrease requirement between the head and the subgoals is satisfied, however the goal does not terminate.

Intuitively, the problem in this example occured due to the fact that infinitely many different atoms are smaller than the boundary. One can try to fix this problem by redefining boundedness as:

An atom A is *bounded* with respect to an ordering $>$, if there exists an atom C such that for all ground instances $A\theta$ of A: $A\theta < C$, and $\{B \in B_P^E \mid B < C\}$ is finite.

Such a definition imposes constraints which are very similar to the ones imposed by standard boundedness in the context of level mappings. However, one thing we loose is that it is no longer a generalisation of groundness. Consider an atom $p(a)$ and assume that our language contains a functor $f/1$ and a constant b. Then one particular well-founded ordering is

$$p(a) > \ldots > p(f(f(b))) > p(f(b)) > p(b).$$

So, $p(a)$ is not bounded with respect to this ordering.

Because of such complications, we felt that the rigidity-based results of the previous section are the preferred generalisations to general orderings.

5   A Methodology for Verifying Order-Acceptability

In this section we present an approach leading towards automatic verification of the order-acceptability condition. The basic idea for the approach is inspired on the "constraint based" termination analysis proposed in [13]. We start off from the conditions imposed by order-acceptability, and systematically reduce these conditions to more explicit constraints on the objects of our search: the quasi-ordering $\geq$ and the interargument relations, R_p, or model I.

The approach presented below has been applied successfully to a number of examples that appear in the literature on termination, such as different versions of *permute* [6, 22, 13], *dis-con* [10], *transitive closure* [22], *add-mult* [25], *combine, reverse, odd-even, at_least_double* and *normalisation* [13], *quicksort* program [29, 2], *derivative* [16], *distributive law* [15], *boolean ring* [20], *aiakl, bid* [9], credit evaluation expert system [29], *flatten* [5], vanilla meta-interpreter *solve* [29] together with wide class of interpreted programs.

In the remainder of the paper, we explain the approach using some of these examples.

We start by showing how the analysis of Example 4, presented before, can be performed systematically. We stress the main steps of a methodology.

Example 11. $\geq$ should be rigid on *Call(P, S)*. To enforce the rigidity, $\geq$ should ignore all argument positions in atoms in *Call(P, S)* that might be occupied by free variables, i.e., the second argument position of *permute* and the first and the third argument positions of *delete*. Moreover, since the first argument of *permute* and the second argument of *delete* are general nil-terminated lists, the first argument of ./2 should be ignored as well.

The decreases with respect to $>$ imposed in the order-acceptability with respect to a set S are:

$$delete(X, [H|T], [H|T1])\theta > delete(X, T, T1)\theta$$
$$delete(El, L, L_1)\theta \text{ satisfies } R_{delete} \text{ implies}$$
$$permute(L, [El|T])\theta > permute(L_1, T)\theta$$

To express the rigidity constraints, we simplify each of these conditions by replacing the predicate argument positions that should be ignored by some arbitrary term—one of $v_1, v_2, \ldots$. The following conditions are obtained:

$$delete(v_1, [H|T]\theta, v_2) > delete(v_3, T\theta, v_4) \tag{1}$$
$$delete(El, L, L_1)\theta \text{ satisfies } R_{delete} \text{ implies}$$
$$permute(L\theta, v_1) > permute(L_1\theta, v_2) \tag{2}$$

Observe that this replacement only partially deals with the requirements that the rigidity conditions expressed above impose: rigidity on functor arguments (the first argument of ./2 should be invariant with respect to the ordering) is not expressed. We keep track of such constraints implicitly, and only verify them at a later stage when additional constraints on the ordering are derived.

For each of the conditions (1) and (2), we have two options on how to enforce it:

Option 1): The decrease required in the condition can be achieved by imposing some property on $\geq$, which is consistent with the constraints that were already imposed on $\geq$ before.

In our example, condition (1) is satisfied by imposing the subterm property for the second argument of ./2 and monotonicity on the second argument of delete. The second argument of ./2 does not belong to a set of functor argument positions that should be ignored. Then, $[t_1|t_2] > t_2$ holds for any terms t_1 and t_2, and by the monotonicity of $>$ in the second argument of delete (1) holds.

In general we can select from a bunch of ordering properties, or even specific orderings, that were proposed in the literature.

Option 2): The required decrease is imposed as a constraint on the interargument relation(s) R of the preceding atoms.

In the permute example, the decrease $permute(L\theta, t) > permute(L_1\theta, t)$ cannot directly be achieved by imposing some constraint on $>$. Thus, we impose that the underlying decrease $L\theta > L_1\theta$ should hold for the intermediate body atoms $(delete(El, L, L_1)\theta)$ that satisfy the interargument relation R_{delete}.

Thus, in the example, the constraint is that R_{delete} should be such that for all $delete(t_1, t_2, t_3)$ that satisfy R_{delete}: $t_2 > t_3$. As we have observed, the interargument relation is valid if it forms a model for its predicate. Thus, one way to constructively verify that a valid interargument relation R_{delete} exists, such that the property $t_2 > t_3$ holds for $delete(t_1, t_2, t_3)$ atoms is to simply impose that $M = \{delete(t_1, t_2, t_3) \mid t_2 > t_3\}$ itself is a model for the delete clauses in the program.

So our new constraint on R_{delete} is that it should include M. Practically we can enforce this by imposing that $T_P(M) \subseteq M$ should hold. As shown in [27], this reduces to the constraints "$[t_1|t_2] > t_2$" and "$t_2 > t_3$ implies $[t|t_2] > [t|t_3]$". These are again fed into our Option 1) step, imposing a monotonicity property on the second argument of ./2 for $>$. At this point the proof is complete.   □

Recall that we do not need to construct actually the ordering, but only to prove that there is one, that meets all the requirements posed.

6   Further Examples

Although the simplicity of the *permute* example makes it a good choice to clarify our approach it does not well motivate the need for general orderings instead of level mappings. Indeed, it is well-known that *permute* can be dealt with using standard acceptability or acceptability with respect to a set [10].

In this section we provide a number of additional examples. Most of them (*distributive law, derivative* and *solve*) illustrate the added power of moving to general orderings. After these we present an alternative version of *permute* in order to discuss an extension of our approach that deals with interargument relations for conjunctions of (body-) atoms.

Before presenting the examples we recall once more the main steps of our approach. First, given a program P and a set S of goals, *compute the set of calls* $Call(P, S)$. Janssens and Bruynooghe [21] show how this can be done through abstract interpretation. Second, *enforce the rigidity of $>$ on $Call(P, S)$*, i.e., ignore all predicate or functor argument positions that might be occupied by free variables in $Call(P, S)$. Given the set of calls, this step can be performed in a completely automatic way. Third, repeatedly *construct decreases with respect to* $>$, such that the rigid order-acceptability condition will hold and check if those can be verified by some of the predefined orderings. While performing this verification step the trade-off between efficiency and power should be considered— using more complex orderings may allow correct reasoning on more examples but might be computationally expensive.

First, we consider the distributive law program. This example originated from [15].

Example 12.

$$dist(x, x).$$
$$dist(x * x, x * x).$$
$$dist(X + Y, U + V) \leftarrow dist(X, U), dist(Y, V).$$
$$dist(X * (Y + Z), T) \leftarrow dist(X * Y + X * Z, T).$$
$$dist((X + Y) * Z, T) \leftarrow dist(X * Z + Y * Z, T).$$

Similarly to the repeated derivation example in the introduction, no linear norm is sufficient for proving termination. The simplest norm, we succeeded to find, providing a termination proof is the following one: $\|X * Y\| = \|X\| * \|Y\|$, $\|X + Y\| = \|X\| + \|Y\| + 1$, $\|x\| = 2$ and the level mapping is $|dist(X, Y)| = \|X\|$. This norm cannot be generated automatically by termination analysers we are aware of.

In order to prove termination of a set of queries

$\{dist(t_1, t_2) \mid t_1$ is an expression in a variable x and t_2 is a free variable$\}$

we use the rigid-acceptability condition. First the quasi-ordering, $\geq$, we are going to define should be rigid on a set of calls, i.e., it should ignore the second argument position of $dist$. Thus, in the decreases with respect to $>$ to follow we replace the second argument of $dist$ with anonymous terms $v_1, v_2, \ldots$.

$$dist((X + Y)\theta, v_1) > dist(X\theta, v_2)$$
$$dist(X, U)\theta \text{ satisfies } R_{dist} \text{ implies}$$
$$dist((X + Y)\theta, v_1) > dist(Y\theta, v_2)$$
$$dist((X * (Y + Z))\theta, v_1) > dist((X * Y + X * Z)\theta, v_2)$$
$$dist(((X + Y) * Z)\theta, v_1) > dist((X * Z + Y * Z)\theta, v_2)$$

The first two decreases are satisfied by any ordering having a subterm property for both arguments of $+/2$ and being monotonic with respect to the first argument position of $dist$. However, in order to satisfy the later two we need to use the recursive path ordering (rpo) [14], with $*$ preceding $+$ with respect to an ordering on functors. If this ordering is used, the following holds for any t_1, t_2 and t_3:

$$t_2 + t_3 > t_2$$
$$t_1 * (t_2 + t_3) > t_1 * t_2$$
$$t_2 + t_3 > t_3$$
$$t_1 * (t_2 + t_3) > t_1 * t_3$$
$$t_1 * (t_2 + t_3) > t_1 * t_2 + t_1 * t_3 \quad \text{(using the properties of rpo)}$$

This proves the third decrease with respect to $>$. The fourth one is proved analogously. □

Now we can return to the motivating Example 1, on computing higher derivatives of polynomial functions in one variable.

Example 13.

$d(der(u), 1)$.
$d(der(A), 0) \leftarrow number(A)$.
$d(der(X + Y), DX + DY) \leftarrow d(der(X), DX), d(der(Y), DY)$.
$d(der(X * Y), X * DY + Y * DX) \leftarrow d(der(X), DX), d(der(Y), DY)$.
$d(der(der(X)), DDX) \leftarrow d(der(X), DX), d(der(DX), DDX)$.

We are interested in proving termination of the queries that belong to the set $S = \{d(t_1, t_2) \mid t_1$ is a repeated derivative of a function in a variable u and t_2 is a free variable$\}$. So S consists of atoms of the form $d(der(u), X)$ or $d(der(u*u+u), Y)$ or $d(der(der(u+u)), Z)$, etc. Observe, that $Call(P, S)$ coincides with S.

We start by analysing the requirements that imposes the rigidity of $\geq$ on $Call(P, S)$. First, the second argument position of d should be ignored, since it might be occupied by a free variable. Second, the first argument position of d is occupied by a ground term. Thus, rigidity does not pose any restrictions on functors argument positions.

Then, we construct the decreases with respect to $>$ that follow from the rigid order-acceptability. The arguments that should be ignored are replaced by terms $v_1, v_2, \ldots$.

$$d(der(X + Y)\theta, v_1) > d(der(X)\theta, v_2) \tag{3}$$

$d(der(X), DX)\theta$ satisfies R_d implies

$$d(der(X + Y)\theta, v_1) > d(der(Y)\theta, v_2) \tag{4}$$

$$d(der(X * Y)\theta, v_1) > d(der(X)\theta, v_2) \tag{5}$$

$d(der(X), DX)\theta$ satisfies R_d implies

$$d(der(X * Y)\theta, v_1) > d(der(Y)\theta, v_2) \tag{6}$$

$$d(der(der(X))\theta, v_1) > d(der(X)\theta, v_2) \tag{7}$$

$d(der(X), DX)\theta$ satisfies R_d implies

$$d(der(der(X))\theta, v_1) > d(der(DX)\theta, v_2) \tag{8}$$

Conditions (3)-(7) impose monotonicity and subset properties to hold on the first argument of d. In order to satisfy condition (8), it is sufficient to prove that for any $(t_1, t_2) \in R_d$ holds that $t_1 > t_2$. That is if $M = \{d(t_1, t_2) \mid t_1 > t_2\}$ then $T_P(M) \subseteq M$. This may be reduced to the following conditions:

$$der(t) > 1 \tag{9}$$
$$t_1 \in R_{number} \text{ implies } der(t_1) > 0 \tag{10}$$
$$der(t_1) > t_2 \ \& \ der(t_3) > t_4 \text{ implies } der(t_1 + t_3) > t_2 + t_4 \tag{11}$$
$$der(t_1) > t_2 \ \& \ der(t_3) > t_4 \text{ implies } der(t_1 * t_3) > t_1 * t_4 + t_2 * t_3 \tag{12}$$
$$der(t_1) > t_2 \ \& \ der(t_2) > t_3 \text{ implies } der(der(t_1)) > t_3 \tag{13}$$

Condition (13) follows from monotonicity and transitivity of $>$. However, (10)-(12) are not satisfied by general properties of $>$ and we need to specify the ordering. The ordering that meets these conditions is the recursive path ordering [14] with der having the highest priority.   □

As a next example we demonstrate that the suggested technique is useful for proving termination of meta-interpreters as well.

Example 14.

$$solve(true).$$
$$solve((A, B)) \leftarrow solve(A), solve(B).$$
$$solve(A) \leftarrow clause(A, B), solve(B).$$

Even though the termination of an interpreted program might be easily proved with level-mappings, the termination proof of the meta-interpreter with respect to it cannot be immediately constructed based on the termination proof of the interpreted program.

Indeed, let P be the interpreted program:

$$p([X, Y|T]) \leftarrow p([Y|T]), p(T).$$

Termination of the set of queries $\{p(t) \mid t \text{ is a list of a finite length}\}$ can be easily proved, for example by a using level mapping $|p(X)| = \|X\|_l$ and the list-length norm $\| \cdot \|_l$. However, when this program is considered together with this meta-interpreter these level-mapping and norm cannot be extended in a way allowing to prove termination, even though there exist a linear level-mapping and a linear norm that provide a termination proof. In the case of this example, the following linear level mapping is sufficient for proving termination:

$$|solve(A)| = \|A\|$$
$$\|(A, B)\| = 1 + \|A\| + \|B\|$$
$$\|p(X)\| = 1 + \|X\|$$
$$\|[H|T]\| = 1 + 3\|T\|$$

The constraint-based approach of [13] is able to derive this level mapping. However, it cannot reuse any information from a termination proof of the interpreted program to do so, and the constraints set up for such examples are fairly complex (n body atoms are interpreted as a , /2-term of depth n and reasoning on them requires products of (at least) n parameters). Most other approaches based on level mappings work on basis of fixed norms, like list-length and term-size, and therefore fail to prove termination of the example.

Applying general orderings allows to define a new ordering for the meta-interpreter together with the interpreted program based on the ordering obtained for the interpreted program itself. More formally, given a quasi-ordering $\geq$, defined for the interpreted program above, define a quasi-ordering $\succeq$ on terms and atoms of the meta-interpreter, as follows (similarly to rpo [14]):

- $t \preceq\succeq s$ if one of the following holds:
  - $t \leq\geq s$
  - $t = (t_1, t_2), s = (s_1, s_2)$ and $t_1 \preceq\succeq s_1, t_2 \preceq\succeq s_2$
  - $t = solve(t_1), s = solve(s_1)$ and $t_1 \preceq\succeq s_1$
- $t \succ s$ if one of the following holds:
  - $t > s$
  - $t = f(\ldots), s = (s_1, s_2), f$ differs from , /2, $solve/1, t \succ s_1$ and $t \succ s_2$

- $t = (t_1, t_2)$ and either $t_1 \succeq s$ or $t_2 \succeq s$.
- $t = solve(t_1), s = solve(s_1)$ and $t_1 \succ s_1$.
- $t = solve(t_1), s = clause(s_1, s_2)$

In our case $\geq$ is a list-length norm based ordering, and $\succeq$ is defined as specified. Then, $p([X, Y|T]) \succ (p([Y|T]), p(T))$. This provides the $\succ$-decrease for the second recursive clause of the meta-interpreter required in the rigid order-acceptability condition. Similarly, the decrease for the first recursive clause is provided by the subterm property that $\succ$ is defined to have, and thus, proving termination.

By reasoning in a similar way, termination can be proved for the meta-interpreter and wide class of interpreted programs: from the small examples, such as *append* and *delete* and up to bigger ones, like *aiakl, bid* [9], credit evaluation expert system [29], or even the *distributive law* program, presented in Example 12. $\qquad\square$

The previous examples do not illustrate our approach in full generality. In general, we may have clauses of the type

$$p(t_1, \ldots, t_n) \leftarrow B_1, B_2, \ldots, B_{i-1}, q(s_1, \ldots, s_m), B_{i+1}, \ldots, B_k.$$

where multiple intermediate body-atoms, $B_1, B_2, \ldots, B_{i-1}$ precede the (mutually) recursive body-atom $q(s_1, \ldots, s_m)$. In such cases the decrease with respect to $>$ between $p(t_1, \ldots, t_n)\theta$ and $q(s_1, \ldots, s_m)\theta$ required by the (rigid) order-acceptability imposes a constraint on $R_{\mathrm{rel}(B_1)}, R_{\mathrm{rel}(B_2)}, \cdots$ and $R_{\mathrm{rel}(B_{i-1})}$. However, our previous technique of using $T_P(M) \subseteq M$ to translate the required decrease to $R_{\mathrm{rel}(B_1)}, R_{\mathrm{rel}(B_2)}, \ldots, R_{\mathrm{rel}(B_{i-1})}$ is not easily generalised. This is because several of the atoms $B_1, B_2, \ldots, B_{i-1}$ together may be responsible for the decrease and the $T_P(M) \subseteq M$ technique is not readily generalised to deal with multiple predicates.

One way to deal with this is based on early works on termination analysis ([31, 25]). Assume that the underlying decrease imposed by

$$B_1\theta, B_2\theta, \ldots, B_{i-1}\theta \text{ satisfy } R_{\mathrm{rel}(B_1)}, R_{\mathrm{rel}(B_2)}, \ldots, R_{\mathrm{rel}(B_{i-1})} \text{ implies}$$
$$p(t_1, \ldots, t_n)\theta > q(s_1, \ldots, s_m)\theta$$

is of the form $u\theta > v\theta$, where u and v are subterms of $p(t_1, \ldots, t_n)$, respectively $q(s_1, \ldots, s_m)$. We then search for a sequence of terms $u, u_1, u_2, \ldots, u_j, v$, such that for each pair of terms, u and u_1, u_1 and u_2, ..., u_j and v, there is a corresponding atom in the sequence $B_1, B_2, \ldots, B_{i-1}$ that contains both of them.

Assume (without real loss of generality) that u and u_1 occur in B_1, u_1 and u_2 occur in B_2, ..., u_j and v occur in B_{i-1}. We then select one of these pairs of terms, say u_{i_1} and u_{i_2} in atom B_{i_3}, and impose the relations:

$u_{i_1} < u_{i_2}$ on $R_{\mathrm{rel}(B_{i_3})}$, and

$u_{i_1} \leq u_{i_2}$ on $R_{\mathrm{rel}(B_{i_3})}$ for all other pairs of terms and corresponding atoms.

Now we can again use the $T_P(M) \subseteq M$ technique to translate such constraints into interargument relations.

Note that this approach involves a search problem: if we fail to verify the proposed inequality constraints, we need to backtrack over the choice of:

- the pair u_{i_1} and u_{i_2} in B_{i_3} with a strict inequality, or
- the sequence of terms $u, u_1, u_2, \ldots, u_j, v$ in $B_1, B_2, \ldots, B_{i-1}$.

A completely different method for dealing with multiple intermediate body-atoms is based on the use of unfold/fold steps to group atoms. We illustrate this second method with an example.

Example 15. The following is the version of the *permute* program that appeared in [22].

$$
\begin{array}{ll}
\text{perm}([], []). & \text{ap}_1([], L, L). \\
\text{perm}(L, [H|T]) \leftarrow & \text{ap}_1([H|L1], L2, [H|L3]) \leftarrow \\
\quad \text{ap}_2(V, [H|U], L), & \quad \text{ap}_1(L1, L2, L3). \\
\quad \text{ap}_1(V, U, W), & \text{ap}_2([], L, L). \\
\quad \text{perm}(W, T). & \text{ap}_2([H|L1], L2, [H|L3]) \leftarrow \\
& \quad \text{ap}_2(L1, L2, L3).
\end{array}
$$

This example is chosen to illustrate applications of Theorem 3 (the well-moded case). We would like to prove termination of the goals $\text{perm}(t_1, t_2)$, where t_1 is a ground list and t_2 a free variable.

Assume the modes $\text{perm}(in, out)$, $\text{ap}_1(in, in, out)$, $\text{ap}_2(out, out, in)$. The order-acceptability imposes, among the others, the following decrease with respect to $>$: $I \models \text{ap}_2(V, [H|U], L)\theta \wedge \text{ap}_1(V, U, W)\theta$ implies $\text{perm}(L)\theta > \text{perm}(W)\theta$. Note that the underlying decrease $L\theta > W\theta$ cannot be achieved by reasoning on $\text{ap}_1/3$ or $\text{ap}_2/3$ alone.

An alternative solution to the one described before is to use the unfold/fold technique to provide a definition for the conjunction of the two intermediate body-atoms. To do this, we start of from a generalised clause, containing the conjunction of atoms both in its head and in its body. In our example we get

$$\text{ap}_2(V, [H|U], L), \text{ap}_1(V, U, W) \leftarrow \text{ap}_2(V, [H|U], L), \text{ap}_1(V, U, W).$$

Next, we unfold both body-atoms , using all applicable clauses, for one resolution step. This gives rise to a generalised program P', defining the conjunction of intermediate body-atoms:

$$
\begin{array}{l}
\text{ap}_2([], [H|T], [H|T]), \text{ap}_1([], T, T). \\
\text{ap}_2([H1|T1], [H2|T2], [H1|T3]), \text{ap}_1([H1|T1], T2, [H1|T4]) \leftarrow \\
\quad \text{ap}_2(T1, [H2|T2], T3), \text{ap}_1(T1, T2, T4).
\end{array}
$$

Now, we need to verify that $M = \{\text{ap}_2(a_1, a_2, a_3), \text{ap}_1(b_1, b_2, b_3) \mid a_3 > b_3\}$ satisfies $T_{P'}(M) \subseteq M$. Using the 2 clauses, this is reduced to "$[t_1|t_2] > t_2$" and "$t_3 > t_4$ implies $[t_5|t_3] > [t_5|t_4]$", for any terms t_1, t_2, t_3, t_4 and t_5, imposing monotonicity and subterm properties on $>$. The proof is completed analogously to the *permute* example.   □

It should be noted that in general unfolding can transform a non-terminating program to a terminating one by replacing infinite branches of the LD-tree with failing ones [7]. Bossi and Cocco [7] also stated conditions on unfolding that impose termination to be preserved.

7   Conclusion

We have presented a non-transformational approach to termination analysis of logic programs, based on general orderings. The problem of termination was studied by a number of authors (see [10] for the survey). More recent work on this topic can be found among others in [12, 13, 17, 19, 23, 26, 28, 30, 32]. The transformational approach to termination has been studied among others in [1, 5, 18, 22, 24]

Our approach gets its power from integrating the traditional notion of acceptability [4] with the wide class of orderings that have been studied in the context of the term-rewriting systems. In theory, such an integration is unnecessary: acceptability (based on level mappings only) is already equivalent to LD-termination. In practice, the required level mappings may sometimes be very complex (such as for Example 1 or Example 12 [15], *boolean ring* [20] or *flattening of a binary tree* [5]), and automatic systems for proving termination are unable to generate them. In such cases, generating an appropriate ordering, replacing the level mapping, may often be much easier, especially since we can reuse the impressive machinery on orderings developed for term-rewrite systems. In some other cases, such as *turn* [8], simple level mappings do exist (in the case of *turn*: a norm counting the number of 0s before the first occurrence of 1 in the list is sufficient), but most systems based on level mappings will not even find this level mapping, because they only consider mappings based on term-size or list-length norms. Meta-interpreters, as illustrated in Example 14, give the same complication. Again, our approach is able to deal with such cases.

Sometimes level mappings and norms provide an advantage over general orderings. This is mostly the case if the termination proof can benefit from arguments based on arithmetical operations on the numerical values provided by the level mapping and norm, as illustrated in Example 2. Note however, that general orderings include orderings based on mappings and norms as a special case. We can allow the latter types of orderings as a special case, resorting to them when other orderings in our workbench fail to produce a proof. If we do resort to them, we may allow arithmetic operations on them. The main reason why we defined interargument relations in a very general way is exactly to allow all the power of numerical orderings, and arithmetic, to be applicable in our context.

Unlike transformational approaches, that establish the termination results for logic programs by the reasoning on termination of term-rewriting systems, we apply the orderings directly to the logic programs, thus, avoiding transformations. This could both be regarded as an advantage and as a drawback of our approach. It may be considered as a drawback, because reasoning on successful instances of intermediate body-atoms introduces an additional complication in our approach, for which there is no counterpart in transformational methods (except for the transformation step itself). On the other hand, we consider it as an advantage, because it is precisely this reasoning on intermediate body atoms that gives more insight in the property of *logic program termination* (as opposed to *term-rewrite system termination*). Another advantage over transformational approaches is that most of these are restricted to well-moded programs and goals, while our approach does not have this limitation.

So, in a sense our approach provides the best of both worlds: a means to incorporate into 'direct' approaches the generality of general orderings.

We consider as a future work a full implementation of the approach. Although we already tested very many examples manually, an implementation will allow us to conduct a much more extensive experimentation, comparing the technique also in terms of efficiency with other systems. Since we apply a demand-driven approach, systematically reducing required conditions to more simple constraints on the ordering and the model, we expect that the method can lead to very efficient verification.

8   Acknowledgements

We thank Robert Kowalski for continuously stimulating us to look outside of our ivory tower of research to search for challenges in cross-fertilisation of different streams of work.

Alexander Serebrenik is supported by GOA: "LP^+: a second generation logic programming language". We thank Maurice Bruynooghe for useful suggestions.

References

[1] G. Aguzzi and U. Modigliani. Proving Termination of Logic Program by Transforming them into Equivalent Term Rewriting Systems. In *Proc. of 13th Conference on Foundations of Software Technologies and Theoretical Computer Science (FST& TCS)*, pages 114–124. Springer Verlag, 1993. LNCS 761.

[2] K. R. Apt. *From Logic Programming to Prolog*. Prentice-Hall Int. Series in Computer Science. Prentice Hall, 1997.

[3] K. R. Apt and S. Etalle. On the unification free Prolog programs. In A. M. Borzyszkowski and S. Sokolowski, editors, *18th Int. Symp. on Mathematical Foundations of Computer Science*, pages 1–19. Springer Verlag, 1993. LNCS 711.

[4] K. R. Apt and D. Pedreschi. Studies in Pure Prolog: Termination. In J. W. Lloyd, editor, *Proc. Esprit Symp. on Comp. Logic*, pages 150–176. Springer Verlag, 1990.

[5] T. Arts. *Automatically proving termination and innermost normalisation of term rewriting systems*. PhD thesis, Universiteit Utrecht, 1997.

[6] T. Arts and H. Zantema. Termination of logic programs using semantic unification. In M. Proietti, editor, *5th Int. Workshop on Logic Programming Synthesis and Transformation*, pages 219–233. Springer Verlag, 1995. LNCS 1048.

[7] A. Bossi and N. Cocco. Preserving universal temination through unfold/fold. In G. Levi and M. Rodríguez-Artalejo, editors, *Algebraic and Logic Programming*, pages 269–286. Springer Verlag, 1994. LNCS 850.

[8] A. Bossi, N. Cocco, and M. Fabris. Norms on terms and their use in proving universal termination of a logic program. *Theoretical Computer Science*, 124(2):297–328, February 1994.

[9] F. Bueno, M. J. García de la Banda, and M. V. Hermenegildo. Effectiveness of global analysis in strict independence-based automatic parallelization. In M. Bruynooghe, editor, *Logic Programming, Proc. of the 1994 Int. Symp.*, pages 320–336. MIT Press, 1994.

[10] D. De Schreye and S. Decorte. Termination of logic programs: The never-ending story. *J. Logic Programming*, 19/20:199–260, May/July 1994.

[11] D. De Schreye, K. Verschaetse, and M. Bruynooghe. A framework for analyzing the termination of definite logic programs with respect to call patterns. In I. Staff, editor, *Proc. of the Int. Conf. on Fifth Generation Computer Systems.*, pages 481–488. IOS Press, 1992.

[12] S. Decorte and D. De Schreye. Termination analysis: some practical properties of the norm and level mapping space. In J. Jaffar, editor, *Proc. of the 1998 Joint Int. Conf. and Symp. on Logic Programming*, pages 235–249. MIT Press, June 1998.

[13] S. Decorte, D. De Schreye, and H. Vandecasteele. Constraint-based termination analysis of logic programs. *ACM Transactions on Programming Languages and Systems (TOPLAS)*, 21(6):1137–1195, November 1999.

[14] N. Dershowitz. Termination. In C. Kirchner, editor, *First Int. Conf. on Rewriting Techniques and Applications*, pages 180–224. Springer Verlag, 1985. LNCS 202.

[15] N. Dershowitz and C. Hoot. Topics in termination. In C. Kirchner, editor, *Rewriting Techniques and Applications, 5th Int. Conf.*, pages 198–212. Springer Verlag, 1993. LNCS 690.

[16] N. Dershowitz and Z. Manna. Proving termination with multiset orderings. *Communications of the ACM (CACM)*, 22(8):465–476, August 1979.

[17] S. Etalle, A. Bossi, and N. Cocco. Termination of well-moded programs. *J. Logic Programming*, 38(2):243–257, February 1999.

[18] H. Ganzinger and U. Waldmann. Termination proofs of well-moded logic programs via conditional rewrite systems. In M. Rusinowitch and J.-L. Remy, editors, *Proc. of CTRS'92*, pages 216–222. Springer Verlag, 1993. LNCS 656.

[19] S. Hoarau. *Inférer et compiler la terminaison des programmes logiques avec contraintes*. PhD thesis, Université de La Réunion, 1999.

[20] J. Hsiang. Rewrite method for theorem proving in first order theory with equality. *Journal of Symbolic Computation*, 8:133–151, 1987.

[21] G. Janssens and M. Bruynooghe. Deriving descriptions of possible values of program variables by means of abstract interpretation. *J. Logic Programming*, 13(2&3):205–258, July 1992.

[22] M. Krishna Rao, D. Kapur, and R. Shyamasundar. Transformational methodology for proving termination of logic programs. *J. Logic Programming*, 34:1–41, 1998.

[23] N. Lindenstrauss and Y. Sagiv. Automatic termination analysis of logic programs. In L. Naish, editor, *Proc. of the Fourteenth Int. Conf. on Logic Programming*, pages 63–77. MIT Press, July 1997.

[24] M. Marchiori. Logic programs as term rewriting systems. In *Proc. of the Algebraic Logic Programming ALP'94*, pages 223–241. Springer Verlag, 1994. LNCS; volume 850.

[25] L. Plümer. *Termination Proofs for Logic Programs*. LNAI 446. Springer Verlag, 1990.

[26] S. Ruggieri. *Verification and validation of logic programs*. PhD thesis, Universitá di Pisa, 1999.

[27] A. Serebrenik and D. De Schreye. Termination analysis of logic programs using acceptability with general term orders. Technical Report CW 291, Departement Computerwetenschappen, K.U.Leuven, Leuven, Belgium, 2000. Available at http://www.cs.kuleuven.ac.be/publicaties/rapporten/CW2000.html.

[28] J.-G. Smaus. *Modes and Types in Logic Programming*. PhD thesis, University of Kent, 1999.

[29] L. Sterling and E. Shapiro. *The Art of Prolog*. The MIT Press, 1994.

[30] C. Taboch. A semantic basis for termination analysis of logic programs. Master's thesis, Ben-Gurion University of the Negev, 1998.

[31] J. D. Ullman and A. van Gelder. Efficient tests for top-down termination of logical rules. *Journal of the Association for Computing Machinery*, 35(2):345–373, April 1988.

[32] S. Verbaeten. *Static verification of compositionality and termination for logic programming languages*. PhD thesis, Department of Computer Science, K.U.Leuven, Leuven, Belgium, June 2000. v+265+xxvii.

Specification, Implementation, and Verification of Domain Specific Languages: A Logic Programming-Based Approach

Gopal Gupta[1] and Enrico Pontelli[2]

[1] Applied Logic, Programming Languages and Systems Lab
Department of Computer Science
University of Texas at Dallas
Richardson, TX, USA 95083
gupta@cs.nmsu.edu
[2] Laboratory for Logic, Databases, and Advanced Programming
Department of Computer Science
New Mexico State University
Las Cruces, NM, USA 88003
epontell@cs.nmsu.edu

Abstract. Domain Specific Languages (DSLs) are high level languages designed for solving problems in a particular domain, and have been suggested as means for developing reliable software systems. We present a (constraint) logic programming-based framework for specification, efficient implementation, and automatic verification of domain specific languages (DSLs). Our framework is based on using Horn logic (or pure Prolog), and eventually constraints, to specify denotational semantics of domain specific languages. Both the syntax as well as the semantic specification of the DSL in question are directly executable in our framework: the specification itself serves as an interpreter for the DSL. More efficient implementations of this DSL—a compiler—can be automatically derived via partial evaluation. Additionally, the executable specification can be used for automatic or semi-automatic verification of programs written in the DSL as well as for automatically obtaining traditional debuggers and profilers. The ability to verify DSL programs is a distinct advantage of our approach. In this paper we give a general outline of our approach, and illustrate it with practical examples.

1 Introduction

Logic programming [27], discovered by Robert Kowalski, is an important paradigm of programming in computer science. Logic is the foundation on which all of computer science rests. Logic programming, a computationally efficient subset of logic, directly relates to almost all core areas of computer science: from databases [28,10] to artificial intelligence and knowledge representation [29], from compilers [52] to operating systems [50], from machine learning [38] to natural language processing [8], and from verification and model checking [42] to

A.C. Kakas, F. Sadri (Eds.): Computat. Logic (Kowalski Festschrift), LNAI 2407, pp. 211–239, 2002.

optimization and constraint programming [51,31]. Indeed, for these reasons we argue that logic programming is the most versatile of all programming paradigms [17]. Logic programming brings to its practitioners a unique unifying perspective to computer science[1]—computer scientists' nirvana, if there is such a thing— and puts Bob Kowalski alongside the greatest of messiahs of computing for bringing this enlightenment to us. Logic programming can also play a pivotal role in software engineering [15], another important area of computer science. In this paper, we show how the task of software engineering can be eased by resorting to *domain specific languages* and how logic programming can be used to naturally and rapidly obtain an implementation infrastructure for domain specific languages.

Writing software that is robust and reliable is a major problem that software developers and designers face today. Development of techniques for building reliable software has been an area of study for quite some time, however, none of the solutions proposed are completely satisfactory. Recently, approaches based on *domain specific languages* (DSL) have been proposed [3,43,25,33,6]. In the DSL approach, a domain specific language is developed to allow users to solve problems in a particular application area. A DSL allows users to develop complete application programs in a particular domain. Domain specific languages are very high level languages in which domain experts can write programs *at a level of abstraction at which they think and reason.* DSLs are not "general purpose" languages, rather they are supposed to be just expressive enough to "capture the semantics of an application domain" [25]. The fact that users are able to code problems at the level of abstraction at which they think and the level at which they understand the specific application domain results in programs that are more likely to be correct, that are easier to write, understand and reason about, and easier to maintain. As a net result, programmer productivity is considerably improved.

The task of developing a program to solve a specific problem involves two steps. The first step is to devise a solution procedure to solve the problem. This steps requires a domain expert to use his/her domain knowledge, expertise, creativity and mental acumen, to devise a solution to the problem. The second step is to code the solution in some executable notation (such as a computer programming language) to obtain a program that can then be run on a computer to solve the problem. In the second step the user is required to map the *steps* of the solution procedure to *constructs* of the programming language being used for coding. Both steps are cognitively challenging and require considerable amount of thinking and mental activity. The more we can reduce the amount of mental activity involved in both steps (e.g., via automation), the more reliable the process of program construction will be. Not much can be done about the first step as far as reducing the amount of mental activity is involved, however, a lot can be done for the second step. The amount of mental effort the programmer has to put in the second step depends on the "semantic" gap between the

---

[1] The role of logic programming as a unifying theory in computer science, however, has not received much attention [23,24].

level of abstraction at which the solution procedure has been conceived and the various constructs of the programming language being used. Domain experts usually think at a very high level of abstraction while designing the solution procedure. As a result, the more low-level is the programming language, the wider the semantic gap, and the harder the user's task. In contrast, if we had a language that was right at the level of abstraction at which the user thinks, the task of constructing the program would be much easier. A domain specific language indeed makes this possible.

A considerable amount of infrastructure is needed to support a DSL. First of all the DSL should be manually designed. The design of the language will require the inputs of both computer scientists and domain experts. Once the DSL has been designed, we need a program development environment (an interpreter or a compiler, debuggers, editors, etc.) to facilitate the development of programs written in this DSL.

In this paper we show how a semantics based framework based on (constraint) logic programming can be used for rapidly developing interpreters/compilers as well as debuggers and profilers for DSLs. In this framework, the syntax and semantics of the DSL are expressed using Horn logic. The Horn logic coded syntax and semantics is executable, automatically yielding an interpreter. Given this semantics-based interpreter for the DSL and a program written in this DSL, the interpreter can be *partially evaluated* [26] w.r.t. the DSL program (e.g., using a partial evaluator for Prolog such as Mixtus [46]) to automatically generate compiled code. Additionally, the semantic specification can be extended to produce a debugger/profiler for the language, as well as used for verifying properties of DSL programs. Given that the interpreter, compiler, and the debugger are all obtained automatically from the syntax and semantic specification, the process of developing the infrastructure for supporting the DSL is very rapid. The most time consuming task is the design of the DSL itself. Observe that the time taken to design the DSL is dependent on how rapidly the DSL can be implemented, since the ability to rapidly implement the language allows its designers to quickly experiment with various language constructs and with their various possible semantics.

Theoretically speaking, one could argue that any complex software system that interacts with the outside world defines a domain specific language. This is because the input language that a user uses to interact with this software can be thought of as a domain specific language. For instance, consider a file-editor; the command language of the file-editor constitutes a domain specific language. This language-centric view can be quite advantageous to support the software development process. This is because the *semantic specification of the input language of a software system is also a specification of that software system*—we assume the semantic specification also includes the syntax specification of the input language. *If the semantic specification of the input language is executable, then we obtain an executable specification of the software system.* In this paper we use the preceding observations to design a language semantics based framework for specifying, (efficiently) implementing, and verifying (rather model checking or debugging in a structured way) DSLs. In our approach both the syntax and semantics are specified using Horn logic/Constraints, and are executable. Efficient (compiled) implementations can be obtained via partial evaluation. The resulting executable specification can also be used for verification, model checking and structured debugging. The ability to automatically verify and debug DSL programs in a structured, automatic way is a distinct advantage of the Horn logic approach, and is absent from other approaches (such as [7]).

An obvious candidate framework for specifying the semantics of a domain specific language is denotational semantics [47]. Denotational semantics has three components: (i) syntax, which is typically specified using a BNF, (ii) semantic algebras, or value spaces, in terms of which the meaning is given, and, (iii) valuation functions, which map abstract syntax to semantic algebras. In traditional denotational definitions, syntax is specified using BNF, and the semantic algebra and valuation functions using λ-calculus. There are various problems with this traditional approach: (i) the syntax is not directly executable, i.e., it does not immediately yield a parser, (ii) the semantic specification cannot be easily used for automatic verification or model checking. Additionally, the use of separate notations for the different components of the semantics implies the need of adopting different tools, further complicating the process of converting the specification into an executable tool. Verification should be a major use of any semantics, however, this has not happened for denotational semantics; its use is mostly limited to studying language features, and (manually) proving properties of language constructs (e.g., by use of *fixpoint induction*). In [49] Schmidt makes a similar observation, and laments the lack of practical impact of denotational semantics, particularly in automatic verification and debugging of programs. Elsewhere we have argued that a major reason for this lack of use of denotational semantics is the very rich[2]—the λ-calculus—that is traditionally used for specifying denotational semantics [14].[3] In this paper, we show how the switch to Horn logic for expressing denotational semantics facilitates the specification, implementation, and automatic verification/debugging of DSL programs.

Traditionally, operational semantics is largely meant for implementors, denotational semantics for language designers, and axiomatic semantics for programmers. Thus, each major type of semantics not only has a different target audience, they all use different types of notation as well. One major reason that has impeded practical uses of semantics, in our opinion, is this use of different semantics and different notations for different uses. The switch to Horn logic (and eventually constraints) for expressing denotational semantics creates a *uniform* description framework and brings flavors of both operational semantics as well as axiomatic semantics in the denotational semantic definition. In switching

---

[2] Here we refer to the ability of λ-calculus to support higher order functions as first class objects; higher order functions make the notation very expressive but computationally harder to automatically process and analyze.

[3] Contrary to intuition, notation has a great impact in ease of use. Two very significant examples are the use of high-level language *vs* assembly language in programming, and the use of the decimal arithmetic notation *vs* the Roman numerals.

the notation, we may sacrifice some of the declarative purity of the traditional denotational definition, but the number of applications that become possible are well-worth this change [14]. As a matter of fact, one can argue that not a whole lot of declarative purity is lost, and analogs of techniques such as fixpoint induction can still be used. Use of "implementational" denotational semantics has been suggested in the past [44].

A Horn logic denotational specification for a language yields a parser and an interpreter automatically. Partial evaluation of the interpreter w.r.t. a program yields compiled code. The interpreter can be used in conjunction with preconditions and postconditions to verify/model-check DSL programs. Thus, the operational semantics flavor allows efficient implementation to be rapidly derived, while the axiomatic semantics flavor permits automatic verification.

Our approach could be applied to develop implementation and verification infrastructure for general purpose languages, however, we feel that general purpose languages are too complex for our techniques to be practical; DSLs on the other hand are simpler, arise quite frequently, and the rapid implementation and verification that becomes possible using our framework perhaps might induce DSL designers to consider our approach for rapid prototyping of their DSLs.

We illustrate the Horn logic denotational framework through two example DSLs: the command language of a file-editor and a language for specifying real-time systems called UPPAAL [30,2]. The rest of the paper is organized as follows: Section 2 introduces the concept of Horn Logic Denotations. Section 3 presents a software engineering perspective of DSL and Horn Logic Denotations. Section 4 presents the derivation of a DSL for file-editing. Section 5 discusses the issues of verification of properties of DSL and presents the derivation of the UPPAAL language for describing real-time systems using Horn Logic Denotations. Section 6 presents related work and Section 7 presents our conclusions. The main contribution of our work is to present a logic programming based framework in which software development is viewed as the activity of defining a DSL, and in which this DSL can be easily specified and implemented and, most significantly, verified as well.

2   Horn Logic Denotations

The denotational semantics [47,48,13] of a language has three components:

- *syntax*: specified as a BNF grammar
- *semantic algebras*: these are the basic domains along with associated operations; the meaning of a program is expressed in terms of these basic domains
- *valuation functions*: these are mappings from patterns of parse trees to values in the domains in the semantic algebra

Traditional denotational definitions express syntax in the BNF format, and the semantic algebras and valuation functions in λ-calculus. However, a disadvantage of this approach is that while the semantic algebra and the valuation functions can be easily made executable, syntax checking and generation of parse trees cannot. A parser has to be explicitly written or generated using a parser-generator. The parse trees generated by the parser will then be processed by the valuation functions to produce the program's denotation in terms of the semantic algebras. These parser and valuation functions constitute an interpreter for the language being defined. An interpreter for a language can be thought of as a specification of its operational semantics, however, using traditional notation (BNF and λ-calculus) it has to be obtained in a complex way.

In contrast, if we use logic programming—with its formal basis in Horn logic, a subset of first-order logic—both syntax and semantics can be specified in the same notation. Additionally, an interpreter is straightforwardly obtained from the denotational specification. The additional advantage that logic programming possesses, among others, is that even syntax can be expressed in it at a very high level—and uniformly in the same language used for the rest of the specification—and *a parser for the language is immediately obtained from the syntax specification*. Moreover, the generation of parse trees requires a trivial extension to the syntax specification. The parsing and parse tree generation facility of logic programming is described in almost every logic programming textbook as *Definite Clause Grammars (DCGs)*. The semantic algebras and valuation functions are also expressed in Horn logic quite easily, since Horn logic allows to define relations, which in turn subsume functions. The semantic algebra and valuation functions are executable, and can be used to obtain executable program denotations. A very significant consequence of this is that the fixpoint of a program's denotation can be computed (assuming that it is finite or finitely expressible—which is not uncommon when the program is enriched with input preconditions, as discussed later on), and such fixpoint can then be used for automatic verification (or model-checking). This implies that verification can also be conveniently done in the framework of Horn logic.

Thus, given a language, both its syntax and semantics can be directly and uniformly specified in logic programming. This specification is executable using any standard logic programming system. What is noteworthy is that different operational models will be obtained both for syntax checking and semantic evaluation by employing different execution strategies during logic program execution. For example, in the syntax phase, if a left-to-right, Prolog style, execution rule is used, then *recursive descent parsing* is obtained. On the contrary, if a *tabling-based* [4] execution strategy is used then *chart parsing* is obtained, etc. Likewise, by using different evaluation rules for evaluating the semantic functions, strict evaluation, non-strict evaluation, etc. can be obtained. By using bottom-up or tabled evaluation, the fixpoint of a program's denotation can be computed, which can be used for verification and structured debugging of the program.

Denotational semantics expressed in a Horn logic notation is executable, but so is denotational semantics expressed in the λ-calculus notation. However, semantics expressed via Horn logic allow for fixpoints of programs to be computed much more intuitively, simply, and efficiently than, we believe, in the case of the λ-calculus. There is a whole body of literature and implemented systems [4,35] for computing fixpoints of logic programs, because of their applicability to deductive databases [45,10,34]. Due to this reason, semantic-based verification (and program debugging) can be much more easily performed in the Horn logic denotational framework than using the λ-calculus based denotational framework, as shown later. This becomes even more prominent when we generalize Horn logic to Constraint Logic Programming—i.e., by adding additional domains (e.g., Real numbers, Sets) and predefined predicates over such domains. This generalization makes specification and verification of very complex systems, e.g., domain specific languages for real-time systems, considerably easier [18].

3 Software Engineering and Domain Specific Languages

As discussed earlier, one way of solving the problem of developing reliable software is to use domain specific languages. Domain specific languages are high-level languages in which domain experts can program at the level of abstraction at which they think and reason. Thus, the semantic gap between the design of a software system and its implementation is considerably reduced, resulting in fewer errors during the coding/implementation stage. Thus, we take a language-centric view of the software development process: to solve problems in a particular domain, a domain specific language should be first developed and then used for writing high-level programs to solve these problems. Of course, designing a language can be quite time-consuming, but we believe that the effort invested in designing the language is worthwhile.

A language-centric view of software engineering allows one to apply language-semantics based techniques for specification, implementation and verification of software systems. In particular, we can use the Horn logic denotational approach for specification, efficient implementation, and verification of the software system.

A language-centric view can also be adopted for developing complex software system. Any complex software system can be understood in terms of how it interacts with the outside world. Thus, to understand a software system, one has to understand its *input language*. The input language is of course nothing but a domain specific language. If we have a denotational specification of this DSL, and if this specification (both the syntax and semantics) happens to be executable, then this denotational specification is *also an executable specification of the software system*. In other words, an interpreter for the DSL of the software system is an implementation of the software system. If this executable denotational specification is written in the proper notation, then it can also be used for proving properties of the DSL (i.e., the software system) as well as the programs written in the DSL.

The Horn logic denotational semantics indeed makes all of the above possible. The syntax specification immediately yields a parser, with the help of the Definite Clause Grammar facility of logic programming systems. The semantic specification yields a back-end for the interpreter. Together with the syntax specification, the semantic specification yields a complete interpreter. Given a program, its denotation can be obtained with respect to the interpreter. This denotation can be run to execute the program. The denotation can be partially evaluated to produce compiled code. Thus, a provably correct compiler is obtained for free. Additionally, appropriate structured queries can be posed to the program's denotation and used for checking properties of the DSL as well as the programs. Bottom-up execution [34] or tabled execution [4] of the denotation yields its fixpoint. This fixpoint of the denotation can be used for model checking. Also, the denotation of a program can be thought of as a declarative specification of the relationship between inputs and outputs of the program, and can be partially evaluated to obtain a more compact relation between the inputs and outputs. This declarative logical denotation can be used to understand programs better: the programmer can find out possible ranges of inputs, given certain outputs, or vice versa.

The interpreter obtained from the Horn logic denotational semantics can also be easily instrumented to obtain traditional debuggers and profilers for the DSL. Typically, valuation predicates are maps from parse trees and the current state to a new state. Hooks can be automatically introduced, after a call to a valuation predicate, to give the user the ability to examine the current state, thus providing debugging facilities. Likewise, execution statistics can be automatically maintained as part of the state and presented to the user at his/her request during the execution, essentially yielding a profiler (observe that this is akin to developing abstract interpreters for the language).

Our logic programming based approach to software engineering is being applied to solve a number of problems. We are currently designing a domain specific language to enable biologists to program solutions to *phylogenetic inference problems* [41]. Phylogenetic inference involves study of the biocomplexity of the environment based on genetic sequencing and genetic matching. Solving a typical problem requires use of a number of software systems, along with a number of manual steps (e.g., judging which sequence alignment for two genes is the "best"), as well as extra low-level coding to glue everything together. A biologist has to be considerably sophisticated in use and programming of computers to solve these problems. We are developing a DSL for phylogenetic inference that will allow Biologists to write/debug/profile programs at their level of abstraction. The task will become much simpler for the biologist, giving them the opportunity to become more productive as well as be able to try out different "what-if?" scenarios.

Our approach is also being used to facilitate the navigation of complex web-structures (e.g. tables and frame-based pages) by blind users (blind-users typically access the WEB using audio-based interfaces). Given a complex structure, say a table, the web-page designer may wish to communicate only the essential parts of the table to a blind-user. In our approach, the web page-writer (or a third party) will attach to the web-page a domain specific language program that encodes the table navigation instructions [39].

4   A Domain Specific Language for File-Editor Commands

In this section we illustrate our Horn logic denotational framework through the use of a simple example. Consider the input language (a DSL) of a file-editor. We show how the logical denotational semantics of this DSL yields an executable specification of the file-editor. We also show how DSL programs can be compiled for efficiency. Later, we show how we can verify certain properties that a file-editor should satisfy (e.g., modifications to one file doesn't change other files).

Consider a simple file editor which supports the following commands: edit I (open the file whose name is in identifier I), newfile (create an empty file), forward (move file pointer to next record), backward (move file pointer to previous record), insert(R) (insert record whose value is in identifier R), delete (delete the current record), and quit (quit the editor, saving the file in the file system). Let us provide the logic denotational semantics for this language. The syntax of the input command language is shown in the BNF below:

```
Program     ::= edit Id cr Statements
Statement   ::= Command cr Statements | quit
Command     ::= newfile | moveforward | movebackward |
                    insert Record | delete
```

Note that cr stands for a carriage return, inserted between each editor command. To keep the example simple we assume that the records consist simply of integers. This BNF can be expressed as a DCG in a straightforward manner as shown in Figure 1. There is a one-to-one correspondence between the rules of the BNF and rules in the DCG. An extra argument has been added to the DCG to hold the recursively synthesized parse tree (note that the management of this additional argument can be easily automated). The DCG specification, when loaded in a Prolog system, automatically produces a parser. We next give the semantic algebras (Figure 2) for

```
program(session(I,S)) --> [edit], id(I),
        [cr], sequence(S).
sequence(seq(quit)) --> [quit].
sequence(seq(C,S)) -->
        command(C), [cr], sequence(S).
command(command(newfile)) --> [newfile].
command(command(forward)) --> [moveforward].
command(command(backward)) --> [moveback].
command(command(insert(R))) -->
        [insert],record(R).
command(command(delete)) --> [delete].
id(identifier(X)) --> atom(X).
record(rec(N)) --> integer(N)
```

Fig. 1: DCG for File Editor Language

each of the domains involved: the file store (represented as an association list of file names and their contents) and an open file (represented as a pair of lists; the file pointer is assumed to be currently on the first record of the second list). The semantic algebra essentially defines the basic operations used by the semantic valuation functions for giving meaning of programs.

The semantic valuation predicates that give the meaning of each construct in the language are given next (Figure 3). These semantic functions are mappings

```
%Define Access and Update Operations
access(Id,[(Id,File)|_],File).
access(Id,[(I,File)|Rest],File1) :-
         (I = Id -> File1 = File;
                    access(Id,Rest,File1)).
update(Id,File,[],[(Id,File)]).
update(Id,File,[(Id,_)|T],[(Id,File)|T]).
update(Id,File,[(I1,F1)|T],[(I1,F2)|NT]) :-
         (Id=I1 --> F2 = File, NT = T;
                    F2 = F1, update(Id,File,T,NT)).
%Operations on Open File representation
newfile(([],[])).
copyin(File,([],File)).
copyout((First,Second),File):-
             reverse(First,RevFirst),
             append(RevFirst,Second,File).
forwards((First,[X|Scnd]),([X|First],Scnd)).
forwards((First,[]),(First,[])).
backwards(([X|First],Scnd),(First,[X|Scnd])).
        backwards(([],Scnd),([],Scnd)).
        insert(A,(First,[]),(First,[A])).
        insert(A,(First,[X|Y]),([X|First],[A|Y])).
        delete((First,[_|Y]),(First,Y)).
        delete((First,[]),(First,[])).
        at_first_record(([],_)).
        at_last_record((_,[])).
        isempty(([],[])).
```

Fig. 2. Semantic Algebras for File Editor

from parse trees and a global state (the file system) to domains (file system, open files) that are used to describe meanings of programs. The above specification gives both the declarative and operational semantics of the editor.

Using a logic programming system, the above specification can serve as an interpreter for the command language of the editor, and hence serves as an implementation of the editor. Thus, this is an *executable specification* of an editor. Although editors are interactive programs, for simplicity, we assume that the commands are given in batches (interactive programs can also be handled by modeling the "unknown" commands through Prolog's unbound variables: we omit the discussion to keep the presentation simple). Thus, if the editor is invoked and a sequence of commands issued, starting with an unspecified file system (modeled as the unbound variable Fin), then the resulting file system (Fout) after executing all the editor commands will be given by the result of the query:

```
?- Comms = [edit,a,cr,newfile,cr,insert,1,cr,insert,2,cr,delete,
   cr,moveback,cr,insert,4,cr,insert,5,cr,delete,cr,quit]),
```

```
prog_val(session(identifier(I),S),FSIn,FSOut) :-
    access(I,FSIn,File), copyin(File,OpenFile),
    seq_val(S,OpenFile,NewOpenFile),
    copyout(NewOpenFile,OutFile),
    update(I,OutFile,FSIn,FSOut).
seq_val(seq(quit),InFile,InFile).
seq_val(seq(C,S),InFile,OutFile) :-
    comm_val(C,InFile,NewFile),
    seq_val(S,NewFile,OutFile).
comm_val(command(newfile),_,OutFile) :-
    newfile(OutFile).
comm_val(command(moveforward),InFile,OutFile) :-
    (isempty(InFile) → OutFile = InFile;
        (at_last_record(InFile) → OutFile=InFile;
        forwards(InFile,OutFile))).
comm_val(command(moveback),InFile,OutFile) :-
    (isempty(InFile) → InFile = OutFile;
        (at_first_record(InFile) →
        InFile = OutFile; backwards(InFile,OutFile))).
comm_val(command(insert(R)),InFile,OutFile) :-
    record_val(R,RV), insert(RV,InFile,OutFile).
comm_val(command(delete),InFile,OutFile) :-
    (isempty(InFile) →
    InFile = OutFile; delete(InFile,OutFile)).
record_val(R,R).
```

Fig. 3. Valuation Predicates

```
program(Tree,Comms,[]),    %produce parse tree
prog_val(Tree,Fin,Fout).   %execute commands
```

The final resulting file-system will be:

$$\text{Fout} = [(a,[rec(1),rec(4)])| \_B],$$
$$\text{Fin} = \_B.$$

The output shows that the final file system contains the file a that contains 2 records, and the previously unknown input file system (represented by Prolog's anonymous variable _B, aliased to Fin). The key thing to note is that in our logical denotational framework, a specification is very easy to write as well as easy to modify. This is because of the declarative nature of the logic programming formalism used and its basis in denotational semantics.

Given the executable implementation of the file-editor, and a program in its command language, we can partially evaluate it to obtain a more efficient implementation of the program. The result of partially evaluating the file-editor specification w.r.t. the previous command-language program is shown in Figure 4. Partial evaluation translates the editor command language program to a sequence of instructions that call operations defined in the semantic algebra.

This sequence of instructions looks a lot like "compiled" code. More efficient implementations of the editor can be obtained by implementing these semantic algebra operations in an efficient way, e.g., using a more efficient language like C or C++, instead of using logic programming. Compilation may not make much sense in case of a file-editor command language; however, there are domain specific languages that have been designed for processing special types of file. For example, the DSL MidiTrans [21] has been designed to manipulate digital music files expressed in the MIDI format. The MidiTrans language can be thought of as an editor-command language, and MidiTrans programs are sequences of commands applied to a MIDI file. In this case compilation (via partial evaluation) is important, in order to achieve efficient execution of MidiTrans programs. Derivation of MidiTrans using Horn logic denotation descriptions is currently in progress [40].

```
access(a, Fin, C),
copyin(C, _),
newfile(D),
insert(rec(1), D, E),
insert(rec(2), E, F),
( isempty(F) → G=F
   ; delete(F, G)),
( isempty(G) → H=G
    ; at_first_record(G) →
      H=G
      ; backwards(G, H)),
insert(rec(4), H, I),
insert(rec(5), I, J),
( isempty(J) → K=J
   ; delete(J, K)),
copyout(K, L),
update(a,L,Fin,Fout).
```

Fig. 4. Compiled code

5   Program Denotation and Verification

Axiomatic semantics is perhaps the most well-researched technique for verifying properties of programs. In Axiomatic Semantics [22] preconditions and postconditions are specified to express conditions under which a program is correct. The notation $(P)C(Q)$ states that if the property P holds before execution of command C, then property Q must hold afterwards. P and Q are typically expressed in a well-defined form of logic. In this section we will explore the use of Horn logic for verifying/checking properties of programs. It is well known that the postconditions of a program are theorems with respect to the denotation of that program and the program's preconditions [47,48]. Given that the program's denotation is expressed in Horn logic, the preconditions can be uniformly incorporated into this denotation. The postconditions can then be executed as queries w.r.t this extended program denotation, effectively checking if they are satisfied or not. In effect, symbolic *model checkers* [5] can be specified and generated automatically. By generalizing Horn logic to constraint logic programming, real-time systems can also be specified and implemented [18] and parallelizing compilers obtained [20].

One way to prove correctness is to show that given the set of all possible state-configurations, S, that can exist at the beginning of the command C, if P holds for a state-configuration $s \in S$, then Q holds for the state-configuration that results after executing the command C in s. If the denotation is a logic program, then it is possible to generate all possible state-configurations. However, the number of such state-configurations may be infinite. In such a case, the precondition P can be specified in such a way that it acts as a *finite* generator of all relevant state-configurations. A model checker is thus obtained from this specification. This model checker can be seen as a debugging aid, since a user can obtain a program's denotation, add preconditions to it and then pose queries to verify the properties that the user thinks should hold.

Consider the specification of the file-editor. Under the assumption that the file system is finite and that the pool of possible records is also finite, we can verify, for instance, that every editing session consisting of an insertion followed by a deletion leaves the original file unchanged. Since the name space of file-names and record-names is infinite, we will use a precondition to restrict their size. The query for verifying this property, along with the appropriate precondition to assure finiteness is shown below. The precondition essentially restricts file names to either a, b or c, and the record names to 1, 2 or 3 (we will show later on how to make this query more general). The member predicate is the standard predicate for checking membership of an element in a list; when its first argument is unbound and the second argument is bound to a list, it acts as a generator of values.

```
?- member(X, [a,b,c]), member(Y, [1,2,3])         %precondition
   program(A,[edit,X,cr,insert,Y,cr,delete,cr,quit],[]),
   prog_val(A,F,G),
   F ≠ G.        %negated postcondition
```

The above query corresponds to verifying whether there exist values for X (file name) and Y (record value) such that inserting and deleting Y in X leads to a resulting file system different from the one we started from. This query should fail, if indeed the result of one insertion and one deletion leaves the file system unchanged. The backtracking mechanism of logic programming goes through all possible values for variables X and Y (finiteness is hence important), and finds that in every case F = G holds, and thus the whole query fails because the final call asserts that F ≠ G. In most practical cases, the restriction of having a finite generator can be readily dismissed as long as the fixpoint of the considered computation can be analyzed in a finite amount of time. The above example could be encoded more simply as:

```
?- program(A, [edit,X,cr,insert,Y,cr,delete,cr,quit],[]),
        prog_val(A,F,G), F ≠ G.
```

If executed on a logic programming system which uses a fair search strategy (e.g., we tested it on the XSB system [45], which uses tabling), the query will produce a failed answer, thus verifying the desired property.

More complex properties can be semi-automatically verified using this semantic definition. Let us study the following property: if an editing session is open for a certain file (let us say file a), then no other file is affected. Proving this property is not straightforward—as it requires being able to infer independence of arguments. This property can be easily tested using a combination of transformation and analysis techniques. We start by partially evaluating the editor specification with respect to the query:

```
?- program(X,[edit,a,cr|Rest],[]),
        prog_val(X,[(a,AIn),(b,BIn),(c,CIn)],[(a,AOut),(b,BOut),(c,COut)]).
```

(we are assume that the file system contains only 3 files; this can be easily generalized). The entry point of the partially evaluated program is the following:

```
entry([edit,a,cr|A], [(a,B),(b,C),(c,D)], [(a,E),(b,F),(c,G)]) :-
        'entry.edit1'(A, B, C, D, E, F, G).
'entry.edit1'(A, B, C, D, E, F, G) :-
        sequence1(A, H),
        seq_val1(H, B, I),
        I=(J,K),
        reverse1(J, L),
        C=F,              %%% **
        D=G,              %%% **
        append3(L, K, E).
```

We have annotated the two unifications (with '**') to show how the partially evaluated program shows that the output files for b and c are indeed identical to the input ones—i.e., those two files are not affected by the editing session. Using a constraint-based execution, which allows to solve equality and inequality constraints, a query like

```
?- (C ≠ F; D ≠ G),
        entry([edit,a,cr|Rest],[(a,B),(b,C),(c,D)],[(a,E),(b,F),(c,G)]).
```

terminates with a failure. Thus, there is no computation which edits file a and modifies also file b or c. This property could be also determined without executing the last query but by simply performing *static analysis*—for *independence detection*—on it [12].

5.1   DSLs: Verification with Constraints

When we generalize Horn logic to Constraint Logic Programming [31] more interesting applications become possible. For example, domain specific languages for realizing real-time systems can be modeled and verified/model-checked using our approach. We illustrate this through an example. Consider the domain specific language UPPAAL [30,2], designed by researchers at Uppsala University and Aalborg University. We specify the syntax and semantics of this DSL using our Horn logic denotational approach, and show how program denotations can be used for automatic verification.

UPPAAL is a domain specific language designed for specifying and verifying concurrent real-time systems. The concurrent real-time system is modeled as a collection of *timed automata* [1]. A timed automaton is a finite state automaton augmented with timers. These timers may be reset to zero on state transitions, and additionally, state transitions may also be conditioned on a given timer satisfying certain properties (e.g., the transition can be made only if a certain amount of time has elapsed on a particular timer). The UPPAAL language provides constructs for defining these automata, along with timing constraints that each timed automaton imposes.

A real-time system is essentially a recognizer of a sequence of timed-events. A sequence of timed-events is correct if the individual events occur in a certain order (syntactic correctness) and the time at which these events occur satisfy the time-constraints laid out by the real-time system specification (semantic correctness). The syntax and semantics of a real-time system can be specified using constraint logic denotations [18]—the key insight is that the specification of a real-time system is a semantic specification of its corresponding timed-language [18]. Time constraints can be modeled as constraints over real numbers [31]. The semantic algebra models the state, which consists of the global time (wall-clock time), and the valuation predicates are maps from sequences of events to the global time. This constraint logic denotational specification is executable and can be used for verifying interesting properties of real-time systems, e.g., *safety* (for instance, if we design a real-time system for a railroad gate controller, we want to make sure that at the time a train is at the gate, the gate can never be open), and *bounded liveness* (for instance, the railroad gate is not closed forever). In the real-time systems modeled, we do not exactly know when an event is actually going to occur, all we know is the relationship between the time at which different events took place. Thus, the exact time at which each event took place cannot be computed from the constraint logic denotation. However, the constraints laid out in the denotation together with constraints that the safety property enforces can be solved to check for their consistency. Essentially, the constraints laid out by the real-time system should entail the constraints laid out by the properties to be verified, if the property indeed holds.

The real-time system that we wish to verify can be specified in the UPPAAL domain specific language. A real-time system that is to be modeled as a timed automaton is expressed as an UPPAAL program. If we give the semantics of the UPPAAL language using constraint denotations, then an executable specification

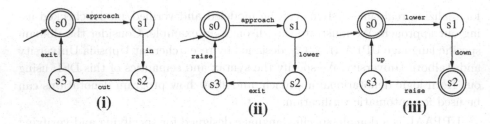

Fig. 5. Train, Controller, and Gate automata

of a timed-automaton system is easily obtained. This executable specification can be run on a constraint logic programming systems, such as $CLP(\mathcal{R})$ [31], and used for verifying properties of the real-time system. The BNF of the UPPAAL language can be found in [30,2]. The DCG of the UPPAAL language is given in Appendix A. The Horn logic semantics of UPPAAL program is given as predicates that map the components of the abstract syntax of the program to a list of tuples of the form $\langle \alpha, \tau, States \rangle$, where α is a particular automaton transition, τ is the time at which that transition took place, and $States$ is the description of the states (of the different timed automaton) from which the transition took place. The postconditions are queries that check for appropriate patterns in this semantics. The semantics is shown in Appendix B. Note that for reasons of practicality our semantic definition uses **assert**, a non-logical feature of Prolog. It is possible to give a completely declarative logical semantics, but this is avoided here for the sake of readability.

The UPPAAL language specifies a real-time system in terms of a collection of timed automata. Each automaton is specified using the **process** construct. The **process** construct identifies the name of the automaton, its states, the initial state (using the **init** statement), and the transitions (using the **trans** construct). The actions associated with each transition—i.e., testing a conditions on clocks, resetting clocks, communicating with other processes—are specified with each transition.

We next specify a real-time system for controlling a gate at a railroad crossing using the UPPAAL Domain Specific Language. The system is composed of three processes, a gate-controller, the gate itself, and the train. The train is modeled by the *timed automaton* shown in figure 5(i). It has four different transitions that are labeled **approach in, out, exit**: (i) The **approach** edge corresponds to the train approaching the gate; (ii) the edge labeled **in** denotes that the train is at the gate; (iii) the edge **out** denotes that the train has just left the gate; and, (iv) and **exit** denotes that the train has left the gate area. The controller is modeled by the timed-automaton in figure 5(ii); it synchronizes with the train process on the **approach** and **exit** edges described above. The controller has two other edges labeled: (i) **lower** denoting starting of the lowering of the gate; and, (ii) raise denoting starting of the raising of the gate. Finally, the gate is modeled by the timed-automaton in figure 5(iii). Time constraints force the train to employ at most 5 units of time to cross the gate area, with a speed which should allow 2 units of time to the gate to lower before the arrival of the train. The controller should be able to react in less than one unit of time to the approach of the train, and the gate should employ no more than one unit of time to completely lower or raise the gate. The UPPAAL program describing this system is presented in Figure 6.

```
// Global Declarations
clock c,e,d;
chan approach,exit,
    lower,raise;
//
// Processes Section
//
process train {
  state s0, s1, s2, s3;
  init s0;
  trans
    s0 → s1 {
      sync approach!;
      assign c := 0;
    },
    s1 → s2 {
      guard c > 2;
    },
    s2 → s3,
    s3 → s0 {
      guard c < 5;
      sync exit!;
    };
}
```

```
process cntl {
    state s0, s1, s2, s3;
    init s0;
    trans s0 → s1 {
      sync approach?;
      assign e := 0;
    },
    s1 → s2 {
      guard e == 1;
      sync lower!;
    },
    s2 → s3 {
      sync exit?;
      assign e := 0;
    },
    s3 → s0 {
      guard e < 1;
      sync raise!;
    };
}
```

```
process gate {
    state s0, s1, s2, s3,
s4;
    init s0;
    trans s0 → s1 {
      sync lower?;
      assign d := 0;
    },
    s1 → s2 {
      guard d < 1;
    },
    s2 → s3 {
      sync raise?;
      assign d := 0;
    },
    s3 → s4 {
      guard d > 1;
    },
    s4 → s0 {
      guard d < 2;
    };
}
// System Description
system train,cntl,gate;
```

Fig. 6. UPPAAL Program

This program can be fed to the executable syntax/semantics specification shown in Appendices A and B. Partial evaluation of this program (massaged for readability) yields the following program:

```
train(s0,approach,s1,T1,T2,T3) :- T3 = T1.
train(s1,epsilon,s2,T1,T2,T2) :- T1 - T2 > 2.
train(s2,epsilon,s3,T1,T2,T2).
train(s3,exit,s0,T1,T2,T2) :- T1 - T2 < 5.
train(X,lower,X,T1,T2,T2).
train(X,raise,X,T1,T2,T2).
```

```
gate(s0,lower,s1,T1,T2,T1).              cntl(s0,approach,s1,T1,T2,T1).
gate(s1,epsilon,s2,T1,T2,T2)             cntl(s1,lower,s2,T1,T2,T2)
   :- T1 - T2 < 1.                          :- T1 - T2 = 1.
gate(s2,raise,s3,T1,T2,T1).              cntl(s2,exit,s3,T1,T2,T1).
gate(s3,epsilon,s4,T1,T2,T2)             cntl(s3,raise,s0,T1,T2,T2)
   :- T1-T2 > 1, T1-T2 < 2.                  :- T1-T2 < 1.
gate(s4,epsilon,s0,T1,T2,T2)             cntl(X,epsilon,X,T1,T2,T2).
   :- T1-T2 < 2.
gate(X,approach,X,T1,T2,T2).
gate(X,exit,X,T1,T2,T2).
```

```
system([],S0,S1,S2,T,T0,T1,T2,[]).
system([X|S],S0,S1,S2,T,T0,T1,T2,[(X,T,[S0,S1,S2])|R]):-
   train(S0, X, S00, T, T0, T00),
   gate(S1, X, S10, T, T1, T10) ,
   cntl(S2, X, S20, T, T2, T20) , TA > T,
   system(S,S00,S10,S20,TA,T00,T10,T20,R).
```

The above constraint denotation of the railroad crossing controller is an executable specification of the composite real-time system. The composite specification can be used for verifying various global properties. For example, we may want to verify the safety property that when the train is at the gate, the gate is always closed. These properties are specified by the designer, and ensure correctness of the real-time system specification. We use the axiomatic semantics based framework discussed earlier to perform this verification. We use preconditions to put restrictions on the events list to ensure finiteness of the computation, and then the properties of interest (postconditions) can be verified. The net effect obtained is that of (deductive) model-checking. Thus, our queries to the program will be of the form:

```
pre_condition(X),
system(X, ...),
not post_condition(X)
```

where post_condition is the verification condition, while pre_condition is the condition imposed on the input—e.g., characterization of the input states of interest and conditions to ensure finiteness. This query should fail, if the post_condition holds true. The pre_condition should be such that it generates all sentences satisfying it. For example, if we want to check that the event "the train is in the gate area" (state s2 of the train process) never occurs before the event "the gate is down" (state s2 of process gate), then a possible precondition is that the transitions to state s2 for the train or to s2 for the gate must occur between two **approach** events. This precondition can be expressed so that it can act as a generator of all possible strings that start with an **approach** and end in **approach** (i.e., thus focusing only on one train at the time). Integrating this precondition in the semantics and partially evaluating it again, we get a modified definition of the **system** predicate as follows:

```
system(_,[],_,_,_,_,_,_,_,[]) :-
system(N,[X|S],S0,S1,S2,T,T0,T1,T2,[(X,T,[S0,S1,S2])|R]) :-
    train(S0,X,S00,T,T0,T00),
    gate(S1,X,S10,T,T1,T10) ,
    contr(S2,X,S20,T,T2,T20) ,
    TA > T, (X = approach ->
                (N = 0 -> M = 1; Rest = []);
                M = N),
    system(M,S,S00,S10,S20,TA,T00,T10,T20,R).
```

The **system** predicate thus acts as a generator, generating all possible strings that begin with **approach** and end in **approach** and that will be accepted by the automata. Now a property can be verified by calling the **system** predicate with uninstantiated input, and checking that the negated property does not hold for every possible meaning of the automata. Suppose, we want to verify that when the train is at the crossing, the gate must be down. This boils down to the following fact: in every possible run of the real-time system, the transition of the train to s2 must occur after the transition of the gate to state s2. The negated property will be that the train gets to s2 before the gate gets to s2. Thus, for example the query

```
?- system(0,X,s0,s0,s0,0,0,0,0,R),
   append(_,[(_,_,[s2,s1,_])|_],R).
```

will fail when run on a constraint logic programming system (we used the CLP($\mathcal{R}$) [31] system). The **append** program is the standard logic program for appending two lists.

Likewise, if we want to verify that the gate will be down at least 4 units of time—i.e., the time between the gate transition to s1 and the transition to s0 is at least 4 time units—then we will pose the following query:

```
?- system(0,s0,s0,s0,0,0,0,0,X,R),
   append(A, [(_,T2,[_,s4,_]),(_,_,[_,s0,_]) |_], R), % Trans. to s0
   append(_, [(_,_,[_,s0,_]), (_,T1,[_,s1,_])|_], A), % Trans. to s1
   T2 - T1 < 4.
```

The above query will fail. Using our constraint-based approach one can also find out the minimum and the maximum amount of time the gate will be closed by posing the following query:

```
?- system(0,s0,s0,s0,0,0,0,0,X,R),
   append(A, [(_,T2,[_,s4,_]) , (_,_,[_,s0,_]) |_], R),
   append(_, [(_,_,[_,s0,_]), (_,T1,[_,s1,_])|_], A),
   N < T2 - T1 < M, M > 0, N > 0.
```

We obtain the answer M < 7, N > 1. This tells us that the minimum time the gate will be down is 1 units, and the maximum time it will be down is 7 units. Other properties of the real-time system can similarly be tested. The ability to easily compute values of unknowns is a distinct advantage of a logic programming based approach, and considerable effort is required in other approaches used for verifying real-time systems to achieve similar behavior.

5.2   Discussion

A major weakness of our approach is that we have to make sure that the verification of properties leads to finite computations. The use of constraint handling and the use of tabling or bottom up computation in the underlying execution model often guarantee such a property (as seen in the examples in Section 5). If it is not, then we have to impose preconditions that ensure this. A popular approach to verifying an infinite state system is to *abstract* it (so that it becomes finite) while making sure that enough information remains in the abstraction so that the property of interest can be verified. The technique of abstraction can be easily adapted in our logical denotational approach: (i) one can give an abstract (logical denotational) semantics for the language, and then run tests on the resulting abstract denotation obtained, using the approach described above. (ii) we can use abstract interpretation tools built for logic programming to abstract the concrete denotation and use that for verifying the properties; in fact, work is in progress in to use non-failure analysis of constraint logic programs [11] to verify properties of real-time systems. A third approach that can be used to remove the finiteness restriction is to use first-order theorem proving. The logical denotation of a program provides an axiomatization w.r.t. the language's semantics. These axioms can then be fed to a theorem prover, along with the preconditions and postconditions, and other additional axioms that may be needed in the postcondition, to perform verification [16].

However, we feel that our approach based on preconditions and postconditions is a pretty good compromise. While we do not verify the system completely, we do verify the program subject to the preconditions, and thus gain more confidence regarding software correctness.

Note that verification can be done more efficiently by inserting preconditions and postconditions in the program's denotation, and then partially evaluating the interpreter obtained for the language with respect to this annotated program denotation. We essentially obtain a compiled version of the program annotated with preconditions and postconditions. We have adopted this technique in both the domain specific languages considered in our examples. It is a lot more efficient to execute this partially evaluated annotated program rather than the original annotated denotation.

The interactive behavior of logic programming provides a simple interactive access to the verification process, encouraging users to "play" with preconditions and postconditions and try different scenarios.

Note also that while the examples that we have included in this paper use only *direct semantics*, *continuation semantics* can also be easily modeled using Horn logic and constraints [14].

6   Related Work

Domain Specific Languages have been becoming increasingly popular. Conferences have been organized on DSLs [43,25,33,6] and several groups have been working on developing frameworks for implementing and analyzing DSLs. This includes the pioneering work of Consel's group in France that has developed a semantics-based framework which has some similarity to ours [7]. However, Consel's framework is based on the traditional lambda calculus, thus syntax analysis and verification, unlike our framework, have to be done outside of the framework. Hudak has proposed the notion of *Domain Specific Embedded Languages (DSEL)* where a Domain Specific Language is built on top of the constructs of an existing General Purpose Language (GPL). As a result, an implementation for the DSEL is easily obtained since the compiler for the GPL also serves as a compiler for the DSEL. The fact that the constructs of the DSEL are built on top of a GPL imposes some constraints on the design of the DSEL. In our approach the DSL designer has complete freedom: as long as the semantics of a construct can be expressed in terms of Horn logic, it can be included in the DSL. Also, in the DSEL framework, the debugger used will be that of the GPL, which might expose the underlying GPL to the DSEL user. Modifying the debugger to hide the details of the GPL while debugging a DSEL program may be quite hard. We believe that the DSEL approach is motivated by the fact that many aspects of the infrastructure needed for a DSL cannot be directly handled in traditional λ-calculus frameworks (e.g., parsing). For these missing aspects, piggy-backing on an existing language simplifies the task of DSL infrastructure development. No such piggy-backing is needed in our approach, since everything can be handled in the logic programming framework.

The major difference of our frameworks from others is that ours is based on logic programming. As a result, a complete interpreter/compiler can be rapidly obtained from the semantic specification. Additionally, verification/debugging can be done in the same framework, since the Horn logic denotation of a DSL program can be viewed as an axiomatization of the problem that the program is supposed to solve. The rapidity with which parsers, interpreters and compilers can be realized is of great importance to the design of domain specific languages. Typically, while a language is being designed, the ability to run programs written in that language so as to better understand the impact of various design decisions is of great significance. The designers can come up with a feature, writes its syntax and semantic specifications, and obtain its implementation in a few hours of work compared to few days or weeks. Our experience indicates that, as a result, the process of language design is greatly accelerated.

Logic programming has been applied in the past to aid and automate different aspects of the software engineering process. These efforts include work by McClusky et al [36,37] on verifying and debugging specifications written in $\mathcal{Z}$ using logic programming, application of logic programming to model checking [42], to component based software engineering [32,9], etc.

7   Conclusions

In this paper we presented a Horn logic and constraint based framework for using denotational semantics for specifying, efficiently implementing, and verifying/debugging Domain Specific Language programs [19]. The three distinct advantages that our Horn logic approach offers are: (i) the syntax specification is conveniently and rapidly expressed using the Definite Clause Grammar facility of logic programming to obtain a parser for the language with little effort; (ii) a uniform framework is created for the specification of all components (syntax and semantics) of the denotational description; (iii) verification/debugging of programs written in the DSL. In this regard, our framework is more advantageous than the frameworks for DSLs developed using the λ-calculus, e.g., in [7].

Our framework can also be used for software development, by taking a language-centric view of the software development process. In the language-centric view of software development, we think of the software system as a processor of programs written in the software system's input language (a domain specific language). An executable semantic specification of this input language is also an executable specification of the software system. This executable specification can be made more efficient by using partial evaluation. The executable specification can also be used for verification and model checking purposes. In this paper, we illustrated our framework by considering two domain specific languages: a file-editor command language and a language for specifying real-time systems. Our framework provides a rapid way of obtaining an executable specification of a domain specific language or a software system. For example, it took us only 2-3 hours to produce the syntax and semantic specification of the UPPAAL language shown in appendix A and B, which we could then use to verify properties on different examples. While one may not use our approach for obtaining a final implementation of a DSL, it is certainly useful for rapidly prototyping and "debugging" the DSL or a software system and for quickly verifying programs written in the DSL. Work is in progress to use our framework for specification, implementation, and verification of other DSLs. Once the DSL has been prototyped, an efficient optimizing implementation can be obtained by using traditional compilation techniques.

Acknowledgments

The authors wish to thank Neil Jones for helpful comments on this work. The authors have been supported by NSF grants CCR 96-25358, CDA-9729848, EIA

98-10732, HRD 98-00209, HRD 96-28450, INT 95-15256, CCR 98-75279 and by a grant from the Fullbright Foundation's US-Spain Research Program.

References

1. R. Alur and D. Dill. The Theory of Timed Automata. *Theoretical Computer Science*, 126, 1994.
2. J. Bengtsson, et al. *UPPAAL: A Tool Suite for Validation and Verification of Real-time Systems*. http://www.docs.uu.se/rtmv/uppaal, 1997.
3. J. Bentley. Little Languages. *CACM*, 29(8):711-721, 1986.
4. W. Chen and D. S. Warren. Tabled Evaluation with Delaying for General Logic Programs. In *Journal of the ACM*, 43(1):20-74, 1996.
5. E. M. Clark, E. A. Emerson and A. P. Sistla. Automatic Verification of finite-state Concurrent Systems Using Temporal Logic Specification. In *ACM TOPLAS*, 8(2), 1986.
6. W. Codenie, K. De Hondt, P. Steyaert and A. Vercammen. From custom applications to domain-specific frameworks. In *Communications of the ACM*,Vol. 40, No. 10, pages 70-77, 1997.
7. C. Consel. Architecturing Software Using a Methodology for Language Development. In *Proc. 10th Int'l Symp. on Prog. Lang. Impl., Logics and Programs (PLILP)*, Springer LNCS 1490, pp. 170-194, 1998.
8. M. A. Covington. Natural Language Processing for Prolog Programmers. Prentice Hall, Englewood Cliffs, NJ, 1994
9. S. M. Daniel. An Optimal Control System based on Logic Programming for Automated Synthesis of Software Systems Using Commodity Objects. *Proc. Workshop on Logic Programming and Software Enginering*. London, UK, July 2000.
10. S. K. Das. *Deductive Databases and Logic Programming*. Addison-Wesley. 1992.
11. S. Debray, P. Lopez-Garcia, and M. Hermenegildo. Non-failure Analysis for Logic Programs. In *International Conference on Logic Programming*. MIT Press, 1997.
12. M. Garcia de la Banda et al. Independence in Constraint Logic Programming. In *Procs. Int. Symposium on Logic Programming*, MIT Press, 1993.
13. C. Gunter. *Programming Language Semantics*. MIT Press. 1992.
14. G. Gupta. Horn Logic Denotations and Their Applications. In *The Logic Programming Paradigm: The next 25 years*, Proc. Workshop on Strategic Research Directions in Logic Prog., LNAI, Springer Verlag, May 1999.
15. G. Gupta. Logic Programming based Frameworks for Software Engineering. *Proc. Workshop on Logic Programming and Software Enginering*. London, UK, July 2000.
16. G. Gupta. *A Horn Logic Denotational Approach to Verification based on First Order Theorem Proving*. Internal report. Dec. 1998.
17. G. Gupta. *Why Logic Programming Matters?* In *Proc. ACM Rio Grande chapter workshop on Computing*. 1994.
18. G. Gupta and E. Pontelli. A Constraint-based Denotational Approach to Specification and Verification of Real-time Systems. In *Proc. Real-time Systems Symposium*, IEEE pp. 230-239, 1997.
19. G. Gupta and E. Pontelli. Specification, Implementation, and Verification of Domain Specific Languages: A Logic Programming-based Approach. Technical Report, NMSU, Mar 1999.

20. G. Gupta, E. Pontelli, R. Felix-Cardenas, A. Lara, Automatic Derivation of a Provably Correct Parallelizing Compiler, In *Proceedings of International Conference on Parallel Processing*, IEEE Press, pp. 579-586, 1998.
21. R. Hartley. *MidiTrans: a MIDI File Transform Language*. Tech. Report, NMSU, 1998.
22. C. A. R. Hoare. An Axiomatic Basis for Computer Programming. In *Comm. of the ACM*. Vol. 12. 1969.
23. C. A. R. Hoare. Unification of Theories: A Challenge for Computing Science. *Proc. COMPASS/ADT*, Springer LNCS 1130, 1995, pp. 49-57.
24. C. A. R. Hoare. Unifying Theories : A Personal Statement. ACM Computing Surveys 28(4):46 (1996).
25. P. Hudak. Modular Domain Specific Languages and Tools. In *IEEE Software Reuse Conf.* 2000.
26. N. Jones. Introduction to Partial Evaluation. In *ACM Computing Surveys*. 28(3):480-503, 1996.
27. R. A. Kowalski. Logic for Problem Solving. North Holland. 1979.
28. R. A. Kowalski: Logic for Data Description. Logic and Data Bases 1977: 77-103
29. R. A. Kowalski: Logic for Knowledge Representation. FSTTCS 1984: 1-12
30. K. Larsen, P. Pettersson, and W. Yi. UPPAAL in a Nutshell. In *Software Tools for Technology Transfer*. 1997.
31. J. L. Lassez and J. Jaffar. Constraint logic programming. In *Proc. 14th ACM POPL*, 1987.
32. K.-K. Lau. The Role of Logic Programming in Next-generation Component-based Software Development. *Proc. Workshop on Logic Programming and Software Enginering*. G. Gupta and I. V. Ramakrishnan (eds), London, UK, July 2000.
33. N. G. Leveson, M. P. E. Heimdahl, and J. D. Reese. Designing Specification Languages for Process Control Systems: Lessons Learned and Steps to the Future. In *Software Engineering - ESEC/FSE*, Springer Verlag, pages 127-145, 1999.
34. J. W. Lloyd. *Foundations of Logic Programming*. Springer Verlag. 2nd ed. 1987.
35. V.W. Marek and M. Truszczyński. Stable Models and an Alternative Logic Programming Paradigm. In K.R. Apt, V.W. Marek, M. Truszcziński, and D. S. Warren, editors, *The Logic Programming Paradigm*. Springer Verlag, 1999.
36. T. L. McCluskey, J. M. Porteous, Y. Naik, C. T. Taylor, S. V A Jones. Requirements Capture Method and its use in an Air Traffic Control Application, The Journal of Software Practice and Experience, 25(1), January 1995.
37. T. L. McCluskey, M. M. West, Towards the Automated Debugging and Maintenance of Logic-based Requirements Models. ASE '98: Proceedings of the 13th IEEE International Conference on Automated Software Engineering, Hawaii. IEEE Press, (pages 105-114). 1998.
38. S. Muggleton. Inductive Logic Programming. New Generation Computing, 1991, 8(4):295-310.
39. E. Pontelli, W. Xiong, G. Gupta, A. Karshmer. *A Domain Specific Language Framework for Non-Visual Browsing of Complex HTML Structures* ACM Int. Conference on Assistive Technologies, 2000.
40. E. Pontelli, G. Gupta, and A. Lara. *Horn Logical Semantics for MidiTrans*. Internal Report, New Mexico State University.
41. E. Pontelli, D. Ranjan, G. Gupta, and B. Milligan. PhyLog: A Domain Specific Language for Describing Phylogenetic Inference Processes. Internal Report, New Mexico State University, 2000.

42. Y. S. Ramakrishnan, C. R. Ramakrishnan, I. V. Ramakrishnan et al. Efficient Model Checking using Tabled Resolution. In *Proceedings of Computer Aided Verification (CAV'97)*. 1997.
43. C. Ramming. *Proc. Usenix Conf. on Domain-Specific Languages*. Usenix, 1997.
44. M. Raskovsky, P. Collier. From Standard to Implementational Denotational Semantics. In *Semantics Directed Compiler Generation*. Springer. pp. 94-139, 1994.
45. K. Sagonas, T. Swift, and D. S. Warren. XSB as an efficient deductive database engine. In *Proc. SIGMOD International Conf. on Management of Data*, 1994.
46. D. Sahlin. *An Automatic Partial Evaluator for Full Prolog*. Ph.D. Thesis, Royal Inst. of Techn. Sweden, 1994.
47. D. Schmidt. *Denotational Semantics: a Methodology for Language Development*. W. C. Brown Publishers, 1986.
48. D. Schmidt. Programming language semantics. In *ACM Computing Surveys*, 28-1, 265-267, 1996.
49. D. Schmidt. On the Need for a Popular Formal Semantics. *Proc. ACM Conf. on Strategic Directions in Computing Research*, Cambridge, MA, June 1996. ACM SIGPLAN Notices 32-1 (1997) 115-116.
50. K. Ueda, T. Chikayama. Design of the Kernel Language for the Parallel Inference Machine. The Computer Journal 33(6):494-500 (1990).
51. P. Van Hentenryck. *Constraint Handling in Prolog*. MIT Press, 1988.
52. D. H. D. Warren. Logic Programming for Compiler-writing. *Software Practice and Experience*, 10, pp. 97-125. 1979.

Appendix A: Definite Clause Grammar for UPPAAL

```
ita(ita(V,P,G)) --> varlist(V), proclist(P), globals(G).
varlist([])     --> { true }.
varlist([X|Y]) --> channel(X), varlist(Y).
varlist([X|Y]) --> variable(X), varlist(Y).

proclist([P])  --> proc(P).
proclist([P|Q]) --> proc(P), proclist(Q).

globals(system(List)) --> ['system'], idlist(List), [';'].
channel(chan(L)) --> [chan], idlist(L), [';'].
variable(var(clock,L)) --> [clock], idlist(L), [';'].
proc(proc(Id,States,Trans)) --> [process], id(Id),
            ['{'],statedecls(States), transdecls(Trans) , ['}'].
idlist([I])   --> id(I).
idlist([I|L]) --> id(I), [','], idlist(L).

statedecls(state(Initial,States)) -->
    [state], idlist(States), [';'], [init], id(Initial), [';'].

transdecls(trans(L)) --> [trans], translist(L) , [';'].
translist([A])   --> trans(A).
translist([A|B]) --> trans(A), [','],translist(B).
trans(t(I1,I2,G,S,A)) -->
    id(I1), ['->'], id(I2), ['{'], opg(G), ops(S), opa(A), ['}'].

opg(noguard) --> {true}.
opg(guard(L)) --> [guard], guardlist(L), [';'].
ops(nosync)      --> {true}.
ops(sync(send,I))   --> [sync], id(I), ['!'],[';'].
ops(sync(receive,I)) --> [sync], id(I), ['?'], [';'].
opa(noassign) --> {true}.
opa(assign(L)) --> [assign], assignlist(L),[';'].

guardlist([L])   --> guard(L).
guardlist([L|R]) --> guard(L), [','], guardlist(R).
assignlist([A])   --> assign(A).
assignlist([A|B]) --> assign(A), [','], assignlist(B).
assign(A) --> clockassign(A).

guard(compare(I,N,Op)) --> id(I), relop(Op), nat(N).
guard(ccompare(I1,I2,N,Op1,Op2)) -->
    id(I1), relop(Op1), id(I2), oper(Op2), nat(N).

clockassign(assign(I,N)) --> id(I) , [':='], nat(N).

relop('<')  --> ['<'].
relop('<=') --> ['<='].
relop('>')  --> ['>'].
```

```
relop('>=') -->   ['>='].
relop('=')  -->   ['=='].
oper(plus)  -->   ['+'].
oper(minus) -->   ['-'].
nat(X) -->  [X], {integer(X)}.
id(X)  -->  [X], {atom(X)}.
```

Appendix B: Logical Denotation of UPPAAL

```
semita( ita([var(clock,Vars),chan(Chan)] , Procs , System) ) :-
    semprocs(Procs,Vars,Chan,Initials),
    semglobals(System,Initials,Vars,Chan).

semglobals(system(List),_,Vars,_) :-
    length(List,N), length(States,N),
    length(Vars,M), length(Clocks,M),
    append(States,[C|Clocks],Args1),
    append(Args1, [[(X,C)|Remainder]], Args),
    Head =.. [system,[X|Y]|Args],
    generate_body(States,List,Clocks,C,X,Body,NewStates,NewClocks),
    append(NewStates,[T1|NewClocks],NewArgs1),
    append(NewArgs1,[Remainder],NewArgs),
    RecCall =.. [system,Y|NewArgs],
    assert((Head :- Body, (T1>C) , RecCall)).

generate_body([State],[Name],Clocks,GClock,Symbol,C,[NState],Clocks1):-
    gen_new_clocks(Clocks,Clocks1,ClocksCode),
    C =.. [Name,State,Symbol, NState,GClock|ClocksCode].
generate_body([State|OtherStates], [Name|OtherNames], Clocks,
            GClock, Symbol, (Call,OtherCalls),
        [NState|NewStates], NewClocks):-
    gen_new_clocks(Clocks,Clocks1,ClocksCode),
    Call =.. [Name,State,Symbol,NState,GClock|ClocksCode],
    generate_body(OtherStates,OtherNames,Clocks1,GClock,
                        Symbol,OtherCalls,NewStates,NewClocks).

gen_new_clocks([],[],[]).
gen_new_clocks([X|Y],[Z|W],[X,Z|Rest]) :- gen_new_clocks(Y,W,Rest).

semprocs([],_,_,[]).
semprocs([proc(Name,States,Trans)|Rest],Vars,Chan,[In1|In2]) :-
    semprocedure(Name,States,Trans,Vars,Chan,In1),
    semprocs(Rest,Vars,Chan,In2).

semprocedure(Name,state(Init,_),trans(List),Vars,Chan,Init) :-
    semtransitions(List,Name,Vars,Chan).

semtransitions([],_,_,_).
semtransitions([t(From,To,Guard,Sync,Assign)|Rest],Name,Vars,Chan) :-
```

```
        (Sync = sync(_,C) ->
                generate_fact(Name,From,To,C,GClock,Vars,Fact) ;
                generate_fact(Name,From,To,epsilon,GClock,Vars,Fact)),
        semguardassign(Fact,Guard,Vars,Assign,GClock),
        semtransitions(Rest,Name,Vars,Chan).

semguardassign(Head,noguard,_,noassign,_) :-
        generate_equalities(Head,Eqs), assert((Head :- Eqs)).
semguardassign(Head,noguard,Vars,assign(AList),GClock) :-
        semopa(AList,Vars,Head,Equalities,GClock,Used),
        difflist(Vars,Used,Remaining),
        additional_equalities(Remaining,Vars,Head,Others),
        assert((Head :- Equalities,Others)).
semguardassign(Head,guard(List),Vars, noassign,GClock) :-
        semopg(List,Vars,Head,Constraints,GClock),
        generate_equalities(Head,Equalities),
        assert((Head :- Constraints,Equalities)).
semguardassign(Head,guard(List),Vars,assign(AList),GClock) :-
        semopg(List,Vars,Head,Constraints,GClock),
        semopa(AList,Vars,Head,Equalities,GClock,Used),
        difflist(Vars,Used,Remaining),
        additional_equalities(Remaining,Vars,Head,Others),
        assert((Head :- Constraints,Equalities,Others)).

semopg([],_,_,true,_).
semopg([compare(Clock,Nat,Op)|Rest],Vars,Head,(C1,C2),GClock) :-
        semguard(Op,Clock,Nat,Vars,Head,C1,GClock),
        semopg(Rest,Vars,Head,C2,GClock).

semopa([],_,_,true,_,[]).
semopa([assign(Var,Nat)|Rest],Vars,Head,(C1,C2),GClock,[Var|Used]) :-
        semassign(Var,Nat,Vars,Head,C1,GClock),
        semopa(Rest,Vars,Head,C2,GClock,Used).

semassign(Var,Nat,Vars,Head,C1,GClock) :-
        extract_variable1(Var,Vars,Head,V),
        C1 = ((GClock - Nat) = V).

semguard(Op,Clock,Nat,Vars,Head,C1,GClock) :-
        extract_variable(Clock,Vars,Head,V),
        C1 =.. [Op,(GClock-V),Nat].

%%%%%%%% Auxiliary predicates

difflist([],_,[]).
difflist([X|Y],Used,Z)      :- member(X,Used), !, difflist(Y,Used,Z).
difflist([X|Y],Used,[X|Z]) :- difflist(Y,Used,Z).

additional_equalities([],_,_,true).
additional_equalities([X|Y],Vars,Head,((V1=V2),Rest)) :-
```

```
        extract_variable(X,Vars,Head,V1),
        extract_variable1(X,Vars,Head,V2),
        additional_equalities(Y,Vars,Head,Rest).

generate_equalities(Head,Eqs) :- Head =..[_,_,_,_,_|List],
                        get_equalities(List,Eqs).

get_equalities([],true).
get_equalities([X1,X2|Rest],((X1=X2),C)) :- get_equalities(Rest,C).

extract_variable(Clock,Vars,Head,V) :- Head =.. [_,_,_,_,_|Clocks],
            search_variable(Vars,Clock,Clocks,V).

search_variable([X|_],X,[Y|_],Y).
search_variable([X|Y],Z,[_,_|Rest],V) :- X \== Z,
            search_variable(Y,Z,Rest,V).

extract_variable1(Clock,Vars,Head,V) :- Head =.. [_,_,_,_,_|Clocks],
            search_variable1(Vars,Clock,Clocks,V).

search_variable1([X|_],X,[_,Y|_],Y).
search_variable1([X|Y],Z,[_,_|Rest],V) :-   X \== Z,
            search_variable1(Y,Z,Rest,V).

generate_fact(Name,StartState,EndState,Symbol,GlobClock,Clocks,FACT) :-
    generate_rest(Clocks,Rest),
    FACT =.. [Name,StartState,Symbol,EndState,GlobClock|Rest].

generate_rest([],[]).
generate_rest([_|Y],[_,_|Rest]) :- generate_rest(Y,Rest).
```

Negation as Failure through Abduction: Reasoning about Termination

Paolo Mancarella, Dino Pedreschi, and Salvatore Ruggieri

Dipartimento di Informatica, Università di Pisa
Corso Italia 40, 56125 Pisa, Italy
{paolo, pedre, ruggieri}@di.unipi.it

Abstract. We study termination properties of normal logic programs where negation as failure is interpreted as a form of abduction, as originally proposed by Eshghi and Kowalski in [EK89]. The abductive proof procedure associated with this interpretation exhibits a better behavior than SLDNF as far as termination is concerned. We first present a strong termination characterization for the Eshghi and Kowalski proof procedure for Datalog programs which is sound and complete. We then extend the characterization to the class of non-Datalog programs, and prove its soundness. Finally we present two instantiations of the general characterization and study the relationships between the classes of programs introduced in the paper.

1   Introduction

Since its early years, the basic logic programming paradigm has been extended in various respects in order to increase its expressive power as well as its effectiveness in different application domains. One of the very first extensions was the introduction of a limited form of negation, namely negation as finite failure [Cla78], and the corresponding extension of the computational mechanism from SLD-resolution to SLDNF-resolution. Negation as failure has been, and is still being, the subject of many research efforts, both from a semantics viewpoint and from a computational viewpoint. Among others, negation as failure has been given an abductive interpretation by Eshghi and Kowalski [EK89]. This interpretation amounts to viewing negative literals in a normal logic program as a form of (abductive) hypotheses that can be assumed to hold, provided they satisfy a canonical set of constraints which express the intended meaning of negation as failure.

Abduction is a form of synthetic inference which allows one to draw explanations of observations. In its simplest form, from $\alpha \rightarrow \beta$ (a general rule) and β (an observation) abduction allows one to assume α as a possible explanation of the observation. In the general case, this form of reasoning from observations and rules to explanations may lead to inconsistencies (as it happens, for instance, if $\neg\alpha$ holds in the previous example). Hence, abductive explanations should be assumed only if they do not lead to inconsistencies. Abduction has found many

A.C. Kakas, F. Sadri (Eds.): Computat. Logic (Kowalski Festschrift), LNAI 2407, pp. 240–272, 2002.

applications in AI, such as fault diagnosis, planning, natural language under-standing, knowledge assimilation, and default reasoning (see e.g. [KKT93] and references therein).

From a semantics viewpoint, the interpretation of negation as failure as ab-duction has a direct correspondence with the stable models semantics of normal logic programs [GL88]. From a computational viewpoint, Eshghi and Kowalski have defined an abductive proof procedure which extends the standard SLDNF proof procedure for negation as failure. In the sequel we will refer to it as the *EK*-proof procedure. As we will discuss later in the paper, computations of the *EK*-proof procedure are the interleaving of two types of phases. The *abductive phase* is standard SLD-resolution, which possibly generates hypotheses corresponding to the negative literals encountered during the computation. The *consistency phase* checks that the generated hypotheses satisfy the constraints associated with negation as failure. In order to perform this checking, a consistency phase may in turn require new abductive phases to be fired. Indeed, the search spaces of SLDNF and the *EK*-proof procedure share many similarities, due to the fact that each consistency phase corresponds to a subsidiary derivation which is fired each time a negative (ground) atom is selected in SLDNF. However, one of the main differences with SLDNF is that, during a computation, the hypotheses generated so far can be used to avoid the recomputation of negative subgoals. Indeed, this is the main reason why the *EK*-proof procedure exhibits a better behavior than SLDNF as far as termination is concerned, in the sense that the former terminates more often than the latter.

The main aim of this work is to formally understand the termination proper-ties of the *EK*-proof procedure. In fact, an abundant literature is available on the subject of termination of logic programs, as witnessed for instance by the sur-veys in [DD94, PRS02]. Several proposed approaches to prove termination deal with normal logic programs and SLDNF-based proof procedures [AB91, AP93]. A natural question then arises which asks whether the proposed methods for proving termination of SLDNF can be extended to deal with the *EK*-proof pro-cedure, the latter being a natural extension of SLDNF. As far as we know, this is still an unanswered problem.

Up to our knowledge, the only work in the literature dealing with a sim-ilar problem, namely termination of abductive based proof-procedures, is the paper of Verbaeten [Ver99], who proposes a method of proving termination of abductive logic programs executed using the SLDNFA procedure of Denecker and De Schreye [DS98]. SLDNFA is a non trivial extension of SLDNF which deals with more general frameworks, namely abductive logic programs. In these frameworks, some predicate symbols are defined as *abducibles*, which never oc-cur in clause heads, but can be assumed during a computation, under suitable consistency requirements. Among others, an interesting feature of the SLDNFA proof procedure is that it solves the floundering abduction problem (i.e. it allows assuming non-ground hypotheses), and it also provides a partial solution to the floundering of negation. However, in SLDNFA negation is not treated abduc-tively, as in the *EK*-proof procedure. Our main interest here is to understand in what respects the abductive treatment of negation as failure allows one to improve the termination properties of normal logic programs.

The paper is organized as follows. In Sect. 2 we give some examples to get the intuition of the behaviour of the *EK*-proof procedure and to compare it informally with SLDNF. After setting up some notations and terminology in Sect. 3, we give a concise but formal account of the *EK*-proof procedure in Sect. 4. The approach of Apt and Bezem to strong termination of logic programs executed using negation as failure, based on the notion of an *acyclicity*, is given in Sect. 5. Next, we present in Sect. 6 a termination characterization for Datalog programs, and prove its soundness and completeness. The termination method for the general case is given in Sect. 7, along with two simplified methods and with a discussion of the relationships between the classes of program and queries associated with the different methods. Section 8 draws some conclusions and scope for future work.

2 Motivating Examples

The aim of this Section is twofold. We provide some examples showing the behaviour of both SLDNF and the *EK*-proof procedure, in order to give the reader an intuition about their similarities and differences. At the same time we provide an informal and intuitive understanding of the *EK*-proof procedure, assuming that the reader has some familiarity with SLDNF. The formal definition of the *EK*-proof procedure will be given in Sect. 4.

Example 1. Consider the simple normal logic program[1]

$$p \leftarrow \sim q.$$

and the goal $\leftarrow p$. The search space generated by SLDNF is shown in Fig.1 (left).

Fig. 1. Search space generated by SLDNF (left) and the *EK*-proof procedure (right)

---

[1] In this paper we use $\sim$ to denote negation as failure.

Notice that a subsidiary SLDNF-derivation is required as soon as the atom $\sim q$ is selected in the main derivation. This subsidiary derivation is needed in order to show that the goal $\leftarrow q$ finitely fails, which is indeed the case since there is no definition for $\leftarrow q$.

The *EK*-proof procedure views negative atoms as hypotheses which can be assumed during a derivation, provided it is consistent to do so. As we will see in Sect. 3, in the original presentation of [EK89], a normal logic program is first transformed into a positive program, by replacing each negative literal of the form $\sim p(t)$ into a positive literal, say not-$p(t)$, not-p being a newly introduced predicate symbol. For simplicity, in this informal discussion we keep the original program unchanged.

The consistency requirements impose that, given an atom A,

(i) A and $\sim A$ do not hold at the same time
(ii) either A or $\sim A$ hold.

The requirement (i) expresses the fact that $\sim A$ has to be understood as the negation of A, hence preventing the assumption of $\sim A$ whenever A holds. On the other hand, the requirement (ii) forces $\sim A$ to hold whenever A does not hold. Computationally, the consistency requirements (i) and (ii) are the source of the interleaving of the abductive and consistency phases. Whenever a negative condition $\sim p$ is selected during an abductive phase (which is basically SLD resolution), the hypothesis $\sim p$ is assumed and a consistency phase is fired in order to ensure that this assumption is consistent with the corresponding requirement (i). This phase amounts to showing that p does not hold, i.e. its aim is to show that all possible derivations for p actually fail. During the consistency phase, whenever the potential failure of a derivation amounts to failing on an hypothesis $\sim q$, a nested abductive derivation is fired, in order to ensure that the requirement (ii) holds, namely that q holds. In the current example, the search space generated by the *EK*-proof procedure is depicted in Fig.1 (right).

The part of the search space enclosed by a double box corresponds to the checking of the consistency requirements. The white little box represents success and the black little box represents failure. Hence a white box at the end of an abductive phase (resp. consistency phase) corresponds to a success (resp. failure) of the phase, whereas a black box at the end of an abductive phase (resp. consistency phase) corresponds to a failure (resp. success) of the phase. Notice that, at each consistency phase, the hypothesis to be checked is added to the current set H of hypotheses.

Also, notice that the answer to the goal comes along with the set of hypotheses collected during the computation (in the previous example the only collected hypothesis is $\sim q$). In the general case, an answer to a goal is a substitution (as in the standard SLDNF) along with the set of collected hypotheses. As it happens with SLDNF, a negative literal (abductive hypothesis) is selected for computation only if it is ground.

The next example shows how the abductive and consistency phases interleave. A nested abductive phase is depicted in a single box.

Example 2. Consider the following program:

$$p \leftarrow \sim q. \qquad\qquad r \leftarrow \sim s.$$
$$q \leftarrow \sim r. \qquad\qquad r \leftarrow t.$$
$$q \leftarrow t.$$

The search space corresponding to the goal $\leftarrow p$ is shown in Fig.2.

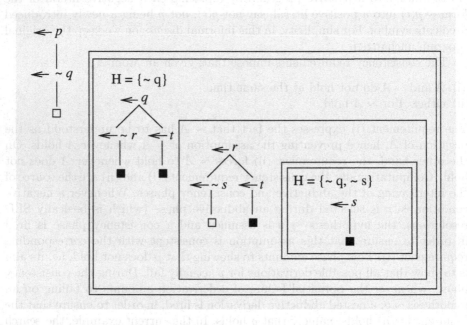

Fig. 2. Nested abductive and consistency phases

Notice that the consistency checking of the hypothesis $\sim q$ needs to explore two branches (corresponding to the two clauses in the definition of q). The right branch is consistent (since there is no definition for t), while the left branch needs a nested abductive phase, in order to make sure that r holds, and hence q cannot be proved. Since there is no clause for t, the only way to prove r is by adding the hypothesis $\sim s$ to the current set of hypotheses, which is checked in turn for consistency.

Let us see an example pointing out the different behaviours of SLDNF and the *EK*-proof procedure.

Example 3. Consider the following program.

$$p \leftarrow \sim q.$$
$$q \leftarrow \sim p.$$

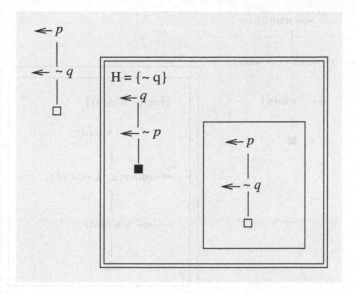

Fig. 3. The search space for the two-loop program

It is easy to see that the goal $\leftarrow p$ does not terminate under SLDNF. On the contrary, it does terminate using the *EK*-proof procedure, as shown by the associated search space of Fig.3.

Notice that, in the consistency phase associated with checking the hypothesis $\sim q$, a nested abductive derivation requires that $\sim p$ does not hold which requires in turn that p holds. This is indeed the case, since the hypotheses collected so far (namely $\sim q$) actually allows the nested abductive phase to succeed on p.

As the previous example points out, the *EK*-proof procedure terminates more often than the SLDNF proof procedure, due to the fact that the hypotheses collected during a computation can be used to avoid the recomputation of negative literals. Let us see a further example.

Example 4. Consider the well known two-person game program:

$$win(x) \leftarrow move(x, y), \sim win(y).$$

Here, $move(x, y)$ is any extensional binary relation over a finite set of game states, where $move(x, y)$ should be read as "there is a move from game state x to game state y". According to this view, $win(x)$ defines x as a winning state if there is a move from x to a state y which is not a winning state.

It is readily checked that, whenever the relation *move* contains a cycle, say $move(a, a)$, then the execution of the goal $\leftarrow win(a)$ does not terminate using SLDNF. On the contrary, executing the same goal $\leftarrow win(a)$ by the *EK*-proof procedure, we get a failure, indicating correctly that a is not a winning state, as shown if Fig.4.

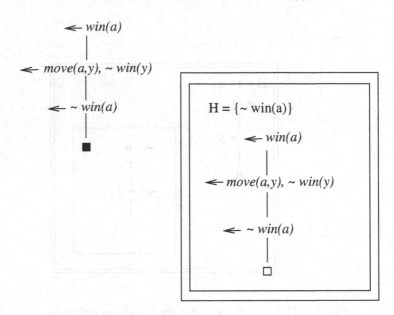

Fig. 4. Search space for the two-person game program

In this paper, we expand on the work on termination of general logic programs, in order to find suitable methods to prove that a general logic program terminates, when executed using the *EK*-proof procedure. We first present a method which applies to the class of Datalog programs, i.e. programs with an associated finite Herbrand Base, and we prove its soundness and completeness. In the general case, i.e. for non-Datalog programs, we provide a new method and two simplifications of it.

3   Preliminaries

We assume that the reader is familiar with the terminology of standard logic programming, as found in [Apt96]. We recall here the conventions and notations adopted in the rest of the paper. We consider a fixed language L in which programs and queries are written. All the results are *parametric* with respect to L, provided L is rich enough to contain every symbol of the programs and queries under consideration. Given the language L, we denote by B_L the Herbrand Base associated with it and by not-B_L be the set

$$\text{not-}B_L = \{\text{not-}p(t) | p(t) \in B_L\}.$$

Then, given a logic program P, the *abductive program* associated with P is the program KB_P obtained from P by replacing each negative literal $\sim p(t)$ by a positive atom not-$p(t) \in$ not-B_L. Notice that an abductive program is always a positive (Horn) program over an extended language, obtained from

L by adding a new predicate symbol not-p, for each predicate symbol $p \in L$. Atoms of the form not-$p(t)$ will be referred to as *abducible* atoms, whereas atoms of the form $p(t)$ will be referred to as *ordinary* atoms. From now onwards, we will denote an abductive program simply by KB, whenever the program P is clear from the context. Moreover, for a definite, normal or abductive program P, by $ground_L(P)$ we denote the set of ground instances of clauses from P. For a goal G, by $ground_L(G)$ we denote the set of ground instances of G. Finally, we denote by $\#$ the set cardinality operator.

We refer the reader to the literature [Dun95, EK89, KKT93] for a thorough discussion about the semantics of abductive programs. Here we concentrate only on computational aspects and in particular on termination properties.

Example 5. Let P be the normal logic program of Example 3. The associated abductive program KB is

$$p \leftarrow \text{not-}q.$$
$$q \leftarrow \text{not-}p.$$

where not-p and not-q are the only abducible atoms.

4   The Eshghi and Kowalski Procedure

In this Section we introduce the formal definition of the *EK*-proof procedure, as presented in [Dun95].[2] As shown in the examples of Sect. 2 a computation is an interleaving of abductive and consistency phases. An abductive phase is basically SLD-resolution. Whenever a ground *abducible* atom is selected for computation there are two possible cases:

- the abducible is already a member of the current set of hypotheses: then the computation proceeds by simply removing the abducible from the current subgoal;
- the abducible is not in the current set of hypotheses: the abducible is added to the current set of hypotheses and a consistency phase is fired, in order to check that the abducible can be safely assumed. If the consistency phase is successful, the abductive phase proceeds by removing the abducible from the current goal and with the set of hypotheses resulting from the consistency phase.

On the other hand, a consistency phase tries to fail all possible ways of proving an atom, say $p(t)$, in order to make sure that it is consistent to assume not-$p(t)$. The computation proceeds basically by exploring the whole SLD-tree corresponding to the goal $p(t)$, looking for failure of all branches. Whenever a ground abducible atom is selected, there are basically two cases:

---

[2]   Dung [Dun95] has shown that the original version of the procedure presented in [EK89] contained a minor error.

- the abducible is already a member of the current set of hypotheses: then the current branch is further explored, if possible, i.c. the abducible is removed from the current subgoal.
- the abducible is not in the current set of hypotheses: an abductive phase is fired, in order to check that the converse of the abducible (i.e. $p(t)$ if the abducible is not-$p(t)$) can be proved. The success of the nested abductive phase makes the current branch of the consistency phase successful. The failure of the nested abductive phase requires to further explore, if possible, the current branch.

The definition given next formalizes this intuitive understanding of the procedure. In the sequel, we simply say *atom* to refer to an ordinary or abducible atom. First, the definition of abductive derivation is given, as a sequence of pairs of the form (G_i, Δ_i) where G_i is a collection of atoms (representing the current subgoal as in ordinary SLD) and $\Delta_i \subseteq$ not-B_L is the set of the hypotheses collected so far. Secondly, the definition of consistency derivation is given, as a sequence of pairs of the form (F_i, Δ_i), where F_i is a set of collections of atoms (each collection representing a node in a different branch of the SLD tree currently under examination) and, as before, $\Delta_i \subseteq$ not-B_L is the set of the hypotheses collected so far. The objective of an abductive phase is to look for an abductive derivation ending up to a pair $(\square, \Delta)$. If this is the case, the original goal succeeds, Δ being the set of hypotheses needed for the success of the computation. The objective of a consistency phase is to look for a consistency derivation ending up to a pair $(\emptyset, \Delta)$. $\emptyset$ represents the fact that all the branches of the SLD tree have been successfully explored. Δ is the set of hypotheses needed.

It is important to notice that an abducible is selected, both in the abductive and in the consistency phases, provided it is ground. This is similar to the behavior of SLDNF, where negative literals can be selected only if they are ground. In the sequel we say that a selection rule[3] is *safe* if it selects an abducible atom only if it is ground.

Definition 1. *Let KB be an abductive program and let R be a safe selection rule.*
An abductive derivation *from* (G_1, Δ_1) *is a (possibly infinite) sequence*

$$(G_1, \Delta_1), (G_2, \Delta_2), \ldots, (G_n, \Delta_n), \ldots$$

such that, for each $i \geq 1$, G_i *has the form* $\leftarrow l, l'$ *where (without loss of generality) R selects l and l' is a (possibly empty) collection of atoms,* Δ_i *is a set of hypotheses (i.e. a subset of neg-B_L), and*

ab1) *if l is an ordinary atom*
        then $G_{i+1} = C$ *and* $\Delta_{i+1} = \Delta_i$
    where C is the SLD-resolvent of some clause in KB with G_i *on the selected atom l.*

---

[3] Given a goal $\leftarrow l_1, \ldots, l_n$ a selection rule simply returns an atom l_i, for some i, $1 \leq i \leq n$.

ab2) *if l is an abducible atom and $l \in \Delta_i$*
$$\text{then} \quad G_{i+1} = \ \leftarrow l' \quad \text{and} \quad \Delta_{i+1} = \Delta_i$$
ab3) *if l is an abducible atom($l = $ not-k) and $l \notin \Delta_i$ and there is a consistency derivation from $(\{\leftarrow k\}, \Delta_i \cup \{l\})$ to $(\emptyset, \Delta')$*
$$\text{then} \quad G_{i+1} = \ \leftarrow l' \quad \text{and} \quad \Delta_{i+1} = \Delta'.$$

In the case where the sequence above is finite, we say that it is an abductive derivation *from* (G_1, Δ_1) *to* (G_n, Δ_n). *An* abductive refutation *is an abductive derivation to a pair* $(\square, \Delta')$.

A consistency derivation *from* (F_1, Δ_1) *is a (possibly infinite) sequence*

$$(F_1, \Delta_1), (F_2, \Delta_2), \ldots, (F_n, \Delta_n), \ldots$$

such that, for each $i \geq 1$, F_i has the form $\{\leftarrow l, l'\} \cup F_i'$ where (without loss of generality) $\leftarrow l, l'$ has been selected (to continue the search), R selects l and

co1) *if l is an ordinary atom*
$$\text{then} \quad F_{i+1} = C' \cup F_i' \quad \text{and} \quad \Delta_{i+1} = \Delta_i$$
where C' is the set of all resolvents of clauses in KB with $\leftarrow l, l'$ on the selected atom l, and $\square \notin C'$.
co2) *if l is an abducible atom, $l \in \Delta_i$ and l' is not empty*
$$\text{then} \quad F_{i+1} = \{\leftarrow l'\} \cup F_i' \quad \text{and} \quad \Delta_{i+1} = \Delta_i$$
co3) *if l is an abducible atom ($l = $ not-k) and $l \notin \Delta_i$*
then if there is an abductive derivation from $(\leftarrow k, \Delta_i)$ to $(\square, \Delta')$
$$\text{then} \quad F_{i+1} = F_i' \quad \text{and} \quad \Delta_{i+1} = \Delta'$$
else if l' is not empty
$$\text{then} \quad F_{i+1} = \{\leftarrow l'\} \cup F_i' \quad \text{and} \quad \Delta_{i+1} = \Delta_i$$

In the case where the sequence above is finite, we say that it is a consistency derivation *from* (F_1, Δ_1) *to* (F_n, Δ_n). $\qquad\qquad\square$

Notice that the definition of the *EK*-proof procedure suffers the same floundering problem as SLDNF, in the case where the selected goal contains only non-ground abducible atoms.

We have already seen examples showing the behavior of the *EK*-proof procedure, and in particular showing that it terminates on some programs where SLDNF does not terminate. We present here some more examples, in order to relate the formal definition with the graphical representation used in Sect. 2.

Example 6. Let us consider again the program of Example 2. The associated abductive program is the following:

$$p \leftarrow \text{not-}q.$$
$$q \leftarrow \text{not-}r.$$
$$r \leftarrow \text{not-}s.$$

The abductive and consistency derivations corresponding to the search space depicted in Fig.2 are shown next. To help the reader, we write

$$(S, \Delta) \xrightarrow{\ \mathbf{r}\ } (S', \Delta')$$

to denote a step of an abductive or consistency derivation by means of rule $\mathbf{r}$ of Def.1.

– **Main abductive derivation**

$$(\leftarrow p, \{\}) \xrightarrow{\ \mathbf{ab1}\ } (\leftarrow \text{not-}q, \{\})$$

$$\xrightarrow{\ \mathbf{ab3}\ }$$

$$(\Box, \{\text{not-}q\})$$

– **First consistency derivation**

$$(\{\leftarrow q\}, \{\text{not-}q\})$$

$$\xrightarrow{\ \mathbf{co1}\ }$$

$$(\{\leftarrow \text{not-}r\}, \{\text{not-}q\})$$

$$\xrightarrow{\ \mathbf{co3}\ }$$

$$(\emptyset, \{\text{not-}q, \text{not-}s\})$$

– **Nested abductive derivation**

$$(\leftarrow r, \{\text{not-}q\})$$

$$\xrightarrow{\ \mathbf{ab1}\ }$$

$$(\leftarrow \text{not-}s, \{\text{not-}q\})$$

$$\xrightarrow{\ \mathbf{ab3}\ }$$

$$(\Box, \{\text{not-}q, \text{not-}s\})$$

– **Second consistency derivation**

$$(\{\leftarrow s\}, \{\text{not-}q, \text{not-}s\})$$

$$\xrightarrow{\ \mathbf{co1}\ }$$

$$(\emptyset, \{\text{not-}q, \text{not-}s\})$$

In the next example, we show a program containing function symbols, and a goal which does not terminate using SLDNF but does so using the *EK*-proof procedure.

Example 7. Consider the following program P

$$p(x) \leftarrow \sim q(f(x)).$$
$$q(f(x)) \leftarrow \sim p(x).$$

and the associated abductive program

$$p(x) \leftarrow \text{not-}q(f(x)).$$
$$q(f(x)) \leftarrow \text{not-}p(x).$$

It is easy to see that any ground goal of the form $\leftarrow p(f(f \ldots f(a) \ldots))$ does not terminate using SLDNF. Consider one instance of the goal in the corresponding abductive program, say $\leftarrow p(f(a))$. The abductive and consistency derivations generated by the goal are the following.

- **Main abductive derivation**

$$(\leftarrow p(f(a)), \{\})$$

$$\xrightarrow{\text{ab1}}$$

$$(\leftarrow \text{not-}q(f(f(a))), \{\})$$

$$\xrightarrow{\text{ab3}}$$

$$(\Box, \{\text{not-}q(f(f(a)))\})$$

- **Consistency derivation**

$$(\{\leftarrow q(f(f(a)))\}, \{\text{not-}q(f(f(a)))\})$$

$$\xrightarrow{\text{co1}}$$

$$(\{\leftarrow \text{not-}p(f(a))\}, \{\text{not-}q(f(f(a)))\})$$

$$\xrightarrow{\text{co3}}$$

$$(\emptyset, \{\text{not-}q(f(f(a)))\})$$

- **Nested abductive derivation**

$$(\leftarrow p(f(a)), \{\text{not-}q(f(f(a)))\})$$

$$\xrightarrow{\text{ab1}}$$

$$(\leftarrow \text{not-}q(f(f(a))), \{\text{not-}q(f(f(a)))\})$$

$$\xrightarrow{\text{ab2}}$$

$$(\Box, \{\text{not-}q(f(f(a)))\})$$

Notice that the last step of the nested abductive derivation applies rule (**ab2**), i.e. it succeeds by exploiting the hypothesis $\text{not-}q(f(f(a)))$ already collected in the current set of hypotheses.

Finally, we show an example where both SLDNF and the *EK*-proof procedure do not terminate.

Example 8. Let P be the following program

$$p(x) \leftarrow \sim p(f(x)).$$

and KB the corresponding abductive framework.

$$p(x) \leftarrow \text{not-}p(f(x)).$$

The goal $\leftarrow p(a)$ does not terminate using SLDNF. The same goal, executed by the *EK*-proof procedure with respect to KB, requires infinitely many nested abductive and consistency derivations, as shown in Fig.5.

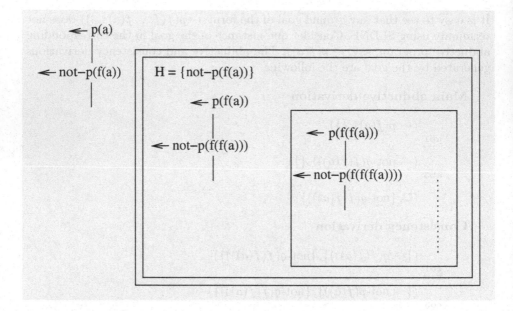

Fig. 5. A non terminating computation

5   Strong Termination of Logic Programs

The problem of universal termination of a program and a goal w.r.t. a set of admissible selection rules consists of showing that every derivation for them via any of the admissible selection rule is finite. Early approaches to the termination problem in logic programming treated universal termination w.r.t. *all* selection rules, called *strong* termination. We extend this notion to abductive programs and goals.

Definition 2. *A normal logic program P and goal G strongly terminate if every SLDNF-derivation of P and G is finite.*

An abductive program KB and goal G strongly terminate if every abductive/consistency derivation reachable from $(G, \emptyset)$ is finite.   □

A largely acknowledged characterization of strong termination for definite logic programs and goals was proposed by Bezem in [Bez89], introducing the class of recurrent programs. The characterization relies on the basic notions of level mappings and ground instances of program clauses.

Definition 3. *A level mapping is a function $| \; | : B_L \to \mathbb{N}$ of ground atoms to natural numbers. $| A |$ is called the level of A.*   □

Intuitively, a program is recurrent if for every ground instance of a clause, the level of the body atoms is smaller than the level of the head.

Example 9. Consider the common logic program defining a predicate $list(x)$ which recognizes when x is a list.

$$list([]).$$
$$list([x|xs]) \leftarrow list(xs).$$

Level mappings are used to measure the "size" of a ground atom (and also of a goal) and show that this size decreases along a derivation, hence showing termination. Intuitively, the "size" of $list$ could be defined as the list-length of its argument, i.e. for x ground term we define $|list(x)| = llen(x)$, where:

$$llen([x|xs]) = llen(xs) + 1,$$
$$llen(f(x_1, \ldots, x_n)) = 0 \text{ if } f \neq [.|.].$$

Note that for a ground list xs, $llen(xs)$ is the length of xs.

Definition 4. *Let $|\ |$ be a level mapping.*

- *A definite program P is recurrent by $|\ |$ iff for every $A \leftarrow B_1, \ldots, B_n \in ground_L(P)$, for $i \in [1, n]$ $|A| > |B_i|$.*
- *P is recurrent if it is recurrent by some $|\ |$.*
- *A goal G is recurrent by $|\ |$ iff there exists $k \in \mathbb{N}$ such that for every $\leftarrow B_1, \ldots, B_n \in ground_L(G)$, for $i \in [1, n]$ $k > |B_i|$.* □

It is readily checked that the program of Example 9 is recurrent by the level mapping defined there.

We summarize the main termination properties of recurrent programs in the following Theorem (see [Bez89] for a proof).

Theorem 1. *Let P be a definite logic program and G a goal.*

If P and G are both recurrent by some $|\ |$ then they strongly terminate.

Conversely, if P and every ground goal strongly terminate, then P is recurrent by some $|\ |$. If in addition P and G strongly terminate, then P and G are both recurrent by $|\ |$. □

Apt and Bezem [AB91] extended the method to normal logic programs and SLDNF-resolution. By introducing the notion of *acyclicity*, a level mapping $|\ |$ is extended to literals by defining $|\sim A| = |A|$ for a ground atom A.

Definition 5. *Let $|\ |$ be a level mapping.*

- *A normal program P is acyclic by $|\ |$ iff for every $A \leftarrow L_1, \ldots, L_n \in ground_L(P)$, for $i \in [1, n]$ $|A| > |L_i|$.*
- *P is acyclic if it is acyclic by some $|\ |$.*
- *A goal G is acyclic by $|\ |$ iff there exists $k \in \mathbb{N}$ such that for every $\leftarrow L_1, \ldots, L_n \in ground_L(G)$, for $i \in [1, n]$ $k > |L_i|$.* □

The proof obligations of acyclicity are a direct extension of those of recurrency. Apt and Bezem [AB91] showed termination soundness and a restricted form of completeness.

Theorem 2. *Let P be a normal program and G a goal.*
If P and G are both acyclic by some $|\ |$ then they strongly terminate.
Conversely, if P and every ground goal strongly terminate and do not flounder, then P is acyclic by some $|\ |$. If in addition P and G strongly terminate and do not flounder, then P and G are both acyclic by $|\ |$. □

Example 10. Consider again Example 3. The program cannot be acyclic since the proof obligation would require for some level mapping $|\ |$ that:

$$|p| > |\sim q| = |q| > |\sim p| = |p|,$$

which is impossible. With an analogous reasoning, we can conclude that the programs of Examples 4 and 7 are not acyclic.

6   A Simple Termination Characterization for Datalog Programs

In this section, we introduce a simple termination characterization of abductive programs under the assumption that B_L is finite, namely that the underlying language does not contain function symbols. Such a class of programs is often referred to as the class of Datalog programs, and it is of interest, e.g. in the deductive databases area.

Consider again Examples 3 and 4. A distinctive feature of the EK-proof procedure is that at each nested consistency derivation, the set of abduced hypotheses *strictly* increases. Since such a set is a subset of B_L, which is finite, this feature implies that there cannot be infinitely many nested consistency/abductive derivations. Strong termination reduces then to show that each of the nested consistency/abductive derivations is finite. The key observation is that finiteness of those derivations depends only on ordinary atoms.

Definition 6. *Let KB be an abductive program. We define KB^{pos} as the definite program obtained by removing all the abducible atoms in KB. Given a goal G, G^{pos} is defined similarly.* □

As an example, let KB be the program from Example 3. We have that KB^{pos} consists of two unit clauses:

$$p.$$
$$q.$$

In order to show termination for ordinary atoms, we can adapt recurrency to abductive programs.

Definition 7 (EK-recurrency). *Let* $|\ |$ *be a level mapping.*

- *An abductive program* KB *is* EK-recurrent *by* $|\ |$ *iff* KB^{pos} *is recurrent by* $|\ |$.
- KB *is* EK-recurrent *if it is* EK-recurrent *by some* $|\ |$.
- *A goal* G *is* EK-recurrent *by* $|\ |$ *iff the goal* G^{pos} *is recurrent by* $|\ |$. □

Intuitively, an abductive program KB is EK-recurrent if its "ordinary part" KB^{pos} is recurrent in the sense of Definition 4. Under the assumption that B_L is finite, EK-recurrency is a sound and complete characterization of strong termination of abductive programs and goals.

Theorem 3. *Let* KB *be an abductive program and* G *a goal.*

(i) If B_L *is finite, and* KB *and* G *are both* EK-recurrent *by some* $|\ |$ *then they strongly terminate.*

(ii) Conversely, if KB *and every* ground goal *strongly terminate, then* KB *is* EK-recurrent *by some* $|\ |$. *If in addition* KB *and* G *strongly terminate, then* KB *and* G *are both* EK-recurrent *by* $|\ |$. □

Proof.

(i). We will show in Theorem 4 a termination soundness result for a class of abductive programs and goals called EK-acyclic. Under the assumption that B_L is finite, EK-recurrent programs and goals are also EK-acyclic, as shown in Lemma 3.

(ii). Consider an SLD-derivation ξ of KB^{pos} and a ground goal G_1^{pos}. We observe that ξ can be mapped into an abductive derivation for KB and G_1 by adopting a (safe) selection rule that selects ordinary atoms in a goal, unless all atoms are abducible. Since KB and G_1^{pos} strongly terminate, KB^{pos} and G_1^{pos} strongly terminate (as definite programs). By Theorem 1, KB^{pos} is recurrent by some $|\ |$, which implies KB is EK-recurrent by $|\ |$. By following the same reasoning, we conclude that also G is EK-recurrent by $|\ |$. □

Example 11. The program KB of Example 3 is EK-recurrent by any level mapping $|\ |$, since KB^{pos} is readily checked to be recurrent. Also, the goal $\leftarrow p$ is EK-recurrent by $|\ |$. Therefore, we conclude that KB and $\leftarrow p$ strongly terminate.

Analogously, the two-person game program of Example 4 and a goal $\leftarrow win(x)$ strongly terminate. In fact, the "ordinary part" of the program is $win(x) \leftarrow move(x, y)$, which is readily checked to be recurrent, e.g. by $|win(t)| = 1$, $|move(s, t)| = 0$.

Notice that part (ii) of the theorem holds also for non-Datalog programs, namely EK-recurrent programs include abductive programs that strongly terminate for every ground goal. However, such an inclusion is strict.

Example 12. The abductive program of Example 8 is readily checked EK-recurrent, but, as shown in that example, it and the ground goal $\leftarrow p(a)$ do not strongly terminate.

7   A General Termination Characterization

In this section, we introduce a sound characterization of strongly terminating abductive programs and goals, which does not require the hypothesis that B_L is finite. Such a general characterization, called EK-acyclicity, is then simplified into the notion of Simply EK-acyclicity, which turns out to strictly include acyclicity in the sense of Bezem. As a result, we have that termination of a normal program w.r.t. SLDNF implies termination w.r.t. the EK-proof procedure.

7.1   EK-acyclic Abductive Programs

First of all, let us extend the definition of level mappings in order to take into account sets of abductive hypotheses.

Definition 8 (Extended level mappings). *An* extended level mapping *is a function* $| \ | : B_L \times 2^{\text{neg-}B_L} \to \mathbb{N}$ *from ground atoms and sets of hypotheses to natural numbers such that:*

$$\forall A \ \forall \ \Delta \subseteq \Delta' \quad |A, \Delta| \geq |A, \Delta'|.$$

For a pair (A, Δ), *we say that* $|A, \Delta|$ *is the level of* (A, Δ). □

Intuitively, the requirement that extended level mappings do not increase when the set of abductive hypotheses increases (i.e. anti-monotonicity) is the declarative counterpart that termination is antimonotonic w.r.t. the set of hypotheses.

We are now in the position to introduce our general characterization, called EK-acyclicity. It exploits two extended level mappings $| \ |^+$ and $| \ |^-$.

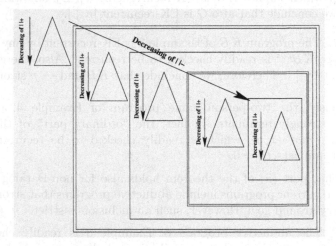

Fig. 6. EK-acyclicity: decrease of $| \ |^+$ and $| \ |^-$ over the axis of the search space

Proof obligations on $|\,|^{+}$ require a decrease from the head to ordinary atoms of clauses. These correspond to the proof obligations of EK-recurrency, and they are needed to prove finiteness of each abductive/consistency derivation of the *EK*-proof procedure.

Proof obligations on $|\,|^{-}$ require a decrease from the head to abducible atoms of clauses. These are needed to prove that there are finitely many nested abductive/consisteny derivations (this is always true when B_L is finite). Since abductive and consistency derivations are interleaved, the decrease can be required only when starting one of them, while a non-increasing requirement can be assumed for the other. We assume a decrease when starting a consistency derivation. Finally, $|\,|^{-}$ is required not to increase on ordinary atoms.

Figure 6 depicts how proof obligations on $|\,|^{+}$ and $|\,|^{-}$ models the decrease along two axis: $|\,|^{+}$ imposes finiteness of a single abductive/consistency derivation; $|\,|^{-}$ imposes finiteness of the number of nested abductive/consistency derivations.

Definition 9 (EK-acyclicity). *An abductive program KB is EK-acyclic by two extended level mappings $|\,|^{+}$ and $|\,|^{-}$ iff for every $\Delta \subseteq \text{not-}B_L$, $A \leftarrow L_1 , \dots , L_n \in ground_L(KB)$, for $i \in [1, n]$:*

ac1) *if $L_i = B$ then*
  (i) $|A, \Delta|^{+} > |B, \Delta|^{+}$,
  (ii) $|A, \Delta|^{-} \geq |B, \Delta|^{-}$;
ac2) *if $L_i = \text{not-}B$ and $L_i \notin \Delta$, then*
  (i) $|A, \Delta|^{-} > |B, \Delta \cup \{L_i\}|^{-}$,
  (ii) $|A, \Delta|^{-} \geq |B, \Delta|^{-}$.

A goal G is EK-acyclic by $|\,|^{+}$ and $|\,|^{-}$ iff there exists $k \in \mathbb{N}$ such that for every $\leftarrow L_1 , \dots , L_n \in ground_L(G)$, for $i \in [1, n]$:

gc1) *if $L_i = B$ then $k > |B, \emptyset|^{+}$ and $k > |B, \emptyset|^{-}$;*
gc2) *if $L_i = \text{not-}B$ then $k > |B, \emptyset|^{-}$.*   □

Proving that a program belongs to the class of the EK-acyclic programs is the proposed termination method. The following result states the soundness of this method.

Theorem 4. *Let KB be an abductive program and G a goal.*
  If KB and G are both EK-acyclic by some $|\,|^{+}$ and $|\,|^{-}$, then they strongly terminate.

Proof. See Appendix A.   □

We give next an example of a non-Datalog program P which is not acyclic, but such that the corresponding abductive program is EK-acyclic (part of the example is a reformulation of a well-known example by Reiter [Rei80]).

Example 13. Let KB be the following abductive program:[4]

$\quad friends([])$.
$\quad friends([x])$.
$\quad friends([x, y|xs]) \quad \leftarrow support\_same(x, y), friends([y|xs])$.
$\quad support\_same(x, y) \leftarrow support(x, z), support(y, z)$.
$\quad support(x, peace) \quad \leftarrow quaker(x), \text{not-}support(x, fight)$.
$\quad support(x, fight) \quad \leftarrow republican(x), \text{not-}support(x, peace)$.
$\quad quaker(john)$.
$\quad republican(john)$.
$\quad quaker(karl)$.
$\quad republican(mary)$.
$\quad quaker(paul)$.

Intuitively, if a person is either *republican* or *quaker*, but not both, she/he (normally) supports fighting or peace, respectively. The question is what happens to a person, say s, who is both *republican* and *quaker*. Computationally, in this case the goals $\leftarrow support(s, peace)$ and $support(s, fight)$ both succeed, the former by assuming not-$support(s, fight)$ (corresponding to the assumption that the person is not abnormal as far as being religious is concerned), and the second by assuming not-$support(s, peace)$ (corresponding to the assumption that the person is not abnormal as far as being republican is concerned). The other definitions in the program above are self-explanatory.

It is easy to see that a goal of the form $friends(xs)$, xs being a ground list of persons, does not terminate using SLDNF in the logic program corresponding to KB. Let us show that KB is EK-acyclic by the level mappings $|\ |^+$ and $|\ |^-$, defined next. In the definitions of the level mappings, we use the list-length function $llen$, as defined in Example 9. Moreover, we use the common int function which given a boolean expression b, returns 1 if b is true and 0 if b is false. Finally, let

$$\tilde{\Delta}(s) = \{\text{not-}support(s, t)|\ t \in \{peace, fight\}\}.$$

The level mappings are defined as follows:

$|friends(l), \Delta|^+ = llen(l) + 1 \qquad |support\_same(s, t), \Delta|^+ = 2$
$|support(s, t), \Delta|^+ = 1 \qquad\qquad\ \ |quaker(s), \Delta|^+ = 0$
$|republican(s), \Delta|^+ = 0 \qquad\quad |support(s, t), \Delta|^- = \#(\tilde{\Delta}(s) \setminus \Delta)$
$|friends(l), \Delta|^- = 2 \qquad\qquad\quad |support\_same(s, t), \Delta|^- = 2$
$|quaker(s), \Delta|^- = 0 \qquad\qquad\ \ |republican(s), \Delta|^- = 0$

Notice that there are no proof obligations as far as unit clauses are concerned. The proof obligations **ac1** *(i)* of Def. 9 are trivially satisfied, for each non unit clause. Similarly, the proof obligations **ac1** *(ii)* and **ac2** of Def. 9 are trivially satisfied as far as the first two non unit clauses are concerned. Indeed, notice that, for each Δ and ground terms s, t, $|support(s, t), \Delta|^- \leq 2$.

---

[4] We use the standard Prolog-like syntax for lists.

Let us consider a ground instance of the third non unit clause
$$support(s, peace) \leftarrow quaker(s), \text{not-}support(s, fight).$$
Let Δ be a set of hypotheses such that $\text{not-}support(s, fight) \notin \Delta$. We calculate:

$$|support(s, peace), \Delta|^-$$

$$=$$

$$\#(\tilde{\Delta}(s) \setminus \Delta)$$

$$>$$

$$\#(\tilde{\Delta}(s) \setminus (\Delta \cup \{\text{not-}support(s, fight)\}))$$

$$=$$

$$|support(s, fight), \Delta \cup \{\text{not-}support(s, fight)\}|^-.$$

Hence, the proof obligation **ac2** *(i)* of Def. 9 is satisfied.

Moreover, $|support(s, peace), \Delta|^- = |support(s, fight), \Delta|^-$, hence also the proof obligation **ac2** *(ii)* of Def. 9 is satisfied.

By totally symmetric arguments, we can prove that the same proof obligations are satisfied as far as the last non unit clause is concerned.

7.2 Simply EK-acyclic Abductive Programs

While acyclicity (in the sense of Apt and Bezem) requires a single level mapping, proving EK-acyclicity requires two (extended) level mappings. It is then natural to simplify the notion of EK-acyclicity by identifying $|\ |^+$ and $|\ |^-$.

Definition 10 (Simple EK-acyclicity). *An abductive program KB is simply EK-acyclic by an extended level mapping $|\ |$ if for every $\Delta \subseteq \text{not-}B_L$, $A \leftarrow L_1, \ldots, L_n \in ground_L(KB)$, for $i \in [1, n]$:*

sac1) *if $L_i = B$ then $|A, \Delta| > |B, \Delta|$;*
sac2) *if $L_i = \text{not-}B$ and $L_i \notin \Delta_i$, then*
  (i) $|A, \Delta| > |B, \Delta \cup \{L_i\}|,$
  (ii) $|A, \Delta| \geq |B, \Delta|.$

A goal G is simply EK-acyclic by $|\ |$ iff there exists $k \in \mathbb{N}$ such that for every $\leftarrow L_1, \ldots, L_n \in ground_L(G)$, for $i \in [1, n]$:

sgc1) *if $L_i = B$ then $k > |B, \emptyset|$;*
sgc2) *if $L_i = \text{not-}B$ then $k > |B, \emptyset|$.*   □

Since simply EK-acyclicity is obtained as an instantiation of EK-acyclicity, it inherits the termination soundness property.

Lemma 1. *Let KB be an abductive program and G a goal.*

If KB and G are both simply EK-acyclic by some $|\ |$, then they are EK-acyclic by $|\ |$ and $|\ |$, and then they strongly terminate.   □

Finally, it is natural to ask ourselves whether EK-acyclicity and simple EK-acyclicity coincide. The answer is negative. EK-acyclicity *strictly* extends acyclicity.

Example 14. Let KB be the following abductive program:

$$p \leftarrow r.$$
$$r \leftarrow \text{not-}p.$$

It is easy to see that KB is EK-recurrent, since KB^{pos} is obviously recurrent. As we will see next, in the case of Datalog programs, the classes of EK-recurrent and EK-acyclic programs coincide. Therefore, KB is EK-acyclic.

However, KB is not simply EK-acyclic. Assume the contrary, and let $\Delta \subseteq$ not-B_L such that not-$p \notin \Delta$. We have:

(1) by the first clause and condition **sac1**:

$$|p, \Delta| > |r, \Delta|.$$

(2) by the second clause and condition **sac2** *(ii)*:

$$|r, \Delta| \geq |p, \Delta|.$$

Obviously, (1) and (2) give a contradiction.

7.3 Acyclic Abductive Programs

As an instantiation of simply EK-acyclicity, we observe that an extended level mapping such that $|A, \Delta|$ depends only on A turns out to be a level mapping. Under such an assumption, simply EK-acyclicity boils down to acyclicity in the sense of Apt and Bezem (modulo renaming of negative atoms into abducible ones).

Definition 11 (Acyclicity). *An abductive program KB is acyclic by a level mapping $|\ |$ if for every $A \leftarrow L_1, \dots, L_n \in ground_L(KB)$, for $i \in [1, n]$:*

aac1) *if $L_i = B$ then $|A| > |B|$;*
aac2) *if $L_i = \text{not-}B$ then $|A| > |B|$.*

A goal G is acyclic by $|\ |$ iff there exists $k \in \mathbb{N}$ such that for every $\leftarrow L_1, \dots, L_n \in ground_L(G)$, for $i \in [1, n]$:

agc1) *if $L_i = B$ then $k > |B|$;*
agc2) *if $L_i = \text{not-}B$ then $k > |B|$.*   □

The following Lemma states that acyclicity implies EK-acyclicity.

Lemma 2. *Let KB be an abductive program and G a goal.*
  If KB and G are both acyclic by a level mapping $|\ |$ then they are both simply EK-acyclic by some extended level mapping $|\ |'$, and then they strongly terminate.

Proof. By considering $|A, \Delta|' = |A|$, the proof obligations of Definition 10 are trivially satisfied. By Lemma 1, KB and G are EK-acyclic and then they strongly terminate.   □

It is immediate to observe that simply EK-acyclicity strictly extends acyclicity, as the following example shows.

Example 15. The simple program:

$$p \leftarrow \text{not-}p.$$

is readily checked to be simple EK-acyclic by defining $|p, \Delta| = 1$ if not-$p \notin \Delta$, and $|p, \Delta| = 0$ otherwise. However, the same program is not acyclic, since the proof obligations require $|p| > |p|$ for some level mapping $|\ |$.

As a consequence of Lemma 2, we obtain a formalized account of the fact that the abductive procedure terminates more often than SLDNF.

Corollary 1. *Let KB_P be an abductive program associated with a normal program P. Let also G_P be the goal associated with a normal goal G.*

If P and every ground goal strongly terminate and do not flounder, and P and G strongly terminate and do not flounder, then KB_P and G_P strongly terminate.

Proof. By Theorem 2, P and G are both acyclic by some level mapping $|\ |$. By Lemma 2, KB_P and G_P strongly terminate.   □

7.4 EK-recurrent Abductive Programs

Finally, let us relate EK-acyclic programs with EK-recurrent programs. As an immediate observation, EK-acyclicity implies EK-recurrency. When B_L is finite, the converse is also true.

Lemma 3. *Assume that B_L is finite. Let KB be an abductive program and G a goal.*

If KB and G are both EK-recurrent by a level mapping $|\ |$ then they are both EK-acyclic by some $|\ |^+$ and $|\ |^-$.

Proof. See Appendix A.   □

The reason of such a dramatic simplification lies in the fact that when B_L is finite, then $|\ |^-$ is naturally defined as the set of abducible atoms that may still be abduced. Such a set is finite and decreasing along the computation of the EK-proof procedure.

Summarizing, when B_L is finite, EK-recurrency and EK-acyclicity coincide. However, they still stricly include simply EK-acyclicity. The program of Example 14 is defined on B_L finite: it is EK-recurrent, and then EK-acyclic, but it is not simply EK-acyclic.

7.5   A Hierarchy of Characterizations

Figure 7 summarizes the hierarchy of the classes of abductive programs discussed in this paper (the meaning of the dashed line will be explained below.) By *strongly terminating* we mean abductive programs P such that P and any ground goal strongly terminate.

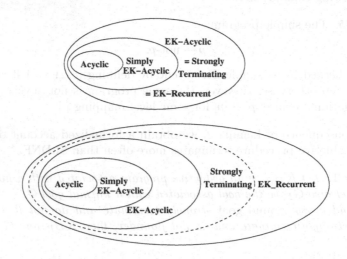

Fig. 7. *A hierarchy of characterization: B_L finite (top) and infinite (bottom).*

When B_L is finite (top of figure 7), the classes of EK-acyclic programs, strongly terminating programs and EK-recurrent programs coincide (Theorem 3 and Lemma 3). Moreover, they strictly include simply EK-acyclic programs (Example 14), which in turn strictly include acyclic ones (Example 15).

When B_L is infinite (bottom of figure 7), we have as before that EK-acyclic programs strictly include simply EK-acyclic programs (just add a clause $q(f(x))$ to Example 14), which again strictly include acyclic ones. Also, we have that EK-recurrent programs include strongly terminating ones (Theorem 3). Such an inclusion is strict (Example 12). Finally, by Theorem 4, strongly terminating programs include EK-acyclic programs. However, these two classes do not coincide.

Example 16. Let KB be the following abductive program:
$$p(x) \leftarrow q(x,y), \text{not-}p(y).$$
$$q(a, f(a)).$$

KB and the goal $\leftarrow p(a)$ strongly terminate. However, the program is not EK-acyclic by any $\mid \mid^+$ and $\mid \mid^-$. Assume the contrary. By Def. 9 **ac2**(*i*), we have for every $n \geq 0$:

$$|p(a), \emptyset|^- > |p(f(a)), \{\text{not-}p(f(a))\}|^- > \ldots > |p(f^n(a)), \cup_{i=1..n}\{\text{not-}p(f^i(a))\}|^-.$$

This is impossible since $|p(a), \emptyset|^- \in \mathbb{N}$.

We observe that a similar incompleteness problem is exhibited by acyclicity for normal logic programs. In fact, the normal program P corresponding to KB and the goal $\leftarrow p(a)$ strongly terminate (w.r.t. SLDNF), but P is not acyclic either.

In both cases, the reason of such an incompleteness problem is floundering. On the one side, floundering prevents the operational semantics (SLDNF or *EK*-proof procedure) from possible non-termination (e.g., in the example above one could always select the abducible non ground atom not-$p(y)$ and loop indefinitely.) On the other side, however, floundering is not taken into account from proof obligations. Moreover, since proof obligations do not take into account safe vs non-safe selection rules, floundering must be avoided both for safe and non-safe selection rules. In fact, the termination completeness result (Theorem 2) of Apt and Bezem [AB91] requires that no SLDNF-derivation of P and G flounders. Therefore, we conjecture that a completeness result extending Theorem 2 can be stated only under the further assumption that no abductive/consistency flounders for the program and the goal at hand. This is the reason why, in Fig. 7 (bottom), the circle of strongly terminating programs is dashed.

Another way to reason about the program above, is to consider the leftmost selection rule. In this case, a proof method could exploit the information provided by the atom to the left of not-$p(y)$, namely $y = f(a)$, thus preventing both floundering and non-termination.

8   Conclusion and Future Work

We studied in this paper the termination properties of the abductive interpretation of negation as failure, in order to provide a formal understanding of the fact that such an abductive procedure terminates more often than the usual SLDNF procedure, and to provide a proof method to reason about termination of abductive programs.

The proof method consists in proving that a program belongs to one of the classes of EK-acyclic, simply EK-acyclic, acyclic, and EK-recurrent programs. These classes are defined declaratively by proof obligations that do not refer to the operational semantics of a program, but rather to the structure of the program itself. The automation of the method is outside the scope of this paper. However, automatic methods have been proposed in the literature for the automatic generation of level mappings, as well as the automatic check of proof obligations, in the case of normal logic programs and of the SLDNF proof procedure [LS97, DDV99, MN01]. We are confident that this automation can be readily applied also to our methods.

In the case of programs over a finite universe, a win-win situation occurs: a dramatically simple method for proving termination of abductive program is both sound and complete, in the sense that it captures all and only the (strongly) terminating abductive programs. The simplicity of the method is due to the fact that a single level mapping (termination function) is needed, which deals only with the ordinary (non-abducible) literals.

264   Paolo Mancarella, Dino Pedreschi, and Salvatore Ruggieri

In the case of programs over an infinite universe the picture gets more involved. First, two separate level mappings are needed, to take into account two distinct dimensions: the depth of the trees and the number of the subsidiary trees. Simplifications of this scheme, such as collapsing the two level mappings into one, are possible, but lead to less powerful proof methods. Second, the proof method is sound, but not complete, due to the possibility of floundering, which, as pointed out in Example 15, prevents a general completeness result as in the case of finite universes. We believe that such a result can be obtained by restricting our attention to non-floundering programs and goals, as in the case of acyclic programs with respect to SLDNF [AB91].

Besides completeness, there are a few more questions that are worth further research.

- The notion of recurrent/acyclic programs was extended in [AP93] to that of acceptable programs, in order to prove termination of a larger class of logic programs, namely the left-terminating programs: those programs which terminate using (Prolog's) left-most selection rule. This class is much larger than the class of strong-terminating programs, which are expected to terminate with every selection rule. It would be interesting to extend the notions above to abductive programs, and devise a method for the left-most abductive procedure.
- In the same paper [AP93], terminating programs are also studied from a declarative semantics point of view. For instance, (normal) acceptable programs exhibit the property that their completion (iff version) has a unique Herbrand model, or equivalently their associated T_P mapping has a unique fixpoint. It would be interesting to study if and how analogous properties may extend to terminating abductive programs, which exhibit a multiplicity of minimal (partial) stable models.
- In the case of the simply EK-acyclic programs, it would be interesting to see whether a meaningful operational (or declarative) semantics exists, which is characterized by this intermediate class of programs.

References

[AB91]   K. R. Apt and M. Bezem. Acyclic programs. *New Generation Computing*, 29(3):335–363, 1991.
[AP93]   K. R. Apt and D. Pedreschi. Reasoning about termination of pure Prolog programs. *Information and Computation*, 106(1):109–157, 1993.
[Apt96] K. R. Apt. *From Logic Programming to Prolog*. CAR Hoare Series Editor. Prentice Hall, 1996.
[Bez89] M. Bezem. Characterizing termination of logic programs with level mappings. In E. L. Lusk and R. A. Overbeek, editors, *Proceedings of the North American Conference on Logic Programming*, pages 69–80. The MIT Press, 1989.
[Cla78] K. L. Clark. Negation as failure. In H. Gallaire and J. Minker, editors, *Logic and Databases*, pages 293–322. Plenum Press, New York, 1978.

[DD94]   D. De Schreye and S. Decorte. Termination of logic programs: the never-
           ending story. *Journal of Logic Programming*, 19-20:199–260, 1994.
[DDV99]   S. Decorte, D. De Schreye, and H. Vandecasteele. Constraint-based termi-
           nation analysis of logic programs. *ACM Trans. on Programming Languages
           and Systems*, 21(6):1137–1195, 1999.
[Der87]   N. Dershowitz. Termination of rewriting. *Journal of Symbolic Computation*,
           8:69–116, 1987.
[DS98]   M. Denecker and D. De Schreye. SLDNFA: An abductive procedure for
           abductive logic programs. *Journal of Logic Programming*, 34(2):111–167,
           1998.
[Dun95]   P. M. Dung. An argumentation-theoretic foundation for logic programming.
           Journal of Logic Programming, 22(2):151–177, 1995.
[EK89]   K. Eshgi and R.A. Kowalski. Abduction compared with negation by failure.
           In G. Levi and M. Martelli, editors, *Proceedings of the 1989 International
           Conference on Logic Programming*, pages 234–254. MIT Press, 1989.
[KKT93]   A.C. Kakas, R.A. Kowalski, and F. Toni. Abductive logic programming.
           Journal of Logic and Computation, 2(6):719–770, 1993.
[LS97]   N. Lindenstrauss and Y. Sagiv. Automatic termination analysis of logic
           programs. In L. Naish, editor, *Proc. of the International Conference on
           Logic Programming*, pages 63–77. The MIT Press, 1997.
[MN01]   F. Mesnard and U. Neumerkel. Applying static analysis techniques for in-
           ferring termination conditions of logic programs. In P. Cousot, editor, *Static
           Analysis Symposium*, volume 2126 of *LNCS*, pages 93–110. Springer-Verlag,
           2001.
[PRS02]   D. Pedreschi, S. Ruggieri, and J.-G. Smaus. Classes of terminating logic
           programs. *Theory and Practice of Logic Programming*, 2002. To appear.
[Rei80]   R. Reiter. A logic for default reasoning. *Artificial Intelligence*, 13:81–132,
           1980.
[Ver99]   S. Verbaeten. Termination analysis for abductive general logic programs.
           In D. De Schreye, editor, *Proc. of the International Conference on Logic
           Programming*, pages 365–379. The MIT Press, 1999.

A   Proofs

A.1   Preliminaries

Function max(). In the following, we assume that the function $max : 2^\omega \to \mathbb{N}$
is defined as follows:

$$
max\ S = \begin{cases} 0 & \text{if } S = \emptyset, \\ n & \text{if } S \text{ is finite and non-empty, and } n \text{ is the maximum of } S, \\ \infty & \text{if } S \text{ is infinite.} \end{cases}
$$

Then $max\ S < \infty$ iff the set S is finite.

Lexicographic ordering. We recall that the lexicographic ordering on pairs of
natural numbers can be defined as follows. We say that $\langle a_1, a_2 \rangle >_{lex} \langle b_1, b_2 \rangle$ if
$a_1 > b_1$ or $(a_1 = b_1$ and $a_2 > b_2)$. We write $\langle a_1, a_2 \rangle \geq_{lex} \langle b_1, b_2 \rangle$ if $\langle a_1, a_2 \rangle >_{lex}$

$\langle b_1, b_2 \rangle$ or $\langle a_1, a_2 \rangle = \langle b_1, b_2 \rangle$. Finally, let us recall that the lexicographic ordering on tuples of natural numbers is well-founded.

Multiset ordering. Moreover, we will use the finite multiset ordering. A multiset on W is an unordered sequence of elements from W. We denote a multiset of elements $a_1, \dots, a_n$ by $bag(a_1, \dots, a_n)$. If W is associated with an irreflexive ordering $>$, we define the ordering $\succ_m$ on the finite multisets induced by $>$ as the transitive closure of the relation

$$Y \succ X \text{ iff } X = Y - \{a\} \cup Z \text{ for } a \in Y \text{ and } Z \text{ such that } a > b \text{ for every } b \in Z,$$

where X, Y, Z are finite multisets of elements from W. A well-known result (cfr., [Der87]) shows that if $(W, <)$ is a well-founded ordering, then the corresponding multiset ordering is well-founded as well. Finally, the multiset union is defined as follows: $bag(a_1, \dots, a_n) \cup bag(b_1, \dots, b_m) = bag(a_1, \dots, a_n, b_1, \dots, b_m)$.

A.2   Termination Soundness of EK-acyclicity

By S we denote the set $\{$ **abd**, **con** $\}$. Intuitively, we will use the symbol **abd** to denote abductive derivations and **con** to denote consistency derivations. We define the functions $is\_abd()$ and $is\_con()$ on S as follows: $is\_abd(\textbf{abd}) = is\_con(\textbf{con}) = 1$, $is\_abd(\textbf{con}) = is\_con(\textbf{abd}) = 0$.

We associate a finite multiset over pairs of natural numbers to states of abductive or consistency derivations, here modelled respectively as triples (G, Δ, s) and pairs (F, Δ), where G is a goal, Δ a set of hypotheses, $s \in S$ and F a set of goals.

Definition 12. *Consider an atom l, a set of hypotheses Δ, two extended level mappings $| \ |^+$ and $| \ |^-$, and $s \in S$. We define*

bo1) *if l is an ordinary atom*

$$|l, \Delta, s|_-^+ = \langle \ max\{2 \cdot |l', \Delta|^- + is\_con(s) \ : l' \in ground_L(l) \ \},$$
$$max\{|l', \Delta|^+ \ : l' \in ground_L(l) \ \} \ \rangle.$$

bo2) *if l is an abducible atom*
    if $s = $ **abd**

$$|l, \Delta, s|_-^+ = \langle \ max\{2 \cdot |l', \Delta \cup \{neg\text{-}l'\}|^- + 1 \ : neg\text{-}l' \in ground_L(l) \ \setminus \Delta\},$$
$$max\{|l', \Delta \cup \{neg\text{-}l'\}|^+ + 1 \ : l' \in ground_L(l) \ \} \ \rangle,$$

    if $s = $ **con**

$$|l, \Delta, s|_-^+ = \langle \ max\{2 \cdot |l', \Delta|^- \ : neg\text{-}l' \in ground_L(l) \ \setminus \Delta\},$$
$$max\{|l', \Delta|^+ + 1 \ : l' \in ground_L(l) \ \} \ \rangle.$$

Now, consider a goal $G = \leftarrow L_1, \ldots, L_n$. The triple (G, Δ, s) is called bounded by $|\ |_-^+$ if ∞ is not an element of the pair $|L_i, \Delta, s|_-^+$ for every $i \in [1, n]$.

For (G, Δ, s) bounded, we define the multiset $\|G, \Delta, s\|$ of pairs of natural numbers as follows:

$$\|G, \Delta, s\| \;=\; bag\,(|L_1, \Delta, s|_-^+, \ldots, |L_n, \Delta, s|_-^+).$$

We say that a pair (F, Δ), where F is a finite set of goals, is bounded by $|\ |_-^+$ iff every $(G, \Delta, \mathbf{con})$ with $G \in F$ is bounded by $|\ |_-^+$. In such a case, we define:

$$\| F, \Delta \| = \bigcup_{G \in F} \|G, \Delta, \mathbf{con}\|.$$

$\square$

We state a simple fact.

Lemma 4. *A goal G is EK-acyclic by $|\ |^+$ and $|\ |^-$ iff $(G, \emptyset, \mathbf{abd})$ is bounded by $|\ |_-^+$.* $\square$

We prove a simple lemma.

Lemma 5. *Consider an abductive/consistency derivation*

$$(G_1, \Delta_1), (G_2, \Delta_2), \ldots, (G_n, \Delta_n) \ldots$$

Then $\Delta_1 \subseteq \Delta_2 \subseteq \ldots \subseteq \Delta_n \ldots$ $\square$

Lemma 6. *Let KB be a program EK-acyclic by $|\ |^+$ and $|\ |^-$, and assume that (G, Δ, s) is bounded by $|\ |_-^+$. Let G' be an SLD-resolvent of G and a clause from KB. Then (G', Δ, s) is bounded by $|\ |_-^+$, and*

$$\|G, \Delta, s\| \quad \succ_m \quad \|G', \Delta, s\|.$$

Proof. Assume that G has the form $\leftarrow l, l_{n+1}, \ldots, l_m$ where (without loss of generality) the ordinary atom l is selected and $m \geq n$. Let $C = h \leftarrow l_1, \ldots, l_n$ be the renamed-apart selected clause, and $\theta = mgu(h, l)$. Then the SLD-resolvent is: $G' = \leftarrow (l_1, \ldots, l_n, \ldots, l_m)\theta$. We observe that:

(1) by Def. 12, $(G\theta, \Delta, s)$ is bounded by $|\ |_-^+$ and

$$\|G, \Delta, s\| \quad \succeq_m \quad \|G\theta, \Delta, s\|.$$

(2) Since KB is EK-acyclic, for every ground instance of $C\theta$, **ac1** and **ac2** hold.

(3) Let $i \in [1, n]$. If l_i is an ordinary atom, then:

$$max\{|l', \Delta|^+ : l' \in ground_L(l\theta) \}$$
$$> \quad \{ \mathbf{ac1}\,(i) \}$$
$$max\{|l'_i, \Delta|^+ : l'_i \in ground_L(l_i\theta) \}$$

$$max\{2 \cdot |l', \Delta|^- + is\_con(s) : l' \in ground_L(l\theta) \}$$
$$\geq \quad \{ \mathbf{ac1}\,(ii) \}$$
$$max\{2 \cdot |l'_i, \Delta|^- + is\_con(s) : l'_i \in ground_L(l_i\theta) \}$$

which imply: $|l\theta, \Delta, s|^+_- >_{lex} |l_i\theta, \Delta, s|^+_-$. If l_i is an abducible atom, then

$$max\{2 \cdot |l', \Delta|^- + 0 : l' \in ground_L(l\theta) \}$$
$$> \quad \{ \mathbf{ac2}\,(i) \}$$
$$max\{2 \cdot |l'_i, \Delta \cup \{\text{neg-}l'_i\}|^- + 1 : \text{neg-}l'_i \in ground_L(l_i\theta) \setminus \Delta\}$$

$$max\{2 \cdot |l', \Delta|^- + 1 : l' \in ground_L(l\theta) \}$$
$$> \quad \{ \mathbf{ac2}\,(ii) \}$$
$$max\{2 \cdot |l'_i, \Delta|^- : l'_i \in ground_L(l_i\theta) \setminus \Delta\}.$$

The first inequality covers the case: $|l\theta, \Delta, \mathbf{abd}|^+_- >_{lex} |l_i\theta, \Delta, \mathbf{abd}|^+_-$. The second one covers: $|l\theta, \Delta, \mathbf{con}|^+_- >_{lex} |l_i\theta, \Delta, \mathbf{con}|^+_-$.

Summarizing:

$$\|G, \Delta, s\|$$
$$\succeq_m \quad \{ \, (1) \, \}$$
$$= \quad \|G\theta, \Delta, s\|$$
$$= \quad bag\,(\,|l\theta, \Delta, s|^+_-, |l_{n+1}\theta, \Delta, s|^+_-, \ldots, \; |l_m\theta, \Delta, s|^+_-)$$
$$\succ_m \quad \{ \, (3) \, \}$$
$$= \quad bag\,(\,|l_1\theta, \Delta, s|^+_-, \ldots, \; |l_m\theta, \Delta, s|^+_-)$$
$$= \quad \|G', \Delta, s\|.$$

□

Lemma 7. *Let KB be a program EK-acyclic by $|\;|^+$ and $|\;|^-$, and*

$$(G_1, \Delta_1), \ldots, (G_i, \Delta_i), (G_{i+1}, \Delta_{i+1}) \ldots$$

an abductive derivation.

If $(G_i, \Delta_i, \mathbf{abd})$ *is bounded by* $| \ |_-^+$ *then* $(G_{i+1}, \Delta_{i+1}, \mathbf{abd})$ *is bounded by* $| \ |_-^+$ *and*

$$\|G_i, \Delta_i, \mathbf{abd}\| \quad \succ_m \quad \|G_{i+1}, \Delta_{i+1}, \mathbf{abd}\|.$$

Moreover, if, for some i, step **ab3** *of the abductive procedure applies, and a consistency derivation is started from* $(\{\leftarrow k\}, \Delta_i \cup \{\text{neg-}k\})$, *then*

$$\|G_i, \Delta_i, \mathbf{abd}\| \quad \succ_m \quad \|\{\leftarrow k\}, \Delta_i \cup \{\text{neg-}k\}\|.$$

Proof. Assume that G_i has the form $\leftarrow l, \mathbf{l}$ where (without loss of generality) l is selected and $\mathbf{l}$ is a (possibly empty) sequence of atoms. We distinguish three cases:

ab1) if l is an ordinary atom, then the conclusion follows from Lemma 6.

ab2) if l is an abducible atom and $l \in \Delta_i$, then:

$$\|G_i, \Delta_i, \mathbf{abd}\| = \|(\leftarrow l, \mathbf{l}), \Delta_i, \mathbf{abd}\|$$
$$\succ_m \quad \{ \text{ Def. 12 } \}$$
$$\|(\leftarrow \mathbf{l}), \Delta_i, \mathbf{abd}\|$$
$$= \quad \{ \text{ Abductive Procedure } \mathbf{ab2} \}$$
$$\|G_{i+1}, \Delta_{i+1}, \mathbf{abd}\|,$$

ab3) if l is a (ground) abducible atom ($l = \text{not-}k$) and $l \notin \Delta_i$ and there is a consistency derivation from $(\{\leftarrow k\}, \Delta_i \cup \{l\})$ to $(\emptyset, \Delta')$, then

$$\|G_i, \Delta_i, \mathbf{abd}\| = \|(\leftarrow l, \mathbf{l}), \Delta_i, \mathbf{abd}\|$$
$$\succ_m \quad \{ \text{ Def. 12 } \}$$
$$\|\leftarrow \mathbf{l}, \Delta_i, \mathbf{abd}\|$$
$$\succeq_m \quad \{ \Delta_i \subseteq \Delta' \text{ (Lemma 5) and Def. 8 } \}$$
$$\|\leftarrow \mathbf{l}, \Delta', \mathbf{abd}\|$$
$$= \quad \{ \text{ Abductive Procedure } \mathbf{ab3} \}$$
$$\|G_{i+1}, \Delta_{i+1}, \mathbf{abd}\|.$$

Moreover, we calculate:

$$\|G_i, \Delta_i, \mathbf{abd}\| = \|\leftarrow l, \mathbf{l}, \Delta_i, \mathbf{abd}\|$$
$$\succeq_m \quad \{ \text{ Def. 12 } \}$$
$$\|\leftarrow l, \Delta_i, \mathbf{abd}\|$$
$$= \quad \{ \text{ Def. 12 } \}$$
$$bag(\langle 2 \cdot |k, \Delta_i \cup \{l\}|^- + 1, |k, \Delta_i \cup \{l\}|^+ + 1\rangle)$$
$$\succ_m \quad \{ \text{ Def. 12 } \}$$
$$\|\leftarrow k, \Delta_i \cup \{l\}, \mathbf{con}\| = \|\{\leftarrow k\}, \Delta_i \cup \{l\}\|.$$

$\square$

Lemma 8. *Let KB be a program EK-acyclic by $|\ |^+$ and $|\ |^-$, and*

$$(F_1, \Delta_1), \ldots, (F_i, \Delta_i), (F_{i+1}, \Delta_{i+1}) \ldots$$

a consistency derivation .
If (F_i, Δ_i) is bounded by $|\ |^{\pm}_-$ then (F_{i+1}, Δ_{i+1}) is bounded by $|\ |^{\pm}_-$ and

$$\|F_i, \Delta_i\| \quad \succ_m \quad \|F_{i+1}, \Delta_{i+1}\|.$$

Moreover, if, for some i, step **co3** *of the abductive procedure applies, and an abductive refutation is started from $(\leftarrow k, \Delta_i)$, then*

$$\|F_i, \Delta_i\| \quad \succ_m \quad \|\leftarrow k, \Delta_i, \mathbf{abd}\|.$$

Proof. Assume that F_i has the form $\{\leftarrow l, \mathbf{l}\} \cup F_i'$ where (without loss of generality) the clause $\leftarrow l, \mathbf{l}$ has been selected (to continue the search), and l is the selected atom:

co1) if l is an ordinary atom, then for C' set of SLD-resolvents of KB and $\leftarrow l, \mathbf{l}$:

$$
\begin{aligned}
\|F_i, \Delta_i\| &= \|\{\leftarrow l, \mathbf{l}\} \cup F_i', \Delta_i\| \\
&= \|\{\leftarrow l, \mathbf{l}\}, \Delta_i, \mathbf{con}\| \cup \bigcup_{G \in F_i'} \|G, \Delta_i, \mathbf{con}\| \\
\succ_m \quad & \{ \text{ Lemma 6 and } KB \text{ finite set } \} \\
& \bigcup_{G \in C'} \|G, \Delta_i, \mathbf{con}\| \cup \bigcup_{G \in F_i'} \|G, \Delta_i, \mathbf{con}\| \\
&= \|C' \cup F_i', \Delta_i\| \\
&= \quad \{ \text{ Abductive Procedure } \mathbf{co1} \} \\
& \|F_{i+1}, \Delta_{i+1}\|, .
\end{aligned}
$$

co2) if l is an abducible atom, $l \in \Delta_i$ and $\mathbf{l}$ is not empty:

$$
\begin{aligned}
\|F_i, \Delta_i\| &= \|\{\leftarrow l, \mathbf{l}\} \cup F_i', \Delta_i\| \\
\succ_m \quad & \{ \text{ Def. 12 } \} \\
& \|\{\leftarrow \mathbf{l}\} \cup F_i', \Delta_i\| \\
&= \quad \{ \text{ Abductive Procedure } \mathbf{co2} \} \\
& \|F_{i+1}, \Delta_{i+1}\|,
\end{aligned}
$$

co3) if l is a (ground) abducible atom ($l = \text{not-}k$) and $l \notin \Delta_i$, then:
  − if there is an abductive derivation from $(\leftarrow k, \Delta_i)$ to $(\Box, \Delta')$, then:

$$
\begin{aligned}
\|F_i, \Delta_i\| &= \|\{\leftarrow l, \mathbf{l}\} \cup F_i', \Delta_i\| \\
\succeq_m \quad & \{ \Delta_i \subseteq \Delta' \text{ (Lemma 5) and Def. 8 } \} \\
& \|\{\leftarrow l, \mathbf{l}\} \cup F_i', \Delta'\|
\end{aligned}
$$

$$\succ_m \quad \{ \text{ Def. 12 } \}$$
$$\|F_i', \Delta'\|$$
$$= \quad \{ \text{ Abductive Procedure } \mathbf{co3} \}$$
$$\|F_{i+1}, \Delta_{i+1}\|.$$

Moreover, we calculate:

$$\|F_i, \Delta_i\| = \|\{\leftarrow l, \mathbf{l}\} \cup F_i', \Delta_i\|$$
$$\succeq_m \quad \{ \text{ Def. 12 } \}$$
$$\|\{\leftarrow l\}, \Delta_i\|$$
$$= \quad \{ \text{ Def. 12 } \}$$
$$bag(\langle 2 \cdot |k, \Delta_i|^-, |k, \Delta_i|^+ + 1\rangle)$$
$$\succ_m \quad \{ \text{ Def. 12 } \}$$
$$\|\leftarrow k, \Delta_i, \mathbf{abd}\|$$

– else if $\mathbf{l}$ is not empty

$$\|F_i, \Delta_i\| = \|\{\leftarrow l, \mathbf{l}\} \cup F_i', \Delta_i\|$$
$$\succ_m \quad \{ \text{ Def. 12 } \}$$
$$\|\{\leftarrow \mathbf{l}\} \cup F_i', \Delta_i\|$$
$$= \quad \{ \text{ Abductive Procedure } \mathbf{co3} \}$$
$$\|F_{i+1}, \Delta_{i+1}\|.$$

$\square$

Theorem 4

Proof. Since G is EK-acyclic by $|\ |^+$ and $|\ |^-$, then by Lemma 4 $(G, \emptyset, \mathbf{abd})$ is bounded by $|\ |^+_-$.

The EK-procedure is non-deterministic. By Lemmata 7 and 8, each non-deterministic choice of the EK-procedure yields a goal/set of goals whose associated multiset decreases according to the $\succ_m$ well-founded ordering. Therefore, the EK-procedure cannot have an infinite computation when the non-deterministic choices are never retracted. Since at each non-deterministic choice there are finitely many alternatives (because KB is finite), by König's Lemma, also when the non-deterministic choices may be retracted the EK-procedure cannot have an infinite computation. $\square$

A.3   EK-recurrency Implies EK-acyclicity

Lemma 3

Proof. Consider the extended level mappings:

$$|A, \Delta|^+ = |A|$$

$$|A, \Delta|^- = \#(B_L \setminus \Delta).$$

Let us show the proof obligations of EK-acyclicity for KB. Consider $\Delta \subseteq \text{neg-}B_L$, $A \leftarrow L_1, \ldots, L_n \in ground_L(KB)$ and $i \in [1, n]$:

ac1) if $L_i = B_i$ then:

$$\begin{aligned}
(i) \quad & |A, \Delta|^+ = |A| \\
& > \quad \{ KB \text{ is EK-recurrent by } |\ | \} \\
& |B_i| = |B_i, \Delta|^+ \\
(ii) \quad & |A, \Delta|^- = \#(B_L \setminus \Delta) = |B_i, \Delta|^-.
\end{aligned}$$

ac2) if $L_i = \text{neg-}B_i$ and $L_i \notin \Delta$ then:

$$\begin{aligned}
(i) \quad & |A, \Delta|^- = \#(B_L \setminus \Delta) \\
& > \quad \{ L_i \notin \Delta \} \\
& \#(B_L \setminus \Delta \cup \{L_i\}) \\
& = |B_i, \Delta \cup \{L_i\}|^- \\
(ii) \quad & |A, \Delta|^- = \#(B_L \setminus \Delta) = |B_i, \Delta|^-.
\end{aligned}$$

Let k be such that the definition of EK-recurrency of G holds. We define $h = max\{k, \#B_L\}$. We show the proof obligations of EK-acyclicity for G using h. Consider $\Delta \subseteq \text{neg-}B_L$, $\leftarrow L_1, \ldots, L_n \in ground_L(G)$ and $i \in [1, n]$:

ac1) if $L_i = B_i$ then:

$$\begin{aligned}
(i) \quad & h \geq k \\
& > \quad \{ G \text{ is EK-recurrent by } |\ | \} \\
& |B_i| = |B_i, \Delta|^+ \\
(ii) \quad & h \geq \#B_L \geq \#(B_L \setminus \Delta) = |B_i, \Delta|^-.
\end{aligned}$$

ac2) if $L_i = \text{neg-}B_i$ and $L_i \notin \Delta$ then:

$$\begin{aligned}
(i) \quad & h \geq \#B_L \\
& > \quad \{ L_i \notin \Delta \} \\
& \#(B_L \setminus \Delta \cup \{L_i\}) \\
& = |B_i, \Delta \cup \{L_i\}|^- \\
(ii) \quad & h \geq \#B_L \geq \#(B_L \setminus \Delta) = |B_i, \Delta|^-.
\end{aligned}$$

$\square$

Program Derivation = Rules + Strategies

Alberto Pettorossi[1] and Maurizio Proietti[2]

[1] DISP, Università di Roma Tor Vergata, Roma, Italy.
adp@iasi.rm.cnr.it
[2] IASI-CNR, Roma, Italy.
proietti@iasi.rm.cnr.it

Abstract. In a seminal paper [38] Prof. Robert Kowalski advocated the paradigm *Algorithm = Logic + Control* which was intended to characterize program executions. Here we want to illustrate the corresponding paradigm *Program Derivation = Rules + Strategies* which is intended to characterize program derivations, rather than executions. During program execution, the *Logic* component guarantees that the computed results are correct, that is, they are true facts in the intended model of the given program, while the *Control* component ensures that those facts are derived in an efficient way. Likewise, during program derivation, the *Rules* component guarantees that the derived programs are correct and the *Strategies* component ensures that the derived programs are efficient. In this chapter we will consider the case of logic programs with locally stratified negation and we will focus on the following three important methodologies for program derivation: program transformation, program synthesis, and program verification. Based upon the *Rules + Strategies* approach, we will propose a unified method for applying these three programming methodologies. In particular, we will present: (i) a set of rules for program transformation which preserve the perfect model semantics and (ii) a general strategy for applying the transformation rules. We will also show that we can synthesize correct and efficient programs from first order specifications by: (i) converting an arbitrary first order formula into a logic program with locally stratified negation by using a variant of the Lloyd-Topor transformation, and then (ii) applying our transformation rules according to our general strategy. Finally, we will demonstrate that the rules and the strategy for program transformation and program synthesis can also be used for program verification, that is, for proving first order properties of systems described by logic programs with locally stratified negation.

1   Introduction

Various models of computation were proposed since the early history of computing. Among others, we may recall the von Neumann machine for imperative languages, term rewriting for functional languages, and resolution for logical languages. In these three different language paradigms, people explored and analyzed different programming methodologies. In particular, in the area of logical

A.C. Kakas, F. Sadri (Eds.): Computat. Logic (Kowalski Festschrift), LNAI 2407, pp. 273–309, 2002.
© Springer-Verlag Berlin Heidelberg 2002

languages, it was realized that both computing and programming can be viewed as a deductive activity.

The idea of computation as deduction may be traced back to the beginnings of the computation theory and recursive function theory, but it emerged clearly within the Theorem Proving community through the pioneering work of Robinson [62] and later, the paper by Kowalski [37], where the author proposed a particular deduction rule, namely, SLD-resolution, to compute in a logical theory consisting of Horn clauses. The deductive approach to computation was still considered to be not very practical at that time, but the situation changed when Warren [75] proposed a Prolog compiler based on SLD-resolution with performance comparable to that of the functional language Lisp. Efficiency is obtained by sacrificing correctness in some cases, but fortunately, that incorrectness turns out not to be a problem in practice.

The idea of programming and program development as a deduction from logical specifications to executable expressions in a formal setting, has its roots in the works by Burstall-Darlington and Manna-Waldinger [10,49] for functional languages and in the works by Clark *et al.*, Hogger, and Kowalski [11,12,32,39] for the case of logical languages. Similar ideas were proposed also in the case of imperative languages and one should mention, among others, the contributions of Dijkstra and Hoare (see, for instance, [21,31]).

In the paper [38] Kowalski proposes the motto: *Algorithm = Logic + Control*, to promote a separation of concern when writing programs: a concern for correctness in the *Logic* component, and a concern for efficiency in the *Control* component. This separation idea for program development goes back to the seminal paper by Burstall and Darlington [10]. The aim is to derive programs which are correct and efficient by applying transformation rules in a disciplined manner according to suitable strategies. In this case the *Logic* component consists of the transformation *rules*, such as unfolding and folding, which are correct because they preserve the semantics of interest, and the *Control* component consists of the *strategies* which direct the use of the rules so to derive efficient programs. Our motto, which can be viewed as an application of Kowalski's motto to the case of program development, is: *Program Derivation = Rules + Strategies*.

As we will illustrate in this chapter, our motto also indicates a way of understanding the relationship among various techniques for program development such as program synthesis, program reuse, and program verification. Some of these techniques based on rules and strategies, are described in [19,20,33,52].

The main objective of this chapter is to provide a unified view of: (i) program transformation, (ii) program synthesis, and (iii) program verification as deductive activities based on the unfolding/folding transformation rules and strategies. We consider the class of logic programs with locally stratified negation. The semantics of a program P in this class is given by its unique perfect model, denoted $M(P)$, which coincides with its unique stable model and its (total) well-founded model [2].

In our setting program transformation, synthesis, and verification can be formulated as follows.

Program Transformation. Given a program P and a goal G with free variables $X_1, \ldots, X_n$, we want to find a computationally efficient program T for a new n-ary predicate g such that, for all ground terms $t_1, \ldots, t_n$,

$$M(P) \models G\{X_1/t_1, \ldots, X_n/t_n\} \quad \text{iff} \quad M(T) \models g(t_1, \ldots, t_n) \qquad (\mathit{Transf})$$

Notice that our formulation of program transformation includes *program specialization* [27,33,44,47] which can be regarded as the particular case where G is an atom with instantiated arguments.

Program Synthesis. Given a program P and a *specification* of the form $g(X_1, \ldots, X_n) \leftrightarrow \varphi$, where: (i) φ is a first order formula with free variables $X_1, \ldots, X_n$, and (ii) g is a new n-ary predicate, we want to derive a computationally efficient program T for the predicate g such that, for all ground terms $t_1, \ldots, t_n$,

$$M(P) \models \varphi\{X_1/t_1, \ldots, X_n/t_n\} \quad \text{iff} \quad M(T) \models g(t_1, \ldots, t_n) \qquad (\mathit{Synth})$$

Program Verification. Given a program P and a *closed* first order formula φ, we want to check whether or not

$$M(P) \models \varphi \qquad (\mathit{Verif})$$

In order to get a unified view of program transformation, program synthesis, and program verification, let us first notice that each of these three tasks starts from a given program P and a first order formula. This formula, say γ, is: (i) the goal G in the case of program transformation, (ii) the formula φ of the specification $g(X_1, \ldots, X_n) \leftrightarrow \varphi$ in the case of program synthesis, and (iii) the closed first order formula φ in the case of program verification. Thus, we can provide a unified treatment of program transformation, program synthesis, and program verification, by viewing them as instances of the following general, two step method for program derivation, which takes as input a given program P and a first order formula γ.

The Unfold/Fold Method for Program Derivation.

We are given a locally stratified program P and a first order formula γ.

Step 1. We construct a conjunction of clauses, denoted by $Cls(g, \gamma)$ such that $P \wedge Cls(g, \gamma)$ is a locally stratified program and, for all ground terms $t_1, \ldots, t_n$,

$$M(P) \models \gamma\{X_1/t_1, \ldots, X_n/t_n\} \quad \text{iff} \quad M(P \wedge Cls(g, \gamma)) \models g(t_1, \ldots, t_n)$$

where $X_1, \ldots, X_n$ are the free variables of γ.

Step 2. We apply unfold/fold transformation rules which preserve the perfect model semantics and we derive a new program T such that, for all ground terms $t_1, \ldots, t_n$,

$$M(P \wedge Cls(g, \gamma)) \models g(t_1, \ldots, t_n) \quad \text{iff} \quad M(T) \models g(t_1, \ldots, t_n)$$

The derivation of program T is made according to a transformation strategy which guides the application of the rules.

Let us now briefly explain how this general unfold/fold method for program derivation will be instantiated to three specific methods for program transformation, program synthesis, and program verification. More details and examples will be given in Sections 2, 3, and 4.

Among the tasks of program transformation, program synthesis, and program verification, the one which has the most general formulation is program synthesis, because the formula φ of a specification is *any* first order formula, whereas the inputs for program transformation and program verification consist of a *goal* (that is, a conjunction of literals) and a *closed* first order formula, respectively.

A method for program synthesis can be obtained from the general unfold/fold method for program derivation in a straightforward way by taking γ as the formula φ of the specification $g(X_1, \ldots, X_n) \leftrightarrow \varphi$. In Section 3 we will see how the conjunction of clauses $Cls(g, \varphi)$ can be constructed by using a suitable variant of the *Lloyd-Topor transformation* [46]. Moreover, we will propose (see Section 2) a general transformation strategy for deriving a suitable program T from program $P \wedge Cls(g, \varphi)$ as required by Step 2 of the unfold/fold method. From the fact that our variant of the Lloyd-Topor transformation and the unfold/fold transformation rules preserve the perfect model semantics, it follows that the equivalence $(Synth)$ indeed holds for this program T.

Similarly, if we consider our general unfold/fold method for program derivation in the case where γ is the goal G, then we derive a program T which satisfies the relation $(Transf)$, and thus, in this case the general method becomes a method for program transformation.

Finally, program verification can be viewed as an instance of our general unfold/fold method in the case where γ is the closed first order formula φ. In particular, the conjunction of clauses $Cls(g, \varphi)$ can be constructed as in the case of program synthesis by starting from the specification $g \leftrightarrow \varphi$. Then, one can prove that $M(P) \models \varphi$ holds by applying Step 2 of our method for program derivation and obtaining a program T which includes the clause $g \leftarrow$.

The contributions of this chapter are the following ones. (i) We describe in some detail our general, two step method based on rules and strategies, for the unified treatment of program transformation, synthesis, and verification, and through some examples, we show that our method is effective for each of these tasks. (ii) We establish the correctness of the transformation rules by giving sufficient conditions for the preservation of perfect model semantics. These correctness results extend results already published in the literature [70]. In particular, we take into consideration also the unfolding and folding rules w.r.t. negative literals, and these rules are crucial in the examples we will present. (iii) We outline a general strategy for the application of the transformation rules and we demonstrate that various techniques for rather different tasks, such as program transformation, program synthesis, and program verification, can all be realized by that single strategy.

The plan of the chapter is as follows. In Section 2 we present a set of transformation rules for locally stratified programs and we give sufficient conditions which ensure their correctness w.r.t. the perfect model semantics. We also present our general strategy for the application of the transformation rules. In Section 3 we present the instance of our two step unfold/fold method for the synthesis of logic programs from specifications provided by first order formulas. In Section

4 we show that also program verification can be performed using our two step method.

2 Transformation Rules and Strategies for Locally Stratified Logic Programs

In this section we recall the basic concepts of locally stratified programs and perfect model semantics. We then present the transformation rules which we use for program transformation, and we provide a sufficient condition which ensures that these rules preserve the perfect model semantics. We also outline a general strategy for applying the transformation rules.

2.1 Preliminaries: Syntax and Semantics of Stratified Logic Programs

We recall some basic definitions and we introduce some terminology and notation concerning general logic programs and their semantics. In particular, we will recall the definitions of *locally stratified* logic programs and their *perfect models*. For notions not defined here the reader may refer to [2,46,59].

Given a *first order language* $\mathcal{L}$, its *formulas* are constructed out of *variables*, *function* symbols, *predicate* symbols, *terms*, *atomic formulas* (also called *atoms*), the formula *true*, the connectives $\neg$ and $\wedge$, and the quantifier $\exists$ (see, for instance, [2,46]). We feel free to write formulas using also the symbols *false*, $\vee$, $\rightarrow$, $\leftrightarrow$, and $\forall$, but we regard them as abbreviations of the equivalent formulas written using the symbols *true*, $\neg$, $\wedge$, and $\exists$ only. Following the usual logic programming convention, we use upper case letters for variables and lower case letters for function and predicate symbols.

A *literal* is an atom (i.e., a *positive* literal) or a negated atom (i.e., a *negative* literal). A *goal* G is a conjunction of n (≥ 0) literals.

General logic programs, simply called *logic programs*, or *programs*, are first order formulas defined as follows. A *program* is a conjunction of *clauses*, each of which is of the form: $G \rightarrow H$, where G is a goal and H is an atom different from *true* and *false*. Normally a clause will be written as $H \leftarrow G$. The atom H is called the *head* of the clause, denoted by $hd(C)$, and the goal G is called the *body* of the clause, denoted by $bd(C)$. A clause $H \leftarrow G$ where G is the empty conjunction *true*, is said to be a *unit* clause and it is written as $H \leftarrow$. When writing goals, clauses, and programs, we also denote conjunctions by using comma ',' instead of $\wedge$. Thus, usually, a goal will be written as $L_1, \dots, L_n$, where the L_i's are literals, a clause will be written as $H \leftarrow L_1, \dots, L_n$, and a program will be written as $C_1, \dots, C_n$, where the C_i's are clauses. When writing programs we will also feel free to omit commas between clauses, if no confusion arises.

A clause is said to be *definite* iff no negated atom occurs in its body. A *definite* program is a conjunction of definite clauses.

Given a term t we denote by $vars(t)$ the set of all variables occurring in t. Similar notation will be used for the variables occurring in formulas. Given a clause

C, a variable in $bd(C)$ is said to be *existential* iff it belongs to $vars(bd(C)) - vars(hd(C))$. Given a formula φ we denote by $freevars(\varphi)$ the set of all variables of φ which have a free occurrence in φ. A clause C is said to be *ground* iff no variable occurs in it. We may freely rename the variables occurring in clauses, and the process of renaming the variables of a clause by using new variables, is called *renaming apart* [46].

The *definition* of a predicate p in a program P, denoted by $Def(p, P)$, is the conjunction of the clauses of P whose head predicate is p. We say that p *is defined in* P iff $Def(p, P)$ is not empty. We say that a predicate p *depends on* a predicate q in P iff either there exists in P a clause of the form: $p(\ldots) \leftarrow B$ such that q occurs in the goal B or there exists in P a predicate r such that p depends on r in P and r depends on q in P. The *extended definition* of a predicate p in a program P, denoted by $Def^*(p, P)$, is the conjunction of the definition of p and the definition of every predicate on which p depends in P. We say that a predicate p *depends on existential variables* in a program P iff in $Def^*(p, P)$ there exists a clause C whose body has an existential variable.

The set of *useless* predicates of a program P is the maximal set U of the predicates of P such that a predicate p is in U iff the body of each clause of $Def(p, P)$ has a positive literal whose predicate is in U. For instance, p and q are useless and r is not useless in the following program:

$$p \leftarrow q, r$$
$$q \leftarrow p$$
$$r \leftarrow$$

By $ground(P)$ we denote the conjunction of all clauses in $\mathcal{L}$ which are ground instances of clauses of P, and by $B_{\mathcal{L}}$ we denote the *Herbrand Base* of $\mathcal{L}$, that is, the set of all ground atoms in $\mathcal{L}$. A stratification σ is a total function from $B_{\mathcal{L}}$ to the set W of countable ordinals. Given a ground literal L which is the atom A or the negated atom $\neg A$, we say that L is in *stratum* α iff $\sigma(A) = \alpha$.

A ground clause $H \leftarrow L_1, \ldots, L_n$ is *locally stratified* w.r.t. a stratification σ iff for every $i = 1, \ldots, n$, if L_i is an atom then $\sigma(H) \geq \sigma(L_i)$, and if L_i is a negated atom, say $\neg A_i$, then $\sigma(H) > \sigma(A_i)$. We say that the program P is *locally stratified* iff there exists a stratification σ such that every clause in $ground(P)$ is locally stratified w.r.t. σ. Let P_α be the conjunction of the clauses in $ground(P)$ whose head is in the stratum α. We may assume without loss of generality, that every ground atom is in a stratum which is greater than 0, so that P_0 may be assumed to be the empty conjunction of clauses.

An *Herbrand interpretation* is a subset of $B_{\mathcal{L}}$. We say that a closed first order formula φ is true in an Herbrand interpretation I, written as $I \models \varphi$, iff one of the following cases holds: (i) φ is the formula *true*, (ii) φ is a ground atom A which is in I, (iii) φ is $\neg\varphi_1$ and φ_1 is not true in I, (iv) φ is $\varphi_1 \wedge \varphi_2$ and both φ_1 and φ_2 are true in I, (v) φ is $\exists X\,\varphi_1$ and there exists a ground term t such that $\varphi_1\{X/t\}$ is true in I.

Given a formula φ and an Herbrand interpretation I, if it is not the case that $I \models \varphi$, we say that φ is false in I and we write $I \not\models \varphi$.

The *perfect model* $M(P)$ of a program P which is locally stratified w.r.t. a stratification σ, is the Herbrand interpretation defined as the subset $\bigcup_{\alpha \in W} M_\alpha$ of $B_\mathcal{L}$, where for every ordinal α in W, the set M_α is constructed as follows:
(1) M_0 is the empty set, and
(2) if $\alpha > 0$, M_α is the *least Herbrand model* [46] of the definite program derived from P_α as follows: (i) every literal L in stratum τ, with $\tau < \alpha$, in the body of a clause in P_α is deleted iff $M_\tau \models L$, and (ii) every clause C in P_α is deleted iff in $bd(C)$ there exists a literal L in stratum τ, with $\tau < \alpha$ such that $M_\tau \not\models L$.

For a locally stratified program P, with $vars(P) = \{X_1, \ldots, X_n\}$, we have that $M(P) \models \forall X_1, \ldots, X_n\, P$.

Our construction of the perfect model differs from the construction presented in [2,59], but as the reader may verify, the two constructions yield the same model.

Recall that perfect models are the usual intended semantics for logic programs with locally stratified negation, and for those programs all major approaches to the semantics of negation coincide [2]. Indeed, as already mentioned, a locally stratified program has a unique perfect model which is equal to its unique *stable model*, and also equal to its total *well-founded model*.

2.2 Unfold/Fold Transformation Rules

In this section we present the rules for transforming logic programs and we provide a sufficient condition which ensures that perfect models are preserved during program transformation.

For the application of the transformation rules we divide the predicate symbols of the language into two classes: (i) *basic* predicates and (ii) *non-basic* predicates. Atoms, literals, and goals which have occurrences of basic predicates only, are called *basic atoms*, *basic literals*, and *basic goals*, respectively. We assume that every basic atom is in a strictly smaller stratum w.r.t. every non-basic atom, and thus, in any given program no basic predicate depends on a non-basic one. Our partition of the set of predicates into basic or non-basic predicates is arbitrary and it may be different for different program derivations.

A *transformation sequence* is a sequence $P_0, \ldots, P_n$ of programs, where for $0 \le k \le n-1$, program P_{k+1} is derived from program P_k by the application of a transformation rule as indicated below.

We consider a set *Preds* of predicates of interest. We also consider, for $0 \le k \le n$, the conjunction $Defs_k$ of the clauses introduced by using the following rule R1 during the whole transformation sequence $P_0, \ldots, P_k$.

R1. Definition Introduction Rule. We get the new program P_{k+1} by adding to program P_k a conjunction of m clauses of the form:

$$\begin{cases} newp(X_1, \ldots, X_s) \leftarrow Body_1 \\ \ldots \\ newp(X_1, \ldots, X_s) \leftarrow Body_m \end{cases}$$

such that:

(i) the predicate *newp* is a non-basic predicate which does not occur in $P_0 \wedge Defs_k$,
(ii) $X_1, \ldots, X_s$ are distinct variables occurring in $Body_1, \ldots, Body_m$, and
(iii) every predicate occurring in $Body_1, \ldots, Body_m$ also occurs in P_0.

R2. Definition Elimination Rule. By *definition elimination* w.r.t. *Preds*, from program P_k we derive the new program P_{k+1} by deleting the definitions of all predicates on which no predicate belonging to *Preds* depends in P_k.

R3. Positive Unfolding Rule. Let C be a renamed apart clause in P_k of the form: $H \leftarrow G_1, A, G_2$, where A is an atom, and G_1 and G_2 are (possibly empty) goals. Suppose that:

1. $D_1, \ldots, D_m$, with $m \geq 0$, are all clauses of program P_k, such that A is unifiable with $hd(D_1), \ldots, hd(D_m)$, with most general unifiers $\vartheta_1, \ldots, \vartheta_m$, respectively, and
2. C_i is the clause $(H \leftarrow G_1, bd(D_i), G_2)\vartheta_i$, for $i = 1, \ldots, m$.

By *unfolding* clause C w.r.t. A we derive the clauses $C_1, \ldots, C_m$. From program P_k we derive the new program P_{k+1} by replacing C with $C_1, \ldots, C_m$.

In particular, if $m = 0$, that is, if we unfold a clause C in program P_k w.r.t. an atom which is not unifiable with the head of any clause in P_k, then we derive the new program P_{k+1} by deleting clause C.

R4. Negative Unfolding Rule. Let C be a renamed apart clause in P_k of the form: $H \leftarrow G_1, \neg A, G_2$. Let $D_1, \ldots, D_m$, with $m \geq 0$, be all clauses of program P_k, such that A is unifiable with $hd(D_1), \ldots, hd(D_m)$, with most general unifiers $\vartheta_1, \ldots, \vartheta_m$, respectively. Assume that:

1. $A = hd(D_1)\vartheta_1 = \cdots = hd(D_m)\vartheta_m$, that is, for $i = 1, \ldots, m$, A is an instance of $hd(D_i)$,
2. for $i = 1, \ldots, m$, D_i has no existential variables, and
3. from $G_1, \neg(bd(D_1)\vartheta_1 \vee \ldots \vee bd(D_m)\vartheta_m), G_2$ we get an equivalent disjunction $Q_1 \vee \ldots \vee Q_r$ of goals, with $r \geq 0$, by first pushing $\neg$ inside and then pushing $\vee$ outside.

By *unfolding* clause C w.r.t. $\neg A$ we derive the clauses $C_1, \ldots, C_r$, where C_i is the clause $H \leftarrow Q_i$, for $i = 1, \ldots, r$. From program P_k we derive the new program P_{k+1} by replacing C with $C_1, \ldots, C_r$.

In particular: (i) if $m = 0$, that is, if we unfold a clause C w.r.t. a negative literal $\neg A$ such that A is not unifiable with the head of any clause in P_k, then we get the new program P_{k+1} by deleting $\neg A$ from the body of clause C, and (ii) if for some $i \in \{1, \ldots, m\}$, $bd(D_i) = true$, that is, if we unfold a clause C w.r.t. a negative literal $\neg A$ such that A is an instance of the head of a unit clause in P_k, then we derive from program P_k the new program P_{k+1} by deleting clause C.

R5. Positive Folding Rule. Let $C_1, \ldots, C_m$ be renamed apart clauses in P_k and $D_1, \ldots, D_m$ be the definition of a predicate in $Defs_k$. For $i = 1, \ldots, m$, let

C_i be of the form: $H \leftarrow G_1, B_i, G_2$. Suppose that there exists a substitution ϑ such that, for $i = 1, \ldots, m$ the following conditions hold:
(1) $B_i = bd(D_i)\vartheta$, and
(2) for every variable X in the set $vars(D_i) - vars(hd(D_i))$, we have that $X\vartheta$ is a variable which occurs neither in $\{H, G_1, G_2\}$ nor in the term $Y\vartheta$, for any variable Y occurring in $bd(D_i)$ and different from X.
By *folding* clauses $C_1, \ldots, C_m$ using clauses $D_1, \ldots, D_m$ we derive the clause E: $H \leftarrow G_1, hd(D_1)\vartheta, G_2$. ¿From program P_k we derive the new program P_{k+1} by replacing $C_1, \ldots, C_m$ with E.
Notice that by definition of rule R1, we have that $hd(D_1) = \ldots = hd(D_m)$.

R6. Negative Folding Rule. Let C be a renamed apart clause in P_k and let $newp$ be a predicate in $Defs_k$ whose definition consists of a single clause D. Let C be of the form: $H \leftarrow G_1, \neg A, G_2$. Suppose that the following conditions hold:
(1) $A = bd(D)\vartheta$, for some substitution ϑ, and
(2) $vars(hd(D)) = vars(bd(D))$.
By *folding* clause C w.r.t. $\neg A$ using clause D we derive the clause E: $H \leftarrow G_1, \neg hd(D)\vartheta, G_2$. ¿From program P_k we derive the new program P_{k+1} by replacing C with E.

R7. Tautology Rule. We derive the new program P_{k+1} by replacing in P_k a conjunction of clauses γ_1 with a new conjunction of clauses γ_2, according to the following rewritings $\gamma_1 \Rightarrow \gamma_2$, where H and A, denote atoms, G, G_1, G_2, G_3, and G_4 denote goals, and C_1, C_2 denote clauses:

(1)	$H \leftarrow A, \neg A, G$	$\Rightarrow$	*true*
(2)	$H \leftarrow H, G$	$\Rightarrow$	*true*
(3)	$H \leftarrow G_1, G_2, G_3, G_4$	$\Rightarrow$	$H \leftarrow G_1, G_3, G_2, G_4$
(4)	$H \leftarrow A, A, G$	$\Rightarrow$	$H \leftarrow A, G$
(5)	$H \leftarrow G_1, \quad H \leftarrow G_1, G_2$	$\Rightarrow$	$H \leftarrow G_1$
(6)	$H \leftarrow A, G_1, G_2, \quad H \leftarrow \neg A, G_1$	$\Rightarrow$	$H \leftarrow G_1, G_2, \quad H \leftarrow \neg A, G_1$
(7)	$C_1, \; C_2$	$\Rightarrow$	$C_2, \; C_1$

R8. Clause Deletion Rule. We derive the new program P_{k+1} by removing from P_k the definitions of the useless predicates of P_k.

R9. Basic Goal Replacement Rule. Let us consider $r \, (> 0)$ renamed apart clauses in P_k of the form: $H \leftarrow G_1, Q_1, G_2, \ldots, H \leftarrow G_1, Q_r, G_2$. Suppose that, for some goals $R_1, \ldots, R_s$, we have:

$$M(P_0) \models \forall X_1 \ldots X_u \, (\exists Y_1 \ldots Y_v \, (Q_1 \vee \ldots \vee Q_r) \leftrightarrow \exists Z_1 \ldots Z_w \, (R_1 \vee \ldots \vee R_s))$$

where:
(i) $\{Y_1, \ldots, Y_v\} = vars(Q_1, \ldots, Q_r) - vars(H, G_1, G_2)$,
(ii) $\{Z_1, \ldots, Z_w\} = vars(R_1, \ldots, R_s) - vars(H, G_1, G_2)$, and
(iii) $\{X_1, \ldots, X_u\} = vars(Q_1, \ldots, Q_r, R_1, \ldots, R_s) - \{Y_1, \ldots, Y_v, Z_1, \ldots, Z_w\}$.
Suppose also that $R_1, \ldots, R_s$ are basic goals and H is a non-basic atom.
Then from program P_k we derive the new program P_{k+1} by replacing the clauses $H \leftarrow G_1, Q_1, G_2, \ldots, H \leftarrow G_1, Q_r, G_2$ with the clauses $H \leftarrow G_1, R_1, G_2, \ldots, H \leftarrow G_1, R_s, G_2$.

We assume that the *equality predicate* $=$ is a basic predicate which is defined in each program by the single clause $X = X \leftarrow$.

R10. Equality Introduction and Elimination. Let C be a clause of the form $(H \leftarrow Body)\{X/t\}$, such that the variable X does not occur in t and let D be the clause: $H \leftarrow X = t, Body$.

By *equality introduction* we derive clause D from clause C. By *equality elimination* we derive clause C from clause D.

If C occurs in P_k then we derive the new program P_{k+1} by replacing C with D. If D occurs in P_k then we derive the new program P_{k+1} by replacing D with C.

The transformation rules from rule R1 to rule R10 we have introduced above, will collectively be called *unfold/fold transformation rules*.

Theorem 1. [**Correctness of the Unfold/fold Transformation Rules**] *Let $P_0, \ldots, P_n$ be a transformation sequence and Preds be a set of predicates of interest. Let us assume that:*

(1) during the construction of $P_0, \ldots, P_n$, each clause introduced by the definition introduction rule and used for folding, is unfolded (before or after its use for folding) w.r.t. a non-basic positive literal in its body, and

(2) during the transformation sequence $P_0, \ldots, P_n$, either the definition elimination rule is never applied or it is applied at the end of that sequence.

Then, for all ground atoms A with predicate in Preds, $M(P_0 \wedge Defs_n) \models A$ iff $M(P_n) \models A$.

Notice that the statement obtained from Theorem 1 by replacing 'positive unfolding' by 'negative unfolding' is not a theorem as shown by the following example.

Example 1. Let P_0 be the program:
1. $p \leftarrow \neg q(X)$
2. $q(X) \leftarrow q(X)$
3. $q(X) \leftarrow r$

By negative unfolding w.r.t. $\neg q(X)$, from clause 1 we get the following clause 4:
4. $p \leftarrow \neg q(X), \neg r$

Then by folding clause 4 w.r.t. $\neg q(X)$, we get the following clause 5:
5. $p \leftarrow p, \neg r$

The final program P_1 consists of clauses 2, 3, and 5. We have that $M(P_0) \models p$, while $M(P_1) \models \neg p$.   □

Our presentation of the transformation rules essentially follows the style of Tamaki and Sato who first introduced the unfold/fold transformation rules in the case of definite programs [74] and proved their correctness w.r.t. the least Herbrand model semantics. Among the rules presented in this section, the following ones were introduced by Tamaki and Sato in [74] (actually, their presentation was a bit different): R1 restricted to $m = 1$, R3, R5 restricted to $m = 1$, R7 restricted to definite clauses, R8, R9 restricted to $r = s = 1$, and R10. Thus, some of our rules may be considered an extension of those in [74].

One of the most relevant features of Tamaki and Sato's rules is that their correctness is ensured by conditions on the construction of the transformation sequences similar to Condition (1) of Theorem 1.

A subset of Tamaki and Sato's rules, namely R3 (positive unfolding) and R5 (positive folding) with $m = 1$, has been extended to general logic programs by Seki and proved correct w.r.t. various semantics, including the perfect model semantics [70,71].

An extension of Seki's rules has been recently proposed by Roychoudhury *et al.* in [64]. In particular, they drop the restrictions that we can fold one clause only and the clauses used for folding are not recursive. The correctness of this extension of Seki's rules is ensured by a rather sophisticated condition which, in the case where recursive clauses cannot be used for folding, is implied by Condition (1) of Theorem 1.

Thus, the positive folding rule presented here is less powerful than the folding rule of [64], because we can only fold using clauses taken from $Defs_k$, and according to the definition introduction rule R1, we cannot introduce recursive clauses in $Defs_k$. However, our set of rules includes the negative unfolding (R4), the negative folding (R5), and the basic goal replacement rules (R9) which are not present in [64], and these rules are indeed very useful in practice and they are needed for the program derivation examples given in the next sections. We believe that we can easily incorporate the more powerful folding rule of [64] into our set of rules, but for reasons of simplicity, we stick to our version of the positive folding rule which has much simpler applicability conditions.

2.3   A Transformation Method

Now we outline our two step method for program transformation based on: (i) the unfold/fold transformation rules presented in Section 2.2, and (ii) a simple, yet powerful strategy, called *unfold/fold transformation strategy*, for guiding the application of the transformation rules. This method is an instance of the general unfold/fold method described in Section 1. Actually, our strategy is not fully specified, in the sense that many transformation steps can be performed in a nondeterministic way, and thus, we cannot prove that it improves efficiency in all cases. However, our strategy can be regarded as a generalization and adaptation to the case of general logic programs of a number of efficiency improving transformation strategies for definite programs presented in the literature, such as strategies for specializing programs, achieving tail recursion, avoiding intermediate data structures, avoiding redundant computations, and reducing nondeterminism (see [53] for a survey). Through some examples, we will indeed show that program efficiency can be improved by applying our unfold/fold transformation strategy.

The Unfold/Fold Transformation Method.

Given a locally stratified program P and a goal G such that $vars(G) = \{X_1, \ldots, X_n\}$, our transformation method consists of two steps as follows.

Step 1. We introduce a new n-ary predicate, say g, not occurring in $\{P, G\}$ and we derive a conjunction $Cls(g, G)$ of clauses such that $P \wedge Cls(g, G)$ is a locally stratified program and, for all ground terms $t_1, \ldots, t_n$,

(1) $M(P) \models G\{X_1/t_1, \ldots, X_n/t_n\}$ iff $M(P \wedge Cls(g, G)) \models g(t_1, \ldots, t_n)$.

Step 2. From the program P, the conjunction $Cls(g, G)$ of clauses, and a set of equivalences to be used for rule R9, by applying the unfold/fold transformation strategy described below, we derive a program T such that, for all ground terms $t_1, \ldots, t_n$,

(2) $M(P \wedge Cls(g, G)) \models g(t_1, \ldots, t_n)$ iff $M(T) \models g(t_1, \ldots, t_n)$

and thus, the relation (*Transf*) considered in the Introduction holds.

Clearly, a program T which satisfies (2) is $P \wedge Cls(g, G)$ itself. However, most often we are not interested in such trivial derivation because, as already mentioned, we look for an efficient program T which satisfies (2).

Now let us look at the above two steps of our transformation method in more detail.

Step 1 is performed by first introducing the clause C_1: $g(X_1, \ldots, X_n) \leftarrow G$ and then replacing this clause by a conjunction $Cls(g, G)$ of clauses as follows: for each non-basic negative literal $\neg p(u_1, \ldots, u_m)$ in G such that p depends on existential variables in P,

(i) we introduce the clause D: $new(Y_1, \ldots, Y_k) \leftarrow p(u_1, \ldots, u_m)$, where

$vars(p(u_1, \ldots, u_m)) = \{Y_1, \ldots, Y_k\}$, and

(ii) we fold clause $g(X_1, \ldots, X_n) \leftarrow G$ w.r.t. $\neg p(u_1, \ldots, u_m)$ using D.

For instance, in Example 2 below, from the initial goal

G: $word(W), \neg derive([s], W)$

we introduce the clause: $g(W) \leftarrow word(W), \neg derive([s], W)$, because the definition of the predicate $derive$ includes clause 3 which has the existential variables B and T. At the end of Step 1, we derive the following two clauses:

16. $g(W) \leftarrow word(W), \neg new1(W)$
17. $new1(W) \leftarrow derive([s], W)$

Step 1 is motivated by the fact that it is often useful, for reasons of efficiency, to transform the definitions of the predicates occurring in negative literals, if these definitions include clauses with existential variables. Indeed, since the unfolding w.r.t. a negative literal, say $\neg p(u_1, \ldots, u_m)$, is defined only if the clauses whose heads unify with $p(u_1, \ldots, u_m)$, have no existential variables, it is desirable to transform $Def^*(p, P) \wedge (new1(Y_1, \ldots, Y_k) \leftarrow p(u_1, \ldots, u_m))$ so to derive a new definition for the predicate $new1$ whose clauses do not have existential variables. Then, this new definition of $new1$ can be used for performing unfolding steps w.r.t. literals of the form $\neg new1(u_1, \ldots, u_m)$ and it may also allow more effective transformations of the clauses where $new1$ occurs.

Step 2 consists in applying the unfold/fold transformation strategy which we describe below. This strategy constructs n program transformation sequences

$S^1, \ldots, S^n$, where for $i = 1, \ldots, n-1$, the final program of the sequence S^i coincides with the initial program of the sequence S^{i+1}. Each transformation sequence corresponds to a *level* which is induced by the construction of the conjunction $Cls(g, G)$ of clauses. We will define these levels according to the following notion of *level mapping* [46].

Definition 1. *A level mapping of a program P is a mapping from the set of predicate symbols occurring in P to the set of natural numbers. Given a level mapping m, the* level *of the predicate p is the number assigned to p by m.*

Given a program P and a goal G, by construction there exists a level mapping of $Cls(g, G)$ such that: (1) the conjunction $Cls(g, G)$ can be partitioned into K subconjunctions: $D^1, \ldots, D^K$, such that $Cls(g, G) = D^1 \wedge \ldots \wedge D^K$, and, for $i = 1, \ldots, K$, the subconjunction D^i of clauses consists of all clauses in $Cls(g, G)$ whose head predicates are at level i, (2) for $i = 1, \ldots, K$ and for each clause $p(\ldots) \leftarrow B$ in D^i, the level of each predicate symbol in the goal B is strictly smaller than the level of p, (3) the predicate g is at the highest level K, and (4) all predicates of $Cls(g, G)$ which occur in P, are at level 0.

The reader may notice that, according to our definition of Step 1 above, K is at most 2. However, we have considered the case of an arbitrary value of K, because this will be appropriate when in Sections 3 and 4 below we consider program synthesis and program verification, respectively.

For the construction of each transformation sequence S^i, for $i = 1, \ldots$, $n - 1$, our unfold/fold transformation strategy uses the following three *subsidiary strategies*: (i) UNFOLD(P, Q), (ii) TAUTOLOGY-REPLACE($Laws, P, Q$), and (iii) DEFINE-FOLD($Defs, P, Q \wedge NewDefs$).

(i) Given a program P, UNFOLD(P, Q) specifies how to derive a new program Q by performing positive and negative unfolding steps (rules R3 and R4).

(ii) Given a program P and a set $Laws$ of equivalences needed for the application of the goal replacement rule, TAUTOLOGY-REPLACE($Laws, P, Q$) specifies how to derive a new program Q by applying the tautology, goal replacement, and equality introduction and elimination rules (rules R8, R9, and R10).

(iii) Given a program P and a conjunction $Defs$ of predicate definitions, DEFINE-FOLD($Defs, P, Q \wedge NewDefs$) specifies how to derive a new program $Q \wedge NewDefs$ by introducing a new conjunction $NewDefs$ of predicate definitions and performing folding steps using clauses occurring in $Defs \wedge NewDefs$ (rules R1, R5, and R6).

The effectiveness of the unfold/fold transformation strategy depends upon the choice of these subsidiary strategies, and much research, mostly in the case of definite programs, has been devoted to devise subsidiary strategies which allow us to derive very efficient programs [53]. For instance, the introduction of new predicate definitions, also called *eureka definitions*, influences the efficiency of the derived programs. Various techniques have been proposed for determining the suitable eureka definitions to be introduced. Here we only want to mention that it is often useful to introduce new predicates whose definition clauses have bodies which are: (i) instances of atoms, so to perform *program special-ization*, (ii) conjunctions of literals that share variables, so to derive programs that simultaneously perform the computations relative to several literals, and (iii) disjunctions of goals, so to derive programs with reduced nondeterminism, because they simultaneously perform the computations relative to several alternative goals.

We omit here the detailed description of the UNFOLD, TAUTOLOGY-REPLACE, and DEFINE-FOLD subsidiary strategies. We will see them in action in the examples given below. Here is our Unfold/Fold Transformation Strategy.

The Unfold/Fold Transformation Strategy.

Input: (i) a program P, (ii) a conjunction $Cls(g, G)$ of clauses constructed as indicated at Step 1, and (iii) a set *Laws* of equivalences for the application of rule R9. These equivalences are assumed to hold in $M(P \wedge Cls(g, G))$.

Output: A program T such that, for all ground terms $t_1, \ldots, t_n$,

$$M(P \wedge Cls(g, G)) \models g(t_1, \ldots, t_n) \text{ iff } M(T) \models g(t_1, \ldots, t_n).$$

Let us partition $Cls(g, G)$ into K subconjunctions: $D^1, \ldots, D^K$, as indicated in Step 2 above.

$T := P$;
for $i = 1, \ldots, K$ **do**
We construct a transformation sequence S^i as follows.
$Defs := D^i$; $InDefs := D^i$;

By the definition introduction rule we add the clauses of *InDefs* to T, thereby obtaining $T \wedge InDefs$.

while *InDefs* is not the empty conjunction **do**

(1) UNFOLD($T \wedge InDefs, T \wedge U$): ¿From program $T \wedge InDefs$ we derive $T \wedge U$ by a finite sequence of applications of the positive and negative unfolding rules to the clauses in *InDefs*.

(2) TAUTOLOGY-REPLACE(*Laws*, $T \wedge U, T \wedge R$): ¿From program $T \wedge U$ we derive $T \wedge R$ by a finite sequence of applications of the tautology and goal replacement rules to the clauses in U, using the equivalences in the set *Laws*.

(3) DEFINE-FOLD(*Defs*, $T \wedge R, T \wedge F \wedge NewDefs$): ¿From program $T \wedge R$ we derive $T \wedge F \wedge NewDefs$ by: (3.i) a finite sequence of applications of the definition introduction rule by which we add to $T \wedge R$ the (possibly empty) conjunction *NewDefs* of clauses, followed by (3.ii) a finite sequence of applications of the folding rule to the clauses in R, using clauses occurring in *Defs* $\wedge$ *NewDefs*. We assume that the definition and folding steps are such that all non-basic predicates occurring in the body of a clause which has been derived by folding, are defined in *Defs* $\wedge$ *NewDefs*.
$T := T \wedge F$; $Defs := Defs \wedge NewDefs$; $InDefs := NewDefs$
end while;
Delete from T the definitions of useless predicates.
end for

Delete from T the definitions of the predicates upon which the predicate g does not depend.

The unfold/fold transformation strategy is correct in the sense that for all ground terms $t_1, \ldots, t_n$, $M(P \wedge Cls(g, G)) \models g(t_1, \ldots, t_n)$ iff $M(T) \models g(t_1, \ldots, t_n)$, if each clause used for folding when executing the DEFINE-FOLD subsidiary strategy is unfolded w.r.t. a positive literal during an execution of the UNFOLD subsidiary strategy. If this condition is satisfied, then the correctness of our transformation strategy w.r.t. the perfect model semantics follows from the Correctness Theorem 1 of Section 2.2.

Notice that the unfold/fold transformation strategy may not terminate, because during the execution of the WHILE loop, *InDefs* may never become the empty conjunction.

Notice also that the iterations of our strategy over the various levels from 1 to K, correspond to the construction of the perfect model of program $P \wedge Cls(g, G)$ derived at the end of Step 1. This construction is done, so to speak, level by level moving upwards and starting from the perfect model of the program P whose predicates are assumed to be at level 0.

Let us now present an example of program derivation using our unfold/fold transformation method.

Example 2. Complement of a context-free language. Let us consider the following program CF for deriving a word of a given context-free language over the alphabet $\{a, b\}$:

1. $derive([\,], [\,]) \leftarrow$ Program CF
2. $derive([A|S], [A|W]) \leftarrow terminal(A),\ derive(S, W)$
3. $derive([A|S], W) \leftarrow nonterminal(A),\ production(A, B),$
    $\qquad\qquad\qquad\qquad append(B, S, T),\ derive(T, W)$
4. $terminal(a) \leftarrow$
5. $terminal(b) \leftarrow$
6. $nonterminal(s) \leftarrow$
7. $nonterminal(x) \leftarrow$
8. $production(s, [a, x, b]) \leftarrow$
9. $production(x, [\,]) \leftarrow$
10. $production(x, [a, x]) \leftarrow$
11. $production(x, [a, b, x]) \leftarrow$
12. $append([\,], A, A) \leftarrow$
13. $append([A|B], C, [A|D]) \leftarrow append(B, C, D)$
14. $word([\,]) \leftarrow$
15. $word([A|W]) \leftarrow terminal(A),\ word(W)$

The relation $derive([s], W)$ holds iff the word W can be derived from the *start symbol* s using the following productions of the grammar defining the given context-free language (see clauses 8–11):

$$s \rightarrow a\,x\,b \qquad x \rightarrow \varepsilon \qquad x \rightarrow a\,x \qquad x \rightarrow a\,b\,x$$

The terminal symbols are a and b (see clauses 4 and 5), the nonterminal symbols are s and x (see clauses 6 and 7), the empty word ε is represented as the empty list $[\,]$, and words in $\{a,b\}^*$ are represented as lists of a's and b's.

In general, the relation $derive(L, W)$ holds iff L is a sequence of terminal or nonterminal symbols from which the word W can be derived by using the productions.

We would like to derive an efficient program for an initial goal G of the form: $word(W), \neg derive([s], W)$, which is true in $M(CF)$ iff W is a word which is *not* derived by the given context-free grammar. We perform our program derivation as follows.

Step 1. We derive the two clauses:

    16. $g(W) \leftarrow word(W), \neg new1(W)$

    17. $new1(W) \leftarrow derive([s], W)$

as indicated in the description of the Step 1 above. The predicate g is at level 2 and the predicate $new1$ is at level 1. All predicates in program CF are at level 0.

Step 2. We apply our unfold/fold transformation strategy. During the application of this strategy we never apply rules R7, R8, R9, and R10. Thus, we use neither the TAUTOLOGY-REPLACE subsidiary strategy nor the deletion of useless predicates. We have that $K = 2$, $D^1 = \{$clause 17$\}$, and $D^2 = \{$clause 16$\}$.

Level 1. Initially program T is CF. We start off by adding clause 17 to T. Both *Defs* and *InDefs* consist of clause 17 only. We will perform four iterations of the body of the WHILE loop of our strategy before *InDefs* becomes the empty conjunction, and then we exit the WHILE loop. Here we show only the first and fourth iterations.

First Iteration.

UNFOLD. By unfolding, from clause 17 we get:

    18. $new1([a|A]) \leftarrow derive([x, b], A)$

DEFINE-FOLD. We introduce the following clause

    19. $new2(A) \leftarrow derive([x, b], A)$

and by folding clause 18 using clause 19 we get:

    20. $new1([a|A]) \leftarrow new2(A)$

which is added to program T.

At the end of the first iteration T is made out of the clauses of CF together with clause 20, *Defs* consists of clauses 17 and 19, and *InDefs* consists of clause 19. Since *InDefs* is not empty, we continue by iterating the execution of the body of the WHILE loop of our strategy.

During the second and third iteration of the WHILE loop, by the definition rule we introduce the following clauses:

    21. $new3(A) \leftarrow derive([\,], A)$

    22. $new4(A) \leftarrow derive([x, b], A)$

    23. $new4(A) \leftarrow derive([b, x, b], A)$

24. $new5(A) \leftarrow derive([\,], A)$
25. $new5(A) \leftarrow derive([x, b], A)$

At the beginning of the fourth iteration *InDefs* is made out of clauses 24 and 25 only. Here are the details of this fourth iteration which is the last one.

Fourth Iteration.

UNFOLD. By unfolding, from clauses 24 and 25 we get:

26. $new5([\,]) \leftarrow$
27. $new5([b|A]) \leftarrow derive([\,], A)$
28. $new5([a|A]) \leftarrow derive([x, b], A)$
29. $new5([a|A]) \leftarrow derive([b, x, b], A)$

DEFINE-FOLD. We fold clause 27 using clause 21, and clauses 28 and 29 using clauses 24 and 25, and we get:

30. $new5([b|A]) \leftarrow new3(A)$
31. $new5([a|A]) \leftarrow new4(A)$

No new definition is introduced during this fourth iteration. Thus, *InDefs* is empty and we exit from the WHILE loop. The transformation strategy terminates for level 1, and program T is made out of CF together with the following clauses:

20. $new1([a|A]) \leftarrow new2(A)$
32. $new2([b|A]) \leftarrow new3(A)$
33. $new2([a|A]) \leftarrow new4(A)$
34. $new3([\,]) \leftarrow$
35. $new4([b|A]) \leftarrow new5(A)$
36. $new4([a|A]) \leftarrow new4(A)$
26. $new5([\,]) \leftarrow$
30. $new5([b|A]) \leftarrow new3(A)$
31. $new5([a|A]) \leftarrow new4(A)$

Level 2. We start off by adding clause 16 to T. Both *Defs* and *InDefs* consist of clause 16 only. Then we execute the body of the WHILE loop.

First Iteration.

UNFOLD. By positive unfolding from clause 16 we derive:

37. $g([\,]) \leftarrow \neg new1([\,])$
38. $g([a|A]) \leftarrow word(A), \neg new1([a|A])$
39. $g([b|A]) \leftarrow word(A), \neg new1([b|A])$

By negative unfolding from clauses 37, 38, and 39 we derive:

40. $g([\,]) \leftarrow$
41. $g([a|A]) \leftarrow word(A), \neg new2(A)$
42. $g([b|A]) \leftarrow word(A)$

DEFINE-FOLD. We introduce the following new definitions:

43. $new6(A) \leftarrow word(A), \neg new2(A)$
44. $new7(A) \leftarrow word(A)$

and by folding clauses 41 and 42 we derive:

45. $g([a|A]) \leftarrow new6(A)$
46. $g([b|A]) \leftarrow new7(A)$

Clauses 43 and 44 are added to *InDefs*. Since *InDefs* is not empty, we continue by a new iteration of the body of the WHILE loop and we stop after the fourth iteration, when *InDefs* becomes empty. We do not show the second, third, and fourth iterations. The final program, whose clauses are listed below, is derived by eliminating all predicate definitions upon which the predicate g does not depend.

40. $g([\,]) \leftarrow$
45. $g([a|A]) \leftarrow new6(A)$
46. $g([b|A]) \leftarrow new7(A)$
47. $new6([\,]) \leftarrow$
48. $new6([a|A]) \leftarrow new8(A)$
49. $new6([b|A]) \leftarrow new9(A)$
50. $new7([\,]) \leftarrow$
51. $new7([a|A]) \leftarrow new7(A)$
52. $new7([b|A]) \leftarrow new7(A)$
53. $new8([\,]) \leftarrow$
54. $new8([a|A]) \leftarrow new8(A)$
55. $new8([b|A]) \leftarrow new10(A)$
56. $new9([a|A]) \leftarrow new7(A)$
57. $new9([b|A]) \leftarrow new7(A)$
58. $new10([a|A]) \leftarrow new8(A)$
59. $new10([b|A]) \leftarrow new9(A)$

This final program corresponds to a deterministic finite automaton in the sense that: (i) each predicate corresponds to a state, (ii) g corresponds to the initial state, (iii) each predicate p which has a unit clause $p([\,]) \leftarrow$, corresponds to a final state, and (iv) each clause of the form $p([s|A]) \leftarrow q(A)$ corresponds to a transition labeled by the symbol s from the state corresponding to p to the state corresponding to q.

The derivation of the final program performed according to our transformation strategy, can be viewed as the derivation of a deterministic finite automaton from a general program for parsing a context free language. Obviously, this derivation has been possible, because the context free grammar encoded by the *production* predicate (see clauses 8–11) generates a regular language.

The final program is much more efficient than the initial program which constructs the complement of a context-free language by performing a nondeterministic search of the productions to apply (see clauses 10 and 11).   □

3   Program Synthesis via Transformation Rules and Strategies

In this section we see how one can use for program synthesis the rules and the strategy for program transformation we have presented in Sections 2.2 and 2.3.

The program synthesis problem can be defined as follows: Given a *specification* S, that is, a formula written in a specification language, we want to derive, by using some *derivation rules*, a *program* T in a suitable programming language, such that T satisfies S.

There are many synthesis methods described in the literature for deriving programs from specifications and these methods depend on the choice of: (i) the specification language, (ii) the derivation rules, and (iii) the programming language.

It has been recognized since the beginning of its development (see, for instance, [11,32,39]), that logic programming is one of the most effective settings for expressing program synthesis methods, because in logic programming both specifications and programs are formulas of the same language, i.e., the first order predicate calculus, and moreover, the derivation rules for deriving programs from specifications, may be chosen to be the inference rules of the first order predicate calculus itself.

Now we propose a program synthesis method in the case of logic programming. In this case the program synthesis problem can be more specifically defined as indicated in the Introduction. Given a locally stratified program P and a specification of the form: $g(X_1, \ldots, X_n) \leftrightarrow \varphi$, where: (i) g is a new predicate symbol not occurring in $\{P, \varphi\}$, and (ii) φ is a formula of the first order predicate calculus such that $freevars(\varphi) = \{X_1, \ldots, X_n\}$, we want to derive a computationally efficient program T such that, for all ground terms $t_1, \ldots, t_n$,

$$M(P) \models \varphi\{X_1/t_1, \ldots, X_n/t_n\} \quad \text{iff} \quad M(T) \models g(t_1, \ldots, t_n) \qquad (Synth)$$

The derivation rules we consider for program synthesis are: (i) a variant of the Lloyd-Topor transformation rules [46], and (ii) the unfold/fold program transformation rules presented in Section 2.2.

Let us begin by presenting the following example of program synthesis. It is our running example for this section and it will be continued in the Examples 4 and 5 below.

Example 3. Specification of List Maximum. Let us consider the following *List-Membership* program:

1. $list([\,]) \leftarrow$
2. $list([A|As]) \leftarrow list(As)$
3. $member(X, [A|As]) \leftarrow X = A$
4. $member(X, [A|As]) \leftarrow member(X, As)$

and $=$ and $\leq$ are basic predicates denoting, respectively, the equality predicate and a given total order predicate over the given domain. For brevity, we do not show the clauses defining these two basic predicates. The maximum M of a list L of items may be specified by the following formula:

$$max(L, M) \leftrightarrow (list(L), member(M, L), \forall X\, (member(X, L) \to X \leq M)) \quad (\Phi)$$

By our synthesis method we want to derive an efficient program *Max* which defines the predicate *max* such that:

$$M(ListMembership \wedge Max) \models \forall L, M\, (max(L, M) \leftrightarrow \varphi_{max})$$

where φ_{max} denotes the right hand side of formula (Φ) above. $\square$

In the rest of this section, we illustrate a synthesis method, called the *unfold/fold synthesis method*, which we now introduce.

The Unfold/Fold Synthesis Method.

Given a locally stratified program P and a specification formula of the form: $g(X_1, \ldots, X_n) \leftrightarrow \varphi$, this method consists of two steps as follows.

Step 1. We apply a variant of the Lloyd-Topor transformation [46], and we derive a conjunction $Cls(g, \varphi)$ of clauses such that $P \wedge Cls(g, \varphi)$ is a locally stratified program and, for all ground terms $t_1, \ldots, t_n$,

(1) $M(P) \models \varphi\{X_1/t_1, \ldots, X_n/t_n\}$ iff $M(P \wedge Cls(g, \varphi)) \models g(t_1, \ldots, t_n)$

Step 2. From the program P, the conjunction $Cls(g, \varphi)$ of clauses, and a set of equivalences to be used for rule R9, by applying the unfold/fold transformation strategy of Section 2.3, we derive a program T such that, for all ground terms $t_1, \ldots, t_n$,

(2) $M(P \wedge Cls(g, \varphi)) \models g(t_1, \ldots, t_n)$ iff $M(T) \models g(t_1, \ldots, t_n)$

and thus, the above relation (*Synth*) holds.

As already mentioned, our unfold/fold synthesis method is a generalization of the two step transformation method presented in the previous Section 2.3, because here we consider a first order formula φ, instead of a goal G. Notice also that, similarly to the transformation method of Section 2.3, the program $P \wedge Cls(g, \varphi)$ itself is a particular program satisfying (2), but usually we have to discard this trivial solution because we look for an efficient program T satisfying (2).

We now illustrate the variant of the method proposed by Lloyd and Topor in [46] which we use for constructing the conjunction of clauses $Cls(g, \varphi)$ starting from the given specification formula $g(X_1, \ldots, X_n) \leftrightarrow \varphi$ according to the requirements indicated in Step 1 above.

We need to consider a class of formulas, called *statements* [46], each of which is of the form: $A \leftarrow \beta$, where A is an atom and β, called the *body* of the statement, is a first order logic formula. We write $C[\gamma]$ to denote a first order formula where the subformula γ occurs as an *outermost conjunct*, that is, $C[\gamma] = \rho_1 \wedge \ldots \wedge \rho_r \wedge \gamma \wedge \sigma_1 \wedge \ldots \wedge \sigma_s$ for some first order formulas $\rho_1, \ldots, \rho_r, \sigma_1, \ldots, \sigma_s$, and some $r \geq 0$ and $s \geq 0$. We will say that the formula $C[\gamma]$ is transformed into the formula $C[\delta]$ when $C[\delta]$ is obtained from $C[\gamma]$ by replacing the conjunct γ by the new conjunct δ.

The LT transformation.

Given a conjunction of statements, perform the following transformations.

(A) Eliminate from the body of every statement the occurrences of logical constants, connectives, and quantifiers other than *true*, $\neg$, $\wedge$, $\vee$, and $\exists$.

(B) Repeatedly apply the following rules until a conjunction of clauses is generated:

(1) $A \leftarrow C[\neg true]$ is deleted.

(2) $A \leftarrow C[\neg\neg\gamma]$ is transformed into $A \leftarrow C[\gamma]$.

(3) $A \leftarrow C[\neg(\gamma \wedge \delta)]$ is transformed into

$$A \leftarrow C[\neg newp(Y_1, \ldots, Y_k)] \wedge newp(Y_1, \ldots, Y_k) \leftarrow \gamma \wedge \delta$$

where $newp$ is a new non-basic predicate and $\{Y_1, \ldots, Y_k\} = freevars(\gamma \wedge \delta)$.

(4) $A \leftarrow C[\neg(\gamma \vee \delta)]$ is transformed into $A \leftarrow C[\neg\gamma] \wedge A \leftarrow C[\neg\delta]$.

(5) $A \leftarrow C[\neg \exists X \gamma]$ is transformed into

$$A \leftarrow C[\neg newp(Y_1, \ldots, Y_k)] \wedge newp(Y_1, \ldots, Y_k) \leftarrow \gamma$$

where $newp$ is a new non-basic predicate and $\{Y_1, \ldots, Y_k\} = freevars(\exists X \gamma)$.

(6) $A \leftarrow C[\neg p(t_1, \ldots, t_m)]$ is transformed into

$$A \leftarrow C[\neg newp(Y_1, \ldots, Y_k)] \wedge newp(Y_1, \ldots, Y_k) \leftarrow p(t_1, \ldots, t_m)$$

where p is a non-basic predicate which depends on existential variables in P, $newp$ is a new non-basic predicate, and $\{Y_1, \ldots, Y_k\} = vars(p(t_1, \ldots, t_m))$.

(7) $A \leftarrow C[\gamma \vee \delta]$ is transformed into $A \leftarrow C[\gamma] \wedge A \leftarrow C[\delta]$.

(8) $A \leftarrow C[\exists X \gamma]$ is transformed into $A \leftarrow C[\gamma\{X/Y\}]$, where Y does not occur in $A \leftarrow C[\exists X \gamma]$.

Given a locally stratified program P and a specification $g(X_1, \ldots, X_n) \leftrightarrow \varphi$, we denote by $Cls(g, \varphi)$ the conjunction of the clauses derived by applying the LT transformation to the statement $g(X_1, \ldots, X_n) \leftarrow \varphi$.

Example 4. *LT transformation of the List Maximum specification.* Let us consider the program *ListMembership* and the specification formula (Φ) of Example 3. By applying the LT transformation to the statement $max(L, M) \leftarrow list(L), member(M, L), \forall X (member(X, L) \rightarrow X \leq M)$ we derive the conjunction $Cls(max, \varphi_{max})$ consisting of the following two clauses:

5. $max(L, M) \leftarrow list(L), member(M, L), \neg new1(L, M)$
6. $new1(L, M) \leftarrow member(X, L), \neg X \leq M$

The program *ListMembership* $\wedge Cls(max, \varphi_{max})$ is a very inefficient, generate-and-test program: it works by nondeterministically generating a member M of the list L and then testing whether or not M is the maximum member of L. $\square$

The following result states that the LT transformation is correct w.r.t. the perfect model semantics [46,55].

Theorem 2. [Correctness of LT Transformation w.r.t. Perfect Models]
Let P be a locally stratified program and $g(X_1, \ldots, X_n) \leftrightarrow \varphi$ be a specification. If $Cls(g, \varphi)$ is obtained from $g(X_1, \ldots, X_n) \leftarrow \varphi$ by the LT transformation, then (i) $P \wedge Cls(g, \varphi)$ is a locally stratified program and (ii), for all ground terms $t_1, \ldots, t_n$, $M(P) \models \varphi\{X_1/t_1, \ldots, X_n/t_n\}$ iff $M(P \wedge Cls(g, \varphi)) \models g(t_1, \ldots, t_n)$.

Step 2 of our unfold/fold synthesis method makes use, as already said, of the unfold/fold transformation strategy presented in Section 2.3, starting from program P, the conjunction $Cls(g, \varphi)$ of clauses, instead of $Cls(g, G)$, and a set of equivalences to be used for the application of rule R9.

The partition of $Cls(g, \varphi)$ into levels can be constructed similarly to the partition of $Cls(g, G)$ in Section 2.3. Indeed, by construction, there exists a level mapping of $Cls(g, \varphi)$ such that: (1) $Cls(g, \varphi)$ can be partitioned into K subconjunctions $D^1, \ldots, D^K$, such that $Cls(g, \varphi) = D^1 \wedge \ldots \wedge D^K$, and for $i = 1, \ldots, K$, the subconjunction D^i consists of all clauses in $Cls(g, \varphi)$ whose head predicates are at level i, (2) for $i = 1, \ldots, K$ and for each clause $p(\ldots) \leftarrow B$ in D^i the level of every predicate symbol in the goal B is strictly smaller than the level of p, (3) the predicate g is at the highest level K, and (4) all predicates of $Cls(g, \varphi)$ which occur in P, are at level 0.

The reader may notice that for all $K \geq 0$ there exists a formula ψ and a predicate g such that K is the highest value of the level mapping of $Cls(g, \psi)$.

Example 5. Synthesis of the List Maximum program. Let us consider again the program *ListMembership* and the formula Φ of Example 3. Let us also consider the conjunction $Cls(max, \varphi_{max})$ consisting of clauses 5 and 6 of Example 4 which define the predicates max and $new1$. We may choose the level mapping so that the levels of *list*, *member*, $\leq$, $=$ are all 0, the level of $new1$ is 1, and the level of max is 2. Thus, the highest level K is 2, $D^1 = \{\text{clause 6}\}$, and $D^2 = \{\text{clause 5}\}$.

We apply our unfold/fold transformation strategy as follows.

Level 1. Initially program T is *ListMembership*. We start off by adding clause 6 to T. Both *Defs* and *InDefs* consist of clause 6 only. Then we execute the body of the WHILE loop as follows.

UNFOLD. We unfold clause 6 w.r.t. $member(X, L)$ and we get:

  7. $new1([A|As], M) \leftarrow X = A, \neg X \leq M$
  8. $new1([A|As], M) \leftarrow member(X, As), \neg X \leq M$

TAUTOLOGY-REPLACE. From clause 7, by applying the goal replacement rule (using the equivalence $\forall A, M\ (\exists X\ (X = A, \neg X \leq M) \leftrightarrow \neg A \leq M)$) we derive:

  9. $new1([A|As], M) \leftarrow \neg A \leq M$

DEFINE-FOLD. By folding clause 8 using clause 6 we derive the clause:

  10. $new1([A|As], M) \leftarrow new1(As, M)$

No new definition has been introduced. Thus, *InDefs* is empty and the transformation strategy terminates for level 1. At this point program T is made out of clauses 1, 2, 3, 4, 9, and 10.

Level 2. We start off the transformation strategy for this level, by adding clause 5 to T. Both *Defs* and *InDefs* consist of clause 5 only. Then we iterate twice the body of the WHILE loop as follows.

First Iteration.

UNFOLD. By some unfolding steps, from clause 5 in *InDefs* we derive:

11. $max([A|As], M) \leftarrow list(As),\ M = A,\ A \leq M,\ \neg new1(As, M)$
12. $max([A|As], M) \leftarrow list(As),\ member(M, As),\ A \leq M,\ \neg new1(As, M)$

TAUTOLOGY-REPLACE. By applying the goal replacement rule, from clause 11 we derive:

13. $max([A|As], M) \leftarrow list(As),\ M = A,\ \neg new1(As, M)$

DEFINE-FOLD. The definition of predicate *max*, consisting of clauses 12 and 13 is nondeterministic, because an atom of the form $max(l, M)$, where l is a ground, nonempty list, is unifiable with the head of both clauses. We may derive a more efficient, deterministic definition for *max* by introducing the new predicate *new2* as follows:

14. $new2(A, As, M) \leftarrow list(As),\ M = A,\ \neg new1(As, M)$
15. $new2(A, As, M) \leftarrow list(As),\ member(M, As),\ A \leq M,\ \neg new1(As, M)$

and then folding clauses 12 and 13 using clauses 14 and 15, as follows:

16. $max([A|As], M) \leftarrow new2(A, As, M)$

Now, (i) T consists of clauses 1, 2, 3, 4, 9, 10, and 16, (ii) *Defs* consists of clauses 6, 14, and 15, and (iii) *InDefs* consists of clauses 14 and 15 only.

Second Iteration.

UNFOLD. By positive and negative unfolding, from clauses 14 and 15 in *InDefs* we get:

17. $new2(A, [], M) \leftarrow M = A$
18. $new2(A, [B|As], M) \leftarrow list(As),\ M = A,\ B \leq M,\ \neg new1(As, M)$
19. $new2(A, [B|As], M) \leftarrow list(As),\ M - B,\ A \leq M,\ B \leq M,\ new1(As, M)$
20. $new2(A, [B|As], M) \leftarrow list(As),\ member(M, As),\ A \leq M,\ B \leq M,$
$\neg new1(As, M)$

TAUTOLOGY-REPLACE. By applying the basic goal replacement rule to clauses 18, 19, and 20, and in particular, by using the equivalence $M(ListMembership) \models true \leftrightarrow B \leq A \vee A \leq B$ (recall that $\leq$ is a total order), we get:

18.1. $new2(A, [B|As], M) \leftarrow B \leq A,\ list(As),\ M = A,\ \neg new1(As, M)$
19.1. $new2(A, [B|As], M) \leftarrow A \leq B,\ list(As),\ M = B,\ \neg new1(As, M)$
20.1. $new2(A, [B|As], M) \leftarrow B \leq A,\ list(As),\ member(M, As),\ A \leq M,$
$\neg new1(As, M)$
20.2. $new2(A, [B|As], M) \leftarrow A \leq B,\ list(As),\ member(M, As),\ B \leq M,$
$\neg new1(As, M)$

DEFINE-FOLD. Now we fold clauses 18.1 and 20.1 using clauses 14 and 15, and we also fold clauses 19.1 and 20.2 using clauses 14 and 15. We obtain:

21. $new2(A, [B|As], M) \leftarrow B \leq A,\ new2(A, As, M)$
22. $new2(A, [B|As], M) \leftarrow A \leq B,\ new2(B, As, M)$

No new definition has been introduced during the second iteration. Thus, *InDefs* is empty and we terminate our unfold/fold transformation strategy also for the highest level 2. We finally eliminate all predicate definitions on which *max* does not depend, and we derive our final program:

16. $max([A|As], M) \leftarrow new2(A, As, M)$
17. $new2(A, [], M) \leftarrow M = A$
21. $new2(A, [B|As], M) \leftarrow B \leq A, new2(A, As, M)$
22. $new2(A, [B|As], M) \leftarrow A \leq B, new2(B, As, M)$

This final program deterministically computes the answers to queries of the form: $max(l, M)$ where l is a ground list. Indeed, while traversing the given list l, the first argument of the predicate $new2$ holds the maximal item encountered so far (see clauses 21 and 22) and, at the end of the traversal, the value of this argument is returned as an answer (see clause 17).   □

4   Program Verification via Transformation Rules and Strategies

In this section we show that the transformation rules and the strategy we have presented in Sections 2.2 and 2.3, can also be used for program verification. In particular, we can prove a property φ of a given locally stratified logic program P by applying the unfold/fold synthesis method of Section 3. For program verification purposes, instead of starting from a specification formula where free variables may occur, the unfold/fold synthesis method is applied starting from the *closed* specification formula $g \leftrightarrow \varphi$, where $freevars(\varphi) = \emptyset$ and g is a predicate symbol of arity 0.

Our method for verifying whether or not φ holds in the perfect model of the program P is specified as follows.

The Unfold/Fold Verification Method.
Given a locally stratified program P and a closed formula φ, we can check whether or not $M(P) \models \varphi$ holds by performing the following two steps.

Step 1. We introduce a new predicate symbol g of arity 0, not occurring in $\{P, \varphi\}$ and, by using the LT transformation we transform the statement $g \leftarrow \varphi$, into a conjunction $Cls(g, \varphi)$ of clauses, such that $M(P) \models \varphi$ iff $M(P \wedge Cls(g, \varphi)) \models g$.

Step 2. From program P, the conjunction $Cls(g, \varphi)$ of clauses, and a set of equivalences to be used for rule R9, by applying the unfold/fold transformation strategy of Section 2.3, we derive a program T such that

$$M(P \wedge Cls(g, \varphi)) \models g \quad \text{iff} \quad M(T) \models g$$

Thus, if T is the program consisting of the clause $g \leftarrow$ only, then $M(P) \models \varphi$, and if T is the empty program, then $M(P) \not\models \varphi$.

Let us now see an example of program verification.

Example 6. The Yale Shooting Problem. This problem has been often presented in the literature on temporal and nonmonotonic reasoning. It can be formulated as follows. Let us consider a person and a gun and three possible *events*: (e1) a *load* event in which the gun is loaded, (e2) a *shoot* event in which the gun shoots, and (e3) a *wait* event in which nothing happens. These events are represented by clauses 6, 7, and 8 of the program *YSP* below. A *situation* is (the result of) a sequence of events. This sequence is represented as a list which, so to speak, grows to the left as time progresses. In any situation, at least one of the following three facts *holds*: (f1) the person is *alive*, (f2) the person is *dead*, and (f3) the gun is *loaded*. These facts are represented by clauses 9, 10, and 11 below. We have the following statements:

(s1) In the initial situation, represented by the empty list [ ], the person is *alive*.
(s2) After a *load* event the gun is *loaded*.
(s3) If the gun is *loaded*, then after a *shoot* event the person is *dead*.
(s4) If the gun is *loaded*, then it is *abnormal* that after a *shoot* event the person is *alive*.
(s5) If a fact F holds in a situation S and it is not abnormal that F holds after the event E following S, then F holds also after the event E. This statement is often called the *inertia axiom*.

The following locally stratified program, called *YSP*, formalizes the above statements, and in particular, clauses 1–5 correspond to statements (s1)–(s5), respectively. Our *YSP* program is similar to the one of Apt and Bezem [1].

  1. $holds(alive, [\,]) \leftarrow$ Program *YSP*
  2. $holds(loaded, [load|S]) \leftarrow$
  3. $holds(dead, [shoot|S]) \leftarrow holds(loaded, S)$
  4. $ab(alive, shoot, S) \leftarrow holds(loaded, S)$
  5. $holds(F, [E|S]) \leftarrow fact(F), event(E), holds(F, S), \neg ab(F, E, S)$
  6. $event(load) \leftarrow$
  7. $event(shoot) \leftarrow$
  8. $event(wait) \leftarrow$
  9. $fact(alive) \leftarrow$
 10. $fact(dead) \leftarrow$
 11. $fact(loaded) \leftarrow$
 12. $append([\,], Y, Y) \leftarrow$
 13. $append([A|X], Y, [A|Z]) \leftarrow append(X, Y, Z)$

Apt and Bezem showed that $M(YSP) \models holds(dead, [shoot, wait, load])$ can be derived in a straightforward way by applying SLDNF-resolution. Let us now consider the following stronger property σ:

$\forall S \, (holds(dead, S)$
$\quad\quad \rightarrow \exists S1, S2, S3, S4 \, (append(S1, [shoot|S2], S4), \, append(S4, [load|S3], S)))$

meaning that the person may be *dead* in the current situation only if a *load* event occurred in the past and that event was followed, maybe not immediately, by a *shoot* event. We would like to prove that $M(YSP) \models \sigma$. Our two step verification method works as follows.

Step 1. We apply the LT transformation starting from the statement $g \leftarrow \sigma$ and we derive $Cls(g, \sigma)$ which consists of the following three clauses:

14. $g \leftarrow \neg new1$
15. $new1 \leftarrow holds(dead, S), \neg new2(S)$
16. $new2(S) \leftarrow append(S1, [shoot|S2], S4), append(S4, [load|S3], S)$

The level of $new2$ is 1, the level of $new1$ is 2, and the level of g is 3. The level of all other predicates is 0.

Step 2. We now apply the unfold/fold transformation strategy of Section 2.3, starting from the program *YSP*, the conjunction of clauses $Cls(g, \sigma)$, and an empty set of equivalences (rule R9 will not be applied). We have that $K = 3$, $D^1 = \{$clause 16$\}$, $D^2 = \{$clause 15$\}$, and $D^3 = \{$clause 14$\}$.

Level 1. Initially program T is *YSP*. We start off by applying the definition introduction rule and adding clause 16 to T. Both *Defs* and *InDefs* consist of clause 16 only. Then we iterate the execution of the body of the WHILE loop of the unfold/fold transformation strategy as follows.

First Iteration.
UNFOLD. By unfolding, from clause 16 we derive:

17. $new2([shoot|S]) \leftarrow append(S4, [load|S3], S)$
18. $new2([E|S]) \leftarrow append(S1, [shoot|S2], S4), append(S4, [load|S3], S)$

DEFINE-FOLD. We introduce the following new predicate definition:

19. $new3(A) \leftarrow append(B, [load|C], A)$

and we fold clauses 17 and 18 using clauses 19 and 16, respectively:

20. $new2([shoot|S]) \leftarrow new3(S)$
21. $new2([E|S]) \leftarrow new2(S)$

At this point (i) program T consists of clauses 20 and 21 together with clauses 1–13, (ii) *Defs* consists of clauses 16 and 19, and (iii) *InDefs* consists of clause 19.

Second Iteration.
UNFOLD. By unfolding clause 19 we derive:

22. $new3([load|S]) \leftarrow$
23. $new3([E|S]) \leftarrow append(S4, [load|S3], S)$

DEFINE-FOLD. By folding clause 23 using clause 19 we derive:

22. $new3([load|S]) \leftarrow$
24. $new3([E|S]) \leftarrow new3(S)$

We need not introduce any new clause for folding. Thus, *InDefs* is empty and the WHILE loop terminates for level 1. At this point program T consists of the following clauses:

20. $new2([shoot|S]) \leftarrow new3(S)$
21. $new2([E|S]) \leftarrow new2(S)$

22. $new3([load|S]) \leftarrow$

24. $new3([E|S]) \leftarrow new3(S)$

together with clauses 1–13.

Level 2. We apply the definition introduction rule and we add clause 15 to T. Both *Defs* and *InDefs* consist of clause 15 only. Then we iterate the execution of the body of the WHILE loop as follows.

First Iteration.

UNFOLD. By unfolding, from clause 15 we derive:

25. $new1 \leftarrow holds(loaded, S), \neg new3(S), \neg new2(S)$

26. $new1 \leftarrow holds(dead, S), \neg new2(S)$

27. $new1 \leftarrow holds(dead, S), \neg new3(S), \neg new2(S)$

28. $new1 \leftarrow holds(dead, S), \neg new2(S)$

TAUTOLOGY-REPLACE. Clauses 27 and 28 are subsumed by clause 26 and they can be deleted.

DEFINE-FOLD. We introduce the following new predicate:

29. $new4 \leftarrow holds(loaded, S), \neg new3(S), \neg new2(S)$

and we fold clauses 25 and 28 using clauses 29 and 15, respectively. We get:

30. $new1 \leftarrow new4$

31. $new1 \leftarrow new1$

Now (i) T is made out of clauses 1–13, 20–24, and 30–31, (ii) *Defs* consists of clauses 15 and 29, and (iii) *InDefs* consists of clause 29. Since *InDefs* is not the empty conjunction, we proceed by a second execution of the body of the WHILE loop of the unfold/fold transformation strategy.

Second Iteration.

UNFOLD. By unfolding, from clause 29 we derive:

32. $new4 \leftarrow holds(loaded, S), \neg new3(S), \neg new3(S), \neg new2(S)$

33. $new4 \leftarrow holds(loaded, S), \neg new3(S), \neg new2(S)$

TAUTOLOGY-REPLACE. Clause 32 is deleted because it is subsumed by clause 33.

DEFINE-FOLD. We fold clause 32 using clause 29, and we derive:

34. $new4 \leftarrow new4$

No new clause is added by the definition introduction rule. Thus, *InDefs* is the empty conjunction and the WHILE loop terminates for level 2. Now, predicates $new1$ and $new4$ are useless and their definitions, that is, clauses 30, 31, and 34, are deleted.

Thus, at the end of the transformation strategy for level 2, the derived program T consists of clauses 1–13 and 20–24.

Level 3. We add clause 14 to program T. By unfolding clause 14 we derive:

35. $g \leftarrow$

Our transformation strategy terminates by applying the definition elimination rule and deleting all definitions of predicates upon which g does not depend.

Thus our final program consists of clause 35 only, and we have proved that $M(YSP \wedge Cls(g, \sigma)) \models g$ and thus, $M(YSP) \models \sigma$.

The reader may check that g cannot be derived from $YSP \wedge Cls(g, \sigma)$ using SLDNF-resolution, because an SLDNF-refutation of g would require the construction of a finitely failed SLDNF-tree for $new1$ and no such a finite tree exists. Indeed, g may be derived by using SLS-resolution, that is, resolution augmented with the *negation as (finite or infinite) failure* rule. However, the applicability conditions of the negation as infinite failure rule are, in general, not decidable and even not semi-decidable. On the contrary, in our approach we use a set of transformation rules which have decidable applicability conditions, assuming that the equivalence of basic goals is decidable (see the goal replacement rule R9).   □

5   Related Work

The idea of program development as a deductive activity in a formal theory has been very fertile in the field of programming methodologies. Early results on this topic are reported, for instance, in [10,11,12,21,32,39,49]. Here we would like to mention some of the contributions to this field, focusing on logic program transformation. In the pioneering work by Hogger [32] program transformation was intended as a particular form of deduction in first order logic. Later, the approach based on the unfold/fold transformations proposed by Burstall and Darlington [10] for functional languages, was adapted to logic languages by Tamaki and Sato [74]. These authors proposed a set of rules for transforming definite logic programs and proved their correctness w.r.t. the least Herbrand model semantics. Since then, several researchers have investigated various aspects of the unfold/fold transformation approach. They also considered its extension to deal with negation [6,29,48,64,70,71], disjunctive programs [30], constraints [4,22], and concurrency [23].

In this chapter we have essentially followed the approach of Tamaki and Sato where the correctness of the transformations is ensured by conditions on the sequence of the transformation rules which are applied during program derivation [74]. The main novelty w.r.t. other papers which follow a similar approach and deal with general logic programs (see, for instance, [64,70,71]) is that our set of rules includes the negative unfolding (R4), the negative folding (R5), and the basic goal replacement rules (R9) which are very useful for the program derivation examples we have presented.

Together with the formalization and the study of the properties of the transformation rules, various strategies for the application of these rules have been considered in the literature. Among others, for case of logic programs we recall: (i) the strategies for deriving *tail recursive* programs [3,17], (ii) the *promotion* strategy for reducing nondeterminism within generate-and-test programs [72], (iii) the strategy for *eliminating unnecessary variables* and thus, avoiding multiple traversals and intermediate data structures [58], and (iv) the strategy for *reducing nondeterminism* during program specialization [56].

The general unfold/fold transformation strategy we have presented in Section 2.3, extends the above mentioned strategies to the case of programs with locally stratified negation. The interesting fact to notice is that the same general strategy can be refined in different ways so to realize not only program transformation, but also program synthesis and program verification. However, in order to be effective in practice, our general strategy requires some information concerning specific computation domains and classes of programs. For instance, information on the computation domains is needed for the application of the goal replacement rule. The merit of a general purpose transformation strategy rests upon the fact that it provides a uniform guideline for performing program derivation in different computation domains.

The work on unfold/fold program transformation is tightly related to other transformation techniques. In particular, *partial evaluation* (also called *partial deduction*) and other *program specialization* techniques à la Lloyd-Shepherdson [16,27,44,47] can be rephrased in terms of a subset of the unfold/fold rules [56,67]. *Compiling control* [7] is another transformation technique which is related to the rules and strategies approach. Compiling control is based on the idea expressed by Kowalski's motto: *Algorithm = Logic + Control,* and it works as follows. Let us consider a logic program P_1 and let us assume that it is evaluated by using a given control strategy C_1. For instance, C_1 may be the Prolog left-to-right, depth-first control strategy. However, for efficiency reasons we may want to use a different control strategy, say C_2. Compiling control works by deriving from program P_1 a new program P_2 such that P_2 with control strategy C_1 is operationally equivalent to P_1 with control strategy C_2. Although the compiling control technique was not originally presented following the rules and strategies approach, the transformation of program P_1 into program P_2, may often be performed by applying a suitable unfold/fold strategy (see, for instance, [53]).

Moreover, during the last two decades there has been a fruitful interaction between unfold/fold program transformation and program synthesis. To illustrate this point, let us recall here the program synthesis methods based on derivation rules, such as the one proposed by Hogger [32] and, along similar lines, those reported in [34,35,42,68,69] which make use of derivation rules similar to the unfold/fold rules. In this regard, the specific contribution of our chapter consists in providing a method for program synthesis which ensures the correctness w.r.t. the perfect model semantics.

Also related to our rules and strategies approach, is the *proofs-as-programs* approach (see, for instance, [8,25] for its presentation in the case of logic programming) which works by extracting a program from a constructive proof of a specification formula. Thus, in the proofs-as-programs approach, programs synthesis is regarded as a theorem proving activity, whereas by using our unfold/fold method we view theorem proving as a particular case of program synthesis.

Our unfold/fold verification method is related to other methods for verifying program properties. The existence of a relation between program transformation and program verification was pointed out by Burstall and Darlington [10] and then formalized by Kott [36] and Courcelle [14] in the case of applicative program schemata. The essential idea is that, since the transformation rules preserve a given semantics, the transformation of a program P_1 into a program P_2 is also a proof of the equivalence of P_1 and P_2 w.r.t. that semantics. In [54] this idea has also been developed in the case of definite logic programs. The method presented in that paper, called *unfold/fold proof method*, allows us to prove the equivalence of conjunctions of atoms w.r.t. the least Herbrand model of a program. In [65] the unfold/fold proof method has been extended by using a more powerful folding rule and in [63,66] the extended unfold/fold proof method has been applied for the proof of properties of parametrized finite state concurrent systems.

A further extension of the unfold/fold proof method has been presented in [55]. By using the proof method described in [55] one can prove properties of the form $M(P) \models \varphi$ where P is a logic programs with locally stratified negation, $M(P)$ is its perfect model, and φ is any first order formula. In the present chapter we basically followed the presentation of [55].

In recent developments (see, for instance, [24]), it has been shown that the unfold/fold proof method can be used to perform *model checking* [13] of finite or infinite state concurrent systems. To see how this can be done, let us recall that in the model checking approach one formalizes the problem of verifying temporal properties of finite or infinite state systems as the problem of verifying the satisfaction relation $T, s \models_{CTL} F$, where (i) T is a state transition system (regarded as a *Kripke structure*), (ii) s is the initial state of the system, and (iii) F is a formula of the CTL branching time temporal logic. In [24] the problem of verifying $T, s \models_{CTL} F$ is reduced to that of verifying $M(P_T) \models sat(s, F)$, where $M(P_T)$ is the perfect model of a locally stratified program P_T defining a predicate sat which encodes the satisfaction relation $\models_{CTL}$. Thus, the unfold/fold proof method described in Section 4 can be used for performing finite or infinite state model checking starting from the program P_T and the atomic formula $sat(s, F)$. An essential point indicated in [24] is that, in order to deal with infinite sets of states, it is useful to consider logic programs extended with *constraints*.

Finally, we would like to mention that the unfold/fold proof method falls into the wide category of methods that use (constraint) logic programming for software verification. In the specific area of the verification of concurrent systems, we may briefly recall the following ones. (i) The method described in [45] uses partial deduction and *abstract interpretation* [15] of logic programs for verifying safety properties of infinite state systems. (ii) The method presented in [26] uses logic programs with linear arithmetic constraints to encode Petri nets. The least fixpoint of one such program corresponds to the reachability set of the Petri net. This method works by first applying some program transformations (different from the unfold/fold ones) to compute a Presburger formula which is a symbolic representation of the least fixpoint of the program, and then proving that a given safety property holds by proving that it is implied by that Presburger formula. (iii) Similarly to [24,26], also the method presented in [18] uses constraint logic programs to represent infinite state systems. This method can be used to verify CTL properties of these systems by computing approximations of least and greatest fixpoints via abstract interpretation. (iv) The methods in [50] and

[61] make use of logic programs (with and without constraints, respectively) to represent finite state systems. These two methods employ *tabulation* techniques [76] to compute fixpoints and they may be used for verifying CTL properties and *modal μ-calculus* [40,57] properties, respectively.

It is difficult to make a precise connection between the unfold/fold proof method and the verification methods listed above, because of the different formalizations and techniques which are used. However, we would like to notice that all verification methods we mentioned above, work by finding, in a more or less explicit way, properties which are *invariants* of the behaviour of a system, and within the unfold/fold proof method, the discovery of invariants is performed by the introduction of suitable predicate definitions which allow folding. This introduction of new definitions is the most creative and least mechanizable step during program transformation.

6   Conclusions

The main objective of this chapter has been to illustrate the power of the rules and strategies approach to the development of programs. This approach is particularly appealing in the case of logic programming and it allows us to separate the correctness requirement from the efficiency requirement during program development. This separation is expressed by our motto: *Program Derivation = Rules + Strategies*. It can be viewed as a variant of Kowalski's motto for program execution: *Algorithm = Logic + Control*.

More specifically, we have considered the unfold/fold transformation rules for locally stratified logic programs and we have outlined a strategy for the application of these transformation rules. As a novel contribution of this chapter we have proposed a general, two step method for performing program transformation, program synthesis, and program verification, and we have presented a powerful unfold/fold transformation strategy which allows one to perform: (1) elimination of multiple visits of data structures, program specialization, and other efficiency improving program transformations, (2) program synthesis from first order specifications, and (3) program verification.

The main advantage of developing several techniques for program derivation in a unified framework, is that we may reuse similar techniques in different contexts. For instance, the program transformation strategy for eliminating unnecessary variables [58] may be reused as a quantifier elimination technique for theorem proving [55]. Moreover, our unified view of program derivation allows us to design a general tool which may be used for machine assisted program transformation, synthesis, and verification.

It should be pointed out that, besides the many appealing features illustrated in this chapter, the transformational approach to program derivation has also some limitations. Indeed, the problems tackled by program transformation have inherent theoretical limitations due to well-known undecidability results. Thus, in general, program derivation cannot be fully mechanical.

Now we mention some approaches by which we can face this limitation and provide techniques which are effective in practice.

(1) We may design *interactive* program transformation systems, so that many ingenious steps can be performed under the user's guidance, while the most tedious and routine tasks are automatically performed by the system. For instance, KIDS [73] is a successful representative of such interactive systems for program derivation. An important line of further development of interactive transformation systems, is the design of appropriate user interfaces and *programmable* program transformers, which allow the user to interact with the system at a very high level. In particular, in such systems the user should be able to program his own rules and strategies. There are some achievements in this direction in the related fields of term rewriting, program synthesis, and theorem proving. For instance, we recall (i) the ELAN system [5] where the user may specify his own strategy for applying rewriting rules, (ii) the Oyster/Clam system [9] where one can make a *plan* to construct a proof or synthesize a program, and (iii) the *Isabelle* generic theorem prover [51], where it is possible to specify customized deductive systems.

(2) We may consider restricted sets of transformation rules or restricted classes of programs, where certain transformation strategies can be performed in a fully mechanical, algorithmic fashion. For logic programs, a number of algorithmic transformation strategies have been developed, such as the already mentioned techniques for partial deduction, eliminating unnecessary variables, and reducing nondeterminism.

(3) We may enhance the program transformation methodology by using techniques for *global programs analysis*, such as abstract interpretation. This approach may remedy to the fact that the transformation rules are designed to make small, local changes of program code, but for their effective application sometimes we need information on the operational or denotational semantics of the whole program. Various techniques which combine program transformation and abstract interpretation have been developed, especially for the task of program specialization (see, for instance, [28,43,60] in the case of logic programs), but also for the verification of concurrent systems (see [45]). We believe that this line of research is very promising.

Finally, we would like to notice that the program derivation techniques we have described in this chapter are essentially oriented to the development of programs *in-the-small*, that is, within a single software module. We believe that one of the main challenges for logic program development is the extension of these techniques for program transformation, synthesis, and verification, to deal with programs *in-the-large*, that is, with many software modules. Some results in this direction are presented in the chapter by Lau and Ornaghi [41] where software engineering methodologies for developing logic programs in-the-large are proposed.

Acknowledgments

We would like to thank Antonis Kakas and Fariba Sadri for their kind invitation to contribute to this book in honor of Prof. Robert Kowalski. Our derivation examples were worked out by using the MAP transformation system mostly developed by Sophie Renault. We also thank the anonymous referees for their constructive comments.

References

1. K. R. Apt and M. Bezem. Acyclic programs. In D.H.D. Warren and P. Szeredi, editors, *Proceedings of the 7th International Conference on Logic Programming, Jerusalem, Israel*, pages 617–633. MIT Press, 1990.
2. K. R. Apt and R. N. Bol. Logic programming and negation: A survey. *Journal of Logic Programming*, 19, 20:9–71, 1994.
3. N. Azibi. *TREQUASI: Un système pour la transformation automatique de programmes Prolog récursifs en quasi-itératifs*. PhD thesis, Université de Paris-Sud, Centre d'Orsay, France, 1987.
4. N. Bensaou and I. Guessarian. Transforming constraint logic programs. *Theoretical Computer Science*, 206:81–125, 1998.
5. P. Borovansky, C. Kirchner, H. Kirchner, and C. Ringeissen. Rewriting with strategies in elan: A functional semantics. *International Journal of Foundations of Computer Science*, 12(1):69–95, 2001.
6. A. Bossi, N. Cocco, and S. Etalle. Transforming normal programs by replacement. In A. Pettorossi, editor, *Proceedings 3rd International Workshop on Meta-Programming in Logic, Meta '92, Uppsala, Sweden*, Lecture Notes in Computer Science 649, pages 265–279. Springer-Verlag, 1992.
7. M. Bruynooghe, D. De Schreye, and B. Krekels. Compiling control. *Journal of Logic Programming*, 6:135–162, 1989.
8. A. Bundy, A. Smaill, and G. Wiggins. The synthesis of logic programs from inductive proofs. In J. W. Lloyd, editor, *Computational Logic, Symposium Proceedings, Brussels, November 1990*, pages 135–149, Berlin, 1990. Springer-Verlag.
9. A. Bundy, F. van Harmelen, C. Horn, and A. Smaill. The oyster-clam system. In M. E. Stickel, editor, *10th International Conference on Automated Deduction, Kaiserslautern, Germany*, Lecture Notes in Computer Science, Vol. 449, pages 647–648. Springer, 1990.
10. R. M. Burstall and J. Darlington. A transformation system for developing recursive programs. *Journal of the ACM*, 24(1):44–67, January 1977.
11. K. L. Clark and S. Sickel. Predicate logic: A calculus for deriving programs. In *Proceedings 5th International Joint Conference on Artificial Intelligence, Cambridge, Massachusetts, USA*, pages 419–420, 1977.
12. K. L. Clark and S.-Å. Tärnlund. A first order theory of data and programs. In *Proceedings Information Processing '77*, pages 939–944. North-Holland, 1977.
13. E. Clarke, O. Grumberg, and D. Peled. *Model Checking*. MIT Press, 2000.
14. B. Courcelle. Equivalences and Transformations of Regular Systems – Applications to Recursive Program Schemes and Grammars. *Theoretical Computer Science*, 42:1–122, 1986.

15. P. Cousot and R. Cousot. Abstract interpretation: A unified lattice model for static analysis of programs by construction of approximation of fixpoints. In *Proceedings 4th ACM-SIGPLAN Symposium on Principles of Programming Languages (POPL '77)*, pages 238–252. ACM Press, 1977.

16. D. De Schreye, R. Glück, J. Jørgensen, M. Leuschel, B. Martens, and M. H. Sørensen. Conjunctive partial deduction: Foundations, control, algorithms, and experiments. *Journal of Logic Programming*, 41(2–3):231–277, 1999.

17. S. K. Debray. Optimizing almost-tail-recursive Prolog programs. In *Proceedings IFIP International Conference on Functional Programming Languages and Computer Architecture, Nancy, France*, Lecture Notes in Computer Science 201, pages 204–219. Springer-Verlag, 1985.

18. G. Delzanno and A. Podelski. Model checking in CLP. In R. Cleaveland, editor, *5th International Conference TACAS'99*, Lecture Notes in Computer Science 1579, pages 223–239. Springer-Verlag, 1999.

19. Y. Deville. *Logic Programming: Systematic Program Development*. Addison-Wesley, 1990.

20. Y. Deville and K.-K. Lau. Logic program synthesis. *Journal of Logic Programming*, 19, 20:321–350, 1994.

21. E.W. Dijkstra. *A Discipline of Programming*. Prentice-Hall, Englewod Cliffs, N.J., 1976.

22. S. Etalle and M. Gabbrielli. Transformations of CLP modules. *Theoretical Computer Science*, 166:101–146, 1996.

23. S. Etalle, M. Gabbrielli, and M. C. Meo. Unfold/fold transformations of CCP programs. In D. Sangiorgi and R. de Simone, editors, *Proceedings of the International Conference on Concurrency Theory, Concur98*, Lecture Notes in Computer Science 1466, pages 348–363, 1998.

24. F. Fioravanti, A. Pettorossi, and M. Proietti. Verifying CTL properties of infinite state systems by specializing constraint logic programs. In *Proceedings of the ACM Sigplan Workshop on Verification and Computational Logic VCL'01, Florence (Italy)*, Technical Report DSSE-TR-2001-3, pages 85–96. University of Southampton, UK, 2001.

25. L. Fribourg. Extracting logic programs from proofs that use extended Prolog execution and induction. In D. H. D. Warren and P. Szeredi, editors, *Proceedings Seventh International Conference on Logic Programming, Jerusalem, Israel, June 18-20, 1990*, pages 685–699. The MIT Press, 1990.

26. L. Fribourg and H. Olsén. A decompositional approach for computing least fixedpoints of Datalog programs with z-counters.

27. J. P. Gallagher. Tutorial on specialization of logic programs. In *Proceedings of ACM SIGPLAN Symposium on Partial Evaluation and Semantics Based Program Manipulation, PEPM '93, Copenhagen, Denmark*, pages 88–98. ACM Press, 1993.

28. J. P. Gallagher and J. C. Peralta. Using regular approximations for generalisation during partial evaluation. In *Proceedings of the 2000 ACM SIGPLAN Workshop on Partial Evaluation and Semantics-Based Program Manipulation (PEPM '00), Boston, Massachusetts, USA, January 22-23, 2000.*, pages 44–51. ACM Press, November 1999.

29. P. A. Gardner and J. C. Shepherdson. Unfold/fold transformations of logic programs. In J.-L. Lassez and G. Plotkin, editors, *Computational Logic, Essays in Honor of Alan Robinson*, pages 565–583. MIT, 1991.

30. M. Gergatsoulis. Unfold/fold transformations for disjunctive logic programs. *Information Processing Letters*, 62:23–29, 1997.

31. C.A.R. Hoare. An axiomatic basis for computer programming. *CACM*, 12(10):576–580, 583, October 1969.
32. C. J. Hogger. Derivation of logic programs. *Journal of the ACM*, 28(2):372–392, 1981.
33. N. D. Jones, C. K. Gomard, and P. Sestoft. *Partial Evaluation and Automatic Program Generation*. Prentice Hall, 1993.
34. T. Kanamori and K. Horiuchi. Construction of logic programs based on generalized unfold/fold rules. In *Proceedings of the Fourth International Conference on Logic Programming*, pages 744–768. The MIT Press, 1987.
35. T. Kawamura. Logic program synthesis from first-order specifications. *Theoretical Computer Science*, 122:69–96, 1994.
36. L. Kott. Unfold/fold program transformation. In M. Nivat and J.C. Reynolds, editors, *Algebraic Methods in Semantics*, pages 411–434. Cambridge University Press, 1985.
37. R. A. Kowalski. Predicate logic as a programming language. In *Proceedings IFIP '74*, pages 569–574. North-Holland, 1974.
38. R. A. Kowalski. Algorithm = Logic + Control. *Communications of the ACM*, 22(7):424–436, 1979.
39. R. A. Kowalski. *Logic for Problem Solving*. North Holland, 1979.
40. D. Kozen. Results on the propositional μ-calculus. *Theoretical Computer Science*, 27:333–354, 1983.
41. K.-K. Lau and M. Ornaghi. Logic for component-based software development. In A. Kakas and F. Sadri, editors, *Computational Logic: From Logic Programming into the Future*. Springer. This volume.
42. K.-K. Lau and S.D. Prestwich. Top-down synthesis of recursive logic procedures from first-order logic specifications. In D.H.D. Warren and P. Szeredi, editors, *Proceedings of the Seventh International Conference on Logic Programming (ICLP '90)*, pages 667–684. MIT Press, 1990.
43. M. Leuschel. Program specialisation and abstract interpretation reconciled. In J. Jaffar, editor, *Proceedings of the Joint International Conference and Symposium on Logic Programming, Manchester, UK, 15-19 June 1998.*, pages 220–234. The MIT Press, 1998.
44. M. Leuschel, B. Martens, and D. de Schreye. Some achievements and prospects in partial deduction. *ACM Computing Surveys*, 30 (Electronic Section)(3es):4–es, 1998.
45. M. Leuschel and T. Massart. Infinite state model checking by abstract interpretation and program specialization. In A. Bossi, editor, *Proceedings of LOPSTR '99, Venice, Italy*, Lecture Notes in Computer Science 1817, pages 63–82. Springer, 1999.
46. J. W. Lloyd. *Foundations of Logic Programming*. Springer-Verlag, Berlin, 1987. Second Edition.
47. J. W. Lloyd and J. C. Shepherdson. Partial evaluation in logic programming. *Journal of Logic Programming*, 11:217–242, 1991.
48. M. J. Maher. A transformation system for deductive database modules with perfect model semantics. *Theoretical Computer Science*, 110:377–403, 1993.
49. Z. Manna and R. Waldinger. A deductive approach to program synthesis. *ACM Toplas*, 2:90–121, 1980.
50. Ulf Nilsson and Johan Lübcke. Constraint logic programming for local and symbolic model-checking. In J. Lloyd et al., editor, *CL 2000: Computational Logic*, number 1861 in Lecture Notes in Artificial Intelligence, pages 384–398, 2000.

51. L. C. Paulson. The foundation of a generic theorem prover. *J. Automated Reasoning*, 5:363–397, 1989.
52. A. Pettorossi and M. Proietti. Rules and strategies for transforming functional and logic programs. *ACM Computing Surveys*, 28(2):360–414, 1996.
53. A. Pettorossi and M. Proietti. Transformation of logic programs. In D. M. Gabbay, C. J. Hogger, and J. A. Robinson, editors, *Handbook of Logic in Artificial Intelligence and Logic Programming*, volume 5, pages 697–787. Oxford University Press, 1998.
54. A. Pettorossi and M. Proietti. Synthesis and transformation of logic programs using unfold/fold proofs. *Journal of Logic Programming*, 41(2&3):197–230, 1999.
55. A. Pettorossi and M. Proietti. Perfect model checking via unfold/fold transformations. In J.W. Lloyd et al., editor, *First International Conference on Computational Logic, CL'2000, London, 24-28 July, 2000*, Lecture Notes in Artificial Intelligence 1861, pages 613–628. Springer, 2000.
56. A. Pettorossi, M. Proietti, and S. Renault. Reducing nondeterminism while specializing logic programs. In *Proc. 24-th ACM Symposium on Principles of Programming Languages, Paris, France*, pages 414–427. ACM Press, 1997.
57. V. Pratt. A decidable μ-calculus. In *22nd Symposium on Foundations of Computer Science*, Washington (DC), 1981. IEEE Computer Society Press.
58. M. Proietti and A. Pettorossi. Unfolding-definition-folding, in this order, for avoiding unnecessary variables in logic programs. *Theoretical Computer Science*, 142(1):89–124, 1995.
59. T. C. Przymusinski. On the declarative and procedural semantics of logic programs. *Journ. of Automated Reasoning*, 5:167–205, 1989.
60. G. Puebla and M. Hermenegildo. Abstract multiple specialization and its application to program parallelization. *J. of Logic Programming. Special Issue on Synthesis, Transformation and Analysis of Logic Programs*, 41(2&3):279–316, November 1999.
61. Y. S. Ramakrishna, C. R. Ramakrishnan, I. V. Ramakrishnan, S. A. Smolka, T. Swift, and D. S. Warren. Efficient model checking using tabled resolution. In *CAV '97*, Lecture Notes in Computer Science 1254, pages 143–154. Springer-Verlag, 1997.
62. J. A. Robinson. A machine-oriented logic based on the resolution principle. *Journal of the ACM*, 12(1):23–41, 1965.
63. A. Roychoudhury, K. Narayan Kumar, C. R. Ramakrishnan, I. V. Ramakrishnan, and S. A. Smolka. Verification of parameterized systems using logic program transformations. In *Proceedings of the Sixth International Conference on Tools and Algorithms for the Construction and Analysis of Systems, TACAS 2000, Berlin, Germany*, Lecture Notes in Computer Science 1785, pages 172–187. Springer, 2000.
64. A. Roychoudhury, K. Narayan Kumar, C. R. Ramakrishnan, and I.V. Ramakrishnan. Beyond tamaki-sato style unfold/fold transformations for normal logic programs. In P. S. Thiagarajan and R. H. C. Yap, editors, *Proceedings of ASIAN'99, 5th Asian Computing Science Conference, Phuket, Thailand, December 10-12*, Lecture Notes in Computer Science 1742, pages 322–333. Springer-Verlag, 1999.
65. A. Roychoudhury, K. Narayan Kumar, C.R. Ramakrishnan, and I.V. Ramakrishnan. Proofs by program transformation. In *PreProceedings of LOPSTR '99, Venice, Italy*, pages 57–64. Università Ca' Foscari di Venezia, Dipartimento di Informatica, 1999.
66. A. Roychoudhury and I.V. Ramakrishnan. Automated inductive verification of parameterized protocols. In *CAV 2001*, pages 25–37, 2001.

67. D. Sahlin. Mixtus: An automatic partial evaluator for full Prolog. *New Generation Computing*, 12:7–51, 1993.
68. T. Sato and H. Tamaki. Transformational logic program synthesis. In *Proceedings of the International Conference on Fifth Generation Computer Systems*, pages 195–201. ICOT, 1984.
69. T. Sato and H. Tamaki. First order compiler: A deterministic logic program synthesis algorithm. *Journal of Symbolic Computation*, 8:625–627, 1989.
70. H. Seki. Unfold/fold transformation of stratified programs. *Theoretical Computer Science*, 86:107–139, 1991.
71. H. Seki. Unfold/fold transformation of general logic programs for well-founded semantics. *Journal of Logic Programming*, 16(1&2):5–23, 1993.
72. H. Seki and K. Furukawa. Notes on transformation techniques for generate and test logic programs. In *Proceedings of the International Symposium on Logic Programming, San Francisco, USA*, pages 215–223. IEEE Press, 1987.
73. D. R. Smith. KIDS: A semi-automatic program development system. *IEEE Transactions on Software Engineering — Special Issue on Formal Methods*, September 1990.
74. H. Tamaki and T. Sato. Unfold/fold transformation of logic programs. In S.-Å. Tärnlund, editor, *Proceedings of the Second International Conference on Logic Programming, Uppsala, Sweden*, pages 127–138. Uppsala University, 1984.
75. D. H. D. Warren. Implementing Prolog – compiling predicate logic programs. Research Report 39 & 40, Department of Artificial Intelligence, University of Edinburgh, 1977.
76. D. S. Warren. Memoing for logic programs. *Communications of the ACM*, 35(3):93–111, 1992.

Achievements and Prospects
of Program Synthesis

Pierre Flener

Information Technology, Department of Computing Science
Uppsala University, Box 337, S – 751 05 Uppsala, Sweden
pierref@csd.uu.se, http://www.csd.uu.se/~pierref/

Abstract. Program synthesis research aims at developing a program that develops correct programs from specifications, with as much or as little interaction as the specifier wants. I overview the main achievements in deploying logic for program synthesis. I also outline the prospects of such research, arguing that, while the technology scales up from toy programs to real-life software and to commercially viable tools, computational logic will continue to be a driving force behind this progress.

1 Introduction

In his seminal book *Logic for Problem Solving* [53], Bob Kowalski introduced the celebrated equation:

$$Algorithm = Logic + Control \qquad (A = L + C)$$

expressing that for an algorithm, the statement of *what* it does — the logic component — can be separated from the manner *how* it is done — the control component. Algorithms and programs in conventional languages feature a merging of these components, whereas pure logic programs only express the logic component, leaving the control component to the execution mechanism. In actual logic programming languages, such as PROLOG, some control directives can be provided as annotations by the programmer. The logic component states only the problem-specific part of an algorithm and determines only its correctness, while the control component only expresses a problem-independent execution strategy and determines only the efficiency of the algorithm.

Kowalski listed several advantages of this encapsulation, which is akin to the abstraction achieved when separating the algorithm and data-structure components of programs. These advantages include the following:

- The logic and control components of algorithms can be successively refined, and improved, independently of each other.
- A default, and thus often sub-optimal, control can be provided for less experienced programmers, who can thus focus their efforts on the logic component.

A.C. Kakas, F. Sadri (Eds.): Computat. Logic (Kowalski Festschrift), LNAI 2407, pp. 310–346, 2002.
© Springer-Verlag Berlin Heidelberg 2002

- The logic component of an algorithm can be mechanically generated from, and verified against, a formal specification, using deduction, without considering the control component. Similarly, the logic component can be mechanically transformed into another one, using deduction, without considering the control component. One thus obtains what is known as program *synthesis*, program *verification*, and program *transformation*, respectively.

The objective of this chapter is to overview the main achievements in deploying logic for program synthesis, and to outline its future prospects. As synthesis nowadays starts scaling up from toy programs to real-life software and to commercially viable tools, it can be argued that computational logic will continue to be a driving force behind these developments.

Scope of this Chapter. In contrast to Kowalski's intention, I here do not focus on the synthesis of logic programs only, but rather take a wider approach and tackle the synthesis of any kinds of programs. Indeed, the target language does not really matter, but what does matter is the use of computational logic in the synthesis process. Similarly, I shall not restrict myself to his advocated use of deductive inference for synthesis, but will also discuss the role of inductive, abductive, and analogical inference in synthesis.

Also, although there is a large overlap in concepts, notations, and techniques between program synthesis and program transformation, verification, and analysis (which is the study of the semantics and properties of programs, such as their termination), I here discuss concepts and techniques relevant to program synthesis only — assuming it can be clearly delineated from those other areas — and refer the reader to the prolific literature on these related research fields.

Having thus both widened and narrowed the scope of this chapter compared to Kowalski's original agenda, the literature to be overviewed is very voluminous and thus cannot possibly be discussed in such a single, short chapter. I have thus made a maybe subjective selection of the landmark research in program synthesis, with particular attention to seminal work and to approaches that scale up for eventual deployment in actual software development. For coverage of more approaches, I thus refer the interested reader to the numerous overviews, surveys, and paper collections periodically published before this one, such as those — in chronological order — by Barr & Feigenbaum [3], Biermann *et al.* [14,15,12,13], Partsch *et al.* [73,72], Smith [79], Balzer [2], IEEE TSE [70], Goldberg [41], Rich & Waters [74,75], Feather [30], Lowry *et al.* [60,61], Steier & Anderson [87], JSC [16], Deville & Lau [27], and Flener [34,37].

Organisation of this Chapter. The rest of this chapter is organised as follows. In Section 2, I describe my viewpoint on what program synthesis actually is, and what it is not, especially in relation to other areas, such as compilation and transformation. Classification criteria are also given. The technical core of this chapter are Sections 3 to 5, where I overview past achievements of logic-based program synthesis.[1] I devote one section each to the three main streams of research, namely transformational (Section 3), constructive (Section 4), and mixed-inference (Section 5) synthesis, exhibiting one or two representative systems for each of them, in terms of their underlying machineries, their actual synthesis processes, and interesting excerpts of sample syntheses. From this sketch of the state-of-the-art, I can then outline, in Section 6, the future prospects of program synthesis, whether logic-based or not, especially in terms of the challenges it faces towards scaling up and eventual transfer of the technology to commercial software development. Finally, in Section 7, I conclude.

2   What *Is* Program Synthesis?

I now describe my viewpoint on what program synthesis actually is, and what it is not. In Section 2.1, I state the objective and rationale of program synthesis, and contrast it with program transformation. Next, in Section 2.2, I propose a classification scheme for synthesisers. Finally, in Section 2.3, I show that the goalposts of synthesis have been moving very much over the years, and that synthesis is in retrospect nothing else but compilation.

2.1   The Goal of Program Synthesis

The grand objective of *program synthesis* — also known as *automatic programming* — research is to develop a program that develops correct programs from specifications, with as much or as little interaction as the specifier wants. Nothing in this formulation is meant to imply that the focus is on programming-in-the-small. Synthesising real-life software only requires a scalable synthesis process. Just like manual programming, synthesis is thus about translating a statement from one language into *another* language, namely from the specification language into the programming language, thereby switching from a statement of *what* the program does and how it should be used to a statement of *how* the program does it, hence ideally not only establishing correctness (the program outputs satisfy the post-condition of the specification, provided the inputs meet its pre-condition) but also achieving a reasonable level of efficiency (outputs are computed within a reasonable amount of time and space).

The rationale for this objective is the notorious difficulty for most programmers of effectively developing correct and efficient programs, even when these programs are small. The benefits of a synthesiser would be higher-quality programs and the disappearance of the program validation and maintenance steps, and instead total focus on specification elaboration, validation, and maintenance, because replay of program development would become less costly. Synthesis would be especially useful in problem domains where there is a huge gap between

---

[1] Citations are not necessarily to the first paper on a specific approach, but to comprehensive papers that may have been published much later. In the latter case, I indicate the year of the original paper in the running text.

the end-user formulation of a problem and an efficient program for solving it, such as for constraint satisfaction problems, for instance.

The hope for synthesisers is as old as computing science itself, but it is often dismissed as a dream. Indeed, we are way off a fully automatic, general-purpose, end-user-oriented synthesiser [75], and pursuing one may well be illusory. Most of the early synthesis projects aimed at starting from informal specifications. For instance, the SAFE project [2] initially went to great efforts to do so, but eventually switched to defining GIST, a very-high-level formal language for conveying formal descriptions of specifications. Nowadays, as a simplification, virtually all synthesisers start from inputs in such formal languages. Another typical simplification through division of work is to focus on the synthesis of the logic component of programs, leaving the design of their data-structure and control components to others. In this chapter, I focus on approaches to logic-based synthesis that embody both of these usual simplifications.

A few words need to be said about the relationship between synthesis and transformation. Whereas program synthesis is here defined as the translation of a statement from a possibly informal specification description language into a program in a necessarily formal programming language, with focus on correctness, *program transformation* is here defined as the equivalence-preserving modification of a program into another program of the *same* language, with focus on achieving greater efficiency, in time or space or both. This makes transformation different from synthesis in purpose, but complementary with it. In practice, they share many concepts and techniques. Optimising transformation can be achieved by changing any of the logic, control, or data-structure components of programs. This raises many interesting issues:

- One can argue that synthesis and transformation should not be a sequence of two separate but complementary tasks, because the correctness and efficiency of algorithms are inevitably intertwined, even if separated in logic and control components. But this division of work is appealing and has been useful.
- If only the text of a program enters transformation, then the rationale of its synthesis steps is lost to the transformation and may have to be rediscovered, in a costly way, in order to perform effective transformation. I am not aware of any transformation approaches that take programming rationale as input.
- In Kowalski's words [53]: "Changing the logic component is a useful short-term strategy, since the representation of the problem is generally easier to change than the problem-solver. Changing the control component, on the other hand, is a better long-term solution, since improving the problem-solver improves its performance for many different problems." A good example of the effect of suitably changing control is the switch from logic programming to constraint logic programming, thereby giving programs with a generate-and-test logic component an often spectacular speedup. Such paradigm shifts may well require a redefinition of what synthesis and transformation are.

No matter which way the purposes of synthesis and transformation are defined, there is an unclear boundary between them, made even more confusing by other considerations, examined in Section 2.3.

2.2   Classification Criteria

A huge variety of synthesis mechanisms exist, so I here propose a multi-dimensional classification scheme for them. The criteria fall into three major categories, grouping the attributes of the synthesis inputs, mechanisms, and outputs.

Synthesis Inputs. The input to synthesis is a *specification* of the informal requirements. Sometimes, a *domain theory* stating the laws of the application domain must also be provided. These inputs have the following attributes:

- **Formality.** An input to synthesis can be written in either an *informal* language (whose syntax or semantics is not predefined), or a *formal* language (whose syntax and semantics are predefined). The often encountered notion of *semi-formal* language is strictly speaking meaningless: controlled natural languages are formal, and UML and the likes are informal even though their graphical parts may have a formal syntax and semantics.
- **Language.** When using a formal input language, a specification can be either *axioms*, or input/output *examples*. Sometimes, the actual language is disguised by a suitable graphical user interface, or it is sugared.
- **Correctness wrt the Requirements.** Informally, a statement S is *correct* wrt another statement T iff S is *consistent* with T (everything that follows from S also follows from T) as well as *complete* wrt T (everything that follows from T also follows from S). Input to synthesis is usually *assumed to be consistent* with the requirements. On the other hand, the input is either *assumed to be complete* or *declared to be incomplete* wrt the requirements. In the former case, the synthesiser need only produce a program that is correct wrt the input. In the latter case, the synthesiser must try to extrapolate the actual complete requirements from the given input. In either case, actual validation against the informal requirements is done by the programmer, by changing the inputs to synthesis until the synthesised program has the desired behaviour. As opposed to the *external* consistency and completeness considered here, *internal* consistency and completeness are not classification attributes, but rather quality criteria that may be mechanically checked before synthesis begins: a statement S is *internally consistent* iff S has at least one model, and *internally complete* iff every symbol in S is either primitive to the language used or defined within S.

Synthesis Mechanisms. The mechanisms of program synthesis can also be classified along a few dimensions:

- **Level of Automation.** Having by definition excluded manual programming, synthesis is either *semi-automatic* or *fully automatic*.
- **Initiative.** In semi-automatic synthesis, the initiative in the interaction can be on either side, making the mechanism *synthesiser-guided* or *user-guided*.
- **Kinds of Inference.** There are many kinds of inference and they can all be used, and combined, towards synthesis. I here distinguish between *purely-deductive* synthesis, which performs only deductive inference and is either

transformational (see Section 3) or *constructive* (see Section 4), and *mixed-inference* synthesis, which features any appropriate mix of deductive, inductive, abductive, and analogical inference (see Section 5).

- **Kinds of Knowledge.** There is a great need for incorporating knowledge into program synthesisers. There are essentially four kinds of useful synthesis knowledge, namely knowledge about the mechanics of *algorithm design*, knowledge about the laws and refinement of *data structures*, knowledge about the laws of the *application domain* (this was called the domain theory above), and *meta-knowledge*, that is knowledge about how and when to use the other kinds of knowledge.
- **Determinism.** A *non-deterministic* synthesiser can generate a family of programs from a specification; otherwise, it is a *deterministic* synthesiser.
- **Soundness.** Synthesis should be a *sound* process, in the sense that it produces an output that is guaranteed to satisfy some pre-determined notion of correctness wrt the input.

Synthesis Outputs. The output of synthesis is a *program*, and usually only the logic component of its algorithm. The classification attribute is:

- **Language.** Technically, the synthesised program can be in any language, because any code can be generated from the chosen internal representation. In practice, the pure parts of the so-called declarative languages are usually chosen as internal and external representation of programs, because they are the highest-level languages compiled today and thus sufficient to make the point. Common target languages thus are *Horn clauses*, *recursion equations*, *λ-expressions*, etc.

These classification attributes are not independent: choices made for one of them affect the available choices for the others.

2.3   The Moving Goalposts of Program Synthesis

The first assemblers and compilers were seen as automatic programming systems, as they relieved the programmers from many of the burdens of binary programming. Ever since, program synthesis research has been trying to be one step ahead of the state-of-the-art in programming languages, but, in retrospect, it is nothing else but the quest for new programming paradigms. To paraphrase Tesler's sentence, which was originally on Artificial Intelligence: *Program synthesis deals with whatever has not been compiled yet.* Of course, as our notion of program evolves, our understanding of compilation has to evolve as well: it is not because today's compilers are largely deterministic and automatic that tomorrow's compilers, that is today's synthesisers, are not allowed to have search spaces or to be semi-automatic.

The main problem with formal inputs to program synthesis is that there is no way to construct them so that we have a formal proof that they capture our informal requirements. In fact, the phrase 'formal specification' is a contradiction in terms, as real specifications can only be informal [57]. An informal correctness proof is needed *somewhere*, as the purpose of software engineering is after all to obtain programs that implement our informal requirements. Writing such formal inputs just shifts the obligation of performing an informal proof from the program-vs-informal-requirements verification to the formal-inputs-vs-informal-requirements verification, but it does *not* eliminate that obligation.

In my opinion, programs and such formal inputs to synthesis are intrinsically the same thing. As synthesis research aims at raising the level of language in which we can interact with the computer, compilation and synthesis are intrinsically the same process. In other words, real programming and synthesis are only being done when going from informal requirements to a formal description, which is then submitted to a compiler. In this sense, focusing synthesis on starting from formal statements is not really a simplification, as claimed above, but rather a redefinition of the task, making it identical to compilation.

I am *not* saying that formal methods are useless. Of course it is important to be able to check whether a formal description is *internally* consistent and complete, and to generate prototypes from executable descriptions, because all this allows early error detection. But one cannot say that such formal descriptions are specifications, and one still knows nothing about whether they are *externally* consistent and complete, namely wrt the informal requirements. Formal inputs to program synthesis are already programs, though not in a conventional sense. But conventions change in time, and the so-called "formal specifications" of today will be perceived as programs tomorrow.

In order to stick to the contemporary terminology and make this chapter independent of agreement or disagreement on this sub-section, I shall nevertheless speak of formal specifications (without the quotes) in the following.

3   Achievements of Transformational Synthesis

In *transformational synthesis*, meaning-preserving transformation rules are applied to the specification, until a program is obtained. Usually, this is done within a so-called wide-spectrum language — such as B, GIST, VDM, Z — containing both non-executable specification constructs and executable programming constructs. I shall use the word 'description' to designate the software representations in such a language, be they formal specifications, programs, or hybrids in-between these two extremes.

Given a logic specification of the following form, where there is no prejudice about which parameters are inputs and which ones are outputs, at run-time:

$$\forall P . \, pre(P) \rightarrow (\, p(P) \leftrightarrow post(P) \,)$$

where *pre* is the pre-condition (an assertion on all the parameters P, assumed to hold when execution of a program for p starts), *post* is the post-condition (an assertion on the parameters P, to be established after execution of a program for p), and p is the specified predicate symbol, transformational synthesis iterates over a single step, namely the application of a transformation rule to some expression within the current description, until a program is obtained.

Transformation rules, or *transforms*, are often represented as rewrite rules with pattern variables:

$$IP \Rightarrow OP \quad [\text{ if } C \,]$$

expressing that under the optional applicability condition C, an expression matching input pattern IP under some substitution θ may be replaced by the instance $OP\theta$ of the output pattern OP.

Transforms are either *refinements*, reducing the abstraction level of the current description by replacing a specification construct by a program construct, or *optimisations*, performing a simplification (reduction in expression size) or a reduction in runtime or space, both at the same abstraction level. Refinements can act on statements or datatype definitions, reducing non-determinism.

A sample refinement is the following unconditional transform of a high-level non-recursive array summation into a recursive expression:

$$S = \sum_{i=l}^{u} A[i]$$
$$\Rightarrow$$
$$\Sigma(A, l, u, S) \leftarrow l > u, S = 0 \quad \% \; \Sigma(A, l, u, S) \text{ iff } S \text{ is the sum of } A[l]..A[u]$$
$$\Sigma(A, l, u, S) \leftarrow \neg \, l > u, +(l, 1, l'), \Sigma(A, l', u, T), +(A[l], T, S)$$

Sample optimisations are the following conditional transform for divisions:

$$x/x \Rightarrow 1 \quad \text{if } x \neq 0$$

and the following accumulator introduction, which amounts to replacing recursion in the non-minimal case of a divide (d) and conquer (c) definition of predicate p by tail-recursion — with the minimal (m) case being solved (s) without recursion — as this can be compiled into more efficient code, like iteration:

$$p(X, Y) \leftarrow m(X), s(X, Y)$$
$$p(X, Y) \leftarrow \neg m(X), d(X, H, T), p(T, V), c(H, V, Y)$$
$$\Rightarrow$$
$$p(X, Y) \leftarrow p(X, Y, I)$$
$$p(X, Y, A) \leftarrow m(X), s(X, J), c(A, J, Y)$$
$$p(X, Y, A) \leftarrow \neg m(X), d(X, H, T), c(A, H, A'), p(T, Y, A')$$
$$\text{if } associative(c) \wedge identity(c, left, I)$$

The latter transform is applicable to the output of the refinement above, because $+/3$ is associative and has a left-identity element, namely 0. This illustrates how transforms can be chained. Of course, the refinement above could immediately have reflected such a chaining.

Other common transforms are *unfolding* (replacing a symbol by its definition), *folding* (the inverse of unfolding), *definition* (introduction of a new symbol via its definition), *instantiation* (application of a substitution), *abstraction* (introduction of a *where* clause, in functional programming), or reflect the laws of the application domain.

Several control issues arise in the rewrite cycle, because the synthesis search space is usually intractable due to the sheer number of transforms. First, who checks the applicability condition? Usually, this is considered a synthesiser responsibility, and thus becomes a task for an automatic theorem proving component thereof. Second, which transform should be applied next, and to which expression? Usually, full automation is abandoned in favour of user-guided interactive application of transforms, with the synthesiser automatically ensuring that applicability conditions are met, as well as correctly applying the chosen transform to the chosen expression, thus taking over all clerical work. Other approaches are based on rule ordering, heuristics, agendas, planning, replay, etc. Third, when to stop transforming? Indeed, many transforms can also be applied during program transformation (as defined in Section 2.1), hence blurring the transition and distinction between synthesis and transformation. Usually, one considers that synthesis *per se* has finished when the current description is entirely within the executable part of the wide-spectrum language, so that synthesis is here defined as the translation from the full wide-spectrum language into its executable subset.

When transforms are too fine-grained, they lead to very tedious and lengthy syntheses. The idea is thus to define macroscopic transforms that are higher-level in the sense that they are closer to actual programming decisions and that they are compositions of such atomic transforms. Examples are *finite differencing* (replacing expensive computations in a loop by incremental ones), *loop fusion* (merging of nested or sequentially-composed loops into one loop), *partial evaluation* (simplifying expressions for fixed arguments), *generalisation* (solving a more general, easier problem), *dynamic programming*, *memoing* (caching results of computations to avoid useless recomputations), *jittering* (preparing the application of other transforms).

To document a synthesis and ease its understanding, the applied sequence of transforms is usually recorded, ideally with the rationale of their usage. This also allows *replay*, though it remains unclear when this is suitable and when not.

I now discuss an entire product-line of representative transformational synthesisers, chosen because of the objective of scaling the technology to real-life software development tasks. Indeed, KIDS and its successors (see Section 3.1) have been successfully deployed in many real-life applications. In Section 3.2, I outline the efforts of the other research centres in transformational synthesis.

3.1 SPECWARE, DESIGNWARE, and PLANWARE

At Kestrel Institute (Palo Alto, California, USA, www.kestrel.edu), Smith and his team have been designing, for over 15 years now, a series of synthesisers, all with the same philosophy, which is specific to them (see below). Their *Kestrel Interactive Development System* (KIDS) [81] extends its predecessor CYPRESS [80] and automatically synthesises correct programs within the wide-spectrum language REFINE, while leaving their transformation to a user-guided rewrite cycle. I here describe the systems of their product-line — SPECWARE (for *Specification Ware*) [86], DESIGNWARE [84], and PLANWARE [18] — as well as how they relate to each other. They amount to more than just recasting, as described in [83], the synthesis and transformation calculus of KIDS in category theory.

The overall Kestrel philosophy is as follows. Consider, for instance, programs that solve constraint satisfaction problems (CSPs) by exploring the entire candidate-solution space, though with pruning of useless subspaces. They have a common structure, called global search, of which the dataflow, control-flow, and interactions between parts can be formally captured in a *program schema*. Similarly, other program schemas can be designed for capturing the methodologies leading to local search programs, divide-and-conquer programs, etc. Such program schemas can then be used in synthesis to significantly reduce the candidate-program space. Some proof obligations arise in such *schema-guided synthesis*, but they are feasible by state-of-the-art automated theorem provers. The synthesised programs are not very efficient, though, since they are just problem-specific instances of program schemas that had been designed for entire problem families, but without being able to take into account the specificities of their individual problems. The synthesised programs can thus be transformed into equivalent but more efficient ones by applying high-level transforms, in a user-guided way. However, this transformation cycle also became the bottleneck of KIDS, because the user really has to be an expert in applying these transforms in a suitable order and to the appropriate sub-expressions. Moreover, the proof obligations of synthesis are only automatable if the entire application domain knowledge is formally captured, which is an often daunting task. Smith used KIDS to rather quickly refine new, breakthrough algorithms for various CSPs [82].

The inputs to synthesis are a formal axiomatic higher-order algebraic specification, assumed to be consistent and complete wrt the requirements, and a domain theory. The synthesis mechanism is purely deductive, interactive or automatic (depending on the system), non-deterministic, and sound. Algorithm design, data structure, and application domain knowledge are exploited. The output is a program in any supported language (e.g., COMMONLISP, C++).

The Transformation System. A category-theory approach to transformation is taken. Viewing specifications as finite presentations of theories, which are the closures of the specification axioms under the rules of inference, a *specification morphism* $S \rightarrow S'$ is a provability-preserving signature morphism between specifications S and S', that is a map between their sort and operator symbols, such that axioms translate into theorems.[2]

For instance, consider the specification of finite containers in Figure 1. It is parameterised on the sort E of the container elements. Containers are either empty, or singletons, or constructed by an infix binary *join* operator.

Also consider the following specification of binary operators:

$$\text{spec } BinOp \text{ is}$$
$$\text{sort } T$$
$$\text{op } \_ \: bop \: \_ : T, T \longrightarrow T$$
$$\text{end}$$

---

[2] For typographic reasons, the '$\rightarrow$' symbol is thus overloaded, being used for both morphisms and logical implication. The distinction should always be clear from context. Under its morphism meaning, this symbol will be typeset here in other directions of the wind rose, to facilitate the representation of graphs of morphisms.

spec *Container* is
    sorts $E, Cont$
    op *empty* : $\longrightarrow Cont$
    op *singleton* : $E \longrightarrow Cont$
    op _ *join* _ : $Cont, Cont \longrightarrow Cont$
    ... other operator declarations ...
    ops $\{empty, singleton, join\}$ construct $Cont$
    axiom $\forall X : Cont . X \ join \ empty = X$
    axiom $\forall X : Cont . \ empty \ join \ X = X$
    ... axioms for the other operators ...
end

Fig. 1. A specification of finite containers

spec *ProtoSeq* is
    sorts E, Seq
    op *empty* : $\longrightarrow Seq$
    op *singleton* : $E \longrightarrow Seq$
    op _ *join* _ : $Seq, Seq \longrightarrow Seq$
    ... other operator declarations ...
    ops $\{empty, singleton, join\}$ construct Seq
    axiom $\forall X : Seq . X \ join \ empty = X$
    axiom $\forall X : Seq . \ empty \ join \ X = X$
    axiom $\forall X, Y, Z : T . (X \ join \ Y) \ join \ Z = X \ join \ (Y \ join \ Z)$
    ... axioms for the other operators ...
end

Fig. 2. A specification of finite sequences

The following specification of associative operators reflects the specification morphism $BinOp \rightarrow Associative$, which is $\{T \mapsto T, bop \mapsto bop\}$:

spec *Associative* is
    import *BinOp*
    axiom $\forall X, Y, Z : T . (X \ bop \ Y) \ bop \ Z = X \ bop \ (Y \ bop \ Z)$
end

Specifications and specification morphisms form a category, called *SPEC*, in which push-outs can be computed. Informally, a *diagram* is a directed graph with specifications as vertices and specification morphisms as arcs.

For instance, the push-out of *Associative* $\leftarrow$ *BinOp* $\rightarrow$ *Container* under morphisms $\{T \mapsto T, bop \mapsto bop\}$ and $\{T \mapsto E, bop \mapsto join\}$ is isomorphic to the specification of prototype finite sequences in Figure 2. Indeed, sequences are containers whose *join* operation is associative. By another morphism, sequence-specific operators can be added to *ProtoSeq*, giving rise to a specification *Sequence* of finite sequences. By another push-out *Commutative* $\leftarrow$ *BinOp* $\rightarrow$ *ProtoSeq*, we can get a specification *ProtoBag* of prototype finite

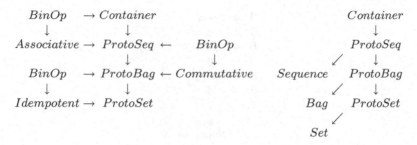

Fig. 3. A chain of commuting diagrams (left) and a taxonomy of containers (right)

bags, to which bag-specific operators can be added, giving rise to a specification *Bag* of finite bags. Indeed, bags are sequences whose join operation is commutative, because element order is irrelevant. Finally, by yet another push-out *Idempotent* ← *BinOp* → *ProtoBag*, we can obtain a specification *ProtoSet* of prototype finite sets, to which set-specific operators can be added, giving rise to a specification *Set* of finite sets. Indeed, sets are bags whose join operation is idempotent, because multiplicity of elements is irrelevant. This process can be captured in the chain of three commuting diagrams of the left of Figure 3. If we graphically add the considered additional morphisms to the central vertical chain, we obtain the *taxonomy* of containers in the right of Figure 3.

A *diagram morphism* $D \Rightarrow D'$ is a set of specification morphisms between the specifications of diagrams D and D' such that certain squares commute. It serves to preserve and extend the structure of specifications, as opposed to flattening them out via co-limits. For instance, a not shown diagram morphism $BAG \Rightarrow BAGasSEQ$ can be created to capture the refinement of bags into sequences, where BAG and $BAGasSEQ$ are diagrams involving specifications *Bag* and *Sequence*, respectively. Diagrams and diagram morphisms also form a category, in which co-limits can be computed, using the co-limits in *SPEC*. The word 'specification' here denotes either a specification or a specification diagram, and 'refinement' refers to a diagram morphism, unless otherwise noted.

In general now, specifications — as theory representations — can capture domain models (e.g., transportation), abstract datatypes (e.g., *BAG*), software requirements (e.g., crew scheduling), algorithm theories (e.g., divide-and-conquer), etc. Tool support and a large library of reusable specifications are provided for structuring and composing new specifications. Also, specification morphisms and diagram morphisms can capture specification structuring (e.g., via imports), specification refinement (e.g., scheduling to transportation-scheduling), algorithm design (e.g., global-search to scheduling), datatype refinement (e.g., $BAG \Rightarrow BAGasSEQ$), expression optimisation (e.g., finite differencing), etc. Again, tool support is provided for creating new refinements, and a large library of useful refinements exists.

$$
\begin{array}{ccc}
A & \Rightarrow Spec_0 & \\
\Downarrow & \Downarrow & \\
B & \Rightarrow Spec_1 & \Leftarrow C \\
& \Downarrow & \Downarrow \\
E & \Rightarrow Spec_2 & \Leftarrow D \\
\Downarrow & \Downarrow & \\
\cdots & \cdots & \cdots \\
& \Downarrow & \Downarrow \\
& Spec_n & \Leftarrow Z \\
& \downarrow & \\
& Code &
\end{array}
$$

Fig. 4. The synthesis process

Finally, *inter-logic morphisms* are provided for translating from the specification logic into the logic of a programming language — thereby performing code generation — or of a theorem-prover or any other supporting tool.

The Synthesis Process. The refinement of a specification $Spec_0$ is an iterative process of calculating push-outs in commuting squares, yielding new specifications $Spec_i$, until the process is deemed finished and an inter-logic morphism is used to generate a program $Code$ from the final specification $Spec_n$. This process is depicted in Figure 4. Here, $A \Rightarrow B$, $C \Rightarrow D$, etc, are refinements stored in a library. With push-outs being calculated automatically, the creative steps are the selection of a refinement and the construction of a *classification arrow* [83,84] between the source diagram (A, C, etc) of a library refinement and the current specification. The leverage can be quite dramatic, with push-outs often generating many new lines, which might have been quite cumbersome, if not difficult, to write by hand.

As the size and complexity of specification and refinement libraries increase, support must be given for this approach to scale up. First, specification libraries are organised in taxonomies, such as Figure 3 above, so as to allow the incremental construction of classification arrows [84]. For instance, to apply the $BAG \Rightarrow BAGasSEQ$ refinement to the current specification S, one can first classify S as a *Container*, then as a *ProtoSeq*, next as a *ProtoBag*, then as a *Bag*, and finally as a *BAG*, rather than classifying S as a *BAG* in one go. The deeper one goes into a taxonomy, the more specification information can be exploited and the more efficient the resulting code. Second, as patterns of useful classification and refinement sequences emerge, parameterised macros, called *tactics*, can be defined to provide higher-level, if not more automatic, operations to the user. For instance, the divide-and-conquer algorithm theory admits two classification tactics, depending on whether the decomposition or the composition operator is manually selected from a library, and thus reused, in a classification step, leaving the other operator to be inferred.

SPECWARE [86] is an abstract machine exporting high-level synthesis and transformation primitives that hide their low-level implementation in terms of category theory operations. Using it, one can more quickly write new synthesisers. First, a new version of KIDS was implemented, called DESIGNWARE [84], extending SPECWARE with domain-independent taxonomies of software design theories plus support for refining specifications using the latter. Then, on top of DESIGNWARE, the PLANWARE [18] domain-specific synthesiser of high-performance schedulers was developed. Both its synthesis and transformation processes are fully automatic, and it even automatically generates the formal specification and application domain knowledge — which are typically thousands of lines — from the information provided by the specifier, who uses a very intuitive domain-specific spreadsheet-like interface, without being aware of the underlying category theory. PLANWARE extends DESIGNWARE with libraries of design theories and refinements about scheduling, together with a specialised tactic for controlling the application of this design knowledge. Other domain-specific synthesisers are in preparation, and will also be built on top of DESIGNWARE.

A Sample Synthesis. A synthesis of a function *sorting* that sorts bags into sequences may start from the following specification:

> spec *Sorting* is
> import *BagSeqOverLinOrd*
> op *sorted* : *Bag, Seq* ⟶ *Boolean*
> def *sorted*$(X, Y) = ord(Y) \land seqToBag(Y) = X$
> op *sorting* : *Bag* ⟶ *Seq*
> axiom *sorted*$(X, sorting(X))$
> end

where *sorted* is used to express the post-condition on *sorting*. Universal quantification consistent with the signature declarations is assumed for unquantified variables. Suppose the specifier wants to apply a divide-and-conquer algorithm design, as embodied in the refinement $DivConq \Rightarrow DivConqScheme$, where the source specification is in Figure 5. Here, a function F from domain D into range R is specified, with post-condition O. Three mutually exclusive predicates p_i (for $i = 0..2$) are defined over D, representing conditions for the existence of decompositions, computed under post-conditions O_{Di} (for $i = 0..2$), with O_{D2} enforcing that its decompositions are smaller than the given term, under well-founded relation $\prec$. Soundness axioms require that the decompositions can be composed, under post-conditions O_{Ci} (for $i = 0..2$), to achieve the overall post-condition O. The target specification of the refinement is in Figure 6. where a schematic definition of the specified function F is introduced, together with composition operators C_i whose post-conditions are O_{Ci}.

Now, to apply the $DivConq \Rightarrow DivConqScheme$ refinement, a classification arrow $Sorting \Rightarrow DivConq$ has to be manually constructed, so that the corresponding push-out can be automatically calculated. The first part of the necessary diagram morphism is straightforward, namely $\{D \mapsto Bag, R \mapsto Seq, F \mapsto sorting, O \mapsto sorted, \prec \mapsto subBag, \ldots\}$. The remaining part gives rise to dual alternatives, which can be captured in tactics, as discussed above: either a set of simple standard decomposition operators is reused from a library

spec *DivConq* is
  sorts $D, R, E, Unit$
  op $F : D \longrightarrow R$
  op $O : D, R \longrightarrow Boolean$
  op $\_ \prec \_ : D, D \longrightarrow Boolean$
  axiom $wellFounded(\prec)$
  op $p_0, p_1, p_2 : D \longrightarrow Boolean$
  op $O_{D0} : D, Unit \longrightarrow Boolean$
  op $O_{D1} : D, E \longrightarrow Boolean$
  op $O_{D2} : D, D, D \longrightarrow Boolean$
  op $O_{C0} : R, Unit \longrightarrow Boolean$
  op $O_{C1} : R, E \longrightarrow Boolean$
  op $O_{C2} : R, R, R \longrightarrow Boolean$
  axiom $p_0(X) \rightarrow O_{D0}(X, \langle \rangle)$
  axiom $p_1(X) \rightarrow \exists M : E . O_{D1}(X, M)$
  axiom $p_2(X) \rightarrow \exists X_1, X_2 : D . O_{D2}(X, X_1, X_2) \wedge X_1 \prec X \wedge X_2 \prec X$
  axiom $O_{D0}(X, \langle \rangle) \wedge O_{C0}(Y, \langle \rangle) \rightarrow O(X, Y)$
  axiom $O_{D1}(X, M) \wedge O_{C1}(Y, M) \rightarrow O(X, Y)$
  axiom $O_{D2}(X, X_1, X_2) \wedge O(X_1, Y_1) \wedge O(X_2, Y_2) \wedge O_{C2}(Y, Y_1, Y_2) \rightarrow O(X, Y)$
  axiom $p_0(X)$ *xor* $p_1(X)$ *xor* $p_2(X)$
end

Fig. 5. Specification of problems that have divide-and-conquer programs

and the corresponding complex composition operators are inferred, or a set of simple standard composition operators is reused and the corresponding complex decomposition operators are inferred. Following the first approach, the bag constructor set $\{emptyBag, singletonBag, bagUnion\}$ could be reused as the basis for decomposition, giving rise to $\{\ldots, p_0 \mapsto emptyBag?, O_{D0} \mapsto \lambda X . X = emptyBag, p_1 \mapsto singletonBag?, O_{D1} \mapsto \lambda X, M . X = singletonBag(M), p_2 \mapsto nonSingletonBag?, O_{D2} \mapsto \lambda X, X_1, X_2 . X = bagUnion(X_1, X_2), \ldots\}$. By deductive inference, the remaining part of the morphism can be obtained, yielding translations to empty sequence construction, singleton sequence construction, and sequence merging for O_{C0}, O_{C1}, and O_{C2}, respectively, ultimately leading thus to a merge-sort algorithm. Under the second approach, the sequence constructor set $\{emptySeq, singletonSeq, seqConcat\}$ could be reused as the basis for composition, ultimately leading to a quick-sort algorithm.

Either way, after calculating the push-out, synthesis could continue by using the $BAG \Rightarrow BAGasSEQ$ datatype refinement, followed by simplification refinements, etc, progressively bringing the specification closer to a programming level, until a code-generating inter-logic morphism for translating the definition of F into a functional program can be applied.

spec *DivConqScheme* is
  import *DivConq*
  op C_0 : $\longrightarrow R$
  axiom $O_{C0}(C_0, \langle\rangle)$
  op C_1 : $E \longrightarrow R$
  axiom $O_{C1}(C_1(M), M)$
  op C_2 : $R, R \longrightarrow R$
  axiom $O_{C2}(C_2(X_1, X_2), X_1, X_2)$
  definition of F is
    axiom $p_0(X) \rightarrow O_{D0}(X, \langle\rangle) \wedge F(X) = C_0$
    axiom $p_1(X) \rightarrow \exists M : E . O_{D1}(X, M) \wedge F(X) = C_1(M)$
    axiom $p_2(X) \rightarrow \exists X_1, X_2 : D . O_{D2}(X, X_1, X_2) \wedge F(X) = C_2(F(X_1), F(X_2))$
  end
  theorem $O(X, F(X))$
end

Fig. 6. Specification of divide-and-conquer programs

3.2   Other Schools

Transformational synthesis is by far the dominant approach to program synthesis, and many dozens of projects have been devoted to it, so I can here only mention the seminal and dominant ones.

At the University of Edinburgh (UK), Burstall & Darlington [22,25] proposed a small, fixed set of domain-independent, low-granularity, and rather optimisation-oriented transforms (namely folding, unfolding, definition, instantiation, and abstraction) for the synthesis and transformation of recursion equations. Laws of the application domain can also be used. They presented a strategy and a semi-automated system for transforming recursive equations, say into tail-recursive ones, with the user making the creative decisions. For synthesis, the objective of applying such transforms often is to construct, through unfolding and other rewriting, a description where recursion may be introduced through folding. The atomic transforms are proven to constitute a correct set for exploring the candidate program space.

At Stanford University (California, USA), at the same time, but independently, Manna & Waldinger [63] discovered the same atomic rules and automatically synthesised LISP programs with their *DEDuctive ALgorithm Ur-Synthesiser* (DEDALUS). The system has over 100 rules, and also generates correctness and termination proofs. See Section 4.1 for a detailed discussion of a redesign of DEDALUS as a constructive synthesiser.

In the UK, much of the early efforts on the synthesis of logic programs were conducted, based on the foundational fold/unfold work mentioned above. Under a first approach, Clark *et al.* [23] execute the specification with symbolic values that cover all possible forms of the type of the chosen induction parameter. For instance, if that parameter is a list, then the empty and non-empty lists are considered. A similar approach was taken by Hogger [49], though with slight differences. Induction on some parameter was only introduced as the need arises. A highly structured top-down strategy for applying folding and unfolding, guided by a recursion schema provided by the specifier, as well as the notion of specification framework for synthesis, were proposed by Lau *et al.* [55,56]. This approach is amenable to mechanisation. Specification frameworks enabled a first-order logic reconstruction of KIDS-like schema-guided synthesis [36,35,38].

Several researchers tried to make synthesis a deterministic process, akin to compilation. For instance, implication formulas with arbitrary bodies may be normalised into normal clauses by the Lloyd-Topor translation [59]. However, this does not always yield useful logic programs, due to the deficiencies of SLDNF resolution, such as floundering. Also, the obtained programs are sometimes hopelessly inefficient. Overcoming these flaws is the objective of program transformation. Another approach was taken by Sato & Tamaki's first-order compiler [77], whose synthesis of partially correct definite programs is fully automatic and deterministic, but may fail, for lack of logical power.

At TU Munich and TU Darmstadt (Germany), Bibel leads synthesis projects since 1974. Their LOPS (*LOgical Program Synthesis*) system [8,9,10], although presented as being a constructive synthesiser, was actually transformational. Synthesis consisted of a four-phased application of heuristics that control special transformations. A novel feature is the breaking of inputs into parts so as to discover in what way they contribute to the construction of the outputs; in this way, loops can be discovered without the need for recursively-expressed background axioms, which would be essentially identical to the synthesised programs. The current MAPS project [11] takes a multi-level approach to synthesis, and is essentially a re-implementation of KIDS within NuPRL, but without optimising transformations yet.

At Stanford University (California, USA), the PSI project led by Green [45] included the transformational engine PECOS [4], which is based on a large, fixed catalog of domain-specific transforms. Cooperation with an efficiency expert, called LIBRA [52], ensured efficient synthesis of efficient programs. A successor system, called CHI [46], was partly developed at Kestrel Institute.

At the University of Southern California (USA), the 15-year-project SAFE/TI (*Specification Acquisition From Experts*, and *Transformational Implementation*) headed by Balzer [2] provided a fixed catalog of domain-specific transforms for refining specifications within the wide-spectrum language GIST, via a knowledge-based approach. Automation issues were tackled by the GLITTER sub-system [31].

At TU Munich (Germany), the long-term CIP (*Computer-aided Intuition-guided Programming*) project of Bauer and co-workers [6,72] led, since 1975, to the wide-spectrum algebraic specification language CIP-L and the interactive environment CIP-S. The main emphasis was on a user-extensible catalog of transforms, starting from a small set of generative rules.

The *Vienna Development Method* (VDM) by Bjørner & Jones [17] is an ISO-standardised comprehensive software development methodology, proceeding by refinement from formal specifications of abstract datatypes in the META-IV wide-spectrum language. Many tools are available, from different sources, but they are not integrated. See www.csr.ncl.ac.uk/vdm for more details.

From Oxford University (UK) comes Z [85], a very successful and soon-to-be-ISO-standardised notation for formal specifications, based on set theory. There is third-party tool support, though not integrated, on top of the HOL theorem prover. Award-winning applications include the IBM CICS project and a specification of the IEEE standard for floating-point arithmetic. See www.afm.sbu.ac.uk/z.

The B formal method was developed by Abrial [1]. A first-order logic specification language with sets is provided to specify and refine systems that are modelled as abstract machines. Tool support for refinement and discharging many of its proof obligations exists. See www.afm.sbu.ac.uk/b.

At the University of California at San Diego (USA), the OBJ language family of Goguen and his team [40] provides wide-spectrum algebraic languages, based on order-sorted equational logic, possibly enriched with other logics. Tool support for refinement exists. See www.cs.ucsd.edu/users/goguen/sys/obj.html.

At the Universities of Edinburgh (UK) and Warsaw (Poland), Sannella & Tarlecki [78] propose EXTENDEDML as a wide-spectrum language for specification and formal development of STANDARDML programs, through refinement. See www.dcs.ed.ac.uk/home/dts/eml.

4 Achievements of Constructive Synthesis

Constructive synthesis — also known as *proofs-as-programs synthesis*, and, a bit misleadingly, as *deductive synthesis* — is based on the *Curry-Howard isomorphism* [50], which says that there is a one-to-one relationship between a constructive proof [7,68] of an existence theorem and a program that computes witnesses of the existentially quantified variables of the theorem. Indeed, the use of induction in proofs corresponds to the use of recursive or iterative composition in programs, while case analysis corresponds to a conditional composition, and lemma invocation to a procedure call.

Assume given a logic specification of the following form:

$$\forall X . \ \exists Y . \ pre(X) \rightarrow post(X, Y) \tag{1}$$

where *pre* is the pre-condition (an assertion on the input parameters X, assumed to hold when execution of the program starts), and *post* is the post-condition (an assertion on X and the output parameters Y, to be established after execution of the program). Note that this specification form naturally leads to the synthesis of total functions, but not of relations. A solution to this is to view relations as functions into Booleans [20]. Constructive synthesis proceeds in two steps:

1. Constructively *prove* the satisfiability of the specification.
2. *Obtain* the procedure, embodied in the proof, of realising the specification.

For the second step, there are two approaches:

- The *interpretative* approach directly interprets the proof as a program, by means of an operational semantics defined on proofs.

– The *extractive* approach mechanically extracts — or: compiles — a program, in a given target language, from the proof.

The two approaches have complementary advantages and drawbacks: interpretation is not as efficient as the execution of a compiled version, but the choice of a target language might obscure computational properties of proofs.

The idea of exploiting constructive proofs as programs is actually way older than its naming as the Curry-Howard isomorphism in 1980: the idea is inherent to intuitionistic logic — see the work of Kleene in the 1940s — and the oldest synthesisers of this approach are QA3 (*Question-Answering system*) by Green [44], and PROW (*PROgram Writer*) by Waldinger & Lee [90], both from the late 1960s. The terminology 'proofs-as-programs' seems to have been coined by Constable in the early 1970s, according to [5].

The bottleneck is of course the state-of-the-art in automated theorem proving (ATP). In essence, the hard problem of synthesis has been translated into the other hard — if not harder! — problem of ATP. The proof space for most conjectures is indeed intractable, and formal specifications tend to be quite complex conjectures. Solutions are thus being worked out to control the navigation through this search space, namely synthesisers with reuse, interactive provers, tactical provers, etc.

I here discuss two representative constructive synthesisers, chosen due to their interesting relationship to each other. Indeed, AMPHION (see Section 4.2) can be seen as an outgrowth of DEDALUS (see Section 4.1), with the objective of scaling the technology to real-life software development tasks, and this was the decisive criterion in my selection. In Section 4.3, I outline the efforts of the other main research centres in constructive synthesis.

4.1   DEDALUS

The *DEDuctive ALgorithm Ur-Synthesiser* (DEDALUS) system of Manna & Waldinger (at Stanford and SRI, California, USA) was originally developed as a transformational synthesiser [63] (see Section 3.2), and then re-designed within the proofs-as-programs paradigm, in a considerably more elegant manner [64,67].

The inputs to synthesis are a formal axiomatic first-order logic specification, assumed to be consistent and complete wrt the requirements, as well as a domain theory. The synthesis mechanism is purely deductive and fully automatable, but an interactive interface with user guidance exists. Only application domain knowledge is exploited. Synthesis is non-deterministic and sound. The outputs of synthesis are a side-effect-free applicative program, as well as implicitly a proof of its correctness and termination.

The Proof System. Constructive logics are not necessarily required for *all* of a constructive synthesis. Indeed, many derivation steps during synthesis actually are only verification steps, and need thus not be constructive at all. Classical logic is thus sufficient, provided it is sufficiently constructive when needed.

Their deductive tableau proof system was developed especially for proofs-as-program synthesis. A *deductive tableau* is a two-dimensional structure, where each row is a *sentence* of the form $\langle a, -, o \rangle$ or $\langle -, g, o \rangle$, where a is an *assertion* and g a *goal*, both in classical first-order logic, while o is an optional *output term* in LISP. The symbol '$-$' denotes the absence of an entry in that column, and is equivalent to *true* for assertions, *false* for goals, and any new variable for output terms. For simplicity, I assume there is only one output parameter in specifications. For instance,

$$\langle -, M \in S \wedge (\forall X . X \in S \rightarrow M \leq X), M \rangle$$

is a sentence capturing a pre-condition-free specification of the $minimum(S)$ function, which returns the minimum element M of integer-set S.

The semantics of a sentence $\langle a, g, o \rangle$, in an interpretation $\mathcal{I}$, is the set of closed terms t that, for some substitution θ, are equal to instance $o\theta$ of the output term, if any, and either the instance $a\theta$ of the assertion, if any, is closed and false or the instance $g\theta$ of the goal, if any, is closed and true, in $\mathcal{I}$.

The semantics of a tableau is the union of the semantics of its sentences. There is thus an implicit conjunction between the assertions of a tableau, and an implicit disjunction between its goals. Note the dual role of assertions and goals: a formula can be transferred between the assertions and goals columns by negating it. Nevertheless, the distinction between assertions and goals provides intuitive and strategic power, and is thus kept.

A set of deduction rules is provided to add new sentences to a tableau, not necessarily in an equivalent way, but at least preserving the set of *computable expressions* (which are quantifier-free expressions in terms of the basic functions of the theory, plus the functions for which programs have already been synthesised, including the function for which a program is currently being synthesised, as this enables recursion formation). Hence the program denoted by a tableau remains unchanged through application of these rules. Each user-provided new rule needs to be first proven *sound* according to this precept.

A *deduction rule* has a set of *required sentences* in the old tableau, representing the applicability condition of the rule, and a set of *generated sentences* in the new tableau, representing the difference between the old and new tableaus.

For instance, the *if-split* rule breaks required sentence $\langle -, \text{if } a \text{ then } g, t \rangle$ into the generated sentences $\langle a, -, t \rangle$ and $\langle -, g, t \rangle$. There are dual splitting rules.

Conditional output terms are normally introduced by four non-clausal resolution rules, reflecting case analysis in informal proofs. For instance, the *goal-goal resolution* rule is as follows:

$$\frac{\langle -, g_1[p], s \rangle \qquad \langle -, g_2[q], t \rangle}{\langle -, g_1\theta[false] \wedge g_2\theta[true], \text{if } p\theta \text{ then } t\theta \text{ else } s\theta \rangle} \quad (GG)$$

where, assuming the required sentences are standardised apart, θ is the most-general unifier for formulas p and q. See below for an example. Similarly, there are the dual *assertion-assertion* (AA), *goal-assertion* (GA), and *assertion-goal* (AG) resolution rules.

There are also rules for *equivalence* (replacing a formula by an equivalent one), theory-independent *equality* (replacing a term by an equal one, using a non-clausal version of paramodulation), *skolemisation* (eliminating existential quantifiers), and *well-founded induction* (allowing formation of terminating recursion in the output term, when the induction hypothesis is actually used).

The Synthesis Process. Synthesis goes as follows, starting from a specification of the form (1), for a function f, in a theory $\mathcal{T}$:

1. Form the initial tableau, with the sentence $\langle -, pre(X) \rightarrow post(X,Y), Y \rangle$ built from the specification, and assertion-only sentences for the axioms of $\mathcal{T}$. Add f to the set of functions of $\mathcal{T}$ and those already synthesised in $\mathcal{T}$.
2. Apply deduction rules to add new sentences to the tableau.
3. Stop with the final tableau when a sentence of the form $\langle false, -, t \rangle$ or $\langle -, true, t \rangle$ appears, where t is a computable expression.

The extracted program then is the function definition $f(X) = t[X]$. It is *correct* wrt specification (1) in the sense that the formula $\forall X . pre(X) \rightarrow post(X, f(X))$ is valid in theory $\mathcal{T}$ augmented with the axiom $\forall X . f(X) = t[X]$. The program is also guaranteed to terminate.

Equivalence-preserving simplification of sentences is automatically performed, as a terminating rewrite process, before synthesis starts and after application of any deduction rule. There are theory-independent logical simplifications, such as replacing formula $a \wedge a$ by a, and theory-specific simplifications, such as replacing integer expression $n + 0$ by n.

The resolution rules have a symmetric nature. For instance, applying the AG rule to an assertion a and a goal g could be replaced by applying the GA rule to g and a. However, typically, one of the two symmetric applications will not advance the proof. The *polarity search control strategy* (not explained here) tries to prevent such unsuitable applications of the resolution rules, and always does so without lengthening the proof nor compromising the completion of the proof.

Two issues around recursion formation deserve discussion. First, there are mechanisms for constructing new well-founded relations (wfr) from old ones, for use in application of the induction rule. However, this makes the wfr search space rather large, and, worse, it is usually difficult to choose in advance the most suitable wfr, which only becomes apparent several steps later. To overcome this, *middle-out reasoning* (originally explored in [48,54]) is performed, here replacing the required wfr by a variable, so as to wait until its desired properties become apparent. Second, there is a *recurrence search control strategy* that tries to match goals and sub-goals so as to form recursion.

Specification-based reuse of existing programs within a theory $\mathcal{T}$ — such as, but not exclusively, already synthesised programs — becomes possible through the addition of formulas of the form $\forall X . pre(X) \rightarrow post(X, f(X))$ to the axioms of $\mathcal{T}$, when starting a new synthesis.

Finally, it is worth stating that the deduction rules are powerful enough to also perform program transformation.

A Sample Synthesis. Rather than showing a full synthesis for a toy function, where the final program is virtually identical to the specification or to some of the necessary axioms in the theory, I decided to exhibit an interesting passage from a more difficult synthesis [66], highlighting the power of the resolution rules.

Consider the specification of a function returning the square-root R of a non-negative rational number N, within a positive rational tolerance ϵ:

$$\epsilon > 0 \rightarrow R^2 \leq N \wedge N < (R + \epsilon)^2$$

within a theory $\mathcal{R}$ for non-negative rationals, including addition $(+)$, squaring (x^2), inequalities $(<, >, \leq, \geq)$, etc.

Suppose synthesis leads to a tableau with the following sentence, after an *if-split* in the initial sentence built from the specification, and after application of the equivalence rule $a < b \leftrightarrow \neg(b \leq a)$:

$$\langle -, R^2 \leq N \wedge \neg \boxed{(R + \epsilon)^2 \leq N}, R \rangle \qquad (2)$$

Let us apply resolution rule (GG) to this sentence and the following standardised-apart copy of itself:

$$\langle -, \boxed{S^2 \leq N} \wedge \neg[(S + \epsilon)^2 \leq N], S \rangle$$

The boxed sub-goals unify under most-general substitution $\{S/R + \epsilon\}$, so the generated sentence is:

$$\langle -,$$
$$R^2 \leq N \wedge \neg false \wedge true \wedge \neg[((R + \epsilon) + \epsilon)^2 \leq N],$$
$$\text{if } (R + \epsilon)^2 \leq N \text{ then } R + \epsilon \text{ else } R \rangle$$

which is automatically simplified into:

$$\langle -, R^2 < N \wedge \neg[(R + 2\epsilon)^2 < N], \text{if } (R + \epsilon)^2 \leq N \text{ then } R + \epsilon \text{ else } R \rangle \qquad (3)$$

Whereas (2) expresses that the square-root of N is in the half-open interval $[R..R + \epsilon[$, in which case R is a suitable output, sentence (3) expresses that the square-root of N is in the wider half-open interval $[R..R + 2\epsilon[$, in which case conditional term 'if $(R + \epsilon)^2 \leq N$ then $R + \epsilon$ else R' is a suitable output. Noting that $R + \epsilon$ is the midpoint of that wider interval, sentence (3) simply says that if a square-root is known to be in wide interval $[R..R + 2\epsilon[$, then it is the first element of either its right half or its left half. In other words, sentence (3) provides an idea for a binary search program, whereas sentence (2) does not. This is very interesting, as this discovery can thus be made mechanically, by a simple application of a resolution rule.

Using DEDALUS, rather intricate programs were synthesised, such as unification [65], as well as interesting new ones [66].

4.2   AMPHION

AMPHION [88] (ase.arc.nasa.gov/docs/amphion.html) was developed by Lowry and his team at NASA Ames and SRI (California, USA). It is of particular interest due to its attention to real-life software engineering considerations, and because it is actually deployed at NASA JPL.

The inputs to synthesis are a formal axiomatic first-order logic specification, assumed to be consistent and complete wrt the requirements, as well as a domain theory. The novelty is that specifications can be conveyed through a menu-driven, domain-independent graphical user-interface. The synthesis mechanism is purely deductive, fully automatic, non-deterministic (though there is no practical difference between alternate programs), and sound. Only application domain knowledge is exploited. The output of synthesis is a side-effect-free applicative program, which can be automatically translated into any other currently supported language (e.g., FORTRAN-77).

The Proof System. The proof system of AMPHION is essentially the deductive tableau system of DEDALUS (see Section 4.1). The automated theorem prover SNARK (*SRI's New Automated Reasoning Kit*) of Stickel and his colleagues was chosen to carry out the proofs. Its initial lack of an induction rule was unproblematic, as discussed below.

The Synthesis Process. AMPHION is domain-independent, but was first deployed in the domain of interplanetary mission planning and data analysis. An axiomatic theory, called NAIF, was formalised for this domain, comprising basic properties of solar-system astronomy as well as formal specifications of the reusable routines of a solar-system kinematics library, developed in FORTRAN-77 at NASA JPL. Synthesised programs in the resulting AMPHION/NAIF are therefore compiled into FORTRAN-77. The options in the graphical user-interface for capturing specifications also depend on the provided domain theory.

Library routines are often difficult to reuse, because of the time needed to master their sheer number, if not because of inadequate specifications, and because competent library consultants may be in short supply. Reluctant or careless programmers may thus well duplicate functionality in the library, thereby losing time and being at the risk of errors. Automated support for correct reuse and composition of library routines would thus come in very handy. But this is precisely what a DEDALUS-like system such as AMPHION can achieve, because reuse is supported, as we have seen in the previous section. Synthesis need thus not bottom out in the primitives of the target language.

Another practical insight concerns the choice of the composition mechanisms — such as conditions and recursion — used during synthesis. Although constructive synthesis can generate them all, recursion formation is by far the most difficult composition. If sufficiently many library routines performing sophisticated calculations are provided, then synthesis need not really "lift" recursion from them but may rather amount to generating an adequate straight-line program — with just sequential and conditional composition — from the specification. AMPHION was designed to synthesise only straight-line code, on the assumption that not too sophisticated proofs would be performed in theories with a large number of axioms. Synthesis is then not bottlenecked by recursion formation.

The synthesised programs can be optimised using the transforms of KIDS (see Section 3.1). Heuristic considerations need to be dealt with when finetuning the domain theory. For instance, a suitable recursive-path ordering and a suitable agenda-ordering function have to be supplied. Also, heuristics, such as the set-of-support strategy, may turn out very beneficial to the prover.

METAAMPHION [62] is a synthesiser synthesiser (*sic*) assisting domain experts in the creation and maintenance of a new instance of AMPHION, starting from a domain theory, and this without requiring any substantial training in deductive inference. This is done by applying AMPHION at the meta-level.

A Sample Synthesis. Considering the scale of synthesis tasks that can be handled by AMPHION, I can here only point to the two on-line sample syntheses at ase.arc.nasa.gov/docs/amphion-naif.html. One of them computes the solar incidence angle at the point on Jupiter pointed to by a camera on the Galileo sonde. A NAIF expert could construct such a program within half an hour, but may not be available to do so. However, after a one-hour tutorial, non-programmer planetary scientists can specify such problems within a few minutes, and synthesis of a correct program usually takes less than three minutes. The synthesised programs are indeed mostly straight-line code, which would however have been quite hard to program for non NAIF-experts.

Other results are the Saturn viewer, developed for use during the time Saturn's ring plane crossed the Earth, or an animation visualising Saturn and its moon Titan as seen from the Cassini sonde on its fly-by, with stars in the background. The latter helped planetary scientists evaluate whether proposed tours of Cassini could satisfy their observational requirements.

4.3   Other Schools

A large number of additional constructive synthesis projects exist, so I can here only skim over the most seminal and important ones.

At Cornell University (New York, USA), Constable and his group designed the PRL [5] and NUPRL [24] interactive proof and functional program development systems, the latter being based on the intuitionistic second-order type theory of Martin-Löf [68].

At the University of Edinburgh (UK), NUPRL was used for the synthesis of deterministic logic programs by Bundy and his team [19]. A first-order subset of the OYSTER proof development system, which is a re-implementation of NUPRL in PROLOG, was also used for logic program synthesis, with special focus on the synthesis of programs that compute relations, and not just total functions. A proof-planner called CLAM was adjoined to OYSTER [21], making it a tactical prover, using Edinburgh LCF [42], which is based on Scott's Logic for Computable Functions. The overall effort also resulted in the WHELK proof development system [91], which performs proofs in the Gentzen sequent calculus and extracts logic programs, the PERIWINKLE synthesiser [54], which systematises the use of middle-out reasoning in logic program synthesis, and many other systems, as the group spawns around the world.

At Uppsala University (Sweden), the logic programming calculus of Tärnlund [89], based on Prawitz' natural deduction system for intuitionistic logic, provided an elegant unified framework for logic program synthesis, verification, transformation, and execution. His team showed how to extract logic programs from constructive proofs performed within this calculus [47], and synthesised a unification algorithm [29], among others.

The INRIA (France) group uses Coquand & Huet's calculus of inductive constructions (COQ), and the Chalmers (Sweden) group exploits Martin-Löf's type theory, both towards the synthesis of functional programs. Their results are compiled in [71,51], for instance.

5   Achievements of Mixed-Inference Synthesis

Considering that human programmers rarely resort to only safe reasoning — such as deductive inference — it would be unwise to focus all synthesis research on only deduction-based mechanisms. Indeed, a growing importance needs to be given to so-called unsafe reasoning — such as inductive, abductive, or analogical inference — if we want synthesis to cope with the full range of human software development activities.

I here discuss one representative mixed-inference synthesiser, namely MULTI-TAC (see Section 5.1), which performs both deductive and inductive inference. In Section 5.2, I outline the efforts of the other main research centres in mixed-inference synthesis.

5.1   MULTI-TAC

MULTI-TAC, the *Multi-Tactic Analytic Compiler* [69] of Minton, who was then at NASA Ames (California, USA), automatically synthesises efficient problem-specific solvers for *constraint satisfaction problems* (CSPs), such that they perform on par with solvers hand-written by competent programmers. While the ability of human experts remains elusive, the results are very encouraging, and popular general-purpose solvers are almost systematically outperformed.

This is so because there is no universally best solver for all CSPs, and, worse, that there is not even a best solver for all instances of a given CSP. Today, the programming of an efficient solver for any instance of some CSP is still considered a black art. Indeed, a CSP *solver* essentially consists of three components, namely a *search algorithm* (such as backtracking search, with or without forward checking), *constraint propagation and pruning rules* (based on consistency techniques, such as node and arc consistency), as well as *variable and value ordering heuristics* (such as most-constrained-variable-first or least-constraining-value-first), with each of these components having a lot of recognised problem-independent incarnations, each of which usually has many problem-specific instantiations. The right combination of components for a given instance of a CSP lies thus in a huge solver space, often at an unintuitive place, and human programmers rarely have the inclination or patience to experiment with many alternatives. On the premise that synthesis time does not matter, say because the

```
procedure solve(FreeVars) :
begin
  if FreeVars = ∅ then return the solution;
  Var ← bestVar(FreeVars, VarOrdRules);
  FreeVars ← FreeVars − {Var};
  PossVals ← possVals(Var, PruneRules);
  while PossVals ≠ ∅ do begin
    Val ← bestVal(Var, PossVals, ValOrdRules);
    PossVals ← PossVals − {Val};
    if fwdChecking = true or Constraints on Var are satisfied by Val
    then begin
      assign(Var, Val);
      if fwdChecking = true then updatePossVals(FreeVars, Constraints);
      if solve(FreeVars) then return the solution;
      if fwdChecking = true then restorePossVals(FreeVars);
      prune(Var, PossVals, PruneRules)
    end;
  end;
  unassign(Var, Val);
  fail
end
```

Fig. 7. Schema for backtracking search

synthesised program will be run many times for different instances, MULTI-TAC undertakes a more systematic exploration of this solver space.

The inputs to synthesis are a formal first-order sorted logic specification of a CSP, assumed to be consistent and complete wrt the requirements, as well as a set of training instances (or an instance generator) reflecting the distribution — in terms of the number of domain variables and the number of constraints between them — of instances on which the resulting solver will normally be run. In the following, I only mention training instances, abstracting thus whether they are given by the user or generated by the given instance generator. The synthesis mechanism is mixed-inference, performing both inductive and deductive inference, and is fully automatic. Algorithm design and data structure knowledge are exploited. Synthesis is non-deterministic and sound. The output of synthesis is a solver in LISP that is finetuned not only for the problem at hand, but also for the given instance distribution.

The Operationalisation System. MULTI-TAC is a schema-guided synthesiser, with a *schema* being a syntactic program template showing how some search algorithm can be parameterised by the other components of a CSP solver. For instance, the *backtracking schema* for backtracking search is approximately as in Figure 7, with the place-holders typeset in boldface. A full discussion of this schema is beyond the scope of this paper, the important issues being as follows. At each iteration, a chosen "best" value is assigned to a chosen "best" variable, with backtracking occurring when this is impossible without violating some constraint. Also, the template is generic in the constraints, the variable and value ordering rules, the pruning rules, and a flag controlling the use of forward checking. Many well-known variations of backtracking search fit this schema. Branch-and-bound and iterative-repair schemas are also available.

The cornerstone of synthesis is the problem-specific instantiation of the rules of the chosen schema. This is done by *operationalisation* of generic heuristics into rules, as described next. For instance, in problems where a subset of the edges of a given graph is sought, the *most-constrained-variable-first* variable-ordering heuristic — stating that the variable with the fewest possible values left should be chosen next — could be operationalised into at least the following rules:

- Choose the edge with the most adjacent edges.
- Choose the edge with the most adjacent edges whose presence in or absence from the sought subset has already been decided.
- Choose the edge with the most adjacent edges whose absence from the sought subset has already been decided.

Operationalisation is thus non-deterministic. The obtained candidate rules have different application costs in terms of evaluation time and different effectiveness in terms of how much the search is reduced, so a trade-off analysis is needed (see *configuration search* below).

MULTI-TAC features two methods for operationalisation of generic heuristics, as described next.

Analytic operationalisation is based only on the problem constraints and ignores the training instances. Each heuristic is described by a meta-level theory that enables the system to reason about the problem constraints. For instance, the meta-theory of the most-constrained-variable-first heuristic describes circumstances where some variable is likely to be more constrained than another one. A good example thereof is that the tightness of the generic constraint $\forall X : S . \ P(X) \rightarrow Q(X)$ is directly related to the cardinality of the set $\{X : S \mid P(X)\}$. From such algorithm design knowledge, candidate search control rules can be inferred.

Inductive operationalisation is based mainly on the training instances, though also uses the problem constraints. Brute-force simplest-first inductive inference is achieved through a generate-and-test algorithm. First, all rules expressible within a given grammar — based on the vocabulary of the problem constraints — are generated, starting with the shortest, that is simplest, rules, until a predetermined upper bound on the number of atoms in the rule is reached, or until a predetermined time bound is reached. The number of rules generated grows exponentially with the size bound, but fortunately the most useful rules tend to be relatively short. The testing step weeds out all the generated rules that do not well approximate the desired effects of the generic heuristics. Towards this, positive and negative examples are inferred from the training instances, and all rules that are more often correct than incorrect on these examples are retained. This is a surprisingly effective criterion.

The analytic method may fail to generate useful short rules, but can infer longer rules. The inductive method often finds excellent short rules, but cannot infer longer rules or may accidentally eliminate a good rule due to the statistical nature of its testing process. The two methods are thus complementary and should be used together to increase the robustness of the system.

The Synthesis Process. Once the generic heuristics have been somehow operationalised into candidate rules, a process called *configuration search* looks for a suitable selection of these rules and for suitable flag values, such that, if plugged into the schema with the problem-specific constraints, they interact nearly optimally in solving instances of the given CSP that fit the given distribution.

Since the space of such possible configurations of rules and flags is exponential in the number of rules and flags, a beam search (a form of parallel hill-climbing) is performed over only a small portion of that space. Given a beam width b, a time bound t, and the training instances, one starts from the single parent configuration that has no rules and where all flags are turned off. At each iteration, child configurations are generated from all parent configurations, by adding one rule from the candidate rules or by activating one flag. Several candidate rules may be retained for a given place-holder in the schema, if this is found to be advantageous; they are then sequenced, so that each rule acts as a tie-breaker for its predecessors. The b configurations that solve the most instances within t seconds enter the next iteration as parent configurations, provided they solve a superset of their own parents' instances. This process continues until no parent configuration can be improved or until the user interrupts it.

Operationalisation and configuration search are able to discover rules for many well-known heuristics from the literature, for each search algorithm.

Once the rules and flags of the chosen schema are instantiated — in a problem-specific and instance-distribution-specific way thus — through operationalisation and configuration search, synthesis proceeds by automatically optimising the winning configuration through refinements (including the choice of adequate data structures), formula simplifications, partial evaluation, and code simplifications (including finite differencing).

A Sample Synthesis. Consider the *Minimum-Maximum-Matching* (MMM) problem: given an integer K and a graph with vertex set V and edge set E, determine whether there is a subset $E' \subseteq E$ with $|E'| \leq K$ such that no two edges in E' share a vertex and every edge in $E - E'$ shares a vertex with some edge in E'. This is an NP-complete problem and can be modelled for MULTI-TAC as follows, representing E' as a set of $m(I, B)$ atoms, where Boolean B is t when edge I of E is in E', and f otherwise:

$$\forall V, E : set(term) . \forall K : int . \; mmm(\langle V, E \rangle, K) \leftrightarrow$$
$$\forall I : E . \, m(I, t) \rightarrow (\forall W : V . \forall J : E . \, I \neq J \wedge e(I, W) \wedge e(J, W) \rightarrow m(J, f))$$
$$\wedge \, \forall I : E . \, m(I, f) \rightarrow (\exists W : V . \exists J : E . \, I \neq J \wedge e(I, W) \wedge e(J, W) \wedge m(J, t))$$
$$\wedge \, cardinality(\{I : E \mid m(I, t)\}) \leq K$$

where problem instances are assumed given through a set of $e(I, W)$ atoms, stating that edge I has vertex W as one of its two endpoints.

In the first constraint, there are two sub-expressions matching the generic expression $\forall X : S . \, P(X) \rightarrow Q(X)$ mentioned for analytic operationalisation, namely the two formulas starting with the universal quantifications on W and J, respectively. From the former, the variable-ordering rule 'Choose the edge with the most endpoints' is inferred, though it is useless, as *every* edge has exactly two endpoints; from the latter, the already mentioned rule 'Choose the edge with the most adjacent edges' is inferred. All variable-ordering rules mentioned above can also be generated by inductive operationalisation.

In three well-documented experiments [69] with different instance distributions for the MMM problem, the solvers synthesised by MULTI-TAC outperformed at least one of two written by competent human programmers, while totally outclassing general-purpose Boolean satisfiability algorithms and CSP solvers, under their default heuristics. Interesting rules were discovered, and MULTI-TAC won by the largest margin on the toughest instance distribution, confirming that massive automated search does often better than human intuition.

5.2   Other Schools

The exclusive use of *inductive* and *abductive* inference in program synthesis, from incomplete specifications, has been studied under two angles, for three decades.

First, in *programming-by-example* (PBE), also and more adequately known as *programming-by-demonstration* (PBD), the specifier provides sample execution traces of the task to be programmed, and the synthesiser generalises them into a program that can re-enact at least these traces. The user thus has to know how to perform the specified task, but there are interesting applications for this, such as the synthesis of macro operations for word processors or operating systems. See [58] for a collection of state-of-the-art papers, especially geared at enabling children and other novices to program. Consult Biermann's surveys [12,13] and edited collections [14,15] for details on underlying mechanisms.

Second, in what should be known as PBE, the specifier provides positive and possibly negative input/output examples of the desired program, and the synthesiser generalises them into a program that covers at least these positive examples, but none of the negative examples. The user need thus not know how to perform the specified task, nor even how to completely specify it, and there are useful applications for this, say for novice programmers. The Machine Learning community is looking extensively into such synthesis, especially its Inductive Logic Programming (ILP) branch. Some surveys and edited collections include [14,15,12,13,27,34] or are dedicated to [79,37] the underlying mechanisms.

Considering the difficulty of correctly extrapolating the desired behaviour from such declared-to-be-incomplete specifications, it is not surprising that purely inductive and abductive synthesis has not been shown yet to scale beyond toy problems. The ensuing uncertainty for the specifier cannot be held against inductive and abductive synthesis, because there also is uncertainty in deductive synthesis, due to the difficulty of formalisation of assumed-to-be-complete specifications. Appropriate combinations of inductive, abductive, and deductive inference do however give leverage in synthesis from incomplete specifications [34].

Even when starting from complete specifications, the use of examples and a combination of deductive and inductive inference can still be interesting, if not necessary, as shown for MULTI-TAC (see Section 5.1). Other successful such combinations are reported by Ellman *et al.* [28], with applications to jet engine nozzle and racing yacht design, as well as by Gratch & Chien [43], towards scheduling ground-based radio antennas for maintaining communication with research satellites and deep space probes.

Program synthesis by *analogical* inference was tackled by Dershowitz [26].

6   Prospects of Synthesis

Program synthesis research is as old as the first computer, and a lot of theoretical research and practical development have gone into its various incarnations. Today, we stand at the dawn of a new era in programming, with languages moving away from the von Neumann model, with powerful tools generating significant amounts of tedious low-level code from higher-level descriptions, and with end-users becoming enabled to program by themselves. It is clear that program synthesis, in its traditional Artificial Intelligence understanding, can provide great leaps forward in this arena, in addition to the simpler advances offered by conventional code generation, such as through visual programming, spreadsheets, etc. The challenge is thus to scale up from techniques demonstrated in research labs on toy problems to the development of real-life software and to enable a technology transfer to commercial software development. I here propose challenges and directions for future research, as far as the inputs (Section 6.1), mechanisms (Section 6.2), and outputs (Section 6.3) of synthesis are concerned.

6.1   Synthesis Inputs

Formalisation Assistance. The acceptance bottleneck for synthesisers will always be the input language, in which the specification and domain theory have to be formalised. Most professional programmers and IT students who became somehow used to low-level languages are clearly reluctant to be re-trained in the more advanced mathematics and logic necessary to interact with synthesisers, despite the appeals of working at a higher level. They may well eventually be bypassed and made obsolete by a synthesis-induced revolution in commercial software development under web-speed market pressures, but that is yet an uncertain outcome. At the same time, end-users — from engineers in other disciplines to computer novices — hope to be enabled to program by themselves, and they will also resist the learning curve. Hence *a significant challenge is to assist users in the formalisation of the specification and domain theory.*

PLANWARE and AMPHION can acquire and formalise them automatically from information provided by the specifiers, due to adequate human-computer-interface engineering. The current trend is thus towards *domain-specific languages* that are intuitive to qualified users, if not identical to the notations they already use anyway, thus masking the underlying mathematics and logic. Turing completeness often needs to be sacrificed, so that highly — if not fully — automated synthesisers can be developed. Research in domain analysis is needed, because the acquisition of a suitable domain theory will always be a bottleneck for synthesisers. Domains have to be identified where the payoff threshold is suitable, in terms of the size and importance of the covered problem class, the existence of a language and interface in which it is easy to describe these problems, and the difficulty of manually writing correct and efficient programs for these problems. This does not mean that the previous trends on general-purpose specification languages and semi-automatic synthesisers must decline.

6.2   Synthesis Mechanisms

Reuse. Most synthesisers are demonstrated on toy problems with little bearing to real-world problems. A main cause is that the granularity of their building blocks is too small. *The challenge is to make synthesis bottom out in reusable, assumed-correct components rather than in the primitives of the target language.*

We have seen that some existing synthesis mechanisms were designed so that libraries of formally-specified reusable components can be used during synthesis.

In KIDS/DESIGNWARE, reuse is attempted before synthesis for each specification, whether it is the initial one or one constructed during synthesis. The number of reuse queries can be significantly reduced by applying heuristics detecting that an *ad hoc* component can be trivially built from the specification. This has the further advantage of keeping the index of the component-base lean and thus accelerating reuse queries. It should be noted that the definition schemas used in algorithm design refinements also represent reused code.

In DEDALUS, reuse is possible, but not especially catered for through heuristics. Fischer & Whittle [33] propose a better integration of reuse into DEDALUS-like constructive synthesisers.

In AMPHION, reuse is the leading principle: as there is no induction rule, the mechanism is *forced* to reuse components that embody iterative or recursive calculations, in its synthesis of straight-line code.

Other than for AMPHION-like approaches, the payoff of reuse versus brute-force synthesis is however still unclear. Much research needs thus to be done towards full-scale synthesis in the style of component-based software development, i.e., bottom-up incremental programming. The synthesis of software architectures, for instance, is still a rather unexplored topic.

Schemas. I believe that *an important challenge is to make formalised algorithm design schemas [36,80,81], design patterns [39], plans [31], or clichés [76] continue to play a major role in scaling synthesis up.* Indeed, they allow the reuse of recognised successful product or process skeletons, which have been somehow, and not necessarily formally, proved off-line, once and for all.

Furthermore, they provide a nice division of concerns by focusing, at any given moment, the user's attention and the available options to just one well-delimited part of the current description, as opposed to, say, having to decide which transform to apply to which expression of the *entire* current description. This also enables users to understand intermediate descriptions and the synthesis process at a suitable level of abstraction.

Inference. As MULTI-TAC shows, inductive inference is sometimes necessary to achieve synthesis of efficient programs, but virtually all research — except PBE and PBD — so far has been on purely-deductive synthesis. Just like human programmers perform all kinds of inference, *the challenge is to further explore mixed-inference synthesis, in order to exploit complementary forms of reasoning.*

Similarly, even within deductive inference, there is no single mechanism that can handle all the proof obligations occurring during synthesis, hence *another challenge is to investigate suitable combinations of deductive proof mechanisms,* thereby achieving multi-level synthesis [11].

Finally, it seems that transformational and constructive synthesis are just two facets of a same deductive approach,[3] so that their reconciliation should be worth investigating.

6.3 Synthesis Outputs

Target Language. In order to facilitate the integration of synthesised programs with otherwise developed code modules, it is important that target languages other than the clean-semantics logic languages, that is the functional and relational ones, are supported. This is not a major research challenge, except if efficiency of the code is an issue, but rather a development issue, but it is often neglected in favour of the more attractive research challenges, thereby missing technology transfer and feedback opportunities.

Efficiency. For some problem classes, such as constraint satisfaction problems (CSPs), the efficiency of programs is crucial, such as those solving NP-complete CSPs with high constrainedness. *The challenge is that effective code optimisation must be somehow integrated with a program synthesiser towards its application in real-world circumstances.*

For instance, in constraint programming, a lot of research has been made about how to craft new variable-and-value-ordering heuristics. However, little is said about the application domain of these heuristics, so programmers find it hard to decide when to apply a particular heuristic, especially that there is no universally best heuristic for all CSPs, and not even for all instances of a given CSP (as we saw in Section 5.1). Adequate heuristics are thus problem-and-instance-specific, and must therefore be dynamically chosen at run-time rather than at programming time. It has also been noted that suitable implied constraints and symmetry-breaking constraints may considerably reduce the search space, but few results are available on how to systematise their inference. Overall, effective constraint programming remains a black art thus. *When targeting constraint programming languages, the challenge is to infer implied constraints and symmetry-breaking constraints and to synthesise problem-specific heuristics, if not solvers, that perform well on all problem instances.*

---

[3] At least the developers of DEDALUS, LOPS, and PERIWINKLE reported difficulties in classifying their systems.

7 Conclusion

After introducing the topic and proposing a classification scheme for program synthesis, I have overviewed past and current achievements in synthesis, across three main research directions, with special focus on some of the most promising systems. I have also laid out a set of directions for future research, believing that they will make the technology go beyond the already-reached break-even point, compared to conventional programming and maintenance.

Program synthesis thus promises to revolutionise accepted practice in software development. Ultimately, acceptance problems due to the necessity for rigorous formalisation are bound to disappear, because programming itself is obviously a formalisation process and synthesis just provides other programming languages or different ways of programming. Similarly, the steps of any followed software lifecycle will not really change, because validation and verification will not disappear, but rather become higher-level activities, at the level of what we today call formal specifications.

Acknowledgements

I wish to thank the anonymous referees for their constructive comments on the previous versions of this paper.

References

1. J.-R. Abrial. *The B-Book: Assigning Programs to Meanings*. Cambridge University Press, 1996.
2. R. Balzer. A 15 year perspective on automatic programming. *IEEE TSE* 11(11):1257–1268, 1985.
3. A. Barr and E.A. Feigenbaum. *The Handbook of Artificial Intelligence, Chapter X: Automatic Programming*, pp. 297–379. Morgan Kaufmann, 1982.
4. D.R. Barstow. A perspective on automatic programming. *AI Magazine*, Spring 1984:5–27. Also in [74], pp. 537–559.
5. J.L. Bates and R.L. Constable. Proofs as programs. *ACM TOPLAS* 7(1):113–136, 1985.
6. F.L. Bauer, B. Möller, H. Partsch, and P. Pepper. Formal program construction by transformations: Computer-aided, intuition-guided programming. *IEEE TSE* 15(2):165–180, 1989. Details in LNCS 183/292, Springer-Verlag, 1985/87.
7. M.J. Beeson. *Foundations of Constructive Mathematics*. Modern Surveys in Mathematics, Volume 6. Springer-Verlag, 1985.
8. W. Bibel. Syntax-directed, semantics-supported program synthesis. *AI* 14(3):243–261, 1980.
9. W. Bibel. Concurrent software production. In [61], pp. 243–261. Toward predicative programming. In [61], pp. 405–424.
10. W. Bibel and K.M. Hörnig. LOPS: A system based on a strategic approach to program synthesis. In [15], pp. 69–89.
11. W. Bibel *et al.* A multi-level approach to program synthesis. In N.E. Fuchs (ed), *Proc. of LOPSTR'97*, pp. 1–28. LNCS 1463. Springer-Verlag, 1998.

12. A.W. Biermann. Automatic programming: A tutorial on formal methodologies. *J. of Symbolic Computation* 1(2):119–142, 1985.
13. A.W. Biermann. Automatic programming. In S.C. Shapiro (ed), *Encyclopedia of Artificial Intelligence*, pp. 59–83. John Wiley, 1992.
14. A.W. Biermann and G. Guiho (eds). *Computer Program Synthesis Methodologies*. Volume ASI-C95. D. Reidel, 1983.
15. A.W. Biermann, G. Guiho, and Y. Kodratoff (eds). *Automatic Program Construction Techniques*. Macmillan, 1984.
16. A.W. Biermann and W. Bibel (guest eds), Special Issue on Automatic Programming. *J. of Symbolic Computation* 15(5–6), 1993.
17. C.B. Jones. *Systematic Software Development using* VDM. Prentice-Hall, 1990.
18. L. Blaine, L. Gilham, J. Liu, D.R. Smith, and S. Westfold. PLANWARE: Domain-specific synthesis of high-performance schedulers. In *Proc. of ASE'98*, pp. 270–279. IEEE Computer Society Press, 1998.
19. A. Bundy. A broader interpretation of logic in logic programming. In R.A. Kowalski and K.A. Bowen (eds), *Proc. of ICLP'88*, pp. 1624–1648. The MIT Press, 1988.
20. A. Bundy, A. Smaill, and G. Wiggins. The synthesis of logic programs from inductive proofs. In J.W. Lloyd (ed), *Proc. of the ESPRIT Symp. on Computational Logic*, pp. 135–149. Springer-Verlag, 1990.
21. A. Bundy, F. van Harmelen, C. Horn, A. Smaill. The OYSTER/CLAM system. In M.E. Stickel (ed), *Proc. CADE'90*, pp. 647–648. LNCS 449. Springer-Verlag, 1990.
22. R.M. Burstall and J. Darlington. A transformation system for developing recursive programs. *J. of the ACM* 24(1):44–67, 1977.
23. K.L. Clark and S. Sickel. Predicate logic: A calculus for deriving programs. In *Proc. of IJCAI'77*, pp. 410–411.
24. R.L. Constable, S.F. Allen, H.M. Bromley, *et al. Implementing Mathematics with the* NUPRL *Proof Development System*. Prentice-Hall, 1986.
25. J. Darlington. An experimental program transformation and synthesis system. *AI* 16(1):1–46, 1981. Also in [74], pp. 99–121.
26. N. Dershowitz. *The Evolution of Programs*. Birkhäuser, 1983.
27. Y. Deville and K.-K. Lau. Logic program synthesis. *J. of Logic Programming* 19–20:321–350, 1994.
28. T. Ellman, J. Keane, A. Banerjee, and G. Armhold. A transformation system for interactive reformulation of design optimization strategies. *Research in Engineering Design* 10(1):30–61, 1998.
29. L.-H. Eriksson. Synthesis of a unification algorithm in a logic programming calculus. *J. of Logic Programming* 1(1):3–33, 1984.
30. M.S. Feather. A survey and classification of some program transformation approaches and techniques. In L.G.L.T. Meertens (ed), *Program Specification and Transformation*, pp. 165–195. Elsevier, 1987.
31. S.F. Fickas. Automating the transformational development of software. *IEEE TSE* 11(11):1268–1277, 1985.
32. B. Fischer, J. Schumann, and G. Snelting. Deduction-based software component retrieval. In W. Bibel and P.H. Schmidt (eds), *Automated Deduction: A Basis for Applications*, vol. III, chap. 11. Kluwer, 1998.
33. B. Fischer and J. Whittle. An integration of deductive retrieval into deductive synthesis. In *Proc. of ASE'99*, pp. 52–61. IEEE Computer Society, 1999.
34. P. Flener. *Logic Program Synthesis from Incomplete Information*. Kluwer Academic Publishers, 1995.
35. P. Flener, K.-K. Lau, and M. Ornaghi. Correct-schema-guided synthesis of steadfast programs. In *Proc. of ASE'97*, pp. 153–160. IEEE Computer Society, 1997.

36. P. Flener, K.-K. Lau, M. Ornaghi, and J.D.C. Richardson. An abstract formal-isation of correct schemas for program synthesis. *J. of Symbolic Computation* 30(1):93–127, July 2000.
37. P. Flener and S. Yılmaz. Inductive synthesis of recursive logic programs: Achievements and prospects. *J. of Logic Programming* 41(2–3):141–195, November/December 1999.
38. P. Flener, H. Zidoum, and B. Hnich. Schema-guided synthesis of constraint logic programs. In *Proc. of ASE'98*, pp. 168–176. IEEE Computer Society, 1998.
39. E. Gamma, R. Helm, R. Johnson, and J. Vlissides. *Design Patterns: Elements of Reusable Object-Oriented Software.* Addison-Wesley, 1994.
40. J. Goguen and G. Malcolm. *Algebraic Semantics of Imperative Programs.* The MIT Press, 1997.
41. A.T. Goldberg. Knowledge-based programming: A survey of program design and construction techniques. *IEEE TSE* 12(7):752–768, 1986.
42. M.J. Gordon, A.J. Milner, and C.P. Wadsworth. *Edinburgh LCF – A Mechanised Logic of Computation.* LNCS 78. Springer-Verlag, 1979.
43. J.M. Gratch and S.A. Chien. Adaptive problem-solving for large scale scheduling problems: A case study. *J. of Artificial Intelligence Research* 4:365–396, 1996.
44. C. Green. Application of theorem proving to problem solving. *Proc. of IJCAI'69*, pp. 219–239. Also in B.L. Webber and N.J. Nilsson (eds), *Readings in Artificial Intelligence*, pp. 202–222. Morgan Kaufmann, 1981.
45. C. Green and D.R. Barstow. On program synthesis knowledge. *AI* 10(3):241–270, 1978. Also in [74], pp. 455–474.
46. C. Green and S. Westfold. Knowledge-based programming self applied. *Machine Intelligence* 10, 1982. Also in [74], pp. 259–284.
47. Å. Hansson. *A Formal Development of Programs.* Ph.D. Thesis, Univ. of Stockholm (Sweden), 1980.
48. J. Hesketh, A. Bundy, and A. Smaill. Using middle-out reasoning to control the synthesis of tail-recursive programs. In D. Kapur (ed), *Proc. of CADE'92.* LNCS 606. Springer-Verlag, 1992.
49. C.J. Hogger. Derivation of logic programs. *J. of the ACM* 28(2):372–392, 1981.
50. W.A. Howard. The formulae-as-types notion of construction. In J.P. Seldin and J.R. Hindley (eds), *To H.B. Curry: Essays on Combinatory Logic, Lambda Calculus and Formalism*, pp. 479–490. Academic Press, 1980.
51. G. Huet and G.D. Plotkin (eds). *Logical Frameworks.* Cambridge Univ. Press, 1991.
52. E. Kant. On the efficient synthesis of efficient programs. *AI* 20(3):253–305, 1983. Also in [74], pp. 157–183.
53. R. Kowalski. *Logic for Problem Solving.* North-Holland, 1979.
54. I. Kraan, D. Basin, and A. Bundy. Middle-out reasoning for synthesis and induc-tion. *J. of Automated Reasoning* 16(1–2):113–145, 1996.
55. K.-K. Lau and S.D. Prestwich. Synthesis of a family of recursive sorting procedures. In V. Saraswat and K. Ueda (eds), *Proc. ILPS'91*, pp. 641–658. MIT Press, 1991.
56. K.-K. Lau and M. Ornaghi. On specification frameworks and deductive synthesis of logic programs. In L. Fribourg and F. Turini (eds), *Proc. of LOPSTR'94 and META'94*, pp. 104–121. LNCS 883. Springer-Verlag, 1994.
57. B. Le Charlier and P. Flener. Specifications are necessarily informal, or: Some more myths of formal methods. *J. of Systems and Software* 40(3):275–296, 1998.
58. H. Liebermann (guest ed), Special Section on Programming by Example. *Comm. of the ACM* 43(3):72–114, 2000.
59. J.W. Lloyd. *Foundations of Logic Programming.* Springer-Verlag, 1987.

60. M.R. Lowry and R. Duran. Knowledge-based software engineering. In A. Barr, P.R. Cohen, and E.A. Feigenbaum (eds), *The Handbook of Artificial Intelligence.* Volume IV, pp. 241–322. Addison-Wesley, 1989.

61. M.R. Lowry and R.D. McCartney (eds). *Automating Software Design.* The MIT Press, 1991.

62. M.R. Lowry, J. Van Baalen. METAAMPHION: Synthesis of efficient domain-specific program synthesis systems. *Automated Software Engineering* 4:199–241, 1997.

63. Z. Manna and R.J. Waldinger. Synthesis: Dreams → Programs. *IEEE TSE* 5(4):294–328, 1979.

64. Z. Manna and R.J. Waldinger. A deductive approach to program synthesis. *ACM TOPLAS* 2(1):90–121, 1980. Also in [15], pp. 33–68. Also in [74], pp. 3–34.

65. Z. Manna and R.J. Waldinger. Deductive synthesis of the unification algorithm. *Science of Computer Programming* 1:5–48, 1981. Also in [14], pp. 251–307.

66. Z. Manna and R.J. Waldinger. The origin of a binary-search paradigm. *Science of Computer Programming* 9:37–83, 1987.

67. Z. Manna and R.J. Waldinger. Fundamentals of deductive program synthesis. *IEEE TSE* 18(8):674–704, 1992.

68. P. Martin-Löf. Constructive mathematics and computer programming. In *Proc. of the 1979 Int'l Congress for Logic, Methodology, and Philosophy of Science*, pp. 153–175. North-Holland, 1982.

69. S. Minton. Automatically configuring constraint satisfaction programs: A case study. *Constraints* 1(1–2):7–43, 1996.

70. J. Mostow (guest ed), Special Issue on AI and Software Engineering. *IEEE TSE* 11(11), 1985.

71. B. Nordström, K. Petersson, and J.M. Smith. *Programming in Martin-Löf's Type Theory: An Introduction.* Clarendon Press, 1990.

72. H.A. Partsch. *Specification and Transformation of Programs.* Springer-Verlag, 1990.

73. H.A. Partsch and R. Steinbrüggen. Program transformation systems. *Computing Surveys* 15(3):199–236, 1983.

74. C. Rich and R.C. Waters (eds). *Readings in Artificial Intelligence and Software Engineering.* Morgan Kaufmann, 1986.

75. C. Rich and R.C. Waters. Automatic programming: Myths and prospects. *IEEE Computer* 21(8):40–51, 1988.

76. C. Rich and R.C. Waters. The Programmer's Apprentice: A research overview. *IEEE Computer* 21(11):10–25, 1988.

77. T. Sato and H. Tamaki. First-order compiler: A deterministic logic program synthesis algorithm. *J. of Symbolic Computation* 8(6):605–627, 1989.

78. D. Sannella and A. Tarlecki. Essential concepts of algebraic specification and program development. *Formal Aspects of Computing* 9:229–269, 1997.

79. D.R. Smith. The synthesis of LISP programs from examples: A survey. In [15], pp. 307–324.

80. D.R. Smith. Top-down synthesis of divide-and-conquer algorithms. *AI* 27(1):43–96, 1985.

81. D.R. Smith. KIDS: A semiautomatic program development system. *IEEE TSE* 16(9):1024–1043, 1990.

82. D.R. Smith. Towards the synthesis of constraint propagation algorithms. In Y. Deville (ed), *Proc. of LOPSTR'93*, pp. 1–9, Springer-Verlag, 1994.

83. D.R. Smith. Constructing specification morphisms. *J. of Symbolic Computation* 15(5–6):571–606, 1993.

84. D.R. Smith. Toward a classification approach to design. *Proc. of AMAST'96*, pp. 62–84. LNCS 1101. Springer-Verlag, 1996.
85. J.M. Spivey. *The z Notation: A reference manual.* Prentice-Hall, 1992.
86. Y.V. Srinivas and R. Jüllig. SPECWARE: Formal support for composing software. In B. Möller (ed), *Proc. of MPC'95*, pp. 399–422. LNCS 947. Springer-Verlag, 1995.
87. D.M. Steier and A.P. Anderson. *Algorithm Synthesis: A Comparative Study.* Springer-Verlag, 1989.
88. M. Stickel, R. Waldinger, M. Lowry, T. Pressburger, and I. Underwood. Deductive composition of astronomical software from subroutine libraries. In A. Bundy (ed), *Proc. of CADE'94*, pp. 341–355. LNCS 814. Springer-Verlag, 1994.
89. S.-Å. Tärnlund. An axiomatic data base theory. In H. Gallaire and J. Minker (eds), *Logic and Databases*, pp. 259–289. Plenum Press, 1978.
90. R.J. Waldinger and R.C.T. Lee. PROW: A step toward automatic program writing. *Proc. of IJCAI'69*, pp. 241–252.
91. G. Wiggins. Synthesis and transformation of logic programs in the WHELK proof development system. In K. Apt (ed), *Proc. of the JICSLP'92*, pp. 351–365. The MIT Press, 1992.

Logic for Component-Based
Software Development

Kung-Kiu Lau[1] and Mario Ornaghi[2]

[1] Department of Computer Science, University of Manchester
Manchester M13 9PL, United Kingdom
kung-kiu@cs.man.ac.uk
[2] Dipartimento di Scienze dell'Informazione, Universita' degli studi di Milano
Via Comelico 39/41, 20135 Milano, Italy
ornaghi@dsi.unimi.it

Prologue

The title of this paper is styled on that of Kowalski's seminal book *Logic for Problem Solving* [32]. This is because in this paper we want to discuss how logic can play a crucial part in next-generation component-based software development, just as Kowalski showed in [32] that logic can be used for programming.

Our starting point is the following quote from the Preface of [32]:

> "In contrast with conventional computing methodology, which employs different formalisms for expressing programs, specifications, databases, queries and integrity constraints, logic provides a single uniform language for all these tasks."

with which we whole-heartedly agree. Unfortunately, despite this potential advantage, it would be fair to say that hitherto Logic Programming has not made any impact on Software Engineering. In fact, it has missed the boat, as far as the latter is concerned.

We believe that for Software Engineering, logical systems stronger and more expressive than Logic Programming are needed. In this paper we want to show that full first-order logic can be used as a basis for developing a *declarative* (model-theoretic) approach to Software Engineering, in particular *component-based software development* [56].

Currently Software Engineering is moving from object-oriented to component-based development (CBD), but it will not succeed, in our view, unless components have suitable declarative semantics. We believe that the declarative nature of logic specifications and programs will give Logic Programming the chance of a second bite at the cherry, to become a force in CBD, which has been hailed as "the Industrial Revolution for IT"!

1   Logic for Programming

Kowalski proposed using predicate logic as a programming language in [57,32], and the rest — as they say — is history. The success of Logic Programming

A.C. Kakas, F. Sadri (Eds.): Computat. Logic (Kowalski Festschrift), LNAI 2407, pp. 347–373, 2002.

languages, principally Prolog, is undoubtedly due to their declarative nature, as observed in another quote from the Preface of [32]:

> "The meaning of programs expressed in conventional languages is defined in terms of the behaviour they invoke within the computer. The meaning of programs expressed in logic, on the other hand, can be defined in machine-independent, human-oriented terms. As a consequence, logic programs are easier to construct, easier to understand, easier to improve, and easier to adapt to other purposes."

In our view, however, the success of Logic Programming languages has been confined to *programming-in-the-small*. We shall not dwell on this, since our main concern here is software development, i.e. *programming-in-the-large*.

2   Logic for Specification

In [32] Kowalski also pointed out the suitability of logic as a specification language. We quote from Chapter 10 (p. 193):

> "The specification of programs, in particular, is an area in which the standard form of logic (or some appropriate extension of Horn clause form) is more suitable than simple clausal form."

Here Kowalski is comparing full first-order logic with clausal form from the point of view of program specification. We agree fully that the former is more suitable than the latter. Indeed, we believe that first-order logic is good for these purposes anyway.

However, somewhat ironically, the use of logic for specification is much more widespread in Formal Methods like Z [55] and B [1] than in Logic Programming itself. In fact within Logic Programming the prevalent view is that logic programs are executable specifications and therefore do not need specifying themselves. For example, here's a quote from the Conclusion of [33]:

> "Logic sufficiently blurs the distinction between program and specification that many logic programs can just as well be regarded as executable specifications."

This implicitly says that "logic programs are obviously correct since they are logical assertions". This is not satisfactory, in our view, since we believe that the meaning of correctness must be defined in terms of something other than logic programs themselves (we are not alone in this, see e.g. [23, p. 410]).

We believe that it is unfortunate that specifications have not received due attention in Logic Programming, and that logic programs have been equated with specifications. Indeed, we take the view that specifications should be strictly distinguished from programs, especially for the purposes of software development.

We have shown in [37,38] that in Logic Programming, not only can we maintain this distinction, but we can also define various kinds of specifications for different purposes.

Our approach is based on a three-tier formalism with model-theoretic semantics illustrated in Figure 1.

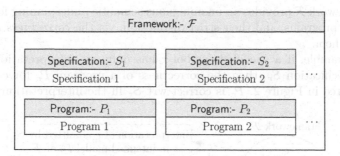

Fig. 1. Three-tier formalism.

– At the top level, we formalise a problem domain as a full first-order logical theory, which we call a *framework* $\mathcal{F}$. $\mathcal{F}$ has an *intended model* $I_{\mathcal{F}}$,[1] i.e. it has model-theoretic and hence *declarative* semantics.

For the purpose of this paper the kind of intended model semantics is not relevant. (In our approach, the intended model $I_{\mathcal{F}}$ of a framework $\mathcal{F}$ is an *isoinitial model* [40].)

In general, a framework $\mathcal{F}$ may be *open*, i.e., it may have no fixed intended models, but a class of possible ones instead. Open frameworks will be considered in Section 3. Here we consider only closed frameworks, i.e. frameworks with fixed intended models.

– In the middle, inside a framework $\mathcal{F}$, we define *specifications* as certain forms of first-order formulas in $\mathcal{F}$. A specification S_r of a new relation symbol r in a framework $\mathcal{F}$ is a set of axioms that defines the new symbol r in terms of the symbols of the framework.

The symbols introduced by specifications will be called *specified symbols*, to distinguish them from the *framework signature* $\Sigma_{\mathcal{F}}$.

In a closed framework with intended model $I_{\mathcal{F}}$, the model-theoretic meaning of a specification S_r of a symbol r is the set of $(\Sigma_{\mathcal{F}} + r)$-expansions[2] of $I_{\mathcal{F}}$ that satisfy S_r. For conciseness, the interpretations of r in such expansions will be called the *interpretations admitted by S_r in $I_{\mathcal{F}}$*.

In an open framework $\mathcal{F}$, S_r associates every intended model I of $\mathcal{F}$ with the set of $(\Sigma_{\mathcal{F}} + r)$-expansions of I that satisfy S_r.

– At the bottom level, inside a framework $\mathcal{F}$, we have the *programs*, either standard or constraint logic programs for computing (specified) relations. P_r denotes a program that computes the specified relation r. (We could equally well use imperative or functional programs here, as long as they are correct or *steadfast* (see Section 3). However, using (constraint) logic programs here has the advantage of a homogeneous formalism as mentioned in the Prologue, which in turn simplifies the treatment of *steadfastness* (see Section 3).)

---

[1] A canonical representative of an isomorphism class.

[2] $(\Sigma_{\mathcal{F}}+r)$ extends $\Sigma_{\mathcal{F}}$ by r, and a $(\Sigma_{\mathcal{F}}+r)$-expansion of $I_{\mathcal{F}}$ is a $(\Sigma_{\mathcal{F}}+r)$-interpretation that coincides with $I_{\mathcal{F}}$ for the symbols in $\Sigma_{\mathcal{F}}$.

The framework $\mathcal{F}$ provides an unambiguous semantic underpinning for specifications and programs, and their strict distinction, via the *correctness relationship* between them.

For example, if a specified symbol r has only one interpretation admitted by its specification S_r, then the correctness of a program P_r for computing r is illustrated in Figure 2. P_r is correct wrt S_r iff the interpretation of r in the

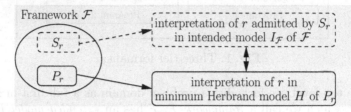

Fig. 2. Strict specifications.

minimum Herbrand model of P_r coincides with the (only) interpretation of r admitted by S_r (in $I_{\mathcal{F}}$).

An example of such a specification is an *if-and-only-if specification* S_r of a new relation r in a framework $\mathcal{F}$:

$$\forall x . r(x) \leftrightarrow R(x)$$

where $R(x)$ is any $\Sigma_{\mathcal{F}}$-formula.

On the other hand, S_r may be *loose*, i.e., it may admit many interpretations for r. For loose specifications, we have the situation in Figure 3. P_r is correct wrt

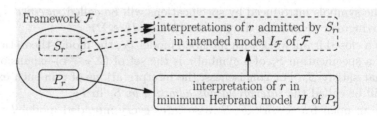

Fig. 3. Loose specifications.

S_r iff the interpretation of r in the minimum Herbrand model of P_r coincides with one of the interpretations of r admitted by S_r (in $I_{\mathcal{F}}$).

An example of such a specification is a *conditional specification* of a new relation r in a framework $\mathcal{F}$:

$$\forall x, y . IC(x) \rightarrow (r(x, y) \leftrightarrow R(x, y))$$

where the *input condition* $IC(x)$ and the *input-output relation* $R(x, y)$ are $\Sigma_{\mathcal{F}}$-formulas.

A conditional specification is like a *pre-post-condition* style of specification as in Z [55] and B [1].

In a framework, all program predicates have specifications. The knowledge of the problem domain, codified by the framework axioms and theorems, together with the specifications, are the basis for developing *formal correctness proofs* [41].

Moreover, they allow us to enhance program reuse through *specification reduction*: a specification S_r reduces to a specification S'_r if every program P that is correct with respect to S_r is also correct with respect to S'_r. Thus, a non-strict specification S_r reduces to a non-strict specification S'_r if the interpretations of r that are admitted by S_r are admitted also by S'_r (strict specifications work as a limiting case). Specification reduction can be treated at the framework level. For example, in a closed framework $\mathcal{F}$, a conditional specification $I(x) \rightarrow (r(x,y) \leftrightarrow R(x,y))$ reduces to $I'(x) \rightarrow (r(x,y) \leftrightarrow R'(x,y))$ if and only if the formula

$$(I'(x) \wedge R'(x,y) \rightarrow I(x) \wedge R(x,y)) \wedge (\neg I(x) \vee R(x,y) \rightarrow \neg I'(x) \vee R'(x,y)) \quad (1)$$

is true in the intended model $I_\mathcal{F}$ of $\mathcal{F}$.

To treat specification reduction in the context of $\mathcal{F}$, the formulas involved, like (1), must not contain program predicates, since the latter do not belong to the framework signature $\Sigma_\mathcal{F}$. This excludes, for example, recursive if-and-only-if specifications. We require that our specifications are *completely declarative* in the context of the framework $\mathcal{F}$, that is, reasoning about them can be done in $\mathcal{F}$, independently of the programs. In this way, we can disregard the implementation details. As a concomitant, frameworks should be strong theories, i.e., they should satisfy the following *richness requirements*:

- The framework language should be *expressive* enough to specify programs naturally in a non-recursive, declarative way. To this end, we use full first-order logic, and we consider frameworks $\mathcal{F}$ with a rich signature $\Sigma_\mathcal{F}$.
- To reason about program correctness and specification reduction, the framework axioms should give a *powerful deductive system*. Moreover, a repository of useful theorems would facilitate theorem proving.

Thus, in order to meet these richness requirements, our frameworks are *full* first-order theories with powerful axioms, like induction schemas or descending chain principles.

Richness requirements and the emphasis on correctness and declarative specifications are the main features distinguishing our approach from algebraic specifications [58,4]. A less relevant difference[3] lies in the kind of intended models we choose. We use *isoinitial models* [40], instead of initial ones. This is in line with the richness requirements: for a closed framework, we require at least *reachability* (a model is reachable if every element of its domain can be represented by a ground term) and *atomic completeness* ($\mathcal{F}$ is atomically complete if $\mathcal{F} \vdash A$ or $\mathcal{F} \vdash \neg A$, for every ground atomic formula A). For reachable models atomic completeness is a necessary and sufficient *isoinitiality condition* [40].

---

[3] As we have said, for the purpose of this paper, what kind of intended model we choose is not a relevant issue.

For the rest, the algebraic approach is close to ours, especially at the framework level. We have in common a model-theoretic semantics, and modularity at the framework level, briefly discussed in the next section, is modelled by theory morphisms, a way to *put theories together* [10,27] that has been largely studied in the algebraic specification community.

Concerning the expressiveness of specifications, it is worthwhile to briefly comment on logics different from first-order classical logic. For example, temporal logic can be used to model time and change in specifications. Temporal logic has been proposed, e.g., in [19], to model concurrent object systems in an algebraic setting. Aspects like concurrency and resources can be implicitly modelled in non-classical logics, where logical connectives may have a non-classical operational interpretation. A notable example is linear logic, that has been used to specify and model concurrent systems [3,31,46]. Finally, compared to first-order logic, higher-order logic has a greater expressive power. It is the basis of various extensions of logic programming, e.g. λProlog [47], and of some logical frameworks, e.g., Isabelle [48], ELF [52], that could be used as a general meta-logic to manage different object logics and theories, as opposed to the categorical approach developed in algebraic specifications.

We do not exclude the use of more expressive logics, in particular temporal logic, in specifications, as long as we can maintain a model-theoretic semantics for frameworks, specifications and program correctness. A model-theoretic semantics is, in our opinion, more declarative than other kinds of semantics, like type-theoretic or proof-theoretic semantics. Moreover, it allows us to introduce *steadfastness*, a model-theoretic notion of *a priori* correctness. Steadfastness and its relevance for correct reusability will be discussed in the next section. So far, we have studied it in the model-theoretic setting of classical logic; the possibility of introducing time and change will be briefly discussed in Section 4.2.

As we will show later, the above features, together with the model-theoretic semantics of frameworks, specifications and programs provide a suitable basis for component-based software development.

3   Logic for Software Engineering

When it comes to Software Engineering, Logic Programming has missed the boat big time. This is primarily due to the view that logic programs are specifications. The quote from the Conclusion of [33] goes on like this:

> "Logic sufficiently blurs the distinction between program and specification that many logic programs can just as well be regarded as executable specifications. On the one hand, this can give the impression that logic programming lacks a programming methodology; on the other, it may imply that many of the software engineering techniques that have been developed for conventional programming languages are inapplicable and unnecessary for logic programs."

Our view is that Logic Programming indeed lacks a programming methodology, notwithstanding [15]. It may well be that many Software Engineering techniques for conventional programming languages are inapplicable to logic programs, but certainly they are not unnecessary.

The lack of emphasis by Logic Programming on Software Engineering is manifested by Logic Programming's bias in the last 20 or so years towards specialised AI and database issues such as non-monotonic logic, which are very distant from Software Engineering problems indeed. This prevented programming language researchers and designers outside Logic Programming from having a stronger positive influence on Logic Programming than they could have done otherwise. Consequently, notions such as modules, parameterisation, polymorphic data types and objects entered Logic Programming relatively recently.

Now we discuss how we might remedy the situation, and make Logic Programming address the issues of Software Engineering.

As we showed in the previous section, we distinguish strictly between specifications and programs within frameworks. This is important for Software Engineering, since it allows us to define *modules* and their *correctness*.

To formalise highly reusable modules, open frameworks are indispensable. Indeed, reusability in a wide context entails that the intended model cannot be fixed in advance, but instead we have to consider a class of possible models.

Intuitively, an open framework contains an as yet incomplete axiomatisation, which can be completed in many ways, by means of different suitable *completion procedures*. An example of a completion procedure is *parameter passing* in parametric frameworks, but we can have other kinds of completion procedures as well, like *internalisation* defined in [39,34].

The symbols of an open framework $\mathcal{F}$ to be closed by the completion procedures are called *open symbols*. We will denote an open framework with open symbols Π by $\mathcal{F}(\Pi)$. A completion operation gives rise to a more specific framework $\mathcal{F}'$, and can be formalised as a suitable theory morphism $m : \mathcal{F} \to \mathcal{F}'$. The ($m$-reducts of the) intended models of $\mathcal{F}'$ are a subset of those of $\mathcal{F}$. We may have *total* completions, giving rise to closed frameworks, that we call *instances* of $\mathcal{F}(\Pi)$, as well as *partial* completions, yielding open *specialisations* of $\mathcal{F}(\Pi)$. For open frameworks, our three-tier formalism is illustrated in Figure 4.

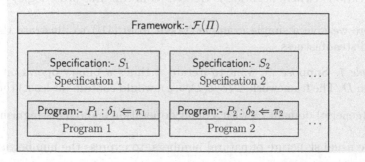

Fig. 4. Three-tier formalism for open frameworks.

Specifications S_1, S_2, ..., define program relations as in closed frameworks (closed frameworks are limiting cases of open frameworks) and may contain parameters from Π.

In each program P_i, δ_i are the *defined predicates* of P_i (they occur in the head of at least one clause), while π_i are the *open* ones (they occur only in the body of clauses). That is, P_i may be an open program. Its specification in $\mathcal{F}(\Pi)$ is a pair $(S_{\delta_i}, S_{\pi_i})$, where S_{δ_i} are specifications of P_i's defined predicates, and S_{π_i} are specifications of its open predicates.

Correctness can be defined in a model-theoretic way, as in the previous section, but we cannot compare minimum Herbrand models and interpretations admitted by specifications in the intended model, for two reasons: (a) minimum Herbrand models interpret the open predicates as empty relations, whereas the latter are supposed to represent generic, though not yet fixed predicates; and (b) an open framework has no fixed intended models, but instead we have to consider a class of possible models. To define correctness of an open program $P : \delta \Leftarrow \pi$ in a class $\mathcal{I}$ of models, we consider its *minimum j-models* where j is a *pre-interpretation*,[4] i.e. an interpretation of the symbols of P that are distinct from δ, namely its sorts, constants, functions and open predicates. Using *minimum j-models*, we base correctness on *steadfastness*.

Steadfastness embodies at once *modularity*, *reusability*, and *correctness*. A *steadfast* program is one that is correct (wrt to its specification) in each intended model of $\mathcal{F}$. Since the (reducts of the) intended models of its specialisations and instances are intended models of $\mathcal{F}$, a steadfast program is a correctly reusable unit in all specialisations and instances of $\mathcal{F}$. It can thus be used to model correct schemas (see [22]).

A formalisation of steadfastness is given in [41] for definite programs, with both a model-theoretic, hence *declarative*, characterisation and a proof-theoretic treatment of steadfastness. Our treatment readily extends to constraint logic programs. However, the extension to normal programs is not automatic, because the existence of the minimum j-model is no longer guaranteed. As far as semantics is concerned, a possible solution could be the introduction of a notion similar to stable models [26], but this would require a different proof theory for steadfastness. The extension of steadfastness to normal programs is an interesting problem, but we do not deal with it here, since our main interest is in specifications (where negation is treated as in full first-order logic) and correctness.

Here we give a simple example (taken from [41]) to illustrate the intuition behind steadfastness.

Example 1. Suppose we want to iterate n times a binary operation $\circ$ on some domain D. The framework, $\mathcal{ITER}(D, \circ, e)$, would contain (at least) the following:

(i) a (generic) domain D, with a binary operation $\circ$ and a distinguished element e;

(ii) the usual structure of natural numbers, to express the number n;

---

[4] Our notion of pre-interpretation generalises that in [42].

(iii) the iteration operation $\times(a, n) = e \circ a \underbrace{\circ \cdots \circ}_{(n \text{ times})} a.$

The specification of the relation *iterate* is:

$$S_{iterate}: \quad iterate(x, n, z) \leftrightarrow z = \times(a, n) \tag{2}$$

Consider the following program $P_{iterate}$:

$$iterate(a, 0, v) \quad \leftarrow unit(v)$$
$$iterate(a, s(n), v) \leftarrow iterate(a, n, w), op(w, a, v)$$

where s is the successor function for natural numbers, and the predicates *unit* and *op* are specified in $\mathcal{ITER}$ by the specifications:

$$S_{unit}: \quad unit(u) \quad \leftrightarrow u = e$$
$$S_{op} \ : \quad op(x, y, z) \leftrightarrow z = x \circ y \tag{3}$$

$P_{iterate}$ is *correct* with respect to the specifications (2) and (3) because it always computes *iterate* correctly in terms of correct computations of *unit* and *op* in *any* interpretation of $\mathcal{ITER}$.

For example, if D is the set of natural numbers, $\circ$ is $+$, e is 0, then $\times(a, n) = 0 + a + \cdots + a = na$, i.e., $S_{iterate}$ specialises to $iterate(x, n, z) \leftrightarrow z = na$. Similarly, S_{unit} specialises to $unit(u) \leftrightarrow u = 0$, and S_{op} to $op(x, y, z) \leftrightarrow z = x + y$.

Now, if P_{unit}^+ computes $u = 0$ and P_{op}^+ computes $z = x + y$ (i.e., they are correct with respect to their specialised specifications), then $P_{iterate} \cup P_{unit}^+ \cup P_{op}^+$ will compute na, i.e., $P_{iterate}$ is correct (wih respect to its specialised specification) in this first interpretation.

As another example, if D is the set of integers, $\circ$ is $-$, e is 0, then $\times(a, n) = 0 - a - \cdots - a = -na$.

If P_{unit}^- computes $u = 0$ and P_{op}^- computes $z = x - y$, then $P_{iterate} \cup P_{unit}^- \cup P_{op}^-$ will compute $-na$ for an integer a, i.e., $P_{iterate}$ is also correct in this second interpretation.

We say $P_{iterate}$ is *steadfast* in $\mathcal{ITER}$.

As an example of a non-steadfast program in $\mathcal{ITER}$, consider the following program $P_{iterate}^*$:

$$iterate(a, 0, v) \leftarrow unit(v)$$
$$iterate(a, n, v) \leftarrow m + m = n, iterate(a, m, w), op(w, w, v)$$
$$iterate(a, n, v) \leftarrow m + s(m) = n, iterate(a, m, w),$$
$$op(w, w, z), op(z, a, v)$$

$P_{iterate}^*$ is more efficient than $P_{iterate}$: the number of recursive calls is linear in $P_{iterate}$, whereas it is logarithmic in $P_{iterate}^*$.

$P_{iterate}^*$ is correct with respect to (2) and (3) if D is the set of natural numbers with $+$ as $\circ$ and 0 as e. However, it is incorrect if D is the set of integers with $-$ as $\circ$ and 0 as e. For instance, for $iterate(a, s(s(s(s(0)))), v)$, $P_{iterate}^*$ computes 0 instead of the correct answer $-4a$. Thus $P_{iterate}^*$ is *not* steadfast in $\mathcal{ITER}$.

However, if we require that e and $\circ$ satisfy the additional (unit and associativity) axioms:

$$\forall x . e \circ x = x$$
$$\forall x, y, z . x \circ (y \circ z) = (x \circ y) \circ z$$

then we can prove that the following properties hold:

$$\begin{cases} \times(a, n) = \times(a, n \div 2) \circ \times(a, n \div 2) \circ a & \text{if } n \text{ is odd} \\ \times(a, n) = \times(a, n \div 2) \circ \times(a, n \div 2) & \text{if } n \text{ is even} \end{cases}$$

and in the subclass $\mathcal{ITER}^*$ of interpretations of $\mathcal{ITER}$ that satisfy the additional axioms, $P^*_{iterate}$ computes correctly, and thus it is steadfast in $\mathcal{ITER}^*$.

For instance, if D is the set of m-dimensional square matrices, with the m-dimensional identity matrix as e, then since matrix multiplication $\times$ is associative, $P^*_{iterate}$ is correct, where op computes matrix products.

To show how frameworks containing steadfast programs allow correct reuse, we continue from this example.

Example 2. The open framework $\mathcal{ITER}(D, \circ, e)$ can be formalised as follows.

Framework $\mathcal{ITER}(D, \circ, e)$;

IMPORT: $\mathcal{NAT}$;

SORTS: D;

FUNS: $e : [\,] \rightarrow D$;
  $\circ : [D, D] \rightarrow D$;
  $\times : [D, Nat] \rightarrow D$;

RELS:

C-AXS:

D-AXS: $\forall x : D . \times (x, 0) = e$;
  $\forall x : D \ \forall n : Nat . \times (x, s(n)) = \times(x, n) \circ x$;

SPECS: $S_{iterate} : iterate(x, n, z) \leftrightarrow z = \times(x, n)$;
  $S_{unit} \quad : unit(u) \leftrightarrow u = e$;
  $S_{op} \quad : op(x, y, z) \leftrightarrow z = x \circ y$;

PROGS: $P_{iterate} : iterate(a, 0, v) \quad \leftarrow unit(v)$
  $iterate(a, s(n), v) \leftarrow iterate(a, n, w), op(w, a, v)$

where $\mathcal{NAT}$ is the closed framework containing first-order Peano Arithmetic.

We distinguish two kinds of axiom: *constraints* (C-AXS) and *definitions* (D-AXS). Constraints are properties to be satisfied by the completion procedures, when the open symbols are closed. Definitions guarantee that, once all the open symbols have been closed, the closed ones ($\times$ in the example) are completely defined, i.e. *total* completions give rise to closed (consistent) frameworks.

In our example, we do not have constraints, i.e. any completion for D, $\circ$ and e will work. This can be proved by considering the following facts: (a) a total completion introduces new Σ-axioms Ax with a reachable isoinitial model I, where Σ contains D, $\circ$, e, and possibly other symbols, but not the defined symbol $\times$; (b) I can be expanded into the reachable $(\Sigma + \times)$-model I' of D-AXS, which interprets $\times$ as the function evaluated according to the recursive equations D-AXS; (c) the atomic completeness of Ax is preserved by D-AXS (due to the evaluability of $\times$).

The intended models[5] of the specialisations and instances of a framework $\mathcal{F}$ are models of $\mathcal{F}$. By the properties of steadfastness, this guarantees that steadfast programs developed in $\mathcal{F}$ are correctly inherited.

For example, we can close the open symbols of $\mathcal{ITER}(D, \circ, e)$ by the following completion by internalisation:

COMPLETION NEG OF $\mathcal{ITER}(Int :: \mathcal{INT}, \circ, e)$:
$\qquad$ CLOSE $\circ$ by $x \circ y = x - y$
$\qquad$ CLOSE e by $e = 0$

In this completion we have used a parameter passing and two internalisations by explicit definitions. The parameter passing implicitly includes the predefined framework $\mathcal{INT}$ for integers, which expands the already imported $\mathcal{NAT}$. Axioms, specifications and programs are inherited. We can prove the formula $\times(x, n) = -nx$, so we can conclude that $S_{iterate}$ specialises to $iterate(x, n, z) \leftrightarrow z = -nx$, that is, our program correctly computes $-nx$. In general, specialisation is equivalence in the more specific context of a completion, but it may also involve specification reduction. Specialisation by reduction improves reusability and correct overriding, as we will discuss later. Since $P_{iterate}$ is open, we have to provide steadfast (i.e. correct)[6] programs for op and $unit$. The latter is trivial, while the former is likely already present in $\mathcal{INT}$. Such programs correctly compose with $P_{iterate}$, by the properties of steadfastness.

We can also consider:

COMPLETION EXP OF $\mathcal{ITER}(Nat, \circ, e)$:
$\qquad$ CLOSE $\circ$ by $x \circ y = x \cdot y$
$\qquad$ CLOSE e by $e = 1$

to get a program for computing the exponential function.

We can specialise $\mathcal{ITER}$ to $\mathcal{ITER}^*$ as follows:

Framework $\mathcal{ITER}^*(D, \circ, e)$;

EXTENDS: $\mathcal{ITER}$;

C-AXS: $\quad \forall x : D \,.\, e \circ x = x$;
$\qquad\qquad \forall x, y, z : D \,.\, (x \circ y) \circ z = x \circ (y \circ z)$;

SPECS: $\quad S_{half} : half(x, y) \leftrightarrow x = y + y$;

PROGS: $\quad P_{iterate} : iterate(a, 0, v) \leftarrow unit(v)$
$\qquad\qquad\qquad iterate(a, n, v) \leftarrow half(n, m), iterate(a, m, w), op(w, w, v)$
$\qquad\qquad\qquad iterate(a, n, v) \leftarrow half(s(n), s(m)), iterate(a, m, w),$
$\qquad\qquad\qquad\qquad\qquad op(w, w, u), op(u, a, v)$

---

[5] More precisely, their reducts.

[6] In a closed framework, steadfastness and correctness coincide for closed programs.

We have inherited all the axioms and specifications, while overriding $P_{iterate}$. The new $P_{iterate}$ is more efficient, but it can be used only if its constraints can be proved after the completion operations. Thus, we can replace $\mathcal{ITER}$ by $\mathcal{ITER}^*$ in the closure EXP, but not in NEG.

Open frameworks and steadfastness conjugate reuse and correctness, and yield 3 levels of *correct reusability*:

- Top level.
  Open frameworks are reusable through completion operations, which allow us to implement framework *composition, specialisation* and *instantiation*. Axioms and theorems are inherited, because completion operations are theory morphisms.
  We require that open frameworks are *correctly constrained*, i.e. its constraints guarantee that consistency is preserved by completion operations (which must satisfy the constraints), and *totally defined*, namely every total completion yields a closed instance.
  At this level, correctness corresponds to constraint satisfaction. Constraints are therefore the first level of guidance for correctly reusing frameworks.
- Specification level.
  Specifications are inherited. Their meaning can be specialised according to the completion operation, by means of specification reduction (introduced in Section 2 for closed frameworks; in an open framework $\mathcal{F}(\Pi)$, S_r reduces to S_r' if, for every intended model I of $\mathcal{F}(\Pi)$, every interpretation of r admitted by S_r in I is also admitted by S_r' in I). For example, in the closure NEG, the specialised $S_{iterate}$ shows that *iterate* computes $-n \cdot x$. Specifications are the second level of guidance for correctly reusing frameworks, because their specialisation describes in a compact and declarative way how the behaviour of steadfast program specialises.
- Bottom level.
  Steadfast programs are inherited, together with their specifications. If $P : \delta \Leftarrow \pi$ with specification (S_δ, S_π) is steadfast in an open framework $\mathcal{F}(\Pi)$, then it is steadfast in *all* the *specialisations* and *instances* of $\mathcal{F}$ by completion operations, that is, it is correctly inherited with respect to the specifications (S_δ, S_π).
  Moreover, its specifications are a guidance for *correctly composing* $P : \delta \Leftarrow \pi$ with other programs Q_i for its open predicates. To guarantee the correctness of the composite program, it suffices to prove that Q_i's are correct with respect to the specifications S_π.

At the top level, there are no substantial differences with respect to algebraic specifications. However, reusability at the specification and bottom (program) level is peculiar to our approach. Specification reduction plays an important role both at the specification level, for specialising specifications while partially or totally completing frameworks, and at the bottom level, to enhance correct program composition.

In the next section, we will discuss how these features of frameworks can help to provide a basis for building reusable components with a declarative semantics.

4   Logic for Component-Based Software Development

CBD [56] has been hailed as the "Industrial Revolution for IT", aimed at delivering Software Engineering from a cottage industry into a "mechanised" manufacturing industry. The goal of CBD is thus to provide the engineering science and tools for constructing software products by plugging components together, like building hardware from kits of component parts. Therefore, the ultimate test for CBD is whether it can allow arbitrary combination, or *third-party assembly*, of software components.

At present the key pre-requisites for CBD to succeed have not been met (see e.g. [9]). The first is a *formal semantics* for components and component reuse. Without formal semantics, it is not possible to achieve a standard, universally understood and accepted definition, which in turn is essential for achieving the ultimate goal of third-party assembly of components.

The second pre-requisite is good component *interfaces*. The interface of a component should be *all we know* about the component. It should therefore provide all the information on what the component does, i.e. its operations, (though not how it does it) and how we can use the component, i.e. its context dependencies. Otherwise, third-party assembly would not be possible. Therefore, an interface should include not just a list of *operations*, but also *context dependencies*. This implies that we need, as a minimum, polymorphism, theory morphism and composition, etc. to describe the semantics of interfaces. Therefore, *pre- and post-conditions* are not enough for specifying interfaces.

Thirdly, we need a good *assembly guide* for selecting the right components. The interface of a reusable component contains a collection of operations. In order to have a good assembly guide, the following pre-requisites should be satisfied:

- We need to know what each component does (correctly). Thus component operations should have *declarative specifications* (we have to know what they do, not how) and composition of components should yield the specification of the operations of the composite.
- We need to know what the reuse of a component within another one (after composition) will yield. This implies that the specifications of component operations should be compositional, namely that the specifications of a composite should indicate when and how we can correctly compose the operations inherited from its components.

This is only possible if we have a notion of correctness of component operations wrt their specifications and require that correctness is preserved by composition (wrt the specification of the composite derived from the specifications of the constituents). This implies that the semantics for components and their interfaces should incorporate a notion of *a priori correctness*, i.e. *pre*-proved correctness of any given component operation wrt its own specification, as well as *pre*-stated conditions that will guarantee that component and operation compositions will preserve correctness. This kind of correctness means *correct reusability* because it preserves *inheritance* and *compositionality*, i.e., programs can be inherited and specifications can be automatically derived from components (in composition) and super-components (when a general super-component is specialised) without destroying correctness.

Thus *a priori* correctness is the key to providing a good assembly guide. It stands in contrast to *a posteriori correctness*. The latter is the usual kind of correctness for verification-based program construction, where correctness of a composite can only be proved *after* the composition has taken place. It therefore cannot provide an assembly guide.

Although there are many strands of existing work in Formal Methods that address correctness, including *a priori* correctness, and composition of modules, collectively they do not meet the above requirements for CBD mainly because their modules are not components in the sense of CBD, such as frameworks [18] or patterns [24] for instance.

4.1   Limitations of Current Software Development Approaches

Now we consider the most relevant approaches to software development, and briefly analyse their potential for CBD, with respect to the prerequisites discussed above.

Object Technology. At present, CBD exists in the form of OO software development, employing current object technology, i.e. tools based on UML [53], together with middleware such as CORBA [28,6], COM [8] and Enterprise Java Beans (EJB) [44].

It lacks formal (declarative) semantics for objects, components, patterns, frameworks, interfaces, component assembly and reuse, component correctness and component assembly correctness. So it cannot provide good interface specifications or a good assembly guide.

Much of current CBD work also suffers from being low-level, consisting in *component-oriented programming* (i.e. a low-level approach akin to programming-in-the-small) because it uses languages like Component Pascal that merely somehow 'upgrade' plain OO programming languages into 'component programming' ones.

Work using CORBA, COM and EJB is rather low-level too, employing as it does what could be called *IDL programming*, i.e. OO programming in C++ or Java, with object integration provided by CORBA/COM/EJB via their respective *interface definition languages* (IDLs).

For CBD to achieve its goal, this low-level, bottom-up approach needs to evolve into a high-level, top-down one, with emphasis on *component assembly*, e.g. architecture description languages [54] and/or 'component assembly' languages.

Another weakness of current CBD is that it relies too much on existing OO (analysis and) design (OOD) methods. These methods use objects (or classes) as the basic unit of design and reuse. However, it is increasingly recognised that classes are not the best focus for design (see e.g. [29,45,18]). Typical design artefacts are rarely just about one object, but about groups of objects and the way they interact.

Frameworks, also known as *OOD frameworks*, are such groups of interacting objects. For example, in *Catalysis* [18], a driver may be represented (in UML) as the framework shown in Figure 5. A driver is a person who drives a car, or in

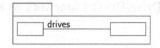

Fig. 5. The Driver framework.

framework terminology, a driver is a framework composed of a car object and a person object, linked by a 'drives' association (or attribute).

Frameworks are increasingly recognised as better units of reuse in software development than objects (see e.g. [29,45]). The reason for this is that in practical systems, objects tend to have more than one role in more than one context, and frameworks can capture this, whereas existing OOD methods (e.g. Fusion [11] and Syntropy [12]) cannot. The latter use classes or objects as the basic unit of design or reuse, and are based on the traditional view of an object, as shown in Figure 6, which regards an object as a closed entity with one fixed role. Such objects are very hard to reuse in practice. On the other hand, frameworks

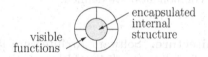

Fig. 6. Objects with one fixed role.

allow objects that play different roles in different frameworks to be composed by composing frameworks. In *Catalysis*, for instance, this is depicted in Figure 7.[7]

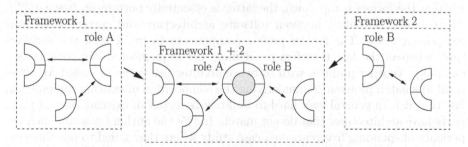

Fig. 7. Objects with multiple roles in different frameworks.

For example, a person can play the roles of a driver and of a guest at a motel simultaneously. These roles are shown separately in the PersonAsDriver and PersonAsGuest frameworks in Figure 8. If we compose these two frameworks,

---

[7] Double arrows denote interactions between (partial) objects.

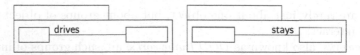

Fig. 8. PersonAsDriver and PersonAsGuest frameworks.

then we get the PersonAsDriverGuest framework as shown in Figure 9. In this

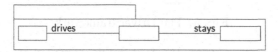

Fig. 9. PersonAsDriverGuest framework.

framework, a person object plays two roles, and is a composite object of the kind depicted in Figure 7. Frameworks are more reusable in practice than objects with fixed roles.

It should be noted that most of the so-called *patterns*, as defined in [24], are frameworks. Also, in UML, it is supposed to be possible to model frameworks and patterns (see e.g. [35]), even though in UML it is not clear how frameworks and patterns (or components) are defined.

Software Architecture. Software Architecture [5] is a relatively new, and as yet immature discipline (see [54]). Although there are architecture description languages, e.g. Wright [2], and architectural design tools, e.g. Rapide [43], research in software architecture has largely been overtaken by the universal adoption of UML (and the Unified Methodology) by software designers.

One difficulty of combining software architecture and current CBD is that whereas the former is top-down, the latter is essentially bottom-up (see e.g. [7]). There is also a conflict between software architecture and current CBD over component reuse. The former prefers components to fit in with the architecture, whereas the latter prefers pre-defined pre-implemented components (see e.g. [50]). Another problem with software architecture is the so-called Architectural Mismatch problem [25] underlying the composition of existing components, viz. that it is in general very hard to build systems out of existing parts if these parts have architectures that do not match. In [25] the authors describe their experience of spending five years on a case study where they failed to put three existing subsystems together and eventually decided to re-design and re-implement these subsystems in order to achieve their composition.

Formal Methods. General-purpose formal methods such as Z [55], VDM [30] and B [1] lack suitable semantics for components, even though they may have been 'upgraded' into versions with objects (e.g. Object Z). They lack semantic characterisations of specifications, objects, components, patterns, frameworks, etc. So they cannot provide good (component) interface specifications.

These methods also do not have meaningful notions of correctness for objects, components, patterns, frameworks, etc, or their composition and reuse. So they cannot provide a good assembly guide.

Existing (semi-)formal OOD methods such as Fusion [11,17] and Syntropy [12] suffer from the same problems with semantics as the above general-purpose formal methods. Besides, they also use classes or objects as the basic unit of design, and as we saw in the previous section, this is not the best approach for next-generation CBD.

4.2   What Can Logic Programming Contribute?

Correct reusability of steadfast programs means *a priori* correctness of their composition. This is a very important feature of steadfastness, and contrasts favourably, for the purposes of CBD, with *a posteriori* correctness normally employed in verification-based approaches to program construction.

Open frameworks containing steadfast programs are suitable as software components in CBD, and we will call them *steadfast components*, since they meet the prerequisites for CBD: *declarative formal semantics*, *interfaces* and *assembly guide* for reuse and composition.

A framework has a model-theoretic, hence declarative, semantics for all its constituents. The constituents of an open framework $\mathcal{F}(\Pi)$ can be identified as the following (see Example 2):

- the problem *signature* Σ, made up of sort symbols SORTS, function symbols FUNS and relation symbols RELS;
- the problem *axioms* AXS (consisting of constraints C AXS and definitions D-AXS);
- a set SPECS of specifications;
- a set PROGS of programs.

To reflect this, we shall write $\mathcal{F}(\Pi) = \langle \Sigma, \text{AXS}, \text{SPECS}, \text{PROGS} \rangle$. The meaning of the problem signature Σ is given by the problem axioms AXS, according to an intended model semantics. Specifications SPECS define program predicates in terms of Σ. An open program $P : \delta \Leftarrow \pi$ (belonging to PROGS) with specification (S_δ, S_π) is interpreted by its j-models, where j ranges over the intended models of $\mathcal{F}(\Pi)$, expanded by the specifications S_π.

An open framework $\mathcal{F}(\Pi) = \langle \Sigma, \text{AXS}, \text{SPECS}, \text{PROGS} \rangle$ has a two-level *interface* with formal semantics:

- The *framework interface* is the problem signature Σ, together with the axioms AXS. It provides a set of known properties that define the meaning of the signature and provide a way of reasoning about the problem domain. The semantics of the framework interface is given by the completion operations and the semantics of the corresponding theory morphisms.

– The *method interface* is the set $\{(S_{\delta_i}, S_{\pi_i})\}$ of specifications of the programs (methods) in PROGS. They state precisely what methods do, in a concise and declarative way. The semantics is based on steadfastness, i.e. correctness within a framework, and specification reduction.

In addition, the interface of a framework $\mathcal{F}(\Pi) = \langle \Sigma, \text{AXS}, \text{SPECS}, \text{PROGS} \rangle$ also contains the following *context dependencies*, that constitute an assembly guide for framework and method reuse and composition:

– At the *framework* level, context dependencies are given by the open symbols Π and their constraints C-AXS $\subseteq$ AXS; only the open symbols can be closed, according to suitable completion operations, that must satisfy the constraints.
– At the *method* level, the specifications S_δ of the defined predicates of a program $P : \delta \Leftarrow \pi$ are a guide for program reuse: P can be correctly reused for a specification S_r of a relation r if δ contains a predicate d with specification S_d such that $S_d[d/r]$ reduces to S_r, where $[d/r]$ indicates the renaming of d by r.
Similarly, the specifications S_π of the open predicates are a guide for program composition: a program $Q : \gamma \Leftarrow \ldots$ correctly composes with P if Q can be correctly reused for the specification S_p of some $p \in \pi$. For the sake of program composition, we can also contextualise specification reduction to the call positions of the open predicates in the clauses of programs, as, for example, in [21]. Contextual reduction is powerful, but it is no longer implementation independent: it can be used to compose two specific programs, while non-contextual reduction applies to any pairs of programs implementing the same specifications.
Of course, reuse and composition may involve suitable renamings of program predicates.

Thus, context dependencies are a guide for correct reuse. An interesting feature is that specification reduction allows us to control inheritance polymorphism, as follows. A framework $\mathcal{G}$ extends a framework $\mathcal{F}$ if it adds new signature, axioms, specifications and methods (i.e., steadfast programs). Framework extension works as a subclassing mechanism, and allows program overriding. In the general case, $P_\mathcal{G}$ correctly overrides $P_\mathcal{F}$ if $S_{\mathcal{G}_\delta}$ reduce to $S_{\mathcal{F}_\delta}$ (i.e., $P_\mathcal{G}$ is also correct wrt $S_{\mathcal{F}_\delta}$) and $S_{\mathcal{F}_\pi}$ reduce to $S_{\mathcal{G}_\pi}$ (i.e., programs that correctly compose with $P_\mathcal{F}$ also correctly compose with $P_\mathcal{G}$). We can also have more flexible overriding mechanisms. For example, it may happen that $P_\mathcal{G}$ works more efficiently, but requires open operations that are not needed by $P_\mathcal{F}$, or have specifications different from those of $P_\mathcal{F}$. In this case, it is reasonable to replace $P_\mathcal{F}$ by $P_\mathcal{G}$, and provide the new required operations. That is, the use of specifications in the context of the problem domain allows us to treat inheritance in a rather flexible way, while maintaining correctness.

Open frameworks have another important property, viz. they can be used to represent classes, where attributes are the open symbols, methods are the steadfast programs, and class invariants are the constraint axioms. A framework

$\mathcal{F}(\Pi)$ representing a class will be called a *class framework*. To build objects of a class framework $\mathcal{F}(\Pi)$, we close its open symbols Π. We may have multiple closures, i.e. many objects of the same class can coexist. Class frameworks have rich features. Attributes may be sorts, functions or relations; for example, relations as attributes can be used to model OO data bases. Framework axioms allow us to specify the abstract data types needed to close the attributes, and to model our general knowledge of the problem domain. Specifications give a formal declarative semantics of method-interface.

This is illustrated below:[8]

$$\begin{array}{cccccc}
\text{Correct} & & \text{Steadfast} & & \text{ADT} & & \text{Methods} & & \text{Correct} \\
& + & & = & \oplus & + & \oplus & = & \text{(composite)} \\
\text{framework} & & \text{programs} & & \text{class} & & \text{specs} & & \text{class} \\
& & & & \text{invariants} & & & &
\end{array}$$

A framework $\mathcal{F}(\Pi)$ can also be used to define a class diagram with possible constraints (as defined, e.g., in UML), and its instances can be seen as the object diagrams instantiating the class diagram. Constraints are satisfied by all the instances, by the way the open symbols are closed. Steadfast programs are like methods that satisfy their specifications in all the instances because of the *a priori* nature of correctness that steadfastness embodies.

In our explanation, we have implicitly assumed that frameworks representing classes and class diagrams have open symbols that can be closed by internalisation, without introducing new signature or axioms. But we can also assume the existence of only partially specified external entities, like data types, frameworks or objects. This is needed to model *OOD frameworks* [39] as components, to be closed by reusing them in different contexts, which have to provide the required external entities.

To illustrate the reuse of frameworks with steadfast methods as steadfast components, and the role of such frameworks as OOD frameworks, we show a simple example.

Example 3. Consider the following open framework $\mathcal{WLIST}(X, wt)$ for computing sums of weights in weighted lists, i.e. lists with weights associated with their elements. We assume that common ADT's, like reals, parametric lists, etc. have been pre-defined (by frameworks). $List(X)$ is the sort of lists with elements of sort X, and a non-empty list l has elements at positions 0 to $len(l) - 1$ (the empty list [ ] has no positions).[9]

---

[8] In the diagram, $a \oplus b$ signifies 'a always satisfies the accompanying specifications b'.

[9] For an axiomatisation, see [39].

Framework $\mathcal{WLIST}(X, wt)$;

FUNS: $wt : [List(X), Nat] \rightarrow Real$;
         $sum : [List(X), Nat] \rightarrow Real$;

C-AXS: $\forall i : Nat \; \forall l : List(X) . \; i \geq len(l) \rightarrow wt(l, i) = 0$;

D-AXS: $\forall l : List(X) . \; sum(l, 0) \qquad\qquad = 0$;
         $\forall k : Nat \; \forall l : List(X) . \; sum(l, k + 1) = sum(l, k) + wt(l, k)$;

SPECS: $lsum(l, w) \qquad \leftrightarrow w = sum(l, len(l))$;
         $lwt([x|a], b, w) \leftrightarrow w = wt(rev(b)|[x|a], len(b))$;

PROGS: P_{lsum} : $lsum(l, w) \leftarrow sumrev(l, [\,], w)$
                 $sumrev([\,], b, 0) \leftarrow$
         $sumrev([x|a], b, w) \leftarrow sumrev(a, [x|b], u),$
                            $lwt([x|a], b, v), w \; is \; u + v$

The framework $\mathcal{WLIST}(X, wt)$ is designed to be reusable with different weighting mechanisms for lists, so we do not fix the weighting mechanism. Instead, we just assume that every position i in a list l has a weight $wt(l, i)$, where $wt(l, i)$ is an open function, to be instantiated by different weighting mechanisms, in different contexts.

Besides $wt(l, i)$, the framework-level interface of $\mathcal{WLIST}$ contains the open sort symbol X of list elements and the defined function $sum(l, i))$.

Relevant properties of $sum(l, i)$, e.g.

$$sum(l, 2) = wt(l, 0) + wt(l, 1) \; ; \; \ldots$$

can be proved as theorems. Theorems are an important component in a framework, as they can help both to explain the meaning of the defined symbols and to reason about specifications and programs. We could also informally but rigorously state explanatory meta-theorems like

$$sum(l, k) = \Sigma_{i=0}^{k-1} wg(l, i)$$

where the (meta) operator Σ is (meta) defined as usual.

The specification-level interface of $\mathcal{WLIST}$ specifies a (defined) program predicate $lsum(l, w)$, which means $w = sum(l, len(l))$, i.e., by the previous meta-theorem, $w = \Sigma_{i=0}^{len(l)-1} wt(l, i)$. The corresponding program P_{lsum} is designed for situations where $wt(l, i)$ may depend on the positions close to i. Thus it uses the open predicate lwt, specified using the weight $wt(rev(b)|[x|a], len(b))$,[10] where $l = rev(b)|[x|a]$ is the list whose weights are to be summed, $i = len(b)$ is the current position in a computation, x is the element at position i in l, and the elements at positions $i+1, i+2, \ldots$ are in a, while those at positions $i-1, i-2, \ldots$ are in b.

The specifications in the interface are the basis for correct reuse through specification reduction.

Here we show a reuse of $\mathcal{WLIST}(X, wt)$ (and $\mathcal{WGRAPH}(X, arc)$, which is a similar framework in which a list represents nodes of a graph and the weights

---

[10] $rev(x)$ means the reverse of x.

represent arcs between adjacent nodes). Since we can have multiple (partial or total) framework completions, we will rename framework symbols and use the usual dot notation, to avoid confusion.

Consider the following completions:

COMPLETION TOWNS OF $\mathcal{WGRAPH}(X, arc)$:
CLOSE X by $\{LON, MAN, MI, \ldots\}$

COMPLETION FLTS OF TOWNS:
CLOSE arc by $arc(x, y, dis) \leftrightarrow (x = MAN \land y = MI \land dis = 2000)$
$$\lor \ldots$$

COMPLETION KMS OF $\mathcal{WLIST}(\text{TOWNS}.X, wt)$:
CLOSE wt by $wt(l, i) = w \leftrightarrow \text{FLTS}.arcwt(l, i, i+1, w) \lor$
$$(w = 0 \land \neg \exists z \,.\, \text{FLTS}.arcwt(l, i, i+1, z))$$

TOWNS has been partially completed to set X to a list of towns. FLTS uses arc to link pairs (x, y) of towns that are connected by a flight, and sets the weight of the link (arc) to be the distance between x and y. It also defines useful specification symbols, like $arcwt(l, i, j, w)$, which indicates that positions i and j in a list l are connected by an arc of weight w.

KMS is used to compute the cumulative distances of connecting flight paths, and to build it we choose $\mathcal{WLIST}(\text{TOWNS}.X, wt)$ because, looking at its interface specification, we see that $sum(l, len(l))$ is the cumulative distance, if we choose wt as indicated in the closure above, i.e., $wt(l, i)$ is the distance from the town at position i to the town at position $i + 1$ if they are connected by a flight, and is 0 otherwise.

We can reduce the specification of lwt to

$$lwt([x], b, 0),$$
$$lwt([x, y|a], b, w) \leftrightarrow \text{FLTS}.arc(x, y, w) \lor$$
$$(w = 0 \land \neg \exists z \,.\, \text{FLTS}.arc(x, y, z))$$

and derive a correct program for it. Steadfastness will guarantee that it correctly composes with P_{lsum}.

We can see the similarity between the closures TOWNS, FLTS and KMS in the example and objects in OO programming. This similarity allows us to consider an open framework as a way to dynamically build specialisations and instances, to be used as objects. A first study of this approach has been given in [34], where we introduce temporal operators. In this way we can specify static methods (they do not change the current instance) and dynamic methods (they may change the current instance). For example, we can model a window, with attributes describing its current dimensions and content. We can specify rows, rectangles, and so on, by first-order formulas, and give static methods to compute such figures. We can also use temporal formulas to *concisely* specify methods that change the current state, e.g. the window dimensions or the figures currently contained (and drawn) in the window. Our notion of steadfastness (*a priori* correctness) applies to static methods, but we do not have yet a satisfactory notion of *a priori* correctness for dynamic methods. Since *a priori* correctness plays an important role in correct reusability, we are currently investigating the possibility of axiomatising explicitly timed objects and programs at a (first-order or higher-order non-temporal) metalogical level where we can define steadfastness, and to use meta-level steadfastness to model steadfastness at the object level of temporal logic.

In summary, steadfastness is defined in terms of interfaces and context dependencies only. It means correct reusability because it is preserved through *inheritance* and *compositionality*. Steadfast components would therefore provide a good assembly guide.

Moreover, because steadfastness is preserved through inheritance and compositionality, steadfast components can be used for both bottom-up and top-down composition. Therefore steadfast components would allow third-party assembly and, we believe, can provide the semantics of components and component composition and reuse, missing from existing object technology, making the latter more declarative and top-down, and thus enhance OOD with suitable semantics for component interfaces.

Epilogue

So where do we go from here? We conclude this paper by outlining our perspective on the role of our approach in next-generation CBD.

Frameworks containing steadfast methods can be used as the basis for the construction of correctly reusable components. We can define various reuse operations, where constraints and specifications are used to ensure correct reuse of the inherited methods.

The development process of a reusable component for a general problem domain is illustrated in Figure 10.

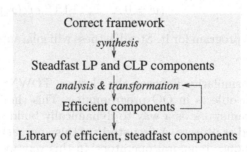

Fig. 10. Developing steadfast components.

In a first phase, we construct an open framework for the chosen problem domain, where we can specify a collection of reusable component operations, and then develop steadfast pure standard logic programs (LPs) and constraint logic programs (CLPs), from their specifications, using logic program synthesis techniques (see [16,36]). In this phase, we can reuse existing developed frameworks.

In the second phase, we apply, iteratively, logic program analysis (e.g. [13]) and transformation techniques (see [51]) to ensure termination and to improve the efficiency of these programs. To be consistent with CBD, we need open termination (informally, an open program $P : \delta \Leftarrow \pi$ with specification (S_δ, S_π) has to terminate in all the pre-interpretations that satisfy S_π in the framework) and transformations that preserve steadfastness. In contexts different from ours, modular termination analysis, e.g., in [14,49], and modular transformations, e.g., in [20], have been studied.

Although the steadfast component operations are implemented by (standard and constraint) logic programs, we can extend the notion of steadfast programs to other programming paradigms, and translate in phase 2 the synthesised logic programs into other (imperative) languages.

Different combinations of these programs then together with the framework form different steadfast components. These components will provide the basic library units for constructing libraries of bigger components, be they patterns or frameworks.

In the wider context of CBD, we see our methodology fitting in with the software development cycle in the manner depicted in Figure 11. The role of

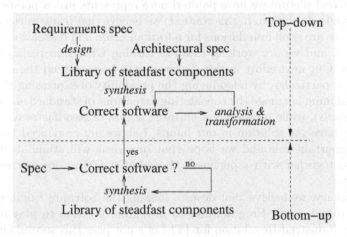

Fig. 11. CBD using libraries of steadfast components.

our methodology will be to provide a library of steadfast components in some chosen programming language, following the process described above. The key contribution of such a library to CBD is that it allows both *top-down* and *bottom-up* styles of development, and indeed a combination of both.

Top-down development will follow the so-called *waterfall model*: given the requirements specification, a design will be made, and software will be synthesised accordingly from the library components in order to meet the requirements. Alternatively we may follow the *software architecture* approach and start with an architectural specification, and synthesise software from the library components. The resulting software is guaranteed to be correct, but it may need to be analysed and transformed to improve efficiency.

Bottom-up development would start from the library of components, and some specification of either the requirements or the architecture. There is no design as such, but instead the development is iterative, in 'pick and mix' style, until the software constructed is seen, or can be verified, to meet the specification. Again, this style is possible because of steadfastness. Composition of steadfast components can show the specification of the composite, and therefore the specification of any software constructed can be compared with the initial specification for the whole system. Guidance as to which components to 'pick and mix' can also be provided by specifications and constraints, as we have discussed before.

If the specifications and the software system under construction have to evolve, then the *spiral model* of software development would be more appropriate. We can achieve this by combining the top-down and the bottom-up development styles described above. In each cycle of the spiral, top-down development can be used to develop software for specifications that have been finalised, whereas bottom-up development can show the gap between interim specifications and the current software system, thus enabling the developer to evolve the specifications or the system appropriately.

The general picture we have painted here represents just a perspective, and not yet a realised solution. In this context, we believe that frameworks and steadfast programs are good foundations for a formalisation and realisation of reusable components, and we are working towards turning CBD into reality in the LP community. Our next effort in this direction will be to extend the specification language (in particular, by introducing the possibility of expressing change) and the programming language (by considering extensions of standard and constraint logic programs), while preserving a suitable notion of steadfastness. We do not pretend to have *the* solution in our hands, but we are convinced that LP can play an important role and we hope that our ideas will stimulate interest in frameworks together with a pertinent theory of specifications, correctness and modularity.

In summary, we believe that despite missing the Software Engineering boat first time round, Logic Programming is in a good position to play an integral part in the Industrial Revolution for IT! Let's not pass this second chance by.

Acknowledgements

We wish to thank the volume editors Fariba Sadri and Tony Kakas for kindly inviting us to contribute to this volume. We are also indebted to the reviewers for their detailed and constructive comments that have considerably improved this paper.

References

1. J.R. Abrial. *The B-Book: Assigning Programs to Meanings.* Cambridge University Press, 1996.

2. R.J. Allen. *A Formal Approach to Software Architecture*. PhD thesis, Carnegie-Mellon University, 1997.
3. J.-M. Andreoli and R.Pareschi. Linear objects: logical processes with built-in inheritance. *New Generation Comp.*, 9:445–473, 1991.
4. E. Astesiano, H.-J. Kreowski, and B. Krieg-Brückner, editors. *Algebraic Foundations of Systems Specifications*. Springer, 1999.
5. L. Bass, P. Clements, and R. Kazman. *Software Architecture in Practice*. Addison-Wesley, 1998.
6. BEA Systems *et al*. CORBA Components. Technical Report orbos/99-02-05, Object Management Group, 1999.
7. J. Bosch and P. Molin. Software architecture design: evaluation and transformation. In *Proc. 1999 IEEE Engineering of Computer Based Systems Symposium*, 1999.
8. D. Box. *Essential COM*. Addison Wesley, 1998.
9. A.W. Brown and K.C. Wallnau. The current state of CBSE. *IEEE Software*, Sept/Oct 1998:37–46, 1998.
10. R. M. Burstall and J. A. Goguen. Putting theories together to make specifications. In R. Reddy, editor, *Proc. IJCAI'77*, pages 1045–1058, 1977.
11. D. Coleman, P. Arnold, S. Bodoff, C. Dollin, H. Gilchrist, F. Hayes, and P. Jeremaes. *Object-Oriented Development: The Fusion Method*. Prentice-Hall, 1994.
12. S. Cook and J. Daniels. *Designing Object Systems*. Prentice-Hall, 1994.
13. A. Cortesi, B. Le Charlier, and S. Rossi. Specification-based automatic verification of Prolog programs. In J. Gallagher, editor, *Proc. LOPSTR 96, Lecture Notes in Computer Science 1207*, pages 38–57. Springer-Verlag, 1997.
14. N. Dershowitz. Termination of rewriting. *J. Symbolic Computation*, 3:69–116, 1987.
15. Y. Deville. *Logic Programming: Systematic Program Development*. International Series in Logic Programming. Addison-Wesley, 1990.
16. Y. Deville and K.-K. Lau. Logic program synthesis. *J. Logic Programming*, 19,20:321–350, 1994. Special Issue: Ten Years of Logic Programming.
17. D.F. D'Souza and A.C. Wills. Extending Fusion: practical rigor and refinement. In R. Malan *et al*, editor, *Object-Oriented Development at Work*. Prentice-Hall, 1996.
18. D.F. D'Souza and A.C. Wills. *Objects, Components, and Frameworks with UML: The Catalysis Approach*. Addison-Wesley, 1999.
19. H.-D. Ehrich. Object specification. In E. Astesiano, H.-J. Kreowski, and B. Krieg-Brückner, editors, *Algebraic Foundations of Systems Specifications*, chapter 12, pages 435–465. Springer, 1999.
20. S. Etalle and M. Gabbrielli. Transformations of CLP modules. *TCS*, 166(1&2):101–146, 1996.
21. P. Flener, K.-K. Lau, and M. Ornaghi. Correct-schema-guided synthesis of steadfast programs. In *Proc. 12th IEEE Int. Automated Software Engineering Conf.*, pages 153–160. IEEE Computer Society Press, 1997.
22. P. Flener, K.-K. Lau, M. Ornaghi, and J. Richardson. An abstract formalisation of correct schemas for program synthesis. *Journal of Symbolic Computation*, 30(1):93–127, July 2000.
23. J.H. Gallier. *Logic for Computer Science: Foundations for Automatic Theorem Proving*. Harper and Row, 1986.
24. E. Gamma, R. Helm, R. Johnson, and J. Vlissades. *Design Patterns – Elements of Reusable Object-Oriented Design*. Addison-Wesley, 1994.

25. D. Garlan, R. Allen, and J. Ockerbloom. Architectural mismatch or why it's hard to build systems out of existing parts. In *Proc. ICSE'95*, pages 179–185, 1995.
26. M. Gelfond and V. Liftschitz. The stable model semantics for logic programming. In R. Kowalski and K.Bowen, editors, *Proc. 5th Int. Conf. and Symp. on Logic Programming*, pages 1070–1080. MIT Press, 1988.
27. J.A. Goguen and R.M. Burstall. Institutions: Abstract model theory for specification and programming. *J. ACM*, 39(1):95–146, 1992.
28. Object Management Group. The Common Object Request Broker: Architecture and specification Revision 2.0, 1995.
29. R. Helm, I.M. Holland, and D. Gangopadhay. Contracts — specifying behavioural compositions in oo systems. *Sigplan Notices*, 25(10), 1990. *Proc. ECOOP/OOPSLA 90*.
30. C.B. Jones. *Systematic Software Development Using VDM*. Prentice Hall, second edition, 1990.
31. N. Kobayashi and A. Yonezawa. Asynchronous communication model based on linear logic. *Formal Aspects of Computing*, 7:113–149, 1995.
32. R. Kowalski. *Logic for Problem Solving*. North-Holland, 1979.
33. R. Kowalski. The relation between logic programming and logic specification. In C.A.R. Hoare and J.C. Shepherdson, editors, *Mathematical Logic and Programming Languages*, pages 11–27. Prentice-Hall, 1985.
34. J. Küster Filipe, K.-K. Lau, M. Ornaghi, and H. Yatsu. On dynamic aspects of OOD frameworks in component-based software development in computational logic. In A. Bossi, editor, *Proc. LOPSTR 99, Lecture Notes in Computer Science*, volume 1817, pages 43–62. Springer-Verlag, 2000.
35. G. Larsen. Designing component-based frameworks using patterns in the UML. *Comms. ACM*, 42(10):38–45, October 1999.
36. K.-K. Lau and M. Ornaghi. A formal approach to deductive synthesis of constraint logic programs. In J.W. Lloyd, editor, *Proc. 1995 Int. Logic Programming Symposium*, pages 543–557. MIT Press, 1995.
37. K.-K. Lau and M. Ornaghi. Forms of logic specifications: A preliminary study. In J. Gallagher, editor, *Proc. LOPSTR 96, Lecture Notes in Computer Science 1207*, pages 295–312. Springer-Verlag, 1997.
38. K.-K. Lau and M. Ornaghi. The relationship between logic programs and specifications — the subset example revisited. *J. Logic Programming*, 30(3):239–257, March 1997.
39. K.-K. Lau and M. Ornaghi. OOD frameworks in component-based software development in computational logic. In P. Flener, editor, *Proc. LOPSTR 98, Lecture Notes in Computer Science 1559*, pages 101–123. Springer-Verlag, 1999.
40. K.-K. Lau and M. Ornaghi. Isoinitial semantics for logic programs. In J.W. Lloyd et al, editor, *Proceedings of the First Int. Conf. on Computational Logic, Lecture Notes in Artificial Intelligence 1861*, pages 223–238. Springer-Verlag, 2000.
41. K.-K. Lau, M. Ornaghi, and S.-Å. Tärnlund. Steadfast logic programs. *J. Logic Programming*, 38(3):259–294, March 1999.
42. J.W. Lloyd. *Foundations of Logic Programming*. Springer-Verlag, second edition, 1987.
43. D.C. Luckham, J.J. Kenney, L.M. Augustin, J. Vera, D. Bryan, and W. Mann. Specification and analysis of system architecture using Rapide. *IEEE Trans, Soft. Eng.*, 21(4):336–355, April 1995.
44. V. Matena and B. Stearns. *Applying Enterprise JavaBeans – Component-based Development for the J2EE Platform*. Addison-Wesley, 2000.

45. R. Mauth. A better foundation: Development frameworks let you build an application with reusable objects. *BYTE*, 21(9):40IS 10–13, September 1996.
46. D. Miller. Forum: A multiple-conclusion specification logic. *TCS*, 165(1):201–231, 1996.
47. G. Nadathur and D.A. Miller. An overview of λProlog. In R.A. Kowalski and A. Bowen, editors, *Proc. 5th Int. Conf. on Logic Programming*, pages 810–827. MIT Press, 1988.
48. L.C. Paulson. Isabelle: The next 700 theorem provers. In P. Odifreddi, editor, *Logic and Computer Science*, pages 361–386. Academic Press, 1990.
49. D. Pedreschi and S. Ruggieri. Verification of logic programs. *J. Logic Programming*, 39(1-3):125–176, 1999.
50. D.E. Perry and A.L. Wolf. Foundations for the study of software architecture. *ACM Software Engineering Notes*, 17(4):40–52, 1992.
51. A. Pettorossi and M. Proietti. Transformation of logic programs: Foundations and techniques. *J. Logic Programming*, 19,20:261–320, 1994. Special Issue on "Ten Years Of Logic Programming".
52. F. Pfenning. Logic programming in the LF logical framework. In G. Huet and G. Plotkin, editors, *Logical Frameworks*, pages 149–181. Cambridge University Press, 1991.
53. J. Rumbaugh, I. Jacobson, and G. Booch. *The Unified Modeling Language Reference Manual*. Addison-Wesley, 1999.
54. M. Shaw and D. Garlan. *Software Architecture: Perspectives on an Emerging Discipline*. Prentice Hall, 1996.
55. J.M. Spivey. *The Z Notation: A Reference Manual*. Prentice Hall, second edition, 1992.
56. C. Szyperski. *Component Software: Beyond Object-Oriented Programming*. Addison-Wesley, 1998.
57. M.H. van Emden and R. Kowalski. The semantics of predicate logic as a programming language. *J. ACM*, 23(4):733–742, October 1976.
58. M. Wirsing. Algebraic specification. In J. Van Leeuwen, editor, *Handbook of Theoretical Computer Science*, pages 675–788. Elsevier, 1990.

Patterns for Prolog Programming

Leon Sterling

Department of Computer Science and Software Engineering,
University of Melbourne,
Victoria, 3010, Australia,
leon@cs.mu.oz.au

Abstract. An approach to Prolog programming based on patterns is presented. Two classes of patterns are identified. *Skeletons* are programs constituting a specific control flow and act as reusable starting components for program development in Prolog. *Techniques* are standard operations that can be performed on a wide range of skeletons. The result of applying a technique to a skeleton is a new program which performs additional Prolog computations while following the control flow of the skeleton. Both classes of patterns are straightforward to understand and reuse due to the high level of abstraction of logic programming languages. Taking a pattern-directed view makes Prolog programs easier to build, for which some anecdotal evidence is given. In honour of Professor Bob Kowalski, the patterns are traced back where possible to Kowalski's original monograph on logic programming.

1 Program Patterns

Patterns have been widely acknowledged as being important in crafting complex systems in areas such as architecture and machine design. During the last decade, design patterns have emerged for software engineering, particularly associated with the widespread espousal of object-oriented programming. To some extent, patterns have been a theme throughout the evolution of programming languages. Subroutines and macros can certainly be viewed as patterns, and were introduced to allow reusability within a single piece of software. Modules and library functions have been developed to allow reuse between software systems.

The history of computer science has shown that progress in software development has come through better abstractions. Logic programming [9] is an abstraction introduced in the 1970s. The key abstraction introduced in logic programming is the logical variable and the use of unification as a uniform means of computation. Unification abstracts away many data manipulation details, making programs more concise, and easier to read and write. The high level of abstraction can make it easy to see connections between programs, and problems can be decomposed and mapped to code in ways not apparent with conventional programming languages.

This paper describes patterns that have emerged within Prolog programming. The patterns constitute reusable components. We discuss how the components

A.C. Kakas, F. Sadri (Eds.): Computat. Logic (Kowalski Festschrift), LNAI 2407, pp. 374–401, 2002.
© Springer-Verlag Berlin Heidelberg 2002

can facilitate program development and maintainability. Because logic programming languages are more abstract, some patterns have been easier to see. Many of the patterns have their origin in Kowalski's pioneering monograph on logic programming [9].

The structure of the paper is as follows. We loosely identify two classes of programming patterns for Prolog programming. Skeletons are discussed in Section 2, while techniques are discussed in Sections 3 and 4. The difference between the techniques discussed in Sections 3 and 4 lies in the type of change made to a program by applying a technique.

Thinking of a logic program in terms of skeletons and techniques arose from research into developing a standard methodology for Prolog programming called stepwise enhancement. Stepwise enhancement can be incorporated into a design method for Prolog, a topic by and large neglected within logic programming. Stepwise enhancement is presented in Section 5, including an example of program design. Finally, related work and conclusions are discussed.

2 Skeletons

A significant feature of logic programming is the coincidence of the declarative and procedural semantics. The first class of patterns we identify are reusable programs, which we have called *skeletons*. Skeletons constitute the essential control flow of a program, and need to be understood procedurally. Good Prolog programming requires you to write code that is declarative, i.e. easy to read, and which executes efficiently under Prolog's execution. They capture efficient execution 'idioms'. Choosing a skeleton is a design decision.

Four useful categories of skeletons are

- data structure traversers
- algorithmic motifs
- grammars
- interpreters.

Skeletons are reused by adding arguments to perform additional computation while the program is being executed. Examples are extending a language interpreter to count operations being performed, or keeping track of intermediate results to avoid infinite loops.

In this section, each category of skeleton is described in turn, giving specific examples, and relating them back to *Logic for Problem Solving* [9] where appropriate. We will use the notation LPS <pp> to refer to specific page numbers <pp> from *Logic for Problem Solving*.

2.1 Data Structure Traversers

The most common data structure for logic programs is the list. Many Prolog programs are based on skeletons for traversing lists. Skeletons for list processing have been described elsewhere, notably in [23] and [25] and indeed LPS 109-112. We give two running examples of other data structures - binary trees and graphs.

```
is_tree(leaf(X))¹.          has_leaf(leaf(X)).
is_tree(tree(L,R)) :-        has_leaf(tree(L,R)) :- has_leaf(L).
   is_tree(L),               has_leaf(tree(L,R)) :- has_leaf(R).
   is_tree(R).
```

Programs 1 and 2 Skeletons for traversing a tree

Programs 1 and 2 are skeleton programs for traversing binary trees with values only at leaf nodes. Program 1, the left-hand program, does a complete traversal of the tree. Note that Program 1, viewed declaratively, is a type definition for binary trees. Program 1 is implicit in the predicate **Tips** from LPS 108. Program 2, the right-hand program, traverses a single branch of a binary tree. Its declarative reading is that a binary tree has a leaf.

Program 3 is a skeleton for traversing graphs. The relation connected(X,Y) is true if node X is connected to node Y in the graph defined by edge/2 facts. The two clauses can be read declaratively. The first clause states that two nodes are connected if there is an edge between them. The second (recursive) clause says that X is connected to Y if there is an edge from X to Z and Z is connected to Y. Program 3 is the transitive closure of the edge relation. Considered as a Prolog program, the program checks whether two nodes are connected via depth-first search inherited from Prolog's computation model.

```
connected(X,Y) :- edge(X,Y).
connected(X,Y) :- edge(X,Z), connected(Z,Y).
```

Program 3 A skeleton for traversing a graph

Program 3 is not exactly found in *Logic for Problem Solving*. That is consistent with Bob Kowalski's emphasis on the expressibility of logic for problem solving rather than expression of algorithmic motifs. For comparison, a doubly recursive predicate for graph traversal, a different less efficient skeleton, is given in LPS, pages 102-103. A collection of facts of the form Go*(A,B)<- Go*(D,X)<- are given, along with the axiom Go*(x,y) <- Go*(x,z), Go*(z,y).

---

[1] The notation in *Logic for Problem Solving* is opposite to the standard Prolog notation used in this paper. In LPS, variables were denoted by lower case letters and predicate symbols, including constants, denoted by words starting with upper case letters. Kowalski used the functor cons to represent binary trees as lists, which he regarded as a special case of binary tree. I prefer the symbols given here.

2.2   Algorithmic Motifs

The essence of an execution idiom is an algorithm. Many algorithms make good skeletons. The prototypical example of an algorithmic motif is the well known Euclidean algorithm for computing the greatest common divisor, d, of two integers, m and n. Knuth gives a good description of the Euclidean algorithm in [8]. Later in the same chapter of his book, Knuth develops the extended Euclidean algorithm, which as well as computing d, is extended to compute two integer multipliers, a and b, such that $a * m + b * n = d$.

Seeing the pattern between the Euclidean algorithm and the extended Euclidean algorithm is precisely the intuition we are trying to capture. Program 4 gives Prolog code for the Euclidean algorithm. In Section 3.4, we will compare it to the extended Euclidean algorithm. The treatment is taken from the Ph.D. dissertation of Arun Lakhotia [10]. More discussion of the program will be given in Section 3.4.

```
gcd(M,N,GCD) :-
    Rem is M mod N,
    gcd(Rem,M,N,GCD).

gcd(0,M,N,N).
gcd(Rem,M,N,GCD) :- Rem > 0, gcd(N,Rem,GCD).
```

Program 4 The Euclidean algorithm

2.3   Grammars

The roots of logic programming lie in grammars for parsing natural language. Grammars are excellent examples of skeletons. The most common grammars within logic programming are definite clause grammars (DCGs). DCGs are in fact syntactic sugar for Prolog, and most Prolog systems translate DCGs directly into Prolog.

Program 5 contains a fragment of a definite clause grammar (DCG) for parsing a Pascal-like programming language. The fragment contains three rules. The first rule says that a (legal) statement is an identifier, followed by :=, followed by an expression. The second and third rules handle if-then-else statements and while statements respectively.

```
statement ⟶ identifier, [:=], expression.
statement ⟶ [if], test, [then], statement, [else], statement.
statement ⟶ [while], test, [do], statement.
```

Program 5 Fragment of a grammar

The parsing problem is prominent in *Logic for Problem Solving*, for example on LPS pages 49-53. The text [17] develops parsers around skeleton grammars.

2.4 Interpreters

Programs and data are syntactically identical in logic programming. This similarity makes it easy to write interpreters in Prolog. Many applications, such as expert system shells, have exploited this feature of Prolog. Interpreters are natural skeletons.

```
solve(true).
solve((A,B)) :- solve(A), solve(B).
solve(A) :- system(A), A.
solve(A) :- clause(A,B), solve(B).
```

Program 6 The vanilla meta-interpreter

The vanilla[2] meta-interpreter (interpreter for Prolog in Prolog) is given in Program 6. The relation `solve(Goal)` is true if `Goal` is true in the program defined by `clause/2` facts. This interpreter makes explicit the choice of clause, but abstracts away other details using Prolog's backtracking and unification. The meta-interpreter in Program 6 has been re-used for many applications - including Prolog tracers, partial evaluators, and rule-based systems.

A meta-interpreter is discussed at length in Chapter 12 of LPS in the context of correct representation of a provability relation. This work was taken further by Bowen and Kowalski in their influential paper on meta-programming [1].

3 Techniques for Extensions

Techniques[3] are the second class of patterns. They capture basic Prolog programming practices, such as building a data structure or performing calculations in recursive code. Unlike skeletons, techniques are not programs but can be conceived as a family of operations that can be applied to a program to produce a program.

Informally, a programming technique interleaves some additional computation around the control flow of a skeleton program. The additional computation might calculate a value or produce a side effect such as screen output. Syntactically, techniques may rename predicates, add arguments to predicates, add goals to clauses, and/or add clauses to programs.

---

[2] This term caught on from the flavors system of Lisp.

[3] An anonymous reviewer criticised the term techniques as too unspecific. The criticism is reasonable, but I have been unable to come up with a better alternative term.

By and large, techniques are not referred to explicitly in *Logic for Problem Solving*. There are several instances of programs that can be interpreted as having been created by applying techniques to skeletons, for example the sorting program on LPS115. However, we won't focus on the comparisons here.

This paper views techniques as operating on programs directly. Lee Naish [14] has taken an alternate view, and describes techniques as instances of higher order predicates. The approaches are compared and contrasted in [15].

In this section we consider a restricted enhancement called an *extension*, which preserves the computational behavior of the skeleton. Several kinds of extension are mentioned in the following subsections.

3.1   Calculate Technique and Build Technique

The *calculate* and *build* techniques both compute while following the control flow of the skeleton. The *calculate* technique calculates a value and the *build* technique constructs a data structure. An extra argument is added to the 'defining' predicate in the skeleton, and an extra goal is added to the body of each recursive clause. In the case of the *calculate* technique, the added goal is an arithmetic calculation; in the case of the *build* technique, the goal builds a data structure, usually by unification. In both cases, the added goal relates the extra argument in the head of the clause to the related extra argument(s) in the body of the clause.

```
prod_leaves(leaf(X),X).             sum_leaves(leaf(X),X).
prod_leaves(tree(L,R),Prod) :-      sum_leaves(tree(L,R),Sum) :-
    prod_leaves(L,LProd),               sum_leaves(L,LSum),
    prod_leaves(R,RProd),               sum_leaves(R,RSum),
    Prod is LProd*RProd.                Sum is LSum+RSum.
```

Programs 7 and 8 Extensions of Program 1 using *calculate*

Two typical examples of the application of the *calculate* technique are given as Programs 7 and 8. Both are extensions of Program 1 which traverses a binary tree with values at its leaves. The left-hand program (7) computes the product of the value of the leaves of the trees. The extra argument in the base case is the value of the leaf node. In the recursive case, the extra goal says that the product of a tree is the product of its left subtree and its right subtree. The predicate is_tree has been renamed to prod_leaves. The right-hand program (8), which computes the sum of the leaves, is very similar. The only differences are the choice of predicate and variable names and the calculation in the extra is/2 goal.

The *calculate* technique applies equally well to Program 6, the meta-interpreter. Program 9 calculates the number of reductions made in solving a goal. solve/1 has been renamed to num_reductions, base values filled in, and extra goals added to recursive clauses. A straightforward exercise is to apply the *calculate* technique to Program 3 to produce a program num which counts the number of nodes in the path that connects two nodes in a graph.

```
num_reductions(true,0).
num_reductions((A,B),N) :-
    num_reductions(A,NA), num_reductions(B,NB), N is NA+NB.
num_reductions(A,1) :-
    system(A), A.
num_reductions(A,N) :-
    clause(A,B), num_reductions(B,NB), N is NB+1.
```

Program 9 Extension of Program 6 using *calculate*

Typical examples of the *build* technique are given in the two programs below. Program 10 builds a path in a tree and is extension of Program 2. Another straightforward exercise is to apply the *build* technique to Program 3 to produce a program path, which constructs the path that connects two nodes in a graph.

```
path_tree(leaf(X),[]).
path_tree(tree(L,R),P1) :- path_tree(L,P), P1 = [1|P].
path_tree(tree(L,R),P1) :- path_tree(R,P), P1 = [2|P].
```

Program 10 Extension of Program 2 using *build*

Program 11 extends Program 6 to construct a proof tree. Proof trees are applied in the case study in Section 5.3. Another example of the *build* technique would be building a parse tree extending the grammar of Program 5, as was used in the testing application reported in [22].

```
solve(true,true).
solve((A,B),Proof) :-
    solve(A,ProofA), solve(B,ProofB), Proof = (ProofA,ProofB).
solve(A,system_goal(A)) :-
    system(A), A.
solve(A,Proof) :-
    clause(A,B), solve(B,ProofB), Proof = A if ProofB.
```

Program 11[4] Extension of Program 6 using *build*

---

[4] This program assumes that if/2 has been declared as an infix operator.

3.2   Accumulators

The accumulator technique adds two arguments to the defining predicate in the skeleton to allow for state variables in a program. The first argument is used to record the current value of the variable in question and the second contains the final result of the computation.

The base case relates the input and output arguments, often via unification. One difference between *calculate* and *accumulate-calculate* is in the need to add an auxiliary predicate. In this call to the auxiliary predicate, the accumulator is initialised, in a manner reminiscent of initial values in object-oriented methods.

Program 12 shows the result of applying the *accumulate-calculate* technique to the tree traversal program, Program 1. It computes the sum of the leaves of a binary tree and is comparable to Program 8. In general, programs written with accumulator techniques will run more efficiently than the equivalent program written with *calculate* and *build* techniques, due to the way tail recursion is implemented in Prolog.

```
sum_leaves(Tree,Sum) :- accum_sum_leaves(Tree,0,Sum).

accum_sum_leaves(leaf(X),Accum,Sum) :- Sum is Accum + X.
accum_sum_leaves(tree(L,R),Accum,Sum) :-
    accum_sum_leaves(L,Accum,Accum1),
    accum_sum_leaves(R,Accum1,Sum).
```

Program 12 Extension of Program 1 using *accumulate-calculate*

Program 13 is an example of the application of the *accumulate-build* technique, also applied to Program 1. The predicate `traversal` builds a traversal of the leaves of the tree. There is no explicit arithmetic calculation, rather lists built by unification in the base clause. There is one trick here. Accumulators build structures in reverse order and hence the right subtree is traversed before the left subtree in order to have the final list in the correct order.

```
traversal(Tree,Xs) :- accum_leaves(Tree,[],Sum).

accum_leaves(leaf(X),Accum,[X|Accum]).
accum_leaves(tree(L,R),Accum,Xs) :-
    accum_leaves(R,Accum,Accum1),
    accum_leaves(L,Accum1,Sum),
```

Program 13 Extension of Program 1 using *accumulate-build*

The well known structure of difference-lists can be explained as an example of a programming techniques in a manner similar to accumulators. An account can be found in *The Art of Prolog* [25].

3.3   Context Parameters

Since logic programming languages do not have global variables, a useful technique is to add an extra argument for the propagation of information. It is assumed that the context variable is grounded before execution begins. For example, Program 14 adds a depth context to the meta-interpreter of Program 6.

```
depth(true,Depth).
depth((A,B),Depth) :- depth(A,Depth), depth(B,Depth).
depth(A,Depth) :- system(A), A.
depth(A,Depth) :-
    clause(A,B), Depth1 is Depth+1, depth(B,Depth1).
```

Program 14 Including depth in a meta-interpreter

Techniques applied to the extension created from the context technique typically use the information in the context variable. For example, a tracer could indent by the depth value to convey depth information on screen. An expert system shell can carry rules that have been used to provide an interactive explanation, as described in Section 5.3.

3.4   Composition

Two extensions of the same skeleton share computational behavior. They can be combined into a single program which combines the functionality of each separate extension. Techniques can be developed independently and subsequently combined automatically. The (syntactic) operation for combining extensions is called *composition*. This is similar in intent to function composition where separate functionalities are combined into a single function.

Program 15 shows the result of composition of Programs 7 and 8, prod_leaves and sum_leaves. Note that the operation of composition is syntactic. The extra arguments in prod_sum_leaves are copied verbatim from their respective programs, as are the extra goals in the recursive clause. An algorithm for composition is described in Chapter 18 of *The Art of Prolog* and Prolog code is given there for performing composition.

```
prod_sum_leaves(leaf(X),X,X).
prod_sum_leaves(tree(L,R),Prod,Sum) :-
    prod_sum_leaves(L,LProd,LSum),
    prod_sum_leaves(R,RProd,RSum),
    Prod is LProd*RProd,
    Sum is LSum+RSum.
```

Program 15 Composition of Programs 7 and 8

A more elaborate example is the extended Euclidean algorithm given as Program 16. The relationship $gcd(M, N, GCD, A, B)$ computes integers A and B such that $A*M + B*N = GCD$. It extends Program 4 for computing the greatest common divisor by adding two accumulators, one for computing A and one for computing B, and three context parameters, one for determining a quotient which is used to save repeated expressions, and one each for computing A and B, to save a result from the previous iteration.

```
gcd(M,N,GCD,A,B) :- gcd_ex(M,N,GCD,0,1,A,1,0,B).

gcd_ex(M,N,GCD,A,AP,FinalA,B,BP,FinalB) :-
    Rem is M mod N,
    Quot is M//N,
    gcd_ex(Rem,Quot,M,N,GCD,A,AP,FinalA,B,BP,FinalB).


gcd_ex(0,Quot,M,N,N,A,AP,A,B,BP,B).
gcd_ex(Rem,Quot,M,N,GCD,A,AP,FinalA,B,BP,FinalB) :-
    Rem > 0,
    NewA is AP  Quot*A,
    NewB is BP  Quot*B,
    gcd_ex(N,Rem,GCD,NewA,A,FinalA,NewB,B,FinalB).
```

Program 16 The extended Euclidean algorithm

At first glance, the code for Program 16 in general and predicate `gcd_ex` in particular looks complicated. There are eleven parameters in the predicate. However, realising that the most of the arguments occur in pairs, and that they are standard programming patterns, leads to a straightforward understanding of the code.

4   Techniques for Enhancements

A more general modification of a skeleton yields an *enhancement*. Examples of enhancements are using a depth bound to cut off a computation, and avoid looping in a search application by checking an accumulator keeping track of previously visited nodes.

To appreciate how adding goals can change program behavior, consider Program 17 which recognizes 'positive trees', that is trees all of whose leaf nodes contain positive values. It is an enhancement of Program 1 for traversing binary trees. The predicate `is_tree` has been renamed to `positive_tree`, and the goal $X > 0$ has been added to the base case. Program 17 is clearly related to Program 1 but behaves differently. If a leaf in the tree has a negative value, the program will fail, and so it has a different meaning from Program 1.

```
positive_tree(leaf(X)) :- X > 0.
positive_tree(tree(L,R)) :-
    positive_tree(L),
    positive_tree(R).
```

Program 17 Enhancement of Program 1

The next three examples give some techniques which make useful, common changes to programs. The first example is imposing a depth bound cut-off. This can be useful for avoiding having a program go into an infinite loop. Program 18 imposes a depth bound cut-off on the meta-interpreter of Program 6. The same technique could be used to place a bound on a tree to only consider branches of a certain depth. That is left as an exercise to the reader.

```
depth(true,Depth).
depth((A,B),Depth) :-
    Depth > 0, depth(A,Depth), depth(B,Depth).
depth(A,Depth) :-
    Depth > 0, system(A), A.
depth(A,Depth) :-
    Depth > 0, clause(A,B),
    Depth1 is Depth-1, depth(B,Depth1).
```

Program 18 Depth cut-off

```
connected(X,Y) :- connected_enh(X,Y,[X]).

connected_enh(X,Y,Visited) :- edge(X,Y).
connected_enh(X,Y,Visited) :-
    edge(X,Z), not member(Z,Visited),
    connected(Z,Y,[Z|Visited]).
```

Program 19 An enhancement keeping track of nodes visited previously

A useful technique is keeping track of the nodes visited. The technique allows the programmer to avoid an infinite loop while traversing a graph with a cycle. The visited nodes, built as an accumulator as in Program 19 on the previous page, can be viewed as a context parameter. The test for membership changes the behavior of the program.

Another useful idea is a result variable, for reporting failure in a meta-interpreter. Program 20 presents the predicate `result(Goal,Result)` which is true if `Result` is the result of solving `Goal`. A value of *yes* denotes success, while *no* denotes failure. The cuts are necessary here to avoid wrong answers on backtracking. Explaining why is beyond the scope of the paper. The **and** predicate is an example of adding clauses to a program. An adaptation of this program serves as a skeleton for the example to be described in Section 5.3.

```
result(true,yes) :- !.
result((A,B),Result) :- !,
    result(A,ResultA),
    result(B,ResultB),
    and(ResultA,ResultB,Result).
result(A,Result) :-
    system(A), !, (A -> Result  yes ; Result = no).=
result(A,Result) :-
    clause(A,B), result(B,Result).
result(A,no) :-
    not clause(A,B).

and(yes,yes,yes).                    and(no,yes,no).
and(yes,no,no).                      and(no,no,no).
```

Program 20 Adding a result variable

5   Program Design Using Patterns

5.1   Systematic Program Construction

Despite attractive features, Prolog has not been widely adopted within software engineering. Standard development practices have not been adapted to Prolog. A major area of weakness is design. Prolog programs have often been viewed as executable specifications. Because specification and implementation are so close, the design phase of software engineering has been often neglected for projects being developed in Prolog. Nothing analogous to design techniques, such as structured analysis for procedural languages or object-oriented design for object-oriented languages, as taught in standard software engineering texts such as [19] and [18], have been developed for logic languages.

The most rigorous presentation of a systematic development of Prolog programs was given by Deville in his excellent monograph [2]. Deville advocates three stages in a methodology, construction of a specification followed by construction of a logic description, which is then transformed to a logic procedure. The approach has been tested only so far for programming-in-the-small. The middle stage, logic descriptions, are arguably at the design level, but remain to be widely tested for their practicality. Deville's approach advocates reaching some of the extensions presented in the previous sections in a different way, but the final programs are the same.

Flach, in Chapter 5 of his book *Simply Logical* [3] has a short section on program development with skeletons which is complementary to the approach presented in this paper.

5.2 Stepwise Enhancement

The method of *stepwise enhancement*, an adaptation of stepwise refinement, was developed to facilitate program development in Prolog. It was originally conceived in the context of Prolog meta-interpreters for building expert systems [21]. The construction of meta-interpreters was extended to more general logic programs as part of the Ph.D. research of Arun Lakhotia [10].

Stepwise enhancement permits a systematic construction of Prolog programs, while exploiting Prolog's high-level features. Stepwise enhancement is an activity for the design phase of a software project. It consists of three steps:

1. Identify a skeleton program to constitute the control flow of the program.
2. Create enhancements to the skeleton using standard programming techniques.
3. Compose the separate enhancements to give the final program.

Developing a program is typically straightforward once the skeleton is decided. Knowing what skeleton to use is less straightforward and must be learned by experience, which is true for any design task. By splitting up the program development into three steps, the design process is simplified and given structure.

A tutorial example of using stepwise enhancement to develop a simple program is given in Chapter 13 of [25]. This paper outlines the development of a program, which computes in a single traversal of a list, the intersection and union of the elements of the list considered as sets. Program 15, presented in this paper, is a similar example. A program computing the sum and product of the leaves of a binary tree in a single traversal of the tree was effectively constructed by stepwise enhancement.

Program 15 is too small an example to be convincing. A more realistic example is given in the following sub-section. Other anecdotal evidence is as follows. A detailed example of code developed using stepwise enhancement is a Prolog debugger, reported in [11]. The approach arose out of the failure of the first author to add features to an existing Prolog debugger from Texas Instruments. Focusing on the patterns needed for each feature simplified the code greatly and allowed code to be shared easily between features.

Stepwise enhancement has also been useful for developing programs for software testing. A skeleton parser for Pascal (of which Program 3 is a part) was instrumented to give def-use chains and block numbering. The experience is reported in [22]. A novice Prolog programmer adapted the program for instrumenting data coverage testing to work on C code rather than Pascal. The programmer was successful due to the structuring of the problem and by being able to adapt patterns.

Stepwise enhancement has been adapted for other logic languages. Michaylov in [12] has developed the idea of stepwise enhancement for CLP($\mathcal{R}$) and has developed an interesting case study with Ordóñez [13].

5.3 Case Study: An Expert System Shell

An extended example of using stepwise enhancement to build an expert system shell with the ability to interactively explain successes and failures is given in Chapter 17 of [25]. That example is reconstructed here as a case study of using patterns. The shell arose from a sustained effort to use Prolog for expert systems, including [21] and [26]. The trickiest part of the shell is incorporating reasoning about failures. There is no doubt my understanding was greatly enhanced by focusing initially on an appropriate skeleton. Communicating the coding insights was facilitated by the pattern approach.

The current presentation extends some of the concepts from stepwise enhancement. We describe the shell using four types of descriptions:

- specifications,

- design descriptions,

- technique applications,

- code components.

Using a mixture of these four 'software engineering entities' effectively creates a design level for Prolog programs. Design for logic languages is a topic that has been largely neglected. A detailed discussion of the features of the design are beyond the present scope. However, I claim it is straightforward to go from the design to the final code, namely Program 17.23 in *The Art of Prolog*. The top-level of that program is reproduced[5] here to make the case study self-contained.

Our notion of a specification of a Prolog program is heavily influenced by Deville [2], and was adapted in [25].

A *Prolog program specification* consists of:

- a program name,

- a list of arguments,

- a list of types corresponding to each of the arguments,

- a (declarative) relation scheme given in precise natural language,

- an elaboration of modes of use,

- an elaboration of multiplicities of solution.

---

[5] An omission from Program 17.23 has been corrected.

Specification	monitor(Goal,Proof)
Types:	Goal: *literal*
	Proof: *proof-tree*
Relation Scheme:	monitor/2 succeeds:

- if a result of *yes* is returned from solving Goal using a solve level meta-interpreter, in which case Proof is a proof tree representing the successful computation, or

- when the end of the computation is reached, in which case Proof is a list of failure branches since the last success.

Modes of use:	Goal is an input while Proof is an output.
Multiplicities:	Succeeds one more time than the number of solutions to Goal.

The top-level specification for our case study on the previous page is for a binary predicate monitor which, given a goal and an (implicit) rule base, gives a proof tree demonstrating that that the goal is implied by the rules, or a failure tree demonstrating that the goal does not follow from the rules. A program that interactively presents the proof or failure tree can be easily written. Note that the presentation of the case study is top-down. The formats of data structures are presented as needed.

A *design description* builds on a specification by adding predicates that the predicate calls, information about the patterns to be used to construct it, and omitting modes of use and multiplicities. Specifically a design description for a program p contains:

- a program name,
- a list of arguments,
- a list of types corresponding to each of the arguments,
- a (declarative) relation scheme given in precise natural language,
- a list of predicates and their arities called by p,
- an enumeration of the clauses in p with a precise description of the 'cases' each clause handles,
- a skeleton s that p is built around,
- a list of techniques that are applied to s to build p.
- the origin for each argument and clause, from either the skeleton or a technique application.

For our running example,

Design Description   `monitor(Goal,Proof)`

Types: `Goal`: *literal*
                       `Proof`: *proof tree*

Relation Scheme: `monitor/2` succeeds:

- if a result of *yes* is returned from solving `Goal` using a solve level meta-interpreter, in which case `Proof` is a proof tree representing the successful computation, or

- when the end of the computation is reached, in which case `Proof` is a list of failure branches since the last success.

Predicates called: `set_search_tree/0`, `filter/2`
                         `solve/4`,   `collect_proof/1`

Clauses: Clause 1: Initialises proof collection with `set_search_tree/0`, then generates solutions to `Goal` using `solve/4` and filters them using `filter/2`
                         Clause 2: Collects the remaining failure branches using `collect_proof/1`

Skeleton used: `monitor(Goal)` covering Clause 1 and Clause 2

Techniques used: *Build* technique to construct `Proof`

The predicates referred to in the design description must be described in turn, sometimes recursively, by specifications, design descriptions, or code components. A design description is degenerate when its skeleton is itself and there are no technique applications. Code components differ from design descriptions by giving explicit code rather than a list of skeletons and techniques. Descriptions of the clauses are listed as necessary. Code components can contain several predicates, which is desirable for mutually recursive code.

Specifically, a *code component* contains:

- a program name,
- a list of arguments,
- a list of types corresponding to each of the arguments,
- a (declarative) relation scheme given in precise natural language,
- a list of predicates (and their arities) called,

– a list of clauses, and a declarative description of what they do,
– a set of clauses.

Proceeding with the case study, here are code components for `monitor/1` and `filter/1` (which is called by `monitor/1`).

Code component	`monitor(Goal)`
Types:	`Goal`: *literal*
Relation Scheme:	`monitor/1` succeeds:

- if *yes* is returned from solving Goal using a 'result' meta-interpreter, or
- when the end of the computation is reached.

Predicates called:	`solve/2`, `filter/1`
Clauses:	Clause 1: Generates solutions to Goal using `solve/2` and filters them using `filter/1`
	Clause 2: Succeeds
Code:	`monitor(Goal) :-`
	`    solve(Goal,Result),`
	`        filter(Result).`
	`monitor(Goal).`

Code component	`filter(Result)`
Types:	`Result`: the atom *yes* or *no*
Relation Scheme:	`filter/1` succeeds if `Result` is *yes* and fails if `Result` is *no*.
Predicates called:	
Clauses:	Clause 1: Succeeds for *yes*
	Clause 2: Fails for *no*
Code:	`filter(yes).`
	`filter(no) :- fail.`

Finally we consider technique applications which are needed to describe the changes to the skeleton code. The level of detail in a technique application description varies, according to where we are in the design phase. Recall, as shown in Sections 3 and 4, that a technique can add extra clauses or extra arguments or both.

A technique application description contains:

- a program name,

- a list of any new arguments and their types,

- the program (skeleton) to which the technique is applied,

- the technique type,

- initialisation clauses for each new argument,

- new predicates called,

- changes needed to each clause.

Before giving examples of technique applications, we turn to the central constituent of the case study. The design description for the extended result meta-interpreter `solve/4` is the most complicated in the case study. It best illustrates how patterns can be used effectively to build up a more complicated program. The rule language, as discussed in *The Art of Prolog* is artificial, and has been chosen for pedagogical reasons. Operator declarations for & and is_true are assumed to be :- op(40,xfy,&). and :- op(30,xf,is_true). An example of a rule which states that a dish should be placed at the top of an oven if it is a pastry and small, is as follows.

```
rule(place_oven(Dish,top),
      pastry(Dish) is_true & size(Dish,small) is_true,p1).
```

The design description on the next page says that `solve/4` is the composition of three applications of techniques to a rule interpreter `solve/2` which returns results. It behaves similarly to Program 20. The design is best explained starting with the skeleton, given as a code component.

Design Description	solve(Goal,Result,Rules,Proof)

Types:	Goal: *literal*
	Result: the atom *yes* or *no*
	Rules: *list of rules*
	Proof: *proof tree*

Relation Scheme: solve/4 succeeds:

- if a result of *yes* is returned from solving Goal using a solve level meta-interpreter, in which case Proof is a proof tree representing the successful computation, or
- when the end of the computation is reached, in which case Proof is a list of failure branches since the last success.

Predicates called:	rule/3,	fact/1
	solve_body/4,	askable/1
	solve_askable/4	

Clauses:	Clause 1: Returns a Result of *yes* when Goal is a fact.
	Clause 2: Calls solve_body when Goal matches a rule in the program.
	Clause 3: Calls solve_askable to handle an askable Goal.
	Clause 4: Returns a Result of *no* when Goal doesn't match a rule or fact.

Skeleton used:	solve(Goal,Result) (Clauses 1, 2, and 4)

Techniques used:	*Context* technique to handle Rules
	Build technique to construct Proof
	Enhancement technique to handle Clause 3

Code component	solve(Goal,Result)
Types:	Goal: *literal*
	Result: the atom *yes* or *no*
Relation Scheme:	Given a set of rules of the form rule(A,B,Name), Goal has Result *yes* if it follows from the rules and *no* if it does not.
Predicates called:	fact/1, solve/2
	rule/3, filter/1
	solve_and/3
Clauses:	Clause 1: Handles facts with solve/2
	Clause 2: Handles rules with solve/2
	Clause 3: solve/2 returns with Result *no*
	Clause 4: Handles conjunctions with solve_body/2
	Clause 5: Handles individual goals with solve_body/2
	Clause 6: solve_and/3 does not proceed if Result is *no*
	Clause 7: solve_and/3 proceeds recursively if Result is *yes*
Code:	

```
solve(Goal,yes) :- fact(Goal).
solve(Goal,yes) :-
    rule(Goal,Body,Name),
    solve_body(Body,Result).
solve(Goal,no).

solve_body(A\&B,Result) :-
    solve(A,ResultA),
    solve_and(ResultA,B,Result).
solve_body(Goal is\_true,Result) :-
    solve(Goal,Result).

solve_and(no,Goal,no).
solve_and(yes,Goal,Result) :-
    solve(Goal,Result).
```

We now give the first technique application, adding rules to the result interpreter.

Technique application	solve(Goal,Result,Rules)
New arguments:	Rules: *list of rules*
Skeleton:	solve(Goal,Result)
Technique type:	*Context*
Initialization:	Rules = [ ]
Clauses:	Clause 1: Rules unchanged Clause 2: Name added to rule list in body Clauses 3-7: Rules unchanged

---

The next technique application adds a proof tree to the result interpreter.

Technique application	solve(Goal,Result,Proof)
New arguments:	Proof: *proof tree*
Skeleton:	solve(Goal,Result)
Technique type:	*Build*
Initialization:	Proof = Proof
Clauses:	Clause 1: Proof = fact(Goal) Clause 2: Proof recursively built Clause 3: Proof = no_match(Goal) Clause 4: Proof recursively built Clause 5: Proof unchanged Clause 6: Proof = unsearched Clause 7: Proof unchanged

---

The final technique application adds a 'query the user' capability [20] to the result interpreter. A specification/design description/code component is needed for solve_askable/2. We leave that detail to [25].

Technique application	solve(Goal,Result)
Skeleton:	solve(Goal,Result)
Technique type:	*Clause enhancement*
Initialization:	
New predicates:	askable/1, solve_askable/2
Clauses:	New clause added between clauses 2 and 3:

$$\text{solve(A,Result) :- askable(A),}$$
$$\text{solve\_askable(A,Result).}$$

We can now complete the top-level of the design with technique applications for our top-level predicates `monitor` and `filter`. To create `monitor/2` from `monitor/1` using the build technique, we need to say how the proof tree is constructed. This is best handled by leaving a hook, or setting up a design description for any additional predicates.

Technique application	monitor(Goal,Proof)
New arguments:	Proof : *proof tree*
Skeleton:	monitor(Goal)
Technique type:	*Build*
Initialization:	init_proof(Proof)
New predicates:	set_search_tree/0, collect_proof/1
Clauses:	Clause 1: add goals initialising the search tree and initialising extra arguments Clause 2: add goal collecting a proof

The effect of the technique application is to replace the two clauses for monitor/1 by the following two clauses. We have included an initial goal init_rules because context parameters must be set in their calling predicates.

```
monitor(Goal,Proof) :-
    set_search_tree, init_rules(Rules), init_proof(Proof),
    solve(Goal,Result,Rules,Proof),
    filter(Result,Proof).
monitor(Goal,Proof) :-
    collect_proof(Proof).
```

The definition of init_rules/1 is init_rules([ ]).

A specification for one of the new predicates is given as an example. Its detail can be filled in later. The situation is similar for collect_proof/1.

Specification	set_search_tree
Types:	
Relation Scheme:	set_search_tree initialises via side-effects the collection of the branches of the search tree.
Modes of use:	
Multiplicities:	Succeeds exactly once

A similar technique application is required for filter/1, and results in the two clauses for filter being replaced by

```
filter(yes,Proof) :- reset_search_tree.
filter(no,Proof) :- store_proof(Proof), fail.
```

That completes a sketch of the design for the case study. The resulting program, at least its top level, is given as Program 21 below. A more detailed version is present in *The Art of Prolog*. Leaving decisions more abstract keeps issues more at the design. In Program 21, a decision has been made about the format of the proof tree that was kept out of the technique application. Arguments can be made as to the best way to proceed. Comments are missing from Program 21, but could be extracted from the design descriptions and program specifications.

Operator declarations:

```
:- op(40,xfy,because).
:- op(30,xfy,with).
:- op(40,xfy,&).
:- op(30,xf,is_true).

monitor(Goal,Proof) :-
    set_search_tree,
    init_rules(Rules), init_proof(Proof),
    solve(Goal,Result,Rules,Proof),
    filter(Result,Proof).
monitor(Goal,Proof) :-
    collect_proof(Proof).

filter(yes,Proof) :- reset_search_tree.
filter(no,Proof) :- store_proof(Proof), fail.

solve(Goal,yes,Rules,fact(Goal)) :- fact(Goal).
solve(Goal,Result,Rules,Goal because Body with Proof) :-
    rule(Goal,Body,Name),
    solve_body(Body,Result,[Name|Rules],Proof).
solve(Goal,Result,Rules,user(Goal)) :-
    askable(Goal), solve_askable(Goal,Result,Rules).
solve(Goal,no,Rules,no_match(Goal)) :-
    not fact(Goal), not rule(Goal,B,Name).

solve_body(A&B,Result,Rules,ProofA&ProofB) :-
    solve(A,ResultA,Rules,ProofA),
    solve_and(ResultA,B,Result,Rules,ProofB).
solve_body(Goal is_true,Result) :- solve(Goal,Result).

solve_and(no,Goal,no,Rules,unsearched).
solve_and(yes,Goal,Result,Rules,Tree) :-
    solve(Goal,Result,Rules,Tree).

solve_askable(A,Result) :-
    not known(A), ask(A,Response), respond(Response,A,
    Result).
```

Program 21 Top-level of an expert system shell

5.4   Software Support

A design method is enhanced by a suitable program development environment.
The only investigation of software tools to facilitate stepwise enhancement has

been the PT[6] environment which supports logic program development via step-wise enhancement. A prototype implementation of PT in C++ is described in [24]. PT's environment can be tailored to either Prolog or CLP(R). Via a mouse-driven interface, a user can create extensions by applying techniques to skeletons. The user is prompted to fill in values for arguments and supply extra goals with the interface stepping through the code to the appropriate places.

The prototype facilitated construction of programs concerned with recursive data structure traversal. The environment allowed the application of four techniques to skeletons: *calculate, build, accumulate-calculate* and *accumulate-build.* Seven skeletons were pre-defined with the environment, with the expectation that the user can add others.

Composition of extensions created in the environment was supported, and limited error checking incorporated. Implicit in PT's interface was a representation of techniques. Each technique was parameterized for each skeleton to know where to add values. For example, the build technique adds an extra argument to each essential predicate in the skeleton. A new goal is given for each rule where the extra argument in the head is determined by the arguments in the body. The prototype was rebuilt in LPA Prolog as part of a student project at Case Western Reserve University, but was not fully completed.

6   Related Work

6.1   Skeletons and Techniques for Declarative Languages

The skeletons and techniques presented in this paper are all taken from Prolog. This pattern-based approach to teaching programming is equally applicable to other logic programming languages, as discussed in Kirschenbaum, Michaylov and Sterling [23]. Our claim is that programming patterns should be identified when a language is first used, in order to encourage systematic, effective program development. This learning approach should be stressed during teaching.

We showed that the skeletons and techniques for Prolog can be extended to a range of styles of logic programming languages. Constraint logic programming languages are exemplified by CLP(R), concurrent logic programming languages by Flat Concurrent Prolog and Strand, and higher order logic program languages by λ-Prolog. Applying the notion of skeletons and techniques to functional programming languages has also been studied.

Gegg-Harrison [6] and [14] has presented skeletons and techniques in terms of higher order predicates. His approach has some elegant predictive power, but is probably only accessible to more advanced students. Naish and Sterling [15] compare and contrast presenting skeletons and techniques as operations on programs or as applications of higher order programming.

---

[6] An unimaginative acronym for Prolog Tool

6.2   Schemas for Logic Programming

There have been several attempts to characterize logic programming patterns using schemas. This paper shares intent with Gegg-Harrison [5], who is interested in schemas to help teach students Prolog programming. The approach to programming via skeletons and techniques is, in my opinion, both simpler and easier to generalize. The skeletons are simpler than schemata because they are not overly general. Students (and programmers) think in terms of specific examples not schemas. We emphasize the specificity by dealing with real but skeletal programs, rather than second-order predicates. Techniques are easily adapted to other skeletons, which is not immediately possible with Gegg-Harrison's schemas.

O'Keefe's text [16] also discusses Prolog programming patterns in terms of schemas. O'Keefe's schemas are different than those proposed Gegg-Harrison, and are geared to expert rather than novice programmers. The schemas use abstract notation, and my preference for teaching[7], is for concrete programs.

6.3   Object-Oriented Patterns

The connection between these logic language patterns and the design patterns espoused in the book by [4] has not been fully examined. Superficially, the OO design patterns are closer to skeletons than techniques, especially in their higher order characterization. Techniques are somewhat akin to methods.

My sense is that the logic programming perspective does not match exactly with classes and instances, but is similar in spirit, especially if a higher order view is taken. Composition is different from functional composition but does combine the effect of two standard programming techniques.

7   Conclusions

Taking a pattern view of programming in general, and programming in logic languages in particular, is helpful. There is no doubt that skeletons and techniques have helped in my teaching of logic program languages. Within the classroom, emphasizing patterns has been valuable for teaching effective Prolog programming. Students are able to follow more complicated Prolog programs and the quality of code in student projects has increased. Graduate students find this approach useful for explaining code to others, and in the cases of meta-interpreters cited earlier, complicated programs were more easily developed.

Design descriptions can help with verification. Some anecdotal experience has been gained how to guide a proof of correctness for programs developed via stepwise enhancement. The proof suggests leveraging the structure of the program development to help the final program. A more detailed exposition of guided verification is future work.

---

[7] Admittedly whether students prefer seeing patterns presented in higher-order notation anecdotally depends on the students. Some prefer abstract notation, while others prefer concrete programs and lots of instances.

Acknowledgements

The views on patterns for Prolog programs expressed in this paper emerged through active discussions over several years with students and colleagues at Case Western Reserve University in Cleveland. The original impetus was the Composers group and was later superseded by the ProSE (Prolog for Software Engineering) group. Particular mention should be made of Marc Kirschenbaum. Discussion has continued with members of the declarative languages research group at the University of Melbourne. The anonymous reviewers made constructive suggestions and triggered the inclusion of the case study in Section 5.3, and the first pass at design descriptions.

References

1. Bowen, K. and Kowalski, R.: Amalgamating Language and Meta-Language, in *Logic Programming*, (eds. Clark, K. and Tarnlund, S.-A.), pp. 153-172, Academic Press, 1982

2. Deville, Y.: *Logic programming: Systematic Program Development*, Addison-Wesley, 1990

3. Flach, P.: *Simply Logical*, John Wiley, 1994

4. Gamma, E., Helm, R., Johnson, R. and Vlissides, J.: *Design Patterns*, Addison-Wesley, 1995

5. Gegg-Harrison, T.: Learning Prolog in a Schema-Based Environment, *Instructional Science*, 20:173-192, 1991.

6. Gegg-Harrison, T. Representing Logic Program Schemata in Prolog, *Proc. 12th International Logic Programming Conference* (ed. L. Sterling), pp. 467-481, MIT Press, 1995

7. Kirschenbaum, M., Michaylov, S. and Sterling, L.S.: Skeletons and Techniques as a Normative View of Developing Logic Programs, *Proc. ACSC'96, Australian Computer Science Communications*, 18(1), pp. 516-524, 1996

8. Knuth, D.: *The Art of Computer Programming*, Vol. 1, Addison-Wesley, 1968

9. Kowalski, R.: *Logic for Problem Solving*, Elsevier-North Holland, 1979.

10. Lakhotia, A.: *A Workbench for Developing Logic Programs by Stepwise Enhancement*, Ph.D. Thesis, Case Western Reserve University, 1989.

11. Lakhotia, A., Sterling, L. and Bojantchev, D.: Development of a Prolog Tracer by Stepwise Enhancement, *Proc. 3rd Intl. Conference on Practical Applications of Prolog*, Paris, pp. 371-393, 1995

12. Michaylov, S.: Skeletons and Techniques for the systematic development of constraint logic programs, *Proc. 6th IEEE Conference on Tools for Artificial Intelligence*, New Orleans, Nov. 1994. Also appears as Technical Report OSU-CISRC-6/94- TR30, Department of Computer and Information Science, The Ohio State University, 1994

13. Michaylov, S. and Ordez, I.: Time and Money: A Case Study in Systematic Development of Constraint Logic Programs, *Proc. 7th Workshop on Logic Programming Environments*, Portland, Oregon, 1995

14. Naish, L.: Higher-order Logic Programming, *Proc. Workshop on Multi-paradigm Logic Programming, JICSLP'96*, Also available as Tech. Report 96/2, Department of Computer Science, University of Melbourne, 1996

15. Naish, L. and Sterling, L.: Stepwise Enhancement and Higher Order Programming in Prolog, *Journal Functional and Logic Programming*, MIT Press, 4, 2000

16. O'Keefe, R.: *The Craft of Prolog*, MIT Press, 1990.
17. Pereira and Shieber: Prolog and Natural Language Analysis, *CSLI Lecture Notes*, Report #10, Stanford, 1987
18. Pressman, R.: *Software Engineering: A Practitioner's Approach*, 5th Ed. McGraw-Hill, 2000
19. Schach, S.: *Classical and Object-Oriented Software Engineering*, 4th Ed. McGraw-Hill, 1999
20. Sergot, M.: A 'Query the User' Facility for Logic Programming, in *Integrated Interactive Computer Systems*, North-Holland, Amsterdam, 1983
21. Sterling, L.S. and Beer, R.D.: Meta-Interpreters for Expert System Construction, *Journal of Logic Programming*, 6 (1-2), pp. 163-178, 1989
22. Sterling, L., Harous, S., Kirschenbaum, M., Leis, B. and White, L.: Developing Software Testing Programs Using Stepwise Enhancement, *Proc. Short Paper sessions, Intl. Conf. Software Engineering*, Melbourne, pp. 8-9, May, 1992
23. Sterling, L. and Kirschenbaum, M.: Applying Techniques to Skeletons, in *Constructing Logic Programs*, (ed. J.M. Jacquet), pp. 127-140, John Wiley, 1993.
24. Sterling, L.S. and Sitt Sen, Chok: A Tool to Support Stepwise Enhancement in Prolog, *Workshop on Logic Programming Environments*, pp. 21-26, ILPS'93, Vancouver, October, 1993
25. Sterling, L.S. and Shapiro, E.Y. *The Art of Prolog*, 2nd edition, MIT Press, 1994.
26. Yalinalp, L..: *Meta-Programming for Knowledge-Based Systems in Prolog*, Ph.D. Thesis, Case Western Reserve University, 1991.

Abduction in Logic Programming

Marc Denecker[1] and Antonis Kakas[2]

[1] Department of Computer Science, K.U.Leuven,
Celestijnenlaan 200A, B-3001 Heverlee, Belgium
Marc.Denecker@cs.kuleuven.ac.be
http://www.cs.kuleuven.ac.be/~marcd
[2] Department of Computer Science, University of Cyprus,
75 Kallipoleos St., Nicosia, Cyprus.
antonis@ucy.ac.cy
http://www.cs.ucy.ac.cy/~antonis

Abstract. Abduction in Logic Programming started in the late 80s, early 90s, in an attempt to extend logic programming into a framework suitable for a variety of problems in Artificial Intelligence and other areas of Computer Science. This paper aims to chart out the main developments of the field over the last ten years and to take a critical view of these developments from several perspectives: logical, epistemological, computational and suitability to application. The paper attempts to expose some of the challenges and prospects for the further development of the field.

1 Introduction

Over the last two decades, abduction has been embraced in AI as a non-monotonic reasoning paradigm to address some of the limitations of deductive reasoning in classical logic. The role of abduction has been demonstrated in a variety of applications. It has been proposed as a reasoning paradigm in AI for diagnosis [8,90], natural language understanding [8,39,4,93], default reasoning [81,29,25,50], planning [28,110,71,59], knowledge assimilation and belief revision [54,76], multi-agent systems [7,64,102] and other problems.

In the context of logic programming, the study of abductive inference started at the end of the eighties as an outcome of different attempts to use logic programming for solving AI-problems. Facing the limitations of standard logic programming for solving these problems, different researchers proposed to extend logic programming with abduction. Eshghi [28] introduced abduction in logic programming in order to solve planning problems in the Event Calculus [65]. In this approach, abduction solves a planning goal by *explaining* it by an ordered sets of events -a plan- that entails the planning goal. This approach was further explored by Shanahan [110], Missiaen et al. [72,71], Denecker [21], Jung [48] and recently in [59,60]. Kakas and Mancarella showed the application of abduction in logic programming for deductive database updating and knowledge assimilation [53,55]. The application of abduction to diagnosis has been studied in [10,11]

A.C. Kakas, F. Sadri (Eds.): Computat. Logic (Kowalski Festschrift), LNAI 2407, pp. 402–436, 2002.

within an abductive logic programming framework whose semantics was defined by a suitable extension of the completion semantics of LP.

In parallel to these studies of abduction as an inferential method, Eshghi and Kowalski [29] and later Kakas and Mancarella in [52,54] and Dung in [25], used abduction as a semantical device to describe the non-monotonic semantics of Logic Programming (in a way analogous to Poole in [81]). In [18,14], abductive logic programming was investigated from a knowledge representation point of view and its suitability for representing and reasoning on incomplete information and definitional and assertional knowledge was shown.

For these reasons, Abductive Logic Programming[1] (ALP) [50,51] was recognized as a promising computational paradigm that could resolve many limitations of logic programming with respect to higher level knowledge representation and reasoning tasks. ALP has manifested itself as a framework for declarative problem solving suitable for a broad collection of problems.

Consequently, at the start of the 90s, a number of abductive systems were developed. In [54], the abductive procedure of [29] for computing negation as failure through abduction was extended to the case of general abductive predicates. Another early abductive procedure was developed in [10] using the completion. [17] proposed SLDNFA, an extension of SLDNF with abduction allowing nonground abductive hypotheses. [21] proposed an extension of SLDNFA with a constraint solver for linear order and demonstrated that this system could be applied correctly for partial order planning in the context of event calculus. Later, the idea of integrating abduction and constraint solving was developed more generally in the ACLP framework [56,61,60]; this procedure is the result of incorporating CLP constraint solving in the abductive procedure of [54]. In [37] an abductive procedure that can be regarded as a hybrid of SLDNFA and the procedure of Console et al has been defined based on explicit rewrite rules with the completion and equality. This has later [66] incorporated constraint solving in a similar way to the ACLP procedure. A bottom up procedure, later combined with some top down refinement, was given in [106] and [42]; the latter system was an implementation using the Model Generator MGTP developed on the multiprocessor machine developed at ICOT. Another recent abductive procedure in LP is that of AbDual [1] which exploits tabling techniques from XSB.

Despite these efforts and the many potential applications for abduction, it has taken considerable time and effort to develop computationally effective systems based on abduction for practical problems. The field has faced (and to some extend continues to do so) a number of challenges at the logical, methodological and implementational level. In the recent past, important progress has been made on all these levels. The aim of this chapter is to give a comprehensive

---

[1] The July/August 2000 volume (Vol. 44) of the journal of Logic Programming is a special issue on Abductive Logic Programming. This contains several papers that open new perspectives on the relationship between abduction and other computational paradigms.

overview of the state of the art of Abductive Logic Programming, to point to problems and challenges and to sketch recent progress.

Bob Kowalski has been one of the founders of Abductive Logic Programming. Recently, he has, together with others, proposed [64] that ALP can be used as a framework in which we can integrate an agent's knowledge on how to reduce its goal to subgoals and thus plan how to achieve this goal, described in the program part of an abductive theory, together with the agent's obligations, prohibitions and other elements that determine its reactive behaviour, described in the integrity constraints part of its abductive theory. In this suggestion ALP plays a central role in capturing the behaviour of an autonomous agent that feeds from and reacts to its environment.

This together with his view of its role in the way that Logic Programming should evolve more generally as a programming language of the future is described elegantly in his short position statement on the future of Logic Programming in this volume.

The rest of the paper is organized as follows. Section 2 briefly reviews the study of abduction in AI and philosophy and situates Abductive Logic Programming within this broad context. Section 3 gives the formal definition of abduction, and reviews the different formal semantics that have been proposed in the literature. Section 4 reviews the different ALP frameworks that have been developed so far analyzing their potential scope to applications and their links to other extensions of LP. The paper ends with a discussion of future challenges and prospects of development for the field of ALP.

2   What Is Abduction?

2.1   What Is an Explanation?

The term abduction was introduced by the logician and philosopher C.S. Pierce (1839-1914) who defined it as the inference process of forming a hypothesis that explains given observed phenomena [77]. Often abduction has been defined broadly as any form of "inference to the best explanation" [47] where *best* refers to the fact that the generated hypothesis is subjected to some optimality criterion. This very broad definition covers a wide range of different phenomena involving some form of hypothetical reasoning. Studies of "abduction" range from philosophical treatments of human scientific discovery down to formal and computational approaches in different formal logics.

In the context of formal logic, abduction is often defined as follows. Given a logical theory T representing the expert knowledge and a formula Q representing an observation on the problem domain, abductive inference searches for an explanation formula $\mathcal{E}$ such that:

- $\mathcal{E}$ is satisfiable[2] w.r.t. T and
- it holds that[3] $T \models \mathcal{E} \rightarrow Q$

---

[2] If $\mathcal{E}$ contains free variables, $\exists(\mathcal{E})$ should be satisfiable w.r.t. T.

[3] Or, more general, if Q and $\mathcal{E}$ contain free variables: $T \models \forall(\mathcal{E} \rightarrow Q)$.

In general, $\mathcal{E}$ will be subjected to further restrictions such as the aforementioned minimality criteria and criteria restricting the form of the explanation formula (e.g. by restricting the predicates that may appear in it). This view defines an abductive explanation of an observation as a formula which *logically entails* the observation. However, some have argued, sometimes with good reasons, that it is more natural to view an explanation as a *cause* for the observation [47]. A well-known example is as follows [92]: the disease *paresis* is caused by a latent untreated form of syphilis. The probability that latent untreated syphilis leads to paresis is only 25%. Note that in this context, the direction of entailment and causality are opposite: syphilis is the cause of paresis but does not entail it, while paresis entails syphilis but does not cause it. Yet a doctor can *explain* paresis by the hypothesis of syphilis while paresis cannot account for an *explanation* for syphilis.

In practice, examples where causation and entailment do not correspond are rare[4]. It turns out that in many applications of abduction in AI, the theory T describes explicit *causality information*. This is notably the case in model-based diagnosis and in temporal reasoning, where theories describe effects of actions. By restricting the explanation formulas to the predicates describing primitive causes in the domain, an explanation formula which entails an observation gives a cause for the observation. Hence, for this class of theories, the logical entailment view implements the causality view on abductive inference.

2.2   Relationship to Other Reasoning Paradigms

As mentioned in the previous section, the definition of abduction is very broad and covers a wide range of hypothetical reasoning inference that could otherwise be formally distinguished. Not surprisingly, there are many different views on what is abduction and how to implement it. Many philosophers and logicians have argued that abduction is a generalization of *induction* [34]. Induction can be defined as inference of general rules that explain certain data. A simple example illustrating inductive inference is the following derivation:

$$\frac{\begin{array}{c} human(socrates) \\ mortal(socrates) \end{array}}{\forall x.human(x) \rightarrow mortal(x)}$$

Hence, induction can also be seen as a form of *inference to the best explanation*.

The term abduction as used in this paper, refers to a form of reasoning that can be clearly distinguished from *inductive inference*. In most current applications of abduction the goal is to infer *extentional knowledge*, knowledge that is specific to the particular state or scenario of the world. In applications of induction, the goal is to infer *intentional knowledge*, knowledge that universally holds

---

[4] See [91] where the relation between causal and evidential modeling and reasoning is studied and linked to abduction.

in many different states of affairs and not only in the current state of the world. For example, an abductive solution for the problem that a certain car does not start this morning is the explanation that its battery is empty. This explanation is extentional. On the other hand, an inductive inference is to derive from a set of examples the rule that if the battery is empty then the car will not start. This is *intentional knowledge*. As a consequence of this distinction, abductive answers and inductive answers have a very different format. In particular, inductive answers are mostly general rules that do not refer to a particular scenario while abductive answers are usually simpler formulas, often sets of ground atoms, that describe the causes of the observation in the current scenario according to a given general theory describing the problem domain. This distinction in the form of the answer induces in turn strong differences in the underlying inference procedures.

Abduction as a form of inference of extentional hypotheses explaining observed phenomena, is a versatile and informative way of reasoning on incomplete or uncertain knowledge. Incomplete knowledge does not entirely fix the state of affairs of the domain of discourse while uncertain knowledge is *defeasible* in the sense that its truth in the domain of discourse is not entirely certain. In the presence of uncertain knowledge, [81] demonstrated how abductive inference can be used for default reasoning. In the presence of incomplete knowledge, abduction returns an explanation formula corresponding to a (non-empty) collection of possible states of affairs in which the observation would be true or would be caused; on the other hand deduction is the reasoning paradigm to determine whether a statement is true in all possible states of affairs. As such, abduction is strongly related to *model generation* and *satisfiability checking* and can be seen as a refinement of these forms of reasoning. By definition, the existence of an abductive answer proves the satisfiability of the observation. But abduction returns more informative answers; answers which describe the properties of a class of possible states of affairs in which the observation is valid.

2.3   Abduction and Declarative Knowledge Representation

An important role of logic in AI is that of providing a framework for *declarative problem solving*. In this, a human expert specifies his knowledge of the problem domain by a descriptive logic theory and uses logical inference systems to solve computational tasks arising in this domain. Although in the early days of logic-based AI, *deduction* was considered as the unique fundamental problem solving paradigm of declarative logic [70] in the current state of the art deduction has lost this unique place as the central inferential paradigm of logic in AI. Indeed, we argue that a declarative problem solving methodology will often lead to abductive problems. Let us illustrate this with an example problem domain, that of university time tabling.

The process of declarative problem solving starts with the *ontology design* phase: during this step, an alphabet of symbols denoting the relevant objects, concepts and relationships in the problem domain must be designed. This alphabet defines the *ontology* of the problem domain. It precedes the *knowledge description* phase during which the expert expresses his knowledge using the symbols of the alphabet. In the example domain of university timetables we have three important types of objects: *lectures, time slots* and *class rooms*. We could represent them using the predicates *lecture*/1, *time_slot*/1 and *room*/1. Important relevant relationships between them refer to when and where lectures take place; these relationships could be represented by predicates *time_of_lecture*/2 and *room_of_lecture*/2.

A key observation is that even though at this stage the knowledge specification has not even started, the choice of the alphabet already determines that certain tasks will be abductive. In particular, the task of computing a correct time table will consist of computing tables for *time_of_lecture*/2 and *room_of_lecture*/2 that satisfy certain logical constraints imposed on correct schedules. This task is not a deductive task: the "correct" tables will not be deducible from the theory. Rather it is an abductive problem — or a model generation problem[5] — a problem of completing the problem description so that the goal (or "observation") that all lectures are scheduled, holds.

The ontology design phase has a strong impact on the specification phase. If the alphabet is complex and does not have a simple correspondence to the objects, concepts, relations and functions of the domain of discourse, this will complicate the knowledge description phase and lead to a more complex, more verbose, less comprehensive and less modular specification. For example, one simple constraint is that each lecture must be scheduled at some time slot and room:

$$\forall l : lecture(l) \rightarrow \exists t, r : time\_slot(t) \land time\_of\_lecture(t, l) \land$$
$$room(r) \land room\_of\_lecture(r, l)$$

Another constraint is that two lectures cannot take place in the same room at the same time:

$$\forall t, r, l1, l2. \; room\_of\_lecture(r, l1) \land room\_of\_lecture(r, l2) \land$$
$$time\_of\_lecture(t, l1) \land time\_of\_lecture(t, l2)$$
$$\rightarrow l1 = l2$$

If we had represented the assignments of rooms and time slots to lectures by balanced binary tree structures, this would have complicated significantly the expression of these requirements which are now expressed directly. Thus, an important aspect of the declarative problem solving methodology, is that the ontology and alphabet is designed in a task independent way such that it naturally matches with the types of objects and relationships that occur in the problem domain.

The above example illustrates that the choice of the alphabet may enforce the use of a specific type of inference to solve a specific computational task, and that, when we follow a declarative approach this will often lead to the problem tasks to be abductive in nature. Vice versa, the a-priori choice of a specific inferential

---

[5] Recall the close relationship between abduction (as viewed in this paper) and model generation, as explained in the previous section.

system such as Prolog or a CLP system to solve a specific computational problem has a strong impact on the choice of the alphabet for that problem domain. In the university time tabling problem, a Prolog or CLP solution will not be based on the use of predicates *time_of_lecture*/2 and *room_of_lecture*/2 but on another, in this case more complex alphabet, typically one in which predicates range over lists or trees of assignments of lectures, time slots and rooms. This alphabet is more complex and is choosen in a task-dependent way, which results in reduced readability and modularity of the problem specification and in a reduced reusability of the specification to solve other types of tasks. The fact that the alphabet in Prolog (and CLP) programming must be chosen in relation to the provided inference system rather than by its match with the human experts conception of the problem domain is one of the fundamental reasons why even pure Prolog programs are rarely perceived as truly *declarative*.

There is clearly a trade-off here. On the one hand, the choice of an alphabet in correspondence with the concepts and relations in the mind of the human expert is a prerequisite to obtain a compact, elegant and readable specification. As a result of this often the computational task of problem solving links tightly to abduction. Putting this more directly we would argue that Declarative Knowledge Representation comes hand in hand with abduction. Abduction then emerges as an important computational paradigm that would be needed for certain problem solving tasks within a declarative representation of the problem domain.

On the other hand, in practice the choice of a representation is not governed merely by issues relating to a natural representation but also and sometimes even more by issues of computational effectiveness. Although the use of a more complex ontology may seriously reduce the elegance of the representation, it may be necessary to be able to use a specific system for solving a problem; in some cases this would mean that the pure declarative problem representation needs to be augmented with procedural, heuristic and strategic information on how to solve effectively the computational problem.

Current research on abduction studies how more intelligent search and inference methods in abductive systems can push this trade-off as far as possible in the direction of more declarative representations.

3   Abductive Logic Programming

This section presents briefly how abduction has been defined in the context of logic programming.

An Abductive Logic Programming theory is defined as a triple (P, A, IC) consisting of a logic program, P, a set of ground abducible atoms A[6] and a set of classical logic formulas IC, called the integrity constraints, such that no atom $p \in A$ occurs in the head of a rule of P.

In the field of Abductive Logic Programming, the definition of abduction is usually specialized in the following way:

---

[6] In practice, the abducibles are specified by their predicate names.

Definition 1. *Given an abductive logic theory* (P, A, IC), *an abductive explanation for a query Q is a set $\Delta \subseteq A$ of ground abducible atoms such that:*

- $P \cup \Delta \models Q$
- $P \cup \Delta \models IC$
- $P \cup \Delta$ *is consistent.*

Some remarks are in order. First, this definition is *generic* both in terms of syntax and semantics. Often, the syntax is that of normal logic programs with negation as failure but some have investigated the use of abduction in the context of extended logic programming [43] or constraint logic programming [56,60,66]. At the level of semantics, the above definition defines the notion of an abductive solution in terms of any given semantics of standard logic programming. Each particular choice of semantics defines its own entailment relation $\models$, its own notion of consistent logic programs and hence its own notion of what an abductive solution is. In practice, the three main semantics of logic programming — completion, stable and well-founded semantics — have been used to define different abductive logic frameworks.

A second remark is that an abductive explanation Δ aims to represent a *nonempty* collection of states of affairs in which the explanandum Q would hold. This explains the third condition that $P \cup \Delta$ should be consistent.

Third, when integrity constraints IC are introduced in the formalism, one must define *how* they constrain the abductive solutions. There are different views on this. Early work on abduction in Theorist in the context of classical logic [81], was based on the *consistency view* on constraints. In this view, any extension of the given theory T with an abductive solution Δ is required to be consistent with the integrity constraints IC: $T \cup IC \cup \Delta$ is consistent. The above definition implements the *entailment view*: the abductive solution Δ together with P should entail the constraints. This view is the one taken in most versions of ALP and is stronger than the consistency view in the sense that a solution according to the entailment view is a solution according to the consistency view but not vice versa.

The difference between both views can be subtle but in practice the different options usually coincide. E.g. it frequently happens that $P \cup \Delta$ has a unique model, in which case both views are equivalent. In practice, many ALP systems [20,61] use the entailment view as this can be easily implemented without the need for any extra specialized procedures for the satisfaction of the integrity constraints since this semantics treats the constraints in the same way as the query.

The above definition aims to define the concept of an abductive solution for a query but does not define *abductive logic programming* as a logic in its own right as a pair of syntax and semantics. However, a notion of *generalized model* can be defined, originally proposed in [52], which suggests the following definition.

Definition 2. *M is a model of an abductive logic framework (P, A, IC) iff there exists a set $\Delta \subseteq A$ such that M is a model of $P \cup \Delta$ (according to some LP-semantics) and M is a classical model of IC, i.e. $M \models IC$.*

The entailment relation between abductive logic frameworks and classical logic formulas is then defined in the standard way as follows:

$$(P, A, IC) \models F \text{ iff for each model } M \text{ of } (P, A, IC), \ M \models F.$$

Note that this definition is also generic in the choice of the semantics of logic programming. This way, abductive extensions of stable semantics [52], of well-founded semantics [79] and the partial stable model semantics [111] have been defined. Also the completion semantics has been extended [10] to the case of abductive logic programs. The completion semantics of an abductive logic framework (P, A, IC) is defined by the mapping it to its completion. This is the first order logic theory consisting of :

- UN, the set of unique names axioms, or Clark's equality theory.
- IC
- $comp(P, A)$, the set of completed definitions for all non-abducible predicates.

A recent study [16] that attempts to clarify further the representational and epistemological aspects of ALP, has proposed ID-logic as an appropriate logic for ALP. ID-logic is defined as an extension of classical logic with inductive definitions. Each inductive definition consists of a set of rules defining a specific subset of predicates under the well-founded semantics. This logic gives an epistemological view on ALP in which an abductive logic program is a *definition* of the set of the non-abducible predicates and abducible predicates are *open predicates*, i.e. not defined. The integrity constraints in an abductive logic framework are simply classical logic *assertions*. Thus the program P represents the human expert's strong *definitional knowledge* and the theory IC represents the human expert's weaker *assertional knowledge*. Therefore in ID-logic, ALP can be seen as a sort of *description logic* in which the program is a TBOX consisting of *one* simultaneous definition of the non-abducible predicates, and the assertions correspond to the ABOX [115].

4   Abductive Logic Programming Frameworks

The framework defined in the previous section is generic in syntax and semantics. In the past ten years, the framework has been instantiated (and sometimes has been extended) in different ways. In order to show the wider variety of motivations and approaches that are found in Abductive Logic Programming, this section aims to present briefly a number of these alternative frameworks, implemented systems and applications. These different instantiations differ from each other by using different formal syntax or semantics, or sometimes simply because they use a different inference method and hence induce a different procedural semantics.

4.1   Approaches under the Completion Semantics for LP

Abduction through Deduction. One of the first ALP frameworks is that of
[10]. The syntax in this framework is that of hierarchical logic programs[7] with
a predefined set of abducible predicates. The formal syntax is an extension of
Clark's completion semantics [9] in which only the non-abducible predicates
are completed. The main aim of this work was to study the relationship
between abduction and deduction in the setting of non-monotonic reasoning.
In particular, many characterizations of non-monotonic reasoning such as
circumscription, predicate completion, explanatory closure implement a sort
of *closure principle* allowing to extract implicit negative information out
of explicit positive information. What is shown in this work is that for a
restricted class of programs, the abductive explanations to a query with
respect to a set of (non-recursive) rules can be characterized in a deductive
way if we apply the completion semantics as a closure principle.

Formally, given a (hierarchical) abductive logic program P with abducibles
A, its completion P_C consists of iff-definitions for the non-abducible predicates. These equivalences allow to rewrite any observation O to an equivalent
formula F in the language of abducible predicates such that $P_C \models O \leftrightarrow F$
where $\models$ is classical logic entailment. The formula F, called the *explanation formula*, can be seen as a disjunctive characterization of all abductive
solutions of O given P. The restriction to hierarchical programs ensures termination of a procedure to compute the explanation formula. The framework
has been extended to handle (a restricted form of)integrity constraints.

The above abductive framework has been used to formalize diagnostic problem solving and classification in nonmonotonic inheritance hierarchies [10,24],
and has been extended to characterize updates in deductive databases [12].
The completion semantics is also the basis for the "knowledge compilation"
optimization of abductive problem solving described in [11].

The IFF Framework. The IFF framework is also based on the completion
semantics. It was initially developed as a unifying framework integrating abduction and view updating [36,37]. The IFF proof procedure is defined by
a rewriting system in which an initial goal is rewritten to a disjunction of
answers. The main rewrite rules are unfolding, namely backward reasoning
with the iff definitions, and propagation, namely forward reasoning with the
integrity constraints. IFF produces answers to goals in the form of conjunctions of abducible atoms and denial integrity constraints. An extension of it
with special treatment of built-in predicates and constraint logic programming was proposed in [120,66]. Another modification of the IFF proof procedure was developed for applications modeling reasoning of rational agents
[64] and management of active rules in databases [96]. The main underlying
LP semantics used in this framework is Fitting's three-valued completion
semantics but correctness results have been proven also for perfect model
semantics and under some restrictions for stable semantics.

---

[7] A hierarchical program is one without recursion.

Prototype implementations of the three instances of the IFF procedure [37,97] exist and have been applied in many experiments. The original IFF proof procedure has been implemented in Java and was applied within a Voyager extension to the problem of interaction and communication amongst multiple agents, as well as cooperative problem solving. It was also used for information integration from multiple sources [95], to the management of information networks [112], and it has been integrated with PROGOL to learn preconditions of actions in the frameworks of the event and situation calculi. The extension presented in [120,66] has been applied to job-shop scheduling [66] and semantic query optimization [121]. The procedure suggested in [96] was implemented in *April*, and was used in the context of applications for active databases and agents. Recently, it has been used to study the problem of resource allocation in a multi-agent environment [102].

4.2   Approaches under Stable and Well-Founded Semantics

In Logic Programming other semantics have been proposed as refinements of the completion semantics. These include the stable model semantics [38] and the well-founded model semantics [116]. The following ALP frameworks use these semantics for their underlying LP framework.

SLDNFA and ID-logic. SLDNFA [17,20] is an abductive extension of SLDNF-resolution [68], suitable for abductive reasoning in the context of (possibly recursive) abductive logic programs under the completion semantics. It was proven sound and, under certain restrictions, complete with respect to the 3-valued completion and well-founded semantics. This procedure came out of the early attempts to implement AI-planning using abductive reasoning in the event calculus. It was one of the first procedures that correctly handles non-ground abduction, i.e. abduction of atoms with variables. The procedure was also used in one of the first experiments of integration of abduction and constraint solving. [21] describes an extension of SLDNFA with a constraint solver for the theory of total order and applies it for partial order planning and in the context of temporal reasoning with incomplete knowledge.

At the logical level, the work evolved into a study of the role of ALP for knowledge representation and of SLDNFA for abductive and deductive reasoning. A number of subsequent experiments with ALP and SLDNFA demonstrated the role of ALP for knowledge representation of incomplete and temporal knowledge [19,113,114,22]. To explain and clarify the representational and epistemological aspects of ALP, [16] proposed ID-logic, an integration of classical logic with inductive definitions under well-founded semantics.

At the computational level, efforts were done to improve the computational performance and expressivity of the original implementation of the SLDNFA procedure. The SLDNFAC system [117] is developed at the K.U.Leuven and implements abduction in the context of ID-Logic, supporting directly general first order classical axioms in the language and higher order aggregates.

The system integrates constraint solving with the general purpose abductive resolution SLDNFA. It is implemented as a meta-interpreter on top of Sicstus prolog and is available from http://www.cs.kuleuven.ac.be/ dtai/kt/systems-E.shtml.

The SLDNFAC system has been used in the context of prototypical constraint solving problems such as N-queens, logical puzzles, planning problems in the blocks world, etc ... for proving infinite failure of definite logic programs [5], failure of planning goals [13] and for semantic interpretation of temporal information in natural language [119]. An extension of the system has also been used in the context of a scheduling application for the maintenance for power units of power plants. This experiment involves the use of higher order aggregates and is described in detail in section 5.1. Recently, [78] compared SLDNFAC with different other approaches for solving constraint problems including CLP, ACLP and the Smodels system [74] and shows that in many problems the system is competitive.

Bottom up Abduction. This approach was proposed originally in [107] and aims to develop efficient techniques for computing abductive solutions under the generalized stable model semantics [52] by translating the abductive logic program to a standard logic program and applying efficient bottom up stable model generators to this translation. This approach is based on a translation of Abductive logic programs into pure logic programs with stable model semantics [107]. Abductive solutions w.r.t. the original abductive logic program correspond to stable models of its translation[8]. To compute abductive solutions, [107] also proposed a procedure for bottom-up stable model computation based on truth maintenance techniques. It is an extension of the procedure for computing well-founded models of [33,94] and dynamically checks integrity constraints during the computation of stable models and uses them to derive facts. Later this bottom up procedure was integrated with a procedure for top-down expectation [108,46]. This top-down procedure searches for atoms and rules that are relevant for the query (and the integrity constraints) and thus helps to steer the search into the direction of a solution. This procedure has been used for a number of applications in the following two domains.

Legal Reasoning: A dynamic notion of similarity of cases in legal reasoning is implemented using abductive logic programming. The input of this system is legal factors, case bases and the current case and position of user (defendant or plaintiff). The system translates the case bases and the current case into an abductive logic program. Using the top-down proof procedure the system then computes important factors and retrieves a similar case based on the important factors and generates an explanation why the current case is similar to the retrieved case which is preferable to user's position [105]. The system has also been extended

---

[8] The correctness of this transformation of abductive logic programs to pure logic programs has been shown to be independent of the stable model semantics, and has been extended to handle integrity constraints [111].

so that legal rules and legal cases are combined together for statutory interpretation [103].

Consistency Management in Software Engineering: This   system computes a minimal revised logical specification by abductive logic programming. A specification is written in Horn clauses which is translated into an abductive logic program. Given an incompatibility between this specification and new information the system computes by abduction a maximally consistent program that avoids this incompatibility [104].

ACLP: Abductive Constraint Logic Programming. The ACLP framework grew as an attempt to address the problem of providing a high-level declarative programming or modeling environment for problems of Artificial Intelligence which at the same time has an acceptable computational performance. Its roots come from the work on abduction and negation as failure in [29] and the early definitions of Abductive Logic Programming [52,53,50]. Its key elements are (i) the support of abduction as a central inference of the system, to facilitate declarative problem solving, and (ii) the use of Constraint Logic Programming techniques to enhance the efficiency of the computational process of abductive inference as this is applied on the high-level representation of the problem at hand.

In an ACLP abductive theory the program, P, and the integrity constraints, IC, are defined over a CLP language with finite domain constraints. Its semantics is given by a form of Generalized Model semantics which extends (in the obvious way) the definition 1 above when our underlying LP framework is that of CLP. Negation in P is given meaning through abduction and is computed in a homogeneous way as any other abducible. The general computation model of ACLP consists of a cooperative interleaving between hypotheses and constraint generation, via abductive inference, with consistency checking of abducible assumptions and constraint satisfaction of the generated constraints. The integration of abductive reasoning with constraint solving in ACLP is cooperative, in the sense that the constraint solver not only solves the final constraint store generated by the abductive reduction but also affects dynamically this abductive search for a solution. It enables abductive reductions to be pruned early by setting new suitable CLP constraints on the abductive solution that is constructed.

The framework of ACLP has also been integrated with Inductive Logic Programming to allow a form of machine learning under incomplete information [62].

The ACLP system [60,49], developed at the University of Cyprus, implements the ACLP framework of ALP for a restricted sub-language of the full ACLP framework. Currently, the system is implemented as a meta-interpreter on top of the CLP language of ECLiPSe using the CLP constraint solver of ECLiPSe to handle constraints over finite domains (integer and atomic elements). The architecture of the system is quite general and can be implemented in a similar way with other constraint solvers. It can be obtained, together with information on how to use it, from the following web address: http://www.cs.ucy.ac.cy/aclp/. Direct comparison experiments [61]

of ACLP with the underlying CLP system of ECLiPSe have demonstrated
the potential of ALP to provide a high-level modeling environment which is
modular and flexible under changes of the problem, without compromising
significantly the computational efficiency of the underlying CLP framework.
ACLP has been applied to several different types of problems. Initial applications have concentrated on the problems of scheduling, time tabling
and planning. Other applications include (i) optical music recognition where
ACLP was used to implement a system that can handle recognition under incomplete information, (ii) resolving inconsistencies in software requirements
where (a simplified form of) ACLP was used to identify the causes of inconsistency and suggest changes that can restore consistency of the specification
and (iii) intelligent information integration where ACLP has been used as a
basic framework in the development of information mediators for the semantic integration of information over web page sources. Although most of these
applications are not of "industrial scale" (with the notable exception of a
crew-scheduling [57] application for the small sized company of Cyprus Airways - see also below 5.2) they have been helpful in indicating some general
methodological guidelines that can be followed when one is developing abductive applications (see [57]). The air-crew scheduling application produced
solutions that were judged to be of good quality, comparable to manually
generated solutions by experts of many years on the particular problem,
while at the same time it provided a flexible platform on which the company
could easily experiment with changes in policy and preferences.

Extended and Preference Abduction. In order to broaden the applicability of ALP in AI and databases, Inoue and Sakama propose two kinds of
extensions of ALP: *Extended abduction* [43] and *Preference abduction* [44].
An abductive program in the framework of extended abduction is a pair
$\langle K, \mathcal{A} \rangle$ of logic programs possibly including negation as failure and disjunctions. Each instance of element of $\mathcal{A}$ is *abducible*. An explanation of a ground
literal G consists of a pair of sets (I, O) of subsets of $\mathcal{A}$ such that $(K \setminus O) \cup I$
is consistent and entails G. An *anti-explanation* of G satisfies the same conditions except that $(K \setminus O) \cup I$ does not entail G. Thus, abduction in this
framework extends standard abduction by defining not only explanation but
also *anti-explanations*, by allowing solutions in which rules from the program
are deleted and by allowing general rules to be abduced or deleted.

Several implementation methods have been proposed for computing extended
abduction. [45] proposed a model generation method with term rewriting.
In [99,41], transformation methods are proposed that reduce the problem of
computing extended abduction to a standard abductive problem. Extended
abduction has several potential applications such as abductive theory revision and abduction in non-monotonic theories, view update in deductive
databases, theory update, contradiction removal, system repair problems
with model checking, and inductive logic programming (see [43,99,41]).

A framework for preference abduction is an abductive logic program $\langle K, \mathcal{A} \rangle$
augmented with a set Ψ of possible priorities between different literals of
the program. For a given goal G, preferred abduction computes a set of

abducible atoms I and a subset ψ of Ψ representing some priority relation, such that $K \cup I$ is consistent and $K \cup I \models_\psi G$, which means that G is true in every *preferred answer set* of the *prioritized logic program* $(K \cup I, \psi)$ [98]. Hence, preferred abduction not only abduces atoms but also the priority relationship. A procedure to compute preference abduction has been proposed in [44].

Preference abduction can be used in resolution of the multiple extension problem in non-monotonic reasoning, skeptical abduction, reasoning about rule preference, and preference view update in legal reasoning [44].

ABDUAL: Abduction in extended LP [1] proposes the ABDUAL framework, an abductive framework based on extended logic programs. An abductive logic program in this framework is a tuple $< P, \mathcal{A}, IC >$, where P is an extended logic program (with both explicit and default negation), IC a set of constraints and $\mathcal{A}$ a set of ground objective literals i.e. atoms or explicitly negated atoms. The declarative semantics of this formalism is based on the well-founded semantics for extended programs.

The procedure presented in [1] integrates a tabling mechanism in the abductive inference procedure. The procedure solves an abductive query in two stages. First, the program is transformed by grounding it and adding for each non-abducible ground atom p a rule $not(p) \leftarrow R$ where R expresses that none of the rules for p applies. The resulting program is called the *dual* program. In the second step, abductive solutions are computed by an evaluation method that operates on the dual program.

The ABDUAL system is currently implemented on top of XSB-Prolog [122]. The system is available from http://www.cs. sunysb.edu/~tswift. Work is currently being done in order to migrate some of the tabling mechanisms of ABDUAL, now taken care of the mcta-interpreter, into the XSB-engine. Work is also underway on the XSB system so that the co-unfounded set removal operation can be implemented at the engine level.

The ABDUAL system has been applied in medical psychiatric diagnosis [31] as a result of an investigation into the logical representation and automation of DSM-IV (Diagnostic and Statistical Manual of Mental Disorders). The current user interface of the *Diagnostica* system (http://medicinerules.com) uses abduction in a simple but clinically relevant way to allow for hypothetical diagnosis: when there is not enough information about a patient for a conclusive diagnosis, the system allows for hypothesizing possible diagnosis on the basis of the limited information available. This is one of the first applications of abduction that is been commercialized.

ABDUAL has also been employed to detect specification inconsistencies in model-based diagnosis system for power grid failure [6]. Here abduction is used to abduce hypothetical physically possible events that might cause the diagnosis system to come up with a wrong diagnosis violating the specification constraints.

Probabilistic Horn Abduction and Independence Choice Logic. Probabilistic Horn abduction [84], later extended into the independent choice logic [86], is a way to combine logical reasoning and belief networks into a simple and coherent framework. Its development has been motivated by the Theorist system [88] but it has been extended into a framework for decision and game-theoretic agents that includes logic programs, belief networks, Markov decision processes and the strategic form of a game as special cases. In particular, it has been shown that it is closely related to Bayesian networks [80], where all uncertainty is represented as probabilities.

An independent choice logic theory is made up of two parts:

- a choice space consisting of disjoint sets of ground atoms. The elements of a choice space are called alternatives.
- an acyclic logic program such that no element of an alternative unifies with the head of a clause.

The semantics is model-theoretic. There is a possible world for each choice of one element from each alternative. What is true in a possible world is given by the stable model of the atoms chosen and the logic program. Intuitively the logic program gives the consequences of the choices. This framework is abductive in the sense that the explanations of an observation g provide a concise description of the worlds in which g is true. Belief networks can be defined by having independent probability distributions over the alternatives. Intuitively, we can think of nature making the choice of a value for each alternative. In this case Bayesian conditioning corresponds exactly to the reasoning of the above framework of independent choice logic. This can also be extended to decision theory where an agent can make some choices and nature others [86], and to the game-theoretic case where there are multiple agents who can make choices.

Different implementations of the ICL and its various special cases exist. These include Prolog-style implementations that find explanations top-down [83,89], bottom-up implementations (for the ground case) that use a probabilistic variant of the conflicts used in model-based diagnosis [85], and algorithms based on efficient implementations of belief networks that also exploit the context-specific independent inherent in the rule forms [87]. Initial studies of application of ICL have centered around problems of diagnosis and robot control.

5   Example Applications of Abduction

ALP as a paradigm of declarative problem solving allows us to formalize a wide variety of problems. A survey of the field reveals the potential application of abduction in areas such as databases updates, belief revision, planning, diagnosis, natural language processing, default reasoning, user modeling, legal reasoning, multi-agent systems, scheduling, and software engineering. In this section, two relatively large-scale applications of ALP are presented in some detail in order to illustrate the main features of declarativeness and modularity of an abductive based approach that have been exposed in the previous sections.

5.1   Scheduling of Maintenance

This experiment is based on a real life problem of a Belgian electricity provider. The problem description is as follows. The company has a network of power plants, distributed over different areas and each containing several power producing units. These units need a fixed number of maintenances during the year. The problem is then to schedule these maintenances so that a number of constraints are satisfied and the risk of power shortage (and hence, import from other providers) is as low as possible. The problem was solved using the SLDNFAC system extended with a restricted yet sufficient form of higher-order aggregates. The system accepts first order constraints which are first compiled to rules using the Lloyd-Topor transformation. Below we given an overview of the problem solution. For a more complete description of the solution and the abductive procedure for reasoning on aggregates, we refer the reader to [117].

The fact that a maintenance M lasts from week B till week E, is represented by the predicate $start(M, B, E)$. This is the only abducible predicate in the specification. Other predicates are either defined or are input data and are defined by a table. Some of the main constraints that need to be satisfied are given below[9].

- Maintenances ($maint(M)$) and their duration ($duration(M, D)$) are given by a table. All maintenances must be scheduled, thus for each maintenance there exists an according $start$ relation. This is specified via a first order logical formula i.e. an integrity constraint as follows:

$$\forall M : maint(M) \rightarrow \exists B, E, D : week(B) \wedge week(E) \wedge duration(M, D) \wedge$$
$$E = B + D - 1 \wedge start(M, B, E).$$

- A table of $prohibited(U, Bp, Ep)$ facts specify that maintenances M for unit U are not allowed during the period $[Bp, Ep]$:

$$\forall U, Bp, Ep, M, B, E :$$
$$prohibited(U, Bp, Ep) \wedge maint\_for\_unit(M, U) \wedge start(M, B, E)$$
$$\rightarrow (E < Bp \vee Ep < B).$$

- For each week the number of the units in maintenance belonging to a plant P should be less than a maximal number Max. A table of $plant\_max(P, Max)$ atoms defines for each plant the maximal number of units in maintenance simultaneously.

$$\forall P, Max, We : plant(P) \wedge plant\_max(P, Max) \wedge week(We)$$
$$\rightarrow \exists OnMaint : card(\{U \mid (unit(U) \wedge unit\_in\_plant(U, P) \wedge$$
$$in\_maint(U, We))\}, OnMaint) \wedge$$
$$OnMaint \leq Max.$$

Note that this constraint uses the cardinality aggregate $card$. The meaning of the above cardinality atom is that the set of units of plant P in maintenance

---

[9] In this and the following section, variable names start with a capital, as standard in logic programming.

in week We contains $OnMaint$ elements. The predicate in_maint is defined by an auxiliary program rule specifying that a unit U is in maintenance during a certain week W if a maintenance M of this unit is going on during W:

$$in\_maint(U, W) \leftarrow maint\_for\_unit(M, U), start(M, B, E), B \leq W, W \leq E.$$

– Another constraint is that the capacity of the units in maintenance belonging to a certain area should not exceed a given area maximum. To represent this, the summation aggregate is needed. A table of $capacity(U, C)$ describes for each unit its maximum capacity.

$$\forall A, Max, We, CM : area(A) \wedge area\_max(A, Max) \wedge week(We) \wedge$$
$$sum(\{(U, C)| (unit(U) \wedge in\_area(U, A) \wedge in\_maint(U, We) \wedge$$
$$capacity(U, C))\}, \lambda(U, Cap)Cap, CM)$$
$$\rightarrow 0 \leq CM \wedge CM \leq Max.$$

In the above constraint, the meaning of the sum aggregate atom is that "the sum of the lambda function over the set expression is CM". It defines CM as the total capacity of area A in maintenance during week We.

The above specification describes some of the necessary properties of a correct schedule. However, not all schedules satisfying these properties are desirable. In particular, schedules that minimise the risk of power shortage are preferable. To this end, the company maintains statistical data about the expected peak load per week. Desirable solutions are those that maximise the *reserve capacity*, that is the difference between the available capacity and the expected peak load. This relation ($reserve(Week, R)$) can then be defined as the difference between available capacity (the sum of capacities of all units not in maintenance during this week) and the estimated peak load:

$$reserve(We, R) \leftarrow peakload(We, Load), total\_capacity(T),$$
$$sum(\{(U, Cap)| (unit(U) \wedge in\_maint(U, We) \wedge$$
$$capacity(U, Cap))\},$$
$$\lambda(U, Cap)Cap, InMaint),$$
$$R = T - Load - InMaint.$$

in which $total\_capacity(T)$ means the sum of all capacities of all units.

In the SLDNFAC system, the query for the optimal solution for the scheduling problem is

```
? minimum(set([R],(exists(W) : reserve(W,R)),M), maximize(M).
```

It expresses that an optimal abductive solution is desired in which the minimal reserve for one year is as high as possible.

The actual problem, given by the company, consists of scheduling 56 maintenances for 46 units in one year (52 weeks). The size of the search space is of the order of 52^{46}. The current implementation reduces the goal and the integrity constraints to a large finite domain constraint store without backtracking points. In the current implementation of SLDNFAC, this reduction phase is completed in less than one minute . Subsequently the CLP solver starts to generate solutions of increasing quality. The current implementation was able to find a solution which is 97% away from the optimal one in 20 minutes.

The same problem was also solved using a CLP system. A comparison between the CLP solution and the ALP solution clearly shows the trade-off between efficiency and flexibility. The pure (optimized) CLP solution will setup its constraint store in several seconds (3 to 4 seconds), and find the same solution as the above specification within 2 minutes (compared to 20 minutes for the SLDNFAC-solver). On the other hand, the CLP solution is a much larger program (400 lines) developed in some weeks of time in which the constraints are hidden within data structures, whereas the above representation in ALP is a simple declarative representation of 11 logical formulae, written down after some hours of discussion.

5.2 Air-Crew Assignment

The second application of abduction that we present is also based on a real-life problem, namely that of crew-assignment for Cyprus Airways. The problem of air crew-assignment is concerned with the assignment of air-crews to each of the flights that an airline company has to cover over some specific period of time. This allocation of crew to flights has to respect all the necessary constraints (validity) and also try to minimize the crew operating cost (quality). The validity of a solution is defined by a large number of complex constraints, which express governmental and international regulations, union rules, company restrictions etc. The quality of the schedule is specified, not only by its cost, but also by the needs and preferences of the particular company or crew at that specific period of time. In addition, an airline is also interested in the problem of re-assignment or of adapting an existing crew assignment to changes in the application environment such as flight delays or cancellations, new flight additions or crew unavailability etc. These changes often affect the quality of an existing solution or even make an existing solution unacceptable.

This problem for (the pilot crew) of Cyprus Airways was solved within ALP using the ACLP system. The problem was represented entirely as an ALP theory $T = (P, A, IC)$. The program part P describes basic data and defines a number of concepts that allow for encoding particular strategies for decomposing the overall goal to subgoals. Different strategies affect efficiency of the problem solving process and the quality of the solutions with respect to the criteria of cost or fairness of assignment. The solution of the problem is captured via an abducible predicate $assigns(Crew, Task)$ (the only member of A) which gives the assignment of crew members to different types of duty tasks (eg. flights, standbys, day-offs, etc.). For details of this and for a more complete description of the problem and its abductive-based solution see [58]. Here we will concentrate more on how the complex validity constraints of the problems are represented in the IC part of the theory.

The problem of air crew-assignment has a large variety of complex constraints that need to be respected. These contain simple constraints such as that a pilot can not be assigned to two overlapping flights but also many other quite complex constraints such as that during any period of 6 days (respectively 14 days) a pilot must have one day off (respectively 2 consecutive days off). Lets us illustrate how some of these would be represented as integrity constraints in IC. The following integrity constraint expresses the requirement that for any pilot there must be at least $MinRest$ hours rest period between any two consecutive duties. $MinRest$ is greater than or equal to 12 and it is calculated according to the previous assignments of the crew. (All variables in the integrity constraints below are universally quantified over the whole formula).

$\neg assign(Crew, Flight) \leftarrow$
  $on\_new\_duty(Crew, Flight),$
  $end\_prev\_duty(Crew, Flight, EndOfDuty),$
  $time\_difference(EndOfDuty, Flight, RestPeriod),$
  $MinRest(Crew, MR), RestPeriod < MR.$

Here $on\_new\_duty(Crew, Flight)$ defines whether the flight, $Flight$, is the beginning of a new duty period for $Crew$ and $end\_prev\_duty(Crew, Flight, EndOfDuty)$ specifies the time of the end of the duty, $EndOfDuty$, for the crew member, $Crew$, which is immediately before the departure time of the flight $Flight$. These are defined in the program P of the theory.

The requirement that each pilot must have at least 2 consecutive days off during any 14 day period is represented by the integrity constraint:

$consec2\_daysoff(Crew, DeptDate, 14) \leftarrow$
  $assign(Crew, Flight),$
  $dept\_date(Flight, DeptDate)$

where $consec2\_daysoff(Crew, DeptDate, 14)$ means that the $Crew$ has two consecutive days off within a time window of 14 days centered around the date $DeptDate$. This is given in the program P with the help of the definition of $dayoff$ as follows:

$consec2\_daysoff(Crew, Date, N) \leftarrow$
  $consec\_days(Date, N, DayA, DayB),$
  $dayoff(Crew, DayA),$
  $dayoff(Crew, DayB)$

$dayoff(Crew, Date) \leftarrow$
  $not\ assign(Crew, flight(Id, Date)),$
  $crew\_at\_base(Date),$
  $further\_free\_hrs(Crew, Date)$

$further\_free\_hrs(Crew, Date) \leftarrow$
    $next\_date(Date, NDate),$
    $assign(Crew, flight(Id, NDate)),$
    $departure(flight(Id, NDate), NDate, DeptTime), DeptTime > 8$

$further\_free\_hrs(Crew, Date) \leftarrow$
    $next\_date(Date, NDate),$
    $assign(Crew, flight(Id, NDate)),$
    $departure(flight(Id, NDate), NDate, DeptTime),$
    $DeptTime > 6, previous\_date(Date, PDate),$
    $assign(Crew, flight(Id, PDate)),$
    $arrival(flight(Id, PDate), PDate, ArrTime), ArrTime < 22$

This expresses the definition of a day-off as a non-working day (0:00 - 24:00), at base, with one of the following additional requirements. Either the crew begins his/her duty after 8am the next morning, or s/he begins work after 6am but finishes before 10pm (22:00) the day before.

During the computation, the satisfaction of this integrity constraint means that whenever a new assumption of assignment of a Crew to a Flight is made we need to ensure that $consec2\_daysoff$ for this Crew member remains satisfied. In some cases this would then dynamically generate extra assignments, of the Crew member to day-offs, to ensure that his/her flight assignments are consistent.

Airlines also have their own requirements on the problem stemming from particular policies of the specific company and crew preferences. The abductive formulation, with its modular representation of the problem, facilitates in many cases a direct representation of these with additional integrity constraints in IC. As an example consider a requirement of Cyprus Airways which states that flight managers should not have more than two duties per week. This can be represented by the following integrity constraint:

$\neg assign(Crew, Flight) \leftarrow$
    $rank(Crew, flight\_manager),$
    $on\_new\_duty(Crew, Flight),$
    $num\_of\_duties(Crew, Flight, week\_period, NDuties),$
    $NDuties > 2.$

Here $num\_of\_duties(Crew, Flight, week\_period, NDuties)$ counts the number of duties $NDuties$ that a crew member has within a $week\_period$ centered around the date of the flight $Flight$.

With regards to the problem of re-assignment under some new information, given an existing solution, a new module is added to the crew-assignment system which exploits the natural ability of abduction to reason with a given set of hypotheses, in this case the (partial) existing solution. This module follows three steps: (1) remove from the old solution all hypotheses which are affected by these changes. This step is in fact optional, helping only in the efficiency, since hypotheses which make the existing solution inconsistent will be eventually removed automatically by the re-execution of the abductive goal in step 3 below,

(2) add the new requirements (changes) of the problem. These may be in the form of integrity constraints or simply as new information in the domain of the application and (3) re-execute the (or part of the) abductive goal of the problem with the set of the hypotheses in step (1) as a given initial set of abducible assumptions.

Given the set of flights which are affected by the change(s), the aim is to re-establish the consistency, and preferably also the quality, of the old solution by re-assigning crew to these flights, without having to recalculate a new solution from the beginning but rather by making the fewest possible changes on the old existing solution, within 48 hours from the time of the change.

The re-assignment module in this application is interactive in the sense that the user can select a crew for a particular flight or decide whether to accept a system proposed selection of crew. Having searched for a crew member, the system informs the user about the particular selection, together with a list of other assignments (secondary changes) on this crew in the old solution, that are affected and would also need to be rescheduled. It then gives him/her the option to reject this choice, in which case the system will look for another possibility. When the selection of a crew is done directly by the user, the system will check if this choice is valid and inform the user of the list (if any) of secondary affected flights, that would also need to be rescheduled, resulting from this choice.

Although Cyprus Airways is a small size airline it contains the full complexity of the problem. During the busy months the flight schedule contains over 500 flight legs per month. The ACLP system was able to produce solutions in a few minutes which were judged by the airline's experts on this problem to be of good quality comparable (and with respect to balancing requirement often better) to the manually generated ones. The system was also judged to be useful due to the flexibility that it allowed to experiment easily with changes in policy and preferences of the company. The re-assignment module was able to suggest solutions on how to adapt the existing roster within at most 5 seconds. It was chosen as the most useful module of the system as it could facilitate the operators to develop and adjust a solution to meet the specific needs and preferences that they have at the time.

6   Links of ALP to Other Extensions of LP

In parallel with the development of the above frameworks and systems for ALP it has become clear that there exist strong links between some ALP frameworks and other extensions of Logic Programming.

ALP has tight connections to Answer Set Programming [32]. Recall that the ABDUAL framework [1] is an extension of Answer Set Programming with abduction. Standard ALP (with one negation) is strongly related Stable Logic Programming [69,75], the restriction of Answer Set Programming [32] to pure logic programs. As mentioned in section 4, an abductive logic framework under the generalized stable semantics can be translated in an equivalent logic program under stable semantics. Consequently, current systems for computing stable models such as SMODELS [75] can be used to compute abduction under the generalized stable semantics. Interestingly, there are significant differences between in computational models that are developed in both areas. Whereas ALP procedures such as SLDNFA, IFF and ACLP are extensions of SLDNF and operate in a top down way on predicate programs, systems like SMODELS are based on bottom up propagation in the propositional grounding of a logic program. More experimentation is needed to assess the strengths and weaknesses of these approaches.

Links have been shown also between ALP and Disjunctive Logic Programming [100,101,124]. The hypothetical reasoning of ALP and the reasoning with disjunctive information of DLP can be interchanged. This allows theories in one framework to be transformed to the other framework and thus to be executed in this other framework. For example, it is possible to transform an ALP theory into a DLP one and then use a system such as the recently developed dlv system [27] to answer abductive queries. Vice versa, [124] showed that abductive proof procedures can be used as for reasoning on DLP programs.

Another type of extension of the LP paradigm is Inductive Logic Programming. Currently, several approaches are under investigation synthesizing ALP and ILP [2,73,123,35]. These approaches aim to develop techniques for knowledge intensive learning with complex background theories. One problem to be faced by ILP techniques is that the training data on which the inductive process operates often contain gaps and inconsistencies. The general idea is that abductive reasoning can feed information into the inductive process by using the background theory for inserting new hypotheses and removing inconsistent data. Stated differently, abductive inference is used to complete the training data with hypotheses about missing or inconsistent data that explain the example or training data using the background theory. This process gives alternative possibilities for assimilating and generalizing this data. In another integration of ALP and ILP, ILP is extended to learn ALP theories from incomplete background data [62]. This allows the framework to perform Multiple Predicate Learning in a natural way.

As we have seen in previous sections several approaches to ALP have recognized the importance of linking this together with Constraint Logic Programming. They have shown that the integration of constraint solving in abductive logic programming enhances the practical utility of ALP. Experiments indicate that the use of constraint solving techniques in abductive reasoning make the abductive computation much more efficient. On the other hand, the integrated paradigm of ALP and CLP can be seen as a high-level constraint programming environment that allows more modular and flexible representations of the problem domain. The potential benefits of this paradigm are largely unexplored at the moment.

7 Challenges and Prospects for ALP

In the past decade, many studies have shown that extending Logic Programming with abduction has many important applications in the context of AI and declarative problem solving. Yet, at this moment the field of ALP faces a number of challenges at the logical, methodological and computational level. In this section we attempt to chart out some of these challenges and point to some promising directions.

7.1 Heterogeneity of ALP

As can be seen in section 4, ALP is a very heterogeneous field. On the one hand, this heterogeneity stems from the fact that logic programming itself shows a complex landscape. On the other hand, it stems from the fact the term *abduction* is defined very broadly and covers a broad class of rather loosely connected reasoning phenomena.

At the conceptual level, abduction is sometimes used to denote concepts at different conceptual levels. For example, in many of the frameworks discussed earlier, abduction is a concept at the *inferential level*: it is a form of logical inference. In other contexts such as in the *abductive semantics* for negation as failure [29], abduction is a concept used at the *semantical level*, as a specific way of formalizing model semantics. This mismatch between different conceptual levels is confusing and a potential hazard for the field.

At the logical level, there are many different formalisms and different semantics. Various forms of abduction have been introduced in different formalisms including pure logic programming, answer set programming and recently a conditional logic programming formalism [30]. The advantage of this is that the field may act as a *forum* for integrating and relating a wide variety of different forms of logical reasoning in otherwise distant areas. A disadvantage is that this heterogeneity may hide a lack of coherence in which efforts of researchers to build effective systems are scattered in a wide variety of incompatible views and approaches. To develop a computational logic, a focused effort at different levels is needed: research on semantics to clarify the declarative meaning, research on knowledge representation to clarify the applications of the logic, research to explore the relation with other logics, and research to investigate how to implement efficient problem solvers. These efforts should link together in a constructive and cross supporting way.

7.2 Epistemological Foundations of ALP

One of the underlying problems of the field is the lack of understanding of the *epistemological foundations* of ALP. Epistemological questions are what kind of knowledge can be represented by an abductive logic framework and vice versa, what does an ALP theory tell us about the problem domain or equivalently, what information about the domain of discourse is expressed by a given ALP theory? Such questions are fundamental to the understanding of any logic. A clear answer is a prerequisite for developing a well-motivated methodology for declarative problem solving using ALP.

The standard definition of ALP as presented in section 3 does not attempt to answer the above questions. The definition 1 of an abductive solution defines a formal *correctness criterion* for abductive reasoning, but does not address the question of how the ALP formalism should be interpreted. Also the (generic) definition 2 of the formal model semantics of ALP does not provide answers. In fact, here ALP inherits the ambiguity of logic programming at the epistemological level, as demonstrated recently in [15]. Here are some fundamental questions:

- To understand the meaning of an ALP framework, at the very least we need to understand the meaning of its symbols. How is negation in ALP to be understood? The extended completion semantics defined for ALP by Console, Thorasso and Theseider Dupré [10] maps negation as failure literals to classical negation. On the other hand, in the generalized stable semantics [52] and in the ABDUAL framework [1], negation as failure literals are interpreted as modal literals $\neg Kp$ in autoepistemic logic or default logic [38].
- What is the relationship between ALP and classical logic? An ALP framework may contain an arbitrary classical logic theory IC of constraints; in ALP's model semantics, models of an ALP framework satisfy the constraints in IC in the standard way of classical logic. This suggests that ALP is an extension of classical logic. On the other hand, ALP is defined as a study of abductive reasoning while classical logic is normally viewed as the study of deductive reasoning. How are these two views reconciled?

The lack of clear epistemological foundations for ALP is one of the causes of ALP's lack of coherence and is a factor blurring the role and status of ALP at the knowledge representation level in the broader context of logic-based AI. An epistemological study of ALP can contribute significantly to the understanding of the field at the logical and methodological level.

7.3   Computational Challenges

The computational challenges of the paradigm are considerable. The challenge of building abductive systems for solving a broad class of problems formalized by high-level declarative representations, is extremely difficult to realise.

At the theoretical level of complexity, formal results show that in general the problem of computing abduction is hard [26]. In the datalog case, the problem of computing abductive solutions is in general intractable. In the general case of ALP frameworks with function symbols, the existence of an abductive solution is undecidable. On the implementational level, the problem of implementing abductive reasoning can be seen as an extension of the implementation of CLP systems in which we need to reason about constraints of general first order logic.

Current systems such as ACLP, SLDNFAC and IFF are based on the integration of CLP techniques in high level abductive procedures. These systems operate by reducing the high level constraints in a, in general, nondeterministic process to a constraint store that can be handled efficiently by specialised constraint systems. Recent experiments with the ACLP and SLDNFAC systems have shown that in those cases where the reduction process is deterministic, these procedures can be very performant. However, when the process is nondeterministic, these procedures can start to trash. The reason for this behaviour is that a number of techniques are built in in the current procedures that delay the creation of choice points and perform deterministic computation first. In many applications such as scheduling, these techniques can avoid making choices altogether. In other cases, such as in planning applications, the arsenal of techniques does not suffice to manage these choice points and the current procedures often make *uninformed selections* of choices leading to uncontrolled depth first execution and *trashing*.

The above analysis suggests different ways to improve the computational techniques of ALP. One way is to further improve the techniques to discover deterministic subgoals and delay creation of choice points. A second way is to incorporate techniques for smarter and *better informed* selection of the choice points and choice of alternatives in the choice point. A third way is an improved control to avoid unrestricted depth first reasoning using techniques similar to loop detection and iterative deepening can be used. With respect to the first two problems, different approaches can be followed. One is to further refine the current integration of Constraint Solving in the abductive inference. In the current systems, the CLP solver is a black box that interacts with the abductive solver by returning a solution at the end, or by reporting consistency or inconsistency of the constraint store at different points during the execution. One direction to be examined is how to exploit the information present in the constraint store to steer the search for an abductive solution and make a better informed selection of goals. An alternative direction is to apply techniques from heuristic search in Artificial Intelligence.

An interesting application domain to study the above techniques for abductive reasoning is AI-planning, due to the strong links between abduction and planning and the fact that recently, techniques from constraint solving and heuristic search have been successfully applied in this domain. What we can learn here is how recent developments of constraint and heuristic methods of search in planning could be applied to the more general case of abductive computation.

A complementary approach to address the computational hardness of ALP would be to develop ALP systems in which the user has the facility to incrementally refine her/his model of the problem in a modular way. Starting from a purely declarative problem description, it should be possible to refine the model by adding more and more additional knowledge about the problem, including non-declarative heuristic and operational control knowledge. Again recent work suggests that this is a promising line of development but there is no systematic study of how such a modeling environment would be designed and build in ALP.

A completely different approach is to exploit the kind of techniques used in bottom up abduction [46] (see section 4) based on the computation of stable models of a ground logic program. Techniques like those used by the smodels system [75] which integrates methods from propositional constraint propagation with bottom up application of semantic fixpoint operators of the 3-valued completion semantics and well-founded semantics. In the current state of the art, it seems that while the latter techniques based on reasoning on propositional theories are more robust, the abductive extensions of SLDNF with CLP may outperform the first ones especially as they can take into account more easily additional problem domain specific information. Therefore, extending the latter procedures along the lines suggested above is a promising research direction.

7.4   Challenges at the Application Level

In the past decade, the potential of the different ALP frameworks have been demonstrated in a wide variety of application domains. However, only a few of the current running applications exceed the level of academic toy examples. Like in many other areas of AI, this potential has not yet been realized in realistic and industrial scale applications. One of the challenges of the domain is to find interesting niche domains with industrial impact in which the current systems can be evaluated and fine-tuned. Experimentation with and evaluation of abductive systems in realistic domains could yield important information at the levels of language constructs, methodology, computational control, integration of heuristic information, etc..

Some prototypical classes of problems that seem good candidates for fine-tuning ALP methods are Scheduling and Planning domains and Knowledge Intensive Learning where machine learning with a rich background knowledge can be performed only if the inductive methods are integrated with abduction [123,73,35].

7.5   A Possible Approach to These Challenges

In this section, we briefly describe our own views on how to approach the above logical and computational challenges.

The underlying logic for ALP is ID-logic [16,23] a logic which is appropriate for ALP in the way that it extends classical logic with inductive definitions of a generalized non-monotone kind. As mentioned earlier in section 3, an abductive logic framework (P, A, IC) has a natural embedding in ID-logic. P represents a definition of the non-abducible predicates while IC represents a set of classical logic assertions. In this view, ALP is the study of abduction in the context of ID-logic. ID-logic was defined in an attempt to cope with the epistemological challenges of logic programming and gives answers to the epistemological questions raised in section 7.2.

At the computational level, we are currently developing a system called the A-system [63,118] integrating features of ACLP and SLDNFAC with special attention to the search in the abductive computation. During the computation, the selection and evaluation of choice points is guided by information obtained from a constraint store associated to the abductive solution. With this information the high level search can avoid deadend branches before entering them. The result is a more robust and modular system which is capable to solve effectively a wider range of problems than the older systems. The application domain of the experiments with the A-system are currently focused on scheduling and planning applications. The A-system is built on top of Sicstus Prolog (version 3.8.5 or above) and is available at *http://www.cs.kuleuven.ac.be/~dtai/kt/*.

8   Conclusion

Abductive logic programming grew out of attempts to use logic programming techniques for a broad class of problems from AI and other areas of Computer Science. At present Abductive Logic Programming presents itself as a "conservative extension" of Logic Programming that allows more declarative representations of problems. The main emphasis till now has been on setting up different frameworks for abduction and showing how they provide a general approach to declarative problem solving.

ALP faces a number of challenges, at the logical, methodological and computational level typical for a field in an initial stage of development. We are now beginning to understand the contributions of this field and to develop solutions for the problems that the field faces.

At the logical level, ALP aims to be suitable for declarative knowledge representation, thus facilitating maintenance, reusability and graceful modifiability. Yet, ALP retains from logic programming the possibility of embedding high level strategic information in an abductive program which allows us to speed up and fine tune the computation. In this respect, ALP is able to combine the advantages of declarative specification and programming to a greater extent than standard logic programming.

The field has also started to recognize the full extent of the problem and the complexity of developing effective and useable ALP systems. The overall task of ALP of providing a high-level general purpose modeling environment which at the same time is computationally effective is an extremely difficult one. But we are beginning to learn how to analyze and break this task down to appropriate subproblems that are amenable to study within our current understanding of the field. The hope remains that within the high-level programming environment that ALP could provide, the programmer will be able to solve problems effectively in a translucent way.

Acknowledgements This work was partly supported by the European Union KIT project CLSFA (9621109).

References

1. J. J. Alferes, L. M. Pereira, T. Swift. Well-founded Abduction via Tabled Dual Programs. In Procs. of the 16th International Conference on Logic Programming, Las Cruces, New Mexico, Nov. 29 - Dec. 4, 1999.
2. H. Ade and M. Denecker. Abductive inductive logic programming. In C.S. Mellish, editor, *Proc. of the International Joint Conference on Artificial Intelligence*, pages 1201–1209. Morgan Kaufman, 1995.
3. J. J. Alferes, J. A. Leite, L. M. Pereira, P.Quaresma. Planning as Abductive Updating. In D. Kitchin (ed.), Procs. of AISB'00, 2000.
4. Balsa, J., Dahl, V. and Pereira Lopes, J.G. Datalog Grammars for Abductive Syntactic Error Diagnosis and Repair. In Proc. Natural Language Understanding and Logic Programming Workshop, Lisbon, 1995.
5. M. Bruynooghe, H. Vandecasteele, D.A. de Waal, and Denecker M. Detecting unsolvable queries for definite logic programs. *The Journal of Functional and Logic Programming*, 1999:1–35, November 1999.
6. J.F.Castro, L. M. Pereira, Z.Vale. Power Grid Failure Diagnosis Certification. Technical Report, University of Lisbon.
7. A. Ciampolini, E. Lamma, P. Mello and P. Torroni. Expressing Collaboration and Competition Among Abductive Logic Agents. In *AI*IA Notizie* - Anno XIII(3), Settembre 2000, pag. 19–24.
8. E. Charniak and D. McDermott. *Introduction to Artifical Intelligence*. Addison-Wesley, 1985.
9. K.L. Clark. Negation as failure. In H. Gallaire and J. Minker, editors, *Logic and Databases*, pages 293–322. Plenum Press, 1978.
10. L. Console, D. Theseider Dupré, and P. Torasso. On the relationship between abduction and deduction. *Journal of Logic and Computation*, 1(5):661–690, 1991.
11. L. Console, L. Portinale and Theseider Dupré, D., Using Compiled knowledge to guide and focus abductive diagnosis. IEEE Transactions on Knowledge and Data Engineering, Vol. 8 (5), pp. 690-706, 1996.
12. L. Console, M.L. Sapino and Theseider Dupré, D. The Role of Abduction in Database View Updating. Journal of Intelligent Information Systems, Vol. 4(3), pp. 261-280, 1995.
13. D. de Waal, M. Denecker, M. Bruynooghe, and M. Thielscher. The generation of pre-interpretations for detecting unsolvable planning problems. In *Proceedings of the Workshop on Model-Based Automated Reasoning (15th International Joint Conference on Artificial Intelligence)*, pages 103–112, 1997.
14. M. Denecker. A Terminological Interpretation of (Abductive) Logic Programming. In V.W. Marek, A. Nerode, and M. Truszczynski, editors, *International Conference on Logic Programming and Nonmonotonic Reasoning*, Lecture notes in Artificial Intelligence 928, pages 15–29. Springer, 1995.
15. M. Denecker. On the Epistemological foundations of Logic Programming and its Extensions. In *AAAI Spring Symposium on Answer Set Programming: Towards Efficient and Scalable Knowledge Representation and Reasoning*, volume technical report SS-01-01. American Association for Artificial Intelligence, AAAI Press, 2001.
16. M. Denecker. Extending classical logic with inductive definitions. In J.Lloyd et al., editor, *First International Conference on Computational Logic (CL2000)*, volume 1861 of *Lecture notes in Artificial Intelligence*, pages 703–717, London, July 2000. Springer.

17. M. Denecker and D. De Schreye. SLDNFA; an abductive procedure for normal abductive programs. In K.R. Apt, editor, *Proc. of the International Joint Conference and Symposium on Logic Programming*, pages 686–700. MIT Press, 1992.

18. M. Denecker and D. De Schreye. Representing incomplete knowledge in abductive logic programming. In *Proc. of the International Symposium on Logic Programming*, pages 147–163. MIT Press, 1993.

19. M. Denecker and D. De Schreye. Representing Incomplete Knowledge in Abductive Logic Programming. *Journal of Logic and Computation*, 5(5):553–578, September 1995.

20. M. Denecker and D. De Schreye. SLDNFA: an abductive procedure for abductive logic programs. *Journal of Logic Programming*, 34(2):111–167, 1998.

21. M. Denecker, L. Missiaen, and M. Bruynooghe. Temporal reasoning with abductive event calculus. In *Proc. of the European Conference on Artificial Intelligence*. John Wiley and sons, 1992.

22. M. Denecker, K. Van Belleghem, G. Duchatelet, F. Piessens, and D. De Schreye. Using Event Calculus for Protocol Specification. An Experiment. In M. Maher, editor, *The International Joint Conference and Symposium on Logic Programming*, pages 170–184. MIT Press, 1996.

23. Marc Denecker, Maurice Bruynooghe, and Victor W Marek. Logic programming revisited : logic programs as inductive definitions. *ACM Transactions on Computational Logic*, 2001. accepted.

24. Theseider Dupré, D.. Characterizing and Mechanizing Abductive Reasoning. PhD Thesis, Dip. Informatica, Università di Torino, 1994.

25. P.M. Dung. Negations as hypotheses: an abductive foundation for Logic Programming. In *Proc. of the International Conference on Logic Programming*, 1991.

26. Thomas Eiter, Georg Gottlob, Nicola Leone. Abduction from Logic Programs: Semantics and Complexity. Theoretical Computer Science 189(1-2):129-177 (1997).

27. Thomas Eiter, Wolfgang Faber, Nicola Leone, and Gerald Pfeifer. Declarative problem-solving using the dlv system. In Jack Minker, editor, Logic-Based Artificial Intelligence. Kluwer Academic Publishers, 2000.

28. K. Eshghi. Abductive planning with Event Calculus. In R.A. Kowalski and K.A. Bowen, editors, *Proc. of the International Conference on Logic Programming*. The MIT press, 1988.

29. K. Eshghi and R.A. Kowalski. Abduction compared with negation as failure. In *Proc. of the International Conference on Logic Programming*. MIT-press, 1989.

30. D. Gabbay, L. Giordano, A. Martelli, and M.L. Sapino. Conditional reasoning in logic programming. *Journal of Logic Programming*, 44(1-3):37–74, 2000.

31. J. Gartner, T. Swift, A. Tien, C. V. Damásio, L. M. Pereira. Psychiatric Diagnosis from the Viewpoint of Computational Logic. In G. Wiggins (ed.), Procs. of AISB, 2000.

32. Gelfond, M., Lifschitz, V. Classical negation in logic programs and disjunctive databases. New Generation Computing, pp. 365-387, 1991.

33. Fages, F. A New Fixpoint Semantics for General Logic Programs Compared with the Well-Founded and the Stable Model Semantics. Proc. of ICLP'90, pp. 442 – 458, 1990.

34. P. Flach and A. C. Kakas (Eds.). Abduction and Induction: Essays on their Relation and Integration. Kluwer Academic Press, 2000.

35. P. Flach and A. C. Kakas. Abductive and Inductive Reasoning: Background and Issues. In Peter Flach and Antonis Kakas, editors, *Abduction and Induction: essays on their relation and integration*. Kluwer, 2000.

36. Fung, T.H. Abduction by deduction. Ph.D. Thesis, Imperial College, London, 1996.
37. T.H. Fung, R.A. Kowalski. The iff procedure for abductive logic programming. In *Journal of Logic Programming* 33(2):151–165, Elsevier, 1997.
38. M. Gelfond and V. Lifschitz. The stable model semantics for logic programming. In *Proc. of the International Joint Conference and Symposium on Logic Programming*, pages 1070–1080. IEEE, 1988.
39. Hobbs, J.R. An integrated abductive framework for discourse interpretation. Symposium on Automated Abduction,Stanford, 1990.
40. K. Inoue. Hypothetical reasoning in Logic Programs. *Journal of Logic Programming*, 18(3):191–228, 1994.
41. K. Inoue. A simple characterization of extended abduction. In: *Proceedings of the First International Conference on Computational Logic, Lecture Notes in Artificial Intelligence*, 1861, pages 718–732, Springer, 2000.
42. K. Inoue, Y. Ohta, and R. Hasegawa. Bottom-up Abduction by Model Generation. Technical Report TR-816, Institute for New Generation Computer Technology, Japan, 1993.
43. K.Inoue and C. Sakama. Abductive framework for nonmonotonic theory change. In: *Proceedings of IJCAI-95*, pages 204–210, Morgan Kaufmann, 1995.
44. K. Inoue and C. Sakama. Abducing priorities to derive intended conclusions. In: *Proceedings of IJCAI-99*, pages 44–49, Morgan Kaufmann, 1999.
45. K. Inoue and C. Sakama. Computing extended abduction through transaction programs. *Annals of Mathematics and Artificial Intelligence*, 25(3,4):339–367, 1999.
46. Iwayama, N. and Satoh, K. Computing Abduction by Using TMS with Top-Down Expectation. Journal of Logic Programming, Vol. 44 No.1-3, pp. 179 – 206, 2000.
47. J.R. Josephson and S.G. Josephson, editors. *Abductive Inference: Computation, Philosophy, Technology.* New York: Cambridge University Press, 1994.
48. C.G. Jung, K. Fischer, and A. Burt. Multi-agent planning using an abductive event calculus. Technical Report DFKI Report RR-96-04, DFKI, Germany, 1996.
49. A. C. Kakas. ACLP: Integrating Abduction and Constraint Solving. In Proceedings of NMR2000, 2000.
50. Kakas, A. C., Kowalski, R. A., Toni, F., Abductive logic programming. *Journal of Logic and Computation* 2(6) (1993) 719–770
51. A. C. Kakas, R.A. Kowalski, and F. Toni. The role of abduction in logic programming. Handbook of Logic in Artificial Intelligence and Logic Programming 5, pages 235-324, D.M. Gabbay, C.J. Hogger and J.A. Robinson eds., Oxford University Press (1998)
52. A.C. Kakas and P. Mancarella. Generalised Stable Models: a Semantics for Abduction. In Proc. 9th European Conference on AI, ECAI90, Stockolm, 1990.
53. A.C. Kakas and P. Mancarella. Database updates through abduction. In *Proc. of the 16th Very large Database Conference*, pages 650–661. Morgan Kaufmann, 1990.
54. A.C. Kakas and P. Mancarella. On the relation of truth maintenance and abduction. In Proc. 1st Pacific Rim International Conference on Artificial Intelligence, PRICAI90, Nagoya, Japan, 1990.
55. A. C. Kakas and P. Mancarella. *Knowledge assimilation and abduction.* International Workshop on Truth Maintenance, Stockholm, ECAI90, Springer Verlag Lecture notes in Computer Science, Vol. 515, pp. 54-71, 1990.
56. Kakas, A. C., Michael, A. Integrating abductive and constraint logic programming. In *Proc. International Logic Programming Conference*, pp. 399-413, 1995.

57. A.C. Kakas and A. Michael. Air-Crew Scheduling through Abduction. Proceedings of IEA/AIE-99, pp. 600–612, 1999.
58. A.C. Kakas and A. Michael. An Abductive-based scheduler for air-crew assingment. Journal of Applied Artificial Intelligence Vol. 15, pp. 333–360, 2001.
59. A.C. Kakas, A. Michael and C. Mourlas. ACLP: a case for non-monotonic reasoning. in Proceedings of NMR98,pp. 46–56, 1998.
60. A.C. Kakas, A. Michael and C. Mourlas. ACLP: Abductive Constraint Logic Programming. Journal of Logic Programming (special issue on Abductive Logic Programming), Vol. 44 (1-3), pp. 129-177, 2000.
61. A.C. Kakas and C. Mourlas. ACLP: Flexible Solutions to Complex Problems. Proceedings of Logic Programming and Non-monotonic Reasoning, LPNMR97, 1997,
62. A.C. Kakas and F. Riguzzi. Abductive Concept Learning. New Generation Computing, Vol. 18, pp. 243-294, 2000.
63. A.C Kakas, Bert Van Nuffelen, and Marc Denecker. A-system : Problem solving through abduction. In *Proceedings of IJCAI'01 - Seventeenth International Joint Conference on Artificial Intelligence*, pp. 591-597, 2001.
64. R.A. Kowalski and F. Sadri, From Logic Programming towards Multi-agent Systems. *Annals of Mathemathics and Artificial Intelligence*, Vol 25, pp. 391-419, 1999.
65. R.A. Kowalski and M. Sergot. A logic-based calculus of events. *New Generation Computing*, 4(4):319–340, 1986.
66. Kowalski, R.A.; Toni, F.; Wetzel, G.; 1998. Executing suspended logic programs. *Fundamenta Informaticae* 34(3):203–224, ISO Press.
67. J. A. Leite, F. C. Pereira, A. Cardoso, L. M.Pereira. Metaphorical Mapping Consistency via Dynamic Logic Programming. In J. Lloyd et al. (eds.), Procs. of First Int. Conf. on Computational Logic (CL 2000), London, UK, pages 1362-1376, LNAI 1861, Springer, 2000.
68. J.W. Lloyd. *Foundations of Logic Programming.* Springer-Verlag, 1987.
69. V.W. Marek and M. Truszczyński. Stable models and an alternative logic programming paradigm. In K.R. Apt, V. Marek, M. Truszczynski, and D.S. Warren, editors, The Logic Programming Paradigm. a 25 Years Perspective, pages pp. 375–398. Springer-Verlag, 1999.
70. J. McCarthy. Situations, actions and causal laws. Technical Report AI-memo 1, Artifical Intelligence Program, Standford University, 1957.
71. Lode R. Missiaen, Marc Denecker, and Maurice Bruynooghe. CHICA, an abductive planning system based on event calculus. *Journal of Logic and Computation*, 5(5):579–602, September 1995.
72. L.R. Missiaen, M. Bruynooghe, and M. Denecker. Abductive planning with event calculus. Internal report, Department of Computer Science, K.U.Leuven, 1992.
73. S. Muggleton. Theory Completion in Learning. In Proceedings of Inductive Logic Programming, ILP00, 2000.
74. I. Niemela and P. Simons. Smodels - an implementation of the stable model and well-founded semantics for normal logic programs. Proceeings of the 4th International Conference on Logic Programming and Non-monotonic Reasoning, pp. 420-429, 1997.
75. I. Niemelä. Logic programs with stable model semantics as a constraint programming paradigm. *Annals of Mathematics and Artificial Intelligence*, 25(3,4):241–273, 1999.
76. M. Pagnucco. The role of abductive reasoning within the process of belief revision. PhD Thesis, Department of Computer Science, University of Sydney, 1996.

77. C.S. Peirce. *Philosophical Writings of Peirce*. Dover Publications, New York, 1955.
78. Nikolay Pelov, Emmanuel De Mot, and Marc Denecker. Logic programming approaches for representing and solving constraint satisfaction problems : a comparison. In *Proceedings of LPAR'2000 - 7th International Conference on Logic for Programming and Automated Reasoning*, 2000. accepted.
79. L.M. Pereira, J.N. Aparício, and J.J. Alferes. Nonmonotonic reasoning with Well-Founded Semantics. In K. Furukawa, editor, *Proc. of the eight international conference on logic programming*, pages 475–489. the MIT press, 1991.
80. J. Pearl. *Probabilistic Reasoning in Intelligent Systems: Networks of Plausible Inference*. Morgan Kaufmann, San Mateo, CA, 1988.
81. D. Poole. A Logical Framework for Default Reasoning. *Artifical Intelligence*, 36:27–47, 1988.
82. D. Poole. A methodology for using a default and abductive reasoning system. *International Journal of Intelligent Systems*, 5(5):521–548, December 1990.
83. D. Poole. Logic programming, abduction and probability: A top-down anytime algorithm for computing prior and posterior probabilities. *New Generation Computing*, 11(3–4):377–400, 1993.
84. D. Poole. Probabilistic Horn abduction and Bayesian networks. *Artificial Intelligence*, 64(1):81–129, 1993.
85. D. Poole. Probabilistic conflicts in a search algorithm for estimating posterior probabilities in Bayesian networks. *Artificial Intelligence*, 88:69–100, 1996.
86. D. Poole. The independent choice logic for modelling multiple agents under uncertainty. *Artificial Intelligence*, 94:7–56, 1997. special issue on economic principles of multi-agent systems.
87. D. Poole. Probabilistic partial evaluation: Exploiting rule structure in probabilistic inference. In *Proc. 15th International Joint Conf. on Artificial Intelligence (IJCAI-97)*, pages 1284–1291, Nagoya, Japan, 1997.
88. D. Poole, R. Goebel, and R. Aleliunas. Theorist: A logical reasoning system for defaults and diagnosis. In N. Cercone and G. McCalla, editors, *The Knowledge Frontier: Essays in the Representation of Knowledge*, pages 331–352. Springer-Verlag, New York, NY, 1987.
89. David Poole. Learning, bayesian probability, graphical models, and abduction. In Peter Flach and Antonis Kakas, editors, *Abduction and Induction: essays on their relation and integration*. Kluwer, 2000.
90. Poole, D., Goebel, R.G., Aleliunas, Theorist: a logical reasoning system for default and diagnosis. *The Knowledge Fronteer: Essays in the Representation of Knowledge*, Cercone and McCalla eds, Springer Verlag Lecture Notes in Computer Science 331–352, 1987.
91. D. Poole, A. Mackworth, R. G. Goebel, Computational Intelligence: a logical approach Oxford University Press, 1998.
92. Stathis Psillos. Ampliative Reasoning: Induction or Abduction. In *ECAI96 workshop on Abductive and Inductive Reasoning*, 1996.
93. Rochefort, S., Tarau, P. and Dahl, V. Feature Interaction Resolution Through Hypothetical Reasoning. In Proc. 4th World Multiconference on Systemics, Cybernetics and Informatics (SCI2000) and the 6th International Conference on Information Systems Analysis and Synthesis (ISAS2000), Orlando, USA July 23-26, 2000.
94. Saccà, D., Zaniolo, C. Stable Models and Non-Determinism in Logic Programs with Negation. Proc. of PODS'90, pp. 205 – 217, 1990.

95. F.Sadri, F. Toni, I.Xanthakos. A Logic-Agent based System for Semantic Integration. 17th International CODATA Conference- Data and Information for the Coming Knowledge Millennium- CODATA 2000, Theme I-3, Integration of Heterogeneous Databases and Data Warehousing.
96. F. Sadri, F. Toni. Abduction with negation as failure for active databases and agents. *Proc. AI*IA 99, 6th Congress of the Italian Association for Artificial Intelligence*, pages 353–362, Pitagora Editrice Bologna, 1999.
97. F. Sadri, F. Toni. Abduction with Negation as Failure for Active and Reactive Rules, In E. Lamma and P. Mello eds., Proc. AI*IA 99, 6th Congress of the Italian Association for Artificial Intelligence, Springer Verlag LNAI 1792, pages 49-60, 2000.
98. C. Sakama and K. Inoue. Representing priorities in logic programs. In: *Proceedings of the 1996 Joint International Conference and Symposium on Logic Programming*, pages 82–96, MIT Press, 1996.
99. C. Sakama and K. Inoue. Updating extended logic programs through abduction. In: *Proceedings of LPNMR '99, Lecture Notes in Artificial Intelligence*, 1730, pages 147–161, Springer, 1999.
100. C. Sakama and K. Inoue. Abductive logic programming and disjunctive logic programming: their relationship and transferability. *Journal of Logic Programming - Special issue on ALP* 44(1-3):71–96, 2000.
101. C. Sakama and K. Inoue. An alternative approach to the semantics of disjunctive logic programs and deductive databases. *Journal of Automated Reasoning* 13(1):145–172, 1994.
102. F. Sadri, F. Toni and P. Torroni. Dialogues for negotiation: agent varieties and dialogue sequences. In Pre-proc. ATAL'01, special track on negotiation. Seattle, WA, August 2001.
103. Satoh, K. Statutory Interpretation by Case-based Reasoning through Abductive Logic Programming. Journal of Advanced Computational Intelligence, Vol. 1, No.2, pp. 94 – 103, 1997.
104. Satoh, K. Computing Minimal Revised Logic Program by Abduction. Proc. of the International Workshop on the Principles of Software Evolution, IWPSE98, pp. 177 – 182, 1998.
105. Satoh, K. Using Two Level Abduction to Decide Similarity of Cases. Proc. of ECAI'98 pp. 398 – 402, 1998.
106. K. Satoh and N. Iwayama. A Query Evaluation method for Abductive Logic Programming. In K.R. Apt, editor, *Proc. of the International Joint Conference and Symposium on Logic Programming*, 1992.
107. Satoh, K. and Iwayama, N. Computing Abduction by Using the TMS. Proc. of ICLP'91, pp. 505 – 518, 1991.
108. Satoh, K. and Iwayama, N. A Query Evaluation Method for Abductive Logic Programming. Proc. of JICSLP'92, pp. 671 – 685, 1992.
109. Satoh, K. and Iwayama, N., "A Correct Goal-Directed Proof Procedure for a General Logic Program with Integrity Constraints", E. Lamma and P. Mello (eds.), Extensions of Logic Programming, LNAI 660, pp. 24 – 44, Springer-Verlag (1993).
110. M. Shanahan. Prediction is deduction but explanation is abduction. In *Proc. of the IJCAI89*, page 1055, 1989.
111. F. Toni. A semantics for the Kakas-Mancarella procedure for abductive logic programming. *Proc. GULP'95*, M. Alpuente and M. I. Sessa, eds., pages 231-242, 1995.

112. F. Toni. Automated Reasoning for Collective Information Management. *Proc. LocalNets, International Workshop on Community-based Interactive Systems*, in conjunction with AC'99, the Annual Conference of the EC I^3 Programme

113. K. Van Belleghem, M. Denecker, and D. De Schreye. Representing continuous change in the abductive event calculus. In *Proc. of the International Conference on Logic Programming*. MIT-Press, 1994.

114. K. Van Belleghem, M. Denecker, and D. De Schreye. The abductive event calculus as a general framework for temporal databases. In *Proc. of the International Conference on Temporal Logic*, pages 301–316, 1994.

115. K. Van Belleghem, M. Denecker, and D. De Schreye. A strong correspondence between description logics and open logic programming. In Lee Naish, editor, *Proc. of the International Conference on Logic Programming, 1997*, pages 346–360. MIT-press, 1997.

116. A. Van Gelder, K.A. Ross, and J.S. Schlipf.r The Well-Founded Semantics for General Logic Programs. *Journal of the ACM*, 38(3):620–650, 1991.

117. Bert Van Nuffelen and Marc Denecker. Problem solving in ID-logic with aggregates: some experiments. In M. Denecker, A. Kakas, and F. Toni, editors, *8th Int. Workshop on Non-Monotonic Reasoning (NMR2000), session on Abduction*, pages 1–15, Breckenridge, Colorado, USA, April 9-11 2000.

118. B. Van Nuffelen and A.C Kakas, A-System: Programming with Abduction. In *Proceedings of LPNMR2001*, LNAI Vol. 2173, pp. 393-396, Springer Verlag, 2001.

119. Sven Verdoolaege, Marc Denecker, and Frank Van Eynde. Abductive reasoning with temporal information. In Ielka van der Sluis Harry Bunt and Elias Thijsse, editors, *Proceedings of the Fourth International Workshop on Computational Semantics*, pages 351–366, 2001.

120. Wetzel, G. *Abductive and Constraint Logic Programming*. Ph.D. Thesis, Imperial College, London, 1997.

121. G. Wetzel, F. Toni. Semantic Query Optimization through Abduction and Constraint Handling. Proc. of the International Conference on Flexible Query Answering Systems, T. Andreasen, H. L. Larsen and H. Christiansen eds., Springer Verlag LNAI 1495 (1998).

122. The XSB Group. The XSB logic programming system, version 2.0. 1999. Available from http://www.cs.sunysb.edu/~sbprolog.

123. A. Yamamoto. Using abduction for induction based on bottom up generalization. In Peter Flach and Antonis Kakas, editors, *Abduction and Induction: essays on their relation and integration*. Kluwer, pp. 267-280,2000.

124. J.H. You, L.Y. Yuan and R. Goebel. An abductive approach to disjunctive logic programming. Journal of Logic Programming (special issue on Abductive Logic Programming), Vol. 44 (1-3), pp. 101-128, 2000.

Learning in Clausal Logic:
A Perspective on Inductive Logic Programming

Peter Flach[1] and Nada Lavrač[2]

[1] University of Bristol
Woodland Road, Bristol BS8 1UB, United Kingdom
Peter.Flach@bristol.ac.uk, http://www.cs.bris.ac.uk/~flach/
[2] Jožef Stefan Institute
Jamova 39, 1000 Ljubljana, Slovenia
Nada.Lavrac@ijs.si, http://www-ai.ijs.si/NadaLavrac/

Abstract. Inductive logic programming is a form of machine learning from examples which employs the representation formalism of clausal logic. One of the earliest inductive logic programming systems was Ehud Shapiro's Model Inference System [90], which could synthesise simple recursive programs like **append/3**. Many of the techniques devised by Shapiro, such as top-down search of program clauses by refinement operators, the use of intensional background knowledge, and the capability of inducing recursive clauses, are still in use today. On the other hand, significant advances have been made regarding dealing with noisy data, efficient heuristic and stochastic search methods, the use of logical representations going beyond definite clauses, and restricting the search space by means of declarative bias. The latter is a general term denoting any form of restrictions on the syntactic form of possible hypotheses. These include the use of types, input/output mode declarations, and clause schemata. Recently, some researchers have started using alternatives to Prolog featuring strong typing and real functions, which alleviate the need for some of the above ad-hoc mechanisms. Others have gone beyond Prolog by investigating learning tasks in which the hypotheses are not definite clause programs, but for instance sets of indefinite clauses or denials, constraint logic programs, or clauses representing association rules. The chapter gives an accessible introduction to the above topics. In addition, it outlines the main current research directions which have been strongly influenced by recent developments in data mining and challenging real-life applications.

1 Introduction

Inductive logic programming has its roots in concept learning from examples, a relatively straightforward form of induction that has been studied extensively by machine learning researchers [70]. The aim of concept learning is to discover, from a given set of pre-classified examples, one or several classification rules with high predictive power. For many concept learning tasks, so-called attribute-value

A.C. Kakas, F. Sadri (Eds.): Computat. Logic (Kowalski Festschrift), LNAI 2407, pp. 437–471, 2002.
© Springer-Verlag Berlin Heidelberg 2002

languages have sufficient representational power. An example of an attribute-value classification rule is the following (regarding contact lens prescriptions, from [97]):

IF Age = Pre-presbyopic AND Astigmatic = No AND Tear-production = Normal THEN Recommendation = Soft

A learned concept definition could consist of several of such rules. Concept learning can be generalised to multi-class classification problems, where one would learn a set of rules for each class. (In contrast, in concept learning we are usually not interested in learning rules for the complement of the concept.)

When objects are structured and consist of several related parts, we need a richer representation formalism with variables to refer to those parts. In the 1970s and '80s machine learning researchers started exploring the use of logic programming representations, which led to the establishment of inductive logic programming (ILP) [79] as a subdiscipline at the intersection of machine learning and computational logic. Recent years have seen a steady increase in ILP research, as well as numerous applications to practical problems like data mining and scientific discovery – see [8,30] for an overview of such applications.

Most of the current real-world ILP applications involve predictive knowledge discovery, in particular the induction of classification and prediction rules from a given database of examples and the available background knowledge. Successful ILP applications include drug design [55], protein secondary structure prediction [78], mutagenicity prediction [93], carcinogenesis prediction [94], medical diagnosis [72], discovery of qualitative models in medicine [48], finite-element mesh design [28], telecommunications [92], natural language processing [73], recovering software specifications [12], and many others.

Focusing on problems such as data mining also led away from pure classification problems, where a teacher would pre-classify the training data and the learning problem consists in coming up with rules predicting the class. In descriptive induction problems, there is no notion of a class and the goal of learning is to come up with rules describing correlations between any descriptors found in the data. A typical example here are association rules [1], which are useful in applications like market basket analysis. Descriptive induction methods have also been studied in a first-order context.

The outline of the chapter is as follows. Sections 2 and 3 introduce the tasks of predictive and descriptive ILP, respectively. In Section 4 we take a closer look at the different knowledge formalisms that are used in ILP, in particular Datalog, Prolog, typed and functional logic languages, and database representations. Section 5 overviews state-of-the-art ILP techniques and systems, and in Section 6 we look at future challenges for ILP research and applications, including a section on research challenges related to computational logic. Section 7 concludes.

2 Predictive ILP

In this section we give a tutorial introduction to the main forms of predictive inductive logic programming. One instance of a predictive ILP problem concerns the inductive construction of an intensional predicate definition (a set of Horn clauses with a single predicate in the head) from a selection of ground instances of the predicate. More generally, there can be several predicates whose definitions are to be learned, also called *foreground* predicates or *observables*. In the general case, this requires suitably defined auxiliary or *background predicates* (simple recursive predicates such as `member/2` and `append/3` notwithstanding). The induced set of rules or *inductive hypothesis* then provides an intensional connection between the foreground predicates and the background predicates; we will sometimes call such rules *foreground* rules. We will also use the terms *facts* to refer to extensional knowledge, and *rules* to refer to intensional knowledge. The terms 'knowledge' or 'theory' may refer to both facts and rules. Thus, predictive induction infers foreground rules from foreground facts and background theory.

Definition 1 (Predictive ILP). *Let P_F and N_F be sets of ground facts over a set of foreground predicates F, called the* positive examples *and the* negative examples, *respectively. Let T_B, the* background theory, *be a set of clauses over a set of background predicates B. Let L be a* language bias *specifying a* hypothesis language $\mathcal{H}_L$ over $F \cup B$ *(i.e., a set of clauses). A predictive ILP task consists in finding a hypothesis $H \subseteq \mathcal{H}_L$ such that $\forall p \in P_F : T_B \cup H \models p$ and $\forall n \in N_F : T_B \cup H \not\models n$.*

The subscripts F and B are often dropped, if the foreground and background predicates are understood. We will sometimes refer to all examples collectively as E.

Definition 1 is under-specified in a number of ways. First, it doesn't rule out trivial solutions like $H = P$ unless this is excluded by the language bias (which is not often the case since the language bias cannot simply exclude ground facts, because they are required by certain recursive predicate definitions). Furthermore, the definition doesn't capture the requirement that the inductive hypothesis correctly predicts unseen examples. It should therefore be seen as a general framework, which needs to be further instantiated to capture the kinds of ILP tasks addressed in practice. We proceed by briefly discussing a number of possible variations, indicating which of these we can handle with the approach proposed in this chapter.

Clauses in T and H are often restricted to definite clauses with only positive literals in the body. Some ILP algorithms are able to deal with normal clauses which allow negative literals in the body. One can go a step further and allow negation over several related literals in the body (called *features* in [65]).

In a typical predictive ILP task, there is a single foreground predicate to be learned, often referred to as the *target predicate*. In contrast, *multiple predicate learning* occurs when $|F| > 1$. Multiple predicate learning is hard if the foreground predicates are mutually dependent, i.e., if one foreground predicate acts as an auxiliary predicate to another foreground predicate, because in that case the auxiliary predicate is incompletely specified. Approaches to dealing with incomplete background theory, such as abductive concept learning [52], can be helpful here. Alternatively, multiple predicate learning may be more naturally handled by a descriptive ILP approach, which is not intended at learning of classification rules but at learning of properties or constraints that hold for E given T (see Section 3). The problems of learning recursive rules, where a foreground predicate is its own auxiliary predicate, are related to the problems of multiple predicate learning.

Definition 1 only applies to boolean classification problems. The definition could be extended to multi-class problems, by supplying the foreground predicate with an extra argument indicating the class. In such a case, a set of rules has to be learned for each class. It follows that we can also distinguish binary classification problems in which both the positive and negative class have to be learned explicitly (rather than by negation-as-failure, as in the definition).

In *individual-centred* domains there is a notion of individual, e.g. molecules or trains, and learning occurs on the level of individuals only. Usually, individuals are represented by a single variable, and the foreground predicates are either unary predicates concerning boolean properties of individuals, or binary predicates assigning an attribute-value or a class-value to each individual. Local variables referring to parts of individuals are introduced by so-called structural predicates. Individual-centred representations allow for a strong language bias for feature construction (see Section 4.2). On the other hand, most program synthesis tasks lack a clear notion of individual. Consider, for instance, the definition of `reverse/2`: if lists are seen as individuals – which seems most natural – the clauses are not classification rules; if pairs of lists are seen as individuals, turning the clauses into boolean classification rules, the learning system will have to rediscover the fact that the output list is determined by the input list.

Sometimes a predictive ILP task is unsolvable with the given background theory, but solvable if an additional background predicate is introduced. For instance, in Peano arithmetic multiplication is not finitely axiomatisable unless the definition of addition is available. The process of introducing additional background predicates during learning is called *predicate invention*. Predicate invention can also be seen as an extreme form of multiple predicate learning where some of the foreground predicates have no examples at all.

An initial foreground H_0 may be given to the learner as a starting point for hypothesis construction. Such a situation occurs e.g., in incremental learning, where examples become available one-by-one and are processed sequentially. Equivalently, we can perceive this as a situation where the background theory also partially defines the foreground predicate(s). This is usually referred to as *theory revision*.

After having considered the general form that predictive ILP problems may take, we now turn our attention to predictive ILP algorithms. Broadly speaking, there are two approaches. One can either start from short clauses, progressively adding literals to their bodies as long as they are found to be overly general (*top-*

down approaches); or one can start from long clauses, progressively removing literals until they would become overly general (*bottom-up* approaches). Below, we illustrate the main ideas by means of some simplified examples.

2.1   Top-Down Induction

Basically, top-down induction is a generate-then-test approach. Hypothesis clauses are generated in a pre-determined order, and then tested against the examples. Here is an example run of a fictitious incremental top-down ILP system:

example	action	clause
+m(a,[a,b])	add clause	m(X,Y)
-m(x,[a,b])	specialise:	try m(X,[])
		try m(X,[V|W])
		try m(X,[X|W])
+m(b,[b])	do nothing	
+m(b,[a,b])	add clause:	try m(X,[V|W])
		try...
		try m(X,[V|W]):-m(X,W)

The hypothesis is initialised with the most general definition of the target predicate. After seeing the first negative example, this clause is specialised by constraining the second argument. Several possibilities have to be tried before we stumble upon a clause that covers the positive example but not the negative one. Fortunately, the second positive example is also covered by this clause. A third positive example however shows that the definition is still incomplete, which means that a new clause has to be added. The system may find such a clause by returning to a previously refuted clause and specialise it in a different way, in this case by adding a literal to its body.

The resulting clause being recursive, testing it against the examples means querying the predicate to be learned. Since in our example the base case had been found already this doesn't pose any problem; however, this requires that the recursive clause is learned last, which is not always under control of the teacher. Moreover, if the recursive clause that is being tested is incorrect, such as m(X,Y):-m(Y,X), this may lead to non-termination problems. An alternative approach, known as extensional coverage, is to query the predicate to be learned against the examples. Notice that this approach would succeed here as well because of the second positive example.

The approach illustrated here is basically that of Shapiro's *Model Inference System* [90,91], an ILP system *avant la lettre* (the term 'inductive logic programming' was coined in 1991 by Muggleton [75]). MIS is an incremental top-down system that performs a complete breadth-first search of the space of possible clauses. Shapiro called his specialisation operator a *refinement operator*, a term that is still in use today (see [59] for an extensive analysis of refinement operators). A much simplified Prolog implementation of MIS can be found in [36]. Another well-known top-down system is Quinlan's Foil [86].

As the previous example shows, clauses can be specialised in two ways: by applying a substitution, and by adding a body literal. This is formalised by the relation of θ-subsumption, which establishes a syntactic notion of generality.

Definition 2 (θ-**subsumption**). *A clause C_1 θ-subsumes a clause C_2 iff there is a substitution θ such that all literals in $C_1\theta$ occur in C_2.*[1]

θ-subsumption is reflexive and transitive, but not antisymmetric (e.g., p(X):-q(X) and p(X):-q(X),q(Y) θ-subsume each other). It thus defines a pre-order on the set of clauses, i.e., a partially ordered set of equivalence classes. If we define a clause to be *reduced* if it does not θ-subsume any of its subclauses, then every equivalence class contains a reduced clause that is unique up to variable renaming. The set of these equivalence classes forms a lattice, i.e., two clauses have a unique least upper bound and greatest lower bound under θ-subsumption. We will refer to the least upper bound of two clauses under θ-subsumption as their θ-LGG (least general generalisation under θ-subsumption). Note that the lattice does contain infinite descending chains.

Clearly, if C_1 θ-subsumes C_2 then C_1 entails C_2, but the reverse is not true. For instance, consider the following clauses:

```
nat(s(X)):-nat(X).
nat(s(s(Y))):-nat(Y).
nat(s(s(Z))):-nat(s(Z)).
```

Every model of the first clause is necessarily a model of the other two, both of which are therefore entailed by the first. However, the first clause θ-subsumes the third (substitute s(Z) for X) but not the second. Gottlob characterises the distinction between θ-subsumption and entailment [47]: basically, C_1 θ-subsumes C_2 without entailing it if the resolution proof of C_2 from C_1 requires to use C_1 more than once.

It seems that the entailment ordering is the one to use, in particular when learning recursive clauses. Unfortunately, the least upper bound of two Horn clauses under entailment is not necessarily unique. The reason is simply that, generally speaking, this least upper bound would be given by the disjunction of the two clauses, but this may not be a Horn clause. Furthermore, generalisations under entailment are not easily calculated, whereas generalisation and specialisation under θ-subsumption are simple syntactic operations. Finally, entailment between clauses is undecidable, whereas θ-subsumption is decidable (but NP-complete). For these reasons, ILP systems usually employ θ-subsumption rather than entailment. Idestam-Almquist defines a stronger form of entailment called T-implication, which remedies some of the shortcomings of entailment [50,51].

---

[1] This definition, and the term θ-subsumption, was introduced in the context of induction by Plotkin [83,84]. In theorem proving the above version is termed subsumption, whereas θ-subsumption indicates a special case in which the number of literals of the subsumant does not exceed the number of literals of the subsumee [68].

2.2   Bottom-Up Induction

While top-down approaches successively specialise a very general starting clause, bottom-up approaches generalise a very specific bottom clause. Again we illustrate the main ideas by means of a simple example. Consider the following four ground facts:

```
a([1,2],[3,4],[1,2,3,4]).    a([2],[3,4],[2,3,4]).
a([a],[],[a])                a([],[],[]).
```

Upon inspection we may conjecture that these ground facts are pairwise related by one recursion step, i.e., the following two clauses may be ground instances of the recursive clause in the definition of a/3:

```
a([1,2],[3,4],[1,2,3,4]):-
    a([2],[3,4],[2,3,4]).
a([a],[],[a]):-
    a([],[],[]).
```

All that remains to be done is to construct the θ-LGG of these two ground clauses, which in this simple case can be constructed by anti-unification. This is the dual of unification, comparing subterms at the same position and turning them into a variable if they differ. To ensure that the resulting inverse substitution is the least general anti-unifier, we only introduce a new variable if the pair of different subterms has not been encountered before. We obtain the following result:

```
a([A|B],C,[A|D]):-
    a(B,C,D).
```

which is easily recognised as the recursive clause in the standard definition of append/3.

In general things are of course much less simple. One of the main problems is to select the right ground literals from a much larger set. Suppose now that we know which head literals to choose, but not which body literals. One approach is to simply lump all literals together in the bodies of both ground clauses:

```
a([1,2],[3,4],[1,2,3,4]):-
    a([1,2],[3,4],[1,2,3,4]),a([a],[],[a]),
    a([],[],[]),a([2],[3,4],[2,3,4]).

a([a],[],[a]):-
    a([1,2],[3,4],[1,2,3,4]),a([a],[],[a]),
    a([],[],[]),a([2],[3,4],[2,3,4]).
```

Since bodies of clauses are, logically speaking, unordered, the θ-LGG is obtained by anti-unifying all possible pairs of body literals, keeping in mind the variables that were introduced when anti-unifying the heads. Thus, the body of the resulting clause consists of 16 literals:

```
a([A|B],C,[A|D]):-
    a([1,2],[3,4],[1,2,3,4]),a([A|B],C,[A|D]),
    a(W,C,X),a([S|B],[3,4],[S,T,U|V]),
    a([R|G],K,[R|L]),a([a],[],[a]),
    a(Q,[],Q),a([P],K,[P|K]),a(N,K,O),
    a(M,[],M),a([],[],[]),a(G,K,L),
    a([F|G],[3,4],[F,H,I|J]),a([E],C,[E|C]),
    a(B,C,D),a([2],[3,4],[2,3,4]).
```

After having constructed this bottom clause, our task is now to generalise it by throwing out as many literals as possible. To begin with, we can remove the ground literals, since they are our original examples. It also makes sense to remove the body literal that is identical to the head literal, since it turns the clause into a tautology. More substantially, it is reasonable to require that the clause is connected, i.e., that each body literal shares a variable with either the head or another body literal that is connected to the head. This allows us to remove another 7 literals, so that the clause becomes

```
a([A|B],C,[A|D]):-
    a(W,C,X),a([S|B],[3,4],[S,T,U|V]),
    a([E],C,[E|C]),a(B,C,D).
```

Until now we have not made use of any negative examples. They may now be used to test whether the clause becomes overly general, if some of its body literals are removed. Another, less crude way to get rid of body literals is to place restrictions upon the existential variables they introduce. For instance, we may require that they are determinate, i.e., have only one possible instantiation given an instantiation of the head variables and preceding determinate literals.

The approach illustrated here is essentially the one taken by Muggleton and Feng's Golem system [77] (again, a much simplified Prolog implementation can be found in [36]). Although Golem has been successfully applied to a range of practical problems, it has a few shortcomings. One serious restriction is that it requires ground background knowledge. Furthermore, all ground facts are lumped together, whereas it is generally possible to partition them according to the examples (e.g., the fact a([a],[],[a]) has clearly nothing to do with the fact a([2],[3,4],[2,3,4])). Both restrictions are lifted in Muggleton's current ILP system Progol [80]. Essentially, Progol constructs a bottom clause for a selected example by adding its negation to the (non-ground) background theory and deriving all entailed negated body literals. By means of mode declarations (see Section 4.4) this clause is generalised as much as possible; the resulting body literals are then used in a top-down refinement search, guided by a heuristic which measures the amount of compression the clause achieves relative to the examples (see the next section on heuristics). Progol is thus a hybrid bottom-up/top-down system. It has been successfully applied to a number of scientific discovery problems.

The examples we used above to illustrate top-down and bottom-up ILP algorithms concerned inductive synthesis of simple recursive programs. While illustrative, these examples are non-typical of many ILP approaches which perform classification rather than program synthesis, use an individual-centred representation, and employ background knowledge rather than recursion. Examples of these kinds of ILP problems will be given in Section 4.

2.3 Heuristics

Shapiro's MIS searched the ordered set of hypothesis clauses in a breadth-first manner. Experience shows that this is too inefficient except for relatively restricted induction problems. In general every ILP system needs heuristics to direct the search. Heuristics are also needed if the data is noisy (contains errors). We can only scratch the surface of the topic here – for overviews see [63, Chapter 8] or [64].

There are basically three approaches to heuristics in machine learning. The statistical approach treats the examples as a sample drawn from a larger population. The (population) accuracy of a clause is the relative frequency of true instances among the instances covered by the clause (which is roughly the same as the number of substitutions that make body and head true divided by the number of substitutions that make the body true). Clearly, population accuracy is a number between 0 and 1, with 1 denoting perfect fit and 0 denoting total non-fit. As this is a population property it needs to be estimated from the sample. One obvious candidate is sample accuracy; when dealing with small samples corrections such as the Laplace estimate (which assumes a uniform prior distribution of the classes) or variations thereof can be applied. Informativity estimates are variants of accuracy estimates, which measure the entropy (impurity) of the set of examples covered by a clause with respect to their classification. One potential problem when doing best-first search is overfitting: if clauses are being specialised until they achieve perfect fit, they may cover only very few examples. To trade off accuracy and generality, the accuracy or informativity gain achieved by adding a literal to a clause is usually weighted with a fraction comparing the number of positive examples covered by each clause. In addition, ILP systems usually include a stopping criterion that is related to the estimated significance of the induced clause.

Bayesians do not treat probabilities as objective properties of an unknown sample, but rather as subjective degrees of belief that the learner is prepared to attach to a clause. The learner constantly updates these beliefs when new evidence comes in. This requires a *prior probability* distribution over the hypothesis space, which represents the degrees of belief the learner attaches to hypotheses in the absence of any evidence. It also requires conditional probability distributions over the example space for each possible hypothesis, which represents how likely examples are to occur given a particular hypothesis. The *posterior probability* of a hypothesis given the observed evidence, which is the heuristic we are going to maximise, is then calculated using Bayes' law. For instance, suppose that initially we consider a particular hypothesis to be very unlikely, but certain evidence to be very likely given that hypothesis. If subsequently we indeed observe that evidence, this will increase our belief that the hypothesis might after all be true. One problem with the Bayesian approach is the large number of probability distributions that are required. Since they influence the posterior probability, they should be meaningful and justifiable. For instance, using a uniform prior distribution (all hypotheses are *a priori* equally likely) may be technically simple but hard to justify.

Finally, there is the compression approach [95]. The idea here is that the best hypothesis is the one which most compresses the data (for instance because the learner wants to transmit the examples over a communication channel in the most efficient way). One therefore compares the size of the examples with the size of the hypothesis. To measure these sizes one needs some form of encoding: for instance, if the language contains 10 predicate symbols one can assign each of them a number and encode this in binary in 4 bits (clearly the encoding should also be communicated but this is independent of the examples and the hypothesis). Similar to the Bayesian approach, this encoding needs to be justified: for instance, if variables are encoded in many bits and constants in few, there may be no non-ground hypothesis that compresses the data and generalisation will not occur.

In fact, there is a close link between the compression approach and the Bayesian approach as follows. Suppose one has to transmit one of n messages but does not know *a priori* which one. Suppose however that one does have a probability distribution over the n messages. Information theory tells us that the theoretically optimal code assigns $-\log_2 p_i$ bits to the i-th message (p_i is the probability of that message). Having thus established a link between a probability distribution and an encoding, we see that choosing an encoding in fact amounts to choosing a prior probability. The hypothesis with the highest posterior probability is the one which minimises the code length for the hypothesis plus the code length for the examples given the hypothesis (i.e., the correct classifications for those examples that are misclassified by the hypothesis). The compression approach and the Bayesian approach are really two sides of the same coin. One advantage of the compression viewpoint may be that encodings are conceptually simpler than distributions.

3   Descriptive ILP

Inductive logic programming started as an offspring of concept learning from examples, with attribute-value classification rules replaced by Prolog predicate definitions. As we have seen, this has naturally led to a definition of induction as inference of a target theory from some of its consequences and non-consequences (Definition 1). However, this definition assumes that the induced hypothesis will be used to derive further consequences. It is much less applicable to induce formulae with a different pragmatics, such as integrity constraints, for which we therefore need a different problem definition. The process of inducing non-classificatory rules is usually called *descriptive* induction, and if the representation formalism involved is clausal logic we may refer to it as descriptive ILP.

The fact that there is a pragmatic difference between intensional database rules and integrity constraints is common knowledge in the field of deductive databases, and the conceptual difference between inducing either of them is a natural one from that perspective. On the other hand, just as the topic of Horn logic is much better developed than the subject of integrity constraints, induction of the latter is a much more recent development than Horn clause induction, and some major research topics remain. For instance, giving up Horn logic means that we loose our main criterion for deciding whether a hypothesis is good or not: classification accuracy. It is not immediately obvious what task the induced constraints are going to perform. One important research problem is therefore to find meaningful heuristics for this kind of induction. Furthermore, it is hard to capture all forms of descriptive ILP in a single definition. The following definition therefore only provides a starting point for discussing different approaches to descriptive ILP.

Definition 3 (Descriptive ILP). *Let E be a collection of evidence and let m_E be a model constructed from E. Let L be a language bias specifying a hypothesis language $\mathcal{H}_L$. A descriptive ILP task consists in finding a hypothesis $H \subseteq \mathcal{H}_L$ axiomatising m_E, i.e., H is true in m_E, and $\forall g \in \mathcal{H}_L$: if g is true in m_E then $H \models g$.*

Definition 3 leaves the form of the evidence unspecified. In the simplest case, the evidence is simply an enumeration of the intended model m_E by ground facts. The evidence may also include an intensional part T, in which m_E would be the truth-minimal Herbrand model of $T \cup E$ (note that in descriptive ILP there is no real need to distinguish between intensional and extensional evidence, since they both end up at the same end of the turnstile). E could also be a collection of models, from which a canonical model m_E is constructed.

In general it can be said that, while predictive induction is driven by entailment, descriptive induction is driven by some notion of consistency or truth in a model. For instance, database constraints exclude certain database states, while intensional rules derive part of a database state from another part. In a sense, integrity constraints are learned by generalising from several database states. It is therefore often more natural to associate the extensional data with one ore more models of the theory to be learned, rather than with a single ground atomic consequence. From this viewpoint induction of integrity constraints is more a descendant of one of the typical problems studied in computational learning theory, *viz.* learning arbitrary boolean expressions from some of its satisfying and falsifying assignments [96,3].

Furthermore, there is often a close link between descriptive induction and nonmonotonic or closed-world reasoning, in that both involve some form of Closed World Assumption (CWA). However, the inductive CWA has a slightly different interpretation: 'everything I haven't seen behaves like the things I have seen' [49]. Sometimes this enables one to treat the data as specifying one pre-ferred or minimal model, and develop the hypothesis from that starting point. Meta-logical properties of this form of inductive reasoning are therefore similar to those of reasoning with rules that tolerate exceptions [37,38].

Table 1. A feature table.

X	female(X)	male(X)	gorilla(X)
	−	−	−
	−	−	+
	−	+	−
richard, fred	−	+	+
	+	−	−
liz, ginger	+	−	+
	+	+	−
	+	+	+

We illustrate descriptive ILP with a simple example, taken from [21]. Let the evidence be given by the following ground facts:

```
gorilla(liz).       gorilla(richard).
gorilla(ginger).    gorilla(fred).
female(liz).        male(richard).
female(ginger).     male(fred).
```

One approach to construct a set of most general satisfied clauses is by means of DNF to CNF conversion [39]. From the evidence we construct a *feature table*, which is a sort of generalised truth-table (Table 1). We assume that a set of literals of interest has been generated in some way. Each column in the feature table corresponds to one of those literals, and each row corresponds to a grounding substitution of all variables in the literal set. In Table 1, the rows without an entry for X indicate that one cannot find a substitution for X such that the three ground atoms obtain the required truth value – these represent the so-called *countermodels*. For instance, the first line indicates that the evidence does not contain a substitution for X such that female(X), male(X) and gorilla(X) are all false. The desired clausal theory can now be found by constructing the prime implicants of the countermodels and negating them. For instance, the first two countermodels together imply that ¬ female(X) ∧ ¬ male(X) is unsatisfiable, i.e., female(X);male(X) is a most general satisfied clause. This yields the following theory:

```
gorilla(X).
male(X);female(X).
:-male(X),female(X).
```

Notice that a more specific hypothesis would be obtained by adding a non-female, non-male non-gorilla to the evidence (or by requiring that the evidence be range-restricted):

```
gorilla(X):-female(X)
gorilla(X):-male(X)
```

Table 2. A 3-dimensional contingency table.

	son(X,Y)/5	¬son(X,Y)/52	son(X,Y)	¬son(X,Y)
parent(Y,X)/11	0 (0.10)	6 (1.06)	5 (0.86)	0 (8.98)
¬parent(Y,X)/46	0 (0.42)	0 (4.42)	0 (3.61)	46 (37.55)
	daughter(X,Y)/6		¬daughter(X,Y)/51	

```
male(X);female(X):-gorilla(X)
:-male(X),female(X)
```

An important difference with the classification-oriented form of ILP is that here each clause can be discovered independently of the others. This means that the approach can be implemented as an any-time algorithm, at any time maintaining a hypothesis that is meaningful as an approximate solution, the sequence of hypotheses converging to the correct solution over time.

In Section 2.3, we discussed the use of heuristics in predictive ILP. The need for heuristics is even more urgent in descriptive ILP, because there are usually large numbers of rules satisfying the requirements (typically because the expensive condition that the rules are the most general ones is relaxed). We outline a possible approach inspired by [44].

Suppose we are considering the literals daughter(X,Y), son(X,Y), and parent(Y,X). As in Table 1 we count the number of substitutions for each possible truthvalue assignment, but instead of a truthtable we employ a multi-dimensional contingency table to organise these counts (Table 2). This table contains the 8 cells of the 3-dimensional contingency table, as well as various marginal frequencies obtained by summing the relevant cells. Using these marginal frequencies we can now calculate expected frequencies for each cell under the assumption of independence of the three literals. For instance, the expected frequency of substitutions that make parent(Y,X) true, daughter(X,Y) false and son(X,Y) false is $11 * 51 * 52/57^2 = 8.98$. These expected frequencies are indicated between brackets. Note that they sum to 57, but not to any of the other marginal frequencies (this would require more sophisticated models of independence, such as conditional independence).

As before, zeroes (i.e., countermodels) in the table correspond to clauses. Prime implicants are obtained by combining zeroes as much as possible, by projecting the table onto the appropriate 2 dimensions. We then obtain the following theory:

```
daughter(X,Y);son(X,Y):-parent(Y,X).  (15.8%)
parent(Y,X):-daughter(X,Y).            (8.5%)
parent(Y,X):-son(X,Y).                 (7.1%)
:-daughter(X,Y),son(X,Y).              (0.9%)
```

Between brackets the expected relative frequency of counter-instances is indicated, which can be taken as a measure of the *novelty* of the clause with respect to the marginal distributions. For instance, the fourth clause has low novelty because there are relatively few substitutions making son(X,Y) true, and the same holds for daughter(X,Y). That no substitutions making both literals true can be found in the data may thus well be due to chance. By the same reasoning, the first clause gets high novelty, since from the marginal frequencies one would expect it to be quite easy to make both literals false.

This analysis interprets clauses in a classical way, since the confirmation of a clause is independent of its syntactical form. If we take a logic programming perspective the approach can be simplified to 2-dimensional tables that assess the dependence between body and head. We refer the interested reader to [44].

4   Knowledge Representation for ILP

Logic is a powerful and versatile knowledge representation formalism. However, its versatility also means that there are usually many different ways of representing the same knowledge. What is the best representation depends on the task at hand. In this section we discuss several ways of representing a particular predictive ILP task in logic, pointing out the strengths and weaknesses of each. As a running example we use a learning problem from [69]. The learning task is to discover low size-complexity Prolog programs for classifying trains as Eastbound or Westbound. The problem is illustrated in Figure 1.

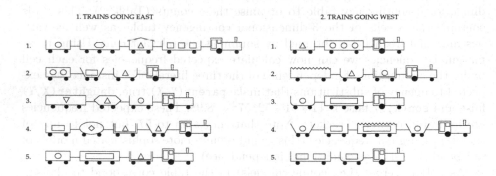

Fig. 1. The ten train East-West challenge.

Each train consists of 2-4 cars; the cars have attributes like shape (rectangular, oval, u-shaped, ...), length (long, short), number of wheels (2, 3), type of roof (none, peaked, jagged, ...), shape of load (circle, triangle, rectangle, ...), and number of loads (1-3). A possible rule distinguishing between eastbound and westbound trains is 'a train is eastbound if it contains a short closed car, and westbound otherwise'.

4.1 Datalog Representations

Datalog is a subset of Prolog in which the only functors are of arity 0 (i.e., constants). This simplifies inference as unification only needs to be performed between two variables, or between a variable and a constant. Similarly, it simplifies the specialisation and generalisation operators in ILP. The drawback is a loss of structure, as aggregation mechanisms such as lists are not available. Structured objects need to be represented indirectly, by introducing names for their parts.

A Datalog representation of the first train in Figure 1 is as follows.

```
eastbound(t1).

hasCar(t1,c11).          hasCar(t1,c12).
cshape(c11,rect).        cshape(c12,rect).
clength(c11,short).      clength(c12,long).
croof(c11,none).         croof(c12,none).
cwheels(c11,2).          cwheels(c12,3).
hasLoad(c11,l11).        hasLoad(c12,l12).
lshape(l11,circ).        lshape(l12,hexa).
lnumber(l11,1).          lnumber(l12,1).

hasCar(t1,c13).          hasCar(t1,c14).
cshape(c13,rect).        cshape(c14,rect).
clength(c13,short).      clength(c14,long).
croof(c13,peak).         croof(c14,none).
cwheels(c13,2).          cwheels(c14,2).
hasLoad(c13,l13).        hasLoad(c14,l14).
lshape(l13,tria).        lshape(l14,rect).
lnumber(l13,1).          lnumber(l14,3).
```

Using this representation, the above hypothesis would be written as

```
eastbound(T):-hasCar(T,C),clength(C,short),not croof(C,none).
```

Testing whether this hypothesis correctly classifies the example amounts to proving the query ?-eastbound(t1) from the hypothesis and the description of the example (i.e., all ground facts minus its classification).

Alternatively, we could represent an example by a ground clause:

```
eastbound(t1):-
    hasCar(t1,c11),cshape(c11,rect),clength(c11,short),
        croof(c11,none),cwheels(c11,2),
        hasLoad(c11,l11),lshape(l11,circ),lnumber(l11,1),
```

```
  hasCar(t1,c12),cshape(c12,rect),clength(c12,long),
    croof(c12,none),cwheels(c12,3),
    hasLoad(c12,l12),lshape(l12,hexa),lnumber(l12,1),
  hasCar(t1,c13),cshape(c13,rect),clength(c13,short),
    croof(c13,peak),cwheels(c13,2),
    hasLoad(c13,l13),lshape(l13,tria),lnumber(l13,1),
  hasCar(t1,c14),cshape(c14,rect),clength(c14,long),
    croof(c14,none),cwheels(c14,2),
    hasLoad(c14,l14),lshape(l14,rect),lnumber(l14,3).
```

From the logical point of view this representation is slightly odd because it doesn't actually assert the existence of train t1 – only that, if t1 existed and had the indicated properties, it would be eastbound. On the other hand, such hypothetical statements are all that is required for an induction algorithm, and we are not interested in rules referring to individual examples anyway. This representation also suggests an alternative way of testing whether a single-clause hypothesis covers an example, namely by a subsumption test.

Note that the body of each ground clause is a set of ground atoms, which can alternatively be seen as a Herbrand interpretation containing all facts describing a single example. Consequently, this setting is often referred to as *learning from interpretations* [19] (notice that this setting does not have to be restricted to Datalog, since the ground atoms in an interpretation may contain complex terms). The key point of this setting is that it allows us to keep all information pertaining to a single example together. In contrast, in the first Datalog representation facts belonging to different examples get mixed in a dataset. This is an important advantage of the ground clause or Herbrand interpretation representation, which increases the efficiency of mining algorithms significantly [5]. The term representations discussed in the next section are similarly individual-centred.

4.2   Term Representations

In full Prolog we can use terms to represent individuals. The following representations uses functors to represent cars and loads as tuples, and lists to represent a train as a sequence of cars.

```
eastbound([car(rect,short,none,2,load(circ,1)),
           car(rect,long, none,3,load(hexa,1)),
           car(rect,short,peak,2,load(tria,1)),
           car(rect,long, none,2,load(rect,3))]).
```

In this representation, the hypothesis given before is expressed as follows:

```
eastbound(T):-member(C,T),arg(2,C,short),not arg(3,C,none).
```

Here we use the built-in Prolog predicate arg(N,T,A), which is true if A is the N-th argument of complex term T.

Strictly speaking, this representation is not equivalent to the previous ones because we now encode the order of cars in a train. We could encode the order of cars in the Datalog representation by using the predicates hasFirstCar(T,C) and nextCar(C1,C2) instead of hasCar(T,C). Alternatively, we can ignore the order of cars in the term representation by only using the member/2 predicate, effectively turning the list into a set. From the point of view of hypotheses, the two hypothesis representations are isomorphic: hasCar(T,C) corresponds to member(C,T), clength(C,short) corresponds to arg(2,C,short), and croof(C,none) corresponds to arg(3,C,none). Thus, Datalog and term representations look very different concerning examples, and very similar concerning hypotheses.

Like the ground Datalog clause representation, the term representation has the advantage that all information pertaining to an individual is kept together. Moreover, the structure of the terms can be used to guide hypothesis construction, as there is an immediate connection between the type of an individual and the predicate(s) used to refer to parts of the individuals. This connection between term structure and hypothesis construction is made explicit by using a strongly typed language [40]. The following representation uses a Haskell-like language called Escher, which is a higher-order logic and functional programming language [67].

```
eastbound :: Train->Bool;
type Train = [Car];
type Car = (CShape,CLength,CRoof,CWheels,Load);
data CShape = Rect | Hexa | ...;
data CLength = Long | Short;
data CRoof = None | Peak | ...;
type CWheels = Int;
type Load = (LShape,LNumber);
data LShape = Circ | Hexa | ...;
type LNumber = Int;

eastbound([(Rect,Short,None,2,(Circ,1)),
          (Rect,Long, None,3,(Hexa,1)),
          (Rect,Short,Peak,2,(Tria,1)),
          (Rect,Long, None,2,(Rect,3))]) = True;
```

The important part here is the type signature. The first line defines eastbound as a function mapping trains to booleans. The lines starting with type define type synonyms (i.e., the type signature could be rewritten without them). The lines starting with data define algebraic datatypes; here, they are simply enumerated types. The actual representation of an example is very similar to the Prolog term representation, except that it is an equation rather than a fact. Notice that functions are more natural to express classification rules than predicates.

The hypothesis is now expressed as follows:

```
eastbound(t) = (exists \c -> member(c,t) &&
                proj2(c)==Short && proj3(c)!=None)
```

Here, the phrase `exists \c ->` stands for explicit existential quantification of variable c, and `proj2` and `proj3` project on the second and third component of a 5-tuple representing a car, respectively. Again, the hypothesis is structurally similar to the Prolog one. However, the main point about strongly typed representations is that the type signature is available to the learning algorithm to guide hypothesis construction.

The term perspective gives us a clear view on the relation between attribute-value learning and first- and higher-order learning. In attribute-value learning, examples are represented by tuples of constants. Hypotheses are built by referring to one of the components of the tuple by means of projection, followed by a boolean condition on that component (e.g., being equal to a constant).[2] First-order representations such as Prolog generalise this by allowing lists and other recursive types, as well as an arbitrary nesting of subtypes (e.g., an individual could be a tuple, one component of which could be a list of tuples). Higher-order representations generalise this further by allowing sets and multisets.[3]

4.3 Database Representations

A third representation formalism for ILP is relational databases. This representation is clearly related to the Datalog representation: in particular, both representations refer to individuals and their parts by means of unique identifiers. However, there is also a close link with the term representation, as each complex type corresponds to a database relation, and the nesting of types corresponds to (chains of) foreign keys in the database.

A relational database representation is given in Figure 2. The train attribute in the CAR relation is a foreign key to *trainID* in TRAIN, and the car attribute in the LOAD relation is a foreign key to *carID* in CAR. Notice that the first foreign key is one-to-many, and the second one is one-to-one. An SQL version of the hypothesis discussed earlier is

```
SELECT DISTINCT TRAIN.trainID FROM TRAIN, CAR WHERE
    TRAIN.trainID = CAR.train AND
    CAR.shape = 'rectangle' AND
    CAR.roof != 'none'
```

---

[2] In practice this projection is not explicitly used, as any condition on a component of the tuple can be equivalently written as a condition on the tuple. The resulting rule will then have the same variable in all literals. Such rules could be called *semi-propositional*, as the only role of the variable is to distinguish hypotheses from examples. This explains why attribute-value learning is often loosely called propositional learning.

[3] A set is equivalent to a predicate; passing around sets as terms requires a higher-order logic.

TRAIN

trainID	eastbound
t1	true

CAR

carID	cshape	clength	croof	cwheels	train
c11	rect	short	none	2	t1
c12	rect	long	none	3	t1
c13	rect	short	peak	2	t1
c14	rect	long	none	2	t1

LOAD

loadID	lshape	lnumber	car
l11	circ	1	c11
l12	hexa	1	c12
l13	tria	1	c13
l14	rect	3	c14

Fig. 2. A relational database representation of the East-West challenge.

This query performs a join of the TRAIN and CAR tables over *trainID*, selecting only rectangular closed cars. To prevent trains that have more than one such car to be included several times, the DISTINCT construct is used.

While this database representation does not seem to add much to the first Datalog representation from Section 4.1, it focuses attention on the fact that we really need a data model to describe the inherent structure of our data. Such a data model could be expressed, e.g., as an entity-relationship diagram (Figure 3), and plays the same role as the type signature in the strongly typed term representation. An alternative would be to use description logics to model the structure of the domain. Some work on learning description logic expressions is reported in [13], but note that this requires a different learning setting as description logic expressions can express concepts (intensional descriptions of classes of individuals) but not single individuals.

Like the first Datalog representation, the database representation has the disadvantage that examples are not easily separable. The term representations and the ground Datalog clause representations are superior in this respect. The term representation works very nicely on tree-structured data, but when the individuals are graphs (e.g., molecules) naming cannot be avoided in this representation either. Moreover, the term representation can be inflexible if we want to learn on a different level of individuals, e.g., if we want to learn on the level of cars rather than trains (the same holds for the ground Datalog clauses).

On the other hand, the strongly typed term representation provides a strong language bias, as hypothesis construction is guided by the structure of the individual. In particular, the strongly typed perspective advocates a distinction between two types of predicates:

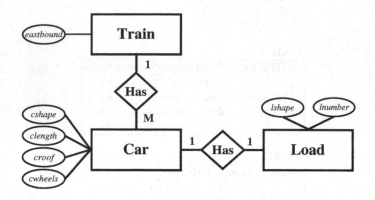

Fig. 3. Entity-relationship diagram for the East-West challenge.

1. *structural* predicates, which introduce variables, and
2. *utility* predicates (also called *properties*), which consume variables.

From the perspective of the entity-relationship data model, utility predicates correspond to attributes of entities, while structural predicates correspond to relationships between entities. This provides a useful language bias even in the Datalog representation; it has been used in [42] to upgrade the naive Bayes classifier to first-order logic.

4.4   Other Approaches to Language Bias

Below, we briefly review other approaches to fight the inherent complexity of ILP by imposing constraints, mostly syntactic in nature, on candidate hypotheses. Such constraints are grouped under the heading of *language bias* (there are other forms of biases that influence hypothesis selection; see [81] for an overview of declarative bias in ILP).

Essentially, the main source of complexity in ILP derives from the local variables in hypothesis clauses. In top-down systems, the branching factor of the specialisation operator increases with the number of variables in the clause. Typing is useful here, since it rules out many potential substitutions and unifications. Furthermore, one can simply put a bound on the number of distinct variables that can occur in a clause. In bottom-up systems, at some point one has to construct θ-LGG's for two or more ground clauses, which introduces many literals with variables occurring in the body but not in the head of the clause (existential variables). The approach of Golem is to restrict the introduction of existential variables by means of ij-determinacy, which enforces that every existential variable is uniquely determined by the preceding variables (i and j are depth parameters) [77].

Mode declarations are a well-known device from logic programming to describe possible input-output behaviour of a predicate definition. For instance, a sorting program will have a mode declaration of `sort(+list,-list)`, meaning that the first argument must be instantiated to a list. Progol uses extended mode declarations such as the following:

```
modeh(*,factorial(+int,-int)).
modeb(*,factorial(+int,-int)).
modeb(*,decr(+int,-int)).
modeb(*,mult(+int,+int,-int)).
```

A `modeh` declaration concerns a predicate that can occur in the head of a hypothesis clause, while `modeb` declarations relate to body literals. A set of mode declarations defines a mode language as follows: the head of the clause contains a predicate from a `modeh` declaration with arguments replaced by variables, and every body literal contains a predicate from a `modeb` declaration with arguments replaced by variables, such that every variable with mode +type is also of mode +type in the head, or of mode -type in a preceding literal. The mode language corresponding to the above mode declarations thus includes the clause

```
factorial(A,B):-decr(A,C),factorial(C,D),mult(A,D,B).
```

The asterisk * in the above mode declarations indicates that the corresponding literal can have any number of solutions; it may be bounded by a given integer. In addition one can apply a depth bound to a variable; e.g., in the clause just given the variable D has depth 2.

Refinement operators can be used as a language bias, since they can be restricted to generate only a subset of the language. For instance, a refinement operator can easily be modified to generate only singly-recursive or tail-recursive clauses. DLAB (declarative language bias) is a powerful language for specifying language bias [21]. Finally, we mention the use of clause schemata as a language bias. These are second-order clauses with predicate variables:

```
Q(X,Y):-P(X,Y).
Q(X,Y):-P(X,Z),Q(Z,Y).
```

Such schemata are used to constrain possible definitions of predicates; in this case it stipulates that any predicate that instantiates Q must be defined as the transitive closure of some other predicate.

5   State-of-the-Art ILP Techniques for Relational Data Mining

We continue to give a brief overview of state-of-the-art ILP techniques for relational data mining. Most of the outlined techniques are described in detail in [32]. This overview is limited to predictive and descriptive ILP techniques resulting in symbolic knowledge representations, excluding non-symbolic first-order approaches such as relational instance-based learning [34], first-order reinforcement learning [31], and first-order Bayesian classifiers [42]. It has been suggested [27] to integrate the two main settings of predictive and descriptive ILP; in this integrated framework the learned theory is a combination of (predictive) rules and (descriptive) integrity constraints that restrict the consequences of these rules.

5.1   Predictive ILP

Learning of classification rules. This is the standard ILP setting that has been used in numerous successful predictive knowledge discovery applications. Well-known systems for classification rule induction include Foil [86], Golem [77] and Progol [80]. Foil is efficient and best understood, while Golem and Progol are less efficient but have been used in many of the successful ILP applications. Foil is a top-down learner, Golem is a bottom-up learner, and Progol uses a combined search strategy. All are mainly concerned with single predicate learning from positive and negative examples and background knowledge; in addition, Progol can also be used to learn from positive examples only. They use different acceptance criteria: compression, coverage/accuracy and minimal description length, respectively. The system LINUS [62,63], developed from a learning component of QuMAS [74], introduced the propositionalisation paradigm by transforming an ILP problem into a propositional learning task.

Induction of logical decision trees. The system Tilde [4] is a top-down decision tree induction algorithm. It can be viewed as a first-order upgrade of Quinlan's C4.5, employing logical queries in tree nodes which involves appropriate handling of variables. The main advantage of Tilde is its efficiency and capability of dealing with large numbers of training examples, which Tilde inherits from its propositional ancestors. Bowers *et al.* describe a decision tree learner that employs higher-order logic [7]. An important difference with Tilde is that Tilde constructs trees with single literals in the nodes, and thus local variables are shared among different nodes. In contrast, the higher-order learner constructs more complex features for each node, such that all variables are local to a node.

First-order regression. A regression task concerns prediction of a real-valued variable rather than a class. The relational regression task can be defined as follows: Given training examples as positive ground facts for the target predicate $r(Y, X_1, ..., X_n)$, where the variable Y has real values, and background knowledge defining additional predicates, find a definition for $r(Y, X_1, ..., X_n)$, such that each clause has a literal binding Y (assuming that $X_1, ..., X_n$ are bound). Typical background knowledge predicates include less-or-equal tests, addition, subtraction and multiplication. An approach to relational regression is implemented in the system FORS (First Order Regression System) [53] which performs top-down search of a refinement graph. In each clause, FORS can predict a value for the target variable Y as the output value of a background knowledge literal, as a constant, or as a linear combination of variables appearing in the clause (using linear regression).

Inductive Constraint Logic Programming. It is well known that Constraint Logic Programming (CLP) can successfully deal with numerical constraints. The idea of Inductive Constraint Logic Programming [89] is to benefit from the number-handling capabilities of CLP, and to use the constraint solver of CLP to do part of the search involved in inductive learning. To this end a maximally discriminant generalisation problem in ILP is transformed to an equivalent constraint satisfaction problem (CSP). The solutions of the original ILP problem can be constructed from the solutions of CSP, which can be obtained by running a constraint solver on CSP.

5.2   Descriptive ILP

Learning of clausal theories and association rules. In discovering full clausal theories, as done in the system Claudien [21], each example is a Herbrand model, and the system searches for the most general clauses that are true in all the models. Clauses are discovered independently from each other, which is a substantial advantage for data mining, as compared to the learning of classification rules (particularly learning of mutually dependent predicates in multiple predicate learning). In Claudien, search of clauses is limited by the language bias. Its acceptance criterion can be modified by setting two parameters: the requested minimal accuracy and minimal number of examples covered. In another clausal discovery system, Tertius [44], the best-first search for clauses is guided by heuristics measuring the "confirmation" of clauses. The Claudien system was further extended to Warmr [16,17] that enables learning of association rules from multiple relations.

First-order clustering. Top-down induction of decision trees can be viewed as a clustering method since nodes in the tree correspond to sets of examples with similar properties, thus forming concept hierarchies. This view was adopted in C0.5 [20], an upgrade of the Tilde logical decision tree learner. A relational distance-based clustering method is presented also in [58]. An early approach combining learning and conceptual clustering techniques was implemented in the system Cola [33]. Given a small (sparse) set of classified training instances and a set of unclassified instances, Cola uses Bisson's conceptual clustering algorithm KBG on the entire set of instances, climbs the hierarchy tree and uses the classified instances to identify (single or disjunctive) class descriptions.

Database restructuring. The system Fender [92] searches for common parts of rules describing a concept, thus forming subconcept definitions to be used in the reformulation of original rules. The result is a knowledge base with new intermediate concepts and deeper inferential structure than the initial "flat" rulebase. The system Index [35] is concerned with the problem of determining which attribute dependencies (functional or multivalued) hold in the given relational database. The induced attribute dependencies can be used to obtain a more structured database. Both approaches can be viewed as doing predicate invention, where (user selected) invented predicates are used for theory restructuring. Various algorithms for discovery of database dependencies can be found in [41,88].

Subgroup discovery. The subgroup discovery task is defined as follows: given a population of individuals and a target property of those individuals we are interested in, find sufficiently large subgroups of the population that have a significantly different distribution with respect to the target property. The system Midos [98] guides the top-down search of potentially interesting subgroups using numerous user-defined parameters. The Tertius system [44] can also perform subgroup discovery. The Warmr system [16,17] can be used to find frequent queries, i.e., conjunctions of literals that have sufficiently many answers.

Learning models of dynamic systems. The automated construction of models of dynamic system may be aimed at qualitative model discovery. A recent qualitative model discovery system [48], using a Qsim-like representation, is based on Coiera's Genmodel to which signal processing capabilities have been added. The system LAGRANGE [29] discovers a set of differential equations from an example behaviour of a dynamic system. Example behaviours are specified by lists of measurements of a set of system variables, and background knowledge predicates enable the introduction of new variables as time derivatives, sines or cosines of system variables. New variables can be further introduced by multiplication.

6   Future Challenges for ILP

This section first presents some application challenges for ILP and continues with the technological advances that will be needed to deal with these challenges. We distinguish between short-term research challenges for ILP and longer-term challenges for ILP and machine learning in general. Finally, we address the connections with the areas of computational logic that may prove to be fruitful in future ILP research.

In our view, the most challenging application areas are in molecular biology, agents, personalised software applications, skill acquisition, natural language processing, information retrieval and text mining, analysis of music and multimedia data, as well as relational knowledge discovery applications in finance, e-commerce, banking, medicine, ecology, and others. For an overview of the state-of-the-art applications of ILP see [32], where also some future application challenges for ILP are indicated.

At present, molecular biology applications of ILP have come closest to practical relevance. Among the early applications was protein secondary structure prediction [78], followed by predicting drug activity through modelling structure-activity relations [77,55] and predicting the mutagenicity of aromatic and heteroaromatic nitro-compounds [94]. In these problems, which are of immediate practical interest, accuracies that are at least as good as the best previously known results have been obtained, as well as understandable and relevant new knowledge. Recent ILP applications in the area of molecular biology include prediction of rodent carcinogenicity bioassays, modelling structure-activity relations for modulating transmembrane calcium movement, pharmacophore discovery for ACE inhibition and diterpene structure elucidation. In the future there is considerable potential for ILP applications using data produced by the human genome project, where the first successful ILP results have already been achieved [56,57].

6.1 Short-Term Research Challenges

ILP as a methodology for first-order learning. ILP has already developed numerous useful techniques for relational knowledge discovery. A recent research trend in ILP is to develop algorithms upgrading well-understood propositional machine learning techniques to first-order representations. Already developed techniques upgrading propositional learning algorithms include first-order decision tree learning [4,7], first-order clustering [20,58], relational genetic algorithms [46,66], first-order instance-based learning [34], first-order reinforcement learning [31] and first-order Bayesian classification [42]. It is expected that the adaptation of propositional machine learning algorithms to the first-order framework will continue also in the areas for which first-order implementations still do not exist. This should provide a full scale methodology for relational data mining based on future ILP implementations of first-order Bayesian networks, first-order neural networks, and other ILP upgrades of propositional machine learning techniques.

Improved robustness, efficiency and scaling-up of ILP algorithms. This involves the development of learning algorithms that are robust with respect to noise, missing information etc., the development of standards for data and knowledge representation, standards for parameter settings, on-line transformers between different data formats, improved efficiency of learners, and the capacity of dealing with large datasets. Improved efficiency and scaling-up of ILP algorithms has to some extent already been achieved e.g., by the system Tilde [4] for induction of logical decision trees. Efficiency may be, on the one hand, achieved by effective coupling of ILP algorithms with database management systems, and on the other hand, by speeding-up the search of the lattice of clauses and speeding up of the testing of clause coverage involving repeated searches for proofs [6]. Speed-ups can also be achieved by employing sampling, stochastic search and stochastic matching procedures that are expected to be further developed in the future. Further speed-ups may be achieved by parallel processing, based on distributing the hypothesis space and testing competing hypotheses against the data independently and in parallel.

Multi-strategy learning and integration. The present data mining applications typically require data analysis to be performed by different machine learning algorithms, aimed at achieving best learning results. Multistrategy learning has shown that best results can be achieved by a combination of learning algorithms or by combining the results of multiple learners. Current simple and popular approaches involve bagging and boosting that employ redundancy to achieve better classification accuracy [9,45,87]. More sophisticated approaches will require the integration of different learners into knowledge discovery tools, standard statistical tools and spreadsheet packages and into software packages routinely used in particular applications. Integrated machine learning will have to be based also on a better understanding of the different types of problem domains and characteristics of learning algorithms best suited for the given data characteristics. Mixing of different rules by the use of logic programming techniques also allows for combining multi-strategy and multi-source learning in a declarative way. Some of the existing techniques are inspired on contradiction removal methods originated in logic programming, others rely on recent work on updating logic programs with each other [2]. Logic program combination techniques may become more important in the near future.

Hierarchically structured learning and predicate invention. Learning from 'flat' datasets nowadays typically results in 'flat' hypotheses that involve no intermediate structure and no constructive induction/predicate invention. Despite substantial research efforts in this area challenging results can still be expected.

Criteria for the evaluation of hypotheses. Except for the standard measure of predictive accuracy, other evaluation measures need to be developed, e.g., ROC-based measures [85] and measures involving misclassification costs. Development of new measures is of particular importance for descriptive ILP systems that often lack such measures for the evaluation of results. Measures of similarity, distance measures, interestingness, precision, measures for outlier detection, irrelevance, and other heuristic criteria need to be studied and incorporated into ILP algorithms.

Criteria for the relevance of background knowledge. Background knowledge and previously learned predicate definitions should be stored for further learning in selected problem areas. One should be aware, however, that an increased volume of background knowledge may also have undesirable properties: not only that learning will become less efficient because of the increased hypothesis space, but given irrelevant information the results of learning may be less accurate. Therefore it is crucial to formulate criteria for evaluating the relevance of background knowledge predicates before they are allowed to become part of a library of background knowledge predicates for a given application area.

Learning from temporal data. ILP is to some extent able to deal with temporal information. However, specialised constructs should be developed for applications in which the analysis of a current stream of time labelled data represents an input to ILP. Experience from the area of temporal data abstraction could be used to construct higher-level predicates summarising temporal phenomena.

6.2   Long-Term Research Challenges

Some of the issues discussed in this section are relevant to ILP only, whereas others are relevant to machine learning in general. Some of these issues have been identified previously by Tom Mitchell in an article published in the Fall 1997 issue of the AI Magazine [71].

Analysis of comprehensibility. It is often claimed that for many applications comprehensibility is the main factor if the results of learning are to be accepted by the experts. Despite these claims and some initial investigations of intelligibility criteria for symbolic machine learning (such as Occam's razor and minimal description length criteria) there are few research results concerning the intelligibility evaluation by humans.

Building specialised learners and data libraries. Particular problem areas have particular characteristics and requirements, and not all learning algorithms are capable of dealing with these. This is a reason for starting to build specialised learners for different types of applications. This may involve also the development of special purpose reasoning mechanisms. In addition, libraries of 'cleaned' data, background knowledge and previously learned predicate definitions should be stored for further learning in selected problem areas. Notice that such libraries are currently being established for certain problem areas in molecular biology. This approach will lead to the re-usability of components and to extended example sets; these can also be obtained by systematic query answering and experimentation as part of 'continuous' learning, discussed next.

Continuous learning from 'global' datasets. Under this heading we understand the requirement for learning from various data sources, where data sources can be of various types, including propositional and relational tables, textual data, and hypermedia data including speech, images and video, including human expert interaction. This involves the issue of globality, i.e., learning from local datasets as well as referential datasets collected and maintained by the world's best experts in the area, referential case bases of 'outlier' data as well as data that is publicly available on the web. Achieving the requirement of continuous and global learning will require also learning agents for permanent learning by theory revision from updated world-wide data, as well as the development of query agents that will be able to access additional information from the internet via query answering (invoked either by experts or by automatically extracting answers from WWW resources, possibly by invoking learning and active experimentation). Query agents may involve dynamic abductive querying on the web.

6.3   Specific Short-Term Challenges Related to Computational Logic

Constraint logic programming. As shown in the overview of techniques for predictive ILP in Section 5.1, the connection between ILP and CLP has already been established through the work on Inductive Constraint Logic Programming. ILP has recognised the potential of CLP number-handling and of the CLP constraint solving to do part of the search involved in inductive learning. Early work in this area by Page and Frisch, Mizoguchi and Ohwada in 1992, and more recent work by Sebag and Rouveirol [89] show the potential of merging ILP and CLP that has to be explored to a larger extent in the future. Due to the industrial relevance of these two areas of computational logic it is expected that the developments at their intersection may result in products of great industrial benefit.

Abduction. Other initiatives spanning different areas of computational logic have also identified the potential for mutual benefits. A series of workshops has been organised on the relation and integration of abduction and induction, resulting in the first edited volume on the topic [43]. Early research in this direction by De Raedt (the system CLINT) and more recent work by Dimopoulos and Kakas [26] show the potential for merging these technologies. A new ILP framework and system, called ACL [52] for abductive concept learning has been developed and used to study the problems of learning from incomplete background data and of multiple predicate learning. More work in this area is expected in the future.

Higher-order logic. Some work towards the use of higher-order reasoning and the use of functional languages has also started, in particular using the declarative higher-order programming language Escher [67] for learning and hypothesis representation [40,66,7]. This work may be a first step towards a larger research initiative in using higher-order features in ILP.

Deductive databases. A tighter connection with deductive database technology has been advocated by De Raedt [22,24] introducing an inductive database mining query language that integrates concepts from ILP, CLP, deductive databases and meta-programming into a flexible environment for relational knowledge discovery in databases. Since the primitives of the language can easily be combined with Prolog, complex systems and behaviour can be specified declaratively. This type of integration of concepts from different areas of computational logic can prove extremely beneficial for ILP in the future. It can lead to a novel ILP paradigm of inductive logic programming query languages whose usefulness may be proved to be similar to those of constraint logic programming.

Other logic programming-based advances. Much work on logic program semantics in the past twelve years, culminating in the definition of well-founded semantics and stable model semantics, and subsequent elaborations could be considered in future ILP research, since they allow dealing with non-stratified programs, and 3-valuedness. Considerable work on knowledge representation and non-monotonic reasoning has been developed using such semantical basis. Also, recent work on constructive negation would allow inducing rules without fear of floundering, and generating exceptions to default negations which could then be generalised. Examples include learning together the positive and negative part of a concept where the learned theory is an extended logic program with classical negation [25,61,60] where a potential inconsistency in such a theory is resolved by learning priorities amongst contradictory rules. Argumentation semantics and procedures are also likely to be useful for composing rules learned separately from several sources, algorithms, or strategies.

The work in logic programming on preferences [10,11] is bound to be of interest when combining rules, and even more so because user preferences might be learned form instances of user choice and rejection. This may turn out to be crucial for information gathering on the basis of user preferences. Fuzzy logic programming may become important in the future for fuzzifying such induced preference rules, as well as generalised annotated programs [54] which allow for different degrees of contradiction to be expressed.

Moreover, the implementational techniques of tabling in logic programming have matured and prove quite useful [99]. In ILP they may save considerable recomputation because results are memoized in an efficient way. Indeed, in ILP each time a clause is abstracted or refined it has to be tested again with the evidence, though many literals in the clause, and surely the background, are the same, so that part of the computation is repeated This is even more important when learned programs become deeper, i.e., not shallow.

7   Concluding Remarks

Research areas that have strongly influenced ILP research are (apart from computational logic): machine learning, data mining and knowledge discovery in databases, and computational learning theory.

ILP has its roots in machine learning, and most of ILP researchers have done machine learning research before entering ILP. Machine learning has always provided the basic research philosophy where experimental evaluation and applications play a key role in the development of novel techniques and tools. This was the case in the early days of ILP and remains so today. Important influences from data mining and knowledge discovery in databases concern mainly the development of new ILP algorithms in the descriptive ILP setting, as well as the emphasis on scaling-up ILP algorithms to deal with large relational databases. Computational learning theory has helped ILP to better understand the learnability issues and provided some basic learning algorithms that were studied and adapted for the needs of ILP.

From the perspective of this chapter it is interesting to analyse the impact of computational logic and logic programming on ILP developments. Both played an extremely important role in early ILP research. Besides providing a framework that helped to develop the theory of ILP, it provided the well-studied representational formalisms and an initially challenging application area of program synthesis. Due to the difficulty of this application task that can not be solved without very strong biases and restrictions on the hypothesis language, program synthesis has become substantially less popular in recent years.

The analysis of theoretical papers in the proceedings of ILP workshops in 1991–1998 by De Raedt [23] indicates that about one third of accepted papers are related to logic programming. The main issues studied in these papers are inference rules, program synthesis, negation, constraint logic programming, abduction, and implementation. One important observation made by De Raedt is that the theory of ILP does not follow recent developments in logic programming and computational logic but, to a large extent, uses the well-established results obtained in early logic programming research. On the other hand, advanced logic programming techniques may become increasingly important once ILP starts seriously addressing difficult learning problems in natural language processing, where recursion, negation, higher-order logic, and other issues requesting a strong theoretical foundation in logic programming will come into play again.

Acknowledgements

We thank two anonymous reviewers for their helpful comments. Part of the material in Sections 2–4 is based on a tutorial given by the first author at the First International Conference on Computational Logic (CL-2000). The section on the state-of-the-art ILP techniques reflects some of the research results achieved in the ESPRIT projects no. 6020 ILP (1992–95) and no. 20237 ILP2 (1996–99). The section on future challenges for ILP has been to a large extent influenced by the panel discussion with panelists Luc De Raedt, Stephen Muggleton and Nada Lavrač, organised by John Lloyd as part of the workshop "Logic Programming and Machine Learning: A Two-way Connection", organised at JICSLP'98 in Manchester in June 1998 under auspices of the CompulogNet area "Computational Logic and Machine Learning". The interested reader can find further directions for ILP research in David Page's invited talk at CL-2000 [82]. This work has been supported by the Network of Excellence in Inductive Logic Programming *ILPnet2*, the EU-funded project Data Mining and Decision Support for Business Competitiveness: A European Virtual Enterprise (IST-1999-11495), the British Royal Society, the British Council (Partnership in Science PSP 18), and the Slovenian Ministry of Science and Technology.

References

1. R. Agrawal, H. Mannila, R. Srikant, H. Toivonen, and A.I. Verkamo. Fast discovery of association rules. In U.M. Fayyad, G. Piatetski-Shapiro, P. Smyth, and R. Uthurusamy (eds.), *Advances in Knowledge Discovery and Data Mining*, pp. 307–328. AAAI Press, 1996.
2. J. J. Alferes, J. A. Leite, L. M. Pereira, H. Przymusinska, and T. C. Przymusinski. Dynamic logic programming, In A. Cohn, L. Schubert and S. Shapiro (eds.), *Proceedings of the Sixth International Conference on Principles of Knowledge Representation and Reasoning*, pp. 98–109. Morgan Kaufmann, 1998.
3. D. Angluin, M. Frazier, and L. Pitt. Learning conjunctions of Horn clauses. *Machine Learning*, 9(2/3): 147–164, 1992.
4. H. Blockeel and L. De Raedt. Top-down induction of first-order logical decision trees. *Artificial Intelligence* 101(1-2): 285–297, June 1998.
5. H. Blockeel, L. De Raedt, N. Jacobs, and B. Demoen. Scaling up inductive logic programming by learning from interpretations. *Data Mining and Knowledge Discovery*, 3(1): 59–93, 1999.
6. H. Blockeel, L. Dehaspe, B. Demoen, G. Janssens, J. Ramon, and H. Vandecasteele. Executing query packs in ILP. In J. Cussens and A. Frisch (eds.), *Proceedings of the Tenth International Conference on Inductive Logic Programming*, Lecture Notes in Artificial Intelligence 1866, pp. 60–77. Springer-Verlag, 2000.
7. A.F. Bowers, C. Giraud-Carrier, and J.W. Lloyd. Classification of individuals with complex structure. In P. Langley (ed.), *Proceedings of the Seventeenth International Conference on Machine Learning*, pp. 81–88. Morgan Kaufmann, 2000.
8. I. Bratko and S. Muggleton. Applications of Inductive Logic Programming. *Communications of the ACM* 38(11): 65–70, November 1995.
9. L. Breiman. Bagging predictors. *Machine Learning* 24(2): 123–140, 1996.

10. G. Brewka. Well-founded semantics for extended logic programs with dynamic preferences. *Journal of Artificial Intelligence Research*, 4: 19–36, 1996.
11. G. Brewka and T. Eiter. Preferred answer sets. In A. Cohn, L. Schubert and S. Shapiro (eds.), *Proceedings of the Sixth International Conference on Principles of Knowledge Representation and Reasoning*, pp. 89–97. Morgan Kaufmann, 1998.
12. W.W. Cohen. Recovering software specifications with inductive logic programming. In *Proceedings of the Twelfth National Conference on Artificial Intelligence*, pp. 142–148. The MIT Press, 1994.
13. W.W. Cohen and H. Hirsh. Learning the CLASSIC Description Logic: Theoretical and Experimental Results. In J. Doyle, E. Sandewall, and P. Torasso (eds.), *Proceedings of the Fourth International Conference on Principles of Knowledge Representation and Reasoning*, pp. 121–133. Morgan Kaufmann, 1994.
14. J. Cussens. Notes on inductive logic programming methods in natural language processing (European work). Unpublished manuscript, 1998. `ftp://ftp.cs.york.ac.uk/pub/ML_GROUP/Papers/ilp98tut.ps.gz`.
15. J. Cussens and S. Džeroski (eds.). *Learning Language in Logic*. Lecture Notes in Artificial Intelligence 1925, Springer-Verlag, 2000.
16. L. Dehaspe and L. De Raedt. Mining association rules in multiple relations. In S. Džeroski and N. Lavrač (eds.), *Proceedings of the Seventh International Workshop on Inductive Logic Programming*, Lecture Notes in Artificial Intelligence 1297, pp. 125–132. Springer-Verlag, 1997.
17. L. Dehaspe, H. Toivonen, and R.D. King. Finding frequent substructures in chemical compounds. In R. Agrawal, P. Stolorz, and G. Piatetsky-Shapiro (eds.), *Proceedings of the Fourth International Conference on Knowledge Discovery and Data Mining*, pp. 30–36. AAAI Press, 1998.
18. L. De Raedt (ed.). *Advances in Inductive Logic Programming*. IOS Press, 1996.
19. L. De Raedt. Logical settings for concept-learning. *Artificial Intelligence*, 95(1): 187–201, 1997.
20. L. De Raedt and H. Blockeel. Using logical decision trees for clustering. In N. Lavrač and S. Džeroski (eds.), *Proceedings of the Seventh International Workshop on Inductive Logic Programming*, Lecture Notes in Artificial Intelligence 1297, pp. 133–140. Springer-Verlag, 1997.
21. L. De Raedt and L. Dehaspe. Clausal discovery. *Machine Learning*, 26(2/3): 99–146, 1997.
22. L. De Raedt. An inductive logic programming query language for database mining (extended abstract). In J. Calmet and J. Plaza (eds.), *Proceedings of the Fourth Workshop on Artificial Intelligence and Symbolic Computation*, Lecture Notes in Artificial Intelligence 1476. Springer-Verlag, 1998.
23. L. De Raedt. A perspective on inductive logic programming. In K. Apt, V. Marek, M. Truszezynski, and D.S. Warren (eds.), *The logic programming paradigm: current trends and future directions*. Springer-Verlag, 1999.
24. L. De Raedt. A logical database mining query language. In J. Cussens and A. Frisch, *Proceedings of the Tenth International Conference on Inductive Logic Programming*, Lecture Notes in Artificial Intelligence 1866, pp. 78–92. Springer-Verlag, 2000.
25. Y. Dimopoulos and A.C. Kakas. Learning non-monotonic logic programs: learning exceptions. In N. Lavrač and S. Wrobel (eds.), *Proceedings of the Eighth European Conference on Machine Learning*, Lecture Notes in Artificial Intelligence 912, pp. 122–138. Springer-Verlag, 1995.
26. Y. Dimopoulos and A.C. Kakas. Abduction and inductive learning. In [18], pp. 144–171.

27. Y. Dimopoulos, S. Džeroski, and A.C. Kakas. Integrating Explanatory and Descriptive Induction in ILP. In M.E. Pollack (ed.), *Proceedings of the Fifteenth International Joint Conference on Artificial Intelligence*, pp. 900–907. Morgan Kaufmann, 1997.
28. B. Dolšak and S. Muggleton. The application of inductive logic programming to finite-element mesh design. In [76], pp. 453–472.
29. S. Džeroski and L. Todorovski. Discovering dynamics: From inductive logic programming to machine discovery. In *Proceedings of the Tenth International Conference on Machine Learning*, pp. 97–103. Morgan Kaufmann, 1993.
30. S. Džeroski and I. Bratko. Applications of Inductive Logic Programming. In [18], pp. 65–81.
31. S. Džeroski, L. De Raedt, and H. Blockeel. Relational reinforcement learning. In J. Shavlik (ed.), *Proceedings of the Fifteenth International Conference on Machine Learning*, pp. 136–143. Morgan Kaufmann, 1998.
32. S. Džeroski and N. Lavrač, eds. *Relational Data Mining*. Springer-Verlag, 2001. In press.
33. W. Emde. Learning of characteristic concept descriptions from small sets to classified examples. In F. Bergadano and L. De Raedt (eds.), *Proceedings of the Seventh European Conference on Machine Learning*, Lecture Notes in Artificial Intelligence 784, pp. 103–121. Springer-Verlag, 1994.
34. W. Emde and D. Wettschereck. Relational instance-based learning. In L. Saitta (ed.), *Proceedings of the Thirteenth International Conference on Machine Learning*, pp. 122–130. Morgan Kaufmann, 1996.
35. P.A. Flach. Predicate invention in inductive data engineering. In P. Brazdil (ed.), *Proceedings of the Sixth European Conference on Machine Learning*, Lecture Notes in Artificial Intelligence 667, pp. 83-94. Springer-Verlag, 1993.
36. P.A. Flach. *Simply Logical – intelligent reasoning by example*. John Wiley, 1994.
37. P.A. Flach. *Conjectures – an inquiry concerning the logic of induction*. PhD thesis, Tilburg University, April 1995.
38. P.A. Flach. Rationality postulates for induction. In Y. Shoham (ed.), *Proceedings of the Sixth International Conference on Theoretical Aspects of Rationality and Knowledge*, pp. 267-281. Morgan Kaufmann, 1996.
39. P.A. Flach. Normal forms for Inductive Logic Programming. In N. Lavrač and S. Džeroski (eds.), *Proceedings of the Seventh International Workshop on Inductive Logic Programming*, Lecture Notes in Artificial Intelligence 1297, pp. 149–156. Springer-Verlag, 1997.
40. P.A. Flach, C. Giraud-Carrier, and J.W. Lloyd. Strongly typed inductive concept learning. In D. Page (ed.), *Proceedings of the Eighth International Conference on Inductive Logic Programming*, Lecture Notes in Artificial Intelligence 1446, pp. 185–194. Springer-Verlag, 1998.
41. P.A. Flach and I. Savnik. Database dependency discovery: a machine learning approach. *AI Communications*, 12(3): 139–160, November 1999.
42. P.A. Flach and N. Lachiche. 1BC: A first-order Bayesian classifier. In S. Džeroski and P.A. Flach (eds.), *Proceedings of the Ninth International Workshop on Inductive Logic Programming*, Lecture Notes in Artificial Intelligence 1634, pp. 92–103. Springer-Verlag, 1999.
43. P.A. Flach and A.C. Kakas (eds.) *Abduction and Induction: Essays on their Relation and Integration*. Kluwer, 2000.
44. P.A. Flach and N. Lachiche. Confirmation-guided discovery of first-order rules with Tertius. *Machine Learning*, 42(1/2): 61–95, 2001.

45. Y. Freund and R.E. Shapire. Experiments with a new boosting algorithm. In L. Saitta (ed.), *Proceedings of the Thirteenth International Conference on Machine Learning*, 148–156. Morgan Kaufmann, 1996.

46. A. Giordana and C. Sale. Learning structured concepts using genetic algorithms. In D. Sleeman (ed.), *Proceedings of the Ninth International Workshop on Machine Learning*, pp. 169–178. Morgan Kaufmann, 1992.

47. G. Gottlob. Subsumption and implication. *Information Processing Letters* 24: 109–111, 1987.

48. D.T. Hau and E.W. Coiera. Learning qualitative models of dynamic systems. *Machine Learning*, 26(2/3): 177–212, 1997.

49. N. Helft. Induction as nonmonotonic inference. In R.J. Brachman, H.J. Levesque, and R. Reiter (eds.), *Proceedings of the First International Conference on Principles of Knowledge Representation and Reasoning*, pp. 149–156. Morgan Kaufmann, 1989.

50. P. Idestam-Almquist. *Generalization of clauses*. PhD thesis, Stockholm University, October 1993.

51. P. Idestam-Almquist. Generalization of clauses under implication. *Journal of Artificial Intelligence Research*, 3: 467–489, 1995.

52. A.C. Kakas and F. Riguzzi. Learning with abduction. In S. Džeroski and N. Lavrač (eds.), *Proceedings of the Seventh International Workshop on Inductive Logic Programming*, Lecture Notes in Artificial Intelligence 1297, pp. 181–188. Springer-Verlag, 1997.

53. A. Karalič and I. Bratko. First-order regression. *Machine Learning*, 26(2/3): 147–176, 1997.

54. M. Kifer and V.S. Subrahmanian. Generalized annotated logic programs. *Journal of Logic Programming*, 1992.

55. R.D. King, S. Muggleton, R. Lewis, and M.J.E. Sternberg. Drug design by machine learning: The use of inductive logic programming to model the structure-activity relationships of trimethoprim analogues binding to dihydrofolate reductase. In *Proceedings of the National Academy of Sciences of the USA* 89(23): 11322–11326, 1992.

56. R.D. King, A. Karwath, A. Clare, and L. Dehaspe. Genome scale prediction of protein functional class from sequence using data mining. In *Proceedings of the Sixth International Conference on Knowledge Discovery and Data Mining*, pp. 384–398. ACM Press, New York, 2000.

57. R.D. King, A. Karwath, A. Clare, and L. Dehaspe. Accurate prediction of protein functional class in the M.tuberculosis and E.coli genomes using data mining. *Yeast (Comparative and Functional Genomics)*, 17: 283–293, 2000.

58. M. Kirsten and S. Wrobel. Relational distance-based clustering. In D. Page (ed.) *Proceedings of the Eighth International Conference on Inductive Logic Programming*, pp. 261–270, Lecture Notes in Artificial Intelligence 1446. Springer-Verlag, 1998.

59. P. van der Laag. *An analysis of refinement operators in Inductive Logic Programming*. PhD Thesis, Erasmus University Rotterdam, December 1995.

60. E. Lamma, F. Riguzzi, and L. M. Pereira. Agents learning in a three-valued logical setting. In A. Panayiotopoulos (ed.), *Proceedings of the Workshop on Machine Learning and Intelligent Agents*, in conjunction with *Machine Learning and Applications, Advanced Course on Artificial Intelligence (ACAI-99)*, Chania, Greece, 1999.

61. E. Lamma, F. Riguzzi, and L. M. Pereira. Strategies in combined learning via Logic Programs. *Machine Learning*, 38(1/2): 63–87, 2000.

62. N. Lavrač, S. Džeroski, and M. Grobelnik. Learning nonrecursive definitions of relations with LINUS. In Y. Kodratoff (ed.) *Proceedings of the Fifth European Working Session on Learning*, Lecture Notes in Artificial Intelligence 482, pp. 265–281. Springer-Verlag, 1991.

63. N. Lavrač and S. Džeroski. *Inductive Logic Programming: techniques and applications*. Ellis Horwood, 1994.

64. N. Lavrač, S. Džeroski, and I. Bratko. Handling imperfect data in Inductive Logic Programming. In [18], pp. 48–64.

65. N. Lavrač and P.A. Flach. An extended transformation approach to Inductive Logic Programming. *ACM Transactions on Computational Logic*, 2(4): 458–494, 2001.

66. C.J. Kennedy. *Strongly typed evolutionary programming*. PhD Thesis, University of Bristol, 2000.

67. J.W. Lloyd. Programming in an integrated functional and logic programming language. Journal of Functional and Logic Programming, 1999(3).

68. D.W. Loveland and G. Nadathur. Proof procedures for logic programming. *Handbook of Logic in Artificial Intelligence and Logic Programming*, Vol. 5, D.M. Gabbay, C.J. Hogger, and J.A. Robinson (eds.), Oxford University Press, pp. 163–234, 1998.

69. D. Michie, S. Muggleton, D. Page, and A. Srinivasan. To the international computing community: A new East-West challenge. Technical report, Oxford University Computing laboratory, Oxford, UK, 1994.

70. T.M. Mitchell. *Machine Learning*. McGraw-Hill, 1997.

71. T.M. Mitchell. Does machine learning really work? *AI Magazine* 18 (3): 11–20, 1997.

72. F. Mizoguchi, H. Ohwada, M. Daidoji, and S. Shirato. Using inductive logic programming to learn classification rules that identify glaucomatous eyes. In N. Lavrač, E. Keravnou, and B. Zupan (eds.), *Intelligent Data Analysis in Medicine and Pharmacology*, pp. 227–242. Kluwer, 1997.

73. R.J. Mooney and M.E. Califf. Induction of first-order decision lists: Results on learning the past tense of English verbs. *Journal of Artificial Intelligence Research* 3: 1–24, 1995.

74. I. Mozetič. Learning of qualitative models. In I. Bratko and N. Lavrač (eds.) *Progress in Machine Learning*, pp. 201–217. Sigma Press, 1987.

75. S. Muggleton. Inductive Logic Programming. *New Generation Computing*, 8(4): 295–317, 1991. Also in [76], pp. 3–27.

76. S. Muggleton (ed.). *Inductive Logic Programming*. Academic Press, 1992.

77. S. Muggleton and C. Feng. Efficient induction of logic programs. In [76], pp. 281–298.

78. S. Muggleton, R.D. King, and M.J.E. Sternberg. Protein secondary structure prediction using logic. *Protein Engineering* 7: 647–657, 1992.

79. S. Muggleton and L. De Raedt. Inductive Logic Programming: theory and methods. *Journal of Logic Programming*, 19/20: 629–679, 1994.

80. S. Muggleton. Inverse entailment and Progol. *New Generation Computing*, 13: 245–286, 1995.

81. C. Nédellec, C. Rouveirol, H. Adé, F. Bergadano, and B. Tausend. Declarative bias in Inductive Logic Programming. In [18], pp. 82–103.

82. D. Page. ILP: Just do it. In J.W. Lloyd (ed.), *Proceedings of the First International Conference on Computational Logic*, Lecture Notes in Artificial Intelligence 1861, pp. 25–40. Springer-Verlag, 2000.

83. G. Plotkin. A note on inductive generalisation. *Machine Intelligence 5*, B. Meltzer and D. Michie (eds.), pp. 153–163. North-Holland, 1970.

84. G. Plotkin. A further note on inductive generalisation. *Machine Intelligence 6*, B. Meltzer and D. Michie (eds.), pp. 101–124. North-Holland, 1971.
85. F. Provost and T. Fawcett. Robust classification for imprecise environments. *Machine Learning* 42(3): 203–231, 2001.
86. J.R. Quinlan. Learning logical definitions from relations. *Machine Learning*, 5(3): 239–266, 1990.
87. J.R. Quinlan. Boosting, bagging, and C4.5 . In *Proceedings of the Thirteenth National Conference on Artificial Intelligence*, pp. 725–730. AAAI Press, 1996.
88. I. Savnik and P.A. Flach. Discovery of multivalued dependencies from relations. *Intelligent Data Analysis*, 4(3,4): 195–211, 2000.
89. M. Sebag and C. Rouveirol. Constraint Inductive Logic Programming. In [18], pp. 277–294.
90. E.Y. Shapiro. *Inductive inference of theories from facts*. Technical Report 192, Computer Science Department, Yale University, 1981.
91. E.Y. Shapiro. *Algorithmic program debugging*. MIT Press, 1983.
92. E. Sommer. Rulebase stratifications: an approach to theory restructuring. In S. Wrobel (ed.), *Proceedings of the Fourth International Workshop on Inductive Logic Programming*, GMD-Studien 237, pp. 377-390, 1994.
93. A. Srinivasan, S. Muggleton, R.D. King, and M.J.E. Sternberg. Mutagenesis: ILP experiments in a non-determinate biological domain. In S. Wrobel (ed.), *Proceedings of the Fourth International Workshop on Inductive Logic Programming*, GMD-Studien 237, pp. 217–232, 1994.
94. A. Srinivasan, R.D. King, S. Muggleton, and M.J.E. Sternberg. Carcinogenesis prediction using inductive logic programming. In N. Lavrač, E. Keravnou, and B. Zupan (eds.), *Intelligent Data Analysis in Medicine and Pharmacology*, pp. 243–260. Kluwer, 1997.
95. I. Stahl. Compression measures in ILP. In [18], pp. 295–307.
96. L. Valiant. A theory of the learnable. *Communications of the ACM* 27: 1134–1142, 1984.
97. I.H. Witten and E. Frank. *Data Mining: Practical machine learning tools and techniques with Java implementations*. Morgan Kauffman, 2000.
98. S. Wrobel. An algorithm for multi-relational discovery of subgroups. In *Proceedings of the First European Symposium on Principles of Data Mining and Knowledge Discovery*, pp. 78–87. Springer-Verlag, 1997.
99. XSB Group Home Page: http://www.cs.sunysb.edu/~sbprolog/.

Disjunctive Logic Programming: A Survey and Assessment

Jack Minker[1] and Dietmar Seipel[2]

[1] Department of Computer Science and
Institute for Advanced Computer Studies
University of Maryland
College Park, Maryland 20742, USA
[2] Department of Computer Science
University of Würzburg
Am Hubland, D – 97074 Würzburg, Germany

Abstract. We describe the fields of disjunctive logic programming and disjunctive deductive databases from the time of their inception to the current time. Contributions with respect to semantics, implementations and applications are surveyed.

In the last decade many semantics have been proposed out of which we highlight what we believe to be the most influential ones and compare them. Basic ideas have been borrowed from the semantics of normal logic programs such as stable model semantics and well–founded semantics, which have been generalized in various ways to obtain semantics of disjunctive logic programs.

We discuss disjunctive systems such as DLV and Smodels, and related non–disjunctive systems such as XSB and DeReS, that have been implemented. We also describe applications of disjunctive logic programming: reasoning about declarative specifications, reasoning about actions, diagnosis (e.g. in medicine or biology), and in data integration that have resource predicates defined by multiple rules. We discuss the future needs to make the field practical: e.g. integrating concepts from databases (such as aggregation), optimization methods, and object orientation.

In Section 12 we discuss the influence that Bob Kowalski had on our work.

1 Introduction

The field of disjunctive logic programming (DLP) had its beginnings in 1982 and is nearing the completion of its second decade. Work prior to 1982 focused primarily on Horn theories of logic programming as described by Kowalski [Kow74]. The first result in the field of disjunctive logic programming (DLP) was by Minker [Min82] who developed a consistent theory for default negation in disjunctive theories, the generalized closed world assumption (GCWA). The paper also set forth the concept of minimal models for computing answers both for positive and negative atoms. The GCWA reduces to the CWA for Horn theories developed by Reiter [Rei78].

A.C. Kakas, F. Sadri (Eds.): Computat. Logic (Kowalski Festschrift), LNAI 2407, pp. 472–511, 2002.
© Springer-Verlag Berlin Heidelberg 2002

There was no work in DLP until 1986 when renewed interest arose as a consequence of a *Workshop on Foundations of Deductive Databases and Logic Programming*, organized by Minker [Min88b]. Following the workshop, Minker and Rajasekar [MR90], developed fixpoint, model theoretic and proof theoretic semantics for DLP. This work extended the results of van Emden and Kowalski [vEK76], for the Horn theory of logic programming. It led to many theoretical developments in disjunctive and normal disjunctive logic programs, including theories of negation and disjunctive deductive databases. Much of this work in the late 1980s and early 1990s was performed at the University of Maryland and is the subject of a research monograph, *Foundations of Disjunctive Logic Programming* [LMR92]. The theoretical results contained in that monograph extend what is known in the theory of logic programs as developed in the monograph by Lloyd [Llo87] and the paper by Apt [Apt90]. The work in DLP has also been shown to be important for representing and implementing nonmonotonic and abductive reasoning. In this paper, we describe the developments that have taken place in disjunctive logic programming since 1982.

The paper is organized as follows. In Section 2, we provide the basic definitions and background needed for the paper. In Section 3, we briefly discuss developments in logic programming that led to the developments in disjunctive logic programming. In Section 4, we discuss the theoretical developments that have taken place in DLP and in the related area of disjunctive deductive databases (DDDBs). One of the major accomplishments in the field has been the implementation of systems to handle normal logic programs, DLPs and DDDBs. This work is discussed in Section 5. We discuss several areas for applications in DLP in Section 6. Finally, in Section 7 we provide a summary and an assessment of the field of DLP. We end the paper with a Tribute to Robert Kowalski whose pioneering research was significant for our research.

2   Background

We assume that the reader has a background in logic programming as described in [Kow78, SS86], or other books on logic programming, and is familiar with the major theoretical results given in [Apt90, Llo87]. A personal perspective on the development of disjunctive logic programming is given in [Min89]. Kowalski [Kow88] provides a personal perspective of the history of the field of logic programming.

Throughout the paper we will refer to different classes of clauses. These are *definite Horn clauses, normal clauses, extended clauses, positive–disjunctive clauses, disjunctive clauses*, and *extended–disjunctive clauses*. Associated with each type of clause is a class of logic programs. These are termed, respectively, *definite logic programs, normal logic programs, extended logic programs, positive–disjunctive logic programs, disjunctive logic programs*, and *extended–disjunctive logic programs*. These logic programs are defined as follows.

Given a first order language $\mathcal{L}$, a *disjunctive logic program* $\mathcal{P}$ consists of logical inference rules of the form

$$r = A_1 \vee \ldots \vee A_k \leftarrow B_1 \wedge \ldots \wedge B_m \wedge not\, C_1 \wedge \ldots \wedge not\, C_n, \qquad (1)$$

where A_i, B_i and C_i are atoms in the language $\mathcal{L}$; $k, m, n \in I\!N_0$, and not denotes negation–by–default, rather than logical negation. A rule r of the form (1) is denoted for short as:

$$r = \alpha \leftarrow \beta \wedge not \cdot \gamma, \qquad (2)$$

where $\alpha = A_1 \vee \ldots \vee A_k$, $\beta = B_1 \wedge \ldots \wedge B_m$, $\gamma = C_1 \vee \ldots \vee C_n$.[1] Sometimes α, β, and γ will be considered as sets (e.g. in Table 3 of Section 4). α is called the *head*, β is called the *positive body*, and $not \cdot \gamma$ is called the *negative body* of r.

- A rule is called a *fact* if $m = n = 0$.
- A rule is called a *definite clause* or a *Horn clause*, if $n = 0$ and $k = 1$, i.e. it neither contains disjunction nor default negation.
- A rule is called *positive–disjunctive*, if $n = 0$, i.e. it does not contain default negation.
- A rule is called *normal*, if $k = 1$, i.e. it does not contain disjunction.
- A rule is called a *denial rule*, if $k = 0$. Denial rules can be used for representing *integrity constraints* and *queries* to disjunctive logic programs.
- A rule is called a *range–restricted* if all variable symbols occurring in the head also occur in the positive body.

A rule of the form (1) is called *extended–disjunctive rule*, if A_i, B_i and C_i are literals in the language, i.e. atoms or atoms preceded by classical negation $\neg$. If a (disjunctive) logic program does not contain any function symbols, then it is called a *(disjunctive) deductive database*.

The Herbrand base $HB_\mathcal{P}$ of a disjunctive logic program $\mathcal{P}$ contains all ground atoms over the language of $\mathcal{P}$. The set of all *ground instances* of the rules and facts in $\mathcal{P}$ is denoted by $gnd(\mathcal{P})$.

Partial Herbrand Interpretations

A *partial (three–valued) Herbrand interpretation* of $\mathcal{P}$ is given by a mapping $I\colon HB_\mathcal{P} \to \{\,t, f, u\,\}$ that assigns a truth value "t" (*true*), "f" (*false*) or "u" (*undefined*) to each ground atom in $HB_\mathcal{P}$. Obviously, I can be represented by a pair $\langle I_t, I_f \rangle$, such that

$$I_t = \{\, A \in HB_\mathcal{P} \mid I(A) = t\,\},$$
$$I_f = \{\, A \in HB_\mathcal{P} \mid I(A) = f\,\}.$$

I is called a *total Herbrand interpretation*, if $I_t \cup I_f = HB_\mathcal{P}$, i.e. if all atoms $A \in HB_\mathcal{P}$ are mapped to one of the classical truth values t or f. In this case, it is sufficient to represent I by its set I_t of *true* atoms alone.

There are two important *partial orderings on truth values*: in the truth ordering $\leq_k$ it holds $f \leq_t u$, $u \leq_t t$, and in the knowledge ordering $\leq_k$ it holds

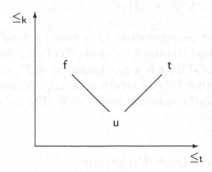

Fig. 1. Truth Ordering and Knowledge Ordering

$u \leq_k f$, $u \leq_k t$, cf. Fitting [Fi91] and Figure 1. These partial orderings have been generalized (pointwise) to partial orderings on partial Herbrand interpretations as follows. For $x \in \{ t, k \}$: $I_1 \leq_x I_2$, iff ($\forall A \in HB_\mathcal{P} : I_1(A) \leq_x I_2(A)$).

The *Boolean operations* "$\vee$", "$\wedge$" and "$\neg$" on truth values are defined based on the truth ordering, cf. Figure 2. The truth value of a disjunction $v_1 \vee v_2$ and a conjunction $v_1 \wedge v_2$ of truth values are constructed by taking the *maximum* and the *minimum* of v_1 and v_2, respectively. "$\vee$" and "$\wedge$" both are commutative and associative, and thus can be generalized to disjunctions and conjunctions, respectively, of more than one truth value. Let M be a partial Herbrand inter-

$\wedge$	t	f	u
t	t	f	u
f	f	f	f
u	u	f	u

$\vee$	t	f	u
t	t	t	t
f	t	f	u
u	t	u	u

$\neg$	
t	f
f	t
u	u

Fig. 2. Boolean operations in three–valued logic

pretation and let $A_i \in HB_\mathcal{P}$ be ground atoms. For a connective $\otimes \in \{ \vee, \wedge \}$ we define $M(A_1 \otimes \ldots \otimes A_k) = M(A_1) \otimes \ldots \otimes M(A_k)$. For $k = 0$, the empty disjunction (i.e. $\otimes = \vee$) evaluates to f, whereas the empty conjunction (i.e. $\otimes = \wedge$) evaluates to t.

Models and Partial Models, Minimality

A total Herbrand interpretation M satisfies a ground rule $r = \alpha \leftarrow \beta \wedge not \cdot \gamma$ if $M(\beta) \wedge \neg M(\gamma) = t$ implies $M(\alpha) = t$. This can be generalized to partial Herbrand interpretations M by requiring that

---

[1] Note that γ is a disjunction, and, according to De Morgan's law, $not \cdot \gamma$ is taken to be a conjunction.

$$M(\beta) \land \neg M(\gamma) \leq_t M(\alpha). \tag{3}$$

A total (partial) Herbrand interpretation M is called a *total (partial) model* of $\mathcal{P}$ if M satisfies of all ground instances $r \in gnd(\mathcal{P})$ of all rules of $\mathcal{P}$. M is called a *partial minimal model* of $\mathcal{P}$ if M is a partial model of $\mathcal{P}$ and there is no other partial model I of $\mathcal{P}$ such that $I \leq_t M$ (truth ordering). A partial minimal model M of $\mathcal{P}$ that is total is called a *minimal model* of $\mathcal{P}$. The set of minimal models of $\mathcal{P}$ is denoted by $\mathcal{MM}_2(\mathcal{P})$.

Semantics of Disjunctive Logic Programs

Each alternative type of logic program leads to a different theory. We are concerned with the semantics of each type of logic program and how one computes in the theory. The computation of negation is particularly important for nonmonotonic reasoning. There are many relationships between logic programming and alternative formulations of nonmonotonic reasoning by circumscription [McCa80], default reasoning [Rei80], and autoepistemic reasoning [MT91, MT93, Moo84], [Moo85]. We do not cover this topic here. For details on work in nonmonotonic reasoning, see [Gin87]. For a discussion of the relationships between nonmonotonic theories and logic programming, see [Min93]. We discuss this topic briefly. See Reiter [Rei78] for an early survey of work in nonmonotonic reasoning.

In the case of logic program theories that are definite, there exists one semantics that is generally accepted as the meaning of the program. This is the unique minimal Herbrand model of the definite theory. When one comes to the alternative types of logic programs, different interpretations may be given to the programs. That is, each theory may or may not provide a unique minimal model; however, even when there is a unique meaning ascribed to the program, the meaning may be different between the alternative approaches. In the rest of this section we define some of the most prominent approaches in detail: stable and partial stable models for disjunctive logic programs, the well–founded model for normal logic programs, and answer sets for extended–disjunctive logic programs. In the following sections we provide a broader overview of the theoretical results that are known in each class of logic programs and we give some examples. We discuss the possible alternative semantics within each class.

Stable and Partial Stable Models. The *Gelfond–Lifschitz transformation* (GL–transformation, [GL88, Prz91]) $\mathcal{P}^M$ of a disjunctive logic program $\mathcal{P}$ w.r.t. a partial Herbrand interpretation M is obtained from the ground instance $gnd(\mathcal{P})$ of $\mathcal{P}$ by replacing in every ground rule $r = \alpha \leftarrow \beta \land not \cdot \gamma \in gnd(\mathcal{P})$ the negative body by its truth value w.r.t. M.[2] We define $r^M = \alpha \leftarrow \beta \land \neg M(\gamma)$ and $\mathcal{P}^M = \{ r^M \mid r \in gnd(\mathcal{P}) \}$. The GL–transformation $\mathcal{P}^M$ is a ground positive–disjunctive logic program that has as additional atoms the truth values t, f

---

[2] If this truth value is "t", then "t" can be deleted from the body. If it is "f", then the whole rule can be deleted from $\mathcal{P}^M$.

and u.[3] Based on $\mathcal{P}^M$ the concepts of stable models (cf. Gelfond and Lifschitz, [GL88]) and partial stable models (cf. Pryzmusinski, [Prz91]) have been defined:

1. A total Herbrand interpretation M is called a *stable model* of $\mathcal{P}$ if M is a minimal model of $\mathcal{P}^M$.
2. A partial Herbrand interpretation M is called a *partial stable model* of $\mathcal{P}$ if M is a partial minimal model of $\mathcal{P}^M$.

It can be shown that stable models are always also partial stable models. That is, the semantics of stable models is always stronger than the semantics of partial stable models. An example will be given in Section 3.

Well–Founded Semantics. For normal logic programs there always exists a (unique) least partial stable model M in the knowledge ordering ([Fi91]). This partial model M coincides with the *well–founded model*, which had been defined by Van Gelder, Ross and Schlipf, and which can be characterized using the following *alternating fixpoint approach* ([VaGe89]):

$$M_0 = \emptyset, \ M_{n+1} = \mathcal{MM}_2(\mathcal{P}^{M_n}).$$

This recursion generates an increasing sequence $(M_{2n})_{n \in \mathbb{N}_0}$ and a decreasing sequence $(M_{2n+1})_{n \in \mathbb{N}_0}$ of sets of atoms, such that $M_{2n} \subseteq M_{2n+1}$, for all $n \in \mathbb{N}_0$. For $M_\cup = \bigcup_{n=0}^\infty M_{2n}$ and $M_\cap = \bigcap_{n=0}^\infty M_{2n+1}$ it holds that $M_\cup \subseteq M_\cap$. The well–founded model M is a partial Herbrand interpretation given by $M = \langle M_\cup, HB_\mathcal{P} \setminus M_\cap \rangle$, i.e. an atom A is *true* under the well–founded model semantics if it is in $M_\cup$ and *false* if it is not in $M_\cap$. An example will be given in Section 3.

Answer Set Semantics. Gelfond and Lifschitz ([GL90, GL91]) have extended the concept of stable models to extended–disjunctive logic programs $\mathcal{P}$, i.e. logic programs that may contain *classical negation*. They propose the so–called *answer set semantics*, which can be defined as follows: $\mathcal{P}$ is transformed to a disjunctive logic program $\mathcal{P}'$ free of classical negation, which is obtained by replacing negative literals $\neg A = \neg p(t_1, \dots, t_n)$ by positive literals $A' = p'(t_1, \dots, t_n)$ over new predicate symbols. Every stable model M' of $\mathcal{P}'$ defines an answer set M of $\mathcal{P}$, which is a set of literals: Let

$$L = \{ A \in HB_\mathcal{P} \mid M'(A) = \mathsf{t} \} \cup \{ \neg A \in \neg HB_\mathcal{P} \mid M'(A') = \mathsf{t} \};$$

if L does not contain any complementary pair A and $\neg A$ of literals, then $M = L$, otherwise $M = HB_\mathcal{P} \cup \neg HB_\mathcal{P}$ is the set of all ground literals.

3   Theory of Logic Programming

Since we treat, primarily, disjunctive logic programs, we sketch, briefly, only the results in logic programming, except for the case of normal and extended logic

---

[3] Note that these truth values must evaluate to themselves under all partial Herbrand interpretations I of $\mathcal{P}^M$.

programs. Logic programming began in approximately 1971 [Kow88]. Theoretical results were obtained first in 1976, with the publication of the landmark paper by van Emden and Kowalski [vEK76] in which they detailed model theoretic, fixpoint, and operational semantics of logic programs as a programming language. They introduced an operator, $\mathcal{T}_{\mathcal{P}}$, and demonstrated that the operator has a fixpoint. The semantics of the fixpoint corresponds to model theory, while operational semantics corresponds to proof theory. The semantics in all three cases are identical. They provided a formal semantics of a definite clause logic formula, viewed as a statement in a programming language. Their use of the least model and least fixpoint constructions, as well as the procedural interpretation, provide the foundations of the field of logic programming. Their ideas also led to the concept of negation. If one subtracts the minimal model of a program from the Herbrand base, the atoms that remain can be considered *false*. This provides a model characterization of the *CWA*, first propounded by Reiter [Rei78] in proof theoretic terms.

Apt and van Emden [AvE82] built upon the theoretical treatment of van Emden and Kowalski. They renamed Hill's inference system [Hil74], LUSH resolution (Linear Resolution with Unrestricted Selection function based on Horn clauses), to be SLD (*SL* resolution for Definite Horn clauses). They also characterized the finite failure set of an atom relative to a program in terms of the van Emden/Kowalski fixpoint operator, $\mathcal{T}_{\mathcal{P}}$ [vEK76]. Lassez and Maher[LM84] then proved that the finite failure set is characterized by the difference between the Herbrand base and the fixpoint operator described by Apt and van Emden. Clark [Cla78] ties these results to the completion of a logic program. He shows the soundness of the negation–as–failure rule for any Horn logic program, $\mathcal{P}$, augmented by $comp(\mathcal{P})$ and equality axioms. He shows that every goal G with a finitely failed SLD–tree is a logical consequence of $comp(\mathcal{P})$ and equality axioms (actually his results extend to general programs using safe computation rules, i.e. rules that select only ground negative literals). Jaffar, Lassez and Lloyd [JLL83] prove the completeness result and show that if a goal G is a logical consequence of $comp(\mathcal{P})$, then there is a finitely failed SLD–tree for G. See Shepherdson [She88], for work on negation, and Lloyd [Llo87] and Apt [Apt90] for the theoretical results in logic programming. Apt and Bol [AB94] and Dix [Dix95d] update the Shepherdson survey on negation in logic programming [She88] and briefly describe theories of negation in disjunctive logic programs.

In 1988, Apt, Blair and Walker [ABW88] extended the class of logic programs to a subset of normal logic programs, termed *stratified logic programs*. Such programs are normal logic programs for which the rules do not have recursion through negation. When this occurs, the predicates can be placed into strata so that one can compute over the strata. Independently, and at the same time, Van Gelder [VaGe88], also described this class of programs. The theoretical results obtained were that there was a fixpoint theory that characterized the semantics of this class of programs, and that there was a unique model that could be obtained by iterating over the strata. Przymusinski [Prz88], showed that the model obtained was the so–called *perfect model*. He also extended the work to include *locally stratified logic programs*.

The semantics of definite and stratified logic programs lead to unique minimal models, which are generally accepted to be the semantics of the two classes of logic programs. However, this is not the case when we come to the class of *normal logic programs*; then there are several possible ways to determine the semantics. Each alternative leads to a different semantics. Van Gelder, Ross and Schlipf [VGRS91], Gelfond and Lifschitz [GL88], and Baral, Lobo and Minker [BLM89,BLM91]* ([Min99])[4], have developed alternative semantics.

Well–Founded and Stable Model Semantics

Van Gelder, Ross and Schlipf [VGRS91], were the first to extend the work by Apt, Blair and Walker [ABW88], to the class of *normal logic programs*. Unlike stratified logic programs, the program may not be stratifiable. This occurs when there is recursion through negation. The *well–founded semantics* (WFS) of Van Gelder et al. is given in terms of three possible truth values: *true, false*, and *unknown*. For the normal logic program

$$\mathcal{P} = \{\, a \leftarrow not\, b,\ b \leftarrow not\, a,\ c \leftarrow a,\ c \leftarrow b \,\}$$

Van Gelder et al. obtain the semantics $I = \langle \emptyset, \emptyset \rangle$. The semantics may be understood as follows: since, from the first two clauses it cannot be decided if either a, or b, are either *true* or *false*, they are determined to be *unknown*. Since a and b are both *unknown*, c must be assigned to be *unknown*.

Chen and Warren [CW93] develop a variant of *SLS*-resolution [Prz88] to obtain a procedural semantics for the WFS. This procedure, called *XOLDTNF*, is sound and complete. Warren and his group at Stony Brook have developed an implementation that handles most cases of the WFS, termed XSB [War99]. The system can handle large sets of data and rules. XSB is a sophisticated extension to PROLOG, containing many of its features. We discuss this and other implementations in logic programming and disjunctive logic programming in Section 5. Zukowski et al. ([ZBF97, ZF99, BDFZ01]) present a transformation–based approach for the bottom–up computation of the well–founded model.

Alternatively, the *stable model semantics* [GL88], has been developed by Gelfond and Lifschitz, as discussed in Section 2. The meaning of the program is taken as the set of positive clauses that are *true* in all minimal models obtained by the GL–transformation. For the program given above, there are two stable models: $\{a, c\}$, and $\{b, c\}$. To be *true* in the stable model semantics, an atom must be *true* in every stable model; to be *false*, it must be *false* in every stable model; to be *unknown*, it must neither be *true* nor *false*. The stable model semantics for the above program $\mathcal{P}$ is thus given by the following partial Herbrand interpretation $I' = \langle \{c\}, \emptyset \rangle$, i.e. a and b are *unknown* and c is *true*. An iterative method for

---

[4] To conserve space, we sometimes write references as, [—]* ([Min99]), to denote that the reference in [—]* can be found in ([Min99]).

finding the stable models of a program has been developed by Fernández, Lobo, Minker and Subrahmanian [FLMS93]. Their approach transforms a normal logic program into a disjunctive logic program with integrity constraints, called the *evidential transformation*. The minimal models of this evidential transformation are the same as the stable models of the original disjunctive logic program. Bell, Nerode, Ng and Subrahmanian [BNNS94] have developed a linear programming based implementation of the stable model semantics. The work of Gelfond and Lifschitz can be extended to include disjunctions of positive atoms in the head of a clause as shown by Przymusinski [Prz91]. The approach by [FLMS93] to find the stable models of normal logic programs extends to the case where there are disjunctions in the head of a clause. Fernández and Lobo [FL93]* ([Min99]) have developed a proof procedure for computing answers to queries under the stable model semantics. Niemela and Simons [NS97] have developed an efficient system, Smodels, that computes the stable model semantics, cf. Section 5.

Other semantics developed at approximately that time, [BLM89,BLM91]* ([Min99]) are not discussed here since it is clear that the two dominant theories for normal logic programs are the WFS and the stable model semantics.

Although in the above example, the *stable* and the *GWFS* semantics are the same, this is not always the case. Various criteria have been specified [Dix92a] to determine which semantics should be chosen. These criteria relate to properties that the semantics satisfy. Based on these properties one may argue the pros and cons of a particular semantics. In addition, motivated by finding semantics with the appropriate properties, several semantics have been developed. A summary of these semantics is given in [Min94]. Although of considerable interest, the well–founded semantics and the stable model semantics remain the dominant semantics in use. Perhaps one of the reasons for this is that efficient systems have been developed for them, namely XSB and Smodels.

Gelfond and Lifschitz [GL90, GL91] introduce classical negation in logic programs, i.e. they represent extended–disjunctive clauses. The semantics proposed for such a logic program, which is called *answer set semantics*, is based on the stable model semantics. They show that an extended–disjunctive program can be viewed as a default theory in which every justification and conclusion is a literal, and every precondition is a conjunction of literals. In [GL91], they show that some facts of commonsense knowledge can be represented by logic programs and disjunctive databases more easily when classical negation is available. Extended–disjunctive programs are shown to be identical to a special case of default theories in the sense of Reiter [Rei80].

4   Theory of Disjunctive Logic Programming

Work in disjunctive theories was pursued seriously after a workshop organized by Minker in 1986 [Min86]* ([Min99]). The field of *disjunctive logic programming (DLP)* started approximately in 1982 with the the paper by Minker [Min82], who devised a consistent theory of negation for *disjunctive deductive databases (DDDBs)*. Shepherdson [She88] showed that Minker's theory of negation for

DDDBs also applied to DLPs. For a historical perspective of DLPs and DDDBs, see [Min88a]. There is a major difference for *deductive databases (DDBs)* and those for DDDBs. Whereas DDBs have a unique minimal model that describes the meaning of the database, DDDBs generally have multiple minimal models.

As shown in [Min82] it is sufficient to answer positive queries over *DDDBs* by showing that the query is satisfied in every minimal model. Thus, for $\mathcal{P} = \{ a \vee b \}$, there are two minimal models, $\{a\}$ and $\{b\}$. The query $\leftarrow a$ is not satisfied in the model $\{b\}$, and hence, a cannot be *true*. However, the query $\leftarrow a \vee b$ is satisfied in both minimal models and hence the answer to the query $\leftarrow a \vee b$ is *yes*. To answer negated queries, it is not sufficient to use Reiter's *CWA* [Rei78] since, as he noted, from the theory $\mathcal{P} = \{ a \vee b \}$, it is not possible to prove a, and it is not possible to prove b. Hence, by the *CWA*, *not a* and *not b* follow. But, $\{ a \vee b, not\ a, not\ b \}$ is not consistent. The *Generalized Closed World Assumption (GCWA)*, [Min82] resolves this problem by specifying that a negated atom be considered *true* if the atom does not appear in any minimal model of the database. This provides a model theoretic definition of negation. An equivalent proof theoretic definition, also in [Min82], is that a ground atom A may be considered to be *false* if, whenever $A \vee \alpha$ may be proven from the database, then α may be proven from the database, where α is an arbitrary ground disjunction of atoms.

For related work on negation in disjunctive theories see [YH85, GPP86, Cha93], [Sak89, RT88, RLM89]. For surveys on negation see [She88, AB94], [Dix95d, Min93].

Fixpoint Approaches

In LPs, it is natural for the fixpoint operator to map atoms to atoms. However, for DLPs, it is natural to map positive disjunctions to positive disjunctions. A set of positive disjunctions is referred to as a *state*. A *model state* is a state all of whose minimal models satisfy the DLP. The concept of a state was defined by Minker and Rajasekar [MR90] as the domain of a fixpoint operator $T_{\mathcal{P}}^s$ whose least fixpoint characterizes the semantics of a disjunctive logic program $\mathcal{P}$. The operator is shown to be monotonic and continuous, and hence converges in ω iterations. The fixpoint computation operates bottom–up and yields a minimal model state logically equivalent to the set of minimal models of the program. The Minker/Rajasekar fixpoint operator $T_{\mathcal{P}}^s$ is an extension of the van Emden/Kowalski fixpoint operator $T_{\mathcal{P}}$. If one considers all model states of a DLP and intersects them, the resultant is a model state, and among all model states it is minimal. Hence, one obtains a unique minimal model in a Horn database, while one obtains a unique model state in a DLP.

In [FM91b, FM95, SMR97] another generalization of the fixpoint operator $T_{\mathcal{P}}$ has been investigated: the operator $T_{\mathcal{P}}^{INT}$ works in sets of Herbrand interpretations rather than states. It generates the set of minimal Herbrand models as its least fixpoint. In [SMR97] a useful relationship has been established between state generation by $T_{\mathcal{P}}^s$ and model generation by $T_{\mathcal{P}}^{INT}$: for a set $\mathcal{I}$ of Herbrand interpretations, the set $T_{\mathcal{P}}^{INT}(\mathcal{I})$ of interpretations is a subset of the set of models of the state $S \cup T_{\mathcal{P}}^s(S)$, if $\mathcal{I}$ is a subset of the set of Herbrand models of the disjunctive Herbrand state S. Furthermore, it is shown that T_P^{INT} is monotonic but not continuous, but that is still converges towards its least fixpoint in at most ω iterations.

Decker [Dec91] develops an alternative fixpoint operator for *DDDBs* which reduces to the Minker/Rajasekar fixpoint operator [MR90]. At each iteration of his operator, he finds partial models of the database. In the limit, he obtains the set of minimal models of the database. If one takes an atom from each minimal model and forms a disjunction, the resulting set of all such disjunctions is equivalent to the minimal model state of the *DDDBs*.

Query Answering

Answering queries in *DDDBs* has been studied by a number of individuals. Grant and Minker [GM86] were among the first to address the problem of computing answers to queries in *DDDBs*. They investigated the case where the database consists exclusively of ground positive disjuncts. Yahya and Henschen [YH85] developed a deductive method to determine whether or not a conjunction of ground atoms can be assumed *false* in a *DDDB* under the *Extended Generalized Closed World Assumption (EGCWA)*. The *EGCWA* is an extension of the *GCWA*. Bossu and Siegel [Boss85]* ([Min99]) developed a deductive method to answer a query by subimplication (a generalization of the *GCWA* that handles databases that have no minimal models). Henschen and Park [Hens86]* ([Min99]) answer *yes/no* questions in a database that consists of an *EDB*, an *IDB* and *ICs* that are all function–free. In addition, they allow negated unit clauses to be part of the database. The axioms in the *IDB* may be recursive. Yahya [Yah97] discusses how to answer queries defined as sets of clauses in implication form in a *DDDB*. Liu and Sunderraman [LS90b] generalize the relational model to represent disjunctive data. They develop a data–structure, called *M–table* to represent the data. Their generalized relational algebra operates on *M-tables*, however, it is sound, but not complete. Yuan and Chiang [YC89] developed a generalized relational algebra that is a sound and complete query evaluation algorithm for *DDDBs* that do not contain recursive *IDB* rules.

Fernández and Minker [FM91b] developed the concept of a *model tree*. They incrementally compute sound and complete answers to queries in *hierarchical DDDBs*. An example of a *model tree* is shown in Figure 3. The model tree represents the two minimal models $\{a_1, a_2, b_1\}$ and $\{a_1, b_2\}$ of the positive–disjunctive database $\{a_1, a_2 \vee b_2, b_1 \vee b_2\}$. A *DDDBs* is hierarchical if it contains no recursion. In [FLMS93] they develop a fixpoint operator over trees to capture the meaning of a *DDDB* that includes recursion. The tree representation of the fixpoint is equivalent to the Minker/Rajasekar fixpoint [MR90]. They compute the model tree of the extensional *DDDB* once for all queries. To answer queries *intensional database* rules may be invoked. Their approach to compute answers generalizes both to stratified and normal *DDDBs*. In [Sei94] a tree data structure for Herbrand states (rather than models) is given, which is called *clause tree*, and it is shown how the fixpoint operator T_P^s can work on clause trees.

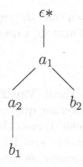

Fig. 3. Model Tree

The above approaches to answering queries in *DDDBs* have the following limitations. [GM86] can only compute answers to queries that contain a disjunctive extensional database. [YH85] can only answer *yes/no* questions. [LS90b] provide sound, but not complete answers to queries. [YC89] essentially compute the fixpoint of the entire *DDB* to answer each query. [FM91b] compute the model tree of the extensional *DDDB* once. To answer queries *IDB* rules may be invoked. However, the models of the extensional disjunctive part of the database do not have to be generated for each query.

Loveland et al. [Llo87, Lov87, SL88, RL90, RLS91] developed a top–down case–based reasoner that uses PROLOG when the database is *near Horn*. Loveland et al. [LRW93] introduced a relevancy detection algorithm to be used with SATCHMO, developed by Manthey and Bry [MB88], for automated theorem proving. Their system, SATCHMORE (SATCHMO with RElevancy), improves SATCHMO by limiting the uncontrolled use of forward chaining. Another approach is by Stickel [Sti88] using a PROLOG *Technology Theorem Prover (PTTP)*.

For disjunctive logic programs a huge amount of work has been done on bottom–up fixpoint evaluations using state generation or model generation. But so far very few top–down approaches exist for disjunctive logic programs. In deductive databases efficient query evaluation is achieved by mixing bottom–up and top–down techniques: The *magic sets technique* incorporates the top–down binding passing known from SLD–resolution into a bottom–up, breadth–first fixpoint computation to achieve a goal–oriented query evaluation, which focuses on relevant derivations as described by Bry [Bry90]. Yahya [Yah00] investigates the problem of efficiently answering positive ground queries to disjunctive deductive databases without default negation. He applies model generation to the *dual database*, which is obtained by reversing the rule arrows in all rules. This generalizes SLD–resolution, and it yields *goal–oriented query processing* which is driven by the facts that are derived from the query goal. Hasegawa et al. [HIOK97, OIH98] have proposed an extension of magic sets for range–restricted disjunctive logic programs. Also Greco, cf. [Gre98, Gre99], presents a rewriting technique for the optimization of bound queries to disjunctive deductive databases. Experiments have shown that the rewriting greatly reduces the number of models to be considered to answer a query.

Complexity Results

Imielinski and Vadaparty [IV89], Vardi [Var82] and Imielinski [Imi91] have investigated the complexity of answering queries in disjunctive logic programs. Chomicki and Subrahmanian [CS90] discuss the complexity of the *GCWA*. For disjunctive theories that are tractable, see [BED94]. For complexity results for disjunctive propositional logic programs see Eiter and Gottlob [EG95, DEGV97]. A summary of complexity results, drawn from [EG95], is given in Table 1.

	Propositional		First Order over Herbrand models no function symbols[5]	
Semantics	Complexity	Ref.	Data Complexity	Ref.
Positive Consequences				
Minimal Models	Π_2^P–complete	[EG93a]	Π_2^P–complete	[EGM94]
Negation				
GCWA	Π_2^P–complete	[EG93a]	Π_2^P–complete	[EGM94]
WGCWA	co–$\mathcal{NP}$–complete	[Cha93]		
Stratified Programs				
Perfect	Π_2^P–complete	[EG93a]	Π_2^P–complete	[EGM94]
Locally Stratified Programs				
Perfect	Π_2^P–complete	[EG93a]	Π_2^P–complete	[EGM94]
Normal Programs				
Stable	Π_2^P–complete	[EG93a]	Π_2^P–complete	[EGM94]
Partial Stable	Π_2^P–complete	[EG93a]	Π_2^P–complete	[EGM94]
Extended Programs				
Stable	Π_2^P–complete	[?]	Π_2^P–complete	[EGM94]
Partial Stable	Π_2^P–complete	[MR94]	Π_2^P–complete	[EGM94]

Table 1. (Taken from [EG93a, EG95]) Complexity of Cautious Reasoning with Disjunctive Logic Programs (with Integrity Constraints)

The development of model theoretic, fixpoint and proof procedures has placed the semantics of DDDBs on a firm foundation. Methods to handle DDDBs have started and are discussed in Section 5. The GCWA and alternative theories of negation have enhanced our understanding of default negation in DDDBs. Complexity results provide an understanding of the difficulties to find answers to queries in such systems.

Disjunctive Deductive Databases with Default Negation

Fernández and Minker [FM95] present a new fixpoint characterization of the minimal models of *DDDBs* and stratified *DDDBs*. They prove that by applying the operator iteratively, in the limit, it constructs the perfect models semantics (Przymusinski [Prz88]) of stratified *DDDBs*. Given the equivalence between the *perfect models semantics of stratified programs* and *prioritized circumscription* [Prz88] their fixpoint characterization captures the meaning of the corresponding circumscribed theory. They present a bottom–up evaluation algorithm for stratified *DDDBs* using the *model–tree* data structure to represent and to compute answers to queries. In [FM92], they develop the theory of *DDDBs* using model trees. Work on updates in *DDDBs* is described in [GHLM93, FGM96].

Four alternative semantics were developed for non–stratifiable normal DLPs at approximately the same time: Ross [Ros89], Baral et al. [BLM90a,BLM90b]* ([Min99]), and two semantics by Przymusinski [Prz90a, Prz90c]. Ross termed his semantics the *strong well–founded semantics*, Baral et al. defined their semantics the *Generalized Disjunctive Well–Founded Semantics (GDWFS)*. They defined a fixpoint operator, and gave model and proof theoretic semantics for such *DDDBs*. Przymusinski [Prz90c] extends *stable model semantics* for normal *DDDBs*. He also defined in [Prz90a] the *stationary semantics*. As in the case of normal *DDBs* it will be necessary to develop effective bottom–up computing techniques to answer queries in these theories.

In addition, other important semantics have been developed. Przymusinski [Prz95] describes a new *semantic framework* for disjunctive logic programs and introduces the *static expansions* of disjunctive programs. The class of static expansions extends both the classes of stable, well–founded and stationary models of normal programs and the class of minimal models of disjunctive programs. Any static expansion of a program $\mathcal{P}$ provides the corresponding semantics for $\mathcal{P}$ consisting of the set of all sentences logically implied by the expansion. The stable model semantics has also been extended to disjunctive programs [GL91, Prz91]. Leone et al., [LRS96], develop an algorithm for solving the (co–$\mathcal{NP}$–hard decision) problem of checking if a model is stable. It runs in polynomial time (in the worst case) on the class of *head–cycle free programs* (discussed below), and in the case of general disjunctive logic programs limits the inefficient part of the computation only to components of the program which are not head–cycle free. Leone et al. [LRS95, LRS97] extend the notion of unfounded sets from normal to disjunctive logic programs and provide a declarative characterization of disjunctive stable models in terms of unfounded sets. They define an algorithm to compute stable model semantics of disjunctive logic programs. [BLR97] extend Disjunctive DATALOG to include integrity constraints and so–called weak constraints that are satisfied if possible.

Several types of *program transformations* have been used for characterizing existing semantics of DLPs and for defining new semantics based on existing ones. Brass and Dix [BD95a, BD99] have used *partial evaluation* and *program simplification* for defining and computing their *disjunctive well–founded semantics* D-WFS; this semantics is of interest as it permits a general approach to bottom–up computation in disjunctive programs. In addition, their transformation approach leads to several confluent calculi ([BD98]) which leads both to a better understanding ([BD97]) and an efficient computation of such semantics ([DFN99]). In [DS98] this approach was extended to first–order programs and coupled with constraint logic programming techniques. A restriction of the transformation approach to normal programs yields an implementation of the WFS which is provably better than the alternating fixpoint procedure and is linear for almost all programs occurring in practice ([BDFZ01]).

Seipel et al. [SMR97b] have characterized the partial stable models of a disjunctive logic program $\mathcal{P}$ as the stable models of a transformed disjunctive logic program $\mathcal{P}^{tu}$, which is called the tu–*transformation*. Fernández et al. [FLMS93] and Seipel [Sei97] have used the *evidential transformation* for characterizing *total stable models*, and *evidential stable models*, respectively. In [Sei00] a disjunctive logic program $\mathcal{P}$ is mapped to a normal logic program $\mathcal{P}^{cd}$ with function symbols for lists, such that the *total stable models* of $\mathcal{P}$ correspond to the stable models of $\mathcal{P}^{cd}$. Moreover, a new semantics for DLPs, which is called *stable state semantics*, is defined based on the stable models of a variant of $\mathcal{P}^{cd}$.

Eiter et al. [ELS97, ELS98] summarize results for partial stable models [Prz91]; maximum stable models (M–stable) which are the maximal partial stable models in the knowledge ordering [Sac96]; regular models of You and Yuan [YY94] which are similar in spirit to M–stable models, but based on a weaker concept[6]; and least undefined stable models (L–stable) [Sac96] which are the partial stable models with the minimal degree of undefinedness. In [YWY97], You et al. presented another semantics for DLPs, called regular extension semantics, for which a generalization of the abductive proof procedure of Eshghi and Kowalski [EK89] is used as a top–down method for query answering [YYG00].

Special Classes of DDDBs and Complexity Issues

As noted previously, there are semantics both for extended *DDBs* and extended *DDDBs*. A user of such a system has the problem of selecting the appropriate semantics for his needs. Which semantics should be used, and under what circumstances? There have been no guidelines developed. However, many complexity results have been obtained for these semantics. Schlipf [Sch95] and Eiter and Gottlob [EG95] summarize complexity results known for alternative semantics. Some of these results, taken from [EG93a, EG95], are listed in Table 1. Further results are reported in [ELS98]. A user may wish to determine the semantics to be used based upon the complexity expected to find answers to queries.

---

[6] For normal databases (without disjunctions), the M–stable models coincide with the regular models.

Ben–Eliyahu and Dechter [BED94] investigate tractable cases of disjunctive theories. They introduced the concept of a *head–cycle free (HCF)* program as follows. A *dependency graph* $G_\mathcal{P}$ is associated with each program $\mathcal{P}$ as follows:

- each rule and each predicate in $\mathcal{P}$ is a node.
- there is a positive (negative) arc from a predicate node p to a rule node r iff p appears positive (negative) in the body of r, and an arc from r to p (resp., and also an arc from p to r) if p appears in the head of r.

The *positive dependency graph* of $\mathcal{P}$ is a subgraph of $G_\mathcal{P}$ containing only positive arcs. A directed cycle in $G_\mathcal{P}$ is called *negative* if it contains at least one negative arc. $\mathcal{P}$ is *head–cycle free (HCF)* if for every two predicate symbols p and q, if p and q are on a positive directed cycle in the dependency graph $G_\mathcal{P}$ then there is no rule in $\mathcal{P}$ in which both p and q appear in the head. They show in [BEPZ96] that answers to queries expressed in this language can be computed in polynomial time. It is shown in [BEP94] that there is an algorithm that performs, in polynomial time, minimal model finding and minimal model checking if the theory is *HCF*. An efficient algorithm to solve the (co–$\mathcal{NP}$–hard) problem of checking if a model is stable in function–free disjunctive logic programs is developed in [LRS96]. The algorithm runs in polynomial time on *HCF* programs and in the case of general disjunctive logic programs, it limits the inefficient part of the computation only to the components of the program which are not *HCF*.

Dix et al. [DGM96] describe *causal* programs, where disjunction is simulated by negation–as–failure. Disjunctive programs are reduced to *stratified nondisjunctive* programs by a series of *shift operations*. They show *causal* semantics belongs to the first level of the polynomial hierarchy unlike minimal model semantics (GCWA), which is Π_2^P-complete for positive disjunctive programs. *Causal semantics* are also *cumulative* and *rational* (see [Dix95]). The class of *positive causal* programs extends the class of *positive HCF* programs [BED94].

Consideration has been given to approximate reasoning. In such reasoning, one may give up soundness or completeness of answers. Efforts have been developed both for deductive and disjunctive deductive databases by Selman and Kautz [SK91, KS92, SK96], who developed lower and upper bounds for Horn (DATALOG) databases and compilation methods, by Cadoli [Cad93], who developed computational and semantical approximations, and by del Val [deVa95], who developed techniques for approximating and compiling databases. See Cadoli [Cad96] for references on compilation, approximation and tractability of knowledge bases.

The complexity results in Table 2 refer to worst case analysis for skeptical reasoning, i.e. to determining if a given literal is *true* in every canonical model (with respect to a particular semantics) of the program. For logic programs with no function symbols, the data complexity over an EDB E is presented. The notation used is the following: $|\mathcal{P}|$ denotes the length of the program $\mathcal{P}$; $|\mathcal{A}|$ denotes the number of ground atoms in the language of $\mathcal{P}$; $|E|$ denotes the total number of symbols that occur in the *EDB E*.

Semantics	Propositional		First Order over Herbrand models		First Order no function symb. over Herbrand models	
	Complexity	Ref.	Complexity	Ref.	Data Complexity	Ref.
Positive Consequences						
Minimal Model	$\mathcal{O}(|\mathcal{P}|)$	[DG84], [IM82]	r.e.–complete	[Smu56], [AN78]	polynomial in $|E|$	[CH82]
Negation						
CWA	$\mathcal{O}(|\mathcal{P}|)$	[DG84], [IM82]	co–r.e.– complete	[Smu56], [AN78]	co–r.e.– complete	[CH82]
Stratified Programs						
Perfect	$\mathcal{O}(|\mathcal{P}|)$		complete arithmetic	[AB90]	polynomial in $|E|$	[CH85]
Locally Stratified Programs						
Perfect	$\mathcal{O}(|\mathcal{P}|)$		Δ_1^1–complete over ω	[BMS92]* ([Min99])	N/A	
Normal Programs						
2–valued completion	co–$\mathcal{NP}$– complete	[KP91]	Π_1^1–complete over ω	[KP91]	co–$\mathcal{NP}$– complete	[KP91]
3–valued completion	$\mathcal{O}(|\mathcal{P}|)$	folklore	Π_1^1–complete over ω	[Fit85]	polynomial in $|E|$	[Fit85]
Stable	co–$\mathcal{NP}$– complete	[MT91]	Π_1^1–complete over ω	[MNR92], [Sch90]	co–$\mathcal{NP}$– complete	[MT91]
Well– Founded	$\mathcal{O}(|\mathcal{A}||\mathcal{P}|)$	folklore	Π_1^1–complete over ω	[VaGe89], [Sch90]	polynomial in $|E|$	[VGRS91], [VaGe89]
Extended Programs						
Stable	co–$\mathcal{NP}$– complete	[MR94]	Π_1^1–complete over ω	[MR94]	co–$\mathcal{NP}$– complete	[MR94]
Well– Founded	$\mathcal{O}(|\mathcal{A}||\mathcal{P}|)$	[MR94]	Π_1^1–complete over ω	[MR94]	polynomial in $|E|$	[MR94]

Table 2. (Adapted from [Sch95]) Complexity of Cautious Reasoning with Horn Logic Programs

Properties of Semantics

A second way to determine the semantics to be used for an application is through their properties. Dix in [Dix92a] proposed criteria useful in determining the appropriate semantics to be used. He developed semantics both for normal *DDBs* [Dix95] and normal *DDDBs* [BD95b] that satisfy some of the properties that he describes. While some properties are adaptations and extensions to those developed by Kraus et al. [KLM90] to compare nonmonotonic theories, *relevance*, *partial evaluation* and *modularity* were newly developed.

A property an arbitrary semantics, *SEM*, might have is that its semantics should not be changed if a tautology is eliminated from its database. Table 3 summarizes other useful properties of semantics of *DDDBs* and specifies for alternative semantics the properties that they satisfy. This table is adapted from tables in [Dix95d, BD98, BD97]. Although complexity results and properties that a semantics satisfy are extremely useful, no generally accepted criteria exist as to why one semantics should be used over another. A semantics may have all the properties one may desire, be computationally tractable and yet not provide answers that a user expected. If for the normal logic program $\mathcal{P} = \{a \leftarrow not\ b,\ b \leftarrow not\ a,\ c \leftarrow a,\ c \leftarrow b\ \}$ of Section 3 the user expected an answer *yes* in response to a query "$\leftarrow c$", and the semantics were the *WFS*, the user would receive the answer *unknown*. However, if the *stable model semantics* had been used, the answer returned would be *yes*. Perhaps the best that can be expected is to provide users with complexity results and criteria so they may decide which semantics meets the needs of their problems.

Relationship to More General Forms of Nonmonotonic Reasoning

Understanding the semantics of disjunctive theories is related to nonmonotonic reasoning. The field of nonmonotonic reasoning has resulted in several alternative approaches to perform default reasoning [McCa80, Rei80, MD80, Moo84], [Moo85]. The articles [Min93, EG95, CS93] cite results where alternative theories of nonmonotonic reasoning can be mapped into extended disjunctive logic programs and databases. Hence, *DDDBs* may be used to compute answers to queries in such theories. In [BE98] priority information on extended logic programs and principles that an approach to handling priorities should satisfy are discussed. The expressive power of a query language over a disjunctive ground database is studied in [BE96]. They show there exist simple queries that cannot be expressed by any preferential semantics (including minimal model semantics and various forms of circumscription), while they can be expressed in default and autoepistemic logic. Default logic, autoepistemic logic and some of their fragments are shown to express the same class of Boolean queries, which turns out to be a strict subclass of the Σ_2^p-recognizable Boolean queries. They prove that under the assumption that the database consists of clauses whose length is bounded by some constant, default logic and autoepistemic logic express *all* of the Σ_2^p-recognizable Boolean queries, while preference–based logics cannot. Eiter and Gottlob [EG97] show that over the standard infinite Herbrand universe,

Property	Condition on a Semantics SEM to satisfy the Property						
	Clark's Compl.	GCWA	WGCWA	Perfect	Stable	WFS, D-WFS	Static
Elimination of Tautologies	If a rule $\alpha \leftarrow \beta \wedge not \cdot \gamma$ with $\alpha \cap \beta \neq \emptyset$ is eliminated from a program $\mathcal{P}$, then the resulting program is SEM–equivalent to $\mathcal{P}$.						
	No	Yes	No	Yes	Yes	Yes	Yes
Generalized Principle of Partial Evaluation (GPPE)	If a rule $\alpha \leftarrow \beta \wedge not \cdot \gamma$, where β contains an atom B, is replaced in a program $\mathcal{P}$ by the n rules $\alpha \cup (\alpha^i - \{B\}) \leftarrow ((\beta - \{B\}) \cup \beta^i) \wedge not \cdot (\gamma \cup \gamma^i)$, where $\alpha^i \leftarrow \beta^i \wedge not \cdot \gamma^i$ $(i = 1, \ldots, n)$ are all rules for which $B \in \alpha^i$, then the resulting program is SEM–equivalent to $\mathcal{P}$.						
	Yes	Yes	Yes	Yes	Yes	Yes	Yes
Positive and Negative Reduction	If (1) a rule $\alpha \leftarrow \beta \wedge not \cdot \gamma$ is replaced in a program $\mathcal{P}$ by $\alpha \leftarrow \beta \wedge not \cdot (\gamma - C)$ where C appears in no rule head, or (2) a rule $\alpha \leftarrow \beta \wedge not \cdot \gamma$ is deleted from $\mathcal{P}$ if there is a fact $\alpha' \leftarrow$ in $\mathcal{P}$ such that $\alpha' \subseteq \gamma$, then the resulting program is SEM–equivalent to $\mathcal{P}$.						
	Yes	N/A	N/A	Yes	Yes	Yes	Yes
Elimination of Non–Minimal Rules	If a rule $\alpha \leftarrow \beta \wedge not \cdot \gamma$ is deleted from a program $\mathcal{P}$ if there is another rule $\alpha' \leftarrow \beta' \wedge not \cdot \gamma'$ such that $\alpha' \subseteq \alpha$, $\beta' \subseteq \beta$, and $\gamma' \subseteq \gamma$, where at least one $\subseteq$ is proper, then the resulting program is SEM–equivalent to $\mathcal{P}$.						
	Yes	Yes	No	Yes	Yes	Yes	Yes
Consistency	$SEM(\mathcal{P}) \neq \emptyset$ for all disjunctive deductive databases $\mathcal{P}$.						
	No	Yes	Yes	Yes	No	Yes	Yes
Independence	For every literal L, L is true in every $M \in SEM(\mathcal{P})$ iff L is true in every $M \in SEM(\mathcal{P} \cup \mathcal{P}')$ provided that the language of $\mathcal{P}$ and $\mathcal{P}'$ are disjoint and L belongs to the language of $\mathcal{P}$.						
	No	Yes	Yes	Yes	No	Yes	Yes

Table 3. (Adapted from [Dix95a]* ([Min99])) Properties of the semantics of disjunctive deductive databases.

disjunctive logic programming and normal logic programming under the (cautious) stable model semantics coincide. See Cadoli and Lenzerini for complexity results concerning circumscription and closed world reasoning [Cad92, CL94]. See Yuan and You [YY93] for relationships between autoepistemic circumscription and logic programming. They use two different belief constraints to define two semantics, the *stable circumscriptive semantics* and *the well-founded circumscriptive semantics*, for autoepistemic theories. The work in [YY93] and on *static semantics* developed by Przymusinski [Prz95] appear to be related. As shown in [BDP96, BDNP98], these approaches, though differently defined, are also related to the D-WFS approach [BD95a, BD99]

DDDBs have also contributed to the *null value* problem. If an attribute of a relation may have a null value, where this value is part of a known set, then one can represent this as a disjunction of relations, where, in each disjunction a different value is given to the argument. For papers on the null value problem both in relational and *DDBs*, see [Cod79, GM86, Lip81, Rei86, Zan84] and [Vas79]* ([Min99]).

Extended–Disjunctive Deductive Databases

Gelfond and Lifschitz ([GL90, GL91]) pointed out the need for another form of negation next to default negation. They called called it *classical negation* and they extended stable model semantics to work with classical negation, i.e., they defined answer set semantics. Alferes, Pereira and Przymusinski ([APP98]) introduced two other definitions of negation, which they summarize as symmetric negations: *strong negation* and *explicit negation*. For logic programs with stable model semantics both coincide with classical negation. Symmetric negation can be used to provide natural solutions to various knowledge representation problems, such as theory and interpretation update, and belief revision. Minker and Ruiz ([MR94]) describe general techniques for extending semantics to extended–disjunctive logic programs, and they apply these techniques to stable models, disjunctive well–founded and stationary semantics. In [RM97, RM98] they study the semantics of extended–disjunctive logic programs that simultaneously contain multiple kinds of default negation.

Extensions of Disjunctive Logic Programming

There are several effective implementations of disjunctive logic programming systems, some of which will be described in more detail in Section 5. These systems will have to be enhanced to be able to handle more sophisticated applications. Several new concepts, introduced for deductive databases have to be extended and incorporated into disjunctive system implementations.

Extensions of disjunctive programs to more general belief programs are considered in [BDP96, BDNP98]. Buccafurri et al. extend Ordered Logic programming to disjunctive theories. They relate the work to knowledge base systems, show the language $\mathcal{DOL}$ *(Disjunctive Ordered Logic)* to be useful for diagnostic processes based on stepwise refinements and study the expressive power and complexity of $\mathcal{DOL}$. Buccafurri et al. [BLR97] also extended disjunctive logic programs by *weak constraints* and defined a semantics which tends to minimize the number of violated instances.

Practical applications of disjunctive logic programs often require the use of extended features like *aggregation operators*. In [Sei99] it has been shown how one can deal with aggregation in the presense of *recursion* and *disjunction*. A suitable, intuitive semantics is defined based on stable model semantics, which is applied to a special *program transformation*, which replaces an aggregation by a suitable construct using *default negation* and the function symbol for lists. Another approach for dealing with aggregation in normal logic programs based on the choice construct was given by [ZW99].

Kifer, Lausen, and Wu, cf. [KLW95] proposed *F–Logic* (Frame Logic) as a database language that accounts in a clean declarative fashion for many object–oriented features such as object identity, complex objects, inheritance, polymorphic types, methods, and encapsulation. F–Logic has a formal semantics and a sound and complete resolution–based proof procedure. Buccafurri, Faber, and Leone [BFL99] have proposed a new knowledge representation language $DLP^<$, which extends disjunctive logic programming with strong negation by inheritance.

5   Implementations of DLP–Systems

In this section we discuss four systems that are relevant to disjunctive logic programming: Smodels developed by Niemela and Simons [NS97], DLV developed by Eiter et al. [ELM+98], XSB developed by Warren et al. [RSS+97, War99], and DeReS developed by Marek and Truszczyński [CMT99].[7]

The system Smodels ([NS97]) was designed to handle range–restricted normal logic programs $\mathcal{P}$ without function symbols, where additionally every variable occurring in a rule must appear in a *domain literal* (i.e., a literal with a non–recursive predicate symbol). Smodels can compute the well–founded semantics as well as the stable model semantics. The inference algorithm for computing stable models is based on bottom–up backtracking search, where a powerful pruning method – related to the WFS – is employed. One of the advantages of Smodels is that it can be implemented to work in linear space. This makes it possible to apply the stable model semantics also in areas where the programs are highly non–stratified and can possess a large number of stable models. In [JNSY00] it is shown how Smodels can be used as a core engine for computing stable models of disjunctive logic programs without function symbols as well. Smodels has been tested using examples from the logic programming literature, combinatorial graph problems, circuit diagnosis, and propositional satisfiability.

---

[7] The systems XSB and DeReS are not disjunctive. However, they can simulate disjunctive systems by shifting all but one literal in the head of a disjunctive clause as negated literals to the body. If this is done for all literals in the head, the systems can partially simulate disjunctive approaches.

The DLV system of Eiter et al. ([ELM+98]) can handle range–restricted disjunctive deductive databases, i.e. disjunctive logic programs without function symbols. DLV takes a new approach to intractability. Instead of attempting to guarantee performance under restrictive assumptions, it relies on the fact that it is often easy to find solutions to instances of hard problem classes, and employs a so–called "guess and check" inference algorithm. The model generator (MG) of DLV exploits heuristic information to construct (guess) one candidate for a stable model at a time, which then is verified by the model checker (MC) against the given problem constraints. In the event that the constraints turn out not to be satisfied, another guess must be made. Considerable success was achieved with DLV in quickly solving NP–complete problems such as finding Hamiltonian paths. Other applications where DLV was applied are planning under incomplete knowledge ([EFLPP00]) and abductive diagnosis ([EFLP98]* ([Min99])). DLV appears to indicate that the effectiveness of "iterative sampling" approaches ([CMT99]) (following a single, possibly heuristically–guided "probe" through the search tree) discovered in the constraint satisfaction literature carries over to logic–based approaches such as disjunctive logic programming.

Both DLV and Smodels have been implemented in C++. They both use intelligent grounding modules which generate a subset $\mathcal{P}'$ of the grounded input program, such that $\mathcal{P}'$ is much smaller than $gnd(\mathcal{P})$ but has the same set of stable models.[8]. Also, both systems use a program simplification method that is based on the WFS for normal logic programs. For DLV, which works with disjunctive deductive databases, a generalization of the notion of unfounded sets, which is fundamental in WFS, is used ([LRS95, LRS96]). The algorithms for computing stable models are then applied to the grounded and simplified versions of the original programs.

The system XSB ([RSS+97]) can compute most cases of the WFS for normal logic programs with function symbols. The inference engine, which is called the SLG–WAM, consists of an efficient tabling engine for definite logic programs, which is extended by mechanisms for handling cycles through negation. These mechanisms are negative loop detection, delay and simplification. They serve for detecting, breaking and resolving cycles through negation. XSB is the only nonmonotonic reasoning system that is a fully–fledged PROLOG–system as well. XSB has been used in systems that contain large sets of rules and data.

The system DeReS ([CMT99]) supports basic automated reasoning tasks for default logic and for logic programming with the stable model semantics. It is shown that a normal logic program $\mathcal{P}$ can be represented by a suitable default theory $\mathcal{D}$, such that the stable models of $\mathcal{P}$ correspond to the so–called *extensions* of $\mathcal{D}$. DeReS uses *relaxed stratification* as a primary mechanism for pruning the search–space. A default theory $\mathcal{D}$ is partitioned into several smaller subtheories, called *strata*, and the extensions of $\mathcal{D}$ are constructed from the extensions of its strata. The approach taken by DeReS is somehow orthogonal to the one taken by Smodels, and it is argued in [CMT99] that next–generation implementations of nonmonotonic systems must combine techniques developed in both projects

---

[8] For Smodels, the intelligent grounding module is called lparse.

in order to be effective in a large range of different applications. DeReS has been tested extensively on the domain of *combinatorial problems*. A benchmarking environment called TheoryBase has been implemented, which can systematically generate parameterized families of default theories that encode graph problems taken from the Stanford GraphBase developed by Knuth.

Other systems that implement disjunctive semantics are the following: The system *near Horn* was implemented in PROLOG by a group headed by Loveland [Llo87, Lov87], [SL88, RL90, RLS91]. Seipel [Sei94] developed a system DIS-LOG that incorporates different disjunctive theories and strategies including the semantics introduced in [LMR92]; DISLOG tries to eliminate redundant computations by using a breadth–first approach. The system DISLOP, headed by Dix and Furbach [ADN97b], aims at extending the *restart model elimination* and *hyper tableau calculi* for DLPs under the D-WFS and stable semantics.

6   Applications

As discussed in Section 4, a problem with disjunctive theories is the complexity of the theory, in general. There was also a sense that there were few applications for disjunctive theories. This impression has changed during the past few years. Below, we discuss several applications that have arisen that require disjunctive theories: data integration, abductive reasoning, knowledge representation, diagnosis, and graph coloring.

6.1   Data Integration

An important part of data integration involves answering queries using various resources rather than by accessing database relations. The process of transforming a query from database relations to resources is often referred to as query folding. For instance, a database of interest to a user may be distributed over a network. It is necessary to bring data distributed over a network to a user's machine so that the data may be manipulated to answer user queries. In a distributed environment it is likely that one will want to save answers to queries in the local user's machine so that if the same or a related query is posed to the distributed database, one can look in the local machine's cached database for answers, rather than have to access data over the network to answer the query. In this situation the resources are the cached relations and the use of these resources is an important aspect of query optimization. In some data integration systems the database relations are themselves virtual and the data must be obtained from the resources. Resources may also be materialized views.

Several researchers have considered various aspects of this problem. Grant and Minker (see [GM00] for references) take a logic–based approach to the problem. We briefly sketch where disjunctions enter into seemingly relational and DATALOG databases. Consider a database that consists of an extensional database (EDB), an intensional database (IDB), a set of integrity constraints (ICs), and a set resources (Res$_{DB}$), where the resources have been obtained by using resource rules. These resources are referred to as materialized views. That is, they have been made explicit in a local computer as a result, for example, of an answer to a conjunctive query. The EDB, IDB, ICs are part of a conventional DATALOG database. A resource r may be defined by several Horn rules as, e.g.,

$$r(X, Y) \leftarrow p(X, Y),$$
$$r(X, Y) \leftarrow q(X, Y) \wedge s(X, Y).$$

Thus, the relation r has been obtained by retrievals from the relations p, q, and s. The assumption is made that these and only these definitions are how r has been formed. This is effectively an iff assumption, that is, r is defined as:

$$r(X, Y) \leftrightarrow (p(X, Y) \vee (q(X, Y) \wedge s(X, Y))).$$

This effectively is the *Clark completion axiom* for the resource r. This then yields the two rules,

$$p(X, Y) \vee q(X, Y) \leftarrow r(X, Y),$$
$$p(X, Y) \vee s(X, Y) \leftarrow r(X, Y).$$

Given the integrity constraint,

$$\leftarrow q(X, a) \wedge s(X, a)$$

the query, $\leftarrow p(X, a)$ can be answered by querying the resource $r(X, Y)$ with $\leftarrow r(X, a)$. Thus, in this instant if the s, p, and q relations are not local to the original query, but the resource r is local, answering the query may be done in an optimized manner.

6.2   Abductive Reasoning

The idea of performing abductive diagnosis based on disjunctive logic programming has been studied by several researchers, e.g. Sakama and Inoue [SaIn00] or Eiter et al. [EFLP98]* ([Min99]). An abductive diagnosis explains a set $\mathcal{O}$ of *observations* based on background knowledge and a set $\mathcal{H}$ of *hypotheses*. In [SaIn00] and [EFLP98]* ([Min99]) the background knowledge is given by an extended disjunctive logic program $\mathcal{P}$, and $\mathcal{H} \subseteq HL_\mathcal{P}$ is a set of ground literals. In [SaIn00], $\Pi = \langle \mathcal{P}, \mathcal{H} \rangle$ is called an abductive logic program, and the elements of $\mathcal{H}$ are called *abducibles*. In [EFLP98]* ([Min99]) an abductive diagnosis problem $\langle \mathcal{P}, \mathcal{H}, \mathcal{O} \rangle$ consists of an abductive logic program $\Pi = \langle \mathcal{P}, \mathcal{H} \rangle$ and a set $\mathcal{O} \subseteq HL_\mathcal{P}$ of ground literals, called *observations*. An *abductive diagnosis* is given by a set $\mathcal{H}' \subseteq \mathcal{H}$ of hypotheses, such that $\mathcal{P}' = \mathcal{P} \cup \mathcal{H}' \models \mathcal{O}$, where $\mathcal{P}' \models \mathcal{O}$, iff for some answer set S of $\mathcal{P}$ it holds $\mathcal{O} \subseteq S$. Then, $\mathcal{E} = S \cap \mathcal{H}$ is called an *explanation* in [SaIn00]. E.g. if the logic program $\mathcal{P}$ consists of the two rules

$$r_1 = wet\_grass \leftarrow rained,$$
$$r_2 = wet\_grass \leftarrow sprinkler\_on,$$

and $\mathcal{H} = \{\, rained,\ sprinkler\_on\,\}$, then the observation $\mathcal{O} = \{\, wet\_grass\,\}$ can be explained by $\mathcal{E} = \{\, rained\,\}$, since the answer set $S = \{\, wet\_grass,\ rained\,\}$ of $\mathcal{P} \cup \mathcal{E}$ contains $\mathcal{O}$. The abductive diagnosis $\mathcal{H}' = \mathcal{E} = \{\, rained\,\}$[9] is called a single–error diagnosis, since $|\mathcal{H}'| = 1$.

In [EFLP98]* ([Min99]) a simple transformation to extended–disjunctive logic programs is given which allows for computing explanations based on the answer set semantics of Gelfond and Lifschitz:

$$dlp(\Pi, \mathcal{O}) = \mathcal{P} \cup \{\, A \vee \epsilon_A \mid A \in \mathcal{H}\,\} \cup \{\, \leftarrow \neg o \mid o \in \mathcal{O}\,\} \cup \{\, \leftarrow o \mid \neg o \in \mathcal{O}\,\}.$$

If S is an answer set of $dlp(\Pi, \mathcal{O})$, then $\mathcal{E} = S \cap \mathcal{H}$ is an explanation. The disjunctive facts $A \vee \epsilon_A$ allow for assuming arbitrary hypotheses, and the denial rules enforce that all observations from $\mathcal{O}$ will hold in S.

Refinements for computing minimal abductive diagnoses or for computing abducibles that should be deleted from the logic program $\mathcal{P}$[10] have also been investigated.

Deduction Vs. Abduction. Abductive reasoning with normal logic programs can be done based on deduction with disjunctive logic programs, cf. Figure 4. Disjunction is introduced by *program completion* which turns normal rules into into disjunctive rules. From the normal rules $r_i = A \leftarrow \beta_i$ defining an atom A

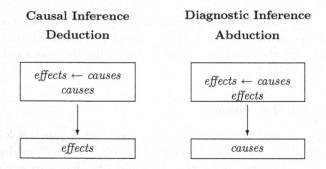

Fig. 4. Deduction vs. Abduction

we conclude the disjunctive rule $r = \beta_1 \vee \ldots \vee \beta_k \leftarrow A$ by program completion.[11] This diagnostic rule r allows one to deduce one of $\beta_1, \ldots, \beta_k$ as an abductive diagnosis (cause) for the observation (effect) A.

---

[9] Here it holds that $\mathcal{H}' = \mathcal{E}$, which need not be true in general.
[10] in addition to the set $\mathcal{H}'$ of abducibles that is added to $\mathcal{P}$
[11] If one of the β_i is a conjunction of more than one atom, then r is not a disjunctive rule of the form (1), but it can be normalized to an equivalent set of disjunctive rules by applying the distributivity law to $\beta_1 \vee \ldots \vee \beta_k$.

6.3 Knowledge Representation

As noted by Baral and Gelfond [BG94],

> Knowledge representation is one of the most important subareas of artifi-
> cial intelligence. If we want to design an entity (a machine or a program)
> capable of behaving intelligently in some environment then we need to
> supply this entity with sufficient knowledge about this environment. To
> do that, we need an unambiguous language capable of expressing this
> knowledge, together with some precise and well–understood way of ma-
> nipulating sets of sentences of the language which will draw inferences,
> answer queries and update both the knowledge base and the desired pro-
> gram behavior.

They note that McCarthy [McCa59] first proposed the use of *logical formulas*
as a basis of a knowledge representation language of this type. In their paper,
they provide many examples of the use of a logic programming formalism to
represent and manipulate knowledge. The following example is used in [Poo89] to
demonstrate the difficulties with representing disjunctive information in Reiter's
default logic. They note that the example has a natural representation in the
language of disjunctive logic programs.

> Normally, a person's left arm is usable, but a person with a broken left
> arm is an exception. and similarly for the right arm. Suppose also that
> we remember seeing Matt with a broken left arm or a broken right arm,
> but we do not remember which.

Baral and Gelfond show how to represent the information in the language of
disjunctive logic programs, where the predicate names are self–explanatory, except that $ab(X, Y)$ denotes that it is 'abnormal that person Y's arm is X'. They
represent the first statement as

$$lh\_usable(X) \leftarrow not\, ab(l, X)$$
$$ab(l, X) \leftarrow lh\_broken(X)$$
$$rh\_usable(x) \leftarrow not\, ab(r, X)$$
$$ab(r, X) \leftarrow rh\_broken(X).$$

The second statement is represented as

$$lh\_broken \lor rh\_broken(X).$$

They then represent the *closed world assumption* for the broken predicates by
the following two rules:

$$\neg lh\_broken(X) \leftarrow not\, lh\_broken(X)$$
$$\neg rh\_broken(X) \leftarrow not\, rh\_broken(X)$$

The last two rules state that if an arm is considered broken by default (*not*), then is is logically considered broken (¬). The disjunctive logic program consisting of the above seven rules has two answer sets:

$$\{ lh\_broken(matt),\ ab(l, matt), rh\_usable(matt),\ \neg rh_broken(matt) \},$$
$$\{ rh\_broken(matt),\ ab(r, matt),\ lh\_usable(matt),\ \neg lh\_broken(matt) \}$$

and therefore infers

$$rh\_usable(matt) \vee lh\_usable(matt)$$

which correspond to the intended specification.

Baral and Gelfond also show how the logical representation of knowledge can be used for more complicated examples.

6.4   Medical Diagnosis

As an example we will consider the following disjunctive deductive database for *medical diagnosis*, which deals with the pair of genes that determine a persons blood–group, cf. Figure 5. Every person has two genotypes, which may be identical. One is inherited from the mother, the other is inherited from the father.

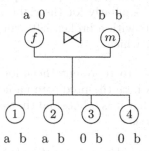

Fig. 5. Inheritance of Blood–Groups

A statement $genotype(P, T)$ means that the person P has the genotype T. The predicates *homozygot* and *heterozygot*, which are defined in the first three rules, below, tell if a person has two identical or two different genotypes, respectively. The rules r_4 and r_5 express that a person must have at least one of the genotypes "a", "b", or "o" and can have at most two different genotypes. r_5 is an integrity constraint, which forbids that a single person has three different genotypes: it has an empty rule head denoting a contradiction, which is derived in that situation. The rules r_6 and r_7 relate the genotype of a person to the genotypes of the parents. Finally, the *phenotype*, i.e. the person's actual blood–group, is a result of the two genotypes. According to the rule r_8 for *phenotype*, four different phenotypes are possible: "a", "b", "ab", and "o". The rules for determining phenotype "a" are given by r_9 and r_{10}.

$r_1 = heterozygot(P, T_1, T_2) \leftarrow$
$\qquad genotype(P, T_1) \wedge genotype(P, T_2) \wedge not\ equal(T_1, T_2).$

$r_2 = heterozygot(P) \leftarrow heterozygot(P, T_1, T_2).$

$r_3 = homozygot(P, T) \leftarrow genotype(P, T) \wedge not\ heterozygot(P).$

$r_4 = genotype(P, a) \vee genotype(P, b) \vee genotype(P, o) \leftarrow person(P).$

$r_5 = \ \leftarrow genotype(P, T_1) \wedge genotype(P, T_2) \wedge genotype(P, T_3) \wedge$
$\qquad not\ equal(T_1, T_2) \wedge not\ equal(T_1, T_3) \wedge not\ equal(T_2, T_3).$

$r_6 = genotype(Child, T_1) \vee genotype(Child, T_2) \leftarrow$
$\qquad parent(Child, Parent) \wedge heterozygot(Parent, T_1, T_2).$

$r_7 = genotype(Child, T) \leftarrow$
$\qquad parent(Child, Parent) \wedge homozygot(Parent, T).$

$r_8 = phenotype(P, a) \vee phenotype(P, b) \vee phenotype(P, ab) \vee$
$\qquad phenotype(P, o) \leftarrow person(P).$

$r_9 = phenotype(P, a) \leftarrow heterozygot(P, a, o).$

$r_{10} = phenotype(P, a) \leftarrow homozygot(P, a).$

Expanding the above rules to include those for phenotypes "b", "ab", "o", and a database of facts, one can then use the stable model semantics to compute answers to queries. This disjunctive logic program is non–stratified: *genotype* depends recursively on itself, and there is a negative dependency between *homozygot* and *heterozygot* involved in the recursion. Therefore it needs to be evaluated by stable model semantics or a semantics that handles default negation with recursion.

6.5   Graph Problems

Eiter et al. [EFLP00] have shown how complex graph problems can be encoded easily using disjunctive logic programming. A directed graph $G = \langle V, E \rangle$ is encoded using an unary predicate *node* for the set V of nodes and a binary predicate *edge* for the set E of edges.

In the following we will describe the problems of *3–colorability* and of *Hamiltonian paths*, which are classical NP–complete problems. Also other graph problems like independent sets and kernels in directed graphs or maximal independent sets and matchings in undirected graphs have been investigated using disjunctive logic programming.

3–Colorability. The problem is to color the edges of a directed graph $G = \langle V, E \rangle$ by three colors (say red, green and blue), such that adjacent nodes always have different colors.

$$g = color(X, red) \lor color(X, green) \lor color(X, blue) \leftarrow node(X),$$
$$c = \leftarrow edge(X, Y) \land color(X, C) \land color(Y, C).$$

In [EFLP00] this program is called a *guess&check* program: the rule g nondeterministically guesses color assignments for the nodes in the graph, and the integrity constraint c checks that these choices are legal, i.e. that no two nodes which are connected by an edge have the same color.

Hamiltonian Path. The problem is to find a path in a directed graph $G = \langle V, E \rangle$ starting at a distinguished node "a" and passing through each node in V exactly once.

$$g = in\_path(X, Y) \lor out\_path(X, Y) \leftarrow edge(X, Y),$$
$$a_1 = reached(a),$$
$$a_2 = reached(X) \leftarrow reached(Y) \land in\_path(Y, X),$$
$$c_1 = \leftarrow node(X) \land not\ reached(X),$$
$$c_2 = \leftarrow in\_path(X, Y) \land in\_path(X, Y') \land Y \neq Y',$$
$$c_3 = \leftarrow in\_path(X, Y) \land in\_path(X', Y) \land X \neq X'.$$

The rule g guesses a subset $E' \subseteq E$ of all given edges to be in the path. The auxiliary rules a_1 and a_2 compute all nodes that are reachable from the starting node "a" and the integrity constraint c_1 checks that there is no node that is not reachable from "a". Finally, the integrity constraints c_2 and c_3 check that there is no two edges in the path that start or end at the same node.

7   Summary and Assessment

During the almost 20 years of its history, the field of disjunctive logic programming and disjunctive deductive databases has made significant progress in the development of theories, implementation and applications. In the area of theory, two significant developments have taken place, the development of semantics, and the development of complexity results. In the area of implementation, we have seen several powerful systems developed: XSB, Smodels, DLV, and DeReS. In the area of applications, we have seen many new applications arise, when initially it was difficult to imagine realistic problems that would need disjunctive theories.

We believe that the following significant developments have taken place in the development of theories for disjunctive logic programming. For disjunctive theories, the work of Minker [Min82] on default negation and that of Minker and Rajasekar [MR90] laid the groundwork for further developments. They showed that a corresponding fixpoint theory for pure disjunctive theories, based on mapping disjuncts to disjuncts, generalized the van Emden/Kowalski fixpoint operator and led to the concept of a minimal state, where a state is a set of disjuncts. The least minimal state for disjunctive theories corresponds to the least minimal model of Horn theories. The work on stratified deductive theories by Przymusinski [Prz88] and by Rajasekar and Minker [RM90] extended the work to stratified theories. The work by Lifschitz and Gelfond who developed answer set semantics for disjunctive theories that include both default and logical negation is also important. This work generalizes the stable model semantics to disjunctive theories. The work by Brass, Dix and Przymusinski on "super logic programs" ([BDP96]) generalizes the well–founded semantics to the disjunctive case. It is clear that the two dominant semantics of logic and disjunctive logic programming are the well–founded and the stable model semantics and their generalizations. The work of Eiter and Gottlob in the development of complexity results is also a significant accomplishment. They show that disjunctive theories capture computationally hard problems that cannot be handled by extended logic programs. This makes it possible to implement extremely complex problems from the complexity class Σ_2^p, such as the *strategic companies* problem ([EFLP00])[12].

The most significant accomplishment in the past 5 years in logic programming and disjunctive logic programming has been the implementation of large scale systems which can handle thousands of rules. Since, as noted in Section 4, most nonmonotonic reasoning systems can be mapped to DLPs, one now has a mechanism to implement nonmonotonic systems. Those systems that have been implemented are: XSB, Smodels, DLV, and DeReS. Although XSB can handle only extended logic programs, it can modify disjunctive theories by writing, for example $a \vee b$ as two clauses, $a \leftarrow not\,b$ and $b \leftarrow not\,a$. In this case, it can obtain disjunctive answers by looking at the minimal models. XSB contains all of the features that are available in PROLOG and extends PROLOG to extended logic programs that can handle the stable model semantics and some aspects of the well–founded. Smodels handles stable model semantics. DLV is a disjunctive system and is being extended to handle large systems. DeReS implements default logic and is being extended for large systems. These systems make it possible to handle large application problems of substantial complexity.

There was a sense that disjunctive theories would not be needed for applications of interest. As noted in Section 6, several recent papers show that this need not be the case. In data integration problems, when one has a resource defined by multiple rules, to determine whether a query can be answered by resource rules only, reduces to a disjunctive set of clauses. As noted by Baral and Gelfond [BG94], large classes of knowledge base system applications are formulated using disjunctive clauses. Abductive reasoning, useful in diagnosis, reduces in many instances to handling disjunctive data. In addition, some problems in cognitive robotics need to be represented by disjunctive data. Many of the disjuncts can be disambiguated by testing sensors to determine the disjunctive condition that may apply, and hence reduce the planning problem to a Horn theory. Problems

---

[12] which is Σ_2^p–complete as a decision problem

that relate to nonmonotonic reasoning may be transformed to disjunctive logic programs, and hence, solved by the existing implementations. These applications show the relevance of disjunctive logic programming to real world problems.

The field of disjunctive logic programming has made large strides in the past several years so that there are now significant semantics available, implementations of large systems, and a wide range of practical applications that need such systems.

Tribute to Bob Kowalski

We are very pleased to have been invited to contribute a chapter in this collection to honor Bob Kowalski. The field of *logic programming* is deeply indebted to Bob's pioneering work. Bob made many contributions to logic programming. He provided the first formalization of logic programming in terms of Horn clauses, a computable subset of first–order logic. Bob's research provided the theoretical framework for logic programming: an inference mechanism and three different, but equivalent semantics (the semantics were developed with Maarten van Emden). His interaction with Alain Colmerauer during the development of PROLOG led to an efficient implementation and an effective inference mechanism. Kowalski's influential dictum "Algorithm = Logic + Control" provided fundamental direction for increasing clarity and scope in the description of algorithms. He showed the relevance of logic programming in legal reasoning, meta–level and commonsense reasoning, representation of temporal knowledge, verification of integrity constraints for databases and abductive reasoning for medical reasoning.

The first author of this paper, Jack Minker, was introduced to logic programming by listening to Bob Kowalski [Kow74] at the IFIP Congress in Stockholm, Sweden. As Minker stated in several papers, he was skeptical about its effectiveness to compete with conventional languages because of his experience with solving problems using a theorem prover. However, after reading Kowalski's paper and realizing that he was talking about a subset of clausal form, namely Horn clauses, he became convinced that logic programming was a viable way to do programming. It has been Minker's privilege to be both a friend and a colleague of Bob Kowalski.

The second author, Dietmar Seipel, started working with PROLOG in 1987 for implementing certain methods for query evaluation in deductive databases. The dual nature of PROLOG– as a declarative specification–style language (e.g. DATALOG for databases) and as a programming language – and the possibility of rapidly prototyping systems became very appealing to Seipel. In 1992 he became interested in disjunctive deductive databases and non–monotonic reasoning. At the ICLP'93 conference in Budapest for the first time he attended a lecture given by Bob Kowalski, and he was fascinated by the convincing style in which Bob Kowalski presented his ideas. At subsequent ICLP conferences Seipel was also able to get to know Bob Kowalski personally.

Abbreviations

AAAI: American Association for Artificial Intelligence
AMAI: Annals of Mathematics and Artificial Intelligence
CADE: International Conference on Automated Deduction
DOOD: Intl. Conf. on Deductive and Object–Oriented Databases
ICLP: International Conference on Logic Programming
ILPS: International Logic Programming Symposium
IJCAI: Intl. Joint Conf. on Artificial Intelligence
KR: Intl. Conf. on Principles of Knowledge Representation and Reasoning
LPNMR: Intl. Conf. on Logic Programming and Nonmonotonic Reasoning
PODS: ACM Symposium on Principles of Database Systems

References

[AB90]   K.R. Apt and H.A. Blair. Arithmetic classification of perfect models of
            stratified programs. *Fundamenta Informaticae*, XIII: pp. 1–18, 1990. With
            addendum in vol. XIV: pp. 339–343. 1991.

[AB94]   K.R. Apt and R.N. Bol. Logic programming and negation: a survey. *Jour-
            nal of Logic Programming*, 19/20: pp. 9–71, 1994.

[ABW88]   K.R. Apt, H.A. Blair, and A. Walker. Towards a theory of declarative
            knowledge. In [Min88b], pp. 89–148. 1988.

[ADN97b]   C. Aravindan, J. Dix, and I. Niemelä. DisLoP: Towards a Disjunctive
            Logic Programming System. Proc. LPNMR'97, Springer, LNAI 1265, pp.
            342–353, 1997.

[AN78]   H. Andreka and I. Nemeti. The generalized completeness of Horn predicate
            logic as a programming language. *Acta Cybernetica*, 4(1): pp. 3–10, 1978.

[APP98]   J.J. Alferes, L.M. Pereira, and T.C. Przymusinski. "Classical" negation
            in nonmonotonic reasoning and logic programming. *Journal of Automated
            Reasoning*, 20, pp. 107–142, 1998.

[Apt90]   K.R. Apt. Logic programming. In J. van Leeuwen, editor, *Handbook of
            Theoretical Computer Science*, pp. 493–574. Elsevier, 1990.

[AvE82]   K.R. Apt and M.H. van Emden. Contributions to the theory of logic
            programming. *Journal of the ACM*, 29(3): pp. 841–862, 1982.

[BD95a]   S. Brass and J. Dix. A general approach to bottom–up computation of dis-
            junctive semantics. In *Nonmonotonic Extensions of Logic Programming*.
            Springer, LNCS 927, pp. 127–155, 1995.

[BD95b]   S. Brass and J. Dix. Disjunctive semantics based upon partial and bottom–
            up evaluation. Proc. ICLP'95, pp. 199–213. MIT Press, 1995.

[BD97]   S. Brass and J. Dix. Characterizations of the disjunctive Stable semantics
            by partial evaluation. *J. of Logic Programming*, 32(3): pp. 207–228, 1997.

[BD98]   S. Brass and J. Dix. Characterizations of the disjunctive well-founded
            semantics: confluent calculi and iterated GCWA. *Journal of Automated
            Reasoning*, 20(1): pp. 143–165, 1998.

[BD99]   S. Brass and J. Dix. Semantics of (disjunctive) logic programs based on
            partial evaluation. *J. of Logic Prog.*, 38(3): pp. 167–213, 1999.

[BDNP01]   S. Brass, J. Dix, I. Niemelae, and T.C. Przymusinski: Comparison of the
            STATIC and the disjunctive well–founded semantics and their computa-
            tion. *Theoretical Computer Science*, 251, 2001.

[BDFZ01]   S. Brass, J. Dix, B. Freitag, and U. Zukowski. Transformation–based bottom–up computation of the well–founded model. *Theory and Practice of Logic Programming*, 1 (5), pp. 497–538, 2001.

[BDNP98]   S. Brass, J. Dix, I. Niemelae, and T.C. Przymusinski: A Comparison of the static and the disjunctive well–founded semantics and its implementation. Proc. KR'98, pp. 74–85. Morgan Kaufmann, 1998.

[BDP96]   S. Brass, J. Dix, and T.C. Przymusinski: Super logic programs. Proc. KR'96, pp. 529–541. Morgan Kaufmann, 1996.

[BE96]   P.A. Bonatti and T. Eiter. Querying disjunctive databases through non-monotonic logics. *Theoretical Computer Science*, 160: pp. 321–363, 1996.

[BE98]   G. Brewka and T. Eiter. Preferred answer sets for extended logic programs. *Journal of Artificial Intelligence* 109(1–2): pp. 297–356, 1999.

[BED94]   R. Ben–Eliyahu and R. Dichter. Propositional semantics for disjunctive logic programs. AMAI 12: pp. 53–87, 1994.

[BEP94]   R. Ben–Eliyahu and L. Palopoli. Reasoning with minimal models: efficient algorithms and applications. Proc. KR'94, pp. 39–50, 1994.

[BEPZ96]   R. Ben–Eliyahu, L. Palopoli, and V. Zemlyanker. The expressive power of tractable disjunction. In *Proc. of the 12th European Conference on Artificial Intelligence (ECAI'96)*, pp. 345–349, 1996.

[BFL99]   F. Buccafurri, W. Faber, and N. Leone. Disjunctive logic programs with inheritance. Proc. ICLP'99, pp. 79–93, 1999.

[BG94]   C. Baral and M. Gelfond. Logic programming and knowledge representation. *Journal of Logic Programming*, 19/20: pp. 73–148, 1994.

[BLR97]   F. Buccafurri, N. Leone, and P. Rullo. Strong and weak constraints in disjunctive datalog. Proc. LPNMR'97. Springer, LNAI 1265, pp. 2–17, 1997.

[BNNS94]   C. Bell, A. Nerode, R. Ng, and V.S. Subrahmanian. Mixed integer programming methods for computing nonmonotonic deductive databases. *Journal of the ACM*, 41(6): pp. 1178–1215, 1994.

[Bry90]   F. Bry. Query evaluation in deductive databases: bottom-up and top-down reconciled. Journal of Data & Knowledge Engineering, 5(4): pp. 289–312, 1990.

[Cad92]   M. Cadoli. The complexity for model checking for circumscriptive formulae. *Information Processing Letters*, 44: pp. 113–118, 1992.

[Cad93]   M. Cadoli. Semantical and computational aspects of Horn approximations. Proc. IJCAI'93, pp. 39–44, 1993.

[Cad96]   M. Cadoli. Panel on "Knowledge compilation and approximation": terminology, questions, references. In *Proc. of the 4th Int. Symp. on Artificial Intelligence and Math. (AI/Math'96)*, pp. 183–186, 1996.

[CH82]   A. Chandra and D. Harel. Structure and complexity of relational queries. *Journal of Computer System Sci.*, 25: pp. 99–128, 1982.

[CH85]   A. Chandra and D. Harel. Horn clause queries and generalizations. *J. of Logic Programming*, 2(1): pp. 1–15, 1985.

[Cha93]   E. Chan. A possible world semantics for disjunctive databases. *IEEE Trans. Data and Knowledge Eng.*, 5(2): pp. 282–292, 1993.

[CL94]   M. Cadoli and M. Lenzerini. The complexity of closed world reasoning and circumscription. *J. of Computer System Sciences*, 43: pp. 165–211, 1994.

[Cla78]   K. L. Clark. Negation as failure. In [GMN78], pp. 293–322. 1978.

[CMT99]   P. Cholewiński, A. Marek, V. W. Mikitiuk, and M. Truszczyński. Computing with default logic. *J. of Art. Intelli.*, 112(1–2): pp. 105–146, 1999.

[Cod79]   E.F. Codd. Extending the database relational model to capture more meaning. *ACM Transactions on Database Systems*, 4(4): pp. 397–434, 1979.

[CS90]   J. Chomicki and V.S. Subrahmanian. Generalized closed world assumption is π_2^0−complete. *Inf. Processing Letters*, 34: pp. 289–291, 1990.

[CS93]   M. Cadoli and M. Schaerf. A survey of complexity results for non–monotonic logics. *Journal of Logic Programming*, 13: pp. 127–160, 1993.

[CW93]   W. Chen and D.S. Warren. A goal–oriented approach to computing the well–founded semantics. *J. of Logic Progr.*, 17(2–4): pp. 279–300, 1993.

[Dec91]   H. Decker. On the declarative, operational and procedural semantics of disjunctive computational theories. In *Proc. of the Second Intl. Workshop on the Deductive Approach to Inf. Syst. and Databases (DAISD'91)*, 1991.

[DEGV97]   E. Dantsin, T. Eiter, G. Gottlob, and A. Voronkov. Complexity and expressive power of logic programming. In *Proc. of the 12th IEEE International Conference on Computational Complexity (CCC'97)*, pp. 82–101, 1997.

[DFN99]   J. Dix, U. Furbach, and I. Niemelä. Nonmonotonic reasoning: towards efficient calculi and implementations. In A. Voronkov and A. Robinson, editors, *Handbook of Automated Reasoning*. Elsevier–Science–Press, 1999.

[DG84]   W.F. Dowling and J.H. Gallier. Linear time algorithms for testing the satisfiability of propositional Horn formulae. *Journal of Logic Programming*, 1: pp. 267–284, 1984.

[DGM96]   J. Dix, G. Gottlob, and V. Marek. Reducing disjunctive to nondisjunctive semantics by shift operations. *Fundamenta Informaticae*, 28(1,2): pp. 87–100, 1996.

[Dix92a]   J. Dix. A framework for representing and characterizing semantics of logic programs. Proc. KR'92, pp. 591–602. Morgan Kaufmann, 1992.

[Dix95]   J. Dix. A classification–theory of semantics of normal logic programs: I. Strong properties and II. Weak properties. *Fund. Informaticae*, XXII(3): pp. 227–255 and 257–288, 1995.

[Dix95d]   J. Dix. Semantics of logic programs: their intuitions and formal properties. An overview. In A. Fuhrmann and H. Rott, editors, *Logic, Action and Information – Essays on Logic in Philosophy and Artificial Intelligence*, DeGruyter, pp. 241–327. 1995.

[DS98]   J. Dix and F. Stolzenburg. A framework to incorporate nonmonotonic reasoning into constraint logic programming. *Journal of Logic Programming*, 37(1,2,3): pp. 47—76, 1998.

[deVa95]   A. del Val. An analysis of approximate knowledge compilation. Proc. IJCAI'95, 1995.

[EFLP00]   T. Eiter, W. Faber, N. Leone, and G. Pfeifer. Declarative problem solving using the DLV system. In J. Minker, editor, Book on *Logic–Based Artificial Intelligence*, Kluwer, 2000.

[EFLPP00]   T. Eiter, W. Faber, N. Leone, G. Pfeifer, and A. Polleres. Planning under incomplete knowledge. in *Proc. of the First International Conference on Computational Logic (CL'2000)*, Springer, LNAI 1861, pp. 807–821, 2000.

[EG93a]   T. Eiter and G. Gottlob. Complexity aspects of various semantics for disjunctive databases. Proc. PODS'93, pp. 158–167. ACM Press, 1993.

[EG95]   T. Eiter and G. Gottlob. On the computation cost of disjunctive logic programming: Propositional case. AMAI 15(3-4): pp. 289–323, 1995.

[EG97]   T. Eiter and G. Gottlob. Expressiveness of stable model semantics for disjunctive logic programs with functions. *Journal of Logic Programming*, 33(2): pp. 167–178, 1997.

[EGM94]   T. Eiter, G. Gottlob, and H. Mannila. Adding disjunction to DATALOG. Proc. PODS'94, pp. 267–278, 1994.

[EK89]   K. Eshghi, R.A. Kowalski. Abduction compared with Negation by Failure. Proc. ICLP'89, pp. 234–254. MIT Press, 1989.

[ELM$^+$98] T. Eiter, N. Leone, C. Mateis, G. Pfeifer, and F. Scarcello. The kr system DLV: Progress report, comparisons, and benchmarks. Proc. KR'98, pp. 406–417, 1998.

[ELS97]   T. Eiter, N. Leone, and D. Saccà. On the partial semantics for disjunctive deductive databases. AMAI 19(1–2): pp. 59–96, 1997.

[ELS98]   T. Eiter, N. Leone, and D. Saccà. Expressive power and complexity of partial models for disjunctive deductive databases. *Theoretical Computer Science*, 206(1–2): pp. 181–218, 1998.

[FGM96]   J.A. Fernández, J. Grant, and J. Minker. Model theoretic approach to view updates in deductive databases. *Journal of Automated Reasoning*, 17(2): pp. 171–197, 1996.

[Fit85]   M. Fitting. A Kripke–Kleene semantics for logic programs. *Journal of Logic Programming*, 2: pp. 295–312, 1985.

[Fi91]   M. Fitting. Bilattices and the semantics of logic programs, *Journal of Logic Programming*, 11: pp. 91–116, 1991.

[FLMS93]   J.A. Fernández, J. Lobo, J. Minker, and V.S. Subrahmanian. Disjunctive LP + integrity constraints = stable model semantics. AMAI 8(3–4): pp. 449–474, 1993.

[FLP99]   W. Faber, N. Leone, and G. Pfeifer. Pushing goal derivation in DLP computations. Proc. LPNMR'97, Springer, LNAI 1265, pp. 177–191, 1997.

[FM91a]   J.A. Fernández and J. Minker. Computing perfect models of disjunctive stratified databases. In *ILPS'91 Workshop on Disjunctive Logic Programming*, 1991.

[FM91b]   J.A. Fernández, J. Minker. Bottom–up evaluation of hierarchical disjunctive deductive databases. Proc. ICLP'91, pp. 660–675. MIT Press, 1991.

[FM92]   J.A. Fernández and J. Minker. Semantics of disjunctive deductive databases. In *Proc. of the International Conference on Database Theory (ICDT'92)*, pp. 332–356, 1992. (Invited Paper).

[FM95]   J.A. Fernández and J. Minker. Bottom–up computation of perfect models for disjunctive theories. *J. of Logic Programming*, 25(1): pp. 33–51, 1995.

[GMN78]   H. Gallaire and J. Minker, editors, Logic and Data Bases, Plenum Press, New York, 1978.

[GHLM93]   J. Grant, J. Horty, J. Lobo, and J. Minker. View updates in stratified disjunctive databases. *J. Automated Reasoning*, 11: pp. 249–267, 1993.

[Gin87]   M.L. Ginsberg, editor. *Readings in Nonmonotonic Reasoning*. Morgan Kaufmann, 1987.

[GL88]   M. Gelfond and V. Lifschitz. The stable model semantics for logic programming. In *Proc. of the 5th Intl. Conf. and Symp. on Logic Programming*, pp. 1070–1080, MIT Press, 1988.

[GL90]   M. Gelfond and V. Lifschitz. Logic programs with classical negation. Proc. ICLP'90, pp. 579–597, MIT Press, 1990.

[GL91]   M. Gelfond and V. Lifschitz. Classical negation in logic programs and disjunctive databases. *New Generation Computing*, 9: pp. 365–385, 1991.

[GM86]   J. Grant and J. Minker. Answering queries in indefinite databases and
            the null value problem. In P. Kanellakis, editor, *Advances in Computing
            Research: The Theory of Databases*, pp. 247–267. 1986.

[GM00]   J. Grant and J. Minker. A logic–based approach to data integration. 2000.
            Submitted for publication.

[GPP86]   M. Gelfond, H. Przymusinska, and T.C. Przymusinski. The extended
            closed world assumption and its relation to parallel circumscription. Proc.
            PODS'86, pp. 133–139, 1986.

[Gre98]   S. Greco. Binding propagation in disjunctive databases. In *Proc. of the
            Intl. Conf. on Very Large Databases (VLDB'98)*, pp. 287–298, 1998.

[Gre99]   S. Greco. Optimization of disjunctive queries. Proc. ICLP'99, pp. 441–455,
            1999.

[Gre99b]   S. Greco. Minimal founded semantics for disjunctive logic programming.
            Proc. LPNMR'99, Springer, LNAI 1730, pp. 221–235, 1999.

[HeWa97]   H. Herre and G. Wagner. Stable models are generated by a stable chain.
            Journal of Logic Programming, 30(2): pp. 165–177, 1997.

[Hil74]   R. Hill. Lush resolution and its completeness. Technical Report DCL
            Memo 78, Department of Artificial Intelligence, Univ. of Edinburgh, 1974.

[HIOK97]   R. Hasegawa, K. Inoue, Y. Ohta, and M. Koshimura. Non–Horn magic
            sets to incorporate top–down inference into bottom–up theorem proving.
            Proc. CADE'97, pp. 176–190, 1997.

[IM82]   A. Itai and J.A. Makowsky. On the complexity of Herbrand's theorem.
            Technical report, Dept. of Computer Science, Israel Institute of Technol-
            ogy, Haifa, 1982.

[Imi91]   T. Imielinski. Incomplete deductive databases. AMAI 3: pp. 259–293,
            1991.

[IS93]   K. Inoue and C. Sakama. Transforming abductive logic programs to dis-
            junctive programs. Proc. ICLP'93, pp. 335–353, 1993.

[IV89]   T. Imielinski and K. Vadaparty. Complexity of query processing in
            databases with OR–objects. Proc. PODS'89, pp. 51–65, 1989.

[JLL83]   J. Jaffar, J.-L. Lassez, and J.W. Lloyd. Completeness of the Negation as
            Failure rule. Proc. IJCAI'83, pp. 500–506, 1983.

[JNSY00]   T. Janhunen, I. Niemelä, P. Simons, and J.-H. You: Unfolding partial-
            ity and disjunctions in stable model semantics. Proc. KR'2000, Morgan
            Kaufmann, 2000.

[KLM90]   S. Kraus, D. Lehmann, and M. Magidor. Nonmonotonic reasoning, pref-
            erential models and cumulative logics. *Journal of Artificial Intelligence*,
            44(1): pp. 167–207, 1990.

[KLW95]   M. Kifer, G. Lausen, and J. Wu. Logical foundations of object–oriented
            and frame–based languages. *J. of the ACM*, 42(4), pp. 741–843, 1995.

[Kow74]   R.A. Kowalski. Predicate logic as a programming language. *Proc. of IFIP
            4*, pp. 569–574, 1974.

[Kow78]   R.A. Kowalski. Logic for data description. In [GMN78], pp. 77–102. 1978.

[Kow88]   R.A. Kowalski. The early years of logic programming. *Communications
            of the ACM*, 31(1): pp. 38–43, 1988.

[KP91]   P. Kolaitis and C. Papadimitriou. Why not negation by fixpoint? *Journal
            of Computer and System Sciences*, 43: pp. 125, 1991.

[KS92]   H.A. Kautz and B. Selman. Forming concepts for fast inference. Proc.
            AAAI'92, pp. 786–793, 1992.

[Lip81]   W. Lipski. On databases with incomplete information. volume 28, pp.
            41–70. ACM, New York, 1981.

[Llo87]   J.W. Lloyd. *Foundations of Logic Programming*. Springer, 2nd ed., 1987.

[LM84]   J.-L. Lassez and M.J. Maher. Closure and fairness in the semantics of programming logic. *Theoretical Computer Science*, 29: pp. 167–184, 1984.

[LMR92]   J. Lobo, J. Minker, and A. Rajasekar. *Foundations of Disjunctive Logic Programming*. MIT Press, 1992.

[Lov87]   D.W. Loveland. Near–Horn PROLOG. Proc. ICLP'87, pp. 456–459, 1987.

[LRS95]   N. Leone, P. Rullo, F. Scarcello. Declarative and fixpoint characterizations of disjunctive stable models. Proc. ILPS'95, pp. 399–413. MIT Press, 1995.

[LRS96]   N. Leone, P. Rullo, and F. Scarcello. Stable model checking for disjunctive programs. In *Prof. of Logic in Databases (LID'96)*, pp. 281–294, 1996.

[LRS97]   N. Leone, P. Rullo, and F. Scarcello. Disjunctive stable models: Unfounded sets, fixpoint semantics and computation. *Information and Computation*, 135: pp. 69–112, 1997.

[LRW93]   D. Loveland, D. Reed, and D. Wilson. Satchmore: Satchmo with relevancy. Technical report, Duke Univ., Durham, North Carolina, USA, 1993.

[LS90b]   K.-C. Liu and R. Sunderraman. On representing indefinite and maybe information in relational databases: A generalization. *Proc. of IEEE Data Engineering*, pp. 495–502, 1990.

[MB88]   R. Manthey and F. Bry. Satchmo: A theorem prover implemented in PROLOG. Proc. CADE'88, 1988.

[McCa59]   J. McCarthy. Programs with common sense. In *Proc. Teddington Conf. on the Mechanisation of Thought Processes*, pp. 75–91, London, 1959. Her Majesty's Stationery Office.

[McCa80]   J. McCarthy. Circumscription – a form of non–monotonic reasoning. *Journal of Artificial Intelligence*, 13(1,2): pp. 27–39, 1980.

[MD80]   D. McDermott and J. Doyle. Non–monotonic logic I. *Journal of Artificial Intelligence*, 13: pp. 41–72, 1980.

[Min82]   J. Minker. On indefinite databases and the closed world assumption. Proc. CADE'82, Also in: Springer, LNCS 138, pp. 292–308, 1982.

[Min88a]   J. Minker. Perspectives in deductive databases. *Journal of Logic Programming*, 5: pp. 33–60, 1988.

[Min88b]   J. Minker, editor. *Foundations of Deductive Databases and Logic Programming*. Morgan Kaufmann, 1988.

[Min89]   J. Minker. Toward a foundation of disjunctive logic programming. In *Proc. of the North American Conference on Logic Programming*, pp. 121–125. MIT Press, 1989. Invited Banquet Address.

[Min93]   J. Minker. An overview of nonmonotonic reasoning and logic programming. *Journal of Logic Programming*, 17(2, 3 and 4): pp. 95–126, 1993.

[Min94]   J. Minker. Overview of disjunctive logic programming. *Journal of Artificial Intelligence & Mathematics*, 12(1-2): pp. 1–24, 1994.

[Min99]   J. Minker. Logic and databases: a 20 year retrospective - updated in honor of Ray Reiter. In H.J. Levesque and F. Pirri, editors, *Logical Foundations for Cognitive Agents: Contributions in Honor of Ray Reiter*, pp. 234–299. Springer, 1999.

[MNR92]   V.W. Marek, A. Nerode, and J.B. Remmel. The stable models of a predicate logic program. In *Proc. of the Joint Intl. Conf. and Symposium on Logic Programming (JICSLP'92)*, pp. 446–460, MIT Press, 1992.

[Moo84]   R.C. Moore. Possible–world semantics for autoepistemic logic. In *Proc. of AAAI Workshop on Non–Mon. Reasoning*, pp. 396–401, New Paltz, 1984.

[Moo85]   R.C. Moore. Semantical considerations on nonmonotonic logic. *Journal of Artificial Intelligence*, 25(1): pp. 75–94, 1985.

[MR90]   J. Minker and A. Rajasekar. A fixpoint semantics for disjunctive logic
            programs. *Journal of Logic Programming*, 9(1): pp. 45–74, 1990.
[MR94]   J. Minker and C. Ruiz. Semantics for disjunctive logic programs with
            explicit and default negation. *Fundamenta Informaticae*, 20(3/4): pp. 145–
            192, 1994. Anniversary Issue edited by H. Rasiowa.
[MT91]   V.W. Marek and M. Truszczyński. Autoepistemic logic. *Journal of the
            ACM*, 38(3): pp. 588–619, 1991.
[MT93]   V.W. Marek and M. Truszczyński. *Nonmonotonic logic: Context–
            dependent reasoning.* Springer, 1993.
[NS97]   I. Niemela and P. Simons. Smodels – an implementation of the stable model
            and well–founded semantics for normal logic programs. Proc. LPNMR'97.
            Springer, LNAI 1265, pp. 420–429, 1997.
[OIH98]   Y. Ohta, K. Inoue, R. Hasegawa. On the relationship between non–horn
            magic sets and relevancy testing. Proc. CADE'98, pp. 333–348, 1998.
[Poo89]   D. Poole. What the lottery paradox tells us about default reasoning. Proc.
            KR'89, pp. 333–340, 1989.
[Prz88]   T.C. Przymusinski. On the declarative semantics of deductive databases
            and logic programming. In [Min88b], Chapter 5, pp. 193–216. 1988.
[Prz89]   T.C. Przymusinski. On the declarative and procedural semantics of logic
            programs. *Journal of Automated Reasoning*, 5: pp. 167–205, 1989.
[Prz90a]   T.C. Przymusinski. Stationary semantics for disjunctive logic programs
            and deductive databases. In *Proc. of the North Amer. Conf. on Logic
            Programming*, pp. 40–62, 1990.
[Prz90c]   T.C. Przymusinski. Extended stable semantics for normal and disjunctive
            programs. Proc. ICLP'90, pp. 459–477, MIT Press, 1990.
[Prz91]   T.C. Przymusinski. Stable semantics for disjunctive programs. *New Gen-
            eration Computing*, 9: pp. 401–424, 1991.
[Prz95]   T.C. Przymusinski. Static semantics for normal and disjunctive logic pro-
            grams. AMAI 14 (Festschrift in honor of Jack Minker): pp. 323–357, 1995.
[Rei78]   R. Reiter. On closed world data bases. In [GMN78], pp. 55–76. 1978.
[Rei80]   R. Reiter. A logic for default reasoning. *Journal of Artificial Intelligence*,
            13: pp. 81–132, 1980.
[Rei86]   R. Reiter. A sound and sometimes complete query evaluation algorithm
            for relational databases with null values. *J. ACM*, 33(2): pp. 349–370,
            1986.
[Rei87]   R. Reiter. Nonmonotonic reasoning. *Annual Reviews of Comp. Sci.*, 1987.
[RL90]   David W. Reed and Donald W. Loveland. A comparison of three PROLOG
            extensions. *Journal of Logic Programming*, 12(1&2): pp. 25–50, 1992.
[RLM89]   A. Rajasekar, J. Lobo, and J. Minker. Weak generalized closed world
            assumption. *Journal of Automated Reasonig*, 5(3): pp. 293–307, 1989.
[RLS91]   D.W. Reed, D.W. Loveland, and B.T. Smith. An alternative characteri-
            zation of disjunctive logic programs. In *Proc. of the Intl. Symposium on
            Logic Programming (ISLP'91)*, pp. 54–68, MIT Press, 1991.
[RM90]   A. Rajasekar and J. Minker. On stratified disjunctive programs. AMAI
            1(1–4): pp. 339–357, 1990.
[RM97]   C. Ruiz and J. Minker. Combining closed world assumptions with stable
            negation. *Fundamenta Informaticae*, 32(2): pp. 163–181, 1997.
[RM98]   C. Ruiz and J. Minker. Logic knowledge bases with two default rules.
            AMAI 22(3-4): pp. 333–361, 1998.
[Ros89]   K. Ross. Well–founded semantics for disjunctive logic programs. Proc.
            DOOD'89, pp. 352–369, 1989.

[RSS+97]   P. Rao, K. Sagonas, T. Swift, D.S. Warren, and J. Friere. XSB: A system for efficiently computing well–founded semantics. Proc. LPNMR'97. Springer, LNAI 1265, pp. 430–440, 1997.

[RT88]   K.A. Ross and R.W. Topor. Inferring negative information from disjunctive databases. *J. of Automated Reasoning*, 4(2): pp. 397–424, 1988.

[Sac96]   D. Saccà. The expressive power of stable models for bound and unbound DATALOG queries. *J. of Comp. and System Sci.*, 54(3): pp. 441–464, 1997.

[SaIn00]   C. Sakama and K. Inoue. Abductive logic programming and disjunctive logic programming: their relationship and transferability, *Journal of Logic Programming*, 44(1–3): pp. 75–100, 2000.

[Sak89]   C. Sakama. Possible model semantics for disjunctive databases. Proc. DOOD'89, pp. 337–351, 1989.

[Sch90]   L. Schubert. Monotonic solution of the frame problem in the situation calculus: an efficient method for worlds with fully specified actions. In H.E. Kyburg, R. Loui, and G. Carlson, editors, *Knowledge Representation and Defeasible Reasoning*, pp. 23–67. Kluwer, 1990.

[Sch95]   J.S. Schlipf. Complexity and undecideability results for logic programming. AMAI 15(3-4): pp. 257–288, 1995.

[Sei94]   D. Seipel. An efficient computation of the extended generalized closed world assumption by support–for–negation sets. In *Proc. of the International Conference on Logic Programming and Automated Reasoning (LPAR'94)*, Springer, LNAI 822, pp. 245–259, 1994.

[Sei97]   D. Seipel. Partial evidential stable models for disjunctive deductive databases. In *Proc. of the Workshop on Logic Prog. and Knowledge Representation LPKR'97 at ILPS'97*, Springer, LNAI 1471, pp. 66–84, 1998.

[Sei99]   D. Seipel. Aggregation in disjunctive deductive databases. In *International Conference on Applications of* PROLOG *(INAP'99)*, 1999.

[Sei00]   D. Seipel. Clausal deductive databases and a general framework for semantics in disjunctive deductive databases. In *Proc. of the International Symposium on Foundations of Information and Knowledge Systems (FoIKS'2000)*, Springer, LNCS 1762, pp. 241–259, 2000.

[She88]   J.C. Shepherdson. Negation in logic prog. In [Min88b], pp. 19–88. 1988.

[SK91]   B. Selman and H.A. Kautz. Knowledge compilation using Horn approximations. Proc. AAAI'91, pp. 904–909, 1991.

[SK96]   B. Selman and H.A. Kautz. Knowledge compilation and theory approximation. *Journal of the ACM*, 43(2): pp. 193–224, 1996.

[SMR97]   D. Seipel, J. Minker, and C. Ruiz. Model generation and state generation for disjunctive logic programs, *J. of Logic Prog.*, 32(1): pp. 48–69, 1997.

[SMR97b]   D. Seipel, J. Minker, and C. Ruiz. A characterization of partial stable models for disjunctive deductive databases, Proc. ILPS'97, pp. 245–259, MIT Press, 1997.

[SL88]   B.T. Smith and D. Loveland. A simple near–Horn PROLOG interpreter. In *Proc. of the 5th Intl. Conf. and Symp. on Logic Progr.*, pp. 794–809, 1988.

[Smu56]   R.M. Smullyan. *Bull, AMS62*, 1956. page 600: Elementary formal system (abstract). page 601: On definability by recursion (abstract).

[SS86]   L.S. Sterling and E.Y. Shapiro. *The Art of* PROLOG. MIT Press, 1986.

[Sti88]   M. Stickel. A PROLOG technology theorem prover: Implementation by an extended PROLOG compiler. *J. of Aut. Reas.*, 4(4): pp. 353–380, 1988.

[Var82]   M.Y. Vardi. The complexity of relational query languages. In *Proc. of the 14th ACM Symp. on Theory of Comp. (STOC'82)*, pp. 137–146, 1982.

[vEK76]   M.H. van Emden and R.A. Kowalski. The semantics of predicate logic as a programming language. *J. of the ACM*, 23(4): pp. 733–742, 1976.

[VaGe88] A. Van Gelder. Negation as Failure using tight derivations for general logic programs. In [Min88b], pp. 1149–176. 1988.

[VaGe89] A. Van Gelder. The alternating fixpoint of logic programs with negation. Proc. PODS'89, pp. 1–10, 1989.

[VGRS91] A. Van Gelder, K.A. Ross, and J.S. Schlipf. The well–founded semantics for general logic programs. *J. of the ACM*, 38(3): pp. 620–650, 1991.

[War99]   D.S. Warren, et al. The XSB programming system. Technical report, State University of New York at Stony Brook, 1999. http://www.cs. sunysb.edu/ sbprolog/xsb-page.html.

[WB93]   C. Witteveen and G. Brewka. Skeptical reason maintenance and belief revision, *Journal of Artificial Intelligence*, 61, pp. 1–36, 1993.

[WVH97]   C. Witteveen and W. van der Hoek. A general framework for revising nonmonotonic theories, Proc. LPNMR'97, Springer, LNAI 1265, pp. 258–272, 1997.

[Yah97]   A.H. Yahya. Generalized query answering in disjunctive deductive databases: Procedural and nonmonotonic aspects. Proc. LPNMR'97. Springer, LNAI 1265, pp. 325–341, 1997.

[Yah00]   A.H. Yahya: Minimal model generation for refined answering of generalized queries in disjunctive deductive databases. *Journal of Data and Knowledge Engineering*, 34(3), pp. 219–249, 2000.

[YC89]   L.Y. Yuan and D.-A. Chiang. A sound and complete query evaluation algorithm for relational databases with disjunctive information. Proc. PODS'89, pp. 66–74. ACM Press, 1989.

[YH85]   A. Yahya and L.J. Henschen. Deduction in non–Horn databases. *Journal of Automated Reasoning*, 1(2): pp. 141–160, 1985.

[YY93]   L.Y. Yuan and J.-H. You. Autoepistemic circumscription and logic programming. *Journal of Automated Reasoning*, 10: pp. 143–160, 1993.

[YY94]   J.-H. You and L.Y. Yuan. A three–valued semantics for deductive databases and logic programs. *J. of Comp. and System Sci.*, 49: pp. 334–361, 1994.

[YYG00]   J.-H. You, L.Y. Yuan, and R. Goebel. An abductive approach to disjunctive logic programming. *J. of Logic Programming*, 44(1–3): pp. 101–128, 2000.

[YWY97]   J.-H. You, X. Wang, and L.Y. Yuan. Disjunctive logic programming as constrained inferences. Proc. ICLP'97, pp. 361–375, 1997.

[Zan84]   C. Zaniolo. Database relations with null values. *Journal of Computer and System Sciences*, 28: pp. 142–166, 1984.

[ZBF97]   U. Zukowski, S. Brass, and B. Freitag. Improving the alternating fixpoint: The transformation approach, Proc. LPNMR'97, Springer, LNAI 1265, pp. 40–59, 1997.

[ZF99]   U. Zukowski and B. Freitag. Well–founded semantics by transformation: The non–ground case, Proc. ICLP'99, pp. 456–470, 1999.

[ZW99]   C. Zaniolo and H. Wang: Logic–based user–defined aggregates for the next generation of database systems. In K.R. Apt, V.W. Marek, M. Truszczyński, and D.S. Warren, editors, *The Logic Prog. Paradigm: Current Trends and Future Directions*, Springer, pp. 401–426, 1999.

Constraint Logic Programming

Mark Wallace

IC-Parc, William Penney Laboratory, Imperial College, London SW7 2AZ
mgw@icparc.ic.ac.uk

Abstract. Constraint Logic Programming (CLP) extends logic programming in two ways. Firstly it admits special predicates called constraints, which are not defined by clauses, but which are handled instead by specific constraint solvers built into the CLP system. This extension has been formalised as the CLP Scheme. Secondly CLP admits other forms of processing than backwards reasoning by unfolding, in particular constraint propagation. This extension has been formalised in terms of Information Systems. These two extensions are now widely applied in industry, in particular to large scale combinatorial optimisation problems. The success of CLP has inspired a great deal of ongoing research into algorithms (especially hybrid and incremental), languages and applications.

1 Introduction

Constraint Logic Programming (CLP) is no more and no less than logic programming. Constraints are formally relations, and an answer to a query is a constraint that entails it. Constraints as answers were already proposed by Kowalski in [41]. Taking this proposition to its logical conclusion, the chapter would have to end here.

In the tradition of modern politics, let me therefore clarify the proposition, and, in so doing, change it. The meaning of Logic Programming (LP) has been summarised by Kowalski et.al [42] in the following paragraph:

> Ordinary LP solves problems by representing problem-solving procedures by means of clauses of the form
>
> $$H \leftarrow L_1 \wedge \ldots \wedge L_m$$
>
> with $m \geq 0$, H and atom and each L_i a literal. Variables in H and L_i are implicitly universally quantified with scope the entire clause. H is called the *head* and $L_1 \wedge \ldots \wedge L_m$ is called the *body* of the clause. Clauses of this form are used backwards to unfold atoms in goals (existentially quantified conjunctions of literals). Negation is interpreted as negation as failure [16].

This restricted view of logic programming excludes built-in predicates, and only admits query evaluation by unfolding. CLP extends this view of LP in

A.C. Kakas, F. Sadri (Eds.): Computat. Logic (Kowalski Festschrift), LNAI 2407, pp. 512–532, 2002.

two ways. Firstly it admits special predicates called *constraints* which are not defined by clauses, and which cannot therefore be processed by unfolding. These constraints are handled by specific *constraint solvers* built into the CLP system.

Secondly CLP admits other forms of processing than backwards reasoning by unfolding. Indeed the specification of constraint solvers and the interaction between different constraint solvers are important aspects of CLP.

1.1 Constraint Domains

CLP incorporates constraints and constraint solvers into LP. We can make the = constraint explicit in LP by introducing equations $T_1 = T_2$ into each clause in order to reduce the arguments in the head to distinct variables. Thus the clause

$$p(a, X, Y, X) \leftarrow q(X, Y)$$

is mapped to:[1]

$$p(A, B, C, D) \leftarrow A = a, B = D, q(B, C)$$

The resulting program includes the single constraint =, whose built-in solver is unification.

CLP results from LP by allowing other constraints than just = to be handled by a built-in solver. The first extension was to handle both = and $\neq$ [17]. This was soon followed by $CLP(\mathcal{R})$ [38] which handled =, $\geq$ and $\leq$. The novel aspect of $CLP(\mathcal{R})$ was that the interpretation of the terms inside the constraint atoms was dictated by the constraints. For example in $CLP(\mathcal{R})$ $3 = 2 + 1$ succeeded, whilst it failed in a traditional LP system where = was handled by unification.

This apparent contradiction was explained in terms of *constraint domains*. In predicate logic the meaning of a formula is captured in terms of an underlying domain of interpretation. Each function and relation in the formula is interpreted as a function and relation respectively over the underlying domain.

In $CLP(\mathcal{R})$ the underlying domain was intuitively taken to be the real numbers, where $3 = 2 + 1$ is true. Whereas LP assumes an underlying Herbrand domain in which $3 = 2 + 1$ is false.

In the mid 1980s it was observed that all the main results for LP - logical semantics, fixed point semantics, soundness and completeness of top-down execution under appropriate restrictions - carried over directly to CLP, as long as the constraints and their solver satisfied certain very intuitive requirements. Thus a whole CLP "Scheme" was introduced, which captured all the CLP languages described above [37].

The main results for the semantics of logic programming over the Herbrand universe all carry over to the CLP Scheme, as summarised in section 3.3 below. Once the necessary properties of the constraints and their solver have been established, the proofs of the results for CLP are simpler than the standard

---

[1] In this paper we shall use a comma rather than a $\wedge$ between literals in the body of a clause.

proofs for logic programming over the Herbrand universe. Thus the CLP Scheme has helped us to understand logic programming better, and also to generalise it in a natural and powerful way. The scheme is described in more detail in section 3 below.

In summary, the CLP Scheme represents problems in terms of clauses, just like LP does. It handles clauses by unfolding, just like LP does. But it allows a different class of constraints than =, and evaluates them using a different constraint solver than unification.

1.2   Constraint Propagation

At the very same time as the emergence of the CLP Scheme, in the mid 1980s, another extension to LP was emerging that is also known as CLP.

In this case no special constraint predicates were introduced, and all predicates in the program were defined by clauses as in LP. The extension to LP was to allow program clauses to be handled by something other than unfolding.

The first example of CLP in this sense was the CHIP system [22]. CHIP allowed clauses to be evaluated not only by unfolding but also by propagation.

Propagation has a long history in AI dating back to its application to vision [82]. Many variations of propagation have been introduced [54, 26], and researchers have developed specialised algorithms for each variety of propagation [50, 53, 33].

Propagation corresponds very broadly to the addition of surrogate subgoals as proposed originally by Kowalski in Chapter 9 of [41]. However the AI tradition of propagation admitted a very specific class of subgoals called *domain constraints*. A domain constraint restricts the possible values that can be taken by a specific variable.

The domain constraint that X can only take values a, b or c would naturally be expressed in LP in terms of membership of a list: $member(X, [a, b, c])$. However domain constraints are standardly written in the form $X::[a, b, c]$.

Domain constraints are combined with other goals to achieve quite specialised evaluation algorithms. By combining a domain constraint on a given variable with other goals involving the variable, domain constraints on other variables may be tightened. This tightening process recurses each time the domain of any variable is reduced, until either no further tightenings are possible, or a domain becomes empty, in which case a failure has been detected.

An example helps, but first we introduce some syntax. The same domain can be associated with several variables simultaneously by writing $[W, X, Y, Z]::[a, b, c]$. A numeric range can be given as a finite domain by writing $X::15..74$. "Tightening" a domain is performed by replacing a domain constraint by another on the same set of variables, but with a new domain which is a strict subset of the old one.

Let us assume, for the purposes of the example, that our propagation algorithms achieve arc-consistency [26]. This means it yields the tightest domains possible by processing the constraints individually.

Consider the query:

$$\leftarrow [X, Y, Z]{::}0..3, X - Y = Z, Y - X = Z, Z > 0$$

- From the goal $X - Y = Z$, no domain tightenings can be deduced because whatever the values of X, Y or Z, there are values for the other two variables which satisfy the constraint. (For example if $X = 0$ the constraint can be satisfied by choosing $Y = 0$ and $Z = 0$. If $Z = 3$, on the other hand, the constraint is satisfied by $X = 3$ and $Y = 0$.) The constraint becomes idle, and awaits further processing.
- From the goal $Y - X = Z$, no domain tightenings can be deduced either, for the same reason. This is somewhat disappointing as the only possible value for Z which could allow both constraints to be satisfied simultaneously is $Z = 0$. This deduction is not made by propagation, however, because the constraints are propagated individually and separately.
- From the goal $Z > 0$, however propagation immediately yields the tightened domain $Z{::}1..3$. Now the domain of one of its variables has been tightened the first two constraints wake up. The first constraint $X - Y = Z$ tightens the domains of X and Y yielding $X{::}1..3$ and $Y{::}0..2$. It then becomes idle again. Now the second constraint $Y - X = Z$ tightens these new domains yielding $Y = 2$, $X = 1$ and $Z = 1$, and becomes idle. The domain reductions wake up the first constraint $X - Y = Z$ again, and it finds that there are no remaining values for the variables that satisfy the constraint. Thus the inconsistency between the constraints is detected at last.

If the domain of any variable becomes empty during propagation, then an inconsistency has been detected. However propagation does not always guarantee to detect inconsistencies between different constraints.

A significant generalisation of propagation is to add a different class of surrogate subgoals than just domain constraints. Such a generalisation was proposed in [47]. Focussing on propagation schemes that just add domain constraints, a range of propagation algorithms and techniques are analysed in [5].

1.3 State of the Art

The differences between LP and CLP summarised above appear technical, and perhaps even marginal. Yet their practical consequences have been dramatic.

The real benefit of logic programming is its ability to correctly capture complex problems, and thus enable these problems to be solved. Unfortunately LP has often failed to deliver these benefits in practice because the natural encoding of a problem in LP rarely maps to an efficient and scalable unfolding procedure.

CLP by contrast has delivered solutions to large complex problems faced by users from many walks of life. Section 2 lists some industrial applications of CLP. It is also a useful tool for researchers, and has been used for example to implement systems for planning [48] and abstract interpretation [18].

An exciting current development is the merge of mathematical programming and Operations Research with CLP. CLP provides an environment where complex algorithms and techniques developed by operations researchers can be captured and reused. CLP also enables these techniques to be generalised, and combined [63].

1.4 Summary of This Chapter

The next section will give an overview of industrial applications of constraint programming. In section 3 we will present the CLP Scheme, and explain how the constraints of logic programming (syntactic equations) can be augmented with other constraints. In section 4 we will present a formalisation of constraint behaviour supported by a variety of examples from current constraint programming platforms. The next section will list some current areas of constraint programming research, and the chapter ends with a short conclusion.

2   Applications

A survey of practical applications of constraint programming appeared in 1996 [81], where annual revenue from constraint technology was already estimated at around 100 million dollars. The annual conference on practical applications of constraint technology [56] is a useful source for ongoing progress. Other sites where applications of the technology are described include the ILOG site [36], the Cosytec site [19], Parc Technologies [60], SICS [72], the Prolog Development Centre [57], Prologia [59], IF-Computer [35], and AIAI [3].

Over the last five years the technology has achieved a level of maturity where its employment in the modelling and delivery of large scale applications is no longer newsworthy. Companies such as Temposoft [77], and i2 [34] make no mention of their use of constraint technology.

The main commercial applications of constraint technology to date have been in the areas of transportation, rostering, manufacturing and planning. These are all areas involving NP-hard problems which require sophisticated algorithms to yield high quality solutions within a reasonable timescale.

In the area of transportation, constraints have been used in many areas of application. Constraint programming has been used to develop timetables and schedules for trains and airlines (eg [64]); it has been used for assigning berths for ships, platforms for trains, slots and stands for aircraft (eg [21]); it has been used for the optimisation of road transport delivering fuel, food, parcels for companies such as Texaco, EDF, Procter and Gamble, Sun Valley, Federal Express, and Unigate; it is used in generic products such as SAPs Advanced Planner and Optimizer; it has also been used for driver and crew planning for airlines, trains and buses (e.g [84]).

Rostering is another application area where constraints are becoming the technology of choice, not only in the transportation industry but also in hospitals (eg [1]), call centres and normal office-based organisations. BT has also claimed to save over 100 million pounds per year by optimising the dispatch of engineers to jobs around Britain.

The use of constraints to optimise manufacturing is also well-established with systems in place in the chemicals industry (eg [73]), aircraft manufacturing, oil refining, food and even tyre production.

Finally constraint programming is used in planning power networks, communications networks, mobile phone systems, wiring for buildings, water systems, and advertising (eg [11]).

There are other very important application areas where as yet the scale of commercial activity remains modest. One successful application is in the design of software to interface complex components (eg [27]).

The validation requirements concern not only the correctness of control software (the lift door must not open while it is moving) but also fairness properties (the lift must eventually satisfy each request). Constraints are already used for hardware verification (eg [23]), but as yet there remain scalability problems for validating substantial software components. The combination of abstract interpretation and powerful constraint solvers could provide the key to fully validating larger systems.

3   The CLP Scheme

3.1   Formalisms

When formalising logic programming it is necessary to specify both its declarative semantics and its operational semantics. The main theorems are, then, mappings between the two.

CLP, like other extensions of logic programming, has extra features for which the declarative semantics needs extending. It also has extra behaviours, for which the operational semantics need extending. The kind of CLP introduced in section 1.1 above, extends LP with a new feature: i.e. constraints. The behaviour of the constraint solvers is encapsulated and needs no formalisation. The kind of CLP introduced in section 1.2 above, however, extends LP with new behaviours, rather than new features.

Logic and model theory provide excellent tools for formalising declarative semantics. For this reason in the current section we shall use logic to formalise the CLP Scheme.

3.2   From Equations to Constraints

Consider the following simple LP:

$$p(X) \leftarrow X = a$$
$$p(X) \leftarrow X = b, Y = a, p(Y)$$

The query

$$\leftarrow p(Z)$$

has computed answers
$Z = a$ and $Z = b$.

A defining property of logic programming is its declarative semantics, which can be directly related to its operational semantics through correctness and completeness theorems. If $\mathcal{P}_1$ is the Clark completion of the above program, the computed answers are correct because
$$\mathcal{P}_1 \models \forall Z.(Z = a \rightarrow p(Z))$$
and
$$\mathcal{P}_1 \models \forall Z.(Z = b \rightarrow p(Z))$$
The computed answers also satisfy the completeness condition that
$$\mathcal{P}_1 \models \forall Z.((Z = a \vee Z = b) \leftrightarrow p(Z))$$

Let us now take a toy CLP instance with a single constraint c. The constraint is defined by the following axiom cT:
$$\forall X, Y.c(X, Y) \leftrightarrow (X = a \wedge Y = b)$$

A toy CLP program over this constraint domain is:

$$p(X) \leftarrow c(X, Z)$$
$$p(X) \leftarrow c(Y, X), p(Y)$$

Answers are computed by unfolding the clauses, accumulating the constraints, and checking the (existential closure of the conjunction of) constraints for consistency. Consider the query

$$\leftarrow p(W)$$

The first computed answer is
$$\exists Z.c(X, Z) \tag{1}$$

(which results from unfolding the first clause). The second computed answer is

$$\exists Y, Z.c(Y, W) \wedge c(Y, Z) \tag{2}$$

which results from unfolding the second clause and then the first. The computation which unfolds the second clause twice accumulates the constraints
$$c(Y, X), c(Z, Y)$$
whose existential closure is inconsistent with the axiom cT, so it fails. Therefore the program halts after producing answers 1 and 2 above.

If $\mathcal{P}_2$ is the Clark completion of the CLP program then the answers are consistent in that, for answer 1:
$$\mathcal{P}_2 \cup \{cT\} \models \forall W.(\exists Z.c(W, Z) \leftarrow p(W))$$
and for answer 2:
$$\mathcal{P}_2 \cup \{cT\} \models \forall W.(\exists Y, Zc(Y, W) \wedge c(W, Z) \leftarrow p(W))$$
Also the computed answers satisfy the completeness condition that:
$$\mathcal{P}_2 \cup cT \models \forall W.(\exists Z.c(W, Z) \vee (\exists Y, Zc(Y, W) \wedge c(W, Z)) \leftrightarrow p(W))$$

These answers seem rather different from the answers computed in LP, but in fact we have only replaced one constraint $=$ with another c.

We cannot in general replace the $=$ constraint by other constraints because it is needed in the computation of programs and queries involving functions and constants. For example with the same constraint c, consider the program:

$$q(X, d) \leftarrow c(X, Z)$$

The query

$$\leftarrow q(V, W)$$

has computed answer
$\exists Z.c(V, Z) \wedge W = d$

The consistency test for a set of constraints $C_1, \ldots, C_n$ during unfolding is formalised as $\mathcal{T} \models \exists \mathbf{X}.C_1 \wedge \ldots \wedge C_n$, where $\mathcal{T}$ is the axiomatisation of the constraint domain, and $\mathbf{X}$ is the set of free variables in $C_1, \ldots, C_n$.

To handle negation correctly we need the negation of a failed goal $\neg G$ to be entailed by the program completion $\mathcal{P}$, and the constraint theory $\mathcal{T}$. In other words $\mathcal{P} \cup \mathcal{T} \models \neg G$. To ensure this result always holds, the constraint theory must also be *satisfaction complete*, which means that every existentially closed conjunction of constraints must be either entailed or disentailed by the constraint theory.

Suppose the constraint theory is not satisfaction complete. For example consider the same program:

$$q(X, d) \leftarrow c(X, Z)$$

but a different constraint theory $\mathcal{T}_3$, which neither entails nor disentails $c(e, f)$. Writing $\mathcal{P}_3$ for the program completion, consistency requires that for every computed answer A from the program, $\mathcal{P}_3 \cup \mathcal{T}_3 \models A$. The query

$$\leftarrow q(e, d)$$

fails against the above program, because it is not the case that $\mathcal{T}_3 \models \exists Z.c(e, Z)$. Negation as failure would therefore sanction the computed answer $\neg q(e, d)$. However it is not the case that $\mathcal{P}_3 \cup \mathcal{T}_3 \models \neg q(e, d)$, which is the condition for soundness of computed answers.

This example shows that negation as failure cannot be soundly applied unless the constraint theory is satisfaction complete.

3.3 Summary of Results

The main results relating the operational to the declarative semantics of the CLP Scheme can be summarised as follows. Consider a program whose completion is P over a constraint domain axiomatised by the satisfaction complete theory $\mathcal{T}$.

1. If the goal G has a successful derivation with answer constraint c, then $\mathcal{P} \cup \mathcal{T} \models c \rightarrow G$.
2. If the goal G has a finite computation tree, with answer constraints $c_1, \ldots, c_n$, then $\mathcal{P} \cup \mathcal{T} \models G \leftrightarrow c_1 \vee \ldots \vee c_n$.
3. If $\mathcal{P} \cup \mathcal{T} \models c \rightarrow G$, then there are derivations for the goal G with answer constraints $c_1, \ldots, c_n$ such that $\mathcal{T} \models c \rightarrow (c_1 \vee \ldots \vee c_n)$.
4. If $\mathcal{P} \cup \mathcal{T} \models G \leftrightarrow c_1 \vee \ldots \vee c_n$ then G has a computation tree with answer constraints $c'_1, \ldots, c'_m$ (and possibly others) such that $\mathcal{T} \models c_1 \vee \ldots \vee c_n \leftrightarrow c'_1 \vee \ldots \vee c'_m$.

These and many further results are presented in an excellent survey of constraint logic programming [39].

4 Constraint Handling

In this section we examine the definition of constraint handling *agents* and facilities for controlling their evaluation. The function of an agent (what result it establishes) should be distinguished from its operational specification (how it establishes the result). The definition of an agent's function should be (as far as possible) orthogonal to its control. This enables the programmer first to define his agents correctly and then to experiment with the control of their behaviour without touching their definitions.

Information Systems (extended to *Constraint Systems* by Saraswat et.al. [67]) provide suitable tools for formalising operational semantics. Therefore in the current section we shall use Constraint Systems to formalise constraint propagation.

4.1 An Architecture for Constraint Handling in CLP

The set of constraints accumulated during a computation is termed the *constraint store*. In the (narrow view of the) CLP Scheme outlined in the previous section, the constraint store is tested for consistency each time a constraint is added.

Going beyond CLP Scheme, different kinds of constraint handling are possible, and indeed there may be multiple constraint stores holding different classes of constraints.

Moreover, when we make explicit both the constraint handling process and the traditional logic program computation by unfolding, it can be helpful to distinguish two execution modes for constraint programs. One mode is the execution of the "host" logic program, where the control is program defined. Examples of such control are sequential and parallel execution of commands, and search with backtracking.

The other mode of execution is constraint-driven. This mode is used for processes which become active as soon as the constraint store satisfies some conditions, and may then become idle for a while before being reactivated again when the constraint store satisfies further conditions. Guarded clauses in languages dating back to Parlog, Concurrent Prolog, GHC and ALPS [70] are early examples exhibiting this mode of execution. Consider, for example, the following "Constraint Handling Rules" [28] as expressed in ECLiPSe [80].

```
plane(Distance,Capacity,Type) ==> Distance>=1000 |
                        long_haul(Capacity,Type).
long_haul(Capacity,Type) ==> Capacity >=200 | Type = jumbo.
```

Logically the constraints state that:
$\forall D, C, T : (plane(D, C, T) \land D \geq 1000 \land C \geq 200) \rightarrow T = \text{jumbo}.$
Each constraint has three parts, the *head*, the *guard* and the *body* distinguished by the syntax `Head ==> Guard | Body`. Let us describe the behaviour of these constraints when executing the query `?- plane(D,C,T), D=1500, C=250.`

1. To handle the first goal `plane(D,C,T)` the system simply sets up the constraint agent $plane(D, C, T)$. The agent checks its guard $D \geq 1000$, to determine whether it is entailed by the current constraint store. The store is currently empty, so the guard is not entailed. Therefore the agent becomes idle.
2. The second goal adds $D = 1500$ to the constraint store. As a consequence the agent wakes up again and checks its guard. The guard *is* now entailed, so the agent posts the new goal `long_haul(C,T)`, and exits. The new goal sets up the agent $long\_haul(C, T)$, which checks its guard $C \geq 200$. This guard is not entailed by the store, so the agent becomes idle.
3. The third goal adds $C = 250$ to the store. The agent $long\_haul(C, T)$ wakes up, and checks its guard, which is now entailed, so it posts the goal `T = jumbo` and exits. This goal adds $T = \text{jumbo}$ to the store, and the execution is finished.

Constraint Handling Rules can be used to implement specific constraint solving behaviour. For example, using rules with two literals on the left hand side, a solver handling a strict partial ordering relation r can be implemented as follows:

```
r(X,Y1), r(Y2,Z) ==> Y1=Y2 | r(X,Z).
r(X1,X2) ==> X1=X2 | fail.
```

Constraint propagation in CSP [49] is another early example from quite a different field of research. Each constraint is an agent, and its behaviour is to tighten the domains of the variables. The behaviour of finite domain constraints was described with an example in section 1.2 above.

Constraint propagation and guarded clauses have subsequently both been captured in the single paradigm of Concurrent Constraint (*cc*) Programming. We usually refer to *commands* when discussing host program execution, but when discussing the parts of the program whose execution is constraint-driven we talk about *agents*. An example of the embedding of agents in a host program is *cc(FD)* where propagation constraints are embedded in logic programming [78].

4.2   Classes of Information

Constraint Systems   Constraints have been very elegantly formalised in [66] as *information systems* and extended to *constraint systems* [67].

Briefly a constraint system is defined by a set of *tokens* (denoting atomic pieces of information) and an entailment relation which specifies when a token is entailed by a finite set of tokens. An *element* of a constraint system is a set of tokens which is closed under entailment. For the closure under entailment of a set S of tokens we will write $\overline{S}$.

Elements represent partial information and we can impose an ordering on them based on how much information they contain. Under this partial ordering, the elements form a complete algebraic lattice. The following introduction is a simplification. For the purposes of this paper, we ignore the differences between information systems and constraint systems.

Constraint Stores and Constraint Agents   Let us formalise a constraint store as an element E of a constraint system that is generated by finitely many tokens, $t_1, \ldots, t_n$. Thus $E = \overline{[t_1, \ldots, t_n]}$. We can formalise the behaviour of constraint agents as operators on constraint systems.

Finite domain propagation is formalized as an operator on a special kind of constraint system whose tokens are just variable domains. Thus $X > Y$, if handled using propagation, maps the store $\overline{[X::1..3, Y::1..3]}$ to the store $\overline{[X::2..3, Y::1..2]}$.

Constraint Handling Rules can also be formalized as an operator on an underlying constraint system. For example the CHR
`long_haul(C,T) ==> C>=200 | T = jumbo`
maps $\overline{[t_1, \ldots, t_n]}$ to $\overline{[T = jumbo, t_1, \ldots, t_n]}$ iff[2] $\overline{[t_1, \ldots, t_n]} \vdash C \geq 200$. Otherwise the store is mapped to itself. The tokens in the underlying system represent the class of primitive constraints, constraints belonging to the underlying constraint domain, as described in section 3.3 above. In this example the underlying tokens might be variable labellings, of the form $Var = val$.

Closure Operators   All constraint agents either map the store to itself, or they *add* information to the store. Formalised as operators on the lattice of constraint systems they are, accordingly, *increasing*. Moreover, and perhaps less obviously, if the original store held more information, then the operator would also produce a new store with at least as much (and possibly more) information. As operators on the lattice of constraint systems they are, therefore, *monotonic*. Finally, since an agent does not become idle until

- in the case of CHR's, no guard is entailed, and
- in the case of propagation, no more domain tightenings are possible

---

[2] The CHR's described in this chapter do not remove the constraints in the head of the rule when they fire, so in a finite computation each rule will eventually fire if its guard is entailed. For *Simplification* rules [28], which replace their heads with their bodies, the semantics are more awkward.

the operator produces no more information if it is applied to its own output. The operator is, therefore, *idempotent*. As an operation on lattices, then, constraint agents can be formalised as *closure operators*. Closure operators are nice because it is very easy to specify how they behave. The specification needs merely to list their fixpoints. A fixpoint is any point which is mapped, by the operator, to itself. Any other point is mapped by the closure operator to the least fixpoint above it. (By monotonicity there cannot be two such fixpoints.)

With this abstraction we have an easy way to tell if two constraint agents (which are logically equivalent) also have the same behaviour: we simply study their fixpoints.

Two Constraint Systems: The Constraints Store and the Constraint Agents Constraint systems also gives us a wonderful insight into constraint behaviour, when we realise that the constraints themselves, viewed as logical formulae, also form a constraint system. This constraint system is more expressive than the one used to formalise the behaviour of the constraint agents. Every token in the underlying constraint system belongs to this one, but this constraint system has extra tokens: one for each constraint expressible in the language.

Taking finite domain propagation as an example, the underlying constraint system has only tokens for domain constraints $X::[a, b, ..., k]$. However the larger constraint system has a token for all constraints, $X - Y = Z$ and $X > Y$ etc.

Simply fixing the class of tokens in the underlying constraint system may severely limit the possible constraint behaviours that can be associated with a constraint. The "best" possible behaviour is to extract from the constraint all logical consequences that are expressible in the underlying constraint system. This is achieved if the fixpoints are all, and only, those points in the underlying lattice that are greatest lower bounds of the original constraint in the larger lattice.

Indeed if the underlying constraint system has only finite domain constraints, and if each constraint is encapsulated as a separate constraint agent, then the most powerful behaviour possible is propagation to achieve arc-consistency. If the underlying constraint system comprised binary inequations ($X >= Y$), then propagation would yield all the entailed binary inequations. Finally if the constraint system comprised all constraints expressible as a disjunction of conjunctions of atoms in the language, then propagation would immediately yield all solutions to any query.

Surprisingly it can be very hard to express quite simple behaviours using CHR's. For example let us express propagation to achieve arc-consistency for a constraint defined by a list of tuples:

It is necessary to compile rules for each entry:

```
short_cons(X,N) ==> short_cons_abc_123(X,N).
short_cons_abc_123(X,N) ==> X\=c | short_cons_ab_123(X,N).
...
short_cons_ab_123(X,N) ==> N\=3 | X=a.
...
```

Table 1. Constraint short_cons

This is also very inefficient. More efficient encodings are possible, but they are not easy to understand, and they cannot compete for performance with specific implementations of finite domains propagation.

Generalised propagation [47] enables the user simply to state the class of tokens in the underlying constraint system, and leave the implementation to generate the most powerful behaviour.

Global Constraints There is a way to get much more powerful constraint behaviour without using a larger class of tokens in the underlying constraint system. This is by encapsulating larger parts of the problem as a single constraint agent.

Consider, for example, the humble disequality constraint $X \neq Y$. Finite domain propagation cannot achieve much useful propagation on separate disequations. Sadly propagation fails to detect the inconsistency of the constraints $[X, Y, Z]::[a, b], X \neq Y, X \neq Z, Y \neq Z$. However the conjunction of all three constraints $X \neq Y \wedge X \neq Z \wedge Y \neq Z$ can be encoded as a single constraint agent. Finite domain propagation on this agent will immediately detect the inconsistency if the domains are reduced to $[X, Y, Z]::[a, b]$.

In general it is not possible to turn any conjunction of disequations into an efficiently implementable constraint agent (since the class of problems expressible with conjunctions of disequations is NP-complete). However it *is* possible to efficiently handle cliques, where a disequation is imposed on *every* pair of variables in the clique. A constraint agent enforcing arc-consistency on the constraint all_different($[X1, X2, \ldots, Xn]$) has been efficiently implemented [61].

This is termed a *global* constraint as it can constrain any number of variables. It can be used in the modelling of any combinatorial problem which includes such cliques. In particular it is very useful for resource allocation problems where tasks which overlap in time cannot be performed by the same resource. Many sophisticated algorithms devised by operations researchers have been captured as global constraints and made available to the constraint programming community [10].

The implementation of global constraints for scheduling has been the subject of a long line of research [2, 14, 7, 45]. For routing and vehicle scheduling problems the *cycle* constraint is very useful [10]. For rostering applications the *sequence* constraint simplifies problem modelling and contributes to the efficiency of the solver [8]. A wide variety of such global constraints have been designed and implemented and they are of tremendous practical importance. A tutorial on the use of global constraints in problem modelling and solving is [74].

A global constraint incorporating a cost function was introduced in [61], and the use of reduced cost fixing to integrate costs into global constraints was presented in [25]. A recent survey of global constraints and their contribution to hybridisation is [52]. A framework for developing and implementing global constraints was recently introduced by Beldiceanu [9].

5   Current Directions

Constraint programming has spawned a variety of research areas, and new topics are continually springing up. This section is a snapshot of just some of the current exciting research.

5.1   Hybrid Algorithms

Motivation Constraint logic programming is making a major impact on two communities: the operations research community who devise sophisticated algorithms for handling particular classes of constraints, and the meta-heuristics community who devise sophisticated search strategies which tune themselves to the problem at hand.

CLP provides an environment in which these widely differing approaches can be cleanly combined. The result is the emergence of a new class of hybridisation techniques, each of which can be used to build a wide variety of hybrid algorithms.

A recent workshop on the integration of AI and OR techniques in constraint programming for combinatorial optimisation problems attracted some 70 participants from a wide variety of backgrounds (CP, and AI and OR) and many different countries [30].

Combining Constructive and Local Search Logic programming has built-in backtracking which makes it easy and natural to express a constructive search algorithm, that explores a search space depth-first.

Constructive search can exploit the constraints very well to avoid exploring irrelevant parts of the search space. However constructive search has a weakness in addressing optimisation problems. The optimisation function typically involves many variables and, until most of them are instantiated, little can be deduced about the value of this function by constraint propagation.

Local search, by contrast, takes a complete labelling of all the problem variables and changes the value of one or more variables to improve it. Local search focusses on optimisation but cannot easily be tuned to handle hard constraints.

By combining the two forms of search in a single algorithm the advantages of each can be exploited, leading to a new kind of search.

An early, and influential, algorithm combining constructive and local search is *weak commitment search* [83]. A technique for preserving completeness in the context of a "chaotic" exploration of the search space is recording *nogoods* [20]. Nogoods were used successfully in conjunction with dynamic backtracking by [31], and in conjunction with weak commitment by [62].

Constructive search can be used within a local search algorithm to find the best neighbour [58] and to find a high quality feasible neighbour in [71]. Local search was used within a constructive search framework in [13].

A tutorial covering hybrid search techniques is [46].

Combined Search for Solving Optimisation Problems Large scale combinatorial optimisation problems involve a cost function, and for performance reasons it is necessary to find solutions quickly that are not only feasible but also of low cost. Usually these cost functions are linear, or can be approximated by a linear or piecewise linear function. Linear programming offers efficient constraint solvers which can quickly return optimal solutions to problems whose cost function and constraints can be expressed using only linear expressions. Consequently most industrial LSCO problems involve one or more linear subproblems which are addressed using linear programming as available in commercial products such as XPRESS [55] and CPLEX [36]).

Whilst global constraints classically return information excluding certain assignments from any possible solution, linear solvers classically return just a single optimal solution. In contrast with global constraints, the information returned by a linear solver for a subproblem does not necessarily remain true for any larger problem in which it is embedded. Thus linear solvers cannot easily be hybridised in the same way as global constraints.

Nevertheless several hybridisation forms have been developed for linear solvers, based on the concept of a "master" problem, for which the optimal solution is found, and other subproblems which interact with the master problem. At each iteration the master problem is solved and this solution passed to the subproblems. Different forms of hybridisation sanction different responses.

If the reponse is to return a new set of constraints to the master problem, this is called *row generation*. Unimodular probing [65] is an integration of a form of row generation into constraint programming.

Another form of hybridisation is called *column generation* [4]. In this case, each subproblem returns one or more solutions which have the potential to improve on the current optimum for the master problem.

A number of applications of column generation have been reported in which the subproblem is solved by constraint programming [40, 76].

Besides optimal solutions, linear solvers can return several kinds of information about the solution. *Reduced costs* are the changes in the cost which would result from changes in the values of specific variables. These are, in fact, underestimates so if the reduced cost is "-10" the actual increase in cost will be greater than or equal to 10. In case the variable has finite domain, these reduced costs can be used to prune values from the domain in the usual style of a global constraint. (A value is pruned from the domain if the associated reduced cost is so bad it would produce a solution worse than the current optimum).

In this way linear programming can be hybridised with other solvers in the usual manner of constraint programming. Indeed the technique has been used very successfully [25].

Finally subproblems can be handled by treating them as "soft" constraints and associating a cost with their violation. Using the power of duality theory in linear programming Langrangian relaxation is a technique that elicits an *ideal* set of penalties [24]. With these penalties it is ensured that the optimal solution to the relaxed problem is also guaranteed to be the optimal solution to the full problem. Lagrangian relaxation has also been applied in constraint programming [69].

5.2 Constraint Databases

Constraint databases represent a new paradigm in the area of database systems [29, 43]. They unify and extend several distinct fields of research: relational, object-oriented, spatial and temporal databases; geographical information systems (GIS) ; and constraint logic programming.

The expressive power of constraint query languages to ensure queries fall into acceptable complexity classes has been a major motivator. Constraint search trees have also been formalised as an extension of traditional tree-based indexing methods [75]. Finally a number of implementations have been built [12] and the field has already spun-off some commercial enterprises.

5.3 Languages for Modelling and Solving Problems

Constraint logic programming is a clean and powerful formalism, but applications of constraint technology have forced issues of problem modelling into a high profile. For the different kinds of people involved, from end users, to application developers, modelling needs are different.

The CHIC-2 project explored in some depth the issues that arise in trying to solve industrial problems, and produced a methodology [15]. On the other hand operations researchers find CLP too powerful, and seek a simpler weaker formalism. One language addressing these needs is OPL [79]. For combinatorial problems search techniques are of fundamental importance, whilst CLP has depth-first search and backtracking built-in. Some researchers are exploring different languages for expressing and controlling search [51, 44]. The constraint programming language ECLiPSE supports hybrid search through its *repair* library [68].

Researchers from the AI community are now exploring ways of mapping logical models of constraint problems (essentially CLP without recursion) automatically to efficient algorithms. This endeavour may still be premature.

5.4 Constraint Graphics

Picture recognition was one of the first applications of constraint propagation. Now it is graphical output rather than input that is motivating a great deal of research.

The use of constraints for implementing graphical user interfaces has made it possible to write graphics that are highly flexible. The shape of the output can adapt to accommodate itself to the size of the displaying medium. Diagrams can be enlarged, shrunk or reshaped, but the constraints can ensure that they still serve the same visual purpose [6, 32]

Constraint-based graphics will find more and more practical applications in the near future.

5.5   Constraint Solving

Constraint solvers themselves are the topic of a great deal of research. Specific solvers for sets, non-linear constraints, terminological constraints and many other generic constraint domains are being developed and integrated. Indeed control of constraint solvers is itself a research topic.

Many global constraints have been developed in the last decade, each one separately. There is currently a move towards developing a toolset for building a wide class of global constraints. It was observed that many global constraints depend upon graph algorithms, and if appropriate data structures for representing and manipulating graphs were available, then new global constraints could be built quickly and efficiently. Current graph algorithm libraries do not meet the needs of constraint programming and so researchers are currently trying to specify what those needs are and what functionality should be supported by such a library [9].

6   Conclusion

Constraint logic programming *is* logic programming. It adds algorithms and new forms of control to the logic programming paradigm, but it loses nothing from Kowalski's original vision.

This author believes it will not be long before the distinction between logic programming and constraint logic programming disappears. Whilst the extra choices offered by the different constraint solvers and propagation techniques in CLP make CLP languages "bigger", their alluring brevity, efficiency and elegance more than compensate.

The collocation of the main international conference for constraint programming and logic programming in 2001 cannot but encourage a closer integration between the two communities.

References

[1] S. Abdennadher and H. Schlenker. INTERDIP - an interactive constraint based nurse scheduler. In *PACLP'99*. The Practical Applications Company, April 1999.

[2] Abderrahmane Aggoun and Nicolas Beldiceanu. Extending CHIP in order to solve complex scheduling and placement problems. *Journal of Mathematical and Computer Modelling*, 17(7):57–73, 1993.

[3] www.aiai.ed.ac.uk/project/statements/sched.html.

[4] L. H. Appelgren. A column generation algorithm for a ship scheduling problem. *Transportation Science*, 3:53–68, 1969.

[5] Krzysztof Apt. The essence of constraint propagation. *TCS: Theoretical Computer Science*, 221, 1999.

[6] Greg J. Badros, Alan Borning, Kim Marriott, and Peter Stuckey. Constraint cascading style sheets for the web. In *Proceedings of the 12th Annual ACM Symposium on User Interface Software and Technology*, pages 73–82, N.Y., November 7–10 1999. ACM Press.

[7] P. Baptiste and C. Le Pape. A theoretical and experimental comparison of constraint propagation techniques for disjunctive scheduling. In C. Mellish, editor, *Proc. IJCAI*, volume 1, pages 600–606, 1995.

[8] N. Beldiceanu. New global constraints in chip. Presented at the CHIP Users' Club 95, 1995.

[9] N. Beldiceanu. Global constraints as graph properties on a structured network of elementary constraints of the same type. In R. Dechter, editor, *Proc. Conf. on Principles and Practice of Constraint Programming, CP'2000*, volume 1894 of *Lecture Notes in Computer Science*, pages 52–66. Springer Verlag, 2000.

[10] N. Beldiceanu and E. Contjean. Introducing global constraints in CHIP. *Mathematical and Computer Modelling*, 12:97–123, 1994. citeseer.nj.nec.com/beldiceanu94introducing.html.

[11] P. Boizumault, P. David, and H. Djellab. A repair algorithm for allocating resources in a mobile telephone network. In *PACLP'99*. The Practical Applications Company, April 1999.

[12] Alex Brodsky. Constraint databases: promising technology or just intellectual exercise? *CSURVES: Computing Surveys Electronic Section*, 28, 1996.

[13] Y. Caseau and F. Laburthe. Heuristics for large constrained vehicle routing problems. *Journal of Heuristics*, 5(3):281–303, 1999.

[14] Yves Caseau and Francois Laburthe. Improved clp scheduling with task intervals. In P. Van Hentenryck, editor, *Proceedings of the 11th International Conference on Logic Programming*, Santa Margherita, 1994. MIT Press.

[15] www.icparc.ic.ac.uk/chic2/chic2_methodology/index.html.

[16] K. L. Clark. Negation as failure. In H. Gallaire and J. Minker, editors, *Logic and Data Bases*, pages 293–322. Plenum Press, 1978.

[17] A. Colmerauer. Equations and Inequations on Finite and Infinite Trees. In *Proceedings of the International Conference on Fifth Generation Computer Systems (FGCS-84)*, pages 85–99, Tokyo, Japan, November 1984. ICOT.

[18] M.-M. Corsini, K. Musumbu, A. Rauzy, and B. L. Charlier. Efficient bottom-up abstract interpretation of Prolog by means of constraint solving over symbolic finite domains. *Lecture Notes in Computer Science*, 714, 1993.

[19] www.cosytec.fr/.

[20] J. de Kleer. A comparison of ATMS and CSP techniques. In *Proc. 11th International Joint Conference on Artificial Intelligence, IJCAI'89*, 1989.

[21] M. Dincbas and H. Simonis. APACHE - a constraint-based, automated stand allocation system. In *Proc. of Advanced Software Technology in Air Transport (ASTAIR'91)*, 1991.

[22] M. Dincbas, P. Van Hentenryck, H. Simonis, A. Aggoun, T. Graf, and F. Berthier. The constraint logic programming language CHIP. In *Proceedings Intl. Conf. on Fifth Generation Computer Systems, Tokyo, Japan, Dec 1988*, pages 693–702. Ohmsha Publishers, Tokyo, 1988.

[23] T. Filkhorn, H.-A. Schneider, A. Scholz, A. Strasser, and P. Warkentin. SVE system verification environment. Technical Report SVE, ZFE BT SE Siemens AG, 1995.

[24] M. Fisher. An applications oriented guide to lagrangian relaxation, 1985.

[25] F. Focacci, A. Lodi, and M. Milano. Embedding relaxations in global constraints for solving TSP and its time constrained variant. *Annals of Mathematics and Artificial Intelligence*, Special issue on Large Scale Combinatorial Optimization, 2001. To appear.

[26] E.C. Freuder. Synthesizing constraint expressions. *Communications of the ACM*, 21:958–966, November 1978.

[27] M. P. J. Fromherz, V. A. Saraswat, and D. G. Bobrow. Model-based computing: Developing flexible machine control software. *Artificial Intelligence*, 114(1-2):157–202, 1999.

[28] T. Fruhwirth. Theory and practice of constraint handling rules, 1998.

[29] V. Gaede, A. Brodsky, O. Guenther, D. Srivastava, V. Vianu, and M. G. Wallace. *Constraint Databases and Applications*. Number 1191 in LNCS. Springer Verlag, 1998.

[30] Carmen Gervet and Mark Wallace. Third international workshop on integration of AI and OR techniques in constraint programming for combinatorial optimization problems. Programme and papers presented at CPAIOR'01: www.icparc.ic.ac.uk/cpAIOR01/, 2001.

[31] Matt Ginsberg. Dynamic backtracking. Technical report, 1992. citeseer.nj.nec.com/ginsberg96dynamic.html.

[32] Weiqing He and Kim Marriott. Constrained graph layout. *Constraints*, 3(4), 1998.

[33] P. Van Hentenryck, Y. Deville, and C.-M. Teng. A generic arc-consistency algorithm and its specializations. *Artificial Intelligence*, 57(2-3):291–321, October 1992.

[34] www.i2.com.

[35] www.ifcomputer.de/consulting/home.html.

[36] ILOG. CPLEX. www.ilog.com/products/cplex/, 2001.

[37] J. Jaffar and J.-L. Lassez. Constraint logic programming. In ACM, editor, *POPL '87. Fourteenth Annual ACM SIGACT-SIGPLAN Symposium on Principles of programming languages, January 21-23, 1987, Munich, W. Germany*, pages 111–119, New York, NY, USA, 1987. ACM Press.

[38] J. Jaffar, S. Michaylov, P. J. Stuckey, and R. H. C. Yap. The CLP(R) language and system. *ACM Trans. Prog. Lang. and Sys.*, 14(3), July 1992.

[39] Joxan Jaffar and Michael J. Maher. Constraint logic programming: A survey. *The Journal of Logic Programming*, 19 & 20:503–582, May 1994.

[40] U. Junker, S. E. Karisch, N. Kohl, B. Vaaben, T. Fahle, and M. Sellmann. A framework for constraint programming based column generation. In *Proceedings of the 5th International Conference on Principles and Practice of Constraint Programming - LNCS 1713*, pages 261–274. Springer-Verlag, 1999.

[41] Bob Kowalski. *Logic for Problem Solving*. North Holland, 1979.

[42] R. Kowalski, F. Toni, and G. Wetzel. Executing suspended logic programs. *FUND-INF: Fundamenta Informatica*, 34, 1998.

[43] G. Kuper, L. Libkin, and J. Paradeans. *Constraint Databases*. Springer Verlag, 2000.

[44] F. Laburthe and Y. Caseau. SALSA: A language for search algorithms. *Lecture Notes in Computer Science*, 1520, 1998.

[45] C. Le Pape and P. Baptiste. Resource constraints for preemptive job-shop scheduling. *Constraints*, 3(4):263–287, 1998.

[46] Claude Le Pape and Mark Wallace. From constraint programming to hybrid problem-solving algorithms. Tutorial at CP98, Pisa. www.icparc.ic.ac.uk/~mgw/cp98_Tutorial.ppt, 1998.

[47] Thierry Le Provost and Mark Wallace. Generalized constraint propagation over the CLP scheme. *Journal of Logic Programming*, 16(3-4):319–359, August 1993.

[48] V. Liatsos and E. B. Richards. Scaleability in planning. In *Proceedings of the 5th European Conference on Planning*, Durham, UK, September 1999.

[49] A.K. Mackworth. Consistency in network of relations. *Artificial Intelligence*, 8(1):99–118, 1977.

[50] A.K. Mackworth and E.C. Freuder. The complexity of some polynomial network consistency algorithms for constraint satisfaction problems. *Artificial Intelligence*, 25:65–74, 1985.

[51] L. Michel and P. Van Hentenryck. Localizer: A modeling language for local search. *Lecture Notes in Computer Science*, 1330, 1997.

[52] M. Milano, G. Ottosson, P. Refalo, and E. Thorsteinsson. Global constraints: When constraint programming meets operations research. Under Submission, 2001.

[53] R. Mohr and T.C. Henderson. Arc and path consistency revisited. *Artificial Intelligence*, 28:225–233, 1986.

[54] U. Montanari. Networks of constraints : fundamental properties and applications to picture processing. *Information Science*, 7(2):95–132, 1974.

[55] Dash Optimization. XPRESS-MP. www.dash.co.uk/, 2001.

[56] www.practical-applications.co.uk/paclp2000/index.html.

[57] ww.pdc.dk/.

[58] Gilles Pesant and Michel Gendreau. A view of local search in constraint programming. In *Principles and Practice of Constraint Programming*, pages 353–366, 1996. citeseer.nj.nec.com/pesant96view.html.

[59] http://prologianet.univ-mrs.fr/us/domaines.htm.

[60] www.parc-technologies.com.

[61] J.-C. Regin. A filtering algorithm for constraints of difference in CSPs. In *Proc. 12th Conf. American Assoc. Artificial Intelligence*, volume 1, pages 362–367. Amer. Assoc. Artificial Intelligence, 1994.

[62] E. Thomas Richards and Barry Richards. Nonsystematic search and no-good learning. *Journal of Automated Reasoning*, 24(4):483–533, 2000. citeseer.nj.nec.com/431873.html.

[63] R. Rodosek, M. G. Wallace, and M. T. Hajian. A new approach to integrating mixed integer programming and constraint logic programming. *Annals of Operations Research*, 86:63–87, 1999. Special issue on Advances in Combinatorial Optimization.

[64] H. El Sakkout, T. Richards, and M. G. Wallace. Minimal perturbance in dynamic scheduling. In Henri Prade, editor, *Proceedings of the 13th European Conference on Artificial Intelligence (ECAI-98)*, pages 504–508, Chichester, August 23–28 1998. John Wiley & Sons.

[65] Hani El Sakkout and Mark Wallace. Probe backtrack search for minimal perturbation in dynamic scheduling. *Constraints*, 5(4):359–388, 2000.

[66] V. Saraswat, Rinard M., and P. Panangaden. Semantic foundations of concurrent constraint programming. In *Proc. 18th ACM POPL*, Jan 1991.

[67] Vijay A. Saraswat, Martin Rinard, and Prakash Panangaden. Semantic foundations of concurrent constraint programming. In *Conf. Record 18th Annual ACM Symp. on Principles of Programming Languages, Orlando, FL, USA, 1991*, pages 333–52. 1990.

[68] Joachim Schimpf and Mark Wallace. Finding the right algorithm - a combinatorial meta-problem. *Electronic Notes in Discrete Mathematics*, 4:80–92, 1999.

[69] M. Sellmann and T. Fahle. Cp-based lagrangian relaxation for a multimedia application. Programme and papers presented at CPAIOR'01: www.icparc.ic.ac.uk/cpAIOR01/, 2001.

[70] E. Shapiro. The family of concurrent logic programming languages. *ACM Computing Surveys*, 21(3), 1989.

[71] Paul Shaw. Using constraint programming and local search methods to solve vehicle routing problems. In *Principles and Practice of Constraint Programming*, pages 417–431, 1998. citeseer.nj.nec.com/shaw98using.html.

[72] www.sics.se/isl/decs/.

[73] H. Simonis. Application development with the CHIP system. In Gabriel Kuper and Mark Wallace, editors, *Proc. 1st Int. Database Workshop on Constraint Database Systems (CDB'95)*, pages 1–21, Friedrichshafen, Germany, 1995. LNCS No. 1034.

[74] H. Simonis. More standard constraint models. Tutorial presented at PAPACT98, 1998.

[75] Peter J. Stuckey. Constraint search trees. In Lee Naish, editor, *Proceedings of the 14th International Conference on Logic Programming*, pages 301–315, Cambridge, July 8–11 1997. MIT Press.

[76] A. V. Moura T. H. Yunes and C. C. de Souza. A hybrid approach for solving large scale crew scheduling problems. In *Proceedings of the Second International Workshop on Practical Asp ects of Declarative Languages (PADL'00)*, pages 293–307, Boston, MA, USA, 2000.

[77] www.temposoft.fr.

[78] P. Van Hentenryck, H. Simonis, and M. Dincbas. Constraint satisfaction using constraint logic programming. *Artificial Intelligence*, 58, 1992.

[79] Pascal Van Hentenryck. *The OPL Optimization Programming Language*. The MIT Press, 1999.

[80] M. G. Wallace, S. Novello, and J. Schimpf. Eclipse - a platform for constraint programming. *ICL Systems Journal*, 12(1):159–200, 1997. www.icparc.ic.ac.uk/eclipse/.

[81] Mark Wallace. Practical applications of constraint programming. *Constraints Journal*, 1(1), 1996.

[82] D. Waltz. Generating semantic descriptions from drawings of scenes with shadows. Technical Report AI271, MIT, Massachusetts, November 1972.

[83] Makoto Yokoo. Weak-commitment search for solving constraint satisfaction problems. In *AAAI, Vol. 1*, pages 313–318, 1994.

[84] Tallys H. Yunes, Arnaldo V. Moura, and Cid C. de Souza. A hybrid approach for solving large scale crew scheduling problems. In *Proc. 2nd International Workshop on Practical Aspects of Declarative Languages (PADL'00)*. Springer Verlag, January 17–18 2000. LNCS 1753.

Planning Attacks to Security Protocols:
Case Studies in Logic Programming

Luigia Carlucci Aiello[1] and Fabio Massacci[2]

[1] Dip. di Informatica e Sistemistica - Univ. Roma "La Sapienza" - Italy
aiello@dis.uniroma1.it
[2] Dip. di Ingegneria dell'Informazione - Univ. Siena - Italy
massacci@dii.unisi.it

Abstract. Formal verification of security protocols has become a key issue in computer security. Yet, it has proven to be a hard task often error prone and discouraging for non-experts in formal methods.

In this paper we show how security protocols can be specified and verified efficiently and effectively by embedding reasoning about actions into a logic programming language.

In a nutshell, we view a protocol trace as a plan to achieve a goal, so that protocol attacks are plans achieving goals that correspond to security violations. Building on results from logic programming and planning, we map the existence of an attack to a protocol into the existence of a model for the protocol specification that satisfies the specification of an attack. To streamline such way of modeling security protocols, we use a description language $\mathcal{AL}_{SP}$ which makes it possible to describe protocols with declarative ease and to search for attacks by relying on efficient model finders (e.g. the smodels systems by Niemela and his group). This paper shows how to use $\mathcal{AL}_{SP}$ for modeling two significant case studies in protocol verification: the classical Needham-Schroeder public-key protocol, and Aziz-Diffie Key agreement protocol for mobile communication.

1 Introduction

The design of secure communication protocols over an insecure medium such as the internet is a daunting task. Notwithstanding the increasingly sophisticated cryptographic primitives for digitally signing messages, encrypting documents, getting notarized timestamps on files etc., most security protocols are often found seriously flawed, even after they make their way up to become a standard.

Interestingly, most of the errors encountered in security protocols are logical error, which do not depend on the strength of the underlying cryptographic algorithms. For instance, if we receive a document digitally signed by Alice, we may think that Alice actually signed this message and sent it to us. However, depending on how the protocol is designed, it might well be that Alice never intended to send that document to us, but rather to a certain Bob, who never asked for it. It is just a malicious hacker who, by intercepting and subtly cutting and pasting messages together, has made such an awkward situation possible.

A.C. Kakas, F. Sadri (Eds.): Computat. Logic (Kowalski Festschrift), LNAI 2407, pp. 533–560, 2002.
© Springer-Verlag Berlin Heidelberg 2002

An interesting collection of examples can be found in the book by Schneider [36, Chap. 3] or the classical articles by Abadi, Needham et al. [7,2].

This phenomenon is somehow surprising because security protocols are not overly complex: academic protocols are seldom above 6 messages, whereas deployed and widely used protocols such as Kerberos or TLS/SSL (the internet secure payment protocol) hardly go beyond twenty ((see [36, Chap. 3] or [7,10] for some characteristic examples), and even a "monster protocol" such the Secure Electronic Transaction protocol (SET) by Visa and Mastercard is substantially composed by 6 suites of "normal" protocols [32]. Nothing even comparable to the intrinsic complexity of current CPU design with billion of gates.

The hardness of the design task can be explained by two different factors. First, security protocols try to achieve difficult and sometimes unclear goals such as entity authentication, confidentiality, proof of receipts etc.in a substantially untrusted medium. It is often not clear what authentication means (see for instance Gollmann [16] vs Lowe [21]).

Second, the medium itself allows for unsuspected interactions, parallelism of actions and events that are difficult to foresee. Consider electronic payment protocols. Even though we think in terms of Alice willing to buy something, and Bob wishing to sell it, Alice and Bob are processes and not persons. Alice (the person) cannot simultaneously go to the grocery and to the bakery. Bob, the grocer, will hardly serve more than one person at a time. Alice cannot really run away with few kilos of pasta to avoid paying Bob. In contrast `Alice` (the shopping softbot of Alice) can practically simultaneously open a connection with `Bob`, the web server of a DVD movies e-shop and `Charlie`, her CD supplier. `Bob`, on his own, can have thousands of these connections who may all be in parallel and ought to be served with minimum delay. He cannot run after `Alice` to grab back his DVD if she "forgets" to pay. Moreover, their orders are channeled through many intermediate untrusted nodes.

It is therefore not a surprise that formal methods have gained such a widespread use in the analysis of security protocols [26,25]. Unfortunately, it turned out that formal verification itself its quite an intensive task as to discourage the application of a formal method by anybody else than the developer of the method itself. As correctly pointed out by Brackin, Meadows and Millen in [6]:

> It became evident that it was difficult for analysts other than the developers of the various techniques to apply them. One reason for this difficulty is that the protocols had to be re-specified formally for each technique and it was not easy to transform the published description of the protocol into the required formal system. Some tool developers began work on translators or compilers that would perform the transformation automatically. The input to any of such translators still requires a formally-defined language, but it can be made similar to the message-oriented protocol description that are typically published in articles, books and protocol standard documents.

The research efforts resulted in languages such as CAPSL [6] and CASPER [22], that are "front-ends" to formal systems, intermediate between formal specifications and the language used in the published descriptions of protocols. Indeed, these languages allow the operational specification of the protocol in terms of messages sent and received, and in terms of the operations made.

Nevertheless, these languages tie the hand of the protocol analyst and bind him to adopt the interpretations of protocol properties made by the designers of the compiler, who usually coincide with the developers of the target formal method. The security analyst must still buy, lock, stock and barrel, the definition of authentication, secrecy, non-repudiation etc. which are hardwired in the tool.

Moreover, the intermediate language proved to be too weak for specifying more complex protocols. For instance, in a public key infrastructure, each agent may have a certificate for its public key, and certificates usually have expiration dates. In the design of a security protocol, a designer may want to specify that the validity period of a certificate must be appropriate: a server may reject a document supposed to be valid for 10 years which is signed with a private key expiring in a month. To overcome this modeling difficulty, front-ends allow the specifiers to hack directly such constraints into the target formal language [22].

So, one would like to combine the best of two worlds: an operational description of a protocol and a declarative specification of its properties.

1.1   Our Contribution

We proposed $\mathcal{AL}_{SP}$ (Action Language for Security Protocols, see [8,9]), an executable specification language for representing security protocols, and checking the possibility of attacks. The intuitions are the following:

- The operational description of a security protocol (what security designers would like) can be quite naturally cast into the general framework of an AI planning problem with simple actions such as sending and receiving. Checks on the protocol actions (such as verifying expiration dates on certificates) are naturally cast into action preconditions. Attacks are just plans to reach security violations.
- The preconditions for the executions of protocol actions and the properties of a protocol should be easily specifiable, as declaratively as possible.
- Modeling nonmonotonic behaviors is essential in this framework, as we may want to say that if something is not specified then it is false by default. Once we modeled the capability of an intruder and – with this capability – no attack is found, then we would like to conclude that no attack exists.
- The number of objects and agents would potentially be unbounded; therefore the language must allow for free variables and function symbols to describe properties of objects, compound objects (such as concatenation of messages) and agents, without forcing the analyst to hardwire each particular object into a particular message of particular protocol steps.
- As soon as we set a bound on the number of objects and agents that are around, it should be possible to check for attacks with fast state-of-the-art systems in a automatic way (that is, debugging should be mostly automatic).

– Decidability and expressiveness of the language matter more than complexity, because we do not verify a protocol on-line (whereas a robot must move in the real world), but we want to specify complex protocols without bit-oriented programming in logic, process algebras or other formal languages.

For all the above reasons, logic programming stands out as an extremely nice formalism upon which to build our specification language $\mathcal{AL}_{SP}$. However, for our formalization of security protocols not everything of logic programming can be bought; therefore $\mathcal{AL}_{SP}$ borrows selected features from logic programming .

$\mathcal{AL}_{SP}$ is based on logic programming with stable model semantics ($\mathcal{LP}_{SM}$) [3,14]. This choice is motivated by three properties guaranteed by $\mathcal{LP}_{SM}$:

– if a fact is true in a stable model, there is a justification for it and no circular justification is allowed;
– if something is not explicitly said, it is false by default;
– it is possible to say that some facts *must* be true in a stable model, and other facts *may* be true in it.

This is particularly appropriate to represent actions and changes, which is needed to model security. For example, consider modeling an intruder. If the intruder decrypted some messages, we want a well-founded justification for the intruder to know the key. Moreover, we want to say that the intruder may disrupt each step of the protocol, but he is not obliged to; he may disrupt some steps and let others remain unchanged.

Logic programming languages — hence $\mathcal{AL}_{SP}$ — allow for a declarative formalization of the operational behavior of the protocol and the possible attacks of an intruder. As mentioned, we borrow this formalization from robotic planning: out of a declarative specification of the world, the proof of the existence of a model for a goal state can be easily transformed into a plan (i.e. a sequence of actions) to achieve it. Conversely, the non-existence of a plan can be checked as an un-satisfiability problem. If no model for a goal state can be found, then we have proven that there is no plan that achieves it.

To achieve decidability for bounded model checking we impose some restriction on the form that free variables occurring in rules may have. Thus we obtain domain restricted logic programs. When a bound on the protocol resources, agents and time is set, we obtain a finite ground model of our specification.

Finally, we search for attacks on the finite ground representation using efficient model finders for the stable model semantics [30,31] which can handle hundreds of thousands of rules in few seconds. This makes $\mathcal{AL}_{SP}$ executable.

1.2 Plan of the Paper

In this paper we show how to model in $\mathcal{AL}_{SP}$ two important case case studies: the classical Needham-Schroeder public-key protocol [29,7] and the Aziz-Diffie key agreement protocol for mobile communication [4,38].

Thus, we first introduce some background on the logic approach to planning (Section 2). Then we shortly introduce the language $\mathcal{AL}_{SP}$ (Section 3) and sketch how it can be used in practice (Section 4). Then we illustrate the formalization in $\mathcal{ACL_{SP}}$ of the Needham-Schroeder protocol (Section 5) and the Aziz-Diffie key agreement protocol (Section 6). We conclude the paper with a brief comparison with related works (Section 7).

2   Logical Approach to Planning

Planning is a research area in AI aiming at the construction of algorithms — called planners — that enable an agent (a robot or a "softbot") to synthesize a course of actions that will achieve its goals (see Weld [39] for a recent survey).

A planner has to be provided with a *background theory*, i.e. a description of generally known properties about the world, and with a *planning problem*:

1. a description of the initial state of the world;
2. a description of the goal state the agent has to achieve;
3. a description of the possible actions that can be performed by the agent. This is often called *domain theory* or *action theory*.

The solution of the problem (if one exists) is a *plan*, i.e. a sequence of actions that, when executed in any world satisfying the initial state description, will achieve the goal.

Actions may have *preconditions*, i.e. requirements to be satisfied in order for the action to be executable. Actions modify the current status of the world; this is described by stating the *"causal laws"*, i.e. how they affect the values of predicates and functions, in the form of the so called *effect axioms*. In addition, the *"laws of inertia"* for the domain are to be stated, i.e. which values are unaffected by each action, so they persist through its execution.

A planning problem in the context of security protocols, where agents exchange messages and are subject to attacks by intruders, is the following:

1. the initial state is described in terms of the keys known to agents and the messages already exchanged (typically none), at the time the protocol starts;
2. the goal state is an unwanted situation where some security violation has occurred (e.g. A receives a message allegedly from B who actually never sent it to A.);
3. actions are exchanges of messages among agents.

A solution of the planning problem, if any, is a sequence of actions leading to an unwanted situation, and thus a plan is an attack to the security of the protocol.

The background theory, in this case, includes the description of how messages are composed and decrypted by agents, the properties of keys, how knowledge is attained by the agents participating in the protocol, etc.

Causal laws and laws of inertia can be cast as constraints on the possible sets of predicates that are admissible for consecutive times t and $t+1$. For instance, if the action predicate $says(A, B, M, t)$ is true, then $said(A, B, M, t+1)$ is true.

In this way, the planning problem becomes the problem of finding a time t such that $Goal(t)$ holds, where $Goal(t)$ is the conjunction of the (relevant) formulas true at time t such that all constraints are satisfied.

The relation between logic programming on the one side, and reasoning about action and planning on the other side, has been studied quite extensively, e.g. by Gelfond and Lifschitz [15], Denecker et al [11] in the context of the Event Calculus, or Subrahmanian and Zaniolo [37]. Kautz and Selman in [17] proposed to cast a planning problem as a model finding problem via an encoding of plans as propositional formulas. We do not adopt their encoding, but share with their proposal the idea that planning can be solved as model finding. Following ideas of Nebel and coworkers [12] and Niemelä [30], our basic intuition is to limit the size of plans (by considering plans whose length l is less than n for some fixed n) and then encode the planning problem as a satisfiability problem of logic programs, by encoding each causal and inertial constraint as a logic programming rule. If we find a stable model for the goal and all formulae, then we have a plan.

Plans can be generated using logic programs with the stable model semantics [14,3]. Stable models capture the two key properties of solution sets to logic programs: they are minimal and grounded, i.e. each atom in a stable model has a justification in terms of the program. Minimality and groundedness make logic programming with stable model semantics ($\mathcal{LP}_{SM}$) particularly suited to modeling actions and change, in particular in security problems, where we want to model exactly what happened (i.e. we do not want to leave room for unwanted models), and where everything has a justification in the model. For example, if an intruder has got a secret key, there is an explanation in the model in terms of actions that he has performed, it cannot have happened for other reasons not captured by the stable model itself.

Even though computing stable models has been proved NP-complete, the techniques for computing stable models for ground programs have advanced and there are systems that can cope with tens of thousands of rules. The system smodels, developed by Niemelä and his group [30,31], is one of them.

In order to introduce it, we present some more notions. Logic programs with variables can be given a semantics in terms of stable models. The stable models of a normal logic program P with variables are those of its ground instantiations P_H with respect to its Herbrand universe. If logic programs are function free, then an upper bound on the number of instantiations is rc^v, where r is the number of rules, c the number of the constants, and v the upper bound on the number of distinct variables in each rule. Hence, to keep the Herbrand Universe of a logic program finite, we need to restrict variables to range over finite domains.

Programs where variables are sorted are domain restricted to the domain of the sort predicates. This property holds for the logic programming language $\mathcal{AL}_{SP}$. Functions are allowed in $\mathcal{AL}_{SP}$ programs, but domain restrictedness is kept by imposing that arguments of functions range over finite domains.

Domain restrictedness is a limitation that still leaves logic programs with expressive power to deal with interesting applications. At the same time, with this limitation, the grounding problem and the search for stable models can be solved efficiently, in particular if the domain is nonrecursive, i.e. D does not contain predicates that are recursively defined in P. $\mathcal{AL}_{SP}$ enjoys this property.

smodels [31,30] is an implementation of $\mathcal{LP}_{SM}$, for range restricted function free normal programs. It consists of two modules: the proper **smodels**, which implements $\mathcal{LP}_{SM}$ for ground programs and **parse**, the grounding procedure, or better **lparse** a more efficient parsing module which works for domain restricted programs with nonrecursive domains. **lparse** automatically detects domain predicates and deals with them very efficiently. In addition, it has some built in arithmetic functions.

The stable model semantics for ground programs as implemented in **smodels** is a bottom-up backtracking search, where only the negative atoms in the program contribute to an increase of the search space, hence it is very efficient.

smodels offers the possibility of including a "choice" rule into logic programs:

$$\{c\} \longleftarrow a, b$$

It reads as: if a and b are both true, then c *may* be in the stable model, but this is not mandatory. Actually, a program containing the choice rule can in fact be translated into a normal program. The language $\mathcal{AL}_{SP}$ borrows the choice rule from **smodels**, as it is useful when representing security problems. For instance, it allows us to easily represent the fact that an agent may send a message, but he is not compelled to do it.

3   The Language $\mathcal{AL}_{SP}$

As already said, $\mathcal{AL}_{SP}$ is logic programming with negation as failure and stable model semantics. We here illustrate the primitives $\mathcal{AL}_{SP}$ offers, i.e. the logic programming rules common to the representation of (almost) all security protocols. $\mathcal{AL}_{SP}$ provides the user with *basic sort predicates* to characterize the basic components of protocols' specifications:

- ag(A) denotes that A is an *agent*
- nonce(N) denotes that N is a *nonce*[1]
- key(K) denotes that K is a *key*[2]
- timestamp(TS) denotes that TS is a *timestamp*.

$\mathcal{AL}_{SP}$ provides the user with *constructors for messages*. Some "classical" constructs are pairing, encryption, hashing, and exclusive-or, which we represent in BAN-like notation [7]:

- $\{M\}_K$ is the encryption of M with the key K;
- $M_1 \| M_2$ is the concatenation of M_1 with M_2;
- $h(M_1)$ is the hash of message M_1;
- $M_1 \oplus M_2$ is the bit-wise xor of M_1 and M_2.

---

[1] Nonce is a security jargon for "Number Used Once"; typically, an unguessable random number.

[2] We may have different keys such as shared, private or agreement keys. We distinguish them with additional predicates.

A *special sort predicate* is msg(M), which denotes that M is a valid (sub)*message* that may appear in a run of the protocol. The predicate msg($\cdot$) specifies how messages are built with message constructors from basic components.

The direct approach would be using msg($\cdot$) and defining messages inductively with constructors. For instance

$$\mathsf{msg}(M_1 \| M_2) \longleftarrow \mathsf{msg}(M_1), \mathsf{msg}(M_2)$$

could be a rule for inductively defining message concatenation. Unfortunately, inductively defined predicates with function symbols have infinitely many ground instances. In our application, we do not need inductive definitions for msg($\cdot$): it is sufficient to use messages that may occur as submessages in a possible run of a protocol. For instance, the concatenation of thousands of nonces will never appear in the Needham-Schroeder public key protocol, and – if it does – it will be ignored by all honest agents. In most protocols, even complex ones, the format and number of valid messages is fixed[3] and can be expressed by few applications of the constructors to elements of the basic types (see [27]).

Therefore we impose two constraints:

Definition 1. *A basic sort predicate is admissible for $\mathcal{AL}_{SP}$ if it is not recursively defined by logic programming rules.*

Definition 2. *A logic programming rule with the special sort predicate msg($\cdot$) in the head is admissible for $\mathcal{AL}_{SP}$ only if basic sort predicates alone occur in the body of the rule.*

If we have finitely many basic objects (agents, nonces, etc.), then we have finitely many messages in $\mathcal{AL}_{SP}$ and therefore we have finite models. This is the only part of $\mathcal{AL}_{SP}$ specifications in which we forbid inductively defined predicates.

The trade off is that the rules defining msg($\cdot$) depend on the particular protocol we are analyzing. We must define each submessage in terms of the atomic components. This tedious part of $\mathcal{AL}_{SP}$ specifications has been automated [18].

$\mathcal{AL}_{SP}$ has predicates for defining *properties of messages*:

- part(M_1, M) denotes that M_1 is a submessage of M;
- invKey(K, K_I) denotes that K_I is the inverse of K;
- symKey(K) denotes that K is a symmetric key;
- sharedKey(K, A, B) denotes that K is a (symmetric) key shared between A and B;
- asymKeyPair($Kpriv, Kpub$) denotes that $Kpriv$ and $Kpub$ are an asymmetric key pair.

Other predicates may be introduced on demand.

Next, we have predicates for *knowledge and ability to compose messages*. From now on we must introduce *time* as an additional argument.

---

[3] The recursive protocol analyzed in [33,35] is an exception.

- $knows(A, M, T)$ denotes that agent A knows message M at time T;
- $synth(A, M, T)$ denotes that A can construct message M at time T.

Then we have predicates for *actions*:

- $says(A, B, M, T)$ denotes the attempt[4] by A to send message M to B at time T;
- $gets(B, M, T)$ denotes the receipt[5] of message M by B at time T;
- $notes(A, M, T)$ denotes the storage of message M by A at time T.

These actions are present in the inductive theory of traces by Paulson and Bella [33,5]. Together with the predicate $knows(A, M, T)$, they are the only predicates typeset in italics, as they are the only ones whose truth value we need to know for extracting attacks from stable models.

We use the predicates $\mathsf{said}(A, B, M, T)$, $\mathsf{got}(B, M, T)$, and $\mathsf{noted}(A, M, T)$, with the obvious meaning that they are true when the corresponding action happened some time before T. We prefer this solution wrt the explicit temporal operators as for instance proposed by Syverson and Meadows [38] because it leads to simpler semantics and gives us the flexibility to explicitly axiomatize when and how information about past runs of the protocol carries on into the current run.

4 $\mathcal{AL}_{SP}$ at Work

In order to verify the security of protocols, building on the above primitives, we write specifications in $\mathcal{AL}_{SP}$, and then use the $\mathsf{smodels}$ systems, according to the following steps:

- we use the $\mathcal{AL}_{SP}$ specification of the general background and action theories;
- we write the $\mathcal{AL}_{SP}$ specification of the protocol dependent part, with choice rules for representing the correct execution of the protocol;
- we define a rule for the security property (attack) we want to check;
- we merge the three specifications, set the maximum execution time of the protocol to t_{max}, and a bound on the number of basic objects (agents, nonces, etc.);
- we use lparse to obtain the finite ground representation of $\mathcal{AL}_{SP}$ specifications;
- we use $\mathsf{smodels}$ to look for a stable model of the ground system.

If no stable model exists, then the attack does not exist for all (possibly parallel) interleaved runs of the protocol up to t_{max}.

If a stable model is found, then we look for the atoms representing actions ($says(A, B, M, T)$, $gets(B, M, T)$, $notes(A, M, T)$) that are true in the model: they give us the sequence of (parallel) actions that constitute the attack.

---

[4] Attempt because the spy might intercept the message and the intended recipient might never see it.

[5] We only specify the recipient in the "get" action as the sender is unreliable. See also [5,33] for a discussion of this modeling choice.

If we are looking for confidentiality attacks, then we must gather the atoms $knows(spy, M, t_{max})$ that are true in the model. They represent the knowledge of the intruder at the end of the protocol.

To speed up the search, we may add extra constraints on the rules that describe the protocol, for instance by limiting the possibility of agents to receive or send messages etc.

In a nutshell, search can be constrained by adding more determinism to the protocol description. Provided these constraints are reasonable and correspond to the "natural" implementation of the protocol, they do not preclude the possibility of finding attacks. Some of these optimizations are described in the subsequent case studies.

5   Needham-Schroeder Public-Key

The Needham-Schroeder Public-Key protocol is a classical workbench for formal analysis. It was introduced by Needham and Schroeder in the 70s and its aim is to allow two agents to exchange two independent secret numbers.

The basic idea is simple: Alice wants to talk to Bob, but doesn't know him directly. So she contacts a trusted server to provide her with the public key of Bob. Then, by using the protocol, Alice and Bob get hold of two shared secrets in the form of nonces which can then be used for subsequent communication[6].

The protocol is interesting because it has been formally analyzed using a belief logic [7], but a substantial weakness[7] has only been detected using model checking within process algebra [19].

The intuitive description of the protocol is the following:

1. Alice contacts Sam, a trusted server, who knows the public key of Bob;
2. Sam replies by sending Bob's public key signed with his private key;
3. Alice sends Bob a fresh nonce and her name encrypted with Bob's public key;
4. Bob reads the message and contacts Sam to get Alice's public key;
5. Sam replies by sending Alice's public key signed with his private key;
6. Then Bob creates a fresh nonce and sends it back to Alice together with her own nonce, all encrypted with Alice's public key;
7. Alice checks her nonce, and then sends back Bob's nonce encrypted with his public key, to show him that she has got hold of it.

---

[6] To be precise, this goal has been ascribed to the protocols by Needham, Abadi and Burrows in [7]. The original paper [29] uses the more vague term of authentication.
[7] Given the rather vague terms used in the original paper, it has been a subject of an intense debate whether Lowe's "attack" is indeed an attack (see [16]).

Formally, it corresponds to the following:

$$A \longrightarrow S : A\|B$$
$$S \longrightarrow A : \{pK(B)\|B\}_{sK(S)}$$
$$A \longrightarrow B : \{N_a\|A\}_{pK(B)}$$
$$B \longrightarrow S : B\|A$$
$$S \longrightarrow B : \{pK(A)\|A\}_{sK(S)}$$
$$B \longrightarrow A : \{N_a\|N_b\}_{pK(A)}$$
$$A \longrightarrow B : \{N_b\}_{pK(B)}$$

Leaving outside the steps involving Sam, which just distributed public keys, the security of the protocol rests upon the following reasoning (borrowed from [7]):

- if Alice sent Bob a number (the nonce N_a) that she has never used for that purpose before, and if she receives from Bob something that depends on knowing that number (the message $\{N_a\|N_b\}_{pK(A)}$), then she ought to believe that Bob's message originated recently, in fact after hers.
- if Alice believes that $pK(B)$ is Bob's public key, then she should believe that any message encrypted as $pK(B)$ can only be decrypted by Bob;
- if Alice believes that her private key $sK(A)$ has not been compromised then any message encrypted with $pK(A)$ can only be decrypted by her;
- thus, upon receiving $\{N_a\|N_b\}_{pK(A)}$, Alice can be assured that Bob is alive, and only her and Bob know N_a and N_b.

The same reasoning can be done for Bob, when he receives $\{N_b\}_{pK(B)}$.

Thus, "each principal knows the public key of the other, and has the knowledge of a shared secret which he believes the other will accept as being shared only by the two principals. [...] From this point, A and B can continue to exchange messages using N_a, N_b and public-key encryption. In this way they can transfer data or other keys securely" [7].

As Lowe has shown [19], this is not exactly the case. There are runs of the protocol where Bob believes that he has been running the protocol with Alice, whereas Alice has been running the protocol with Charlie and has never heard about Bob.

For simplicity sake, as in Lowe's analysis, we omit messages to and from S.

The first step is the specification in $\mathcal{AL}_{SP}$ of the valid messages of the protocol, to guarantee that the $\mathcal{AL}_{SP}$ specification is admissible (see Definition 2 or [8,9] for further discussion). To this extent, we must define each sub-message in terms of the atomic components:

$$\mathsf{msg}(\{N\|A\}_K) \longleftarrow \mathsf{key}(K), \mathsf{isPubKey}(K), \mathsf{nonce}(N), \mathsf{ag}(A)$$
$$\mathsf{msg}(\{N\|N'\}_K) \longleftarrow \mathsf{key}(K), \mathsf{isPubKey}(K), \mathsf{nonce}(N), \mathsf{nonce}(N')$$
$$\mathsf{msg}(\{N\}_K) \longleftarrow \mathsf{key}(K), \mathsf{isPubKey}(K), \mathsf{nonce}(N)$$
$$\mathsf{msg}(N\|A) \longleftarrow \mathsf{nonce}(N), \mathsf{ag}(A)$$
$$\mathsf{msg}(N\|N') \longleftarrow \mathsf{nonce}(N), \mathsf{nonce}(N')$$
$$\mathsf{msg}(N) \longleftarrow \mathsf{nonce}(N)$$
$$\mathsf{msg}(A) \longleftarrow \mathsf{ag}(A)$$

This step is entirely mechanical and tedious. To avoid it, a translator from protocol descriptions in CASPER into $\mathcal{AL}_{SP}$ has been recently implemented at the Department of Informatica e Sistemistica [18] and a graphical interface is under way.

Next, we need rules to model the ability of agents to manipulate messages. We start by inductively defining the *parts of a message* on the basis of our constructors:

$$\begin{aligned} \mathsf{part}(M, M) &\longleftarrow \mathsf{msg}(M) \\ \mathsf{part}(M, M_1 \| M_2) &\longleftarrow \mathsf{msg}(M), \mathsf{msg}(M_1), \mathsf{msg}(M_2), \\ &\qquad \mathsf{part}(M, M_1) \\ \mathsf{part}(M, M_1 \| M_2) &\longleftarrow \mathsf{msg}(M), \mathsf{msg}(M_1), \mathsf{msg}(M_2), \\ &\qquad \mathsf{part}(M, M_2) \\ \mathsf{part}(M, \{M_1\}_K) &\longleftarrow \mathsf{msg}(M), \mathsf{msg}(M_1), \mathsf{key}(K), \\ &\qquad \mathsf{part}(M, M_1) \end{aligned}$$

In the sequel, for sake of readability, we omit all sort predicates and use the convention that A, B, C, etc. stand for agents, N stands for nonces, T stands for time, K stands for keys, and M stands for messages.

Keys have particular properties, which can be modeled provided the resulting rules are admissible according to Definition 1. For instance, we need to state that

1. public and private keys go in pairs,

$$\begin{aligned} \mathsf{isPubKey}(Kp) &\longleftarrow \mathsf{asymKeyPair}(Ks, Kp) \\ \mathsf{isPrivKey}(Ks) &\longleftarrow \mathsf{asymKeyPair}(Ks, Kp) \end{aligned}$$

2. each private key is the inverse of the corresponding public key, and vice versa,

$$\begin{aligned} \mathsf{invKey}(Ks, Kp) &\longleftarrow \mathsf{asymKeyPair}(Ks, Kp) \\ \mathsf{invKey}(Kp, Ks) &\longleftarrow \mathsf{asymKeyPair}(Ks, Kp) \end{aligned}$$

3. each agent has a public/private key pair.

$$\mathsf{asymKeyPair}(sK(A), pK(A)) \longleftarrow \mathsf{ag}(A)$$

Since Herbrand Equality (i.e. the unique name assumption) is implicit in our model, we obtain that each agent's public (private) key is different from all other asymmetric keys. We can explicitly impose these constraints:

$$\begin{aligned} &\longleftarrow \mathsf{asymKeyPair}(Ks, Kp), \mathsf{asymKeyPair}(Ks, Kp'), Kp \neq Kp' \\ &\longleftarrow \mathsf{asymKeyPair}(Ks, Kp), \mathsf{asymKeyPair}(Ks', Kp), Ks \neq Ks' \end{aligned}$$

If the above rules are the only rules about asymmetric keys, by stable model semantics we have that a public key cannot be another agent's private key. This constraint (which is not necessarily true for all crypto-systems, e.g. RSA [36]) can also be added:

$$\begin{aligned} &\longleftarrow \mathsf{asymKeyPair}(Ks, Kp), \mathsf{asymKeyPair}(Kp, Kp') \\ &\longleftarrow \mathsf{asymKeyPair}(Ks, Kp), \mathsf{asymKeyPair}(Ks', Ks) \end{aligned}$$

Shared keys can be modeled in a similar fashion (see [8,9]).

Next, we define what an agent can infer from other messages and how he can construct messages; that is we *model knowledge*. Most of these rules are protocol independent. The reader may find a comprehensive description in [8,9].

For instance, we may need to specify that if you get something then you obviously know it.

$$knows(A, M, T) \longleftarrow got(A, M, T)$$

Beside sending and receiving messages, we need rules to peel constructors off. For the N-S protocol, we just need rules for concatenation and encryption:

$$knows(A, M_1, T) \longleftarrow knows(A, M_1 \| M_2, T)$$
$$knows(A, M_2, T) \longleftarrow knows(A, M_1 \| M_2, T)$$
$$knows(A, M, T) \longleftarrow knows(A, \{M\}_K, T),$$
$$knows(A, K_I, T), \mathsf{invKey}(K, K_I)$$

In some cases concatenation is modeled as an associative operator. This can be captured by the following rule:

$$knows(A, (M_1 \| M_2) \| M_3, T) \longleftarrow knows(A, M_1 \| (M_2 \| M_3), T)$$

In first-order logic programs, this rule may lead to non termination. We would avoid this problem, as we use the ground representation for actual search.

However, we drop the rule altogether as it is not appropriate for modeling well-implemented protocols: ISO Distinguished Encoding Rules (DER) distinguishes precisely between the concatenation $A \| (B \| C)$ and the concatenation $(A \| B) \| C$ even from a bitwise point of view. Since the formal verification of badly implemented protocols have little sense we decided to leave it out.

Then we can model message composition as follows:

$$synth(A, M, T) \longleftarrow knows(A, M, T)$$
$$synth(A, \{M\}_K, T) \longleftarrow synth(A, M, T),$$
$$knows(A, K, T)$$
$$synth(A, M_1 \| M_2, T) \longleftarrow synth(A, M_1, T),$$
$$synth(A, M_2, T)$$

Now we can build the first part of the *protocol independent action theory* in $\mathcal{AL}_{SP}$. Again, some successor state axioms are identical for all protocols and we refer to [8,9] for further details. For instance, we have axioms to model what happens when a message is received:

$$got(B, M, T + 1) \longleftarrow gets(B, M, T)$$
$$got(B, M, T + 1) \longleftarrow got(B, M, T)$$

The first axiom models a causal law (getting something now causes it to be got afterwards) and the second one models the law of inertia (once you got something, you got it). We need identical axioms for the $notes(A, M, T)$, $says(A, B, M, T)$, etc.

We have not found the need for "forgetful" agents in the protocols we have seen so far [10], thought there might be protocols for which we may need to modify this law of inertia.

Next, we define the preconditions for getting and receiving messages that are independent of the protocol that we want to analyze. For instance, message reception:

$$\{gets(B, M, T)\} \longleftarrow says(A, B, M, T)$$

We use the choice rule (see Section 2) to specify that if A attempts to send a message M to B at time T then B *may* receive it. There are stable models where the message is delivered (the normal execution of the protocol) and stable models where B does not receive the message. A possible interpretation is that in these latter models, the intruder has intercepted the message, or that the communication lines went down. Thus, we do not need to explicitly model the action of message interception as done in [24,27,38].

Modeling the intruder according the classical Dolev-Yao model [13] is simple: he may get any message in transit and he may say any message (but in both cases he needs not to). We do not need to model the ability of intercepting messages as we have already modeled faulty channels by specifying that messages may not be delivered. Therefore, there will be stable models of the protocol where the intruder does nothing (the correct runs) and stable models where he is busy. Formally

$$\{gets(spy, M, T)\} \longleftarrow says(A, B, M, T)$$
$$\{says(spy, B, M, T)\} \longleftarrow \mathsf{synth}(spy, M, T)$$

As we mentioned, we may add more constraints on the action preconditions to cut meaningless attacks and cut the search in the verification stage. For instance, we may strengthen the action preconditions:

$$\{gets(spy, M, T)\} \longleftarrow says(A, B, M, T), A \neq spy, B \neq spy$$
$$\{says(spy, B, M, T)\} \longleftarrow \mathsf{synth}(spy, M, T), B \neq spy$$

In security protocols the notion of *freshness* plays a key role. The whole reasoning in the Needham-Schroeder protocol rests on the nonces being freshly generated. To model freshness, we introduce at first a fluent $used(N, T)$ which is true when message M has been used by somebody before time T. We use the fluent $usedPar(M, T)$ when two agents try to use the same message in parallel, or when an agent tries to send the same message to two different agents in parallel. Out of these two axioms we have rules to denote when something is fresh, i.e. when the fluent $fresh(M, T)$ holds. Since the treatment of freshness is a bit subtle, we refer to [8,9] for further details.

Finally, we are left with the rules specifying the *protocol's action*. We just need to "copy" them from the protocol description making just explicit all freshness checks:

$$\{says(A, B, \{N_a \| A\}_{pK(B)}, T)\} \longleftarrow fresh(N_a, T)$$
$$\{says(B, A, \{N_a \| N_b\}_{pK(A)}, T)\} \longleftarrow got(B, \{N_a \| A\}_{pK(B)}, T),$$
$$fresh(N_b, T)$$
$$\{says(A, B, \{N_b\}_{pK(B)}, T)\} \longleftarrow said(A, B, \{N_a \| A\}_{K_b}, T),$$
$$got(A, \{N_a \| N_b\}_{pK(A)}, T)$$

As we have eliminated the exchanges with S, we have directly used the functions $pK(A)$ and $pK(B)$ to identify the corresponding public keys. In the full protocol, where agents do not know each other's public keys in advance, the check that the public key is appropriate must be made explicit:

$$\{says(B, A, \{N_a \| N_b\}_{K_a}, T)\} \longleftarrow got(B, \{N_a \| A\}_{K_b}, T),$$
$$isPubKey(K_b), invKey(K_b, sK(B))$$
$$isPubKey(K_a), got(B, \{K_a \| A\}_{sK(S)}, T),$$
$$fresh(N_b, T)$$

Once again, we can restrict the search by imposing further operation constraints on each action precondition. It is up to the security analyst to decide which checks are reasonable, depending on the way he thinks the protocol will be implemented. For instance, we can impose that an agent never knowingly sends a message to himself by setting:

$$\{says(A, B, \ldots, T)\} \longleftarrow \ldots A \neq B$$

for all the above rules.

This is a typical limitation common to all formal approaches to the verification of security protocols. Obviously, Alice might be fooled into running the protocol with herself (a classical "mirror attack"), but this typically happens because she is running two protocol instances in parallel, one instance as initiator and one instance as responder. So she sends her messages to Bob, but Bob never sees them: the intruder intercepts the messages and feeds them back to Alice, who might then believe that they come from Bob. These attacks are not prevented by this optimization.

These additional constraints substantially reduce the size of the ground program. Since each constraint eliminates some possible models from consideration, its introduction must be evaluated on a case by case basis, to be sure that we only eliminate models which do not correspond to meaningful attacks.

Last but not least, is the *goal of the protocol*. This depends on what the security analyst is interested in verifying. The procedure to specify an attack to a confidentiality or authentication goal is simple [8,9]:

1. we consider the view point of the agent for which the property must be verified;
2. we list all messages that he has sent or received up to the point of the protocol (typically the end) that we want to verify;
3. for authentication properties, we add the *negation* of the event(s) that we expected to have happened if the protocol was correct (e.g. Bob should have got some message but in reality has not);

4. for confidentiality properties, we say that the spy knows the messages that ought to have remained secret;
5. add additional checks that the security analyst may deem necessary (e.g. constraints on time or on nonces).

We obtain a rule of the form $attacks(T) \longleftarrow \ldots$ and we can finally ground the specification and look for stable models where $attack(t_{max})$ is true (see Section 4). The intuition behind this rule and indeed behind what an attack is can be also explained in the vernacular:

1. Look at the problem from the perspective of an agent A wishing to securely buy an item from a merchant B.
2. A has sent all appropriate messages to the network, allegedly to B or to another bunch of trusted guys and has received all appropriate answers (and thus we list all messages that he has sent or received up to now).
3. For sake of example, suppose that A wants to be sure that the message about B's bank coordinates did actually come from B, i.e. B's message is *authentic*. If the protocol is correct, there is no run (i.e. stable model) of the protocol in which A could have run for so long without apparent errors and without B actually issuing this message. So, to look for a an authentication bug we add the negation of the event whose authenticity we wish to verify. If there is a model for *attack*, then in this model B didn't actually send his bank coordinates, even though A received it, allegedly from B. Something fishy is going on...
4. Looking for a secrecy bug is similar: in all our intended model the intruder is not supposed to get A's credit card number. So we should add the negation of the event (not getting the credit card number) that we wish to verify. Then, loosely speaking, we cancel double negation and just ask for a model where the spy knows the secret.
5. Additional checks may be necessary to avoid attacks that the security analysist may deem uninteresting. For a secrecy attack we may want B to be trusted (lousy merchants may well lose credit card numbers without need of buggy protocols) whereas for authentication or non-repudiation attack we may want the security of the protocol guaranteed within a certain temporal interval (after which the low level connection may time-out or certificates be no longer relevant.

Let's exemplify this procedure in the Needham-Schroeder protocol. At first we may consider the authentication guarantee that the protocol offers to Alice, the initiator of the protocol: if Alice sent $\{N_a \| A\}_{pK(B)}$ to B, received $\{N_a \| N_b\}_{pK(A)}$ and sent $\{N_b\}_{pK(B)}$, she can be sure that Bob actually sent $\{N_a \| N_b\}_{pK(A)}$ to her.

$attack(T) \longleftarrow$

$\quad \left. \begin{array}{l} \mathsf{said}(A, B, \{N_a \| A\}_{pK(B)}, T), \\ \mathsf{got}(A, \{N_a \| N_b\}_{pK(A)}, T), \\ \mathsf{said}(A, B, \{N_b\}_{pK(B)}, T), \end{array} \right\}$ %The protocol is correct for A

$\quad not\ \mathsf{said}(B, A, \{N_a \| N_b\}_{pK(A)}, T)$ %yet B didn't participate

$\quad A \neq spy, B \neq spy$ \qquad\qquad %and all agents are honest

The authentication guarantee from B's viewpoint is stated in dual form:

$$attack(T) \longleftarrow$$
$$\left. \begin{array}{l} \mathsf{got}(B, \{N_a \| A\}_{pK(B)}, T), \\ \mathsf{said}(B, A, \{N_a \| N_b\}_{pK(A)}, T), \\ \mathsf{got}(B, \{N_b\}_{pK(B)}, T), \end{array} \right\} \text{ \%The protocol is correct for } B$$
$$\left. \begin{array}{l} not \ \mathsf{said}(A, B, \{N_a \| A\}_{pK(B)}, T), \\ not \ \mathsf{said}(A, B, \{N_b\}_{pK(B)}, T) \end{array} \right\} \text{\%yet } A \text{ didn't participate at all}$$
$$A \neq spy, B \neq spy \qquad \text{\%and all agents are honest}$$

In some protocols we may also be worried about attacks in which only some steps are missing. In other words, we may consider attacks in which A participated only in a part of the protocol: e.g. in e-commerce protocol we want A to get the goods *and* to pay them. Obviusly, we have an attack if B completed the run successfully, apparently with A and A neither paid not got the goods; but we also have an attack if A got the goods but "forgot" to pay.

In this example, we can weaken the attack, by eliminating either the literal (i) $not \ \mathsf{said}(A, B, \{N_a \| A\}_{pK(B)}, T)$ or the literal (ii) $not \ \mathsf{said}(A, B, \{N_b\}_{pK(B)}, T)$ from the body of the rule. This means that we accept as valid attacks those in which A indeed participated in the protocol but only in part.

Of course the meaning of the attacks that is possibly found is different:

1. if a model where $attack(t)$ is found and both (i) and (ii) are true in the precondition, it means that we have found an attack where A never participated in the protocol at any stage. So A doesn't know at all that B even exists. This is indeed Lowe's attack [19].
2. If no model is found with both (i) and (ii), but a model is found with (i) true, it means that A actually never started the protocol run with B. However, for some unfatomable reasons she sent the last message. Therefore she knows N_b.
3. If no model is found with both (i) and (ii), but a model is found with (ii) true, it means that A actually started the protocol run with B but didn't complete it (at least she didn't completed it with B). Now we can only conclude that she knows N_a.

It is up to the security analyst to decide which attack is worth looking for. However, notice that the analyst does not need to specify *how* the attack is found by combining the protocol actions. He must only specify *what* should not happen. It is the task of the model finder to find the appropriate model that satisfies these declarative constraints.

Confidentiality properties can be equally well specified by imposing that the protocol completed and yet the spy happened to get the messages that ought to be secret. We can specify them either with respect to a particular agent (the run completed correctly for one agent and yet the spy knows the secret) or for all honest participants (the runs are correct for all participants, and yet the spy knows the secret). Whereas the first case is usually coupled with a lack of authentication (the spy grabbed some secret message because the protocol failed for the other agent), the last case is an example of a total break of the protocol.

In case of the Needham-Schroeder protocol, a confidentiality attack from the viewpoint of B is the following:

$$attack \longleftarrow$$
$$\left. \begin{array}{l} got(B, \{N_a\|A\}_{pK(B)}, T), \\ said(B, A, \{N_a\|N_b\}_{pK(A)}, T), \\ got(B, \{N_b\}_{pK(B)}, T), \end{array} \right\} \text{\%The protocol is correct for } B$$
$$knows(spy, N_b, T) \qquad \qquad \text{\%yet } spy \text{ knows } N_b$$
$$A \neq spy, B \neq spy \qquad \qquad \text{\%and all agents are honest}$$

We can formalize the protocol and this attack in $\mathcal{AL}_{SP}$ and run smodels to see what happens. Indeed, we have used the Casper2ALsp translator by Lorenzon [18] to generate the $\mathcal{AL}_{SP}$ specification of the protocol from the Casper specification used by Lowe [20]. We have added some general rules for trimming down useless steps (e.g. there is no sense for the intruder to send a message to somebody if the intruder itself intercepts this very message, etc.), put some restriction on freshness similar to those imposed by Lowe on its CSP encoding and run smodels by setting a bound on time to 4, 5, and 6.

The result is shown in Figure 1. Each $says(A, B, M, T)$ action in the final stable model corresponding to the attack is indicated by T. A --->B : M, $gets(A, M, T)$ actions are indicated by T. -> A:M and the $notes(A, M, T)$ is indicated by T. # A:M. The ellipsis indicates that we have eliminated some obviously spurious messages[8] that have been also sent by the intruder.

Since we have no control on smodels search heuristics, it is often the case that the attack (i.e. the stable model) is not minimal and that there are some spurious actions. In a nutshell, the attack found by smodels is still an attack but the intruder might have wasted some time (i.e. the plan is not optimal).

A total break of the confidentiality of the protocol would be represented by

$$attack \longleftarrow$$
$$\left. \begin{array}{l} said(A, B, \{N_a\|A\}_{pK(B)}, T), \\ got(B, \{N_a\|A\}_{pK(B)}, T), \\ said(B, A, \{N_a\|N_b\}_{pK(A)}, T), \\ got(A, \{N_a\|N_b\}_{pK(A)}, T), \\ said(A, B, \{N_b\}_{pK(B)}, T), \\ got(B, \{N_b\}_{pK(B)}, T), \end{array} \right\} \text{\% } \begin{array}{l} \text{The protocol is correct} \\ \text{for both } A \text{ and } B \end{array}$$
$$knows(spy, A, N_b)T \qquad \qquad \text{\%yet } spy \text{ knows } N_b$$
$$A \neq spy, B \neq spy \qquad \qquad \text{\%and all agents are honest}$$

6   Aziz-Diffie Key Agreement

The Aziz-Diffie key agreement protocol for mobile communication [4] as simplified by Meadows and Syverson [38] aims at establishing a shared key between a mobile unit A and a base station B.

---

[8] For instance, when the intruder sends to B a message encrypted with A's public key that B can't obviously read.

```
massacci{goldrake}: nice-filter.sh ns-pk-trial.lp domain.lp generic.lp 4
****** Model Checking ns-pk-trial.lp up to 4 steps **********
Pre-processing Domain
     Original program has 41 rules
     Ground program has 20924 rules
 - Searching for attacks with smodels
******* NO attack found in  1.250 second (after 0 choices)*******
massacci{goldrake}: nice-filter.sh ns-pk-trial.lp domain.lp generic.lp 5
****** Model Checking ns-pk-trial.lp up to 5 steps **********
Pre-processing Domain
     Original program has 41 rules
     Ground program has 26129 rules
 - Searching for attacks with smodels
******* NO attack found in  1.700 second (after 0 choices)*******
massacci{goldrake}: nice-filter.sh ns-pk-trial.lp domain.lp generic.lp 6
****** Model Checking ns-pk-trial.lp up to 6 steps **********
Pre-processing Domain
     Original program has 41 rules
     Ground program has 31334 rules
 - Searching for attacks with smodels
******* ATTACK found in  4.140 second ******
with 108 choices of which 0 are wrong ones *******
1.  A ---> I : {na,A}pk_I
1.        -> I : {na,A}pk_I
...
2.  I ---> B : {na,A}pk_B
2.        -> B : {na,A}pk_I
...
3.  B ---> A : {na,nb}pk_A
3.        -> A : {na,nb}pk_A
...
4.  A ---> I : {nb}pk_I
4.        -> I : {nb}pk_I
...
5.  I ---> B : {nb}pk_B
5.        -> B : {nb}pk_B
...
6.        # B : {nb}pk_B
...
******* The SPY Learned *******
na
nb
nm
```

Fig. 1. smodels running on Needham-Schröder

This protocol is called *key agreement protocol* because both A and B "contribute" to the generation of the key, and thus they have to agree on its value (and hence the name of the protocol). The agreement is typically done by having A and B each proposing a share of the key and the final key composed by applying some function to the two shares. In this case, the function is simple an exclusive-or of the two shares, but more complicated forms of key agreement can be found in the literature [36, Cap.22].

The informal description of the protocol is the following:

1. The mobile unit Alice sends her certificate and a fresh nonce to the base unit Bob.
2. Bob checks the certificate and replies with his certificate, a fresh share of the agreement key K_B (encrypted with Alice's public key) and binds the encrypted share and the nonce, by signing them with his private key.
3. Alice checks that everything is correct and generates her fresh share of the agreement key K_A, binds K_A and K_B together by signing the pair and sends it to Bob.

If the protocol successfully completes, then Alice and Bob agree on the key $K_A \oplus K_B$ for further communication. The first nonce is used by Alice as a guarantee that Bob's share of the key is fresh, under the obvious assumption that Bob's signature key has not been compromised. Bob's share of the key plays also the role of a nonce, guaranteeing that Alice's share is fresh.

With respect to the original protocol, we have omitted the possibility of choosing the encryption algorithm. From the viewpoint of the formal analysis all algorithms are equivalent (as we abstract most of their details away), so this is usually modeled with an extra message field which would just make the present description more complex.

Formally, it boils down to three messages:

$$A \longrightarrow B : Cert_A \| N$$
$$B \longrightarrow A : Cert_B \| \{K_B\}_{pK(A)} \| Sign_{BforA}\{K_B, N\}$$
$$A \longrightarrow B : \{K_A\}_{pK(B)} \| Sign_{AforB}\{K_A, K_B\}$$

where A is the mobile unit, B is the base unit, N a fresh nonce. The message $Cert_X$ is an abbreviation for $\{X, pK(X), T_{not-before}, T_{not-after}, \dots\}_{sK(CA)}$, a certificate issued by a trusted certification authority CA. We also use the abbreviations

$$Sign_{BforA}\{K_B, N\} \doteq \{h(\{K_B\}_{pK(A)} \| N)\}_{sK(B)}$$
$$Sign_{AforB}\{K_A, K_B\} \doteq \{h(\{K_A\}_{pK(B)} \| \{K_B\}_{pK(A)})\}_{sK(A)} .$$

The first step is always the modeling of the cryptographic primitives and the theory of knowledge and messages. To this extent we borrow from Section 5 all the corresponding rules and add more rules for modeling exclusive-or and the hash function.

The first rules about message composition are obvious:

$$\mathsf{part}(M, M_1 \oplus M_2) \longleftarrow \mathsf{msg}(M), \mathsf{msg}(M_1), \mathsf{msg}(M_2), \mathsf{part}(M, M_i)$$
$$\mathsf{part}(M, h(M_1)) \longleftarrow \mathsf{msg}(M), \mathsf{msg}(M_1), \mathsf{part}(M, M_1)$$

Reasoning about knowledge is subtler, as it heavily exploits the stable model semantics of logic programs:

$$knows(A, M_1, T) \longleftarrow knows(A, M_1 \oplus M_2, T), knows(A, M_2, T)$$
$$knows(A, M_2, T) \longleftarrow knows(A, M_1 \oplus M_2, T), knows(A, M_1, T)$$

First, we should notice that we only mention xor, and not the hash function. Infact, we have no rule for knowing the content of a message out of its hash. Thus, there is no way to derive $knows(A, M, T)$ from the sole knowledge of $knows(A, h(M), T)$, as it should be.

Second, the stable model semantics rules out unwanted models of the xor-rules that are very difficult to cope with when using monotonic logic formalisms. Suppose that we asked for a model with the additional fact that $knows(A, M_1 \oplus M_2, T)$. The correct interpretation is that A doesn't know anything else. In any monotonic logic we would have the model in which A knows also M_1 and M_2. This knowledge would be self sustained: intuitively we will use the first rule to derive that M_1 is there because M_2 is there and the second to rule to conclude that M_2 is there because M_1 is there. Here, $knows(A, M_1, T)$ and $knows(A, M_2, T)$ are not grounded in the premise $knows(A, M_1 \oplus M_2, T)$.

When using exclusive-or, it is useful to add some of its simplest algebraic properties, as many attacks exploit them [35]. Commutativity is one of them and the simplest way to cope with it is to add the axiom:

$$knows(A, M_1 \oplus M_2, T) \longleftarrow knows(A, M_2 \oplus M_1, T)$$

It is convenient to use abbreviations in the actual $\mathcal{AL}_{SP}$ code. To this extent we can use a relational translation: in every rule where an abbreviation $f(m_1, \ldots, m_n)$ occurs as symbol (or where its use can make the rule more readable), replace the abbreviation with a fresh variable M, add a new atom $is\_f(M, m_1, \ldots, m_n)$, and then define is_f appropriately. For instance for $Sign_{A for B}\{K_B, N\}$ we can use the following:

$$is\_sign(\{h(\{K_B\}_{pK(A)}\|N)\}_{sK(B)}, B, A, K_B\|N).$$
$$is\_sign(\{h(\{K_A\}_{pK(B)}\|\{K_B\}_{pK(A)})\}_{sK(A)}, A, B, K_A\|K_B).$$

The rules for sending and receiving actions are identical to the general case described in [8,9] and sketched in Section 5. So we are only left with the axioms for the protocol dependent parts.

Since we have an explicit notion of time, we can verify that certificates have not expired when writing down action preconditions for the choice rules.

To this extent, we introduce a defined fluent $\mathsf{validCert}(A, B, K_B, Cert, T)$ which specifies whether at time T, the agent A considers $Cert$ a valid certificate for the public key K_B of B.

$\mathcal{AL}_{SP}$ gives the security analyst the flexibility to specify the validity conditions. For instance, certificates are emitted by a suitably trusted certification authority, they must refer to a public key, and the current time should be within the validity period of the certificate.

$$\text{validCert}(A, B, K_B, \{B\|K_B\|T_{nb}\|T_{na}\}_{sK(CA)}, T) \longleftarrow$$
$$\text{trusts}(A, CA), \text{isPubKey}(K_B), T_{nb} \leq T, T \leq T_{na}$$

During the model-checking phase, the grounder `lparse` will directly compile away the cases where the certificate is expired.

To start the protocol, A picks up a valid certificate for her public key and generates a fresh nonce:

$$\{says(A, B, Cert_A\|N, T)\} \longleftarrow mobile(A), base(B),$$
$$\text{validCert}(A, A, pK(A), Cert_A, T),$$
$$\text{fresh}(N, T)$$

Notice that the certificate must be valid for A, as in principle A might trust different certification authorities than B.

The agent B responds when the message he receives is valid, and has appropriately generated his fresh share of the key. He also attaches a valid certificate:

$$\{says(B, A, Cert_B\|\{K_B\}_{pK(A)}\|\{h(\{K_B\}_{pK(A)})\}_{sK(B)}, T)\} \longleftarrow$$
$$mobile(A), base(B),$$
$$got(B, Cert_A\|N, T)$$
$$\text{validCert}(B, A, pK(A), Cert_A, T)$$
$$\text{validCert}(B, B, pK(B), Cert_B, T)$$
$$\text{fresh}(K_B, T)$$

The last step of the protocol is carried forward by A:

$$\{says(A, B, \{K_A\}_{pK(B)}\|\{h(\{K_A\}_{pK(B)}\|\{K_B\}_{pK(A)})\}_{sK(A)}, \}) \longleftarrow$$
$$mobile(A), base(B),$$
$$said(A, B, Cert_A\|N, T)$$
$$got(A, Cert_B\|\{K_B\}_{pK(A)}\|\{h(\{K_B\}_{pK(A)})\}_{sK(B)}, T)$$
$$\text{validCert}(A, A, pK(A), Cert_A, T)$$
$$\text{validCert}(A, B, pK(B), Cert_B, T)$$
$$\text{fresh}(K_A, T)$$

Notice that by adding the fluent validCert$(A, A, pK(A), Cert_A, T)$ we impose that A replies only if the certificate she sent to B is still valid at the time in which the third message is issued.

Other checks can be encoded in different ways. For instance, a security analyst may impose that a certificate is valid only if the timespan $[T_{nb}, T_{na}]$ is not larger than a predefined constant. It is rather straightforward to incorporate this check into the definition of the validCert(A, B, K, C, T) fluent.

Another analyst may impose tougher constraints on the timeliness of messages: A only replies to B if B's message comes back within a certain time limit

t_{lim} from her initial request. In such a way the protocol implementation may avoid checking the validity of A's certificate a second time, by imposing that the timespan must exceed t_l.

$$\mathsf{validCert}(A, B, K_B, \{B\|K_B\|T_{nb}\|T_{na}\}_{sK(CA)}, T) \longleftarrow$$
$$\mathsf{trusts}(A, CA), \mathsf{isPubKey}(K_B), T_{nb} \leq T, T + t_{lim} \leq T_{na}$$

Forcing these checks as preconditions on protocol actions is particularly tricky in process algebras approaches which have only an indirect notion of time. In our case it is rather simple to incorporate this check. We revise the action preconditions by replacing "Said" with "Says" and adding the time constraints.

$$\{says(A, B, \{K_A\}_{pK(B)}\|\{h(\{K_A\}_{pK(B)}\|\{K_B\}_{pK(A)})\}_{sK(A)}, \}) \longleftarrow$$
$$mobile(A), base(B),$$
$$says(A, B, Cert_A\|N, T_i)$$
$$got(A, Cert_B\|\{K_B\}_{pK(A)}\|\{h(\{K_B\}_{pK(A)})\}_{sK(B)}, T)$$
$$\mathsf{validCert}(A, B, pK(B), Cert_B, T)$$
$$T_i + t_{lim} \leq T,$$
$$fresh(K_A, T)$$

These three rules are not sufficient to completely model the protocol. Indeed, the protocol description specifies that B accepts the key only after having made a number of additional checks. Thus, from the viewpoint of B the protocol can be considered completed only after these extra checks have been made.

The final "agreement step" is formalized with an action $notes(X, K_{AB}, T)$ that takes place after all messages are sent and checks made, to mark the event that X noted the final agreement key for future use.

$$\{notes(B, K_A \oplus K_B, T)\} \longleftarrow mobile(A), base(B),$$
$$got(B, Cert_A\|N, T),$$
$$said(B, A, Cert_B\|\{K_B\}_{pK(A)}\|\{h(\{K_B\}_{pK(A)})\}_{sK(B)}, T),$$
$$got(B, \{K_A\}_{pK(B)}\|\{h(\{K_A\}_{pK(B)}\|\{K_B\}_{pK(A)})\}_{sK(A)}, T).$$

We have used the messages exactly as they appear in the protocol description. We could use a similar rule for A, which would however be redundant.

For this complex protocol, it makes sense to define events which compromise the current value of the key agreement pair to see whether future runs of the protocol can be compromised. This is done with an oops-rule following the technique introduced by Paulson [33]: we take all short term secrets, all nonces and key which appear in the messages exchanged during a successful protocol run and let the spy note their value.

$$\{notes(spy, N\|K_A\|K_B, T)\} \longleftarrow$$
$$said(A, B, Cert_A\|N, T),$$
$$said(B, A, Cert_B\|\{K_B\}_{pK(A)}\|\{h(\{K_B\}_{pK(A)})\}_{sK(B)}, T),$$
$$said(A, B, \{K_A\}_{pK(B)}\|\{h(\{K_A\}_{pK(B)}\|\{K_B\}_{pK(A)})\}_{sK(A)}, T),$$
$$noted(B, K_A \oplus K_B, T)$$

The loss of old agreement keys is an additional event wrt the "normal" attacks that the spy can perform on the protocol by just intercepting and manipulating messages. When adding this rule, we want to test the robustness of the protocol if past keys can be lost to the spy.

If we add the oops-rule we must slightly change the definition of attack, otherwise trivial attacks will always be found during the verification phase: complete a run of the protocol and then pipe all secret values to the spy with an oops rule. In contrast, what really matters when checking an attack is the following: suppose that the protocol run completed successfully, and the spy didn't get the secret value by means of an oops rule, were the value compromised nonetheless?

In this way, we only block the oops rule for the current run of the protocol, but we do not forbid older protocol runs to be compromised and that compromised runs might be used by the spy to compromise the current run.

$$
\begin{aligned}
attack \longleftarrow\ & mobile(A), base(B), A \neq spy, B \neq spy, \\
& \mathsf{said}(A, B, Cert_A \| N, T), \\
& \mathsf{got}(A, Cert_B \| \{K_B\}_{pK(A)} \| Sign_{B for K_B, N}\{, \}T), \\
& \mathsf{said}(A, B, \{K_A\}_{pK(B)} \| Sign_{A for K_A, K_B}\{, \}T), \\
& not\ \mathsf{noted}(spy, N \| K_A \| K_B, T), \\
& knows(spy, K_A \oplus K_B, T).
\end{aligned}
$$

The intuition is the following: we have an attack if we have completed a run of the protocol, the current agreement keys have not been compromised by some unfortunate oops-action and yet the spy knows the agreement key.

7 Discussion

Throughout the paper we have referred to the differences with some of the state-of-the-art approaches for protocol verification which have been automated. Here we just summarize the main differences.

We have already pointed out that there are many connections between our proposal and Paulson's inductive method [33,34,5]. Indeed, we have in common the operational semantics for the specification of protocols. In the inductive method one models a protocol as a set of traces and then uses interactive theorem proving to prove that the protocol is secure, i.e. prove that *all* traces satisfy a desired guarantee. The price to pay is that inductive theorem proving is interactive and requires expert knowledge, even if current tools substantially help in shortening the verification efforts. Our approach is based on model finding and thus we look for *one* trace that satisfies a given property, i.e. a security violation. Thus, we can substantially automate the search for attacks.

The NRL Protocol Analyzer (NPA) shares with us the choice of the programming paradigm, as we both use logic programs. A key difference is that we use the logic programming language $\mathcal{AL}_{SP}$ as specification language whereas, Prolog is used as implementation language for the NPA [24,27]. The protocol description and the specifications for the NPA are based on state variables and rules for changing state variables with an explicit modeling of the words learned by the intruder. This aspect of NPA is closer to state exploration tools such as Murphi [28]. Security specifications, whose violation may lead to an attack, must be written in a different language either with temporal operators as done by Syverson and Meadows [38] or by using the CAPSL intermediate language [6]. Such specifications are declarative but not executable [38].

Our current formalization does not cope with an infinite search space, which can be treated by NAP at the price of becoming interactive rather than fully automatic. Infinite state space (such as an infinite number of agents or nonces) can be modeled in our approach by minor modifications, but the price to pay is that we would also lose decidability: we could use iterative deepening on t_{max} and the number of basic objects, as this allows us to retain the benefits of the bounded model checking completeness.

We believe that, wrt other model checking approaches, the use of a declarative specification language greatly simplifies the presentation of actions and events [20,21,27,28,38]. Indeed, $\mathcal{AL}_{SP}$ is a good compromise between three contrasting needs: being close to the description of protocols as specified in the security literature, specifying security properties at a high level of abstraction, automating the analysis of the protocols and the search for bugs (i.e. security attacks). Gollmann in [16, pag. 53] writes:

> High level definitions of entity authentication may obscure the precise goals an authentication protocol should achieve. On the other hand, a low level description of the cryptographic mechanisms employed in the protocol may obscure their intended purpose.

Our specification language $\mathcal{AL}_{SP}$ is a step towards making these ends meet.

We plan to apply our verification methodology to more complex protocols such as SET [23] and test to what extent, in terms of the size of specifications, can we use only general purpose tools such as `smodels` for verifying $\mathcal{AL}_{SP}$ specifications. To ease comparison and integration with other approaches, a translator from CASPER specifications [22] to $\mathcal{AL}_{SP}$ specifications has been built [18].

Acknowledgements

We thank P. Baumgartner and U. Furbach for many useful comments on an earlier formalization of this work, I. Niemela and T. Syrianen for support in using `smodels`. This work is partly supported by ASI, CNR, and MURST grants. F. Massacci acknowledges the support of a CNR Short Term Mobility fellowship and the CNR-201-15-9 fellowship.

We dedicate this paper to Bob Kowalski on his 60th birthday, for his seminal contributions to the applications of computational logic to practical problems.

References

1. M. Abadi and R. M. Needham. Prudent engineering practice for cryptographic protocols. Research Report SRC-125, Digital System Research Center, 1994.

2. M. Abadi and R. M. Needham. Prudent engineering practice for cryptographic protocols. *IEEE Transactions on Software Engineering*, 22(1):6–15, January 1996. Preliminary version in [1].

3. K. Apt. Logic programming. In J. van Leeuwen, editor, *Handbook of Theoretical Computer Science*. Elsevier Science Publishers (North-Holland), Amsterdam, 1990.

4. A. Aziz and W. Diffie. Privacy and authentication for wireless local area networks. *IEEE Personal Communications*, 1(1):25–31, 1994.

5. G. Bella and L. C. Paulson. Kerberos version IV: Inductive analysis of the secrecy goals. In *Proceedings of the Fifth European Symposium on Research in Computer Security (ESORICS'98)*, volume 1485 of *Lecture Notes in Computer Science*, pages 361–375. Springer-Verlag, 1998.

6. S. Brackin, C. Meadows, and J. Millen. CAPSL interface for the NRL Protocol Analyzer. In *IEEE Symposium on Application-Specific Systems and Software Engineering Technology (ASSET-99)*. IEEE Computer Society Press, 1999. A complete specification of the Clark-Jacob Library [10] is available at http://www.cs.sri.com/~millen/capsl/.

7. M. Burrows, M. Abadi, and R. Needham. A logic for authentication. *ACM Trans. Comput. Syst.*, 8(1):18–36, 1990.

8. L. Carlucci Aiello and F. Massacci. An executable specification language for planning attacks to security protocols. In P. Syverson, editor, *IEEE Computer Security Foundation Workshop*, pages 88–103. IEEE Computer Society Press, 2000.

9. L. Carlucci Aiello and F. Massacci. Verifying security protocols as planning in logic programming. *ACM Transactions on Computational Logic*, Vol. 2, No. 4, pages 542–580, 2001.

10. J. Clark and J. Jacob. A survey of authentication protocol literature: Version 1.0. Technical report, University of York, Department of Computer Science, November 1997. Available on the web at http://www-users.cs.york.ac.uk/~jac/.

11. M. Denecker, L. Missiaen, and M. Bruynooghe. Temporal Reasoning with Abductive Event Calculus. In *Proceedings of the Tenth European Conference on Artificial Intelligence (ECAI'92)*, 1992.

12. Y. Dimopoulos, B. Nebel, and J. Koehler. Encoding planning problems in non-monotonic logic programs. In S. Steel and R. Alami, editors, *Proceedings of the Fourth European Conference on Planning (ECP'97)*, volume 1348 of *Lecture Notes in Artificial Intelligence*, pages 169–181. Springer-Verlag, 1997.

13. D. Dolev and A. Yao. On security of public key protocols. *IEEE Transactions on Information Theory*, IT-30:198–208, 1983.

14. M. Gelfond and V. Lifschitz. The stable model semantics for logic programming. In R. Kowalski and K. Bowen, editors, *Proceedings of the Fifth International Conference on Logic Programming (ICLP'88)*, pages 1070–1080. MIT-Press, 1988.

15. M. Gelfond and V. Lifschitz. Representing Actions and Change as Logic Programs. *Journal of Logic Programming*, 17:301–322, 1993.

16. D. Gollmann. What do we mean by entity authentication? In *Proceedings of the Fifteenth IEEE Symposium on Security and Privacy (SSP'96)*, pages 46–54. IEEE Computer Society Press, 1996.

17. H. Kautz and B. Selman. Planning as satisfiability. In *Proceedings of the Tenth European Conference on Artificial Intelligence (ECAI'92)*, pages 359–363. John Wiley & Sons, 1992.

18. L. Lorenzon. Un traduttore da CASPER ad $\mathcal{AL}_{SP}$. Master's thesis, Facoltà di Ingegneria, Univ. di Roma I "La Sapienza", March 2000. In Italian.

19. G. Lowe. Breaking and fixing the Needham-Schroeder public-key protocol using CSP and FDR. In T. Margaria and S. B., editors, *Tools and Algorithms for the Construction and Analysis of Systems (TACAS'96)*, volume 1055 of *Lecture Notes in Computer Science*, pages 147–166. Springer-Verlag, 1996.
20. G. Lowe. Some new attacks upon security protocols. In *Proceedings of the Ninth IEEE Computer Security Foundations Workshop (CSFW'96)*, pages 162–169. IEEE Computer Society Press, 1996.
21. G. Lowe. A hierarchy of authentication specifications. In *Proceedings of the Tenth IEEE Computer Security Foundations Workshop (CSFW'96)*, pages 31–43. IEEE Computer Society Press, 1997.
22. G. Lowe. Casper: A compiler for the analysis of security protocols. *Journal of Computer Security*, 6(18-30):53–84, 1998.
23. Mastercard & VISA. *SET Secure Electronic Transaction Specification: Business Description*, May 1997. Available electronically at http://www.setco.org/set_specifications.html.
24. C. Meadows. The NRL Protocol Analyzer: An overview. *Journal of Logic Programming*, 26(2):113–131, 1994.
25. C. Meadows. Open issues in formal methods for cryptographic protocol analy sis. In *Proceedings of DISCEX 2000*, pages 237–250. IEEE Computer Society Press, 2000.
26. C. A. Meadows. Formal verification of cryptographic protocols: A survey. In *Advances in Cryptology - Asiacrypt'94*, volume 917 of *Lecture Notes in Computer Science*, pages 133–150. Springer-Verlag, 1995.
27. C. A. Meadows. Analyzing the needham-schroeder publik key protocol: A comparison of two approaches. In E. Bertino, H. Kurth, G. Martella, and E. Montolivo, editors, *Proceedings of the Fourth European Symposium on Research in Computer Security (ESORICS'96)*, volume 1146 of *Lecture Notes in Computer Science*, pages 351–364. Springer-Verlag, 1996.
28. J. Mitchell, M. Mitchell, and U. Stern. Automated analysis of cryptographic protocols using Murphi. In *Proceedings of the Sixteenth IEEE Symposium on Security and Privacy (SSP'97)*, pages 141–151. IEEE Computer Society Press, 1997.
29. R. M. Needham and M. Schroeder. Using encryption for authentication in large networks of computers. *Communications of the ACM*, 21(12):993–999, 1978.
30. I. Niemelä. Logic programs with stable model semantics as a constraint programming paradigm. *Annals of Mathematics and Artificial Intelligence*, 25(3-4):241–273, 1999.
31. I. Niemelä and P. Simmons. Smodels – an implementation of Stable Model and Well-founded Semantics for Normal Logic Programs. In *Proceedings of the Fourth International Conference on Logic Programming and Nonmonotonic Reasoning (LPNMR'97)*, volume 1265 of *Lecture Notes in Artificial Intelligence*, pages 420–429. Springer-Verlag, 1997.
32. D. O'Mahony, M. Peirce, and H. Tewari. *Electronic payment systems*. The Artech House computer science library. Artech House, 1997.
33. L. C. Paulson. The inductive approach to verifying cryptographic protocols. *Journal of Computer Security*, 6:85–128, 1998.
34. L. C. Paulson. Inductive analysis of the internet protocol TLS. *ACM Transactions on Information and System Security*, 2(3):332–351, 1999.
35. P. Ryan and S. Schneider. An attack on a recursive authentication protocol. a cautionary tale. *Information Processing Letters*, 65(15):7–16, 1998.
36. B. Schneier. *Applied Cryptography: Protocols, Algorithms, and Source Code in C*. John Wiley & Sons, 1994.

37. V. S. Subrahmanian and C. Zaniolo. Relating Stable Models and AI Planning Domains. In *Proceedings of the International Conference on Logic Programming (ICLP-95)*, 1995.
38. P. Syverson and C. Meadows. A formal language for cryptographic protocol requirement. *Designs, Codes and Cryptography*, 7:27–59, 1996.
39. D. S. Weld. Recent Advances in AI Planning. *Artificial Intelligence Magazine*, (Summer 1999):93–123, 1999.

Multiagent Compromises, Joint Fixpoints, and Stable Models

Francesco Buccafurri[1] and Georg Gottlob[2]

[1] DIMET, Universitá di Reggio Calabria, I-89100 Reggio Calabria, Italy,
bucca@ing.unirc.it
[2] Institut für Informationssysteme, Technische Universität Wien,
A-1040 Wien, Austria,
gottlob@dbai.tuwien.ac.at

Abstract. We assume the requirements or desires of an agent are modeled by a logic program. In a multi-agent setting, a joint decision of the agents, reflecting a compromise of the various requirements, corresponds to a suitable joint model of the respective logic programs. In this paper, an appropriate semantics for selecting joint models representing compromises is proposed: *the joint fixpoint semantics*. The intended joint models are defined to be the (minimal) joint fixpoints of the agent programs. We study computational properties of this new semantics showing that determining whether two (or more) logic programs have a joint fixpoint is NP complete. This remains true even for entirely positive logic programs. We also study the complexity of skeptical and credulous reasoning under the joint fixpoint semantics. The former is proven to be co-NP complete, while the latter is Σ_2^P complete. We show how the joint fixpoints of a set of logic programs can be computed as stable sets.

1 The Joint Fixpoint Semantics for Finding Compromises

Assume there are three agents, Mary, Larry, and Brenda, who discuss about dinner. Mary and Larry care much about food. Brenda is very tolerant about food. She is picky about drinks, however. Here are their respective requirements:

Mary: I would like to have soup. I'd like to have either meat or fish this evening. I don't like potatoes. Spinach is okay. Carrots are okay, too (but I don't necessarily care for any of those). Concerning drinks, I have no real preference among beer, red wine, and white wine.

Larry: Soup is fine (but not a must). However, if we have soup, I want to eat meat. Fish is okay. I'd like to have either spinach or potatoes. Carrots (in addition) are okay for me, if somebody wants them. Every drink (among beer, red or white wine) is fine.

Brenda: Whatever you decide about food is okay for me. However, I care much about drinks. If we eat fish I insist on white wine, and if we eat meat, red wine is okay (but not a must).

A.C. Kakas, F. Sadri (Eds.): Computat. Logic (Kowalski Festschrift), LNAI 2407, pp. 561–585, 2002.

Requests and consents of the above form can be expressed in logic programming with negation as failure (*not*), with an absurdity sign $\perp$ and with an additional modality *okay*(p), meaning that p is *tolerated*. Modal atoms *okay*(p) can only appear in the head of a rule.[1] This means that p is not requested, but accepted if necessary in order to reach a compromise. A program written in this enriched language is referred to as a *Compromise Logic Program (COLP)*. The desires and consents of Mary, Larry, and Brenda are represented by the following COLPS P_m, P_l, and P_b, respectively:

P_m :		P_l :	
$\perp$ ←	potatoes	potatoes ←	*not* spinach
okay(spinach) ←		spinach ←	*not* potatoes
okay(carrots) ←		*okay*(soup) ←	
soup ←		meat ←	soup
fish ←	*not* meat	*okay*(fish) ←	
meat ←	*not* fish	*okay*(carrots) ←	
okay(redwine) ←		*okay*(redwine) ←	
okay(whitewine) ←		*okay*(whitewine) ←	
okay(beer) ←		*okay*(beer) ←	

$$P_b :$$

okay(spinach) ←	
okay(carrots) ←	
okay(soup) ←	
okay(potatoes) ←	
okay(fish) ←	
okay(meat) ←	
okay(redwine) ←	meat
whitewine ←	fish
okay(beer) ←	

What we are looking for is a good semantics, which allows us to determine the intuitively intended models representing the acceptable compromises satisfying all requirements of the agents taking into account also their consents (i.e., the *okay* statements). To this aim, let us first more or less informally specify some desiderata of such a semantics.

Requirements:

1. Every intended model should be a model of each single agent's program (when *okay*-clauses are disregarded and $\perp$ is interpreted as *false*).
2. For each agent COLP P, each intended model M, and each atom $p \in M$, one of the two following conditions should hold:

---

[1] We make this restriction for simplicity here. Our semantics could be extended to programs containing *okay* literals in rule bodies, too.

(a) p is supported in the classical sense by M in P, i.e., there is at least one rule of P with head p and body true in M; or

(b) p is supported by some other agent, and $okay(p)$ is supported by M in P. (This is the case when the agent corresponding to P accepts p by compromise.)

3. M should be as small as possible, i.e., no unnecessary atoms should be contained in M.

4. For any agent program P, the body atoms of a clause of P whose head is $\perp$ cannot be simultaneously satisfied by M.

It is easy to see that these requirements are *not* fulfilled, if we consider any semantics that operates on the union of all agent programs (i.e., on the single program obtained by putting together all agent programs). In fact, by performing such a union, we would unite all *okay* statements and thus risk to be more liberal than intended. Any satisfactory approach to fulfill the above requirements must thus operate on the *set* of the agent programs and not on their union.

The first contribution of this paper is to present a semantics for "compromise logic programming" that satisfies all the requirements and appears to be extremely natural, intuitive, and clear-cut. This semantics is referred to as the *Joint Fixpoint Semantics (JFP Semantics)*. Interestingly, it completely relies on the well-known fixpoint semantics for logic programs with negation [14]. The JFP semantics, and, in particular, the new *okay* modality, is fully explained in terms of classical logic program constructs.

We define a function σ mapping a COLP into a classical logic program as follows.

– For each COLP P, we have:

$$\sigma(P) = \{\sigma(r) \mid r \text{ is a rule of } P\}.$$

– Each classical rule r (i.e., rule in whose head neither *okay* nor $\perp$ appears) is invariant under σ, i.e., $\sigma(r) = r$.

– For each modal rule $r = okay(p) \leftarrow body$, we have:
$\sigma(r) = p \leftarrow p, body.$

– For each rule $r = \perp \leftarrow body$ appearing in some agent program P_i, let abs_i be a new atom occurring in no other program P_j, $j \neq i$, and let $\sigma(r) = abs_i \leftarrow body.$

A *fixpoint* of a (classical) LP P is a supported model of P. A formal definition will be given in Section 2. Recall that each positive LP has a unique minimal fixpoint. A program with negation in rule bodies may have several minimal fixpoints. We denote by $FP(Q)$ the set of all fixpoints of a LP Q.

If $T = \{Q_1, \ldots, Q_n\}$ is a set of (classical) LPs defined over the same set of atoms, then $JFP(T)$ denotes the set of *joint fixpoints* of $Q_1 \ldots, Q_n$:

$$JFP(T) = JFP(Q_1, Q_2, \ldots, Q_n) = FP(Q_1) \cap FP(Q_2) \cap \cdots \cap FP(Q_n).$$

By $MJFP(T)$ or $MJFP(Q_1, \ldots, Q_n)$ we denote the set of all set-minimal elements of $JFP(T)$.

We are now ready for specifying the *joint fixpoint semantics for COLPs*. We do this, by assigning to each set $S = \{P_1, P_2 \ldots, P_n\}$ of COLPs a set of intended models $\mathcal{M}(S)$ by:

$$\mathcal{M}(S) = MJFP(\sigma(S)) = MJFP(\sigma(P_1), \sigma(P_2), \ldots, \sigma(P_n)).$$

The following proposition is easy to verify (we do not give a formal proof here).

Proposition 1. *The joint fixpoint semantics for COLPs satisfies all requirements* $1 - 4$.

To illustrate the joint fixpoint semantics, consider the programs $\sigma(P_m)$, $\sigma(P_l)$, and $\sigma(P_b)$ of our example programs:

$\sigma(P_m)$:			$\sigma(P_l)$:		
abs_m	$\leftarrow$	potatoes	potatoes	$\leftarrow$	*not* spinach
spinach	$\leftarrow$	spinach	spinach	$\leftarrow$	*not* potatoes
carrots	$\leftarrow$	carrots	soup	$\leftarrow$	soup
soup	$\leftarrow$		meat	$\leftarrow$	soup
fish	$\leftarrow$	*not* meat	fish	$\leftarrow$	fish
meat	$\leftarrow$	*not* fish	carrots	$\leftarrow$	carrots
redwine	$\leftarrow$	redwine	redwine	$\leftarrow$	redwine
whitewine	$\leftarrow$	whitewine	whitewine	$\leftarrow$	whitewine
beer	$\leftarrow$	beer	beer	$\leftarrow$	beer

$\sigma(P_b)$:		
spinach	$\leftarrow$	spinach
carrots	$\leftarrow$	carrots
soup	$\leftarrow$	soup
potatoes	$\leftarrow$	potatoes
fish	$\leftarrow$	fish
meat	$\leftarrow$	meat
redwine	$\leftarrow$	redwine, meat
whitewine	$\leftarrow$	fish
beer	$\leftarrow$	beer

It is easily verifiable that $\sigma(P_m)$, $\sigma(P_l)$ and $\sigma(P_b)$ admit an unique minimal joint fixpoint that is $M = \{\text{soup}, \text{meat}, \text{spinach}\}$.

Examples of joint fixpoints that are not minimal are $M_1 = \{\text{soup}, \text{meat}, \text{spinach}, \text{carrots}\}$ and $M_1 = \{\text{soup}, \text{meat}, \text{spinach}, \text{redwine}\}$.

Note that a set of COLPs can have multiple intended models. For example, if we replace the rule $\bot \leftarrow$ potatoes by the rule $okay(\text{potatoes}) \leftarrow$ in the program P_m we obtain that the programs $\sigma(P_m)$, $\sigma(P_l)$ and $\sigma(P_b)$ admit as minimal joint fixpoint also the model $M' = \{\texttt{soup}, \texttt{meat}, \texttt{potatoes}\}$ in addition to M.

We have thus introduced a completely new semantics for describing compromises of agents who declare their requirements and their consents. This semantics is based on a new use of the classical machinery of fixpoints of logic programs, in particular, all minimal joint fixpoints of the logic programs associated to the given COLPs.

Note that our translation from COLPs to classical programs provides a new meaning to clauses of the form $p \leftarrow p$. In the classical single-program fixpoint semantics, such clauses have the somewhat questionable meaning "p can be opted to be part of a fixpoint at any time". In our multiagent context, such clauses correspond to modal atoms $okay(p)$ and have the following precise meaning: "if p is required by *another* agent, then let it be".

Here is another, slightly more involved example, where it is shown that realistic constraints of members of a closed chat forum or net-meeting can be modeled via COLP programs. Consider a chat forum involving a fixed set of users who all know each other (this is called a "closed" forum). Suppose each user can specify complex requirements concerning the presence of other users in the forum. The goal is to find the possible scenarios compatible with all users requirements in order to arrange electronic forum meetings. Each user can ask to enter in the forum or simply declare that she/he is available to chat (if someone requires her/him). Further, she/he can either require or accept the presence of other users specifying also possible conditions under which such users are required or accepted, respectively. Let Ann, Bob, Connie and Dan be four users. Here are their respective requirements:

Ann: I want to enter in the forum. I accept the presence of Dan, but I do not require him. I know that Bob and Connie are expert in soccer, but they are fans of the two main competing teams, respectively. Thus, if soccer is a subject of the forum, I accept the presence of Bob and Connie, but only if they are both in the forum (to guarantee a fair discussion).

Bob: I do not require to enter in the forum, but I accept to do this if other users want to contact me. I accept the presence of Ann, but if soccer or music are subjects of the forum, I require her presence (due to her expertise in these topics). I could accept Dan in the forum, but only on working days, to avoid the interference of his unruly son. As for me, also Connie could enter, but only if Dan is not in the forum: I hate their long lively discussions.

Connie: I require to enter in the forum only on Sundays. However, on the other days I'm available to chat. I accept anyone in the forum, if the topic is soccer.

Dan: I'm available to chat in the forum and I accept the presence of all the users. But, if I'm involved in the forum, I would like to meet Ann in it. I like her very much.

Note that a new modality *okay_group* appears in the COLP programs below. A derived atom $okay\_group(p_1, ..., p_n)$ expresses that the group of arguments $p_1, ..., p_n$ is *tolerated* without implying that $p_1, ..., p_n$ are tolerated separately.

However, rules with *okay_group* head atoms can be equivalently expressed by use of normal COLP rules, therefore the *okay_group* modality can just be considered a convenient abbreviation that does not require a proper extension of the COLP semantics. In particular, each rule

$$okay\_group(p_1, p_2, \ldots, p_k) \leftarrow \text{body}$$

can be equivalently rewritten as the following set of regular COLP rules

$$okay(p_1) \leftarrow p_2, p_3, \ldots, p_k, \text{body}$$
$$okay(p_2) \leftarrow p_1, p_3, \ldots, p_k, \text{body}$$
$$\ldots$$
$$okay(p_k) \leftarrow p_1, p_2, p_3, \ldots, p_{k-1}, \text{body}.$$

Therefore, the translation of a rule "$okay\_group(p_1, p_2, \ldots, p_k) \leftarrow \text{body}$" into classical LP is as follows:

$$p_1 \leftarrow p_1, p_2, p_3, \ldots, p_k, \text{body}$$
$$p_2 \leftarrow p_1, p_2, p_3, \ldots, p_k, \text{body}$$
$$\ldots$$
$$p_k \leftarrow p_1, p_2, p_3, \ldots, p_k, \text{body}.$$

The desires and consents of Ann, Bob, Connie and Dan are represented by the following COLPS P_{Ann}, P_{Bob}, P_{Connie} and P_{Dan}, respectively.

P_{Ann} :
in_forum(Ann) ←
okay(in_forum(Dan)) ←
okay_group(in_forum(Bob), in_forum(Connie)) ← subject(soccer)

P_{Bob} :
okay(in_forum(Bob)) ←
okay(in_forum(Ann)) ←
in_forum(Ann) ← in_forum(Bob), subject(soccer) ∨ subject(music)
okay(in_forum(Dan)) ← *not* day(Sunday)
okay(in_forum(Connie)) ← *not* in_forum(Dan)

P_{Connie} :
in_forum(Connie) ← day(Sunday)
okay(in_forum(Connie)) ←
okay(in_forum(X)) ← user(X), subject(soccer)

P_{Dan} :
okay(in_forum(Dan)) ←
okay(in_forum(X)) ← user(X)
in_forum(Ann) ← in_forum(Dan)

Note that we assume that a request of a user U to insert another user V in the forum is active only if U is in the forum. This implies that the COLP rule corresponding to the request of U of inserting V has the literal in_forum(U) in the body (as it happens for the 3th rule of P_{Ann} and the 3th rule of the program P_{Dan}).

The knowledge about each user is enriched by a common knowledge base, defining the relations user, day and subject. Further the constraint that a chat forum must contain at least two users is also included:

$$
\begin{aligned}
&\text{user(Ann)} \leftarrow \\
&\text{user(Bob)} \leftarrow \\
&\text{user(Connie)} \leftarrow \\
&\text{user(Dan)} \leftarrow \\
&\text{subject(soccer)} \leftarrow \\
&\text{day(Monday)} \leftarrow \\
&\bot \leftarrow not \text{ multiple\_chat} \\
&\text{multiple\_chat} \leftarrow \text{in\_forum(X)}, \text{in\_forum(Y)}, X \neq Y
\end{aligned}
$$

The above COLP programs can be easily translated into classical logic programs. As explained before, the rule of P_{Ann} :
$okay\_group(\text{in\_forum(Bob)}, \text{in\_forum(Connie)}) \leftarrow \text{subject(soccer)}$
is translated into the rules:
   in_forum(Bob) ← in_forum(Bob), in_forum(Connie), subject(soccer)
   in_forum(Connie) ← in_forum(Bob), in_forum(Connie), subject(soccer).

Classical logic programs obtained by translating P_{Ann}, P_{Bob}, P_{Connie} and P_{Dan} are the following:

$\sigma(P_{\text{Ann}})$:
in_forum(Ann) ←
in_forum(Dan) ← in_forum(Dan)
in_forum(Bob) ← in_forum(Bob), in_forum(Connie), subject(soccer)
in_forum(Connie) ← in_forum(Bob), in_forum(Connie), subject(soccer)

$\sigma(P_{\text{Bob}})$:
in_forum(Bob) ← in_forum(Bob)
in_forum(Ann) ← in_forum(Ann)
in_forum(Ann) ← in_forum(Bob), subject(soccer)
in_forum(Ann) ← in_forum(Bob), subject(music)
in_forum(Dan) ← in_forum(Dan), not day(Sunday)
in_forum(Connie) ← in_forum(Connie), not in_forum(Dan)

$\sigma(P_{\text{Connie}})$:
in_forum(Connie) ← day(Sunday)
in_forum(Connie) ← in_forum(Connie)
in_forum(X) ← in_forum(X), user(X), subject(soccer)

$\sigma(P_{\text{Dan}})$:
in_forum(Dan) ← in_forum(Dan)
in_forum(X) ← in_forum(X), user(X)
in_forum(Ann) ← in_forum(Dan)

To each of the above programs consider added the rules obtained by translating the common knowledge base. On this knowledge base, it can be easily verified that the minimal joint fixpoints of the above programs are $\text{CHAT}_1 = \{\text{in\_forum(Ann)}, \text{in\_forum(Dan)}\}$ and $\text{CHAT}_2 = \{\text{in\_forum(Ann)}, \text{in\_forum(Bob)}, \text{in\_forum(Connie)}\}$ (where we have omitted atoms coming from the common knowledge base) representing the two possible (alternative) populations of the chat forum compatible with desires and consents of all the users.

The computationally interesting tasks associated with the joint fixpoint semantics are the following:

1. **Joint Fixpoint Existence.** Determining whether a set of LPs has a joint fixpoint (of course, there is a minimal JFP iff there is a JFP). This corresponds to determining whether a set of agents can reach a compromise at all.
2. **Skeptical reasoning under the JFP semantics.** This means determining whether some atom p occurs in all minimal JFPs of some logic programs $P_1, \ldots, P_n$. Note that this is equivalent to determining whether p occurs in all JFPs of $P_1, \ldots, P_n$. In this case, any compromise will force all agents to adopt p. This is of course an interesting information worth to be known.
3. **Credulous Reasoning.** This means, determining whether some atom p occurs in *at least one* minimal JFP. In practice this means that a compromise containing p may be chosen.

In Section 4 we study the complexity of these three problems. In particular, we show that

- JFP existence is NP complete even for pairs P_1, P_2 of *purely positive* programs (in which neither the symbol *not*, nor the absurdity symbol appear). This is rather astonishing, because each positive program has a unique least fixpoint, and one could have thought that a joint fixpoint could be constructed from least fixpoints of P_1 and P_2.
- Skeptical JFP reasoning is co-NP complete and thus exactly as hard as inferencing in classical propositional logic, or as reasoning under the stable model semantics [9, 20, 21, 19].
- Credulous JFP reasoning is Σ_2^p-complete, and thus exactly as hard as credulous reasoning in default logic [18, 8, 11], or as circumscriptive reasoning [16, 4, 11], or as *disjunctive* logic programs under the stable model semantics [5].

In Section 5 we construct a polynomial-time translation between the JFP semantics and the stable model semantics for LPs with negation [9]. The advantage of such a translation is that existing engines [7, 17] (that are rather efficient in practice) for computing stable models can be used to compute joint fixpoints. In particular, the tasks *JFP existence* and *skeptical JFP reasoning* can be easily translated to analogous LP tasks according to the stable model semantics. This enables the construction of simple frontends for JFP reasoning to systems such as S-models [17], the dlv system [7], or others.

Before proceeding with our technical exposition, let us discuss related work. To the best of our knowledge, we are not aware of similar approaches. The work in the area of Belief-Desire-Intention is mainly based on various modal logics [24, 25, 26]. Closest to our work is perhaps [22]. This approach is based on logic programs too and considers diagnostic agents that need to reach a common diagnosis. So the problem is similar to our setting but their methods to solve it are not. There is also the CaseLP approach in [15] based on logic programs, but the authors do not consider the problem to compute common conclusions between the agents.

Various methods for giving semantics to logic programs with *conflicting rules* have been defined in the literature (e.g. Ordered Logic Programming [2, 3], the PARK model [10], or Courteous Logic Programming for prioritized conflict handling [12]).

An interesting extension of logic programming to provide multi-agent functionality is presented in [13]. This model is, however, very different from ours and has completely different aims. Its goal is not to reach common conclusions or compromises, but to achieve a "thinking component" of an agent via a proof proceedure the combines abductive backward reasoning with a forward reasoning method that uses constraint checking methods in the style of Constraint Logic Programming. An agend can observe changes as inputs and react to them under time resource bounds, using an "agent cycle" that alternates between thinking operations, choices, and actions. In summary, this proof-theoretic model of dynamic agent interaction with time parameters cannot be reasonably compared to our method of model-theoretically defining the concept of a compromise of agent desires that are (statically) defined through a set of logic programs.

Finally, there is the IMPACT project [23], a multiagent framework the underlying semantics of which is also based on logic programs. Although the authors do not consider explicitly the problem of reaching common conclusions, it seems that their use of (flat) modalities might be used to encode some of the examples considered in this paper.

But in all the above cases, our use of a joint fixpoint of a set of logic programs is new and has not been considered before.

This paper is a short version of the full report [1], where more technical proof details are given.

2   Preliminaries on Logic Programming

This section recalls basic concepts of propositional logic programming.

2.1   Basic Definitions

A propositional logic program $\mathcal{P}$ is defined on a finite set of propositional variables $Var(\mathcal{P})$. An *atom* or *positive literal* of $\mathcal{P}$ is an element $a \in Var(\mathcal{P})$; a *negative literal* is the negation *not* a of an atom.

A *program clause* or *rule* r is

$$a \leftarrow b_1 \wedge \cdots \wedge b_k \wedge not\ b_{k+1} \wedge \cdots \wedge not\ b_m \qquad m \geq 0.$$

where $a, b_1, \cdots, b_k$ are positive literals and *not* $b_{k+1}, \cdots, not\ b_m$ are negative literals. a is called the *head* of r, while the conjunction $b_1 \wedge \cdots \wedge b_k \wedge not\ b_{k+1} \wedge \cdots \wedge not\ b_m$ is its *body*.

A (propositional) *logic program* $\mathcal{P}$ consists of a finite set of program clauses whose propositional variables are all in $Var(\mathcal{P})$. (Note, however, that $Var(\mathcal{P})$ may contain atoms that do not occur in $\mathcal{P}$). We denote by $Var^*(\mathcal{P})$ the set of atoms of $Var(\mathcal{P})$ appearing in $\mathcal{P}$.

A logic program is *positive* if no negative literal occurs in it.

An *(Herbrand) interpretation* for a program $\mathcal{P}$ is a subset of $Var(\mathcal{P})$. A positive literal a (resp. a negative literal *not* a) is *true* w.r.t. an interpretation I if $a \in I$ (resp. $a \notin I$); otherwise it is *false*. A rule is *satisfied* (or is *true*) w.r.t. I if its head is true or its body is false w.r.t. I. An interpretation I is a *(Herbrand) model* of a program $\mathcal{P}$ if it satisfies all rules in $\mathcal{P}$.

For each program $\mathcal{P}$, the *immediate consequence operator* $T_{\mathcal{P}}$ is a function from $2^{Var(\mathcal{P})}$ to $2^{Var(\mathcal{P})}$ defined as follows. For each interpretation $I \subseteq Var(\mathcal{P})$, $T_{\mathcal{P}}(I)$ consists of the set of all heads of rules in $\mathcal{P}$ whose bodies evaluate to true in I. Note that $T_{\mathcal{P}}$ is well-defined also for programs with negations in rule bodies.

An interpretation I is a *fixpoint* of a logic program $\mathcal{P}$ if I is a fixpoint of the associated transformation $T_{\mathcal{P}}$, i.e., if $T_{\mathcal{P}}(I) = I$. Note that each fixpoint of $\mathcal{P}$ is also a model of $\mathcal{P}$, but the converse does not hold in general. For example the program consisting of the single rule $q \leftarrow p$ has as unique fixpoint the empty set; however, the interpretation $M = \{p, q\}$ is a model of $\mathcal{P}$. The set of all fixpoints of $\mathcal{P}$ is denoted by $FP(\mathcal{P})$.

Let I be an interpretation of $\mathcal{P}$ and let $a \in Var(\mathcal{P})$ be an atom. We say that a is *supported* by I (in $\mathcal{P}$) if there is a rule of $\mathcal{P}$ with head a whose body evaluates to true in I, i.e., if $a \in T_{\mathcal{P}}(I)$. From the definition of fixpoint it immediately follows that an interpretation I of $\mathcal{P}$ is a fixpoint of $\mathcal{P}$ iff I coincides with the set of all atoms supported by I.

For any interpretation $I \subseteq Var(\mathcal{P})$, we define $T_{\mathcal{P}}^0(I) = I$ and for all $i \geq 0$, $T_{\mathcal{P}}^{i+1}(I) = T_{\mathcal{P}}(T_{\mathcal{P}}^i(I))$. If $\mathcal{P}$ is a positive program, then $T_{\mathcal{P}}$ is monotonic and thus has a least fixpoint $lfp(\mathcal{P}) = T_{\mathcal{P}}^\infty(\emptyset)$. This least fixpoint coincides with the least Herbrand model $lm(\mathcal{P})$ of $\mathcal{P}$, i.e.. $lm(\mathcal{P}) = lfp(\mathcal{P})$. For non-positive programs $\mathcal{P}$,

T_P is in general not monotonic, and P does not necessarily have a least fixpoint (it may even have no fixpoint at all). It was shown in [14] that it is NP complete to determine whether a non-positive logic program has a fixpoint.

2.2   Stable Models

In this section we recall the notion of stable models for propositional logic programs and we report some results from [6] that we shall use in the following.

Let P be a logic program and $I \subseteq Var(P)$ be an interpretation. The *Gelfond-Lifschitz transformation* (or simply *GL-transformation*) of P w.r.t. I, denoted by P^I is the program obtained by P by removing all rules containing a negative literal *not b* in the body such that $b \in I$, and by removing all negative literals from the remaining rules.

Definition 1 ([9]). *Given a logic program P and an interpretation $M \subseteq Var(P)$, M is a stable model of P if $M = T_{P^M}^\infty(\emptyset)$.*

A logic program P admits in general a number (possibly zero) of stable models. We denote by $SM(P)$ the set of all stable models of the program P.

Example 1. Let P be the program consisting of the following set of clauses: $\{a \leftarrow not\ b, b \leftarrow not\ a\}$. It easy to verify that P admits two stable models, that are $M_1 = \{a\}$ and $M_2 = \{b\}$. Indeed, $P^{M_1} = \{a \leftarrow\}$ and $P^{M_2} = \{b \leftarrow\}$.

Definition 2 ([6]). *Let P_1 and P_2 be programs. We say that P_2 potentially uses P_1 (denoted $P_2 \triangleright P_1$) if each predicate that occurs in some rule head of P_2 does not occur (positively or negatively) in P_1.*

Given a set of atoms M, the *program of M* is the set of rules $\{a \leftarrow\ |\ a \in M\}$. With a little abuse of notation, when the context is clear, we denote the program of a set of atoms M by the same symbol M.

Proposition 2 ([6]). *Let $P = P_1 \cup P_2$ be a program such that $P_2 \triangleright P_1$. Then:*

$$SM(P) = \bigcup_{M \in SM(P_1)} SM(M \cup P_2).$$

Proposition 3 ([6]). *Let $P = P_1 \cup P_2$ be a program such that $Var^*(P_1) \cap Var^*(P_2) = \emptyset$.[2] Then:*

$$SM(P) = \bigcup_{M_1 \in SM(P_1), M_2 \in SM(P_2)} \{M_1 \cup M_2\}.$$

---

[2] Recall that $Var^*(P)$ denotes the set of atoms actually appearing in P.

3 Joint Fixpoints

In this section we introduce the Joint Fixpoint Semantics for logic programs.

Let $\mathcal{P}_1, \mathcal{P}_2, \ldots \mathcal{P}_n$ be logic programs such that $Var(\mathcal{P}_1) = Var(\mathcal{P}_2) = \cdots = Var(\mathcal{P}_n)$. We define the set $JFP(\mathcal{P}_1, \mathcal{P}_2, \ldots, \mathcal{P}_n)$ of *joint fixpoints* by:

$$JFP(\mathcal{P}_1, \mathcal{P}_2, \ldots, \mathcal{P}_n) = FP(\mathcal{P}_1) \cap FP(\mathcal{P}_2) \cap \cdots \cap FP(\mathcal{P}_n).$$

In words, $JFP(\mathcal{P}_1, \mathcal{P}_2, \ldots, \mathcal{P}_n)$ consists of all common fixpoints to the programs $\mathcal{P}_1, \ldots, \mathcal{P}_n$.

Moreover, we define the set $MJFP(\mathcal{P}_1, \ldots, \mathcal{P}_n)$ of *minimal joint fixpoint* as:

$$MJFP(\mathcal{P}_1, \ldots, \mathcal{P}_n) = \{F \in JFP(\mathcal{P}_1, \ldots, \mathcal{P}_n) \mid$$
$$\nexists F' \in JFP(\mathcal{P}_1, \ldots, \mathcal{P}_n) \wedge F' \subset F\}.$$

$MJFP(\mathcal{P}_1, \ldots, \mathcal{P}_n)$ consists of all minimal common fixpoints to the programs $\mathcal{P}_1, \ldots, \mathcal{P}_n$.

Since, as mentioned, it is NP complete to determine whether a *single* non-positive program has a fixpoint, determining whether a set of programs containing at least one non-positive program has a joint fixpoint is trivially NP hard. Moreover, since this problem is easily seen to be in NP, it is NP complete.

In this paper we are also interested in joint fixpoints of *positive* programs. In particular, we will investigate the issue whether a set of positive programs has a minimal JFP and we will study different forms of *reasoning* with joint fixpoints.

The following example shows that a set of positive logic programs may have zero, one, or more joint fixpoints.

Example 2.

- If $\mathcal{P}_1 = \{p \leftarrow\}$ and $\mathcal{P}_2 = \{q \leftarrow\}$, then $JFP(\mathcal{P}_1, \mathcal{P}_2) = MJFP(\mathcal{P}_1, \mathcal{P}_2) = \emptyset$.
- If $\mathcal{P}_1 = \{p \leftarrow q\}$ and $\mathcal{P}_2 = \{p \leftarrow s\}$, then $JFP(\mathcal{P}_1, \mathcal{P}_2) = MJFP(\mathcal{P}_1, \mathcal{P}_2) = \{\emptyset\}$.
- If $\mathcal{P}_1 = \{p \leftarrow\}$ and $\mathcal{P}_2 = \{p \leftarrow p\}$, then $JFP(\mathcal{P}_1, \mathcal{P}_2) = MJFP(\mathcal{P}_1, \mathcal{P}_2) = \{\{p\}\}$.
- If $\mathcal{P}_1 = \{p \leftarrow p,\ q \leftarrow q\}$ and $\mathcal{P}_2 = \{p \leftarrow q,\ q \leftarrow p\}$, then $JFP(\mathcal{P}_1, \mathcal{P}_2) = \{\emptyset,\ \{p, q\}\}$ and $MJFP(\mathcal{P}_1, \mathcal{P}_2) = \{\emptyset\}$.

We will also consider *credulous and skeptical reasoning* under joint fixpoints. Let $S = \{\mathcal{P}_1, \ldots, \mathcal{P}_n\}$ be a set of logic programs over the same set of propositional variables Var. Let p be an atom in Var.

- p is a *credulous MJFP-consequence* of S if for some minimal joint fixpoint $I \in MJFP(\mathcal{P}_1, \ldots, \mathcal{P}_n)$ it holds that $p \in I$.
- p is a *skeptical MJFP-consequence* of S if for all minimal joint fixpoints $I \in MJFP(\mathcal{P}_1, \ldots, \mathcal{P}_n)$ it holds that $p \in I$.

We define the following decision problems:

PROBLEM JFP (*JFP* existence):

Instance: A set of positive logic programs $\mathcal{P}_1, \ldots, \mathcal{P}_n$ defined over the same set of propositional variables.

Question: Is $JFP(\mathcal{P}_1, \ldots \mathcal{P}_n) \neq \emptyset$, i.e., do the programs $\mathcal{P}_1, \ldots, \mathcal{P}_n$ have a joint fixpoint?

The problem JFP$_2$ is the restriction of JFP to instances consisting of two positive programs:

PROBLEM JFP$_2$ (JFP existence restricted to the case of two programs):

Instance: A pair of positive logic programs $\mathcal{P}_1$ and $\mathcal{P}_2$.
Question: Is $JFP(\mathcal{P}_1, \mathcal{P}_2) \neq \emptyset$, i.e., do the programs $\mathcal{P}_1$ and $\mathcal{P}_2$ have a joint fixpoint?

PROBLEM MJFP^s (skeptical reasoning under the JFS semantics):

Instance A set of positive logic programs $S = \{\mathcal{P}_1, ..., \mathcal{P}_n\}$ defined over the same set of propositional variables Var and an atom $p \in Var$.
Question Is p a skeptical MJFP-consequence of S?

PROBLEM MJFP^c (credulous reasoning under the JFS semantics):

Instance A set of positive logic programs $S = \{\mathcal{P}_1, ..., \mathcal{P}_n\}$ defined over the same set Var of propositional variables and and an atom $p \in Var$.
Question Is p a credulous MJFP-consequence of S?

Also in this case, we define the restrictions of MJFP^s and MJFP^c to the case in which S contains only two programs. We denote such decision problems by MJFP$_2^s$ and MJFP$_2^c$, respectively.

4   Complexity Results

Theorem 1. *The problems* JFP *and* JFP$_2$ *are NP complete.*

Proof. 1.) Membership. It suffices to prove membership for the more general problem JFP. To verify that a set S of positive logic programs on a set of propositional variables Var has a joint fixpoint, it suffices to guess an appropriate interpretation $I \subseteq Var$ and check that $T_{\mathcal{P}}(I) = I$ for each $\mathcal{P} \in S$. The latter is obviously feasible in polynomial time. The problem JFP is thus in NP.

2.) Hardness. It suffices to prove hardness for the less general problem JFP$_2$. We prove that JFP$_2$ is NP hard by a reduction from 3SAT. Let ϕ be a 3DNF formula over a set of atoms $A = \{a_1, \ldots, a_n\}$ of the form: $\phi \equiv (q_1^1 \vee q_2^1 \vee q_3^1) \wedge \cdots \wedge (q_1^m \vee q_2^m \vee q_3^m)$, where q_k^i, $1 \leq k \leq 3, 1 \leq i \leq m$ is a (positive or negative) literal over A. We will transform ϕ into a pair of positive logic programs $\mathcal{P}_1(\phi)$ and $\mathcal{P}_2(\phi)$ such that $\mathcal{P}_1(\phi)$ and $\mathcal{P}_2(\phi)$ have a joint fixpoint iff ϕ is satisfiable.

$\mathcal{P}_1(\phi)$ and $\mathcal{P}_2(\phi)$ are both defined over the following set Var of propositional variables:

$$Var = A \cup \{a'|a \in A\} \cup \{fail\}.$$

For each atom $a \in A$, let $\tau(a) = a$ and let $\tau(\neg a) = a'$.

Program $\mathcal{P}_1(\phi)$ consists of the following rules:

$$
\begin{array}{llll}
\text{Program } \mathcal{P}_1(\phi): & c_i & \leftarrow & 1 \leq i \leq m \\
& a_i & \leftarrow a_i & 1 \leq i \leq n \\
& a_i' & \leftarrow a_i' & 1 \leq i \leq n \\
& \mathit{fail} & \leftarrow a_i, a_i' & 1 \leq i \leq n
\end{array}
$$

Program $\mathcal{P}_2(\phi)$ consists of the following rules:

$$
\begin{array}{llll}
\text{Program } \mathcal{P}_2(\phi): & c_i & \leftarrow \tau(q_j^i) & 1 \leq i \leq m, 1 \leq j \leq 3 \\
& a_i & \leftarrow a_i & 1 \leq i \leq n \\
& a_i' & \leftarrow a_i' & 1 \leq i \leq n
\end{array}
$$

It is obvious that $\mathcal{P}_1(\phi)$ and $\mathcal{P}_2(\phi)$ can be computed in time polynomial in the size of ϕ.

It can be seen that ϕ is satisfiable iff $\mathcal{P}_1(\phi)$ and $\mathcal{P}_2(\phi)$ have a joint fixpoint (for a detailed proof see the full version of the paper). □

Theorem 2. *The problems* MJFP^s *and* MJFP_2^s *are co-NP complete.*

Proof. 1.) Membership. It is sufficient to prove membership for the more general problem MJFP^s. We proceed by showing that the complementary problem is in NP. Let S be a set of positive programs over the same set of propositional variables Var and denote by $\tilde{M} = \bigcap_{M \in MJFS(S)} M$ the intersection of all the minimal joint fixpoints of S. Since an atom p is a skeptical consequence of S iff $p \in \tilde{M}$, we have to prove that deciding whether $p \notin \tilde{M}$ is in NP.

In order to check if $p \notin \tilde{M}$, it is sufficient to guess a set of atoms $M \subseteq Var$ and verifying that:

- $p \notin M$, and
- M is a joint fixpoint of S.

Both the above items are clearly feasible in polynomial time. Thus, checking if $p \notin \tilde{M}$ is in NP. As a consequence, the problem MJFP^s is in co-NP.

2.) Hardness. It suffices to prove hardness for the less general problem MJFP_2^s. We prove that MJFP_2^s is co-NP hard by a reduction from the complement of the problem JFP (joint fixpoint existence). Indeed, as stated in Theorem 1, the problem JFP is NP complete.

The complement of the problem JFP is the following decision problem. *Instance:* a set $S = \mathcal{P}_1, \dots \mathcal{P}_n$ of positive programs over the same set of propositional variables Var. *Question:* Is $JFP(S) = \emptyset$? We reduce this problem to MJFP_2^s. Let x be an atom not occurring in Var and let $Var' = Var \cup \{x\}$. Clearly, x is a skeptical MJFP-consequence of the programs $\mathcal{P}_1, \dots, \mathcal{P}_n$ over the set of propositional variables Var' if and only if $JFP(\mathcal{P}_1, \dots, \mathcal{P}_n) = \emptyset$. Thus, the complement of the JFP problem is polynomially reducible to the MJFP_2 problem. □

Now we analyze the complexity of the problems $MJFP^c$ and $MJFP^c_2$. First we give some preliminary definition and results.

A *positive propositional disjunctive logic program* (DL^+-*program*) is a positive propositional theory in DNF. We denote the i-th rule of a DL^+-program consisting of $t > 0$ rules by:

$$h_1^i \vee \cdots \vee h_{n_i}^i \leftarrow body(r_i)$$

where $n_i > 0$, $body(r_i)$ denotes a (possibly empty) conjunction of positive literals, and r_i is a label not occurring in $Var(\mathcal{P})$ identifying the rule i, for each $1 \leq i \leq t$.

The models $M(\mathcal{P})$ of the DL^+-program $\mathcal{P}$ precisely coincide to classical models of the program seen as positive propositional theory in DNF. The same happens for the minimal models $MM(\mathcal{P})$.

Definition 3. *Let $\mathcal{P}$ be a DL^+-program consisting of $t > 0$ rules. $R_\mathcal{P}$ is a (disjunction-free) program over the set of propositional variables $Var(\mathcal{P}) \cup \{r_1, ..., r_t\}$ consisting of the following set rules:*

$$R_\mathcal{P} = \{r_i \leftarrow h_j^i \mid 1 \leq i \leq t \wedge 1 \leq j \leq n_i\}.$$

Moreover, we define the DL^+-program $\mathcal{P}^* = \mathcal{P} \cup R_\mathcal{P}$.

Lemma 1. *Let $\mathcal{P}$ be a DL^+-program. Then:*

$$MM(\mathcal{P}^*) = \bigcup_{M \in MM(\mathcal{P})} MM(M \cup R_\mathcal{P}).$$

Proof. It follows from Proposition 2, since $R_\mathcal{P} \rhd \mathcal{P}$. $\qquad\square$

We recall that the minimal model semantics assigns to $\mathcal{P}$ the set $MM(\mathcal{P})$ of minimal models of $\mathcal{P}$. A propositional formula ϕ is a *credulous consequence* under the minimal model semantics of $\mathcal{P}$ if for some $M \in MM(\mathcal{P})$ it holds that $M \models \phi$. Observe that the problem of deciding whether a propositional formula is a credulous consequence under the minimal model semantics of a positive disjunctive program is Σ_2^P-complete [5, 6].

Lemma 2. *Given a DL^+-program $\mathcal{P}$ and an atom $p \in Var(\mathcal{P})$, p is a credulous consequence under the minimal models semantics of $\mathcal{P}$ if and only if it is a credulous consequence under the minimal models semantics of $\mathcal{P}^*$.*

Proof. It immediately follows from Lemma 1. $\qquad\square$

Definition 4. *Let $\mathcal{P}$ be a DL^+-program consisting of $t > 0$ rules. We define the set $JUST^r(\mathcal{P}^*)$ as the set of models M of $\mathcal{P}^*$ such that each atom in $M \cap \{r_1, ..., r_t\}$ is supported by M (in $\mathcal{P}^*$). $JUST^r(\mathcal{P}^*)$ is said the set of rule-justified models (or simply r-justified models) of $\mathcal{P}^*$.*

Moreover, we define the set $MJUST^r(\mathcal{P}^*)$ of minimal r-justified models of $\mathcal{P}^*$ as:

$$MJUST^r(\mathcal{P}^*) = \{M \in JUST^r(\mathcal{P}^*) \mid \nexists M' \in JUST^r(\mathcal{P}^*) \wedge M' \subset M\}.$$

Lemma 3. *Let $\mathcal{P}$ be a DL^+-program. Then:*

$$MM(\mathcal{P}^*) = MJUST^r(\mathcal{P}^*).$$

Proof. Let $t > 0$ be the number of rules of the program $\mathcal{P}$.

($\subseteq$) By contradiction let $M \in MM(\mathcal{P}^*)$ and $M \notin MJUST^r(\mathcal{P}^*)$. Since M is a model of $\mathcal{P}^*$ it must holds that:

(i) either $M \notin JUST^r(\mathcal{P}^*)$, or
(ii) $M \in JUST^r(\mathcal{P}^*)$ but it is not minimal.

Consider case (i). If M is not in $JUST^r(\mathcal{P}^*)$, there exists an atom in $M \cap \{r_1, ..., r_t\}$, say r_i ($1 \leq i \leq t$), that is not supported by M. Thus, each rule of $\mathcal{P}^*$ with r_i occurring in the head has body false in M. As a consequence, each of such rules is satisfied in $M \setminus \{r_i\}$. Moreover, any other rule of $\mathcal{P}^*$ is satisfied in $M \setminus \{r_i\}$ as well, since no rule of $\mathcal{P}^*$ contains r_i in the body and M is a model of $\mathcal{P}^*$. Hence $M \setminus \{r_i\} \subset M$ is a model of $\mathcal{P}^*$. This contradicts the hypothesis that M is a minimal model of $\mathcal{P}^*$.

Consider now case (ii). Since M is not minimal there exists $M' \in JUST^r(\mathcal{P}^*)$ such that $M' \subset M$. Since M' is a model of $\mathcal{P}^*$ and M is a minimal model of $\mathcal{P}^*$, we have reached a contradiction.

($\supseteq$) By contradiction let $M \in MJUST^r(\mathcal{P}^*)$ and $M \notin MM(\mathcal{P}^*)$. Since M is a model of $\mathcal{P}^*$, $M \notin MM(\mathcal{P}^*)$ implies that there exits a model M' of $\mathcal{P}^*$ such that $M' \subset M$. Clearly, it holds that:

(i) either $M' \in JUST^r(\mathcal{P}^*)$, or
(ii) $M' \notin JUST^r(\mathcal{P}^*)$.

Case (i) contradicts hypothesis, since M is a minimal r-justified model of $\mathcal{P}^*$ and $M' \subset M$.

Consider now case (ii). Let $R = \{r_1, ..., r_t\} \cap M'$. Since $M' \notin JUST^r(\mathcal{P}^*)$ there exits some atom in R not supported by M'.

Let $\bar{R}$ be the set of all the atoms of R not supported by M'. Clearly, $\bar{R} \neq \emptyset$. We claim that $M' \setminus \bar{R}$ is a model of $\mathcal{P}^*$. Indeed, each rule of $\mathcal{P}^*$ with an atom of $\bar{R}$ occurring in the head has body false in M' (since $\bar{R}$ is a set of atoms not supported by M'). Consequently, each of such rules is satisfied also in $M' \setminus \bar{R}$. On the other hand, any other rule of $\mathcal{P}^*$ is satisfied in $M' \setminus \bar{R}$, since M' is a model of $\mathcal{P}^*$ and no rule of $\mathcal{P}^*$ contains atoms of $\bar{R}$ in the body. Thus, $M' \setminus \bar{R}$ is a model of $\mathcal{P}^*$.

By definition of $\bar{R}$, any atom in $R' = R \setminus \bar{R}$ is supported by M'. Further, since atoms of $\{r_1, ..., r_t\}$ do not occur in the body of the rules of $\mathcal{P}^*$, any atom in R' is supported by $M' \setminus \bar{R}$ too. But $R' = \{r_1, ..., r_t\} \cap (M' \setminus \bar{R})$. Moreover, as proven above, $M' \setminus \bar{R}$ is a model of $\mathcal{P}^*$. Therefore, by Definition 4, $M' \setminus \bar{R} \in JUST^r(\mathcal{P}^*)$. Since $M' \subset M$ we have reached a contradiction, as M is a minimal r-justified model of $\mathcal{P}^*$. $\square$

Definition 5. *Let $\mathcal{P}$ be a DL^+-program consisting of $t > 0$ rules. We define the two programs $\mathcal{P}_h$ and $\mathcal{P}_b$ associated to the program $\mathcal{P}$ in the following way: The program $\mathcal{P}_h$ is the union of the sets of rules S_h^1 and S_h^2 defined as follows:*

$$S_h^1 = \{r_i \leftarrow h_j^i \mid 1 \leq i \leq t \wedge 1 \leq j \leq n_i\}$$
$$S_h^2 = \{x \leftarrow x \mid x \in Var(\mathcal{P})\}$$

The program $\mathcal{P}_b$ is the union of the sets of rules S_b^1 and S_b^2 defined as follows:

$$S_b^1 = \{r_i \leftarrow body(r_i) \mid 1 \leq i \leq t\}$$
$$S_b^2 = \{x \leftarrow x \mid x \in Var(\mathcal{P}) \cup \{r_1, ..., r_t\}\}.$$

Lemma 4. *Let $\mathcal{P}$ be a DL^+-program. Then:*

$$JFP(\mathcal{P}_h, \mathcal{P}_b) = JUST^r(\mathcal{P}^*).$$

Proof. Let $t > 0$ be the number of rules of the program $\mathcal{P}$.
($\subseteq$) We proceed by contradiction by supposing that $M \in JFP(\mathcal{P}_h, \mathcal{P}_b)$ and $M \notin JUST^r(\mathcal{P}^*)$. The latter implies that:

(i) either M is not model of $\mathcal{P}^*$, or
(ii) M is a model of $\mathcal{P}^*$ but there exists an atom in $\{r_1, ..., r_t\} \cap M$ not supported by M.

Case (i). If M is not a model of $\mathcal{P}^*$ there exits a rule of $\mathcal{P}^*$ not satisfied in M. Such a rule can belong either to $\mathcal{P}$ or to $R_{\mathcal{P}}$ (see Definition 3).

In the former case (i.e., there is a rule not satisfied in M belonging to $\mathcal{P}$), let r_i (for some $1 \leq i \leq t$) be the identifier of a rule of $\mathcal{P}$ not satisfied in M. Such a rule has body true in M and head false in M. Thus, h_i^j is false in M, for each $1 \leq j \leq n_i$ and $body(r_i)$ is true in M. Since M is a fixpoint of $\mathcal{P}_b$, due to the rule $r_i \leftarrow body(r_i)$ belonging to $\mathcal{P}_b$, $r_i \in M$. On the other hand, h_i^j false in M, for each $1 \leq j \leq n_i$, implies that each clause of $\mathcal{P}_h$ with head r_i has body false in M. Thus, the atom $r_i \in M$ is not supported by M in $\mathcal{P}_h$. But this is a contradiction, since M is a fixpoint of $\mathcal{P}_h$ and thus each atom in M must be supported by M in $\mathcal{P}_h$.

In the latter case (i.e., there is a rule not satisfied in M belonging to $R_{\mathcal{P}}$), since $R_{\mathcal{P}}$ coincide with the set of rules S_h^1 of $\mathcal{P}_h$, M would not a model of $\mathcal{P}_h$. But this is a contradiction, since M is a fixpoint of $\mathcal{P}_h$.

Consider now case (ii) above. Let $x \in \{r_1, ..., r_t\} \cap M$ be an atom not supported by M in $\mathcal{P}^*$. Since a rule with head x belongs to $\mathcal{P}_h$ if and only if it belongs to $\mathcal{P}^*$, $x \in M$ is not supported by M in $\mathcal{P}_h$ too. This contradicts the hypothesis that M is a fixpoint of $\mathcal{P}_h$.

($\supseteq$) We proceed by contradiction by supposing that $M \in JUST^r(\mathcal{P}^*)$ and $M \notin JFP(\mathcal{P}_h, \mathcal{P}_b)$. $M \notin JFP(\mathcal{P}_h, \mathcal{P}_b)$ implies that at least one of the following items holds:

(i) M is not fixpoint of $\mathcal{P}_h$, or
(ii) M is not a fixpoint of $\mathcal{P}_b$.

Both items can be shown to be contradictory (for details see the full version).

□

Corollary 1. *Let $\mathcal{P}$ be a DL^+-program. Then:*

$$MJFP(\mathcal{P}_h, \mathcal{P}_b) = MJUST^r(\mathcal{P}^*).$$

Proof. It immediately follows from Lemma 4.   □

Lemma 5. *Given a set of positive logic programs S over the same set of propositional variables Var, and a set $F \subseteq Var$, deciding whether F is a minimal joint fixpoint of S is in co-NP.*

Proof. We show that the complementary problem is in NP. To verify that F is not a minimal joint fixpoint of S, we guess a set $F' \subseteq Var$ and check that:

1. either F' is a joint fixpoint of S and $F' \subset F$, or
2. F is not a joint fixpoint of S.

Both the above tasks are feasible in polynomial time. Thus, the statement immediately follows.   □

Theorem 3. *The problems $MJFP^c$ and $MJFP_2^c$ are Σ_2^P-complete.*

Proof. 1.) Membership. It suffices to prove membership for the more general problem $MJFP^c$. Given a set of positive programs S on a set of propositional variables Var and an atom $p \in Var$, to verify that p is a $MJFP$-credulous consequence of S, we guess a subset $F \subseteq Var$ and check that:

(1) F is a minimal joint fixpoint of S, and
(2) $p \in F$.

By virtue of Lemma 5 the task (1) is in co-NP, while the task (2) is trivially polynomial. Therefore $MJFP^c$ is in Σ_2^P and $MJFP_2^c$ is in Σ_2^P as well.

2.) Hardness. It suffices to prove hardness for the less general problem $MJFP_2^c$.

First, consider the following decision problem. *Instance:* a positive program $\mathcal{P}$ and an atom $p \in Var(\mathcal{P})$. *Question:* there exists a model $M \in MJUST^r(\mathcal{P}^*)$ (i.e., a minimal r-justified model of $\mathcal{P}$) such that $p \in M$? By Lemma 3, since the credulous reasoning under minimal model semantics is Σ_2^P-complete, the above decision problem is Σ_2^P-complete too.

We prove Σ_2^P-hardness of $MJFP_2^c$ by reduction from the above decision problem.

From Corollary 1 it follows that given an atom $p \in Var(\mathcal{P})$ there exists a model in $MJUST^r(\mathcal{P}^*)$ containing p if and only if there exists a joint fixpoint $M \in \{\mathcal{P}_a, \mathcal{P}_b\}$ such that $p \in M$. The latter is clearly the problem $MJFP_2^c$ with instance on the set of programs $\{\mathcal{P}_a, \mathcal{P}_b\}$ and the atom p.

Thus, $MJFP_2^c$ is Σ_2^P-hard. Since $MJFP_2^c$ is a restriction of the problem $MJFP^c$, we conclude that $MJFP^c$ is Σ_2^P-hard as well.   □

5   Joint Fixpoints and Stable Models

In this section we give the translation from Logic Programming under the Joint Fixpoint Semantics to Logic Programming under Stable Model Semantics. First we need some preliminary definitions and results.

Definition 6. *Let $\mathcal{P}$ be a program and let M be a set of atoms in $Var(\mathcal{P})$. We denote by $[M]_{\mathcal{P}}$ the set $\{a_{\mathcal{P}} \mid a \in M\} \cup \{a'_{\mathcal{P}} \mid a \in Var(\mathcal{P}) \setminus M\} \cup \{sa_{\mathcal{P}} \mid a \in M\}$.*

Definition 7. *Let $\mathcal{P}$ be a positive program. We define the program $\Gamma(\mathcal{P})$ over the set of atoms $Var(\Gamma(\mathcal{P})) = \{a_{\mathcal{P}} \mid a \in Var(\mathcal{P})\} \cup \{a'_{\mathcal{P}} \mid a \in Var(\mathcal{P})\} \cup \{sa_{\mathcal{P}} \mid a \in Var(\mathcal{P})\} \cup \{fail_{\mathcal{P}}\}$ as the union of the sets of rules S_1, S_2 and S_3, defined as follows:*

$$S_1 = \{a_{\mathcal{P}} \leftarrow not\ a'_{\mathcal{P}} \mid a \in Var(\mathcal{P})\} \cup \{a'_{\mathcal{P}} \leftarrow not\ a_{\mathcal{P}} \mid a \in Var(\mathcal{P})\}$$

$$S_2 = \{sa_{\mathcal{P}} \leftarrow b^1_{\mathcal{P}}, ..., b^n_{\mathcal{P}} \mid a \leftarrow b_1, ... b_n \in \mathcal{P}\}$$

$$S_3 = \{fail_{\mathcal{P}} \leftarrow not\ fail_{\mathcal{P}}, sa_{\mathcal{P}}, not\ a_{\mathcal{P}} \mid a \in Var(\mathcal{P})\} \cup$$
$$\{fail_{\mathcal{P}} \leftarrow not\ fail_{\mathcal{P}}, a_{\mathcal{P}}, not\ sa_{\mathcal{P}} \mid a \in Var(\mathcal{P})\}.$$

Lemma 6. *Let $\mathcal{P}$ be a program. Then:*

$$SM(\Gamma(\mathcal{P})) = \bigcup_{F \in FP(\mathcal{P})} \{[F]_{\mathcal{P}}\}.$$

Proof. ($\subseteq$) Let X be a stable model of $\Gamma(\mathcal{P})$. We prove that there exists a set of atoms $F \subseteq Var(\mathcal{P})$ such that:

(1) $X = [F]_{\mathcal{P}}$, and
(2) F is a fixpoint of $\mathcal{P}$ (i.e., $F \in FP(\mathcal{P})$).

First we show that Item (1) holds. To this end we prove that:

(a) $fail_{\mathcal{P}}$ does not occur in X,
(b) for any $a \in Var(\mathcal{P})$, either $a_{\mathcal{P}}$ or $a'_{\mathcal{P}}$ occurs in X but not both, and
(c) $a_{\mathcal{P}} \in X$ if and only if $sa_{\mathcal{P}} \in X$, for any $a \in Var(\mathcal{P})$.

Item (a). The only rules with $fail_{\mathcal{P}}$ in the head are those of S_3. If $fail_{\mathcal{P}} \in X$, these rules do not belong to the GL-transformation $\Gamma(\mathcal{P})^X$ of $\Gamma(\mathcal{P})$ w.r.t. X. Hence X cannot be the least fixpoint of $T_{\Gamma(\mathcal{P})^X}$.

Item (b). We proceed by contradiction. Thus we suppose there exists an atom $a \in Var(\mathcal{P})$ such that either:

$-\ a_{\mathcal{P}} \notin X$ and $a'_{\mathcal{P}} \notin X$, or
$-\ a_{\mathcal{P}} \in X$ and $a'_{\mathcal{P}} \in X$.

In the former case (i.e., $a_{\mathcal{P}} \notin X$ and $a'_{\mathcal{P}} \notin X$) the rules $a_{\mathcal{P}} \leftarrow$ and $a'_{\mathcal{P}} \leftarrow$ belong to the GL-transformation $\Gamma(\mathcal{P})^X$ of $\Gamma(\mathcal{P})$ w.r.t. X. Indeed, the rule $a_{\mathcal{P}} \leftarrow not\ a'_{\mathcal{P}}$ belonging to S_1 is transformed into the rule $a_{\mathcal{P}} \leftarrow$ (since $a'_{\mathcal{P}} \notin X$) and the rule $a'_{\mathcal{P}} \leftarrow not\ a_{\mathcal{P}}$ belonging to S_1 is transformed into the rule $a'_{\mathcal{P}} \leftarrow$ (since $a_{\mathcal{P}} \notin X$). As a consequence, X is not a fixpoint of $T_{\Gamma(\mathcal{P})^X}$ (contradiction).

In the latter case (i.e., $a_{\mathcal{P}} \in X$ and $a'_{\mathcal{P}} \in X$), the GL-transformation $\Gamma(\mathcal{P})^X$ of $\Gamma(\mathcal{P})$ w.r.t. X eliminates both rules $a_{\mathcal{P}} \leftarrow not\ a'_{\mathcal{P}}$ and $a'_{\mathcal{P}} \leftarrow not\ a_{\mathcal{P}}$ belonging to S_1. Indeed, their body is false w.r.t X. On the other hand, such rules are the only rules occurring in $\Gamma(\mathcal{P})$ with $a_{\mathcal{P}}$ or $a'_{\mathcal{P}}$ in the head. Hence, $\Gamma(\mathcal{P})^X$ does not contain any rule with $a_{\mathcal{P}}$ or $a'_{\mathcal{P}}$ in the head. This contradicts the hypothesis that X is a fixpoint of $T_{\Gamma(\mathcal{P})^X}$.

Item (c). Let $P_1 = S_1 \cup S_2$ and $P_2 = S_3$. Given a set of atoms $M \subseteq Var(\Gamma(\mathcal{P}))$, we say that M satisfies the *fixpoint condition* if the following holds: for any $a \in Var(\mathcal{P})$, $a_{\mathcal{P}} \in M$ if and only if $sa_{\mathcal{P}} \in M$. Note that Item (c) states that X satisfies the *fixpoint condition*.

The following claim can be proven (see the full version for details):

Claim 1. *Let $M \in SM(\mathcal{P}_1)$. Then, $SM(M \cup \mathcal{P}_2) = \{M\}$ if M satisfies the fixpoint condition, $SM(M \cup \mathcal{P}_2) = \emptyset$, otherwise* [3].

Using the above claim, we prove now that X satisfies the *fixpoint condition* (as stated in Item (c)), that is $a_{\mathcal{P}} \in X$ if and only if $sa_{\mathcal{P}} \in X$, for any $a \in Var(\mathcal{P})$.

First observe that $\mathcal{P}_2 \rhd \mathcal{P}_1$ (according to Definition 2) and, further, $\Gamma(\mathcal{P}) = \mathcal{P}_1 \cup \mathcal{P}_2$. Thus, by Proposition 2, $SM(\Gamma(\mathcal{P})) = \bigcup_{M \in SM(\mathcal{P}_1)} SM(M \cup \mathcal{P}_2)$.

Since $X \in SM(\Gamma(\mathcal{P}))$, there exits a stable model $Y \in SM(\mathcal{P}_1)$ such that $X \in SM(Y \cup \mathcal{P}_2)$. Thus $SM(Y \cup \mathcal{P}_2) \neq \emptyset$. By Claim 1, it follows that both $SM(Y \cup \mathcal{P}_2) = \{Y\}$ and Y satisfies the *fixpoint condition* (otherwise $SM(Y \cup \mathcal{P}_2)$ would be $\emptyset$). This implies that $X = Y$ and hence that X satisfies the *fixpoint condition*. This concludes the proof of the Item(1).

We have thus proven that there exits a set of atoms $F \subseteq Var(\mathcal{P})$ such that $X = [F]_{\mathcal{P}}$. Now we prove that Item (2) holds, i.e., that F is a fixpoint of $\mathcal{P}$.

Recall that F is a fixpoint of $\mathcal{P}$ if and only if it coincides with the set of all atoms of $Var(\mathcal{P})$ supported by F (recall that an atom a is supported by F if there exists a rule in $\mathcal{P}$ with head a and body true in F).

Thus it suffices to prove that:

(i) if a belongs to F then a is supported by F in $\mathcal{P}$ and

(ii) if $a \in Var(\mathcal{P})$ is supported by F in $\mathcal{P}$ then a belongs to F.

The proof of these two items is given in the full version of the paper.

($\supseteq$) Let F be a fixpoint of $\mathcal{P}$. We have to show that $[F]_{\mathcal{P}}$ is a stable model of the program $\Gamma(\mathcal{P})$.

---

[3] Note that $M \cup \mathcal{P}_2$ denotes the set of rules $\{a \leftarrow\ |\ a \in M\} \cup \mathcal{P}_2$.

Let Π be the GL-transformation of $\Gamma(\mathcal{P})$ w.r.t. $[F]_{\mathcal{P}}$. It is immediately verifiable that Π is the union of the following sets of rules:

$$S'_1 = \{a_{\mathcal{P}} \leftarrow \ | \ a \in F\}$$
$$S'_2 = \{a'_{\mathcal{P}} \leftarrow \ | \ a \in Var(\mathcal{P}) \setminus F\}$$
$$S'_3 = \{sa_{\mathcal{P}} \leftarrow b^1_{\mathcal{P}}, \ldots, b^n_{\mathcal{P}} \ | \ a \leftarrow b^1, \ldots b^n \in \mathcal{P}\}$$
$$S'_4 = \{fail_{\mathcal{P}} \leftarrow sa_{\mathcal{P}} \ | \ a \in Var(\mathcal{P}) \setminus F\}$$
$$S'_5 = \{fail_{\mathcal{P}} \leftarrow a_{\mathcal{P}} \ | \ a \in Var(\mathcal{P}) \setminus F\}$$

We proceed by contradiction by supposing that $[F]_{\mathcal{P}}$ is not a stable model of $\Gamma(\mathcal{P})$.

$[F]_{\mathcal{P}}$ is not a stable model of $\Gamma(\mathcal{P})$ if and only if $T^{\infty}_{\Pi}(\emptyset) \neq [F]_{\mathcal{P}}$. This implies that:

(i) either $T^{\infty}_{\Pi}(\emptyset) \not\subseteq [F]_{\mathcal{P}}$, or
(ii) $T^{\infty}_{\Pi}(\emptyset) \subset [F]_{\mathcal{P}}$.

In the full paper we show that both these cases are impossible.   □

An immediate consequence of the above lemma is that there is a one-to-one correspondence between the set of fixpoints of a given program $\mathcal{P}$ and the set $SM(\Gamma(\mathcal{P}))$ of stable models of the program $\Gamma(\mathcal{P})$.

Now suppose we have a set of positive programs $\mathcal{P}_1, \ldots, \mathcal{P}_n$ over the same set of propositional variables. We find a program $J(\mathcal{P}_1, \ldots, \mathcal{P}_n)$ associated to the set of programs $\mathcal{P}_1, \ldots, \mathcal{P}_n$ such that the stable models of $J(\mathcal{P}_1, \ldots, \mathcal{P}_n)$ correspond to the joint fixpoints of $\mathcal{P}_1, \ldots, \mathcal{P}_n$. $J(\mathcal{P}_1, \ldots, \mathcal{P}_n)$ is constructed by performing the union of all the programs $\Gamma(\mathcal{P}_i)$, for $1 \leq i \leq n$, with another program $C(\mathcal{P}_1, \ldots, \mathcal{P}_n)$ that we next define. Informally, under stable model semantics, rules of programs $\Gamma(\mathcal{P}_1)$, $\Gamma(\mathcal{P}_2)$, ... , $\Gamma(\mathcal{P}_n)$ have the effect of generating all the fixpoints of $\mathcal{P}_1$, $\mathcal{P}_2$, ... , $\mathcal{P}_n$, respectively, while rules of $C(\mathcal{P}_1, \ldots, \mathcal{P}_n)$ select among these all fixpoints that are simultaneously fixpoints of $\mathcal{P}_1$, $\mathcal{P}_2$, ... , $\mathcal{P}_n$.

Definition 8. *Given a set of positive programs $\mathcal{P}_1, \ldots, \mathcal{P}_n$ over the same set of atomic propositions Var, $C(\mathcal{P}_1, \ldots, \mathcal{P}_n)$ is the program over $Var' = \bigcup_{1 \leq i \leq n}\{a_{\mathcal{P}_i} \ | \ a \in Var\} \cup \{fail\}$ defined as follows:*

$$C(\mathcal{P}_1, \ldots, \mathcal{P}_n) = \{fail \leftarrow not \ fail, a_{\mathcal{P}_i}, not \ a_{\mathcal{P}_j} \ | \ 1 \leq i \neq j \leq n\}.$$

Moreover, the program $J(\mathcal{P}_1, \ldots, \mathcal{P}_n)$ over $\bigcup_{1 \leq i \leq n} Var(\Gamma(\mathcal{P}_i)) \cup \{fail\}$ is defined as:

$$J(\mathcal{P}_1, \ldots, \mathcal{P}_n) = \Gamma(\mathcal{P}_1) \cup \cdots \cup \Gamma(\mathcal{P}_n) \cup C(\mathcal{P}_1, \ldots, \mathcal{P}_n).$$

The next theorem states that there is a one-to-one correspondence between the set of joint fixpoints of the programs $\mathcal{P}_1, \ldots, \mathcal{P}_n$ and the set of stable models of the program $J(\mathcal{P}_1, \ldots, \mathcal{P}_n)$.

Theorem 4. *Let $\mathcal{P}_1, \ldots, \mathcal{P}_n$ be positive logic programs over the same set of atomic propositions Var. Then:*

$$SM(J(\mathcal{P}_1, \ldots, \mathcal{P}_n)) = \bigcup_{F \in JFP(\mathcal{P}_1, \ldots, \mathcal{P}_n)} \{\cup_{1 \leq i \leq n}[F]_{\mathcal{P}_i}\}.$$

where $JFP(\mathcal{P}_1, \ldots, \mathcal{P}_n)$ is the set of the joint fixpoints of $\mathcal{P}_1, \ldots, \mathcal{P}_n$.

Proof. By virtue of Lemma 6 it holds that:

$$SM(\Gamma(\mathcal{P}_i)) = \bigcup_{F \in FP(\mathcal{P}_i)} \{[F]_{\mathcal{P}_i}\}.$$

for each $1 \leq i \leq n$. We denote by $\mathcal{P}_u = \bigcup_{1 \leq i \leq n} \Gamma(\mathcal{P}_i)$. Since $Var^*(\Gamma(\mathcal{P}_i)) \cap Var^*(\Gamma(\mathcal{P}_j)) = \emptyset$, for any $1 \leq i \neq j \leq n$, we can apply Proposition 3 obtaining that:

$$SM(\mathcal{P}_u) = \bigcup_{F_1 \in FP(\mathcal{P}_1), \ldots, F_n \in FP(\mathcal{P}_n)} \{[F_1]_{\mathcal{P}_1} \cup \cdots \cup [F_n]_{\mathcal{P}_n}\}. \tag{1}$$

As $C(\mathcal{P}_1 \cdots \mathcal{P}_n) \triangleright \mathcal{P}_u$ holds (according to Definition 2), from Proposition 2 it follows that:

$$SM(J(\mathcal{P}_1, \ldots, \mathcal{P}_n)) = \bigcup_{M \in SM(\mathcal{P}_u)} SM(M \cup C(\mathcal{P}_1 \cdots \mathcal{P}_n)). \tag{2}$$

Consider now a stable model M in $SM(\mathcal{P}_u)$. We say that M satisfies the *join condition* if: $a_{\mathcal{P}_i} \in M$ implies $a_{\mathcal{P}_j} \in M$, for any $1 \leq j \neq i \leq n$ and for any $a \in Var$.

In the full version we prove the following claim:

Claim 2. Let $M \in SM(\mathcal{P}_u)$. $SM(M \cup C(\mathcal{P}_1 \cdots \mathcal{P}_n)) = \{M\}$ if M satisfies the join condition. $SM(M \cup C(\mathcal{P}_1 \cdots \mathcal{P}_n)) = \emptyset$, otherwise.

By applying Claim 2, from (2) it follows that:

$$SM(J(\mathcal{P}_1, \ldots, \mathcal{P}_n)) = \bigcup_{M^{jc} \in SM^{jc}(\mathcal{P}_u)} \{M^{jc}\}. \tag{3}$$

where $SM^{jc}(\mathcal{P}_u)$ denotes stable models of $SM(\mathcal{P}_u)$ satisfying the join condition.

Consider now a stable model $M^{jc} \in SM^{jc}(\mathcal{P}_u)$. Since $SM^{jc}(\mathcal{P}_u) \subseteq SM(\mathcal{P}_u)$, from (1) it follows that $M^{jc} = [F_1]_{\mathcal{P}_1} \cup \cdots \cup [F_n]_{\mathcal{P}_n}$, for some $F_1 \in FP(\mathcal{P}_1), \ldots$, $F_n \in FP(\mathcal{P}_n)$. On the other hand, since M^{jc} satisfies the join condition, it follows that $F_1 = F_2 = \cdots = F_n$. Thus, $M^{jc} = \bigcup_{1 \leq i \leq n} [F]_{\mathcal{P}_i}$, for some joint fixpoint $F \in JFP(\mathcal{P}_1, \ldots, \mathcal{P}_n)$. Hence, (3) becomes:

$$SM(J(\mathcal{P}_1, \ldots, \mathcal{P}_n)) = \bigcup_{F \in JFP(\mathcal{P}_1, \ldots, \mathcal{P}_n)} \{\bigcup_{1 \leq i \leq n} [F]_{\mathcal{P}_i}\}.$$

as stated in the theorem.   □

6   Conclusion and Future Work

In this paper we have introduced a new model-theoretic semantics for defining compromises among desires and consents of agents represented by logic programs. Rather than joining the theories of different agents and considering models or fixpoints of a single joint logic program (possibly incorporating modalities), we advocated that the right approach is most likely to consider joint fixpoints of separate logic programs. To our best knowledge, the idea of using joint fixed points of logic programs is new and has never been explored by others. We think that this is a quite appealing idea, which uses existing concepts and machinery in a diverse rendering. The effectiveness of our method was demonstrated on two small nontrivial examples. In this context, we also described a new way of specifying requests and consents of agents by logic programs. A novel feature is the *okay* modality and its translation into a self-implication of an atom in a classical logic program.

Our new semantics for describing requests and consents of multiple agents naturally induced us to study the computational properties of reasoning with joint fixed points and with minimal joint fixed points. We proved the surprising result that determining whether two plain positive propositional logic programs have a joint fixpoint is already NP complete. Translated into our agent-compromise framework this means that determining whether there exists a compromise between two agents whose requests and consents are formulated in the simplest possible rule-based language (just definite propositional Horn clauses, without negation or disjunction or similar constructs) is a hard problem. For those who agree that our semantics can faithfully describe standpoints of agents, this NP hardness result says something about determining compromises in the real world. We also analyzed the complexity of credulous and skeptical reasoning under the minimal joint fixpoint semantics. We think that our complexity studies and results are of independent interest, whether one agrees with our interpretation of joint fixpoints as compromises or not.

While this paper offers a new approach of defining static agent compromises and some related complexity studies, it does certainly not describe a framework for defining agent dynamics, interaction, negotiation, and similar most relevant issues. This was not our goal. We hope, however, that a full framework of agent dynamics can be constructed on the top our very basic formalization of compromise. Actually,we do not see any reason why this should not be possible. What also seems to be feasible is the incorporation of our notion of compromise into existing frameworks such as [23]. This is left for future research.

Acknowledgments

Research supported by FWF (Austrian Science Funds) under project Z29-INF and by the Italia-Austria cooperation project *Enhancing Nonmonotonic Systems to Deal with Quantitative Information*. We are grateful to Jürgen Dix anfd Thomas Eiter for helping us to find related work.

References

[1] Buccafurri, F., Gottlob, G.: Multiagent Compromises, Joint Fixpoints and Stable Models. Technical Report DBAI-TR-2000-36 (2000) available from the authors
[2] Buccafurri, F., Leone, N., Rullo, P.: Stable Models and their Computation for Logic Programming with Inheritance and True Negation. Journal of Logic Programming **27**(1), Elsevier Science (1996) 5–43

[3] Buccafurri, F., Leone, N., Rullo, P.: Semantics and Espressiveness of Disjunctive Ordered Logic. Annals of Mathematics and Artificial Intelligence Journal. J.C. Balzer AC, Science Publisher **25** (1999) 311–337

[4] Eiter, T., Gottlob, G.: Propositional Circumscription and Extended Closed-World Reasoning are Π_2^p-Complete. Theoretical Computer Science **114**(2) (1993) 231–245

[5] Eiter, T., Gottlob, G.: On the Computational Cost of Disjunctive Logic Programming: Propositional Case. Annals of Mathematics and Artificial Intelligence, **15**(3-4) (1995) 289–323

[6] Eiter, T., Gottlob, G., Mannila, H.: Disjunctive Datalog. ACM Transactions on Database Systems **22**(3) (1997) 315–363

[7] Eiter, T., Leone, N., Mateis, C., Pfeifer, G., Scarcello, F.: A Deductive System for Non-Monotonic Reasoning. Proceedings of the 4th International Conference on Logic Programming and Nonmonotonic Reasoning (LPNMR '97). Lecture Notes in Computer Science, Vol. 1265. Springer-Verlag, Dagstuhl, Germany (1997) 364–375

[8] Eiter, T., Gottlob, G., Cadoli, M.: Default Logic as a Query Language. Transactions on Knowledge Data Engineering **9**(3) (1997) 448–463

[9] Gelfond, M., Lifschitz, V.: The Stable Model Semantics for Logic Programming. Proceedings of the 5th International Conference on Logic Programming. MIT Press, Cambridge, (1988) 1070–1080

[10] Gottlob, G., Moerkotte, G., Subrahmanian, V.S.: The PARK Semantics for Active Rules. Proceedings of the International Conference on Extending Database Technology, EDBT'96, Lecture Notes in Computer Science. Springer Verlag, (1996) 35–55

[11] Gottlob, G.: Complexity Results for Nonmonotonic Logics. Journal of Logic and Computation **2**(3) (1992) 397–425

[12] Grosof, B.: Prioritized Conflict Handling for Logic Programs. Proceedings of the International Logic Programming Symposium, ILPS'97, MIT Press, Cambridge, (1997) 197–211.

[13] Kowalski, R., and Sadri, F.: From LP Towards Multi-Agent Systems. Annals of Mathematics and Artificial Intelligence **25**(3-4) (1999) 391–419

[14] Kolaitis, P.G., Papadimitriou, C.H.: Why not Negation by Fixpoint? Journal of Computer and System Sciences **43**(1) (1991) 125–144

[15] Martelli, M., Mascardi V., Zini, F.: Towards Multi-Agent Software Prototyping. Proceedings of The Third International Conference and Exhibition on The Practical Application of Intelligent Agents and Multi-Agent Technology (PAAM 98), London, UK, (1998) 331–354

[16] McCarthy, J.: Circumscription - a Form of Nonmonotonic Reasoning, Artificial Intelligence **13** (1980) 27–39

[17] Niemelä, I., Simons, P.: Smodels - an Implementation of the Stable Model and Well-founded Semantics for Normal Logic Programs. Proceedings of the 4th International Conference on Logic Programming and Non-Monotonic Reasoning (LPNMR '97), Lecture Notes in Computer Science, Vol. 1265. Springer-Verlag, Dagstuhl, Germany (1997) 420–429

[18] Reiter, R.: A Logic for Default Reasoning. Artificial Intelligence **13** (1980) 81–132

[19] Saccá, D.: The Expressive Power of Stable Models for Datalog Queries with Negation. Proceedings of the ILPS'93 Workshop on Structural Complexity and Recursion-Theoretic Methods in Logic Programming, Washington D.C., USA (1993) 150–162

[20] Schlipf, J.S.: The Expressive Powers of Logic Programming Semantics, Proceedings of the ACM Symposium on Principles of Database Systems (1990) 196–204

[21] Schlipf, J.S.: A Survey of Complexity and Undecidability Results in Logic Programming. Proceedings of the ILPS'93 Workshop on Structural Complexity and Recursion-Theoretic Methods in Logic Programming, Washington D.C., USA (1993) 93–102

[22] Schroeder, M., De Almeida Mora, I., and Pereira L.M.: A Deliberative and Reactive Diagnosis Agent based on Logic Programming. Intelligent Agents III: Lecture Notes in Artificial Intelligence **1193**, Springer-Verlag, J.P. Muller, M.J. Wooldridge and N. Jennings ed., (1997) 293–307

[23] Subrahmanian V.S., Bonatti P., Dix, J., and Eiter T., Kraus S., Özcan, F., and Ross, R.: Heterogenous Active Agents. MIT-Press (2000)

[24] Wooldridge, M., Jennings, N.R.: Formalizing the Cooperative Problem Solving Process. Readings in Agents, M. Huhns and M. Singh ed., Morgan Kaufmann (1997) 430–440

[25] Wooldridge, M., Jennings, N.R.: Agent Theories, Architectures and Languages: A survey. Intelligent Agents, M. J. Wooldridge and N. R. Jennings ed., Lecture Notes in Artificial Intelligence, Springer-Verlag **890** (1995) 1–39.

[26] Wooldridge, M., Jennings, N.R.: Intelligent Agents: Theory and Practice. Knowledge Engineering Reviews **10**(2) 1995

Error-Tolerant Agents

Thomas Eiter[1], Viviana Mascardi[2], and V.S. Subrahmanian[3]

[1] Institut für Informationssysteme, Technische Universität Wien, Favoritenstraße 9–11,
A-1040 Wien, Austria.
eiter@kr.tuwien.ac.at

[2] Dipartimento di Informatica e Scienze dell'Informazione, Università di Genova,
Via Dodecaneso 35, I-16146, Genova, Italy.
mascardi@disi.unige.it

[3] Institute for Advanced Computer Studies, Institute for Systems Research and CS Department,
University of Maryland, College Park, Maryland 20742.
vs@cs.umd.edu

Abstract The use of agents in today's Internet world is expanding rapidly. Yet, agent developers proceed largely under the optimistic assumption that agents will be error-free. Errors may arise in agents for numerous reasons — agents may share a workspace with other agents or humans and updates made by these other entities may cause an agent to face a situation that it was not explicitly programmed to deal with. Likewise, errors in coding agents may lead to inconsistent situations where it is unclear how the agent should act. In this paper, we define an agent execution model that allows agents to continue acting "reasonably" even when some errors of the above types occur. More importantly, in our framework, agents take "repair" actions automatically when confronted with such situations, but while taking such repair actions, they can often continue to engage in work and/or interactions with other agents that are unaffected by repairs.

1   Introduction

Agents are a rapidly growing area of research in artificial intelligence and databases, with an ever increasing range of applications, spanning e-commerce servers to web search engines. Numerous paradigms for agents have been proposed in the AI literature [11,30,27]. In past work, two of the authors have been working on a framework called *IMPACT* (Interactive Maryland Platform for Agents Collaborating Together) [14,4,26] in which they develop a theory by which existing legacy code bases and data sources can be "agentized". In their framework, each agent has a state (composed of whatever resides in its data structures and message box). Whenever the agent's state changes, the agent must take actions in accordance with some clearly specified operating principles so as to ensure that the resulting state satisfies some integrity constraints. Examples of state changes include receipt of a message, a clock tick, a receipt of a service request, receipt of a response to a service request, update of a data source, and many others. Eiter *et al.*[14] show strong connections between the agent theory they propose with classical methods for logic programming, nonmonotonic reasoning. They further show how Shoham's AOP ("agent oriented programming") system [24] can largely be simulated within *IMPACT*, and that large parts of the well known belief, desires, and

A.C. Kakas, F. Sadri (Eds.): Computat. Logic (Kowalski Festschrift), LNAI 2407, pp. 586–625, 2002.

intentionality architecture (BDI) can be captured within their framework. Most of these frameworks all agree on the fact that an agent decides on what to do in response to a state change, and then does it. However, two major problems need to be addressed.

1. First, most agent frameworks (cf. [11,30,27]) including *IMPACT* assume that the rules used are sufficient to appropriately respond to all requests that arrive. Unfortunately, this assumption that the agent developer covered "all possibilities" is rather optimistic and as unreasonable as an assumption that all programs in C (or any other programming language) are bug-free. Hence, there is a question of what to do when an agent is confronted with a situation for which it does not know how to act.
2. Second, in the case of legacy systems, we note that the legacy system's existing GUI and the agent both access and update the same data. Thus, the legacy GUI may alter the agent's state in ways that the agent may find unacceptable.

An agent is said to be *corrupted* if either (i) changes caused by external entities have caused the agent's current state to violate one or more integrity constraints, or (ii) the agent is unable to find a "valid"[1] set of actions to execute in its current state (which may, perhaps, have been caused by a coding error). In this paper, we tackle the first problem above — the second is considered only to the extent that nonexistence of a status set is because of an integrity constraint violation.

This paper presents a theory, architecture and algorithms so that agents may exhibit two important properties.

1. **Recovery.** Agents must be able to recover from being "corrupted" to being "uncorrupted."
2. **Continuity.** Agents must continue to process some (though perhaps not all) requests while continuing to recover. This is important when an agent is servicing lots of requests.

The organization of this paper is as follows. In Section 2, we present a brief overview of *IMPACT*'s agent architecture (see [14,4,26] for more details). To this architecture, we add one component — an *error recovery component* whose architecture is described in Section 3. In Section 3, we provide a formal set of definitions specifying what requests are affected (or may be affected) when an agent is known to be corrupted in a certain way. Unaffected requests may continue to be processed by a corrupted agent, even while the corrupted agent attempts to recover. Then, in Section 4, we describe special repair data structures and repair actions which are to be used by the recovery component. The latter may be selected from a repair action library, which provides a host of different realizations for repair. In Section 5, we discuss how an agent can, using the results and tools of the previous section, recover from an error. We not only show how *IMPACT* agents may use our recovery methods, but also present a modification of the Kowalski-Sadri agent cycle [20] as in [14,26] which incorporates the desired properties of recovery and continuity. In section 6, we discuss how our work may be applied to three different agent frameworks out there in the literature: Kowalski and

---

[1] With respect to the semantics of the agent. In this paper, we will assume that either the feasible, rational or reasonable status set semantics of agents [14,26] is used.

Sadri's framework, the *BDI* (Belief, Desires, Intentionality) framework, and the work of Wooldridge. Other related work is discussed in Section 7. Directions for future work are discussed in Section 8.

2 *IMPACT* Preliminaries

As different application programs reason with different types of data, and even programs dealing with the same types of data often manipulate them in a variety of ways, it is critical that any notion of agenthood be applicable to arbitrary software programs. Agent developers should be able to select data structures that best suit the application functions desired by users of the application they are building. Figure 1 shows the architecture of a full-fledged *IMPACT* software agent. It is important to note that all agents have the same architecture and hence the same components, but the *content* of these components can be different, leading to different behaviors and capabilities offered by different agents.

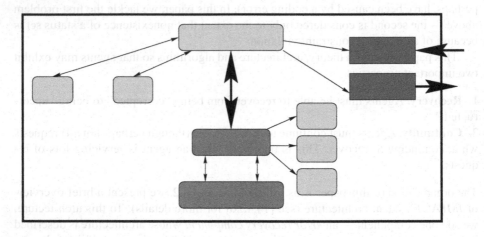

Fig. 1. Basic Architecture of *IMPACT* Agents

Agent Data Structures. As all agents are built "on top" of some existing body of code, we first need an abstract definition of what that body of code looks like.

• First, we need a specification of the data types or data structures, T, that the agent manipulates. As usual, each data type has an associated *domain* which is the space of objects of that type. For example, the data type countries may be an enumerated type containing names of all countries. At any given point, the *instantiation* or *content* of a data type is some subset of the space of the data-objects associated with that type.

• The above set of data structures is manipulated by a set of functions, F, that are callable by external programs. Such functions constitute the *application programmer interface* or API of the package on top of which the agent is being built. An agent includes a specification of all signatures of these API function calls (i.e., types of the inputs to such function calls and types of the output of such function calls).

We use a unified language to query software packages by leveraging from T and $\mathcal{F}$. If $f \in \mathcal{F}$ is an n-ary function defined in that package, and $t_1, \ldots, t_n$ are *terms* (either values, i.e., constants, or variables) of appropriate types, then $S : f(t_1, \ldots, t_n)$ is a *code call*. This code call says "Execute function f as defined in package S on the stated list of arguments." For evaluation, the code call must be ground, i.e., all arguments t_i must be values. We assume that it returns, as output, a *set* of objects— if a single object is returned, it can be coerced into a set anyway.

A *code call atom* is an expression cca of the form $in(t, cc)$ or $notin(t, cc)$, where t is a term and cc is a code call. For ground t, cca succeeds (i.e., has answer true) if t is in (resp., not in) the set of values returned by cc, and it fails (i.e., has answer false) otherwise. If t is a variable X, then cca returns each value from the result of cc, i.e., its answer is the set of ground substitutions θ for X such that $cca\theta$ returns true. A uniform view of ground and non-ground case identifies the answer true with the set $\{\emptyset\}$ of the void substitution and the answer false with the empty set of substitutions.

For each code call atom cca, we denote by $\sim cca$ the logically negated code call atom, i.e., $\sim in(t, cc) = notin(t, cc)$ and $\sim notin(t, cc) = in(t, cc)$. We extend this naturally to sets X of code call atoms by $\sim X = \{\sim cca \mid cca \in X\}$.

A *code call condition* is a conjunction of code call atoms and *constraint atoms*, which may involve decomposition operations. An example of a constraint atom is $V.x > 25$, where $V.x$ accesses the x field of a variable V ranging over records that have an x field. It checks whether the stated condition is true; in general, constraint atoms are of the form $t_1 \ op \ t_2$ where op is any of $=, \neq, <, \leq, >, \geq$ and t_1, t_2 are terms.

Code call conditions provide a simple, but powerful syntax to access heterogeneous data structures. For example, the code call condition

```
in(X, oracle : select(emp, sal, >, 100000)) &
in(Y, image : select(imdb, X.name)) & in("Mary", imagedb : findpeople(Y))
```

is a complex condition that joins data across Oracle and an image database. It first selects all people who make over 100K from an Oracle database and for each such person, finds a picture containing that person with another person called Mary. It generalizes the notion of join in relational databases to a join across a relational and image database.

Each agent is also assumed to have access to a message box data structure, together with some API function calls to access it. Details of the message box in *IMPACT* may be found in [14,26].

At any given point in time, the actual set of objects in the data structures (and message box) managed by the agent constitutes the *state* of the agent. We shall identify a state $\mathcal{O}$ with the set of ground code calls which are true in it.

Actions. The agent has a set of *actions* $\alpha(X_1, \ldots, X_n)$, where $X_1, \ldots, X_n$ are variables for parameters, that can change its state. Such actions may include reading a message from the message box, responding to a message, executing a request, cloning a copy of the agent and moving it to a remote host, updating the agent data structures, etc. Even doing nothing may be an action. Expressions $\alpha(t)$, where t is a list terms of appropriate types, are *action atoms*. They represent the sets of (ground) actions which result if all variables in t are instantiated by values. Only such actions may be executed by an agent. Every action α has a precondition $Pre(\alpha)$ (which is a code call condition), a set of effects (given by an add list $Add(\alpha)$ and a delete list $Del(\alpha)$ of code call atoms) that describe how the agent state changes when the action is executed, and an *execution method* (which can be implemented in any programming language or scripting language that the user deems appropriate) consisting of a body of physical code that implements the action.

Notion of Concurrency. The agent has an associated body of code implementing a *notion of concurrency* $\mathbf{conc}(AS, \mathcal{O})$. Intuitively, it takes a set of actions AS and the current agent state $\mathcal{O}$ as input, and returns a single action (which "combines" the input actions together) as output. Various possible notions of concurrency are described in [14,26]. They all have the property that the changes to the state $\mathcal{O}$ are restricted to the code call atoms occurring in the add and delete lists of the actions in AS. We make the same assumption in this paper.

Action Constraints. Each agent has a finite set of *action constraints* which are rules of the form "If the state satisfies some code call condition, then actions $\{\alpha_1, \ldots, \alpha_n\}$ cannot be concurrently executed." In the present paper, we disregard actions constraints, sine they can be easily eliminated (see [14]).

Integrity Constraints. Each agent has a finite set $\mathcal{IC}$ of *integrity constraints* ic that states $\mathcal{O}$ of the agent must satisfy (written $\mathcal{O} \models ic$ resp. $\mathcal{O} \models \mathcal{IC}$), of the form $\psi \Rightarrow \chi_a$ where ψ is a code call condition, and χ_a is a code call atom or constraint atom. Informally, ic has the meaning of the universal statement "If ψ is true, then χ_a must be true."[2] For example, a functional dependency $A1\ A2 \rightarrow B$ on a relation r in some database package db can be expressed as an integrity constraint

$$\texttt{in(T1 , db : all(r))\&in(T2 , db : all(r))\&(T1.A1 = T2.A1)\&(T1.A2 = T2.A2)} \Rightarrow \texttt{T1.B = T2.B}$$

where $\texttt{all(r)}$ returns all tuples in the relation r. Throughout this paper, we assume that the integrity constraints are consistent, i.e., there exists at least one agent state $\mathcal{O}_0$ which satisfies all integrity constraints in $\mathcal{IC}$. It may happen, though, that a set of integrity constraints is not consistent. Determining such an inconsistency is, in general, an undecidable problem, and thus can not be done by an automated check. However, a software agent usually has a legal initial state $\mathcal{O}_0$ when it is deployed, and this state is known (or, it might be one out of a collection of possible states). The state $\mathcal{O}_0$ must satisfy all integrity constraints. Thus, in the specification of integrity constraints, only those may be accepted which hold on $\mathcal{O}_0$.

Agent Program. Each agent has a set of rules called the *agent program* specifying the principles under which the agent is operating. These rules specify, using deontic modalities, what the agent may do, must do, may not do, etc. Expressions $\mathbf{O}\alpha(t)$, $\mathbf{P}\alpha(t)$, $\mathbf{F}\alpha(t)$, $\mathbf{Do}\,\alpha(t)$, and $\mathbf{W}\alpha(t)$, where $\alpha(t)$ is an action atom, are called *action status atoms*. These action status atoms are read (respectively) as $\alpha(t)$ is *obligatory, permitted, forbidden, done*, and the obligation to do $\alpha(t)$ is *waived*. If A is an action status atom, then A and $\neg A$ are called *action status literals*. An *agent program* $\mathcal{P}$ is a finite set of rules of the form:

---

[2] For simplicity, we omit here and in other places safety aspects (see Appendix B and [14,26] for details).

$$A \leftarrow \chi \,\&\, L_1 \,\&\, \cdots \,\&\, L_n \qquad\qquad (1)$$

where A is an action status atom, χ is a code call condition, and $L_1, \ldots, L_n$ are action status literals. Due to space constraints, we do not repeat the semantics of agent programs here. A brief overview is given in Appendix A, while comprehensive details are given in [14,26].

3 Architecture and Formal Definitions

In this section, we discuss how to extend the architecture in Fig. 1 to handle the cases where agent errors cause, due to violated integrity constraints, non-existence of valid status sets, and where an agent's state can be autonomously updated by a third party.

3.1 Architecture

We assume that there is some mechanism that notifies the agent when its state has been changed by a third party. Thus, we may assume in abstraction that every agent a receives messages of the following forms:

1. ask(b, cca), where agent b is asking agent a the answer to a code call atom cca = in(t, cc) resp. cca = notin(t, cc), where t is a term and cc is ground.
2. tell(b, cca, ans), where agent b is telling agent a the answer ans to a code call atom cca of the previous form.
3. done(cca, ans$^+$, ans$^-$), where cca is a code call atom and ans$^+$, ans$^-$ are sets of ground substitutions. Its meaning is that a third party (which may not be an agent) has updated agent a's state so that the answer to cca has changed — the new answer is the old one minus the substitutions in ans$^-$ plus the substitutions in ans$^+$.

Errors occur in the agent in one of two situations. In the first, incoming messages of the form ask(·) or tell(·) trigger errors as there is no valid status set associated with the incoming message.[3] In the second, another entity sends the agent a message of the form done(·) and the update violates the integrity constraints of the agent, leaving it in a state which is invalid.

We deal with these two situations as follows. When an agent developer builds an *IMPACT* agent, she needs to perform the following tasks in order to specify how her *IMPACT* agents must recover when corrupted. She must specify

---

[3] The reader may wonder why an ask(·) message can cause an error. All incoming messages to an agent cause a change in the agent's state because the message updates the agent's message box. No "sensible" integrity constraint should be violated because of an ask(·) message. However, it is possible for an agent developer to write patently absurd integrity constraints. For instance, the syntax of ICs allows an agent developer to write rules such as "If the message box contains a message from agent B, then $\mathbf{F}a$" as well as "If the message box contains a message from agent B, then $\mathbf{P}a$". This causes an agent to become corrupt whenever a message from agent B arrives. The problem can be avoided by adding restrictions to the syntax of agent programs (e.g. certain types of *regular* agent programs introduced in [15] avoid this problem). In addition, requiring that ICs not mention code call atoms involving ask(·) messages would also help alleviate this problem.

1. a set $\mathcal{RA}$ of *repair* actions having some properties (see Section 3); and,
2. an objective function (to be maximized) used to evaluate the cost of a state. The idea is that the agent code's repair component will automatically use repair actions to compute a state (which satisfies the integrity constraints or generates a valid status set).

Once the user specifies the various components of an agent as described in Section 2 and specifies the above parameters, the *IMPACT* Agent Development Environment should automatically convert the agent components plus the repair components into an executable body of Java bytecode which may then be deployed.

The continuity property of agents may be preserved by requiring that whenever an agent's state is corrupted by the actions of an external agent, the agent continues to process requests for its services as long as those requests are not "affected" by the ongoing repairs to the corrupted part. For example, an agent managing 30 relations in a relational database may find that external changes have corrupted one relation. In this case, queries that do not access that one relation may be processed by the agent while the corrupted relation is being repaired.

We proceed as follows. In Section 3.2, we address the problem of specifying, given an agent a and a "corrupted"[4] code call atom cca resp. a set of such code call atoms, what other code call atoms may be potentially corrupted. The method we apply is based on a syntactic analysis of the agent's integrity constraints. We then introduce in Section 3.3 the notion of "suspiciousness" for code call atoms. Using this notion, we are able to determine which decisions that an agent tries to make are affected by these potentially corrupted code calls. This will be central for recovery in Section 5.

3.2   Corrupted Code Call Atoms

When a set X of code call atoms is known to be corrupted, we would like to know what other code call atoms and integrity constraints are affected by this. In this section, we define a procedure called corrcca(X) that takes X as input, and returns, as output, the set of code call atoms in integrity constraints which are (potentially) corrupted by X. We first need some preliminary definitions. The first introduces the notion of subsumption for code call atoms.

Definition 3.1 (Code Call Subsumption). *A set of code call atoms X is subsumed by a set of code call atoms Y, written $X \lhd Y$, if each* cca $\in X$ *is an instance of some* cca$' \in Y$ *or its complement, i.e.,* cca $=$ cca$'\theta$ *or* cca $= \sim$cca$'\theta$ *for some substitution θ. If X (resp., Y) is a singleton set $\{$cca$\}$, we omit parentheses and write* cca$\lhd Y$ *(resp., $X \lhd$ cca).*

Here, and in the rest of the paper, we implicitly assume that code call atoms are standardized apart before unification.

---

[4] By "corrupted" we mean that the current result of the code call atom may lead to an inconsistency in one or more integrity constraints. A code call atom could turn out to be corrupted either because an external entity has modified the state in an "uncontrolled" way, or due to a "propagation" of corruptedness, as described in Section 3.2.

Example 3.1 (Subsumption). The code call atoms in(a, cc1) and notin(Y,cc1), where cc1 is ground, are both subsumed by in(X, cc1). Thus, {in(a, cc1), notin(Y, cc1)} ◁ {in(X, cc1), notin(a, cc2)}.

We next define how to associate with any code call condition χ, a set $CCA(\chi)$ of code call atoms. Informally, $CCA(\chi)$ is the set of code call atoms occurring somewhere in χ.

Definition 3.2 (Code-Call Atoms Set $(CCA(\chi))$). *For any code call condition χ, the code call atom set $CCA(\chi)$ is inductively defined as follows:*

$$CCA(\chi) = \begin{cases} \{\text{cca}\}, & \textit{if } \chi \textit{ is a code call atom } \text{cca}; \\ \emptyset, & \textit{if } \chi \textit{ is a constraint atom}; \\ CCA(\chi_1) \cup CCA(\chi_2), & \textit{if } \chi \textit{ is a code call condition } \chi_1 \,\&\, \chi_2. \end{cases}$$

For any integrity constraint $ic : \psi \Rightarrow \chi_a$, define $CCA(ic) = CCA(\psi) \cup CCA(\chi_a)$.

Corr(ic, cca) defined below describes the set of potentially corrupted code call atoms given that code call atom cca is corrupted.

Definition 3.3 (*Corr(ic, cca)*). *For any integrity constraint ic and code call atom cca,*

$$Corr(ic, \text{cca}) \ = \ \bigcup \left\{ CCA(ic\theta) \ \middle| \ \begin{array}{l} \text{cca } \textit{and some } \text{cca}' \in CCA(ic) \cup {\sim}CCA(ic) \\ \textit{unify with most general unifier (mgu) } \theta \end{array} \right\}.$$

If cca is considered corrupted, then each code call atom occurring in $ic\theta$ is considered corrupted as well. Notice that unifiers and most general unifiers (mgu's) θ are easily computed, since there are no nested terms.

Example 3.2 (Corruptedness). Let us consider the integrity constraint

$$ic : \text{in(X, cc1)} \,\&\, \text{in(X, cc2)} \Rightarrow \text{in(X, cc3)}.$$

Then we have $CCA(ic) = \{\text{in(X, cc1), in(X, cc2), in(X, cc3)}\}$ and, furthermore, $Corr(ic, \text{in(p, cc1)}) = \{\text{in(p, cc1), in(p, cc2), in(p, cc3)}\}$.

We may now define the procedure corrcca(X) which computes, given a set X of code call atoms considered corrupted, the set of all code call atoms considered corrupted as follows.

proc corrcca(X : set of code call atoms) : set of code call atoms;

1.   *old* := $\emptyset$; *new* := X;
2.   **while** *new* $\neq$ *old* **do**
3.   *old* := *new*;
4.   **for each** $ic \in \mathcal{IC}$, cca $\in$ *old* **do**
5.   *new* := *new* $\cup$ *Corr(ic, cca)*;
6.   **endwhile**;
7.   **return** *old*.

end proc

Notice that corrcca implements a monotone, inflationary operator over the set of code call atoms, and terminates on finite input X. Furthermore, the output can be compacted by removing subsumed code call atoms from new.

The reason why we have to iteratively apply the $Corr$ operator in the above procedure is because errors might be masked. For illustration, consider the following four integrity constraints:

$$ic_1 : \text{in}(X, cc1) \,\&\, \text{in}(Y, cc2) \Rightarrow X = Y,$$
$$ic_2 : \text{in}(W, cc3) \,\&\, W = c \Rightarrow \text{in}(a, cc1),$$
$$ic_3 : \text{in}(Z, cc4) \Rightarrow Z > 8,$$
$$ic_4 : \text{in}(Z, cc4) \,\&\, \text{in}(J, cc5) \Rightarrow Z < J.$$

Suppose that in the current state all and only the following code call atoms are true:

$$\text{in}(a, cc1), \; \text{in}(b, cc2), \; \text{in}(c, cc3), \; \text{in}(10, cc4), \text{ and } \text{in}(20, cc5).$$

In the current state ic_1 is violated. Then, both $\text{in}(a, cc1)$ and $\text{in}(b, cc2)$ are potentially corrupted, since their evaluation returns a result which causes a violation of an integrity constraint; at least one of them reflects a condition on the current state which is not coherent with the agent's setting. The other integrity constraints are not violated in the current state. As we know that $\text{in}(a, cc1)$ is potentially corrupted, its correct evaluation may well have been false rather than true (though this is not necessary !). If in fact $\text{in}(a, cc1)$'s correct evaluation should have been false, then it may well be the case that $\text{in}(c, cc3)$ is also corrupted. This is because $\text{in}(c, cc3)$ should evaluate to false in order to satisfy ic_2.

We do not know whether $\text{in}(a, cc1)$ or $\text{in}(b, cc2)$ is the cause of the violation. Hence, we cannot exclude the possibility that the problem is with $\text{in}(a, cc1)$ and that it propagates to $\text{in}(c, cc3)$. Thus, to be on the safe side, we consider an integrity constraint (potentially) corrupted whenever it contains a potentially corrupted code call.

The integrity constraints ic_3 and ic_4 are not violated in the current state, and there is no reason to suspect that the code call atoms appearing in them are corrupted. This is because they are completely unrelated to the corrupted atoms.

The soundness of this approach is expressed by the following proposition which states that a coherent state can be reached from an incoherent one only by changing the return values of (some) corrupted code call atoms, and by maintaining the return values of the uncorrupted ones.

For any agent state $\mathcal{O}$, let $\mathcal{VGI}(\mathcal{O})$ be the set of ground instances of integrity constraints from $\mathcal{IC}$ which are violated in the state $\mathcal{O}$, and let $\mathcal{CGI}(\mathcal{O}) = \bigcup_{ic \in \mathcal{VGI}} CCA(ic)$ be the set of code call atoms in $\mathcal{VGI}(\mathcal{O})$.

Proposition 3.1. *Let Y be any set of code call atoms such that* corrcca$(\mathcal{CGI}(\mathcal{O})) \lhd Y$. *Then, there exists an agent state $\mathcal{O}'$ such that $\mathcal{O}' \models \mathcal{IC}$ and, for any ground code call atom* cca, $\mathcal{O}$ *and* $\mathcal{O}'$ *differ on* cca *only if* cca $\lhd Y$.

This means that $\mathcal{O}$ can be turned into $\mathcal{O}'$ by modifying the return result for some corrupted code call atoms, and without changing the results of non-corrupted code call atoms.

Proof. We define a suitable $\mathcal{O}'$ as follows. Recall that at least one agent state exists which satisfies all integrity constraints, and let $\mathcal{O}_0$ be an arbitrary such agent state. For any ground code call atom cca, we define

$$\mathcal{O}' \models \text{cca} \iff \begin{cases} \mathcal{O}_0 \models \text{cca}, & \text{if cca} \lhd Y; \\ \mathcal{O} \models \text{cca}, & \text{otherwise.} \end{cases}$$

Notice that $\mathcal{O}'$ is well-defined, and differs from $\mathcal{O}$ only on ground cca's which are subsumed by Y. Let ic be any ground instance of some integrity constraint in $\mathcal{IC}$. Then, one of the following two cases applies:

(1) There exists some cca $\in CCA(ic)$ such that cca$\lhd Y$. Then, by definition of corrcca, $CCA(ic) \lhd Y$ holds. Hence, for each cca $\in CCA(ic)$, we have $\mathcal{O}' \models$ cca iff $\mathcal{O}_0 \models$ cca. Since $\mathcal{O}_0 \models ic$, it follows $\mathcal{O}' \models ic$.

(2) For no cca $\in CCA(ic)$ it holds that cca$\lhd Y$. This implies $C\mathcal{GI}(\mathcal{O}) \cap CCA(ic) = \emptyset$; hence, $\mathcal{O} \models ic$. Similarly, we conclude that $\mathcal{O}' \models$ cca iff $\mathcal{O} \models$ cca. It follows $\mathcal{O}' \models ic$.

Hence, in both cases $\mathcal{O}' \models ic$. Therefore, $\mathcal{O}' \models \mathcal{IC}$, which proves the result. ∎

To continue the previous example, let us consider the state where the code call atoms

$$\text{in}(a, cc1), \ \text{in}(c, cc3), \ \text{in}(10, cc4), \ \text{and in}(20, cc5)$$

are true and all the other code call atoms are false. This is a consistent state, and we can reach it by simply changing the return value of cc2 so that in(b, cc2) becomes false.

The implementation of corrcca(X) which we have described is cautious and considers, in general, a larger set of code call atoms corrupted than may be semantically necessary. By applying a case by case distinction, we could get a refined picture in which a minimal set of code calls is identified as (potentially) corrupted. In the example above, in(c, cc3) is viewed as corrupted, as well as in(a, cc1), but we were able to reach a coherent state without changing the values of *all* these code call atoms. Unfortunately, computing a minimal set of code call atoms which need to be changed leads to intractability, which is the gist of the following result.

Theorem 3.1. *Given the sets $\mathcal{GI}$ and $\mathcal{VGI}(\mathcal{O})$ of ground and violated ground integrity constraints in the current agent state $\mathcal{O}$, respectively, and a ground code call atom* cca, *deciding whether* cca *is in some smallest (w.r.t. inclusion) set of ground cca's X such that, by changing values of cca's in X only, a consistent state $\mathcal{O}'$ results is* NP-*hard.*

Proof. (Sketch) A variant of the satisfiability problem can be reduced to this problem. Suppose $C = \{C_1, \ldots, C_m\}$ is a set of clauses $C_i = L_{i,1} \lor L_{i,2} \lor L_{i,3}$ where each $L_{i,j}$ is a propositional atom a or its negation $\neg a$. The software package S maintains truth assignments to propositional atoms, and the API tvars() returns all variables set to true. Suppose a_0 is a distinguished atom such that an assignment in which a_0 is true satisfies C iff all other atoms are false. Now let $\mathcal{O}$ be the agent state in which all atoms are true, and set up for each clause C_i an integrity constraint $\sim\tau(L_{i,1})$ & $\sim\tau(L_{i,2}) \Rightarrow \tau(L_{i,3})$ where $\tau(L_{i,j}) = \text{in}(a, \text{tvars}())$ if $L_{i,j} = a$ and $\tau(L_{i,j}) = \text{notin}(a, \text{tvars}())$ if $L_{i,j} = \neg a$. Then, some of these integrity constraints are violated by $\mathcal{O}$. The cca in(a_0, tvars()) belongs to some smallest change of ground code call atoms X that turns $\mathcal{O}$ into a consistent state $\mathcal{O}'$ iff C has a satisfying assignment in which a_0 is false. Since deciding the latter, under the above assumption, is NP-hard, and since $\mathcal{GI}$ and $\mathcal{VGI}(\mathcal{O})$ are easily constructed in polynomial time, the result follows.   ∎

3.3   Suspicious Code Call Atoms

Changing an appropriate subset of the ground instances of corrupted code call atoms will recover the agent to an "uncorrupted" state. This will be done in the agent cycle by a repair procedure. However, while this repair is going on, some message(s) might arrive. Rather than simply queuing the message(s) until the agent has recovered, it should:

1. find out whether processing the message interferes with the repair process, and
2. proceed with handling it if this is not the case.

For this purpose, we introduce the notion of "affected" action atom and rule, and the notion of "suspicious" code calls. Informally, the evaluation of an action atom is affected by a repair if it accesses a code call atom which is possibly changed by the repair process. The deontic status (is it permitted? forbidden? to be done? etc) of an action atom might change after the repair is completed. This also might have an impact on other action atoms whose deontic status is determined by running the agent program. In particular, a rule in the program that involves an affected action atom or a corrupted code call atom might propagate affectedness to other action atoms. The code call atoms in the body of such a rule are considered "suspicious" because they allow an affected rule to fire.

If we treat at least all corrupted code calls as being suspicious, then any unsuspicious code call may be safely evaluated in the current agent state. This is because (i) it is not affected by whatever corrupted the state and (ii) it will not be affected by any attempt to repair the corrupted part of the state. Hence, unsuspicious atoms may be safely evaluated even during the repair process. In particular, if the agent processes a message ask(b, cca), say, during which it naturally evaluates the code call atom cca, then the processing of this message does not interfere with the repair of the state as long as cca is unsuspicious. On the other hand, if cca is suspicious, then processing of a message should be delayed to avoid potentially incorrect results. A similar rationale applies when processing messages of the form tell(b, cca, ans).

As in the case of corrupted code call atoms, we determine suspicious code call atoms by a syntactic analysis of the agent program. We define a procedure suscca(X) which takes as input, a set X of code call atoms which subsumes all corrupted ground code call atoms of agent a and returns, as output, a set of suspicious code call atoms. The procedure operates in two phases. In the first phase, it determines what code call atoms are corrupted. In the second phase, it backward propagates possible integrity constraint violations that may arise after the completed repair.

We first define direct affectedness of an action atom by a code call atom.

Definition 3.4 (Directly Affected Action Atom). *An action atom $\alpha(t)$ is directly θ-affected by some code call atom* cca, *if there exists a* cca$'$ $\in$ $CCA(Pre(\alpha(t)))$ $\cup$ $\sim\!CCA(Pre(\alpha(t)))$ *which unifies with* cca *via mgu θ. We say that $\alpha(t)$ is directly affected if it is directly θ-affected for some θ.*

Informally, $\alpha(t)$ is directly θ-affected, if the status evaluation of its ground instances involves overlaps with the ground instances of the code call atom cca. If cca is corrupted, the value of the precondition of $\alpha(t)$ might change by the repair.

We next define affectedness of action atoms from a rule, given sets of affected action and code call atoms.

Definition 3.5 (Affected Rule and Action Atom). *Let*

$$r : A \leftarrow \chi \& L_1 \& \cdots \& L_n$$

be a rule, and let $AC(r)$ be the set of all action atoms occurring in r. Let X and Y be sets of action and code call atoms, respectively. Then r is θ-affected by X, Y if either

1. *some* cca $\in CCA(\chi) \cup \sim CCA(\chi)$ *unifies with some* cca$' \in Y$ *with mgu θ, or*
2. $\alpha(t) \in AC(r)$ *is directly θ-affected by some* cca$' \in Y$, *or*
3. $\alpha(t) \in AC(r)$ *unifies with some $\alpha'(t') \in X$ with mgu θ.*

The set $\Theta AFF(r, X, Y)$ is the union of all $AC(r\theta)$ such that r is θ-affected by X, Y. The set $\Theta CCA(r, X, Y)$ is the union of all $CCA(r\theta)$ such that r is θ-affected by X, Y. The rule r is affected by X, Y, if it is θ-affected for some θ. We define $AFF(r, X, Y) = AC(r)$ if such a θ exists and $AFF(r, X, Y) = \emptyset$ otherwise.

Informally, the affectedness set $\Theta AFF(r, X, Y)$ contains the actions atoms into which the affectedness of the actions atoms in X propagates, assuming that the code call atoms in Y are corrupted. Clearly, $AFF(r, X, Y)$ subsumes $\Theta AFF(r, X, Y)$ and takes a coarser view in which more ground atoms are affected, which we may choose for simplicity or efficiency.

We remark that by taking the particular semantics applied to an agent program into account, the definition of $\Theta AFF(r, X, Y)$ may be further refined. For instance, in the case of reasonable status set semantics [26], only the action atom of $A\theta$ needs to be added to $\Theta AFF(r, X, Y)$ if $\alpha(t)$ is from the body of r.

Example 3.3 (Affectedness). Consider an agent which manages the advertisement policy of a department store by classifying customers as high, medium or low spenders. The classification may be used to send appropriate advertisements to customers (clearly, in practice more sophisticated classifications could be applied). A rule in the agent program could be:

$r : \mathbf{Do}\,(\text{high\_spender}(C)) \leftarrow \text{in}(C, \text{oracle} : \text{select}(\text{person}, \text{sal}, >, 100000)) \&$
$\qquad\qquad\qquad \mathbf{Do}\,(\text{new\_customer}(C))$

This rule says that when a new customer is entered into the database, she is assumed to be a high-spender customer if she has a high salary. The pre, add, and del lists of new_customer are

$Pre(\text{new\_customer}(P)) = \text{notin}\,(P, \text{oracle} : \text{all}\,(\text{customers}))$,
$Add(\text{new\_customer}(P)) = \text{in}\,(P, \text{oracle} : \text{all}\,(\text{customers}))$,
$Del(\text{new\_customer}(P)) = \emptyset$.

Some examples of θ-affectedness of r for pairs X, Y are:

1. $\langle \emptyset, \{\text{in}(\text{mary}, \text{oracle}:\text{select}(\text{person}, \text{sal}, >, 100000))\}\rangle$: The code call atom in Y unifies with $\text{in}(\text{C}, \text{oracle}:\text{select}(\text{person}, \text{sal}, >, 100000))$ under mgu $\theta = \{C = \text{mary}\}$.
2. $\langle \emptyset, \{\text{in}(\text{george}, \text{oracle}:\text{all}(\text{customers}))\}\rangle$: $\alpha(t) = \text{new\_customer}(C)$ is directly θ-affected by Y since its code call atom unifies with $\sim CCA(Pre(\alpha(t))) = \{\text{in}(\text{C}, \text{oracle}:\text{all}(\text{customers}))\}$ under mgu $\theta = \{C = \text{george}\}$.
3. $\langle \{\text{high\_spender}(\text{steve})\}, \emptyset \rangle$: the action atom unifies with the one in the head of r under mgu $\theta = \{C = \text{steve}\}$.

The above notions help us to determine which action atoms may be affected when building the status set of the agent. Depending on the semantics applied, however, there are different ways to include an action status atom into a status set:

- Under rational and reasonable status set semantics, an action status atom $Op(\alpha)$ may only belong to a status set S if it occurs in a rule, or if it is derived by some action or deontic closure rule (cf. Def. A.3 in the appendix);
- under feasible status set semantics, any $Op(\alpha)$ may be included (even in some cases where it occurs in no rule).

We respect this by assuming that in the latter case, the program $\mathcal{P}$ contains dummy rules $\mathbf{P}(\alpha(X)) \leftarrow \mathbf{P}(\alpha(X))$ for every action name α. Such rules can easily be added without changing the semantics of the program. We are now in a position to define how to compute a set of suspicious code call atoms from a given set of code call atoms known to be suspicious — the procedure $\text{suscca}(X)$ defined in Table 1 does this.

Informally, suspicious code call atoms are determined as follows. In Phase 1 of the procedure, we iteratively determine which code call atoms are affected by syntactically examining the rules of the agent program and starting with the knowledge that the code call atoms in the input to the algorithm are known to be corrupted. The code call atoms in the body of each rule which is found to be affected become suspicious. At the end of Phase 1, all code call atoms *possibly* affected by the corrupted code call atoms are determined — as this might lead to the agent taking actions which vary dramatically from what the agent developer originally intended, these code call atoms may have unintended consequences that need to be addressed. Specifically, these corrupted code call conditions might trigger unintended actions and this needs to be taken care of.

We further have to take into account the fact that such an action α might interfere with some other (yet unconsidered) action β through an integrity constraint, i.e., some effects of α and β occur together in an integrity constraint. In such a case, the joint execution of α and β might not be possible. If, on the corrupted state, β were executed, then on the repaired state β could no longer be executed if α must be executed in it.

We illustrate this by an example. Suppose the add list of α contains the code call atom $\text{in}(\text{a}, \text{cca1})$, while the add list of β contains $\text{in}(\text{b}, \text{cca2})$, and there is an integrity constraint $ic : \text{in}(\text{a}, \text{cca1}) \Rightarrow \text{notin}(\text{b}, \text{cca2})$. Assume that in the current (corrupted) state, both $\text{in}(\text{a}, \text{cca1})$ and $\text{in}(\text{b}, \text{cca2})$ are false, and that α is not executed but β is, where ic is not an incriminated integrity constraint involving corrupted code call atoms.

proc suscca(X: set of code call atoms) : set of code call atoms;
  /* X subsumes all corrupted ground code call atoms */

  /* Phase 1: propagation of corruptedness */
1. $old := \emptyset; S := X; A := \emptyset;$
2. **while** $S \cup A \neq old$ **do**
3. $old := S \cup A;$
4.   **for each** $r \in \mathcal{P}$ **do**
5.   **if** $\Theta AFF(r, A, X) \neq \emptyset$ **then**
6.   **begin** $S := S \cup \Theta CCA(r, A, X);$
7. $A := A \cup \Theta AFF(r, A, X);$
8.   **end**;
9. **endwhile**;
  /* Find action atoms which may cause troubles with IC */
10. $B := \emptyset;$
11. **for each** $\alpha(t) \in A$ **do**
12. $C := \bigcup \left\{ CCA(ic\theta) \;\middle|\; \begin{array}{l} ic \in \mathcal{IC}, \text{ some } cca \in CCA(Add(\alpha) \& Del(\alpha)) \text{ and} \\ cca' \in CCA(ic) \cup \sim CCA(ic) \text{ unify with mgu } \theta \end{array} \right\};$
13. $B := B \cup \left\{ \beta(\boldsymbol{X}\theta) \;\middle|\; \begin{array}{l} \text{some } cca \in CCA(Add(\beta(\boldsymbol{X})) \& Del(\beta(\boldsymbol{X}))) \\ \text{and } cca' \in C \cup \sim C \text{ unify with mgu } \theta \end{array} \right\};$
14. **endfor**;
  /* Phase 2: back propagate poss. IC-violation by atoms B */
15. $old := S;$
16. **while** $S \cup B \neq old$ **do**
17. $old := S \cup B;$
18.   **for each** $r \in \mathcal{P}$ **do**
19.   **if** $\Theta AFF(r, B, \emptyset) \neq \emptyset$ **then**
20.   **begin** $S := S \cup \Theta CCA(r, B, \emptyset);$
21. $B := B \cup \Theta AFF(r, B, \emptyset);$
22.   **end**;
23. **endwhile**;
  /* return S plus precond's of affected action atoms in B */
24. **return** $S \cup \{cca \mid cca \in CCA(Pre(\alpha(t))) \wedge \alpha(t) \in B\}.$

end proc

Table 1. Procedure suscca

Furthermore, suppose that in the repaired agent state, α is executed. Then β could not be executed simultaneously unless ic is violated. Hence, in the repaired state, the agent would compute a status set according to which β is not executed. But this means that as for the status of $\mathrm{in}(b, cca2)$, the action taken by the agent on the corrupted state is (possibly) different from the one taken on the repaired state, which is undesired.

To eliminate such cases, the procedure suscca computes action atoms $\beta(\boldsymbol{X}\theta)$ which could lead to this problem. In Phase 2, it then computes action atoms which may be used in a derivation of these action atoms. This is done by analyzing in which rules of the program such atoms occur. Here $\Theta AFF(r, B, \emptyset)$ means that some $\alpha(t) \in B$ unifies with some action atom $\beta(t')$ in the body of rule r. No suspicious code call atoms in the rule body need to be considered since in this analysis, the effects of possible changes of the result of a code call atom are not relevant (they have already been considered earlier in Phase 1). Nonetheless, as in Phase 1, the code call atoms in affected rules become suspicious, since their value might contribute to deriving a problematic action atom.

After the back propagation, we take care of the fact that for an action atom $\alpha(t) \in B$ the code calls in $Pre(\alpha)$ might be evaluated when computing the status set. Thus, all these code calls are also considered to be suspicious if α was found to be affected.

Example 3.4 (Suspiciousness). Let us consider a simple agent s_ag that has the integrity constraint ic from Example 3.2. Suppose the agent program consists of the following rules, and rational status semantics is applied:

$r1 : \mathbf{Do}\,(\mathsf{a}_1(\mathsf{X})) \leftarrow \mathrm{in}(\mathsf{X}, \mathsf{cc1})\,\&\,\mathsf{X} \neq \mathsf{q}\,\&\,\mathbf{F}(\mathsf{a}_2(\mathsf{q})),$
$r2 : \mathbf{F}(\mathsf{a}_2(\mathsf{q})) \leftarrow \mathbf{P}(\mathsf{a}_1(\mathsf{q})),$
$r3 : \mathbf{F}(\mathsf{a}_2(\mathsf{s})) \leftarrow \mathrm{in}(\mathsf{s}, \mathsf{cc3})\,\&\,\neg\mathbf{Do}\,(\mathsf{a}_3),$
$r4 : \mathbf{Do}\,(\mathsf{a}_4) \leftarrow \mathrm{not}\,\mathrm{in}(\mathsf{q}, \mathsf{cc3}).$

Let $Pre(\mathsf{a}_i(\mathsf{X})) = \{\mathrm{in}(\mathsf{X}, \mathsf{cci})\}$, $Add(\mathsf{a}_i(\mathsf{X})) = \{\mathrm{in}(\mathsf{q}, \mathsf{cci})\}$, and $Del(\mathsf{a}_i(\mathsf{X})) = \{\mathrm{in}(\mathsf{X}, \mathsf{cci})\}$, for $i \in \{1, 2\}$, and furthermore $Pre(\mathsf{a}_j) = \{\mathrm{in}(\mathsf{q}, \mathsf{ccj})\}$, $Add(\mathsf{a}_j) = \emptyset$, and $Del(\mathsf{a}_j) = \{\mathrm{in}(\mathsf{q}, \mathsf{ccj})\}$, for $j \in \{3, 4\}$.

Suppose we are told that $\mathrm{in}(\mathsf{p}, \mathsf{cc1})$ is corrupted, and we want to find out the suspicious code call atoms given this information. As already seen, $Corr(ic, \mathrm{in}(\mathsf{p}, \mathsf{cc1})) = \{\mathrm{in}(\mathsf{p}, \mathsf{cc1}), \mathrm{in}(\mathsf{p}, \mathsf{cc2}), \mathrm{in}(\mathsf{p}, \mathsf{cc3})\}$.

Let us call suscca(X) with $X = Corr(ic, \mathrm{in}(\mathsf{p}, \mathsf{cc1}))$. We iteratively augment the initial sets $S := Corr(ic, \mathrm{in}(\mathsf{p}, \mathsf{cc1}))$ and $A := \emptyset$ until we reach a fixpoint.

1. In the first iteration, rule $r1$ is θ-affected for $\theta = \{X = p\}$, and we add to A the action atoms $\mathsf{a}_1(\mathsf{p})$ and $\mathsf{a}_2(\mathsf{q})$. The set S remains unchanged, since code call atom $\mathrm{in}(\mathsf{X}, \mathsf{cc1})\theta = \mathrm{in}(\mathsf{p}, \mathsf{cc1})$ from the body of $r1\theta$ already occurs in S. Rule $r2$ is now affected since because $\mathsf{a}_2(\mathsf{q})$ from A occurs in its head; thus, the action atom $\mathsf{a}_1(\mathsf{q})$ is added to A, while S remains unchanged. Rules $r3$ and $r4$ are not affected.
2. In the second iteration, rule $r1$ is newly affected for $\theta = \emptyset$, because $\mathsf{a}_2(\mathsf{q})$ from S occurs in its body, and for $\theta = \{X = q\}$, since $\mathsf{a}_1(\mathsf{q})$ unifies with the atom in its head. As a consequence, $\mathsf{a}_1(\mathsf{X})$ is newly added to A, and $\mathrm{in}(\mathsf{X}, \mathsf{cc1})$ and $\mathrm{in}(\mathsf{q}, \mathsf{cc1})$ are added to S. Rule $r2$ is not newly affected, and no further rule is affected.

A further iteration brings now change, and phase 1 of suscca(X) terminates. We have $S = \{\mathrm{in}(\mathsf{p}, \mathsf{cc1}), \mathrm{in}(\mathsf{p}, \mathsf{cc2}), \mathrm{in}(\mathsf{p}, \mathsf{cc3}), \mathrm{in}(\mathsf{X}, \mathsf{cc1}), \mathrm{in}(\mathsf{q}, \mathsf{cc1})\}$ and, furthermore, $A = \{\mathsf{a}_1(\mathsf{X}), \mathsf{a}_1(\mathsf{p}), \mathsf{a}_1(\mathsf{q}), \mathsf{a}_2(\mathsf{q})\}$.

In computing B, we have $C := CCA(ic)$ for $\alpha(t) = \mathsf{a}_1(\mathsf{X})$, since $\mathsf{a}_1(\mathsf{X})$'s delete list contains $\mathrm{in}(\mathsf{X}, \mathsf{cc1})$, which occurs in ic. Thus, B is set to $\{\mathsf{a}_1(\mathsf{X}), \mathsf{a}_2(\mathsf{X}), \mathsf{a}_3\}$ on the next line. The further actions in A only add subsumed actions to B; we obtain $B = \{\mathsf{a}_1(\mathsf{X}), \mathsf{a}_1(\mathsf{p}), \mathsf{a}_1(\mathsf{q}), \mathsf{a}_2(\mathsf{X}), \mathsf{a}_2(\mathsf{p}), \mathsf{a}_2(\mathsf{q}), \mathsf{a}_3\}$.

Phase 2 of suscca(X) then looks for the rules which are affected by $(B, \emptyset)$. Note that the only way for a rule to be affected by $(B, \emptyset)$ is to contain an action status atom unifying with an action status atom in B.

1. $r1$ is affected by $(B, \emptyset)$, but nothing new is added to S and B.
2. Also $r2$ is affected by $(B, \emptyset)$, but nothing new is added to S and B.

3. $r3$ is affected by $(B, \emptyset)$, because $a_2(X)$ unifies with its head for $\theta = \{X = s\}$. Thus, $in(s, cc3)$ is added to S and $a_2(s)$ is added to B.

4. $r4$ is not affected by $(B, \emptyset)$.

The while loop terminates; we have $S = \{ in(p, cc1), in(p, cc2), in(p, cc3), in(X, cc1), in(q, cc1), in(s, cc3) \}$. The return value of S, evaluated adding the preconditions of action status atoms in B, is $S = \{ in(p, cc1), in(p, cc2), in(p, cc3), in(X, cc1), in(q, cc1), in(s, cc3), in(q, cc2), in(q, cc3), in(X, cc2), in(s, cc2) \}$. Omitting subsumed code call atoms, the result is the following set of code call atoms: $S = \{ in(X, cc1), in(X, cc2), in(p, cc3), in(q, cc3), in(s, cc3) \}$.

The following theorem states that the procedure suscca(X) — where X is an input set of code call atoms — returns, as output, a set Y of code call atoms having the following property: If an arbitrary code call atom cca (or its complement) is not unifiable with any code call atom in Y, then decisions based on cca are not affected by ongoing attempts to repair the code call atoms in X. That is, action decisions and resulting state changes that involve cca are isolated from the corrupted code call atoms, and would be the same if the state were repaired before running the agent program.

For example, if agent a should reply to a message ask(b, in(jeff, db : persons)) querying a table persons, it might do so if the corrupted code call atoms are restricted to in(X, db : cars) where cars is a different table which is currently being repaired, provided that answering this message doesn't refer to cars.

We need some preliminary definitions. For a (fixed) agent program $\mathcal{P}$ and a given ground code call atom cca, the *influence set* IS of cca is the smallest set of (ground) actions that contains (1) all actions directly affected by cca and (2) all actions in $AC(r)$ where $r : A \leftarrow \chi \& L_1 \& \ldots \& L_n$ is any ground instance of a rule in $\mathcal{P}$ such that either cca $\in CCA(\chi)$ or $AC(r) \cap IS \neq \emptyset$. The influence set of an arbitrary code call atom, denoted $IS(\text{cca})$, is the union of all $IS(\text{cca}')$ where cca$'$ is a ground instance of cca.

Theorem 3.2. *Let $\mathcal{O}$ be an agent state and let $\mathcal{O}_r$ be a repair of $\mathcal{O}$. Let X be any set of code call atoms such that* corrcca$(\mathcal{CGI}(\mathcal{O})) \lhd X$. *Suppose* cca *is a code call atom not unifiable with any* cca$' \in$ suscca(X) *nor* $\sim$cca$'$, *and suppose S is a valid status set on $\mathcal{O}$ disregarding* $\mathcal{VGI}(\mathcal{O})$. *Then there exists a valid status set S' w.r.t. $\mathcal{O}_r$ and $\mathcal{IC}$ such that* $Op(\alpha) \in S'$ *iff* $Op(\alpha) \in S$ *holds for all modalities Op and* $\alpha \in IS(\text{cca})$.

Proof. By our assumption, some status set S' exists on $\mathcal{O}'$, leading to a state $\mathcal{O}'_r = $ **conc**(**Do** $(S'), \mathcal{O}_r)$. It holds that no action $\alpha(t) \in IS(\text{cca})$ belongs to $IS(\text{cca}')$ for any ground code call cca$'$ on which $\mathcal{O}$ and $\mathcal{O}_r$ are different. Otherwise, since cca$'$ must be a corrupted code call atom, cca$'$ is subsumed by X, and by virtue of Phase 1 of suscca, it follows that cca would have an instance which is subsumed by suscca(X). This is in contradiction to the hypothesis on cca. Thus, the value of a status atom $Op(\alpha(t))$ in the status sets S and S' is computable by accessing only (1) ground code call atoms on which $\mathcal{O}$ and $\mathcal{O}_r$ coincide, and (2) using only other action status atoms $Op'(\alpha'(t'))$ such that $\alpha'(t') \notin IS(\text{cca}')$ for every ground code call atom cca$'$ on which $\mathcal{O}$ and $\mathcal{O}_r$ are different.

Let AF be the set of all (ground) actions which instantiate action atoms in the sets A and B computed by suscca(X). We define the status set S'' by

$$S'' := \{Op(\alpha) \in S' \mid \alpha \in AF\} \cup \{Op(\alpha) \in S \mid \alpha \notin AF\}.$$

That is, for affected actions we take the status from S' and for non-affected actions from S. We show that S'' is a Sem-status set on $\mathcal{O}_r$, leading to $\mathcal{O}_r'' = \mathbf{conc}(\mathbf{Do}\,(S''), \mathcal{O}_r)$. Since it coincides with S on the $IS(\mathtt{cca})$, the result follows.

We first show that S'' is a feasible status set, i.e., satisfies conditions $(S1)$–$(S4)$ of Def. A.4. The key fact is that every ground instance r of a rule in $\mathcal{P}$ satisfies either $AC(r) \subseteq AF$ or $AC(r) \cap AF = \emptyset$

Since S and S' satisfies all rules of $\mathcal{P}$, it is thus clear that also S'' satisfies each rule of $\mathcal{P}$. Hence, condition $(S1)$ is satisfied. Since, for any ground action α, all action status atom $Op(\alpha)$ in S'' belong either to S or to S' and S, S' are feasible status sets, it is clear that S'' satisfies the conditions $(S2)$ and $(S3)$.

As for $(S4)$, a case analysis yields that every ground instance ic of an integrity constraint in $\mathcal{IC}$ is satisfied by $\mathcal{O}_r''$: (i) Assume first that $CCA(ic)$ contains some corrupted code call. Then all code calls in ic are corrupted, and only actions α where in $\alpha \in AF$ may change the value of any these code calls. Thus, for no such action $\mathbf{Do}\,(\alpha)$ can belong to $S \setminus S'$. Since $\mathcal{O}_r' \models ic$, it follows that also $\mathcal{O}_r'' \models ic$. (ii) Assume next that no code call in ic is corrupted, but some action $\alpha \in AF$ specifies a change of some code call in ic. Then, by Phase 2 in procedure $\mathrm{suscca}(X)$, we have $\beta \in AF$ for every action β that specifies a change of some code call atom in ic. Again, since $\mathcal{O}_r' \models ic$ it follows that $\mathcal{O}_r'' \models ic$. (iii) If neither (i) nor (ii) applies, then every code call atom in ic is uncorrupted and may be changed only by actions $\alpha \notin AF$. Since (i) does not apply, ic is not violated in state $\mathcal{O}$, and thus $\mathbf{conc}(\mathbf{Do}\,(S), \mathcal{O}) \models ic$. It follows that $\mathcal{O}_r'' \models ic$. Summarizing, we have that ic is satisfied in the state $\mathcal{O}_r''$. Hence, $\mathcal{O}_r'' \models \mathcal{IC}$, and thus condition $(S4)$ is satisfied. This shows that S'' is a feasible status set w.r.t. $\mathcal{O}_r$.

If Sem is rational status set semantics, we must further show that S'' is grounded, i.e., no proper subset $T'' \subset S''$ satisfies $(S1$–$S3)$. Suppose such a T'' exists; we shall derive a contradiction. Assume first that T'' is smaller than S'' on the action status atoms set over actions $\alpha \notin AF$. Then,

$$T := \{Op(\alpha) \in S \mid \alpha \in AF\} \cup \{Op(\alpha) \in T'' \mid \alpha \notin AF\}$$

is a smaller status set $T \subset S$ which satisfies $(S1)$–$(S3)$ on state $\mathcal{O}$: Indeed, note that each ground instance of rule satisfies either $AC(r) \subseteq AF$ or $AC(r) \cap AF = \emptyset$, and obviously T is deontically and action consistent and action closed. This would mean that S is not a rational status set on $\mathcal{O}$ (disregarding $\mathcal{VGI}(\mathcal{O})$), which is a contradiction to the hypothesis. Hence, T'' must coincide with S'' w.r.t. the status of actions not in AF, and thus T'' is smaller w.r.t. AF. Then, the status set

$$T' := \{Op(\alpha) \in T'' \mid \alpha \in AF\} \cup \{Op(\alpha) \in S' \mid \alpha \notin AF\}$$

is a smaller status set $T' \subset S'$ which satisfies, by similar arguments, $(S1)$–$(S3)$ on state $\mathcal{O}_r$. This means that S' is not a rational status set on $\mathcal{O}_r$, which is a contradiction. Thus, such a T'' can not exist, which proves that S'' is indeed a rational status set.

If Sem is reasonable status set semantics, we must show that S'' is a rational status set of the reduct $\mathcal{P}' = red^{S''}(\mathcal{P}, \mathcal{O}')$. In fact, since every reasonable status set is also rational, S'' is w.r.t. $\mathcal{O}_r$ a feasible status set for $\mathcal{P}$ and thus also for $\mathcal{P}'$. Observe that the reduct preserves the key property that either $AC(r) \subseteq AF$ or $AC(r) \cap AF = \emptyset$. By similar arguments as above, we thus obtain that S'' is grounded for $\mathcal{P}'$. Consequently, S'' is a reasonable status set of $\mathcal{P}$ w.r.t. $\mathcal{O}_r$. ∎

In particular, this formal result assures us that in case an agent program admits a single status set in each state (which, e.g., is true for the *IMPACT* target class of regular agent programs [15]), then the actions taken in reply to a message *must* also be taken if the corrupted state were repaired before.

4 Agent State Repair

Recall that an agent's state is characterized by the contents of its data structures. In order for an agent to automatically handle integrity constraint violations (or lack of a status set), we will add a special set of data structures to each agent called repair *data structures*. These data structures will have their own specialized API function calls.

4.1 The repair Data Structures

The repair data structures contain:

1. A buffer waitbuf consisting of messages that are waiting to be serviced because they involve accesses to part of the agent state that is "corrupted."
2. A buffer repbuf consisting of corrupted code call atoms.
3. A buffer icbuf consisting of (instances of) integrity constraints that are currently undergoing repairs.
4. An auxiliary buffer susbuf which contains the suspicious code call atoms.
5. A set cons_state consisting of all ground code call atoms true in a distinguished consistent state.
6. A set curr_state consisting of all ground code call atoms true in the current state.

The repair data structures support the following API functions:

suspicious(cca) : This function takes a code call atom cca as input, and returns true if cca is implied by the set of code call atoms contained in repbuf under a notion of inference fixed by the concrete implementation of the function. There are many ways to implement suspicious(cca). For example, it may:
    1. check whether cca is physically present in repbuf or
    2. check whether cca is an instance of a code call atom in repbuf, or
    3. check whether cca is implied by repbuf using some set of axioms and some set of implication rules.
suscca(X): This is the procedure defined in Section 3.3.
add_repbuf(cca) : This function "inserts" the code call atoms corrupted by cca into the repair buffer, such that after insertion, suspicious(cca$'$) returns true if cca$'$ is from suscca(repbuf), and returns false otherwise. Its implementation depends on the one of suspicious(cca), and different possibilities exist (see Section 5.1).

It is important to note that the repair data structures and API calls can be included as part of the *IMPACT* agent development environment (see [15,26]) and do not need to be programmed over and over again for each agent by the agent developer.

4.2 Repair Action Library

In addition to the repair data structures, we augment the agent with a set of "repair" actions. Each agent has a set of actions that may be used to "repair" the agent state. The repair actions can be implemented as a straightforward extensible dynamic linked library (DLL) provided by the *IMPACT* agent development environment.

Definition 4.1. *Suppose* a *is an agent and* $\mathcal{O}, \mathcal{O}'$ *are two states of agent* a. *Let* $\mathcal{RA}$ *be the repair action library of agent* a. *Then* $\mathcal{O}'$ *is said to be:*

1. $\mathcal{RA}_0$-reachable *from* $\mathcal{O}$ *iff* $\mathcal{O} = \mathcal{O}'$,
2. $\mathcal{RA}_{i+1}$-reachable *from* $\mathcal{O}$, $i \geq 0$, *iff there is a state* $\mathcal{O}''$ *such that* $\mathcal{O}''$ *is* $\mathcal{RA}_i$-*reachable from* $\mathcal{O}$ *and there is an action* α *in* $\mathcal{RA}$ *which is executable in* $\mathcal{O}''$ *and the execution yields* $\mathcal{O}'$.

State $\mathcal{O}'$ *is* $\mathcal{RA}$-reachable *from* $\mathcal{O}$ *iff* $\mathcal{O}'$ *is* $\mathcal{RA}_i$-*reachable from* $\mathcal{O}$, *for some* $i \geq 0$.

Intuitively, when we say a state $\mathcal{O}'$ is $\mathcal{RA}$ reachable from a given state $\mathcal{O}$, this means that there is a sequence of repair actions which allow $\mathcal{O}$ to be transformed into $\mathcal{O}'$. The following example illustrates this.

Example 4.1 (Simple Grid Scenario). Let us consider a simple scenario where a *grid* agent manages three robots moving on an n×n grid, n ≥ 2. The repair actions $\mathcal{RA}_{grid}$ are composed of the actions for moving a robot in one direction (north, south, east, west). We describe the go_north action; the others are similar. We assume that the underlying software has a Pos(Robot) API function which may returns the position of the specified robot at the time the function call is made.

> **Name**: go_north
> **Schema**: (Robot)
> $Pre(\text{go\_north}) = \text{in}(P, \text{grid} : \text{Pos}(\text{Robot})) \& P.y \neq n$
> $Add(\text{go\_north}) = \text{in}(P', \text{grid} : \text{Pos}(\text{Robot})) \& P'.x = P.x \& P'.y = P.y + 1$
> $Del(\text{go\_north}) = \text{in}(P, \text{grid} : \text{Pos}(\text{Robot}))$

Let $\mathcal{O}$ be the state

$$\mathcal{O} = \{\text{in}((0,0), \text{grid} : \text{Pos}(\text{r1})), \text{in}((0,0), \text{grid} : \text{Pos}(\text{r2})), \text{in}((0,0), \text{grid} : \text{Pos}(\text{r3}))\}.$$

Then

$$\mathcal{O}' = \{\text{in}((0,1), \text{grid} : \text{Pos}(\text{r1})), \text{in}((0,0), \text{grid} : \text{Pos}(\text{r2})), \text{in}((0,0), \text{grid} : \text{Pos}(\text{r3}))\}$$

is $\mathcal{RA}_1$-reachable from $\mathcal{O}$, while

$$\mathcal{O}'' = \{\text{in}((0,1), \text{grid} : \text{Pos}(\text{r1})), \text{in}((0,0), \text{grid} : \text{Pos}(\text{r2})), \text{in}((1,1), \text{grid} : \text{Pos}(\text{r3}))\}$$

is $\mathcal{RA}_3$-reachable from $\mathcal{O}$. Both $\mathcal{O}'$ and $\mathcal{O}''$ are $\mathcal{RA}$-reachable from $\mathcal{O}$.

Definition 4.2. *A set* $\mathcal{RA}$ *of repair actions is said to be* complete w.r.t. *an agent state* $\mathcal{O}$ *iff there exists an* $\mathcal{RA}$-reachable state $\mathcal{O}'$ *such that* $\mathcal{O}' \models \mathcal{IC}$. *Furthermore,* $\mathcal{RA}$ *is said to be* complete w.r.t. *an agent* a, *iff* $\mathcal{RA}$ *is complete w.r.t.* $\mathcal{O}$ *for every state* $\mathcal{O}$ *of* a.

Intuitively, $\mathcal{RA}$ is complete for an agent iff whatever possible state the agent is in, there is always some way of executing repair actions so that a consistent (w.r.t. integrity constraints) agent state is obtained. When an agent developer specifies his or her repair actions, it is critical that they be complete w.r.t. the rest of the agent.

Example 4.2 (Grid Scenario Continued). Suppose that in the previous scenario an integrity constraint exists stating that a position can be occupied by at most one robot.

$\mathcal{RA}_{grid}$ is *complete* w.r.t. $\mathcal{O}$, since there exists a state $(\mathcal{O}'')$ which is $\mathcal{RA}_{grid}$-reachable from $\mathcal{O}$ and satisfies the integrity constraints. $\mathcal{RA}_{grid}$ is also *complete* w.r.t. agent *grid*, it is alway possible to move, in any agent state, the robots in such a way that they occupy three different positions.

The set of repair actions in the grid example is domain-dependent. In order to provide the system developer with already defined strategies, we propose some domain-independent sets of repair actions which can be adopted whatever the context is. They use the repair data structures introduced in Section 4.1.

Example 4.3 (Initialized State Repair Actions $\mathcal{RA}_{init}$). We assume that an agent a is in an initial state $\mathcal{O}_{init}$ at the time of deployment. $\mathcal{O}_{init}$ is assumed to satisfy the integrity constraints. We may then set cons_state-set = $\mathcal{O}_{init}$. Then $\mathcal{RA} = \{ra\}$ is complete w.r.t. $\mathcal{O}_{init}$ if we define action ra to be defined as follows:

Name: ra
Schema: ()
$Pre(ra) = \{in(0, repair : curr\_state()) \& in(I, repair : cons\_state())\}$
$Add(ra) = \{in(I, repair : curr\_state())\}$
$Del(ra) = \{in(0, repair : curr\_state())\}$

Here, two functions curr_state() and cons_state() are used which are provided by the repair package. The former returns, as output, the set of all ground code call atoms which are true in the current state, and the latter the set of all ground code call atoms true in a distinguished state $\mathcal{O}_0$ that satisfies the integrity constraints (see Section 2).

The action ra can be applied in any state: we assume that the ground code call atoms characterizing the current state $(in(0, repair : curr\_state()))$ and the consistent state $\mathcal{O}_0$ $(in(I, repair : cons\_state()))$ can always be retrieved. Then, the current state is changed to $\mathcal{O}_0$.

Example 4.4 (Preferred State Repair Actions $\mathcal{RA}_{pref}$). Preferred state repair actions are exactly like the above except that the agent developer initializes the cons_state-set with a state $\mathcal{O}_{pref}$ which is known to satisfy the integrity constraints.

Example 4.5 (Rollback Repair Actions $\mathcal{RA}_{roll}$). In rollback-based repair, at any given instant t of time, the agent tracks its last known consistent state $\mathcal{O}_{lk}$ and sets cons_state-set equal to $\mathcal{O}_{lk}$. This is done by the mkrepair function which identifies the proper repair actions to perform for reaching a consistent state, and updates cons_state accordingly. When integrity constraints are violated, repairs cause the agent state to be reset to the last known consistent state. Thus, the set of repair actions consists of the single action ra, which is exactly like that in Examples 4.3 and 4.4. What is different, though, is the content of cons_state, which dynamically changes during the agent's life cycle. This strategy is usable only when actions are reversible (e.g., an agent that executes a fax action will probably find it impossible to recall the fax).

Example 4.6 (IC-Oriented Repair $\mathcal{RA}_{ic}$). This repair strategy can be applied under the condition that each integrity constraint with a comparison atom in the head has at least one code call atom in its body. Suppose a is an agent having integrity constraints $ic_i : \psi_i \Rightarrow \chi_i$, where $i \in \{1, \ldots, n\}$. We now construct repair actions ra_i for them:

Name: ra_i
Schema: ()
$Pre(ra_i) = \emptyset$
$Add(ra_i) = \{\chi_i\}$, if χ_i is a code call atom, and $Add(ra_i) = \emptyset$ otherwise.
$Del(ra_i) = \emptyset$, if χ_i is a code call atom, and $Del(ra_i) = \{cca\}$, for some cca $\in CCA(\psi_i)$ otherwise.

Example 4.7 (IC-Repair with Protected Atoms $\mathcal{RA}_{icp}$). A slight variant of the preceding strategy, called $\mathcal{RA}_{icp}$, may include a list of "protected" code call atoms. The repair actions ra_i are similar except that ra_i's delete list may contain only non-protected code call atoms if χ_i is a comparison atom. Prior to deployment of an agent, the system must check that each integrity constraint with a comparison atom in the head has at least one non-protected code call atom in its body.

The following results give us some idea about the difficulty of checking completeness. For concrete statements about complexity, we need some assumptions about the complexity of evaluating code calls and the domains of different data types. The assumptions we make are similar to those in the comprehensive analysis of the complexity of agent programs in [13], and request that the size of an agent state is bounded by a polynomial in the size of the problem input (e.g., this can be ensured by assuming that the number of arguments in code calls is bounded by a constant, and that the number of values is polynomial in the input size), and that each code call to an agent state can be evaluated in polynomial time. For further ramifying assumptions concerning state changes, we refer to [13].

Theorem 4.1. *1. Checking the completeness of a given set of repair actions $\mathcal{RA}$ w.r.t. a given agent state $\mathcal{O}$ is PSPACE-complete under the above assumptions and undecidable in general.*
  2. Checking completeness of a given set of repair actions $\mathcal{RA}$ w.r.t. a given agent a is PSPACE-complete under the above assumptions and undecidable in general.

Proof. (Sketch) The PSPACE upper bound is a consequence of the fact that the size of the agent state is bounded by a polynomial. The PSPACE lower bounds are explained by the fact that Turing machines with polynomial work space can be easily encoded to this problem. However, checking completeness of a set of repair actions with respect to an agent is harder than checking w.r.t. an agent state. Even if the latter is polynomial, the completeness test w.r.t. an agent might be undecidable. This can be shown by reducing to this problem e.g. the one of deciding whether a given SQL-query returns true over all possible instances of a relational database, which is undecidable (cf. [1]).   ∎

An extensible library of complete sets of repair actions may easily be incorporated within *IMPACT*. The agent developer - once she has specified her agent's integrity constraints, agent program, etc., can automatically select $\mathcal{RA}_{init}, \mathcal{RA}_{roll}, \mathcal{RA}_{ic}$ repair action strategies. In this case, the relevant repair actions may automatically be computed and filled in for the agent by the *IMPACT* Agent Development Environment.

5   Error Tolerant Agent Cycle

In this section, we specify a solution to the problem of how an agent can recover from corrupted states while continuing to process requests that are unaffected by ongoing repairs. Note that at any point in time, the agent's state may be under repair or not.

If it is not under repair and a message of the form ask($\cdot$) or tell($\cdot$) arrives, then we attempt to process the request as usual (nothing needs to be done to account for the repairs). Two possibilities now arise. Either the message yields a valid status set, or not. In the first case, we are done. Otherwise, we need to add the message to waitbuf and start repairing the state.

If, on the other hand, the agent's state is being repaired, we need to check whether ongoing repairs will interfere with processing of the current request. This can be done by checking whether the code call atom in the message is affected by the ongoing repairs. If so, we must add the message to the waitbuf buffer. Otherwise we can process it, secure in the knowledge that repairs being made to the agent state are not going to affect decisions depending on the current value of code call atom. Note that the two cases where the state is not under repair, and the state is under repair without affecting the incoming message, are both captured by the condition suspicious($cca\theta$) = false. In fact, if the state is not under repair, repbuf is empty, and nothing can be "derived" from it (in particular, $cca\theta$ cannot be derived). Otherwise, repbuf is not empty but again $cca\theta$ cannot be "derived" since it is not involved with the ongoing repairs. These two cases are dealt with uniformly. We need a few simple definitions.

Definition 5.1 (*Sem-* and **Sem-***Sem*-**Compatible Update**). *Let $\mathcal{P}$ be an agent program. Then, an agent state $\mathcal{O}$ is Sem-compatible with $\mathcal{P}$, if a has a Sem-status set w.r.t. $\mathcal{O}$. Furthermore, $\mathcal{O}$ is Semi-Sem-compatible with $\mathcal{P}$, if it is not Sem-compatible but $\mathcal{P}$ has a status set w.r.t. $\mathcal{O}$ modulo condition $(S4)$ of a feasible status set (cf. Definition A.4 in Appendix A).*

We now show how the agent decision cycle given in [14,26] may be modified so as to handle the requirements of recovery and continuity. The modified decision cycle, et_agent_cycle ("et" stands for error tolerant), defined in Table 2 uses a special procedure mkrepair that takes, as input, an agent state as well as repbuf, icbuf, waitbuf, and (i) assembles a list of ground action status atoms whose serial execution is guaranteed to change the agent state to one satisfying all integrity constraints and (ii) executes this list and causes that waitbuf is flushed, i.e., all buffered messages are handled.

proc et_agent_cycle(a:agent; $\mathcal{O}$:agent-state; msg:message);

1.   **if** $msg = $ ask(b, cca) or $msg = $ tell(b, cca, ans) **then**
2.   **if** $msg = $ ask(b, cca) **then** ans $:= \{id\}$
         /* take identity as dummy substitution: ccaθ = cca if $\theta = id$ */
3.   **if** suspicious(ccaθ) = **true** for some $\theta \in$ ans **then** $insert$(waitbuf, msg);
            /* add affected msg to waitbuf (state is under repair) */
4.   **else** /* no state repair or doesn't affect msg */
5.   **if** some Sem-status set S w.r.t. $\mathcal{IC} \ominus$ icbuf exists on $\mathcal{O} + msg$ **then**
6.   execute the action **conc**($\{\alpha \mid \mathbf{Do}(\alpha) \in S\}, \mathcal{O} + msg$)
7.   **else** /* no status set exists - error condition */
8.   **if** some Semi-Sem-status set S' exists on $\mathcal{O} + msg$ **then**
               begin /* switch to new (corrupted) state; needs repair */
9. $\mathcal{O}' := \mathbf{conc}(\{\alpha \mid \mathbf{Do}(\alpha) \in S'\}, \mathcal{O} + msg)$;
10.   icbuf $:= \emptyset$; repbuf $:= \emptyset$;   /* reinitialize buffers */
11.   **for each** instance ic' of an $ic \in \mathcal{IC}$ s.t. $\mathcal{O}' \not\models ic'$ **do**
12. $insert$(icbuf, ic');   /* add int.cons. requiring repair */
13.   **for each** cca$' \in CCA(ic')$ **do** add_repbuf(cca$'$);
                    /* add poss. corrupted cc-atoms in ic' to repbuf */
14. $insert$(waitbuf, msg);
15.   mkrepair($\mathcal{O}'$, repbuf, icbuf, waitbuf)
16.   **end**
17.   **else** /* $msg = $ done(b, cca, ans$^+$, ans$^-$) */
18.   **begin** $X := \{ic \mid ic \in \mathcal{IC} \ominus$ icbuf and $\mathcal{O} + msg \not\models ic\}$;
19.   **if** $X \neq \emptyset$ or no Sem-status set for $\mathcal{O} + msg$ w.r.t. $\mathcal{IC} \ominus$ icbuf exists **then**
20.   **begin** add_repbuf(cca);
21.   **for each** $ic \in X$ **do** $insert$(icbuf, ic);
22.   mkrepair($\mathcal{O}$, repbuf, icbuf, waitbuf)
23.   **end**
24.   **else** compute a Sem-status set S for $\mathcal{O} + msg$ w.r.t. $\mathcal{IC} \ominus$ icbuf and
                execute the action **conc**($\{\alpha \mid \mathbf{Do}(\alpha) \in S\}, \mathcal{O} + msg$)
25.   **end**
end proc

Table 2. Modified agent decision cycle

Here, icbuf contains instances of violated integrity constraints, repbuf represents (perhaps a superset) of the set of corrupted code calls, and waitbuf contains messages which need to be serviced/handled. The expression $\mathcal{IC} \ominus$ icbuf denotes the set of all integrity constraints which are ground instances of some integrity constraint in $\mathcal{IC}$ but not in icbuf. Note that they can be described at the non-ground level. Furthermore, $\mathcal{O} + msg$ describes the agent state that updates the state $\mathcal{O}$ with the message msg.

Let us see how the above algorithm captures our requirements of Recovery and Continuity. Recovery is supported via (i) Steps 8-16 and (ii) Steps 19-23 of the algorithm, where (i) handles the case when a message that yields no valid status set is encountered, and (ii) is used when an external update causes integrity constraint violations.

Continuity is supported as well. In Step 6, execution of actions according to S can be safely done by Theorem 3.2, even though possible repairs are going on. In two cases, however, processing the message is deferred: In Step 3, when it is realized that the current state repair might interfere with the processing of the message, and in Step 12, after it is realized that the agent program *per se* violates some integrity constraints, and thus the state needs repair.

When the state has been repaired, the messages are flushed from the waitbuf buffer. That is, they are processed one by one and new status sets are computed.

5.1   Different Methods to Implement suspicious and add_repbuf

In this section, we propose a couple of alternative ways of implementing the functions suspicious and add_repbuf.

A First Implementation   As mentioned earlier, there are many ways to implement add_repbuf and suspicious. One simple way is given below. It is important to note that add_repbuf and suspicious must be mutually compatible.

proc suspicious1(cca)   **proc** add_repbuf1(cca)
   if cca ◁ susbuf **then return** true   repbuf := repbuf ∪ corrcca(cca)
   else return false.   susbuf := suscca(repbuf)
end proc   **end proc**

When inserting a message's code call atom into repbuf, we compute all other corrupted code call atoms (using the function corrcca defined in Section 3.3) and add them to repbuf. Starting from repbuf we also evaluate the suspicious code call atoms and put them in an auxiliary buffer, susbuf.

This procedure has the advantage that when evaluating suspicious1, all that is needed is a simple subsumption check which is executable in time proportional to the product of the length of the table and the longest code call atom stored in it. However, it has the disadvantage that whenever a message is to be inserted, all corrupted and suspicious code calls must be computed. Hence, insertion is an expensive and space consuming operation. The use of suspicious1 and add_repbuf1 is appropriate if we expect the agent's state to be corrupted infrequently in comparison to the number of messages that can be processed without being concerned about corruption of the agent state.

A Second Implementation   Another implementation of suspicious and add_repbuf would work as follows. When a code call atom (in a message) causes problems, then we insert the code call atoms corrupted by it into repbuf without computing the suspicious code call atoms. Later, when a new message is received, we explicitly determine if it is affected using the suscca function.

proc suspicious2(cca)   **proc** add_repbuf2(cca)
   if cca ◁ suscca(repbuf) **then**   **if** not(cca ◁ repbuf) **then**
      return true   repbuf := repbuf ∪ corrcca(cca)
   else return false.   **end proc**
end proc

Unlike the first implementation, this one spends minor effort when inserting code call atoms into repbuf. However, for each arriving request, it attempts to check if that request is affected by the ongoing repairs. Thus, in using this application, we may find that repbuf is large (as lots of things are inserted into it) and hence the time for checking if a given request is affected by the ongoing repairs as in repbuf can be significant. Thus, this method is worth using if the number of repairs is large and there are few requests.

5.2   Implementing mkrepair

The mkrepair procedure (it is a procedure rather than a function in programming language terminology as it has side effects) takes as input, a current agent state $\mathcal{O}$ and values of repbuf, icbuf, and waitbuf. The procedure does the following:

1. It finds a state $\mathcal{O}_{new}$ that satisfies all the agent's integrity constraints (and in particular repairs those in icbuf).
2. It resets icbuf and repbuf to $\emptyset$ as the integrity constraints are now repaired and as the code calls causing problems are now no longer causing problems.
3. It then iteratively reinvokes et_agent_cycle with the messages in waitbuf (they will no longer trigger errors as the repairs that caused them to originally be placed in waitbuf are now fixed).
4. It resets waitbuf to $\emptyset$ as the waiting messages are now handled.

Steps (2)–(4) above are simple to handle and understand, and hence, in the rest of this section, we focus on step (1).

It is easy to see that Step (1) may be formulated as a classical AI planning problem. Specifically, we have a current state and a set of goal states (those where $\mathcal{IC}$ is satisfied) and a set $\mathcal{RA}$ of repair actions — we wish to find a sequence of (some) appropriate actions in $\mathcal{RA}$ that yield a goal state. When $\mathcal{RA}$ is a complete set of actions, it is possible that there are multiple consistent states that the agent can transition to. In this situation, the agent should transition to a "best" repair state w.r.t. some state evaluation function. This again is a classical AI planning problem [21]. Hence, in this section, we confine ourselves to specify how such a cost function to evaluate states may be set up. Solutions already proposed in the AI literature [21] may be easily adopted to actually find a "best" state w.r.t. such a cost function.

Definition 5.2. *A state evaluation function,* $\text{sef}_a(\mathcal{O})$*, associated with agent* a *is one that takes as input, an agent state* $\mathcal{O}$*, and provides as output, an integer.*

Definition 5.3. *A state* $\mathcal{O}'$ *of an agent* a *is optimal w.r.t. an agent state* $\mathcal{O}$ *iff*

1. *$\mathcal{O}' \models \mathcal{IC}$,*
2. *$\mathcal{O}'$ is $\mathcal{RA}$-reachable from $\mathcal{O}$, and*
3. *there is no other agent state $\mathcal{O}^\star$ satisfying 1 and 2 such that $\text{sef}_a(\mathcal{O}') < \text{sef}_a(\mathcal{O}^\star)$.*

Example 5.1 (Optimal Agent State). Let us reconsider Example 4.1. We may set sef($\mathcal{O}$) to be the sum of the Hamming distances between the positions of the three robots. Suppose we have an API function "hdist(P_1, P_2)" which computes the Hamming distance between two points P_1, P_2 in the integer plane. Then we can formally set

$$\text{sef}(\mathcal{O}) = \text{hdist}(R_1, R_2) + \text{hdist}(R_2, R_3) + \text{hdist}(R_3, R_1).$$

The results of the code call atoms in(R_1, grid : Pos(r1)), in(R_2, grid : Pos(r2)), and in(R_3, grid : Pos(r3)) describe the agent state. Assume a 5×5 grid and suppose the current agent state is

$$\mathcal{O} = \{\text{in}((0,1), \text{grid} : \text{Pos}(r1)), \text{in}((0,0), \text{grid} : \text{Pos}(r2)), \text{in}((1,1), \text{grid} : \text{Pos}(r3))\}.$$

Then,

$$\mathcal{O}' = \{\text{in}((0,4), \text{grid} : \text{Pos}(r1)), \text{in}((0,0), \text{grid} : \text{Pos}(r2)), \text{in}((4,4), \text{grid} : \text{Pos}(r3))\}$$

is an optimal state w.r.t. $\mathcal{O}$ as it satisfies *grid*'s integrity constraint, it can be reached from $\mathcal{O}$ through a series of actions from { go_north, go_south, go_east, go_west } and, as the robots are located on three corners of the grid, the sum of their Hamming distances is maximal. Note that more than one state may be optimal. For example,

$$\mathcal{O}'' = \{\text{in}((4,0), \text{grid} : \text{Pos}(r1)), \text{in}((4,4), \text{grid} : \text{Pos}(r2)), \text{in}((0,0), \text{grid} : \text{Pos}(r3))\}$$

is another optimal state w.r.t. $\mathcal{O}$.

The goal of mkrepair is to take a state $\mathcal{O}$ that violates the agent's integrity constraints, and to find a sequence of repair actions which yields an optimal state $\mathcal{O}'$.

This is easily seen to be an AI planning problem. However, there is one major difference. Whereas in AI planning problems, the cost of a plan is typically taken to be the sum of the costs (or some monotonic function of the costs) of the actions in the plan, in this case, the repair actions are not being assessed any cost. Instead, each state has an associated "value" captured by the state evaluation function, and we want to find a reachable state satisfying the integrity constraints that has the maximal value.

We now specify how we may define the value of a state.

Definition 5.4 (Variable Specification). *Suppose χ is a code call condition involving an integer variable X. Then $X : \chi$ is a* variable specification.

We assume the existence of a specialized package math which supports a number of standard arithmetic functions, including a binary "sum" operation on integers and a binary "hdist" function on points (pairs of integers).

Example 5.2 (Variable Specification). The expression

$\text{HDR}_1\text{R}_2 : \text{in}(R_1, \text{grid:Pos}(r1)) \& \text{in}(R_2, \text{grid:Pos}(r2)) \& \text{in}(\text{HDR}_1\text{R}_2, \text{math:hdist}(R_1, R_2))$

is a variable specification of HDR_1R_2, while

$V : \text{in}(\text{Res}_1, \text{math:sum}(\text{HDR}_1\text{R}_2, \text{HDR}_2\text{R}_3)) \& \text{in}(V, \text{math:sum}(\text{Res}_1, \text{HDR}_3\text{R}_1))$

is a variable specification of V. Their intended meaning is to specify the Hamming distance between Robot R1, R2 and the sum of the three Hamming distances, respectively.

Definition 5.5 (Math Code Call Conditions and Specifications). *A* math code call condition with input variables $\mathbf{X} = X_1, \ldots, X_n$ and output variable X *is a code call condition which is safe modulo* $\mathbf{X}$,[5] *contains* X *and involves only code call atoms accessing* math. *A* math variable specification with input variables $\mathbf{X}$ and output variable X *is a variable specification whose associated code call condition is a math code call condition with input variables* $\mathbf{X}$ *and output variable* X.

Example 5.3. The variable specification

$$V \; : \; \mathtt{in}(\mathtt{Res}_1, \mathtt{math} : \mathtt{sum}(\mathtt{HDR}_1\mathtt{R}_2, \mathtt{HDR}_2\mathtt{R}_3)) \;\&\; \mathtt{in}(V, \mathtt{math} : \mathtt{sum}(\mathtt{Res}_1, \mathtt{HDR}_3\mathtt{R}_1))$$

is a math variable specification with input variables $\mathtt{HDR}_1\mathtt{R}_2$, $\mathtt{HDR}_2\mathtt{R}_3$, $\mathtt{HDR}_3\mathtt{R}_1$ and output variable V.

Definition 5.6 (Objective Function Specification). *An* objective function specification *is a pair* $\langle X : \chi_{math}, \{VS_1, \ldots, VS_n\} \rangle$ *where:*

1. *each VS_i is a variable specification of the form $X_i : \chi_i$, and*
2. *$X : \chi_{math}$ is a math variable specification with input variables $X_1, \ldots, X_n$ and output variable X.*

Example 5.4 (Objective Function Specification). We continue the grid example and describe an objective function which assigns higher values to states where the three robots are further apart. Such an objective function specification may look like $\langle V : \chi_{\mathtt{math}} \rangle, \{VS_1, VS_2, VS_3\}$, where

$$\chi_{\mathtt{math}} = \mathtt{in}(\mathtt{Res}_1, \mathtt{math}:\mathtt{sum}(\mathtt{HDR}_1\mathtt{R}_2, \mathtt{HDR}_2\mathtt{R}_3)) \;\&\; \mathtt{in}(V, \mathtt{math}:\mathtt{sum}(\mathtt{Res}_1, \mathtt{HDR}_3\mathtt{R}_1))$$

$$
\begin{aligned}
VS_1 = \;\; & \mathtt{HDR}_1\mathtt{R}_2 : \mathtt{in}(\mathtt{R}_1, \mathtt{grid}:\mathtt{Pos}(\mathtt{r1})) \;\&\; \mathtt{in}(\mathtt{R}_2, \mathtt{grid}:\mathtt{Pos}(\mathtt{r2})) \;\&\; \\
& \mathtt{in}(\mathtt{HDR}_1\mathtt{R}_2, \mathtt{math}:\mathtt{hdist}(\mathtt{R}_1, \mathtt{R}_2)), \\
VS_2 = \;\; & \mathtt{HDR}_2\mathtt{R}_3 : \mathtt{in}(\mathtt{R}_2, \mathtt{grid}:\mathtt{Pos}(\mathtt{r2})) \;\&\; \mathtt{in}(\mathtt{R}_3, \mathtt{grid}:\mathtt{Pos}(\mathtt{r3})) \;\&\; \\
& \mathtt{in}(\mathtt{HDR}_2\mathtt{R}_3, \mathtt{math}:\mathtt{hdist}(\mathtt{R}_2, \mathtt{R}_3)), \\
VS_3 = \;\; & \mathtt{HDR}_3\mathtt{R}_1 : \mathtt{in}(\mathtt{R}_3, \mathtt{grid}:\mathtt{Pos}(\mathtt{r3})) \;\&\; \mathtt{in}(\mathtt{R}_1, \mathtt{grid}:\mathtt{Pos}(\mathtt{r1})) \;\&\; \\
& \mathtt{in}(\mathtt{HDR}_3\mathtt{R}_1, \mathtt{math}:\mathtt{hdist}(\mathtt{R}_3, \mathtt{R}_1)).
\end{aligned}
$$

Intuitively, an objective function specification measures the value of agent state $\mathcal{O}'$ by

1. setting $v_i = \max\{X_i\theta \mid \chi_i\theta \text{ is ground and } \mathcal{O}' \models \chi_i\theta\}$;
2. grounding out the values of the X_i's in χ_{math} and setting $v = X\gamma\theta \mid \chi_i\gamma\theta$ is ground and is true w.r.t. $\mathcal{O}'$, where $\gamma = \{X_i = v_i \mid 1 \leq i \leq n\}$;
3. returning v.

Example 5.5 (Value of the Objective Function). We continue Example 5.1 by considering $\mathcal{O}$, $\mathcal{O}'$ and $\mathcal{O}''$. Then, for $\mathcal{O}$ we have that $v_1 = 1, v_2 = 2, v_3 = 1$ and thus $v = 4$. For $\mathcal{O}'$, instead, we have that $v_1 = 4, v_2 = 8, v_3 = 4$ and thus $v = 16$. The value of $\mathcal{O}''$ is also 16 since $v_1 = 4, v_2 = 8, v_3 = 4$.

---

[5] Informally, this means that after assigning $X_1, \ldots, X_n$ values, the code call condition can be reordered so that an evaluation from left to right is possible (see Appendix B and [14,26]).

6   Relevance to Other Agent Frameworks

In this paper, we have shown how to define an "error tolerant" agent decision cycle that can apply to *IMPACT* agents when they are corrupted. This decision cycle allows the agent to continue processing unaffected requests and conditions, while repairing the state so that affected requests may be processed effectively. A natural question to ask is how the results of this paper may be applied to other agent frameworks. In this section, we show how this may be done in the context of the following three agent frameworks: the Kowalski-Sadri agent framework [18,20], the Belief-Desires-Intentionality framework due to Rao and Georgeff [22] and the rational agent framework due to Wooldridge [29]. For further frameworks, this is briefly discussed in Section 7.2.

6.1   Kowalski and Sadri's Unified Agent Architecture

Kowalski and Sadri [18,19] analyze the similarities and differences between rational and reactive agent architectures and propose a unified architecture which aims to capture both as special cases. An agent's reasoning is captured via a proof procedure and a logic programming style search engine is used to reduce goals to subgoals in a "rational" manner. The complete proof reduction procedure given in the papers is based on the observation that in many cases it is possible to replace a goal G by an equivalent set of condition-action rules R. The problem of controlling the reasoning process so that it works correctly with bounded resources is also addressed.

The resulting cycle governing the architecture is the following:

1. observe any input coming from the environment at time T;
2. record all input;
3. resume the execution of proof procedure (applied to the current goal statement) by first propagating the input[6];
4. continue applying the proof procedure for a total of n inference steps;
5. select an atomic action respecting time constraints;
6. execute any such action and record the results.

The extension of such a cycle to take error-tolerance into account may appear complex at first glance because *integrity constraints* dynamically evolve during the execution of the cycle itself: goal reduction replaces goal statements with simpler goal statements which have the form of integrity constraints. In the case of *IMPACT* agents, the integrity constraints are established once for all, and we made the same assumption for our error-tolerant extension of the *BDI* architecture.

Fortunately, despite the use of the same phrase ("integrity constraint") Kowalski and Sadri's *integrity constraints* have a different meaning than ours: they just represent a condition to be checked on the current state, but they do not need to be necessarily satisfied. As shown in various examples from [18] and [19], the proof procedure continues to execute when their integrity constraints are not satisfied, leading to a new goal which takes the unsatisfied integrity constraints into account.

---

[6] The *propagation of input* replaces the current goal statement with a simpler one, taking into account the observed input and the integrity constraints characterizing the agent's behavior.

Thus, to avoid confusion, let us suppose that a set of *Static Integrity Constraints* are included in the knowledge base of Kowalski and Sadri's agents, and let us suppose that these *Static Integrity Constraints* have the same meaning as *IMPACT*'s *Integrity Constraints*: they are established once and for all, and if they are violated, a repair procedure must immediately start.

The Unified Agent Architecture cycle may now be modified as outlined below.

1. observe any input coming from the environment at time T;
2. record all input;
3. check if the new inputs cause some violation to the *Static Integrity Constraints*: if they are violated then start a repair procedure as a concurrent thread;
4. evaluate if resuming the proof procedure of the current goal statement leads to some conflict with the current repair procedure; if at least one *error-tolerant* atomic action (namely, an action which is unrelated to the current repairs) turns out to be executable
   (a) continue applying the proof procedure for a total of n inference steps;
   (b) select any *error-tolerant* atomic action respecting time constraints;
   (c) execute any such action and record the results.
   else,
   (a) interrupt processing inputs and complete the repair procedure.

The key obstacle in applying this definition is to determine what it means for a "conflict" to occur between the proof procedure and a repair procedure. This can be addressed in many ways. One way is to determine which atoms are affected by the repair procedure and which ones are affected by the proof procedure and if there is an intersection between the two sets, then declaring a conflict. A notion of affectedness similar to that in our paper can be used. An alternative solution is to simulate in advance what should occur by going on with the proof procedure and using some syntactic check.

6.2   Rao and Georgeff's BDI Architecture

The *BDI* architecture [22] is based on the notion of agents as *intentional systems* [12]; for an excellent introduction, see [30]. The architecture is characterized by the following structures, as depicted in Figure 2:

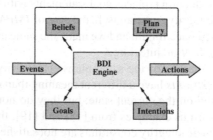

Fig. 2. The *BDI* Architecture

- **beliefs**, which represent the knowledge of the agents;
- **goals**, which are beliefs, or conjunctions and disjunctions of beliefs, which must be achieved or tested in the current state;
- **plans**, which contain the procedural knowledge of agents. They are characterized by a trigger, a context, a body; a maintenance condition, a set of "success actions" and a set of "failure actions"; and
- **intentions**, which are partially instantiated plans.

A typical *BDI* engine is characterized by the following cycle

1. observe the world and the agent's internal state, and subsequently update the *event queue*;
2. generate possible new plans whose trigger event matches an event in the event queue and whose context is satisfied;
3. select one from this set of matching plans for execution;
4. push the selected plan onto an existing or new *intention stack*, according to whether or not the event is a (sub)goal;
5. select an intention stack, take the topmost plan and execute the next step of this current plan: if the step is an action, perform it, otherwise, if it is a subgoal, post it on the event queue.

In order to extend this agent cycle to handle error-tolerance, we must modify steps 2, 3 and 5 of the above cycle. In particular, we must choose an event from the event queue only if it is safe to process it. Likewise, we must select a plan for execution only if it is safe to execute it, and we must select an intention stack only if the next step in its topmost plan can be safely executed.

Let us suppose that some integrity constraints hold while some other integrity constraints are currently violated, and a repair is being done on the current state to recover to a correct state. In this case, we may modify steps 2,3, and 5 of the *BDI* agent cycle as follows:

Step 2: *When is it safe to choose an event from the event queue?* We say that an event is *error-tolerant* if there is at least one *error-tolerant* plan (see definition below) among the plans whose trigger event matches the chosen event and whose context is satisfied.

Step 3: *When is it safe to select a plan for execution?* In order to decide if a plan is *error-tolerant* (namely, it can be safely executed without leading to inconsistencies due to the repairs which are being made on the state), it is necessary to evaluate the consequences of executing it (before actually executing it). If pushing the selected plan onto an existing (resp. new) intention stack, and selecting this newly modified (resp. created) stack[7] leads to executing an action which could be affected by some repair, the plan is not *error-tolerant*. Giving details of which kind of actions are affected by a repair is out of the scope of this paper. However, the good news is that our definitions of affectedness and corruptedness may be adapted (with some work) to the *BDI* framework.

Even if an *error-tolerant* plan is chosen in step 3, it is possible that an *unsafe* intention stack is chosen in step 5. This may causes problems because the action to be

---

[7] We can ignore the other intention stacks at this point, since they will be analyzed in step 5 of the cycle.

performed may interfere current repairs. Thus, it is also necessary to consider error-tolerance of intention stacks.

Step 5: *When is it safe to select an intention stack?* As in the previous case, here too, it is necessary to evaluate the consequences of executing the next step of the topmost plan in the stack (before actually doing so). If the action to execute is potentially affected by some repair, the intention stack cannot be selected (it is not *error-tolerant*). If at least one plan can be selected for execution in step 3, then there is at least one error-tolerant intention stack to chose (the one modified in step 3).

If at a certain moment there are no error-tolerant events in the event queue, the execution cycle must stop until the repairs have been completed. If no repairs are currently made, all the events in the event queue are error-tolerant. Given the definitions above, the "error-tolerant" *BDI* cycle is outlined below:

1. observe the world and the agent's internal state, and subsequently update the *event queue*. if some violation of the integrity constraints occurs, start a repair procedure as a concurrent thread;
2. if at least one error-tolerant event exists in the event queue
   (a) choose an error-tolerant event from the event queue;
   (b) generate possible new plans whose trigger event matches the chosen event and whose context is satisfied;
   (c) select one from this set of matching plans for execution, provided that the plan is error-tolerant;
   (d) push the selected plan onto an existing or new *intention stack*, according to whether or not the event is a (sub)goal;
   (e) select an error-tolerant intention stack, take the topmost plan and execute the next step of this current plan: if the step is an action, perform it, otherwise, if it is a subgoal, post it on the event queue.
3. else interrupt processing events and complete the repair procedure.

6.3   Wooldridge's Computational Multi-agent System

In chapter 4 of his PhD thesis, Wooldridge [29] gives a formal model intended to capture diverse aspects of a variety of agent systems. It is based on some assumptions:

- agents have significant but finite computational resources;
- agents have a set of explicitly represented *beliefs* and are able to reason about these beliefs in accordance with the computational resources afforded to them;
- beliefs are expressed in some *logical* language;
- in addition to being believers, agents can *act*: in particular, they are capable of *communicative actions*;
- finally, agents are able to *revise* their beliefs by means of a belief revision function.

Each agent in the system continuously executes the following cycle:

1. interpret any message received;
2. update beliefs according to previous action and message interpretation;
3. derive deductive closure of belief set;

4. derive set of possible messages, choose one and send it;
5. derive set of possible actions, choose one and apply it.

Wooldridge defines two execution models for multi-agent systems: a synchronous model, and an asynchronous one. All agents in the synchronous model begin and end an execution cycle together. In the more realistic asynchronous model, where execution is interleaved, at most one agent is allowed to act at any fixed point of time.

A naive error-tolerant extension of his agent cycle may be defined as follows:

1. interpret any message received;
2. update beliefs according to previous action and message interpretation;
3. check if the new beliefs violate the agent's integrity constraints: if they are violated then start a repair procedure as a concurrent thread;
4. derive deductive closure of belief set: if the deductive closure does not contain beliefs which interfere with the integrity constraints under repair, then
   (a) derive set of *error-tolerant* messages, choose one and send it;
   (b) derive set of *error-tolerant* actions, choose one and apply it;
5. else interrupt processing received messages and complete the repair procedure.

As usual, we are assuming that each agent has a set of static integrity constraints to be satisfied in any state. By *error-tolerant* messages and actions we mean those messages and actions which do not interfere with the current repair procedure. Determining when a belief "interferes" with an ongoing repair may be defined by adapting the notion of affectedness given in our paper to the case of Wooldridge's syntax.

7   Related Work

To our knowledge, there has been no work on error tolerance in agent systems. As a consequence, we compare our work with related work in other areas. In the previous section, we have already shown how many of the ideas proposed in this paper for *IM-PACT* agents also apply to other agent systems.

7.1   Inconsistency in Databases

Sources of information and services are often required to satisfy integrity constraints (ICs). When the ICs are not satisfied, the source is in an inconsistent state and no interaction between the source and its users should take place until recovery from inconsistency has been completed. Though it is clear that excluding users from interacting with the "consistent part" of an inconsistent data source is beneficial in practice, research on providing consistent services over inconsistent data sources has not been as widespread.

Reasoning about inconsistent databases has been studied extensively in the context of "paraconsistent" databases, and in the cases of reasoning with multiple knowledge bases [6,25,5]. However, there was no notion of an agent decision cycle – for an agent that is a continuously running process to steadily execute requests even while corrupted, the decision cycle must be modified so that error tolerant processing methods can be incorporated into the decision cycle. This is one of the key contributions of this paper.

An important effort to deal with consistent query answering in information systems with inconsistent ICs was done by Bry [8]. He proposed an approach which makes it possible to recognize whether an answer to a query has been derived from possibly corrupted data. He exploits a notion of local inconsistency, formalized in terms of *minimal logic*[8]. Data which cause an IC violation is considered potentially corrupted. An answer which cannot be established (i.e., which is not derivable in minimal logic) without using some potentially corrupted data is called *inconsistent*. Conversely, an answer is *consistent* if it can be computed without using data involved in IC violation. He shows that minimal logic suffices as a foundation of query answering in positive, definite or disjunctive, deductive databases. However, the problem is not addressed in the context of an agent system that accesses external data sources via code calls and where rules involve actions and deontic modalities. Also, the way consistent and inconsistent answers should be computed is not addressed. This represents a significant difference between Bry's approach and ours, as we have provided algorithms to evaluate corrupted and affected items, and formally proved that these items correspond to the intuitive notion of "corruptedness" and "suspiciousness" resp. "affectedness".

Arenas, Bertossi, and Chomicki [2] provide a logical characterization of consistent query answering in relational databases that may be inconsistent with the given ICs. An answer to a query posed to a database that violates the ICs is "consistent," if it is the same as that obtained from any minimally repaired version of the database. A method for computing such answers and an analysis of their properties is provided: on the basis of a query Q, the method computes, using an iterative procedure, a new query $T_\omega(Q)$ whose evaluation in an arbitrary database (consistent or inconsistent) state returns the set of consistent answers to the original query Q. $T_\omega(Q)$ is based on the notion of *residue* in the context of semantic query optimization. The soundness of the approach is proven, as well as its completeness for particular ICs (*binary ICs*). Termination of computing T_ω is also guaranteed under proper conditions. A variant of the T_ω operator is described in [9], which is proven to be sound, terminating and complete for some classes of ICs extending those in [2]. In [3] the *Annotated Predicate Calculus* (APC) is adopted, a logic where inconsistent information does not unravel logical inference and where causes of inconsistencies can be reasoned about. The inconsistent database is embedded in APC which is then used to define database repairs and query answers. This approach has been used to help understand the results of [2] and to provide a more general algorithm that covers classes of queries beyond [2]. The main difference between the approach in [2] and ours is the way how consistent answers are evaluated. In fact, [2] *rewrites* a query so as to take into account the ICs, and then evaluates the answers of the rewritten query, which are proved to be consistent answers of the original one. What we do, instead, is to evaluate whether processing the incoming message involves "unsafe" data: if not, we process the message as it is (as shown, this yields in this case the same results as if the ICs would not be violated), otherwise we defer it. A further complication in our work is that when an external request is made of an agent, the agent state may get modified while the repairs are going on.

---

[8] Minimal logic is a constructivistic weakening of classical logic defined in terms of the natural deduction proof system by Gentzen, deprived of the absurdity rule.

As for repair of constraint violations, an interesting approach has been proposed in [16], where basic concepts from model-based diagnosis are adopted to discover minimal sets of simultaneous reasons for violations of (different) constraints. These reasons indicate possible repair actions that guarantee elimination of violations. The adopted repair actions depend on the "repair strategy" which the user can choose. The proposed strategies are domain independent and range from minimal undo or consistent completion of a violating transaction up to user interaction with the repair process. A sound and complete algorithm for enumerating possible minimal repair transactions for an inconsistent database is also proposed. Our repair strategies are similar to those of [16] in that they allow the user to choose the strategy which is most suitable for her application from an application independent library of strategies, eventually specifying priorities or preferences for use during the repair. The interaction between the user and the repair process is briefly sketched in [16], assuming that a suitable environment exists. We believe that *IMPACT can be* such an environment as user interaction with the repair process can be easily performed in *IMPACT*'s multi-agent setting.

7.2 Agent Frameworks

The problems tackled and solved in this paper, namely how to let an agent go on working even when its state is corrupted, and how to ensure that an agent recovers from a corrupted state to an uncorrupted state, are critical for the agent community. Agents find application in domains such as telecommunication [28], process control (e.g. [10]), electronic commerce and many others (see http://agents.umbc.edu/) where the reliability of a multiagent system is a key issue. In these domains, as well as many others, *continuity* and *recovery* properties should be supported so as to guarantee a high-quality service. Error tolerance is a must. We are not aware of any research on agent architectures, environments or formalisms which allow the development of error-tolerant agents. However, we believe that this is an important aspect in the endeavor of building rational agents, which should make good (but not necessarily perfect) decisions about what to do in any given situation [30]. In particular, if it turns out that there is an inconsistency, then the agent should still be able to go ahead and take decisions and actions which *seem to make sense*. Of course, there must be some underlying assumptions – for example, that the integrity constraints are correct. We could imagine that some integrity constraint is not correct, and withdrawal or modification of that integrity constraint could remedy the situation. However, if the agent has the choice between modifying, on the one hand, the agent state and, on the other hand, its integrity constraints, which are part of its specification, given that other agents or entities might have unprevented access to its state, the former seems to be more plausible to us. However, the agent designer could be informed of violations of the integrity constraints, and decide whether a change of the integrity constraints is needed.

Our notions of corruptedness and affectedness are auxiliary technical concepts which helped to formalize the intuition that actions which are unrelated to errors may be still executed; the peculiarities of the framework, however, make this a nontrivial task.

Fortunately, the results of the preceding section show how our techniques for error-tolerance may be adapted to different types of agent architectures. In addition, there are many other works in the agent community that are related to that proposed here.

Shoham [24] was perhaps the first to propose an explicit programming language for agents, based on object oriented concepts, and based on the concept of an agent state. Shoham [24, Section 3] states that a complete AOP ("agent oriented programming") system will have three components.

1. a restricted formal language for describing mental state;
2. an interpreted agent programming language with primitive commands such as RE-QUEST and INFORM; and,
3. an "agentifier".

We have already shown, in [14], that *IMPACT* agents can express most of Shoham's AOP framework. Hence, the results of this paper may be applied to Shoham's AOP framework in this way.

Hindriks *et al.* [17] have developed a deontically based agent programming framework. In their framework, an agent's mental state consists of a set of goals and a set of beliefs. An *agent program* in their framework consists of a quadruple $(T, \Pi_0, \sigma_0, \Gamma)$ where T is a transition function specifying the effects of basic actions, Π_0 is an initial set of goals, σ_0 is an initial set of beliefs, and Γ is a set of rules of the form

$$Head \leftarrow Guard \mid Body.$$

In general, $Head$ is a (potentially) complex formula describing a goal. The syntax of goals supported by Hindriks *et al.* [17] allows goals to be elementary actions, but also includes sequential compositions of actions, disjunctive goals, and/or conjunctive goals. The $Guard$ is a logical formula, while the $Body$ has the same structure as the head. While not everything in Hindriks *et al.* [17] can be expressed in *IMPACT* (and vice versa), their agent decision cycle is very similar to ours, and hence, the results on error tolerance may be applied to their agent decision cycle in much the same way as it is applied in this paper to *IMPACT*'s agent cycle. This is also the case for agent decision making frameworks such as the initial frameworks of Rosenschein [23] who was perhaps the first to say that agents act according to states, and which actions they take are determined by rules of the form "When P is true of the state of the environment, then the agent should take action A." Their decision cycle too, is similar to ours. When a state change occurs, determine what to do based on the rules involved. Hence, in such a decision cycle, our notions of affectedness can be directly used to only allow rules involving unaffected atoms to be used to process requests and the same repair mechanism proposed by us may be used to conduct repairs to the agent state. This also applies to the IRMA system by Bratman *et al.* [7], where the agent generates different possible courses of actions (Plans) based on the agent's intentions. These plans are then evaluated to determine which ones are consistent and optimal with respect to achieving these intentions. A cycle similar to ours may be used there - in particular, only plans that involve "unaffected" atoms may be used.

8 Conclusion

Software agents provide a powerful new paradigm for distributed, collaborative, and mobile applications. Software agent systems that build on top of legacy software in a principled way, and that support automatic coupling of simple and complex actions to changes in their environment, have a wide variety of applications in e-commerce. Nonetheless, it is dangerous to assume that just because agents are prototyped using a declarative language such as in *IMPACT*, they will be free of errors. Prolog programs over the years have not been error-free. The history of programming has shown that bugs in code must always be accounted for.

In an *IMPACT* based agent system, and for that matter, in any agent system that builds on top of legacy code, bugs may arise for one of several reasons. First, the agent developer may have written rules that do not account for all possible states of the agent that arise. Second, the agent may not be in full control of its state — this is true in legacy applications where the agent is just one vehicle to access the legacy application's state. Third, the legacy code on top of which the agent is being built may itself have bugs, causing unexpected agent states to arise.

In this paper, we have taken a modest first step toward addressing this extraordinarily difficult problem. Specifically, we have proposed for the first time (to our knowledge) an agent decision algorithm that has two good features. First, it incorporates a method for the agent to recover from a "corrupted" state to an "uncorrupted" one. Second, it allows the agent to continue processing requests during such a recovery/repair process, as long as such requests are unaffected by the ongoing repairs.

Our work may be seen as a contribution in the endeavor of building rational agents [30]. We have shown how our methods may be applied to various agent frameworks, and in particular to the BDI model. An important aspect is reasoning about the behavior of agents, which for the BDI model has been amply discussed and demonstrated by Wooldridge using $\mathcal{LORA}$ (*$\mathcal{L}$ogic $\mathcal{O}$f $\mathcal{R}$ational $\mathcal{A}$gents*) [30]. It remains an interesting issue to see how error-tolerance can be modeled in $\mathcal{LORA}$, or which extension is needed for that. Observe that $\mathcal{LORA}$ builds on top of classical logic; thus, if the agent state and integrity constraints would be modeled as sets of classical facts and axioms, from a violation of an integrity constraint we could conclude everything; this may be avoided using methods from paraconsistent logic or suitable belief operators.

Our contribution in this paper is admittedly not a panacea for all problems involving bugs in agent programs. It handles the case when agent's don't have status sets due to violation of integrity constraints. Such violations may occur because third parties are manipulating the agent's state without the agent having any veto on such updates. It also arises when the agent's rules are not adequate to deal with such IC violations. However, these scenarios only represent a small microcosm of the space of errors that can arise when agents are programmed. This forms a rich avenue for future research.

The results of this paper may be extended in future work in many different ways. For instance, rather than considering action atoms as affected, we could view action *status* atoms as affected, and determine suspicious code call atoms on the basis of a syntactic analysis of the agent programs similar as described in the this paper. Due to the interplay of the various semantics components of feasible status sets including deontic consistency, action closure and integrity constraints, this would provide a more refined approach. However, its study would also be substantially more complex.

Acknowledgments. We thank the reviewers for their constructive comments which helped to improve this paper. This work was supported in part by the Austrian Science Fund projects P13871-INF and Z29-INF, by the Army Research Lab under contract number DAAL01-97-K0135, by ARO grant DAAD190010484, and by Darpa/AFRL grant F306029910552.

A   Appendix: Feasible, Rational, and Reasonable Status Sets

This appendix provides in succinct form the definition of various concepts of status sets from [14,26], to which the reader is referred for more information.

Definition A.1 (Status Set). A *status set* is any set S of ground action status atoms over the values from the type domains of a software package $\mathcal{S}$. For any operator $Op \in \{\mathbf{P},$ $\mathbf{Do}, \mathbf{F}, \mathbf{O}, \mathbf{W}\}$, we denote by $Op(S)$ the set $Op(S) = \{\alpha \mid Op(\alpha) \in S\}$.

Definition A.2 (Operator $\mathbf{App}_{\mathcal{P}, \mathcal{O}_S}(S)$). *Let $\mathcal{P}$ be an agent program and $\mathcal{O}$ be an agent state. Then, $\mathbf{App}_{\mathcal{P}, \mathcal{O}_S}(S) = \{Head(r\theta) \mid r \in \mathcal{P}, R(r, \theta, S)$ is true on $\mathcal{O}\}$, where the predicate $R(r, \theta, S)$ is true iff (1) $r\theta : A \leftarrow \chi \& L_1 \& \cdots \& L_n$ is a ground rule, (2) $\mathcal{O} \models \chi$, (3) if $L_i = Op(\alpha)$ then $Op(\alpha) \in S$, and (4) if $L_i = \neg Op(\alpha)$ then $Op(\alpha) \notin S$, for all $i \in \{1, \dots, n\}$.*

Definition A.3 (A-Cl(S)). *A status set S is deontic and action closed, if for every ground action α, it is the case that $(DC1)$ $\mathbf{O}\alpha \in S$ implies $\mathbf{P}\alpha \in S$, $(AC1)$ $\mathbf{O}\alpha \in S$ implies $\mathbf{Do}\,\alpha \in S$, and $(AC2)$ $\mathbf{Do}\,\alpha \in S$ implies $\mathbf{P}\alpha \in S$.*

For any status set S, we denote by $\mathbf{A}\text{-}\mathbf{Cl}(S)$ the smallest set $S' \supseteq S$ such that S' is closed under $(AC1)$ and $(AC2)$, i.e., action closed.

Definition A.4 (Feasible Status Set). *Let $\mathcal{P}$ be an agent program and let $\mathcal{O}$ be an agent state. Then, a status set S is a feasible status set for $\mathcal{P}$ on $\mathcal{O}$, if $(S1)$-$(S4)$ hold:*

$(S1)$ $\mathbf{App}_{\mathcal{P}, \mathcal{O}_S}(S) \subseteq S$;
$(S2)$ For any ground action α, the following holds: $\mathbf{O}\alpha \in S$ implies $\mathbf{W}\alpha \notin S$, and $\mathbf{P}\alpha \in S$ implies $\mathbf{F}\alpha \notin S$.
$(S3)$ $S = \mathbf{A}\text{-}\mathbf{Cl}(S)$, i.e., S is action closed;
$(S4)$ The state $\mathcal{O}' = \mathbf{conc}(\mathbf{Do}\,(S), \mathcal{O})$ which results from $\mathcal{O}$ after executing (according to some execution strategy **conc**) the actions in $\mathbf{Do}\,(S)$ satisfies the integrity constraints, i.e., $\mathcal{O}' \models \mathcal{IC}$.

Definition A.5 (Groundedness; Rational Status Set). A status set S is *grounded*, if no status set $S' \neq S$ exists such that $S' \subseteq S$ and S' satisfies conditions $(S1)$–$(S3)$ of a feasible status set. A status set S is a *rational status set*, if S is a feasible status set and S is grounded.

Definition A.6 (Reasonable Status Set). Let $\mathcal{P}$ be an agent program, let $\mathcal{O}$ be an agent state, and let S be a status set. Then:

1. If $\mathcal{P}$ is positive, i.e., no negated action status atoms occur in it, then S is a *reasonable status set* for $\mathcal{P}$ on $\mathcal{O}$, iff S is a rational status set for $\mathcal{P}$ on $\mathcal{O}$.
2. The reduct of $\mathcal{P}$ w.r.t. S and $\mathcal{O}$, denoted by $red^S(\mathcal{P}, \mathcal{O})$, is the program which is obtained from the ground instances of the rules in $\mathcal{P}$ over $\mathcal{O}$ as follows.
   (a) Remove every rule r such that $Op(\alpha) \in S$ for some $\neg Op(\alpha)$ in the body of r;
   (b) remove all negative literals $\neg Op(\alpha)$ from the remaining rules.
   Then S is a *reasonable status set* for $\mathcal{P}$ w.r.t. $\mathcal{O}$, if it is a reasonable status set of the program $red^S(\mathcal{P}, \mathcal{O})$ with respect to $\mathcal{O}$.

B   Appendix: Safety

A variable is a *root variable*, if it does not involve deconstruction of an object. Given any variable Y (possibly involving deconstruction), its root $root(Y)$ is the variable which refers to the non-decomposed object.

Definition B.1 (Safe Code Call (Condition)). *A code call* $S : f(d_1, \ldots, d_n)$ *is safe iff each d_i is ground. A code call condition* $\chi_1 \& \ldots \& \chi_n$, $n \geq 1$, *is safe iff there exists a permutation* π *of* $\chi_1, \ldots, \chi_n$ *such that for every* $i = 1, \ldots, n$ *the following holds:*

1. *If* $\chi_{\pi(i)}$ *is a comparison* s_1 *op* s_2*, then*
   1.1 *at least one of* s_1, s_2 *is a constant or a variable* X *such that* $root(X)$ *belongs to* $RV_\pi(i) = \{root(Y) \mid \exists j < i \text{ s.t. Y occurs in } \chi_{\pi(j)}\}$*;*
   1.2 *if* s_i *is neither a constant nor a variable* X *such that* $root(X) \in RV_\pi(i)$*, then* s_i *is a root variable.*
2. *If* $\chi_{\pi(i)}$ *is a code call atom of the form* $in(X_{\pi(i)}, cc_{\pi(i)})$ *or* $notin(X_{\pi(i)}, cc_{\pi(i)})$*, then the root of each variable* Y *occurring in* $cc_{\pi(i)}$ *belongs to* $RV_\pi(i)$*, and either* $X_{\pi(i)}$ *is a root variable, or* $root(X_{\pi(i)})$ *is from* $RV_\pi(i)$*.*

Intuitively, a code call is safe, if we can reorder the code call atoms occurring in it in a way such that we can evaluate these atoms left to right, assuming that root variables are incrementally bound to objects.

Definition B.2 (Safety Modulo Variables). *Suppose* χ *is a code call condition, and let* **X** *be any set of root variables. Then,* χ *is said to be safe modulo* **X** *iff for an (arbitrary) assignment* θ *of objects to the variables in* **X***, it is the case that* $\chi\theta$ *is safe.*

References

1. S. Abiteboul, R. Hull, and V. Vianu. *Foundations of Databases*. Addison Wesley, 1995.
2. M. Arenas, L. Bertossi, and J. Chomicki. Consistent query answers in inconsistent databases. In *Proc. PODS'99*, pp. 68–79. ACM Press, 1999.
3. M. Arenas, L. Bertossi, and M. Kifer. Applications of annotated predicate calculus to querying inconsistent databases. In J. Lloyd et al. (editors), *Proc. CL'2000/DOOD'2000*, pp. 926–941, LNCS 1861. Springer, 2000.

4. K. Arisha, T. Eiter, S. Kraus, F. Ozcan, R. Ross, and V.S. Subrahmanian. IMPACT: A platform for collaborating agents. *IEEE Intelligent Systems*, 14(2):64–72, March/April 1999.
5. C. Baral, S. Kraus, J. Minker, and V.S. Subrahmanian. Combining multiple knowledge bases consisting of first order theories. *Computational Intelligence*, 8(1):45–71, 1992.
6. H. Blair and V.S. Subrahmanian. Paraconsistent logic programming. *Theoretical Computer Science*, 68:135–154, 1989.
7. M. Bratman, D. Israel, and M. Pollack. Plans and resource-bounded practical reasoning. *Computational Intelligence*, 4(4):349–355, 1988.
8. F. Bry. Query answering in information systems with integrity constraints. In S. Jajodia, W. List, G. McGregor, and L. Strous, editors, *Integrity and Internal Controls in Information Systems, vol. I: Increasing the confidence in information systems, Proceedings 1997 IFIP WG 11.5 Working Conference on Integrity and Control in Information Systems*. Chapman & Hall, December 1997.
9. A. Celle and L. Bertossi. Querying inconsistent databases: algorithms and implementation. In J. Lloyd et al. (editors), *Proc. CL'2000/DOOD'2000*, pp. 942–956, LNCS 1861. Springer, 2000.
10. J. M. Corera, I. Laresgoiti and N. R. Jennings. Using archon, part 2: Electricity transportation management. In *IEEE Expert*, 11(6):71-79, 1996.
11. K. Decker, K. Sycara, and M. Williamson. Middle agents for the internet. In *Proc. 15th International Joint Conference on Artificial Intelligence (IJCAI'97)*, pp. 578–583. Morgan Kaufmann, 1997.
12. D. C. Dennet. *The Intentional Stance*. MIT Press, 1987.
13. T. Eiter and V.S. Subrahmanian. Heterogeneous active agents, II: Algorithms and complexity. *Artificial Intelligence*, 108(1-2):257–307, 1999.
14. T. Eiter, V.S. Subrahmanian, and G. Pick. Heterogeneous active agents, I: Semantics. *Artificial Intelligence*, 108(1-2):179–255, 1999.
15. T. Eiter, V.S. Subrahmanian, and T. Rogers. Heterogeneous active agents, III: Polynomially implementable agents. *Artificial Intelligence*, 117(1):107–167, 2000.
16. M. Gertz and U. Lipeck. An extensible framework for repairing constraint violations. In S. Jajodia, W. List, G. McGregor, and L. Strous, editors, *Integrity and Internal Controls in Information Systems, vol. I: Increasing the confidence in information systems, Proceedings 1997 IFIP WG 11.5 Working Conference on Integriy and Control in Information Systems*, pp. 89–111. Chapman & Hall, December 1997.
17. K. V. Hindriks, F. S. de Boer, W. van der Hoek, and J. J. C. Meyer. Formal semantics for an abstract agent programming language. In *Proc. International Workshop on Agent Theories, Architectures, and Languages (ATAL'97)*, LNCS/LNAI 1365, pp. 215–230. Springer, 1998.
18. R. Kowalski and F. Sadri. Towards a unified agent architecture that combines rationality with reactivity. In *Proc. International Workshop on Logic in Databases (LID'96)*, LNCS/LNAI 1154, pp. 137–149. Springer, 1996.
19. R. Kowalski and F. Sadri. An agent architecture that unifies rationality with reactivity. Technical Report, Imperial College, London, UK, 1997.
20. R. Kowalski and F. Sadri. From logic programming towards multi-agent systems. *Annals of Mathematics and Artificial Intelligence*, 25(3/4):391–491, 1999.
21. N. J. Nilsson. *Principles of Artificial Intelligence*. Morgan Kaufmann, 1980.
22. A. Rao and R. Georgeff. Modeling rational agents within a BDI-architecture. In R. Fikes and E. Sandewall, editors, *Proc. Second International Conference on Knowledge Representation and Reasoning (KR-91)*, pp. 473–484. Morgan Kaufmann Pub, 1991.
23. S. J. Rosenschein. Formal theories of knowledge in AI and robotics. *New Generation Computing*, 3(4):345–357, 1985.
24. Y. Shoham. Agent-oriented programming. *Artificial Intelligence*, 60:51–92, 1993.

25. V.S. Subrahmanian. Paraconsistent disjunctive deductive databases. *Theoretical Computer Science*, 93(1):115–141, 1992.
26. V.S. Subrahmanian, P. Bonatti, J. Dix, T. Eiter, S. Kraus, F. Ozcan, and R. Ross. *Heterogeneous Agent Systems: Theory and Implementation*. MIT Press, 2000.
27. K. Sycara and D. Zeng. Multi-agent integration of information gathering and decision support. In Wolfgang Wahlster, editor, *European Conference on Artificial Intelligence (ECAI '96)*, pp. 549–556. Wiley & Sons, 1996.
28. R. Weihmayer and H. Velthuijsen. Intelligent agents in telecommunications. In N. R. Jennings and M. J. Wooldridge, editors, *Agent Technology: Foundations, Applications and Markets*, pp. 203–217. Springer, Berlin, Germany, 1998.
29. M. Wooldridge. *The Logical Model of Computational Multi–Agent Systems*. PhD thesis, Department of Computation, UMIST, Manchester, UK, October 1992.
30. M. Wooldridge. *Reasoning about Rational Agents*. MIT Press, 2000.

Logic-Based Hybrid Agents

Christoph G. Jung[1] and Klaus Fischer[2]

[1] infor business solutions AG
christoph.jung@infor.de
[2] DFKI GmbH,
Klaus.Fischer@dfki.de,
http://www.dfki.de/~kuf

Abstract. Hybrid agents integrate different styles of reactive, deliberative, and cooperative problem solving in a modular fashion. They are the prime device of (Distributed) Artificial Intelligence and Cognitive Science for realising a broad spectrum of simultaneous functionalities in application domains such as Artificial Life, (Tele-)Robotics, Flexible Manufacturing, and Automated Transportation. This article presents a design methodology for hybrid agents which combines complementary approaches of Software Engineering and declarative Cognitive Robotics at five interconnected specification stages: Architecture, Computational Model, Theory, Inference, and Implementation. Although we give an introduction to the complete methodology of agent design in the first section, we concentrated on presenting a logic-based approach to describe deliberative processes within a hybrid agent architecture in the rest of the article. The interested reader can find the details of the overall framework as well as the proofs of the theorems in [JF01].

1 A Design Methodology for Hybrid Agents

Before bounded rationality became a common denominator for AI and Cognitive Science, the appropriate notion of rationality, and hence the choice of agent design methods, was a highly controversial subject. While early symbolists concentrated on building perfect knowledge-based systems (see Nilsson [Nil84]), the *New AI* community has argued against any expensive data-structures and computations (see Brooks [Bro91]). Both research streams can be seen as extreme, because they focus either on high-level tasks or low-level control. Their systems are optimised for particular classes of domains. Because of their inability to adjust to varying needs and resources, these systems show severe drawbacks in broad domains, such as an automated loading dock, the RoboCup Soccer simulation, or the ROTEX work-cell (Figure 1) for which agents have been designed according to the concepts presented in this article.

Agent Engineering: It is equally difficult to force an inherently myopic reactive system to exhibit goal-oriented behaviour as it is difficult to force an inherently complex planning algorithm to exhibit responsive behaviour. Hybrid agents have been developed to integrate the reactive, but myopic mechanisms proposed by

A.C. Kakas, F. Sadri (Eds.): Computat. Logic (Kowalski Festschrift), LNAI 2407, pp. 626–654, 2002.

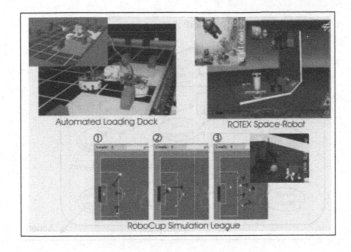

Fig. 1. Representative Scenarios for Broad Agents

Rodney Brooks with optimal, but expensive deliberation facilities, such as planning. A particular example of a hybrid agent architecture is INTERRAP (Figure 2). INTERRAP has a *layered* structure for the combination of a reactive *behaviour-based layer*, a deliberative *local planning layer*, and a *social planning layer*. Each layer is associated with computations on a particular level of representation. Each layer supplements its subordinate layers in order to enforce the achievement of more abstract and more persistent goals and decisions.

With respect to bounded rationality, hybrid agents provide a resource-adaptive trade-off between computational costs and solution quality, that is to say between reactive, deliberative, and social abilities. As such, they have already proven quite successful in constructing broad agents for real-world and virtual-world domains (see the assessment of [Mül99]).

In order to fill their designated role in industrial-strength systems, however, hybrid models face a fundamental engineering problem in that they lack a clear design methodology. Up to now, their description is usually given in an informal *architectural* manner. This pragmatic method of specification introduces very crude and abstract concepts and leaves many design issues open. Hence, the space of possible *implementations* does not necessarily reflect the original objectives, such as a practical trade-off between reactivity, deliberation, and social abilities.

Moreover, by integrating a variety of modules from various backgrounds, hybrid models are not easily comprehensible. This complicates the identification of appropriate programming constructs and impedes their customisation to various domains. We have experienced these difficulties with previous INTERRAP implementations.

Cognitive Robotics: Formal *logic* has always been used in the tradition of *theories of rationality*. Research on agent-based systems also tries to build on logic-based

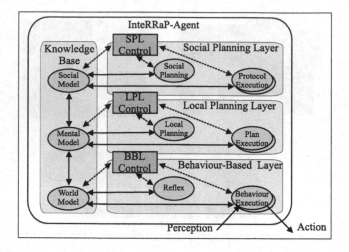

Fig. 2. Hybrid INTERRAP Agents

formalisms, for example Cohen & Levesque [CL90], Shoham [Sho90], and Rao & Georgeff [RG91] describe agents in temporal and epistemic logic, deviating from earlier informal descriptions in [GL87]. Kowalski & Sadri [KS96b] rely on the power of first-order logic augmented with *abduction* as the declarative basis of a *unified* agent. Especially the latter approach envisages a logic programming (LP) perspective [Kow79] in which the high-level agent axiomatisation is straightforwardly implemented by a special *inference procedure*.

The logic-based specification of agents[1] is nowadays summarised under the umbrella title Cognitive Robotics [Bow87]. It aims at a coherent, concise, and verifiable design whose declarative concepts can immediately serve as intuitive programming constructs. However, the conceptual level is too high for deriving practical systems: straightforward implementations via inference procedures are either not feasible or build on restricted expressiveness; the operational considerations to 'make the theory run' are seldom discussed. To our knowledge, no such monolithic 'rationality engine' has ever been able to master settings that are comparable to those of hybrid systems.

The Design Space of Agents: From what we have just discussed, it is apparent that Agent Engineering and Cognitive Robotics are rather complementary: both ways of specification introduce useful concepts for agents, either on the theoretical side — the logic-based representations of Cognitive Robotics — or on the architectural side — the modular structures of Agent Engineering. Both are lacking in some aspects of design issues, either in declarative or in opera-

---

[1] There are differences between logic theories for specifying agent computations, such as [Kow79], and logic theories for describing and verifying agent behaviour, such as [RG91]. We do not engage in a discussion of the latter issue, but rather stay with the first perspective to agent design.

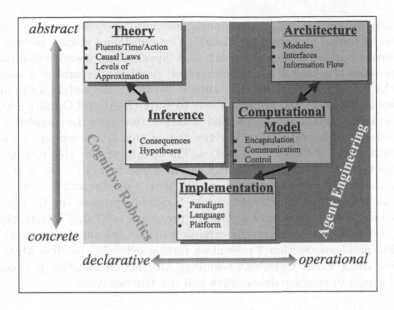

Fig. 3. The Design Space of Agents

tional respect. Hence, a design methodology that reconciles both approaches in a preferably formal setting seems promising.

Such a methodology would provide a well-understood collection of interrelated methods (or *specification stages*) bridging theory and practice. In doing so, such a methodology also addresses a matter that both Agent Engineering and Cognitive Robotics have largely neglected up to now, namely how to derive sound implementations in effective programs. The methodology that we are looking for runs under the slogan **"Agent = Logic + Architecture"**[2] and is the basis for reconstructing INTERRAP as an agent-oriented programming tool for a broad spectrum of applications.

In Figure 3, we have arranged the specification stages in the common *design space of agents*. This design space is defined by two independent *dimensions of specification*, namely the degree of abstraction and the degree of declarativity. Architectural Engineering turns out to be a rather abstract and operational enterprise while Cognitive Robotics covers the declarative side of the design space. Agent implementations are most concrete; although they are a too low-level medium for research, their connection to the higher-level specification is nevertheless of justified interest.

To complete the design space of agents, the point of concern is to find an operational complement to the inference stage that is able to capture the architectural features of hybrid agents, for example their *modularisation*, in formal

---

[2] Derived from the path-setting motto of Kowalski: **"Algorithm = Logic + Control"**

and computational terms. We call such descriptions *computational models* as inspired by formal programming [Hoa69]. Computational models are written in dedicated specification languages, such as Z [Spi92]. They describe the state and the operation of a kind of agent 'interpreter' running inferences in a particular logic. As *formal specifications*, they already became a successful tool in modern Software Engineering and are just about to enter (D)AI and Cognitive Science.

The design methodology presented in this section gives the complete picture to the design of hybrid agents. For the rest of this article we put a focus on the contribution of Cognitive Robotics. The details of how this relates to the other parts of the design methodology can be found in [JF01]. The next section introduces two calculi: the state-based Situation Calculus and narrative Event Calculus. We describe how Event Calculus (originally proposed in [KS86]) can be adopted for the specification of a planning procedure (cf [Esh88, Mis91, Sha97a]) for hybrid agents and present our extension to this calculus to deal with some technical problems. Section 3 presents a further extension to allow abstraction planning using Event Calculus reasoning. Abstraction planning is crucial for hybrid agents to combine deliberative and reactive behaviour.

2   Cognitive Robotics

Figure 4 shows the first order specification that was introduced by [FK97] using completed clausal programs, that is to say by relying on equivalence definitions and disjunctive goals. During completion, clauses that represent *facts* become existentially quantified positive literals including equality statements. Furthermore, *integrity constraints* are introduced which are universally quantified implications. The computational service that is modelled with this logic is to verify for given P : *Program*; Δ : *Facts*; G : *Goal*; and IC : *Constraints* the entailment of the goal G, that is to say $Comp(P \wedge \Delta) \wedge CET \models \exists G^3$. Additionally, integrity constraints need to be theorems $Comp(P \wedge \Delta) \wedge CET \models IC^4$.

Kowalski & Sadri [KS96b] propose this logic as an appropriate foundation to transfer the features of logic programming to the design of agents. They achieve this by requiring an agent to act deliberatively as the result of tracing evidences back to a background theory of the world (by the logic program) as well as to act reactively as the result of trying to maintain its mandatory integrity (by the constraints stating, for example, 'never bump into a wall'). Although a plausible argument, this is too general for situated agents: just as we would not describe an agent as a Turing machine, but as a specific program running upon it, it is necessary to have a closer look at a logical agent's background theory, that is to say its logic program, in order to determine its architecture more precisely.

---

[3] $Comp(P \wedge \Delta)$ means that P and Δ are transformed according to Clark's completion. CET are the usual clauses for the equational theory. $Comp$ can be straightforwardly extended to equivalence definitions and facts.

[4] Another possibility to treat integrity constraints would be to check their *consistency*. Theoremhood of constraints turns out to be semi-decidable, while consistency is not [FK97].

$SubGoal ::= \top \mid Literal \wedge SubGoal$
$Facts ::= \top \mid Constant(Term^*) \wedge Facts$
$Goal ::= \bot \mid \exists SubGoal \vee Goal$
$Definition ::= \tilde{\forall} Constant(Variable^*) \equiv Goal$
$Program ::= \top \mid Definition \wedge Program$
$Constraint ::= \tilde{\forall} Facts \supset Goal$
$Constraints ::= \top \mid Constraint \wedge Constraints$

Fig. 4. First-Order Equivalence Definitions with Constraints

There is a substantial amount of research devoted to finding such declarative foundations of situated representation and reasoning. Although the umbrella title *Cognitive Robotics* [LLL+94, Bow87] was coined in the early 90's, the original ideas can be traced back to the very fundamental ideas of McCarthy & Hayes in the late 50's [McC58, McC63, MH69]. Back then, McCarthy & Hayes proposed to introduce a notion of *time* into logic in order to describe how the state of the world (in the form of information particles, called *fluents*) evolves as being *caused* by *actions*. By axiomatising these concepts, an agent is able to logically trace or explain the frequent observations about the world that it is perceiving and to logically anticipate or plan the future state of affairs including its own actions.

It was not until the publication of [Rei91] that the fundamental *frame problem* posed back in [MH69] found a first satisfying solution in terms of a first-order theory (see Section 2.1). This raised the interest in Cognitive Robotics and led to a number of alternative formalisms for realising the McCarthy & Hayes postulate. Today, researchers tend to generalise their ideas about state constraints, side effects, continuous trajectories, and natural actions across those core calculi. Current implementations show a considerable expressiveness and performance when reasoning about partially observable blocks worlds [Rei99] or robot navigation [Sha97a].

So why should we bother about Agent Engineering at all if there already exists a prototyping methodology for agents? The answer is: because Cognitive Robotics is still incomplete. As conceptually clean as the separation of declarative theory and computational inference is, these concepts are not concrete enough to derive implemented agent systems, for example in the automated loading dock and the RoboCup simulation. The more practical agent design is based on the pragmatic and operational guidelines of hybrid architectures and computational models.

So why should we care about Cognitive Robotics at all if we concentrate on traditionally engineered agents? The answer is because it provides the most convenient supplement when it comes to specify the core of primitive modules, that is to say to specify the reasoning processes inside an operational agent framework. For both a unified agent, say a decision maker situated in a dynamic environment, as well as a particular module, say the local planning process operating inside the hybrid INTERRAP agent, the same aspects of situated representation and reasoning are relevant: for both the agent and a process, the world (including other agents and processes) is a partially observable and dynamic environment that is to be rationally explained and controlled. This shows the intimate relation between Cognitive Robotics and Agent Engineering and motivates a common logic framework.

The main aim of the rest of this article is to define such a theory and its underlying inferences respectively which can be applied in a unified decision making agent as well as in a decision making module of a hybrid agent. While concentrating on planning, this does not mean that other INTERRAP functionalities cannot be handled by this logic-based approach. The details of the overall framework and the proofs for the given theorems can be found in [JF01].

2.1   The State-Based Situation Calculus

The first approach to use a predicate logic formalisation for representing action and change in a situated agent (called *reasoning program* or *advice taker*, back then) was by McCarthy & Hayes [McC58, McC63, MH69]. Fluent predicates are annotated with additional situation arguments in order to trace their validity over time $at(box_1, truck, s_0)$[5]. An implicit temporal relation between situations is given by a function do which maps situations to successor situations that have been caused by the execution of actions $do(pickup(rob_1, box_1), s_0)$. Change is expressed as an implication of the applicability of actions, that is to say the validity of their preconditions:

$$(SIT) \quad \tilde{\forall} holding(Box, Rob, do(pickup(Rob, Box), S)) \subset$$
$$\tilde{\exists} ahead(Rob, Box, S) \wedge at(Box, Area, S) \wedge handempty(Rob, S)$$

Given a description of an initial situation $I : Facts$, such as

$$I ::= ahead(rob_1, box_1, s_0) \wedge at(box_1, truck, s_0) \wedge handempty(rob_1, s_0)$$

and a goal $G : Goal$, such as $G ::= holding(box_1, rob_1, S)$, this *Situation Calculus* is able to reason about the connection of a situation with a goal, that is to say it can both analyse and synthesise plans: $I \wedge SIT \models \tilde{\exists} G$. This early formalisation was implemented by Green [Gre69] and, as shown by [GLR91], its expressiveness exceeds that of typical planning algorithms of today [FN71, BF95, KS96a]. For example, it is possible to reason about partial initial situations as well as conditional and universal effects of actions. At the same time, a key problem behind the Situation Calculus was revealed [MH69] that is the problem of determining persistent facts (non-effects) which do not change when applying an action, for example the location of other boxes and the category of their content.

---

[5] We use lower-case letters to distinguish individual constants box_1 from individual variables Box_1.

In the Situation Calculus, these frame fluents have to be treated in the same way as the changing fluents by additional axioms (FRA):

$$\tilde{\forall} at(Box_1, Area, do(pickup(Rob, Box_2), S)) \subset$$
$$\tilde{\exists} at(Box_1, Area, S) \land \neg Box_1 \doteq Box_2$$
$$\tilde{\forall} at(Box_1, Area, do(label(Rob, Box_2), S)) \subset \tilde{\exists} at(Box_1, Area, S)$$

(FRA) $\quad \tilde{\forall} category(Box_1, Cat_1, do(label(Rob, Box_2, Cat_2), S)) \subset$
$$\tilde{\exists} category(Box_1, Cat_1, S) \land \neg Box_1 \doteq Box_2$$
$$\tilde{\forall} category(Box_1, Cat_1, do(pickup(Rob, Box_2), S)) \subset$$
$$\tilde{\exists} category(Box_1, Cat_1, S)$$

This *frame problem* is nowadays well-recognised as one of the classical problems of AI. Besides its philosophical aspect, it has great engineering repercussions: for specifying a problem domain such as the automated loading dock in the Situation Calculus, it is a tedious task to specify all the non-effects in the form of separate axioms, that is to say one for each fluent and each action. Small changes in fluent and action representation amount to great changes in the axiomatisation. In order to make the logic-based approach to decision making practical, a different formalisation has to be found in which the concise specification of effects implicitly also determines the non-effects. Such a solution to the frame problem should not restrict expressiveness as is the case in traditional planning algorithms.

Equivalences, such as those used in the Clark completion, play an important role in the calculus proposed by Reiter [Rei91]. By combining all the explicit evidence for a fluent being changed into a single definition, we derive Successor-State-Axioms (SSA). From these equivalences, the independence of fluents and actions can then be logically derived, such as the persistence of *category* over any action other than *label*:

(SSA)
$$\tilde{\forall} category(Box, Cat, do(A, S)) =$$
$$\tilde{\exists} A \doteq label(Rob, Box, Cat)$$
$$\lor \tilde{\exists} category(Box, Cat, S)$$
$$\land \neg(\tilde{\exists} A \doteq label(Rob, Box, Cat_2) \land Cat \doteq Cat_2)$$

The formulation of Reiter is the basis of the GOLOG language [LLL+94]. However, it has the drawback of not separating its basic reasoning principle from the domain representations of fluents and actions. In SSA, both aspects are intermingled. To enable the extraction of such a domain-independent logic program, we have to switch from a fluent representation by means of predicates to a fluent representation by means of manipulable objects, hence terms of our theory. The appropriate technical notion is called *reification* and has been applied by Kowalski [KS94] to obtain a variant of the Situation Calculus $(SITK)$ which looks like a domain-independent version of SSA:

$(SITK)$
$$\tilde{\forall} holds(F, do(A, S)) \equiv \tilde{\exists} initiates(A, F, S) \lor$$
$$\tilde{\exists} holds(F, S) \land \neg terminates(A, F, S)$$

In $SITK$, the *holds* predicate is introduced to describe whether a given fluent, now as an element of the universe, is true in a particular situation. We can now separate an initial situation description

$$I ::= holds(ahead(rob_1, box_1), s_0) \wedge holds(at(box_1, truck), s_0) \wedge$$
$$holds(handempty(rob_1), s_0) \wedge holds(category(box_1, toys), s_0)$$

and a goal $G ::= holds(holding(rob_1, box_1), do(pickup(rob_1, box_1), s_0))$ from the background theory $SITK$ and a domain description DOM. DOM determines the positive and negative effects of domain actions by means of the predicates *initiates* and *terminates*.

$$\tilde{\forall} initiates\ (A, F, S) \equiv$$
$$\tilde{\exists} F \dot{=} holding(Rob, Box)$$
$$\wedge\ A \dot{=} pickup(Rob, Box) \wedge\ holds(at(Box, Area), S)$$
$$\wedge\ holds(ahead(Rob, Box), S) \wedge\ holds(handempty(Rob), S)$$
$$\vee\ \tilde{\exists} F \dot{=} category(Box, Cat) \wedge\ A \dot{=} label(Rob, Box, Cat)$$
$$\vee \dots$$
(DOM)
$$\tilde{\forall} terminates(A, F, S) \equiv$$
$$\tilde{\exists} F \dot{=} at(Box, Area)$$
$$\wedge A \dot{=} pickup(Rob, Box) \wedge\ holds(at(Box, Area), S)$$
$$\wedge holds(ahead(Rob, Box), S) \wedge\ holds(handempty(Rob), S)$$
$$\vee \tilde{\exists} F \dot{=} category(Box, Cat_1) \wedge\ A \dot{=} label(Rob, Box, Cat_2)$$
$$\vee \dots$$

This gives us the desired framework $SITK \wedge DOM \wedge I \models \tilde{\exists} G$. In recent years, the reification technique has been extended to also cover possible combinations of fluents in partial situation descriptions [HS90, Thi99]. Their *Fluent Calculus* uses a particular equational theory (the multi-set theory $AC1$ [GHS+92]) to axiomatise changes in partial situations using *state update axioms (SUA)*. It can be shown that this treatment allows for computational advances when inferring the frame.

2.2   The Narrative-Based Event Calculus

State-based approaches to Cognitive Robotics, such as the Situation Calculus, are characterised by their implicit notion of time and their explicit focus on global states. It has been argued, especially in the context of natural language systems and narrative understanding [All84, KS86], that this is a major reason for the frame problem to appear — states enforce the distinction of what is relevant for the reasoning from what is not. Furthermore, states are a cognitively non-plausible representation for a human hearer or reader: in narratives and discourse, an overall description of the initial world state is seldom given, nor a complete sequence of actions. Rather, the important parts of the story are introduced piecewise and presented with incomplete temporal annotations ("first, there was a box labelled with 'toys' standing on the truck ... one robot picked it up ... guess what its category was after the other robot labelled it with 'guns'."). The hearer or reader of the story then has to reason under the assumption that all the relevant information has been given to him. Sometimes, he has to withdraw wrong conclusions when getting more information (non-monotonic reasoning).

The role of an interactive hearer or reader is a natural picture for a situated agent within a multi-agent system, too. The agent cannot perceive every detail of the world, but is frequently gathering bits of information whose temporal ordering could be unclear. From these bits, the agent must derive preliminary conclusions and decisions. Hence, the agent is not able to project a complete state representation of the world into past and future, but only the relevant parts of the agent's vague estimation of it. That is why narrative-based logics of action, which were originally developed in discourse understanding and temporal databases to avoid global states, turn out to be useful formalisms for Cognitive Robotics, too.

One of these formalisms is the *Event Calculus* which has been introduced in [KS86] and brought into a form quite similar to *SITK* by [Sha89, KS94]:

$$ECK ::= ECK1 \wedge ECK2, ECK3 \wedge ECK4 \wedge ECK5$$

$(ECK1)$ $\quad \tilde{\forall} holds(F, T_1) \equiv \quad \tilde{\exists} happens(E, A, T_2) \wedge initiates(A, F, T_2) \wedge$
$$T_2 \dot{<} T_1 \wedge \neg clipped(F, T_2, T_1)$$

$(ECK2)$ $\quad \tilde{\forall} clipped(F, T_1, T_2) \equiv \quad \tilde{\exists} happens(E, A, T_3) \wedge terminates(A, F, T_3) \wedge$
$$T_1 \dot{\leq} T_3 \dot{\leq} T_2{}^6$$

$(ECK3)$ $\quad \tilde{\forall} T_1 \dot{<} T_2 \wedge T_2 \dot{<} T_3 \supset \tilde{\exists} T_1 \dot{<} T_3$

$(ECK4)$ $\quad \tilde{\forall} T_1 \dot{<} T_1 \supset \tilde{\exists} \bot$

$(ECK5)$ $\quad \tilde{\forall} happens(E, A_1, T_1) \wedge happens(E, A_2, T_2) \supset \tilde{\exists} A_1 \dot{=} A_2 \wedge T_1 \dot{=} T_2$

The ontological entities in *ECK* are fluents, *events* (as unique tokens of a certain type of action), and time points. Similar to Kowalski's approach in *SITK*, there exists a *holds* predicate which denotes that a certain fluent is valid at a particular point in time. The axiom of change *ECK*1 realises a restricted version of the law of strict inertia: A fluent holds at a particular point in time T_1 iff there exists an event E_1 that happened (the *happens* predicate) at an earlier point in time T_2 (the before relation $\dot{<}$ in infix notation) and that has successfully initiated the fluent — unless the fluent ceased to persist in the meantime (it is *clipped*: *ECK*2) as the result of being terminated by some other event E_2 that happened in the period of time between T_2 and T_1. *ECK*3 and *ECK*4 are the background constraints to obtain temporal order as a transitive and anti-symmetric relation. *ECK*5 describes events to be unique and instantaneous action appearances over time.

---

[6] $T_1 \dot{\leq} T_2$ is an abbreviation for $T_1 \dot{<} T_2 \vee T_1 \dot{=} T_2$

Given an initial situation[7] and a narrative

$$I ::= holds(on(box_1, truck), t_0) \wedge holds(category(box_1, toys), t_0)$$

$$\Delta ::= happens(e_1, label(rob_2, box_1, guns), t_1) \wedge t_0 \dot{<} t_1 \wedge$$
$$happens(e_2, pickup(rob_1, box_1), t_2) \wedge t_0 \dot{<} t_2 \wedge t_1 \dot{<} t_3 \wedge t_2 \dot{<} t_3$$

and the identical domain description DOM as in the $SITK$ case[8], we can now infer

$$ECK1 \wedge ECK2 \wedge DOM \wedge I \wedge \Delta, ECK3 \wedge ECK4 \wedge ECK5 \models$$
$$\tilde{\exists} holds(category(box_1, guns), t_3).$$

This result is due to the completion of the situation I and the narrative Δ that was not mandatory in the Situation Calculus. In $SITK$, a closed-world assumption can connect partial states to global situations, but is not able to deal with incomplete temporal information. In the same way as the Situation Calculus is regarded as the theory behind *state-space planners* [McC85], the completion of $\dot{<}$ into a partial order thus closely relates the Event Calculus to algorithmic *partial-order planning* [Esh88, Mis91, Sha97a].

However, the notion of a correct plan in ECK is different from the common intuition. Typically, a solution plan is one which satisfies the goal in all of its linearisations, that is to say its extensions to totally ordered plans. By minimising the $\dot{<}$ relation, ECK specifies the validity of effects under the existence of a single successful linearisation. Suppose we add another action and some initial facts

$$\Delta' ::= \Delta \wedge \ happens(e_3, pickup(rob_2, box_1), t_4) \wedge t_0 \dot{<} t_4 \wedge t_4 \dot{<} t_3$$

$$I' ::= I \wedge \ holds(handempty(rob_1), t_0) \wedge holds(handempty(rob_2), t_0) \wedge$$
$$holds(ahead(rob_1, box_1), t_0) \wedge holds(ahead(rob_2, box_1), t_1)$$

we then infer $G ::= \tilde{\exists} holds(holding(rob_1, box_1), t_3) \wedge holds(holding(rob_2, box_1), t_3)$ which is not intuitive.

For partial-order planning with the Event Calculus, an alternative formalisation $ECS ::= ECK1 \wedge ECS1 \wedge ECS2, ECK3 \wedge ECK4 \wedge ECK5$ has been proposed by [Sha89, Mis91, Sha95]. Instead of qualifying persistence-destroying events inside the persistence interval, they are now required to happen outside the interval bounds.

(ECS1) $\tilde{\forall} clipped(F, T_1, T_2) \equiv \tilde{\exists} happens(E, A, T_3) \wedge terminates(A, F, T_3) \wedge$
$$\neg out(T_3, T_1, T_2)$$
(ECS2) $\tilde{\forall} out(T_3, T_1, T_2) \equiv \tilde{\exists} T_3 \dot{<} T_1 \vee \tilde{\exists} T_2 \dot{<} T_3$

---

[7] According to $ECK1$, each *holds* expression must have an associated initiator. In the Event Calculus, the initial situation is thus normally described by a particular 'dummy' event in Δ and DOM which introduces all the initial fluents. We have omitted this for the purpose of simplification.

[8] The correspondence of situations and time points has been used to compare ECK and $SITK$ [KS94].

ECS restricts its models in such a way that a solution plan has to be correct in all of its linearisations. In the absence of relevant temporal information, such as in our previous example, *ECS* would not predict that the box is kept by any of the robots — this is what we expect from any hearer who requires more information in order to resolve a story. But this restriction comes at the high price of a computationally intractable semantics!

For our example, we can construct two minimal *ECS* models which differ in the validity of statements: one in which rob_1 successfully picks up box_1, thus rendering the action of rob_2 non-effective, and one in which the opposite is the case. To give this a semantic basis, we deploy the notion of three-valued models (cf. [Kun87]). The minimal three-valued *ECS* model of our example hence leaves the truth values for preconditions and effects of both *pickup* actions 'undefined' (0.5).

Undefinedness gives a natural interpretation to the *ECS* behaviour. Nevertheless, it is computationally intractable: in a minimal three-valued model, the conditions for $\models^1$ and $\models^0$ turn out to be computable, but $\models^{0.5}$ describes the case in which an inference procedure cannot decide and does not halt[9]. In other words, inference procedures will steadily loop ('flounder') between the minimal two-valued models. Especially during planning within ignorant agents, such as the forklifts in the loading dock, such cases could appear rather often and 'paralyse' the agents forever.

Different semantics, such as stable models [GL88] and well-founded models [GRS88], have been proposed to allow for more useful inferences, at the same time keeping the expressiveness of the LP framework. We could adopt such semantics for *ECS* as well. However, this would require special inference procedures, which would be difficult to implement using standard platforms for logic programming, such as constraint-based languages.

Instead, we have taken in [JFB96] the pragmatic approach to refine the calculus in order to allow for unique two-valued models, again. At first sight, this is in conflict with a purist view on Cognitive Robotics. It is however justified as long as the calculus keeps its intuitive form, that is to say the extensions have a declarative reading. This argument will be used again when talking about representational extensions in the following section.

The crucial observation of [JFB96] was that, instead of running into mutual dependencies, some sort of pessimistic worst-case analysis has to be performed by the calculus, that is to say to apply the most conservative notion of a partially specified planning solution that is available. A first approach is thus to omit the precondition checks invoked by the *clipped* axioms. This way, any action, even if its preconditions are not valid, could threaten the persistence of some fluent and requires efforts from the agent in order to re-establish the wanted effect. Such efforts could be to strengthen temporal constraints or to insert repair actions. This scheme does not however allow the incorporation of immediate countermeasures to 'neutralise' adversary actions in advance. To be able to do things

---

[9] $\models^1 \equiv \models, \models^0 \equiv$ **not** $\models$, and $\models^{0.5} \equiv$ **undefined**

like that would be desirable in non-cooperative multi-agent system applications [EM91].

We now define

$$ECJ ::= ECJ1 \wedge \ldots \wedge ECJ4 \wedge ECS3 \wedge ECK3 \wedge \ldots \wedge ECK5$$

which just focuses its worst-case analysis on mutual dependencies, and thus is able to reason about the preconditions of persistence destroyers as well. ECJ predicates, such as $holds$, are extended to keep book about the visited events in a causal chain C (using a list representation, for example $C \doteq cons(e_1, cons(e_2, \ldots)))$), the current worst case B, and the event E that is currently under consideration:

$$
(ECJ1) \quad
\begin{aligned}
\tilde{\forall} holds(F, T_1, C, B, E) \equiv {}& \tilde{\exists} member(E, C) \wedge B \doteq \dot{1} \\
\vee {}& \tilde{\exists} \neg member(E, C) \wedge happens(E_2, A, T_2) \\
& \wedge initiates(A, F, T_2, cons(E, C), B, E_2) \\
& \wedge T_2 \lessdot T_1 \wedge flip(B, B_2) \\
& \wedge \neg clipped(F, T_2, T_1, C, B_2, E)
\end{aligned}
$$

$$
(ECJ2) \quad
\begin{aligned}
\tilde{\forall} clipped(F, T_1, T_2, C, B, E) \equiv {}& \\
\tilde{\exists} happens(&E_2, A, T_3) \\
\wedge terminates(&A, F, T_3, cons(E, C), B, E_2) \\
\wedge \neg out(&T_3, T_1, T_2)
\end{aligned}
$$

$$(ECJ3) \quad \tilde{\forall} flip(B_1, B_2) \equiv \tilde{\exists} B_1 \doteq \dot{1} \wedge B_2 \doteq \dot{0} \quad \vee \quad \tilde{\exists} B_1 \doteq \dot{0} \wedge B_2 \doteq \dot{1}$$

$$
(ECJ4) \quad
\begin{aligned}
\tilde{\forall} member(E, C) \equiv {}& \tilde{\exists} C \doteq cons(E, C_2) \vee \\
& \tilde{\exists} C \doteq cons(E_2, C_2) \wedge member(E, C_2)
\end{aligned}
$$

ECJ allows the same kind of reasoning as ECS unless one is trying to prove the precondition of some event E in $ECJ1$ which has already been entered into that list (the $member$ predicate in $ECJ4$). Then, we have detected some causal cycle and the worst case assumption must be applied: the worst case is indicated by the additional parameter B which can take either of the values $\dot{0}$ and $\dot{1}$. For example, on the one hand, the worst case for wanting to demonstrate the validity of an effect is that the precondition of its initiator does not hold ($\dot{0}$). On the other hand, the worst case for demonstrating the persistence of some fluent is that a possible destroyer successfully terminates that fluent ($\dot{1}$). Hence, B is flipped ($ECJ3$) each time it crosses a negation in the calculus. The ultimate goals for ECJ start with an empty causal chain nil and refer to a 'dummy' consumer E, for example $holds(category(box_1, guns), t_3, nil, \dot{0}, E)$. Also the domain description DOM is correspondingly extended:

$$
(DOM) \quad
\begin{aligned}
\tilde{\forall} initiates(A, F, T, C, B, E) \equiv {}& \tilde{\exists} F \doteq holding(Rob, Box) \\
& \wedge A \doteq pickup(Rob, Box) \\
& \wedge holds(at(Box, Area), T, C, B, E) \wedge \ldots \\
\\
\tilde{\forall} terminates(A, F, T, C, B, E) \equiv {}& \tilde{\exists} F \doteq at(Box, Area) \\
& \wedge A \doteq pickup(Rob, Box) \\
& \wedge holds(at(Box, Area), T, C, B, E) \wedge \ldots
\end{aligned}
$$

The proof of the well-definedness of ECJ uses the following argumentation: any undefined value in a minimal three-valued ECJ model can only affect the defined predicates *holds, clipped, initiates,* and *terminates* and results in an infinite sequence of undefined *holds* values that incrementally build up a causal chain. For any given narrative, this chain then must have a cycle. From the definition of the calculus, it follows that the appropriate *holds* value must be either 1 or 0 (Proposition 1). Since this prohibits any proper minimal three-valued model for ECJ, we can derive the uniqueness of an appropriate minimal two-valued model (Theorem 1). Using a similar argumentation, Theorem 2 shows that any statement valid in the worst case ($\dot{0}$) is also valid in the optimistic case ($\dot{1}$). The proofs can be found in [JF01].

Proposition 1 (Three-Valued Minimal Models of ECJ). *Any minimal three-valued (Herbrand) model M of ECJ is already a two valued model of ECJ.*

Theorem 1 (Unique Minimal Two-Valued Model of ECJ). *ECJ has a unique minimal two-valued (Herbrand) model*

$$M \models_2 Comp(ECJ1 \wedge \ldots \wedge ECJ4 \wedge ECS3 \wedge \Delta \wedge I \wedge DOM) \wedge$$
$$CET \wedge ECK3 \wedge ECK4 \wedge ECK5$$

Theorem 2 (Treatment of Worst Case in ECJ). *Let M be the minimal (Herbrand) model of ECJ:*

$$M \models \tilde{\forall} holds(F, T, C, \dot{0}, E) \supset holds(F, T, C, \dot{1}, E)$$

Due to its expressiveness and computational properties, ECJ has been successfully applied in the context of the original INTERRAP architecture and the automated loading dock by standard LP techniques [JFB96]. Especially the ability to treat partially-ordered multi-agent plans has been a key requirement to encode the delivery tasks and the necessary coordination between forklifts. [Sha97a] has shown that abductive inferences with the Event Calculus closely mirror the behaviour of partial-order planning algorithms, giving a declarative meaning to concepts such as protected links, threats, clobberers, and the promotion and demotion of clobberers. In recent years, several alternative narrative-based formalisms have been developed for dealing with the frame problem. The *temporal action language (TAL)* [DGKK98, San94], for example, grew out of an evaluation framework for action logics. It is currently applied in the off-line verification of an unmanned airborne vehicle. However, it has not yet been integrated into on-line decision making.

3 Abstraction in the Event Calculus

With the core formalisms of *SSA, SUA, ECJ,* and *TAL*, the practical impact of Cognitive Robotics has been sufficiently demonstrated and the frame problem seems to be solved today. Research now focuses on other aspects, such as indeterminate effects [Sha97b, BT97, Lin95], simultaneous actions [Sha97c, BT94, LS95], the modelling of continuous actions [Sha90, HT96], and the incorporation of state-constraints and side-effects of actions (the *ramification problem* [Thi97, KM97]).

These extensions develop increasingly sophisticated, thus increasingly expensive reasoning machines without worrying about the foremost requirement of situatedness both for agents as well as for particular reasoning modules inside agents: the need for making early and approximate decisions. Our experiments in [JFB96], for example, have demonstrated that an *ECJ*-based planner is able to navigate a forklift's behaviour-based layer, but only if the timing requirements are not too tight. Otherwise, the planner takes too long at computing future details, such as complete navigation paths, for influencing the fast reactions at the behaviour-based layer in time.

Instead of being occupied with details, a reasoner should be able to first treat the important issues of the problem, hence to solve its problem approximately. Later, this solution sketch should be refined into a detailed result. This is the idea of anytime algorithms [BD94]. In a logic-based setting, abstract representations are intuitive means to indicate which features of the original problem specification are most important and to hide other information for later incorporation [tTvH98]. For planning systems, this has been most reasonably argued by [Sac74]. Because abstract representations are organised in a decomposition hierarchy, we often speak of hierarchical planning. In hierarchical planning, abstraction can be applied to fluents (*situation abstraction*) and narratives (*action abstraction*). The latter subsumes the former if regarding initial situations and goals as 'dummy' actions with no preconditions or no effects, respectively.

Abstraction planning is useful for interleaving planning and action in real-time architectures [WHR96]. Figure 5 shows an extract of a forklift's representation hierarchy in which two *transport* actions are performed concurrently. From an abstract viewpoint, *transport* is defined as an opaque action with preconditions and effects that describes the movement of the robot and the delivered box. Hereby, *transport* loses information about particular fluents which have to do with the robot's positioning (areas of the loading dock, their reachability) and with the robot's ability to pick and drop a box. The *transport* macro also loses information about its complex temporal sub-structure that consists of two sequential sub-actions which are macros by themselves (*search* the box and deliver it to a free destination, *searchFree*).

transport allows one to quickly connect a delivery goal with the current situation. Using this decision as a kind of 'promise' for being able to solve the goal, a planner could already commit to certain actions, for example by influencing a forklift's behaviour-based layer to move the robot to the initial area of the box, while still refining *transport* on the next level of representation, for example to insert *pickup* and *drop* actions and to develop a complete navigation path to the destination.

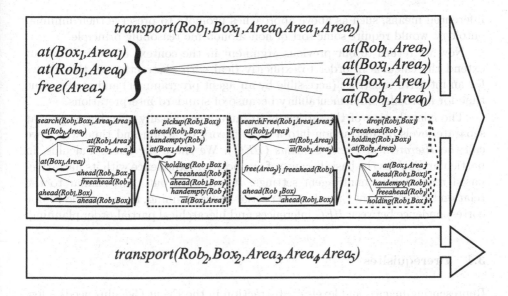

Fig. 5. An Abstraction Hierarchy

Thus, both for a planning module inside INTERRAP and for a single decision-making agent, abstract representations are a useful tool. Put in a more general context, any rational agent and any situated reasoning process must always be aware that its representations are in fact abstractions of the real world. To cater for this aspect, a declarative foundation for abstraction hierarchies in Cognitive Robotics has to be found. One prerequisite, the composition of primitive actions into macro actions, has already been discussed for most of the core calculi [LRL97, San94, Dav96, EHT96]. In these extensions, macros are not allowed to have effects by themselves. Causal reasoning is still performed at the most concrete level of representation. Shanahan [Sha97a] goes further by introducing effect axioms also for macro events. Still, his macros are not to be called abstract, since their effects must be logically equivalent to the lower level axiomatisation. By this design, macros do not really loose information which gives no advantage for enabling approximate reasoning.

It is the loss of information that makes real abstractions a non-trivial concept for logic-based treatment. In the example of Figure 5, the conclusion $at(Box_1, Area_2)$ is provable at a high level of abstraction. But this conclusion cannot be necessarily made at the next lower level of abstraction, since, for example the delivering robot could already be occupied with some other box ($\neg holds(handempty(Rob_1), \ldots)$) alternatively written as the *dual* fluent $holds(\overline{handempty}(Rob_1), \ldots))$ which we have not taken into account before and which requires additional efforts, for example to drop the carried box, in order to install the wanted result. Hence, treating macros by purely semantical or inferential means, such as above approaches promote to preserve their minimal ontology, would require some sort of non-monotonic reasoning principle.

Now we return to our previous argument in the context of *ECJ*. Why not extend the calculus in order to explicitly deal with abstractions if this allows for an intuitive construct (accessible by an agent programmer) and at the same time for a broader implementability because of standard interpretations?

The contribution of this article is to introduce causally-effective macros at separate levels of abstraction into a logic theory of action and time which we call the *Hierarchical Event Calculus (HEC)*. We chose the Event Calculus, in particular *ECJ*, as the basis because of our positive experience with its narrative-based reasoning in multi-agent settings. It will turn out that, similar to the relation between Event Calculus and partial-order planning, there is a one-to-one correspondence between *HEC* inferences and hierarchical partial-order planning.

3.1   Prerequisites

Representing macros and levels of abstraction in the Event Calculus needs a few prerequisites which we would like to discuss before giving their formalisation. From these, it will be apparent that *HEC* keeps an intuitive reading, whilst unveiling and addressing a deeper problem in reasoning about causality that is also inherent to single-level approaches, such as *ECS*.

Duration: In *ECK*, *ECS*, and *ECJ*, events are ideally regarded as instantaneous. When switching to macro actions, such as *transport*, this idealisation does not hold anymore.

Since macros are complex compositions of temporal substructures, for example they are possibly long-lasting configurations of underlying reactive processes, they must have a positive duration. Therefore, events must be assigned a time interval consisting of a start time point and an end time point. The end time is greater or equal to the start time.

Preconditions: In *ECK*, *ECS*, and *ECJ*, preconditions are valid iff they are provably present at the start time of the respective instantaneous event which is equal to its end time. In *HEC*, events represent opaque substructures with duration. Thus, it is not possible to prove preconditions just at the start of some action, such as to check *free*($Area_2$) just at the beginning of a *transport*.

Worst-case assumptions are the right tool to deal with the absence of further information at this level of reasoning: in the worst case, preconditions are needed by some sub-event of the macro which is located quite at the end (for example *searchFree* in *transport*). Hence, it is safe to speak of a valid precondition iff it has been demonstrably initiated before the start of the macro and is not clipped until its very end. For example, we need to ensure that until the end of *transport*, no concurrent activity is able to put a different box on the last free space of the envisaged shelf, hence does not terminate *free*($Area_2$).

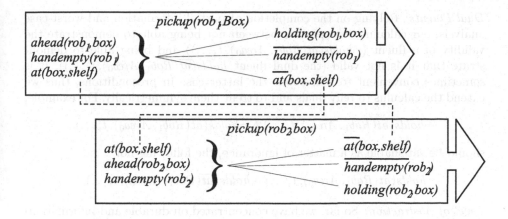

Fig. 6. Causal Cycles Lead to Partially Undefined Models

Effects: When do effects become visible? Similar to the consumption of a precondition, the effect of a macro (for example $at(Rob_1, Area_2)$ in *transport*) could be produced by some sub-event relatively late with respect to the overall duration (here: *searchFree*). Thus, we cannot assume that effects are visible before the very end of some action.

On the other hand, effects could as well be caused by some sub-event rather early in the course of the macro, such as $at(Rob_1, Area_0)$ being terminated by *search*. Therefore, the persistence of preconditions is violated right from the beginning of some initiating action. On the other hand, terminating effects violate the persistence of preconditions right from the beginning of a destroyer event. Using these conservative rules, we take as much care as possible of the further refinement of an abstract plan.

Causality: Interestingly, a special version of the above worst-case assumptions has already been presented in the *ECK* and *ECS* calculi. *ECK* and *ECS* state that initiators have to happen before ($\dot{<}$) the consumption of their effects while destroyers already influence simultaneous settings ($\dot{\leq}$).

The inherent possibility of running into causal cycles with that design leads to the computational intractability of *ECS* by partially undefined minimal models. A possible fix is the requirement that no two actions can happen simultaneously [KS94]. For *HEC*, this restriction is too strong, since actions have durations and could be interleaved (Figure 6).

Hence, we employ the solution of *ECJ* not as a purely practical issue to reestablish well-definedness, but also as a deeper question with respect to the applied causality principle: what *ECJ* already anticipated and what is taken over to *HEC* is, in a nutshell, the naive physical stance that excludes any effect from altering its own cause, any event from influencing the validity of its own preconditions.

Dual Fluents: Relying on the completion of partial information and worst-case analysis, our calculus distinguishes between not being able to demonstrate the validity of a fluent ($\neg holds(at(Rob_1, Area_0), t, \ldots)$) and being able to demonstrate that it is not valid (the dual fluent $holds(\overline{at}(Rob_1, Area_0), t, \ldots)$). It is sometimes convenient to talk about the latter case in preconditions, thus we extend the calculus to reify duals and to treat them symmetrically. For example,

$$\neg holds(at(Rob_1, Area_0), t, \ldots) \wedge \neg holds(\overline{at}(Rob_1, Area_0), t, \ldots)$$

should be satisfiable as a matter of ignorance, the following not

$$holds(at(Rob_1, Area_0), t, \ldots) \wedge holds(\overline{at}(Rob_1, Area_0), t, \ldots).$$

Level of Abstraction: So far, we have concentrated on durable and information-losing macros. Once obtained, the representation of levels of abstraction nearly comes for free: predicates are simply annotated with abstraction-level terms, for example one term referring to *transport* and corresponding fluents, one level referring to *search*, *searchFree*, *pickup*, and *drop* and their respective fluents. In this way, we can express fluents which are valid at a particular level of abstraction ($holds(at(Box_2, Area_2), t, \ldots, l_2)$) where this does not necessarily imply that they are valid at a different level ($holds(at(Box_2, Area_2), t, \ldots, l_3)$). The reasoning at different levels is however not completely separated: an operation which performs the (de-)composition of representations is added and installs the connection between abstract macros and primitive sub-events, between high-level fluents and more concrete state descriptions. This (de-)composition performs bidirectionally, hence serves as a declarative foundation for decomposing approximate plans into refined decisions and for reconstructing high-level intentions from piecewise observations.

3.2   The Hierarchical Event Calculus

We now incrementally formalise the Hierarchical Event Calculus
$$HEC ::= HEC1 \wedge \ldots \wedge HEC5 \wedge ECJ3 \wedge ECJ4,$$
$$HEC6 \wedge \ldots \wedge HEC12 \wedge ECK3 \wedge ECK4$$

In the following $HEC1$ definition, *holds* takes seven arguments which denote the envisaged fluent, two subsequent time-points between which we would like the fluent to persist, a causal chain, the worst case flag, the event whose preconditions are currently under consideration, and the current level of abstraction. It is to read as follows: the fluent holds at a particular level of abstraction immediately before the beginning of the indicated interval and it is exclusively affected by the event under consideration throughout the whole interval. $HEC1$ provides a special interface to an initial situation I by using the predicate *initially* (see, for example [Sha97a]). Since we assume the initial situation to happen at the very earliest time-point in the narrative, a special version of persistence (*iclipped*) is used. The effects of actions are introduced by a single predicate (*causes*) that is defined in the domain axiomatisation DOM. Both *initially* and *causes* operate on fluents and dual fluents.

$$\tilde{\forall} holds(F, T_1, T_2, C, B, E, L) \equiv$$
$$\tilde{\exists} T_1 \dot{\leq} T_2 \wedge member(E, C) \wedge B \dot{=} \mathbf{i}$$
$$\vee \ \tilde{\exists} T_1 \dot{\leq} T_2 \wedge \neg member(E, C) \wedge initially(F, L)$$
$$(HEC1) \qquad \wedge \ flip(B, B_2) \wedge \neg iclipped(F, T_2, C, B_2, E, L)$$
$$\vee \ \tilde{\exists} T_1 \dot{\leq} T_2 \wedge \neg member(E, C)$$
$$\wedge \ happens(E_i, A_i, T_3, T_4, L) \wedge T_4 \dot{<} T_1$$
$$\wedge \ causes(A_i, F, T_3, T_4, cons(E, C), B, E_i, L)$$
$$\wedge \ flip(B, B_2) \wedge \neg clipped(F, T_3, T_2, C, B_2, E, L)$$

The *clipped* predicate in *HEC2* is also extended by the current level of abstraction *L*. Since it is defined over fluents and dual fluents, a destroyer is now identified by its causing the dual fluent — the *dual* predicate defined in *HEC3* uses the function symbol *not* to switch between the two fluent versions — and by its not being disjoint (the *disjoint* predicate defined in *HEC4*) with the proper persistence interval. Since any event should not be able to alter its own preconditions, a destroyer furthermore must be different from *E*. This coincides with our above remark about *holds* in which only *E*, if any event, is able to affect the fluent throughout the persistence interval.

$$\tilde{\forall} clipped(F, T_1, T_2, C, B, E, L) \equiv$$
$$(HEC2) \qquad \tilde{\exists} happens(E_t, A_t, T_3, T_4, L) \wedge \neg E_t \dot{=} E \wedge dual(F, F_-)$$
$$\wedge \ causes(A_t, F_-, T_3, T_4, cons(E, C), B, E_t, L)$$
$$\wedge \ \neg disjoint(T_1, T_2, T_3, T_4)$$
$$(HEC3) \qquad \tilde{\forall} dual(F, F_-) \equiv \tilde{\exists} F \dot{=} not(F_-) \vee \tilde{\exists} F_- \dot{=} not(F)$$
$$(HEC4) \qquad \tilde{\forall} disjoint(T_1, T_2, T_3, T_4) \equiv \tilde{\exists} T_2 \dot{<} T_3 \vee \tilde{\exists} T_4 \dot{<} T_1$$

HEC5 defines *iclipped* which checks the defect of persistence between the very beginning of the narrative and any time-point T_1. The temporal constraints in *HEC2* simplify in this case and forbid a destroyer to start after T_1.

$$\tilde{\forall} iclipped(F, T_1, C, B, E, L) \equiv$$
$$(HEC5) \qquad \tilde{\exists} happens(E_t, A_t, T_3, T_4, L) \wedge \neg E_t \dot{=} E \wedge dual(F, F_-)$$
$$\wedge \ causes(A_t, F_-, T_3, T_4, cons(E, C), B, E_t, L) \wedge \neg T_1 \dot{<} T_3$$

The following axioms (*HEC6* – *HEC9*) relate neighbour levels of abstraction. We assume that there exist (de-)composition operations *decomposeMacro* and *decomposeHolds* which are defined in *DOM* and which describe the correspondence of higher-level representations (macro actions and abstract fluents) with more primitive occurrences (sub-events and more concrete fluents). Intuitively, there should be an equivalence between *happens* and *decomposeMacro* which we do not immediately express as a definition. Rather, we use two separate constraints (*HEC6* and *HEC8*) for 'maintaining the integrity' of the given abstraction hierarchy. Abstract *holds* statements are subject to information loss. Hence, lower-level fluents will imply the occurrence of higher-level ones (*HEC9*), but not vice versa. For the opposite direction, we determine a weaker relation (*HEC7*) which just focuses on the initial situation *I* and requires a *decomposeInitially* definition in *DOM* analogous to *decomposeHolds*.

$(HEC6)$ $\tilde{\forall}happens(E, A, T_1, T_2, L) \supset \tilde{\exists}decomposeMacro(E, A, T_1, T_2, L)$

$(HEC7)$ $\tilde{\forall}initially(F, L) \supset \tilde{\exists}decomposeInitially(F, L)$

$(HEC8)$ $\tilde{\forall}decomposeMacro(E, A, T_1, T_2, L) \supset \tilde{\exists}happens(E, A, T_1, T_2, L)$

$(HEC9)$ $\tilde{\forall}decomposeHolds(F, T_1, T_2, nil, \dot{0}, E_1, L) \supset$
$$\tilde{\exists}holds(F, T_1, T_2, nil, \dot{0}, E_2, L)$$

Finally, we add three constraints $HEC10$, $HEC11$, and $HEC12$ which state that each event has a positive duration and is unique with respect to its action type, its duration, and its level of abstraction, and that the initial situation must be consistent with respect to dual fluents. The background theory of $<$ is borrowed from ECK ($ECK3$ and $ECK4$).

$(HEC10)$ $\tilde{\forall}happens(E, A, T_1, T_2, L) \supset \tilde{\exists}T_1 \dot{\leq} T_2$

$(HEC11)$ $\tilde{\forall}happens(E, A_1, T_1, T_2, L_1) \wedge happens(E, A_2, T_3, T_4, L_2) \supset$
$$\tilde{\exists}A_1 \dot{=} A_2 \wedge T_1 \dot{=} T_3 \wedge T_2 \dot{=} T_4 \wedge L_1 \dot{=} L_2$$

$(HEC12)$ $\tilde{\forall}initially(F, L) \wedge initially(F_-, L) \wedge dual(F, F_-) \supset \tilde{\exists}\bot$

3.3 Domain Representation and (De-)Composition

A narrative in HEC (see our example in Figure 5) is a set of facts of the form

$$\Delta ::= happens(e_1, transport(rob_1, box_1, parking, truck, shelf_3), t_1, t_2, l_2) \wedge$$
$$happens(e_2, transport(rob_2, box_2, parking, shelf_1, truck), t_3, t_4, l_2) \wedge$$
$$happens(e_3, search(rob_1, box_1, parking, truck), t_5, t_6, l_3) \wedge \ldots \wedge$$
$$t_1 \dot{\leq} t_5 \dot{\leq} t_6 \dot{\leq} t_2 \dot{<} t_7 \dot{\leq} t_8 \wedge t_3 \dot{\leq} t_4 \dot{<} t_7 \wedge \ldots$$

Before we had to encode the initial situation I within the narrative and the domain description DOM, this is now much easier to specify using the *initially* predicate:

$$I ::= initially(at(box_1, truck), l_2) \wedge initially(at(rob_1, park), l_2) \wedge$$
$$initially(free(shelf_3), l_2) \wedge initially(at(box_1, truck), l_3) \wedge$$
$$initially(handempty(rob_1), l_3) \wedge \ldots$$

Domain-dependent situation abstraction is encoded by means of the following definition of *decomposeHolds* (and an analogous definition of *decomposeInitially*) in $DOMSAB$. It relates particular fluents at higher levels of abstraction to fluents at a more primitive or the same level of abstraction. For example, the occupancy of areas within the loading dock can be inferred from more concrete positioning data with respect to landmarks (*atPos*). For example, *ahead* can be derived from positioning and orientation. The decomposition of most of the primitive fluents is simply $\top$.

$$\tilde{\forall} decomposeHolds(F, T_1, T_2, C, B, E, L) \equiv$$
$$\tilde{\exists} L \doteq l_3 \wedge F \doteq at(Object, truck)$$
$$\wedge holds(atPos(Object, \dot{1}, \dot{1}), T_1, T_2, C, B, E, l_4)$$

(DOMSAB) $$\vee \tilde{\exists} L \doteq l_4 \wedge F \doteq ahead(Rob, Box) \wedge X_1 \doteq X_2 \wedge Y_2 \doteq \dot{+}(Y, 1)$$
$$\wedge holds(atPos(Rob, X_1, Y_1), T_1, T_2, C, B, E, L)$$
$$\wedge holds(orient(Rob, north), T_1, T_2, C, B, E, L)$$
$$\wedge holds(atPos(Box, X_2, Y_2), T_1, T_2, C, B, E, L)$$
$$\dots$$

As for HEC's ancestor calculi, DOM contains the causal effects of actions $DOMCAU$. These are defined through a single *causes* predicate which assigns both fluents ($at(Box, Area_1)$) and dual fluents ($not(at(Rob, Area_0))$) as the result of executing an action under particular (positive or negative) preconditions. *causes* distinguishes actions according to different levels of abstraction, that is to say the same action type, such as *pickup*, could have more abstract preconditions and effects at a higher level than at a lower level of abstraction, such as the *atPos* fluent which does not become apparent until level l_4.

$$\tilde{\forall} causes(A, F, T_1, T_2, C, B, E, L) \equiv$$
$$\tilde{\exists} L \doteq l_2 \wedge A \doteq transport(Rob, Box, Area_0, Area_1, Area_2)$$
$$\wedge F \doteq at(Box, Area_2) \wedge holds(at(Rob, Area_0), T_1, T_2, C, B, E, L)$$
$$\wedge holds(at(Box, Area_1), T_1, T_2, C, B, E, L)$$
$$\wedge holds(free(Area_2), T_1, T_2, C, B, E, L)$$
$$\vee \tilde{\exists} L \doteq l_2 \wedge A \doteq transport(Rob, Box, Area_0, Area_1, Area_2)$$
$$\wedge \neg Area_0 \doteq Area_1 \wedge F \doteq not(at(Rob, Area_0))$$

(DOMCAU) $$\wedge \dots$$
$$\vee \tilde{\exists} L \doteq l_3 \wedge A \doteq pickup(Rob, Box)$$
$$\wedge F \doteq holding(Rob, Box) \wedge holds(at(Box, Area), T_1, T_2, C, B, E, L)$$
$$\wedge holds(handempty(Rob), T_1, T_2, C, B, E, L)$$
$$\wedge holds(ahead(Rob, Box), T_1, T_2, C, B, E, L)$$
$$\vee \tilde{\exists} L \doteq l_4 \wedge A \doteq pickup(Rob, Box)$$
$$\wedge F \doteq not(atPos(Box, X_1, Y_1)) \wedge$$
$$holds(atPos(Box, X_1, Y_1), T_1, T_2, C, B, E, L)$$
$$\wedge \dots$$

The final task of DOM is to encode abstraction within the temporal narrative by defining the *decomposeMacro* predicate ($DOMAAB$). A successful decomposition of a macro is most straightforwardly described as the occurrence (*happens*) of corresponding sub-events at the next level of abstraction and the validity of temporal constraints between their duration. In our example, the *transport* macro decomposes into a sequence, that is to say a completely ordered set, of sub-actions. It is possible that actions just decompose into more refined versions of themselves, such as it is the case for *pickup* and *drop* from level l_3 to l_4.

$$\tilde{\forall} decomposeMacro(E, A, T_1, T_2, L) \equiv$$
$$\tilde{\exists} L \dot{=} l_2 \wedge A \dot{=} transport(Rob, Box, Area_0, Area_1, Area_2)$$
$$\wedge happens(E_1, search(Rob, Box, Area_0, Area_1), T_1, T_3, l_3)$$
$$\wedge happens(E_3, searchFree(Rob, Area_1, Area_2), T_4, T_2, l_3)$$
$$\wedge T_1 \dot{\le} T_3 \dot{\le} T_4 \dot{\le} T_2$$

(DOMAAB)
$$\tilde{\exists} L \dot{=} l_3 \wedge A \dot{=} pickup(Rob, Box)$$
$$\wedge happens(E_1, pickup(Rob, Box), T_1, T_2, l_4)$$
$$\tilde{\exists} L \dot{=} l_3 \wedge A \dot{=} drop(Rob, Box)$$
$$\wedge happens(E_1, drop(Rob, Box), T_1, T_2, l_4)$$
$$\dots$$

Using the expressiveness of first-order logic, the (de-)composition predicates can be converted into a powerful description tool. For example, arbitrarily interleaved activities, such as the two delivery macros in Figure 5, can be described in $DOMAAB$ by loose temporal relations

$$\tilde{\exists} happens(E_1, transport(\dots), T_3, T_4, l_2) \wedge happens(E_2, transport(\dots), T_5, T_6, l_2) \wedge$$
$$T_1 \dot{\le} T_3 \dot{\le} T_4 \dot{\le} T_2 \wedge T_1 \dot{\le} T_5 \dot{\le} T_6 \dot{\le} T_2$$

As [Dav96] has shown, $DOMAAB$ implements the fundamental concepts of a procedural programming language including concurrent statements, sequential statements, recursion, and even conditionals. For example, the *search* macro can be procedurally refined as

$$\tilde{\exists} holds(at(Rob, Area_1), T_1, T_2, l_3) \wedge holds(ahead(Rob, Box), T_1, T_2, l_3)$$
$$\vee \tilde{\exists} happens(E_1, moveArea(Rob, Area_1), T_1, T_3, l_4) \wedge$$
$$happens(E_2, look(Rob, Box, Area_0, Area_1), T_4, T_2, l_3) \wedge T_1 \dot{\le} T_3 \dot{\le} T_4$$

where *moveArea* and *look* are lower-level navigation 'routines'.

This property of $DOMAAB$, namely the treatment of plans or narratives as procedures, is the key to specify the complex intentions of agents. This is of course not too surprising, since the definitions just lift the expressiveness of the underlying logic programming. One may argue that the use of HEC is therefore a trivialisation to the general application of logic programming to agent design. As already argued in [McC63], the difference is that a logic 'procedure' and a logical 'application of the procedure' are now represented as reified terms of our theory of time and action and hence subject to ongoing reasoning about explicit causal and temporal relationships. This holds for the prediction of abstract situations from given observations such as needed to build a knowledge base module, for the task of a planning module to synthesise an intention from designer-given pieces of behaviour, and for the plan's on-line interpretation in interaction with the environment within intention execution modules.

The final part of a HEC specification are the overall goals to be achieved which are defined as a set of conservative *holds* expressions (sceptical mode $\dot{0}$, causal chain *nil*, 'dummy' consumer E_1, E_2) referring to different levels of abstraction

$G ::= holds(at(box_1, shelf_3), t_7, t_8, nil, \dot{0}, E_1, l_2) \wedge$
$$holds(at(box_1, shelf_3), t_7, t_8, nil, \dot{0}, E_2, l_3)$$
We then derive the framework $DOM \wedge I \wedge \Delta \models_{HEC} \tilde{\exists} G$.

3.4   Well-Definedness and Other Properties

As we have explained in the case of ECJ, it is important to establish the computational tractability of HEC with respect to partially undefined models. Since the technique of dealing with mutual dependencies has been carried over to HEC, the arguments and proofs are similar, if not identical. First, we have to show that undefined predicates result in an infinite sequence of undefined *holds* values incrementally building up a causal chain. The events referred to in that sequence are introduced via *happens* facts in the narrative Δ. When a causal cycle is present the definedness of intermediate *holds* predicates, hence the collapse of the infinite sequence, can be shown (Proposition 2). This construction also carries over to the worst-case behaviour of HEC (Theorem 4) from which we finally can derive in Theorem 5 that dual fluents are treated as intuitively expected: it is not possible to demonstrate the persistence of both a fluent and its dual within the same pessimistic context. The details of the proofs of the proposition and the theorems can be found in [JF01].

Proposition 2 (Three-Valued Minimal Models of HEC). *Any minimal three-valued (Herbrand) model M of HEC is already a two valued model.*

Theorem 3 (Unique Minimal Two-Valued Model of HEC). *HEC' has a unique minimal two-valued (Herbrand) model*

$$M \models_2 Comp(HEC1 \wedge \ldots \wedge HEC5 \wedge ECJ3 \wedge ECJ4 \wedge \Delta \wedge I \wedge DOM) \wedge$$
$$CET \wedge ECK3 \wedge ECK4 \wedge HEC6 \wedge \ldots \wedge HEC12$$

Theorem 4 (Treatment of Worst Case in HEC). *Let M be the minimal (Herbrand) model of HEC:*

$$M \models \tilde{\forall} holds(F, T_1, T_2, C, \dot{0}, E, L) \supset holds(F, T_1, T_2, C, \dot{1}, E, L)$$

Theorem 5 (Treatment of Dual Fluents). *Let M be the minimal (Herbrand) model of HEC:*

$$M \models \tilde{\forall} holds(F, T_1, T_2, C, \dot{0}, E, L) \wedge Dual(F, F_-) \supset \neg holds(F_-, T_1, T_2, C, \dot{0}, E, L)$$

4   Conclusion

Hybrid agents integrate different styles of reactive, deliberative, and cooperative problem solving in a modular fashion. They are the prime device of (Distributed) Artificial Intelligence and Cognitive Science for realising a broad spectrum of simultaneous functionalities in application domains such as Artificial

Life, (Tele-)Robotics, Flexible Manufacturing, and Automated Transportation. This article we proposed a design methodology for hybrid agents which combines two complementary approaches of Software Engineering and declarative Cognitive Robotics at five interconnected specification stages: architecture, computational model, theory, inference, and implementation. While we gave an introduction to the complete methodology of agent design in the first section, we concentrated on presenting a logic-based approach to describe deliberative processes within a hybrid agent architecture in the rest of the article. The interested reader can find the details of the overall framework as well as the proofs of the theorems in [JF01].

A common declarative framework for describing the reasoning of unified agents as well as of particular processes inside a hybrid agent has to handle the representation of fluents, time, actions, and their inherent causal relationships in an 'executable' first-order logic where possible. We presented the Hierarchical Event Calculus (HEC) as an expressive theory that is derived from the narrative-based formalisms of [KS86, Sha97a, Dav96]. Like the calculi of [LRL97, Sha97a, Dav96], HEC reifies a procedural sub-language which is able to synthesise and analyse the complex intentions of agents, such as behaviours, plans, and protocols. Unlike [LRL97, Sha97a, Dav96], HEC explicitly deals with multiple levels of abstraction that incorporate macro events with their own duration, own effects, and own preconditions. This is to address the foremost requirement of situatedness, which is the making of approximate inferences and decisions.

For this purpose, HEC relies on standard logic programming for broad implementability and exhibits useful properties, such as well-definedness, in reasoning about incomplete information. Just as the Situation Calculus is regarded as the theory behind state-space planning, the Event Calculus has been shown to declaratively mirror the computation of partial-order planning à la UCPOP [Wel94], HEC provides a formal basis for expressing the abstraction planning of, for example, hierarchical transition networks [EHN94], and, in general, for expressing all the INTERRAP processes, such as mental models, reflexes, and protocol execution in an inferential setting.

5   Acknowledgements

We are grateful to Alastair Burt, who gave valuable comments on earlier versions of this text and made the effort of proof reading the English.

References

[All84]   J. F. Allen. Towards a general theory of action and time. *Artificial Intelligence*, 23:123–154, 1984.

[BD94]   M. Boddy and T. L. Dean. Deliberation scheduling for problem solving in time-constrained environments. *Artificial Intelligence*, 1(67):245–285, 1994.

[BF95]   A. L. Blum and M. L. Furst. Fast planning through planning graph analysis. In C. S. Mellish, editor, *Proceedings of the International Joint Conference on Artificial Intelligence (IJCAI)*, pages 166–1642, Montreal, Canada, August 1995. Morgan Kaufmann.

[Bow87]   C. M. Bowling, editor. *Principles and Elements of Thought Construction, Artificial Intelligence, and Cognitive Robotics*. Csy Pub, 1987.

[Bro91]   R. A. Brooks. Intelligence without reason. Technical Report 1293, MIT AI Laboratory, April 1991.

[BT94]   S. Bornscheuer and M. Thielscher. Representing concurrent actions and solving conflicts. In B. Nebel and L. Dreschler-Fischer, editors, *Proceedings of the German Annual Conference on Artificial Intelligence (KI)*, volume 861 of *LNAI*, pages 16–27, Saarbrücken, Germany, September 1994. Springer.

[BT97]   S. Bornscheuer and M. Thielscher. Explicit and implicit indeterminism: Reasoning about uncertain and contradictory specifications of dynamic systems. *Journal of Logic Programming*, 31(1–3):119–155, 1997.

[CL90]   P. R. Cohen and H. J. Levesque. Intention is choice with commitment. *Artificial Intelligence*, 42(3):213–261, 1990.

[Dav96]   J. Davila. Reactive Pascal and the Event Calculus. In U. Siegmund and M. Thielscher, editors, *Proc. of the FAPR'96 Workshop on Reasoning about Actions and Planning in Complex Environments*, volume 11 of *Technical Report AIDA*, 1996.

[DGKK98] P. Doherty, J. Gustafsson, L. Karlsson, and J. Kvarnström. TAL: Temporal action logics language specification and tutorial. *Linköping Electronic Articles in Computer and Information Science*, 3(15), 1998. URL: http://www.ep.liu.se/ea/cis/1998/015/.

[EHN94]   K. Erol, J. Hendler, and D. Nau. Htn planning: complexity and expressivity. In *Proc. of the 12th National Conference on Artifical Intelligence (AAAI-94)*, volume 2, Seattle, Washington, 1994. AAAI Press.

[EHT96]   K. Eder, S. Hölldobler, and M. Thielscher. An abstract machine for reasoning about situations, actions, and causality. In R. Dyckhoff, H. Herre, and P. Schroeder-Heister, editors, *Proceedings of the International Workshop on Extensions of Logic Programming (ELP)*, volume 1050 of *LNAI*, pages 137–151, Leipzig, Germany, March 1996. Springer.

[EM91]   C. Elsaesser and R. MacMillan. Representation and algorithms for multi-agent adversarial planning. Technical report, The MITRE Corporation, 1991.

[Esh88]   K. Eshghi. Abductive planning with event calculus. In *Proc. of the Fifth International Conference on Logic Programming*, pages 562–578, 1988.

[FK97]   T. H. Fung and R. A. Kowalski. The IFF Proof Procedure for Abductive Logic Programming. *Journal of Logic Programming*, 33(2):151–165, 1997.

[FN71]   R. E. Fikes and N. J. Nilsson. Strips: A new approach to the application of theorem proving to problem solving. *Artifical Intelligence*, 2(3/4):189–208, 1971.

[GHS⁺92] G. Große, S. Hölldobler, J. Schneeberger, U. Sigmund, and M. Thielscher. Equational Logic Programming, Actions, and Change. Technical Report AIDA–92–14, FG Intellektik, TH Darmstadt, 1992. Appeared in *Proc. Joint International Conference and Symposium on Logic Programming JIC-SLP'92*.

[GL87]   M. P. Georgeff and A. L. Lansky. Reactive reasoning and planning. In *Proc. of the 6th National Conference on Artificial Intelligence*, 1987.

[GL88]   M. Gelfond and V. Lifschitz. The stable model semantics for logic pro-
           gramming. In R. A. Kowalski and K. Bowen, editors, *Proceedings 5th Inter-
           national Conference on Logic Programming*, pages 1070–1080, Cambridge,
           Massachusetts, 1988. MIT Press.

[GLR91]   M. Gelfond, V. Lifschitz, and A. Rabinov. What are the limitations of the
           situation calculus? In S. Boyer, editor, *Automated Reasoning, Essays in
           Honor of Woody Bledsoe*, pages 167–181. Kluwer Academic, 1991.

[Gre69]   C. Green. Applications of Theorem Proving to Problem Solving. In *Pro-
           ceedings of IJCAI'69*, 1969.

[GRS88]   A. van Gelder, K. Ross, and J.S. Schlipf. Unfounded sets and well–founded
           semantics for general logic programs.   In *Proceedings of the 7th ACM
           SIGACT-SIGMOD-SIGART Symposium on Principles of Database Systems*,
           pages 221–230, 1988.

[Hoa69]   C. A. R. Hoare. An axiomatic basis for computer programming. *Communi-
           cations of the ACM*, 12:576–580 and 583, 1969.

[HS90]   S. Hölldobler and J. Schneeberger. A new deductive approach to planning.
           New Generation Computing, 8:225–244, 1990.

[HT96]   C. S. Herrmann and M. Thielscher. Reasoning about continuous processes.
           In B. Clancey and D. Weld, editors, *Proceedings of the AAAI National Con-
           ference on Artificial Intelligence*, pages 639–644, Portland, OR, August 1996.
           MIT Press.

[JF01]   C. G. Jung and K. Fischer. Theory and practice of hybrid agents. Technical
           Report RR-01-01, DFKI GmbH, Germany, 2001.

[JFB96]   C. G. Jung, K. Fischer, and A. Burt. Multi-agent planning using an abduc-
           tive event calculus. Technical Report RR-96-4, DFKI GmbH, Saarbrücken,
           Germany, 1996.

[KM97]   A. C. Kakas and R. Miller. Reasoning about actions, narratives, and ramifi-
           cations. *Electronic Transactions on Artificial Intelligence*, 1(4):39–72, 1997.

[Kow79]   R. A. Kowalski. *Logic for Problem Solving*, volume 7 of *Artificial Intelligence
           Series*. Elsevier Science Publisher B.V. (North-Holland), 1979.

[KS86]   R. A. Kowalski and M. Sergot. A logic-based calculus of events. *New Gen-
           eration Computing*, 4(1):67–95, 1986.

[KS94]   R. A. Kowalski and F. Sadri. The situation calculus and event calculus
           compared. In M. Bruynooghe, editor, *Proceedings of the International Logic
           Programming Symposium*, pages 539—553, Ithaca, New York, 1994. The
           MIT Press.

[KS96a]   H. A. Kautz and B. Selman. Pushing the envelope: Planning, propositional
           logic, and stochastic search. In B. Clancey and D. Weld, editors, *Proceedings
           of the AAAI National Conference on Artificial Intelligence*, pages 1194–1201,
           Portland, OR, August 1996. MIT Press.

[KS96b]   R. A. Kowalski and F. Sadri. Towards a unified agent architecture that
           combines rationality with reactivity. In D. Pedreschi and C. Zaniolo, editors,
           Logic in Databases, volume 1154 of *Lecture Notes in Computer Science*.
           Springer-Verlag, 1996.

[Kun87]   K. Kunen. Negation in Logic Programming. *Journal of Logic Programming*,
           4:231 – 245, 1987.

[Lin95]   F. Lin. Embracing causality in specifying the indirect effects of actions. In
           C. S. Mellish, editor, *Proceedings of the International Conference on Artifi-
           cal Intelligence*, pages 1985–1991, Montreal, Canada, August 1995. Morgan
           Kaufmann.

[LLL+94]   Y. Lespérance, H. J. Levesque, F. Lin, D. Marcu, R. Reiter, and R. B. Scherl. A Logical Approach to High-Level Robot Programming: A Progress Report. In B. Kuipers, editor, *Control of the Physical World by Intelligent Systems: Papers from the '94 AAAI Fall Symposium*, pages 79–85, New Orleans, 1994.

[LRL97]   H. Levesque, R. Reiter, and Y. Lespérance. Golog: A logic programming language for dynamic domains. *Journal of Logic Programming*, 31:59–84, 1997.

[LS95]   F. Lin and Y. Shoham. Provably correct theories of action. *Journal of ACM*, 42(2):293–320, 1995.

[McC58]   J. McCarthy. Programs with Common Sense. In *Proceedings of the Symposium on the Mechanization of Thought Processes*, volume 1, pages 77–84, London, November 1958.

[McC63]   J. McCarthy. *Situations and Actions and Causal Laws*. Stanford Artificial Intelligence Project, Memo 2, 1963.

[McC85]   J. McCarthy. Formalization of STRIPS in situation calculus. Technical report, Formal Reasoning Group, Department of Computer Science, Stanford University, 1985.

[MH69]   J. McCarthy and P. J. Hayes. Some philosophical problems from the standpoint of artificial intelligence. *Machine Intelligence*, 4:463–502, 1969.

[Mis91]   L. Missiaen. *Localized Abductive Planning with the Event Calculus*. PhD Dissertation, K.U. Leuven, Leuven, September 1991.

[Mül99]   J. P. Müller. The right agent (architecture) to do the right thing. In J. P. Müller, M. P. Singh, and A. S. Rao, editors, *Intelligent Agents V — Proceedings of the Fifth International Workshop on Agent Theories, Architectures, and Languages (ATAL-98)*, Lecture Notes in Artificial Intelligence. Springer-Verlag, Heidelberg, 1999.

[Nil84]   N. J. Nilsson. Shakey the robot. Technical report, SRI AI Center, April 1984.

[Rei91]   R. Reiter. The frame problem in the situation calculus: A simple solution (sometimes) and a completeness result for goal regression. In V. Lifschitz, editor, *Artificial Intelligence and Mathematical Theory of Computation*, pages 359–380. Academic Press, 1991.

[Rei99]   R. Reiter. Knowledge in action: Logical foundations for describing and implementing dynamical systems. URL: http://www.cs.toronto.edu/cogrobo/, 1999.

[RG91]   A. S. Rao and M. P. Georgeff. Modeling Agents Within a BDI-Architecture. In R. Fikes and E. Sandewall, editors, *Proc. of the 2rd International Conference on Principles of Knowledge Representation and Reasoning (KR'91)*, pages 473–484, Cambridge, Mass., April 1991. Morgan Kaufmann.

[Sac74]   E. D. Sacerdoti. Planning in a Hierarchy of Abstraction Spaces. *Artificial Intelligence*, 5:115–135, 1974.

[San94]   E. Sandewall. *Features and Fluents. The Representation of Knowledge about Dynamical Systems*. Oxford University Press, 1994.

[Sha89]   M. Shanahan. Prediction is deduction but explanation is abduction. In *Proceedings of the IJCAI 89*, page 1055, 1989.

[Sha90]   M. Shanahan. Representing continuous change in the event calculus. In *Proceedings of the ECAI 90*, pages 589–603, August 1990.

[Sha95]   M. Shanahan. A circumscriptive calculus of events. *Artificial Intelligence Journal*, 77:249–284, 1995.

[Sha97a] M. Shanahan. Event calculus planning revisited. In *Proc. of the Fourth European Conference on Planning*, 1997.

[Sha97b]   M. Shanahan. Noise and the Common Sense Informatic Situation for a
           Mobile Robot. In *Proc. AAAI'96*, pages 1098–1103, 1997.

[Sha97c]   M. Shanahan. *Solving the Frame Problem: A Mathematical Investigation of
           the Common Sense Law of Inertia*. MIT Press, 1997.

[Sho90]   Y. Shoham. Agent-oriented programming. Technical report, Stanford Uni-
           versity, 1990.

[Spi92]   M. Spivey. *The Z notation (second edition)*. Prentice Hall International,
           Hempel Hempstead, England, 1992.

[Thi97]   M. Thielscher. Ramification and causality. *Artificial Intelligence*, 89(1–
           2):317–364, 1997.

[Thi99]   M. Thielscher. From Situation Calculus to Fluent Calculus: State update
           axioms as a solution to the inferential frame problem. *Artificial Intelligence
           Journal*, 1999. (To appear).

[tTvH98]   A. ten Teije and F. van Harmelen. Characterising approximate problem-
           solving: From partially fulfilled preconditions to partially achieved function-
           ality. In H. Prade, editor, *Proc. of the 13th Biennial European Conference
           on Artificial Intelligence (ECAI'98)*, pages 78–82, 1998.

[Wel94]   D. Weld. An introduction to least-commitment planning. *AI Magazine*,
           15(4):27–62, 1994.

[WHR96]   R. Washington and B. Hayes Roth. Incremental Abstraction Planning for
           Limited-Time Situations. In *New Directions in AI Planning*, pages 91–102.
           IOS press, 1996.

Heterogeneous Scheduling and Rotation

Thomas Sjöland[1,2], Per Kreuger[1], and Martin Aronsson[1]

[1] SICS, The Swedish Institute of Computer Science AB, Sweden
[2] IMIT/KTH, The Royal Institute of Technology, Kista, Sweden

Abstract. This article highlights an application in the area of decision support for planning transports in a railway company utilising constraint logic programming and a flexible design which has been successfully tested on real world data.

We discuss the problem formulation for the co-ordination of distinct sub-problems, the allocation of track resources to transports, the allocation of vehicles to transports, and the allocation of personnel to perform the transportation tasks in a railway company and the development of a *heterogeneous constraint model* which is usable also for other production planning problems.

Using constraints as the key technology, we discuss approaches to find interfacing principles to combine several solvers.

1 Introduction

This paper describes a practical application of constraint logic programming [31, 49] developed during a few years by a group at SICS AB in co-operation with the strategic development unit of SJ and Green Cargo AB, a company handling goods transports for the Swedish railway. The paper is an overview of the project, the architectural considerations that were of interest in the system design, and a discussion on use of the techniques. More details can be found in the different reports produced in the project [4, 32, 36, 37, 39, 52]. References to other work in this area are introduced in the text.

1.1 Organisation of This Paper

The paper starts with an introduction to the project in section 2. The problem of resource allocation is discussed in section 3 followed by section 4 on the scheduling sub-problem and section 5 on the rotation sub-problem. In section 6 we discuss architectures for co-ordination problems, with section 6.2 on the particular co-ordination problem occurring in railway planning. The concept of abstraction is discussed in section 7. In section 8 we discuss the main techniques: constraint programming (section 8.1), and OR-techniques (section 8.2). For the latter case we discuss network flows, and Lagrange-relaxation. The section on techniques is finalised in section 8.3 with a discussion on the relation of OR-techniques to constraint programming.

A.C. Kakas, F. Sadri (Eds.): Computat. Logic (Kowalski Festschrift), LNAI 2407, pp. 655–675, 2002.

2   The Project

The problem is characterised by a more or less fixed track net and by the division into sub-problems that are traditionally used in production planning in the railway industry.

The project has built an interactive tool that contains specialised solvers for sub-problems and mechanisms to subdivide, abstract and refine problem specifications. In a general perspective the fundamental mechanisms can be the core of a framework for decision support systems for a large class of complex technical systems. The used platform consists of SICStus Prolog [20] for some novel global constraints, CPLEX for OR-based solvers, and Mozart-Oz [29] for co-ordination of the solvers.

The software produced in the project can be understood as a support system for a manager responsible of the planning task. A fundamental property is that planning steps can be iterated since the input and output data have the same format. This allows successive planning steps where new orders are added to those that have already been given resources, even though this approach excludes the finding of optimal plans/schedules. This type of problem solving strategy where a sub-problem is partially solved in order to constrain the search space for a subsequent planning step is sometimes named *iterative* planning.

One goal of the project is to enable a uniform access model of the information in a set of spaces which might use e.g. different constraint models. From the perspective of the user (or a control program) the different spaces should ideally appear as a single one. Furthermore the access model should offer a common information model and a uniform language for access and modification of the spaces.

2.1   Decision Support

Decision support systems for planning activities in companies have been built using logic programming systems [4, 36, 38, 39, 54]. Essential to the success of such tools is the use of constraints and the construction of intuitive user interfaces as well as modifiability. Production plans can be interactively improved and optimised, leading to dramatic cuts in overheads.

Planning of the complicated and numerous activities of a supplier of transport services must for many reasons use manual decisions at decisive points. A decision support system is not intended to replace the expert who makes these decisions with a program, but rather to release him/her of the burden of routine decisions and to supply as good a decision background as possible.

The problem can also be divided into sub-problems. Each problem solving component could be seen as a separate *planning agent* (see section 6). This clarifies the decision process where users with different areas of responsibility co-operate, each with limited knowledge of the detailed models of the others, and according to common (agreed or centrally dictated) criteria build a working tactical plan.

In spite of this there are also significant gains to be made in the co-ordination of decisions that clearly affect several parts of the activity. Planning components should be capable of communicating suggested solutions and local costs, and working with different levels of abstraction. With this approach it is natural that a user inspects the results and controls the direction in which the system should proceed, which methods to apply etc.

3 Resource Allocation

Resources can in general model a wide variety of entities, for instance processing equipment in a production process, a packet router in a communication network, personnel, vehicles, track links, shunting yards, buffer areas in a transport net for goods, etc.

An important goal of the overall planning is to diminish the total cost for using resources. This puts the focus on the problem of co-ordinating the planning processes involved in time-tabling and allocation of resources in railway nets [39, 4]. The three most important of these resources are *track time slots*, *engines* and *travelling personnel*.

3.1 Railway Networks

A railway network is a graph where the nodes are *locations*, places where significant *operations* can occur, and the arcs are *tracks*. The operations are for instance meeting between trains using the same part of the net in different directions, overtaking of slower trains by faster ones, waiting for safe security distances to be achieved, unloading of cargo, reassignment of engines, cars and personnel etc. There is internal state in the nodes, which for some sub-problems can be abstracted away, such as information about exactly which tracks are connected and how they can be used. The arcs are either directed or undirected. Allowed paths in the network are predefined.

The network representation used in the project contains for each station a maximum number of trains allowed to be simultaneously present at the station. This limit is expressed as a cumulative constraint [1].

3.2 Production Planning in the Railway Industry

Production planning in the railway industry involves the planning of train movements given a specification of (train-)*trips*. In order to be executable, each trip must get allocated track time slots for certain time intervals, vehicle resources that can perform the movement and traveling personnel, foremost engine drivers.

Trips model individual trains traversing the network. Suitable paths for a given trip are given by the user. The set of trips that are needed to satisfy a certain transport requirement, the *train orders*, is decided in advance and represented for instance as a number of *trip specifications* stating *demands* on time points of departure and arrival.

In the project a specification language is used to express the trip specifications. The paths that are to be traversed by a given trip is completely determined by such a specification. The language allows the expression of more or less exact time specifications and for stops at arbitrary places in the path of a train, and the specification of all the information required by the different planning components, including recurrent (for instance hourly, daily or weekly) trips. A graphical tool was developed to support this process.

A *task* represents the traversal of a track by an individual trip. With each task is associated a unique identifier and the departure time and waiting duration at the origin of the traversal. Each task has a *traversal duration* representing the minimum time distance between the departures of any two trips traversing a track in opposite directions and another duration called *headway*, the minimum duration after a trip departs from or arrives at a location in the network before a following trip running in the same direction on the same track may depart from or arrive at that location. These parameters are determined from the length of the track and the speed parameters of the track and the trip.

In general one would like to generate specifications starting from descriptions of transportation needs given as flows. Methods to solve such problems have been developed in operations analysis. For an excellent survey see [14].

4   Scheduling

A *scheduling problem* consists of a number of *tasks* utilising resources. A task has restrictions on *start time*, *stop time* and *time extension*. Often the tasks are *partially ordered*. A totally ordered subset of tasks is often called a *job*. Each task uses one or more resources during certain time intervals.

A *schedule* is the result of assigning values to the time points and durations associated with each task in a plan so that no limitations on resource usage are violated. A *plan specification* denotes a (set of) schedule(s) in terms of a given network and a specification of the required set of train trips to be performed. This specification allows limiting the arrival, departure and waiting durations for arbitrary locations in the path of a trip. The result of this phase of the planning is a completely determined time table.

The *railway scheduling problem* can be concisely stated thus:

> Schedule a set of train trips over a fixed network of pre-determined paths where trains travel through a network with mixed double and single tracks connecting nodes where trains can meet and overtake while maintaining reasonable bounds on waiting time.

Scheduling is in general a very difficult computational problem [26]. Nevertheless the many practical applications for methods in this area make it fairly well studied [28, 3]. Railway scheduling is normally treated with OR-techniques [22], but recently such problems have been successfully modelled and solved with constraint programming [39, 53]. Many of the best approaches to solving scheduling problems during the latest ten years have been introduced as global constraints

[6, 7, 16, 17, 19]. We refer to [39] for more details of the finite domain constraint model used in the prototype scheduler used in the project.

4.1   Job-Shop Scheduling

The simple case where the network consists only of double tracks can be modelled as a job-shop scheduling (JSS) problem [5, 6, 17, 18] viewing train trips as jobs and tracks as resources. Each train trip traversing a track represents a task where the traversal duration is taken as the task extension. Thus the trip scheduling problem can be viewed as a job-shop scheduling problem with release times and either sequence dependent durations [12, 13] or sequence dependent setup times with fixed durations [35, 40, 55, 56, 62].

5   Rotation

Rotation is the problem of assigning resources (engines, personnel etc.) to perform transportation tasks. Some types of tasks can be understood as cyclic processes or flows. One aspect of a resource rotation problem is the determination of the movement of the resources as *circuits*, that is cyclic routes in a graph. Another is the allocation of individual resources to tasks, often called *rostering*. The references [11, 27, 46, 51, 57, 58, 59, 60] put the problem in context.

5.1   Rotation of Engines

A distinct sub-problem is that of determining *engine rotations* describing the route of each engine through the net. The solution makes sure that each trip is allocated an engine from departure to arrival. This also involves determining *passive transports* of engines where an engine is moved from the place of arrival for one trip to the place of departure of the next trip of its rotation. This *passive* transport can either occur through the engine itself moving via free track time slots to the place of departure of its next task (empty train, a.k.a. "deadhead") or through the engine under certain conditions joining an already determined trip (multiple trains, a.k.a. "twohead"). The latter is often preferred since the cost of such a passive transport is most often lower than for "deadheads". This problem can be solved with traditional optimisation techniques given that a fully determined timetable has been generated beforehand. If not, the problem becomes significantly harder.

If an arc in the graph represents a *turning* of an engine from one trip to another, the model is a classical network flow (see section 8.2 below) only if the decision whether the arc satisfies the model can be made locally, that is independent of other tasks (trips) than the two that the arc connects. In practice this is rarely the case. In production planning for the railway industry two important rotation problems occur that do not have this property:

- The problem to generate engine rotations without a fixed schedule
- The problem to generate circuits of a determined "length" for instance working periods with daily rest periods at fixed locations

How hard it is to solve such problems depends strongly on the conditions being posed on the arcs of the graph. If the condition can be determined locally the problem can be modelled as a *network flow*. For certain problem structures, such as determining rotations without considering different engine types, there exist very efficient optimising solvers [2, 25] (see section 8.2 below). For instance it takes just a few minutes to produce a full scale engine rotation plan when you do not consider engine types. Considering different engine types, the problem has a drastically different complexity [41] and an otherwise comparable example takes up to five hours. In addition to the demands that are put on the engine rotations there are constraints for the circuits (service periods) that are parts of the rotations. These are for instance limited in length, typically requiring one of two full days and nights, which complicates the problem considerably.

5.2 Rotation of Personnel

Finally *personnel rotations* must be generated. In the same way as in the case with the engines the personnel must be at the right place at the right time in order for the trip to be executable. Also personnel must sometimes travel "passively" for instance homewards for their daily rest. Furthermore there are additional limitations on the personnel rotations. These depend on legislation, formal agreements and locally varying praxis and were not treated by this project.

6   Co-ordination of Planning Agents

Since many co-ordination problems are NP-hard in themselves and the interaction is complex, problem decomposition and careful analysis of the interdependencies between sub-problems are necessary to handle real world problem sizes.

Co-ordination problems are well known from for instance the car industry, and are often referred to as *supply-chain management* [8, 42]. The problem is to reduce as much as possible the storage of expensive semi-products and components. The method to buy components from sub-contractors and to hold minimal storage drastically reduces the cost of production but it also tends to increase the sensitivity of the systems to disturbances. A certain co-ordination of production plans is therefore often necessary to uphold security of delivery.

6.1 Agent Models

By sub-dividing a planning system into sub-problem solvers and specifying the interactions between the different parts of the system a distributed software model is achieved. Such models are nowadays often named *agent models*, especially if the different parts have a certain degree of independence. One reason to use this design principle is to clarify the communication between different actors (internal and external) and different organisational units. Another is to reduce the impact of the inherent complexity of producing a plan.

In general it is possible to make a division into agents in several alternative dimensions. The choice of division is controlled partly by performance demands on the planning and partly by organisational demands on the architecture of the system. In principle the model could also be distributed to physically separated locations in a computer network [23]. In the case where the purpose is to considerably increase the performance by running the software on several computers it is required that the problem can be divided in such a way that parallel computation is enabled. In an agent model where a plan manager is responsible for the total cost optimisation, the different agents could be made more independent.

6.2   Co-ordination in Railway Planning

The above described railway transportation problems can be seen as three separate resource allocation problems. Traditionally the three sub-problems are solved in sequence in a *waterfall model* containing a certain amount of manual feedback.

The need to co-plan the use of different resources for each task puts the co-ordination problem into focus. Firstly because of the size of the problem there is a need to co-ordinate the construction of sub-plans for each of the three resource problems, and secondly there are significant gains to be made by loosening the strict order between the planning steps that are today the dominating approach to solving the total problem. One example of this circumstance is the following:

Assume that a plan specification contains a certain slack in the time specifications for departures and arrivals. Assume also that a solution to the track allocation is fixed. This means that certain departures are determined to time-points that occur in close proximity after some of the arrival times for points of departure for other trips at the same station. Then the same engine cannot be used to serve certain sequences of tasks which in turn can destroy the possibility to efficiently use the vehicle resources.

To keep as much as possible of the slack in departure times in the general case evidently gives room to generate better rotations. Unfortunately the very efficient traditional methods (network flows) to generate rotations break down when the times are allowed to vary. This holds in general when the question of whether a trip can be followed by another in a circuit cannot be determined locally, that is with knowledge only about these two tasks.

Therefore it is necessary to use heuristic methods to generate rotations that can be used to restrict (partially order) specifications in such a way that the track time slot plans that are generated in accordance with this limited specification allow us to form the circuits that are, in some sense, locally good. Optimal rotations can then be generated for these track time slot plans in a traditional way.

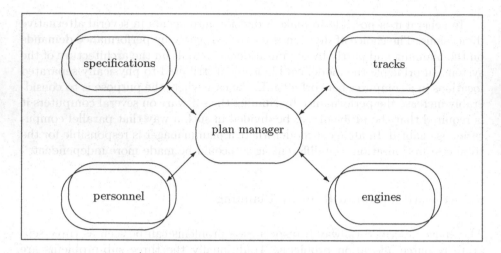

Fig. 1. Agent Model Based on Resource Types

Modelling Train Planning with an Agent Model The rotation planner for engines, together with the track allocation planner and their interfaces can be seen as a minimal agent model, where the subdivision of planning agents is based on *resource types* (figure 1). It divides the system as follows: The *service producers* generate train orders and negotiate contracts with customers, *track allocation planners* supply track resources (generate time table), the *engine planners* supply engines (generate engine rotations) the *personnel planners* supply personnel (generate personnel rotations) and the *plan manager* co-ordinates the negotiations and maintain the total plan. The main aspect of agent modelling used by the project is the translation between different representations for different sub-problems. The agents are not running independently and automatically.

Other approaches to division of the planning/scheduling problem might be useful, for instance *regional* where different planning agents schedule the local plans on a regional level, *train types* or *customer groups* based on different responsibilities for the service salesmen.

7   Abstraction for Reducing Complexity

In order to achieve the gains that can be made by co-ordinating the shared-resource usage of the local activities, it is necessary to handle problems with different degrees of detail. The need arises to in a uniform and unambiguous way move the point of view between these different levels. Typically a planner in the agent model handles a specialised form of plan abstractions for the relevant sub-plans representing limitations, cost estimates etc.

One way to attack the problem is to abstract from the given solutions to a common problem description that keeps as much as possible of the locally good properties of the sub-plans. An abstract (less fine-grained) model is needed to estimate the total costs at the strategic and central level and concrete and detailed local cost measures for each sub-problem. The aim is to limit the local choices so that they at least meet the elementary demands on the central level. Another approach is to simplify the problem by for instance combining simple resources to more complex ones in order to reduce the total set of tasks in a given problem. In order for such abstraction techniques to be meaningful, an abstracted problem should of course be simpler to solve than the problem you would have had if you had combined the original problem descriptions to begin with.

Descriptions of constraint spaces with different levels of detail should be formally related. Such a formalisation must also allow a computationally robust implementation. The abstraction of constraint expressions from different spaces must guarantee that important information is not lost, or could be regained with relative ease.

One practical way to handle the complexity is to abstract from the concrete track net. This is done in the project by using the concept of headway to lift the number of nodes in the net to just contain stations and crossings that actually contain 5 000-10 000 exchanges, sensors and signals. For each given path it was considered appropriate to schedule 10-100 points.

7.1   Task Hierarchies

When dividing a resource problem into smaller parts the need arises to merge sub-plans generated locally with incomplete knowledge about the resource conflicts that occur when they are to be co-ordinated.

The approach of the project [37] is one that builds on a concept of task that is organised in a hierarchy. Each primitive task and job is represented as a *task structure* with an unambiguous sub-structure. A *problem structure* is represented partly by such a *task structure*, partly by a (partial) *order relation* on the individual tasks and their parts and finally partly by a formal representation of the *resources* used by the tasks. *Abstractions* and *concretisations* are defined as mappings on problem structures.

7.2   Abstraction of Time in the Scheduling Problem

Time points in the constraints are represented as finite domain variables in the scheduler used in the project [39]. This means that the scheduling problem is discrete. Since different parts of the network might have different loads there is a possibility of generating a large number of redundant solutions with this approach.

The traversal time parameter for an arc in the abstract network should cover the longest possible time between the two nodes in the concrete network. This might prohibit the finding of a schedule if the abstraction is applied on parts of the network where there is much traffic. Two possible abstractions are investigated in [32]:

- Use fewer time points in the intervals described by the finite domain variables.
- Use a simpler network such that only those nodes where significant operations such as overturns, meetings and reallocation of engines or personnel are allowed, are taken into account. A later phase can generate times for stops at intermediate nodes.

A conclusion from these experiments is that the time required for scheduling is up to four times shorter for the best type of abstraction than for the concrete scheduling. Furthermore, the abstract scheduling requires less memory than the concrete scheduling.

7.3 Planning Strategies

Mechanisms for abstraction and concretisation can in principle be combined in complex patterns, called strategies. Such strategies can be used both to enable planning of bigger problems that are possible to handle as a unit and to reduce the required time for the planning by dividing the problem into smaller pieces.

A strategy can be used for instance to co-ordinate the results of several track resource planning sessions. This is interesting for instance if remote trains travel through a geographical area where also local traffic occurs, and can also be used to merge solutions when planning tracks in geographically closely related areas. Strategies need not to be limited to abstractions and concretisations, and can furthermore be used to control the co-ordination between the different sub-problems.

Planning Language In order to make it practical to use strategies it is required that a strategy can easily be defined. This becomes possible with the aid of a planning language.

Such a language offers possibilities to use mechanisms for abstraction and concretisation. It also supports constructions to express conditional behaviour, so that if one part of a strategy is failing, a new attempt is made to solve this part of the problem in another way. Finally a strategy that is entered as an expression in the language needs to be stored and again be read into the system.

It is worth noting that a planning language is useful not just for solution of the problem at hand in the transport sector, but that it can simplify the solution of many types of larger planning problems.

8 Techniques

8.1 Constraint Programming

Constraint programming (CP) [31, 61] is based on the idea of an abstract space of statements (restrictions or conditions), a constraint space.

Some of these statements can be understood as fully determined. Take for instance the claim that a given train will depart from Avesta 15.05 Thursday April 15th in the year 2001. Other statements are less exact for instance that a steel manufacturer needs to transport between 320 and 380 kilotons of steel from Hofors and Hellefors to Malmö next year. Both these statements can be represented as conditions in a constraint programming system. These are named *constraints* or restrictions on the value space for the variables contained by the statement.

It is certainly non-trivial to determine in a space of such statements how for instance these two statements are related given some mathematical model of a planning problem but under certain circumstances is is possible to make calculations with such abstract objects and to determine for instance logical consistency, that is to decide whether the statements are possibly both true or not.

It is also possible to compute one or several *witnesses*, that is assignments of values to all variables in a space. This is called to *enumerate the search space* for a given problem and in general it contains the utilisation of a search procedure. Such witnesses can in the production planning domain for instance be concrete production plans.

If many such plans are generated they can be compared with respect to different measures of *cost*. To find the best plan is modelled as an optimisation problem in the constraint system.

Much of the search when enumerating the search space for a given problem can often be eliminated with a technique named *constraint propagation*. This means briefly that each statement that is not completely determined is considered as a temporarily interrupted computation which can be made to interact with other similar concurrent computations. Computations are interrupted when the information that is needed to determine a value is missing but they continue once the information is later available.

A constraint programming system can be seen as a set of parallel processes which communicate, interact and are synchronised via shared variables in a dataflow graph. Whether it is possible to compute solutions for a given problem or not is to a large extent depending on the expressive power of the language being used to express statements about the problem. To formulate a mathematical model of some real process in such a language is in general a very hard problem. In spite of this there have been good results by using constraint techniques to model and solve known hard planning problems for instance many classical scheduling and resource allocation problems.

Consider the example with a departure time. If it is known one might like to represent it as a number. Assume now that it is not known, but that there is nevertheless some information available about it, for instance that it must be between 11 and 12 some given day and that it must follow after the arrival time for some other trip.

This is a very strong restriction of the value for the departure time. Yet it contains an ambiguity which separates it in a fundamental way from the totally determined one.

A number of constraint statements can for instance express the relation between this departure time and other departure times (or arrivals) and can be said to represent a specification of a production plan. The more determined it is, the closer it is to a finished plan with totally determined times.

In principle it is possible to construct a production plan by successively adding more and more information to a space containing conditions (a constraint space).

Finite Domains The constraint programming systems that have been most actively developed the last ten years are those that handle *finite domains*. In such a system each variable can take on values from a finite set of discrete values. This type of variable is natural to use to model discrete entities such as the number of engines or personnel that have been allocated to a given task. They are, however, unnecessarily restrictive when the modelling concerns values that can be assumed to vary over continuous domains (with an infinite number of possible values), for instance time.

Global Constraints A global constraint is a way to express properties of many variables in one statement.

The first type of constraint that was studied in constraint programming was constraints that relate two variables, for instance $<, \leq, \neq, =$ etc. In contrast to these simple binary constraints the focus has in recent years more and more been on complicated constraints between an unlimited number of variables. Examples of such constraints are such that relate variables with the value of a linear sum or such that maintain pairwise dis-equality of an arbitrarily large set of variables.

Such constraints can in principle often be encoded in terms of a set of simpler binary constraints which semantically have the same meaning. This is rarely practical, however, since an efficient solution is often too computationally complex to be realised by simply considering the variables in a pairwise fashion. The expression *global constraints* for this type of constraint was introduced in [9] and refers to arguments that can be made over a multitude of variables related with a non-binary condition.

Global constraints are abstractions of more complicated properties of problems and enables computations on a more detailed model. Many times methods from operations analysis or algorithm theory, which operate on graphs, can efficiently and naturally be integrated into a constraint programming system as global constraints. This is an active and very promising research area in constraint programming. For a systematic description of a large number of global constraints see [10].

Constraint solving is often limited by a prohibitively large search space, for instance by the enumeration of many redundant variants. The use of meta-operations such as constraint relaxation, redundant modeling [21] etc. could be utilised to improve the search behaviours of a solver. Another approach is to use abstraction to speed up search problems. This has been investigated in AI for general search problems [33, 34, 63].

Prolog [20], the dominating logic programming language, now standardised, is developed by adding new expressive possibilities, for instance constraints, object orientation, functional and meta-logical extensions and embeddings, parallel execution models and interoperability with other systems such as databases, GUI toolkits, Java etc.

Mozart-Oz [29] is especially targeted at modern intra/inter-net applications. It is designed to handle concurrency and multi-paradigm programming. This language utilises logical variables as in logic programming, but bases its operational semantics not on SLD-resolution as Prolog does, but on a rewrite semantics driven by entailment as in concurrent constraint programming [50]. This approach, while more general and flexible than that of Prolog, naturally embeds logic programming as one of its programming paradigms [30] together with higher-order functional and object-oriented programming. Constraint programming is also well supported [43, 44]. If needed, the user can explicitly program the search.

8.2   OR-techniques

Techniques from operations analysis, for instance linear programming (LP) and integer programming (IP) handles models efficiently where most of the variables are continuous and where a simple and well defined cost function well captures the "goodness" of different solutions to a given problem. OR-techniques are often based on massive computations where input data is given in the form of a complete problem description.

Linear Programming Linear programming is used to model optimising problems where the cost function can be expressed as a linear sum over continuous variables and where the conditions are linear inequalities over these.

A linear program:

$$c_1 x_1 + \cdots + c_n x_n \tag{1}$$

is maximized where

$$a_{11} x + \cdots + a_{1n} x_n \leq b_1$$
$$\vdots \tag{2}$$
$$a_{m1} x_1 + \cdots + a_{mn} x_{n \leq b_m}$$

and

$$x_1 \geq 0, \ldots x_n \geq 0 \tag{3}$$

Simplex is the oldest and most well known algorithm to solve this type of problem. Despite that Simplex in most applications has very good complexity properties (polynomial time complexity) there is for certain classes of problems specialised algorithms which are even more efficient. An example of such an algorithm is *network flow optimisation* (see below).

The main disadvantage with Simplex is that it works only if all the conditions are linear and the variables are continuous. The latter requirement excludes all disjunctive conditions (decision problems) where the value of a function depends on a boolean variable. The research field studies the problems that occur when you loosen the first demand. In OR it is called non-linear programming and will not be further covered here. The problems that can be formulated when variables are allowed to vary over discrete values are studied in the area of integer programming. Sometimes problems where both types of variables occur are called *mixed integer programming*.

Network Flows is a collecting concept for many types of linear programming algorithms which handle optimisation of flows in networks. The area is well researched and many problems are classified. Three important sub-problems in network flow optimisation are *shortest path*, *maximal flow* and *minimal cost*. When computing the shortest path the issue is to find the shortest path between some or all points in a network. Maximal flows encode problems where the flow between pairs of points in the network should be maximised. In minimal cost problems costs are assigned for the flow between different points and the cost of sending flows from one or more points in the network to one or more destinations is minimised.

Since this area is large, the algorithms are fairly dissimilar. For minimal cost problems specialised variants of *Simplex* are often used.

Integer Programming Many times introducing integer variables can be a-voided by using more or less advanced modelling tricks that encode a problem with integer demands as a linear problem. This often demands a comparatively specialised mathematical competence and is far from always possible.

Allowing integer conditions gives a significantly more free modelling, but search must instead be introduced in the algorithms. The search mechanisms that have been developed to solve this type of problem use the cost function in a direct way and solve *linear relaxations* (for parts) of the real problem in each step (iteration).

Many heuristic methods have been developed to make the search converge faster for certain classes of problems. Given a concrete problem, to determine whether it can be modelled as an instance of one of these well studied problem classes also requires specialised mathematical competence.

Lagrange-Relaxation is a technique which can be seen as systematically refor-mulating integer demands as parameters in the cost function in a corresponding

	LP (linear progr.)	IP (integer progr.)	CP (constraint progr.)
domains	continuous	integer/mixed	integer/(finite set), intervals
cost function	optimisation	optimisation, search	domain limitation
scalability	polynomial compl.	some problem classes	good for decision problems
search	SIMPLEX	problem dependence	method integration

Table 1. Some Properties of a Selection of Techniques

linear program. These parameters are then adjusted by solving the relaxed problem with respect to the parameterised cost function. In each step the parameters are adjusted based on the results from the preceding iteration.

Lagrange-relaxation has successfully been used to solve for instance very large vehicle rotation problems [41] and it is also one of the most important techniques to solve pairing problems (see below). For a general introduction to Lagrange-relaxation and also descriptions of a number of so called local search mechanisms which are not treated in this article see [47].

Pairing Algorithms Most optimising systems for personnel planning in the transport sector (that is for travelling personnel) work in two steps:

1. Produce a number of possible circuits, that is jobs containing tasks (legs) that can be executed in order by for instance one person; Each circuit should also (sometimes by adding passive transports) describe a cycle in the track net graph, that is for instance starting and ending in the same location.
2. Solve an optimising problem that contains in choosing among the above generated circuits a subset such that all tasks are a part of at least one cycle and so that a global cost is minimised.

Step two is from a mathematical point of view simple to formulate, even if the size of the problems can many times make them hard to solve. In order to reach as good results as possible you must therefore in step one generate as many candidates as you can handle computationally in step two. It is however in practice often impossible to consider all possible circuits, so the selection that is being made is of utmost importance for the result.

Step two can simplified be described as constructing a matrix, with the tasks as rows and the circuits generated in step one as columns. In the meeting points between the tasks and circuits there is the value 1 if the task is a part of the circuit, and 0 otherwise. Furthermore it is required that each row shall sum up to at least the number of persons needed to perform the job. The task for the optimisation algorithm is now to assign boolean (0/1) values so that the cost is minimised.

There are special algorithms for 0/1-matrices that are very efficient and which can handle large data sets.

Step one is not as simple, and it is here that the commercial solvers differ. This is the step that is named *pairing*. It is important that a good selection of alternative circuits is generated in this step, since these are the only candidates considered in the search for solutions.

The circuits should also satisfy conditions that encode laws and union agreements, which are often hard to represent in a correct and efficient way. It is far from clear that agreements and legislation are mathematically consistent and there is always room for interpretations that often vary locally. Since agreements also change with time, it is important that they are represented in such a way that they are easy to maintain.

In addition a number of heuristically motivated generation conditions are represented and cost parameters, which limit the choice of circuits to those that are considered reasonable.

These two sets of conditions are then used in different methods to generate candidates for circuits for step two. Two main methods are used in this context: *Integer programming* with *Lagrange-relaxation* and *column generation* (see above and for instance [24, 48]). This is still an active area of research within OR.

8.3   OR-techniques Vs. Constraints

OR-methods are very efficient when the model of the real problem suits well into some well known class of problems and the problem is pure, that is independent of a context which is hard to describe or too complex. They are therefore often less suitable at an early stage of the planning process when many parameters are yet unknown. On the other hand they have a given place once the search space of the problem has been shrunk with other methods and when you want to compare results of strategic choices in well delimited sub-problems. You can see many of these methods as planning primitives, methods that can be used to investigate properties of the problem.

In contrast, the techniques that have been developed in constraint programming, using finite domains, work well also when a majority of the variables model naturally discrete entities, when the cost function is hard to determine and when the model contains complicated (for instance non-linear) conditions. As mentioned, many of the best approaches to solving scheduling problems during the latest ten years have been introduced as global constraints [6, 7, 16, 17, 19].

Constraint techniques offer the possibility to maintain a dynamically changing space of statements that represent all currently possible (sub)-plans given the constraints from customer demands, resource limitations and cost considerations. It is for instance possible to choose to optimise parts of a plan late and incrementally and leave the rest of the plan only partially determined. Another advantage is that it is possible to incorporate techniques from operations analysis into the constraint paradigm in the form of global constraints. This makes constraint programming an *integrative* project, where techniques from different areas are collected and made available to modelling experts without requiring from them a detailed algorithmic competence. In this way these two classes of techniques can be said to complement each other. Much current research deals with finding suitable combinations of OR-techniques and constraints.

9   Conclusion

We gave an overview of a project concerning the use of constraint techniques to solve production planning problems in the railway domain. We specified and discussed the problems of scheduling and allocation of transports. In particular we outlined some considerations relevant to the design of a co-ordination model, which loosens the strict sequentiality of current approaches. We also discussed the use of abstraction techniques to reduce complexity and compared constraint programming to techniques from operations research. The project has resulted in the investigation of a number of new techniques and methods that are useful also outside this particular problem area.

10   Acknowledgements

Jolanta Drott and her group at SJ and Green Cargo AB presented the co-ordination problem and provided real-world data and much valued feedback. The co-operation with the Mozart-Oz teams at SICS/Kista, Catholic University of Louvain and at the University of Saarbrücken and the SICStus/Quintus Prolog development team of SICS/Uppsala is invaluable.

Other contributors to the project have been Per Holmberg, Simon Lindblom, Emil Åström, Mats Carlsson, Volker Scholtz, Jan Olsson, Tina Wilhelmsson, Henrik Eriksson and Waldemar Kocjan.

References

[1] Aggoun, A., Beldiceanu, N.: Extending CHIP in Order to Solve Complex Scheduling and Placement Problems. In *Mathematical Computer Modelling* 17(7): pp. 57–73, Pergamon Press Ltd. 1993.

[2] Ahuja, R.K., Magnanti, T.L., Orlin, J.B.: *Network Flows*. Prentice Hall, 1993.

[3] Applegate, D., Cook, W.: A Computational Study of the Job-Shop Scheduling Problem. In *ORSA Journal of Computing*, 3(2): 149-156, 1991.

[4] Aronsson, M., Kreuger, P., Lindblom, S., Holmberg, P.: ACOOR Rapport 1 – TUFF: Systemöversikt och arkitektur. SICS Technical Report T2000/06 (in Swedish)

[5] Baker, K.R.: *Introduction to Sequencing and Scheduling* Wiley & Sons, 1974.

[6] Baptiste, P., Pape, C.L.: A Theoretical and Experimental Comparison of Constraint Propagation Techniques for Disjunctive Scheduling. In the *Proceedings of the Fourteenth International Joint Conference on Artificial Intelligence* Montreal, Quebec, pp. 400–606, 1995.

[7] Baptiste, P., Le Pape, C., Nuijten, W.: Incorporating Efficient Operations Research Algorithms in Constraint Based Scheduling. In *Proceedings of the First International Joint Workshop on Artificial Intelligence and Operations Research*, Timberline Lodge, Oregon, 1995.

[8] Beck, J.C., Fox, M.S.: Supply Chain Co-ordination via Mediated Constraint Relaxation. In *Proceedings of the First Canadian Workshop on Distributed Artificial Intelligence*, May 15 1994.

[9] Beldiceanu, N., Contejean, E.: Introducing Global Constraints in CHIP. In *Mathematical Computer Modelling* 20(12): 97–123, Pergamon Press Ltd. 1994.

[10] Beldiceanu, N.: Global Constraints as Graph Properties on Structured Networks of Elementary Constraints of the Same Type. Research Report R:2000-01, SICS, 2000.

[11] Bodin, L., Golden, B.: Classification in Vehicle Routing and Scheduling. *Networks*, 11(97–108), 1981.

[12] Bianco, L., Ricciardelli, S., Rinaldi, G., Sassano, A.: Scheduling Tasks with Sequence-dependent Processing Times. In *Naval Research Logistics* 35:177–184, 1988.

[13] Brucker, P., Thiele, O.: A Branch & Bound Method for the General-shop Problem with Sequence Dependent Setup-Times. In *OR Spektrum*, 18:145-161, 1996.

[14] Bussieck, M.R., Winter, T., Zimmermann, U.T.: Discrete Optimization in Public Rail Transport. In *Mathematical Programming*, 79:415–444, 1997.

[15] Caseau, Y., Laburthe, F.: Disjunctive Scheduling with Task Intervals. Technical Report 95-25, Laboratoire d'Informatique de l'Ecole Normale Supérieure LIENS, Département de Mathématiques ed d'Informatique, 45 rue d'Ulm, 75232 Paris Cedex 05, France, 1995.

[16] Caseau, Y., Laburthe, F.: Improving Branch and Bound for Job-Shop Scheduling with Constraint Propagation. Technical Report, Laboratoire d'Informatique de l'Ecole Normale Supérieure LIENS, Département de Mathématiques ed d'Informatique, 45 rue d'Ulm, 75232 Paris Cedex 05, France, 1996.

[17] Carlier, J., Pinson, E.: An Algorithm for Solving the Job-Shop Scheduling Problem. In *Management Science* 35(2): 164-176, 1989.

[18] Carlier, J., Pinson, E.: A Practical Use of Jackson's Preemptive Schedule for Solving the Job-Shop Problem. In *Annals of Operations Research*, 26: 269-287, 1990.

[19] Carlier, J., Pinson, E.: Adjustments of Heads and Tails for the Job-Shop Scheduling Problem. In the *European Journal of Operational Research*, 78:146-161, 1994.

[20] Carlsson, M. et. al: *SICStus Programming Manual* at
http://www.sics.se/sicstus.html

[21] Cheng, A.B.M.W., Lee, J.H.M., Wu, J.C.K.: Speeding up Constraint Propagation by Redundant Modeling. In *Second International Conference on Principles and Practice of Constraint Programming CP'96*, volume 1118 of *LNCS*, pp. 91–103, Cambridge, Massachusetts, USA, Aug 1996. Springer-Verlag. Available in
http://www.cse.cuhk.edu.hk/˜isl/dPub2.html#Li.

[22] Cordeau, J.-F., Toth, P., Vigo, D.: *A Survey of Optimization Models for Train Routing and Scheduling.* In *Transportation Science*, Nov 1998.

[23] Dalfiume, A., Lamma, E., Mello, P., Milano, M.: A Constraint Logic Programming Application to a Distributed Train Scheduling Problem. In *Proceedings of the conference on the practical applications of prolog*, pp. 163–182, 1995.

[24] Desrosiers, J., Soumis, F., Desrochers, M.: Routing With Time Windows by Column Generation. *Networks*, 14:545–565, 1984.

[25] Drott, J., Hasselberg, E., Kohl, N., Kremer, M.: A Planning System for Locomotive Scheduling. Technical Report, Swedish State Railways, Stab Tågplanering, Stockholm, Sweden and Carmen Systems AB, Jul 1997.

[26] Fox, M.S., Sadeh, N.: Why Is Scheduling Difficult? In *Proceedings of the European Conference on Artificial Intelligence*, pp. 754–765, 1990.

[27] Golden, B.L., Assad, A.A.: Vehicle Routing with Time-Window Constraints: Algorithmic Solutions. *American Journal of Mathematical and Management Sciences*, 6, 1986.

[28] Gosselin, V.: Train Scheduling Using Constraint Programming Techniques. In *13th Conference on AI, Expert Systems and Natural Language*, Avignon, 1993.

[29] Haridi, S., Van Roy, P., Brand, P., Schulte, C.: Programming Languages for Distributed Applications. Invited paper in *New Generation Computing*, Vol.16, No.3, pp. 223–261, 1998. Ohmsa Ltd. and Springer-Verlag., Tokyo.

[30] Haridi, S., Van Roy, P., Brand, P., Schulte, C., et.al.: http://www.mozart-oz.org/.

[31] Van Hentenryck, P.: *Constraint Satisfaction in Logic Programming. Programming Logic Series*. The MIT Press, Cambridge, MA, 1989.

[32] Holmberg, P.: *The Use of Abstractions to Solve Large Scheduling Problems*. M. Sc. Thesis. KTH, The Royal Institute of Technology, Stockholm, Sweden, 2000.

[33] Holte, R.C., Mkadmi, T., Zimmer, R.M., MacDonald, A.J.: Speeding Up Problem Solving by Abstraction: A Graph Oriented Approach. *Artificial Intelligence*, 85:321–361, 1996.

[34] Holte, R.C., Perez, M.B., Zimmer, A.J., MacDonald, R.M.: Hierarchical a*: Searching Abstraction Hierarchies Efficiently. 1995.

[35] Jordan, C., Drex, A.L.: A Comparison of Constraint and Mixed-integer Programming Solvers for Batch Sequencing with Sequence-dependent Setups. In *ORSA Journal on Computing* 7: 160-165, 1995.

[36] Kreuger, P., Aronsson, M., Holmberg, P., Lindblom, S.: ACOOR Rapport 2 – Översikt av tekniker och metoder. SICS Technical Report T2000/07 (in Swedish)

[37] Kreuger, P., Aronsson, M., Lindblom, S.: Task Structure Abstraction. SICS Technical Report T2001:05

[38] Kreuger, P., Carlsson, M., Sjöland, T., Åström, E.: Sequence dependent task extensions for trip scheduling. SICS Technical report T2001:14.

[39] Kreuger, P., Carlsson, M., Olsson, J., Sjöland, T., Åström, E.: The TUFF Train Scheduler – Trip Scheduling on Single Track Networks. In *The Proceedings of the Workshop on Industrial Constraint-Directed Scheduling, at the Third International Conference on Principles and Practice of Constraint Programming*, Schloß Hagenberg, Linz, Austria, 1997. Davenport, A. (ed.).

[40] Lockett, A.G., Muhlemann, A.P.: A Scheduling Problem Involving Sequence Dependent Changeover Times. In *Operations Research* 20: 895-902, 1972.

[41] Löbel, A.: *Optimal Vehicle Scheduling in Public Transit*. Ph. D. thesis, TU Berlin, 1998. Shaker-Verlag, Aachen.

[42] Martin, C.: *Logistics and Supply Chain Management* Financial Times Pitman Publishing, 1992

[43] Müller, M., Popov, K., Schulte, C., Würtz, J.: *Constraint Programming in Oz.* DFKI, Saarbrücken, Germany, 1995

[44] Müller, M., Würtz, J.: *Finite Domain Programming in Oz.* DFKI, Saarbrücken, Germany, 1995.

[45] Oliveira, E., Smith, B.M.: *A Job-Shop Scheduling Model for the Single-Track Railway Scheduling Problem* University of Leeds, UK, 2000.

[46] Potvin, J.-Y., Rousseau, J.-M.: A Parallel Route Building Algorithm for the Vehicle Routing and Scheduling Problem with Time Windows. *European Journal of Operational Research*, 66:331–340, 1993.

[47] Reeves, C., (ed.). *Modern Heuristic Techniques for Combinatorial Optimization.* McGraw-Hill International (UK) Ltd., 1995.

[48] Ribeiro, C.C., Soumis, F.: A Column Generation Approach to the Multiple-Depot Vehicle Scheduling Problem. *Operations Research*, 42(1):41–52, 1994.

[49] Rossi, F., et.al.: Constraint Logic Programming (a survey). In J. Siekmann, (ed.) *Proc. of the ERCIM Working Group on Constraints/Compulog Net Area on Constraint Programming Workshop*, Cyprus. *LNAI*, oct 1999. Springer-Verlag.

[50] Saraswat, V.A.: *Concurrent Constraint Programming Languages.* Ph.D. Thesis 1989, MIT Press, 1993.

[51] Savelsbergh, M.W.P.: Local Search in Routing Problems with Time Windows. *Annals of Operations Research*, 4:285–305, 1985.

[52] Scholtz, V.: *Knowledge-Based Locomotive Planning for the Swedish Railway.* Master's Thesis, Institut für Informatik, Universität Stuttgart and Swedish Institute of Computer Science (SICS), Nov 1998. ISRN: SICS-T–2000/05-SE.

[53] Simonis, H.: A Problem Classification Scheme for Finite Domain Constraint Solving. In *CP'96 Applications Workshop*, COSYTEC SA, Orsay, France.

[54] Simonis, H.: Calculating Lower Bounds on a Resource Scheduling Problem. In *Proceedings of the Workshop on Applications at the International Conference of Constraint Programming CP'96*, 1996.

[55] Simonis, H.: Modeling Machine Set-up Time in CHIP. In *Proceedings of the Workshop on Applications at the International Conference of Constraint Programming CP'96*, 1996.

[56] So, K.T.: Some Heuristics for Scheduling Jobs on Parallel Machines with Setups In *Management Science* 36: 467-475, 1990.

[57] Solomon, M.M.: On the Worst-case Performance of Some Heuristics for the Vehicle Routing and Scheduling Problem with Time Window Constraints. *Networks*, 16:161–174, 1986.

[58] Solomon, M.M.: Algorithms for the Vehicle Routing and Scheduling Problem with Time Window Constraints. *Operations Research*, 35(2):254–265, March-April 1987.

[59] Solomon, M.M., Desrosiers, J.: Time Window Constrained Routing and Scheduling Problems. *Transportation Science*, 22(1):1–13, 1988.

[60] Thompson, P.M., Psaraftis, H.N.: Cyclic Transfer Algorithms for Multi-Vehicle Routing and Scheduling Problems. *Operations Research*, 41(5):935–946, 1993.

[61] Tsang, E.: *Foundations of Constraint Satisfaction*. Academic Press, 1993.
[62] White, C.H., Wilson, R.C.: Sequence Dependent Set-up Times and Job Sequencing. *International Journal of Production Research* 15, pp. 191–202, 1977.
[63] Yang, Q.: *Intelligent Planning – A Decomposition and Abstraction Based Approach*. ISBN 3-540-61901-1. Springer-Verlag, Berlin, 1997.

Author Index

Lecture Notes in Artificial Intelligence (LNAI)

Lecture Notes in Computer Science